THE HANDBOOK OF INTERNATIONAL
FINANCIAL TERMS

THE HANDBOOK OF INTERNATIONAL FINANCIAL TERMS

PETER MOLES

AND

NICHOLAS TERRY

OXFORD

Oxford University Press, Great Clarendon Street, Oxford OX2 6DP

Oxford New York

Athens Auckland Bangkok Bogota Buenos Aires Calcutta
Cape Town Chennai Dar es Salaam Delhi Florence Hong Kong Istanbul
Karachi Kuala Lumpur Madrid Melbourne Mexico City Mumbai
Nairobi Paris São Paolo Singapore Taipei Tokyo Toronto Warsaw

and associated companies in
Berlin Ibadan

Oxford is a registered trade mark of Oxford University Press

Published in the United States by
Oxford University Press Inc., New York

British Library Cataloguing in Publication Data
Data available

Library of Congress Cataloging in Publication Data
Moles, Peter.
Handbook of international financial terms/Peter Moles and Nicholas Terry.
Includes bibliographical references (p.   ).
ISBN 0-19-828885-9 (alk. paper)
1. International finance—Terminology—Handbooks, manuals, etc.
2. Finance—Terminology—Handbooks, manuals, etc   I. Terry Nicholas.   II. Title.
HG3881.M578   1996   96-31008
332'. 03—dc20

3 5 7 9 10 8 6 4

Printed in Great Britain
on acid-free paper by
Biddles Ltd.
Guildford and King's Lynn

CONTENTS

PREFACE

For many people, the picture that they have of a financial market-place is provided by television and cinema. In such forms, the world of finance can appear exciting, glamorous, and almost totally incomprehensible. The commonest images comprise rooms hidden away from the public gaze, filled with people at desks crammed with computer screens and telephones. The lack of comprehension comes from not only the language being used but also the purpose of all this activity and the working practices of those involved. Life in this environment seems complicated and fast moving. A place where individual careers and incomes, and the fortunes of entire institutions, can be won and lost.

The Handbook of International Financial Terms is designed to provide a ready reference to these financial markets. Its scope is both broad and international, covering a very wide range of activities undertaken by the major global financial centres. To this extent, it can be seen as an extension of the *Oxford Dictionary of Finance*. It will have appeal to both formal and informal finance students, and help them to a better understanding of what financial markets do, how they do it, and the particular language that is used. *The Handbook of International Financial Terms* has been written with the purpose of assisting those students following courses in finance as both a free-standing introduction, and a handy refresher or decoder to accompany standard finance textbooks. It is with this group in mind that some entries contain suggestions for further reading.

For the practitioner, this handbook should be a ready reference and, possibly, a source of inspiration as well as providing definitions of items. Such professionals will be able to save on search time and draw confidence from having their existing understanding confirmed. It is written with the intention of providing one of the most comprehensive and technically advanced collections of terms currently available in a single volume. As such, *The Handbook of International Financial Terms* represents a convenient reference work suited to the needs of practitioners. The notion of the practitioner here is intended to be inclusive in its coverage. For example, practitioners could be: traders, analysts, money and fund managers, bankers, advisers, corporate treasurers, lawyers, accountants, and related professionals.

The authors have the strongly held conviction that there is a place for one book which contains information ranging from the fundamental to the highly sophisticated. Unlike a textbook which works thematically, *The Handbook of International Financial Terms* is a source book for looking up specific items and definitions in a quick and efficient manner. The logic behind this approach is to provide readers with an understanding of the use of the term, and how and where it is used in the market concerned. Once this is achieved, the reader has the awareness to expand the search thematically using cross-references. For those less familiar with the subject, or for those wishing a contextual approach, there is the next section entitled 'Getting Going with the A—Z of Entries'.

The Handbook of International Financial Terms features up-to-date terminology from the different markets around the world. Particular attention is given to derivatives (futures, options, and other risk management products), which is an area that has grown significantly in recent years. Consequently, there has been an explosion in new terms and concepts. The authors have sought to do justice to the modern practice of financial risk management as well as financial innovations. Therefore, the handbook contains a large number of foreign terms, details about how these different derivative products are interrelated, and indications of why they are used.

How to use the Handbook

The main text of the Handbook contains the entries listed alphabetically. Clear definitions for each of the individual terms are provided together with formulae, where appropriate. If warranted, examples or illustrations are also given in order to aid understanding. Other related terms (for example, opposites are denoted by opp.) are indicated, as well as other referenced terms which may be of interest (denoted by 'see'). Items which appear elsewhere are denoted using semi-bold. A typical entry would appear as follows:

> **Finance** (i) The study, specialization in, or use of money. Hence, *financial officer*, and *financial economics*. (ii) The markets, activities, and businesses involved directly with money rather than with real **assets** (cf. **financial institution**). This is an economy's *financial sector*. (iii) **Funds** or a **loan** (cf. **capital**). See **financial instrument**. (iv) Those persons who have specific responsibility for advising about or managing money (cf. **finance director**). Hence a *financial expert*. (v) Alternative term for **capital** (cf. **liabilities**).

Finance is a generic term and is therefore not market or activity specific. Where a term is used in a particular market, or refers to a particular activity, or location this is also shown (in parentheses). For example: **collateralized mortgage obligation (CMO)** (Bonds; USA). Thus the instrument is a collateralized mortgage obligation, the acronym for which is CMO, and it belongs to the bond markets or traded term debt markets in the United States of America. If the reader had wanted to know the meaning of CMO, this is found by looking in the List of Abbreviations and Acronyms, which gives the meaning of the letters, allowing the term to be looked up in the alphabetical section. This follows the section entitled 'Getting Going with the A to Z of Entries', which is provided to assist the less knowledgeable reader by setting the entries in context and is designed to give a short overview of the main entries.

Acknowledgements

The authors would like to express their gratitude to many people for offering suggestions, most of which have been readily adopted. A very special thanks is due to Bernard Manson who diligently read and commented on an early draft of the Handbook. His recommendations and suggestions were extremely useful in firming up the approach finally taken. The following are also worthy of our thanks:

Andrew Adams; Seth Armitage; the *Bank Relationship Consultancy*; Lloyd Beat; Jonathan Crook; Adrian Fitzgerald; Steve Lunt; Kenneth Lyall; Andrew McCosh; David Middleton; Mark Runiewicz; Simon Wheatley; and Simon Witney-Long.

Thanks are also due to the staff at various exchanges and institutions around the world, who kindly responded to our requests for information.

We would like to thank Moody's Investors Services and Standard and Poor's for allowing us to reproduce the details of their credit rating scales as part of this Handbook.

A special thanks to David Musson at Oxford University Press who believed in this undertaking, provided ideas and helpful comments, and prodded when necessary. A heavy burden fell on Edwin Pritchard who had the task of editing the manuscript. His diligence has greatly improved the final result.

Finally, as is usual in these matters, all errors and omissions remain entirely the responsibility of the authors. Although great care has been taken over the detail in this work, mistakes can occur with a project of this type. The authors would greatly appreciate learning of any such mishaps, and any more general comments on the structure of the book and suggestions about the future.

Peter Moles and Nicholas Terry

Edinburgh University Management School
University of Edinburgh
7 Bristo Square
Edinburgh EH8 9AL
Scotland
United Kingdom

Tel.: Int + 44 (0) 131 650 8065 / 3823
Fax: Int + 44 (0) 131 650 6501

e mail: P.Moles@ed.ac.uk
e mail: J.GOLDRING@ed.ac.uk

March 1996

In this publication, occasional reference is made to certain terms which are Trademarked by companies. It should be noted that such references have been made for information purposes only and the use of any such names without mention of the Trademark should not be taken as any kind of challenge whatsoever to the Trademark.

GETTING GOING WITH THE A TO Z OF ENTRIES[1]

Finance specialists should find it possible to explore the main body of entries comprising *The Handbook of International Financial Terms* (*THIFT*) without too much difficulty. The large number of definitions provides an opportunity to enhance and confirm their existing knowledge and understanding, as well as to become more aware of the wide implications of international finance. What follows is a descriptive overview of financial markets and instruments intended to offer the non-specialist several ways into the A to Z listing. By gaining access to the entries (highlighted in bold), the non-specialist should be able to demystify much of the behaviour of modern financial markets. In particular this *Handbook* provides a guide to what is traded; why it is traded; where, how, and by whom it is traded. The domestic/regional markets and sectors which comprise the international or global financial market-place share, to a varying degree, common problems, organizational structures, and regulations and, in different ways, these shared and separating characteristics also influence the behaviour of the individual markets.

Financial markets trade what are called financial claims or instruments, and markets are interested in 'Who is doing the issuing?' and 'Who is doing the buying?', and 'Why?' in both cases. That is, how do individuals, households, companies, governments, and countries pay for what they do; are any of these groups spending more than they receive (often referred to as deficit units or net borrowers); or receiving more than they spend (surplus units or net lenders). This is best seen in terms of the flow of funds between different sectors of an economy shown in Figure 1. The flow of funds within a country will see borrowing and lending between the different sectors: the state sector, the personal sector, and the industrial and commercial sector. This will take place either directly or be channelled through the financial markets. In addition, in an open economy, the domestic sectors and the domestic financial markets are connected to the international financial markets whether to borrow or lend.

A major question of interest is how, if they are borrowers, are they raising funds in the financial markets? For example, is it via loans or overdrafts from **intermediary** institutions who specialize in finance, or by issuing various kinds of financial

---

[1] Note this section is designed to provide an introduction to the main text and is not meant to provide a rigorous framework for the alphabetical list of entries. The coverage of topics is highly selective and designed to put the financial markets in context. As a result many areas of importance have had to be omitted, or not given true prominence. A reader wishing for a rigorous discussion of issues in international finance should consult one of the many excellent books on the subject.

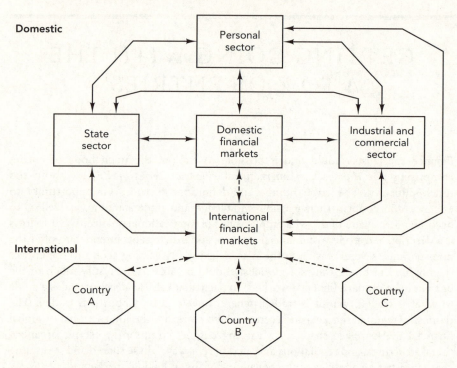

Figure 1. Flow of funds and financial markets

instruments or claims directly to surplus units, usually with the help of institutions which act to facilitate transactions. Or if they are lending, what sorts of claims and promises from borrowers or intermediary institutions are they prepared to accept? To obtain a basic understanding of the different nature of these claims, see **equity, debt, instrument**, and **loans**, and for an example of how the lender–borrower relationship is priced, see the **term structure of interest rates**. From a market perspective, perhaps the most important part of this lender–borrower relationship is how these financial claims are priced or valued. Moreover, participants are exposed to changes in value as market prices change and seek to know and benefit from or protect themselves from these changes in the relative valuation of assets over time and under varying economic conditions.

The different categories of financial instrument within this flow of funds are linked with a common concern about money and how it circulates (e.g. between the personal sector and private sector industrial and commercial **companies**). This is done in such a way as to satisfy the functions of **money**. These functions reflect the ability of particular forms of money (e.g. gold pieces, notes, coins, and credit cards) to: act as a payment in settlement of a transaction or debt; act as a unit of account; and act as a store of value. Different economies, and therefore the markets located within individual countries, have used differing institutional arrangements in an attempt to ensure a smooth flow of funds between sectors. Differences in culture and country specific requirements also help explain why a variety of financial markets and agents have emerged. Collectively, this array of disparate markets and institutions is often referred to as the international monetary system. Within this system, we can distinguish basic functional categories such as the **capital markets**, the **money markets**, the **currency markets** or **foreign exchange markets**, and the **commodities** markets.[2] In order to assist in the flow of funds in the **cash markets** or the **physical markets**, markets in **contingent claims** have been developed. These **derivative** markets have emerged to manage and transfer the various risks inherent from financial exposures.[3]

Within a single country or economic system, individual arrangements are normally associated with specific customs and practices. For example, the **London Stock Exchange** and the **Bank of England** for the UK are at the core of the **City**, and the **New York Stock Exchange** and the **Federal Reserve** for the USA make up **Wall Street**. When combined, these markets and institutions provide the basis for the creation of a domestic financial system, within which **financial institutions** operate. As well as existing to fulfil the functions of money, these systems provide a valuation for financial assets (or equivalently, the required rate of return), markets in which such claims may be traded, and efficiencies that reduce transaction costs. These aspects of the flow of funds reveal the **opportunity costs** of using money in one way, rather than another, and the relative values of different assets, and the choice of instruments, thus effecting the process of saving and investing. One important function of markets is **price discovery**, where the continual revaluation process provides signals to economic agents as to how funds should be allocated to financial assets and, as a result, helps in the efficient allocation of resources.

At the heart of the domestic financial systems that go to make up the global system are **financial institutions**. They help ensure that the flow of funds works in an efficient manner. Their role is to act either as facilitators or intermediators (or occasionally both). Facilitators help smooth transactions between surplus units and deficit units. They help structure, sell, advise, and generally assist in completing transactions for borrowers and lenders. Intermediators have a more complex function in that they transform claims from borrowers in ways that make them more attractive to lenders. For example, they attempt to overcome situations where more wish to borrow than wish to lend; such a situation is often called a **liquidity** crisis. Where the reverse situation arises, a market could be described as being over-funded. Financial institutions exist in part to reconcile such imbalances, which can

---

[2] Commodities are in principle a separate factor of production, being consumption assets. However, they share some characteristics with money and financial assets, notably that trading in major commodities is carried out on organized exchanges and commodities are treated as an investment class. One only has to look at the financial pages of a newspaper to see that the gold and crude oil price are placed alongside the stock market indicators, the cost of money, and exchange rates.

[3] It is interesting to note the growth of derivatives as a transfer mechanism and their absolute necessity as an overlay to the cash markets. In those countries that have recently made the transition from a command to a market economy, the financial sector has started with the establishment of a stock exchange and a debt market, but then have moved rapidly to establish derivatives markets.

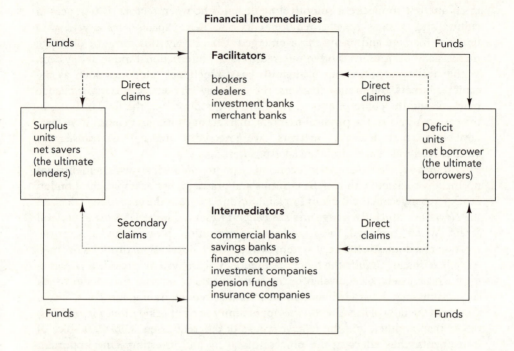

Figure 2. Flow of funds II—the role of financial intermediaries

be caused by the straightforward timing differences in the availability of funds from lending units and the demand for funds from borrowing units. The imbalance in the demand and supply of loanable funds can also be as a result of the **mismatch** in the quality of potential borrowers, and the expectation of lenders. Hence, the importance of **credit ratings** and the existence of **quality spreads**. In such cases, financial institutions may act on behalf of borrowers and lenders in markets, using their name and resources to overcome such difficulties. This process is referred to as financial **intermediation**.

A more familiar transaction might involve a financial institution, such as a **bank, building society, savings and loan association,** or a **savings bank**. Depositors place funds into a bank in return for a promise to repay the amount on demand, a rate of interest, and the provision of certain services, such as a **current** or **checking accounts**. In order to justify paying interest and providing services, the bank must make its deposits work in some profitable way. One way would be for the bank to lend money to a business in order to enable it to invest in, say, new products. The bank will charge **interest** on the loan at a rate above that paid to the depositor; this difference in interest rates is called the **margin**. Margins in general reflect the perceived **risk** associated with the **debtor** firm. The amount at risk or **exposure** can, in part, be offset by the bank accepting a claim on the firm's **assets** via a **lien** which can be exercised if the firm fails to meet the interest charges, or fails to repay the original sum borrowed, the **principal**. When assets are pledged in this manner, the loan would be called a **secured loan**. Negotiable claims upon a borrower which are transferable to third parties are known as **securities**.[4] A situation in which a borrower breaks some or all of the borrowing terms attached to the debt is usually called **default**. What happens thereafter will depend upon the precise terms of the loan agreement and certain provisions within that contract called **covenants**.

Although financial intermediation is carried out in a variety of different ways, there are many shared characteristics, especially in relation to the overall structure of the markets in which they operate, and the products and services that they issue, offer, and trade. Intermediators provide surplus units with immediate **diversification** and the benefits from the pooling of deposits and the creation of **portfolios**.[5] Correctly undertaken, diversification reduces risks and therefore the required return to lenders. Facilitators do not lend directly but assist in finding investors, in structuring the resultant transactions, and, in many cases, in providing a secondary market where existing claims can be transferred between surplus units. Since the requirements of borrowers and lenders do diverge radically, the ability to resell financial claims in the market is of paramount importance. Facilitating institutions, known variously as **agents, brokers, broker-dealers, dealers**, or **traders** (for example, **stockbrokers** who handle various kinds of stocks, or commodity brokers who specialize in commodities markets) act to match up buyers and sellers. Trading in financial assets is either arranged through an **organized exchange** or is carried in the **over-the-counter** (OTC) markets.

Financial markets involve financial claims based either on borrowing and lending or represent ownership rights (these two categories of claims are shown at the top of Figure 3). Differences in these contractual positions lead to **debt** claims which have known monetary or contractual payoffs or various types of **equity** or **share capital** where the payoffs involve varying degrees of participation in the profits or value of the firm, asset, or instrument. Debt instruments may be either provided by intermediating institutions when it is usually non-negotiable (variously known as **loans, advances**, or **credit facilities**) or issued directly to lenders as transferable **securities**. These money claims may also vary according to factors such as the frequency and type of interest payments, their repayment date or **maturity**, and the type of contract. Such claims can be also backed by physical assets, as with **asset-backed** or **mortgage-backed securities**, or the borrower's **credit worthiness**. The credit worthiness, credit standing, or financial solidity is effectively a promise to repay based on the current and future **cash flow** or **earnings** of the issuer, or a third-party **guarantor**. There are also **hybrid** instruments which combine features of

---

[4] **Securitization**, one of the major trends of the capital markets, involves the substitution of negotiable claims for bilateral contracts. As such, it has led to a number of intermediate stage instruments, such as **sub-participation** of **loans**, or **asset sales** where the legal basis is still a loan, but the lender's rights can be transferred.

[5] It should be noted that they also provide administrative services, such as valuation, payment, money transfer, and so on.

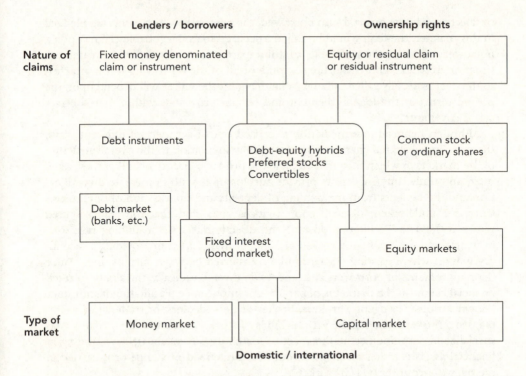

Figure 3. Classification of financial markets by type

more than one **class** of claim, such as **convertibles**. The equity of a firm comes in various forms, including: **common stock** or **ordinary shares**, alternatively known as **equities**; and **preferred stock** or **preference shares**. These differ according to factors such as contracted or expected **dividends, capital appreciation**, and their priority and share of assets in **liquidation** or when sold.

The financial markets are also characterized by the **maturity** of the claims being traded. The **money markets** involve transactions where the financial claims are typically of twelve months or less in maturity, or **duration**. Money markets trade, for example, **banker's acceptances, certificates of deposit, commercial paper, treasury bills, bills of exchange, loan notes, repurchase agreements, foreign exchange**, and, internationally, **eurocurrencies**. Where the time involved exceeds one year, or thereabouts, the transactions are grouped under the heading of **capital markets**. These provide **new issue** and **secondary markets** in both **fixed income** (or **notes and bonds**) and in **equities**. It is rare (but not unknown) for the **bond markets** to trade fixed claims beyond thirty years until **maturity**.[6] Many financial institutions

---

[6] Government bond markets in the USA and the UK offer 30-year bonds; those of France, Germany, and Japan tend to have shorter, 10-year maturities, although longer-dated issues exist. On the whole, corporate bonds tend not to exceed the maturity of the government debt markets in the country of issue.

are participants in more than one type of market, although individual organizations may specialize in particular instruments, sectors, or classes. The rationale for the existence of different instruments is to provide the most appropriate means to meet the requirements of those needing to satisfy **liabilities** in the near or distant future, and to appeal to those with funds available over a roughly equal period. The surge in financial innovation, in the form of new instruments, derivatives, and trading methods, has been a direct response to questions of **asset-liability management** and gaps in the available instruments. These gaps come about due to, amongst other factors, legal and regulatory constraints, unfavourable or undesirable risk-reward characteristics, and taxes.[7] Innovations which address a wide economic need can themselves become established instruments (for example, **interest rate swaps** and **cross-currency swaps** which were developed in the early 1980s have become established as a fourth type of derivative); other innovations, which address more specific economic or individual requirements, have been seven-day wonders.[8]

The financial markets in which these claims are traded operate either to recycle existing claims between surplus units in the **secondary market** with the help of financial institutions or by creating new claims or **new issues** via the **primary market** (see Figure 4). An **initial public offering** (IPO) is one of the ways a company can first offer its shares to a wide range of investors. Once the company has received its funds in exchange for its shares, they become **listed** or **quoted** on an exchange and can be bought and sold in what is termed the **secondary** or **after-market**. Investors, or more correctly **speculators**, that anticipate an increase in the value of shares between the time that they are first issued, and when they are traded in the secondary market are called **stags** in the UK. The analogy to animals continues as market participants who are optimistic about future asset values are known as **bulls**; and those who are pessimistic are known as **bears**. Hence expressions such as 'the equities bull market of the early to mid-1980s'.

The formalities associated with organized stock markets can differ; for example, the London Stock Exchange has at the time of writing a **quote** or **price-driven** dealing system; whereas, the New York Stock Exchange (NYSE) is **order-driven** using **specialists** to handle the flow of **orders**. Moreover, the **Big Board** (NYSE) located on **Wall Street** maintains a physical **trading floor**, as compared to London's screen-based trading system. Derivatives exchanges have tended to favour **open outcry** in **pits** where **floor brokers**, supplemented by **locals**, provide a frenzied trading atmosphere shouting offers or signalling frantically between buyers and sellers. This results in differences in the way financial instruments are bought and sold, and the procedure for establishing the prices at which trades take place. Regardless of the technical methods used, these represent formal, or not so formal, **auction** systems designed to establish the market (or fair) price to both buyer and seller, and are as a result, therefore, often referred to as a **double-auction** process. The

[7] At the operational level, the key role of information technology as a means of processing ever larger volumes of data should not be underestimated.

[8] For instance, the **leveraged swap** and the **wedding band swap** do not appear to have become established as a new type of instrument.

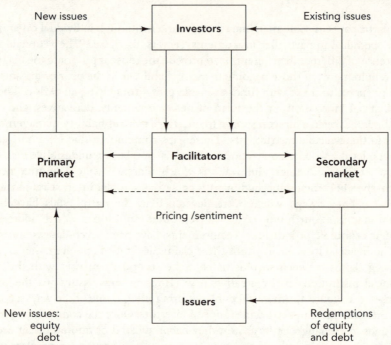

Figure 4. Primary and secondary markets

two-way prices provided by intermediaries comprise both **bid** and **offer** quotes. The market price can be established by **specialists** whose function is to smooth transactions and in so doing may trade on behalf of themselves and also operate a **book** in which customers' unexecuted orders are maintained. Alternatively, markets allow in a **dual capacity** under which **intermediaries** can act either **principal**, or **agent**, or both. The names given to **traders** and instruments may also differ; for example, in the USA, shorter-term company debt issues are called **commercial paper**, and in the UK the same sort of issue would be called commercial **bills**.

As a result of the nature of their claims, equity and bond markets have a separate identity within the capital markets and they often have distinct dealing and **settlement** systems. This, in turn, has produced specialist traders and specific methods for assessing each market. Another difference is the importance of government issues in the bond markets which act as a **benchmark** for the pricing and **terms and conditions** of non-government debt issues. When large amounts of debt are sought by governments **auctions** or **tenders** are used. For other issuers, several financial intermediaries may act together to establish the basis of the funding under an arrangement called **syndication**. Such a process may well include the introduction of additional parties to provide **underwriting** or **distribution** capabilities based on the intermediary's **placing power**. In the international markets, the **eurobond market** is now the principal source of cross-border, debt-based transactions rather than **foreign bonds** in domestic markets. A recent innovation has been the introduction of **global** debt issues and equity offerings where the securities are distributed and traded both internationally and in the major domestic markets.

Financial institutions such as **investment banks, commercial banks**, or **money center banks** perform functions and offer products and services that are recognizable around the world. The differences emerge with regard to their specialized functions and often unique solutions to particular operations demanded by the individual domestic financial and regulatory systems. For example, the UK has particular money market institutions known as **discount houses** and **accepting houses**. The capital markets in the UK are dominated by the **London Stock Exchange** for both equities and bonds while the **London International Financial Futures and Options Exchange** (LIFFE) handles **exchange-traded** derivatives. The financial services sector includes institutions which are **financial conglomerates** or **universal banks, securities houses**, often with specialist in-house **investment banks, merchant banks, investing institutions**, and **international banks**. Serving the domestic and international markets are a number of specialized institutions such as **leasing** companies, **finance houses**, and **venture capital** firms. The extent to which these businesses are carried out by separate institutions has been eroded by the emergence of **financial conglomerates, universal banks**, or **allfinanz**. The trend towards **globalization** has ensured that in the world's three main financial markets, of New York, Tokyo, and London, the same relatively small number of world-class **bulge bracket** financial institutions can be found, together with a larger number of specialized, **boutique**, national, or regional institutions that undertake similar functions.

The operations of these markets are divided into three core businesses: banking, investment, and insurance. The banking industry can take several different forms, as previously mentioned, and is influenced by regulatory and legal restrictions, such as the **Glass–Stegal Act** in the USA, and by a desire for individual institutions to be differentiated in order to gain comparative advantage. The differences between, say, commercial banks and investment banks are most visible when comparing the products and services offered, which reflects how they generate **earnings**. Clearing banks which accept **deposits** and create **loans** and **credit** do so in return for a **margin**; whereas investment banks offer more specialized products and services for which they receive **fees** and **commissions**. Commercial banking is therefore often considered a **spread**-driven, relationship business, as compared to the fee-driven, **transaction**-orientated investment banking business.[9] **Universal banks** that operate in both businesses have, therefore, opportunities for the cross-selling of services. For individuals, the merging of, insurance, investments, and banking has led to the idea of **bancassurance**, the one-stop provider of all customers' retail financial services needs. For the wealthy individual, the **private bank** provides a personalized full range of services.

---

[9] This simplistic asset-building intermediation versus transaction facilitating distinction ignores the increasing fee-based activities of commercial banks.

Commercial banks prosper and grow according to how well they attract deposits, using interest rates, product diversity, convenient location, and quality of service. Simultaneously, they must be prudent in creating credit and accepting lending opportunities based on **credit worthiness, credit rating**, or **credit scoring**. Investment banks thrive by increasing the number and size of transactions, selling financial products, and providing advice to firms and governments. Examples of the sort of help on offer include: valuation; drawing up a **prospectus** which accompanies a share or debt issue; and producing an **offer document** in pursuit of a corporate **merger** or **acquisition**; and structuring the finance in a **project**. Investment bankers not only offer advice about the timing and pricing of proposed transactions, they can be essential in arranging the financing of the deal. This would be the case in transactions called **leveraged buy-outs** or LBOs. In addition to such single-purpose deals, investment banks offer a range of ongoing dealing and advisory services that are aimed at the **chief financial officer** and treasury departments of larger firms. These products include tailor-made: **options, caps, floors and collars, forward rate agreements, interest rate swaps, foreign exchange transactions** and **cross-currency swaps, swaptions, commercial paper, banker's acceptances, medium-term notes, floating rates notes** and **repurchase agreements**, and **commodity swaps**.

The rationale for many of these relatively complex financial arrangements give them special appeal to large, multinational organizations because they are likely to be exposed to significant **interest rate risk** and **currency risk**. These, and other, sources of risk need to be managed or **hedged**, otherwise changes in the **macroeconomic** factors outside the control of the individual organization may cause otherwise profitable operations to be uneconomic. The mechanism by which firms and banks get together to do deals, or put in place **risk management** strategies, is not provided by a formal and recognizable market-place (as is the case with the buying and selling of equities). Instead, it is based on institutional reputation. How such reputations are established often appears unclear, although past success with similar transactions seems to be important. It is common for particular departments within institutions to be known for certain things, for example, correctly analysing stock market sentiment, or accurately predicting trends in economic variables like inflation, and growth rates. Such activities rely extensively on **forecasting** techniques based on **models**. This may help explain why the representatives of such institutions participate in television and radio programmes and are regarded as 'experts'.

Risk is central to financial markets, it arises either from the nature of the contract, as it does with **interest rate risk** if it is a debt claim, for instance, or the risk might arise from the **counterparty** on the other side, whose ability to perform their contractual obligation may be impaired. The relationship between the risks taken by investors, either surplus units or via financial institutions such as banks, and the returns that they expect is normally explained within something called the **risk-return trade-off** or **risk-reward**.

In other words, the way in which banks, for instance, price money is made according to how they view the relationship between the risk of the borrower and

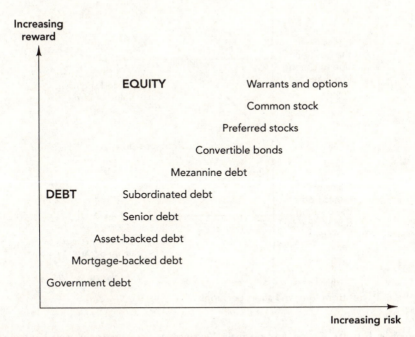

Increasing reward

EQUITY   Warrants and options

Common stock

Preferred stocks

Convertible bonds

Mezannine debt

DEBT   Subordinated debt

Senior debt

Asset-backed debt

Mortgage-backed debt

Government debt

Increasing risk

Figure 5. Risk-reward trade-off for financial instruments

return they are getting. As far as the bank is concerned, the deposit is a **liability**, and the loan to the business is an **asset**. To influence lenders' attitudes to risk and reward, bank regulators will often limit the extent to which such assets can be created on the basis of given liabilities. Such controls often begin with devices known as **cash** and **liquidity reserves**, but can extend to international agreements like the **Basle Capital Convergence Accord** which defines capital requirements in terms of **risk-adjusted assets** in relation to the bank's **capital base**. These types of arrangements are intended to prevent, amongst other things, depositors losing confidence in an institution such that they precipitately attempt to withdraw funds (known as a 'run on the bank'). When the assets of a bank fail to achieve the expected **rate of return** (however measured) they are called **non-performing assets**.

At the organizational level, many risks can be modified using **derivatives** and the growth of these **off-balance sheet** instruments is one of the most salient features of finance in the last thirty years.[10] The basic elements making up derivatives are

[10] Derivatives allow individual firms to change the nature of a particular risk by transferring all or part to another party better able to assume the risk. Accordingly, derivatives act as a risk-transfer mechanism and, at the macro level, do not eliminate risk. However, since in many cases, one party's exposure is the mirror image of the other's, risk is effectively extinguished. For instance, commodity producers and consumers can both benefit from dealing in futures contracts: one to hedge future sales,

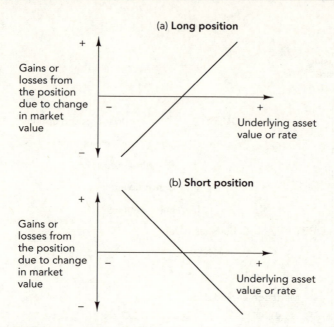

Figure 6. Payoff from long and short positions

forwards, futures, swaps, and **options**. Derivatives are extremely useful in transferring risks from the cautious or prudent to the more speculative or those better able to accept such risks. A useful way to visualize exposures is via the payoff diagram, also known as a **risk profile** (as shown in Figure 6). A **long position** (*a*) is equivalent to holding the underlying asset, a gain is made if the price rises, a loss if it falls. The opposite, the **short position** (*b*) is equivalent to having sold the asset, the gain comes from a repurchase at a lower price, the loss occurs if the price has risen in the meantime. These kinds of exposures have a **linear** or symmetric relationship to the underlying asset, instrument, commodity, rate, or spread relationship.[11] When considering these positions in terms of forwards, futures, and swaps, the long position is contractually obliged to buy the underling asset while the short is obliged to deliver.

The exposure is either positive, in the case of a **long position** (*a*), or negative, in the case of a **short position** (*b*). These risks can be eliminated by combining opposite positions in such a way as to **hedge** an underlying exposure. This is shown in Figure 7 when a long exposure to an underlying asset (i), which has a

the other future purchases. As a result, derivatives provide an important economic function in reducing price uncertainties. The US regulatory agency, the **Commodity Futures Trading Commission** requires that before authorizing the setting up of a new derivatives contract its sponsors, amongst other things, demonstrate an economic purpose.

[11] This last element is required because there are a number of contracts where the payoff is the change in the spread between two different assets.

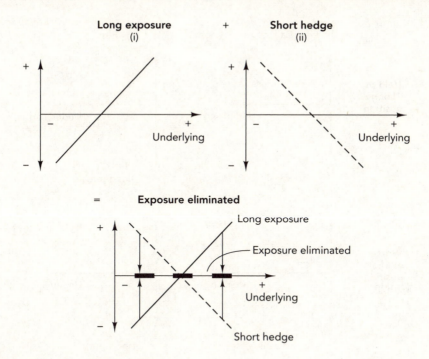

Figure 7. The principle of hedging

risk of loss if prices fall, is combined with a short position or short hedge (ii), which gains in value when prices fall.[12] As a result, the risk of loss on the position is eliminated.[13]

Options or option-like positions, however, have **asymmetric** or non-linear characteristics in that the risks taken by the buyer and the seller are very different. The four possible positions, held or purchased **call** or **put** and written or sold call or put, are shown in Figure 8. The difference between calls and puts relates to the direction of the gains or losses; the call is equal to the advantageous pay off from the long position and provides the holder with the right but not the obligation to buy at a pre-agreed price or rate. The put provides the advantageous payoff from the short position in that it gives the holder the right to sell at a pre-agreed price or rate. This is illustrated in Figure 9 where the linear payoff profiles have been snapped apart to show the option positions that go to make them up.

For option buyers or **holders** (the long position), the risk in the option position is limited to the amount of premium paid and the gain is unlimited; for the seller, or **writer** (the short position), the gain is limited and the loss unlimited. In exchange

---

[12] For example, a long asset position (e.g. a bond holding) which is hedged via a derivative contract (e.g. a sold or short futures position in an interest rate futures contract).

[13] The efficiency of the hedge or the degree to which the positions offset each other will dictate how much of the risk is eliminated.

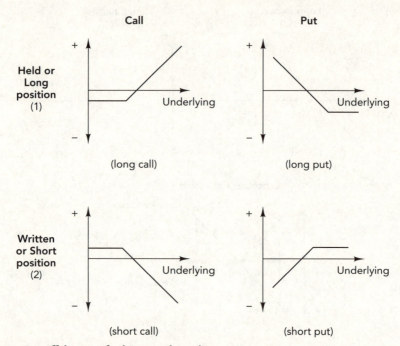

Figure 8. Pay-off diagram for linear and non-linear exposures

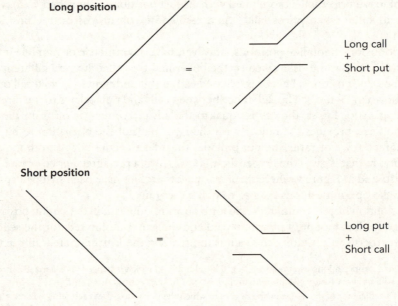

Figure 9. The component process

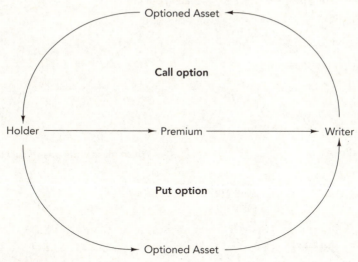

Figure 10. The option flow

for the potential gain, the holder pays a known premium to the writer in exchange for the right to buy or sell (as per Figure 10). The writer receives a known payment against the chance of being exercised against. One of the key developments of the last thirty years has been the evolution of contingent-claims analysis and, in particular, **option pricing models**. These provide methods for determining the theoretical or **fair value** of non-linear payoff instruments based on arbitrage pricing and **replication** strategies.

Much of the mystique of options relates to the way in which such non-linear claims are priced. Many transactions rely on **put-call parity** relationships and how they allow different ways to create the same payoff. Using these methods, **synthetics** can be created by combining different elements of these packages. For instance, a **synthetic call** is equal to a long position plus a long put. The building block process required to create a synthetic call is shown in Figure 11.

One way of considering the complex choices available with **option strategies** is to view them in terms of a **decision tree**. The required position and its risk is governed both by the direction of the protection required, that is whether the optioned instrument will rise or fall in value, and whether the asset is to be owned or not (So a **covered call** has a different risk to a **naked call** position). Hence a call is suitable if the holder wishes to benefit from or protect themselves from an increase in asset value. However, given the same **bullish** directional view on the asset price, writing a put provides an immediate inflow of premium against the potential risk of having to buy the asset at the **strike price** if the value should fall. Both strategies provide a potential gain, however because of the asymmetrical payoffs from the different sides of option positions provide very different risks. A covered put, however, is an income-generating strategy allowing the writer to reduce the cost of a future

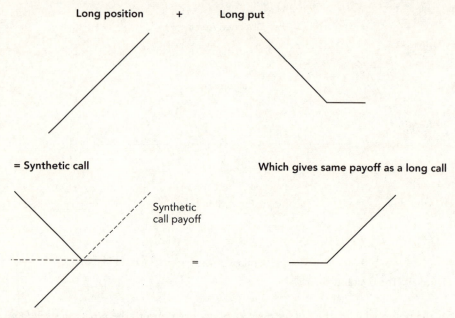

Figure 11. Creating a synthetic call

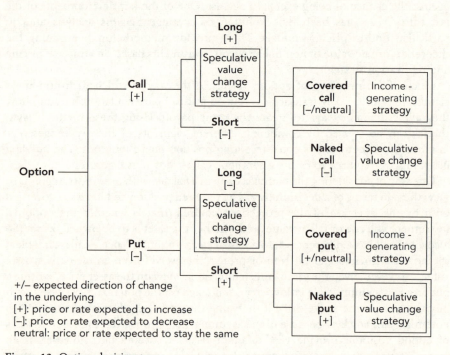

+/− expected direction of change
in the underlying
[+]: price or rate expected to increase
[−]: price or rate expected to decrease
neutral: price or rate expected to stay the same

Figure 12. Option decision tree

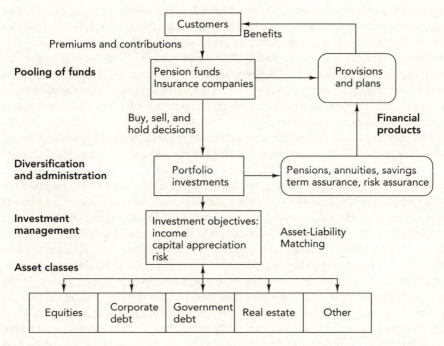

Figure 13

purchase. A covered call provides the opportunity for the writer to reduce the costs of ownership by receiving premium income up-front.

Institutional investors are defined by what they do, and how they use the financial markets. The largest participants are **pension funds** and insurance companies. The key function of such funds is to organize or pool customers' savings in order to provide either long-term benefits or insurance against specific contingencies. In the case of these particular institutions their investment activities are carried out with specific outcomes which can be related to time or events which give them a distinct preference for certain types of asset **classes**. As a consequence they have a particular approach to asset-liability management. Their function is summarized in Figure 13, which shows the flow of funds between customers and the key functions undertaken by such institutions, such as pooling funds, administration, diversification, investment management, and the provision of appropriate financial products.

Next to **pension funds** in supplying funds to the securities markets are **insurance companies**. This business is usually divided according to the main types of contract they issue. Those that specialize in covering accident risks, such as theft and fire damage, are known as insurers; whereas, those that specialize in providing benefits on death are called assurers or, in the UK, life offices. Institutions that write both kinds of policies are referred to as composites or general insurers. Many life insurance companies in both the UK and USA are not strictly speaking companies (although they may have wholly-owned subsidiaries that are incorporated), rather they are mutual institutions and owned by their policy-holders. The reasons for this are largely historical but the fact that such a legal status persists suggests that the advantages are seen as enduring. The main benefits from mutual status can be found in a commonality of interest between the customer and the institution and fewer threats to independence leading to **short-termism**. Many insurers and assurers offer pension schemes, and to this extent the two types of institutional investors are operationally linked.

For pension funds, insurance, and assurance organizations the investing strategies adopted are likely to be influenced by the nature and timing of the liabilities they are contracted to meet. Managing such a business is, therefore, concerned with assessing the risks of a particular event occurring, and the requirement to pay out a given sum, or a specified amount over a stated period, such as under a retirement plan. Managing the liabilities-side of the business falls to a group of specialized professionals called **actuaries**. The asset-side is the responsibility of **fund managers** and **analysts** who must ensure an adequate flow of returns to meet all liabilities and obligations, as and when they fall due. The management task, therefore, is somewhat similar to that of **matching** the assets and liabilities in banks, although the nature of the products and the maturities involved are distinct. The main reasons for investing in securities is to generate a regular stream of income, and to preserve and enhance capital values over time. To this extent, institutional investors see participation in company funding markets as a strictly financial relationship. Not one that offers them the opportunity to become involved in making individual company decisions, for example deciding what products to develop. It may be argued that such an arrangement produces a limiting set of objectives for company managers, not least the desire to smooth **dividends** over several years of results in order to deliver on the stable regular income requirement. Such a policy may well assist in managing the insurance business but could work against the strategic reinvestment needs of the company. Firms are increasingly required to justify value creation and, in particular, pursue strategies that enhance shareholder value.

Institutional fund managers can become more than normally interested in the strategic and commercial decisions of the companies in which they hold stakes. This arises because certain corporate actions have the potential for producing significant changes in share prices. Sudden (i.e. unexpected) movements in market values can be caused by events such as: a **takeover** bid being made or received by a company; an announcement by a company of its intention to make a **rights issue**, or offer a **bonus issue** of shares; and information that might indicate that a company is in financial distress; or a **proxy contest** between contesting visions for the firm. Any one of these events can prompt investors to seek clarification directly from the company involved. Given the importance of institutional fund managers, they are likely to demand—and get—an opportunity to question company executives about the reasons behind particular corporate decisions and conditions. The exchange of information between executives and investment managers has to be handled with care so as to avoid offending stock exchange listing rules, such as London's **Yellow Book**, and violating **insider dealing** legislation.

When the growth ambitions of companies takes the form of wishing to acquire other businesses via a **merger** or an **acquisition**, investors are confronted with several **portfolio** considerations. For example, questions arise about continuing with a stake in the proposed transaction (e.g. shares in the enlarged company), or accepting **cash** in exchange for the shares held in the existing company. The critical consideration is usually the share price offered by the bidder, raising therefore the issue of company valuation. Under 'normal' portfolio selection conditions, valuation will be seen in relation to the rest of the market, so that an understanding of how the market arrives at a price is important, and here fundamental concepts like the **efficient markets hypothesis** can be useful. In the case of **mergers and acquisitions**, however, the investor needs to assess whether a sufficient price adjustment has occurred, in light of the claims made for the future performance of the new company. Such gains are often expressed in terms of business **synergies**. There are several methods available for deriving a valuation, including the **dividend discount model**. This makes use of the **discounted cash flow** approach which seeks to assess value in terms of the firm's future **cash flows**. Such elaborate models have become increasingly common in recent years due to the availability of sophisticated spreadsheets and ever more powerful personal computers.

Several approaches to examining portfolio selection and management exist, including **fundamental analysis** and **technical analysis**. Each of these approaches gives a different emphasis to the underlying performance of the issuer, security, sector, or market as compared to its historical, current, and expected future behaviour. Within these approaches, however, there are common assessment tools such as **earnings analysis** and **yield analysis**. Single number measures like the **price-earnings ratio** (PER) and **yield-to-maturity** are often applied to determine value and decisions as to when to **trade**. The intensity with which such techniques are employed by institutional investors, especially given the requirement for quarterly reviews of portfolio performance, has given rise to accusations of **short-termism**. Moreover, the rigorous application of **portfolio theory** by fund managers has led to worries about an over-emphasis upon the pursuit of the efficient pricing of **risk**.

If the investor should choose to accept the cash on offer in a takeover, which would normally include a **premium** for control, then another decision immediately follows. Namely, what alternatives are available for using the funds released from the sale? These include reinvestment in the same sector and selecting another company. Such a decision could also prompt a review of the overall investment strategy causing, perhaps, a fundamental reappraisal in policy, and creating a search for other things to trade, and a desire to (re-)assess the investment characteristics currently on offer. At various times a fundamental **policy switch** might result leading to **block trading** by the institution.

Individual investors with cash to invest may consider alternative ways of pooling investments, such as **investment trusts, commodity fund, mutual funds,** and

personal equity plans. If the equity market remains the preferred choice a number of different types of stocks and shares are available. This choice includes **blue chips, recovery stocks,** and **growth stocks.** Blue chips are the largest and most stable of quoted common stocks and provide a balance between risk and reward. These companies usually are major constituents of the various stock **indexes** used to track market performance. Recovery shares, or **penny stocks** as they are sometimes known, are companies that have fallen on hard times for various reasons. The shares become very cheap, everyone writes them off, but many recover. Access to management information is most important, and, if correctly selected, the rewards are high as the price recovers sharply. The risk is that the management fails to turn the company around, ultimately resulting in the **liquidation** or **bankruptcy** of the company, and the shares drift lower and lower as the inevitable end approaches. Growth shares are considered to have the greatest potential to increase in size. The problem here is whether management can retain control if it is expanding rapidly or if business conditions are uncertain. Many technological stocks fall into this category, as do biotechnology-based businesses. Many depend on the quality of the inventions and potential market demand. In addition, if the growth is dependent upon a particular **trend,** what happens if that trend falters, or is reversed? Growth shares tend to be relatively expensive so timing the investment decision is important.

The range of financial instruments available for issue and trading has grown significantly in recent years which reflects several trends in international finance. Innovation in the design of securities and other instruments, especially **derivatives,** has led to a shift in the way corporates view the money and capital markets. Such markets are now seen as providing opportunities for making best use of surplus funds and meeting financial obligations in the most efficient way. This has caused a reappraisal of the role of finance in business, incorporating the notion that finance is no longer an enabling function but one that can contribute to strategic decisions. In other words, the finance specialist should be able to develop financial arrangements that accommodate the future, as well as the more traditional recording, verifying, and reporting of the past. This type of operation is usually referred to as the treasury function. The sort of activities that occur here are sometimes called **financial engineering.** These changes to the traditional ways in which companies, and to some extent governments, interact with financial markets are normally referred to as the trend to **securitization.**[14] This phenomenon includes the increasing ability for borrowers to deal directly with the capital markets, via markets such as the **euromarkets,** rather than through financial intermediaries and to be offered customized and tradable products. Previously they would have had to use standardized and untradable products. As the latter are provided by banks and other financial intermediaries, it has been argued that **disintermediation** is taking place

---

[14] This is true in the USA with the development of **asset-backed** and **mortgage-backed securities.** These in turn have spawned a number of derivatives such as **interest only** (IO) and **principal only** (PO) securities.

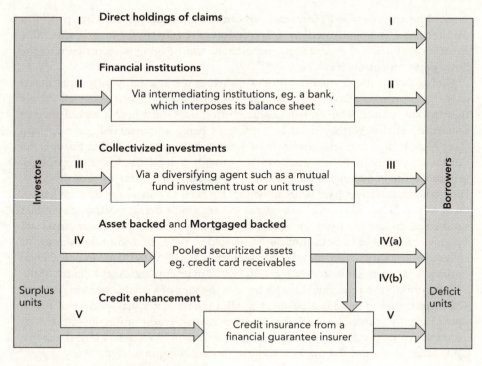

Figure 14. Methods of intermediation

in the international financial markets. In terms of the flow of funds between investors (surplus units) and borrowers (deficit units), the traditional function of institutions, as shown in Figure 14, is to superimpose their balance sheet between the two sides (II). This is being replaced by an increase in the direct holding of claims (I) or the use of collectivized investment vehicles, such as **mutual funds**, which in turn invest directly in financial claims (III). Another aspect of disintermediation has been the growing ability to undertake securitization of assets which were hitherto the domain of intermediaries (IV*a*). Examples are the issuance of **asset-backed securities** and **mortgage-backed securities**. Equally, the provision of specialized credit enhancement or credit insurance allows unusual assets to be packaged and sold as securities (V), some of which are asset-backed or mortgage-backed (IV*b*). Most commentators expect these trends, which have been evident for many years now, to continue in the future. Developments such as securitization and disintermediation have also led to different ways of looking at aspects of **corporate** financial structure, including such things as levels of **leverage**, and the **cost of capital**.

A major component of the international markets is the market for exchanging different **currencies**. This market for **foreign exchange** is the largest financial market in the world and operates non-stop twenty-four hours a day, seven days a week. The major traded currencies (approximately equal to the **Group of Ten** countries) are supplemented by markets for all freely available or **convertible** currencies. Trade and investment, speculation, and hedging all contribute to the flows between currencies.[15]

Globalization allows financial products such as credit arrangements and **mortgages** to be traded across geographical boundaries. For this to occur effectively these products must have certain characteristics: they must have a high degree of uniformity of design; they must be capable of being administered centrally; and there must be a strong relationship between user and provider. Within Europe, the **European Union** (EU) has attempted to provide a legal framework capable of generating the confidence levels necessary to sustain the trading of such products. For example, directives have been drawn up designed to encourage the suppliers of financial products and services to view the EU as a **single market**. Although product similarities do already exist, for example in savings products, UK **unit trusts** are roughly comparable to both **mutual funds** sold in the USA and **undertakings for collective investments in transferable securities** (UCITS) available in continental Europe. The intention is to create an integrated market-place. At the centre of the EU's contribution to the globalization trend is the idea of a single operating licence. This is intended to provide a passport to all member states, irrespective of which state originally granted the authority to act as a bank, **credit union**, investment, or insurance company. Regulation is thus now increasingly seen as a global activity, comparable to that of the markets and institutions being regulated.

It is, however, perhaps in the area of securities trading, rather than with savings products, that convergence in the world's financial markets is most striking. Following major restructuring and changes in practices (for instance, New York in 1975, the so-called '**May Day**' changes, and the **Big Bang** of 1986 in London), markets around the world have recognizable similarities. This has combined with the activities of institutional investors of the major economies to produce **asset allocation** strategies of a genuinely global nature. For example, most of the larger funds will own shares in foreign managed and owned **listed** and private companies. Such participation requires access to up-to-date information and familiarity with different trading, **settlement**, and regulatory systems.[16] Whilst some of these needs can be offset using devices like **American Depository Receipts** (ADRs), and portfolio management techniques like **programmed trading**, an understanding of the individual markets remains essential to successful investing; although important international differences remain, for example, in government debt issuing methods, and the various uses of **auctions**, and in the area of supervising activities such as contested company takeovers. The nature and style of the **Securities and Exchange**

[15] Surveys of the currency markets in the three major financial centres suggests that turnover in the mid-1990s was in excess of US$ 1.3 trillion a day.

[16] As markets have globalized, settlement procedures have become more uniform. For instance, the **account** system that used to operate on the London Stock Exchange has given way to rolling settlement. The time-scale between transaction date and settlement is also gradually being harmonized, with a two-or three-day cycle becoming the accepted international standard.

Commission operating in the USA can be contrasted sharply with that of the UK's **Securities and Investments Board**.

Despite these differences, the increasingly internationalized world of finance has witnessed a trend towards less, rather than more, regulation. The relaxation of rules governing what financial institutions can do, and the granting of additional powers to market players which has occurred in both the USA and the UK has combined to produce an atmosphere of **liberalization**. When mixed with advances in technology, the trends towards less regulation and more freedom to cross geographical boundaries have dramatically increased the pace and intensity with which funds are moved around markets. Such a condition has prompted concern about the underlying stability of international financial markets and how they respond to 'shocks' (i.e. unexpected events), what economists like to call **systemic risk**. Such concerns are seen as the preserve of central banks, and bodies like the **Bank for International Settlements** (BIS), and the **Group of Thirty** (G30). They are primarily interested in being able to manage the potential adverse effects of difficulties or failure within the new areas of financial dealings; for example, **off-balance sheet** activities which are perceived to have higher **interconnection risks**. In today's highly integrated financial markets, turbulence (such as a loss of confidence in a particular product, market, or institution) could lead to the repositioning of massive amounts of funds and currencies in a **flight to quality**. Such market inflows and outflows have the potential for threatening individual country stability, and ultimately undermining the integrity of the international financial system. What is at stake here are the three main elements of any financial system: **liquidity, efficiency** (or pricing), and confidence.

Whether it is equities or bonds, whether it is in New York, Tokyo, or London, securities trading is dominated by **institutional investors**. Although both American and Japanese individuals own directly more company shares and bonds than does the average European who prefers **fixed interest** investments, market sentiment in each of the major markets is set by institutional preferences. The asset allocation decisions of large institutional investors, where a relatively small group of like-minded investment managers make large changes to their portfolios, gives rise to concerns about the existence of a domino effect where problems in one market or sector may cascade into other areas. Examination of the 1987 Crash has led to the development of a **cascade theory** about the links between the stock market and the related derivatives markets. The growth of global markets has increased the concern among the different national regulators about global interconnection or **systemic risk**.

All financial markets are subject to some degree of self-prophecy, resulting from the similarities of the major institutional investors and the activities of market analysts or experts. Usually owned by banks and **brokers**, analysts supply information and opinion to market users. Investors and speculators respond to this **data** about the prospects for particular issues and markets. For example, investment managers make, buy, sell, or hold decisions about individual company shares based on an interpretation of the information supplied, as well as information that they themselves have collected. Such information is likely to concentrate on perform-ance indicators such as earnings, profits, dividends, and growth prospects. These **portfolio** choices are also made in relation to industry and securities market considerations as well as individual **market capitalization** or **company value**.

Examples of shocks to the financial system are clearly visible, including: the stock market 'crashes' of 1929 and 1987, **Herstatt Bank**, sterling's ejection from the **Exchange Rate Mechanism** (ERM) in 1991, and the **Barings** bank collapse of 1995. Such events often generate responses calling for specific regulatory action but it is difficult to see how the law can predict precisely the source of future difficulties. It is likely that the reshaping of the world's financial markets and players will continue, and at a rapid pace, thereby placing an increasing burden of respons-ibility on both the market supervisors, as well as the managers inside organizations that use and provide financial instruments, to be aware of the true nature of these activities.

It is with the above in mind that a key purpose of this Handbook is to provide an explanation of the often daunting, confusing, and multiple terminology used.[17] The international financial system has evolved enormously over the last half-century as has the whole field of finance. The size and scope of the entries is a reflection of the range and complexity involved. The purpose behind this overview has been to 'set the scene' for the non-specialist and place the entries within a wider, thematic context. We trust this will assist the general user in making use of this extensive reference source.

---

[17] One conclusion we came to is that there are often four or more terms for the same thing!

ABBREVIATIONS AND ACRONYMS

NB: The large majority, but not all, the abreviations included here are subsequently defined.

α		alpha
A, Aa, Aaa, AA, AAA		*See* Credit ratings
AA		always afloat
		against actuals
AB	Sweden	Aktiebolag (stock company)
ABA	USA	American Bankers' Association
		American Bar Association
ABC	USA	accrual or accretion bond
ABEDA		Arab Bank for Economic Development in Africa
ABI	UK	Association of British Insurers
	USA	American Bureau of Shipping
ABLA	USA	American Business Law Association
ABO	USA	accumulated benefit obligation
ABS		asset-banked security
ACA	UK	Associate of the Institute of Chartered Accountants
ACCA	UK	Associate of the Chartered Association of Certified Accountants
ACCESS		American and Canadian Connection for Efficient Securities Settlement
ACE	USA	American (Stock Exchange) Commodities Exchange
ACH	USA	Automated Clearing House
ACP		African, Caribbean, and Pacific (countries)
ACR		average claim rate
ACRS	USA	Accelerated Cost Recovery System
ACSA	USA	American Cotton Shippers' Association
ACT	UK	advance corporation tax
	UK	Association of Corporate Treasurers
A–D		advance–decline (indicator)
ADB	USA	adjusted debit balance
		Asian Development Bank
ADEF	France	Standard & Poor's Agence d'Évaluation Financière
ADIBOR		Abu Dhabi interbank offered rate
ADP		alternative delivery procedure
ADR	USA	American depository receipt
ADRS	USA	Asset Depreciation Range System
ADST	UK	Approved Deferred Share Trust
AE	USA	account executive, *see* registered representative

AFB	France	Association Française des Banques (French Banking Association)
AFBD	UK	Association of Futures Brokers and Dealers
AfDB; AFDB		African Development Bank
AFESD		Arabian Fund for Economic and Social Development
AFFM	Australia	Australian Financial Futures Market Limited
AFI	UK	Association for Futures Investments
AFIC		Asian Finance and Investment Corporation
AFMA	Australia	Australian Financial Markets Association
AFOF	UK	authorized futures and options fund
AFSB	France	Association Française des Sociétés de Bourse
AFTE	France	Association Française des Trésoriers d'Entreprise (French Association of Corporate Treasurers)
AFUDC		allowance for funds used during construction
AG	Germany	Aktiengesellschaft (stock company)
		Arabian Gulf (crude)
AH		Anno Hijra *see* Hijra years
A/H		Antwerp or Hamburg
AI		accrued interest
AIBD		Association of International Bond Dealers, now the International Securities Market Association
AIBOR		Amsterdam interbank offered rate
AICPA	USA	American Institute of Certified Public Accountants
AID	USA	Agency for International Development
AIDC	Australia	Australian Industries Development Corporation
AIM	Netherlands	Amsterdam Interprofessional Market
	UK	Alternative Investment Market
AIRS	Australia	Australian interest rate swaps (terms)
AIS		accrued interest scheme
AITC	UK	Association of Investment Trust Companies
AKA	Germany	Ausfuhrkredit GmbH
AKTB	Sweden	Aktiebolgaget (joint stock company)
AKV	Germany	Deutscher Auslandskassenverein AG
AL		average life
ALADI		Asociación Latino-Americana de Integración
ALCO		asset-liability management committee
ALFI	Luxembourg	Association Luxembourgeoise des Fonds d'Investissement (Luxembourg Fund Managers' Association)
ALMAC; ALMC		asset-liability management committee
ALPS		adjustable long-term puttable securities
AMA		asset management account
AMBAC	USA	American Municipal Bond Assurance Corporation
AMEX	USA	American Stock Exchange
AMFA	USA	American Managed Futures Association
AMPS	USA	auction market preferred stock
ANRPC		Association of Natural Rubber Producing Countries
ANSI	USA	American National Standards Institute

AOI	Australia	All Ordinaries Share Price Index
AOM	Australia	Australian Options Market
AON		all or none (order)
APCS	UK	Association of Payment Clearing Services
APB	USA	Accounting Principles Board
	UK	Audit Practice Board
APCIMS	UK	Association of Private Client Investment Managers and Stockbrokers
API	USA	American Petroleum Institute
APO		average price option, *see* Asian option
APR		annual percentage rate
APS	USA	auction preferred stock
APT		arbitrage pricing theory
	UK	Automated Pit Trading
APT+	UK	Automated Pit Trading Plus
APV		adjusted present value
Arb	USA	arbitrageur
ARBL	USA	assets repriced before liabilities
ARC	USA	adjustable rate consumer loan
ARCH		autoregressive conditional heteroscedasticity
ARCRU		Arab currency related unit
ARIEL	UK	Automated Real-Time Investments Exchange
ARIMA		autoregressive integrated *or* interactive moving average model
ARM	USA	adjustable rate mortgage
ARMA		autoregressive moving average model
ARMPS	USA	auction-rate market preferred stock
ARMS		autoregressive models
ARO		average rate option, *see* Asian option
ARP; ARPS	USA	adjustable rate preferred stock
ARR		accounting rate of return
ARTA		automatic reporting to tax authorities
ASA	USA	American Standards Association
	USA	American Soybean Association
ASAS	Netherlands	Amsterdam Security Account System
ASB	UK	Accounting Standards Board
ASC	Australia	Australian Securities Commission
ASCI	Netherlands	Act on the Supervision of Credit Institutions
ASCT	Australia	Australian Society of Corporate Treasurers
AsDB		Asian Development Bank
ASE	USA	American Stock Exchange
	Canada	Alberta Stock Exchange
ASEAN		Association of South East Asian Nations
ASPA	USA	American Soybean Processors' Association
ASPRINS	Australia	All Ordinaries Share Price Riskless Index Notes
ASRO		average spot rate option
		average strike rate option
AST		automated screen trading
ASTM		American Society for Testing Materials

ASTRO		average strike rate option
ASU		Asian Clearing Union
ASX	Australia	Australian Stock Exchange
ATDON- SHINC		any time day or night Sundays and holidays inclusive
ATI	Austria	Austrian Traded Index
ATIC	Italy	Associazione Tesorie Istituzione Creditize (Association of Bank Treasurers), *see* Milan interbank offered rate
ATK		aviation turbine kerosene
ATM		automated teller machine
		at the money
	Netherlands	Amsterdam Treasury Bond Market
ATP		aid trade provision
ATPC		Association of Tin Producing Countries
ATS		Automated Trading System
		automatic transfer service
ATX	Austria	Austrian Traded Index
AUS	Australia	Australian Stock Exchange
AUTIF	UK	Association of Unit Trusts and Investment Trusts
AVC	UK	additional voluntary contributions
AVG		asset value guarantee
β		beta
B, Ba, Baa, BB and BBB		*see* credit ratings
BA	USA	banker's acceptance
Back.		backwardation
BACS	UK	Bankers' Automated Clearing Services Limited
BAKred	Germany	Bundesaufsichtsamt für das Kreditwesen
BAN	USA	bond anticipation note
B&H		buy and hold
BAPEPAM	Indonesia	*see* Jakarta Stock Exchange
BATF		banker's acceptances tender facility
BAX		banker's acceptances
BBA	UK	British Bankers' Association
BBAIRS	UK	British Bankers' Association interest rate swap (terms)
BBF	Brazil	Bolsa Brasileira de Futuros
BBM	Brazil	Bolsa Brasileira de Mercedorios (Brazilian Merchantile Exchange)
BCG	USA	Boston Consulting Group (matrix), *see* Bostan matrix
BD		bank draft
		bills discontinued
B/D; B-D		broker-dealer
BDA		bank deposit agreement, *see* guaranteed investment contract
BDR		bearer depository receipt
BDT	France	billet de trésor
BE		bill of exchange
BECS		bearer eurodollar collateralized securities, *see* FLAGS
BEI	Banque	Européenne d'Investissement, *see* European Investment Bank

Belfox	Belgium	Belgian Futures and Options Exchange
BERD		Banque Européenne de Reconstruction et de Développement *see* European Bank for Reconstruction and Development
BERO	UK	bearer exchange rate option
BES	UK	business expansion scheme
BF		bought forward
		butterfly
BFCE	France	Banque Française du Commerce Extérieure
BFE	UK	Baltic Futures Exchange, *see* London Futures and Options Exchange (London Fox)
BFSR		bank financial strength, *see* credit ratings
B/H		Bordeaux/Hamburg
BHC		bank holding company
BIBOR	Bahrain	Bahrain interbank offered rate
	Belgium	Brussels interbank offered rate
BIC		Bank Investment Contract, *see* guaranteed investment contract
BIFFEX	UK	Baltic International Freight Futures Exchange
billion		thousand million (1,000,000,000)
BIMBO		buy-in and management buy-out
BIRD		Banque Internationale de Reconstruction et de Développement *see* International Bank for Reconstruction and Development
BIS		Bank for International Settlements
BL; B/L		bill of lading
BLEU	Belgium/ Luxembourg	Belgo-Luxembourg Economic Union
BLOX	UK	Block Order Exposure System
BM&F	Brazil	Blosa de Mercadoria e Futuros
BMBA	UK	British Merchant Bank and Securities House Association
BO		buyer's option
		butterfly
BOATS		Bunds-Obligations Assimables du Trésor securities
Bobl	Germany	medium-term interest rate future
BOC		Bank of China
BOE	UK	Bank of England
BOI	Italy	Bank of Italy
BOJ	Japan	Bank of Japan
BOLO		borrower's option, lender's option
BOLT	India	Bombay Stock Exchange On-line Trading (system)
BOLTS		bull oil-linked transactions
BOM		beginning of the month
BONUS		borrower's option for notes or underwritten standby
BOP		balance of payments
BOPM		binomial option pricing model
BOS		bond-over-stock option, *see* stock-over-bond warrant
BOSS	Germany	Börsen-Order-Service-System
BOT		balance of trade

		bought or purchased
		board of trustees
	Italy	Buono Ordinaro del Tesoro
BOTCC		Board of Trade Clearing Corporation
BOUNDS	USA	buy-right option unitary derivatives
BOVESPA	Brazil	Bolsa de Valores de Sâo Paulo
BP; BIP		basis point (0.01%)
BPC		bearer participation certificate
BPD		barrels per day
BPR		business process re-engineering
BPT	Italy	Buoni Pluriemali del Tesoro
BR		bills receivable
BRI		Banque de Reconciliation Internationale *see* Bank for International Settlements
BS		balance sheet
	UK	British Standard
BSC	UK	Building Societies Commission
BSE	India	Bombay Stock Exchange
BSOPM		Black–Scholes option pricing model
BTAN	France	Bons à Taux Annuel Normalisé
BTE	Italy	Buoni Tesoro Denominati in Euroscudi (Treasury bonds denominated in European currency units)
BTF		basis trade facility
BTP	Italy	Buoni del Tesoro Poliennali
BTU	UK	British Thermal Unit
Buba/BuBa	Germany	Bundesbank
Bubl	Germany	Bundesobligationen
Bunds	Germany	Bundesbonds (government bonds)
BURP	USA	book unreported profits
BV	Netherlands	Besloten Vennootschap (limited company)
BVRJ	Brazil	Bolsa de Valores do Rio de Janeiro (Rio de Janeiro Stock Exchange)
BW	USA	bid wanted
BX		box spread
C, Ca, Caa, CC and CCC		*see* credit ratings
CA		Chartered Accountant
CAC	Australia	Corporate Affairs Commission
	France	Compagnie des Agents de Change, *see* Société des Bourses Françaises
		Cotation Assistée en Continue
CAD		cash against documents (delivery)
		capital adequacy directive
CAF		currency adjustment factor
CAMEL		capital, assets, management, earnings, liquidity
CAMPS	USA	cumulative auction market preferred stock
C&F		cost and freight

C&I		cost and insurance
CANPR	Canada	Canadian prime rate
CANS	UK	Company Announcements Samizo
CAP		Common Agricultural Policy (European Union)
CAPM		Capital Asset Pricing Model
CAPS	USA	convertible adjustable preferred stock
	USA	capped index options
CAR		compound annual return
CARDS	USA	certificates of amortizing revolving debt securities
CARS	UK/USA	certificates of automobile receivables
		collateralized automobile receivables securities
CATS	USA	certificate of accrual on Treasury securities
CBA		cost–benefit analysis
CBCA	Canada	Canadian Business Corporations Act
CBD		cash before delivery
CBO	USA	collateralized bond obligation
CBOE	USA	Chicago Board Options Exchange
CBOT	USA	Chicago Board of Trade
CBRS	Canada	Canadian Bond Rating Service
CBT	USA	Chicago Board of Trade
CBV	France	Conseil des Bourses de Valeurs (Stock Exchange Council)
CCA	USA	Comex Clearing Association
	France	Compagnie des Commissionaires Agrées (commodity brokers' association)
	UK	current cost accounting
CCC	USA	Commodity Credit Corporation
CCCCCC (6 Cs)		capacity, capital, character, collateral, conditions, compliance
CCH	USA	Commerce Clearing House
CCIFP	France	Chambre de Compensation des Instruments Financiers de Paris
CCNS	UK	Commercial Company News Service
CCPO	UK	cumulative convertible participation preference ordinary shares
CCS		cross-currency swap
CCT		Common Customs Tariff, see Common External Tariff
	Italy	Certificati di Credito del Tesoro (a Cedola Variabile)
CD		certificate of deposit
CDA		controlled disbursement account
CDIC	Canada	Canadian Deposit Insurance Corporation
CDN	Canada	Canadian Dealing Network
	France	certificats de dépôts négotiables (transferable certificates of deposit)
C$		Canadian dollars
CEC	USA	Commodities Exchange Centre Inc.
	USA	Commodities Exchange Commission
CEDEL		Centrale de Livraison de Valeurs Mobilières
CEO		Chief Executive Officer

CEPS	USA	convertible exchangeable preferred stock
CET		Common External Tariff
CEV		constant elasticity of variance
CEW		Currency exchange warrant
CF		carried forward
		condor
CFA		Communauté Financière Africaine
CFC	USA	Chartered Financial Counsellor
		(United Nations) Common Fund for Commodities
CFD	UK	contract for differences
CFI		court of first instance
CFO		Chief Financial Officer
		cancel former order
CFP		capital fulcrum point
	USA	certified financial planner
		Communauté Financière Pacifique
CFTC	USA	Commodity Futures Trading Commission
CFX		credit for export
CGB		Canadian Government Bonds
CGBR		Central Government Borrowing Requirement
CGO	UK	Central Gilts Office
CGT		capital gains tax
CH		clearing house
CHAPS	UK	Clearing House Automated Payments System
CHIPS	USA	Clearing House Interbank Payments System
Cía	Spain	Compañía (company)
CIBOR	Denmark	Copenhagen interbank offered rate
Cie	France	Compagnie (company)
CIF		cost, insurance, freight
	USA	corporate income fund
CII	UK	Chartered Insurance Institute
CIMA	UK	Chartered Institute of Management Accountants
CIP		cash index participation
CIS		Commonwealth of Independent States (formerly the Soviet Union)
CISCO	UK	City Group for Smaller Companies
CLASS		Canadian London Automated Settlement Service
CLD		called
CLEO	USA	collateralized lease equipment obligations
CLOB		Central Limit Order Book
CLOU		currency-linked outperformance unit
CMB	USA	cash management bill
CME	USA	Chicago Mercantile Exchange
CMHC	Canada	Canadian Mortgage and Housing Corporation
CMMPS	USA	convertible money market preferred stock
CMO	USA	collateralized mortgage obligation
	UK	Central Moneymarkets Office (of the Bank of England)
CMP	USA	capital market preferred stock

CMS		constant maturity swap
CMT		constant maturity treasury (bond)
	France	Conseil du Marché à Terme
CMV		current market value
CN		credit note
CNAR		compound net annual return
CNMV	Spain	Comisión del Mercado de Valores, *see* Bolsa del Madrid (Madrid Stock Exchange)
CNS	USA	continuous net settlement
CO		cash order
		condor
CO.; Co.		company
COATS	Canada	Canadian Over-the-Counter Automated Trading System
COB		close of business
	France	Commission des Opérations de Bourse
COBRA		Capture of Bond Repost and Analysis
COCERAL		Committee for Trade in Cereals and Animal Feeds in the European Union
COD		cash on delivery
		collect on delivery
CODA		cash or deferred arrangement
COFACE	France	Compagnie Française pour l'Assurance du Commerce Extérieur
COFI	USA	cost of funds index
COFI swap	USA	cost of funds index swap
COGECA		General Committee for Agricultural Cooperation in the European Union
COINS	USA	continuously offered intermediate notes
COLTS	USA	continuously offered long-term securities
Comex	USA	New York Commodity Exchange
CONSOB	Italy	Commissione Nazionale per le Societá e la Borsa
Consol	UK	consolidated stock
COP		certificate of participation
COPIBOR	Denmark	Copenhagen interbank offered rate
COPS		covered option securities
		continuously offered payment rights
CORES	Japan	Computer-assisted Order Routing and Execution System
CORES-F	Japan	Computer-assisted Order Routing and Execution System for Futures
COSI	Denmark	Copenhagen Stock Exchange International
COTO		cash-or-title option
COUGARS; COUGRS	USA	certificates of government receivables
CP		commercial paper
CPA	USA	Certified Public Accountant
CPD	USA	Commissioner of Public Debt
CPFF		cost, plus a fixed fee
CPI	USA	consumer price index

CPN		coupon
CPO	Spain	Certificados de Participación Ordinarios
CPP		current purchasing power
CPR		conditional prepayment rate
CPS		commercial property schemes
CQS		Consolidated Quotation Service *see* tape
CR		current rate
CRB (Index)	USA	Commodities Research Bureau (Price Index)
CRD	USA	Central Registration Depository
CREIL		commercial real-estate index linked swap
CRIB		cross-indexed basis (swap), *see* differential swap
CROP	USA	Compliance Registered Option Principal, *see* Registered Option Principal
CRR	USA	contemporaneous reserve accounting
CRS	UK	Computer Readable Services
CRT		composite rate tax
CSCE	USA	(New York) Coffee, Sugar and Cocoa Exchange
CSDA		contractual settlement day accounting
CSE	USA	Cincinnati Stock Exchange
CSPI	Japan	corporate service price index
CTA		Commodity Trading Advisor
CTCI	USA	computer-to-computer interface
CTD		cheapest to deliver
CTE	Italy	Certificati di Credito del Tesoro Denominati in Euroscudi
CTO	Italy	Certificati del Tesoro con Opzione
CTR	Italy	Certificati del Tesoro Reali
CTS	Italy	Certificati di Credito del Tesoro a Sconto
CTT	UK	capital transfer tax
CUBES	USA	Coupons Under Book Entry Safekeeping
CULS	UK	convertible unsecured loan stock
CUPS		currency protected swap
CUSIP	USA	Committee on Uniform Securities Identification Procedures, *see* also CUSIP Number System
CV		convertible
		conversion/reversal
CVM	Brazil	Commissão de Valores Mobiliaros
CWO		cash with order
CXL		cancel
D		default, defaulted *see* credit ratings
DA		deposit account
		discretionary account
D/A		documents against acceptance
D&B	USA	Dun and Bradstreet
DARTS	USA	Dutch auction rate term securities
DATES	USA	daily adjustable tax exempt security
DAX	Germany	Deutsche Aktienindex (German stock index)
Dax	Germany	Deutsche Aktienindex

DB		double
DBRS	Canada	Dominion Bond Rating Service Limited
DCE		domestic credit expansion
DCF		discounted cash flow
DDA		demand deposit account
DDB	USA	double-declining-balance method, *see* depreciation
DDM		dividend discount model
D/E		debt–equity (ratio), *see* ratio analysis
DEAR	USA	daily earnings at risk, *see* Risk Metrics
DERV		diesel engine road vehicle
DG		diagonal spread
DGCCRF	France	Direction Générale de la Concurrence, de la Consommation et de la Répression des Fraudes
DI		divergence indicator
DIBOR	Ireland	Dublin interbank offered rate
DIDMCA	USA	Depository Institution Deregulation and Monetary Control Act
DIE	UK	Designated Investment Exchange
DIFF	USA	futures contract on short-term interest rate differentials traded on the Chicago Merchantile Exchange
diff		interest rate differential
DIN	Germany	Deutsche Industrie Norm
DINB	USA	Deposit Insurance National Bank
DINGO	Australia	discounted investment in negotiable government obligations
DIP	USA	debtor in possession (facility)
DIRF		differential interest rate fix
DJIA	USA	Dow-Jones Industrial Average
DJTA	USA	Dow-Jones Transportation Average
DJUA	USA	Dow-Jones Utility Average
DK, DKed		don't know (don't know the trade)
DKV	Germany	Deutscher Kassenverein AG
DM		Deutschmarks
		discounted margin
DN		debit or debit note
		delta neutral (position)
DNR		do not reduce
dollar repo		dollar repurchase agreement
DOT	USA	Designated Order Turnaround (system)
D/P		documents against payment
DPM	USA	Designated Primary Market-maker
DPP	USA	direct participation program
DRS		delayed rate setting
DRT		disregard tape
DS		days after sight
		diagonal straddle
DSE	Ireland	Dublin Stock Exchange
DSO		days sales outstanding, *see* ageing schedule
DSR		debt service ratio

DTA		double taxation agreement
DTB	Germany	Deutsche Terminbörse GmbH
DTC	USA	depository transfer checks
	USA	Depository Trust Company
DTI	UK	Department of Trade and Industry
DTR		double taxation relief
DUNS	USA	Data Universal Numbering System
DVP		delivery versus (or against) payment
DWZ	Germany	Deutsche Wertpapierdaten-Zentrale GmbH
EAFE		Europe, Asia, and the Far East
E&O; E&OE		errors and omissions; errors and omissions excepted
EAR		earnings at risk, *see* value at risk
EASD		European Association of Securities Dealers
EASDAQ		European Association of Securities Dealers Automated Quotations
EASy	UK	Exchange Access System
EAT		earnings after tax
EBA		Ecu Banking Association
EBIT		earnings before interest and taxes
EBITDA		earning, before interest, tax, depreciation, and amortization
EBRD		European Bank for Reconstruction and Development
EBS	Switzerland	Elektronische Börse Schweiz
EBT		earnings before taxes
EC		European Community
ECCOFEX		European Commission Co-ordinating Committee on Options and Futures Exchanges
ECLA		Economic Commission for Latin America
ECM	USA	Emerging Companies Marketplace, *see* American Stock Exchange
ECP		eurocommercial paper
ECR		earnings credit rate
ECSC		European Coal and Steel Community
ECU		European Currency Unit
EDC	Canada	Export Development Corporation
EDF		European Development Fund
EDGAR	USA	Electronic Data Gathering And Retrieval
EDI		electronic data interchange
EDPC		enhanced derivative product company
EDR		European depository receipt
EDS	UK	Electronic Data Services
EDSP		exchange delivery settlement price
EDTC		electronic depository transfer cheque
EEA		European Economic Area
		Exchange Equalization Account
EEC		European Economic Community
EFA		electricity forward agreement
EFCC	Netherlands	European Futures Clearing Corporation

EFF		extended finance facility
EFFAS		European Federation of Financial Analyst Societies
EFFP		exchange of futures for physical
EFIC	Australia	Export Finance and Insurance Corporation
EFP		exchange for physical
EFPOS		electronic funds at point of sale
EFT		electronic funds transfer
EFTA		European Free Trade Association
EFTPOS		electronic funds transfer at point of sale
EFTS		electronic funds transfer system
EHS	Germany	Electronisches Handels-system, *see* Electronic Trading System
EIB		European Investment Bank
EIF		European Investment Fund
EIP		Equity Index Participation
ELN		equity-linked notes
EMA		European Monetary Agreement
EMCF		European Monetary Cooperation Fund
EME		European Mercantile Exchange
EMFA		European Managed Futures Association
EMH		efficient markets hypothesis
EMI		European Monetary Institute
EMMPS	USA	exchangeable money market preferred stock
EMP		end of month payment
EMS		European Monetary System
EMTN		euro medium-term note
EMU		European Monetary Union
EOA		effective on or about
EOC		economic order quantity
EOE	Netherlands	European Options Exchange
EOM		end of the month
EOQ		economic order quantity
EOS		enter open stop
EPIC	UK	Exchange Price Information Computer
		equity, participation indexed certificate
EPN		equity participation note
EPR		earnings–price ratio, *see* price–earnings multiple
EPS; eps		earnings per share
EPU		European Payments Union
ERA		exchange rate agreement
		extension refinancing agreement
ERDF		European Regional Development Fund
ERI	UK	Exchange Rate Index
ERISA	USA	Employee Retirement Income Security Act
ERM		Exchange Rate Mechanism
ESAF		Enhanced Structural Adjustment Facility
ESAP		economic structural adjustment programme
ESCB		European System of Central Banks

ESF		Exchange Stabilization Fund
ESOP	USA	Employee Stock Ownership Plan
ETC		electronic trade confirmation
	USA	equipment trust certificate
ETF		electronic transfer of funds
ETLT		equal to, or less than
ETM	USA	escrowed to maturity
ETR		estimated total return
ETS		electronic trading system
EU		European Union
EUA		European Unit of Account
EUCLID 90		*see* Euroclear
EURATOM		European Atomic Energy Community
Eximbank	USA	Export-Import Bank
EXTRA		export tender risk avoidance
EYES		equily yield-enhanced security
FABC	USA	Form for Analyzing Bank Capital
FAC		fast as can
FALCONS	Netherlands	fixed-term agreements for long-term call options on Netherlands securities
FAN		fixed assurance note
FANMAC	Australia	First Australia Mortgage Acceptance Corporation
Fannie Mae	USA	Federal National Mortgage Association
FAO		Food and Agricultural Organisation
FAS#	USA	Financial Accounting Standard (number)
FASB	USA	Financial Accounting Standards Board
FASCONS	Netherlands	fixed-term agreements for short-term call options on Netherlands securities
FAST	Australia	Flexible Accelerated Security Transfer, See Stock Exchange Automated Trading System (SEATS)
	UK	Fast Automated Screen Trading
FAZ	Germany	Frankfurter Allgemeine Zeitung (index)
FCA	UK	Fellow of the Institute of Chartered Accountants
	USA	functional cost analysis
FCC	USA	Federal Communications Commission
	France	fonds commun de créances
FCCA	UK	Fellow of the Chartered Association of Certified Accountants
FCIA	USA	Foreign Credit Insurance Association
FCII	UK	Fellow of the Chartered Insurance Institute
FCM	USA	futures commission merchant
FCOJ; fcoj		frozen concentrated orange juice
FCP		fonds commun de placement
FDIC	USA	Federal Deposit Insurance Corporation
FECBBA	UK	Foreign Exchange Committee of the British Bankers' Association
FECDBA	UK	Foreign Exchange and Currency Deposit Brokers Association
Fed	USA	Federal Reserve

FEDI		financial electronic data interchange
FEE		Fédération des Experts Comptables Européens
FELABAN		Federación Latino-Americano de Bancos
FERARI		floating eurodollar repackaged assets of the Republic of Italy
FERC	USA	Federal Energy Regulatory Commission
FERM		foreign exchange risk management
FET	USA	Federal Excise Tax
FF	USA	federal funds
FFCS	USA	Federal Farm Credit System
FGI		Financial guarantee insurance
FGIC	USA	Financial Guarantee Insurance Corporation
FHA	USA	Federal Housing Association
	UK	Finance Houses Association
FHEX		Fridays and holidays excluded
FHLB	USA	Federal Home Loan Banks
FHLBB	USA	Federal Home Loan Bank Board
FHLMC	USA	Federal Home Loan Mortgage Corporation
FIA	USA	Futures Industry Association
FIBOR	Germany	Frankfurt interbank offered rate
FIBV		Fédération Internationale des Bourses de Valeurs (International Federation of Stock Exchanges)
FICB	USA	Federal Intermediate Credit Bank
FID	UK	foreign income dividend
FIFO		first in, first out (stock or inventory valuation method)
FIGS	USA	future income and growth securities, *see* zero-coupon convertible
FII	UK	franked investment income
FIMBRA	UK	Financial Intermediaries, Managers and Brokers Regulatory Association, *see* Personal Investment Authority
FIN		full investment note
FINEX	USA	New York Financial Exchange, part of the New York Cotton Exchange
FIPS		foreign interest payment securities
FIRREA	USA	Financial Institutions Reform, Recovery and Enforcement Act of 1989
FIRS		Fonds d'Intervention et de Régulation du Marché du Sucre
FIRST	USA	fixed floating interest rate short tranche, *see also* collateralized mortgage obligation
		fixed interest rate substitute transaction
FIV		forward intrinsic value (of an option)
fixed rate CD		fixed rate certificate of deposit
FLAGS	UK	*see* flags
FLB	USA	Federal Land Bank
FLI	Australia	Fifty Leaders Index
FMA	France	France MATIF Automatique
FNMA	USA	Federal National Mortgage Association
FO		futures *v.* options
FOB		free on board

FOC		free of charges
FOCUS	USA	Financial and Operations Combined Uniform Single (report)
FOF	UK	futures and options funds
FOK		fill or kill (order)
FOM	Finland	Finnish Options Market
FOMC	USA	Federal Open Market Committee
Footsie	UK	FT-SE 100 Index
FOR		free on rail
Forex		foreign exchange
FOTPI		future obligation to pay interest
FOTRA	UK	free of tax to residents abroad
FOX	Finland	Finnish Options Index
	UK	forward with optional exit, *see* breakforward
	UK	London Commodity Futures and Options Exchange
FP		fully paid
FPR		fixed price reoffer
FRA		forward rate agreement
FRABBA	UK	Forward Rate Agreement British Bankers' Association (terms)
FRAPS	USA	fixed rate auction preferred stock
FRB	USA	Federal Reserve Bank
	USA	Federal Reserve Board
FRC	UK	Financial Reporting Council
FRCD		floating rate certificate of deposit
FRCMO	USA	floating rate collateralized mortgage obligation
FRD	USA	Federal Reserve District
FRED	UK	Financial Reporting Exposure Draft
Freddie Mac	USA	Federal Home Loan Mortgage Corporation
FREIT	USA	finite life real-estate investment trust
FRENDS		floating rate enhanced debt security
FRMCO	USA	floating rate collateralized mortgage obligation, *see* collateralized mortgage obligation
FRN		floating rate note
FRRP	UK	Financial Reporting Review Panel
FRS	UK	Financial Reporting Standard
	USA	Federal Reserve System
FRSB	UK	Financial Reporting Standards Board
FS		final settlement
FSA		forward switching agreement
		forward spread agreement
	UK	Financial Services Act, 1986
	SA	Financial Services Industry Association
FSAVC	UK	free-standing additional voluntary contributions
FSB	UK	final salary basis
FSBR	UK	financial statement and budget report
FSC	USA	foreign sales corporation
FSLIC	USA	Federal Savings and Loan Insurance Corporation
FTA	Netherlands	Financiel Termijnmarkt Amsterdam (Amsterdam Financial Futures Market)

FTC	USA	Federal Trade Commission
FTP		full two-way payment
FT-SE	UK	Financial Times-Stock Exchange (index)
FUTOP	Denmark	Garantifonden for Danske Optioner og Futures, *see* Guarantee Fund for Danish Options and Futures
FV		future value
FVO		for valuation only, *see* for your information
FX		foreign exchange
FXA		forward exchange agreement
FY		financial *or* fiscal year
FYE		financial *or* fiscal year-end
FYI		for your information
GAAP	USA	Generally Accepted Accounting Principles
GAAS	USA	Generally Accepted Auditing Standards
GAB		General Agreement to Borrow
GAFTA	UK	Grain and Feed Trade Association, *see* London Futures and Options Exchange
GAINS	USA	growth and income securities, *see* zero-coupon convertible
GAN	USA	grant anticipation note
GAO	USA	General Accounting Office
GARCH		generalized autoregressive conditional heteroscedasticity (model)
GASB	USA	Governmental Accounting Standards Board
GATS		General Agreement on Trade in Services
GATT		General Agreement on Tariffs and Trade
GD		good for the day (type of order)
GDP		gross domestic product
GDR		global depository receipt
GDS		global depository stock or share
GE		Germany
GECU		geared equity capital unit
GEM	USA	growing equity mortgage
GEMM	UK	gilt-edged market-maker
GEMMA	UK	Gilt-Edged Market-Makers' Association
GFOF	UK	geared futures and options fund
GIC		guaranteed investment contract
Ginnie Mae	USA	Government National Mortgage Association
GLMC		general ledger multi-currency (system)
GLOBEX		*see* Reuters
GmbH	Germany	Gesellschaft mit beschränker Haftung (limited liability company)
GMC	USA	guaranteed mortgage certificate
GNF		global note facility
GNIF		global note issuance facility
GNMA	USA	Government National Mortgage Association
GNP		gross national product
GO	USA	general obligation bond

GOFFEX	Germany	German Options and Financial Futures Exchange, *see* Deutsche Terminbörse GmbH
GOFRA		gold forward rate agreement
GOVPX	USA	Government (securities) Pricing Information System
GPM	USA	graduated payments mortgage
		gross processing margin
GRA		guaranteed refinancing agreement
GRIPS		guaranteed return index participation securities
GROI		guaranteed return on investment certificate
GRS		guaranteed return structures
GSCI	USA	Goldman Sachs Commodity Index
GT		gut (spread)
GTC		good till cancelled
GTM		good this month
GTR		good till revoked
GTW		good this week
GUN		grantor underwritten note
G3		Group of Three
G5		Group of Five
G6		Group of Six
G7		Group of Seven
G10		Group of Ten
G15		Group of Fifteen
G24		Group of Twenty-four
G30		Group of Thirty
H		high (of time series)
		higher (credit rating within a rating category)
H1		first half
H2		second half
HELIBOR	Finland	Helsinki interbank offered rate
HHI	USA	Herfindahl–Herschman index
HIBOR; HKIBOR	Hong Kong	Hong Kong interbank offered rate
HKCE	Hong Kong	Hong Kong Commodities Exchange
HKFE	Hong Kong	Hong Kong Futures Exchange
HKSE		Hong Kong Stock Exchange
HLT		highly leveraged transaction
HMMC	Finland	Helsinki Money Market Centre
HOPM		higher of proceeds or market
HP		hire purchase
HR		human resources
HRM		human resources management
HS		horizontal straggle
HSE	Finland	Helsinki Stock Exchange
HSI	Hong Kong	Hang Seng Index
HUD	USA	Department of Housing and Urban Development
HY		Hijra years

HZ		horizontal (spread)
IAA	Brazil	Instituto do Azúcar e do Alcool
IACS		International Association of Classification Societies
IADB		Inter-American Development Bank
IAPC		International Auditing Practices Committee
IAR		index-amortizing rate (swap)
IAS		International Accounting Standards
IASC		International Accounting Standards Committee
IB		iron butterfly
IBAA	USA	Independent Bankers' Association of America
IBBR		interbank bid rate
IBC	Brazil	Instituto Brasiliero de Café
IBEC		International Bank for Economic Cooperation
IBEL	UK	interest bearing eligible liabilities
IBES	USA	institutional brokers' estimate system
IBF	USA	international banking facility
IBIS	Germany	Integriertes Borsenhandels-und Informations-System
	Germany	Interbanken Information System
IBMBR		interbank market bid rate
IBNR		incurred but not yet reported
IBRD		International Bank for Reconstruction and Development
IC		investment certificate
ICA	UK	Institute of Chartered Accountants
ICC	USA	Interstate Commerce Commission
	USA	Intermarket Clearing Corporation
		International Chamber of Commerce
ICCH	UK	International Commodities Clearing House
ICCO		International Cocoa Organization
ICDA		International Certificate of Deposit Association
ICE		inverted curve enhancement
ICERC		Inter-Agency Country Exposure Review Committee
ICMA	UK/USA	Institute of Cost and Management Accountants
ICO		International Coffee Organization
ICON		indexed currency option note
ICS		International Chamber of Shipping
ICSID		International Center for the Settlement of Investment Disputes
IDA		International Development Association
IDB	USA	industrial development bond
	UK	inter-dealer broker
IDR		international depository receipt
IEA		International Energy Agency
IET	USA	Interest Equalization Tax
IFA	USA	independent financial adviser
IFC		International Finance Corporation
IFD	UK	Inspector of Foreign Dividends
IFMA	UK	Institutional Fund Managers Association

IFO/ifo		in favour of
IFOX	Ireland	Irish Futures and Options Exchange
IFS		international financial statistics
IFSC	Ireland	International Financial Services Centre
IGLU		indexed growth-linked unit
IHT	UK	inheritance tax
IIB		international instrument bank, *see* investment bank
IIC		Inter-American Investment Corporation
IIF		International Institute of Finance
IMF		International Monetary Fund
IMI	USA	International Market Index
IML	Luxembourg	Institut Monétaire Luxembourgeoise
IMM	USA	International Monetary Market (part of the Chicago Mercantile Exchange)
IMO		International Maritime Organization
IMRO	UK	Investment Management Regulatory Organisation
Inc.	USA	incorporated
INRO		International Natural Rubber Organization
INS	UK	Institutional Net Settlement (service)
INSEE	France	Institut National de la Statistique et des Études Économiques
INSTINET	USA	Institutional Networks Corporation
INTEX	Bermuda	International Futures Exchange
IO	USA	interest only STRIP (stripped mortgage backed security)
IOC		immediate or cancel (order)
IOM	USA	Index and Options Market
IO/PO	USA	interest only/principal only securities
IOSCO		International Organization of Securities Commissions
IOU		I owe you
IP		Institute of Petroleum
IPA		issuing and paying agent
IPC	UK	Investor Protection Committee
IPD	UK	Investment Property Databank
IPE	UK	International Petroleum Exchange
IPMA		International Primary Markets Association
IPO	USA	initial public offering
IPS		indexed principal swap
IR	UK	Inland Revenue
IRA	USA	Individual Retirement Account
IRB	USA	industrial revenue bond
IRC		interest rate collar
	USA	Internal Revenue Code
IRG		interest rate guarantees
IRI	Italy	Istituto per la Ricostruzione Industriale
IRN		increasing rate note
IRO		interest rate option
IRP		instantly repackaged perpetual
IRPT		interest rate parity theory (of exchange rates)
IRR		internal rate of return

		implied repurchase rate
IRRM		interest rate risk management
IRS		interest rate swap
	USA	Internal Revenue Service
IS		inter-commodity spread
ISBN		International Standard Book Number
ISCC		International Securities Clearing Corporation
ISD		implied standard deviation, *see* implied volatility
ISDA		International Swaps and Derivatives Association
ISE	UK	International Stock Exchange in London, *see* London Stock Exchange
	Turkey	Istanbul Stock Exchange
ISIN		International Security Identification Number
ISLA		International Stock Lenders' Association
ISMA		International Securities Markets Association
ISO		International Organization for Standardization
		International Standards Organization
ISRO	UK	International Securities Regulatory Organization, *see* Securities and Futures Authority
ISSN		International Standard Serial Number
IT	UK	investment trust
ITC	USA	investment tax credit
ITF		interest to follow
ITIC	China	International Trust and Investment Corporation
ITM		in the money (option)
ITS	USA	Intermarket Trading System
IV		implied volatility
IWA		International Wheat Agreement
IWC		International Wheat Council
JA		joint account
JBRI	Japan	Japan Bond Research Institute
JCR	Japan	Japan Credit Rating Agency Limited
JDB	Japan	Japan Development Bank
JEC	UK	Joint Exchanges Committee
Jeep	USA	graduated payment mortgage
JGB	Japan	Japanese Government Bond
JR		jelly roll
JR; Jr		junior
JSC	UK	Joint Standing Committee (of banks and brokers)
JSCC	Japan	Japan Securities Clearing Corporation
JSE	South Africa	Johannesburg Stock Exchange
	Indonesia	Jakarta Stock Exchange
K		kilo *or* thousand
KCBT	USA	Kansas City Board of Trade
KD		Kuwaiti dinar
KfW	Germany	Kreditanstalt für Wiederaufbau

KIBOR	Kuwait	Kuwait interbank offered rate
KIO	Kuwait	Kuwait Investment Office
KISS	Germany	Kurs-Informations-Service-System
KK	Japan	kabushiki kaisha (limited company)
KLCE	Malaysia	Kuala Lumpur Commodity Exchange
KLOFFE	Malaysia	Kuala Lumpur Options and Financial Futures Exchange
KLSE	Malaysia	Kuala Lumpur Stock Exchange
KSE	Korea	Korea Stock Exchange
KYC	USA	know your customer (rule)
L		low (of time series)
		lower (credit rating within a rating category)
LAB	UK	local authority bond
LABS	USA	liquid asset-backed securities index
LACMI		Latin American Capital Markets Institute
LAUTRO	UK	Life Assurance and Unit Trust Regulatory Organization
LBI 100		London and Bishopsgate 100 index
LBO		leveraged buy-out
L/C		letter of credit
LCAC	UK	Listed Companies Advisory Committee
LCE	UK	London Commodity Exchange
LDC		less developed country
LCH	UK	London Clearing House
LCL		lower control limit
LCM		lower of cost or market
LDFRA		long-dated forward rate agreement
LDMA	UK	London Discount Market Association
LDP	UK	London daily prices
LDT	UK	licensed deposit taker
		leveraged derivatives transaction
LEAPS	USA	long-term equity anticipation security
LED		LIBOR eurodollar spread
LEPO		low exercise price option
LHS		left-hand side
LIBID		London interbank bid rate
LIBO; LIBOR		London interbank offered rate
LICOM	UK	London interbank currency options market
LIFFE	UK	London International Financial Futures and Options Exchange
LIFO		last in, first out (stock or inventory valuation method)
LIMEAN		London interbank mean rate
LIONS	Netherlands	leveraged income obligations via new shares
	USA	Lehman investment opportunity notes
LIVES		latest investment vehicles for ex-warrant swaps
LME	UK	London Metal Exchange
LOB	USA	lease obligation bond
LOBO		lender's option, borrower's option
LOC; L/C		letter of credit

LOCM		lower of cost or market
loco		location
LOMI		letter of moral intent
LOTS	Canada	Limit Order Trading System
	UK	LIFFE Order Transit System
LP	USA	limited partnership
LQS	UK	large quote size
LRR	USA	lagged reserve requirement, *see* contemporaneous reserve accounting
LSE	UK	London Stock Exchange
	Portugal	Lisbon Stock Exchange
LTD., Ltd.		limited company
LTFX		long-term foreign exchange
LTGIS		long-term gap income sensitivity
LTOM	UK	London Traded Options Market, *see* London Financial Futures and Options Exchange
LTP		limited two-way payments, *see* walk away clause
LTPR	Japan	long-term prime rate, *see* bank debenture
LTV		loan to value
LUXIBOR	Luxembourg	Luxembourg interbank offered rate
LYONS	USA	liquid yield option notes securities, *see* zero coupon convertible bond
M	USA	a thousand
M0; M1; M2; M3; M4; M5		money supply series, *see* money supply
MAE		mean absolute error
M&A		mergers and acquisitions
M&L	USA	matched and lost
MAPS		maturity adjustable preferred stock
MARPS	USA	market auction rate preferred stock
MATIF	France	Marché à Terme International de France
MBA		Master of Business Administration
MBI		management buy-in
MBIA	USA	Municipal Bond Insurance Corporation
MBB		mortgage-backed bond
MBO		management buy-out
MBS		mortgage-backed security
MCA		Monetary Compensatory Account
M-CATS	USA	municipal certificates of accrual on tax-exempt securities, *see* certificates of accrual on treasury securities
MCSE	Russia	Moscow Central Securities Exchange, *see* Russian exchanges
MCT	UK	mainstream corporation tax
MD		months after date
		managing director, *see* chief executive officer
ME	Canada	Montreal Exchange
MECS		marketable eurodollar collateralized securities
MEFF	Spain	Mercado Español de Futuros Financieros

Merc	USA	Chicago Mercantile Exchange
MERIT		Managed Exchange Rate Insurance Technique
MESA		mutual ECU settlement account
MFN	USA	most favoured nation
MFTA	USA	Managed Futures Trade Association
MIB	Italy	Milano Indice di Borsa
MIBOR	Italy	Milan interbank offered rate
	Spain	Madrid interbank offered rate
MICEX	Russia	Moscow International Currency Exchange, *see* Russian exchanges
MICR		magnetic ink character recognition
MidAm	USA	MidAmerica Stock Exchange
MID	Italy	Mercato Interbancario dei Depositi, *see* interbank market
MIDAS	Germany	Market-Maker Information and Trading System
MIF	Italy	Mercato Italiano dei Futures
MIFE	Philippines	Manila International Futures Exchange
MIG#	USA	Moody's Investment Grade (number)
MIGA		Multilateral Investment Guarantee Agency
mille		thousandth, i.e. 0.1%
milliard		thousand million; a.k.a. billion
million		1,000,000
MIOR	Italy	Milan interbank offered rate
MIP		monthly investment plan
		marine insurance policy
		maximum investment plan
MIRAS	UK	mortgage interest relief at source
MIS	USA	Moody's Investors Service
MISE	Russia	Moscow International Stock Exchange, *see* Russian exchanges
MIT		market if touched
	USA	municipal investment trust
MITT		market index target term security, *see* equity-linked note
MITI	Japan	Ministry of International Trade and Industry
MJDS		multi-jurisdictional disclosure system
MLA	UK	mandatory liquid assets, *see* reserve requirements
MLP	USA	master limited partnership
MLR	UK	minimum lending rate
MM	USA	million
		Modigliani–Miller hypothesis
MMC	UK	Monopolies and Mergers Commission
MMDA	USA	money market deposit account
MMDR	USA	money market deposit rate
MMI	USA	Major Market Index
MMMF	USA	money market mutual fund
MMP	USA	money market preferred (stock)
MNC		multinational company, *see* transnational corporation
MNE		multinational enterprise, *see* transnational corporation

MOB	USA	municipal over bond (spread)
MOC		market-on-close order
MOF	Japan	Ministry of Finance
		multi-option facility
MOFERT	China	Ministry of Foreign Economic Relations and Trade
MOFF		multi-option financing facility
MONEP	France	Marché des Options Négociables de Paris
Moody's	USA	Moody's Investors Service
MOTO	USA	mortgage over Treasury option
MPC	USA	mortgage participation certificate
MPL		maximum publication level
MPT		modern portfolio theory
MQS	UK	minimum quote size
MSB	USA	Mutual Savings Bank
MSCI	USA	Morgan Stanley Capital International (indices)
MSE	USA	Midwest Stock Exchange
	Australia	Melbourne Stock Exchange
	Philippines	Manila Stock Exchange
MSP		matched sale–purchase (agreement)
MSRB	USA	Municipal Securities Rulemaking Board
MSS	UK	Maximum Stock Exchange Automated Quotations Execution Facility Size
MSVR		Mandatory Securities Valuation Reserve
MTC		Markets and Trading Commission
MTFA		medium-term financial assistance
MTN		medium-term note
MTTCD		multi-tranche tap certificate of deposit
MTTN		multi-tranche tap note
MVN	France	Marché des Valeurs Nouvelles
MVP		minimum variance portfolio
NA	USA	National Association (federally chartered bank)
NACHA	USA	National Automated Clearing House Association
NACT	USA	National Association of Corporate Treasurers
NAFTA		North American Free Trade Area
NAPF	UK	National Association of Pension Funds
NAPM	USA	National Association of Purchasing Managers
NASD	USA	National Association of Securities Dealers Inc.
NASDAQ	USA	National Association of Securities Dealers Automated Quotations system
NASDIM	USA	National Association of Securities Dealers and Investment Managers
NAV		net asset value
NBS	USA	National Bureau of Standards
NBV		net book value, *see* ratio analysis
NC		no charge
NCCMA	USA	National Corporate Cash Management Association
NCI		New Community Instrument

NCSC	Australia	National Companies and Securities Commission, *see* Australian Securities Commission
NCV		no commercial value
NDP		net domestic product
NEDC (Neddy)	UK	National Economic Development Council
NEMS	USA	National Exchange Market System
NFA	USA	National Futures Association
NGO		non-governmental organization
NH		not held
NIB		Nordic Investment Bank
NIBOR	USA	New York interbank offered rate
		Nassau interbank offered rate
NIC		newly industrialized country
NIE		newly industrialized economy
NIF		note issuance facility
NII		net interest income
Nikkei	Japan	equity index, *see* Nikkei 225 Index
NIM		net interest margin
NINOW	USA	non-interest bearing negotiable order of withdrawal, *see* negotiable order of withdrawal
NIP		normal investment practice
NIS	Japan	Nippon Investors Service Inc.
NIT		negative income tax
NL	USA	no load (on a mutual fund)
		no liability
NLB		Nikkei-linked bond
NMMC	Australia	National Mortgage Market Corporation
NMS	USA	National Market System
	UK	normal market size
N/N		not to be noted (on a banker's acceptance/bill of exchange)
NNP		net national product
NOB	Norway	Norwegian Options Market, *see* Oslo Stock Exchange
	USA	note over bond (spread)
NOW	USA	negotiable order of withdrawal
NP		no protest
N/P		notes payable
NPA	USA	non-performing assets
NPL	USA	non-performing loans
NPV		net present value
	USA	no-par value (of common stock)
NQB	USA	National Quotations Bureau
		no qualified bidders
NQS	UK	normal quote size
NR		not rated
NRV		net realizable value
NSC	UK	National Savings Certificate
NSCC	USA	National Securities Clearing Corporation

NSE	Japan	Nagoya Stock Exchange
NSF		not sufficient funds
NSJ	USA	non-sticky jump bond
NSTS	USA	National Securities Trading System
NTA	Japan	National Taxation Authority
		net tangible assets
NTM		near the money (option)
NTP		not to press (for delivery)
NTU	USA	normal trading unit, see round lot
NV	Netherlands	Naamloze Vennootschap (limited company)
NYBOR	USA	New York interbank offered rate
NYCE	USA	New York Cotton Exchange
NYCSCE	USA	New York Coffee, Sugar and Cocoa Exchange
NYCTN, CA	USA	New York Cotton Exchange, Citrus Associates
NYFCC	USA	New York Futures Clearing Corporation
NYFE	USA	New York Futures Exchange
NYMEX	USA	New York Mercantile Exchange
NYSE	USA	New York Stock Exchange
NZFOE	New Zealand	New Zealand Futures and Options Exchange
OAPEC		Organization of Arab Petroleum Exporting Countries
OAS		option-adjusted spread
OAT	France	obligations assimilables du Trésor
OB		or better
OBF		offshore banking facility
OBM	USA	Office of Budget and Management
OBO		order book official
OBS		off-balance sheet
OBU		offshore banking unit
OBV		on-balance volume
OCC	USA	Office of the Comptroller of the Currency
	USA	Options Clearing Corporation
OCO		one cancels the other (order)
OD		overdrawn
ODFI		originating depository financial institution
ODR	Japan	official discount rate
OECD		Organization for Economic Cooperation and Development
OEIC	EU; UK	open-ended investment company
OEX	USA	S&P 100 stock index option
OFT	UK	Office of Fair Trading
OID		original issue discount
OIP		original issue premium
OLEM	USA	other loans especially mentioned
OLS		ordinary least squares
OM; OML	Sweden	Optionsmarklarna (Swedish Options and Futures Market)
OMB	USA	Office of Management and Budget
OMLX	UK	London Securities and Derivatives Exchange, see OM London
OMO		open market operations

OMX	Sweden	Index of the Stockholm Stock Exchange
OOB		open order book
OPALS	USA	optimized portfolios as listed securities
OPCVM	France	Organismes de Placement Commun en Valeurs Mobilières
OPD	USA	opening delayed
OPEC		Organization of Petroleum Exporting Countries
open repo (RP)		open repurchase agreement
OPIC		Overseas Private Investment Corporation
OPL		overall premium limit
OPM		option pricing model
		other people's money
OPRA		Options Price Reporting Authority
OREO	USA	other real estate owned
ORT	France	obligations renouvelables du Trésor
OSC	Canada	Ontario Securities Commission
OSE	Japan	Osaka Securities Exchange
	Norway	Oslo Stock Exchange
OSP		official selling price
OTC		over the counter
OTM		out of the money (option)
OTOB	Austria	Österreichische Termin-und-Optionenbörse
OTS	USA	Office of Thrift Supervision
OTT		over-the-top option *or* warrant
OW	USA	offer wanted (on a particular security)
PA		power of attorney
	USA	Public Accountant
PAC		put and call (options)
	USA	planned amortized class bond
P&L		profit and loss account (or statement)
P&S		purchase and sale statement
PARR		purchased accelerated recovery right
PART		participating interest rate agreement
PAYE		pay (tax) as you earn
PBGC	USA	Pension Benefit Guarantee Corporation
PBIT		profit before interest and taxes, *see* earnings before interest and taxes
PBOC	China	People's Bank of China
PBOT	USA	Philadelphia Board of Trade
PBT		profit before taxes, *see* earnings before taxes
P/BV		market-to-book ratio, *see* ratio analysis
PC		participation certificate
PCBDA	USA	Put and Call Brokers and Dealers Association
PCI		public credit institution
pcKISS	Germany	Kurs-Informations-Service-System
PDF		probability density function
PDR; P/D ratio		price–dividend ratio

PEACS	Canada	payment enhanced capital securities
PEP	UK	personal equity plan
		protected equity participation (note)
PE ratio; PER; P/E ratio		price–earnings ratio
PERCS		preference equity redemption cumulative stock
PERLS		principal exchange rate linked securities
PERMIC		principal exchange rate mortgage investment conduit
PERQ	USA	preferred equity redeemable quarterly-pay shares, *see* preference equity redemption cumulative stock
PEST		political, economic, sociological and technological (analysis)
PET		potentially exempt transfer
PETS		short-term equity participation securities, *see* short-term equity participation unit
		package equity trust securities
PFD		preferred stock
PFI	UK	private finance initiative
PHI		permanent health insurance
PHLX	USA	Philadelphia Stock Exchange
PI		profitability index
PIA	UK	Personal Investment Authority
PIBOR	France	Paris interbank offered rate
PIBS	UK	permanent interest bearing shares
PIC	UK	property income certificate
PICC	China	People's Insurance Company of China
PIK bond *or* note	USA	pay-in-kind bond *or* note
PIMBS	UK	programme for the issuance of mortgage-backed securities
PIN		personal identification number
PINC		property investment certificate
PIP		performance indexed paper
	Canada	penalty interest payment
		protected index participation (note)
Pip		$1/100^{th}$ of 1% (0.0001)
PIRA		participating interest rate agreements
PLC or plc	UK	public limited company
PLL		provision for loan losses
PMI		primary mortgage insurance
PMSR		purchased mortgage servicing nights
PMT		Post-Market Trading
PN	USA	project note
		promissory note
PO	USA	principal only STRIP (stripped mortgage backe security) (based on a mortgage-backed issue)
POA		power of attorney
POCM	Netherlands	public order correspondent member
POD		pay on delivery

POM	Netherlands	public order member
PP; pp.		per pro (per procurationem)
PPI	USA	producer prices index
PPP		purchasing power parity (theory)
PPS	USA	prior preferred stock
PRA		participation rate agreement
	Canada	Purchase and Resale Agreements, *see* repurchase agreement (repo)
PRIME	USA	prescribed right to income and maximum equity
PRO	USA	planned reduction obligation
PRT	UK	Petroleum Revenue Tax
PSA	USA	Public Securities Association
PSBR	UK	public sector borrowing requirement
PSDR	UK	public sector debt reduction
PSE	USA	Pacific Stock Exchange
PSL		private sector liquidity, *see* money supply
P/T	Italy	pronti-contro-termine (repurchase agreement)
PTD		payable through draft
PTY		private
Pty Ltd.	Australia; South Africa	Proprietary Limited (company)
PUC	USA	Public Utilities Commission
PUF		prime underwriting facility
PUMA		pooled unlisted mortgage asset (fund)
PV		present value
PVBP		price value of a basis point
PVF		par value forward
PX-50	Czech Republic	Prague Stock Exchange index
Q		quarterly
Q1, Q2, Q3, Q4		first, second, third, fourth quarter
QCB		qualifying corporate bond
QET		quote extension time
QIB	USA	qualified institutional buyers
QII	USA	qualified institutional investor
QPAM	USA	qualified professional asset manager
QT		questionable transaction
QTIP	USA	qualified terminable interest property trust
QTM		quantity theory of money
QUANGO	UK	quasi-autonomous non-governmental organization
QUANTO		quantity adjusting option
RA		ratio (spread)
RAAP		real asset accounting principle
RAES	USA	Retail Automatic Execution System

RAFT		revolving acceptance facility by tender
RAM	USA	reverse annuity mortgage
		risk analysis model
		random access memory
RAN	USA	revenue anticipation note
R&D		research and development
RAROC	USA	risk-adjusted return on capital
RCF		revolving credit facility
RCH		recognized clearing house
RCMM	USA	Registered Competitive Market Maker (National Association of Securities Dealers)
RCPR		regional cheque-processing centre
REAL	USA	real yield securities
REFCORP	USA	Resolution Funding Corporation
REIT	USA	real-estate investment trust
REMIC	USA	real-estate mortgage investment conduit
repo		repurchase agreement
reverses	USA	reverse repurchase agreement
revolver		revolving credit facility
REX/REXP	Germany	Frankfurt Stock Exchange index of first section securities
RFC	USA	regulated futures contract
RFQ		request for quotes
RHP		return to hedged portfolio, *see* implied repurchase agreement rate
RIBOR	Italy	Rome interbank offered rate
RICO	USA	Racketeers Influence and Corrupt Organizations Act
RIE	UK	recognized investment exchange
RIMSE	Russia	Russian International Stock Exchange, *see* Russian exchanges
RIPS		reverse indexes principal swap
RLS		recursive least squares
RM		règlement mensuel
RMA		risk management adviser, *see* risk management
RMB	China	renminbi
RNS	UK	Regulatory News Service
ROA		return on assets
ROB	Italy	riserva obbligatoria (compulsory reserves), *see* reserves
ROC		return on capital, *see* ratio analysis: return on capital employed
ROCE		return on capital employed
		return on common equity
ROE		return on equity
ROI		return on investment *or* return on invested capital
ROP	USA	registered options principal
ROS		return on sales
	Germany	Renten-Offerten-System
RP		repurchase agreement
		remarketed preferred (stock)
RPB	UK	recognized professional body

RPI	UK	retail price index
RPIX	UK	retail price index excluding mortgage interest
RR		risk reversal
RRP		reverse repurchase agreement
RRR		required rate of return
RSA		rate-sensitive assets
RSE	Russia	Russian Stock Exchange, *see* Russian exchanges
RSI		relative strength indicator
RSL		rate-sensitive liabilities
RT	USA	royalty trust
RTC	USA	Resolution Trust Corporation
RUF		revolving underwriting facility
RVP		receive versus (against) payment
SA	Spain	Sociedad Anónima (public company)
	Belgium, France, Luxembourg	Société Anonyme (limited company)
	Portugal	Sociedade Anónima (public company)
SAA		strategic asset allocation
SABRES		share adjusted broker remarketed equity security
SACE	Italy	Sezuione Speciale per l'Assicurazione del Credito all'Esportazia
SAR	USA	stock appreciation rights
SAEC	China	State Administration of Exchange Control
SAEF	UK	Small-order Automatic Execution Facility
SAFE		synthetic agreement for forward exchange
SAFEX	South Africa	South African Futures Exchange
Sallie Mae	USA	Students Loan Marketing Association
S&L	USA	savings and loan association
S&P	USA	Standard and Poor's Corporation
S&P 100	USA	Standard and Poor's 100 Stock Index
S&P 500	USA	Standard and Poor's 500 Stock Index
S&P 600	USA	Standard and Poor's 600 Stock Index
S&P ADEF	France	Standard and Poor's Agence d'Évaluation Financière
S&P-AR	Australia	S&P Australian Ratings
S&P MidCap	USA	Standard and Poor's MidCap 400 Index
SAP		Statutory Accounting Principles
SAPCO		single asset property company
SARs	UK	rules governing the substantial acquisition of shares
SARL	France	Sociéte à Responsabilité Limitée (private limited liability company)
	Italy	Società a Responsabilità Limitata (private limited liability company)
SAS	France	Société Anonyme Simplifiée (simplified joint stock company)
	UK	Statement of Auditing Standards
SAYE	UK	Save As You Earn

SB	USA	Savings Bond
		short bill
SBA	USA	Small Business Administration, *see* small business investment company
SBF	France	Société des Bourses Françaises
SBIC	USA	small business investment company
SBLC	UK	Stock Borrowing and Lending Committee
SBM		soyabean meal
SCAPI	France	société en commandité par actions de participations immobilières
SCIT	UK	Split capital investment trust
SCM	Ireland	small companies market
SCMC		Société de Compensation des Marchés Conditionels
SCORE	USA	special claim on residual equity
SCOUT		shared currency option under tender
SCP	UK	sterling commercial paper
SD		standard deduction
SDA		swap differential agreement
SDB	USA	special district bond, *see* municipal bond
SDBL		sight draft, bill of lading attached
Sdn Bhd	Malaysia	Sendirian Berhad (public company)
SDR		Special Drawing Rights
SDRT	UK	Stamp Duty Reserve Tax
SDS		same-day settlement
SE		shareholders' equity
SEAQ	UK	Stock Exchange Automated Quotations
SEAQI	UK	Stock Exchange Automated Quotations International
SEATS	UK	Stock Exchange Alternative Trading Service
	Australia	Stock Exchange Automated Trading System
SEBI	India	Securities and Exchange Board of India
SEC	USA	Securities and Exchange Commission
SEDOL	UK	Stock Exchange Daily Official List
SEEC	UK	Stock Exchange Executive Council
SEK	Sweden	Svensk Exportkredit
SELA		Sistema Económico Latino-Americano (Latin American Economic System)
SEMB	UK	Stock Exchange Money Brokers
SEPON	UK	Stock Exchange Pool Nominees Limited
SEQ	USA	sequential pay collateralized mortgage obligation
SES	Singapore	Stock Exchange of Singapore
SESDAQ	Singapore	Stock Exchange of Singapore Dealing and Automated Quotations System
SESI	Singapore	Stock Exchange of Singapore Index
SET	Thailand	Securities Exchange of Thailand
SF		sinking fund
SFA	UK	Securities and Futures Authority
SFAS	USA	Statement of Financial Accounting Standard
SFE	Australia	Sydney Futures Exchange

	UK	Scottish Financial Enterprise
SFECH	Australia	Sydney Futures Exchange Clearing House, *see* clearing house
SG		strangle
SG&A		selling, general, and administrative costs
SHEX		Sundays and holidays excluded
SHIELD	UK	synthetic high-income equity-linked debt
SHINC		Sundays and holidays included
SIA	USA	Securities Industry Association
	Italy	Società Interbancaria Automatica
SIAC	USA	Securities Industry Automation Corporation
SIB	UK	Securities and Investments Board
SIBOR	Singapore	Singapore interbank offered rate
SICAF	France	société d'investissement à capital fixe
SICAV	France	société d'investissement collectif à capital variable
SICC	USA	Standard Industrial Classification Code
SICOVAM	France	Société Interprofessionnelle pour la Compensation des Valeurs Mobilières
SIGN	USA	stock index growth note, *see also* equity-linked note
SIM	Italy	Società di Intermediazione Mobiliani
SIMEX	Singapore	Singapore International Monetary Exchange
SIPC	USA	Securities Investor Protection Corporation
SIT		Society of International Treasurers
SITC		Standard International Trade Classification
SL	USA	sold
SLC		standby letter of credit
SLD	USA	sold last sale
SLGS	USA	state and local government series
SLMA	USA	Student Loan Marketing Association
SLO		stop limit order *or* stop-loss order
SLOB	USA	secured lease obligation bond
SMBS	USA	second-mortgage backed securities
SME		small and medium-sized enterprises
SMI	Switzerland	Swiss Market Index
SMILE	Switzerland	Swiss Market Index Liierte Emission
SMM	USA	single monthly mortality
SMR	Malaysia	standard Malaysian rubber
SMTN		sterling medium-term notes
SN	USA	stock number
Snake		*see* European Monetary System
SNCF		securities note commitment facility
SNIF		short-term note issuance facility
SOB		stock over bond (warrant)
SOEC	UK	Small Order Execution System
SOES	USA	Small Order Execution System
SOFA		shared option forward agreement
SOFFEX	Switzerland	Swiss Options and Financial Futures Exchange
SOMA		surveillance of market activity, *see* Stock Watch
SOP		standard operating procedures

SORP	UK	Statement of Recommended Practices
SOYD		sum-of-years depreciation, *see* depreciation methods
SP		intra-commodity spread
SpA	Italy	Società per Azioni (limited company)
SPAN		standard portfolio analysis of risk
SPARS	USA	single point adjustable rate stock
SPECS	Canada	special equity claim securities
SPEL	USA	stock performance exchange-linked investments
SPI	Australia	All Ordinaries Share Price Index
	Switzerland	Swiss Performance Index
SPIDR; SPDR	USA	Standard and Poor's Index Depository Receipts
SPINS	USA	Standard and Poor's 500 Index Linked Notes
SPMC		special purpose mortgage company
SPOT	USA	single property ownership trust
SPQR		small profits, quick returns
SPRI	Belgium	Société de Personnes à Responsabilité Limitée (limited partnership)
SPT	USA	single property trust
SPV		special purpose vehicle
SQ	Japan	special quotation
SR		strip
SR, Sr		senior
SRA		sale and repurchase agreement, *see* reverses
SRF		structured receivables financing
SRO		self-regulating organization
SROP	USA	senior registered options principal
SSAP	UK	Statements of Standard Accounting Practice
SSE	Australia	Sydney Stock Exchange
ST		synthetic or combination
		straddle
STA	USA	Society of Technical Analysts
STAAAC		something to be avoided at all costs
STAGS	UK	sterling transferable accruing government securities
STAIR	USA	short-term appreciation and investment return (trust)
STAIRS	USA	step tax-exempt appreciation and income security
STAMP	France	Système de Transactions Automatisées du MONEP, *see* Marché des Options Négociables de Paris
STARS		securities transferred and repackaged
	USA	short-term auction rate stock
STEERS	USA	Structured Enhanced Returns Trusts
STEP	USA	short-term equity participation (unit)
STGIS		short-term gap income sensitivity
STI	Singapore	Straight Times Industrial (index)
STIBOR	Sweden	Stockholm interbank offered rate
STRAPS	USA	stated rate auction preferred stock
STRIP	USA	stripped mortgage-backed securities
STRIPES		securities transferred and repackaged into pound equivalent securities

STRIPS	USA	separate trading of registered interest and principal of securities
STRM	USA	stabilized term reduction mortgage obligation
STRMS	USA	stabilized mortgage reduction term security
SURF		step-up recovery floating rate note
SVT	France	Spécialistes en Valeurs du Trésor
SWIFT		Society for Worldwide Interbank Financial Telecommunications
SWING	UK	sterling warrants into gilt-edged stock
swissy; swissies		Swiss francs
SWOT		strengths, weaknesses, opportunities, threats
SYCOM	Australia	Sydney Computerized Overnight Market
SYTM		simple yield-to-maturity
T-		treasury
T+3		three-day settlement (transaction day, plus 2 business days)
T+5		five-day settlement (transaction day, plus 4 business days)
T+10		ten-day settlement (transaction day, plus 9 business days)
TA		trade acceptance transfer agent
TAA		tactical asset allocation
TAB	USA	tax anticipation bill
TAC	USA	targeted amortization class
TAG	France	taux annuel glissant
TAIX		Taipei Stock Exchange
TALISMAN	UK	Transfer, Accounting, Lodgement for Investors, Stock Management for Jobbers
TAM	France	taux annuel monétaire
TAN	USA	tax anticipation note
TAURUS	UK	Transfer and Automated Registration of Uncertificated Stock
TBA		to be announced
T-bill		treasury bill
TBN		to be nominated
TCBOT	USA	Twin Cities Board of Trade
TCE	Japan	Tokyo Commodity Exchange
TCN	France	titre de créance négociable
TCO	Canada	Trans Canada Options Inc.
TD		time deposit
TE		tandem
TECP	USA	tax-exempt commercial paper
TEDIR	USA	(New York) Tax-Exempt Daily Interest Rate index
TED spread	USA	US Treasury bill and eurodollar futures contract spread relationship
TEFRA	USA	Tax Equity and Fiscal Responsibility Act of 1982
TEN		Trans-European Networks
10K	USA	annual statement filed with the Securities and Exchange Commission
TENOR	USA	(New York) Tax-Exempt Note Rate index

10Q	USA	quarterly statement filed with the Securities and Exchange Commission
term repo (RP)		term repurchase agreement
TESSA	UK	tax-exempt special savings account
TFE	Canada	Toronto Futures Exchange
THS	France	transaction hors séance
TIBOR	Japan	Tokyo interbank offered rate
TIFFE	Japan	Tokyo International Financial Futures Exchange
TIGER; TIGR	USA	treasury investment growth receipt
TIOP	France	taux interbancaire offert à Paris, *see* Paris interbank offered rate
TIPs	Canada	Toronto 35 Index Participation Units
TL		traded last
TLC		transferable loan certificate
TLI		transferable loan instrument
TME	France	taux moyen des emprunts d'État
TMMMM	France	taux moyen mensuel du marché monétaire
TMO	France	taux moyen obligatoire
TMP	France	taux moyen pondéré
TNC		transnational corporation
TOCH	South Africa	Traded Options Clearing House, *see* clearing house
TOCOM	Japan	Tokyo Commodity Exchange for Industry
TOM	South Africa	Traded Options Market, part of the Johannesburg Stock Exchange
TOPIC	UK	Teletext Output of Price Information by Computer
TOPIX	Japan	Tokyo Stock Price index
TOPS		trust obligation participating securities
TPF	Germany	Ticker Plant Frankfurt
TPI	UK	tax and prices index
TR	USA	treasury receipt
TRAN	USA	tax revenue anticipation note, *see* revenue anticipation note; tax anticipation note
TRAX		*see* International Securities Markets Association
TRUF		transferable revolving underwriting facility
TSA	UK	The Securities Association, *see* Securities and Futures
TSE	Canada	Toronto Stock Exchange
	Japan	Tokyo Stock Exchange
TT		telegraphic transfer
TT&L	USA	Treasury tax and loan account
TTC		tender to contract (option)
Turbo	USA	long bond yield-decrease warrant
TUS	Italy	Tasso Ufficiale di Sconto (official discount rate)
TVA	French	(value added tax)
UBIT	USA	Unrelated Business Income Tax
UCC	USA	Uniform Commercial Code
UCITS		undertaking for collective investments in transferable securities

UCL		upper control limit
UCOM	USA	United Currency Options Market
UESDA	UK	underwritten enhanced scrip dividend alternative
UIT	USA	unit investment trust
ULS	UK	unsecured loan stock
UN		United Nations
UNCITRAL		United Nations Commission for International Trade Law
UNCTAD		United Nations Conference on Trade and Development
UPC	USA	Uniform Practice Code
UQ		unquoted
US	USA	United States (of America)
USA	USA	United States of America
USBS	USA	United States Bureau of Standards
USC	USA	United States Code
U-Schatze	Germany	Unverzinsliche Schatzanweisungen
USDA	USA	United States Department of Agriculture
USGG	USA	United States government guaranteed
USGS	USA	United States government securities
USIT	USA	unit share investment trust
USM	UK	Unlisted Securities Market
USU	USA	unbundled stock unit
UTA	UK	Unit Trust Association
UW		underwriter
VA	USA	Veterans' Administration, *see* Federal Housing Association
VAN		value added network
VAR		value at risk
VARIMA		volatility autoregressive integrated moving average
VAT		value added tax
VCR		variable coupon renewable note
VCTS	UK	Venture Capital Trust Scheme
VD	USA	volume deleted (on consolidated tape)
Veep	USA	vice president
VL	USA	value line investment survey
VOL		volume
VP		vice president
VRA		volatility rate agreement
VRC		voting right certificate
VRDO	USA	variable rate demand obligation
VRM	USA	variable rate mortgage
VRN		variable rate note
VRP	USA	variable rate preferred stock
VS		vertical straddle
VSE	Canada	Vancouver Stock Exchange
VSS		volatility subsidized swap
VT		vertical spread
VTC	USA	voting trust certificate

WA		with average
WABO	USA	we are buyers of
WACC		weighted average cost of capital
WASO	USA	we are sellers of
WCCC	Canada	West Canada Clearing Corporation
WCDTC	Canada	West Canada Depository Trust Company
WCE	Canada	Winnipeg Commodity Exchange
WD	USA	when distributed
WDV		written-down value
Whoops	USA	Washington Public Power Supply System
WI		when, as and if, issued
WIBOR	Austria	Wien (Vienna) interbank offered rate
WINGS	USA	warrants into negotiable government securities
WIP		work in process or progress
WIWI	USA	when issued, when issued
World Bank		International Bank for Reconstruction and Development
WPPSS	USA	Washington Public Power Supply System
WR		warehouse receipt
WSCI	USA	Wiltshire Small Capitalization Index
WSE	Canada	Winnipeg Stock Exchange
WT		warrant
W/Tax		withholding tax
WTC		Wheat Trade Convention, *see* International Wheat Council
WTI	USA	West Texas Intermediate (crude oil)
WTO		World Trade Organization
WW		with (cum) warrants
X		ex
XAC	USA	index allocated principal collateralized mortgage obligation
XD		ex-dividend
X-Dis	USA	ex-distribution, *see* distributed
XR		ex-rights
XT		xmas tree
XW		ex-warrant
YCAN		yield curve adjustable notes
YCN		yield curve note
YLD		yield
YTAL		yield to average life
YTB	USA	yield to broker
YTC		yield to call
YTEL		yield to equivalent life
YTM		yield to maturity
YTOD	USA	yield to operative date, or life
YTP	USA	yield to put
YTW		yield to worst
Z		zero

ZBA		zero balance account
ZCB		zero-coupon bond
ZDP	UK	zero dividend preference share
ZEBRAS	UK	zero-coupon eurosterling bearer or registered accruing securities
ZECRO		zero-cost ratio option
Zeds		zero-strike price option
ZR	USA	zero-coupon issue

INTERNATIONAL CURRENCIES
AND CURRENCY CODES

Country	Currency	SWIFT Code
Afghanistan	afghani	AFA
Albania	lek	ALL
Algeria	Algerian dinar	DZD
Andorra	French franc	FRF
	Spanish peseta	ESP
Angola	New Kwanza	AOK
Antigua	East Caribbbean $	XCD
Argentina	Argentinian peso	ARS
Armenia	dram	
Aruba	florin	AWG
Australia	Australian $	AUD
Austria	schilling	ATS
Azores	Portuguese escudo	PTE
Bahamas	Bahama $	BSD
Bahrain	Bahrain dinar	BHD
Balearic Is.	Spanish peseta	ESP
Bangladesh	taka	BDT
Barbados	Barbados $	BBD
Belarus	Belarus rouble	SUR
Belgium	Belgian fr.	BEF
Belize	Belize $	BZD
Benin	Communauté Financière Africaine fr.	XAF
Bermuda	Bermudian $	BMD
Bhutan	ngultrum	BTN
Bolivia	boliviano	BOB
Botswana	pula	BWP
Brazil	real	BRR
Brunei	Brunei $	BND
Bulgaria	lev	BGL
Burkino Faso	Communauté Financière Africaine fr.	XAF
Burma	kyat	BUK
Burundi	Burundi fr.	BIF
Cambodia	riel	XAF
Cameroon	Communauté Financière Africaine fr.	XAF
Canada	Canadian $	CAD
Canary Is.	Spanish peseta	ESP

Country	Currency	SWIFT Code
Cape Verde	Cape Verde escudo	CVE
Cayman Is.	Cayman Islands $	KYD
Cent Afr. Rep.	Communauté Financière Africaine fr.	XAF
Chad	Communauté Financière Africaine fr.	XAF
Chile	Chilean peso	CLP
China	yuan	CNY
CIS	rouble	RUS
Colombia	Colombian peso	COP
Comoros	French fr.	KMF
Congo	Communauté Financière Africaine fr.	XAF
Costa Rica	colon	CRC
Côte d'Ivoire	Communauté Financière Africaine fr.	XOF
Croatia	kuna	
Cuba	Cuban peso	CUP
Cyprus	Cyprus £	CYP
Czech Republic	koruna	CZK
Denmark	Danish krone	DKK
Djibouti Rep.	Djibouti fr.	DJF
Dominica	East Caribbean $	XCD
Dominican Rep	Dominican Rep. peso	DOP
Ecuador	sucre	ECS
Egypt	Egyptian £	EGP
El Salvador	colon	SVC
Equatorial Guinea	Communauté Financière Africaine fr.	XAF
Estonia	kroon	
Ethiopia	Ethiopian birr	ETB
Falkland Is.	Falkland Is. £	FKP
Faroe Is.	Danish kroner	DKK
Fiji Is.	Fiji $	FJD
Finland	markka	FIM
France	French fr.	FRF
Fr. Central Africa	Communauté Financière Africaine fr.	
Fr. Guiana	local fr.	FRF
Fr. Pacific Is.	CFP fr.	
Gabon	Communauté Financière Africaine. fr.	XAF
Gambia	dalasi	GMD
Germany	mark	DEM
Ghana	cedi	GHC
Gibraltar	Gibraltar £	GIP
Greece	drachma	GRD
Greenland	Danish krone	DKK
Grenada	East Caribbean $	XCD
Guadeloupe	local fr.	FRF
Guam	US $	USD
Guatemala	quetzal	GWP

Country	Currency	SWIFT Code
Guinea	local fr.	GNF
Guinea-Bissau	GB peso	GWP
Guyana	Guyanese $	GYD
Haiti	goude	HTG
Honduras	lempira	HNL
Hong Kong	HK $	HKD
Hungary	forint	HUF
Iceland	Icelandic krona	ISK
India	Indian rupee	INR
Indonesia	rupiah	IDR
Iran	Iran rial	IRR
Iraq	Iraqi dinar	IQD
Irish Republic	punt	IEP
Israel	shekel	ILS
Italy	Italian lira	ITL
Jamaica	Jamaican $	JMD
Japan	yen	JPY
Jordon	Jordanian dinar	JOD
Kenya	Kenya shilling	KES
Kiribati	Australian $	AUD
Korea North	won	KPW
Korea South	won	KRW
Kuwait	Kuwaiti dinar	KWD
Laos	new kip	LAK
Latvia	lats	LVL
Lebanon	Lebanese £	LBP
Lesoto	maluti	LSL
Liberia	Liberian $	LRD
Libya	Libyan dinar	LYD
Liechtenstein	Swiss fr.	CHF
Lithuania	litas	LTL
Luxembourg	Luxembourg fr.	LUF
Macao	pataca	MOP
Madagascar	Madagascar fr.	MGF
Madeira	Portuguese escudo	
Malawi	kwacha	MWK
Malaysia	ringgit	MYR
Maldive Is.	rufiya	MVR
Mali Republic	Communauté Financière Africaine fr.	XAF
Malta	Maltese lira	MTL
Martinique	local fr.	FR.F
Mauritania	ouguiya	MRO
Mauritius	Mauritius rupee	MUR
Mexico	Mexican peso	MXP
Miquelon	local fr.	

Country	Currency	SWIFT Code
Monaco	French fr.	FRF
Mongolia	tugrik	MNT
Montserrat	East Caribbean $	XCD
Morocco	dirham	MAD
Mozambique	metical	MZM
Namibia	South African rand	ZAR
Nauru Is.	Australian $	AUD
Nepal	Nepalese rupee	NPR
Netherlands	guilder	NLG
Netherlands Antilles	Antilles guilder	ANG
New Zealand	New Zealand $	NZD
Nicaragua	gold cordoba	NIO
Niger Rep.	Communauté Financière Africaine fr.	XAF
Nigeria	naira	NGN
Norway	Norwegian krone	NOK
Oman	Omani rinai	OMR
Pakistan	Pakistani rupee	PKR
Panama	balboa	PAB
Papua New Guinea	kina	PGK
Paraguay	guarani	PYG
Peru	new sol	PEN
Philippines	Philippines peso	PHP
Pitcairn Is.	£ sterling	
	New Zealand $	NZD
Poland	zloty	PLZ
Portugal	escudo	PTE
Puerto Rico	US $	USD
Qatar	Qatar riyal	QAR
Reunion, Is. de la	French fr.	FRF
Romania	leu	ROL
Rwanda	local fr.	RWF
St Christopher	East Caribbean. $	
St Helena	St Helena £	SHP
St Lucia	East Caribbean. $	XCD
St Pierre	French fr.	FRF
St Vincent	East Caribbean. $	XCD
San Marino	Italian lire	ITL
São Tomé	dobra	SUR
Saudi Arabia	Saudi riyal	SAR
Senegal	Communauté Financière Africaine fr.	XAF
Seychelles	Seychelles rupee	SCR
Sierra Leone	leone	SLL
Singapore	Singapore $	SGD
Slovakia	koruna	SKK
Slovenia	tolar	SIT

Country	Currency	SWIFT Code
Solomon Is.	Sololon Is. $	SBD
Somali Rep	Somali shilling	SOS
South Africa	rand	ZAR
Spain	peseta	ESP
Spanish ports in N. Africa	Spanish peseta	ESP
Sri Lanka	Sri Lankan rupee	LKR
Sudan Rep.	Sudan dinar	
Surinam	Surinam guilder	SRG
Swaziland	lilangeni	SZL
Sweden	Swedish krona	SEK
Switzerland	Swiss fr.	CHF
Syria	Syrian £	SYP
Taiwan	Taiwan $	TWD
Tanzania	Tanzanian shilling	TZS
Thailand	baht	THB
Togo Rep.	Communauté Financière Africaine fr.	XAF
Tonga Is.	pa'anga	TOP
Trinidad and Tobago	Trinidad and Tobago $	TTD
Tunisia	Tunisian dinar	TND
Turkey	Turkish lira	TRL
Turks and Calcos	US $	USD
Tuvalu	Australian $	AUD
Uganda	new shilling	UGX
Ukraine	karbovanets	SUR
UAE	dirham	AED
United Kingdom	£ sterling	GBP
United States	US $	USD
Uruguay	peso Uruguayo	UYP
Vanuatu	vatu	VUV
Vatican	Italian lira	ITL
Venezuela	bolivar	VEB
Vietnam	dong	VND
Virgin Is. -British	US $	USD
Virgin Is. -US	US $	USD
Western Samoa	tala	WST
Yemen (Rep. of)	Yemeni rial	YER
Yemen (Rep. of)	Yemeni dinar	YED
Yugoslavia	new dinar	YUN
Zaire Rep.	zaire	ZRZ
Zambia	kwachal	ZMK
Zimbabwe	Zimbabwe $	ZWD

A

A, Aa, Aaa, AA, and **AAA.** See credit ratings.

AAA, Aaa, or **Triple-A.** Shorthand term (taken from the credit rating system) used informally to indicate top credit worthiness.

A1, A-1, or **A1 risk.** (i) Used to indicate the best kind of insurance risk at Lloyds of London, hence *A1 at Lloyds.* For a vessel it has to be 'maintained in good and efficient condition'; or if a person or an asset, it is in best condition, hence *an A1 life.* (ii) The upper tier suffix to categories for **Moody's Investors Services** ratings, e.g. A1, is higher than A2 and A3. The alternative method used by some agencies is for pluses (+) and minuses (−), or higher (H) and lower (L) (iii) The rating method used by **Standard and Poor's,** the rating categories are $A - 1+, A - 1, A - 2, A - 3$, etc.

aajir (Islam). The **lessor** in a risk-sharing transaction, a practice permitted under Islamic law (the shira). See **ijara.**

abandon or **abandonment.** Leaving an **option** to expire unexercised (cf. **cabinet trade; exercise**).

ABC Agreement (USA). The legal basis for a firm to finance the purchase of a membership of the New York Stock Exchange for an employee since only individuals can be members. A typical agreement will specify what happens should the employee cease to be employed and how the seat is to be disposed of: by assignment to or buying of a new seat for a designated employee; or the sale of the seat to reimburse the firm.

ABC securities (USA). A non-interest-paying convertible where the **dividends** on the **underlying** issue of **common stock** are passed through to the holders if the price of the common stock rises more than a predetermined amount.

ability to pay or **service.** Generally a condition of an issuer of **long-term** debt to meet the principal and interest payments (cf. **default**). See **credit analysis; credit ratings.**

abnormal return. The return on an asset or security beyond that predicted by market movements alone (cf. **alpha coefficient; specific risk; stock specific risk**). See also **anomaly; risk premium.**

above par. A security which is trading above its redemption value or **par value.** Purchasers of such securities will make a **capital loss** if held to **maturity** (cf. **premium; discount**). Many corporate bonds are redeemed at a premium over par (cf. **redemption**).

above-the-line activities. A corporate or banking obligation that must appear on the **balance sheet** (cf. **below-the-line activities**). Sometimes known as *on-balance sheet.* See **financial lease.**

absolute. Not made with reference to any other price or rate.

absolute priority rule (USA). A condition of the pre-1978 US bankruptcy proceedings which gave creditor claims priority over claims by owners and required that these claims be paid out in order of priority. Much modified by the Bankruptcy Reform Act of 1978. See **Chapter 11.**

absolute rate. (i) An interest rate expressed as a percentage rather than in reference to a benchmark (cf. **reference rate**). Also sometimes called an *absolute yield.* (ii) A **euronote** term referring to the rate of interest payable on an instrument which is not expressed in relation to a specific reference rate, such as **London interbank offered rate.** (iii) An interest rate in an **interest rate swap** or a **cross-currency swap** which is expressed as a fixed percentage return rather than in relation to a reference rate (cf. **coupon rate**).

absolute swap rate. The fixed rate side of an **interest rate swap** or a **cross-currency swap** expressed as an **absolute rate** rather than in relation to a **benchmark** rate plus a **spread** (cf. **coupon rate**).

absorb. To allocate or apportion an item. See also **marginal costing.**

absorbed cost or **expense.** Indirect costs of doing business, such as insurance and local taxes.

absorption costing. A method of accounting which includes the total costs incurred in undertaking the activity. It allocates the full cost to the line of business rather than the marginal cost of undertaking the activity.

A/B structure. Description of a two-tranche transaction: the A tranche is usually in the form of **senior** debt, while the B tranche is **subordinated**. It is commonly used as a method of **credit enhancement** for **asset-backed** issues where the loss rates are generally known. The junior, or subordinated tranche absorbs the expected losses allowing the senior tranche to have low **default risk** and thus obtain a relatively high **credit rating**. Also sometimes called a *senior/subordinated structure*.

Accelerated Cost Recovery System (ACRS) (USA). The depreciation schedules established for tax purposes by the Economic Recovery Act of 1981 and subsequently modified by the Tax Reform Act of 1986. There are seven classes which are determined in relation to their **asset depreciation range** (ADRS), which is based on their upper and lower expected useful lives. The ACRS uses the mid-point of the ADRS. Taxpayers may elect for an alternative **straight line** depreciation schedule based on the relevant ADR class.

ACRS classes depreciation method for tax purposes:

3-year
5-year   } Double declining
7-year   } balance method
10-year

15-year } 150% declining
20-year } balance method

Real-property straight-line method with:
  residential   27.5 years
  non-residential   31.5 years

accelerated depreciation. Any depreciation method that writes off an asset in book terms faster than its loss of economic value. See **depreciation methods**.

accelerated supply (Commodities). The effect of gold being made available in advance of production through lending and leasing arrangements between producers and holders (often provided by **central banks**).

acceleration clause, covenant, or **provision.** A condition found in debt and **derivatives** contracts that requires immediate repayment in the event of **default**. Typically a **breach of covenant** or term of the loan will trigger a default and hence the acceleration clause. See **technical default**.

acceptance (acceptor). (i) The signing of a **bill** in formal acknowledgement of the obligation to honour the bill. The drawee puts the word 'accepted' together with a date for payment if a **time bill** and signs, thus becoming the *acceptor*. Acceptances are normally of two types: **banker's acceptances** where the acceptor is a bank; and **trade acceptances** where the acceptor is a company. (ii) A bill which has been accepted. (iii) Agreement to the terms of an offer (cf. **offer for sale**; **tender**). For instance, when tendering **stock** in an acquisition or a repurchase, sellers complete 'forms of acceptance' when agreeing to the terms of the transaction.

acceptance credit (Banking). A facility by which a bank provides finance for the sale of goods or services, usually used in international trade (cf. **banker's acceptance**). The bank will extend a credit to an acceptable **counterparty** as the (foreign) buyer against which the seller or exporter can draw a **bill of exchange** (cf. **discounted**).

accepting house (Banking; UK). A bank or specialized institution which agrees to endorse **acceptances** (cf. **bankers acceptances**; **bills**).

Accepting Houses Committee (Banking; UK). The group of seventeen leading London merchant banks with strictly controlled membership approved by the **Bank of England**. The Accepting Houses Committee merged with the Issuing Houses Committee in 1988 following **Big Bang** to create the **British Merchant Banks and Securities Houses Association**.

acceptor. Drawee of an **acceptance**.

accommodation bill. A banker's acceptance or **bill of exchange** which is guaranteed by a third party who undertakes to honour the obligation in the event that the writer or acceptor fails to honour his pledge. This might arise, for instance, where the accommodation party is the parent or affiliate to the acceptor, which is based in a different jurisdiction to the contracting party. Sometimes also known as a *windbill*.

accommodation endorser. A third party who undertakes to guarantee a transaction. For instance, the holding company of a group might thus guarantee the loans raised by a subsidiary. In the event of **default**, the accommodating party becomes liable for the obligation (cf. **guarantee**).

accommodation paper. An acceptance, such as a **banker's acceptance** or **bill of exchange** which is made up of a number of different transactions, typically **trade acceptances** or trade bills.

accord de place (French). Memorandum of understanding.

accordion swap. Another name for a **concertina** swap.

account (Equities; UK). The name given to the London Stock Exchange old method of settlement based on a number of accounting periods for the settlement of transactions. The year was divided into twenty-five periods; most were of two weeks' duration but some were of three weeks' to even up the calendar. Most UK-registered securities were settled for the account which was the second Monday following the end of the account period and known as the *account day* (cf. **contango; new time**). The exchange moved to a ten-day (T+10) rolling settlement basis in 1994, which was then reduced to a five-day (T+5) settlement period in line with the **Group of Thirty** recommended international standard on 26 June, 1995.

account. (i) A balance held with a financial institution to facilitate transactions, such as a bank account or securities account. The account may allow the beneficiary to transact business on a credit basis (in the case of a bank account, by overdrawing on the amount deposited) with the grantor institution providing the funds. (ii) Used in the accounting sense of an entry recording a transaction in a ledger. (iii) Evidence of a credit or debit held at a financial institution. For instance, a *current account*, *deposit account*, or *loan account* held with a bank.

account day (Equities; UK). The day on which all transactions undertaken within the **London Stock Exchange's** old **account** system were settled (cf. **contango**). It was normally the second Monday following the end of the account. See **rolling settlement**.

account executive. Term for the employee empowered to handle a client's **account** and therefore act as an **agent**. In the USA and UK such employees have to be accredited to the appropriate regulatory body. Hence the account executive is sometimes known as a *registered representative*.

accounting balance sheet. See **balance sheet**.

accounting period. The period of time covered by a set of accounts and/or the tax year. Also sometimes referred to as the *financial* or *fiscal year* (FY).

Accounting Principles Board (APB) (USA). Forerunner to the **Financial Accounting Standards Board**.

accounting rate of return (ARR). Method of evaluating the profitability of a project or firm based on accounting numbers (cf. **discounted cash flow; internal rate of return; net present value**). It is the incremental annual profit divided by the amount of the investment as a percentage.

Accounting Standards Board (ASB) (UK). Statutory body established by the Companies Act (1989) as the operating arm of the **Financial Reporting Council** to set accounting standards (cf. **Financial Accounting Standards Board** (USA)). The Board consults on proposals, then issues **financial reporting standards** which are to be followed by companies. The Board has legal powers of enforcement. Given the time required to implement new proposals, it also has a subcommittee called the **Urgent Issues Task Force** which addresses questions of interpretation and other topical problems related to financial reporting. The ASB also promulgates *Statements of Recommended Practice* (SORP) proposing best practice in financial reporting.

accounts. (i) The reported **balance sheet, profit and loss statement**, and **cash flow statement** of an organization. Also known as the *financial statements*. (ii) An organization's internal financial reports and ledgers.

accounts payable. Short-term debts owed by a firm to its creditors for goods and services received (cf. **current liabilities**).

account sweeping. See **concentration banking**.

accounts receivable. Short-term assets consisting of debtors for goods and services supplied (cf. **current assets**).

accounts receivable financing. A type of finance against **collateral** where funds are provided against the firm's receivables (cf. **asset-backed**). The lender takes a floating **lien** on the invoices as security. The advantages to the company are that such loans remain private and do not disturb the firm's relationship with the customer. Sometimes also known as *confidential factoring* or **invoice discounting**. See **factoring**.

accounts receivable turnover ratio (USA). A financial **ratio** that shows the number of times in the accounting period the **accounts receivable** have been collected. It is the ratio of sales to trade debtors.

account trading (UK). Former facility available for transactions on the **London Stock Exchange** due to the **account** method of **settlement** that allowed trading within an account without the need to provide funds in settlement. It was also possible to **rollover** positions from one account to another for a fee (cf. **contango market**). Since the exchange has moved to **rolling settlement**, this facility is no longer available. See also **daytime trading**.

accredited investor (USA). A member of a limited **partnership** who is excluded from the maximum of thirty-five partners under the **Securities**

and Exchange Commission's Regulation D because of the individual's high net worth.

accreting interest rate cap (accreting cap). An interest rate cap where the notional principal amount is increased over time. The opposite would be an amortizing interest rate cap, where the notional principal amount decreased over time. See also deferred cap; forward cap.

accreting swap. An interest rate swap or cross-currency swap in which the notional principal increases towards maturity (cf. amortizing swap). Frequently used in cases where a borrower expects to draw down funds over a period of time (for instance in response to a project's funding requirements) but wants to fix in advance his cost of funds. It is priced by calculating the cost of deferring the different tranches of the principal. Also called an *accreting principal swap, accumulation swap, construction loan swap, drawdown swap, staged drawdown swap,* or *step-up swap.* See deferred swaps.

accretion. (i) The writing to profit of the increase in the value of an asset over a period of time. For securities, it tends to indicate an increase in the principal amount over time in a predictable or determined manner (cf. amortization). Hence bonds which are trading at a discount to par accrete to their principal value as they move towards maturity. (ii) In portfolio analysis, the resultant increase in value of bonds which are at a discount as they move to par at maturity; bonds at a premium are amortized to par.

accretion bond. See accrual bond.

accretion directed bond (AD bond) (USA). A collateralized mortgage obligation where the redemption of principal is linked to payments from an accrual bond.

accrual basis, concept, method, or **accruals.** Accounting method or convention whereby income and expenditure items are recognized over time when earned or incurred and whether paid or not. When drawing up accounts for a given period, the intention is to include costs and revenues which are partly earned or charged to the period to provide a fairer indication of the profitability of activities, that is costs and revenues are matched for the reporting period. The alternative cash basis method takes account only of cash movements.

accrual or **accretion bond (ABC).** (USA). The last payment made under a collateralized mortgage obligation and where interest is added to enhance the principal value. Sometimes called a *Z bond.*

accrual note. See range floating rate note.

accrual rate. The interest rate used to calculate accrued interest, normally the coupon rate adjusted for the day count. See interest basis; interest rate calculations.

accrual swap. Interest rate swap where one party pays the floating rate at the reference rate while the other will pay the floating rate plus a significant spread. However, this party is only required to pay if the reference rate remains within pre-agreed lower and upper boundaries (cf. minimax floating rate note). Also known as a *fairway swap* or a *range swap.*

accrued income scheme (UK). Inland Revenue procedure that allocates the accrued interest on an asset to the vendor and reduces the amount of tax due on the coupon or interest payment to the purchaser by the same amount.

accrued interest (AI). (i) The amount of interest earned but not yet due for payment (cf. arrearage; arrears). (ii) The amount of interest that a buyer of a security pays to a seller when the transaction takes place between coupon payment dates or before maturity in the case of single-period instruments such as certificates of deposit which pay interest or any other instrument with coupons or predictable dividends. The buyer of a bond pays the seller the agreed price plus interest accrued since the last interest payment date up to and including the value date. Where bonds are traded ex-coupon the accrued interest is computed using the next coupon to be paid and is negative (cf. accumulated interest). See interest basis; interest rate calculations.

accrued interest option (USA). The right of the short futures position holder to determine when in the delivery period to make delivery of the underlying into the contract. The timing will be influenced by the cost of carry, dealers either opting for early delivery if they have negative carry or late delivery if they are gaining from positive carry. While in theory this would lead the futures contract to trade to either the earliest or latest date depending on the cost of carry situation, the fact that most dealers in the Treasuries market use overnight repurchase agreements to finance their position means that in practice there may be some uncertainty for the long position holder as to when delivery may take place.

accumulated benefit obligation (ABO) (USA). An actuarial calculation of the outstanding contractual liabilities to existing employees and pension recipients based on the assumed immediate winding-up of the pension plan.

accumulated depreciation. The total amount of **depreciation** on an asset since the asset was acquired. Accumulated depreciation is normally shown for most categories of assets on a **balance sheet**. Combined with the amount in the **profit and loss account**, it allows a calculation of the estimated age of the assets to be made.

accumulated earnings tax. Tax levied on firms which retain an unreasonable level of **earnings**. See **payout ratio**.

accumulated interest. This is the amount of past interest that is due but not paid. Accumulated interest is often the result of a **default** on the part of the issuer or borrower (cf. **arrearages**). See also **accrued interest; interest basis**.

accumulated profit. Profit that is retained in the accounts after **dividends**, tax, and transfers to **reserves**.

accumulating shares (Equities; UK). Payment of **dividends** in the form of additional units of **stock**. See **scrip dividend**.

accumulation. In securities markets it means the purchase of a security in a series of small transactions in order to avoid adversely moving the price or rate, i.e. to minimize the **market impact,** which is the cost of undertaking large transactions. It is also used in the sense of a firm accumulating reserves rather than paying out **dividends** on its profits.

accumulation area. A **technical analysis** term for a price range at which buyers step into the market thereby preventing prices falling any further (cf. **resistance level**). See **breakout**.

accumulation or **accumulating swap**. See **accreting swap**.

accumulation unit (UK). A **unit trust unit** that automatically reinvests **dividends** from the **underlying** portfolio rather than paying these out as income to the holder.

achat au comptant (French). Cash transaction.

acid test ratio. A financial **ratio** calculated by dividing cash and near-cash equivalents, such as marketable securities, on a particular day by current liabilities on the same day. It is used to measure the ability of an organisation to meet its short-term obligations. Sometimes called the *quick ratio*. See **ratio analysis**.

acknowledgement (Banking). A **confirmation** of a transfer of funds to a correspondent bank which

details the amounts received and **settlement** details.

acquired surplus (USA). In a **pooling of interests** merger, the portion of **net worth** of the successor corporation that is not **capital stock**.

acquiree. Term for a company that is being taken over (cf. **target**).

acquiror. Term for a company that is buying something, another firm, assets, etc. (cf. **predator**).

acquisition. The purchase of a company or an asset. Acquisitions can be either of the **target** company's outstanding **common stock** or of the firm's assets; that is its **tangible assets** and **goodwill** (cf. **merger**).

acquisition accounting. The accounting treatment methods and conventions used when one company acquires another or two firms merge. There are basically two methods: the purchase of assets or pooling of interests.

across the board. A term to describe a general movement of a market that affects all sectors (cf. **systematic risk**).

actif (French). **assets** (cf. **left-hand side**). The opposite is *passif*: **liabilities** (cf. **right-hand side**).

acting in concert. See **concert party**.

action (Equities; France). French term used for a share or stock. Thus *actionnaire*: a shareholder.

active bond crowd (Bonds; USA). Those members of the **New York Stock Exchange** who handle the most actively traded **bond** issues (cf. **cabinet crowd**).

active box (USA). Term for the available collateral for backing **broker's loans** or **margin positions**. It derives its name from the holding location of securities held in **safekeeping** for clients or the firm itself. Securities pledged as **collateral** must be owned by the **broker** or **hypothecated** by the client to the **broker** who in turn pledges them to the lender.

active management. An approach to fund, or other asset or liability, management which seeks actively to manage the **position** in order to increase returns or reduce costs (cf. **passive management**). It is thus a **portfolio** strategy of positively managing assets by adjusting the constituent parts of the portfolio in response to perceived favourable conditions in different markets or securities (cf. **indexing**). See **anomaly; asset allocation;**

policy switch; strategic asset allocation; tactical asset allocation.

active market. A market where buying and selling is above average levels.

active stocks. The most liquid and traded **common stocks** or other securities traded in a market over a given period. Normally these are the largest issues, or special situations such as a **takeover** announcement.

activity. (i) In **portfolio** management, the excess of **turnover** of the portfolio above the net cash flow. It is a measure of the amount of trading made by a portfolio manager. (ii) In markets, the amount of business that is taking place (cf. **heavy**; **thin**).

actuals. (i) **Commodities markets** term for exchange of the physical commodity as opposed to the **futures** or **forward contracts** (cf. **cash market**; **spot market**). (ii) Used for those **futures** and **forward** contracts where actual physical delivery of the **underlying** takes place as compared with a **cash settled** contract (cf. **against actuals**; **exchange for physical**; **physical delivery**; **tender**). (iii) Also sometimes used to describe the *actual outcome* of what has happened to a particular variable in relation to a projection or target.

actual total loss. An insurance **write-off** in respect of a claim.

actuarial return. The assumed future rate of return or **yield** applied by an actuary to assets and liabilities in a pension plan.

actuarial yield. The total yield earned from cash flows. When applied to **serial bonds** it refers to the total **yield** assuming the **bond** is held to **maturity** and all **coupon** and principal repayments are made according to the terms of the issue.

actuary. A professionally-trained expert concerned with applying a mathematical approach to the solution of long-term financial problems, particularly relating to pensions, insurance, and investment. This is used to price various kinds of insurance **risks** or investments, as with valuing and advising on pension funding and provisioning. Employed mainly by life assurance and insurance companies with the responsibility for managing the **liabilities** side of the business, rather than **fund managers** or **investment analysts**, who look after the **asset** side of the business. Actuaries play an important role in assessing the way in which **pension funds** operate, especially with regard to such issues as: discretionary benefits payable to pensioners; **minimum solvency requirements**; contributions holidays; and the

effects of changing benefits for future pensioners. See **indexation**.

Additional Voluntary Contributions (AVC) (UK). Additional payments by an individual into a defined contribution scheme by which the future income benefits of a pension scheme can be enhanced. Traditionally, this option has been available to the self-employed and the employer side of occupational pension schemes. Under UK legislation extra payments can now be made by individuals to pension providers. See **portable pensions**.

add-on interest rate (USA). A method of calculating interest on **amortizing** loans, usually used with consumer credit, where the **simple interest** is calculated on the opening balance. The add-on rate is thus normally lower than the **annual percentage rate** and is comparable to the **currow yield**. It is calculated by:

$$\frac{\text{Principal} \times \text{add-on interest rate} \times \text{period of the loan}}{\text{Repayment frequency}}$$

Thus a US$10,000 loan repaid over five years with an add-on interest rate of 6% per annum and computed monthly and repaid quarterly would pay:

$$\frac{\text{US\$10,000} \times 6\% \times 60}{20} = \text{US\$1,800}$$

This is equal to an annual percentage rate of 17.5%.

adjudication. The giving of a judgement in a court of law.

adjustable long-term puttable securities (ALPS). A proprietorial name for a **dual currency bond**.

adjustable peg (Forex). See **crawling peg**.

adjustable rate bond. See **floating rate note**.

adjustable-rate consumer loan (ARC) (Banking; USA). A **variable rate consumer loan**.

adjustable rate convertible bond (USA). A convertible bond where the **floating rate coupon** is set equivalent to the **dividend** on the firm's common stock. The intention was to create a debt instrument for interest purposes. However, the US Internal Revenue Service has treated the coupon payments as distributions made after tax, thus eliminating the tax benefit to the issuer.

adjustable rate mortgage (ARM) (USA). A mortgage loan whose interest rate is periodically changed to reflect changes in market interest rates. The rate of interest is normally set in relation to a reference rate, which is usually US **treasuries**, on a quarterly **reset,** but there is normally a maximum **limit** or **margin** on how much the rate may be adjusted in any period (typically 0.25–0.50%). In addition, some variants include a **cap** on the interest rate as well (cf. **interest rate cap**). To make the mortgages attractive to buyers the mortgage will normally have a lower rate of interest than that prevailing on traditional fixed rate mortgages, and sometimes will have a low initial rate, commonly known as a *teaser rate.* Also known as a *floating rate mortgage* or *variable rate mortgage.*

adjustable rate note. See **floating rate note.**

adjustable rate preferred stock (ARPS) (USA). A type of **preferred stock** with a **floating rate** dividend which is reset periodically in line with market rates based on a **reference rate** (usually US **treasury bills,** the ten-year or the twenty-year treasury rate) plus a specified **margin** (cf. **spread**).

adjustable rate securities. See **dual coupon; floating rate.**

adjustable tender securities. See **puttable securities.**

adjusted basis. A method of valuing assets for capital gains tax purposes which takes account of stock splits or scrip issues to ascertain gains or losses.

adjusted certificate of deposit rate (Banks; USA). A method of pricing loans based on the rate for **certificates of deposit** (CD) and adjusting to reflect the banks' cost of funds. The basic CD rate is increased by the cost of deposit insurance by the **Federal Deposit Insurance Corporation** and any **reserve** requirement at the **federal Reserve:**

$$\text{Adjusted CD rate} = \frac{\text{Basic cost of certificate of deposit}}{(1 - \text{reserves requirement})} + \text{cost of insurance}$$

Thus the loan rate using this method, where the prevailing CD rate was 3% and insurance costs were 0.1% and the reserves requirement 2%, would be

$$\frac{3\%}{(1 - 2\%)} + 0.1\% = 3.16\%$$

adjusted debit balance (ADB) (USA). A method for working out the **position** on a **margin** account under **Regulation T** of the Federal Reserve Board.

adjusted duration. See **duration.**

adjusted exercise or **strike price.** (i) A modification to the **exercise** or **strike** price and number of shares in a **stock option** to reflect **capitalization** changes. For instance, if a stock valued at 100 has a

1 for 4 **bonus** or **scrip issue,** then the stock price will fall to 80, and the number of shares in the option increase accordingly, so that if the original option was for 100 shares the new number would be 125. (ii) A method of varying the **exercise price** to ensure standardization of **put** and **call options** on **Ginnie Mae bonds.** Contracts are traded on a standard Ginnie Mae issue, so that the **exercise price** is adjusted for different yielding pools of mortgages to give the same **yield** to the holder.

adjusted forecast. Simple forecast, such as linear extrapolation of a trend which is then adjusted for, for instance, the point at which the economy has reached in the **business cycle.**

adjusted present value (adjusted net present value; APV). A method of analysing investments or projects which includes valuing the side-effects of undertaking the project. The approach involves an initial assessment of the *base case* of the project, based on an all-**equity** financing, and then adding the associated side-effects of accepting the project, such as funding costs, **tax shields,** or other factors.

adjusted r-squared or **adjusted r²**. See **coefficient of determination.**

adjusted strike price. A change made to the strike price of an **option** as a result of a special event, such as a **stock split** or **stock dividend.** There is usually a contractual difference in the treatment of a cash disbursement, such as a **dividend,** and the creation of additional units of the **underlying** (cf. **leakage; total return**). In the latter case, the **market capitalization** will be unaltered but the price of individual units will fall by a predictable amount.

adjusting. See **dynamic replication.**

adjustment bond (USA). A **bond** exchange made by companies in financial distress restructuring their liabilities. In order to avoid the costs of bankruptcy proceedings bondholders agree to allow the company to meet interest payments as and when it can (cf. **income bonds; junk bonds**). See **assented securities.**

adjustment credit (Banking; USA). Short-term loan made by the **Federal Reserve System** to smaller banks within the system to meet short-term lending needs.

adjustment swap. Another term for an **off-market swap.**

administration order (UK). A court order made in relation to an insolvent or financially distressed company (cf. **bankruptcy**). The administration order was introduced by the Insolvency Act, 1986 in imitation of the USA's **Chapter 11,** as a way of preserving a company's business and allowing it to reorganize or undertake an orderly winding up of its affairs. A firm subject to an administration order by a court will be placed under the control of an **administrator** and will be protected from any legal moves by creditors to wind up the business.

administrative receiver (UK). An individual appointed by the holder of a floating **lien** on a firm to recover the debt due to the creditor. Such an individual has wide discretion as to how such a debt may be recovered, including keeping the business running as a going concern or winding up the firm.

administrator (UK). A person appointed to execute an **administration order** or act as an **administrative receiver.** Such an individual is usually a specialist from a firm of insolvency practitioners. To act legally, the administrator must be in possession of letters of administration issued by the relevant court.

ad valorem (Latin). By value.

advance. (i) (Banking) A short-term **loan** made by a bank to a customer (cf. **advances option; committed facility; revolving credit facility; rollover**). (ii) An anticipatory payment.

advance corporation tax (ACT) (UK; France; Australia). The tax paid by companies on their **dividends** to **shareholders.** It is levied at the basic (or lowest) rate of income tax and represents both the **tax credit** on the dividend to shareholders and an advance payment of **corporation tax.** See also **franked income; imputation; unrelieved advance corporation tax.**

advance–decline (A–D). A technical analysis method which measures the ratio of **stocks** which have risen in value against those which have fallen (cf. **sentiment indicator**). A positive number is **bullish;** a negative one **bearish.** By plotting the ratio over time, the trend provides an indication of the general mood of the market while the trend's slope gives an indication of the strength of the movement.

advanced premium forward (Commodities). A series of **forward** contracts which have a constant **spread** between the spot and forward dates. Also called a *flat rate forward* or *stabilized contango forward.*

advance fee fraud. A method of defrauding individuals or firms by making false representations concerning the ability to arrange a transaction. The fraudster obtains a fee in advance of the deal to help the process and then disappears without

trace. Many firms anxious to raise finance have been duped in this fashion; few recover the amounts paid over.

advance guarantee. A call option.

advance refunding (Bonds; USA). A practice of raising new funds under favourable market conditions and reinvesting the proceeds until it is time to redeem existing issues. The rationale is to avoid the problems that might arise if refunding is left to the **maturity** of the debt.

advances option. A clause in a **note issuance facility** that gives the holder the **option** to purchase **promissory notes** at a predetermined rate or to make a short-term advance, normally at the same rate, instead of buying the note.

adventure. A speculative type of investment often, by implication, equated with foreign investment. See **venture capital.**

adverse selection. An activity undertaken by a firm or individual that conveys information of a negative (or adverse) kind about their product or service (cf. **free rider; signalling**).

advised line of credit (Banking). A **credit facility** in which the bank has confirmed the terms and conditions to the customer. Such facilities tend to be provided by banks to potential borrowers with whom they wish to do business as an indication of goodwill and intent. Terms on such facilities vary and may be **best efforts, confirmed** or **unconfirmed,** depending on the bank's preferences. See also **credit line.**

advising bank. Term used for the bank which informs the beneficiary of the opening of a **documentary credit.**

advisory broker (UK). A **broker-dealer** who gives clients advice as to which **shares** to buy and sell. The decision, however, remains entirely with the client. A **broker** who decides transactions based on his own internal analysis for a client is known as a *discretionary broker.*

advisory funds. Funds placed with an intermediary to invest at its own discretion on behalf of a client.

affiliate. A company which is less than fully owned by another. The exact definition of affiliate will depend on the context. The requirement to **consolidate** such a company in the group accounts will depend on the local accounting standards, as will its inclusion in any group taxation. In general, a company will be an affiliate if it is less than 50% owned by the parent or **equity** accounted rather than included in the **consolidated balance sheet**.

affiliated person (USA). Term for an individual able to exert direct influence on the conduct of a company's business. Generally taken to mean a stock-holding in excess of 10%.

affirmative covenant. A covenant that requires positive actions on the part of the covenanted. For instance, the requirement to distribute **financial statements**.

African Development Bank (AfDB; AFDB). International agency involved with lending to Africa and patterned on the **International Bank for Reconstruction and Development** (World Bank). It was established in 1964 and is based in Abidjan, Ivory Coast, and includes non-African states as members. It is a known borrower in the international markets.

after-acquired clause (Bonds; USA). A term in an issue of secured debt which provides for any additional securable assets acquired after the debt obligation has come into being to be included as security to the debt. In effect, it restricts the borrower's ability to raise other secured debt on newly acquired assets.

after date. A condition in a **banker's acceptance** or **bill of exchange** indicating the period after which the bill or acceptance becomes due (cf. **after sight**). The alternative is *at sight*, where payment is due immediately.

after-hours trading. Transactions made after the close of official business on an exchange. See **kerb market**.

aftermarket or **secondary market.** That part of a market that trades securities previously issued securities up to their **maturity**. It is considered to be important to have an active aftermarket in order to stimulate demand for new issues. In the eurobond market, it is used sometimes for the period between the launch of an issue and the ending of restrictions on trading (cf. **grey market; global note**).

after sight. Refers to a bill that becomes payable after the **acceptor** has written his acceptance on the bill.

after-tax basis. A method of calculating the returns on taxable and tax-exempt securities. The taxable security's **yield** is adjusted by the holder's tax rate. Although the method is simple in principle, complications arise if the holder has different tax rates for **capital gains** and income and, in addition, the possibility exists of using any off-

setting tax deductions against the income which makes a like-for-like analysis complicated, especially if the securities to be compared are trading at different levels in relation to their **par value** (cf. **discount; premium**). The result is that for different individuals and companies, the after-tax rate may diverge significantly. Also called *after-tax return* or *after-tax yield*.

against actuals (AA). Commodities market term for an **offset** transaction involving the use of the **cash market** rather than doing the opposite transaction in the **futures** market (cf. **cash and carry; exchange for physical**).

against the box (USA). Market term for a covered **short sale** where the seller owns the security sold (hence it is in the box, the storing place of securities held in **safekeeping**). Such a short is designed to earn additional returns on a **long position** by taking advantage of temporary price declines. Note, however, the seller maintains his original holding, the deliverable securities being borrowed in the market.

aged fail (USA). Term for a **bad delivery** which remains unsettled after a month (cf. **fail; outtrade**). The costs of such trading failures have then to be treated as a charge against reserves.

ageing schedule. A breakdown of the **receivable** account or creditors by time **buckets** by the date of invoice (cf. **credit risk**) (see Table).

Days	Amount	Percentage of outstanding	Cumulative total
1–7	2,500	8.4	8.4
8–14	3,200	10.8	19.2
15–30	11,000	27.0	56.2
31–60	8,500	28.6	84.9
61–90	3,800	12.8	97.6
91+	700	2.4	100.0
	18,700	100.0	

agencies (Bonds; USA). Market name for **federal agency** issues such as **Federal National Mortgage Association** (Fannie Mae); **Government National Mortgage Association** (Ginnie Mae); **Students Loan Marketing Association** (Sallie Mae).

agency. (i) (Banking; USA). Name given to foreign banks' operations in the US market that do not have branch status. (ii) (USA) One of the federal agency issues. See **agencies**. (iii) The relationship between a principal and his agent who is commissioned to undertake actions on behalf of the principal. See **agency problem**.

agency accounts (USA). A type of account held with financial institutions which undertake a defined set of activities on behalf of customers (cf. **paying agent**).

agency bill. A bill drawn on the foreign branch of a bank in a particular country.

agency broker (UK). A type of **broker** in the UK market who undertakes to carry out transactions for a **commission** on behalf of clients with **market-makers** (cf. **broker-dealer**).

agency costs. See **agency problem**.

agency deals. A relationship between institutional investors and **broker-dealers** covering such things as an agreed **commission** structure for the dealing service and set **fees** for brokerage house research.

agency fee. The fee paid to an **agent** for undertaking actions on behalf of a **principal**. See also **agency problem; commission**.

agency problem. According to **principal-agent** theory or analysis the two sides of a financing arrangement can be characterized as principals, those that supply money and capital, and agents, those that carry out the actions intended to meet the expectations of principals. In the context of money and capital markets, principals would comprise banks, investing institutions, and individual shareholders. The managers of the organizations into which the funds flow would be regarded as agents. The central idea behind this analysis, first formalized by Jensen and Meckling (1976), is that principals and agents are likely to have different objectives such that conflicts of interest arise given that principals rely on agents to make day-to-day decisions about the application of the deposited or invested funds. For example, investors may assume that the business will make capital expenditure decisions consistent with the implied rates of return and **risk** as measured by such indicators as the **beta coefficient**. Agents as managers may, however, perceive there to be different opportunities available that can lead to different rates of return and risk being undertaken by the business in practice. The 'problem' for lenders and investors is that they are unlikely to learn of any such divergencies until after the decisions have been made; that is, too late to reverse any decisions with which they do not agree as being consistent with the implied contract. Clearly, managers hope to meet the expectations of their principals but in addition may have other reasons for choosing a particular course of action; for example, rapid growth strategies that could increase the remuneration available to them as agents. As a result, principals may have an incentive to engage in what are known as *agency costs* to monitor the actions and behaviour of agents. Lenders, for instance,

may insist upon the regular receipt of accounting information in order to ensure the business is not going to breach any of the **covenants** attached to the loans. Investors as principals may well feel they have to scrutinize annual reports and accounts and follow the general financial or trade press in order to ensure they are aware of any announcements that could adversely affect the **common stock** or **ordinary share** price or **dividend** performance of their investments. This commitment to time, energy, and possibly the use of specialist expertise may have a direct fee cost, or at the least an **opportunity cost**. The analysis proposes various ways of trying to align the interest of principals and agents closer together within the context of specific funding relationship. See **asymmetric information; venture capital**. See M. C. Jensen and W. H. Meckling (1976), 'Theory of the Firm: Managerial Behaviour, Agency Costs, and Ownership Structure', *Journal of Financial Economics*, 3: 305–60.

agency relationship. The explicit and implicit contractual relationship between the **principal**, as owner, and the **agent**, as manager. See **agency problem**.

agent. (i) Individual or firm acting on behalf of another, the **principal**, to undertake some task. (ii) A **broker-dealer** who is acting on behalf of another party, the principal, and is not buying the securities or transacting for his own account but merely finding another party who is willing to enter into the opposite transaction (cf. **placing agent**). Such an agent does not have title to the principal's assets and owes a duty of trust. See **agency problem**. (iii) The manager of a firm. See **director**.

agent bank. (i) For floating rate securities an agent bank's main responsibility is to fix the appropriate interest rate when the **coupon** is reset (cf. **reference rate**). For short-term **euronotes** and **certificates of deposit**, the agent bank may also arrange issue and payments (cf. **issuing and paying agent**). See **floating rate note**. (ii) In banking, in a **syndicated loan**, or other kind of joint facility, the bank responsible for collecting interest and principal repayments from a borrower and passing this to the lending banks.

agent de change (French). **Stockbroker** or securities house.

agenti di cambio (Italy). **Stockbroker**.

aggregate exercise price. An option's strike price multiplied by the number of units of the **underlying** in the **contract**. Note that in some **option contracts** the aggregate exercise price is the strike price multiplied by the **face value** of the **underlying**.

aggregate risk. The total credit risk of one party with respect to another. The term is often used in the foreign exchange market to indicate both the current transactional risk from spot deals and out of value forward transactions.

aggregation. The netting of assets and liabilities between counterparties in the case of default or early termination of an agreement.

aggregation risk. The complex risk interdependencies that can arise when derivative instruments are based on more than one type of market or risk.

agio. (i) The premium over par value. Thus a price of 102 would have an agio of 2 (cf. disagio); (ii) A fee paid for undertaking a transaction. (iii) Uncommon term for spread.

agreement among underwriters or **agreement among managers.** Euromarket term for the purchase group agreement. See also subscription agreement; selling group agreement.

agreement corporation (Banking; USA). See Edge Act bank.

agreement value. The value of an interest rate swap or cross-currency swap for early termination purposes. It is based on the cost (or benefit) of replacing the swap at current market rates.

air pocket security (USA). A market description for a security where there are few buyers causing it to behave like an airplane hitting an air pocket (cf. penny stocks).

Aktie (German). Share (cf. common stock). Hence *Aktiengesellschaft*, stock company.

à la criée (French). Open outcry.

Aladdin bond. A type of refunding in which the terms and conditions of the new issue are set according to a predetermined formula.

alien corporation (USA). A company incorporated outside the USA and territories. See foreign corporation.

all-equity net present value (all-equity NPV). An approach to capital budgeting or investment appraisal in corporate finance that assumes the firm is totally financed by equity. This is used to establish the net present value of a project or investment, which is then modified by the benefits or costs of the firm's existing or intended capital structure. See adjusted present value.

Allfinanz (Germany). A term used to describe a fully integrated financial institution offering a complete range of products and services. See also bancassurance.

allied member. An owner of a member firm of the New York Stock Exchange who is not a member of the exchange.

alligator spread. Any type of option spread position made unprofitable under virtually all outcomes by high transaction costs (cf. butterfly spread). It derives its name from the voracity of the alligator which devours its prey while still alive.

all-in cost. The cost of acquiring, holding, or issuing a security or obtaining a loan that includes all the incidental costs of the transactions such as commissions, listing fees, taxes, and so forth. Usually arrived at by subtracting (adding) from (to) the price and (or) adding (subtracting) to (from) the interest payments these incidental items. In some markets the difference between the quoted price and the all-in cost can be quite substantial, for instance when warehousing commodities.

all-in premium. A warrant price as a percentage of the market price of the underlying if exercised.

allocation. See allotment.

allonge. An addition to a banker's acceptance or bill of exchange used to provide room for additional endorsements.

All-Ordinaries Share Index (Equities; Australia). Capitalization-weighted arithmetic index of the largest 245 common stocks quoted on the Australian Stock Exchange.

All-Ordinaries Share Price Riskless Index Note (ASPRIN) (Australia). Debt securities paying little or no interest where the returns are linked to the performance of the All-Ordinaries index. They are a combination of zero-coupon bonds and stock index call options on the index, where the difference between the par value and the zero is used to fund the option premium (cf. equity-linked notes). See also liquid yield option note.

all or none (AON). (i) An instruction to a broker that no part the transaction should be undertaken unless all of it is made at the agreed price. Inability to undertake the transaction does not automatically terminate the instruction (cf. fill or kill; good till cancelled). (ii) A type of underwriting agreement where the issue is cancelled if the under-

writer or **underwriting syndicate** is unable to sell the entire issue.

all-or-nothing option. A type of **exotic option** which pays either a predetermined amount or nothing, depending on whether it is **in the money** or not. See **digital option**.

allotment. (i) The allocation of a new issue of securities by the **lead manager** among **syndicate** members. This occurs after the issue's subscription period and after its final terms have been fixed. The syndicate members then allocate the securities to their investor clients. (ii) The allocation of securities in varying proportions according to the amount subscribed for in response to an **over-subscription** in the event of an **initial public offering** (USA) or **offer for sale** (UK) of new securities. Successful applicants receive a *letter of acceptance* specifying the details of the transaction. (iii) The award of bids in a **tender** (cf. **auction**).

allotment letter (UK). See **provisional allotment letter**; **renounceable documents**.

allowance for loan losses (Banking). See **reserve for credit losses**.

all-risks insurance. Standard marine insurance terms. Although termed all-**risks** there are significant exclusion clauses, such as war and piracy. Separate cover is required for these risks.

All Share Index. (Equities; UK). See **FT-Actuaries All Share Index**.

alpha or **alpha coefficient** (α). The risk-adjusted excess return on an asset or portfolio above that which is implied by its risk-adjusted return in the **Capital Asset Pricing Model** (CAPM). The CAPM relationship of risk to return is:

$$E(R_j) = R_f + \beta_j(E(R_m) - R_f)$$

where $E(R_j)$ is the expected return on the asset or portfolio j; R_f the risk-free rate; β_j the asset or portfolio's systematic risk; $(E(R_m) - R_f)$ the market risk premium. Alpha is the difference between the expected return as predicted by the CAPM and the actual return: $\alpha = R_j - E(R_j)$. The term is used in a general market sense for a firm's exceptional performance or performance above that anticipated for the risks taken (cf. **risk–reward**). See also **stock specific risk**.

alpha share. Defunct categorization of **ordinary shares** on the **London Stock Exchange** used between 1986 and 1991 for the most actively traded **stocks**. Listed stocks were divided into alpha, **beta**, **gamma**, and **delta** categories based on the availability of continuous prices, the number of

market-makers, the volume of turnover and market **capitalization** of the issues. The categorization has been replaced by the **normal market size** system.

alternative currency option. An option where the **underlying** is in one currency, but the payoff of this underlying is determined in another currency: for example, an option on a convertible in US dollars on a Japanese company's **common stock**. See **dual currency option**; **quantity adjusting option**.

alternative delivery procedure (ADP). Settlement of a **futures** or **option** contract between the **long** and the **short position** holders where the **delivery** or procedures are varied against the standard contract rules as specified by the exchange.

Alternative Investment Market (AIM) (Equities; UK). The formally regulated equity successor small firms market which replaced the **London Stock Exchange's Unlisted Securities Market** on 19 June 1995. In order to get a **quotation** the following conditions must be met: (1) be a **public limited company**; (2) accounts must meet a recognized standard (cf. **Financial Reporting Standards Board**); (3) issue a **prospectus**; (4) meet the **European Union's** Public Offer of Securities Regulation; (5) have a **nominated adviser**; and (6) have a **nominated broker**. AIM does not require a company to have a track record or issue a profits forecast (cf. **main market**). At least three different categories of company can be attracted: (1) growth companies with little or no track record which require a sizeable amount of capital for expansion or product development; (2) growth companies with a strong regional presence, which may not need large amounts of capital but think they can tap into local investors; and (3) private or family-owned companies which may not want capital but want to raise profile and provide additional liquidity for shares.

alternative option. See **rainbow option**.

alternative order. An instruction to a **broker-dealer** giving him a choice of actions. Typically an instruction to buy (or sell) a range of alternative securities.

alternative performance. A condition of a **cross-currency swap** agreement where, in the event that the two currencies are not re-exchanged at **maturity** but are sold on the market, the gains from the difference between the **spot rate** and the contractual rate are passed to the party which has made a loss.

amalgamation. See **merger**.

Amazon bond (Brazil). **Bonds** issued by the Brazilian government to foreign investors to fund conservation of the Amazonian rain forest.

amendment. A legally binding change made to an agreement when properly signed (cf. **waiver**).

American depository receipt (ADR) (USA). A receipt issued by a US bank evidencing it holds a foreign security on behalf of holders (cf. **European depository receipts**). It is used to trade foreign securities in the domestic US market by issuing **depository receipts** evidencing ownership of securities, principally **common stocks**, held by a depositary in the issuing firm's country. This is done in order to circumvent the problems of direct listing inherent in US securities regulations and to simplify **dividend** payments. The terms and conditions on the ADR, its **settlement**, transfer, and negotiability are the same as those for US securities, a harmonization desired by investors. In addition, some investors who are not permitted to invest in foreign securities are allowed to own ADRs. The first ADR was issued in the US market in 1920.

American excise. The right with an American-style **option** to exercise prior to the **expiry date** (cf. **European exercise**). In some circumstances this may be valuable.

American option. See American-style option.

American Stock Exchange (Amex; ASE) (USA). 86 Trinity Place, New York, NY 10006 (tel. 1 212 306 1000; fax 1 212 306 1802). Established in 1790. Second stock exchange based in New York and listing companies that are usually smaller and younger than on the **Big Board** (the **New York Stock Exchange** (NYSE)). Formerly known as the *curb exchange* since, until 1921, trading took place out on the street. The exchange has less stringent requirements for listing than the NYSE and also trades **options** and **futures**. It also established a direct link with the **Toronto Stock Exchange** in 1985 for primary market issuance (cf. **initial public offering**).

American Stock Exchange Composite Index (Equities; USA). Broad market average **index** of **common stocks** listed on the **American Stock Exchange**.

American-style option. A **put** or **call option** that may be exercised at any time over an extended period up to its **expiry date**, unlike a **European-style option** which is exercisable only at expiry. Because in certain circumstances it may be advantageous to **exercise** an option early, American options may trade at a higher price than corresponding European options. Conditions which may lead to optimal early exercise are:

1. A deeply **in-the-money** put. By not exercising, the holder forgoes the possible interest on the **underlying** surrendered since the underlying's value is not likely to recover. The exact point is known as the *critical asset price*. This might apply even in cases where there was a small intervening cash flow on the underlying (such as a **dividend**), the loss of which would have to be balanced against the gain in interest. The critical asset price or break-even point can be worked out approximately as the ratio of the underlying to the **strike price**, **time to expiry**, and interest rates.

2. A deeply in-the-money call and where there may be either one or more cash flows on the underlying which may or may not have been known with certainty when the option was written or bought; or where the known cash flow may be higher than what was predicted. An example would be a call on a **stock** which was going to pay a dividend before expiry or might announce a special dividend. In this case the option's **time value** is nearly zero and it may prove optimal to exercise early and forgo this. The holder should exercise at the last possible moment that would allow him to take advantage of the situation.

3. Where the risk of **default** of the option writer is high or rising, holders may exercise if the position is near to, at or just in the money, so as to preserve value.

Most **exchange-traded** stock **options** are the American-style, while **over-the-counter** options tend to be the European-style. Often called an *American option*.

American terms (Forex). The **foreign exchange market** quotation of currencies as the base against the US dollar. That is, the **foreign exchange rate** is expressed as one unit of the currency against units of US dollars. Sterling is normally quoted this way, for example the quote might be £1 = US$ 1.5523 (£/US$). The practice dates back to the time when sterling played a significant role in international trade as well as the complications of the old pre-decimal coinage. Also called *US terms*. The opposite, where the US dollar is the **base currency**, is known as **European terms**. The expression of the exchange rate is often abbreviated in reports. For instance, the rate between the Deutschemark and the US dollar is usually expressed as DM/US$ (i.e. as a **ratio**), although this is not universal practice and some people use the opposite (i.e. US$/DM, that is, a US$ variable amound = DM1) for the same method of quoting the exchange rate, so beware.

Americus Trust (Equities; USA). A five-year **trust** set up to repackage **common stocks** into different component parts made up of a **warrant** unit for the **underlying** stocks and a holding unit of the stocks but with a **covered call**. The warrant unit is a growth element since if the stock price exceeds the warrant **strike price**, then holders of the warrants will exercise and purchase the stocks. Holders of the stock unit receive **dividends** and capital appreciation up to the strike price. The idea is that the units will appeal to different types of investors, or can be held in different combinations providing different payoffs depending on expectations, e.g. a holding in two stock units and one warrant unit. The idea has been developed in **preference equity redemption cumulative stocks**, **prescribed right to income and maximum equity**, and **special claim on residual equity**.

Amman Financial Market (Jordan). PO Box 8802, JO-Amman (tel. 962 660170; fax 962 686830).

amortization or **amortising**. (i) The provision to repay debt over a period often through establishing a **sinking fund**. (ii) The gradual reduction of a **premium** over time, or the repayment of borrowings in a series of instalments, or the notional spreading of a **front-end fee** over the life of an issue (cf. **accretion**). See **balloon**; **grace period**; **straight line method**. (iii) A transaction or security where the **principal** reduces over the life of the agreement on the basis of pre-agreed redemption or in response to the reduction in the **underlying** pool of assets. Typically, **mortgage-backed securities** amortize before their final **maturity**. See also **collateralized mortgage obligation**. (iv) The writing off or reduction in value of an intangible asset over time (cf. **depreciation**).

amortizing cap. See **amortizing interest rate cap**.

amortizing collar. An **interest rate collar** in which the notional **underlying** principal amount is reduced over the life of the collar. As with the **amortizing cap**, such a structure will reduce the cost of the collar given the dynamics of **option pricing**.

amortizing interest rate cap (amortizing cap). An **interest rate cap** where the **notional principal** amount is reduced over time. The opposite would be an **accreting interest rate cap**, where the notional principal amount increased over time. Since a cap is a series of **options** with the same **strike price**, such an arrangement will reduce the cost of a cap given the dynamics of **option pricing**. See also **deferred cap**; **forward cap**.

amortizing mortgage. A mortgage arrangement where the borrower repays both interest and **principal** over the term of the mortgage (cf. **annuity**).

amortizing option. Type of **exotic option** where the **notional principal** amount decreases over the life of the option.

amortizing swap. A swap in which the notional **underlying** principal is reduced towards **maturity** (cf. **accreting swap**).

amortizing swaption. A swaption which has a declining notional **underlying** principal. This is used to match up with an **amortizing** security or underlying.

amount at risk. See replacement cost (cf. **value at risk**).

Amsterdam Financial Futures Market. See Amsterdam Stock Exchange.

Amsterdam Interprofessional Market (AIM) (Netherlands). **Block** trading system used on the Amsterdam Stock Exchange introduced in 1986.

Amsterdam Securities Account System (ASAS) (Netherlands). Method used on the Amsterdam Stock Exchange for trading foreign securities in their original form in their home currency and settlement system, rather than creating **depository receipts**.

Amsterdam Stock Exchange or **Amsterdamse Effectenbeurs**. (Netherlands). Amsterdamse Effectenbeurs, Beursplein 5 PO Box 19163, 1000 GD Amsterdam (tel. 31 20 23 9711). Beursplein 5, 1012 JW, Amsterdam; postal address: PO Box 19163, 1000 GD, Amsterdam, The Netherlands (tel. 31120 5234567; tlx 31 20 12302). The exchange is divided into a first tier, known as the Official Market, and second tier, Official Parallel Market for small and medium sized companies, and an Open Order Book (OOB) for trading government bonds, as well as trading foreign securities through the **Amsterdam Securities Account System** and **block** trading via the **Amsterdam Interprofessional Market**. There are three kinds of members: (i) Banks and broker-banks, who are registered with the **central banks**; (ii) **Brokers** who are not credit institutions; and (iii) Hoekman firms, which act as **specialists** (cf. **jobber**). The exchange's history goes back to 1602 when it started trading **shares** in the United East India Company.

Amsterdam Treasury Bond Market (ATM) (Netherlands). Interprofessional market in Dutch **government bonds** and in **futures** contracts on bonds on the Financiel Termijnmarkt Amsterdam (Amsterdam Financial Futures Market).

Amtlicher Handel (German). First section, or official market (cf. **Geregelter Markt**).

Analitico (Italy). **Capital gains tax** computed on gains reported in year-end tax reports. Holders could alternatively choose a lower flat rate tax paid when selling on all dealings known as a *forfettario*.

analysis of variance. A method of determining the causes of any deviation between the budgeted or expected outcome and the actual outcome of a particular decision, investment, project, or other activity.

analyst. An individual employed to undertake research into markets, companies, securities, and so forth (cf. **quant**). The type of research undertaken normally defines the area of expertise, e.g. a *credit analyst, equity analyst, technical analyst*. Sometimes known as a *researcher*.

analytical model. Formal mathematical **model** used to derive a theoretical or 'fair value' of an asset, security, or instrument. Because the model uses an equilibrium or **arbitrage-free condition** to derive the price or rate, such models are deterministic and are often called 'closed-form' in the theoretical literature since the derived value does not depend on additional, external factors. The **Black–Scholes option pricing model** is probably the best known analytical model in finance.

analytic approximation model. Estimation models used for valuing securities which combine features of analytic models with estimation techniques to arrive at a price. Typically such models aim to modify the values from analytic models which make assumptions about either the distribution of future prices or returns, payments, or **leakages** from the **underlying** value or changes in some other parameter used.

Andean Pact. Association grouping Bolivia, Ecuador, Columbia, Peru, and Venezuela set up in 1978 to further trade and economic intergration.

and interest. A term used to denote that accrued **interest** will be included in the purchase price of a security.

anergy. Unwinding the failed effects of **synergy**. See **mergers and acquisitions**.

angels. Individuals and companies which back high-risk ventures in the hope of high returns. Angels provide **seed capital** for high-risk business ventures.

Anglo-Saxons (French). Derogatory term used to describe the supposed preference in English-speaking economies for free market pricing and solutions.

Anlagefonds (German). **Mutual funds.**

Anleihe (Germany). A bond or loan obligation (cf. **Schuldschein**).

announcement date. The date a transaction becomes public. This may not be the date the transaction is **settled** or becomes effective (cf. **dated date**). For securities, also called the *launch date*.

annual accounts. Audited **financial statements** published by an organization, partnership, or incorporated business in compliance with statutory requirements. In most countries, semi-annual but unaudited statements are also required for listing purposes; and in a few countries the requirement is for quarterly unaudited statements.

annual basis. A method of interpreting economic statistics to give the annualized result of a time series based on fewer than a year's observations. Often used in reports on newly issued economic statistics to indicate the effect of a trend. Such extrapolations need to be treated with caution, especially since seasonal variations can seriously distort the result. Sometimes commentators favour an annualized three-month average to avoid the worst distortions of annualizing a single month's figures.

annual depreciation. The amount of **depreciation** reported in a firm's **financial accounts** for the year. See also **depreciation methods**.

annual equivalent. The yield on a bond that pays interest more than once a year, presented as an annual figure. Used, for example, to compare yields of semi-annual with annual bonds. The conversion formulae are:

1. To obtain the annual equivalent yield of a security with more than one coupon period per annum:

$$\left[\left(1+\left\{\frac{\text{Yield(expressed as an annual rate in decimals)}}{n = \text{(the coupon frequency per annum)}}\right\}\right)^n -1\right] \times 100\%$$

where the coupon is paid n times a year. For example, a bond yielding 10% with a semi-annual coupon, the annual equivalent yield is 10.25%:

$$\left[\left(1+\left\{\frac{0.10}{2}\right\}\right)^2 -1\right] \times 100 = 10.25\%$$

2. To obtain the periodic (annualized) yield of a security with an annual (equivalent) yield:

$$[(\{1+\text{yield expressed as an annual rate in decimals}\}^{1/n}) -1] \times 100 \times n\%$$

where the coupon is to be paid n times a year. For example, a bond yielding 10.25% with an annual coupon, the semi-annual equivalent (annualized) yield is 10%:

$$[(\{1 + 0.1025\}^{1/2}) - 1] \times 100 \times 2$$

The formula holds only when the tenor of the security is on an exact number of years. **Day count** conventions introduce a minor innacuracy to the results.

annual general meeting or **annual meeting (AGM).** A meeting of **common stock** holders of a company which generally takes place once a year to approve the financial results presented by the **board of directors**, to elect new directors and to vote on and agree any other matters that need shareholder approval (cf. **extraordinary general meeting**). Shareholders who cannot attend in person may vote by **proxy** (cf. **cumulative voting**; **majority voting**; **supermajority**).

annualized forward premium, annualized forward discount (Forex). The **premium** or **discount** between the **spot exchange rate** and the **forward** rate stated as an annualized percentage of the spot rate.

annually compounded yield. The **yield** calculated on the assumption that interest is reinvested annually at the yield rate (cf. **compound interest**).

annual percentage rate (APR). A method, specified by law, for calculating the nominal annual rate of return. This is to enable individuals to compare instruments with different ways of computing interest (weekly; monthly; quarterly; annually) (cf. **compounding interest**). See **annual equivalent**.

annual report. The report on an incorporated company's affairs that must be sent to **shareholders** after the end of the financial year. Such reports include an audited statement of the company's affairs as well as reports from the management of the company. The preparation and publication of such documents is seen by most companies as an important way of communicating with their stakeholders and may include many sections not required by law.

annual return (UK). A filing made with the Registrar of Companies by incorporated businesses to comply with the reporting provisions of the various Companies Acts. It includes, *inter alia*, a copy of the audited **financial statements** of the company, details of the company's share capital and assets, prior charges, directors, the company secretary, and **shareholders**.

annuity. (i) A fixed set of cash flows for a given period featuring the same periodic cash flow and the same frequency of payments. (ii) The value of a lump sum required to replicate (i). It assumes a constant discount, reinvestment, or compounding rate on the cash flows.

The present value of an annuity stream ($PV_{annuity}$) is found by:

$$PV_{annuity} = \text{Periodic Cash Flow} . \left[\frac{1 - \dfrac{1}{(1 - i)^n}}{i} \right]$$

The future value of an annuity stream ($FV_{annuity}$) is found by:

$$FV_{annuity} = \text{Periodic Cash Flow} . \left[\frac{(1 - i)^n - 1}{i} \right]$$

The term in square brackets is the annuity factor for the number of periods n at the periodic rate of interest i. The annuity factor (a) is sometimes written in shorthand as $at\rceil$. (iii) A financial contract between an insurance company and a person who, upon paying a lump sum, receives a periodic payment either for a fixed period (when it is known as an *annuity certain*) or for the life of the individual (known as a *life annuity*). It is an investment paying a predictable annual income, often until the investor dies. The annual payments can be so structured that they increase or decrease over the life of annuity so that they match known financial commitments. Purchasing an annuity is one way in which pension arrangements can be enhanced as it will provide a steady periodic payment. See **Additional Voluntary Contributions**.

annuity bond or **note.** A bond where the principal and interest are **amortized** over the life of the bond to give a stream of payments, normally equal. Variations (which are not strictly annuities) can include **balloon** repayments at maturity and a **grace period** at the start.

annuity due. An annuity where the cash flows occur at the start of each period rather than the end. That is, the first payment is 'due' now.

annuity finance or **loan.** A type of debt, which may be either at a **fixed rate** or a **floating rate** where the borrower repays both principal and interest at each interest payment date, thus reducing the principal amount of the loan over time. The alternative structure where the loan is all repaid at **maturity**, is known as a **bullet**. Intermediate structures where part of the loan is repaid during the life of the loan and the balance at maturity are called **balloons**.

annuity income shares (UK). A class of **ordinary shares** issued by a **split capital investment trust** (cf. **common stock**; **preferred stock**). They offer high income but no repayment of principal at maturity, since this is amortized in the payments (cf. **amortization**; **current yield**).

annuity swap. (i) A type of **amortizing swap** agreement that creates regular cash flows from irregular ones. May be used, for example by a highly seasonal borrower to help match cash flows to loan payments. To make such an arrangement work, the **notional principal** amount is adjusted over the tenor of the swap to take account of the differences in the payment streams. (ii) A **cross-currency swap** which has no exchange of principal.

anomaly. A misalignment in value for a security or a market which gives an **arbitrage** opportunity. Hence, *anomaly switching,* which involves replacing a part of a **portfolio** or a security in a portfolio with another of a similar nature in order to exploit a temporary misalignment of values. See **switch**; **technical analysis.**

ante date. To give a document a date prior to the date at which it is drawn up (cf. **ex ante**; **ex post**).

antei sōsa (Japan). **Stabilization.**

anticipated holding period (USA). A statement of the expected time in which assets procured under a **limited partnership** are likely to be held. In effect it gives an indication of how long the partnership is expected to last.

anticipation rate. See **refunding rate**.

anticipatory hedge. Term for a **hedging** transaction undertaken to protect a transaction that will occur at a future date (cf. **long hedge**; **producer's hedge**; **short hedge**).

anticipazioni a scandeza fissa o straordinarie (Lombard rate) (Banking; Italy). Fixed-term, collateralized advances made by the **Bank of Italy** to provide funds to banks (cf. **Tasso Sulle Anticipazioni Straordinarie**). See also **Lombard Rate.**

anticipazioni ordinarie (Banking, Italy). Short-term avances for **liquidity** purposes provided by the **Bank of Italy** based on the prevailing **discount** rate, known as the **Tasso Ufficiale di Sconto.**

antidilution clause. A provision in a **warrant** or **convertible** issue that allows for an adjustment in the terms should there be a **stock split**, **dividend**, or **new issue**. Its effect is to safeguard the price of the warrant and its holder's claim to **equity**.

anti-takeover measures. Any of a range of defences put in place by a company vulnerable to a takeover. See **poison pill**; **radar alert**; **self-uglification**; **shark repellent**.

antitrust laws. Generally those national laws designed to prevent the creation and operation of monopolies and restraint of trade.

API gravity (American Petroleum Institute gravity). A measure of **crude oil** viscocity. See **contract grade**; **energy futures.**

application for listing. Procedures and vetting of companies or securities when they initially seek a listing on a **stock exchange**.

application form. Document provided by intermediaries for the purpose of making an application in a **tender** or securities offer (cf. **prospectus**).

applied proceeds swap (USA). A sale of securities where the consideration is used in purchasing other securities. See **swap**.

appraisal. The determination of the degree to which a sample of a given **commodity** varies from the standard **contract grade**, used to determine **premiums** or **discounts** as appropriate for **delivery** purposes. Also known as *grading.* See also **alternative delivery procedure.**

appraisal ratio. A measure of an analyst's forecasts. It seeks to measure the degree the forecast varies against the actual outcome.

appreciation. An increase in value of an asset over time (cf. **depreciation**). Often used in the context of changes in **foreign exchange rates**.

appropriation. (i) Accounting procedure allocating the profits earned by an organization in its accounts. (ii) The right of a debtor to specify the allocation of payments owned to a particular debt owed to a creditor.

approved deferred share trust (ADST) (Equities; UK). A trust whose beneficiaries are the employees of the firm setting up the trust which purchases and holds shares in the originating company (cf. **employee stock ownership plan**). Such trusts are approved by the Inland Revenue and offer tax advantages, allowing the deferral of the tax on **dividends**.

approved list. A list of securities or credits that an individual or institution has defined as being suitable investments. Sometimes the list is based on categories, such as **credit ratings**, or on specific **obligors** or types of instruments. Approved lists may be constrained due to regulatory requirements, such as the need to have the securities **listed** on a recognized exchange. Every security salesman wants to know his client's approved list! See also **investment grade**.

Arab Bank for Economic Development in Africa (ABEDA). Bank modelled on development agency lines set up in 1973 to promote development in African countries.

Arab currency related unit (ARCRU). Little-used **basket** currency developed along the lines of the **European Currency Unit** and the **special drawing right**.

Arab Fund for Economic and Social Development (AFESD). Fund modelled on the **World Bank** established in 1968 to further economic development in Arab countries.

Arabian Light. See **marker crude**.

Arab Monetary Fund. Established along the lines of the **International Monetary Fund** in 1977 for the Arab world. Its members are Algeria, Saudi Arabia, Bahrain, Egypt, Iran, Yemen, Jordan, Qatar, Kuwait, Libya, Lebanon, Mauretania, Morocco, Oman, Somalia, Sudan, Syria, Tunisia, the United Arab Emirates, and the Palestinian Liberation Organization (PLO).

arbitrage. Initially taken to mean buying cheap and selling dear. Now taken to mean the purchase of a security in one market and the sale of that security, or its equivalent, in the same or other markets in order to exploit a temporary misalignment of prices at little or no **risk**. This misalignment can occur because of conditions unique to each market (cf. **anomaly**). It is possible, therefore, to arbitrage between the **cash**, **security**, **options**, and **futures** markets. Hence a person or institution involved in arbitrage activities is known as an *arbitrageur*. Although market participants talk of arbitrage, in many cases this refers to **spread** strategies where expectations of changes in price, spread, **yield**, or other relationships aim to secure a profit. Such arbitrage is not risk free but the behaviour of these different markets is highly interdependent (cf. **correlation**; **inter-commodity spread**; **intra-commodity spread**). It can also be applied to transactions aimed at benefiting from differences in regulations between countries, a condition known as *regulatory arbitrage*, or to exploit differences in taxation (*tax arbitrage*) (cf. **offshore**). See **covered interest arbitrage**; **index arbitrage**; **Risk arbitrage**; **riskless arbitrage**; **switch**; **trader**.

arbitrage bonds. See **advance refunding**.

arbitrage channel. (i) The range within which two financial instruments that are linked by risk-free arbitrage can diverge due to **bid-offer** spreads,

tax effects, or other technical factors such as uncertainty over the **delivery** price (cf. **cost of carry**). (ii) The upper and lower bounds by which **futures** can deviate from their **fair value** or theoretical value before **arbitrage** can take place, due to imperfections in the markets such as difficulties in **short selling** the **underlying**, transaction costs, and problems in closing out positions to match the final **settlement price**.

arbitrage-free condition. A precept of financial economics that in an efficient market with no transaction costs, short selling, and perfect divisibility, two assets with identical payoffs should trade at the same price (cf. **anomaly**). If they do not, it is possible to sell one and buy the other and make a risk-free or **arbitrage** profit. The idea that two assets with the same payoffs should sell for the same price, is called the *law of one price*. See **covered interest arbitrage**; **put–call parity**.

arbitrage pricing theory (APT). An asset-pricing theory based on arbitrage and diversification arguments. The approach proposes a **model** of the expected return on assets given that there are no arbitrage opportunities allowing investors to create risk-free wealth. The model is an attempt to provide a consistent and robust method for pricing the risk associated with different assets, based on the idea that each asset's return is a function of such factors as interest rates, yield structures, and the return on a market portfolio. The main problem with the model is defining exactly the set of factors that make up the determinants of expected asset returns. As such it is intended to represent an alternative to the **Capital Asset Pricing Model**. Stephen Ross developed the theory in 'The Arbitrage Theory of Capital Asset Pricing', *Journal of Economic Theory*, 13 (Dec. 1976), 343–62.

arbitrageur. A market participant who undertakes **arbitrage** as an investment strategy. The term is increasingly used to describe those institutions which undertake **equity** arbitrage in particular. This is a high-**risk** activity involving buying and selling **stocks** during price moving events. Such arbitrageurs are frequently active during takeovers, where they both buy and sell the securities of the participants involved, betting on the eventual outcome of the transaction.

arbitration. A process of resolving commercial disputes without recourse to lengthy, costly, and possibly chancy legal process by asking an independent third party (known as an *arbitrator*) to decide on the outcome. Many contracts stipulate the use of arbitration as a first means of settling differences. Arbitration can be either binding or not, the former compelling the two parties to abide by the arbitrator's decision. Arbitrators have evolved a sophisticated set of procedures to handle the process.

ARCRU currency unit. See Arab currency related unit.

arithmetic average or **mean.** The average of a set of numbers obtained by adding the numbers together and dividing by the number of observations:

$$\text{Arithmetic average (mean)} = \frac{1}{n}\sum_{i=1}^{n} x_i$$

Also just called the *mean*. See also **geometric average**.

arithmetic Brownian motion. See Wiener process.

arithmetic scale. A method of representing price movements where the vertical (price) axis uses an arithmetic scale (for instance, divided into units of 20). An alternative approach is to use a **semilogarithmic** scale, where the intervals represent equivalent value changes.

arm's length transaction. A transaction between related counterparties which is equivalent to those which would have been reached by independent parties (cf. **conflict of interest; transfer pricing**). It is often a requirement, for instance, for establishing market values in connection with a tax liability, the exact definition depending on the jurisdiction.

arrangement. A method of partially satisfying the debts owed to creditors, either through an informal agreement or supervised by the courts, which normally involves the assets of the debtor being paid out pro rata to the amounts owed. Also known as a *composition*. See also **Chapter 11; voluntary arrangement**.

arrangement fee. A **commission** paid to an intermediary for arranging a transaction (cf. **spread**). See **front-end fee**.

arranger. A financial intermediary who puts in place a major, one-off transaction. The term is mostly used for types of transaction where the intermediary does not act as an **underwriter** (cf. **best efforts**).

arrearages. The due but unpaid **dividends** on preferred stocks (cf. **cumulative**).

arrears. Overdue or unpaid interest and/or principal (cf. **default; problem asset**).

arrears rate reset swap or **arrears swap.** See in-arrears swap.

around (Forex). Abreviation of *around par* and used by traders when quoting the **forward** or **swap points'** spread (**discounts** or **premiums**) to the current **spot rate** (or **par** rate). Thus a Deutschmark quote of 'ten-ten around' would mean a ten-point spread either side of the current spot rate. A trader can only use around when the forward market is close to the current spot rate (i.e. the interest rate differential between the two currencies is negligible, or very small).

Article 65 of the Securities Exchange Law (Japan). Legislation introduced during the US occupation of Japan after the end of the Second World War by the MacArthur administration and patterned on the **Glass–Steagall Act**, separating commercial banking from securities activities and thus preventing Japanese banks from conducting securities business (cf. **universal banking**). Like the US equivalent, this is slowly being unwound as banks are being allowed to conduct securities activities.

Articles 85 and 86 of the Treaty of Rome. Two articles of the Treaty of Rome which deal with competition and monopoly power and have been used by the **European Community** to regulate **mergers and acquisitions**. See **Merger Control Directive**.

articles of association. See articles of incorporation.

articles of incorporation (Equities; USA). The document lodged with the relevant authority by those setting up a corporation. Once approved by the authority, a **certificate of incorporation** is issued. Taken together, these two documents represent the **charter** that gives legal status to the corporation. The charter contains detail regarding such things as company name, purpose, authorized **share capital**, and number and identity of directors. In the UK the document containing this type of information is known as the **memorandum of association**. Rules controlling the internal operation of the company are called **bylaws** in the USA, and as the articles of association in the UK (cf. **memorandum and articles of association**).

articles of partnership (USA). The written contract drawn up establishing a **partnership** (cf. **general partner; limited partner; unlimited liability**). See also **master limited partnership**.

ascending tops. A bullish **chart analysis** pattern where each succeeding peak is higher than the previous one and where a **resistance** line can be drawn linking them together. The chartist will expect the time series to continue rising up to this level with each new upswing. Also observable

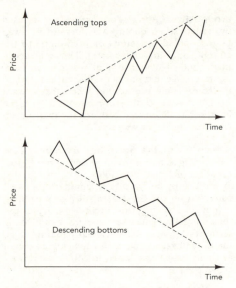

Ascending tops

as a **bearish** pattern of descending bottoms when the troughs of the series become lower with time.

A Shares. Class of ordinary shares or common stock which has no voting rights. Sometimes called *participation certificates*. See also **non-voting shares.**

Asian Development Bank (ADB; AsDB). Regional international agency patterned on the International Bank for Reconstruction and Development (**World Bank**) and based in Manilla, the Philippines, and providing funds to the Asian region (cf. **African Development Bank; European Bank for Reconstruction and Development; Inter-American Development Bank**).

Asian dollars or **Asian dollar market.** US dollar deposits held in Asia and the interbank market, principally US dollars, in the Asian time zones.

Asian Finance and Investment Corporation (AFIC). A subsidiary of the Asian Development Bank which invests in private sector projects or business (cf. **International Finance Corporation**).

Asian option. A type of **path-dependent option** or *look back* option where the buyer has the right to **exercise** at the average rate or price of the under-lying over the period of the option. There are two variants: method one sets the **strike price** as the average of the underlying against a fixed strike price, while method two gives the **expiry** price of the underlying against the average price over the option period. Asian options are less expensive than ordinary **European-style** options because

the **volatility** of an average is lower. As a result, sometimes called an *average rate option, history dependent option, moving strike option,* or **path-dependent option.**

asked, asked price, ask price, asking price, or **ask.** American term for **offer** or offer price (cf. **bid**). It is the price at which a security will be sold or the interest rate at which a loan will be made. It is numerically the higher **quote** in a two-way price. Now also commonly used internationally and in the UK.

as-of adjustments (Banking; USA). Ex-post cor-rections made to a bank's **reserves** position due to the receipt of delayed information or the dis-covery of errors. Banks are required to report to the **Federal Reserve** on a timely basis and, in consequence, after-the-fact adjustments have to be made.

assay. The test of purity of a metal to meet the standards of a **commodities** exchange (cf. **con-tract grade**). See also **alternative delivery proce-dure.**

assented securities. Typically bonds for which a suggested reorganization of interest and principal payments has been accepted or the **common stock** or **ordinary shares** tendered in acceptance of a **takeover** (cf. **non-assented**).

asset. (i) Any item owned or right possessed by a firm or individual which has an economic, com-mercial, or exchangeable value. (ii) The entries recorded on the left-hand side of a **balance sheet** (cf. **liabilities**).

asset allocation. A means of allocating assets by class or market based on an investment objective. See **strategic asset allocation; tactical asset allo-cation.**

asset analysis. A method of assessing securities which measures their potential performance on the basis of asset utilization. The financial statistics used include: **net asset value; return on capital employed;** and **takeover ratio.**

asset-backed. Generic term for securities or financing methods where the **underlying** obliga-tion and the source of interest and principal repay-ment is the cash flow from a particular financial asset or a portfolio (pool) of financial assets. Ex-amples of asset-backed securities include **receiva-bles** from commercial loans, credit cards, auto loans, real estate, inventory financing, and other securities (cf. **mortgage-backed**). The key factor in putting together such securities is the ability to **differentiate or pool specific income producing assets** so as to establish a legitimate legal claim or **lien** thereon. See **pass-through**; **pay-through bond**.

asset-backed commercial paper. An issue of **commercial paper** (CP) by a **special purpose vehicle**, which in turn holds a pool of assets (**mortgages**; **receivables**, and so forth). The CP is used to fund their purchase. See also **asset backed**; **securitization**.

asset-backed finance. Banking term for finance where assets are specifically pledged in support of the loan in contrast to normal bank lending against cash flow (cf. **factoring**).

asset-backed security (ABS). A security where the principal and interest is secured on predictable income-producing assets (cf. **asset-backed**).

asset-based. Any form of lending which involves a pledge of the **underlying assets**. See **asset-backed security**; **debenture**; **lien**; **mortgage-backed securities**.

asset-based monetary aggregate. A measure of **money supply** based not on notes and coins but on the price behaviour of certain assets, such as property prices, exchange rates, and other securities. The intent is to create a basis for setting **monetary policy** that is not only transparent in its calculation but one which reflects financial transfers within and outside an economy.

asset-based swap or **asset swap.** An interest rate swap or cross-currency swap designed to modify the cash flows from an **underlying** asset. The opposite, where obligations are being modified, is known as a *liabilities swap*.

asset bubble. Systematic overvaluation of an asset (or sometimes a market) beyond that implied by historical precedent and **fundamental analysis**.

asset class. See **class**.

asset constraint. Any restriction imposed on the freedom of choice of **assets** in a **portfolio**, for instance, restrictions imposed on investments in particular countries, industries, or processes. Such constraints may form part of the allocation decision for ethical or environmental reasons.

asset coverage test. A **covenant** that restricts the amount of further indebtedness by a borrower in a loan **facility** or security issue to some fixed ratio of **assets** to debt. The test usually specifies what constitutes assets (normally net tangible assets) and debt (normally **long-term** debt).

Asset Depreciation Range System (ADRS) (USA). A schedule of the range of useful lives drawn up by the US Internal Revenue Service in determining the amount of tax **depreciation** allowable, used in conjunction with the **Accelerated Cost Recovery System**. The method gives an upper and lower range to the expected useful life of the assets within the different classes.

asset engineering. Any of a range of restructuring activities by firms which reduce the asset base. See **bifurcation**; **divestment**; **leasing**; **management buy-out**.

asset finance. A range of financing techniques which include **factoring**, **hire purchase**, **leasing**, and **receivable financing**. The salient characteristic is that the funding is advanced against an asset in many cases, the firm's trade debtors.

asset financing. Methods of financing based around the pledging of assets to raise debt. Such methods include **asset-backed** and **mortgage-backed** as well as **forfaiting** and **receivables** financing.

asset-liability gap. Differences between contractual liabilities and covering assets (cf. **current assets**; **acid-test ratio**). Such gaps may be a product of timing mismatches between payments and receipts or mismatches of a more fundamental structural nature, such as funding long-term assets with short-term borrowing.

asset-liability management. The area of **risk management** which primarily manages the **interest rate risk** mismatches between receipt and payment flows of primarily financial **assets** and **liabilities**. It requires analysis of the tenor and certainty of future cash flows. A common approach to analysing mismatches is the **funding gap** methodology based on the idea that **sensitivity** to interest rate changes arises from the need to fund net asset balances. The method assigns to each asset and liability a **maturity** of (*a*) its final

Asset liability management

Period	Quarter 1	Quarter 2	Quarter 3	Quarter 4
Assets	200	100	100	100
Liabilities	(150)	(150)	0	0
Funding gap	50	(50)	100	100
Direction of sensitivity	—	—	—	—
Cumulative gap	50	0	100	200
Direction of cumulative sensitivity	—	0	—	—
Effect of 1% rate rise	−0.5	0	−1.0	−2.0
Effect of 1% rate fall	+0.5	0	+1.0	+2.0

repayment date and (*b*) the next date on which its interest rate is reset to a market rate. The funding gap is the net outstanding asset (positive) or liability (negative) **position** in each time period. Such periods are often referred to as *buckets*. The gap in a given period indicates the sensitivity of the value of the portfolio to a rise in interest rates in that period. For example, if the portfolio consisted of a £100 fixed interest loan maturing in twelve months, a £100 **floating rate note** repricing in three months and a £150 **floating rate** deposit repricing in six months have the funding gaps shown in the Table.

Note that for a variety of reasons, the funding gap method only gives an approximate prediction of interest rate sensitivity. A more accurate approach uses **cash gaps**. See also **asset-liability management committee**; **assets repriced before liabilities**; **gearing**; **leverage**.

asset-liability management committee (ALCO; ALMC). Senior management committee in a financial institution responsible for policy on **asset-liability management** and **risk control**. Typically the ALMC would meet monthly and would set broad policy guidelines for asset-liability mismatches, balance sheet usage, permitted trading positions, **liquidity**, and so forth. Sometimes the committee is also responsible for authorizing new lines of business and the required control systems.

asset-liability sensitivity. See **gap analysis**.

asset liquidity. The ability quickly to realize assets for cash (cf. **current assets**; **liquidity risk**). See **acid-test ratio**; **forced sale**.

asset management. (i) Investment service provided by financial institutions to their clients. (ii) Management of the (financial) assets of an organization to obtain the best results (cf. **liability management**). Also commonly called *investment management*.

asset management account (USA). Generic term for accounts held with financial intermediaries which combine some of the functions of investment accounts with traditional banking functions.

asset manager. An individual or institution responsible for managing assets. The opposite would be a *liabilities manager*.

asset mix. The percentage of each type or class of asset in a **portfolio**. For instance, a portfolio might have a 50 : 30 : 20 mix of **common stock**, **preferred stock** or **preference shares**, and **bonds**.

asset-or-nothing option. See **binary option**.

asset play. The market's term for an investment strategy based on buying **stocks** where the market price is low relative to the corporation's assets.

asset sales. (i) Disposals of assets or business units made by a company. These can take the form of trade sales, to another company, or a **management buy-out**. Also known as a 'disposal'. (ii) (Banking) The practice of **sub-participation** of commercial **loans** by banks. Many banks originate loans with the express intention of then selling them on. The unit responsible for such activity is usually known as the asset sales group or unit.

asset securitization. The process of turning assets into securities. There are four basic ways that this is done: via a **mortgage**, a **pass-through**, a **pay-through**, or unitization. See also **collateralized mortgage obligation**.

asset sensitive or **asset sensitive gap.** (Banking). A condition where a bank's assets are repriced (the interest rate is reset) before its **liabilities**. The converse is known as *liability sensitive*. See **asset-liability management**; **assets repriced before liabilities**; **gap analysis**.

asset settlement. See **deliverable**; **physical delivery**.

asset specificity. The degree to which the value of a specific or set of tangible or intangible assets is connected to their current use. There is a potential loss of value in next best use.

assets repriced before liabilities (ARBL) (USA). A US banking term for the difference in size between assets and liabilities to be repriced at market interest rates. If the ARBL is positive, this implies that the bank is *asset sensitive*; if the ARBL is negative, this means that the bank is *liability sensitive* (cf. **rate sensitive assets**). In the UK, known as *interest rate exposure* (cf. **gap**; **maturity gap exposure**). See also **asset-liability management**.

asset stripping. The acquisition of a business with the intention of reselling at a profit some or all of its **assets** or component businesses. In this situation, the sum is hopefully worth less than the parts. Individuals or firms which specialize in this type of activity are known as *asset strippers* and there is a degree of opprobrium attached to the activity. In a more respectable guise it is known as *unbundling*.

asset swap. Term used for **cross-currency swap** and **interest rate swap** transactions specifically hedging individual assets. Such swaps alter the net cash flows to the holder of the asset. For instance, a **receive fixed swap** together with a floating rate note will turn the asset into a **synthetic**

fixed rate bond. Different types of swaps may be required: for example, **callable swaps** or **puttable swaps** may be used to match with **call provisions** and **put provisions** that are embedded in the underlying asset. See also **bond swap; switch**.

asset utilization. Measures as to how efficiently a firm uses its **assets**. See **ratio analysis**.

asset value. (i) The market value of an asset. (ii) The recorded value of an asset in a set of accounts. See **book value**. (iii) Another term for **net worth**.

assign. The requirement of an **option writer** to meet the obligation on the **exercise** of an **option**: to sell the asset in the case of a **call option** writer, or to buy the asset in the case of a **put option** writer. When a writer has been so designated he is said to have been *assigned*.

assignment. (i) General term for the passing of a contractual obligation to a third party. In the UK, to be legally binding, it has to be absolute, in writing, and communicated to the party owed the right. (ii) Term for one of the methods used in the asset sales market to trade loans (cf. **less developed countries debt market**). The other common method is through a **sub-participation agreement** (cf. **silent sub-participation**). (iii) Used in the swaps market when a **swap** contract (a bilateral agreement between parties) is sold (assigned) by one party to another, normally for a lump sum, reflecting the market value of the swap contract. Such a transaction usually requires the approval of the original party, but the right to assign is increasingly a standard feature of swap contracts. The major problem is that the new **counterparty** assumes the **credit risk** of the remaining party. Institutions under regulatory pressure have increasingly resorted to **cancellation** or **netting** rather than assignment for this reason. (iv) In the **exchange-traded options markets**, the exchange makes an assignment to a counterparty to take **delivery** (in the case of a **put**) or provide the **underlying** (in the case of a **call**) when an **option** is **exercised**. Such counterparties are chosen by the exchange **clearing house** at random from all the writers of that **class** of option.

assimilation (Equities; USA). Term for the **seasoning** of a new issue when all the new securities have been sold to investors. Also known as *absorbed*.

associate company. A partly-owned company where, in general, the interest is less than 50%.

Association Française des Banques (AFB) (Banking; France). French bankers' association.

Association Luxembourgeoise des Fonds d'Investissement (ALFI) (Luxembourg). A trade association set up to represent the interests of managed funds in the Grand Duchy.

Association of Futures Brokers and Dealers (AFDB) (UK). Former **self-regulating organization** which was responsible for the conduct of practitioners in the **futures** industry and accountable for ensuring adherence to its rule book to the **Securities and Investments Board**. Now incorporated into the **Securities and Futures Authority**.

Association of International Bond Dealers (AIBD). The self-regulatory organization of dealers in **Eurobonds** formed in 1969 with its headquarters in Zurich. One of its activities was to set standards for trading and settlement in the market. Following regulatory and compliance changes required under the UK's Financial Services Act, 1986, it became a designated exchange and is now known as the **International Securities Market Association**. See also **International Primary Markets Association**.

Association of Payment Clearing Services (APCS) (Banking; UK). The umbrella organization responsible for the money transfer and payments system within the UK. Under its aegis are the **Bankers' Automated Clearing Services** and the **Clearing House Automated Payment System**.

Association of South East Asian Nations (ASEAN). Comprises Brunei, Indonesia, Malaysia, Philippines, Singapore, and Thailand. Originally set up to coordinate defence requirements in the region.

assumption agreement. An agreement by a new party to take on the liability of another party (cf. **assignment**).

assurance. Type of insurance contract for an eventuality which will definitely occur but where the timing is uncertain. It is used particularly in life assurance (insurance) (cf. **risk management**). The purchaser is known as the *assured* or policy holder; the seller, as the *underwriter*.

asymmetrical margining. A condition of a two-way **margin** agreement where one party may be required to provide a higher margin than the other party to reflect differences in **credit worthiness** or other features of the transaction.

asymmetrical treatment (Bonds; USA). For difference in treatment allowed by issuers of **asset-backed securities** between the Internal Revenue Service and the **Financial Accounting Standards Board**. The former will allow the obligation to be treated as a debt for tax reporting purposes while the latter will allow complete accounting removal from the balance sheet (cf. **defeasance**).

asymmetric information. Usually regarded as part of the **agency problem** because managers (**agents**) are said to be in possession of share price-sensitive information and other intimate knowledge of the organization for which they work which is not available to outsiders, including investors and lenders. For such principals the existence of this one-sided possession of valuable information creates a dilemma. Do they attempt to extract this information directly or do they rely on the formal arrangements for the dissemination of information? In practice, most investors use generalized proxies for this information, such as **dividend** announcements and brokers' reports. See also **adverse selection; efficient markets hypothesis; moral hazard.**

asymmetric payoff or **profile.** The characteristic of certain types of securities and **derivative** instruments to provide payoffs which are not the same depending on whether the market rises or falls. For instance, **bonds** with **call provisions** will not rise much above the **yield-to-call** since there is a high probability that the issuer will redeem the bonds early (cf. **negative convexity**). Similar asymmetries arise in **options** where the holder has a fixed cost but a potentially unlimited gain. Also called a *non-linear profile*. See also **symmetric payoff; skewness.**

as-you-like option or **warrant.** A type of warrant which is a **double option**, that is the holder has the right to make the warrant either a **call** or a **put** on the **underlying**. It has the same disadvantages as the double option. See also **chooser option.**

at a discount. See discount.

at a premium. See premium.

at best. An instruction to a dealer to buy or sell securities at the most favourable price ruling at the time the transaction takes place (cf. **limit order**).

at call. See call money.

Athens Stock Exchange (Greece). 10 Sophocieus Street, GR-Athens 10559 (tel. 30 1 32 11 301; fax 30 1 32 13 938). The exchange was established in 1876 for trading Greek company **common stocks.**

Atlantic-style option. See Bermudan-style option.

at limit. See limit order.

at-market. A transaction effected at the prevailing market price or rate (cf. **at best; at the market**). The opposite would be 'off-market'.

at-or-better. An instruction to a dealer to buy or sell securities at the given price or rate, or better if possible.

at par. A transaction, such as a security's redemption, at the **face value** or **par value** (cf. **discount; premium**). See also **redemption price.**

ATS account (USA). Account to trade on a **screen-based automated trading system.**

at sight. Term on a **banker's acceptance** or bill of exchange indicating that payment is due on presentation (cf. **after date; after sight**).

attached. When a **warrant** has remained attached to the securities with which they were originally issued (cf. **cum**).

attachement. A lien made on assets or earnings provided by a court to enforce the repayment of an outstanding debt.

at the close. A buy or sell order to be executed during the last few seconds of a trading session, usually in order that the transaction price is the same as the **closing price.**

at the market. Instruction to transact at the prevailing market price, whatever it is.

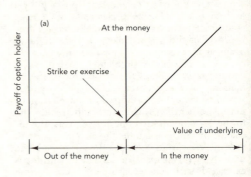

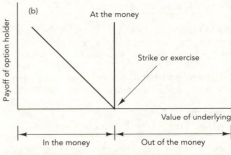

At the money. (a) For a call option (b) For a put option

at the money or **on the money.** Description of an **option** whose **strike price** or rate is equal to the market price or rate of the **underlying** (cf. **exercise price; in the money; out of the money**).

at-the-money forward (Forex). **Currency option** where the **exercise price** is the same as the forward foreign exchange rate at the time the option is written. This is unlikely to be the same rate as the **spot rate** at the time.

at the open or **at the opening.** A buy or sell order to be executed during the first few seconds of a trading session, usually in order that the transaction price is the same as the **opening price** (cf. **opening rotation**). See also **market-on-close order.**

auction. (i) An organized method of establishing the market price for some asset, property, security, or instrument. It is a central feature of financial markets which involve the purchase and sale of many kinds of **assets, securities, instruments,** or **commodities** in which a number of potential buyers and sellers compete on price or rate, the highest bidder, lowest offeror being successful (cf. **winner's curse**). There are a number of different ways auctions can be organized. They can be either one-off operations, as with a new issue, or continuous, as with secondary trading. In practice, most financial market trading is organized as a *two-sided market* involving buyers and sellers, the usual examples being stock exchanges. Such markets are, as a result, often called *double-auction systems* since both sides are effectively engaging in an auction, with sellers soliciting purchasing bids and buyers selling offers. Organized exchanges maintain a system to regulate transactions across time. To ensure an 'orderly market', there are fixed criteria for determining transaction precedence based on: (i) the highest bid and lowest offer; (ii) large size before small, with random selection if two trades are the same size and the precedence time criterion is not applicable; and (iii) exchange rules normally stipulate public orders have precedence over members' own orders. Most exchanges consider the need to have a **specialist** as a **market-maker** to operate such a system successfully and are *order-driven* markets, although, as with the **London Stock Exchange** and **over-the-counter** (OTC) trading, *quote driven* markets also exist. The **derivatives** exchanges have a different auctioning method in that a large number of buyers and sellers congregate in one physical location and determine transactions via *open-outcry*, which involves buyers (sellers) finding sellers (buyers) willing to enter into a transaction at an agreed price (cf. **floor; limit order board; pit**). For the OTC markets, the auction principle is less applicable, since the price is negotiated between the buyer or seller directly or with a finan-

cial intermediary, acting as **principal**. However, such a market is effectively also an auction since most market participants are aware of the price or rate at which transactions take place and a number of intermediaries are involved in providing price indications or **quotes** at which they will undertake transactions.

New issue markets are organized on slightly different lines. Auctions, or **tenders**, can take different forms. The most common method is a *competitive auction* or *bidding* process designed to award the auctioned asset to the highest bidder. The two most common methods are the *English auction*, or competitive auction, where the amount on offer is allocated on the basis of the highest bid, then sequentially lower bids until the entire amount on offer is successfully allotted (cf. **tail**). The other major method is via a *Dutch auction*, which allocates the securities on offer to all participants in the auction at the lowest price required to successfully allot the amount on offer. This type of auction is also sometimes referred to as a *unitary price auction*. Such an auction ensures a market clearing price for a new issue. In addition, with new issues, the selling party sometimes also sets a *non-competitive auction* where allotment is based on criteria other than price competitiveness. For instance, it might be based on size, previous activity, or other factors.

Although auctions generally are designed to allocate securities to the highest bidder or to establish a market clearing price, the competitive pricing mechanism can also be used to redeem or retire financial instruments, in such case; it is often called a *reverse auction or tender*. Auctions are also used formally or informally to sell assets or businesses. Usually such auctions are organized on the basis of a sealed-bid and allocate the asset to the highest bidder (cf. **second price auction**). See also **silent auction; tender panel**.

(ii) (USA) Market term for the **US Treasury's** primary issuance of securities. **Treasury bills** are generally auctioned once a week, while **bonds** are auctioned once a quarter (aka *the quarterly refunding*) but the frequency has increased with the size of the US budget deficit. In the UK, generally known as a **tender**, although US-style auctions have been introduced.

auction market. A financial market where all transactions take place in a given location (cf. **floor; pit**). Organized exchanges are auction markets. It involves a system of trading securities through **brokers**, **agents**, or **market-makers** where buyers compete with other buyers while sellers compete with other sellers for the best prices. Most trades are executed for final investors on both sides since the **specialists** buy and sell on their own behalf (cf. **head-to-head; principal-to-principal; quote driven; direct search market**).

auction market preferred stock (AMPS) (Equities; USA). Another name for **auction-rate preferred stock**.

auction-rate note. A type of **variable rate note** where the **coupon** rate is reset by a **dutch auction** process.

auction-rate preferred stock (ARPS) (Equities; USA). A type of **floating rate preferred stock** in which the **dividend** is reset by **dutch auction** based on a **reference rate** (normally US **treasury bills**, plus the required investor **margin**), which is usually held every forty-nine days. To avoid problems with the market, normally parts of an issue will be auctioned at different dates. In addition, such **preferred stocks** normally have a **backstop** or maximum dividend rate and are **puttable** to the issuer or a **remarketing agent** at each dividend determination date. There are many different names for this instrument: *auction market preferred stock* (AMPS), *dutch auction rate transferable securities* (DARTS), *money market preferred stock* (MMP), *short-term auction rate stock* (STARS). Such issues are considered **equity** for financial reporting and tax purposes. They also have the attraction of allowing an issuer to make his name known in the market. Because the securities are frequently repriced in line with current interest rates, such issues have been seen as a low-cost form of equity finance.

audit. (i) External scrutiny of a firm's **financial statements** or financial records or workings by independent accountants (the **auditors**) to ensure they can be described as a 'true and fair view' of the business. (ii) Similarly, any inspection of a particular activity which could be done by an internal working party (*internal audit*) and pollution control (*environmental audit*). See **audit trail**.

Auditing Practices Board (Accounting; UK). Standards-setting body for auditing practice in the UK. It sets *Statement of Auditing Standards* (SAS) for how items should be audited.

auditor's opinion, report, or **statement.** A letter written by an auditing firm of accountants that certifies the scope and accuracy of the report. A qualified opinion may indicate difficulties in auditing to the required standard and/or missing information. The opinion is a useful supplement to the published information in that it may highlight any departure from accepted standards. In the USA sometimes called an *auditor's certificate*.

audit trail (Securities). The name given to the ability of a stock market's surveillance department to trace the ultimate beneficiaries of security transactions. Also known as a *paper trail* or *smoking gun*.

au jour le jour (Money markets; France). Overnight money.

Ausfuhrkredit GmbH (AKA) (Banking; Germany). Export finance and credit guarantee corporation owned jointly by German banks.

Auslandsbuchforderungen (Switzerland). A type of short-term security similar to **commercial paper** which avoids Swiss stamp duty by being in book-entry form.

Auslandskassenverein (AKV) (Germany). See **Deutsche Auslandskassenverein**.

Auslandsobligationen (Switzerland). Foreign bond public or private issues made in the Swiss domestic market. In English-language reports normally called Swiss franc foreign bonds (maturities in excess of eight years) and notes (maturities of two to eight years), or market.

Aussie bonds. Australian dollar-denominated eurobonds.

Aussie Mac (Australia). See **National Mortgage Market Corporation**.

Australian Financial Futures Market (AFFM) (Australia). A division of the Australian Stock Exchange. 20 Bond Street, Sydney, NSW 2000 (tel. 61 (0) 2 227 0000; fax 61 (0) 2 251 5525). Established in 1976.

Australian Options Market (AOM) (Australia). Part of the Australian Stock Exchange. 20 Bond Street, NSW 2001 (tel. 61 (0) 2 227 0000; fax 61 (0) 2 251 5525). Established in 1976.

Australian Securities Commission (ASC) (Australia). The national regulator responsible for administering companies and securities law. Regulatory body for the securities industry. Formerly the National Companies and Securities Commission (cf. **Commission des Opérations de Bourse** (France); **Securities and Exchange Commission** (USA); **Securities and Investments Board** (UK)).

Australian Stock Exchange Limited (ASX) (Australia). Exchange Centre, 20 Bond Street, Sydney NSW 2000; Postal Address: PO Box H224 Australia Square NSW 2000 (tel. (02) 227 0000; fax: (02) 227 0961; tlx: STOCKEX AA 20630). The successor combination established on 1 April 1987, of the six independent regional stock exchanges in the state capital cities of Australia which were Sydney, Brisbane, Adelaide, Hobart, Melbourne, and Perth. See **all-ordinaries share index**; **Stock Exchange Automated Trading System**.

Austrian Traded Index (ATI) (Austria). Market-capitalization weighted **index** of the largest **common stocks** traded on the Vienna Stock Exchange. It is calculated in real time while the exchange is in session.

Autex system (USA). An electronic notification system for large blocks of securities (cf. **block; lot**).

authentication. The physical endorsement of a certificate by an **agent** in order to give it legal effect (cf. **bearer bond; book-entry security; issuing agent; issuing and paying agent**).

authority bond (Bonds; USA). A **bond** issue made by an agency or corporation set up to administer a public revenue-generating project. Such issues have some of the characteristics of **income bonds**.

authorized capital (Equities; UK). See **authorized stock**.

authorized dealer or **intermediary.** A financial institution that is permitted to engage in certain lines of business or act in a particular market: for instance, a broker who is authorized to transact business on an exchange, or a bank which is granted **central bank** permission to engage in foreign exchange.

authorized financial advisor (UK). Financial intermediary authorized under the **Financial Services Act, 1986** to proffer investment advice (cf. **execution-only broker**).

authorized futures and options fund (AFOF) (UK). **Investment** and **unit trusts** regulated by the **Securities and Investments Board** and allowed to market to the public in the UK. Such funds may either invest in **futures** or **options** or both. They hold a mixture of **derivatives** and securities and deposits, although some are fully invested in derivatives and thus offer **geared** or **leveraged** exposure to the **underlying**.

authorized stock, shares, or **share capital.** The number of shares that a firm may issue as specified in its **corporate charter** (USA) or **articles of incorporation**.

autocorrelation. Used to describe the **correlation** between the error terms in a regression. Its effect is to invalidate one of the key assumptions underpinning the **ordinary least squares** procedure, thereby requiring corrective action to the procedure (cf. **multicollinearity**). See **heteroscedasticity**.

Automated Clearing House (ACH) (USA). A US term for the computer **clearing** and **settlement** system, operated under the control of the Federal Reserve Board made up of thirty-two regional interbank networks.

Automated Pit Trading (APT) (UK). The London International Financial Futures and Options Exchange's screen-based trading system started in November 1989, which offers extended after-hours trading beyond that of the exchange's floor trading sessions (cf. **open outcry; screen-based**).

Automated Real-Time Investments Exchange (ARIEL) (UK). A now defunct, computer-based trading system set up in 1974 as a competitor to the **London Stock Exchange**.

automated screen trading (AST). Electronic interchange of orders through computers allowing continuous (24-hour) trading. A typical system is the one operated by Reuters for **foreign exchange** (cf. **GLOBEX**).

automated teller machine (ATM). An unmanned terminal usually activated by a magnetically coded card, which can be used to dispense cash, take instructions on fund transfers, and summarize information on the status of an account. The user authenticates his transactions by identifying himself with a personal identification number (PIN). Also known as a *cash dispenser*, although the system can do more than just provide cash advances.

Automated Trading System (ATS) (New Zealand). Screen-based trading system in use by the New Zealand Futures and Options Exchange.

automatic exercise. The practice that **options** which are **in the money** at **expiry** are automatically **exercised** by the **clearing house** or the **counterparty** without specific instructions (cf. **cabinet trade**). The assumption is that the holder would want to exercise since he stands to make a profit. Clearing houses now routinely exercise all *in-the-money* options at expiry without requiring an exercise notice. NB: only those options manifestly in the money are automatically exercised; options **at the money**, or just in the money may not be triggered by the automatic exercise routine. Automatic exercise can be suppressed by filing a supression notice with the clearing house (at expiry). Also known as *exercise by exception*.

automatic stay. A court or legally enforced **moratorium** on actions against a plaintiff. For example, this is a condition that arises if a firm files for **Chapter 11** in the USA, or enters **insolvency** proceedings in the UK.

automatic transfer service (ATS) (Banking). Facility provided by a bank to transfer surplus **funds** automatically from a current account or non-interest bearing **checking account** into an interest paying or savings account. See **concentration banking**.

automobile receivables. See **asset-backed securities**; **certificates of automobile receivables securities**.

autoregressive conditionally heteroscedastic model (ARCH). See **homoscedastic**.

autoregressive integrated or **interactive moving average models (ARIMA).** See **moving average models**.

autoregressive models (ARMS). See **moving average models**.

autoregressive moving average models (ARMA). See **moving average models**.

availability clause (Banking). A term in a multi-currency **credit facility** which stipulates that the lender is only obliged to provide a particular currency, if generally and freely available. As a result it is sometimes known as a *currency availability clause*.

availability float. See **float**.

available earnings. See **earnings per share**; **ratio analysis**.

availability risk. The risk that **funds** will not be made available to a firm. It results from any mismatching **assets** and **liabilities** (cf. **flight-to-quality**). See **asset-liability management**; **bankruptcy**; **credit worthiness**; **financial leverage**; **gap analysis**; **insolvency**; **leverage**; **liquidity risk**.

aval. (i) A bank guarantee for debt purchased by a **forfaiting** transaction. (ii) Third party guarantee provided on a **banker's acceptance**, **bill of exchange**, or **promissory note**, usually by a bank. (iii) The signature that authenticates the guarantee.

average. (i) (USA). Term sometimes used for **index**. Hence the **Dow-Jones** average. (ii) One of a range of statistics used to describe a series of numbers (cf. **arithmetic average**; **geometric average**; **mean**; **median**).

average cap. See **average rate cap**.

average collection period ratio. A measure of a firm's control on extending **credit** to buyers. It is the total **receivables** divided by the sales or **turnover** per day. See **ratio analysis**.

average down or **averaging down.** The practice of buying or selling large volumes of a security in stages as its market price falls. This means that the average cost of the block of securities falls with each additional purchase. See **averaging**.

average equity. A term for a customer's average daily balance on a trading account. See **margin requirement**.

average life. A method of calculating the average maturity of **bonds** or borrowings which are amortized. It is calculated by taking the sum of the amount repaid in each period times the period and dividing by the total issue size. Thus a bond which repays from year 7 with four equal annual instalments will have an average life of 8.5 years against a maturity of 10 years (see Table).

Year (i)	Amount (ii)	Sum (i×ii)
7	25	175
8	25	200
9	25	225
10	25	250
	100	850

Average life $= 850 \div 100 = 8.5$ years. Note that average life is a different concept from the **duration** method, which is also known as the discounted mean term, for working out the **discounted** average **tenor** of payments of interest and principal payments.

average price or **average rate option (APO; ARO).** See **Asian option**; **path-dependent options**.

average rate cap or **average cap.** A type of **cap** based on the average interest rate over the period (usually six months) rather than on the rate prevailing on the cap **exercise** date. It is the cap market's equivalent to a **path-dependent option** (cf. **Asian option**).

average spot rate option (ASPRO) (Forex). An **Asian option** type **currency option** where the holder receives the difference between the **strike** or **exercise** price and the average spot currency rate over the life of the option.

average rate option. A type of **Asian option** where the **underlying's** average spot price or rate over the option period is used to determine whether the option has value or not at **expiry**. The two sides to the transaction agree the underlying's sampling frequency and the source of the data at the outset. The payout is then based on this average against the **strike rate**.

average strike option. **Asian option** where the **strike price** or rate is based on an **average** of the spot price or rate over the option's life. See also average rate option.

average strike rate option (ASTRO) (Forex). An Asian option type **currency option** where the holder receives the difference between the **spot** exchange rate at **expiry** and where the **strike** or **exercise** price is the average spot currency rate over the **life** of the option.

average tax rate. The actual rate paid on profit or income by a firm, as opposed to the current corporate tax rate (cf. **tax shield**). It is a measure of the ability of the company to avoid paying taxes, through using tax off sets and allowances. It is calculated by dividing the tax paid by total taxable income (cf. **earnings before taxes**). See **ratio analysis**.

average up. Same as **average down** but where the average cost of the block of securities rises with each additional purchase. See **averaging**.

average yield. The average of a sample of **yields** of a number of different **bonds** or the average of a single bond's yield over a period of time. The former is used to obtain a benchmark or performance indicator. See also **index construction**.

averaging. An investment method which involves periodic purchases of a security or portfolio to obtain an average price. Often used by private investors. Called *dollar averaging* in the USA and *pound-cost averaging* in the UK.

away. Used by **brokers-dealer** to indicate a **quote** or transaction that is a better price than he is willing to give.

away from the market (USA). Term for a transaction instruction in which the price is not the current market price and therefore cannot be executed. Such instructions are kept in the **specialist's** book pending a movement in price subject to any conditions such as **fill or kill** (cf. **limit order**).

azione (Italy). **Common stock.**

azioni di risparmio (Italy). Savings **shares.** Senior category of **equity** introduced in 1974 which ranks above **common stocks** and **preferred stocks** but which does not carry any **voting rights** (cf. **participation certificate**).

azione pregiata (Equities; Italy). **Blue chip stock.**

B

B, Ba, Baa, BB and BBB. See credit ratings.

baby bond. (i) (**Bonds**; USA) A market term for a **bond** where the denomination of the **certificates** is smaller than the market norm. Such issues, which entail additional administrative costs, are designed to appeal to individual investors. (ii) (UK). Tax-exempt bonds aimed at savings for children issued by friendly societies.

back bond or **virgin bond.** A **bond** created by exercising an **option** or **warrant**.

back contract. The **futures** contract on an exchange with the longest **expiry date** currently being traded (cf. **back month; nearby**).

backdate or **backdating.** (i) A procedure for putting a date on a document or instrument earlier than the date it was compiled or issued to make it effective from that date. (ii) (Banking). A process used in **clearing** for the settlement of failed transactions. Since the paying party has had use of the funds in the interim, the payee is compensated by receiving the lost interest.

back door listing. The admission to listing on an exchange that is done without publicity, often in the context of an initial **private placement**.

backed note. (i) A shipping term for a receiving note bearing the endorsement of a ship broker or agent. It is an authority for goods to be brought in barges (or other means of transshipment) alongside a ship, and for the officer in charge of the vessel to take them on board. (ii) Short for **asset-backed security** or **mortgage-backed security**.

back-end load. Fees and management charges made when holders of **mutual funds** or **trust** units sell their holdings (cf. **front-end loading; no-load fund**). See also **single pricing**.

back-end set swap. See in-arrears swap.

backing away (USA). A **market-maker's** inability to transact in the minimum market quantity for a given security. It is seen as an unethical practice under market rules.

backlog. Unfulfilled orders.

back month. The traded **futures contract** which is the last to **expire** (cf. **back contract**). If the date is February and the **expiration cycle** is March, June, September and December, then the back month contract is the December one.

back office. The area of a financial firm documenting and controlling the firm's financial flow. Typically the back office functions include **confirmation** and **settlement**. Historically, the back office would have been hidden from the public while the **front office** dealt with clients. The back office is now also involved with regulatory matters, especially **compliance**. See also **middle office**.

back office crunch. A situation that can arise when trading is particularly heavy where a firm's **back office** is unable to handle the volume of transactions.

back price or **backwards price** (UK). A condition of the market where one **market-maker's** **offer** price is lower than another's **bid** price (cf. **backwardation**).

back spread. (i) An **option strategy** which involves selling a near-to or **at-the-money call** (or **put**) **option** and using the **premium** to buy a larger number of **out-of-the-money** calls (puts) with a higher (lower) **exercise price**. The attractions of such a strategy is predicated on a significant upward (downward) movement in the price of the **underlying** making the purchased options become **in the money**. One of the purchased options is used to fulfil the written option obligation while the others represent the profit. Such a position will only work if a significant upward (downward) move in the underlying is anticipated. (ii) Sometimes taken to mean a **credit spread**. See **ratio spread; option strategies**.

backstop. Used in the euronote market when an **underwriter**, usually a bank, makes a commitment to buy notes at a predetermined **margin**, normally given in relation to **London interbank offered rate**, if notes cannot be placed at or below this rate with money market investors (cf. **remarketing agent**). See **back-up line; committed facility**.

back-to-back credit. A second **trade credit** provided on the strength of the first (usually non-transferable) credit.

back-to-back loan. One of two loans in different currencies but initially with the same value and **maturity** where party A lends to party B and simultaneously party B lends to party A.

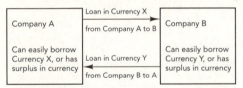

Company A	Loan in Currency X from Company A to B	Company B
Can easily borrow Currency X, or has surplus in currency	Loan in Currency Y from Company B to A	Can easily borrow Currency Y, or has surplus in currency

Back-to-back loan

Usually used as a method of circumventing currency regulations when borrowing foreign currency. The payment flows are the same as those for **spot** and **forward** currency transactions. Back-to-back loans were the precursors of **cross-currency swaps** which have largely replaced the technique, although where the free exchange of currency is restricted, or regulatory or tax **arbitrage** is involved, they might still be used. They may also be used in specialized **credit enhanced** transactions. Also known as a *parallel loan*.

back-to-back swap. The result of combining two **interest rate swaps** or **cross-currency swaps** such that one set of the two opposing payment flows is completely eliminated. This is used as an alternative to **termination** in some cases, although the obligations of all the parties are retained and, in general, an agreement which ends the contracts with a compensating lump sum is usually preferred since it then removes all **credit risk** to both sides.

back up. (i) Used to describe those market conditions where **yields** are rising and prices are falling. (ii) Used in the **US bond markets** to describe a **bond swap/switch** which reduces **maturity** or **duration**. That is, the longer-dated bond is sold in favour of a shorter maturity one (cf. **pay-up**).

back-up line (USA). Common term for a **standby credit facility** used to ensure funds are available to meet maturing **commercial paper** repayments in the event of market disruption. Note that such a **facility** is not the same as a **guarantee** since in the event of a problem with the borrower's **conditions precedent**, the lender may not advance funds.

backwardation. (i) (Commodities; Forex). The amount that the **spot** price, plus any carrying costs, exceeds **forward** prices. Backwardation occurs when demand for the spot or near-delivery maturity **futures** is higher than that for later dates. In commodity markets, this can be sometimes due to the availability of deliverable amounts of the physical commodity (cf. **contango**). Also called a *discount market*. (ii) (Equities; UK). On the **London Stock Exchange** it is the percentage charge paid by the seller for the right to delay delivery from one **account period** to the next. (iii) Also sometimes used, especially in the **eurobond** markets, when a **bid** price by one **dealer** is above another **market-maker's offer** price (cf. **triple witching hour**). It is normally the result of tumultuous market conditions. Also called *backward price*.

backwardation swap. Commodity **swap** where the payments are based on the **spot** price and a **futures** or **forward** price with a **margin**. It allows a producer or consumer of the commodity to fix the **spread** between the two markets and thus his cost of **hedging** (cf. **contango swap**).

backward price (UK). A situation in which a **market-maker's two-way prices** are out-of-line such that an immediate profit could be made by buying and selling simultaneously, that is the best **bid** is higher than the best **offer**. This can happen when stock **index futures** and **options** expire (cf. **triple witching hour**; **witching hour**). Sometimes known simply as *backs* or *back price*. See **arbitrage**.

bad debt. A receivable or loan that is likely to be unrecoverable and needs to be provided against or treated as a loss. There are various technical definitions of what constitutes a bad debt, depending on accounting conventions, regulatory treatment and the conservatism of the institution provisioning. In the USA, bank loans with more than ninety days' arrears become **problem loans** (cf. **problem assets**).

bad delivery. The presentation, at **settlement**, of the **certificates** related to the securities transaction which are not acceptable (cf. **good delivery**). This is not the same as a **fail**, which is non-delivery at settlement (cf. **aged fail**; **partial delivery**).

baden (Japan). The direct lines between the trading floor and a **broker's** offices.

baibai kaiten ritsu (Japanese). The turnover ratio in a particular security. It is the turnover or **volume** in a particular period divided by the average number of outstanding units.

baibai tan'i (Japanese). Trading unit (cf. **basket**). See **lot**; **odd lot**.

bail bond. Not a security, but a guarantee or **collateral** provided to a court to allow an individual or an asset, such as a ship, to be released from custody pending a hearing or a trial.

balance concentration (Banking). System by which a bank transfers funds from the different bank accounts in a group of companies to minimize overdrawn positions and for investment purposes. Also called *balance sweeping, concentration banking, target balancing* or *zero balance*. See also **cross-border one-currency concentration**.

balanced mutual fund (USA). A mutual fund pursuing an **investment strategy** which seeks to balance growth, **risk** and income, and which may lead to the purchase of **preferred stocks** and **bonds** as well as **common stocks**.

balance of payments. (BOP) The total net effect, positive or negative (surplus or deficit), of the **trade balance, invisible balance,** and **capital account** (cf. **current account**).

balance-of-term yield. The yield that a longer-dated **bond** must have on the **maturity** of a shorter bond in order that the proceeds may be reinvested to produce equal returns on the two securities (cf. break-even analysis). See **reinvestment risk**.

balance of trade. See trade balance.

balance sheet. A statement of an organization's financial position at a certain time showing all its **assets** and **liabilities** (cf. **financials**). Together with the **profit and loss account** and a **cash flow statement**, it makes up the three parts of a report on an organization for a set period that allow detailed analysis of the organization's condition (cf. **credit analysis**). Such financial statements are periodic statutory reporting requirements for limited companies and also for tax assessment purposes by all firms. The balance sheet will have three main components: the assets, liabilities, and capital. The statement can be seen as the wealth of the owners (assets less liabilities) (cf. **net worth**), or of the capital or funding used to support the assets (cf. **leverage**). Known also as a *statement of condition* or a *statement of financial position*.

balance sheet hedge. A translation exposure hedge, for instance a foreign currency borrowing, used to reduce the impact of changes in foreign currencies when converted into the **base currency** upon **consolidation**.

balance sheet ratios. See ratio analysis.

balancing charge (UK). The difference between the resale or scrap value of an asset on disposal and its value for tax accounting purposes. If the resale value is higher a balancing charge or if less than the written-down value an additional allowance is made to taxable profits.

balcony bracket or **group** (USA). Term used for a **junior** class of **underwriter** below the major

bracket (cf. **special bracket underwater**). Sometimes called *second tier*.

balloon, balloon-payment, or **balloon maturity.** A principal amount paid on **maturity** of a **sinking fund** or amortising issue or debt that is significantly larger than the **sinking fund** repayments. For example, an issue could have six payments of 10 %, followed by a balloon of 40 % at maturity. Also *balloon interest*, a higher rate of interest on the later maturing parts of **serial bond** issues. See **amortization; bullet; grace period**.

ballot. Method of allocating securities in an **auction** or **tender** when the amount bid for is in excess of the amounts available (cf. **over-subscribed**). Successful applicants are chosen at random by balloting. The alternative method of allotment is to scale back all bidders **pro rata**, or according to some predetermined criteria. Given the potential for abuse, there are normally strict regulations as to how **lead managers** may allocate securities.

Baltic Exchange (UK). A commodities, freight-chartering, and maritime exchange engaged in bringing together available ships and cargoes. With the advent of air-freight and charters, the exchange has diversified into providing a similar function. It is now part of **London Fox**.

Baltic Freight Index. An **index** of the cost of transport.

Baltic International Freight Futures Exchange (BIFFEX) (UK). See **London Fox**.

banca del monte (Banking; Italy). **Savings bank**.

banca di credito ordinario (Banking; Italy). Commercial bank.

banca popolari (Banking; Italy). Cooperative bank.

bancassurance. The process of selling financial products to bank or building society customers through these institutions' retail outlets. It involves the view that existing customers will be open to cross-selling and the value of a financial supermarket. The thinking behind the grouping of such businesses is seen in terms of increased selling opportunities and economies in distribution channels, especially within the retail sector. This is based on the fact that a typical **commercial bank** satisfies a small proportion of its personal customers' requirements for investment, insurance, and related products. The absence of an equivalent English term is indicative of the relative slowness of banks in the UK and USA to develop and market a truly integrated range of retail financial services, although regulatory barriers have a part to play. Perhaps **financial supermarket** or **financial conglomerate** is the closest these markets have to the concept. The equivalent German term is *Allfinanz*.

band. (i) A range within which a price or rate is allowed to fluctuate. The best-known bands are the parities set by the **Exchange Rate Mechanism** for currency fluctuations. (ii) Term used for the maturities of **treasury bills**, local authority bills, and **eligible bills** purchased or sold by the **Bank of England** when carrying out **open-market-operations** (cf. **intervention rate**). Band 1 are those bills maturing 1–14 days; band 2: 15–33 days; band 3: 34–63 days; and band 4: 64–91 days. The Bank will purchase bills in the bands with ever increasing maturities in order to meet a money market shortage. Recent changes to the way the Bank operates mean that it will also buy **treasury bills** with maturities within the bands.

Bangalore Stock Exchange Ltd (India). 1st Floor, 'M' Block, Unity Building, J C Road, IN-Bangalore 560 002 (tel. 91 812 220 163; tlx 8452874).

Bangkok Stock Exchange (Thailand). See **Stock Exchange of Thailand**.

bank basis. The way in which accrued interest on **certificates of deposit**, **eurocommercial paper**, **floating rate certificates of deposit**, and **floating rate notes** is calculated. The rate of interest is multiplied by the number of days in the interest period divided by the **basis** or computational year. Interest earned is the same as **money market basis**. See **interest rate calculations**.

bank bill. Commercial bill accepted by a bank (cf. **banker's acceptance**; **trade bill**). Such bills are usually sold at a **discount** to a **discount house**.

bank bill of exchange (Australia). **Bill of exchange** traded in the Australian domestic market. The rate on such bills is a key money market interest rate, known as the *bank bill rate*.

Bank Capital Adequacy Requirements. See **Basle Capital Convergence Accord**.

bankcertifikat (Banking; Sweden). Certificate of deposit.

bank collection float. The time between when a cheque is deposited and when it is cleared and can be drawn against (cf. **clearing**; **float**).

bank debenture (Japan). **Bonds** by the long-term banks in Japan: Industrial Bank of Japan, Long-Term Credit Bank of Japan, Nippon Credit Bank,

Norinchukin Bank, Shoko Chukin Bank, and Bank of Tokyo. These banks were the only ones authorized to raise such long-term funds, which were then used to make term loans to customers. Traditionally, the rate on such issues determined the **long-term prime rate**, which was set at a **margin** over the **coupon** on such debentures.

bank deposit. Money placed on deposit with a bank.

bank deposit agreement (BDA). See **guaranteed investment contract**.

bank deposit notes. See **certificates of deposit**.

bank discount basis, bank discount interest rate, or **bank discount method or bank discount yield.** The annualized **simple interest** rate based on the **par value** of the security. It is the method used to quote the interest on non-interest bearing **money market** instruments such as **commercial paper**. It is calculated by taking the issue price and solving for the interest rate, using the following formula:

$$\left[\frac{FV}{MP} - 1\right] \times \frac{Basis}{T_{sm}}$$

where *FV* is the face value or redemption amount; *MP* the market price; T_{sm} the days from settlement to maturity; *Basis* the number of days in the accounting year. Thus a commercial paper issue with 90 days from **settlement** to **maturity** trading at 98.5, where the **basis** is a 360-day year would have a bank discount basis **yield** or interest rate of 6.09%. See also **discount**; **interest rate calculations**; **money market yield**; **interest to follow**.

bank draft. See **banker's draft**.

banker's acceptance (BA) (Money markets; USA). US name for a short-term negotiable discount note, draft, or bill, drawn on and accepted by banks which are obliged to pay the **face value** upon **maturity** (cf. **bill**; **certificate of deposit**; **commercial paper**; **treasury bill**; **trade acceptance**). Under US regulations funds raised via BAs must be used for the financing of trade.

banker's acceptances tender facility (BATF). A facility provided by a group of banks via a **tender panel** to **bid** for a borrower's **banker's acceptances**.

banker's acceptance swap. An interest rate swap where the **floating rate** leg reference rate is the **banker's acceptances** (BA) rate. The BA rate is a common **benchmark** for the Canadian market.

Banker's Automated Clearing House (BACS)
(Banking; UK). One of the two systems used by British banks for **clearing**, the other being **Clearing House Automated Payments System**. Of the two, BACS handles routine, standard payments which are pre-loaded onto the system.

banker's draft. A payment drawn upon the bank itself. The credit is thus that of the bank rather than the customer. It is equivalent to cash in most transactions. A variation is a *banker's payment*, which is a draft drawn in favour of another bank. Also known as a *banker's cheque* or a *bank draft*.

bank financial strength rating. (BFSR) See credit ratings.

Bank for International Settlements (BIS). An international bank for European **central banks**, based in Basle, Switzerland, it is the oldest international financial institution in the world, founded in January 1930 at the Hague Conference of creditor countries as a response to the need for an international organization to promote central bank cooperation. It has three main functions: to promote international monetary cooperation for which it provides the secretariat for the **Committee on Banking Regulations Supervisory Practices**; it provides banking, **agency**, and trustee functions for over eighty central banks; and it acts as a **clearing house** for the eurocurrency markets. It is a major source of data on international lending and developments in the **eurocurrency market**. It is sometimes called the central bankers' club since the heads of the principal nations' central banks meet regularly to discuss matters of mutual concern (cf. **group of ten**). For instance, it was a committee of the BIS that set out the technical standard on **capital adequacy** requirements for regulating banks in all member countries (cf. **Basle Capital Convergence Accord**). Often called the *central bankers' central bank*.

bank guarantee. A repayment **guarantee** provided by a bank as a means of improving the **credit worthiness** of a transaction.

bank holding company (BHC) (USA). A holding corporation that, while not a bank itself, has a bank as one of its major subsidiaries (cf. **Edge Act bank**). Its other subsidiaries may be engaged in non-banking financial activities such as mortgage lending, leasing, credit card operations, and securities business. Typically most major US banks are owned by bank holding companies.

bank holiday. Days, other than weekends, when banks are closed for business, and by implication settlement of transactions is not possible (cf. **business day**; **clearing**).

banking book. A bank's portfolio of loans and off-balance sheet items which are long-term investments as defined by the regulating authorities (cf. **risk-adjusted assets**; trading book).

bank insurance fund (Banking;. USA). See **Federal Deposit Insurance Corporation**.

Bank Investment Contract (BIC). See guaranteed investment contract.

bank line (USA). American term for a **credit facility** or **line of credit**, usually taken to mean **uncommitted**.

bank loan. Money lent by a bank to a customer (cf. **loan**). If **collateral** has been provided by the borrower, it is a secured loan; if not it is unsecured. The bank will judge the **credit worthiness** of the borrower before deciding whether to request security or not.

Bank of Canada (Canada). Founded in 1934 as a private institution it subsequently passed into government ownership in 1938. Responsibility for policy is vested in the Board of Directors under the Bank of Canada Act and consists of a governor, a senior deputy-governor, and twelve directors with varied backgrounds from Canada's different provinces and regions. The directors are appointed by the *Ministry of Finance* for three-year terms and they appoint the governor and senior deputy-governor who serve seven-year terms. The Bank is responsible for carrying out **monetary policy** on behalf of the government and to regulate credit and currency in the best interests of the economic life of the nation as well as operate in the foreign exchange market to control the value of the Canadian dollar. It implements its policy via **reserve requirements**, which require banks to have deposits with the Bank, and through **open-market operations**, almost exclusively made with government securities.

Bank of China (BOC). *The Republic of China's* state bank responsible for **foreign exchange** management.

Bank of England (BOC) (UK). The **central bank** set up in 1694 as a private bank to provide banking services to the government of the day. It was nationalized in 1946 and currently has responsibility for the regulation of the banking system and control of the domestic money and bond markets, including overseas traders operating in such markets and activities as the **eurocurrency** markets out side the UK. It shares responsibility for regulating banks and other financial institutions in the UK (cf. **Securities and Investments Board**). Note that **building societies** as mutual societies are regulated by the Building Societies Commission and not the Bank. It is banker to the government and manages, on behalf of the Treasury, the issue of new government debt and the secondary market in government bonds (cf. **gilt-edged**). It is also responsible for the issue of sterling notes but not coins, this being the responsibility of the Royal Mint. The governing body of the Bank is its Court of Directors, which is made up of a governor, deputy-governor, and sixteen directors. It controls **monetary** conditions through day-to-day actions in the **money markets**, principally through its **intervention rate**, the rate at which it adds or subtracts liquidity to the market, as well as by requiring banks to maintain **reserve requirements**, although this is not used as a policy instrument. See also **open-market operations**.

Bank of England Stock Register (UK). See **Central Gilts Office**.

Bank of Italy (BOI) (Italy). Italy's **central bank**, which was established in 1893 when four banks of issue were merged. Policy is determined by a Board which consists of fourteen directors, one of whom is then elected governor with the approval of the President of the Republic. The governorship has no term while the directors have three-year terms, although eligible for renomination. It was made an independent institution in spring 1993 and has been granted complete autonomy in setting monetary policy, interest rates, and **reserves** criteria. Jointly with the **Commissione Nazionale per le Società e la Borsa** it is responsible for regulating Italy's financial markets and institutions.

Bank of Japan (BOJ) (Japan). Japan's **central bank**. It has responsibility for monetary policy; however, regulation of the banking sector rests with the Ministry of Finance. The controlling body is the seven-member Policy Board appointed by the Cabinet and approved by the Diet. Traditionally, the governor of the Bank is elected chairman of the Policy Board and, usually, holds the position for five years. One non-voting member is appointed from the Ministry of Finance and the Economic Planning Agency while there are four voting sectoral specialists, one from agriculture, one from commerce and industry, one from city banking, and one from municipal banking, who serve four-year terms. The Policy Board formulates monetary policy to achieve a stable value for the yen, and since 1978 it provides at the start of each quarter estimated value for the **money supply** (technically M2 and **certificates of deposit**) for the quarter. Following deregulation of the banking system in 1988, the BOJ stopped setting rates and now uses **open-market operations**. Its three instruments for altering monetary conditions (with the approval of the Ministry of Finance) are: changes to the official discount rate, lending pol-

icy (via **administrative guidance**), and **reserve requirements**.

bank quality (USA). A term often used interchangeably for **investment grade** securities, i.e. issues rated triple-B (Baa) or above.

bank rate (Banking). A generic term for the rate or price at which a **central bank** is prepared to advance money to the banking system (cf. **discount rate**; **discount window**; **intervention rate**; **minimum lending rate**). See **Lombard rate**.

bank return. Report prepared by a bank for its **regulator**. It normally states the amount and type of **assets** on the bank's **balance sheet** (cf. **eligible assets**).

bank run. A sudden and unexpected withdrawal of **deposits** on a bank due to concerns about its stability (cf. **bankruptcy**). See **liquidity risk**.

bankruptcy. Common usage term for describing a state of **financial distress** or difficulty in a firm or individual, that is the condition when an entity cannot meet its fixed commitments on borrowings, which has to be resolved by legal process. In the UK, individuals become bankrupt; firms insolvent (cf. **crash**; **insolvency**; **liquidation**; **voluntary liquidation**). Bankruptcy proceedings arise following a court order (a *bankruptcy order*) allowing a **receiver** to be appointed to manage the assets of the individual with a view to paying off their debts. See also **Chapter 11**.

bankruptcy filing. To seek legal protection from creditors through the courts, as in **Chapter 11**, or for creditors to force a **liquidation** of the firm, as in **Chapter 13**.

Bankruptcy Reform Act of 1978 (USA). The key legislation governing the management of a firm's or municipality's restructuring when it can no longer meet its fixed liabilities. The process is court supervised and allows a number of alternatives to be considered by the court, specifically aimed at securing the most desirable outcome for the firm. This significantly altered the existing absolute priority rule, giving preference to secured creditors in all cases, in favour of a more general restructuring aimed at maintaining the entity as a going concern as well as streamlining the procedures for bringing cases to court. Of greatest benefit to firms or municipalities entering bankruptcy proceedings is the court-supervised restructuring, allowed under **Chapter 11** of the Act, giving court protection against existing creditor claims during the restructuring period (cf. **debtor in possession**).

bankruptcy risk. See **default risk**.

Bankschuldverschreibungen (German). **Bearer bonds** issued by banks. As a class it also includes **certificates of deposit**. See also **Pfandbriefe**.

bank trust department (Banking; USA). The **agency** services part of a bank acting as **trustee** for **bond** issues, pension and profit-sharing plans, transfer **agent**, and other activities.

Bank voor Nederlandsche Gemeenten Bonds (BNG) (Bonds; Netherlands). The central financing bank for the Netherlands' municipalities.

bank wire (Banking; USA). An interbank communications system for advising of transactions and the dissemination of important information (cf. **Clearing House Interbank Payment System**; **fed wire**).

banque d'affaires (French). **Investment bank** (USA) (cf. **merchant bank (UK)**).

Banque de France (France). The **central bank**, it was established by Napoleon in 1800 and, like the **Bank of England**, it was initially a private institution, being nationalized in 1946. It was made independent again in 1994 to increase its credibility and as part of the run up to **European Monetary Union**. It is responsible for **monetary policy** and undertakes **open-market operations** for both technical and policy reasons either via short term repurchase agreements or through official repurchase facilities or, on a limited basis, changes to **reserve requirements**. Its **currency intervention** fund is known as the 'Fonds de Stabilisation des Changes' and is important in the context of the Franc's participation in the **Exchange Rate Mechanism** (cf. **Exchange Stabilization Fund**).

Banque Française du Commerce Extérieure (BFCE). A specialized bank which makes medium- to long-term loans in aid of exports or other foreign activities. It is quasi-government owned and is a regular borrower in the international markets in its own name.

barbell. A spread or **portfolio** position made up of short-maturity and long-maturity fixed income securities with nothing in the middle. Thus a combination of a two-year and a thirty-year bond position would be considered a barbell (cf. **ladder portfolio**). See also **yield curve swap**.

bar chart. See **point and figure chart**.

Barclays Commodity Trading Advisors Index. A performance index of, principally US-domiciled, **Commodity Trading Advisors**.

bareboat charter. See **capital lease**; **financial lease**.

bargain (UK). A contract to buy or sell securities on the **London Stock Exchange**. Some bargains are **marked** and their prices reported in the financial press. Also known in some markets as a *deal* or *transaction*.

bargain hunter. A type of investor who is on the look-out for assets underpriced relative to their risks. A *bottom fisher* is a bargain hunter who monitors market conditions, aiming to buy at the lows of the market.

Barings (UK). Synonymous for management failure to control the **risk** from **proprietary trading** in **derivative** instruments. The bank crashed in February 1995 as a result of gross overtrading, mostly on stock index futures and options on the Nikkei 225 Index and Japanese Government Bonds, carried out by Nick Leeson, Barings' senior **trader** in their Singapore office. The bank had, unwittingly, allowed a position to develop in the market where it had over 20 % of the outstanding contracts in the market with a **notional principal** amount of over US$27 bn and the losses wiped out the bank's entire **equity**. Hence, the *Barings Leeson*, or *to do a Barings*. Also just called *The Disaster*.

barometer. (i) A security used for gauging the mood or behaviour of a market (cf. **benchmark**). A good barometer security will behave like a typical security in that market (cf. **index**). (ii) A digest of economic and market data that gives guidance as to the trend in an economy or market.

Barone-Adesi and Whaley option pricing model. An option pricing model that provides an analytic approximation solution to the valuation of **American-style options** on stocks which pay continuous **dividends**. See *Journal of Finance*, 42 (June 1987), 301–20.

barrel. Standard unit of crude oil (crude), equal to 42 US gallons, 36 imperial gallons, 158.97 litres, or 0.136 tons. See **contract grade**; **marker crude**.

barrels per day (BPD). A measure of oilfield production capacity and activity.

barrier. See **trigger**.

barrier option. Term for a **path-dependent option** which is either cancelled or activated if the price of the **underlying** reaches a pre-set level regardless of the price at which the underlying may be trading at the **expiry** of the option. The *knock-out* type is cancelled if the underlying price or rate trades through the trigger; while the *knock-in* becomes activated if the price moves through the trigger. As a result they are sometimes known as a *trigger option*. The attraction of the barrier option is that by setting limits on the movement of the underlying the buyer can reduce the amount of **option premium** to be paid, although this will depend how close the trigger is set to the current spot price or rate and how much **volatility** there is. Greater volatility tends to reduce (increase) the premium of knock-out-(in) options since there is a greater chance the price will trade through the barrier point. Note that when a barrier option becomes effective it is normally **European-style**. Also sometimes referred to as a *fourchette option*.

Barrier option

Type	Conditions required to make option effective	Option type at exercise date when triggered
up-and-out	Option cancelled if underlying goes *above* the pre-set level before expiry.	Call
up-and-in	Option is worthless *unless* the underlying *moves above* the pre-set level at some point before expiry.	Put
down-and-out	Option cancelled if underlying goes *below* a pre-set level before expiry.	Put
down-and-in	Option is worthless unless the underlying *moves below* the pre-set level at some point before expiry.	Call

The four principal types are shown in the Table. The up-and-in and down-and-in would be classed as *knock-in* options, the up-and-out and down-and-out, as *knock-out* options. Such options are sometimes described as *clever* or *intelligent* since they are either activated or extinguished if the price moves beyond the trigger level.

barrier price or **rate.** The price or rate at which a **barrier option** is either activated or cancelled. If the option is of the *knock-in* type, it is known as the *instrike*, if of the *knock-out* type, the *outstrike*.

Barron's confidence index (Bonds; USA). A spread **index** measuring the difference between high and low credit quality **bonds**. The measure assumes that in **bearish** times investors will prefer high-quality issues (the **index** will widen) whereas in **bullish** phases, investors will invest in lower-quality issues (the index will narrow) since better conditions will increase the safety factor for such issues (cf. **default risk**).

barrow boy (UK). Derogatory term used to describe a **trader**. The term comes from street mar-

ket entrepreneurs and their stalls, or barrows. Such individuals are possibly vulgar and certainly streetwise.

barter. (i). A very old type of trading arrangement which dispenses with the use of money. Parties agree to exchange goods or services with each other. Sometimes still used in international trade (cf. **disagio**). (ii) To barter is to negotiate (cf. **auction**).

base currency (Forex). The currency against which the value of another is expressed. It is the other currency which is varied as the foreign exchange rate changes. Most exchange rates are quoted against the US dollar, for which there are two methods: **American terms** (the foreign currency is the base and the US dollar varied) and **European terms** (US dollar the base). This does not apply for **crosses**, where the heavier currency, that is the currency with fewer units in any exchange, is normally the base currency. For instance, with the Deutschmark and the Japanese yen, the Deutschmark is the base currency. With crosses, the quote is also normally given for 100 units of the base currency to avoid the confusion of too many decimal places. Thus a quote for the Deutschmark–Danish kroner cross would be 369.69, that is $6.0895 \div 1.5507 \times 100$.

base date. The date from which an **index** or other time series is referenced. This is normally set at a round number such as 100 or 1,000. Values for the idex subsequently are expressed in relation to this base date. See **index construction**.

base lending rate or **base rate** (Banking; UK). The published interest rate which is used by UK banks to determine the rate they will lend to their customers. It is the key rate that the **Bank of England** seeks to influence through its **open-market operations** activities (cf. **intervention rate**). Normally, the press will report on the **clearing bank** base rate, which is a **fine rate**.

base market value. A method of working out the weights for **stocks** in a portfolio when **index-matching**. (cf. **indexing**).

base metals (Commodities). The market in non-precious metals.

base metal futures. The exchange-traded market in futures on base metals. Also called simply *metals*, but this term could also include **precious metals**. An example is the contract for lead traded on the **London Metal Exchange** (LME).

Lead
Refined pig lead assaying not less than 99.97 % purity in pigs weighing not more than 55 kg. each.

All lead delivered must be of brands listed in the LME-approved list of lead brands.

Contract unit: 25 tonnes
Price basis: US$ per tonne
Minimum price movement: US$0.25 per tonne
Delivery dates: Daily for 3 months forward, then every Wednesday for the next three months and then every third Wednesday of the month for the next nine months. (A total of 15 months forward.)
Ring trading times: 12.05–12.10; (official) 12.45–12.50; 15.20–15.25; 16.00–16.05.

base/quoted convention (Forex). Quoting a foreign exchange on the basis of base currency/quoted currency, i.e. expressing the US dollar versus sterling, which is normally quoted in **American terms** as £/$ when abbreviating the relationship £1 = US$ x.xxxx

base rate (Banking). An alternative pricing method used in the **eurocurrency** market for pricing loans. The base rate is normally the higher of two funding rates to the lenders, such as **London interbank offered rate** or the **fed funds rate**. (ii) (UK) The **reference rate** used by banks in the UK for pricing loans to their customers (cf. **prime rate**). Changes in base rates are widely advertised in the national newspapers. It is also used in reference to manipulation of short-term interest rates via **open-market operations** by the **Bank of England** (BOE) to influence monetary conditions. The BOE signals changes in the monetary stance via its lending rate to the wholesale money market and hence the 'base rate' at which financial institutions lend out money (cf. **discount rate; intervention rate; minimum lending rate**).

base rate agreement (Money markets; UK). A forward rate agreement where the reference rate is the bank's base (lending) rate.

base period. The time over which a set of price or yield relationships are monitored to ascertain their behaviour (cf. **correlation**).

base weighted. A method of creating an index in which the values are related to a base period, point, or year.

base year. The start point in an **index** or series. The starting values are calculated to give a round number, typically 100 or 1,000, and later calculations are adjusted up or down in relation to this starting-point. The base year concept is also sometimes used in performance appraisal.

basic financial statements. See financial statements.

basis. (i) (Futures) The difference in price between the price of the **underlying** asset and its **futures** price (cf. **convergence**). In a **contango** market where the futures prices are higher than the **spot** or cash price, the basis will be negative; while in a **backwardated** market (where the cash price is higher), the basis will be positive (cf. **yield curve**). This is sometimes referred to as *over futures* or *under futures*, as in '25 basis points over futures'. Changes in the cash-futures relationship due to changes in expectations affecting **hedging** and **speculation** activity will take place over time. The basis computed from the fair or theoretical valuation of the futures price is known as the *carry basis*, while the *value basis* or *excess basis* is the difference between the carry basis and the actual futures price (cf. **price discovery**).

Basis

Cash Market	Futures	Basis	Description	Market type
98.75	99.13	−0.38	under futures	Contango
99.75	99.13	+0.63	over futures	Backwardated

- *Theoretical basis (cost of price carry)*:
  Cash market: 98.75
  Cost of carry at 6% for 1 month: 0.49
  Theoretical of 'fair value' of futures: 99.24
  Carry basis: −0.49
  Actual market price of futures contract: 99.13
  Value basis or excess basis: 0.12

Changes to the basis leads to *basis risk*: the risk associated with variation in the basis over time. It is said that if:

- the relative prices (or rates) between the cash market and its related futures in which the spot market price increases by *more* than the futures price this is a *strengthening of the basis*;
- the relative prices (or rates) between the cash market and its related futures in which the spot market price increases by *less* than the futures price this is a *weakening of the basis*.

See also **basis risk**.

(ii) (Derivatives; securities) (*a*) A method of computing interest, as in *bond basis* or *eurobond basis*; the method for calculating the **coupons** on bonds, money market or loan interest. For methods see **interest rate calculations**. (*b*) Used to describe the **yield-to-maturity** of a bond.

(iii) General term used synonymously with **spread** for the price or rate relationship between different markets (cf. **cross-hedge**).

basis convergence. See convergence.

basis grade. See contract grade.

basis market. See quote.

basis point (BP). One hundredth of 1% (0.01%; 1/100 of 1%). **Yield spread** usually quoted in basis points of 0.01%. Usually used in the **money markets** where quoted prices are derived from exact **yields** or when prices are quoted in terms of yields (cf. **big figure**; **handle**). Typically, prices of such instruments as **commercial paper, eurocommercial paper, floating rate notes,** and **treasury bills** are expressed in basis points as well as the prices of **short-term interest rate futures.** Beware also of confusion with prices of some term securities such as **US treasuries** where information services sometimes quote just part of a price, which is expressed as a fraction but could be mistaken for a basis point quote. For example a US Treasury quoted at 95.28 is in fact priced at $95\frac{28}{32}$ (95.875%). It is also important to differentiate between the value of a basis point and a **point,** which is 1%; the **pip** which is one-hundredth of a 1% of the value of a security (1/100 × value) and commonly used in a **foreign exchange rate** quote; and the **tick** which is the smallest price change allowed in an **exchange-traded** security or derivative contract; this can be equal to a basis point, or may equally well be a fraction. Also known as the *minimum price fluctuation*. See also **price value of a basis point.**

basis price. (i) The price expressed in terms of **yield** or return on an investment See **yield basis.** (ii) The **striking price.**

basis risk. (i) (Bonds) The **risk** of a change in price as a result of a change in **yield-to-maturity.** (ii) (Futures) The risk of an unfavourable change in the relationship between a **futures price** and its **underlying** resulting in a **futures** gain less than a **cash market** loss, or a futures loss greater than a cash market gain if the transaction is **closed out** before **expiry** or the two sides are not a perfect match (cf. **cross hedge; imperfect hedge**). This arises for two reasons. The value of a future is determined by the time-value-of-money (known in the markets as *cost of carry* or *carrying cost*) and market expectations about the future course of the underlying (cf. **convenience yield**). This latter will influence the **basis** although the principal determinant will be changes in interest rates which then impact the cost of carry. As a result, the basis will be negative with a normal, upward sloping **yield curve** and positive for downward, inverted ones. Changes in the shape of the yield curve will thus affect the basis. Changes in the basis are sometimes referred to as a *strengthening of the basis* or as a *weakening of the basis*.

basis swap or **basis rate swap.** A type of interest rate swap in which the two payments are on a different floating rate **basis,** such as the US domestic bank lending rate prime against **London interbank offered rate** (LIBOR) or six-month LIBOR against three-month LIBOR. There are two types:

simple basis swap within one currency and *cross-currency basis swap*. Such swaps are useful as a way of reducing interest rate mismatch between assets and liabilities or for reducing the cost of funding (for instance, issuing **commercial paper** in the US domestic market and using a basis swap to convert the liability to LIBOR). A basis swap can be seen as a combination of interest rate swaps and **cross-currency swaps.** For instance, a simple basis swap is equivalent to pairing two simple interest rate swaps such that the payment flows are converted from a floating rate basis to fixed and then back to a fixed rate basis but based on a different **index** or **reference rate.** Also known as a *floating/floating swap* or a *money market swap*.

basis trade facility (BTF). A feature offered on some financial futures exchanges allowing a position in futures to be exchanged for the **underlying.** It is similar to the **commodities markets's against actuals, exchange for physical.**

basis transaction. (i) A **cash and carry** transaction (or the reverse), hence *basis trading* which aims to make a profit on changes in the **basis** over time. (ii) The exchange of an asset or portfolio against a **futures** position. See **exchange for physical.** (iii) Any **arbitrage** transaction aimed at making a riskless profit between the cash and **futures** or **options** markets. Such transactions aim to profit from the misalignment of prices in the two markets (i.e. the **basis**). See **spread.**

basket. A group of different securities, generally all of one class which are bought and sold as one unit or form the **underlying** to a **derivative instrument** (cf. **lot; program trading**). See **rainbow option.**

basket delivery (Futures). The delivery system for **futures contracts** that have several **underlying** cash instruments. Basket delivery is common in **bond futures** since it greatly increases the supply of deliverable securities and prevents **ramping** or **squeezes** (cf. **corner the market; notional bond**).

basket option or **warrant.** A type of **option** or **warrant** where the **underlying** is a **basket** of assets. It is often seen in the **foreign exchange market,** where it allows the holder to buy or sell a specific basket of currencies against the base currency. The option is simply priced by adding the **premiums** from the individual components by weight. If the individual assets comprising the basket are highly volatile, it is possible that the option value begins to differ from the protection sought as prices diverge.

Basle Capital Convergence Accord (Banking). An agreement brokered by the **Bank for International Settlements** and signed by the **Group of**

Ten in 1988 creating a set of **capital adequacy** rules for banks operating in member states (cf. **Basle Committee on Banking Regulations and Supervisory Practices**). The creation of minimum capital requirements is intended to strengthen the underpinning of the world banking system and to allow banks to compete on an equal capital basis. The agreement defines capital; provides a method for measuring **risk** by estimating **credit risk** in terms of loan equivalent **principal**; and specifies a minimum ratio of 8% of capital to risk assets for banks. The method used to determine risk assets is to assign assets to risk categories based on their credit exposures (central governments, its agents, banks, and corporate and individual categories) and specific capital is required to support lending to each of these groups. The Accord allowed the local regulator, if it wished, to require a higher ratio than the 8% minimum. There was a transition period from the agreement to the end of 1992 allowing affected institutions to make the necessary changes to meet the minimum requirements. The effect of the Accord has been to make banks either put more capital behind their riskier assets thereby requiring them to recapitalize their balance sheets, or to change the balance between the pricing of their lending activities and the acceptance of the risks involved, or both. The current guidelines require that 50% of a bank's capital is represented by tier 1, or core capital, defined as issued equity and published reserves, post tax. The rest may be tier 2, which is effectively a combination of long-term or perpetual subordinated debt, loan loss reserves, **preferred stock**, and some types of **hybrid instruments**. In addition, each capital tier is further divided into an upper and lower category with maximums allowed in each. The requirement is for a minimum 8% capital adequacy with at least 4% in tier 1, and the balance in tier 2, but in practice banks maintain levels somewhat above the minimum requirement so as to give themselves some freedom of action and to compensate for factors such as movements in **foreign exchange rates**. The ratio is also known as the *Cooke ratio*, after the chairman of the committee which put forward the standard. Subsequent guidelines have extended the Accord to cover **market risk**.

Basle Committee on Banking Regulation and Supervisory Practices (Banking). Standing committee within the **Bank for International Settlements** charged with promoting more effective bank regulation and supervision.

Basle Concordat (Banking). An agreement within the framework of the **Bank for International Settlements** setting out the regulatory framework between **central banks** and which regulator was responsible for what. The basic rule is that the regulator in the country of origin would have the prime responsibility for the institution. To ensure adequate regulatory supervision in an international context, it also provided for regular exchanges of information between the regulatory authorities of different jurisdictions.

Basle Stock Exchange (Switzerland). Aeschenplatz 7, CH-4002 Basel (tel. 41 (0) 61 2720 555; fax 41 (0) 61 2720 626). Established in 1876.

Bausparkassen (German). Associations for savings and housing finance (cf. **building society**; **savings and loan association**).

Bay Street (Canada). (i) The financial district in Toronto, and by implication, the (Canadian) financial sector (cf. **Street**; **Wall Street**). (ii) The **Toronto Stock Exchange**.

bazaar. (i) A generic term for secondary debt markets, particularly used to describe those markets that trade sovereign debt (cf. **less developed countries debt market**). (ii) Often used to describe markets which are thinly regulated or opaque to outsiders.

beamer (Bonds; USA). Term for a low **coupon mortgage-backed** annuity.

bean counter. Colloquial name for an accountant (cf. **number tumbler**).

bear. An investor or trader who takes the view that prices are likely to fall and accordingly sells securities or goes **short**, thereby anticipating a profit by buying them back later at a lower price (cf. **short sale**). Hence a *bear trend*, where prices are generally falling (cf. **bull**).

bear-bull bond. A **bond** issue in two tranches, the redemption prices of which are linked to some **index**, such as the FT-SE 100. One slice [bear] has redemption proceeds which fall as the index falls, and the other slice [bull] has redemption proceeds which rise as the index rises. The issuer is neutral on the index and has a net **fixed rate** issue. Sometimes called a *bull-bear bond*.

bear certificate of deposit (bear CD). Certificate of deposit where the return is linked to the fall in price of an index or rate (cf. **bull certificate of deposit**).

bear closing or **bear covering.** See short covering.

bearer. Any instrument or asset where title is established by possession of the certificate, coupon or talon, or transfer of the title deed. Hence a *bearer security*, where ownership is transferred upon presentation of the certificate. The opposite is a *registered security*, where ownership is recorded in a register, either physically or electronically.

bearer bond, form or **security.** A negotiable security in **physical** form, not registered on the books of the issuer, that is presumed in law to be owned by the holder. Title to bearer securities is effected by **delivery** (cf. **registered security**). Interest and principal repayment is made on the presentation of the **coupons** to a **paying agent** (cf. **clipping**).

bearer certificates. See bearer security.

bearer depository receipt (BDR). Issued in order to promote trading in a foreign security (cf. **American depository receipt; European depository receipt**). See **bearer bond**.

bearer eurodollar collateralized securities (BECS) (Bonds). A repackaged or **synthetic** security denominated in US dollars created by holding a **floating rate note** issued by the UK and attaching an **interest rate swap**, thus creating a **fixed rate** payment stream to holders of the BECS package (cf. **synthetic fixed rate bond**).

bearer exchange rate option (BERO) (UK). Over-the-counter currency options first offered by Barclays Bank and targeted at smaller corporate clients. The instrument is designed to mimic the performance of similar **exchange-traded currency options**.

bearer participation certificate (BPC). A non-voting security which is issued in bearer form and includes the right to receive a **dividend** and any liquidation proceeds. It can also contain the right to subscribe for new shares, if issued (cf. **permanent interest bearing shares; titre participatif**). See also **common stock; equity; ordinary share; participation certificate; preferred stock; warrants**.

bear floating rate note (bear FRN; bear floater). A type of **floating rate note** where the coupon increases disproportionately in relation to increases in interest rates (cf. **leaverage**). It is the opposite structure to a **reverse floating rate note**, in that the coupon payment is calculated as a multiple of the **reference rate** less a fixed amount. For example, such an instrument might pay three times **London interbank offered rate (LIBOR)** less 18%. If LIBOR was 7%, then the note would pay a coupon of 21% − 18%, or 3%; if LIBOR moved to 7.25% (an increase of 3.6%), the new coupon would be 3.75% (an increase of 25%). See also **hybrid reverse floating rate note**.

bear hug. A takeover bid offering such benefits to the **target** company **shareholders** that an other-wise resistant management accepts it, rather than risk shareholder protest.

bearish. To believe that prices will fall or rates will rise, i.e. to have a negative view on the outlook for prices or rates. See **bear**.

bear market. A market perceived to be on a trend of falling prices (cf. **bull market**). A market where bears would prosper (i.e. a falling market).

bear note. See bull-bear bond.

bear position. A short position, that is one designed to take advantage of falling prices (cf. **bull position; short sale**). See **short**.

bear raid. A market manipulation practice of selling **short** at prices below that of previous deals in order to encourage the price to trade down so as to be able to repurchase at a profit. Sometimes the bear raids are accompanied by (unfounded) rumours designed to cause the price to fall. In some jurisdictions bear raids are illegal.

bear slide. A steep fall in prices created by a **bear raid**.

bear spread or **bear money spread** (Options). A strategy used in the option markets which reduces the amount of **option premium** required to profit from an expected decline in the **underlying**, by simultaneously buying and selling two **options** that differ only in their **strike prices** (cf. **bull spread; horizontal spread; money spread; vertical spread**). There are two types: **call spread** and **put spread**. The first involves the sale of the call spread by selling a call option with a low strike price and purchasing another one with a higher strike. The put spread involves selling a put with a low strike price and purchasing a higher strike price put. This latter is more bearish in effect since the potential gain is the difference in the two strike prices less the difference in the two option premiums (cf. **credit spread; debit spread**). The two strategies are also **volatility** trades since the call spread will be more rewarding if the underlying's price is unchanged. The different possible bear spreads are: *vertical spread*–describes

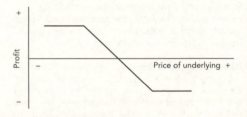

Payoff of bear spread at expiry

option positions with the same **expiry date** but different **exercise prices**; *calendar spread*—describes option positions with the same exercise price but different expiry dates; *diagonal spread*—describes option positions which are both a **vertical** and a **calendar spread**. Sometimes also called a *bear straddle* if undertaken with **futures** (it involves the purchase and sale of different contracts on the expectation that the far date will rise faster than the near date). See also **option strategies**.

bear spread (Bonds). A strategy of taking a **long position** at the short end of the **yield curve** and simultaneously a **short position** (to finance the long position) at the long end of the yield curve. The expectation is that the yield curve will steepen and the position can then be **closed out** at a profit.

bear spreading (Futures). Selling the **nearby contract**, i.e. the one due to **expire** next, and buying a deferred contract (cf. **bull spreading**). This is usually required in order to **roll forward** an existing **long position**. Also known as *selling the spread*.

bear squeeze or **bear trap**. See **short squeeze**.

bed and breakfast (UK). The strategy of selling a security one day, at some critical time, and buying it back on the following day, in order to establish a **capital gain** or **capital loss** for tax reasons. The advantages of this type of tax avoiding strategy have recently been reduced by changes in the tax legislation. See **dividend rollover investment**.

Beige Book (USA). Market name given to the report on the state of the US economy prepared by one of the banks in the **Federal Reserve System** in advance of the **Federal Open Market Committee** meetings. Also known as the *tan book*.

Belgian Futures and Options Exchange (Belfox) S.C./C.V. (Belgium). Palais de la Bourse—Beurspaleis, Rue Henry Maus Straat no. 2, Bruxelles 1000 (tel. (322) 512 80 40; fax (322) 513 83 42). Futures and options exchange for the Belgian market which was established 23 January 1990.

bell. The signal for the opening and closing of a trading session on an exchange.

bells and whistles. The additional features of a **derivatives** instrument or securities issue intended to attract investors or reduce issue costs or both (cf. **equity kicker**; **kicker**; **put provision**). The opposite (simple) structure is known as a **plain vanilla** or **straight**.

bell-wether bond. One of a number of bond issues intended to measure the performance of the market (cf. **benchmark bonds**).

below par. See **discount**.

below-the-line activities. A corporate or banking obligation that does not have to appear on the **profit and loss account** because, for example, of accounting convention or tax law (cf. **above the line**). It can be used to disguise the true state of a company's borrowings and so increase its debt capacity or a bank's exposure and so increases its ability to issue debt. Also known as *off-balance sheet*. Other examples of off-balance sheet activities include: **note issuance facilities**; **revolving underwriting facilities**; **repurchase agreements**, **currency options**, **interest rate swaps** and **cross-currency swaps**, and **futures contracts**. See also **operating lease**.

benchmark. (i) A standard against which performance can be measured (cf. **benchmark bond**). (ii) A surrogate for **liabilities**. (iii) (Futures) A standard specification for **commodity futures** contracts as to purity, grade, content, etc. (iv) A base price or yield used for measuring value (cf. **benchmark issue**; **spread**). See also **reference rate**. (v) Sometimes used to describe a neutral strategy.

benchmark bonds. Those bonds which are considered to act as key indicators of market conditions (cf. **bell-wether**). In Japan, if several similar issues exist, there is a consensus as to which ten-year **Japanese Government Bond** is considered to be the benchmark issue. Such a **bond** normally trades at a **premium** to other governments. See **on the run**.

benchmark error. The use of an inappropriate benchmark in assessing performance.

benchmark issue or **security.** The setting of a standard for the return on a particular security that serves as a guide for further issues.

beneficial owner. That individual or institution to whom the benefits of owning a security ultimately accrue. See **nominee**.

benefit stream. Income or payments that are received over a number of periods (cf. **annuity**). See **cash flow**.

Benelux. Belgium, the Netherlands, and Luxembourg.

benign neglect. Government approach to the management of the internal economic conditions which takes no account of the external parity of the country's currency. See **float**.

Bermudan-style option. A cross between the **American-style option** which can be exercised at any point throughout its life and European-style options which can only be exercised at **expiry**. The Bermudan option can be exercised at specific dates during its life. As a result the option is also known as an *Atlantic style, limited exercise,* or *quasi-American style option.*

best advice (UK). A requirement placed on financial advisors by the Financial Services Act, 1986 to provide the best investment alternative in a given situation, with due consideration of the circumstances of the client.

best efforts. (i) When an issue is not **underwritten** (cf. **underwrite; firm commitment**). The **lead manager** will use his 'best efforts' to ensure placement, although this is not guaranteed to the issuer until the transaction takes place (cf. **best efforts basis**). Or in the sense of a **purchase fund** agent for a **bond** issue where an attempt is made to buy securities in the **aftermarket** to satisfy the conditions of a **purchase fund**, but no guarantees are given that any securities will be acquired. (ii) It can also be used to describe where managers handling a **private placement** or **public issue** try to find buyers or sellers of a security on behalf of a client (cf. **purchase-and-sale**).

best efforts basis or **best efforts underwriting.** (i) A method of securities distribution often seen in the new issues markets where the **managers** or the **market-maker** will sell an issue, or block of securities, on the basis of what can be sold instead of **underwriting** the entire transaction (cf. **bought deal**). In the secondary market most often seen when the securities in question are **illiquid** or of doubtful **credit worthiness**. (ii) In the **money markets** refers to a firm order for a given amount to be executed at the best price available over a set period. It can also be taken to mean a flexible amount (up to some limit) at a set rate.

best execution rule (UK). On the **London Stock Exchange** a **broker-dealer** who is not a **market-maker** in a particular security is only allowed to trade in it as a **principal** if the broker-dealer can better the price currently on offer by a market-maker in a comparable size on **Stock Exchange Automated Quotations**.

best price. See at best.

Best Rating Service (USA). A **credit rating** agency specializing in analysing insurance companies. The highest rating is 'A+'. Used by purchasers of insurance company products, such as annuities, to gauge the firm's soundness.

beta. (β) A measure of the sensitivity of an asset to changes in the market, i.e. its **market risk**. Technically, the correlation of the asset price with the net value of all assets in the market. A beta of 0.5

means that a 1% change in the market index results in a 0.5% change in the value of the asset. See **alpha, Capital Asset Pricing Model; residual risk; specific risk; systematic risk.**

beta shares (Equities; UK). The now defunct category of **ordinary shares** that are traded with reasonable frequency on the **London Stock Exchange** (cf. **gamma shares; delta shares**). For details see **alpha shares; normal market size.**

beta trading. A method of **hedging foreign exchange risk** in **currency options** by taking the **volatility risk** of one currency with another. For instance, to hedge a US dollar/Belgian franc **position** by a US dollar/Deutschmark position. The beta risk is the probability that the **volatility** of the two currencies (Belgian franc and Deutschemark) will diverge.

better-of-two-assets options. An option where the **exercise** is into the more advantageous of two specified **underlyings**. For example a **call option** that pays out either on the **New York Stock Exchange** or **National Association of Securities Dealers Automated Quotations** composite **stock** indices. This would give the holder the benefit of any large/small company differences in performance over the **life** of the option. When there are more than two assets, they are known as a **rainbow option.**

bible. A complete set of records of a transaction prepared for archive and reference purposes.

bid. (i) The price or **yield** at which a buyer wishes to purchase a particular security (cf. **asked price; offer**). (ii) The price or yield at which a buyer commits to purchase a security, as when a **broker** or investor bids at an **auction, offer for sale,** or **tender**. (iii) The interest rate at which a **counterparty** will pay interest on an instrument (cf. **fixed rate payer; interest rate swap**). (iv) An offer made to acquire another company (cf. **tender offer**). See also **mergers and acquisitions.**

bid-asked price (USA). American term for a quote that has both a **bid** and an **offer** price. See **two-way price.**

bid-asked spread (USA). The difference between the **offer** price and the **bid** price. Also known as the *dealer's spread, dealing spread, gross spread,* or *specialist's quote.* See **spread.**

bid deadline. The time at which a **bid** or instruction to buy (or sell) must be received in an **auction** or **tender** (cf. **share buy-back**).

bidder. A participant in an **auction**; that is, one who places a **bid.**

bidding-up. (i) The willingness of a buyer of a large amount of a security to pay an above-market price to obtain his **position** (cf. **market impact**). (ii) The process of a buyer having to raise his purchase price continually to match the rising offered price in the market (cf. **paying up**).

bid and offer prices. The prices at which parties enter into transactions. It applies in particular to financial intermediaries who aim to make the difference at which they buy and sell, the *bid-offer spread* or *turn* (cf. **liquidity**). The relationship of who buys and sells is shown in the Table.

	Dealer or broker	Customer
Bid	Buying price (by broker or dealer)	Selling price
Offer (ask)	Selling price (by broker or dealer)	Buying price

See **bid-asked price**; **two-way price** (cf. **spread**).

bid market. See **oversold**.

bid-offer price. A dealer **quote** that has both a bid and an **offer** price or rate. See **spread** (cf. **liquidity**).

bid only. A security for which the **dealer** will not **offer** to sell. Normally this would be in anticipation of a shortfall in the supply of the security so that the dealer would be unsure if and when the security could be bought to effect **delivery**. Sometimes referred to as *bid without*.

bid price or **bid rate.** The price or (interest) rate at which assets or securities are purchased (cf. **offer price**). See **bid**.

bid-spread price. This is the **offer** price less the bid price. Sometimes known as the *dealer's spread*, the *specialist's quote*, or the *gross spread*.

bid wanted (BW) (USA). A term that often appears on market quotations for lesser traded securities and which is an indication that the holder wants to sell and is soliciting prospective bids. Buyers may respond with a counter-offer and the final price is worked out by negotiation (cf. **direct search market**).

bid yield. See **bid**.

biennial bond. A bond where the first **coupon** is deferred for the first two years.

bifurcation (USA). A divestiture of a part of a company in order to improve the focus of the business (cf. **divestment**; **spin-off**. This might

arise because one area of activity or business line was in a cyclical, mature phase whilst the other was in a growth phase. By splitting the two, investors can better value the two parts and management can concentrate on managing the two types of business in more efficient ways, without being distracted by problems in the other area. Also sometimes known as a *demerger* or *unbundling* (cf. **conglomerate**).

Big Bang (UK). Used to describe the series of deregulatory alterations to the rules and trading practices that took place, or took effect, on 27 October 1986 at the **London Stock Exchange**, and which brought them more into line with other major **stock exchanges** overseas. These changes centred upon the introduction of: negotiated **brokerage commissions** (cf. **broker**), the introduction of **dual capacity** allowing members both to make markets and act as brokers (cf. **capacity**), and multi-functional and diversely owned members (cf. **liberalization**; **universal banking**). The term is also frequently used in a more general sense to describe the major changes to the financial markets that took place in the UK in the mid-1980s.

Big Blue (Equities; USA). Market nickname for International Business Machines Inc. (IBM).

Big Board. Nickname for the **New York Stock Exchange** (cf. **kerb**; **Little Board**; **stock exchange**).

big figure. (i) The whole number part of a price, for example 95 of a price of 95.50. In the USA, known as the *handle*. (ii) In the **foreign exchange** markets it is that part of the quote which is the same for both the **bid** and **offer** for the currencies. Therefore for a Deutschmark/US dollar two-way quote of 1.4520/30, the big figure is 1.45 and is often implied or taken to be known by market participants since a trader may make a price by quoting just the 20/30.

Big Four. (i) (Banking; UK). The four largest retail or high-street banks in the UK: Barclays, Lloyds, Midland, and NatWest. (ii) (Japan). The four largest securities firms in Japan: Daiwa Securities, Nikko Securities, Nomura Securities, and Yamaichi Securities.

big ticket. Slang term often used to denote a large transaction (cf. **lot**).

bilateral clearing or **netting.** Agreements between two **counterparties** that the mutual obligations of both will be settled by a single net payment. Thus if party A owes party B 600,000 and B owes A 500,000, then A will make a net payment of 100,000 to B. See also **multilateral netting**; **netting**.

bill. Any of a range of short maturity finanancing instruments issued by firms, agencies, or governments. See **banker's acceptance**; **bill of exchange**; **documentary credit**; **treasury bill**.

bill arbitrage (Money markets; UK). This refers to the ability of companies to issue **bills** at a favourable rate and redeposit the proceeds with banks at a profit. A condition that has arisen due to a lack of availability of **eligible bills** for the **Bank of England's open market operations**. It is also known as *roundtripping*.

bill broker (UK). Also known as a *discount broker*.

billet de trésor (French). **Commercial paper**.

billion. 1,000,000,000.

bill of exchange. A **negotiable instrument**, used mainly in international trade, instructing one person (the *drawee*) to pay a certain sum of money to another named person (the *drawer*) or to bearer on demand or at a certain future time. The drawee gives his acceptance of the undertaking by endorsing the face of the bill with his signature. If the drawee or **acceptor** of the bill is a bank, the bill is a **bank bill** (known in the USA as a **banker's acceptance**); if it is a trader, the bill is a **trade acceptance** or bill. All such bills are normally issued with 90-day **maturity**, and their marketability depends on the standing of the drawee or acceptor; the nature of transactions being financed; and whether the bill is **eligible** for rediscounting with the **central bank**. A bill issued by a company is also known as a *commercial bill* or a *trade bill*. See **discount**; **protest**; **stale**.

bill of lading (BL; B/L). A document of title over goods in transit and widely used in international trade. It provides evidence of the receipt of the goods by the shipper; is the basis of a contract between the exporter and the shipper; and may convey title to the goods being shipped. It is a necessary document for issuing **banker's acceptances** in the USA.

bill rate or **bill discount rate.** The discount rate applicable to **bills of exchange** (cf. **eligible bill**). See **interest rate calculations**.

bills pass (Money markets; USA). See **coupon pass**; **Federal Reserve**.

binary option. An exotic type of **option** where the payout is typically **all or nothing**, depending on the **underlying** at **expiry**. Such payouts may be **path-dependent**, as with **barrier options**. See also **digital option**.

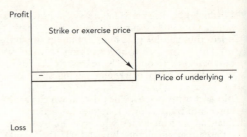

Payoff of a binary call option at expiry

binomial distribution. A discrete probability distribution where there are at any time only one of two possible outcomes. For instance, repeated tossing of a coin would create a series of heads (H) or tails (T) with each successive trial. The binomial distribution computes the probability for such events. Market practitioners have considered that asset price changes take place in a discrete fashion and can thus be accurately represented by a tree or lattice of such events. See also **binomial pyramid**.

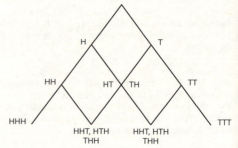

Binomial distribution

Binomial jump diffusion process. A combined binomial lattice with **jump process** used for **option pricing** which aims to take into account the non-stationarity of the **underlying** stochastic process. See also **jump diffusion process**.

binomial option pricing model (BOPM). An **option pricing model** in which the movements in the price or rate of the **underlying** can only take two values in the next time period for each value it may have in the previous period. The model makes use of the **binomial distribution** as the stochastic process generating the asset price movement over time. The life of the option is divided into steps or time intervals at which the asset price is allowed to vary by a fixed proportion set equal to its expected **volatility** at that point in time. The value of the option payoff is computed by working backwards from the pairs of outcomes in the probability tree of lattice towards the present. As with all option pricing models, it derives a 'fair value' based on risk-neutral, **arbitrage-free**

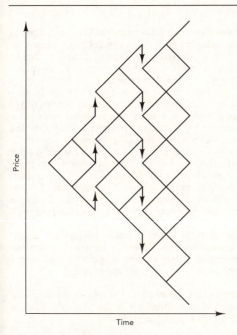

Binomial jump diffusion process

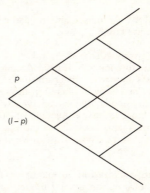

Binomial tree

binomial tree. The possible changes in asset price or rate used in determining **option** value in a discrete, **jump**, or step type of **option pricing model**. More complicated trinomial or polynomial trees are also possible allowing a larger number of alternative price movements to the **underlying** in any given period. It is interesting to note that simulations using the **binomial option pricing model** against the **Black-Scholes option pricing model**, which uses continuous price adjustment, suggests very little difference to the option's fair value. However, for **exotic options**, where the option payout may be linked to a part of the probability distribution, the use of the binomial approach provides a clearer indication of the likely probability of **exercise**. The binomial tree is also called a *lattice*, *probability tree*, or simply *tree*.

black box risk. See **model risk**.

black box syndrome. Problems with using advanced **analytical models** and stochastic **hedging models** where the underlying mathematical and statistical assumptions are only partially understood. This applies particularly to the complex **exotic options** such as **currency-protected options** and other multi-currency **rainbow option** types.

Black–Derman–Toy option pricing model. Interest rate **option pricing model** based on an extension of the **binomial option pricing model's** approach which allows for the change in the interest rate **volatility** over time.

Black Friday (USA). *Black* (day) has become a generic term for a sharp fall in prices. The origins date back to the market panic, spawned by the attempt by market manipulators to corner the **gold market**, on Friday 24 September 1869.

Black–Karasinki option pricing model. Interest rate **option pricing model** using a lognormal **volatility** distribution for the **underlying**.

conditions. Variations to the basic approach include trinomial or multinomial steps where the asset price or rate can assume three or more different values. The model can also cope with changes in volatility over time. Because it can be set to account for trigger points, either for **barrier options** or **ladder options**, the BOPM has found increasing favour with market participants in pricing **exotic options** with non-standard payoffs. The original concept was established in 1979 by J. Cox, S. Ross, and M. Rubinstein, 'Option Pricing: A Simplified Approach', *Journal of Financial Economics* 7: 229–63.

binomial pyramid. The cumulating density function of a **binomial distribution**. The initial part looks as in the figure. See also **binomial tree**; **binomial option pricing model**; **digital option**.

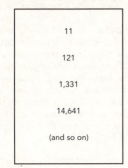

11
121
1,331
14,641
(and so on)

Binomial pyramid

black knight. An unwelcome predator (cf. grey knight; white knight).

Black Monday (USA). (i) Monday 28 October 1929. The Dow-Jones Industrial Average fell by 13%. This is the start of what came to be known as the *Great Crash*, which ushered in the Great Depression. (ii) Monday 19 October 1987, which saw the Dow-Jones Industrial Average fall 508 points in the day. It also saw falls in the major stock markets across the globe. Also known as the *1987 Crash*.

Black's approximation. An addition to the basic Black–Scholes option pricing model for pricing American-style options on stocks.

Black–Scholes option pricing model. The first theoretically correct option pricing model that provides a means to derive a *fair value* of option contracts for European-style options on traded assets paying no dividend in the option period. It involves using information on the underlying, the strike price, volatility, time to expiry, and the present risk-free interest rate. First formulated by Fischer Black and Myron Scholes in 'The Pricing of Options and Corporate Liabilities', *Journal of Political Economy*, 81 (May–June 1973), 637–54. It is the model most frequently used to trade options. Although in theory quite restrictive, the model has proved robust in use and, for most trading and investment purposes, can adequately approximate the values of many different types of options.

Black's option pricing model. A model for the pricing of European-style options on futures or forward priced assets derived in a straightforward way from the Black–Scholes option pricing model.

Black Wednesday or **Golden Wednesday** (UK). 16 September 1992, the day that the UK left the Exchange Rate Mechanism. As a result, sterling fell about 15% against the Deutschmark. To some it was a black, or catastrophic event, to others, a release, hence golden.

blanket recommendation. A broker's circular sent to all its clients recommending a course of action.

blank transfer (Equities; UK). Share transfer certificate which has been signed by the registered holder but where the date and name of the recipient are left blank. Such a certificate allows the holder to become the registered owner upon completing the missing details (cf. bearer participation certificate). It is used when securities are used to collateralize loans or to disguise the name of the beneficial owner.

blended interest rate swap. The quotation of a complex interest rate swap (IRS) which may include an accreting, amortizing, or deferred structure, where the payment rate on the swap is a weighted-average combination of two or more rates from the individual, simple swaps transactions. For instance, a blended five-year pay-fixed step-down swap where the notional principal is initially 100 for three years and then 50 for the last two years would be made up from a simple IRS with a notional principal of 100 for three years at 8%, combined with a three-year deferred swap for 50 for a further two-years at 8.50%. The customer therefore pays a weighted average rate of 8.29% for both the swaps as a single payment, plus or minus any spread required by the counterparty.

blind pool (USA). Limited partnership agreement where the assets to be acquired are not specified. Contrast with a specified pool where the assets are specifically delineated.

block. An abnormally large amount of securities, more than a round lot in the particular market. See liquidity; market impact.

blocked account (Banking). Deposits that may not be withdrawn or transferred. These can arise due to court or administrative orders (cf. country risk).

blocked currency. A currency whose domestic monetary authority restricts its geographical mobility and price variability.

block house. Financial intermediary specializing in bringing together buyers and sellers of blocks of securities (cf. block trading).

Block Order Exposure System (BLOX) (UK). A service available through Stock Exchange Automated Quotations that will allow subscribers to quote for and trade large amounts of securities. Designed for institutional investors and customers of London Stock Exchange members, and intended to reduce dealing time and costs (cf. Small-order Automatic Execution Facility).

block positioner (USA). A financial intermediary, typically a broker-dealer who acts as counterparty to a block sale. Because of the market risk of such large transactions, block positioners must be registered with the Securities and Exchange Commission and, if members, the New York Stock Exchange. To guarantee a profit from the transaction a broker-dealer will need to use all his powers of risk management and distribution to hedge and to sell off his position.

block sale, trade, or **transaction.** (i) A trade in a specific security (or portfolio of securities) which is larger than normal for the particular market, given the ruling market conditions (cf **lot**). (ii) It can also be used to describe a transaction in which the sponsoring managers of a **certificate of deposit** or **floating rate certificate of deposit** issue buy the entire issue on behalf of themselves for distribution at their discretion. (iii) An issue of new securities where the **lead manager** does not **syndicate** the transaction but undertakes to **underwrite** the entire issue (cf. **bought deal**).

block trading. A technique used by **portfolio** managers in order to achieve a major shift in the nature of the portfolio (cf. **block trade**). On occasion this buying and selling of whole or parts of the portfolio is effected without the precise character of the underlying securities being known.

block volume. The number of **block** transactions over a given period. That is, abnormally large transactions in a particular stock or market (cf. **lot**).

block voting. The practice of a number of shareholders acting together to cast their votes in a single block (cf. **proxy contest**).

Bloomberg. A financial services **quote vendor** which provides a real-time price and information service for market participants. The system also allows users to manipulate and investigate market and other data on securities, **foreign exchange**, a **portfolio**, and so on, via a suite of analytical programmes.

blotter. A foreign exchange **trader's** own record of his transactions showing his **positions**.

blow-out (Slang). Said to occur when an issue of securities is sold very rapidly.

Blue Book (UK). Name given to the official statistics relating to the UK's national income and expenditure.

blue chip. The type of **equity** that is considered to be of the highest quality, which involves little risk of a sharp decline to either income/earnings or capital value; the **common stock** or **ordinary shares** of companies that are regarded as stable investments in terms of **capital gain** and **dividend** payments. Originally a US term but now widely used internationally (cf. **investment grade**). The term comes from the colour of the best diamonds; or the colour on the highest value poker chip.

blue list (Blue List of Current Municipal Offerings) (Bonds; USA). A list published daily giving details of, mostly, **municipal** and **tax-exempt bond** issues, including price, yield, and other pertinent data, such as **call** or **put** provisions.

blue screen (UK). The situation where **market-makers** on the London market are marking their prices up or leaving them the same (cf. **red screen**).

blue sky laws (USA). The term given to the various states' legislation on investor protection intended to prevent securities fraud. Such laws cover securities issuances where the selling is confined to within the boundaries of a single state and exempt from **registration** with the **Securities and Exchange Commission**. This applies mostly to small **equity** issues (cf. **initial public offering; new issue; private placement**).

board broker (USA). The member of a US exchange responsible for keeping records of investors' **limit orders** using **open outcry** or a **market-maker** system rather than the **specialist** system; used extensively on the **Chicago Board Options Exchange**, where he is known as an *order book official*. See **public limit order**.

board lot. The standard trading quantity on an exchange based on a multiple of a single security. Thus an exchange might set 100 units of **common stock** as a board lot. See **lot**.

board of directors. Key decision-making body consisting of the **directors** of a company. Company law requires that certain validating actions are made by, and are recorded as having been made, at a meeting of a quorum of directors of a company, although individual directors may be given specific executive powers (cf. **finance director; chief executive officer**).

Board of Governors of the Federal Reserve System (USA). See **Federal Reserve**.

Board of Trade Clearing Corporation (BOTCC) (Derivatives; USA). The **clearing house** of the **Chicago Board Options Exchange** (cf. **International Commodities Clearing House**).

board order. A **limit order** that is handled by a **board broker** or an **order book official**.

boardroom. (i) A place where the **board of directors** holds its meetings. (ii) Also takes the meaning in the USA of a room where a **broker's** clients can watch current activity in the market (cf. **ticker**).

boilerplate. Shorthand used to describe the terms and conditions in contracts which are standard market practice.

boiler room. High-pressure selling of securities. Firms engaged in this activity aim to give the impression of great activity and a sense of urgency.

bolsa (Portuguese; Spanish). An exchange.

Bolsa Brasileira de Futuros (BBF) (Brazil). Brazil's **futures** exchange.

Bolsa de Bogota SA (Colombia). Carrera 8 No. 13–82, Piso 7, A A 3584, Co-Bogota (tel. 57 1 243 6501: fax 57 1 281 1850).

Bolsa de Comercio de Buenos Aires (Buenos Aires Stock Exchange) (Argentina). Sarmiento 299, 1353 Buenos Aires (tel. 54 (0) 1 311 5231/2/3, 54 (0) 1 311 1174 7860; fax 54 (0) 1 312 9332). Established 10 July 1854.

Bolsa de Comercio de Santiago (Chile). Casilla 123-D, CL-Santiago (tel. 56 2 689 2001; fax 56 2 672 8046).

Bolsa de Madrid (Equities; Spain). Principal **stock exchange** in Spain although there are others in Barcelona, Bilbao, and Valencia. Spanish financial markets are regulated by the Comisión del Mercado de Valores (CNMV).

Bolsa de Medellin SA (Colombia). Carrera 50 No. 50–48 Piso 2, Co-Medellin (tel. 57 4 260 3000: fax 57 4 251 1981).

Bolsa de Mercadorias and Futuros (BM & F) (Commodities and Futures Exchange) (Brazil). Praça Antonio Prado 48, 01010 São Paolo SP 01010–901 (tel. 55 (0) 11 239 5511; fax 55 (0) 11 35 2541). Established in 1985.

Bolsa de Valores de Lisboa (Lisbon Stock Exchange) (Portugal). Edifício da Bolsa—R Soeiro Pereira Gomes, 1600 Lisboa (tel. 351 1 795 20 31/8; fax 351 1 795 20 21). The main **stock market** in Portugal. **Derivative instruments** are traded from the **Bolsa de Oporto**. Regulation is carried out by the Bank of Portugal, the **central bank**.

Bolsa de Valores de São Paulo (BOVESPA) (Brazil). Largest and most important of the ten **stock exchanges** in Brazil. Its main **index** is the BOVESPA Index. See also **emerging markets**.

Bolsa de Valores do Porto (Oporto Securities Exchange) (Portugal). Palacio da Bolsa, Rua de Ferreira Borges, PT-4000 Porto (tel. 351 2 318546; fax 351 2 316859). **Futures** and **options** exchange based in Oporto. The Lisbon and Oporto exchanges agreed to split cash instruments and derivatives trading. Oporto is thus the **derivatives** exchange.

Bolsa de Valores do Rio de Janeiro (BVRJ) (Rio de Janeiro Stock Exchange) (Brazil). Praça XV de Novembro 20, 20010 Rio de Janeiro (tel.

55 (0) 21 271 1001; fax 55 (0) 21 221 2151). Established in 1845.

Bolsa Mexicana de Valores (Mexico). Paseo de la Reforma 255, Colonia Cuauhtemoc, MX-06500 Mexico DF (tel. 525 726 67 35; fax 525 705 47 98).

Bolsa Nacional de Valores SA (Costa Rica). Apartado 1736, PO Box 1736, CR-1000 San Jose, Costa Rica (tel. 506 22 80 11; fax 506 55 01 31).

Bombay Stock Exchange (BSE) (Equities; India). Phiroze Jeejeebhoy Towers, Dalal Street, Bombay, 400 001 India (tel. 91–22–265–5860; fax 91–22–265–8121). The principal **stock exchange** in India, although there are other exchanges. It is regulated by the **Securities and Exchange Board of India**. It has a computerized trading system called the BSE On-line Trading system (BOLT).

bond. (i) A security evidencing debt. Usually used for debt instruments with an **original maturity** of more than one year. It can be in **physical** form or **book entry** (cf. **certificate**). The issuer of a bond normally undertakes, amongst other things, to pay the holder a fixed principal amount on a stated future date and a stream of interest payments during the life of the bond (cf. **plain vanilla**; **straight**; **zero-coupon bond**). Also called a *certificate of indebtedness*.

The key features (which may not be features of all types of bonds or of a particular issue) are:

- *principal value*: the denomination or value of the bond. For trading purposes this is taken as a percentage value per hundred nominal or face or par value.
- *maturity* or *redemption date*: the date at which the bond is repaid.
- *coupon*: the amount of interest that is paid on the bond; this is usually expressed in terms of a percentage rate per 100 nominal, when it is known as the *coupon rate*, which is paid on designated dates.
- *bullet* or *straight*: bond without any additional features and where the principal is all repaid at maturity.
- *call provision*: the right of the issuer to seek early repayment before the stated maturity date, usually after a stated period.
- *put provision*: the right of the holder to seek early repayment before the stated maturity date, usually after a stated period.
- *convertible*: the right of the holder to convert the bond into another instrument of the issuer (usually the issuer's common stock, but it can also be other bonds).
- *amortization*: a part of the issue may be redeemed prior to the final maturity date: *sinking fund*: involves the issuer in a compulsory repurchase of a part of the issue; *purchase*

fund: allows the issuer to make repurchases in the market prior to maturity; *serial* involves either part repayment of the principal of each bond or retiring a portion of the issue according to a predetermined schedule.

- *security*: *unsecured*, the issuer has a general obligation to repay; *secured*, the issuer pledges specific asset(s) as collateral, of which the two most common types are *mortgage-backed* (the issue is supported by a specific mortgage on an asset or pool of assets) and *asset-backed* (the issue is supported by a specific asset or a pool of such assets).

- *covenants* or *protective covenants*: terms and conditions attached to the bond contract for the protection of bond holders. *Affirmative covenants* require the issuer to undertake specific actions. *Negative covenants* require the issuer to desist from specific actions. *Negative pledge* means no new debt can be issued which takes priority over existing bondholders' claims: An *event of default* occurs if the issuer fails to meet a covenant term as laid out in the bond contract.

- *ranking*: the seniority of the bond in relation to other claims of the issuer. The principal categories are: *secured* (holder benefits from a prior claim on the assets of the issuer); *general obligations* or *unsecured* (general obligations of the issuer ranking alongside common creditors); *junior* (any claim that is deferred in respect of other issues of a similar class or category); *subordinated* (a category of bonds which is deferred as to class and repayment conditions).

- *indenture* or *trust deed*: the contract between the issuer and bond buyers which specifies both parties obligations. This usually makes use of a *trustee*, to represent the holders' interests.

See **interest rate calculations; yields**.

(ii) (USA) In the US **treasury** market it means a fixed-rate debt instrument with a life-span of more than ten years (cf. **note**). It should be noted that in the UK a bond is normally unsecured, whereas a **debenture** is secured against some asset, while in the USA the usage is the reverse (cf. **unsecured loan stock**). See also **interest rate calculations**.

(iii) It can also be used in terms of a guarantee provided by one party to another as part of a contract. For example, a *completion bond*, which is given by the contractor as a guarantee that the contract will be carried out to the end. *Performance bond* is another name for **margin**.

bond agreement (USA). The contract covering a private placement.

bond analysis. Two ways of looking at fixed interest securities: (i) as either a long-term investment held until maturity or for at least five years; or (ii) as shorter-term investments which can be bought and sold as interest rates rise and fall. In either case, getting the timing of the transaction right is very important. Factors that influence the approach include: tax position; expectations about inflation and interest rates; the behaviour of the different classes of bonds, corporate and government; and **yield** analysis. See also **term structure of interest rates**.

bond anticipation note (BAN) (Money markets; USA). Issued by US local government authorities to receive interim project finance in anticipation of funding through a **bond** issue.

bond basis. The method used to compute accrued interest on some **bonds** and on some short-term money market instruments. It is used, for example, in the **eurobond** market where accrued interest is calculated on a bond basis and is equal to the **coupon** rate multiplied by the number of elapsed **bond days** divided by 360. It should be noted that there are two variants, known as 30/360 and 30/360E, the first method being used in the USA, while the 'E' stands for European and is used in a number of Continental European countries. The difference relates to the way months with thirty-one days are calculated when working out the accrued interest. (cf. **money market basis**). Also sometimes known as the *360-day year convention* and seen written as 360/360. In some markets, such as that for **US treasuries**, the coupon payments are computed on the basis of the actual number of days in a given year, often written as actual/actual. For details of the different methods, see **interest rate calculations**.

bond broker (USA). A broker who carries out **bond** transactions on an exchange (cf. **active bond crowd; cabinet crowd; bond crowd**). Also used for any **trader** in the **over-the-counter** (OTC) **bond markets** (which includes **US treasuries** and **agencies**).

bond buyback. A company repurchase of its own **bonds**, normally those standing at a **discount** in the market. Because retiring a liability incurs no **capital gain**, the repurchaser has effectively capitalized the future interest cost as a gain. Sometimes such buybacks are linked to an **exchange offer** since the company is concerned with its after-tax cost of **debt**.

Bond Buyer's Index (Bonds; USA). Daily **fixed-rate bond** indices published by *The Bond Buyer*. There are two principal indices: an **index of long-term municipal bonds** rated single-A or above; and an index of double-A rated municipals.

Bond Buyer Municipal Bond Index, The
(USA). Much watched **index of municipal bonds**
which is also used as the **underlying** for a **futures**
and **option on futures** contract at the Chicago
Board of Trade.

bond conversion. A right in a **bond indenture**,
or **trust deed**, allowing the holder to convert from
the existing issue into another **bond** (perhaps already extant) or a bond which has different terms,
for instance a longer **maturity**. Such a right might
be included in an issue in order to increase marketability (cf. **bells and whistles**). It can also mean the
opposite, where the issuer has the right, upon giving notice, of conversion to vary the bond's terms
and conditions. Also sometimes called a *convertible*.

bond covenant. A contractual term in a **bond**
issue imposing a restriction on the issuer. See
covenants.

bond crowd (USA). Exchange brokers who undertake **bond** transactions. The area where bonds are
traded is separate to that of **equities**, hence the
expression.

bond days. The number of days that have passed
between the date on which a **bond** was issued and
the date being used in the assessment, normally on
the assumption of 360 days in the year and 30 days
in the month. The formula for the number of
elapsed days is given by:

$$\{(Y_2-Y_1)\times 360\} + \{(M_2-M_1)\times 30\} + (D_2-D_1)\}$$

Where $Y_1; M_1; D_1$ is the earlier date and $Y_2; M_2; D_2$
is the later date. See **interest rate calculations**.

bond equivalent yield. See **equivalent bond
yield**.

bond fund. A fund that is invested in **bonds** (cf.
money market fund).

bond futures. Bond futures are **futures contracts**
to buy or sell a **notional bond** at a fixed future date
at a price agreed today. Also called *long-term interest rate futures*.

Futures transaction	Contractual obligation
Buyer	To purchase a 'notional bond' at the specified futures price
Seller	To sell a 'notional bond' at the specified futures price

bondholder. The owner of a **bond**.

bond house. A firm whose main activities involve **underwriting**, distributing, and dealing in
bonds.

bond indenture (USA). The contract covering a
public offering of bonds (cf. **registration**).

bond index. An index which uses a set of bonds.

bond index swap. Interest rate swap where one
side's payments are linked to a **bond index** or
benchmark bond's performance and the other to
a **floating rate** based on **money market rates** (cf.
basis swap; coupon swap).

bonding. The process of management trying to
make themselves appealing to financiers.

bond interest term securities (BITS) (Money
Markets; USA). See **variable rate demand obligations**.

bond-like option. Any of a number of guaranteed return structures such as **equity-linked notes**
where the principal is protected.

bond market. (i) That part of the capital market
that deals in negotiable term instruments rather
than loans, short-term instruments or **equities**. (ii)
The market in which a particular type of bond is
traded. For instance, the government bond market, the corporate bond market, the **eurobond**
market.
Some key bond markets (or sub-markets) are:

DOMESTIC MARKETS

- *government bonds*: obligations issued by a government, either as bonds or notes.
- *agencies of government*: obligations issued by
  an agency of the government and benefiting
  from its full faith and credit.
- *municipal and local government bonds*: obligations of municipalities, states, or regions
  within a country.
- *asset-backed* and *mortgage-backed bonds*: obligations where the issue is backed by an asset,
  pool of assets, or mortgages.
- *corporate bonds*: obligations issued by industrial and commercial firms.

INTERNATIONAL MARKETS

- *eurobonds*: obligations issued on the international eurobond market.
- *foreign bonds*: obligations issued by foreign
  entities in a domestic market; these can be
  any of the above three categories, as well as,
  supranational institutions.
- *global bonds*: bonds which are offered in more
  than one market simultaneously.

TYPES OF BONDS

- *fixed rate bonds*: bonds with fixed coupons.
- *variable rate notes*: bonds or notes with coupons that are reset periodically in line with
  market conditions.

- *convertible bonds*: bonds which give the holder the right to convert to a different instrument.
- *short-term* or *shorts*: bonds with a short maturity.
- *medium-term* or *medium*: bonds with an intermediate maturity.
- *long-term* or *longs*: bonds with a long maturity.

bond option. An option on a bond (cf. **call option**; **put option**). There are exchange-listed options on some government bonds, while **over-the-counter** options are traded on a variety of government and non-government bonds.

bond-over-stock warrant. See stock-over-bond warrant.

bond power (Bonds; USA). An **assignment** form used for the transfer of ownership.

bond price elasticity. See bond risk; duration.

bond price linked bull-bear bond. A type of bull-bear bond where the redemption is linked to movements in an **underlying bond**, typically a government bond.

bond price quotation. The quotation of **bonds** as a percentage of **par**. A quote of 85 would mean a price of 85% of the **par value** of the bond (that is, the bond is priced in the market at **discount**) and a quote of 110 would mean a price of 10 per cent above par value (that is at a **premium**). This convention gets around the fact that individual issues may have different unit sizes. To simplify trading, such quotes are also **clean prices**; that is, without the **accrued interest** due on completion of the transaction (cf. **dirty price**). See also **income bond**.

bond rating. See credit ratings.

bond ratio. See debt-equity ratio; ratio analysis.

bond refunding. See refunding.

bond risk. A measure of bond price sensitivity based on **modified duration** and the **full price** of a bond, expressed as a ratio of the price change for a 1% change in yield. It is calculated by:

$$Bond\ risk = \frac{Modified\ duration\ (bond\ volatility) \times Full\ price\ of\ the\ bond}{100}$$

If a bond has a **clean price** of 96.375 and accrued interest of 1.75, and a modified duration of 5.75, the bond risk will be:

$$5.6422 = \frac{5.75 \times (96.375 + 1.75)}{100}$$

bond swap. A transaction involving the sale of one **bond** and the simultaneous purchase of another (cf. **switch**). There are several common reasons for bond swaps: *duration* (where the **duration** of the purchased bond is either lengthened or shortened); *quality* (where the new (old) bond has a better (worse) **credit worthiness**; *tax* (to crystallize a **capital gain** (or **loss**) but at the same time maintaining the **position**); *yield* (the new bond has a higher **yield** than the old (cf. **pick-up**)).

bon du trésor (French). **Treasury bill.**

bond value or **straight value.** The value a bond with **option** features (for example a **convertible** or **call provision**) would have without the embedded option.

bond volatility. See duration (cf. volatility).

bond warrant. See debt warrant.

bond washing. Selling **bonds, equities,** or other securities before **coupon** or **dividend** payment in order to convert income into **capital gains** (cf. **zero-coupon bond**). See also **coupon stripping**.

bond with put. See put provision; retractable bond.

bond with warrant. A **hybrid** instrument giving the holder a combination of a straight debt instrument plus an option instrument on either the issuer's **equity** or additional debt instruments. Variations include warrants on third party equity (cf. **covered warrant**); or the warrant is **exercisable** into the issuer's **preferred stock**, rather than common stock.

bond yield. Generally the internal rate of return on a **bond**. For details of different types see **yield** (cf. **interest rate calculations**).

bond yield index mismatch floating rate note (Mismatch FRN). A type of **mismatch bond** where the **reference rate** is based on changes in **yield** of a **bond index**. A variation on the structure uses a specific type of government bond (e.g. the thirty-year US **treasury bond**).

bonos del estado (Spain). Medium-term government **bond** issues.

Bons à Taux Annuel Normalisé (BTAN) (France). **Treasury bills** and **treasury notes**.

Bons à Taux Fixe (BTF) (France). Fixed rate government bonds. See **obligations assimilables du Trésor**.

bonus issue (Equities). An issue of **shares** to existing holders requiring no payment, which has the effect of increasing the company's **issued capital** by converting **reserves** into **shares**. Also known as a *scrip issue* (UK) or *capitalization issue* (USA).

book. (i) Common term for a **market-maker's** total **long** and **short positions** (cf. **mismatched book**). Hence *running a book*. (ii) In new issues, to *build a book* or *book-building* means to identify investors in advance to fix the price of an issue and determine who will commit to buy the issue when launched. The degree of commitment may vary from **firm order** to **indication** (cf. **ringing**). (iii) To record in the accounts an item or transaction. (iv) An organization's ledgers and accounting records. (v) Also used as a generic term for a firm's business records. (vi) *Books* is the name given to the **Bank of England's directors's** daily policy meeting. (vii) Short for **public order book**.

book building. The process by which the **lead manager** to a new issue ascertains demand and hence the offer price for the securities. Investors are asked to indicate the amount and price at which they would subscribe for securities. They are offered the incentive to participate in this shadow **auction** process by being offered the guarantee that they will be able to receive securities at the price they informally indicate, or be allowed to increase the price in order to be assured of the quantity they require. Thus the lead manager is given information on the likely demand for the issue and the price at which the issue can be successfully brought to the market. Book building is principally used for **equity** issues where there is some difficulty over establishing the market price and/or demand. It has become increasingly the major means of setting the issue price for large **initial public offerings** or **secondary public offerings**. See also **circle**.

book cost. The price paid for an asset (cf. **book loss; marked-to-market**).

booked. Recorded or entered into the accounts or ledgers.

book-entry security. Those securities whose details of ownership are kept in records by some central authority rather than having **physical** form (or being evidenced by **certificates**). For example, US **treasury bonds** are book-entry securities. See **nominative; registered security** (cf. **bearer bond**).

book gain, loss, or **profit.** The notional profit or loss coming from the difference between the cost of a security and its current market price. Sometimes called *unrealized loss, gain,* or *profit*. See marked-to-market.

book runner. A term for a **lead manager**. The manager who is in charge of managing a new issue, especially the allocations (cf. **book**). Hence *book running* or *running the books*.

book value (Accounting). (i) The original purchase price, less the cumulative **depreciation** of an asset (cf. **market value; sunk cost**). (ii) The **net assets** or worth of the firm:

	Total assets (fixed assets and current assets)
plus	Intangible assets
less	Current liabilities
less	Long-term liabilities
	Value of equity
less	Preferred stock
=	Net Worth

Net worth divided by the number of **issued shares** gives the *book value per share*. (iii) The nominal value of the **common stock**. (iv) From the investor's viewpoint, it means the value of a security as given in the accounting records of the holder. Often taken to mean the price at which the security was acquired (cf. **book cost; marked-to-market**).

book yield. Where the **yield** of a security is computed using its **book value** rather than its market value.

boom. A period of expansion, high economic activity, and, usually, rising asset values (cf. **bear market; bull market; recession**).

boot (USA). A taxable gain deemed to arise from an exchange of securities where one of the components has a built-in profit. For instance, a **stock** for stock and debt securities (**bonds** or **notes**) exchange, where the latter are issued at a **discount**. A gain may arise if the **secondary market** price of the debt securities is above the exchange price.

booth. Compartment situated at the edge of the trading floor where members can access information or communicate with their office.

bootstrap. (i) Colloquial term for a **two-tier tender offer**. This involves making an offer to acquire a controlling interest in a company at one price with the expectation of being able to make a second, but lower, offer for the remaining outstanding **equity** of the company. In some countries, such as the UK, bidders have to make an offer for all the share capital of a company at the same price. However, in other countries, multiple price offers are permitted (e.g. Germany and the United States). (ii) A method of deriving prices or valuations by repeated iterations using the results from the earlier calculations as inputs to the following ones. Many financial valuation problems are susceptible to bootstrap methods rather than analytic solutions. An example of the bootstrap method would be deriving the **zero-coupon yield curve** from **straight bonds**. Hence the expression *bootstrapping*.

bootstrapping operations (USA). Another and early name for **management buy-outs**.

borrow. (i) (Commodities) A market participant who buys a commodity in the cash or **spot market** and at the same time makes a **forward** sale is said to have 'borrowed' the commodity (cf. **borrowing**). (ii) (Securities) Market practice of holders of securities making them available to **counterparties** for a given period (usually for a **fee**) to allow them to take a **short position** in the security or to effect **settlement** (cf. **against the box; delivery; flat**). See **borrow versus cash; borrow versus pledge**.

borrowed reserves (USA). Reserves made available to member banks of the **Federal Reserve System**. See **net borrowed reserves**.

borrower. One who borrows money for a purpose (cf. **issuer**). A borrower enters into a contractual obligation with the lender or provider of funds to repay the funds, plus interest. Generically, the contractual obligation is called debt if in the form of a loan; and securities if a capital market instrument. Also known as the *obligor*.

borrower option. An interest rate cap on a forward rate agreement (cf. **lender option**).

borrower's limit. A debt limit set by a lender for the maximum amount of **credit** exposure that the lender will take with an individual borrower. The Bank of England sets guidelines that this maximum limit must not exceed 10% of the lending institution's capital base. Most borrowers' limits will be subsumed within other **risk management** limits, such as **country risk limits, maturity** limits, etc.

borrower's option for notes or underwritten standby (BONUS). A type of global note issuance facility.

borrower's option/lender's option (BOLO). A type of issue where the issuer has the choice, at some future date, to select a new **coupon** rate. The holder may then choose to have the bond redeemed or to accept the new interest rate. The opposite structure is known as **lender's option/borrower's option**. See **retractable bond**.

borrowing (UK). Term for the **future's spread** transaction on the **London Metal Exchange** involving the purchase of near-dated contracts and selling longer **expiry** contracts.

borrow versus cash (USA). Securities lending where the borrower provides a cash payment at the outset. This is returned when the borrowed securities are returned with the fee for borrowing.

borrow versus pledge (USA). Securities lending where the borrower provides acceptable collateral, usually in the form of other securities. These are returned when the borrowed securities are returned together with the borrowing fee.

borsa (Italian). Stock exchange.

Borsa di Milano (Italy). See **Italian Stock Market; Milan Stock Exchange**.

Börse (German). Stock exchange.

Börsenhandel (Switzerland). Official **stock market**.

Börsen-Order-Service-System (BOSS) (Germany). Electronic order routing system used on the **Frankfurt Stock Exchange**.

Börsenumsatzsteur (Germany). Tax levied on turnover.

Börsenvorstand (Germany). Stock exchange council.

Bostadsobligationer (Sweden). Mortgage-backed bonds.

Boston matrix. An influential approach to business strategy used to identify the strengths, opportunities, weaknesses, and threats to firms proposed by the Boston Consulting Group. The basic relationship is as in the Figure.

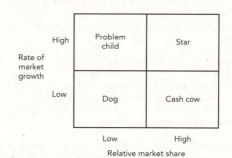

Boston matrix

Boston option. Name given to **zero-cost** or deferred **premium options**, such as a **breakforward** contract. When used in the **currency markets**, it is made up of two different contracts: a **forward foreign exchange** purchase or sale contract and an **option** to reverse the **forward** at a set rate. The cost or **premium** for the option is embedded in the **forward rate** (which is set at a less favourable rate than the true forward rate). Also known as a *capitalised option* or a *forward reverse option*.

Boston Stock Exchange (USA). One of the nine stock exchanges in the United States. See **American Stock Exchange**; **New York Stock Exchange**.

BOT (USA). Notational shorthand for 'bought'. The opposite is SL, for sold. Can also mean Balance of Trade, Board of Trade, or Board of Trustees.

bottom. A low point in security prices over a given period. Also used to describe a resistance level in prices after a market fall or the process of price recovery. The expression the *bottom dropped out* indicates a significant and unexpected breach of such a resistance point.

bottom fisher (USA). See **bargain hunter**.

bottom line. A firm's earnings or profits. Hence to pass through to the bottom line is to be credited with a profit.

bottom straddle. See **straddle**.

bottom vertical combination. See **strangle**.

bought deal. (i) A procedure used in handling new issues where a **lead manager** acting on its own or together with **co-managers** commits to **underwrite** an entire offering of securities on agreed fixed terms (cf. **block trade**; **primary underwriter**). A common type of transaction in the **eurobond** and domestic US debt markets (cf. **fixed price reoffering**). See **best efforts**; **offer for sale**. (ii) A **management buy-out** or **buy-in** transaction where all the finance is provided by a single institution (often with the intention of syndicating the **risk** at a later stage).

boundary condition. Statement that can be made about the minimum and maximum range of values within which **options** must trade to avoid riskless **arbitrage**. This will depend on whether it is an **American-style** or **European-style** option. For details see **option pricing**.

bounded-payoff option. A foreign exchange option where the payoff is limited to a particular range of outcomes (cf. **cylinder**). See **vertical spread**.

Bourse (French). French for a stock exchange, but used in other languages also (e.g. Portuguese and

Spanish). In some countries the bourse is also responsible for arranging the (currency) **fix**.

Bourse de Commerce (French). Chamber of Commerce.

Bourse de Genève (Switzerland). 8 rue de la Confédération, Case Postale, CH-1211 Geneva 11 (tel. 41 22 310 06 84; fax 41 22 311 25 76).

Bourse de Luxembourg. See **Luxembourg Stock Exchange**.

Bourse de Montréal (Canada). See **Montreal Exchange**.

Bourse de Paris (France). See **Paris Bourse** (Paris Stock Exchange).

Bourse des Valeurs de Abidjan (Ivory Coast). Avenue Marchand, 01 BP 1878, CI-Abidjan 01 (tel. 225 21 57 83; fax 225 22 16 57).

Bourse des Valeurs de Casablanca (Morocco). 98 Bd Mohammed V, MA-Casablanca (tel. 212 227 45 62; fax 212 220 03 65).

boutique. A small financial firm specializing in a small product range. Thus there are **bond** boutiques, **mergers and acquisitions** boutiques, and so forth. The claimed advantages of such firms are their close internal communications and deep, specialized expertise.

box (USA). Name for the storage location for **physical** form securities held in **safekeeping**. It originates with the pigeonhole or box used to store the **certificates** (cf. **in-the-box**).

Box–Jenkins model. Time-series forecasting model used in econometrics. It is named after its two originators, who pioneered much of modern econometric time-series analysis; their approach lets the data specify the model that bests represents the generating process for the series.

box management (UK). Term for the powers given to managers of **unit trusts** to hold units in the trust themselves (cf. **mutual fund**; **undertaking for collective investments in transferable securities**). Normally new units are created or cancelled in the trust when investors buy or sell. However, trust managers have the option to *run a box* using their own capital, thus avoiding the dealing charges inherent in buying and selling the **underlying** assets in the market, with the attendant costs. Box management works as follows: a unit holder redeems his units and receives the **bid price** (say 97); however, the management knows that they have regular investors who buy units every month and will be purchasing units in a day or two's time (cf. **pound cost averaging**). Instead of selling the appropriate proportion of the fund in the market, the managers buy the units from the seller and hold them 'in the box' until such time as new buyers appear. At this point, say, the **offer** price of the units is now 102; the fund managers have made the difference of 5 on each unit (102 offer less 97 bid), less any costs. Box management greatly increases the profitability of unit trust management, since not only does the fund get initial and management fees, it is making a turn on the units. Note that box management requires a flow of two-way business in the units.

box spread (Derivatives). (i) A type of arbitrage in the **options markets** using **calendar spreads** where both a **bull spread** and a **bear spread** are established in order to produce a riskless profit (cf. **horizontal spread; vertical spread**). One spread is effected using **put options** and the other using **call options**. The spreads can be either *debit spreads* (a call bull spread versus put bull spread) or *credit spreads* (a call bear spread versus put bull spread). (ii) A more general term for any offsetting combination of bull and bear **spreads**.

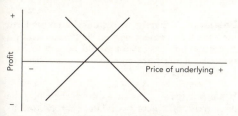

Box spread: payoff for box spread holder at expiry

bracket. A class of **underwriter** in a primary market issue. The **commission** earned by and status of the underwriter is determined by the size of the commitment taken, and from largest to smallest; special bracket, major, sub-major, and minor (cf. **co-lead manager; co-manager; lead manager; selling group**).

Brady bonds. Named after Nicholas Brady, who was US Secretary to the Treasury, these are refinancings of **less developed country** debt in conjunction with the **World Bank**. They were an official attempt to deal with the problems of debtor countries and to find an acceptable solution to endless **rescheduling**. Some of the issues are backed as to principal by non-negotiable long-dated **zero-coupon bonds** issued by the **US Treasury**. See **Mex-Ex Issue**.

Brady commission and **report** (USA). A commission set up by the then President Ronald Reagan to investigate the causes of the October 1987 stock market crash and headed by Nicholas Brady. See **Presidential Task Force on Market Mechanisms**.

Brady plan. The initiative announced by Nicholas Brady, US Secretary to the Treasury, on 10 March 1989 for a new approach to the **less developed country** (LDC) debt crisis involving both the **International Monetary Fund** and the **World Bank**. The plan set out an agenda requiring an accelerated reduction in the debt burden of LDC nations through concerted assistance by the multinational agencies and through the cooperation of the lender banks. See also **Brady bonds**.

Bratislava Stock Exchange (Slovak Republic). Hlavne namestie 8, PO Box 151, CS-81499 Bratislava (tel. 42 7 332 974; fax 42 7 335 725). Principal **stock exchange** set up in Bratislava to service the needs of the Slovak Republic established after the dissolution of the Czechoslovakian union.

breach of covenant. An infraction by a borrower of one of the **covenants** in the terms and conditions of a debt contract. Normally the precursor of **default**. See **affirmative covenants; Negative covenants; technical default**.

breadth. A description of a market by reference to the number of potential buyers (cf. **thin**).

breadth of the market (Equities; USA). A measure of the extent to which individual **stocks** follow the general market movement. See **advance–decline**.

break. Used to describe a period of rapid or sharp price change. See **breakout level**. Sometimes used only when prices fall, *bulge* being used for price rises. (ii) Used to describe a discontinuity in market trading or a price series (cf. **jumps**). (iii) A fortuitous occurrence, such as being accidentally long and the market subsequently rising. (iv) The termination of a syndicate, called *breaking the syndicate*. Members are then freed to trade the securities at any price they choose (cf. **fixed price reoffer**).

breakaway. A movement in securities prices outside a narrow band established by a **line pattern** (where prices remain relatively constant for a period of time indicating that buyers and sellers are fairly evenly matched). A breakaway that leads to a rise in prices is known as a *breakup* and for a fall a *breakdown*. See **technical analysis**.

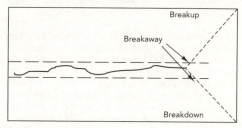

Breakaway

break clause (Banking). A clause within a **facility** which absolves the lender from advancing funds in case of market disruption (cf. **currency availability clause**). Also known as *force majeure*.

break-even analysis. (i) A method of examining investments to establish under what conditions the returns of different securities would be equal (cf. **break-even yield**). (ii) A means of comparing two securities of different maturities. See **balance-of-term yield**. (iii) Used in investment appraisal to estimate the minimum revenue level required to pay all fixed charges and direct costs (cf. **cash flow**).

break-even exchange rate. After allowing for currency fluctuations, the exchange rate that would equalize the returns on similar **bonds** in different markets. Thus for a sterling bond with a yield of 10% and US dollar bond with a yield of 6%, the break-even exchange rate would require an appreciation of the US dollar (or sterling depreciation) of approximately 4%.

break-even point. (i) (Options). The value that the **underlying** has to reach such that the buyer of an **option** recovers the cost of the contract, known as the **premium**. For a **put option** this would be the **exercise price** minus the premium, and for a **call option** it would be the exercise price plus the premium; for a **short position** in a **covered call**, the underlying purchase price minus the premium; for a **short put** covered by **short stock position** the **short sale** price of the underlying plus the premium. (ii) The point in a project or investment where income exactly matches costs.

break-even rate or **yield.** The **yield** at which the returns on two securities are equalized. The returns are computed taking into account the horizon date and the capital appreciation or depreciation because of the change in the yields.

break-even time (Bonds). A value indicator for a convertible security. It is taken to be the time required for the **premium** over the **conversion value** to be removed by the convertible's **yield** advantage. It is equivalent to the **conversion premium** divided by the **convertible income advantage**.

breakforward (Forex). A kind of synthetic **option** or combination popular in the **foreign exchange market** since the buyer pays no up-front **premium**; this is hidden in the rate obtained (cf. **zero-cost option**). It is made up of two different contracts: a **foreign exchange forward** purchase or sale contract and an option to reverse the **forward** at a set rate. The cost or premium for the option is **embedded** in the **forward rate** which is set at a less favourable rate than the true forward rate to pay for the option to cancel the forward at the predetermined **exercise price** (cf. **embeddo**).

  Buy currency: call option = Purchased forward + purchased put
  Sell currency: put option ≐ Sale forward + purchased call

It is also known as a *Boston option*.

breaking a leg. See **lift a leg**.

breaking the syndicate. The termination of the **underwriting agreement** or **purchase and sale agreement**. Normally, the agreement will stipulate when this would occur, but in **securities underwriting** early termination by mutual consent is quite common. Once the **syndicate** is broken, the **underwriters** are free to sell the security at whatever price they choose. Prior to this they must attempt to sell the securities at the **offering price**. Two conditions are likely to break the syndicate: either a successful **distribution** of the issue has occurred, or the underwriters cannot place securities at the offer price. See **fixed price reoffering**.

breakout. A chartist or **technical analysis** term for a price movement beyond that predicted by a **pattern**. Thus a breakout would be said to have occurred if the price moved above a **resistance** level. See **breakaway**.

breakout level. This is said to occur when the price trend of a security deviates sharply from its established trend (cf. **break**; **breakaway**). See **chartist**; **technical analysis**.

break point. This is said to occur when a new issue trades in the **aftermarket** at a **discount** larger than the **selling concession**. See **breaking the syndicate**.

breakup value. The realizable value if an asset or business is sold piecemeal. The opposite assumption is *going-concern value*.

Brent crude oil. A type of crude oil produced in the UK sector of the North Sea and used as a **benchmark** grade for trading purposes in Europe, and as the **underlying** for the crude oil **futures** and **options** contracts on the International Petroleum Exchange. See **marker crude**.

Bretton Woods. System of fixed rate **exchange rate** parities agreed in 1944 as part of a post-war international monetary system. The same conference also saw the creation of the International Monetary Fund and the International Bank for Reconstruction and Development (World Bank).

bridge agreement. A cross-settlement system agreed between the two major **clearing houses** for the **euromarkets** (cf. **over the bridge**). It attempts to reconcile the processing differences between Euroclear (which runs on overnight processing) and the **Centrale de Livraison de Valeurs Mobilières**, which uses same-day processing in order to allow a simultaneous interchange between the two.

bridge finance or **bridging finance** or **bridging loan.** A form of interim financing, usually used in the property market or in **mergers and acquisitions** (cf. **acquisition accounting; investment bank; merchant banking**).

Britannias (UK). A range of gold coins in £100, £50, £25, and £10 denominations issued by the Royal Mint since October 1987 and designed to compete with **maple leafs** and **krugerrands**.

British American Depository Receipts (British ADRs) (Equities; UK). **American depository receipts** traded in the British market.

British Bankers Association (BBA) (UK). The trade association of banks located in the UK, principally London. Among other activities, it sets model contracts for financial instruments and publishes daily market interest rates in major eurocurrencies (cf. **future rate agreements**). The BBA is responsible for collecting and disseminating **London interbank offered rate** quotes, which act as an **index** or **reference rate** on many of these contracts, hence *BBA terms*.

British Corporation and County Stocks (Bonds; UK). Old name for negotiable British local authority securities.

British Merchant Banks and Securities Houses Association (UK). Successor organization to the **Accepting Houses Committee**, the group of seventeen banks active in discounting or accepting **bills of exchange**, and the Issuing Houses Committee set up in 1988 following changes to the way the London market operated, principally after the **Big Bang**.

broad money. See **money supply**.

broad tape (USA). See **consolidated tape**.

broken dates. Any non-regular value date and/or maturity date. See **odd dates**.

broken period. The normal maturities for eurocurrency deposits or **forward foreign exchange** transactions are based on the 'calendar-month' convention where maturities are for the same day in the relevant month. Transaction periods which fall outside these are known as broken periods (cf. **fixed dates; odd date**).

broker. An individual or firm acting as an **agent** for buyers and sellers and charging a **commission**, known as **brokerage**, but who does not take a **position** on his own account in the transaction (cf. **broker-dealer; inter-dealer broker**). See also **agency broker; deal; market-maker**.

brokerage. Another term for the **commission** charged by a **broker**.

broker-dealer. (i) Generally, an individual (or firm) acting as an **agent** for buyers and sellers and charging a **commission**, known as **brokerage**, but who—at the same time—trades for his own account and may also be a **market-maker** (cf. **broker**). (ii) (UK) Specifically a member of the **London Stock Exchange** who may act as either an **agent** or **principal**, or both. See also **agency broker; capacity; dual capacity**.

brokered deposit (Banking). A **deposit** which has been obtained through the use of an intermediating **broker** rather than directly from a customer.

brokered market. Market where financial intermediaries act as **brokers, broker-dealers, dealers**, or middle-men for finding buyers and sellers (cf. **specialist**). See also **direct search market**.

broker loan rate or **call loan rate** (USA). The rate charged by banks to **brokers** on borrowings used to finance client **positions**. Because the collateral that covers the borrowings is the same as that used for **margin**, broker loans are usually **demand loans**. The process is sometimes known as rehypothecation. See **call loan**.

broker-trader. See broker-dealer.

brown goods. Consumer durable items, such as record and tape players and cameras (cf. **white goods**). Used by investment analysts to describe areas of specialization by retailing stocks (as in *brown goods sector*).

Brownian motion. A way of describing the random movement of asset prices in competitive markets. See **efficient markets hypothesis; geometric Brownian motion; Wiener process**.

Brussels Stock Exchange (Belgium). Stock exchange for Belgian **common stocks**.

B Shares. (i) A second, usually **junior**, **class** of **common stocks** or **ordinary shares** issued by firms. Firms will have an A class and a B class. In such a case, the B shares might have restricted or reduced voting rights, pay smaller dividends, or be limited in other ways compared to the A shares (cf. **participation certificate**; **restricted shares**). See also **A shares**; **C shares**. (ii) (China) The common stocks of Chinese companies that are denominated in hard currencies (cf. **H shares**).

Buba (Germany). Market shorthand for the **Bundesbank**.

bubble. See **asset bubble**.

bucket analysis. See **cash buckets**.

buckets. See **asset-liability management**; **cash buckets**; **maturity gap**.

bucket shop. Colloquial term for a **discount brokerage** firm. Also used for a type of illegal **broker** operation where customers' orders are not immediately carried out but are delayed until the firm can indulge in **risk-less arbitrage** between the market price and the instructed price.

bucket trading (USA). A type of illegal trading activity in the **futures markets** where a **broker** and a **market-maker** (known as the *bagman*) conspire to make profits at the expense of public market orders.

Budapest Stock Exchange (Hungary). Deak Ferenc Utca 5, HU-1052 Budapest (tel. 36 1 1175 226; fax 36 1 1181 737). Set up in July 1989, it covers both **debt** and **equity** instruments. To be a **broker** on the exchange requires the firm to be a specialized investment bank.

budget. (i) Projected target for revenues and expenditures of an organization over a set period. See also **business plan**. (ii) (UK). 'The Budget' is the Chancellor of the Exchequer's presentation of the government's revenue and spending plans for the coming financial year. This now takes place in November, when a unified revenue and expenditure statement is laid before Parliament.

buffer stock. A supply of a **commodity** held by an organization either to alleviate potential market shortages or to control the market price. The history of buffer stocks has been very mixed, from the attempts by commodity producers to increase prices, to the United States' Strategic Petroleum Reserve. The idea behind a producer buffer stock is to buy in supply when prices are depressed and to sell out when prices rise. However, since most producer countries are desperately short of revenues, the effect has been to encourage over-supply since market signals are distorted. See also **convenience yield**.

buffer stock financing facility (Banking). A loan facility used to finance a **buffer stock** programme. It is normally secured on the **commodity** being purchased.

building society (Australia; Ireland; New Zealand; UK). A mutual institution whose primary business traditionally comprises taking retail deposits and lending funds on domestic mortgages. In the UK, societies have been given powers under the Building Societies Act, 1986 to diversify their activities into such areas as **cheque** accounts, unsecured lending, **overdrafts**, credit cards, **unit trusts**, pensions, **Personal Equity Plans**, estate agency, and property development. The Act limits the amount of such activities to a fraction of their total assets. Regulatory oversight in the UK is the responsibility of the Building Societies Commission. See **savings and loan association** (cf. **Bausparkassen**; **Caisse d'épargne**; **Caja de Ahorro**).

bulge. A rapid, but temporary rise and fall in market or security prices.

bulge bracket. Name given to leading investment banks in the **capital markets**. To qualify for bulge bracket status, firms must be dominant players in key activities such as **underwriting**, **mergers and acquisitions**, securities **distribution**, and so forth.

bull. An investor or trader who takes the view that prices are likely to rise and buys securities, hoping to make a profit by subsequently selling at a higher price (cf. **bear**). A *bull trend* is a series of generally increasing prices, also called a *bull run*.

bull-bear bond. A two-**tranche** issue of securities with each tranche linked to the particular performance of an **index**, **commodity**, or security. The **bull** (**bear**) tranche increases (decreases) in value with upward (downward) movements in the **underlying**. Since the two tranches offset each other, the issuer has little risk. The attraction of the security is to holders who have a view on the performance of the linked payments. Also known as a *bear-bull bond*.

bull certificate of deposit. (bull CD) Certificate of deposit where the return is linked to the rise in price of an **index** or rate (cf. **bear certificate of deposit**).

bulldog bond (UK). Used to describe a **foreign bond** (i.e. a **bond** issued by an **obligor** who is not domiciled in the UK) issued in the UK domestic market (cf. **samurai**; **matador bond**; **yankee bond**). Not to be confused with similar issues which may be offered in the eurosterling sector of the **eurobond** market. In the case of bulldogs, these feature semi-annual payment of **coupon** interest and are quoted on the **London Stock Exchange**.

bullet or **bullet maturity.** A loan or an issue of securities with no **amortization** (cf. **balloon; purchase fund; serial security; sinking fund**). Sometimes seen written as *bullit*. See **straight** (cf. **plain vanilla**).

Bulletin Board (Equities; UK). Trial method used on the **London Stock Exchange** in 1992 for thinly traded **ordinary shares** in very small companies which had only one **market-maker**. Prices at which transactions were on **offer** would be posted on the bulletin board (cf. **wabo; waso**). It has now been replaced by the **Stock Exchange Alternative Trading Service**. See also **Alternative Investment Market**.

Bulletin de la Côte Officielle (Equities; France). Daily official list of stock market prices published by the **Société des Bourses Françaises**.

bull floating rate note or **bull floater.** See **reverse floating rate note**.

bullion (Commodities). Term often used for the wholesale precious metals and their markets (that is in the form of ingots) rather than the market in coins. Bullion includes both gold, silver, and other precious metals, but the term in general use is often taken to mean the market in gold.

bullish. To believe that prices will rise or rates will fall, i.e to have a positive view on the outlook for prices or rates (cf. **bearish; bear**). See **bull**.

bull market. A market perceived to be on a trend of rising prices and general optimism (cf. **bear market**); conditions under which **bulls** would prosper (i.e. a rising market).

bull note. See bull-bear bond; reverse floating rate note.

bull position. A long position, that is one designed to take advantage of rising prices (cf. **bear position; short position**).

bull spread or **bull money spread** (Options). A strategy used in the **option markets** which reduces the amount of **option premium** required to profit from an expected rise in the **underlying** by simultaneously buying and selling two options that differ only in their **strike prices** with a view to making a profit on the difference in outcomes (cf. **bear spread; horizontal spread; money spread; vertical spread**). There are two types: **call spread**, this involves buying a call with a low strike price and selling or writing a call with a higher strike; and **put spread**, which involves selling a high strike

put and purchasing a lower strike one (cf. **credit spread; debit spread**). The former is more bullish in effect since the potential gain is the difference in the two strike prices less the difference in the two **option premiums**. The two strategies are also **volatility** trades since the put spread will be more rewarding if the underlying's price is unchanged. The different possible bull spreads are: *vertical spread* (describes option positions with the same **expiry date** but different **exercise prices**); *calendar spread* (describes option positions with the same exercise price but different expiry dates); and *diagonal spread* (describes option positions which are both a vertical spread and a **calendar spread**). Sometimes also called a *bull straddle* if undertaken with **futures** (this involves the purchase and sale of different contracts on the expectation that the near date will rise faster than the distant date). See **option strategies**.

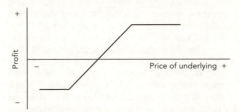

Payoff of bull spread at expiry

bull spread (Bonds). A strategy of taking a **short position** (to finance the **long position**) at the short end of the **yield curve** and simultaneously a **long position** at the long end of the yield curve. The expectation is that the yield curve will flatten and the position can then be **closed out** at a profit.

bull spreading (Futures). A strategy based on buying the **nearby** contract and selling the longer-dated contract (cf. **buying the basis**). Also known as *buying the spread* or *borrowing*. See **carrying**.

bunching. (i) Used in securities trading where buying or selling orders are combined for convenience of execution. (ii) An effect of trading activity where the frequency of observed prices is related to rounding. Whole numbers are most commonly observed, followed by halves, quarters, eighths, sixteenths, and so on in decreasing frequency.

Bundesanleihen (Bunds) (Bonds; Germany). Federal Republic **bond** issues, principally with an **original maturity** of 10 years (cf. **straight**). The **Coupon** is paid annually and **accrued interest** computed on a 30/360 day basis. See **interest rate calculations**.

Bundesaufsichtsamt für das Kreditwesen (BAKred). (Federal Banking Supervisory

Authority) (Banking; Germany). The federal agency which oversees banking activities. It has joint responsibility for the banking system with the **Bundesbank**.

Bundesbahnposten (Bonds; Germany). **Bonds** issued by the Federal Republic, the Federal Railway (Bundesbahn), and the Post Office (Bundespost). Equivalent to state-guaranteed issues in other countries. Latterly has included the Treuhand, the institution charged with financing and privatizing the former East German state sector.

Bundesbank (Deutsche Bundesbank) (Buba) (German Federal Bank) (Germany). The Federal Republic of Germany's **central bank**, which is based in Frankfurt, and is responsible for determining and implementing monetary policy. To do so it uses four main instruments: the **discount rate**, i.e. normal loans to the banking system; the **Lombard rate**, used for overnight deposits and short-term funding of the banking system; **open-market operations**; and **reserve requirements**. Its duties are defined by the Bundesbankgesetz, 1957 and 1967 with a special obligation to maintain stable prices by regulating the supply of money, credit, and currency intervention. The Central Bank Council is the supreme policy-making body made up of a Directorate, whose members are nominated by the federal government and appointed by the President, and the eleven Presidents of the Länder banks of the different states, who are in turn appointed by the Bundesrat, the upper chamber of Parliament, and represent the Länder. This structure reflects the federal nature of the Bundesbank and is reminiscent of the **Federal Reserve System** in the USA. Appointment to the Board is for eight-years and members cannot be removed from office by the government. Federal government representatives may attend the regular Board meetings, which usually take place every second Thursday, but may not vote. While the Council makes policy, executive responsibility rests with the Directorate. While the Directorate can normally influence policy within the Council due to their executive role, they do not have a majority and can be overidden by a majority of the Länder bank Presidents. The Bundesbank is not responsible for supervision of the financial system, this being the responsibility of the **Bundesaufsichtsamt für das Kreditwesen** (the Bank Supervisory Authority), although the two cooperate closely. Compared to many other central banks, the Bundesbank does enjoy and exercise considerable autonomy; in fulfilling its legal obligations under its constitution, it is independent of the federal government but is required to support its policies in so far as they do not conflict with its primary aim of monetary stability as defined in the 1957 Act. The eleven Länder banks on the Council are:

Baden-Württemberg
Bavaria
Berlin
Brandenburg
Bremen
Hamburg
Hesse
North-Rhine Westphalia
Rhineland-Palatinate
Saarland
Schleswig-Holstein

The Länder banks situated in the states are the principal administrative bodies of the Bundesbank and typically comprise credit, banking, economic analysis, statistics, foreign exchange, bond, and administration activities.

Bundesbond (Germany). Federal republic debt issues. The most common ones, known as *bunds* have an original maturity of ten-years, although there have been some longer-term issues and *bubls*. Formerly offered to a fixed **syndicate** of domestic and foreign **underwriters** who took a fixed share of each issue, they are now offered via competitive **auction**.

Bundeschätzchen (Germany). See **Unverzinsliche Schatzanweisungen**.

Bundeskartellamt (Federal Cartel Office). (Germany). Government office charged with overseeing competition and anti-monopoly activity (cf. **Monopolies and Mergers Commission**).

Bundeskassenobligation (Germany). Federal government **medium-term note** issues, typically with maturities of two to six years. They are continuously offered to the market through the **Bundesbank**.

Bundesobligationen (Bubl) (Germany). A five-year federal government bond issue issued on a **tap** basis and used by the **Bundesbank** when undertaking **open-market operations**. Interest is paid annually and calculated on the 30/360-day method.

Bundesschatzbriefe (Bonds; Germany). Federal Republic savings bonds.

Bundesschatzanweisungen (Schatz) (Bonds; Germany). Federal government **note** issues with an **original maturity** of two to six years. They are **straight bonds** with an annual **coupon based** on a 30/360-day year. See **Unverzinsliche Schatzanweisungen**.

Bundesschatzbriefe (Federal savings bond). (Germany). German government debt issues targeted at the private investor. Such issues are available on a continuous basis but are restricted to domiciled individuals and not for profit institutions. There are a number of different varieties available, the most common being the six- and seven-year issues. Holders have the right to put the bonds back to the government after a specified period although there is a secondary market.

bundling. Combining one or more types of securities for the purpose of issuance or trading (cf. **unbundling**). A common example of bundling is the issue of **bond with warrants**. See also **packages; stapled security.**

bunds. See Bundesbond, Bundesanleihen.

bunny bond. A **bond** issue under which the holder has the choice of receiving interest payments either in cash or as more bonds of the same issue. Sometimes called a *multiplier bond*. Because the issue offers the holder an **option** on interest rates, the **coupon** on such securities is normally lower than that for equivalent **straight** bonds. If interest rates fall, the holder will want to receive more bonds, if it rises, the holder will want cash (cf. **reinvestment rate**). See also **pay-in-kind bond.**

Buono del Tesoro Poliennali (BTP) (Bonds; Italy). **Treasury bonds:** fixed **coupon** issues with maturities typically between three and ten years, although longer issues have been made (cf. **Buono Ordinario del Tesoro**). They are issued monthly by competitive **auction**. Coupons are paid semi-annually and interest is accrued on a 30/180-day basis (30/360). See **interest rate calculations.**

Buono Ordinario del Tesoro (BOT) (Money markets; Italy). **Treasury bill** with usually an initial **maturity** of either three, six or twelve months.

Buoni Pluriennali del Tesoro (BPT) (Italy) Government long-term fixed rate bonds.

Buoni Tesoro Denominati in Euroscudi (BTE) (Bonds; Italy). **European Currency Unit** denominated Italian government **treasury bond** issued in the domestic market.

buoyant. A market or economy which is generally resistant to bad news (cf. **heavy market; thin**). See **bull market.**

burning head. A **takeover** defence involving reducing the attractiveness of the **target** by selling or otherwise impairing the company's most attractive assets. Also known as *self-uglification.*

burn-out (USA). The using up of a **tax shield** such that additional income is now taxed.

burn-out turnaround. Rescue finance for a financially troubled company that has the effect of significantly diluting existing **shareholders'** claims. For instance, a company may issue a large number of new **shares** which result in existing shareholders losing control of the company.

burn rate. The rate at which a project or firm with a negative **cash flow** consumes available finance. It is an estimate of the time when additional funding or **financial distress** is likely to arise (cf. **Death Valley curve**). The calculation is used to evaluate the soundness, or otherwise, of **high-tech** or **venture capital** type firms. It has been likened to measuring the distance between a lemming and the edge of the cliff.

bushel. Measure of volume in **commodities**. It is equal to 35.238 litres.

business angels. Individuals prepared to provide **seed capital** for **high-risk**, start-up business ventures. The term *angel* is also applied to backers of stage shows in the theatre business. It derives from the intention to do good rather than make a quick return on the money.

business cycle. Observed changes to economic conditions which move from prosperity through recession to depression and hence back to recovery and further prosperity. Also known as the *economic cycle*. See, for example, **Kondatrieff wave.**

business day. A day in which financial markets are open in a specified country or city. Business days are generally synonomous with days in which banks are open for business. Transaction procedures which stipulated a given number of business days between the **trade date** and the **value** or **settlement date** would count only business days, ignoring Saturdays and Sundays and any 'bank holidays' (or legal holidays) in between. Also sometimes referred to as a *clearing day*. In the **euromarkets**, generally taken to be a day in which the London and New York financial markets are open; but it can also mean any day in which two eurocurrencies' domestic markets are open.

business ethics. The standards of individual and corporate conduct for business (cf. **rules of fair practice**). See **corporate governance.**

Business Expansion Scheme (BES) (UK). A government-sponsored scheme begun in 1983 as an attempt to provide a source of **equity** finance for expanding companies and to provide new investment opportunities for investors. The scheme was a replacement for, and extension of, the Business Start-up scheme, which allowed individual investors to claim tax relief on equity investments in certain **unquoted** newly commenced companies (cf. **quoted**). The BES widened the range of 'qualifying' companies and relaxed some of the previous restrictions in an attempt to broaden the appeal of the Scheme. The giving of relief to individual investors is designed to achieve three things: to encourage the making of **risk** investments that the individual would not otherwise have; to enable the investment to be retained for a longer-term view; and to compensate for the likely lack of returns, in **dividends**, but where there is potential for significant **capital gain** as the business prospers. This is said to be of more interest to higher-rate income tax-payers. The government's original intention was that individuals should seek out and make their own separate investments but in general this has failed because the opportunities, while they may have existed, have not been focused on the potential investors. The way in which the scheme has brought companies and individuals together has been through investment funds approved by the Inland Revenue for investing under the scheme. These funds pool individual investors into a **mutual fund** and invest and manage the money on their behalf. No new schemes have been allowed since the end of 1993. It has now been superseded by the **Enterprise Investment Scheme**.

business interruption policy. An insurance policy designed to cover a firm for consequential losses due to an interruption to its business activities.

business judgement rule (USA). A defence doctrine used to protect a firm's managers from liability when adverse outcomes are the result of poor business judgement rather than dishonesty or fraud.

business plan. A strategic document setting forth the expected or intended future development of a company or line of business over a given period (cf. **budget**). Such a plan will include detailed sections analysing the firm's market(s), methods of accessing and penetrating the market, financial projections, including cash flow analysis, projected profit and loss and balance sheet statements, as well as any other material facts such as key staff and other operating information. The plan is designed to provide the business with a strategic framework against which to measure objectives and set priorities. In some cases, the intention is to provide sufficient and accurate details of the future of the business to allow outsiders to assess the viability and scope for external finance. It is also known as the *corporate plan*.

business risk. The possibility that a firm may not be able to meet ongoing operating expenditures (cf. **financial distress**). It is the fundamental inalienable **risk** of a business or line of business

which is not diversifiable. Sometimes called *operating risk* or *specific risk*. See also **Capital Asset Pricing Model**; **Default**.

business segment reporting. An accounting standard requiring the reporting entity to provide a breakdown of activities by type, subsidiary, line of business, and so forth, to facilitate comparison. Sometimes known as *line of business reporting*.

business strategy. An analysis and statement of the key drivers governing the choices made by a firm or line of business.

bust a trade (USA). To cancel or break a transaction that has already been executed.

busted. (i) Often used to describe **bond** issues that have defaulted on interest payments or repayment of the **principal**, but usually both. There is now an active collectors' market for these so-called busted **bond certificates** (cf. **scripophily**). Sometimes called *old bonds*. (ii) The term can also be applied to **convertibles** when they possess a negligible **conversion value** because the market price of the underlying security has fallen way below the **conversion price** (cf. **out of the money**).

busted convertible. Market term for a **convertible bond** with negligible likelihood of being able to be converted into the **equity** of the issuer at a profit (cf. **out of the money**).

butterfly. A **swap** involving the replacement of long- and short-term securities with a security of an intermediate **maturity** that produces the same or a better **yield**. Sometimes known as a *dumb-bell*. See **longs**; **mediums**; **shorts**.

butterfly spread. An option strategy that possesses both limited risk and restricted profit potential (cf. **iron butterfly**). It is produced either by combining a **bull spread** and a **bear spread** on the same **underlying** or using a **straddle** and a **strangle**. Four **strike prices** are involved, with the lower two being used in the bull spread and the higher two in the bear spread (cf. **sandwich spread**). The strategy may be set up using **call** or **put options**. There are four different ways of combining the options to produce the same position.

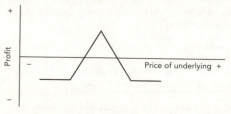

Butterfly spread: Payoff of written butterfly at expiry

buy and hold (B&H). (i) An investment policy of selecting securities and subsequently holding them for investment purposes rather than trading them for an immediate profit. The actual **holding period** will depend on the investor's horizon, which could extend to the **maturity** of the issue. (ii) Phrase used in brokers' reports on individual companies which contain a recommendation to a potential investor. The inference here is that the share is worth buying provided the investor has some patience for what is expected to be attractive growth prospects, rather than immediate jumps in share price and **dividends**. Alternatively, the broker could recommend *Sell* or *Hold* for existing shareholders, or simply *Buy*. See **fundamental analysis; technical analysis**.

buy and write. An options strategy that involves writing **options** against a security which is held (cf. **covered call; covered put**). It assumes that the **underlying** will not change significantly in price, thus the **writer** gains the **premium** as additional income. Some types of funds offering a guaranteed return use this strategy to enhance their returns. Also known as *buy-write*.

buy at best. See **market order**.

buy-back. (i) A repurchase of a previously sold security (cf. **purchase fund**). A firm's repurchase of its own shares is often referred to as a *share buy-back*. See **stock repurchase plan**. (ii) The elimination of a **position** in the market by repurchase (cf. **cover; closing transaction; repurchase agreement**).

buy-back valuation (Forex). The price at which a **foreign exchange forward** transaction can be unwound before its **maturity**.

buy earnings. An investment strategy that is based on purchasing low, but rising, **earnings per share common stocks** or **ordinary shares** based on the expectation that the stock value will provide a significant **capital gain** in the future.

buyer's credit. A term loan facility, normally arranged by the vendor of an asset, to enable the buyer to finance the purchase and commonly used in the international trade of capital goods. In many cases, the lender assumes the credit risk on the purchaser. Official export agencies are active providers to this market and offer funds at a concessionary rate.

buyers' market. A market condition where there are more buyers than sellers at current prices (cf. **buyers over**). The opposite would be a *sellers' market* (cf. **sellers over**).

buyers over. A market situation where there is unsatisfied buying demand (cf. **sellers over**).

buy hedge. See **long hedge**.

buy-in. (i). The buying of a security at market prices to complete delivery of a failed transaction. If the original seller fails to make **good delivery**, the buyer can, upon notification to the seller, effect a buy-in through a third party, such as a **clearing house**. (cf. **sell-out**). The costs of such action, to rectify a **failed delivery**, are borne by the defaulting party (cf. **aged fail**). (ii) In the **options** markets, a procedure for closing a **short position** that involves *buying-in* the same option as has been sold, the only difference being in the **premium** paid (cf. **cover**). (iii) To acquire a **controlling interest**. See **buy-in and management buy-out; management buy-in**. (iv) A feature of some **settlement** systems where the **clearing house** effects a purchase in the open market in order to complete a failed delivery. Normally the seller has a grace period in which to make good the fail after which the clearing house will issue a *buy-in notice* giving its intent to purchase on behalf of the buyer. The seller is then required to make good the difference between the transaction price and any additional costs from the buy-in. Also called a *buying-in notice*. The opposite condition, when the buyer fails to honour his side of the bargain, is known as a *sell-out*.

buy-in and management buy-out (BIMBO). A method of purchasing a business involving both the existing management and outside managers. The latter are often chosen by the group of financiers funding the deal. See **management buy-out; management buy-in**.

buying ahead. When **bonds** are bought using a **sinking fund**, either in excess of present requirements or before the sinking fund due date. It should be noted that buying a surplus of bonds because of an **option to double** is not viewed as buying ahead.

buying forward. See **forward** (cf. **futures**).

buying hedge. When an investor buys a **futures contract** to protect against rising prices and to lock in the **yield** at which an expected cash flow can be invested. It is also called a *long hedge*.

buying on margin. The practice of buying securities using a **broker's** willingness to advance a part of the cost of purchase (cf. **margin; margin requirements**).

buying price (UK). The price at which an investor can acquire **units** in a **unit trust**. Also called the *offer price*.

buying the basis. Another term for a **cash-and-carry** transaction.

buying the spread. A strategy used when higher selling prices are anticipated by going long on the front contract month in a particular **future** and selling the deferred contract month (cf. **bear spread**). See **bull spread**.

buy-in notice. The instruction sent announcing a buy-in.

buy minus (USA). An instruction to buy at a price lower than the current market price when the instruction was given.

buy on rumour. An investment maxim linked to market behaviour which requires *buy on the rumour, sell on the fact*.

buy-op (buying-in operation) (USA). See **stock repurchase plan**.

buy order. An instruction to an **agent**, **broker**, or other intermediary to buy on your behalf (cf. **market order; limit order; sell order; stop-loss**).

buy-out. The act of taking a company private. The current **shareholders** are made an offer, i.e. they are bought out by the new owners or management. See **leveraged buy-out; management buy-out**.

buy-right option unitary derivatives (bounds) (Equities.; USA). A type of **stock option** introduced by the **American Stock Exchange** which has a lower **premium** than a simple **option** and is aimed at retail investors. It works on the same principle as a **participating forward**, where an option and a forward purchase (sale) are blended together.

buy-sellback forward (USA). Effectively securities lending, except the securities are initially sold and at the same time a **forward** sellback at a predetermined price is agreed with the vendor. See **repurchase agreement**.

buy/sell on close. Used in the **option** markets when buying or selling an **option** at the end of a trading session at a price within the closing range (cf. **buy on opening**).

buy/sell on opening. To buy or sell an **option** at the start of a trading session at a price within the opening range (cf. **buy on close**).

buy stop. A **stop order** instruction that automatically becomes a **market order** to purchase if the price reaches the **stop price** (cf. **sell-stop order**). Also known as a *suspended market order*.

buy the book (USA). An instruction to a **broker** to purchase all available securities from **market-makers** at the current market price. It is an attempt by a **block buyer** to minimize the effect of **market impact**.

buy-write. Market jargon for a **covered call**.

bylaws (USA). In the organization of a firm, that part of a company's **charter** which details the number of officers of the company, their titles, and functions.

C

C, Ca, Caa, CC, and **CCC.** See **credit ratings**.

cabinet crowd (Bonds; USA). Those members of the **New York Stock Exchange** who handle the infrequently traded **bond** issues (cf. **active bond crowd; foreign bond; foreign crowd; liquidity**).

cabinet stock or **bond** (USA). Term for an infrequently traded **stock** or **bond**. It derives from the storage racks, or cabinets, where **limit order** instructions are kept by the **specialist**.

cabinet trade or **transaction.** The purchase or sale of an **out-of-the-money option** at **expiry** in order to establish a loss for reporting purposes (cf. **wasting asset**).

cable. In the **foreign exchange** markets, **spot** deals between sterling and US dollars. Derives from the time when such transactions took place over the direct cablegram link between New York and London.

cacall (call on a call). Type of **compound option** where the payoff is on a **call** option at **expiry** (cf. **caput; exotic option**).

Cadbury Code of Corporate Governance (UK). Model code of best practice conduct governing senior executive remuneration and terms of contract produced by the **Cadbury Committee**.

Cadbury Committee on the Financial Aspects of Corporate Governance or **Cadbury Committee** (UK). Technically the *Report of the Committee on the Financial Aspects of Corporate Governance*, it is concerned with questions of corporate governance and establishes a Code of Best Practice (cf. **Greenbury Committee**). See **agency problem; corporate governance**.

cage (USA). The cash management section of a **back office**. The cash disbursement section is colloquially known as the *window*.

caisse d'épargne (Banking; France). **Savings bank** (cf. **building society; savings and loan association**).

caja de ahorro (Banking; Spain). Savings bank.

calendar. A list of new issues scheduled to come to a market in the near future. It is normal for it to be designated by a particular group of securities, such as debt. Sometimes called *visible supply*.

calendar/month convention. The convention used in the **euromarkets** to establish the **maturity** of **short-term** financial transactions. The basic principle is that the start and end dates are the same calendar day in the appropriate month for the tenor of the transaction (cf. **end-end; odd dates**). Thus a three-month deposit with a start date on the fifteenth of January will have a **maturity date** of the fifteenth of April, weekends and holidays excepting. In the case of weekends and holidays, the transaction will mature on the next business day, unless that business day would take the transaction into the following calendar month. In the latter case, the transaction would mature on the last business day of the month.

calendar spread. An **options** strategy which involves the purchase of a later expiring **option** and the sale of an earlier expiring one on the same **underlying** (cf. **spread; straddle; strangle**). Generally, the holder aims to gain if the price differential widens; the **time decay** of the earlier expiring option will also erode at a faster rate. There are a number of different variants: *bearish calendar spread* will have a lower strike price on the purchased option; *bullish calendar spread* will have a higher strike price; *diagonal spread* will have different strike prices as well as expiration dates; *horizontal spread* will have the same strike price for both options; *neutral calendar spread* will have the same strike price; *reverse calendar spread* involves buying the earlier expiring option and selling the later expiring one (cf. **credit spread**). Calendar spreads are also called *horizontal* or *time spreads*. The opposite where the longer-dated option is sold and the near-dated purchase is known as a *reverse calender spread*. See **option strategies**.

call. (i) The act of redeeming a **bond** early at the borrower's discretion, hence *callable* (cf. **call provision**). (ii) The next payment due on a **partly paid** security (cf. **gearing; leverage**). (iii) In banking, the act of demanding early repayment of a loan, hence *to call a loan* (cf. **default**). (iv) Short for a **call option**, a contract giving the holder the right to receive or call the **underlying**. (v) A UK commodities futures markets term for the opening or closing period of the daily trading session, hence *opening (closing) call*. It comes from the **open outcry** method of determining prices used in commodities markets, where prices are literally called out. (vi) Short for **margin call**.

callable. Capable of being called or redeemed; usually in the context of an early redemption of a security incorporating a **call provision**. It generally involves paying a premium to **par** (cf. **declining call schedule**; **optional redemption provision**). Hence a *callable bond*.

callable at a premium (Bonds). A term in a **bond** indenture which provides for a **premium** to **par** value in the event that an issuer **exercises** a **call provision**. Normally such premiums are on a declining **call schedule** (cf. **call premium**).

callable common stock (USA). An issue of common stock in a **subsidiary** where the parent corporation holds an **option** to repurchase the issue, typically increasing with time. Such callable common stock issues are also often packages including **warrants** allowing holders to purchase the common stock of the parent.

callable for tax reasons. A provision in the terms of issue of a security, normally seen in **eurobonds** which are paid without any withholding tax, providing the issuer with the right to early redemption in the case where changes in tax law would require the issuer to 'gross up' the interest payments to compensate for any withholding tax in the event of the imposition of such a tax.

callable swap. A type of **swap** in which one **counterparty** has the right to terminate the agreement at one or more points before the **maturity** of the swap. The counterparty with the right to terminate is effectively the holder of one or more **swaptions**. The **option premium** is reflected in the terms of the swap. Some definitions of a callable swap give the right to terminate to the **fixed rate payer** and not the **fixed rate receiver**. Because the agreement then becomes null and void, it is sometimes known as a *cancellable swap* or a *retractable swap*. Swaps where the receiver may terminate are known as **puttable**.

callable Treasury receipts (Bonds; USA). A zero-coupon Treasury receipt where the **underlying** US Treasury obligation features a **call provision**. In order to match the payment structure, the Treasury receipt also has a **call** feature. In the event of an **exercise** of the call on the underlying Treasury, the receipt is also called.

callable warrant. A warrant where the issuer has the right to **call** the warrant during a certain period, normally after some delay. The intention

is to force early **exercise**, either to limit the **option** value of the warrant or to create additional **underlying**, for instance, to have more **stock** issued (and for the issuer to get the proceeds!) (cf. **dilution**).

call an option. To exercise a call **option**.

call date. The date a **call** becomes effective or must be met (cf. **settlement date**).

call deferment (USA). A time during which a **bond** cannot be called, usually a period of five years for the issues of utilities and ten years for issues of industrial companies.

call deposit (Banking). Money either on **overnight deposit** or deposited for up to a week. Also known as a *demand deposit*.

called away. Used to describe **bonds** where the issuer has exercised his **call provision**, or the exercise of **calls** and **puts** against the **writer**, or delivery on a **short sale**.

called-up capital. The proportion of issued common **stock** or **ordinary shares** that have been paid up. Thus a company may issue shares for 100, with 25 paid up and the balance which may be called by the company as and when required (cf. **partly paid**).

call feature. A commonly used phrase for a **call provision** in a **bond** issue.

call loan or **demand loan** (USA). A bank loan that has no final **maturity**, but is usually repayable on demand. In the UK, known as an *overdraft*.

call loan rate. See broker loan rate.

call market. System of trading where transactions are made when the security or asset is 'called' for trading (cf. **continuous market**).

call monetization. Process by which an issuer obtains the **option premium** value of **embedded options** in debt issues. Typically, the issuer will offer a **bond** with a **call provision**, allowing him to repay the bond early on particular dates. In order for the issuer to get the up-front value of this option, he may **write** a **swaption** or other interest rate option which mirrors the issuer's early redemption provision (cf. **covered call**). Thus if the written option is exercised against him, he may in turn exercise his rights to call the issue. The attractions depend on the securities markets pricing the value of the call provision less than the swaps or interest rate options markets.

call money. (i) Deposits placed for overnight, or up to seven days. Also known as a *demand deposit*, *money at call*, or *money at short notice*. (ii) (USA) Loans or deposits that pay interest but may be withdrawn at short notice, often used by **brokers** to finance their operations (cf. **broker loan rate**). (iii) Another term for the **premium** for a **call option**. Call premiums are known as *call money* and **put** premiums as *put money*.

call notice. The period of notice required by an issuer when **exercising** a **call provision** before the call can be effective. In the **euromarkets**, the call notice period for **floating rate notes** is generally 30–45 days; for **fixed rate bonds** 45–90 days.

call of more option. See **option to double**.

call option. (i) (Derivatives) An option to buy a specified **underlying asset** at a specified price on a specified date or dates or at any time during a specified period (cf. **put option**). Often shortened to *call*. See **American-style**; **European-style**; **option pricing**.

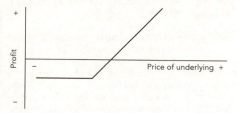

Payoff of call option for buyer at expiry

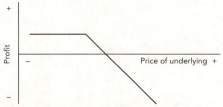

Payoff of call option for writer at expiry

(ii) (Bonds) An **embedded option** in a **bond** giving the issuer the right to redeem prior to **maturity**. Normally the dates at which the issuer can exercise his right to **call** are specified in the **bond indenture** (cf. **Atlantic-style**). See **call provision**; **declining call schedule**.

callover. See **open outcry** (cf. **ring session**).

callover price. See **opening price** (cf. **closing price**).

call premium. (i) (Bonds) A payment made to holders of securities that is above the **face** or **par value** of the securities if the issuer redeems before maturity. This **premium** may be constant over the life-span of the issue or, more typically, declines towards **maturity** (cf. **declining call schedule**). (ii) The premium paid on a **call**. Also known as *call money*.

call price. (i) The price at which a **call provision** may be **exercised** in a **bond** (cf. **redemption price**). Also sometimes called the **exercise** or **strike price** (cf. **options**). (ii) The **premium** or purchase price of a **call option**. Also known as *call money*.

call protection. Term for the period in a **bond** with a **call provision** before which the issuer can **exercise** his **call**. Sometimes called *call deferment* or *cushion*.

call protection warrant. A warrant that matures over the long term but which in the short term can be exercised only by surrendering a **host bond**, thus avoiding an immediate **call** structure on that bond (cf. **harmless warrant**).

call provision. A term in a security giving the issuer the right to redeem the issue before **maturity**. The specific terms and conditions under which the issuer may exercise his **option** and at what price are normally detailed in the **indenture** or the **prospectus** (cf. **declining call schedule**). See **embedded option**.

call risk. The risk that a **call provision** in a debt instrument will be **exercised**. See also **reinvestment risk**.

call schedule. The permitted dates and prices at which a **call provision** may be **exercised** by an issuer (cf. **declining call schedule**; **redemption price**).

call seller. See **writer**.

call spread. A bullish **option strategy** designed to reduce the cost of the **premium** or **risk** in **writing** options by buying a **call** at a given **strike price** and simultaneously selling the same call at a higher strike price. This limits the amount of profit (loss) that the buyer (seller) can make if the **underlying** price moves above the higher strike price but the premium received (paid) from the second option partly offsets the cost (risk) of the first option. Such a structure may appeal to a buyer who thinks that the price of the underlying is unlikely to move above the second strike price. The same combination but where prices are expected to fall is known as a *put spread*. See also **bear spread**; **bull spread**.

call yield premium. An extra yield on a callable **bond** paid by an issuer over the yield on a non-callable bond in order to compensate investors for the risk of the bond being called, or not being called if trading to call (cf. **yield-to-call**; **yield-to-maturity**). See **interest rate calculations**.

cambiste (French). Foreign exchange and money market dealer.

Canadian agencies (USA). The agencies of Canadian banks established in the United States.

Canadian Bond Rating Service (CBRS) (Canada). 1 Westmount Square, Suite 1350, Westmount, Québec, H3Z 2P9, Canada (tel. (514) 937 9557; fax (514) 937 0676). Provides short- and long-term ratings for Canadian corporate and municipal securities. Publications include *Corporate Ratings Manual* and *Government Ratings Manual* as well as real-time electronic information.

Canadian Bond Rating Service

	Long-term debt[a]	Short-term debt[a]	Government debt[b]	Investment funds[a, c]
Highest quality	A++	A–1+	AAA	AAAi
Very good quality	A+	A–1	AA	AAi
Good quality	A	A–2	A	Ai
Medium quality	B++	A–3	BBB	BBBi
Lower medium quality	B+		BB	BBi
Poor quality	B	A–4	B	Bi
Speculative quality	C		C	Ci
Default	D		D	
Rating suspended		Suspended		Suspended

[a] Higher (H) and lower (L) indicate relative quality within a rating.
[b] A plus (+) and minus (−) indicate relative quality within a rating.
[c] The suffix (i) indicates investment fund ratings and is not comparable with corporate or government debt ratings.

Canadian Business Corporations Act (CBCA) (Canada). Key Canadian legislation governing the activities of corporations in Canada. It is supplemented by provincial legislation.

Canadian Mortgage and Housing Corporation (CMHC) (Bonds; Canada). Issuer of mortgage loan insurance on pooled mortgages resold in the capital markets (cf. **collateralized mortgage obligation**).

Canadian provincial bonds (Canada). Bonds issued by one of the ten provinces of Canada. Such bonds are also offered in the US domestic market denominated in US dollars, or on the international

market in a variety of different currencies. See **eurobond**.

cancel (CXL). (i) To redeem a security. (ii) To countermand an instruction to an intermediary.

cancel former order (CFO). Instruction to terminate a previous order. Typically used to nullify limit orders (cf. **good till cancelled**).

cancellable forward. See **breakforward**.

cancellable swap. See **callable swap**; **swaption**.

cancellation. A method used to terminate a transaction prior to **maturity**. The two parties agree the current value of the contract and the party who would lose from cancellation receives a compensating payment from the other. See **call**.

cancellation price (UK). The price at which a unit trust will redeem (or cancel) its units (cf. **bid**; **single pricing**).

candlestick chart. A chartist method of representing price movements developed by the Japanese in the nineteenth century. The wicks of the candle represent the highs and lows during the trading period, and the candle the price range between the opening and closing. Thus candle charts embody three sets of information: intra-session **volatility**, opening–closing price ranges, and the **closing price**.

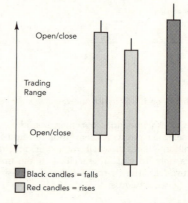

Candlestick chart

cantonal bond (*Schweizerobligation*) (Switzerland). Bonds issued by the twenty-two cantons of the Swiss Confederation. They normally have a slightly higher **yield** than similar issues by the Confederation, since they are not federal obligations. Such issues may have maturities out to fifteen years, but frequently are **callable** after an initial period (usually five years). Interest is paid annually.

cap. (i) (Markets) A limit placed on the upward movement of a price or on the interest or **coupon** rate. Can be a characteristic of a particular issue or required by the market regulators (cf. **limit**). See **circuit breakers**. (ii) (Derivatives) Any feature that sets a maximum return, payout, or cost. See **interest rate cap; capped floating rate note.**

capacity. The separation of the functions of **jobber** or **market-maker** and **broker** or **agent** is termed *single capacity*. A single entity fulfilling both roles of agent and **principal** is said to be *dual capacity*. See also **local; specialist.**

cap and collar security. See **minimax floating rate note.**

capital. (i) Funding for business organizations. Usually used with reference to the **equity** of a firm but can include the debt. Leads to the idea of different **classes** of capital. The distinction is based on the level and type of **risk** to which the providers of funds are exposed. **Shareholders** are normally known as the *risk-bearing* class of capital because if the business fails they rank last in the distribution of assets. However, all the variation in distributable profits are reserved for such investors. See **fixed capital; working capital: market capitalization.** (ii) Another term for **net worth**. That is the total **assets** less **liabilities** (cf. **equity**). (iii) The investment or equity held in an entity, less the fixed liabilities. Hence *invested capital* (cf. **partnership; limited company**). (iv) The liabilities of an enterprise. This consists of owners' funds and retentions *equity, equity capital* or *stock capital*, and debt or *loan capital*. (v) A factor of production, the others being labour, land, and enterprise.

capital account. (i) The record of an economy's annual investment and other capital flows. Sometimes called *capital flows* (cf. **hot money**). (ii) The accounting entries for expenditures on land, buildings, plant and machinery, and so forth (cf. **fixed assets**). (iii) For partnerships and sole traders, the surplus of total **assets** less **liabilities** (cf. **equity**).

capital adequacy. A goal of prudential supervision of financial institutions by their regulators to ensure that their capital is sufficient to absorb likely losses. These losses can arise in two main areas: customer- or credit-related losses, such as defaults on the interest or principal of loans (cf. **bad debt; problem assets**); and market-related, such as the risk arising from volatile interest rates and currency and securities prices (cf. **market risk**). Such provisions are sometimes called *capital allocation*. See **Basle Capital Convergence Accord; Capital Adequacy Directive; capital adequacy**

rules; insurance; Second Banking Directive; securities.

Capital Adequacy Directive (CAD). European Union (EU) directive issued on 15 March 1995 set out in the **Second Banking Directive** to harmonize the regulatory structure of deposit-taking institutions within the EU. The rules are largely the same as those which emerged from the **Basle Capital Convergence Accord** covering the capital requirements of credit institutions and investment firms: (i) common standard for **capital adequacy** of investment firms in respect to **market risks** incurred in their trading book activities: position risk, counterparty and settlement risk, and currency risk; (ii) common basis for capital adequacy for credit institutions in respect of market risks in their trading book activities and currency risk; (iii) to provide that both credit institutions and investment firms are subject to the same regulatory regime in respect of their exposures to market risks (level playing field). The institution's own **capital** (as defined) must be equal to: (*a*) the capital requirement in respect to the **trading book** (position risk, **settlement** and **counterparty risk**, and risks from large exposures); (*b*) capital requirement in respect of currency exposure in all its lines of business; (*c*) the capital requirement imposed by the **solvency ratio directive** (SRD) with respect to non-trading activities; (*d*) any capital requirements imposed by the competent regulatory authority in respect of risks not covered by the CAD or the SRD.

capital adequacy rules (UK). The rules used to regulate the financial resources of banks (by the **Bank of England**), building societies (by the Buildings Societies Commission), and other investment businesses (by the **Securities and Investments Board**) operating in the UK. There are four main requirements, relating to: minimum financial resources; additional financial resources based upon specific *economic risks* such as holding securities, and sometimes known as *risk–asset ratios*; definitions of capital according to gross capital, net current assets, adjusted capital, and liquid capital; and reporting and disclosure requirements, such as audited annual reports. The levels of capital required vary depending upon the nature of the business being undertaken. See also **Basle Capital Convergence Accord**.

capital allowances (UK). Tax relief allowances against profits as laid out by the Inland Revenue and statutes. For tax purposes the Revenue ignores accounting **depreciation** but provides a tax credit against various categories of capital expenditure based on a predetermined formula. The current rate for plant and machinery is a 40% allowance in the first year, followed by a declining 25% balance thereafter. The effect on taxable income of an asset acquired at 1,000 for the first four years is therefore as in the Table.

FY period	Value for tax purposes	Capital allowance against tax liability
Purchase price	1,000.0	
1	600.0	400.0
2	450.0	150.0
3	337.5	112.5
4	253.1	84.4

capital appreciation fund. See growth fund.

capital asset. Any of a range of assets used in an organization which have the character of permanancy rather than being rapidly replaced; examples include land, buildings, investments, and plant and machinery (cf. **fixed asset**). The other main type is **current assets** (cf. **current liabilities**).

Capital Asset Pricing Model (CAPM). An economic model of the behaviour of asset prices under conditions of risk. The model is intended to promote an **equilibrium** relationship for pricing the risk associated with holding assets. It predicts that expected rates of return will be directly related to a single common factor: the return on the market portfolio. These returns are a function of (i) the known risk-free rate, (ii) the asset's or security's beta, and the (iii) **market risk premium**:

$$E(R_j) = R_f + \beta_j(E(R_m) - R_f)$$

where $E(R_j)$ is the expected return on the jth asset or security; R_f the risk-free rate; β_j is the jth asset or security's beta or systematic risk element; and $(E(R_m) - R_f)$ the market risk premium. As such, it is an 'indirect', exogenous method of observing and predicting returns. Risk is divided into **systematic risk** and **residual risk**; the latter can be diversified away by investors through holding an efficiently diversified portfolio, but all assets have systematic risk to a greater or lesser extent. The amount of systematic risk is measured by the asset's or portfolio's beta (β). The model predicts that investors require to be compensated for taking on systematic risk and that this needs to be priced into asset or security returns. Residual risk, because it can be eliminated by diversification, is thus not priced (cf. **stock specific risk**). See also **Arbitrage Pricing Theory**.

capital base. (i) (Banking) Used to determine the underlying financial strength of banks in relation to the types of activities they undertake. It is normally defined as: **paid-up capital**, including **ordinary** and non-redeemable **preference shares**; **subordinated debt**, without restrictive **covenants**, usually limited to a proportion of the total capital base and where short-term loan capital is written off to zero according to the **straight line method**;

minority interest share holdings (these can be included provided certain conditions are met); and **reserves** subject to consideration by the relevant monetary authority. Sometimes deferred tax provisions can be included although such reserves are scrutinized by the **central bank**. In the UK this authority is the **Bank of England**; in the USA it is the **Federal Reserve**; and internationally agreed rules are contained in the **Basle Capital Convergence Accord** (cf. **Cook ratio**). See also **risk–asset ratio**. (ii) The **net worth** of a firm.

capital-based supervision (Banking). A method of regulating banks and other financial institutions which focuses on the degree to which **capital** supports their activities. The best criterion is that the institution is *well capitalized* indicating it has capital ratios well above the minimum regulatory standard, down to *critically under-capitalized*, where the **capital adequacy** of the institution is at risk. The latter condition would attract additional regulatory supervision and restrictions on the institution's activities (cf. **capital impairment**).

capital budget. Planned future expenditures on **capital assets**. See **budget**; **business plan**.

capital budgeting. The process of analysing and choosing between different **long-term** investments. Also known as *investment appraisal* (cf. **discounted cash flow**).

capital commitments. (i) Agreed but not disbursed expenditures on **capital assets**. (ii) (USA) The funds invested by **market-makers** in securities held in **inventory** in which they make markets.

capital employed. The total money committed to a firm which allows it to operate. Made up of fixed capital and working capital and equivalent to debt, taxes, and equity. As such, can be seen to represent one side of the balance sheet; the other representing what the firm has done with this capital. Otherwise known as *net operating assets*. See **return on capital employed**.

capital expenditure. Spending on **capital assets**. In accounting methodologies, such assets are not treated as a charge against profits, but are represented at cost on the **balance sheet** and their value is **depreciated** through the **profit and loss account** over time.

capital flight. Describes one of the effects of a weak currency. In that, international investors decide to move **capital** from one market to another because of concerns about the long-term value of **dividends** and interest. See also **hot money**.

capital formation. Used by economists to describe the **net investment** in fixed assets that represent additions to the stock of **capital**. Net capital formation excludes **depreciation**; gross capital formation includes it. In official statistics, it is used to measure the total amount of capital expenditure by the different sectors of an economy, usually on an annual basis.

capital fulcrum point (CFP). The indifference point between buying a **warrant** rather than the **stock** in a company. It is an indication of the required annual growth in the firm's stock to the **expiry** date of the warrant. The smaller the CFP, the lower the **risk** in holding the warrants. For example, a French company has a current share price of 735 fr. The warrants **exercise price** is 720 fr. (that is they are currently **in the money**), while the warrants are trading for 50 fr. each (15 fr. of **intrinsic value** and 35 fr. of **time value**) and have three years to expiry. The current warrant price is 720 fr. + 50 fr. − 735fr. = 35fr., which is a 4.76% CFP (cf. **premium**).

capital fund. See growth fund.

capital gain or **loss.** The gain (loss) made when an asset is sold above (below) its purchase price (cf. **marked-to-market**). Gains are often subject to some form of **capital gains tax**, e.g. in the UK.

capital gains return or **yield.** The **appreciation** in value as a result of the change in price for an asset or security, excluding any income expressed as a return or **yield**. See also **zero-coupon bond**.

capital gains tax (CGT). The tax imposed on profits made from realized purchases and sales of capital assets (cf. **capital gain**). Sometimes the gain can be adjusted for changes in the nominal value arising from inflation and therefore includes an **indexation** provision. CGT is usually charged at a lower rate than taxes on income (**dividends** and interest payments).

capital gearing. At its simplest the **ratio** of debt to equity in a **balance sheet**. It is both a measure of the extent that debt has been used to fund the assets of a business and also the **risk** inherent in the **capital structure** of the firm (cf. **highly leveraged transaction; low leverage**). Higher levels of capital gearing lead to a higher likelihood that a company will not be able to meet the attendant interest costs. That is, the company has a higher proportion of fixed charges, the higher the ratio of borrowed money relative to **shareholders' equity**. In the USA, it would be known as *capital leverage*. It is also called *equity gearing*. For the formula, see **ratio analysis**.

capital goods. That stock of goods that have themselves been produced in order to allow the production of other goods for consumption. Nor-mally used to describe durable goods such as plant and equipment, land and buildings (cf. **capital**).

capital growth. A rise in the value of invested assets. Returns for investments can come from either income or **dividends** received or through an increase in the value of the holding (cf. **capital gain**). Different **classes** of asset provide a different mix between growth and income, depending on the preferences of investors.

capital impairment (Banking). A condition where a deposit-taking institution has insufficient **capital** to meet loan losses and **capital adequacy** requirements set by regulators.

capital intensive. Those industries which require a large investment in **fixed assets**. Typical examples are steel, electricity generation, and so forth. Also called *heavy industry*.

capital investment. Decisions about and purchases of **capital assets** (cf. **capital budgeting**).

capitalization. (i) A company's outstanding long-term **debt** and **equity**, earned surplus and capital surplus. See also **market valuation**. (ii) Transactions to provide debt and equity. (iii) **Bonus** or **scrip issue**. (iv) Deriving the **present value** of a series of cash flows (cf. **discounting; net present value**). See **discounted cash flow**.

capitalization issue. The conversion of a company's **reserves** into issued capital which is then distributed to **shareholders**. Also frequently called a *bonus issue* or *scrip issue*.

capitalization rate. The rate of return expected by holders of an **asset** or security. At its simplest it is the **income** and any change in value of the asset over the anticipated holding period:

$$\text{Expected return} = \frac{\text{Income} + \text{End price} - \text{Purchase price}}{\text{Purchase price}}$$

and is also known as the *market capitalization rate* since it reflects the market or consensus required rate of return from the asset.

capitalization ratio. See leverage.

capitalization-weighted index. An index where the constituents' effect on the index is weighted according to their market **capitalization**. The effect is to give more significance to the firms with the greater market value. The alternative method is to use a *price index* where each share is given equal weight by price. Most performance indices use the capitalization-weighted method since this is a truer reflection of what **investment managers** can actually achieve.

capitalized option. See Boston option.

capitalized value. See capital value.

capital lease or **capitalized lease obligations**
(USA). A type of lease which gives the lessor
effective ownership of the leased asset and must,
therefore, be included on the **balance sheet** (cf.
above the line; below the line; off-balance sheet).
Typically, contractual terms which fall into this
category give the leasor a peppercorn purchase; or
transfer the asset at the **maturity** of the lease; or the
lease lasts for over 75% of the economic life of the
asset; or the lease payments are equivalent to a loan
for 90% or more of the asset's value. Also known as a
financial lease, full payout lease, or *demise hire.*

capital leverage (USA). See **capital gearing;**
leverage.

capital loss. The loss made when a capital asset
is below its purchase price (cf. **marked-to-market**).
See **capital gain.**

capital market. The market in capital. This is
usually taken to be the **equity** markets and those
for **long-term debt** (cf. **bond market**).

capital market line. See **modern portfolio
theory.**

capital market preferred stock. See auction
rate preferred stock; preferred stock.

capital markets. Collective term for various
types of markets where money can be raised
from investors. They comprise: share markets;
bond markets; commercial paper markets; domestic and international (**euromarkets**); the **primary
market** and the **secondary market.** The markets
for the purchase and sale of medium-to long-term
financial instruments such as **bonds** and **equities,**
commodities, and the **derivative instruments** created on the same.

capital market securities. Those securities
which have **long-term** characteristics, typically
taken to be more than one year. See **bonds;**
equities.

capital note. A bond issue, carrying either a fixed
or a **variable rate** coupon, the latter being also
known as *capital floating rate notes* where at maturity there is mandatory conversion into the **common stock** of the issuer. The attraction to buyers is
that it is an equity substitute, which generally
offers a higher **yield** than the common stock
until maturity.

capital ratio. The ratio of a firm's own funds, or
capital to assets (cf. **leverage**). See **capital
adequacy; capital structure.**

capital rationing. Restrictions imposed on the
availability of **capital** or **funds** to undertake investments. This can be imposed externally, through
the discipline of the market place via the rate of
interest, or through the unwillingness of investors
to provide funds to certain types of firms or activities, or through regulation. This process of rationing is sometimes termed *hard* since the individual
firm cannot vary the outcome. Or rationing may
be imposed internally by the management of
firms, who limit by amount or type investments
in any given period. This latter form of rationing is
sometimes called *soft,* since it is discretionary to
management. See also **capital structure.**

capital reconstruction. Any of a range of financing transactions aimed at significantly altering the
shape of a firm's **liabilities** (cf. **recapitalization;**
recontracting). There are three basic ways in
which this can happen: increases/decreases
in the amount of **equity,** increases/decreases in
debt, and lengthening/shortening debt maturities (cf. **buy-out; debt-equity swap; going private;**
**highly-leveraged transaction; refunding; stock
repurchase plan**).

capital reserves. Profits attributable to shareholders but not available for distribution (cf. reserves). Also known as *undistributable reserves* in
the UK.

capital risk. The risks arising to a firm's **capital**
from its operations.

capital shares (Equities; UK). That class of **shares**
in a split fund which is entitled to benefit from the
portfolio's **capital growth.** The other category is
known as *income shares.*

capital stock (USA). The **stock** authorized by a
corporation's **charter** or **articles of incorporation.**
Also sometimes used for **common stock.**

capital structure. The relative distribution
of a company's overall finance between **debt**
and **equity:** that is, the firm's loans, **bonds,**
debentures, preferred stock, and **common stock**
or **ordinary shares,** earned surplus and retained
income (cf. **debt–equity ratio; capital gearing;**
cost of capital; gearing (UK); **leverage** (USA);
weighted average cost of capital). See **ratio analysis.**

capital turnover. The ratio of sales or turnover
divided by **net worth.** See **ratio analysis.**

capital value. (i) The current or market value of
a future income stream (cf. **discounted cash flow;**
internal rate of return; present value). (ii) The
accounting value of a **capital asset** in the **balance
sheet** excluding accumulated depreciation.

caplet. Name given to a part of an **interest rate cap**. Effectively it is a single period interest rate cap or **option** (cf. **fraption**).

capped. (i) **Floating rate** interest being restricted to a range below a fixed ceiling (cf. **interest rate cap/floor; floor**). (ii) The maximum payout on **capped options**. (iii) Provision in certain **option** structures for automatic **exercise** if the **underlying** trades through a given point (cf. **trigger**).

capped floating rate certificate of deposit or **variable rate certicate of deposit (capped FRCD).** A floating rate certificate of deposit where the **variable rate interest** has a maximum rate (i.e. it is *capped*). As with the **capped floating rate note**, with this type of structure the holder forgoes the possibility of receiving a return above the **cap rate** should the market interest rate exceed the cap rate. When the probability of the capped rate becoming effective is high, such issues normally are issued and trade at a **discount**.

capped floating rate note (capped FRN). Floating rate note with an upper limit on the **coupon** rate (cf. **floor**). With this structure the holder forgoes the possibility of receiving a full market rate of interest should the interest rate exceed the cap rate, usually in exchange for a greater **margin** to the reference rate (cf. **embedded option**). See also collared floating rate note; delayed cap floating rate note; minimax floating rate note.

capped heaven-and-hell bond. A variation on a **heaven-and-hell bond** where the potential rewards to the holder are **capped**.

capped index option (CAPS) (USA). A type of **option** where the payout is **capped** such that it may not exceed US$30 per CAPS. The option has a European-style exercise, except that in the event where the **underlying** closes more than US$30 above (below) the **strike price** for **calls** (**puts**), the option is automatically exercised (cf. **trigger**). See **barrier option**.

capped option. An **exotic option** where the payout on the **underlying** has a **cap** at a specific value. Such a capped payout option will cost less than a simple option since the **risk** to the writer is bounded at a fixed point. It is tantamount to a **vertical spread**.

capped prime loan (Banking; USA). A loan where the **reference rate** is a bank's **prime rate** but with an absolute upper limit. See **interest rate cap**.

capped swap. A type of **interest rate swap** or cross-currency swap where the **floating rate** payments are **capped**, thus limiting the risk of the floating rate payer to adverse movements in interest rates.

cap rate. The **strike rate** on an **interest rate cap** (cf. **floor rate**). For instance, it is the maximum interest rate paid or received on an **interest rate collar** or a **capped floating rate note**.

caption. An **option** on an **interest rate cap** (cf. **cacall; caput; floortion**). It is a type of **compound option** that is an option on an option. This is a useful way of reducing the **option premium** if the likelihood of **exercise** is perceived as limited. For instance, a company may be bidding for another in which case it will need to finance the acquisition. It may wish to limit its **interest rate risk** by buying an interest rate cap on the purchase consideration. Since the outcome is uncertain, the firm has not added to its bid costs the full cost of interest rate protection if it is unsuccessful, but can proceed in the knowledge that it can protect itself if successful.

captive finance company or **subsidiary.** A wholly owned subsidiary of any organization that acts as a lender for **working capital** (credit lines) or **fixed capital** purposes. The borrowers can be either the owner or other credit-worthy borrowers.

captive insurance company. An insurance company set up by one or more corporations to insure the activities of the owners. Such captive insurance companies are common when there are tax benefits or mutual insurance is a lower-cost alternative than going through the market.

captive venture capital fund. See venture capital.

caput (call on a put). Type of compound option where the payoff is on a **put** option at **expiry** (cf. **cacall; exotic**).

cap with accretion or **amortization.** Interest rate cap where the **notional principal** increases or decreases during the period covered by the cap agreement. The arrangement is designed to protect a changing amount of **underlying floating** or variable rate debt.

carat. An international measure used for valuing diamonds. It is equal to 200 milligrams.

carried interest. Returns on capital instruments that if delayed can be paid in subsequent periods. Often applied to **preferred stocks** or preference and known as **cumulative** interest.

carries. See carrying.

carry. The cost of financing a physical commodity or of financing a particular market **position**. It is normally seen as the rate of interest earned from the securities held less the cost of funds borrowed for their purchase. When the interest earned is greater than the cost then there is a **positive carry**, and when the cost of borrowings is greater than the returns there is a **negative carry** (cf. **discount**; **premium**). In order to **break even** on a position with a negative carry, the selling price must be above the purchase price by, at least, the amount of the **rolled-up interest**. See **cash and carry**; **cost of carry**; **yield curve**.

carryback and **carryforward.** The ability to set losses against gains for the purpose of establishing a tax position. In the case of a carryback, losses which cannot be set against current income may be set against prior financial years' profits; with carryforward, unutilized losses may only be set against future years' income.

carrying or 'carries' (UK). Term given to either lending or borrowing operations on the **London Metal Exchange** (cf. **carry**; **cost of carry**). When *borrowing* a near-dated contract is bought and at the same time a longer-dated contract is sold; when *lending* a near-dated contract is sold and at the same time a longer-dated contract is bought. See **horizontal spread**.

carrying charge. A payment made to a lender or investor where the interest due is delayed or violated in some way.

carrying cost. See **cost of carry**.

carrying cost model. See **cost of carry**.

carrying market. The market for non-perishable commodities (cf. **softs**). That is, it is possible to hold, store, and later sell such commodities without loss of quality (cf. **warehouse stocks**).

carryover. (i) (Securities) Delaying **delivery** or payment on a transaction from one **settlement** date to the next (cf. **fail**). Also known as *contango* in the UK. Generally a carryover has the consent of the **counterparty**. (ii) That proportion of the production of a soft **commodity** that is available to be carried over into the next growing season (cf. **warehouse stocks**).

carryover day. The day at which a transaction has to be carried over from one **settlement date** to the next.

cartel. A formal version of **collusion** among firms for the setting of prices, output levels, and market shares. Such agreements comprise a set of rules that can be enforced by law. At present,

cartels are illegal in both the USA and UK because they are held to create monopoly conditions in industry.

Cartel Office (Germany). Office charged with overseeing restrictive practices, monopolies, anticompetitive activities, and competition policy.

Carter bonds (USA). Foreign currency **US treasuries**, denominated in Deutschmarks and Swiss francs issued when Jimmy Carter was President of the United States during the late 1970s. See also **Brady bonds**.

cascade shareholdings. A form of **pyramiding** of ownership involving controlling interests in a company being used to acquire control of subsidiaries further down the chain. In the Figure, company A has a minority stake in firms X and Y which also have outside shareholders B and C. There are **cross-holdings** between X and Y of 10%. A then effectively controls firm Z via X and Y, neither of which is majority owned and therefore not consolidated with A.

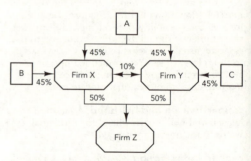

Example of a cascade shareholding structure

cascade theory. A model of the destabilizing effects of **portfolio insurance** methods on market prices. It postulates that wide swings in prices may be the result of automatic sell orders generating **market impact** price falls in **futures** and/or the **underlying** which then trigger further sell orders with other portfolio insurers, thus causing a further drop in futures and the underlying, thus repeating the whole process in a descending cascade. The regulator's solution has been to impose **circuit breakers**.

cash. (i) Money or demand deposits. (ii) Readily realizable deposits or securities, generally considered to be **default-free**. (iii) Those financial instruments which are exchangeable for cash, such as stocks, bonds, **commodities**, as opposed to **derivatives** such as **futures**, **forwards**, and **options**, where additional payments to obtain ownership of the **underlying** need to be made (cf. **spot market**).

cash account (USA). An account with a **broker** which is settled on a **cash basis** (cf. **margin account**).

cash against delivery or **documents (CAD)**. A **settlement** method used when buying an asset to mitigate **counterparty risk** by requiring simultaneous exchange of assets against the payment. The **counterparty** instruction which stipulates the opposite, as seller, is known as *documents versus (against) payment or presentation* (DVP).

cash and carry. The simultaneous purchase of a commodity or financial instrument for physical delivery and the sale of the same commodity or instrument for delivery at a future date (cf. **reverse cash and carry**). Also used in the securities markets where the purchase is financed either by a loan or through a **repurchase agreement**. The strategy aims to gain either due to **futures** prices being expensive to cash or through an anticipated narrowing of the **basis**, at which point the positions are **closed out** at a profit. Also known as *buying the basis*.

cash and new. On the **London Stock Exchange** when securities that have been purchased (sold) during the **account period** are sold (purchased) free of commission at the end of the account and then immediately repurchased (resold) for the next account period. Unlike a **contango** or **backwardation**, the two prices used in the one linked deal are not the same. Such transactions are no longer possible now that the exchange has moved to **rolling settlement**. See **new time dealings**.

cash basis. An accounting method which only recognizes receipts and payments when they are actually made (cf. **accrual basis**).

cash bucket. A method of pooling different cash flows into a single time bucket to facilitate analysis and interpretation. It is a starting-point for many **risk management** techniques and **asset-liability management**. It is also frequently used in preparing budgets and forecasts for project appraisal purposes. See **maturity buckets**.

cash card. See **debit card**.

cash commodity. The actual **commodity** in which one party will take **physical delivery** rather than **derivative instruments** based on the **underlying** (cf. **cash settled**).

cash commodity markets. Organized markets for buying and selling **commodities** which date back to the Renaissance. The Antwerp exchange was the original model for Thomas Gresham's **bourse** set up in 1571 in London (later known as the Royal Exchange).

cash cow. A firm in mature markets requiring only maintenance investments to maintain operations and generate surplus cash flow. One of the four parts of the Boston Consulting Group's strategy matrix (the others are **dog**, **star**, and **problem child**). Cash cows are suitable for **leveraged buy-outs** and **equity buy-backs**. See **Boston matrix**.

cash crop. See **commodities**; **soft commodities**.

cash cycle. The process of turning over cash in manufacturing from purchasing raw materials, making finished goods, and selling them, and then receiving payment after extending deferred payment or **credit** terms.

cash deal or **cash dealing** (UK). A next-day **settlement** transaction on the **London Stock Exchange**. When the Exchange settled on an **account** basis, buyers and sellers had to wait to the end of the account to settle up. With a cash deal, accelerated settlement was possible. The LSE has now moved to five-day $(T + 5)$ **rolling settlement**.

cash deficiency agreement. An undertaking, usually seen in **project finance**, where the **sponsor** agrees to provide additional funds to cover any cash flow shortfalls. Used to ensure there are enough funds to meet the project's fixed charges.

cash delivery (USA). Term meaning same-day **settlement** as opposed to **regular way delivery**, which is the next business day.

cash dividend. A normal **dividend** by a company paid in cash, as opposed to a **stock dividend** (cf. **enhanced scrip dividend**).

cash equivalents. Financial instruments which are readily marketable and are effectively cash substitutes (cf. **cash instruments**).

cash flow. (i) The receipts and payments made by a business. (ii) The contractual payments on a security or a portfolio of securities. (iii) Used as a synonym for new money.

cash flow budget or **projection.** A forecast of future expected or anticipated **cash flows** from a business or line of activity. See **budget**; **business plan**.

cash flow match or **matching.** The efficient timing of positive and negative cash flows for a **portfolio** of assets and a given set of liabilities. It is essentially a method of **immunization** where the cash flows from a portfolio or security are matched to known or expected outgoings. See **asset-liability management**; **dedication**.

cash flow projection. A prediction of the cash or borrowing needs or surpluses in a business over a given time period (cf. **budget; business plan**). Cash management would aim to ensure that the financial requirement of the business would not exceed available funding less some safety margin (cf. **overtrading**).

cash flow statement. A financial statement that is often provided alongside the **balance sheet** and the **profit and loss account** (or income statement) that shows the sources and uses of cash within the reporting period. There are two basic definitions of cash flow: (i) *gross cash flow* (made up of after-tax profit plus depreciation plus any increase (decrease) in deferred taxes, and (ii) *net cash flow* which is the same as gross cash flow but which also deducts any **dividend** payments. Because the cash flow statement shows the movement of funds for the reporting organization, it is also known as the *flow of funds statement* or a *source and application of funds statement.*

cash flow stream. A series of future cash flows (cf. **annuity**). Often called a *cash stream.*

cash flow swap. See roller-coaster swap.

cash-for-stock (Mergers and acquisitions). A **take-over** which is financed by purchasing, for cash, the target company's **equity**. The alternative is a stock-for-stock exchange, or a partial cash offer (cf. **vendor placing**).

cash-futures arbitrage. The process by which **arbitrage** maintains the price of the cash market and the **futures** price close to the theoretical **fair value** (cf. **basis; basis risk**). Traders will seek to exploit any mispricings between markets.

Cash-futures arbitrage

If futures are (in relation to their fair or theoretical value):	Futures market: action	Cash market: action	Known as:
Expensive	Sell futures	Buy cash (or cash instrument)	Buying the basis
Cheap	Buy futures	Sell cash (or cash instrument)	Selling the basis

The arbitrageur activity in the two markets buying cheap assets and selling expensive ones will tend to bring the future price back to its correct price level. See **cash and carry; reverse cash and carry.**

cash gaps. The area of **risk management** which primarily manages the **interest rate risk** mis-

matches between receipt and payment flows of primarily financial **assets** and **liabilities**. It requires analysis of the tenor and certainty of future cash flows in order to quantify the *gap*, or difference, between the values of interest-rate-sensitive assets and interest-rate-sensitive liabilities. The gap can thus be defined to be equal to the market value of rate-sensitive assets less the market value of rate-sensitive liabilities. These gaps are usually measured over a number of time periods (buckets), for instance one, two, three, six, nine, twelve months and longer. For example a one-year gap report might appear as in the Table.

Cash gaps

	Periods						total
	1	2	3	6	9	12	
(£m)							
Assets	10	35	15	20	20	10	110
Liabilities	5	40	20		25	0	90
Gap	5	(5)	(5)	20	(5)	10	20
Cumulative gap	5	0	(5)	15	10	20	
Effect of 1% rise in interest rates	(0.05)	0	0.05	(0.15)	(0.10)	(0.20)	(0.20)
Effect of 1% fall in interest rates	0.05	0	(0.05)	0.15	0.10	0.20	0.20

Although assets equal liabilities, changes in interest rates will affect the overall values of assets and liabilities differently. There is in effect interest rate risk in the maturity mismatch. Refinements to a basic gap report can include **sensitivity analysis**, refunding, **liquidity** and time decay, and so forth.

cash index participation (CIP) (USA). A type of long-term **option** on a **stock index**. See **long-term equity anticipation securities.**

cash instruments. Those financial instruments, such as **stocks, bonds,** or **spot foreign exchange,** which are generally bought and sold for immediate delivery as opposed to **derivative instruments,** such as **forwards, futures, swaps,** or **options,** where the payment on the **underlying** is deferred to a later date. See **cash markets.**

cash management. The planning, monitoring, and control of **liquidity**. It includes the day-to-day management of an organization's cash balances, short-term borrowings and investments, domestic and foreign money transfers, and **payables and receivables.** Also called *treasury management.* See **account; bill of exchange; documentary credit; facility; letter of credit; money market instruments; promissory note.**

cash management bill (CMB) (Money markets; USA). A special issue of short-term US **treasury bills** issued, as its name suggests, to provide additional funds for the US government. Such issues used to be for very short **maturities** but longer-maturity CMBs have been issued in recent years.

cash market. Markets where **delivery** and settlement of a transaction is immediate, or within a few days, as compared with **forward markets**, where delivery and settlement are delayed (cf. **actuals; cash settlement; continuous net settlement; regular delivery**). Also known as a *spot market*.

cash on delivery (COD). See **cash against delivery; delivery versus payment**.

cash-or-nothing option. A type of **binary option** which pays out a fixed amount if the **underlying** is above (for a **call**) or below (for a **put**) the **strike price**. See also **digital options**.

cash or physical. A provision in some financing agreements for extractive industries allowing the borrower to elect to make cash or deliver physical amounts of the **commodity** to the equivalent value of the repayments of interest and/or principal. See also **project finance; take-or-pay contract**.

cash-or-title option (COTO) (Switzerland). A type of **option** issued in the Swiss market to take advantage of a tax loophole on the payment of **dividends** (cf. **enhanced scrip dividend**). Holders of the options were offered a range of alternatives: exercise of the option into shares of the issuer without paying withholding tax; sale on the secondary market, which attracted no tax liability; or receiving the dividend. This latter alternative was subject to federal withholding tax. The Swiss authorities have now moved to close the loophole making COTOs unattractive. See **low exercise price option**.

cash price. The price for the **underlying** in the **cash market**, that is for immediate **delivery**, rather than in the **forward** or **futures market** (cf. **basis; cost of carry**).

cash ratio. (i) A **ratio analysis** test of a firm's immediate **liquidity**. It is the ratio of **cash** and marketable securities to current **liabilities**. See **acid test ratio**. (ii) (Banking) The ratio of cash (notes and coins) to total liabilities held by a bank to meet customer withdrawals. Also known as the *liquidity ratio*. See also **capital adequacy**. (iii) In the UK, the requirement for banks to hold interest free deposits at the **Bank of England** (cf. **reserve requirements**).

cash redeemable liquid yield option notes (cash redeemable LYONS). A type of liquid yield option note (a **zero-coupon convertible**) where the issuer has an **option** to redeem the notes in cash at the prevailing market price of the firm's **common stock**, rather than issuing new equity.

cash secured put. A written **put** position where the writer deposits cash equal to the **exercise price** of the **puts** with the **clearing house** or intermediary (cf. **covered call; covered put**). It is a way of avoiding problems with **margin accounts**.

cash security. See **cash market**.

cash settled. A means of settling up futures and **options** contracts where the parties pay the differences between the purchase or sale and the **expiry** price rather than provide or receive the **underlying**. In certain types of contracts such as **stock index futures** this is essential given the difficulties of delivering the **index** basket to the other party. Increasingly, futures and options are now cash settled; the buyer then purchases the relevant underlying in the **spot market** if the buyer wants delivery. Also known as a *non-deliverable contract*.

cash settlement. The settlement of a transaction in the **cash market** in accordance with normal market practice. For example, in the US domestic **money markets**, cash settlement means payment in **fed funds** on the same day of the transaction (cf. **spot; tom/next**). Also referred to as a *cash deal* or *transaction* as opposed to a deferred settlement transaction, typical of the **derivatives** markets.

cash settlement contract. See **cash settled**.

cash unit trust. See **money market mutual fund**.

cassa di risparmio (Banking; Italy). **Savings bank**.

casualty loss (USA). A sudden and unexpected insurance loss due to a specific event.

category. A grouping of investments by type for analytic purposes. See **class**.

cats and dogs (Equities; USA). Market jargon for speculative shares (cf. **penny stocks**).

caveat emptor (Let the buyer beware) (Latin). A principle of unregulated markets and dealings between professionals (cf. **bazaar**).

cedulas hipotecarias (Bonds; Spain). Mortgage-backed bonds.

ceiling. See **capped; interest rate cap**.

ceiling agreement or **ceiling rate agreement.**
See **interest rate cap.**

Cellar–Kefauver amendment of 1950 (USA).
The amendment made to the **Clayton Act** that
extended the antitrust legislation to acquisitions of
assets as well as complete businesses.

central bank. The bank or financial institution
with responsibility for a country's monetary
policy. A central bank will normally also act
as lender of last resort and may also be the
regulator for the financial system (cf. **discount
rate; open-market operations; reserve requirements**). Activities include issuance of bank notes,
accepting **deposits** and making loans to commercial banks, managing the national debt and the
country's **foreign exchange** reserves, acting as
banker to the government and other state agencies, and conducting relations with other foreign
central banks (cf. **Bank for International Settlements**).

central bank discount rate. See discount rate
(cf. **Minimum Lending Rate**).

central bank intervention (Forex). See intervention.

central bank swap lines. Agreements between
central banks for undertaking **intervention**.

**Centrale de Livraison de Valeurs Mobilières
(CEDEL).** One of the two clearing houses used by
the **euromarkets**. Established in 1970, it is owned
by several of the major European banks, and is
based in Luxembourg (cf. **Euroclear**).

Central Gilts Office (CGO) (Bonds; UK). The
Bank of England's electronic clearing house for
gilt-edged transactions established in 1986 following the reforms known as **Big Bang**.

**Central Government Borrowing Require-
ment (CGBR)** (UK). The total borrowing requirement by the central government which is the
public sector borrowing requirement less any
borrowings undertaken by local authorities and
state-owned corporations.

Central Limit Order Book (CLOB) (Equities; Singapore). Electronic, screen-based, market system
used for trading. See **Stock Exchange of Singapore.**

central limit theorem. A statement about the
nature of a stochastic distribution that says that as
long as the distribution has a finite variance it will
approximate to a **normal distribution**. This is a
very useful theorem for analysing stochastic processes in that it allows the legitimate use of the

normal or **lognormal distribution** for analytic
purposes. See **geometric Brownian motion;
Black–Scholes option pricing model; Wiener
process.**

Central Moneymarkets Office (CMO) (Money
markets; UK). The **Bank of England's** electronic
clearing house for sterling **money market** instruments, such as **certificates of deposit** and commercial paper. It is the short-end of the market
equivalent to the **Central Gilts Office**.

central parity or **rate** (Forex). The central currency rate that must be maintained by members of
the **Exchange Rate Mechanism** in relation to the
European Currency Unit. When the currency
diverges from this central rate by a predetermined
amount, countries are expected to take corrective
action through either intervention or changes in
domestic monetary conditions to maintain the
parity with other currencies (cf. **divergence indicator**).

Central Registration Depository (CRD) (USA).
National Association of Securities Dealers sponsored computerized register of details of registered representatives. (cf. **account executive**).

central treasury or **centralized treasury.** Aggregation of the **cash management** and financial
activities of a group of companies into a single
location or function. Typically, the individual companies of the group are relieved of the responsibility of managing their cash flow position, this
function being undertaken by the central treasury
on their behalf. In effect, the treasury acts as a
banker to the group. The attraction for many large
firms is that the centralization of treasury activities
allows for both **netting** and natural offsets from
positions. The opposite treasury approach is to
allow each unit to undertake its own transactions
as required. In such a situation, the group as a
whole will not be able to offset naturally occurring
opposing positions, nor will senior management
have as much information on the group's activities. For these reasons, the decentralized approach is less often used.

certainty equivalent. The value of a guaranteed
cash flow that would make an investor indifferent
as to the choice between this safe payment or cost
and an alternative risky, cash flow (cf. **risk averse;
risk neutral; risk seeker; utility**). See also expected value.

certificat d'investissement (French). **Participation certificate.**

certificate. A document providing evidence of
fact, claim, or entitlement (cf. **certificate of deposit**). See also **warehouse warrant**.

certificated stock or **certified stock.** See physical security.

certificate of accrual on Treasury securities (CATS) (Bonds; USA). A form of **strip** where the **coupon** payments and **principal** on a **US treasury** are repackaged to trade as seperate zero-coupon securities. The **underlying** is a claim on a single portion of the US Treasury security's cash flow: the principal and each coupon have been removed and are held in a trust (or depository) and receipt certificates issued for each cash flow in order to make CATS a capital appreciation-only investment with a single final payment at maturity. See **corpus Treasury receipt; coupon Treasury receipt; physical strip; separate trading of registered interest and principal of securities; treasury investment growth receipt; zero-coupon eurosterling bearer or registered accruing securities.**

certificate of amortizing revolving debt securities (CARDS) (Bonds; USA). A type of **asset-backed, pass-through** security where the **underlying** assets are credit card receivables.

certificate of automobile receivables securities (CARS) (Bonds; UK/USA). A type of **asset-backed** issue where the **underlying** assets are the auto-financing receivables from car buyers.

certificate of deposit (CD). Issued by banks, or other deposit-taking institutions, these negotiable instruments provide evidence of an interest-bearing or **discount** time **deposit** of fixed maturity with the issuing bank. CDs may be in **bearer** form or **registered**; and some are non-negotiable. Maturities are normally up to ninety days but can be longer, with five years usually the maximum. This is the case under **Bank of England** rules in the London market, the principal international market for CDs. The rate of interest may be paid at maturity, as with short-term CDs or with **term** CDs, reset periodically or fixed to maturity (cf. **floating rate certificate of deposit; fixed rate certificate of deposit**). Issues can be in a wide variety of currencies, the principal issuing activity being in US dollars, sterling, yen, or **European Currency Units.** The formula for calculating the interest on a **secondary market** purchase for an interest-bearing CD is:

$$Price = FV \left[\frac{1 + \dfrac{C \times T}{Basic \times 100}}{1 + \dfrac{MMY \times T_s m}{Basis \times 100}} \right]$$

Where *FV* is the face value of CD; *C* the coupon (or interest) on the CD; T_{im} the time from issue to maturity, in days; *MMY* the money market yield; T_{sm} the time from settlement to maturity, in days; *Basis* the number of days in the computation year,

either 365 for sterling, or 360 for most other currencies (for details, see **interest rate calculations**). For a 5 million CD issued with a 10% coupon with an original maturity of 180 days and a current maturity of 90 days sold at a money market yield of 8.5% based on a 360-day basis, the purchase price would be:

$$5,140,758.87 = 5,000,000 \left[\frac{1 + \dfrac{10 \times 180}{360 \times 100}}{1 + \dfrac{8.5 \times 100}{360 \times 100}} \right]$$

See also **floating rate note.**

certificate of participation (USA). Security providing a part share in a lease or mortgage on a property where the **counterparty** is the federal or state government, or one of its agencies.

certificate of quality. A document providing proof of the grade or quality of a **commodity** for trading purposes on an **exchange** (cf. **assay**). Contracts traded on **commodities exchanges** are to a given specification; a certificate of quality provides details of the quality of any particular lot being traded. If the commodity is of lesser (higher) quality, then an appropriate price adjustment has to be made. See **contract grade.**

Certificats de Trésorerie (Belgium). Treasury bills.

certificates of government receivables (COUGARS) (Bonds; USA). Zero-coupon receipts offered by AG Becker Inc. created by stripping US Treasury bonds. See **separate trading of interest and principal of securities.**

certificates of indebtedness. See treasury certificate.

Certificati del Tesoro con Opzione (CTO) (Bonds; Italy). A government **bond** with a final **maturity** of six years, but incorporating a **put** provision after three years to redeem the bond at **par. Coupon** interest is paid semi-annually on a 30/180-day **basis.** See **interest rate calculations.**

Certificati del Tesoro Reali (CTR) (Bonds; Italy). Index-linked bonds.

Certificati di Credito del Tesoro (CCT). Floating rate **notes** issued by the Italian government. Their reference rate is that for **treasury bills,** known as **Buoni Ordinari del Tesoro.** CCTs were first issued in 1979 and have an initial maturity between five and ten years. Issues with maturities over five years pay the **coupon** semi-annually and accrue interest on a 30/180-day **basis.** CCTs are offered every month in an English-style **auction.**

Certificati di Credito del Tesoro a Cedola Variabile (CCT) (Bonds; Italy). Floating rate notes where the coupon is linked to the rate on Buoni Ordinari Del Tesoro.

Certificati di Credito del Tesoro a Sconto (CTS) (Bonds; Italy). Deep discount government bonds.

Certificati di Credito del Tesoro Convertibili (Bonds; Italy). A floating rate note which is convertible at the holder's option into a fixed rate on predetermined terms one year after issue.

Certificati di Credito del Tesoro Denominati in Euroscudis (Bonds; Italy). Five- and ten-year maturity treasury bonds denominated in European Currency Units in the domestic market.

Certificati di deposito (Money markets; Italy). Certificate of deposit.

certification. The marking on the transfer deed, upon the sale of registered securities, to show that the certificate has been lodged with the registry authority or with the appropriate exchange. This is necessary when the seller is not disposing of all the holding, or when the securities are purchased by more than one person. New certificates will then be issued to reflect the new ownership.

Certified Accountant (UK). Member of the Chartered Association of Certified Accountants.

Certified Public Accountant (CPA) (USA). Member of the Institute of Certified Public Accountants. A specialist legally recognized as being capable of examining the financial records of US companies for share listing, taxation, and auditing purposes. See due diligence.

chain rule. An arithmetic rule comprising the formation of a series of equations which are connected together and dependent each on the preceding one, like the links in a chain. See, for example, Retail Prices Index (cf. index construction).

chairman. That member of the board of directors who conducts meetings. In some models of management, the chairman is responsible for external relations and broad issues of strategy while the chief executive officer (CEO) or managing director (MD) handles day-to-day internal, operational matters. In some firms, both positions are combined. See corporate governance.

Chambre Agent General Index (Equities; France). Broad-based, arithmetically weighted index of common stocks quoted on the Paris bourse.

Chambre de Compensation des Instruments Financiers de Paris (CCIFP) (France). The Options and futures clearing house for the Marché à Terme International de France and the marché des options négotiables de Paris.

channel. A chartist or technical analysis term for a movement in prices where it is possible to draw parallel lines from the highs and lows, such that the price series appears to be channelled in a particular direction (cf. flag; pennant; triangle pattern). Any breakout of the price through these lines is considered a significant breach of a resistance point, if upward, or support point, if downward. See also arbitrage channel.

chaos theory. A mathematical model developed to explain complex phenomena that postulates complex feedback interactions between the component variables. In financial markets, the model has been used to try and describe the stochastic behaviour of assets prices in new and meaningful ways. Thus, rather than attempt to explain the observed pricing phenomenon in terms of market forces, technical factors, and economic variables, chaos would seek to redefine market behaviour in terms of, for instance, market stability/instability patterns and other factors, drawn from the theory.

chaotic behaviour. The suggestion that financial markets, and business activity at large, no longer obey the received wisdom based on custom and practice. It implies, for example, that share prices do not behave rationally and certainly not in a sufficiently systematic way to allow for the sustainability of such theories as the efficient markets hypothesis.

Chapter 7 (USA). That part of the Bankruptcy Reform Act of 1978 which concerns the liquidation of a firm.

Chapter 11 (USA). The section in the Bankruptcy Reform Act of 1978 under which a firm may seek court protection from its creditors while it undergoes a reorganization. It gives the court considerable control over the firm's affairs, but also provides a breathing space for the business to trade out of its troubles. The court supervises any capital reconstruction, which may involve creditors surrendering some of their claim and receiving new securities (cf. assented securities). Two key elements have characterized the process: violation of absolute priority, where junior debt and equity holders participate in the restructuring process; and the ability of the court to enforce a *cram down* when a majority of creditors have reached agreement. Once the various claims are resolved and the business can survive, it emerges from Chapter 11 protection to resume normal activities. While in Chapter 11 a firm may raise additional funds called **debtor-in-possession** financings which have priority over existing claimholders. In a pre-packaged Chapter 11 filing, the company already has a reorganization plan that must have the prior approval of over 50% of debtholders who represent two-thirds of the outstanding claims.

Chapter 13 (USA). The section in the **Bankruptcy Reform Act of 1978** under which a firm may be **liquidated** or **wound up** (cf. **bankruptcy**).

Chapter 17 (Germany). German money market term. This allowed the **Bundesbank** to use government funds deposited with it to provide temporary **liquidity** to the markets. In exchange, government institutions enjoyed favourable borrowing rates. New **European Union** regulations abolished this facility at the end of 1993.

charge. See **lien**.

charge-off (Banking; USA). Lending or other credit-related losses that are **written off** as unrecoverable. Bank examiners categorize loans as: *other loans especially mentioned* (OLEM): specific problem assets in a bank's portfolio; *substandard*: these have inadequate value protection based on the borrower's capacity to repay or the collateral; *doubtful*: substandard loans where the repayment is highly unlikely; *loss*: uncollectable loans where an actual charge-off is made. See **net charge-offs**.

chart analysis or **chartism.** The analysis of market trends using graphs and charts to predict future market movements. The approach is based on the view that asset price behaviour is predictable and that market participants will react in a given way that can be observed from price trends. The technique is also sometimes called *technical analysis*, although this has a wider meaning (cf. **fundamental analysis**). See **flag**; **filter**; **head and shoulders**; **line**; **pennant**; **quantitative analysis**; **technical analysis**; **triangle pattern**.

Charter (USA). A corporation's **articles of incorporation**.

Chartered Accountant (CA) (UK). A member of the Institute of Chartered Accountants in England and Wales, the Institute of Chartered Accountants of Scotland or the Institute of Chartered Accountants in Ireland. There are two grades: *Associate of the Institute of Chartered Accountants* (ACA) and *Fellow of the Institute of Chartered Accountants* (FCA).

chartered bank (Banking; USA). A bank which is constituted by a charter. This may be either at the

level of the individual state, when the bank is known as *state chartered* or at the federal level, when it is known as *nationally chartered*. See **National Association**.

chart gap. See **technical analysis**.

chartist. One who practises **technical analysis** using charts. See **chart analysis**.

chattel mortgage. A mortgage with a lien on personal property (cf. **fixed charge**; **floating charge**).

cheapest to deliver (CTD). The least-cost **bond** that can be provided in **settlement** by a **short position** holder (seller) in a **bond futures** contract (cf. **interest rate futures**). Bond futures are based on a **notional bond** and allow any bond from a **basket** to be used to settle the seller's obligation at the **expiry** of the contract. Differences in price for the different bonds in the basket mean that, at any point in time, there is a particular security which minimizes the amount of the bonds that have to be delivered by the futures seller. Since the bonds have different **coupon rates** and may trade at different prices in the market, at settlement, each deliverable bond's price is computed at the same **yield** as the notional bond specified in the **futures** contract. The difference in price between the notional bond and the actual bond used to settle the contract is then adjusted by this **delivery factor** such that a higher (lower) coupon bond relative to the notional bond will decrease (increase) the amount of the **underlying** that has to be made available. Different bonds will have different delivery factors and it will be in the interest of the provider to give-up the least expensive alternative for **delivery**. As a result, at any point in time the market price for the bond future is based on the current CTD bond. Variations in interest rates and the shape of the **yield curve** will change the CTD bond over time, since normally quite a wide range of bonds are included in the basket. If we have the following situation with two bonds available for delivery:

Bond	Coupon rate	Maturity	Conversion factor
A	9.875%	15	1.1700
B	6.125%	25	0.8150

OUTCOME 1

If the futures price, for instance, has an **exchange delivery settlement price** (EDSP) of 116.50:

Bond	Futures price	Delivery price (EDSP × conversion factor)	Market price of bond
A	116.50	116.50 × 1.1700 = 136.31	136.31
B	116.50	116.50 × 0.8150 = 94.95	96.13

The cheapest to deliver is bond A.

OUTCOME 2

The EDSP in this case is 92.12

Bond	Futures price	Delivery price (EDSP × conversion factor)	Market price of bond
A	92.12	92.12 × 1.1700 = 107.78	108.12
B	92.12	92.12 × 0.8150 = 75.08	75.08

The cheapest to deliver is bond B.

cheap money. See easy money.

checkable. See check.

check account or **checking account.** (Banking; USA). An **account** held with a depository institution such as a **bank** against which **cheques** may be written for immediate withdrawal that (usually) pays nominal or no interest. Sometimes includes an **overdraft** facility.

checking. The system that allows security deals to be reported to the appropriate **clearing house** by both parties. Only **matched bargains** can be settled (cf. **out-trade**).

checking the market (USA). A process of sounding out different **market-makers** as to their quotes (cf. **picture**; **real market**).

cheque (USA: **check**). A bill of exchange or a **draft** on a bank that is drawn against funds held at the institution to pay a specified sum to the recipient. A cheque is **negotiable** if endorsed. The process of settling cheque transactions is known as **clearing**.

cherry picking. (i) Selecting only the most attractive cases or parts that appeal to the buyer or investor out of a **pool** of **assets** or business. (ii) The process of a **receiver** deciding to enforce only those contracts where it stands to gain; while disputing those where it stands to lose for the benefit of the company in receivership or **liquidation** (cf. **insolvency**).

Chicago Board of Trade (CBOT; CBT) (US). 141 West Jackson Boulevard, Chicago, IL 60604 (tel. 1 312 435 3500; fax 1 312 341 3306). Established in 1848, it is the main US centre for **financial futures** trading. It started in 1848 as an exchange for handling the growing Midwest grain trade and its **futures contracts** date back to the 1850s. It diversified into financial futures on US **treasury bonds** in the 1970s.

Chicago Board Options Exchange (CBOE) (US). 400 South LaSalle, Chicago, IL 60605 (tel. 1 312 786 5600; fax 1 312 786 7409/7413). Established in 1973, it is the largest US centre for the trading of linked **options** in over 150 **common** stocks, such as **stock index options**, based on S&P 100 and S&P 500 Indices, and options on sub-indices.

Chicago Mercantile Exchange (CME) (US). 30 South Wacker Drive, Chicago, IL 60606 (tel. 1 312 930 1000; fax 1 312 930 8219). Established in 1874 as a competitor to the **Chicago Board of Trade** formerly called the Butter and Egg Board, it became the CME on 1 December 1919. It handles mainly **commodity future** trading in live cattle, feeder cattle, live hogs, pork bellies, broiler chickens, and lumber **futures contracts**. In addition, it operates the **International Monetary Market**, where the first currency futures were traded in 1972. The main financial contracts are rolling spot, index futures on the Goldman Sachs Commodity Index, Russell 2,000, **Nikkei 225**, and the **Major Market Index**.

Chicago school. See monetarism.

Chief Executive Officer (CEO). The senior manager responsible for the day-to-day activities of a company.

Chief Financial Officer (CFO) (USA). The senior manager responsible for the financial affairs of a corporation. See also **comptroller**; **treasurer**.

Chief Operating Officer (USA). The officer responsible for the day-to-day management of the corporation.

chinese walls. The internal information barriers set up within diversified financial firms to prevent **conflicts of interest** (cf. **firewalls**). They typically involve the setting up of barriers or procedures to limit the dissemination of information or decision-making influence between divisions (such as proprietary trading and those acting for issuers and investors). Hence, if **market-makers** are part of a financial services conglomerate then they must be separately established as companies or partnerships so that any transactions within the conglomerate are effected at arm's length. See also **compliance**; **insider dealing**.

choice. Used to describe the situation when the best **bid price** and the best **offering price** are the same (cf. **backwardation**; **locked**).

chooser option. A type of **option** which gives the holder the right to decide up to some point prior to **expiry** whether the option is a **call** or a **put**. The regular chooser option has both the put and call at the same **strike price**, while the complex chooser option has different strikes on each side. The payout is similar to that of an **option strategy straddle** but at less cost since the holder must decide which way to go prior to expiry. Pricing and **hedging**

depends on the **put–call parity** theorem and the fact that the holder will always select the more valuable alternative. Also known as an *as-you-like-it option*, *double option*, or *preference option*.

Christmas tree spread (XT). Complex **option** strategy involving six options with three **strike prices** which provides limited **risk** but, eqully, limited potential. A **long** position in a christmas tree spread can be established by buying a **call** (**put**) at the lowest (highest) strike price, selling three calls (puts) at a higher (lower) strike price, and buying two calls (puts) at an even higher (lower) strike price. This might be an attractive strategy if for instance, **volatility** is not constant across all strikes (cf. **volatility smile**).

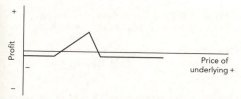

Payoff of a Christmas tree spread using call options

chūki kokusai (Bonds; Japan). **Medium-term** government bond, typically of five years' **original maturity**.

chummy trading (USA). Artificially inflating the volume of **securities** traded in order to encourage more activity by other traders. Sometimes called *chumming*. See **ramp**.

churning. Unnecessary buying and selling in order to generate **commission**.

Cincinnati Stock Exchange (USA). One of the nine stock exchanges in the United States. See **American Stock Exchange; New York Stock Exchange**.

circle. Before fixing the price of a new issue **underwriters** may test market sentiment by approaching investors that are likely to be interested in the offer. When a potential buyer has been circled it means he has made a commitment to buy at an agreed price. If the price turns out to be different, then he has first refusal at the actual price. See **book**.

circuit breakers. A method of preventing very large fluctuations in securities prices by requiring market traders to agree upper and lower limits beyond which no further deals take place (cf. **limit; suspension**). Such methods of stopping trading in volatile markets have become standard features of many exchanges following the October 1987 stock market crash (cf. **Black Monday; cascade theory**).

circus. A transaction that involves both an **interest rate swap** and a **cross-currency swap**. That is, one side will be **floating rate** in one currency and the other will be **fixed rate** in the other currency. Also termed a *cross-currency coupon swap*.

circus option. Another term for a **cross-currency swaption**.

Citiplus. Name given by Citibank to a **participating forward**.

citizen bonds (USA). A type of **book-entry municipal bond**.

City (UK). The City of London, the financial district of London, also known as the *square mile* (cf. **Bay Street; Wall Street**).

city bank. (i) (Japan). One of the thirteen major national banks in Japan (cf. **Keiretsu**). (ii) A **money centre bank**.

City Code on Takeovers and Mergers (Take-over Panel) (UK). A set of voluntary rules governing the behaviour of the parties to **takeover** and **merger** transactions first established in 1968. The rules are administered by the Panel on Takeovers and Mergers (the Takeover Panel) in conjunction with the **Rules Governing Substantial Acquisitions of Shares**. The Code is implemented by the Takeover Panel which, since the introduction of the **Financial Services Act 1986**, is part of the **Securities and Futures Authority** as a self-regulating organisation. It embodies four principles: that all **shareholders** of the same **class** (such as ordinary shareholders) should be treated equally; that shareholders should be given sufficient information to form a proper judgement about the transaction; that high standards of care in the wording of all documents and advertisements should be maintained; that the **board of directors** of the **target** or merged company must act in the best interests of their shareholders; and that the creation of a **false market** in the shares should be avoided. One of its most significant rules requires a **bidder**, once the proportion of shares controlled exceeds 30%, to make a general offer to all remaining shareholders, at the highest price paid for the shares in the past twelve months. Detailed rules on the timing and content of announcements, the offer period, and other operational matters are also covered by the Code, namely:

1. the prevention of discrimination between shareholders in the target company to be acquired, including a fair and transparent information policy;
2. the principle that intent is more important than the precise legal interpretation and is open to

modification by the Takeover Panel in any individual circumstance; and

3. the principle of practical orientation, which means the Code is flexible and adaptable to changing circumstances.

The most important operational rules derived from the above principles are:

(*a*) A party with less than 30% of the outstanding shares is only permitted to expand its stake by a maximum of 10% within a seven day period. Exceptions are (i) the bidder has already made a tender offer for the shares; (ii) the intention to bid has been declared; (iii) the bidder is about to make an offer which is recommended by the Board of Directors of the target company; and (iv) the shares are to be acquired from a single vendor who owns more than 10% of the target and who wishes to sell more than 10% of the holding.

(*b*) When the bidder has acquired shares within the three-month period prior to the offer being made, the tender price is allowed to be lower than the highest price paid in this period. If, however, (i) the bidder has purchased shares in the twelve-month period prior to the offer and has acquired more than 10% in this period; or (ii) has accumulated more than the 30% threshold requiring the bidder to make a full offer for the target, the bidder is obliged to offer at least the highest price paid during the preceding twelve months.

(*c*) Whenever a company reaches a threshold of 30% of the shares in a company, it is obliged to make a cash tender offer for the remaining outstanding shares, the offer to be kept open until it becomes unconditional.

(*d*) A company with an existing stake of 29.9% in a target and having made no offer is only allowed to increase its stake within seven days and it may only exceed the 30% threshold by making one purchase.

(*e*) The only route to increasing the stake in the target above the 29.9% and having made a tender which is not recommended by the target company's Board is for the bidder to receive acceptances or by purchases in the market after the first closing date, that is, twenty-one days after the tender is declared.

City scribbler (UK). A derogatory term for an economic or policy analyst. The phrase was coined by Nigel Lawson when Chancellor of the Exchequer in response to adverse City criticism of UK government policies.

claim. (i) Rights over assets used by another organization or individual (cf. **lien**). See **lease**. (ii) An application to make good a loss made under an insurance policy or guarantee.

class. Securities which are similar in type. For example: **bonds** would form one class; **fixed rate**

and **floating rate** two (sub)classes; **foreign bonds** would also be called a class. **Options**, which are similar, would also be a class. See also **fungible**.

classical system of company taxation. Tax treatment of corporations which treats them as separate entities to their **shareholders** and which leads to double taxation, first at the company level and then as income received by shareholders (cf. **imputation**). See **advance corporation tax; double taxation; mainstream corporation tax; unrelieved advance corporation tax**.

classified stock (USA). The issuance of different types of **common stock** by a corporation. For instance, voting and non-voting **stock**.

class of options. The **options** of the same type, either **calls** or **puts**, on the same **underlying**.

class voting. The procedure whereby each **class** of **liability** votes separately. Also known as *series voting*.

clawback. (i) A provision within a **project finance** agreement requiring the **sponsor** to repay profit distributions if there is a subsequent shortfall in later periods. (ii) Taxation method which recoups part of the cost of universal social benefits by including them as taxable income.

Clayton Act of 1914 (Mergers and takeovers; USA). Along with the Sherman Act of 1890, the keynote legislation defining **antitrust law** in the USA. The Clayton Act concerned the ability of firms to merge or acquire each other in such a way as substantially to reduce competition in an industry. The test as to acceptability used in the legislation is whether competition in the industry is reduced. Parts of the Act also applied to restraint of trade and monopoly conditions.

clean float (Forex). A policy which allows market forces to determine a currency's **foreign exchange rate**. Alternatives to such benign neglect include managed foreign exchange and **crawling peg** policies (cf. **Exchange Rate Mechanism**). Also known as *free float*.

clean index principal swap. See **index principal swap**.

clean pot (USA). Term used when the **pot**, that is the securities available for distribution in a new issue, is empty (cf. **distributed**).

clean price or **cleaned price**. (i) A price quoted for a **bond**, excluding **accrued interest** (cf. **dirty price; full price**). See also **ex-dividend**. (ii) It can also mean a price without any dealing **commission**.

clean-up call provision (bonds). (i) A condition of an **asset-backed security** issue where the issuer has the right to redeem the outstanding balance once the pool of assets falls below a certain minimum. The reasoning behind such a provision is to allow the issuer to avoid excessive costs in servicing a small fraction of the total issue and to give investors some assurance that they will not be left with a significant long tail-end residual **maturity** on their security. (ii) A provision within a **convertible** giving the issuer the right to force **conversion** when a given percentage of the issue has already been turned into **equity**.

clear or **clearing**. The process of **settlement** of transactions. The term *clear* or *clearing* is normally applied to the interbank payment system while *settle* or *settlement* is most often used for the securities markets. Confusingly, a **clearing house** may process either type of transaction. A transaction which does not clear is said to **fail** (cf. **aged fail**; **buy-in**; **sell-out**).

clear a position. To close out a **long** or **short** position, leaving no **position** (cf. **flat**; **matched book**).

clearing bank (Banking). (i) (USA) Any bank that **settles** corporate, **agency**, or federal securities on behalf of customers (cf. **fed wire**; **regular delivery**). See **clearing house bank**. (ii) (UK) One of twelve major banks which are actively involved in deposit-taking and lending within the banking system and are members of the Bankers' Clearing House Association.

clearing day. Any day of the week, except Saturday and Sunday and any legal bank holidays. Sometimes called a *business day*.

clearing fee. Charges made by a **clearing house** for settling transactions.

clearing float. The time required for a **cheque** to be cleared and the **funds** available. Often just called *float*.

clearing house. An organization that registers, monitors, matches, and, in the case of some markets (such as **futures** and **exchange-traded options**), acts as the **counterparty** to transactions and effects **settlement**. It may also be an organization that settles and acts as trustee for **bearer securities** in the international markets (cf. **Centrale de Livraison de Valeurs Mobilières**; **Euroclear**). See also **clearing system**.

Clearing House Automated Payments System (CHAPS) (Banking; UK). A network of linked computers operated by UK clearing banks providing rapid transfer of large balances (cf.

Bankers' Automated Clearing Services; Society for World-wide Interbank Financial Telecommunications).

clearing house bank (Banking; USA). A member bank of the **Federal Reserve System**.

clearing house funds. Funds held at and payments made through a **clearing house**. In the USA refers to payments made through **clearing house interbank payments system**, which are settled the same day through the **fed wire**. For *New York clearing house funds*, payments and receipts are made in **fed funds** on the next business day after clearing.

Clearing House Interbank Payments System (CHIPS) (Banking; USA). The New York Clearing House Association members' computerized **settlement** system for dollar transactions. Net positions between the various participating institutions are settled through the **fed funds** transfer system on the same day. Particularly useful in the **euromarkets**, transactions can be bundled and net payments agreed due to the advance notice nature of **spot** settlement.

clearing margin. The amount of **margin** required to be deposited by a **clearing member** with a **clearing house** to support its trading activity with the exchange (cf. **marked-to-market**). See **initial margin**; **maintenance margin**; **variation margin**.

clearing member. An exchange member who is also a member of the **clearing house** that settles trades made on the exchange. Note, to trade on an exchange you need to be a member, but not necessarily a clearing member. In **futures** markets, the clearing member is involved in guaranteeing its transactions with the clearing house, receiving and making **delivery** of the **underlying**, and management of the **margin** accounts with the clearing house.

clearing price. See settlement price.

clearing system. A transaction or depository system for efficient physical delivery of the **underlying** against **cash**. The two international security clearing systems are the **Centrale de Livraison de Valeurs Mobilières** and **Euroclear**, which handle securities such as **bonds**, **eurocommercial paper**, **American depository receipts**, and **equities**.

clientele effect. An explanation of why firms pay dividends at particular levels over time. It emphasizes the role to be played by the **portfolio** requirements and tax status of particular groups of investors. For example, **institutional investors**

prefer dividend flows to be both stable and predictable as this helps in the management of their liabilities. Such investors may also be exempt from income taxes on dividends, which provides an incentive for firms to be generous in their payout policies. The idea has been taken to its logical conclusion by BOC plc in the UK, where dividend payments where announced in advance of the financial year! See also **dividend policy.**

clipping or **clipping the coupon.** Physically detaching the **coupons** from **bearer bonds** to present for payment (cf. **paying agent; talon**).

cliquet option. See **barrier option.**

clone fund (USA). Term for an **investment company** set up to mimic an existing and successful competitor.

close. The last part of the trading session on an exchange. Definitions as to what constitutes the *closing period* vary (cf. **at the close; at the opening**). See also **closing range.**

close a position. Same as **close out.**

close company (Equities; UK). A company that is effectively controlled by, or where 50% of the assets in a winding-up would accrue to, five or fewer **shareholders** or shareholders who are also **directors** of the company. Such companies have special restrictions on distributions and other transactions which could be seen to benefit the controlling group directly. In the USA, known as a *closed company* or *corporation.*

closed corporation (USA). See **close company.**

closed economy. An economy that does not participate in international trade, such that it has no imports or exports. Although no such economy exists in practice, it provides a useful simplifying assumption to the analysis of how financial flows behave; for example, the relationship between consumption and **investment.** Sometimes called a *Robinson Crusoe economy.*

closed-end fund or **investment company** (USA). Alternative name for an **investment trust.** It is a type of **mutual fund** where the number of shares issued is fixed and they cannot be redeemed (cf. **open-end; unit trust**). Instead, shares in the fund are traded on the open market and may differ from the underlying **net asset value** per share (cf. **discount; premium**). See **investment trust company.**

closed-end mortgage. A type of mortgage against which no additional debt may be raised (cf. **open-end mortgage**).

closed mortgage-backed security. See mortgage-backed security.

closed out. When a futures **counterparty** fails to meet **margin requirements**, the **broker** will automatically **close out** his position and repay the outstanding margin left from the **initial margin.** The position is said to have been closed out. See also **margin call; variation margin.**

closed position. See **close out** (cf. **flat; match**).

closely held corporation (USA). A company where control is in the hands of a few **shareholders** (cf. **controlling interest**). It is not a privately held corporation since a **minority** of the stock may be traded.

close out. (i) Generally used to describe any transaction of an equal and opposite nature designed to neutralize an existing position. Also known as *liquidate.* (ii) For a **futures** position this involves selling a bought or **long** position and buying a sold or **short** position; in either cases, the close-out negates all contractual liability (cf. **open interest**). (iii) In the case of **forward contracts** it means the issuer of the contract agreeing to cancel or delay the completion of the contract (the latter is usually known as an extension or **rollover**).

close price. See **closing price.**

close up. When a dealer narrows the **bid-asked spread** (cf. **narrowing the spread**).

closing. (i) The process of completing a new issue or transaction on the **closing date.** (ii) It can also refer to the completion of a deal such as a reversal of a **switch**, a **long** position, or a **short** position (cf. **clear a position; close out**).

closing a market. See **narrowing the spread.**

closing date. The date on which the proceeds from a new issue or other transaction are paid by the **lead managers** and the securities are delivered to holders, in either definitive or **global note** form (cf. **global bond**). For eurosecurities this normally occurs ten to fifteen days after effecting the **subscription agreement.**

closing out. See **closed out.**

closing price. The price, or **spread** of prices, at which transactions are made just before the **close** of official business in a particular market (cf. **after-hours trading; opening price**). Such prices tend to be those reported in the financial press and used in portfolio valuation. Technical rules prevent manipulation of the closing price. See also **exchange delivery settlement price.**

closing purchase. An **option writer's** purchase of an exchange-traded **option** to cancel his initial obligation.

closing quote. The last **bid** and **offer** price recorded by a **market-maker** at the close (cf. **closing price**).

closing range. Normally the high and low price for the last fifteen minutes to half an hour of a trading session on an exchange (cf. **close**). Sometimes just called the *range*. See **closing price** (cf. **daily price limit**).

closing sale. An **option holder's** sale of an exchange-traded **option** with the same conditions as his holding to cancel his initial **position** (cf. **closing purchase**).

closing transaction. The ending of an **open** position by its corresponding offsetting transaction (cf. **close out**). For example, closing purchase transactions reduce **short** positions and closing sale transactions reduce **long** positions. See **closing purchase**; **closing sale**.

club deal (Banking). A **syndicated loan** facility in which each participant has an equal commitment and/or where the borrower has specified the participating lenders. Club deals are not normally sold down by the **lead managers** to other banks. Such transactions can often be done with little or no publicity (cf. **private placement**).

clustering of prices. The tendency of market prices to trade at certain levels. It is a phenomenon of the pricing mechanisms of markets that price changes cluster at round numbers, halves, quarters, eighths, and so forth, in descending order of frequency. For **futures** prices, the most common change is just one **tick**, the minimum price fluctuation allowed by the exchange.

cocktail currency. Used in **forward currency** contracts when the forward rate is fixed with respect to a basket of currencies.

cocktail swap. See **multi-legged swap**.

coefficient of determination (r^2; *r*-squared). A statistical measure of the 'goodness of fit' in a regression equation. It gives the proportion of the total variance of the forecasted variable that is explained by the fitted regression equation, i.e. the independent explanatory variables. If the model has more than one explanatory variable, the *adjusted* r^2 compensates for the upward bias in the result from using additional predictor variables.

co-finance. A method of lending which involves official and private lenders in the same transaction.

It is quite often used in development projects. The **lead manager** is often the official lender. The attraction of co-financing arrangements is that they reduce the amount of resources that need to be committed by the official lender while for the private lenders they have an official body as sponsor and umbrella.

COFI swap (USA). See **cost of funds index swap**.

coincident indicator. See **indicator**.

coinsurance. See **reinsurance**.

cointegration. An econometric or financial model for time-series analysis designed to predict whether two or more variables are linearly related (cf. **factor model**). If the values of these variables are plotted over time, we would expect them to move together. However, observations on these two variables may have a trend over time or may be drifting apart and are therefore not consistent with the modelling process. Nevertheless a linear regression of y_t on x_t may appear to fit the data very well and to give high *t*-statistics. Cointegration is a property of a data series which implies that the time series move together.

Formally, a series is integrated order d, denoted as $I(d)$, if after differencing it d times, it is stationary. A stationary time series is a series with a constant **mean** and **variance** over time and a **covariance** which depends on the time gap between the values rather than the period in time to which the observations relates. Consider a vector (x_t) consisting of n variables. These variables are said to be cointegrated if (i) each of the variables is integrated order $I(d)$, and (ii) there exists a vector $z_t = \alpha^1 X_t \sim I(d - b)$, where $b > 0$. The term α^1 is known as the cointegrating vector and the fact that the variables within X_t are cointegrated is denoted $X_t \sim CI(d, b)$. The cointegrating vector represents the long-run relationship between the variables in X_t and is therefore referred to as a long-run equilibrium relationship. Engle and Granger (1987) showed that, if we consider a vector which consists of two variables (y_t, x_t) which are $CI(1,1)$, then there exists an error correction model (ECM) representation of the form:

$$\Delta y_t = \alpha + \sum_{i=0}^{n} \beta_{1i}\Delta x_{t-1} + \sum_{i=1}^{n} \beta_{2i}\Delta y_{t-1} + \beta_3 z_{t-i} + \varepsilon_t$$

where $\varepsilon_t \sim iid(0, \sigma_\varepsilon^2)$. The ECM explains changes in y_t in terms of (lagged values) of changes in y_t itself, (lagged values) of changes in x_t, and the difference between y and its equilibrium value in the previous period.

A conventional approach to using cointegration (following the development of a theoretical model) is to test each variable for the order of integration $I(d)$. If the variables are all integrated to the same order (*d*), then test for the existence of a cointegrating vector. If this exists, formulate the ECM representation of the model, estimate the coefficients, and perform nested significance tests to delete non-significant coefficients to derive a parsimonious equation.

Many tests exist for testing for the order of integration of a time series. A common test is the Augmented Dickey–Fuller (ADF) test. To test the null hypothesis: $H_0: x_t \sim I(1)$ against $H_1: x_t \sim I(0)$, using the ADF test one would use ordinary least squares regression to estimate:

$$\Delta x_t = \delta_0 + \delta_1 t + \delta_2 x_{t-1} + \sum_{i=1}^{n} \delta_i \Delta x_{t-i} + \eta_t$$

where as many Δx_{t-i} terms as necessary are added to make η_t stationary. The *t*-statistic from the null hypothesis that $\delta_2 = 0$ would be compared to the critical values as given by Fuller (1976: 373, in the bottom part of table 8.5.2). If the *t*-statistic is closer to zero (the critical values are negative) than the critical value, then the null hypothesis cannot be rejected. Next, the restriction $\delta_1 = \delta_2 = 0$ has to be tested because stationarity requires that Δx_t is not time trended. In order to determine this, the F-statistic would be calculated from the restriction $\delta_1 = \delta_2 = 0$ and compared with the value for ϕ_3 in Dickey and Fuller (1981: 1063, table vi). If this F-statistic is less than the critical value, the null hypothesis cannot be rejected, and, provided the null that $\delta_2 = 0$ cannot also be rejected, then one would conclude that X_t is integrated of order $1 : I(1)$. When the number of variables in the X_t vector exceeds two, it is possible that multiple cointegrating vectors exist. To test different null hypotheses, each stating the number of cointegrating vectors, one might use the Johansen Maximum Likelihood procedure (Johansen 1988) as provided in many software routines using this modelling procedure. Cointegration offers an alternative approach to modelling time series data to that provided by ordinary least squares methods.

For details of the methods and signficance tests, see: D. A. Dickey and W. A. Fuller (1981), 'The likelihood ratio statistics for autoregressive time series with a unit root', *Econometric*, 49: 1057–72; R. F. Engle and C. W. Granger (1987), 'Cointegration and error correction: representation, estimation and testing', *Econometrica*: 50: 251–76; W. A. Fuller (1976), *Introduction to Statistical Time Series* (Wiley & Sons, New York); S. Johansen (1988), 'Statistical analysis of cointegrating vectors', *Journal of Economic Dynamics and Control*, 12: 231–54.

co-lead manager. The title given to an **underwriter** who has joint **lead manager** status and may be sometimes involved in an active role in structuring the transaction, although generally not **book running**, which is the lead manager's role. Such a **manager** will usually be a party to the **praecipuum**. (cf. **bracket**; **co-manager**; **selling group**).

collar. (i) A ceiling and floor interest rate placed upon the variability of the coupon rate on a **floating rate note** or the interest on a loan. (ii) The simultaneous purchase of an **interest rate cap** and sale of an **interest rate floor** in order to reduce the cost of the former. A collar where the **option premium** paid on the cap equals the floor premium received is known as a *zero-cost collar.* A collar is equivalent to a **vertical spread**. See also **participating forward**; **range forward**. (iii) Also used interchangeably to describe a **cylinder** (cf. **risk reversal**).

collared floating rate note (collared FRN) (Bonds). A **floating rate note** where there is both a maximum and a minimum permissible **coupon** rate. See **minmax floating rate note**.

collared forward (Forex). Type of **collar** or vertical spread created by buying and selling **puts** and **calls** on the forward foreign exchange rate. See also **breakforward**; **participating forward**; **range forward**.

collared offer (Equities; USA). A **tender offer** for stock which has an upper and a lower bound on the amount of stock to be made available by the tendering company.

collar hedge. A type of participating **hedge** where the value of a fixed rate **portfolio** is insured as to a minimum value whilst surrendering part of the potential gain. See also **participating collar**; **portfolio insurance**.

collar option. See **cylinder**.

collar swap. A swap involving a **fixed rate** against a **floating rate** when the latter has an upper and lower limit (cf. **collar**). See **minmax floating rate note**.

collateral. (i) A form of security against a borrowing other than a **guarantee** used to secure the ability of the borrower to repay (cf. **self-financing**). Often used to allow fund-raising against illiquid assets, such as property, or where the transaction costs of liquidating an asset would be substantial (which is called a *collateralized loan*). In most cases the amount of collateral required is significantly above the amount of the loan to take account of the potential costs of realizing the asset's value in the case of enforcement by the lender (cf. **factoring**). Sometimes referred to as a secondary lien or security rather than a primary lien or security, such as a guarantee, since it is the asset itself and not the borrower which makes the borrowing possible. See **asset-backed**; **collateralized bond**

obligation; **collateralized mortgage obligation**. (ii) Used in the **futures market** to secure the **credit worthiness** of the **clearing house** when undertaking trades (cf. **performance bond**). See **initial margin; maintenance margin; variation margin**.

collateralized automobile receivable securities (CARS) (Bonds). **Asset-backed bond** where the **underlying** are the inventory finance for car dealers.

collateralized bond obligation (CBO) (USA). A **synthetic security** created by issuing **bonds** secured on the **principal** and interest payments from a pool of **junk bonds**.

collateralized lease equipment obligations (CLEO) (Bonds; USA). **Asset-backed Securities** where the **underlying** are pools of lease receivables.

collateralized mortgage obligation (CMO) (Bonds; USA). A type of **mortgaged-backed bond** where the repayments of **principal** are separated into different **maturity** streams (cf. **asset-backed**). CMOs were developed to mitigate the problems of unpredictable repayment inherent in mortgage-backed securities. With a CMO the **pool** is divided sequentially by repayments (or **tranches**) and the **bonds** are designated by A-Class CMO (fast pay), B-Class CMO (medium pay), C-Class CMO (slow pay), and so on and may be divided into as many tranches as required. Redemption of the A-Class has to take place before the B-Class starts redemption and so on. Investors can choose the tranche(s) which most meets their expected maturity requirements. The final tranche is known as the **Z bond** CMO which is a **zero-coupon bond** until the other classes are redeemed and then becomes an interest and principal repaying security. A different approach is taken by the **Y bond** CMO which has the repayment profile of a bond with a **sinking fund** and, as a consequence, takes precedence over the other classes. There is also a **floating rate** CMO.

collateralized mortgage obligation equity (CMO equity) (USA). The residual entitlement to the cash flows in a **collateralized mortgage obligation** issue where the mortgage cash flows exceed the interest and principal repayments on the CMO **bond** series (A, B, C, etc., Y and Z bond). Also known as *CMO residual* or *z bond*.

collateralized mortgage obligation swap (CMO swap) (USA). **Interest rate swap** where the **notional principal** is linked to the repayment patterns on a **collateralized mortgage obligation** tranche.

collateralized swap. An **interest rate swap** or **cross-currency swap** where one of the parties provides **collateral** to safeguard the interest of the other. In such an arrangement, the amount of collateral required would need to cover the replacement of the transaction in the event of default, not the full amount; thus more collateral would be required for the cross-currency swap.

collateral risk. The **risk** that the lender will not be able to exercise his **lien** on the assets as security for the loan in the event of **default** (cf. **Chapter 11**).

collateral trust bond (USA). A **bond** issue that is secured by other securities which are normally held by a trustee under an **indenture** (cf. **defeasance**). Used, for example, by **parent** or **holding** companies to borrow against assets or securities held by **subsidiaries**.

collecting bank. See **remitting bank**.

collection. An instruction to a bank to submit a bill for payment, on behalf of a customer, for which it receives a fee but is not liable for non-payment (cf. **documentary credit**).

collection account. A specific account set up in an **asset-backed** security transaction to record receipts and payments on the pool of **underlying** assets.

collection float. The delays in obtaining funds from customers due to posting, processing, and **clearing** cheques.

collection ratio. A ratio that is used to measure the speed at which a business collects its debts. It is calculated by dividing total sales by 365 days to give an average daily sales rate and dividing this into the **accounts receivables** (cf. **ageing schedule**). Also known as the *average collection period*.

collective wisdom. Describes the body of knowledge said to encapsulate the standard ways in which financial markets will behave under various conditions. For example, when UK-listed companies make an **initial public offering** of **shares** it is normally expected that the price will be set at a slight **discount** to value in order to ensure a buoyant **aftermarket**. To this extent 'wisdom' may be nothing other than expected practice. It can also be influenced by historically observed trends as well as local market conditions. For instance, the discount to **net assets** seen with **investment trusts**. See **market forces**.

collusion. Sometimes overt but often covert arrangements between firms to agree pricing policies or general market behaviour, or both. For example, firms could agree to split-up a market such that each firm promises to stay within a particular sector, leaving it free to pursue its own strategies without fear of competition from other members of the colluding group. When such agreements are made formal they are called **cartels**. The incentives to break the rules can be high, not least because they rely on self-policing, which tends to make collusion unstable over longer periods of time. See also **concert party**.

Colombo Stock Exchange (Sri Lanka). 2nd Floor, Mackinnons Building, York Street, LK-Colombo 1 (tel. 94 1 446581; fax 94 1 445279).

colour. Market jargon for information and opinions. To give colour is to provide information on the current state of a market, sector, or security (cf. **taking a view**).

co-manager. An **underwriter** to a primary issue who is in the **manager bracket** but not having an active role in technical aspects of the transaction other than the issue's pricing (cf. **co-lead manager**; **lead manager**; **selling group**).

combination. An **option strategy** which involves both **put** and **call** options, usually on different terms. There are three basic kinds: **straddles** which involve only buying options, **ratio spreads** which involve different amounts on either side, and **box spreads** which include written options in the position (cf. **calendar spread**; **vertical spread**). See **option strategies**.

combination bond (USA). An **authority bond** issue which also carries the **full faith and credit** of the authority's **sponsor**.

combination matching. A portfolio strategy involving both the processes of **dedication** and **immunization**. A combination-matched portfolio is an immunized, **duration**-matched portfolio under which the first years of liabilities are **cash flow** matched. It is said to be useful when short-term liabilities are known with some certainty but long-term ones are uncertain.

combination spread A **long** position in a **call** or **put option** together with a **short** or written position in a put or call. A **bear spread** is designed to benefit from a fall in the price of the underlying; a **bull spread** from a rise, and a **calendar** spread from differences in **expiry dates**.

combination yield curve swap. Complex **interest rate swap** where one side of the transaction is based on the performance of one **reference rate** and the other is a package or combination of two or more reference rates. A single currency combination yield curve swap might entail one side paying six-month **London interbank offered rate** while the other pays a mixture of the two-year

rate, the five-year rate, the seven-year rate, and the ten-year rate. **Cross-currency swap** versions of the combination yield curve swap are also possible.

combined financial statement. See **consolidated accounts**.

combined leverage. See **leverage**.

combo. An option strategy involving a written **call** together with a purchased **put** at a lower **strike price** (cf. **risk reversal**; **straddle**; **strangle**). Also known as *splitting the strike*.

(*a*) **Payoff of a combo at expiry**

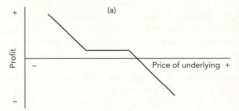

(*b*) **Payoff of splitting the strike at expiry**

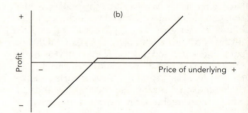

A written put at one strike price together with a purchased call at a higher strike price.

Comex. See **New York Commodity Exchange**.

comfort letter. An undertaking, which does not have the force of a contract, in which the party expresses its intention to meet certain conditions or take certain actions. For example, the parent company might issue a comfort letter expressing its intention (but not contracting) to support the subsidiary should it run into difficulties. See **letter of comfort**.

Comisión Nacional del Mercado de Valores (Spain). Regulatory agency for securities markets (cf. **Commission des Opérations de Bourse** (France); **Securities and Investments Board** (UK); **Securities and Exchange Commission** (USA)).

commercial bank. A bank which undertakes a range of banking services to companies and individuals. Examples of such services are: providing checking facilities; taking deposits; making loans; and supplying and receiving notes and coins. Such banks may offer additional trustee services and a range of securities advisory and transaction facilities (cf. clearing bank). In the USA, such banks are called money center banks or member banks; and in Continental Europe, they are known as credit banks. They are usually distinguished from investment banks or merchant banks. Where such institutions offer a full range of products and services such as foreign exchange, securities trading, and funds transfer to the widest possible client base, such as individuals, small and large firms, internationally as well as domestically, the description universal bank might apply. The distribution method used by such banks varies as between countries; for example, in the UK the system used relies upon an extensive branch network (hence *branch banking*); whereas in the USA, commercial banks can operate from one location, or a cluster of branches centred around different areas of the same state, or adjacent states (hence *unit banking*). Whatever the country, these institutions are regulated and supervised by a central bank. Sometimes called *joint-stock banks*.

commercial bank bond (Germany). See Bankschuldverschreibungen.

commercial bill or draft. See bill.

Commercial Company News Service (CCNS) (UK). London Stock Exchange's information service for company and economic news.

commercial credit company (USA). A financial institution which specializes in providing loans and leasing transactions to the business sector.

commercial hedgers. End users of commodities who participate in the markets in order to hedge the cost of their raw materials (cf. buying hedge; short hedge).

commercial loan sales. See asset sales (cf. subparticipation).

commercial paper (CP) (Money markets). A generic term for short-term promissory notes issued on an unsecured basis and depending on the credit worthiness of the issuer for repayment. Obligors may include sovereign states, sovereign agencies and other entities, state agencies and entities, state-owned companies, companies, financial institutions and banks or their holding companies. In the USA, such issues may not exceed a 270-day maturity, unless registered with the Securities and Exchange Commission (cf. medium-term notes). In other markets, such as the UK or Germany, the maturities may be up to 365 days. Gen-

erally issues are traded on the money markets and sold to investors via dealers. Issues which are sold on the international market are called eurocommercial paper (cf. euronotes). Each market has specific regulations governing the issuance and investment in commercial paper but it is generally seen as a professional (wholesale) market with large denomination transactions. It can be issued on a discount basis, or a discount-to-yield.

commercial real-estate index linked swap (CREIL). A type of index-linked swap where the underlying is an index of commercial property.

Commerzbank index (Equities; Germany). Arithmetic average index of the largest sixty companies.

commingling. The practice of mixing together monies or other assets held in different customer accounts by intermediaries for investment and/or administrative purposes. Although a convenience to the intermediary, some practices are forbidden in most jurisdictions, such as mixing proprietary and client money. See mutual fund.

Commissão de Valores Mobiliaros (CVM) (Brazil). Regulatory commission for the securities markets in Brazil.

commission. (i) A fee paid, usually for securities dealing, issuing, broking transactions, or arranging, as a fixed amount on either a flat or an annual basis (cf. concession). A fee is usually paid on a success basis by the principal to an independent intermediary for finding a counterparty or customer. (ii) Fee paid to a salesperson for success. A person uniquely remunerated on this basis, is deemed to be *commission only*. (iii) Another term for the round turn (cf. bid-offer spread).

Commissionarie (Italy). Commission brokers.

Commission Bancaire (Banking; France). Regulatory authority for the banking industry.

commission broker. A broker, who normally works on the floor of an exchange, who acts as an agent to execute trades in stocks, bonds, commodities, futures, or exchange-traded options (cf. crowd). See also local.

Commission des Opérations de Bourse (COB) (France). An autonomous administrative agency set up in 1967 for regulating the activities of exchanges (French: *Bourses*) and patterned after the United States' Securities and Exchange Commission. The agency has broad investigative, regulatory, and, where necessary, punitive powers. Its main functions as a regulatory agency are: oversight of published financial and other material related to issues and issuers; authorizing mutual funds; monitoring transactions (especially **insider dealing** and price manipulation, both of which are illegal practices in France) and market practice; and investigating complaints. Final decision-making is vested in a nine-member **board of directors**.

commissioned bank (Japan). A bank that is a party to a securities issue with some of the duties and functions of a **trustee**.

Commissione Nazionale per le Societáe la Borsa (CONSOB) (Italy). Regulatory authority set up in 1974 for regulating **quoted** companies, auditing practices and financial markets. Together with the **Bank of Italy**, the **central bank**, and the Consiglio di Borsa (Italian Stock Exchange Council), it is responsible for regulating the Italian Stock Market. See also **Commission des Opérations de Bourse** {France}; **Securities and Investments Board** {UK}; **Securities and Exchange Commission** {USA}.

commission house. See agency broker.

commission merchant. See floor broker.

commitment fee. A fee paid in a **committed facility** on undrawn funds as payment to the lenders in recompense of their obligation to advance funds as some future date. In some cases the fee is only payable on the undrawn portion of the loan. See also **underwriting**.

committed or **committed facility** or **committed line of credit** (Banking). Usually a **standby facility** where the lender has entered into an obligation to provide funds when the borrower asks (cf. **uncommitted**). This arrangement means that the lender has to provide funds whether it is convenient or not as long as the **conditions precedent** are in place. See **line of credit**.

Committee on Banking Regulations and Supervisory Practices. See Basle Committee (cf. **Bank for International Settlements**).

Committee on Uniform Securities Identification Procedures (CUSIP) (USA). An agreement by market participants to assign unique identification numbers to securities in order to facilitate identification and **settlement**. See also **CUSIP Number System**.

commodities; commodity. ('produce'). Generic term for traded raw materials and foodstuffs. The commodities markets cover a wide range and are generally divided into different types: hard commodities, which are further divided into precious metals and base metals; soft commodities or **softs**, which are generally perishables such as grains, coffee, or sugar; and energy, which consists of oil, natural gas, and other energy products. Commodities are traded both in **over-the-counter** markets and through organized exchanges. These latter typically have a degree of specialization, some concentrating on hard commodities, others on energy products or precious metals. The markets are divided into **cash** or physical **spot** markets and **forward** or **futures** markets (cf. **contract grade**). A breakdown of the principal categories is as follows.

- *Hard commodities*: base metals, including copper, tin, lead, nickel, zinc, aluminum (ingots, alloy); precious metals, including gold (bullion, coins), silver, platinum, palladium.
- *Soft commodities* ('softs') or *agriculturals*: cocoa, frozen orange juice, robusta coffee, coffee, sugar (raw, white), potatoes, cattle (feeder, live), pigs (hogs, pork bellies), lamb, broiler chickens, soybean (beans, meal, oil), grains (wheat, corn, barley, rice, oats), orange juice, coconut oil, palm oil, copra, cotton, wool, rubber.
- *Energy products*: oil (crude, heating, unleaded gasoline), natural gas, jet kerosene, electricity.
- *Miscellaneous*: freight, insurance, lumber.

SOME GENERAL COMMENTS ON PRICE MOVEMENTS:

The supply of agricultural products is highly seasonal and is affected by the weather. Significant price influences come from the activities of various trade organizations such as the International Coffee Organization. Price subsidies by governments or supra-governmental bodies are important; particularly within the **European Union**.

In terms of price behaviour there are real differences between the commodities markets and other financial markets:

1. There is a significant cost to holding the commodity due to warehousing, insurance, interest costs, and, possibly, freight charges. Except when availability is tight, cash commodities usually trade at a discount to forward positions, reflecting the costs of holding physical commodities, principally the costs of storage, insurance, and lost interest on the holding (a condition often called *normal backwardation*).

2. There exists the real possibility of price squeezes (either deliberate or unintentional) due to shortages of deliverable commodity to warehouses involved in **settlement** at the expiration of futures/forward contracts;

3. Commodities may be subject to significant *convenience yields* since there are usually only limited alternatives. Unlike financial assets which are held as investments in their own right, there is a value to a user of having an assured supply of a commodity for commercial use. For this reason they are sometimes known as *consumption assets*.

The general **market forces** dynamics of the different commodities markets are as follows: price movements are determined by demand less supply, less run-down in stocks, plus technical position with the positive or negative effect of speculative activity, depending on expectations of future price behaviour, shortages, and so on. The technical position of commodities markets is complicated due to the potential limits on the amount of the commodity that is deliverable or available at recognized warehouses, together with the costs associated with delivering additional stock to meet contractual obligations. In the forward or futures markets, most exchanges impose daily price **limits** on daily movements and positions in the market. Because of the cost of warehousing the underlying, the normal expectation is for the future price to be higher than the spot price. With soft commodities there is a natural annual cycle as the growing season advances and the new supply position becomes clearer.

Important indices: Reuters (base date: 18 September 1931 = 100); Dow-Jones (base date: 31 December 1974 = 100); Goldman Sachs Commodity Index (GSCI); Commodities Research Bureau price index (CRB) {USA} (base year 1967 = 100); Economist (The) Commodity Price Index (base year 1985=100).

Commodities Exchange Commission (CEC) (USA). A grouping of the New York Commodity Exchange, New York Mercantile Exchange, New York Coffee, Sugar and Cocoa Exchange, New York Cotton Exchange, and the New York Futures Exchange.

Commodities Research Bureau Price Index (CRB Index) (USA). Index of commodities prices compiled by the Commodities Research Bureau and on which a **futures contract** is traded. It has a **base year** of 100 in 1967.

commodity-backed bond. A bond issue where the interest payments or the principal redemption value are tied to the price of a commodity. Also sometimes called a *commodity-linked bond* since the transaction is **cash-settled**. In theory, it is supposed to provide a **hedge** against inflation since commodity prices are expected to maintain their real value. Variations on the structure include **bull-bear bonds** and bonds with **embedded options**, usually guaranteeing a minimum return, but offering unlimited **upside**.

commodity-based. (i) Any security or structure which has a link to the behaviour of **commodities**. (ii) Applied to an economy which is dependent on commodities for its foreign earnings.

commodity broker. See broker; broker-dealer; commission broker.

Commodity Credit Corporation (CCC) (USA). A federal agency of the Department of Agriculture responsible for price support programmes for **soft commodities**. The agency will advance **non-recourse** loans against produce **collateral** to farmers participating in its price support programmes.

commodity currency. The **currency** that forms the quotation in **foreign exchange**. The **base currency** is the currency against which it is measured. Most currencies are quoted in **European terms**, where the non-dollar currency is the commodity currency. A few currencies are quoted in **American terms**, where the US dollar is the commodity currency.

commodity derivative. Any of a number of **derivative** contracts on an individual commodity, a commodity **basket**, or a commodity index. These may be **exchange traded** or **over the counter**. See also **commodity futures; commodity option; commodity swap**.

commodity exchange. An organized market for the buying and selling of **commodities**. The exchanges can be of two sorts, either **cash markets**, where the physical product is bought and sold for immediate delivery (cf. **actuals**); or **futures markets** which deal in deferred **settlement** and are used for managing the **price risk** for producers and consumers through **arbitrage, hedging, speculation**, or **spreading** transactions. See **stock exchange; over the counter**.

Commodity Exchange (comex) (US). 4 World Trade Center, New York, NY 10048, (tel. 1 212 938 2900; fax 1 212 432 1154). Established on 5 July 1933. Major contracts are gold, silver, copper, and aluminium. There is also a **stock index future** contract on the **Euro-Top 100 Index**.

commodity fund. Pooled fund which invests in commodity futures and **options**.

commodity futures. Futures contracts on commodities (cf. **spot market**). These have standard terms and conditions as to amounts, purity, type, location, and other specifications allowing for the development of a liquid market (cf. **assay; contract grade**). For example, below are the nickel contract traded on the **London Metal Exchange**, and the dry milk contract traded on the **New York Coffee, Sugar and Cocoa Exchange**. See also **base metals; energy futures; soft commodities**.

LME PRIMARY NICKEL: SPECIFICATION

- *Quality*: The nickel delivered under this contract must be Primary Nickel of minimum 99.80% purity with chemical analysis conforming to the current ASTM specification.

- *Shapes and weights*: All nickel delivered must be: (*a*) of the production of those producers named in the LME-approved list: (*b*) in the form of either cathodes or pellets or briquettes. In the case of cathodes, deliveries shall be made in the form of sizes cut to either 100 mm × 100 mm (4 in. × 4 in.), 50 mm × 50 mm (2 in. × 2 in.) or 25 mm × 25 mm (1 in. × 1 in.) size tolerances in accordance with internationally accepted trade practice. Each warrant shall consist of only one size. All nickel delivered shall be packed in sound steel drums with a net weight of minimum 150 kg. and maximum 500 kg. Each warrant shall consist of drums of uniform size and weight. The gross and net weights must be clearly marked/stamped on each individual drum together with the producer's or brand name.

- *Warehouse inspection of drummed primary nickel*: Nickel in original producer drums with Ring Dealing or Associate Clearing Member guarantee. Nickel in original producer drums with producer seal intact can be placed on LME Warrant without opening every drum under certain conditions, namely: (*a*) that the ring Dealing or Associate Clearing Member warranting the material certifies in writing that all the nickel in any one delivery is from one source known to that Member; (*b*) that the certificate should identify the nickel with drum numbers or other markings specific to the certified volume; and (*c*) that the warehouse opens one drum in ten from each batch so certified. The one drum in ten is to be selected at random from the batch. Provided that this inspection confirms that the contents of the opened drums conform to the producer markings for both product and weight, the warehouse is permitted to enter the other drums into the stock unopened.

  The warehouse should mark each drum with its distinguishing mark or seal identifying the warehouse and indicating that the drums were entered into stock uninspected.

  The warehouse will be required to retain the Member certification on record for a minimum of six months after withdrawal of the nickel from that LME-listed warehouse. Any complaint which might arise after withdrawal can be taken via the Member concerned, with the help of the warehouse, with the Member who provided the original certification.

  All other nickel in drums: All other drummed nickel to be placed on LME Warrant must, without exception, be opened and emptied on arrival by the LME-listed warehouse and the nickel inspected, repacked, and resealed in original drums where possible. This includes: producer nickel in original producer drums where there is no written Member guarantee; producer nickel in unmarked drums; producer nickel in original drums which are in unsafe condition and/or where the seals are broken; repacked producer nickel; producer nickel which has been withdrawn from LME-listed warehouse and is subsequently presented for re-warranting. The warehouse will be responsible for resealing all inspected drums using their own numbered seals. All costs incurred will be for account of the party instructing the warehouse to place the material on Warrant.

- *Size of lot*: 6 tonnes.

- *Warrants*: Warrants shall be for 6 tonnes each (2% either more or less). Each parcel of 6 tonnes shall be the product of one producer in one country, and shall consist of one shape and size and shall lie in one warehouse. Each warrant must state the name of the producer, the shape, the dimension of cathodes where applicable, the gross and net weights, and the numbers of the drum seals making up each parcel.

- *Major currency*: US dollars.

- *Minimum price movement*: US$1 per tonne.

- *Delivery dates*: Daily for three months forward; then every Wednesday for the next three months; and then every third Wednesday of the month for the next nine months. (A total of fifteen months forward.)

NYCSCE: NON-FAT DRY MILK FUTURES CONTRACT. CALLS FOR DELIVERY OF EXTRA GRADE OR BETTER NONFAT DRY MILK FOB WESTERN REGION,

- *Trading unit*: 44,000 lbs in 25-kilo bags.

- *Trading hours*: 2.15 p.m. to 3.15 p.m. New York time.

- *Price quotation*: Cents per pound.

- *Delivery months*: February, May, July, September, November.

- *Ticker symbol*: MU.

- *Minimum fluctuations*: 5/100 cent per lb, equivalent to $22.00 per contract.

- *Daily price limits*: (from previous day's settlement price) 6.00 cents with variable limits effective under certain conditions. No price limits on two nearby months.

- *Standards*: Non-fat dry milk shall meet the requirements of USPHS/FDA Extra Grade or better. It shall be manufactured using low heat and shall have a moisture content of not more than 4.00%. On the Exchange business day following the last trading day the non-fat dry milk shall not be less than one day or more than 150 days old.

- *Last trading day*: First Friday of the delivery month.

- *Notice day*: First Exchange business day following the last trading day.
- *Position limits*: 1,000 contracts net on the same side of the market in any one month and in all months combined. 250 contracts net on the 2nd Friday before the last trading day of an expiring contract. Combine published 'futures equivalent' ratios of option positions. Exemptions may apply for hedge, straddle, and arbitrage positions. Contact the Exchange for more information.

Commodity Futures Trading Commission (CFTC) (USA). The federal regulatory agency charged by Congress with overseeing the activities of futures trading, in particular **commodity futures**, created by the Commodity Futures Trading Act of 1974. It is responsible for the trading practices of the individual futures and commodity exchanges, authorizes new commodity contracts, and has, like the **Securities and Exchange commission**, investigative and disciplinary powers. All the commissioners are presidential appointees who are confirmed by Congress.

commodity index futures. Futures contracts on an **index** of **commodities** (cf. **spot market**). These are similar to **stock index futures** in that they are **cash settled**. The example below is a contract traded on the **Chicago Mercantile Exchange** and is based on a futures index produced by Goldman Sachs Inc. Specific commodity futures are also traded (cf. **base metals; energy futures; soft commodities**).

GSCI$^{TM/SM}$ FUTURES

- *Ticker symbol*: GI.
- *Trading unit*: $250 times the GSCI Nearby Index (e.g. $190.4 \times \$250 = \$47,600$).
- *Price quote*: Index points.
- *Minimum price fluctuation (tick)*: 0.10 Index points, equivalent to $25 per contract.
- *Daily price limit*: None.
- *Contract months*: February, April, June, August, October, December.
- *Trading hours (Chicago time)*: 8.15 a.m.–2.15 p.m.
- *Last day of trading*: The fourth business day of the contract month.
- *Settlement*: Cash settled to the final GSCI. Nearby Index on the last trading day.

OPTIONS ON GSCI$^{TM/SM}$ FUTURES

- *Ticker symbols*: Calls: GI; puts: GI.
- *Underlying contract*: One GSCI futures contract.
- *Strike prices*: 2 GSCI points e.g. 190, 192, etc. (Half-interval strike prices for contract month nearest maturity, e.g. 190, 191, 192, etc.).
- *Premium quotations*: US dollars per Index point.

- *Minimum price fluctuation (tick)*: .10 Index points ($25 per contract) (cabinet = $12.50) (A trade may occur at the value of a half-tick (cabinet).)
- *Daily price limit*: None.
- *Contract months*: February, April, June, August, October, December, and serial months.
- *Trading hours (Chicago time)*: 8.15 a.m.–2.15 p.m.
- *Last day of trading*: February bi-monthly cycle contracts: the fourth business day of contract month; serial months: first Friday of serial month that is business day.
- *Minimum performance bond*: No performance bond required for put or call option buyers, but the premium must be paid in full; option sellers must meet additional performance bond requirements as determined by the Standard Portfolio Analysis of Risk (SPAN®) performance bond system.
- *Exercise procedure*: An option may be exercised by the buyer up to and including the last day of trading. To exercise, the clearing member representing the buyer submits an Exercise Notice to the Clearing House by 7.00 p.m. on the day of the exercise. Any long in-the-money option position not liquidated or exercised prior to termination of trading will be automatically exercised. (Consult your broker for specific requirements.)

Note: The GSCI$^{TM/SM}$ Nearby Index is owned by and proprietary to Goldman Sachs.

commodity-linked bond. Any of a range of **bonds** where the returns are linked to the performance of an **underlying** that is a **commodity**, a commodity **index**, or the **spread** between two commodities.

commodity-linked interest rate swap. Type of **interest rate swap** contract where one party pays a variable rate while the **counterparty** pays a fixed rate where the payments are linked to the price of a commodity, for example:

$$\text{Payment} = |\text{Fixed commodity price} - (\text{spot commodity price})_t|$$

The effect of such an arrangement is to make the counterparty's payment inversely related to the movement in the commodity price. If the commodity price had a significant negative impact on the firm, such a transaction would link the cost of its borrowings to the variability in the cash flows from changes in the spot commodity price. See also **commodity swap**.

commodity option. An option on a **commodity**. The **exchange-traded** options are usually of the **option on futures** type, while the **over-the-counter** options are either **cash settled** or require

physical delivery. Pricing such options is the same as pricing a non-dividend paying **stock** (cf. **convenience yield**). See **option pricing**.

commodity paper. A form of financing involving the pledging of raw materials as security for the debt. Evidenced either by a **bill** of lading or by a **trust receipt** by the holder.

commodity price-for-interest-swap or **commodity swap.** A type of **swap** contract in which the payment streams are a **commodity** price times a **notional principal** amount and where one leg is fixed and the other floating. **Settlement** involves the fixed rate payer paying the floating rate payer if the commodity price is below the fixed rate and vice versa if above. As such it has the same effect as a **forward** or un-margined **futures** contract position. The most common type involves cash payments for settling the differences, although some swaps require physical delivery. Such commodity swaps have been in existence since the 1970s and are a useful supplement to the normal **hedging** instruments available in the **commodities markets** allowing producers and consumers to hedge their **market risk**. In such a situation, the consumer of the commodity would normally be the fixed payer (that is paying a variable amount for the product) while the producer a floating rate payer (that is receiving a fixed amount for the product). Key requirements for commodity swaps are: market size, with a two-way flow of business between consumers and producers, and a homogeneous product. Areas where such swaps have been effectively undertaken, either through bilateral agreements or intermediated by financial institutions, are: oil, **gold**, base metals, and soya beans. See also **flat rate forward**.

commodity semi-fixed swap. Commodity swap where the **fixed rate payer** agrees to pay one of two **fixed rates** on the **notional principal** amount depending on the price performance of the **floating rate** side. If the floating rate should trade through a **trigger price**, the fixed rate payer pays the higher price. The alternative, where the fixed rate payer initially pays the higher price and pays the lower price if the floating rate side moves above a predetermined point. To create the structure, the originator of the swap incorporates a **binary option** into the transaction. See **semi-fixed swap**.

commodity swap. (i) An agreement between two parties to exchange a given amount of a commodity at two **warehouses** to avoid transportation costs (cf. **exchange for physical**). (ii) Type of **interest rate swap** where the parties agree to exchange a fixed price for a commodity for a variable price. There are several types of swaps: *fixed-for-floating commodity swaps* have one party paying (receiving) a fixed price on a notional physical quantity of the commodity against receiving (paying) the current **spot price**; *basis commodity swaps* involve exchanges in the price of a commodity based on two different **reference rates** (thus an oil producer might wish to hedge the price differentials between **West Texas Intermediate** and **Brent crude** through such a swap); *backwardation* and *contango commodity swaps* aim to lock in the differentials between the spot price and a forward of futures price. These have the same effect as a **yield curve swap**. See also **commodity-linked interest rate swap**.

Commodity Trading Advisor (CTA) (USA). Individual or firm registered with the **Commodities Futures Trading Commission** to provide advice on investments in **commodities**.

commodity trust unit (USA). Exchange-traded securities allowing the holders to have direct exposure to commodities through indirect ownership over a longer time-frame than would be available through **commodity futures** contracts.

commodity warrant. A **warrant** giving the holder the right to receive a fixed amount of a given **commodity**. Such issues are generally **cash settled** and are issued either by producers or by financial intermediaries to investors. Such warrant issues generally have a much longer **expiry date** than **exchange-traded options** on commodity futures. Not to be confused with a **warehouse warrant**.

Common External Tariff (CET). A single rate of duty imposed on imports coming from third countries by a group of states. For example the **European Union** uses a CET or Common Customs Tariff (CCT) on goods cleared into the Community.

Common Market. See **European Union**.

common shareholders' equity (Banking). Given the use of **subordinated** capital, this is the **core capital** of a bank.

common shares (Canada; USA). **Common stock** (cf. **ordinary shares**). See also **preferred stock**.

common stock (common share or **ordinary share).** Ownership rights, usually issued in the form of a certificate that represents participation in the ownership of an enterprise. Holders normally benefit from voting privileges on company resolutions, the payment of **dividends**, limited access to the firm's financial statements, proportionate share of the **assets** in any liquidation or sale, subscription privileges for new shares (**pre-emptive rights**), and **limited liability** (cf. **bearer**

participation certificate; participation certificate; preferred stock). An individual or institution who owns stock is called a *shareholder* or *stockholder*. Sometimes misleadingly called *equity*. A *common stock certificate* is a **certificate** evidencing ownership of a quantity of common stock.

common stock equivalents. Certain types of securities, such as **convertibles, equity warrants,** and **stock options** that are substantially equivalent to **common stock**. A **controlling interest** in a firm can be built up using common stock equivalents.

common stock fund (USA). A **mutual fund** which invests uniquely in **common stocks** (cf. **balanced mutual fund**).

common stock ratios. See **ratio analysis**.

common stock with a put. See **puttable stock**.

Commonwealth bond (Australia). A Treasury bond issued by the federal government. Maturities range out to twenty-five years and, like **gilt-edged**, they pay interest semi-annually on a 365-day year basis.

Commonwealth Development Corporation (UK). A **joint venture** agency set up in 1953 between UK companies, banks, and the **Bank of England** to provide loans to UK companies operating in the Commonwealth.

Commonwealth of Australia notes and **bonds** (Australia). Commonwealth government **treasury note** and **bond** issues offered in the domestic market.

communal bond. (i) See **municipal bond**. (ii) (Germany) Bond issues by the largest German banks. See **Kommunalobligationen**.

community bank (Banking). A local bank. See **savings bank**.

commutation. An agreement to receive an up-front payment in exchange for foregoing future income rights, for example on an occupational pension.

Compagnie des Agents de Change (Equities; France). See **Société des Bourses Françaises**.

Compagnie des Agents de Change 40 Index (CAC-40) (France). Principal market **index** for French **common stocks** traded on the **Paris Bourse** of the forty leading **stocks** in their sectors. It is the most watched index of French equities and has **futures** and **options** contracts written on it. It has a **base date** of June 1988.

Compagnie Française pour l'Assurance du Commerce Extérieur (COFACE) (France). Set up in 1947 by the French government to administer their export finance and guarantee programmes. It provides protection to exporters for commercial and political risks, including in some cases **foreign exchange risk**. The agency's capital is held by the major French banks.

company. A body corporate, where regulation is governed by statute and is likely to have **share capital**. It is a form of business organization which in law has a separate legal existence to that of the owners. Such a company or *corporation* may be incorporated (*inc*) giving it the right to own assets and act as if it were a person. If the company benefits from **limited liability**, it is known as a **limited company**; alternatively, where the liability of its owners is not restricted to the paid-up capital and guarantees, it is an unlimited company. If it is listed on a recognized **stock exchange**, shares in it may be bought by the public; if restrictions exist on ownership it is generally known as a private company (*pty*).

There are several ways within different countries of creating companies; probably the most common method is by some form of official and formal registration. Important features of any legal framework for the operation of companies are whether **capital** can be raised directly from the public, and the extent to which company **directors** can be held personally liable for company debts. These two characteristics are usually captured by a word meaning 'public', and a phrase or abbreviation indicating limited liability in the company name. Hence, in the UK the postscript *plc*; in the US, *inc.*; *GmBH* in Germany; in France *SARL*; in Italy *SpA*; and in Australia *PTY*. Companies can have share capital, with limited liability but those shares being publicly traded. Such entities are called **private companies**. See also **close company; charter; joint stock company; memorandum and articles of association**.

Company Announcements Samizo (CANS) (UK). An information service which gives full text company announcements, directly from companies, via **Teletext Output of Price Information by Computer**.

Company Bulletin Board Service (Equities; UK). Experimental market in very small capitalization issues on the **London Stock Exchange** undertaken between April and November 1992 (cf. **wabo; waso**). Subsequently replaced by the **Stock Exchange Alternative Trading Service** and the **Alternative Investment Market**.

company doctor. A specialist practitioner drafted into a troubled **company**, at the request of management or the creditors, with the responsibility of improving performance so that the company might continue, or be sold for the best price. See **turnaround**.

comparative advantage. The relative advantage one institution has in terms of cost of funds in a particular market, due to **credit worthiness**, regulations, or familiarity. Thus, a US corporation would, all things being equal, tend to have a comparative advantage in issuing in the US domestic market compared to a similar foreign corporation (cf. **yankee**).

comparison ticket (USA). The acknowledgement of a transaction's details prior to **settlement** (cf. **confirmation**; **out-trade**).

compensating balance (Banking). A deposit that must be made with a lender when borrowing. It may be part of the loan agreement or an informal market practice (as in Japan).

compensation fund (UK). An insurance fund maintained by the **London Stock Exchange** to recompense investors should a **member firm** be unable to meet its obligations (cf. **hammered**).

compensation trading. See barter.

compensatory finance. The term given to a facility provided by the **International Monetary Fund** under their adjustment programmes to help compensate for changes in value of a member country's export earnings. The facility has usually been provided in the case of changes in price for **commodity** exports rather than manufactured products or services.

competent authority (UK). For matters relating to economic and financial affairs, it is the Secretary of State for Trade and Industry (President of the Board of Trade).

competitive auction. A system for issuing securities, normally government debt issues (cf. **non-competitive bid**). Under an English-style (*discriminatory price auction*), bidders buy securities at their **bid price** if they bid above the **tender** or **stop price** [if they bid below they receive any unsold securities]. Under a **Dutch auction** type all bidders receive the same price (*unitary price auction*), that is, bidders buy securities at the stop price if their bid is above the stop price. It should be noted that UK **gilt-edged** securities are sold using a Dutch auction.

competitive bid. (i) The process of seeking auction or **tender** bids for the issuance of securities, either by individual investors or via **underwriting syndicates** (cf. **bought deal**). (ii) (USA) The bid made at a **US Treasury Auction** at a specific **price**

for an agreed amount (cf. **competitive auction**; **non-competitive bid**). (iii) Any competitive tendering for a contract. Colloquially known as a *beauty parade*.

competitive devaluation. Currency devaluation aimed at improving the competitiveness of exports and reducing the competitiveness of imports. The intent of **devaluation** is to improve the **balance of payments** position, but here it is not because of a **fundamental disequilibrium**, but rather as a way of ensuring the comparative price advantage of exports, or the relative unattractiveness of import prices. Clearly, a spiral of such exchange rate changes could occur with each country trying to maintain international price competitiveness and ensure a share of world trade. The long-term effect of the continuance of such policies would be to beggar everybody as buyers would come to expect lower prices, caused by exchange rate adjustments, with suppliers finding domestic costs not being covered and going out of business. It is to avoid such outcomes that bodies like the **International Monetary Fund** and the **World Trade Organization** (formerly the **General Agreement on Tariffs and Trade**) exist. Such a policy is sometimes called *beggar-thy-neighbour*.

competitive offering. An issue of securities made by a **competitive auction**.

completion program (USA). The transfer of oil and gas reserves by a wildcatter to a **limited partnership** once the find is proven to be commercially viable. A relatively low-**risk** investment strategy since the partnership does not take the risk of a dry hole.

completion risk. The risk in **project finance** that the project will not be completed (and hence generate positive cash flows).

completion undertaking. An undertaking for a **project finance** borrower either to complete a project to specification at or before a certain date or to repay the borrowing if the project is not completed.

complex chooser options. A variant on the **chooser option** where the two alternatives in the option may have different **strike** or **exercise prices** and/or **expiry dates**. Thus the call alternative may have a strike at 100 and expiry in six months, the put at 80 with expiry in four months. The holder has to decide which alternative the option will become prior to the expiry of the earlier alternative.

complex conversion. A type of **conversion** embedded in a **bond** issue which incorporates both **bond conversion** and **currency conversion** (cf. **embeddos**).

complexity theory. A theory that builds on existing economic, behavioural, and management theories by integrating the findings of the physical sciences, computer science, mathematics, and the theory of evolution. It is applicable to the properties, behaviour, and evolution of complex organizational, technological, and economic systems with special reference to unpredictability of chaotic systems and the dynamic, creative, evolutionary, innovative, and non-equilibrium conditions observed in the world.

compliance. Methods for ensuring that financial market operators meet any legal and supervisory requirements. These could include: avoidance of conflicts of interest, fraud, and abuse of **insider information**. It may also refer to the systems that monitor trading behaviour and the setting of minimum standards of training and competency (cf. **Stock Watch**). Most financial institutions have a **compliance officer** whose responsibility it is to ensure that the internal systems are working and are capable of withstanding external scrutiny. See also **chinese walls; firewalls; securities and Exchange Commission;** Securities and Investments Board.

compliance department. The department within exchanges charged with monitoring market activity to ensure adherence to the exchange's rules and regulations and to the law (cf. **Stock Watch**).

compliance officer. A person responsible for ensuring that the staff of a financial firm conduct their personal and professional dealings according to house rules. See **insider dealing**.

composite (Equities; UK). Term given to an insurance company which engages in a number of lines of insurance activity (e.g. life insurance and general insurance).

composite index. An **index** created by adding together different types of securities. In the UK, the **Financial Times-Actuaries All Share Index** is a composite index since it includes most market sectors. In the USA, the **New York Stock Exchange composite index** is likewise. Normally a composite index will show the broad market change while the **sector** or industry indices will give details of specific performance. Composite indices are often used for **indexing**.

compound annual return (CAR). The return obtainable through compounding of interest expressed on an annual basis (cf. **compound yield**). See **annual percentage rate; compound interest; decompounding; interest rate calculations; yield-to-maturity**.

compound growth rate. The growth rate based on reinvestment of the income. Also known as the *price relative*. See **compound interest**.

compound interest. Interest calculated as if it was partially paid on an intermediate and that partial payment was then reinvested to the actual payment date, generating additional *interest on interest* (cf. **simple interest**). Thus a sum of £100 invested at 10% p.a. will give £110 at the end of the first year; £121 at the end of the second year; and £133.10 in the third, and so forth. The effective interest rate, expressed as a decimal, will depend on the number of compounding intervals in the year based on the following formula:

$$\text{Effective interest rate} = \left[1 + \left(\frac{\text{Nominal rate}}{\text{Frequency (n)}}\right)\right]^n - 1$$

Compound option

Number of compounding periods in the year	Effective interest rate
1 (once per annum; annually)	10
2 (semi-annual)	10.25
3	10.33
4 (quarterly)	10.38
6 (bi-monthly)	10.43
12 (monthly)	10.47
52 (weekly)	10.51
365 (daily)	10.52
Continuously compounded rate	10.52

The compounded rate or effective interest rate is not to be confused with the **flat rate**. Thus a monthly interest rate of 1% would have a flat annual rate of (1% × 12) or 12%, but the compounded annual equivalent rate would be significantly higher $[(1 + 0.01)^{12} - 1] \times 100\%$, or 12.683%. See also **decompounding; interest rate calculations**.

compound interest rate option. Compound option where the **underlying** is an interest rate option.

compound net annual return (CNAR). The after-tax basis, compound annual return.

compound option. Type of **option** where the **underlying** is itself an option (i.e. it is an option on an option) (cf. **cacall; caput**). It offers a **leveraged position** on the underlying of the option into which it can be **exercised** and is priced not in relation to the option position on exercise, but in relation to the underlying itself. The **leverage** comes from the fact that the **volatility** of compound options is increased by the underlying option. It is used to **hedge** contingent exposures where there is some uncertainty whether the underlying option is required, as might be the case in a bid to undertake a project and where, for instance, the **foreign exchange exposure** needed to be hedged. A compound option could reduce the cost of obtaining protection at the bidding stage but this might be at the expense of a higher **all-in cost** if successful due to the additional cost of the **option premium** on the second option leading to the paying of two option premiums. See also **caption**; **floortion**.

compound or **compounded value**. The return from an investment where the interest and any principal are reinvested before maturity. Also known as the **internal rate of return** or the **yield** (cf. **yield-to-maturity**).

comptant (France). Term for **cash** or **spot settlement** of a transaction.

comptroller. The senior financial officer in an organization. See also **finance director**; **treasurer**.

Comptroller of the Currency (USA). The official responsible for regulating the national banking system (and hence nationally **chartered banks**) by chartering, examining, supervising and, if necessary, issuing reports on the condition of individual banks or liquidating them. It is an office of the United States Treasury Department. Together with the **Federal Reserve** and **Federal Deposit Insurance Corporation** (FDIC) it is one of the main bank regulators in the USA. Note that state chartered banks may or may not be regulated by the Comptroller.

compulsory liquidation or **winding-up** (UK). The forced winding-up of a company by court order (cf. **administration order**; **members' voluntary liquidation**). This is normally due to the action of one or more creditors seeking payment. It is the only means by which a creditor can bring about the winding-up of the company and a distribution of its value (cf. **bankruptcy**; **default**; **insolvency**).

computer leasing receivable security (Bonds). Asset-backed security where the **underlying** are computer leases.

Computer Readable Services (CRS) (UK). London Stock Exchange's online market price information system.

computer-to-computer interface (CTCI) (USA). Computer link between transactions undertaken on the **National Association of Securities Dealers Automated Quotation System** and brokers' in-house systems.

concentration. The degree to which an industry or activity is undertaken by a small group of firms.

concentration banking. Using a bank to act as a recipient of balances transmitted from several deposit accounts or other banks. See **multi-currency cash concentration**; **single currency cash concentration**.

concentric merger (Mergers and acquisitions). A type of **merger** where the two companies coming together share some common expertise that may possess mutually advantageous spin-offs. For example, managerial or technological know-how that may not be industry or product-specific (cf. **congeneric merger**; **conglomerate merger**; **horizontal merger**; **vertical merger**).

concertina swap. A type of **interest rate** or **cross-currency swap** transaction aimed at replacing the existing swap with another, at **market swap**.

concert party. (i) (UK) Said to occur when a group of **traders** or institutions agree to pursue a particular course of action in order to further the aims of one or more of them. Those in the party that do not share directly in the common goal receive a fee for their involvement. Concert parties typically arise when an entity or individual wishes to acquire a larger stake in a firm without disclosing the fact, as required under the Companies Act, 1985 (cf. **controlling interest**). An example would be when the adviser to a company wishing to take another company over requests other market operators to acquire shares in the **target** company on its behalf such that no individual holding breaches the disclosure limit (currently 3% of outstanding **ordinary shares**). This would, it is hoped, have the effect of not requiring the acquiring company to declare openly its interest in the other company, consequently increasing the share price and thus making the target company more expensive to acquire (cf. **mergers and acquisitions**). See **City Code on Takeovers and Mergers**. (ii) It can also have the much more innocent meaning of a grouping of investors who share a common purpose that may be better served by coordinating their market actions (cf. **investment club**).

concession. When some aspect of securities trading is available at a discount as a fixed amount on either a **flat** or an **annual basis** (cf. **commission**).

Concordat. See Basle Capital Convergence Accord.

conditional bargain (UK). A transaction which is dependent on a certain event, e.g. **shareholders'** approval. Such transactions typically take place in response to activities such as a **vendor placing**. The **London Stock Exchange** has to give prior agreement to such transactions in order to prevent the development of a false market.

conditional bond. See performance bond.

conditional bond sales. Another term for a repurchase agreement.

conditional forward purchase contract. See breakforward.

conditionality. A condition of balance of payments assistance to a country by the International Monetary Fund (IMF) which stipulates that one of the conditions governing the provision of IMF support is that policy steps are taken to resolve the underlying problem.

conditional order. Any instruction to a broker or agent which is dependent on some event to become effective. Thus a stop-loss would only be activated if the price went below some set value (or above, in the case of a purchase instruction). Conditional orders can be of four basic types: price, timing, outcome, and activity. The price condition would involve setting a transaction price, as with the stop-loss. The timing condition sets the length of time the order may be valid, or when it is to be executed (cf. at the close; good until cancelled). The outcome condition defines the desired end-result of the instruction. Thus a one-cancels-the-other instruction has the first of two instructions being carried out automatically cancelling the unexecuted one. The activity condition defines how the transaction is to be (or should be) executed. For instance, the principal can stipulate whether part of an order is to be executed or that the order is to be executed after a certain volume of trading has occured (cf. do not reduce; fractional discretion order).

conditional prepayment rate (CPR). A calculation made for prepayment models typically used for mortgage-backed securities where the paydown rate is stated in annualized terms and which assumes constant monthly prepayments as a percentage of the remaining principal balance.

conditional sale/purchase. A transaction which is subject to prior conditions before becoming absolute. This is typical of mergers and acquisitions where due diligence is required before the transaction is finalized. In some cases, there may be a price adjustment to reflect new information uncovered during the course of the investigation, for instance, adjustments to the value of stock or inventory being acquired.

conditional sale lease. See hire purchase (cf. lease).

conditions precedent. The contractual actions required to be complied with by a party to a transaction before it can be implemented (e.g. a borrower of funds before the funds are made available). The condition normally requires the contractor to satisfy the conditions of the contract, including evidence that all legal conditions have been met (for instance, that the contractor is legally able to enter into the contract). Conditions precedents normally apply at the start of the transaction and at any subsequent point where the risk of the contracting party may change (e.g. when additional or re-borrowings are made) (cf. breach of covenant; default; revolving credit facility; rollover).

condor (CO). An option combination designed to take a view on future volatility without having a directional view on the underlying (cf. vertical spread). It is similar in approach to a butterfly (which is based on a straddle), except that the written options are at two different strikes, and the condor is based on a strangle. While strangles have the potential for unlimited profit as long as the price of the underlying moves out of a certain range, the condor restricts potential profit but, since the up-front premiums on the strangle leg are reduced from premiums from the written options, the amount the price of the underlying has to move for the strategy to be in profit is also less. A long position involves the simultaneous purchase of a call (or put) at one strike price, together with writing two further calls (or puts) at equally higher strikes and purchasing a call (or put) at an even higher price. The purchased and written options are reversed for a short position. It can also be set up using futures as one element of the spread. Also known as a *tabletop*. See option strategies.

(*a*) Payoff for condor buyer at expiry

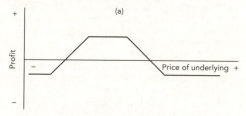

(*b*) Payoff for condor writer at expiry

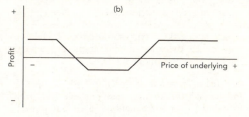

conduct of business rules (UK). The set of rules and regulations established by **self-regulating organizations** for how members carry out their business.

conduit. A **single purpose company** (SPV) used to facilitate one or more financial transactions. The SPV is typically used to avoid taxes or to allow the **securitization** of assets.

Confederation bond (Switzerland). Bonds issued by the Swiss federal government. Issues range up to fifteen years, pay **coupons** annually, and, generally, have a **call provision** for the last five years.

confidence interval. An estimate, based on stochastic modelling, of the probability or chance of a given price or rate. Such estimates are important tools for **risk management** and **hedging**.

confirmation. Part of the **settlement** process which involves the immediate dispatch once a transaction has been undertaken of a memorandum giving all the details of the trade and the relevant **clearing** procedures (cf. **out-trade**). It is designed to catch mistakes and reduce the number of trades that **fail**. A very important part of transactions management in the case of **derivatives** which trade for future delivery. Also called a *comparison ticket*.

confirmed (USA). A settlement plan that is consented to by all **creditors** for a firm in **Chapter 11** (cf. **assented securities**).

confirmed and irrevocable. A condition on a trade financing, **documentary credit**, or **letter of credit** where the correspondent bank confirms the transaction and undertakes to honour the payment, if valid. It means that any dispute (and point of jurisdiction) is with the correspondent bank and not the issuing bank. It reduces the risk to the exporter.

confirmed letter of credit or **confirmed credit** (Banking). A **letter of credit** (LOC) or **bill** which has been issued by one bank and confirmed by another, where both banks are obligated to honour drafts drawn in accordance to the credit. An unconfirmed LOC is an obligation only of the bank issuing the credit. In the case of international trade, an exporter will want the LOC issued by a bank in the importer's country confirmed by a bank acting as the **correspondent** to the foreign bank when there are doubts about the foreign bank's ability to honour the LOC.

confict of interest. A situation where a firm or individual acting in more than one role finds itself in conflict over the benefits of a transaction (cf.

moral hazard). Typical examples include firms acting both for an issuer and as an investor in the issue or a **broker** and **market-maker**. See **chinese walls**; **dual capacity**; **single capacity**.

conformed copy. A copy of a document where the necessary binding features, such as the participant's signature, have been typed or written in.

congeneric merger (Mergers and acquisitions). A **merger** between firms in related or complementary businesses (cf. **conglomerate merger**; **horizontal merger**; **vertical merger**).

congested market. A market suffering from an oversupply of new issuance (cf. **window**). Such gluts have led to rationing systems, for instance, the one operated in the UK by the **Bank of England** for company issues (cf. **visible supply**).

conglomerate. A holding company with subsidiaries with unrelated interests.

conglomerate merger. A merger between two firms where there is little industrial logic or synergy. Often such mergers are driven by financial rather than strategic considerations (cf. **congeneric merger**; **horizontal merger**; **vertical merger**).

congratulatory trading (Japan). Transactions undertaken between parties to mark a relationship (cf. **chummy trading**).

consecutives. **Futures contracts** that are next in line for **expiry**. See **expiration cycle**.

Conseil des Bourses de Valeurs (CBV) (France). The Stock Exchange Council for the Societés des Bourses de Valuers is the French stockmarket's supervisory and regulatory authority (cf. **Commission des Opérations de Bourse**). Based on a twelve member Board, it is responsible for establishing the overall rules for market operations, called the *Règlement Général du Conseil des Bourses de Valeurs*, subject to regulatory approval. It covers matters such as the entry requirement for new member firms, listing, delisting, suspension, takeovers, as well as a professional code of conduct.

Conseil du Marché à Terme (France). Governing body for the **Marché à Terme International de France**. It is a subsidiary body to the **Chambre de Compensation des Instruments Financiers de Paris**.

Consejo Superior de Bolsas (Spain). The supervisory body for Spanish financial markets (cf. **Commission des Opérations de Bourse** (France); **Securities and Exchange Commission** (USA); **Securities and Investments Board** (UK)).

consent decree (USA). An arrangement used to settle a prosecution brought by the government as guardian of the law and another party, usually a commercial firm. With a consent decree, the government agrees to drop the prosecution and the firm to desist or cease from the activities which brought the prosecution. However, in accepting the consent decree, the firm does not accept responsibility for past breaches of the law from the now discontinued activities (cf. **no-action letter; safe harbour**).

consequential-loss policy. See **business-interruption policy.**

conservator (USA). An official appointed to manage the affairs of an insolvent **savings and loans association** (cf. **Resolution Trust Corporation**).

consideration. (i) The amount paid for an asset or security. It is net of additional charges such as commission and taxes. (ii) In law, the promise by one party in a contract that is the price for obtaining the promise of the other party (cf. **counterparty**).

Consiglio Di Borsa (Italy). Degli Affrai 6, IT-20123 Milano (tel. 39 2 72426 1; fax 39 2 72 00 43 33).

consol (Bonds; UK). See **consolidated stock.**

consolidate. The bringing together or grouping of items. (i) (Accounting) It is the process of grouping the accounts of different legal entities so that the whole position, the consolidated position, can be treated as a whole. The process applies to subsidiaries which are more than 50% owned by the parent or holding company (cf. **equity accounting; minority interest**). The key principle when consolidating a group is adjust the accounts so as to eliminate intra-group activity, that is, any double counting of payables and receivables between the members of the group and any intra-group borrowing and lending. See **consolidated accounts.** (ii) Any financial transaction aimed at reducing the number of separate securities in issue outstanding in the market without, at the same time, making any repayment to holders (cf. **scrip issue**). For instance, the gilt-edge securities known as consolidated stock or consols were a consolidation of a number of smaller issues. Consolidation arises when the value of individual units or the total **market capitalization** of an issue is too small in relation to market norms. It is also sometimes effected for administrative purposes since payments can be regularized for a number of issues, thus reducing servicing costs. (iii) To merge (cf. **acquisition; merger; takeover**). (iv) A reduction in the number of firms in an industry. It is usually applied when the number of firms is being reduced

through a wave of **mergers and acquisitions**. This might arise from a number of causes such as the maturity of the industry, changes in competition, technology, and so forth. (v) A market, sector, or individual security, is said to consolidate when prices remain stable (cf. **falling market; resistance area; rising market; sideways moving market; support level**). See also **consolidation.**

consolidated accounts. (Accounting). Accounts consisting generally of a *consolidated balance sheet* and a *consolidated profit and loss account*, showing the financial condition of a company (either the **parent** or **holding company**) and its subsidiaries. Consolidation must take place if the **parent company** has over 50% or more of the subsidiary. Less than 50% may require consolidation on an equity basis (cf. **controlling interest; equity accounting**). Consolidation rules differ between countries but normally net out intra-group transactions. Known in the USA as the *consolidated financial statements.*

consolidated bonds (USA). **Bonds** issued by the Federal Farm Credit System (cf. **agencies**).

consolidated mortgage bond (USA). A type of **mortgage bond** in which several properties are being financed.

Consolidated Quotation Service (CQS) (USA). See **consolidated tape.**

consolidated quotation system. See **tape.**

consolidated stock (Consol) (UK). An irredeemable (**one-way stock option**) **gilt-edged** security with either a 2.5% or 4% fixed **coupon**. First issued during the Napoleonic Wars, together with **War Loan**, they form the bulk of the **undated** sector of the British National Debt. Irredeemables are useful for comparing yields on a safe (government) security with those on higher risk equities and their **yield** is sometimes used for the **risk-free rate** of interest. Under the UK's **generally accepted accounting principles**, the yield on the 2.5% Consols is used for deriving the difference between the theoretical income and the calculated diluted **earnings per share**. Consol is sometimes used as a general term for a *perpetuity.* Also known as *consolidated annuities.*

consolidated tape (Equities; USA). A market transaction reporting system managed by the National Association of Securities Dealers Automated Quotations which combines **stocks** listed on the New York Stock Exchange, the American Stock Exchange, and selected issues traded on the regional stock exchanges.

consolidation. (i) An accounting term for the bringing together of the **financial statements** or accounts of a number of legally connected subsidiaries to show the group or consolidated results. The consolidation principle involves netting out intra-group trading activity. (ii) The act of turning several different issues of securities or debts by a borrower into one issue or debt obligation. (iii) Transaction aimed at reducing the number of shares outstanding to increase their market value (cf. **penny stocks; scrip issue**). Holders of existing shares are asked to exchange their existing holdings for fewer shares but with a higher **face value** or **par value**. (iv) A **merger**.

consortium. A group working together for a common purpose. Typically, consortia involve the setting up of a **special purpose vehicle** or a **joint venture** where there is no one controlling interest. Consortia are often involved in projects or as a means of **risk** sharing. See also **concert party**.

consortium bank. A banking subsidiary or affiliate set up by a group of banks, not necessarily of the same nationality, where no one bank holds a majority interest. At one time consortium banks were common in the **euromarkets** as they were seen as a means of gaining experience in that market while sharing the **risks**, but the concept fell out of favour when it became apparent that there were often **conflicts of interest** between the different **shareholders** and the majority have subsequently become wholly owned subsidiaries of one of the owners, have been closed, or have been sold off to third parties.

consortium loan. Another term for a **syndicated credit**.

constant dollar plan. See averaging.

constant elasticity of variance (CEV). An adjustment made to **option pricing models** designed to accommodate the empirically observed fact that **variance** is mean reverting and not proportional to time.

constant elasticity of variance option pricing model. An option pricing model that allows the volatility to be proportionate to the price. The assumption is that the higher the price, the greater the market's valuation of the asset's earning power and the smaller the **minimum price fluctuation** for the asset becomes in relation to value.

constant maturity swap (CMS). An index of swaps for a given unchanging **maturity**.

constant maturity treasury (CMT) (Bonds; USA). An **index** of US Treasury **yields** published by the Federal Reserve based on an unchanging **maturity**.

constant maturity treasury option (CMT option) (USA). An **interest rate cap** or **floor** based on the **index** yield of a given **constant maturity treasury**.

constant maturity treasury swap (CMT swap) (USA). **Interest rate swap** where the fixed rate payment is based on the **index** for a given maturity constant maturity treasury tenor.

construction trust. A method of funding used in **project finance** where the **sponsor** agrees to provide the finance once the project is operational. It has been particularly used by utility companies in the USA to finance major capital investments.

consumer credit. Short-term finance provided to the public to buy goods or services, that is unsecured personal **loans, credit cards, debit cards, hire purchase, lease finance**, and so on.

consumer debenture (USA). A **bond** issue sold directly to the public.

consumer finance company. A financial institution which lends money to consumers, usually for the purchase of durable goods (such as cars) (cf. **consumer credit**). See also **hire purchase**.

consumer instalment loan (USA). See **consumer credit; amortizing loan**.

consumer price index (CPI) (USA). The US indicator of consumer inflation trends published monthly (cf. **produce prices index**). The index is actually made up of two parts: an urban price index and a wage earners index (cf. **retail price index {UK}**). See **economic indicators**.

consumer's hedge. See long hedge.

consumption assets. See commodities.

contagion. A feature of the behaviour of financial markets where adverse developments in one specific company spread through the industry or sector.

contango (i) (Commodities). The amount by which the **forward** price exceeds the **spot** price. Because of the significant carrying costs, storage, finance, and insurance involved in holding the physical product, this is the expected condition for **commodity futures** markets. Also known as a *positive term structure market*, a *premium market*, or *forwardation*. The opposite condition is known as *backwardation*. (ii) (Equities; UK). On the **London Stock Exchange** under the old **account** method used for **settlement**, it was the percentage charge paid by the buyer for the right to delay payment from the current **account period** to the next. See **cash and new**; **new time dealings**. (iii) In the futures market, it is the **cost of carry** where the contract is at a **premium** to the **cash** or **spot** market (cf. **backwardation**). (iv) (Netherlands). Term given to the Netherlands equivalent of the **Lombard rate**.

contango day. See new time dealings.

contango market (France). Special deferral procedures used on the **Paris Bourse** to allow deferral of **delivery** of securities from one regular monthly settlement (*marché règlement mensuel* (RM)) to the next. This market determines the financing rate at which buyers can obtain funds and sellers can borrow the securities required to meet their obligations at the month end, and thus to **rollover** their positions to the following month.

contango swap. **Commodity swap** where one party (A) pays a rate based on the current difference between the **spot price** and the six-month **futures contract** while the **counterparty** (B) pays the spot rate plus a predetermined margin. Thus party (A) has locked in a spread over the spot rate and been protected from any flattening or inverting of the commodity **yield curve**. The opposite transaction aimed at protecting against a change in a **discount** market is known as a *backwardation swap*.

contango theory. A theory of the commodities term **structure** which proposes that the forward or futures price must exceed the expected spot price (cf. **backwardation**). See also **convenience yield**; **expectations theory**; **liquidity preference**.

contemporaneous reserve accounting (CRR) (Banking; USA). The requirement to maintain **reserves** with the **Federal Reserve** as set by **Regulation D** where the computational and maintenance periods largely overlap. The Fed switched to CRR from a lagged reserve requirement in 1984.

contested takeover. Mergers and **acquisitions** situation where the **target** company is being **bid** for by more than one other company.

continental depository receipt. See European depository receipt (cf. global depository receipt).

contingency order. See contingent order.

contingent. Any form of transaction, contract, or instrument which depends on an event or prior conditions to become effective.

contingent annuity. A form of contract where the payment, in the form of an **annuity**, depends on some specific event.

contingent bargain (UK). The sale of one security at the same time as the purchase of another security. **Settlement** must, therefore, take place at the same time. Used to wind up or wind down **positions** (cf. **delivery against payment**; **free delivery**).

contingent claim. (i) The generic name given to an **option** or security that has a feature of choice, such as a **warrant**, **convertible**, or **rights issue**. The exercise of the choice is dependent upon the holder fulfilling the requirements of the **option writer** (or grantor), such as paying the **exercise price** in the case of **calls** or delivering **stock** in the case of **puts**. (ii) **Rights** that become operable if certain conditions are not met. For instance, a lender's right to place a **lien** on a borrower's assets if payments are not received (cf. **default**). (iii) Any financial asset or liability where there is a degree of uncertainty as to its occurring. For instance, sales or purchases in a foreign currency which are expected to occur but have not yet been contracted for. (iv) Another term for **derivatives**.

contingent immunization. A mixed portfolio objective that aims to provide a degree of gain potential while at the same time providing a minimum return designed to meet a set of liabilities. It involves active portfolio management that uses a contingent **immunization** structure and which aims to provide a minimum return but allows the manager some scope for higher than average or market returns. For example, if ruling interest rates are 10% the immunization plan might be used to lock in a return of 8%. There is thus a 2% safety net which would allow managers to actively seek higher returns. If returns decline this **triggers** the immunization strategy once the potential return drops to the 8% level. If there is an expectation of higher interest rates, then the manager could shorten the **duration** of the portfolio thereby giving a greater total return providing **yields** rise as expected.

contingent interest payment. Interest that depends on a specific event or the performance or behaviour of an **underlying** asset or market.

contingent liability. A liability or obligation whose occurrence is not certain. Typically guarantees fall into this category, but many other types of activity are uncertain. For example, a bid to purchase an asset in a foreign currency would create a contingent foreign currency liability which would crystallize if the bid was successful.

contingent option. Option which requires a given price or rate to become effective (cf. **knock-in; trigger**). See **barrier options**.

contingent order or contingency order. An instruction to sell one security and buy another, where the deal is dependent on the first order being carried out. Sometimes called a *net order* or a *not held order*.

contingent premium option. Type of option where no **premium** is paid when purchased, but where the premium is contingent on the option expiring **in the money**. Such an option is more expensive than a conventional option since the premium is only paid if exercised. Also confusingly called a *contingent option*. See also **money-back warrant**.

contingent swap. A type of **swap** where the terms are predetermined but are only applied when interest rates reach a pre-specified level or on the actions of a third party such as the exercising of a **warrant**. Similar to a **swaption** in pricing, but cheaper since it requires the specific event to occur. For issuers seeking to **hedge** against such events, a way of reducing the **premium** required. Also called an *option swap*. See **drop-lock swap; spread-lock swap**.

contingent value rights (USA). A special type of security issued when firms merge designed to provide **stockholders** with downside price protection. As such they are similar to **put warrants**.

contingent voting rights. The right of certain classes of securities to have voting rights in certain circumstances. For instance, **preferred stock** holders may be enfranchised if their **dividend** payments are delayed (cf. **arrearages**).

continuation. Contractual arrangement between a **broker** and his client where the latter agrees to undertake through the broker a series of transactions in return for reduced **commission** charges.

continuous compounding. An assumption used in many **analytical models** about the nature of interest (cf. **option pricing; time value of money**). Continuous compounding is when the frequency of the compounding of interest is progressively reduced in interval. At the limit it is being continuously compounded. The formula is:

$$FV = PV \cdot e^{Rn}$$

where *FV* is the future value; *PV* the present value of the amount; *e* the mathematical constant (= 2.71828); *R* the interest rate (expressed as a decimal); and *n* the compounding frequency. For an investment of 100 continuously compounded at

a rate of 10% for a year the future value would be 110.5171. This compares to compounded rates based on actual periods (see Table). In practice, continuous compounding and daily compounding should give nearly equal results.

Continous compounding

Compounding interval or frequency in the year	Value of 100 invested at the end of 1 year at 10% per annum
1	110.0000
2	110.2500
4	110.3813
12	110.4713
52	110.5065
365	110.5155

continuous dividend adjustment model. A modification made to the **Black–Scholes option pricing model** to allow for **dividends**. The approach is to use a continuous dividend-adjusted stock price rather than the actual stock price (cf. **leakage**).

continuous leakage option. An **option** on an **underlying** which pays out interest or **dividends** during the life of the option (cf. **leakage**).

continuously offered intermediate notes (COINS). A type of euro medium-term note programme used by US companies through an offshore subsidiary.

continuously offered long-term securities (COLTS) (Bonds; USA). A **World Bank** (International Bank for Reconstruction and Development) medium-term note programme which allows the bank to continuously offer amounts with maturities from nine months to thirty years in the US domestic market. A similar programme also operates in the international capital markets. The World Bank offers to issue securities to meet specific demands of investors as to instrument, maturity, and **coupon rate**. Intermediaries act as **placing agents** on the programme (cf. **dealer**).

continuously offered payment rights (COPS) (Money markets; Switzerland). A short-term borrowing programme set up by the **World Bank** (International Bank for Reconstruction and Development) in the Swiss domestic market through the major banks to offer a money market instrument to local investors.

continuous market. A market which has uninterrupted trading (cf. **call market**). See also **dealer; market-maker; quote driven; specialist**.

continuous net settlement (USA). Process of settlement at the end of each **business day** for transactions undertaken that day (cf. **rolling settlement**). It involves the **clearing house** or system providing members with a record of transactions made during the settlement period together with the amount of the net transfer of funds to be made to settle the account (cf. **full two-way payments clause**).

continuous swap. Package consisting of a **swap** and a long-dated **forward contract**. The combined position will have a constant **maturity** or **term** (cf. **tenor**).

continuous tender panel. A type of **tender panel** arrangement allowing the **underwriters** of the **facility** the right to subscribe up to the limits of their commitment for short-term **promissory notes** issued by the obligor during the tender period, subject to availability (cf. **euronotes**). Such an arrangement allows the underwriters to benefit from their ability to place the securities even if not members of the tender panel.

contra-broker. The **broker-dealer** on the other side of the transaction.

contract. (i) A general term for a legal agreement between two **counterparties** and used specifically to refer to a simple financial transaction such as an exchange of two currencies or a swap. A contract specifies the full details of the transaction. In a trading environment, the verbal agreement usually establishes the binding contract, the **contract note** or **confirmation** merely evidences it. In UK law, to be binding a contract must have three elements: offer; acceptance, and consideration. (ii) A binding agreement to make or take delivery of a financial instrument at a specified date at an agreed price (cf. **forward contract**). Can be applied to currencies, securities, **options**, **commodities**, **futures**, and metals (cf. **contract grade**). The contract is also likely to specify quantities, grades and rules of **settlement**. The form evidencing the agreement is known as a *contract note*. (iii) (Futures). The trading unit on a **futures exchange**. Each contract relates to a specific amount and other criteria relating to the **underlying** (cf. **cash instruments**; **lot**). (iv) In financial economics the explicit and implicit arrangement that defines the role of **agent** and **principal**. See **agency problem**.

contract bond. See performance bond.

contract financing. See factoring; project finance.

contract for differences (CFD) (UK). Term in the **Financial Services Act, 1986** used to define cash-settled agreements or instruments (cf. forward; futures option; swaps). Short CFDs are used by **short sellers** to avoid having to borrow securities or to pay stamp duty on repurchases; while long CFDs allow a direct exposure to the market, a sector, or an individual security. Contracts are **marked-to-market**, with an **initial margin** ranging from 5% or more of the value of the position with interest being charged when setting up a long position or credited in a short position. Unlike a forward contract, there is no final **maturity**, the position being closed out at the discretion of the position taker. See **derivatives**.

contract grade (Commodities). The specifications as to purity or type in a **futures** contract. In the event that the seller delivers a lower/higher grade an adjustment to the price will be made. For instance, the **London Metal Exchange** specifies the following as being the contract grade for its nickel **futures contract**: 'Quality: The nickel delivered under this contract must be Primary Nickel of minimum 99.80% purity with chemical analysis conforming to the current ASTM (American Society for Testing Materials) specification.' The exchange also specifies the shapes and weights and producers whose production can be used to settle the contract.

contract market (USA). Qualifying exchange under the Commodity Futures Trading Commission Act of 1976.

contract month. The calendar month in which a specific **futures contract** can be satisfied by accepting or making **delivery**. Also called the *cash settlement month* or the *delivery month*.

contract note. A document sent from one **counterparty** to another providing details of a transaction or trade. Typically includes the full title of the security, price, transaction tax (if applicable), money value of the transaction, **commission**, **delivery** or **settlement** instructions, and so forth. Also known as a *confirmation* or a *bought note*, if related to a purchase; a *sold note* if a sale (cf. **comparison ticket**).

contract size. The amount of the **underlying** in an **option** contract. For **common stock** or ordinary shares this is usually 100 shares; for **stock index options**, it is the level of the **index** times a multiplier; for **options on futures**, it is typically one **futures** contract.

contract specification. The legal agreement or contract which sets out the details of a **futures** or **options** contract. For instance, **deliverable stock**, **settlement**, hours when trading may take place, and so forth (cf. **contract grade**).

contractual notional amount. See notional principal.

contracyclical trading. A trading strategy that appears to be the opposite of that demanded by ruling market conditions. For example, if all other traders believe that interest rates will fall, this strategy would imply selling. Such an investor is called a *contrarian*.

contribution margin. The amount of contribution to the overall income of a business a given activity provides above those costs of undertaking it that would not be incurred if the activity ceased. Sometimes called *marginal contribution*.

contributory. In the winding up or **liquidation** of a firm, all those who have a **liability** towards the assets.

controlled amortization. A method of serial redemption of a security, such as an **asset-backed** issue, where the structure of the issue ensures that the repayments are pre-specified. Normally the process involves some third party guaranteeing reinvestment rates on that part of the principal that would normally be pre-paid when the underlying obligation was repaid. Such an approach has the attraction for investors of predictability; equally issuers can reduce their interest cost. See also **collateralized mortgage obligation.**

controlled commodities (USA). Those **commodities** which are regulated by the Commodities Exchange Act.

controller or **comptroller** (USA). The chief accountant with responsibility for budgeting, accounting, and auditing in a firm (cf. **treasurer**).

controlling interest. Strictly speaking, an ownership stake of any business which is 50% or more. In practice it means a sufficiently large stake in a company by an individual **shareholder** to allow effective control. In principle, a stake of 50% plus one share gives a blocking majority, but in practice effective control can be had with a smaller holding. Key holding levels are 25%, which can block changes in the articles of the company, 51%, which gives voting control, and 76%, which permits changes to the articles. In a **company** setting it usually means holding a majority of the **voting rights** which usually comes from the ownership of **equity**. The ability to capture ownership, or **acceptances** or pledges, of around this percentage of the voting equity in a company can be crucial in such situations as **contested takeovers.** See **minority interest.**

control risk. The **risk** that managerial controls are inadequate or may be overridden by employees (cf. **fraud**). See also **risk management.**

convenience yield (Commodities). An unobservable component of the **cash market** and **futures** or **forward** market relationship for **commodities** (cf. **basis**). Essentially, it is the cost that users of commodities are willing to accept to insure themselves against shortfalls in supply at some future date. That is, it reflects the market's expectations concerning the future availability of the commodity. The greater the chance of shortages occurring during the life of the contract, the higher the convenience yield. A proxy measure can be derived from holdings of the physical product, since if holdings are high, there is relatively little chance of shortages occuring in the near future and the convenience yield tends to be negligible in the valuation of **derivatives** on the commodity. Conversely, low supplies of the physical commodity tend to create high convenience yields. Because most financial instruments are substitutes, forward and futures contracts on financial instruments have negligible or zero convenience yields and are valued at the **cost of carry**. See **backwardation**; **contango.**

conventional gilts (Bonds; UK). Those government bond issues which are **straight bonds** (cf. **gilt-edged**). The distinction is required because the UK government issues **floating rate gilts**, **convertible bonds**, and **index-linked** as well as the **undated** or **irredeemables** (cf. **consols**). Conventional gilts have both a fixed **coupon** and **maturity.**

convergence. The process by which **futures** prices move towards **cash** prices as the **contract** moves towards **expiry**. Since futures are not settled until expiry, the holder does not have to provide the bulk of funds to cover the purchase. This **time-value** is reflected in the price at which the future sells (cf. **basis**). As the contract approaches expiry, this time-value diminishes to zero. In **cash-settled** contracts, the futures price equals the cash price at **settlement**. Otherwise it would be possible to sell the **underlying** and purchase the futures (or vice versa) and make a risk-free profit. As futures get near to their expiry date, convergence reduces the usefulness of such contracts for **hedging** purposes and market participants then **switch** to later-expiring contracts. See **basis risk.**

conversion. (i) (Securities) In the securities markets this is the **exercise** of the right to acquire securities according to specified terms by surrendering an existing security. (ii) (Derivatives). In the **options markets**, an **arbitrage** strategy involving the buying of the **underlying**, offset by the setting up of a **synthetic short position** in the option (the purchase of a **put** and the sale of a **call**). The overall **position** would then be unaffected by price movements in the underlying. Such a trade would be seen as appropriate when small differences appear

between the **long** position in the underlying and
the synthetic short position in the option. Such a
strategy provides a guaranteed profit from, for
instance, holding a put and the underlying and
selling a call where both the put and the call have
the same strike price and expiry date. The rationale for the position is that one of the three elements was mispriced upon entry into the
transaction. At expiry, if the underlying price is
above (below) the strike, the call (put) is exercised
and the underlying is delivered in either case,
resulting in a zero position and a net gain (cf. **pin
risk**). The opposite condition to the above is also
possible and is known as a *reversal* or a *reverse
conversion*. (iii) The exchange of an **asset** or **liability** denominated in one currency for a similar
asset or liability in another currency. This is generally an accounting exercise that takes place when
subsidiaries using a foreign currency are consolidated into the **base currency** of the holding company. See **translation risk**.

conversion account. The bookkeeping account
related to a foreign currency item in the accounts
of a firm or organization whose operational currency is different.

conversion bond warrant. A warrant that gives
the holder the right to either (*a*) **exercise** the
warrant into a **bond**, or (*b*) exercise the warrant
into the bond by surrendering a set security
(usually the **host bond**) as consideration for the
proceeds (cf. **harmless warrant**).

conversion date. The date at, or from which, the
right to exchange a **convertible** security starts.

conversion discount. See **conversion premium**.

conversion equity warrant. A warrant that
gives the holder the right to either (*a*) **exercise**
the warrant into **equity**, or (*b*) exercise the warrant
into equity by surrendering a set security (usually
the **host bond**) as consideration for the proceeds.

conversion factor. See **delivery factor**.

conversion factor hedge. See **duration-based
hedge ratio**.

conversion issue (Bonds). A new issue of **bonds**
made at the **maturity** of another issue by the same
authority. It is likely that the terms of the new issue
will be designed to encourage investors to exchange the maturing issue for the new one (cf.
new money). See **rolling debt**.

conversion parity (Bonds). The price at which a
convertible bond must sell for it to match the
current market value of the **common stock** or
ordinary shares to be given upon **conversion**.

conversion premium or **discount** (Bonds). The
ratio of the market value of a **convertible** security
to its **conversion value**, expressed as a percentage.
If the market value is greater than the conversion
value then the ratio is at a **premium**; if it is lower, a
discount. It should be noted that the **accrued
interest** needs to be considered because this is
given up when going from the **bond** to the **equity**.

conversion price (Bonds). The price of the underlying **common stock** fixed in a **convertible** (cf.
exercise price).

conversion ratio (Bonds). The number of units
of **stock** or **shares** into which a **convertible** security may be converted. For example, assuming a
convertible has a principal value of US$1000 and
the conversion price for the shares of US$50, the
conversion ratio is 20. That is the holder receives
20 units of **common stock** upon **conversion**.

conversion value (Bonds). The market value of a
convertible once converted, given by multiplying
the **conversion ratio** by the current market price
of the **underlying** security.

convertibility. The ability to be exchanged. See
convertible currency; **marketability**; **negotiable
instrument**.

convertible (Bonds). (i) Usually applied to a **bond**
or **preferred stock**, which can be exchanged for
other securities, normally, but not always, the
equity of the issuer (cf. **hybrid**). The **option** to
convert usually rests with the convertible holder
and can be denominated in a currency other than
that of the equity. The terms of conversion are
determined at the time of the convertible issue
but may alter through time due to **capitalization**
changes or at certain trigger prices of the equity.
Convertible issues are attractive in that generally
they offer a **yield** pick-up from the issuer's equity, a
greater certainty of receiving interest, and they
normally rank ahead of **equity** in any winding up
of the company. Also known as a *conversion issue*
or, in the UK, as *convertible loan stock*.
   Convertible bonds may be issued with features
seen in other types of bonds such as **call** and **put
provisions**. In some cases they are **extendible** and
step-up coupons have also been used. A large
number of convertibles also include, in the **bond
terms**, the **130% rule**. A number of convertible
bonds have been issued where the **obligor** of the
translated security is not the issuer. These have
features in common with **covered call** writing.
The rationale behind these types of convertible is
to fund the issuer's stake at lower cost (cf. **negative
carry**); the **option premium** being taken in the
form of the lower **coupon** on the convertible.
   Convertible option cost per common stock or
ordinary share (rights premium):

$$\frac{(\text{Market value of convertible}) - (\text{Value as straight bond})}{\text{Number of shares on conversion per 100 nominal}}$$

Effective conversion price per common stock or ordinary share:

$$\frac{\text{Current market price of convertible}}{\text{Number of common stock on conversion per 100 nominal}}$$

Conversion **premium/(discount)** = effective conversion price − current stock price.

(ii) In the **gilt-edged market** a convertible bond can be exchanged into one or more longer-dated bonds on the basis of fixed nominals on specific dates. The amount of nominal decreases as time passes if holders do not exercise the **conversion right**. See **convertible gilt-edged security; conversion issue**. (iii) (Forex) In the **currency markets**, the ability to buy and sell one currency against another without restrictions. Also called *free convertibility.*

convertible adjustable preferred stock (CAPS) (USA). A form of **adjustable rate preferred stock** which is **convertible** into **common stock**. One variant includes a cash alternative.

convertible arbitrage. An attempt to derive an immediate profit from the simultaneous purchase and sale of related securities upon conversion. It involves the buying of a **convertible bond** which is trading at a price below its **conversion value**, and the **short sale** of its **equity**. The equity received from the **conversion** offsets the **short sale**.

convertible auction market preferred stock (USA). A type of **auction market preferred stock** which is **convertible** into **common stock** (cf. **convertible adjustable preferred stock**). Also sometimes seen in the form of *convertible adjustable rate preferred stock.*

convertible bond. See convertible.

convertible capital bonds (Bonds; UK). A type of offshore issue by a UK company designed to access the international markets and similar to a normal **convertible**, except that the obligation is issued by an offshore company (cf. **special purpose vehicle**).

convertible currency (Forex). A currency that may be freely or partially exchanged, or converted, into another. That is, there are few or no restrictions on the right of individuals, companies, or institutions to purchase and sell the currency.

convertible exchangeable preferred stock. Convertible preferred stock that has either an issuer's or investors' **option** to change the issue into a **convertible bond** with the same conversion terms. Such a conversion feature issue facilitates tax planning since the convertible bond interest is tax deductible to the issuer.

convertible floating rate note (convertible FRN) (Bonds). A **floating rate note** (FRN) that can be exchanged into either (i) a **fixed-rate bond**; (ii) another FRN with a different **maturity**, or different **currency** denomination; or (iii) the **equity** of the issuer, or other entity. This latter is sometimes known as a *capital note* if conversion is mandatory (cf. **mandatory convertible bond**).

convertible gilt-edged security. A type of **gilt-edged** which allows the holder to convert into a longer **maturity** issue at a predetermined price, often an extant security. Such securities are offered as a way of increasing the attractiveness of new issues when market conditions are difficult (cf. **bells and whistles**). Pricing of such issues (partially) includes the value of the **embedded option** to holders and, as a result, will tend to have a lower **yield** than similar dated issues, the difference being the value of the **option**. Since such issues are generally free of **credit risk**, they offer a pure interest rate play. In addition, to facilitate **distribution**, the offer price tends to undervalue the option on interest rates.

convertible income advantage (Bonds). The additional yield or income obtainable by holding a **convertible** as opposed to the **common stock** of an issuer.

convertible into equity. See convertible.

convertible loan stock (UK). See convertible.

convertible money market preferred stock (CMMPS) (USA). A type of **money market preferred stock** which allows the holder to convert into **common stock** of the issuer.

convertible mortgage. A lending method secured on property where the lender has the right to either early repayment at a **premium** or conversion of part of the loan into a **share** of the value of the property. Typically used to reduce the funding cost of such finance.

convertible notes (Australia). A type of note issue which allows the holder to convert into the **ordinary shares** of the issuer. Equivalent to **convertible unsecured loan stock** (UK).

convertible option. A type of **foreign exchange option** where the holder is mandatorily converted into a forward foreign exchange contract if the currency moves beyond a pre-agreed price. Such an **option** is cheaper than a normal option since it restricts the range within which the writer has to pay out. See also **barrier option** (cf. **trigger**).

convertible preferred stock. An issue of **preferred stock** or preference shares which is **convertible** into **common stock** at the holder's **option**. Such issues normally include some deferment provisions on the ability to convert. Known in the UK as a *convertible preference share*.

convertible reset bond or **debenture** (USA). A **convertible** issue featuring a **coupon** reset provision such as to make the issue trade at **par** at some predetermined date. Such an issue is designed to protect holders against a deterioration in the issuer's **credit worthiness** and/or financial prospects.

convertible revolving credit (Banking). **Revolving credit facility** that can, at the request of the borrower, be converted into a fixed-term facility.

convertible stock note. See **convertible**.

convertible unsecured loan stock (CULS) (UK). A type of **convertible** issued in the UK domestic **bond** market. Such an issue is not necessarily **subordinated**. It is a straight issue with the **embedded option** to surrender the proceeds in exchange for **shares** in the issuer. Typically such issues often carry subordination or are **preferred stock** (known in the UK as preference shares).

convertible with premium puts. A type of **convertible bond** where the holder has the right to redeem the bonds prior to final **maturity** at a **premium** to par. Such early redemption normally provided the holder with a return closer to that of a **straight bond** equivalent (having the characteristics of a **deep discount bond**) and is a way of increasing the marketability of the issue, since the holder is protected against the underperformance of the **common stock**. In principle, the convertible would be converted into **equity**, but many issues made in the **eurobond** market in the 1980s just before the October 1987 **crash**, subsequently underperformed and left many issuers with a large (and unexpected) **contingent liability** for the premium and no increase in equity!

convexity. (i) A measure of the sensitivity of the **duration** of a **bond** to its **yield**. It is effectively a multiple of the second derivative of the price with respect to the yield, divided by the bond's **full price**. Convexity measures how much duration changes with changes in yield. Duration and convexity act to predict the price movement of a bond to changes in interest rates. *Positive convexity,* means that for a given change in yield the bond will increase more in price than it will fall in price

for the same change in yield. *Negative convexity* means the opposite occurs: for a given increase in yield the bond will increase less in price and it will fall more in price for the same increase in yield. **Straight bonds,** the fixed side of an **interest rate swap**, will have positive convexity. Negative convexity is to be found in instruments with **embedded options**, for instance, **mortgage-backed securities**. (ii) Used also to describe the rate of change in an **option's delta** in relation to changes in the value of the **underlying**, that is the **gamma** sensitivity of an option.

Cooke ratio (Banking). The minimum capital ratio as laid down by the **Basle Capital Convergence Accord**. It is so named after the Cooke committee, that is the Committee on Banking Regulations and Supervisory Practices, which developed the standard. See **capital adequacy**.

cooling-off period (USA). (i) The time between the **registration** of an issue and when it can be offered to the public. During this period, the **lead manager** will issue the preliminary **prospectus** and hold a **due diligence** meeting (cf. **red herring**). Different types of issue are subject to different delays. (ii) (UK) The time that must elapse before another offer for the purchase of a company may be made following a failed **takeover bid** (cf. **lapsed option**). Normally, this is twelve months as recommended by the **City Code on Takeovers and Mergers**.

Copenhagen Stock Exchange (Kobenhavns Fondsbors) (Denmark). Nikolaj Plads 6, Postbox 1040, DK-1007 Kobenhavn K (tel. (4533) 93 33 66; fax (4533) 12 86 13).

Coppock index A form of **moving average** which gives greater weight to the latest observations. Also known as an *exponential moving average*.

core capital (Banking). **Tier 1** capital as defined by the **Basle Capital Convergence Accord** as implemented by the local bank regulator.

core deposits (Banking). Those, usually retail, **deposits** at a bank that are maintained with predictable continuity.

core holding. That part of a **portfolio** that is regarded as a **long-term** holding and is crucial to the portfolio manager's investment strategy (cf. **noyaux durs**).

corner-the-market. Occurs when a market participant buys a large proportion of a security and may result in **short sellers** having to pay higher prices in order to cover their **short position**. Also called a *ramp*.

corporate bond. Bond issued by a company or corporation.

corporate bond equivalent (USA). The computation of **yield** on a security which has another interest calculation method; for instance, the yield on a **treasury bill** expressed as a **bond** yield. See interest rate calculations; **equivalent bond yield**.

corporate bylaws. See **bylaws**.

corporate charter (USA). The legal basis upon which companies are registered and operated. In the UK the same documents are called the **memorandum and articles of association**.

corporate control (Mergers and acquisitions). The rights, such as a majority of votes at company meetings, used for control of a firm's assets (cf. **controlling interest**).

corporate finance. (i) That part of the theory of finance concerned with explaining the behaviour of companies in the following policy areas: **capital structure**; **capital budgeting**; **dividends**; taxation; and **mergers and acquisitions**. (ii) Departments of **investment banks** or **merchant banks** concerned with advisory services about such matters. Hence a *corporate financier*, an individual who provides corporate finance advice. (iii) A **business segment** defined by **commercial banks** for the provision of larger-scale loans to companies as opposed to individual lending.

corporate financing review (USA). The review of a firm's underwriting arrangements and terms and conditions in which **National Association of Securities Dealers** members are involved to determine whether they are fair and reasonable.

corporate governance. The organization of the management of a company to promote the interests of **stockholders**. It usually involves pro-active collective **shareholder** pressure on managements to ensure that equitable decisions are made on matters which may affect the value of equity holdings, such as voting rights, pre-emptive rights, disposals, capital raising, the nomination of directors, **dividend** policy, and so forth. Often involves the solicitation of **proxies** by shareholder activists.

The direction of companies can be based upon statutory requirements with legal redress and penalties for non-compliance. Alternatively, the way in which companies are run can be set by so-called 'best practice'. There is not a universal structure used by all countries, rather there are major differences as between markets and relevant authorities. What can be said is that the controversy surrounds such issues as the role of non-executive **directors**; how executive remuneration packages should be designed, operated, and made known to share-holders; when directors can talk to investment analysts; when they can exercise options to buy or sell shares in the company they direct; and whether the roles of a **chairman** should be combined or split away from those of managing director or **chief executive**. In the UK, these issues have been dealt with by the **Cadbury Committee on the financial aspects of corporate governance**, which made several recommendations regarding the disclosure of information and the powers and responsibilities of non-executive directors (cf. **Greenbury Committee**). See **agency problem** (cf. **agent**; **principal**); **compliance**.

corporate governance standards (USA). Standards set by the **National Association of Securities Dealers Automated Quotations** in respect to the structure and management of firms **quoted** on the market.

corporate income fund (CIF) (USA). A type of **investment company** which differs from a **mutual fund** by the fact that it has a **portfolio** which is fixed at the time it is launched.

corporate raider. See **raider**.

corporate restructuring. See Chapter 11; re-structuring.

corporate service price index (CSPI) (Japan). A measure of wholesale price inflation compiled by the **Bank of Japan**.

corporate settlement (USA). Same as **regular delivery** (cf. **skip-day settlement**).

corporate tax equivalent (Bonds; USA). The equivalent **yield** required on a taxable **bond** at **par** when compared to a tax-exempt bond, such as a **municipal**. The formula is:

$$\text{Taxable equivalent yield} = \frac{\text{Tax} - \text{exempt yield}}{1 - \text{Tax rate}}$$

For example, a tax-exempt bond with a yield of 5%, a tax rate of 25%, will be equivalent to a taxable bond with a yield of 6.67%.

corporate venturing. (i) The practice of a large company either taking a speculative stake in a venture or retaining a holding after a divestiture, usually a **management buy-out**. (ii) A **venture capital** fund set up or funded by a company, rather than a financial institution. A company can have several reasons for trying to identify new business opportunities, not least as providing a supply of potential longer-term acquisitions, and as a means of developing indirectly new products and markets. This activity whilst common in the US is relatively unknown elsewhere. See also **business angels**.

corporation. Another term for a **company**.

corporation bills (UK). Notes issued by local governments in the UK. These are also known as *local government promissory notes*.

corporation tax. The tax which is assessed on profits made by companies or corporations (cf. **advance corporation tax; mainstream corporation tax**).

Corpus Treasury receipt (Corpus TR). A zero-coupon certificate with the **underlying** security of principal payments on particular **US Treasury** securities. Holders of these certificates receive **principal** payments at **maturity** but no intervening income. Sometimes called *principal Treasury receipts* (cf. **coupon Treasury receipt; physical strip; separate trading of registered interest and principal of securities; Treasury receipt**).

correction. A downward move in a generally rising price trend.

correlation. A statistical technique for determining the extent to which variations in the values of one variable are associated with variations in the value of another. Statistics has made this idea more precise, and has devised methods of capturing the degree of association, the most frequently used of which is the **correlation coefficient** (cf. **covariance**). If the sign of the coefficient, measured for a set of pairs of values of two variables, is negative, this indicates that relatively high values of one variable tend to be associated with relatively low values of the other, and vice versa; this is known as an *inverse association*. If the sign of the coefficient is positive, this indicates that relatively high values of both variables tend to occur together, as do relatively low values. In this context, relatively means above and below the two series averages. The actual value of the number indicates the strength of the association. The limits to these values, in the case of the correlation coefficient, are +1 and −1, such that a value close to +1 shows that high-to-high and low-to-low values are very likely; and values close to −1, that high-to-low, and low-to-high values are very likely. Conversely, a value close to zero, whether positive or negative, indicates that relatively high values of one variable are equally likely to be associated with relatively low values of the other. Therefore, an increasing element of association (inverse association) is shown as the coefficient varies from zero to +1 (−1). The usefulness of correlation analysis can be found in hypothesis testing about the possible relationships between variables and, practically, for **cross-hedging** purposes to establish the optimal **hedge ratios** as well as assisting in the **diversification** of **portfolios**. Correlation is useful as a means of testing hypotheses. For example, it

could be asserted that the more information that a company releases about itself beyond that required by statute, the higher would be its **price–earnings ratio**. Data on different companies' non-statutory disclosure policy could be collected together with data on the performance of share prices. It would then be possible to show how closely the two variables (information disclosure and share price performance in relation to earnings) were associated in practice, and hence how much confidence could be placed in the hypothesis (or at least to show that it is not totally wrong). In terms of the correlation coefficient described here, several limitations exist. The most significant is that the coefficient value itself proves little about causation. It is possible for values to be associated without there being a causal connection as between variables. One possible reason for this is that both variables are determined by some third variable, and changes in this third variable cause changes in the other two to be associated without, at the same time, there being any causal relationship as between them. A significant special case of this is in respect of time, where two variables may have a strong time-trend which leads to high correlations without there necessarily being causation. Alternatively, a high correlation may come about by chance, such as the observed relationship between the position in trees where birds nest and levels of economic activity. Therefore, correlation does not show causation, although it can provide some useful benchmarks for further study. See **multiple correlation; partial correlation; regression analysis**.

correlation coefficient. A statistical measure, which can take the range of +1 to −1, of the degree of interdependence between two variables. It is equivalent to the normalized **covariance** of two variables. A positive correlation is any positive value up to +1 when the two series are perfectly correlated; a negative correlation is any value down to −1. Two series with no correlation will have a value close to zero. It is possible to assign confidence limits to the estimate of interrelation. Correlation coefficients are widely used for estimating the efficiency of **cross-hedges**. They are defined as:

$$r = \frac{\sum_{i=1}^{n}(x_i - \mu_x)(y_i - \mu_y)}{\left[\sqrt{\sum_{i=1}^{n}(x_i - \mu_x)^2}\right]\left[\sqrt{\sum_{i=1}^{n}(y_i - \mu_y)^2}\right]}$$

where n is the number of observations; x_i the value of the ith observation of series x; μ_x the mean of the total set of observations of series x; y_i the value of the ith observation of series y; μ_y the mean of the total set of observations of series y.

correlation forecasting. Using the results of **correlation** to predict how variables may change in value in the future in relation to each other. If variables can be shown to be strongly and weakly associated, it is tempting to conclude that if information is available about the future values of one of the variables, reliable forecasts can be derived about the other. Whilst such a conclusion can be helpful in business and market forecasting, it should be remembered that correlation analysis has limitations; not least it does not prove causation, which is likely to be much more useful to discover, and is sensitive to the quality of historical information. See **econometrics**.

correlation risk. (i) The risk that the relationship of two markets, two assets, or two sectors as measured by historical **correlation** used to calculate **hedge ratios** will not stay constant (cf. **crosshedge**). (ii) The risk of a positive relationship between two variables in a complex **derivative** instrument where the pricing must take account of the likely interaction of the variables. An example would be the problems involved in hedging **currency protected swaps** where the payout is conditional on both changes in the **exchange rate** and the relationship of interest rates between the two currencies. The degree to which these elements move in tandem will create correlation risk for the hedger, since a rise in the one variable may at the same time increase the other in ways that cannot be effectively hedged out.

correspondent. A financial institution that regularly performs services for another in a location or market to which the other does not have direct access (cf. **nostro**; **vostro**).

corridor. (i) Term for an **option strategy** in the **interest rate caps** and **floors** market which involves buying a lower price cap (higher-priced floor) and simultaneously selling a higher (lower) priced one. Also known as a *cylinder* or a *vertical spread*. Variations could include **horizontal spreads** or **time spreads**. (ii) An **interest rate collar** on an **interest rate swap** created by using two **swaptions** (options-on-swaps), the exact payoff depending on the type and **strike price** of the swaptions.

corset. (i) (Forex) Limits to the freedom of movement in exchange rates as a result of controls (cf. **crawling peg**; **Exchange Rate Mechanism**; **managed float**). (ii) (Banking; UK) Term for the now abolished Supplementary Deposit Scheme operated between 1973 and 1980 by the **Bank of England** to control the **money supply**.

cost basis. The original purchase or transfer price of an asset (cf. **book value**; **marked-to-market**). Sometimes known as *original cost basis*.

cost-benefit analysis. Decision-making assessment technique which seeks to equate a choice to the resultant costs involved and benefits gained. It can be used as a **capital budgeting** or investment appraisal technique in conjunction with **discounted cash flow** methods, as a method of incorporating social costs into a decision. The technique is frequently used in assessing social projects, such as public infrastructure investments. In its broadest use it aims to capture aspects of particular projects which would not normally be considered in a commercial or finance evaluation.

cost company arrangement. A project finance condition where the project participants receive the output free of charge in exchange for meeting all the operating and other expenses of the project.

cost curve (Commodities). Used for the analysis of primary producers, this is a graphical representation of the unit operating costs of different extractors against cumulative output. It shows which producers are most vulnerable to a reduction in the commodity price. See **fundamental analysis**.

cost effective. The ratio of the gain to the cost in a project or investment. See **cost-benefit analysis**; **net present value**; **profitability index**.

cost of capital. At its simplest, the average of the costs of a company's various types of capital: **common stock** (or **ordinary shares**) or **equity**, Preferred stock, debentures, loan stock, and reserves. Analytically, the concept can become important when considering the different ways in which such claims can be serviced. For example, the retirement of debt and the issuing of more equity. It is also significant in deciding capital expenditure plans as an individual company's cost of capital is likely to be critical in producing a justification for proceeding with individual projects within the traditional **discounted cash flow** criteria. Conventionally, the concept is expressed as the **weighted average cost of capital**. This is the discount rate which combines the capital costs of all the various types of capital claims which a company issues. It is regarded as a convenient measure to use because it captures in a single discount rate all the returns necessary to service the company's capital claims. It is normally calculated when applied to investment decisions according to the following:

$$\text{WACC} = \frac{\text{Debt market value}}{\text{Total market value}} \times \frac{\text{Debt required}}{\text{return}}$$
$$+ \frac{\text{Equity market value}}{\text{Total market value}} \times \frac{\text{Equity required}}{\text{return}}$$

where the debt market value is the amount of debt servicing required on the amount borrowed to fund the project, discounted at the rate payable over the period of the project; the equity market value is the amount of discounted free cash flow available to shareholders once the debt providers have been satisfied, again over the life of the project, and the total market value is the combined debt and equity market value. The debt and equity required returns are given and are based on the risk of the particular project and conditions currently ruling in both equity and debt markets. The cost of capital can influence not only capital project selection but **capital structure** and **restructuring** as well as **dividend policy.**

cost of carry. (i) The loss from funding at a higher cost than the returns from the **position.** Also known as *negative carry.* See **carry.** (ii) A model of the **fair value** of **futures.** It takes the cost of holding the cash position (which will include funding, storage costs, and so forth) and delivering it into the contract as the **arbitrage** free price at which futures should trade. See also **basis; basis risk.**

cost of finance. See **all-in cost; cost of capital; cost of funds; weighted-average cost of capital; yield.**

cost of funds (i) (Banking). The cost of borrowing funds for a financial institution in a particular market. See **interbank rate; London interbank offered rate; Paris interbank offered rate** (ii) Used in a general sense for the cost of raising additional finance (cf. **cost of capital**). See **weighted-average cost of capital**.

cost of funds index (COFI) (Banking; USA). An index of funding costs for **savings and loans associations** based in the 11th Federal Reserve District (Arizona, California, and Nevada) and frequently used as a benchmark for **adjustable rate mortgages** (cf. **COFI swap**).

cost of living index. See **consumer price index** retail price index.

cost-plus contract. An arrangement where the provider of goods or services is remunerated on the basis of its costs plus an agreed profit **margin.** An alternative would be a **fixed price contract**.

cost push inflation. A rise in prices due to increased costs in manufacturing and service industries. Normally this is due to excessive wage increases, but it may also be based on changes in commodity prices and currency rates.

Côte Officielle (Equities; France). The stock exchange's official price list published each business day. Also sometimes used to refer to the **Paris Bourse** rather than the unofficial **coulisse** market (cf. **over the counter**).

coulisse (France). Unlisted securities trading (cf. **National Association of Securities Dealers Automated Quotations**).

Council of Economic Advisors (USA). A panel of economists appointed by the President to advise on economic policy.

Council of Europe Social Development Fund (Council of Europe). A European supranational entity that borrows funds for member countries in response to social needs. Was formerly known as the Council of Europe Resettlement Fund.

counterpart or **counterparty.** The legal entity who is the other party to a transaction (cf. **contrabroker**). Some financial intermediaries make the distinction between a counterparty being a professional and a customer being non-professional.

counterparty risk. The credit risk assumed when undertaking a transaction with another party that they will be unable or unwilling to honour their commitments. Sometimes measured as the cost of replicating or restoring the transaction with another party (cf. **opportunity cost; daylight exposure limit; value at risk**).

counter-trade. A generic term for commercial mechanisms for reciprocal trade including: **barter,** counter-purchase, offset, buy-back, evidence accounts, and switching trading. The common characteristic of these arrangements is that export sales to a particular market are made conditional upon undertakings to accept imports of similar value from that market. Used as a way of promoting trade with **less developed countries**, and intended to avoid, or mitigate, the problems associated with **sovereign debt**. A number of specialist intermediaries have appeared prepared to exchange the output/produce received by the seller for money/currency, and then place the output/**commodities** with the ultimate user for a **disagio** fee.

countervailing credits. See **back-to-back loan.**

country fund. A type of **investment company** which specializes in investing in one specific country, typically an **emerging market**.

country limit. A credit limit placed on the amount of **country risk** that a **counterparty** is willing to assume with one country (cf. **sovereign risk**).

country risk. The risk associated with undertaking transactions or holding **assets** of a particular country. These may be political, legal, **settlement** difficulties, or regulatory changes (cf. **credit risk**). Problems might arise over the repatriation of profits or assets in a country; nationalization or expropriation of assets; and the tax treatment of foreign-owned assets or businesses. A distinction could perhaps be made between country risk, the risk associated with a country; and **sovereign risk**, the risks associated with the state of the country. It can also be an **indirect risk** when the impact of such changes affects a third party or the value of securities issued by the country or its enterprises abroad (cf. **eurobonds; foreign bonds**). See **risk management; sovereign immunity**.

country selection. International portfolio **asset allocation** which is based upon investing (via their capital markets) in those countries that are likely to be best performers in any given period. See **emerging markets; strategic asset allocation; tactical asset allocation**.

coupon (Bonds; Money markets). (i) The nominal annual rate of interest expressed as a percentage of the **principal** value. Variously called the *coupon interest rate, coupon rate of interest* or *coupon rate*. (ii) A certificate attached to a **bearer security** that has to be produced before the **paying agent** delivers payment of interest, hence the term *coupon bond*. A bond will have one coupon for each interest payment. See **interest rate calculations; talon**. (iii) Generic term for **bond** and **note** securities in the **US treasury market**. (iv) The fixed rate payment side of an **interest rate swap** or a **cross-currency swap**. Hence, a *coupon swap*.

coupon accrual swap. See **accrual swap**.

coupon equivalent yield. See **equivalent bond yield**.

coupon interest bond (USA). See **municipal multiplier security**.

coupon issues or **coupon securities** (Bonds; USA). Term applied to any security issue by the US Government which pays a **coupon**; that is, note and bond issues.

coupon pass (USA). Market's term for a permanent injection or drain of liquidity by the **Federal Reserve** (cf. **desk; funds**). Unlike its normal **open-market operations** which involve **repurchase agreements**, the coupon pass involves the outright sale or purchase of securities.

coupon period. The frequency with which coupon interest is paid; normally annually or semi-annually for fixed interest securities; for **floating rate notes** it may be any frequency.

coupon rate. The rate of interest on a **bond** expressed as a percentage of its **face value**. Thus a bond which paid an $8\frac{3}{4}$% coupon would pay 8.75 per 100 nominal, or multiples thereof depending

on the size of the **certificates**. It is convention to express the coupon rate as an annual percentage, regardless of the frequency with which the coupons are paid.

coupon stripping (Bonds). The process of restructuring a conventional **bond** in order to generate a series of **zero-coupon bonds**. It can be achieved either by (i) detaching the **coupons** from the principal, or (ii) issuing receipts representing the individual coupons payments and principal on a security held by a trustee (cf. **physical strip; separate trading of registered interest and principal of securities**).

Coupons Under Book Entry Safekeeping (CUBES) (Bonds; USA). Facility allowing holders of **physical stripped coupons** to convert them to book-entry securities. See **separate trading of registered interest and principal securities**.

coupon swap. A fixed coupon for floating interest rate swap (cf. **basis swap; cross-currency swap**).

Coupon Treasury receipt (Coupon TR) (Bonds; USA). A **zero-coupon** certificate with the underlying security of **principal** payments on particular US Treasury securities. They represent a claim for a single payment of **coupon** interest from an **underlying US Treasury note** or **bond** to the face value of the certificate (cf. **Corpus Treasury receipt; physical strip; separate trading of registered interest and principal of securities; Treasury receipt**).

court (French). **Short**.

courtage (French). **Brokerage**.

courtier (French). **Broker**.

covariance. A statistical measure of the co-movement between two series. It is an indication of the measure of interdependence of the two sets of data. The **correlation coefficient** is a more easily interpreted version of the same relationship. Covariances are important in **modern portfolio theory** since, given a large enough **portfolio**, the effect of individual price variances is dominated by the matrix of covariances (cf. **variance-covariance matrix**).

covariance asset. A type of investment that has a low **covariance** with a **portfolio's** main components. It has the effect of reducing the variation in return of the portfolio. Examples of such assets include foreign currency **stocks** and **bonds**, and **commodities**.

covenant of equal value. See **negative pledge**.

covenant protection. The degree of investor or lender protection provided by **covenants**. (cf. **boilerplate**).

covenants. Provisions within a borrowing agreement (**bond indenture**; **trust deed**) that the borrower will take certain actions (**affirmative covenants**) or refrain from taking certain actions (**negative** or restrictive covenants) in order to safeguard the interests of the lender. **Breach of covenant** may lead the lender to call the loan or place the security into **default** (cf. **acceleration clause**; **technical default**). See **negative pledge**; **pari passu**.

cover. (i) (As in *to cover*). To offset one **position** with an equal and opposite transaction (that is, to offset a **long** (short) position with a short (long) covering transaction). (ii) In **auctions** and **tenders**, the number or, more usually, the amount of bids submitted compared with the number or amount actually awarded. (iii) Short form for the **dividend cover**. (iv) To take out insurance ('to take out cover'). (v) To procure the instrument or **commodity** in order to honour a contractual obligation (cf. **naked option**; **writer**). (vi) The security or lien provided in a borrowing. (vii) Another term for a **hedge**.

coverage. Used in assessing **credit worthiness** and indicates the margin of safety for repayment of debt. Calculated as the **ratio** of operating income plus interest to long-term and short-term investment needs over the period of the debt. Also known as *interest cover*. See **ratio analysis**.

coverage test. A covenant that limits the raising of more debt if the borrower's interest **cover** would in consequence fall below some specified minimum **ratio**.

covered arbitrage (Forex). See **covered interest arbitrage**.

covered bear. A short sale against a long hedge position. Also called a *protected bear position*.

covered call or **covered option**. A short position in a **call option** for which the **option writer** has adequate quantities of the deliverable **underlying** to satisfy an **exercise** of the call by the holder (cf. **covered put**; **delta hedge**). For example, an equity investor might hold the shares and write the call, hoping to profit from the premium income so gained. If the call is exercised, he can provide the shares to meet his obligation. Also known as a *buy and write* or *buy-write*.

covered interest arbitrage (Money markets; Forex). A method of investing or borrowing in foreign currency assets or liabilities where the exchange rate risk is eliminated by covering the

exposure in the **forward foreign exchange market**; that is, to borrow in one currency, convert it into another currency through the **spot foreign exchange market**, then sell the second currency for **forward** delivery against the first for the maturity of the borrowing (cf. **foreign exchange swaps**). For example, borrowing US dollars for three months and exchanging this for French francs while at the same time entering into a same-date forward transaction to sell the francs and receive back dollars. Such a transaction is designed to exploit anomalies between the forward foreign exchange market and the **money markets** in different countries either to raise returns, since there are **yield** pick-up opportunities from investing in the foreign assets; or to reduce the cost of the liability. It can also be used as a means of funding a **position** in a currency where the **money markets** are restricted or inefficient. For instance, a bank may pay a **premium** to borrow in some currencies, but not for undertaking foreign exchange. The bank would avoid paying the premium on the borrowing by using covered interest arbitrage. See **arbitrage**.

covered interest rate parity. The setting of the **forward** rate for **foreign exchange** by a **market-maker** so as to prevent market participants engaging in **covered interest arbitrage**.

covered margin. The **margin** on two instruments denominated in different currencies after taking into account the cost of **forward** foreign exchange protection.

covered option securities (COPS) (Bonds; money markets). Securities with **embedded** written **currency options** allowing the issuer to repay in an alternative currency at a set rate. Holders are compensated for writing the option by receiving a higher rate of interest. Some COPS have maturities of less than a year and are therefore **money market instruments**. See **dual currency bond**.

covered option writer. An individual or institution which **writes covered calls** or **options**. That is, in the case of calls, they hold the **underlying** when writing the option; in the case of puts, they are prepared to receive the underlying (cf. **buy and write**; **covered put**).

covered position. A position in a security that is matched by an opposite position in another similar security; or a position in a **derivative** that is matched by a position in the **underlying**, thereby neutralizing the initial position (cf. **cross-hedge**; **hedge**; **naked position**).

covered put (Derivatives). A **short position** in a **put option** for which the **option writer** has adequate eligible assets to take delivery of the **under-**

lying in the event of the **put** being exercised (cf. **writer**). It is the opposite transaction to a **covered call**.

covered short. A **short sale** against a security held. Such a **hedge** transaction may be necessary if it is not possible or desirable to actually sell the security. Known in the USA as *selling short against the box*.

covered straddle. A situation where the straddle **option writers** has a covering position in the **underlying** asset.

covered warrant. Warrants issued by an obligor where the **exercise** is into the debt or, more commonly, the **equity** of a third party. This is similar to **covered call writing**. The logic is to earn income from the **premium** against an already extant holding. Sophisticated issuers of covered warrants will offer such instruments when **volatility** is overpriced by the **stock options** market. Typically such warrants have a longer **expiry** than similar **exchange-traded** options.

covered writing (Derivatives). The writing of a **call option** covered by an existing **long position** in the **underlying** (cf. **covered call**). As a trading strategy it is intended to enhance overall returns by generating up-front premium income from selling the options. Sometimes only part of the underlying is held.

covering short. See **cover**.

Cox–Ingersoll–Ross option pricing model. An **option pricing model** for interest rates options making use of the term structure of interest rates. It is based on the **expectations theory** of the term structure and models the expected returns from holding the **underlying** for different periods in order to be able to derive the **fair value** of an **option** on an interest rate sensitive security. See J. C. Cox, J. E. Ingersoll, and S. A. Ross (1985), 'A Theory of the Term Structure of Interest Rates' *Econometrica*, 53: 385–407.

crack spread. The difference between the price of crude oil and its refined products, or their futures prices, created by *cracking the crude*. It is, in effect, oil refiners' **margin** (cf. **commodity swap**; **crush spread**).

crack spread option. Option on the **spread** between the price of crude oil and its refined products. There is an **exchange-traded** option contract on the **New York Merchantile Exchange** for this **spread option**.

crack spread swap. Commodity swap similar to an **interest rate swap** allowing one of the parties to

pay a fixed **crack spread**, thus protecting their refining **margin**, against a floating margin to the crack spread.

cram down (USA). The imposition on the dissenting minority of **creditors** of a **restructuring** of a firm in **Chapter** 11 by the court (cf. **assented securities**).

crammed down paper (Bonds; USA). Term for a type of **junk bond**, such as **pay-in-kinds**, which pays interest in the form of additional securities.

crash. (i) Generic description for any sudden and dramatic large fall in the prices of securities, currencies, or **commodities** (cf. **break**; **jumps**). The US stock market had a *Great Crash* in 1929 and world-wide securities markets experienced similar difficulties in 1987. Interestingly, when prices fall trading screens change to the colour red, not black! See also **Black Monday**. (ii) A systems failure. This can seriously disrupt trading or **settlement**. (iii) Another term for **bankruptcy** or **insolvency**, particularly of a bank or other financial institution (cf. **hammered**).

crawling peg (Forex). Method of managing the external value of a **currency** which involves frequent adjustments to the **exchange rate** in line with domestic conditions. Typically, under such a managed currency, the **central bank** will buy and sell **foreign exchange** so as to control the speed and direction of change in value (cf. **fixing**). Also known as a *sliding peg*.

CRB Futures Price Index Futures (USA). See **commodity index futures**.

creation price (UK). The price at which a **unit trust** manager can create new **units** in the trust. See also **single pricing**.

creative accounting. (i) The misuse of accounting conventions to disguise poor operating performance or to enhance stated earnings. See **below-the-line**. (ii) The practice of using deferred purchase schemes by UK local authorities to circumvent budget limits set by the central government.

credit (i) The financial status or reputation of an individual or organization. (ii) Outstanding sums made available to suppliers or customers by firms. See **ageing schedule**; **current assets**; **current liabilities**; **payables**; **receivables**. (iii) Short-term borrowings made available to finance consumer spending (cf. **consumer credit**). (iv) The right-hand side of a ledger T balance, showing **assets** or receipts. (v) Generic term for borrowers, usually of a short-term nature. (vi) Any transaction offering immediately usable funds. For instance, a

credit spread where the net of the two **options'** **premiums** is received (cf. **debit spread**). (vii) Money paid into an account. (viii) Goods or services provided on terms of deferred payment (cf. **creditors**). (ix) The capacity of an entity to repay borrowed money, hence a *good credit* or a *bad credit*. See **credit ratings; credit scoring; credit worthiness**.

credit analysis or **appraisal.** The process of assessing actual and potential borrowers for **credit worthiness**. When assessing credit, the lender or investor will want to be certain or reasonably sure that the borrower will be able to repay or meet the pre-set criteria. To this end, a number of different formulas have been developed. Two common ones in use are: the *6 Cs: capability*, that is the willingness to repay; *capacity*, the ability to repay; *collateral*: security of the loan or investment; *capacity*: the wealth of the borrower; *conditions*: the macro- or micro-economic environment; *compliance*: meeting all lending regulations, and so on. Another system is known as *CAMEL* which is an acronym for *capital, assets, management, earnings*, and *liquidity*. Credit analysis generally looks at the **fundamentals** of a business or borrower, the **cash flow**, and other determinable aspects. Some methods of credit analysis involve statistical methods such as **credit scoring** or **Z scores**. Credit scoring aims to produce a statistical profile of undesirable borrowers or investments against which new credits are assessed. Those which are below an acceptable threshold are turned down. Credit scoring, Z scores, and other **bankruptcy** prediction methods are aimed at inter-temporal predictions of those individuals or firms which are potentially likely to **default** on their obligations. Techniques are based on sophisticated multivariate statistical treatment of data on the potential credit or investment and aim to segregate those **risks** which are satisfactory from those which are unacceptable. An individual who is a specialist in assessing credit is known as a *credit analyst*. See also **fundamental analysis; technical analysis**.

credit broker. An intermediary that arranges loans with a lender for borrowers in return for a commission.

credit bureau. See credit reference agency.

credit card receivable securities. A type of asset-backed security where the **underlying** assets are the outstandings on consumer credit cards. See **certificates of amortizing revolving debt securities**.

credit card trust. A special purpose trust used as the **conduit** for repackaging credit card receivables into securities. See **certificates of amortizing revolving debt securities**.

credit control or **credit management**. Internal policies and procedures used by firms and lenders to control and manage their **credit risks** (cf. **risk management**).

credit creation. See lending multiple.

credit crunch. A period where lenders are unwilling to extend or renew advances to existing or potential borrowers. Such conditions increase the likelihood of **default** by borrowers since they may find it impossible to obtain new **funds**. See also **business cycle**.

credit culture (Banking). The attitude or approach to handling **credit risk** within a bank (cf. **risk averse; risk neutral; risk seeker**). See also **risk-adjusted return on capital**.

credit cylinder. An option strategy based on a cylinder which provides the writer with a net **premium** up-front (cf. **box spread; credit spread; debit spread**).

credit default option. An option that has a payoff linked to the **credit worthiness** or payment performance of the **underlying**. The option protects the holder against a **default** over a specified time period, the payout being conditional on some **event of default** or non-payment by the credit. Such options are used in international trade as a means of insuring the **credit risk**.

crédit de mobilisation de créances commerciales (French). Banker's acceptance (cf. **documentary credit**).

credit derivative. Any instrument where the payoff is linked to changes in the **underlying's** credit standing. The aim is to allow buyers and sellers of the instruments to **hedge** or **speculate** on changes in credit **class**. They fall into three broad categories: those which provide single name default protection; those which give multiple name default protection; and those which offer multiple name price-rating protection. See **credit default option**.

credit enhanced debt securities. Debt issues which have had their **credit worthiness** increased via **credit enhancement**.

credit enhanced undated floating rate note (credit enhanced perpetual FRN). A perpetual floating rate note that is credit enhanced to make it more attractive. This normally involves some form of exit guarantee to the holder in the event of a credit downgrade for the issuer.

credit enhancement. Techniques used for increasing the **credit standing** of (usually) asset-backed securities, debt, or other credit-sensitive transactions. There are basically three mechanisms used, internal enhancement, insurance, and collateralization:

- *Junior/senior tranches*. In this method, the borrowing is divided into tranches. The most junior of the tranches will take all the initial losses (if any). As a result, the senior tranches will have a reduced, anticipated **default** rate which means that they will have a relatively high credit standing.
- *Insurance*. A third party will agree for a fee to **underwrite** any credit losses. The insurance company may be a general insurer or specialist institution, known as a monoline insurance company.
- *Over-collateralization*. The debt will be backed by a larger amount of **underlying** or pooled assets than the money raised, the surplus being used to ensure that enough is left in the **pool** to pay off the debt. In effect, the originator has provided **equity** in the form of assets to back up the debt.
- *Margin*. This involves a technique similar to that used in the **futures** exchanges. The party subject to credit enhancement will post **collateral** to the value of the difference between the market value and the original value.

credit equivalent. Method used in the **Basle Capital Convergence Accord** for converting off-balance sheet items into loan or credit value equivalents for **capital adequacy** purposes.

Credit export (Belgium). The export credit financing consortium set up and owned by Belgian banks.

credit exposure. The amount at risk in a particular credit situation (cf. **credit risk**).

credit facility or **credit line.** A short-term borrowing arrangement with a bank or other lender (for instance a **broker-dealer**) which may take many forms (cf. **overdraft**; **revolving facility term loan**).

credit for export bond. Asset-backed security where the **underlying** is a pool of export credits.

credit-insurance. A policy covering bad debts on receivables. Also known as *credit guarantee* or *trade indemnity* or *insurance*.

credit limit. The amount of credit that an organization is willing to extend to an individual or organization. Also called a *credit line*. See **daylight exposure limit**.

creditor. An individual or organization to whom money is owed (cf. **payables**; **receivables**).

creditors' committee. A working group formed to represent the interests of creditors in **insolvency**, **bankruptcy**, or informal work-out situations with a debtor. See also **administrative receiver**; **liquidator**; **receiver**.

creditors' meeting. Meeting held by the creditors of a firm when the latter is not in a position to repay to decide on the best approach to salvaging value from the situation (cf. **chapter 11**; **default**; **financial distress**; **moratorium**; **workout**).

creditors' voluntary liquidation (UK). A method available under the Insolvency Act, 1986 for winding-up a company's affairs (cf. **administration order**). Also called a *creditors' voluntary winding-up*.

credit quality. See **credit worthiness**; **credit ratings**.

credit rating agency. An organization that specializes in **credit analysis**. The results may be publicly available or provided to users directly when **credit referral** is undertaken. Also known as a *rating agency*.

credit ratings. Formal scoring of a company's **credit worthiness** provided by a specialist institution. The detailed criteria by which Moody's Investors Services and Standard and Poor's assess and assign credit rating for both the **short term** (that is out to one year) and the **long term** is given below:

1. **LONG-TERM RATINGS**

Moody's Investors Services Rating Definitions
'Aaa Bonds which are rated Aaa are judged to be of the best quality. They carry the smallest degree of investment risk and are generally referred to as "gilt edged". Interest payments are protected by a large or by an exceptionally stable margin and principal is secured. While the various protective elements are likely to change, such changes as can be visualized are most unlikely to impair the fundamentally strong position of such issues.

Aa Bonds which are rated Aa are judged to be of high quality by all standards. Together with the Aaa group they comprise what are generally known as high-grade bonds. They are rated lower than the best bonds because margins of protection may not be as large as in Aaa securities or fluctuation of protective elements may be of greater amplitude or there may be other elements present which make the long-term risk appear somewhat larger than the Aaa securities.

A Bonds which are rated A possess many favourable investment attributes and are to be considered as upper-medium-grade obligations. Factors giving security to principal and interest are considered adequate, but elements may be present which suggest a susceptibility to impairment some time in the future.

Baa Bonds which are rated Baa are considered as medium-grade obligations (i.e., they are neither highly protected nor poorly secured). Interest payments and principal security appear adequate for the present but certain protective elements may be lacking or may be characteristically unreliable over any great length of time. Such bonds lack outstanding investment characteristics and in fact have speculative characteristics as well.

Ba Bonds which are rated Ba are judged to have speculative elements; their future cannot be considered as well-assured. Often the protection of interest and principal payments may be very moderate and thereby not well safeguarded during both good and bad times over the future. Uncertainty of position characterises both in this class.

B Bonds which are rated B generally lack characteristics of the desirable investment. Assurance of interest and principal payments or of maintenance of other terms of the contract over any long period of time may be small.

Caa Bonds which are rated Caa are of poor standing. Such issues may be in default or there may be present elements of danger with respect to principal or interest.

Ca Bonds which are rated Ca represent obligations which are speculative in a high degree. Such issues are often in default or have other marked short-comings.

C Bonds which are rated C are the lowest rated class of bonds, and issues so rated can be regarded as having extremely poor prospects of ever attaining any real investment standing.

Moody's bond ratings, where specified, are applied to senior bank obligations and insurance company senior policyholder and claims obligations with an original maturity in excess of one year. Obligations relying upon support mechanisms such as letters-of-credit and bonds of indemnity are excluded unless explicitly rated.

Obligations of a branch of a bank are considered to be domiciled in the country in which the branch is located. Unless noted as an exception, Moody's rating on a bank's ability to repay senior obligations extends only to branches located in countries which carry a Moody's sovereign rating. Such branch obligations are rated at the lower of the bank's rating or Moody's sovereign rating for the bank deposits for the country in which the branch is located.

When the currency in which an obligation is denominated is not the same as the currency of the country in which the obligation is domiciled, Moody's ratings do not incorporate an opinion as to whether payment of the obligation will be affected by the actions of the government controlling the currency of denomination. In addition, risk associated with bilateral conflicts between an investor's home country and either the issuer's home country or the country where an issuer branch is located are not incorporated into Moody's ratings.

Moody's makes no representation that rated bank obligations or insurance company obligations are exempt from registration under the US Securities Act of 1933 or issued in conformity with any other applicable law or regulation. Nor does Moody's represent that any specific bank or insurance company obligation is legally enforceable or is a valid senior obligation of a rated issuer.

Moody's ratings are opinions, not recommendations to buy or sell, and their accuracy is not guaranteed. A rating should be weighed solely as one factor in an investment decision and you should make your own study and evaluation of any issuer whose securities or debt obligations you consider buying or selling.'

BANK FINANCIAL STRENGTH RATING DEFINITIONS

'Moody's Bank Financial Strength Ratings represent Moody's opinion of a bank's intrinsic safety and soundness and, as such, exclude certain external credit risks and credit support elements that are addressed by Moody's traditional debt and deposit ratings. Unlike Moody's traditional debt ratings, Bank Financial Strength Ratings do not address the probability of timely payment. Instead, Bank Financial Strength Ratings can be understood as a measure of the likelihood that a bank will require assistance from third parties such as its owners, its industry group, or official institutions. Bank Financial Strength Ratings do not take into account the probability that the bank will receive such external support, nor do they address risks arising from sovereign actions that may interfere with a bank's ability to honour its domestic or foreign currency obligations.

Factors considered in the assignment of Bank Financial Strength Ratings include bank-specific-elements such as financial fundamentals, franchise value, and business and asset diversification. Although Bank Financial Strength Ratings exclude the external factors specified above, they do take into account other risk factors in the bank's operating environment, including the strength and prospective performance of the economy, as well as the structure and relative fragility of the financial system, and the quality of banking regulation and supervision.

The definitions for Moody's Bank Financial Strength are as follows:

A
Banks rated A possess exceptional intrinsic financial strength. Typically, they will be major institutions with highly valuable and defensible business franchises, strong financial fundamentals, and a very attractive and stable operating environment.

B
Banks rated B possess strong intrinsic financial strength. Typically, they will be important institutions with valuable and defensible business fran-

chises, good financial fundamentals, and an attractive and stable operating environment.

C

Banks rated C possess good intrinsic financial strength. Typically, they will be institutions with valuable and defensible business franchises. These banks will demonstrate either acceptable financial fundamentals within a stable operating environment, or better than average financial fundamentals within an unstable operating environment.

D

Banks rated D possess adequate financial strength, but may be limited by one or more of the following factors: a vulnerable or developing business franchise; weak financial fundamentals; or an unstable operating environment.

E

Banks rated E possess very weak intrinsic financial strength, requiring periodic outside support or suggesting an eventual need for outside assitance. Such institutions may be limited by one or more of the following factors: a business franchise of questionable value; financial fundamentals that are seriously deficient in one or more respects; or highly unstable operating environment.

Intermediate Categories

Where appropriate, a "+" may be appended to ratings below the "A" category to distinguish those banks that all into intermediate categories.

Standard & Poor's Debt Rating Definitions

'The range of instruments available in the international capital market has exploded in recent years. S&P has expanded its range of ratings service accordingly. We now offer ratings covering:

- long-term debt;
- commercial paper;
- certificates of deposit;
- money market funds;
- mutual bond funds;
- insurance companies' claims-paying ability.

A Standard & Poor's corporate or municipal debt rating is a current assessment of the creditworthiness of an obligator with respect to a specific obligation. This assessment may take into consideration obligors such as guarantors, insurers, or lessees.

The debt rating is not a recommendation to purchase, sell, or hold a security, inasmuch as it does not comment as to market price or suitability for a particular investor.

The ratings are based on current information furnished by the issuer or obtained by S & P from other sources it considers reliable. S & P does not perform an audit in connection with any rating and may, on occasion, rely on unaudited financial information. The ratings may be changed, suspended, or withdrawn as a result of changes in, or unavailability of, such information, or based on other circumstances.

The ratings are based, in varying degrees, on the following considerations:

1. Likelihood of default—capacity and willingness of the obligor as to the timely payment of interest and repayment of principal in accordance with the terms of the obligation;
2. Nature of and provisions of the obligation;
3. Protection afforded by, and relative position of, the obligation in the event of bankruptcy, reorganization, or other arrangement under the laws of bankruptcy and other laws affecting creditors' rights.

LONG-TERM RATING DEFINITIONS

Investment grade

AAA Debt rated "AAA" has the highest rating assigned by Standard & Poor's. Capacity to pay interest and repay principal is extremely strong.

AA Debt rated "AA" has a very strong capacity to pay interest and repay principal and differs from the highest rated issues only in small degree.

A Debt rated "A" has a strong capacity to pay interest and repay principal although it is somewhat more susceptible to the adverse effects of changes in circumstances and economic conditions than debt in higher rated categories.

BBB Debt rated "BBB" is regarded as having an adequate capacity to pay interest and repay principal. Whereas it normally exhibits adequate protection parameters, adverse economic conditions or changing circumstances are more likely to lead to a weakened capacity to pay interest and repay principal for debt in this category than in higher rated categories.

Speculative grade

Debt rated "BB", "B", "CCC", and "C" is regarded as having predominantly speculative characteristics with respect to capacity to pay interest and repay principal. "BB" indicates the least degree of speculation and "C" the highest. While such debt will likely have some quality and protective characteristics, these are outweighed by large uncertainties or major exposures to adverse conditions.

BB Debt rated "BB" has less near-term vulnerability to default than other speculative issues. However, it faces major ongoing uncertainties or exposure to adverse business, financial, or economic conditions which could lead to inadequate capacity to meet timely interest and principal payments. The "BB" rating category is also used for debt subordinated to senior debt that is assigned an actual or implied "BBB-" rating.

B Debt rated "B" has a greater vulnerability to default but currently has the capacity to meet interest payments and principal repayments. Adverse business, financial, or economic conditions will likely impair capacity or willingness to pay interest and repay principal. The "B" rating category is also used for debt subordinated to senior debt that is assigned an actual or implied "BB" or "BB-" rating.

CCC Debt rated "CCC" has a currently identifiable vulnerability to default, and is dependent upon favourable business, financial, and economic conditions to meet timely payment of interest and repayment of principal. In the event of adverse business, financial, or economic conditions, it is not likely to have the capacity to pay interest and repay principal. The "CCC" rating category is also used for debt subordinated to senior debt that is assigned an actual or implied "B" or "B-" rating.

CC The rating "CC" typically is applied to debt subordinated to senior debt that is assigned an actual or implied "CCC" rating.

C The rating "C" typically is applied to debt subordinated to senior debt which is assigned an actual or implied "CCC-" debt rating. The "C" rating may be used to cover a situation where a bankruptcy petition has been filed, but debt service payments are continued.

CI The rating "CI" is reserved for income bonds on which no interest is being paid.

D Debt rated "D" is in payment default. The "D" rating category is used when interest payments on principal payments are not made on the date due even if the applicable grace period has not expired, unless S & P believes that such payments will be made during such grace period. The "D" rating also will be used upon the filing of a bankruptcy petition if debt service payments are jeopardized.

Plus (+) or minus(−): The ratings from "AA" to "CCC" may be modified by the addition of a plus or minus sign to show relative standing within the major rating categories.

c The letter "c" indicates that the holder's option to tender to security for purchase may be cancelled under certain prestated conditions enumerated in the tender option documents.

i The letter "i" indicates the rating is implied. Such ratings are assigned only on request to entities that do not have specific debt issues to be rated. In addition, implied ratings are assigned to governments that have not requested explicit ratings for specific debt issues. Implied ratings on governments represent the sovereign ceiling or upper limit for ratings on specific debt issues of entities domiciled in the country.

L The letter "L" indicates that the rating pertains to the principal amount of those bonds to the extent that the underlying deposit collateral is federally insured and interest is adequately collateralized. In the case of certificates of deposit, the letter "L" indicates that the deposit, combined with other deposits being held in the same right and capacity, will be honored for principal and accrued pre-default interest up to the federal insurance limits within 30 days after the closing of the insured institution or, in the event that the deposit is assumed by a successor insured institution, upon maturity.

p The letter "p" indicates that the rating is provisional. A provisional rating assumes the successful completion of the project being financed by the debt being rated and indicates that payment of debt service requirements is largely or entirely dependent upon the successful and timely completion of the project. This rating, however, while addressing credit quality subsequent to completion of the project, makes no comment on the likelihood of, or the risk of default upon failure of, such completion. The investor should exercise his own judgment with respect to such likelihood and risk.

* Continuance of the rating is contingent upon S & P's receipt of an executed copy of the escrow agreement or closing documentation confirming investments and cash flows.

N.R. Not rated.

Debt Obligations of Issuers outside the United States and its territories are rated on the same basis as domestic corporate and municipal issues. The ratings measure the creditworthiness of the obligor but do not take into account currency exchange and related uncertainties.

Bond Investment Quality Standards: Under present commercial bank regulations issued by the Comptroller of the Currency, bonds rated in the top four categories ("AAA", "AA", "A", "BBB" commonly known as "investment grade" ratings) are generally regarded as eligible for bank investment. In addition, the laws of various states governing legal investments impose certain rating or other standards for obligations eligible for investment by savings banks, trust companies, insurance companies, and fiduciaries generally.

RATING OUTLOOK DEFINITIONS

An S & P Rating Outlook assesses the potential direction of an issuer's long-term debt rating over the intermediate to longer term. In determining a Rating Outlook, consideration is given to any changes in the economic and/or fundamental business conditions. An Outlook is not necessarily a precursor to a rating change or future CreditWatch action.

Positive indicates that a rating may be raised.

Negative means a rating may be lowered.

Stable indicates that ratings are not likely to change.

Developing means ratings may be raised or lowered.

N.M. means not meaningful.

CD RATING DEFINITIONS

Long-term investment grades

AAA The highest degree of safety with overwhelming repayment capacity.

AA Very high degree of safety with strong capacity for repayment, but these issues are somewhat more susceptible in the long term to adverse economic conditions than those rated in higher categories.

BBB A satisfactory degree of safety and capacity for repayment, but these issues are more vulner-

Comparison of long term Ratings across different rating agencies

ASPAC Australian Ratings (Australia)	Canadian Bond Rating Service (Canada)	Dominion Bond Rating Service (Canada)	Duff & Phelps (USA)	Fitch Investors' Service (USA)	IBCA Banking Analysis (UK)	Japan Bond Research Institute (Japan)	Japan Credit Rating Agency (Japan)	McCarthy Crisanti & Maffei (USA)	Moody's Investor Service (USA)	Nippon Investor Service (Japan)	Standard & Poor's (USA)
AAA	A++	AAA	AAA	AAA	AAA	AAA	Aaa	AAA	Aaa	AAA	AAA
AA+	A+H	AAH	AA+	AA+	AA+	AA+	Aa+	AA+	Aa1	AA+	AA+
AA	A+	AA	AA	AA	AA	AA	Aa	AA	Aa2	AA	AA
AA-	A+L	AAL	AA-	AA-	AA-	AA-	Aa-	AA-	Aa3	AA-	AA-
A+	AH	AH	A+	A+	A+	A+	A+	A+	A1	A+	A+
A	A	A	A	A	A	A	A	A	A2	A	A
A-	AL	AL	A-	A-	A-	A-	A-	A-	A3	A-	A-
BBB+	B++H	BBBH	BBB+	BBB+	BBB+	BBB+	Bbb+	BBB+	Baa1	BBB+	BBB+
BBB	B++	BBB	BBB	BBB	BBB	BBB	Bbb	BBB	Baa2	BBB	BBB
BBB-	B++L	BBBL	BBB-	BBB-	BBB-	BBB-	Bbb-	BBB-	Baa3	BBB-	BBB-

Note that these are generally accepted comparisons but will not be the same in all cases.

able to adverse economic conditions or changing circumstances than higher rated issues.

Long-term speculative grades

CDs rated in these categories have predominantly speculative characteristics in their ability to repay interest and principal. "BB" indicates the lowest degree of speculation and "C" the highest.

BB This designation reflects less near-term vulnerability to default than other speculative issues. However, the issues face major ongoing uncertainties or exposures to adverse economic or financial conditions threatening capacity to meet interest and principal payments on a timely basis.

B This designation indicates that the issues have a greater vulnerability to default but currently have the capacity to meet interest payments and principal repayments. Adverse business, financial, or economic conditions will likely impair capacity to pay interest and repay principal.

CCC Issues rated "CCC" have currently identifiable vulnerability to default, and are dependent upon favourable business, financial, and economic conditions to meet timely interest and principal repayments. Adverse business, financial, or economic developments would render repayment capacity unlikely.'

2. SHORT-TERM RATINGS

Moody's Investors Services Rating Definitions

'Moody's short-term debt ratings are opinions of the ability of issuers to repay punctually senior debt obligations which have an original maturity not exceeding one year. Obligations relying upon support mechanisms such as letters-of-credit and bonds of indemnity are excluded unless explicitly rated.

Moody's employs the following three designations, all judged to be investment grade, to indicate the relative repayment ability of rated issuers.

PRIME-1 Issuers rated Prime-1 (or supporting institutions) have a superior ability for repayment of senior short-term debt obligations. Prime-1 repayment ability will often be evidenced by many of the following characteristics:

- Leading market positions in well-established industries
- High rates of return on funds employed.
- Conservative capitalization structure with moderate reliance on debt and ample asset protection.
- Broad margins in earnings coverage of fixed financial charges and high internal cash generation.
- Well-established access to a range of financial markets and assured sources of alternate liquidity.

PRIME-2 Issuers rated Prime-2 (or supporting institutions) have a strong ability for repayment of senior short-term debt obligations. This will normally be evidenced by many of the characteristics cited above but to a lesser degree. Earnings trends

and coverage ratios, while sound, may be more subject to variation. Capitalization characteristics, while still appropriate, may be more affected by external conditions. Ample alternate liquidity is maintained.

PRIME-3 Issuers rated Prime-3 (or supporting institutions) have an acceptable ability for repayment of senior short-term obligations. The effect of industry characteristics and market compositions may be more pronounced. Variability in earnings and profitability may result in changes in the level of debt protection measurements and may require relatively high financial leverage. Adequate alternate liquidity is maintained.

NOT PRIME Issuers rated Not Prime do not fall within any of the Prime rating categories.

Obligations of a branch of a bank are considered to be domiciled in the country in which the branch is located. Unless noted as an exception, Moody's rating on a bank's ability to repay senior obligations extends only to branches located in countries which carry a Moody's sovereign rating. Such branch obligations are rated at the lower of the bank's rating or Moody's sovereign rating for bank deposits for the country in which the branch is located.

When the currency in which an obligation is denominated is not the same as the currency of the country in which the obligation is domiciled, Moody's ratings do not incorporate an opinion as to whether payment of the obligation will be affected by actions of the government controlling the currency of denomination. In addition, risks associated with bilateral conflicts between an investor's home country and either the issuer's home country or the country where an issuer's branch is located are not incorporated into Moody's short-term debt ratings.

Moody's makes no representation that rated bank or insurance company obligations are exempt from registration under the US Securities Act of 1933 or issued in conformity with any other applicable law or regulation. Nor does Moody's represent that any specific bank or insurance company obligation is legally enforceable or a valid senior obligation of a rated issuer.

When an issuer represents to Moody's that its short-term debt obligations are supported by the credit of another entity or entities, then the names of such supporting entities are listed with the name of the issuer, or indicated with a footnote reference, in Moody's publications. In assigning ratings to such issuers. Moody's evaluates the financial strength of the affiliated corporations, commercial banks, insurance companies, foreign governments or other entities, but only as one factor in the total rating assessment. Moody's makes no representation and gives no opinion on the legal validity or enforceability of any support arrangements.

Moody's ratings are opinions, not recommend-ations to buy or sell, and their accuracy is not guaranteed. A rating should be weighed solely as one factor in an investment decision and you should make your own study and evaluation of any issuer whose securities or debt obligations you consider buying or selling.'

Standard and Poor's Rating Definitions

COMMERCIAL PAPER RATING DEFINITIONS

A Standard & Poor's commercial paper rating is a current assessment of the likelihood of timely payment of debt having an original maturity of no more than 365 days.

Ratings are graded into several categories, ran-ging from 'A-1' for the highest quality obligations to 'D' for the lowest. These categories are as follows:

A-1 This highest category indicates that the degree of safety regarding timely payment is strong. Those issues determined to possess extre-mely strong safety characteristics are denoted with a plus sign (+) designation.

A-2 Capacity for timely payment on issues with this designation is satisfactory. However, the rela-tive degree of safety is not as high as for issues designated 'A-1'.

A-3 Issues carrying this designation have ade-quate capacity for timely payment. They are, how-ever, more vulnerable to the adverse effects of changes in circumstances than obligations carry-ing the higher designations.

B Issues rated 'B' are regarded as having only speculative capacity for timely payment.

C This rating is assigned to short-term debt obligations with a doubtful capacity for payment.

D Debt rated 'D' is in payment default. The 'D' rating category is used when interest payments or principal payments are not made on the date due, even if the applicable grace period has not expired, unless S & P believes that such payments will be made during such grace period.

A commercial paper rating is not a recommenda-tion to purchase, sell, or hold a security inasmuch as it does not comment as to market price or suitability for a particular investor. The ratings are based on current information furnished to S & P by the issuer or obtained by S & P from other sources it considers reliable. S & P does not per-form an audit in connection with any rating and may, on occasion, rely on unaudited financial in-formation. The ratings may be changed, sus-pended, or withdrawn, as a result of changes in, or unavailability of, such information, or based on other circumstances.

CD RATING DEFINITIONS

Short-term investment grades

A-1 This highest category indicates that the degree of safety regarding timely payment is strong. Those issues determined to possess extremely

strong characteristics are denoted with a plus sign (+) designation.

A-2 Capacity for timely payment on issues with this designation is satisfactory. However, the rela-tive degree of safety is not as high as for issues designated 'A-1'.

A-3 Issues carrying this designation have ade-quate capacity for timely payment. They are, how-ever, more vulnerable to the adverse effects of changes in circumstances than obligations carry-ing the higher designations.

Short-term speculative grades

B Issues rated 'B' are regarded as having only speculative capacity for timely payment.

C This rating is assigned to short-term debt obligations with a doubtful capacity for payment.

D Debt rated 'D' is in payment default. The 'D' rating category is used when interest payments or principal payments are not made on the date due, even if the applicable grace period has not expired, unless S & P believes that such payments will be made during such grace period.

Plus (+) or minus (−) Ratings from 'AA/A-1+' to 'CCC/C' may be modified by a plus or minus sign, reflecting the relative standing within the major rating categories.

N.R. Indicates no rating has been requested, that there is insufficient information on which to base a rating, or that S & P does not rate a particular type of obligation as a matter of policy.

A CD rating is not a recommendation to purchase, sell, or hold a security inasmuch as it does not comment as to market price or suitability for a particular investor. The ratings are based on cur-rent information furnished to S & P by the issuer or obtained by S & P from other sources it con-siders reliable. S & P does not perform an audit in connection with any rating and may, on occasion, rely on unaudited financial information. The rat-ings may be changed, suspended, or withdrawn as a result of changes in, or unavailability of, such information, or based on other circumstances.

MONEY MARKET FUND RATING DEFINITIONS

Money market fund ratings assess the safety of principal. Symbols are as follows:

AAAm Safety is excellent. Superior capacity to maintain principal value and limit exposure to loss.

AAm Safety is very good. Strong capacity to maintain principal value and limit exposure to loss.

Am Safety is good. Strong capacity to maintain principal value and limit exposure to loss.

Bm Safety is uncertain. Limited capacity to maintain principal value and limit exposure to loss.

G The letter 'G' follows the rating symbol when a fund's portfolio consists primarily of U.S. govern-ment securities.

Plus (+) or minus (−) sign The 'AAm' and 'Am' ratings may be modified to show relative standing within the funding categories.

Comparison of short term ratings across different rating agencies

ASPAC Australian Ratings (Australia)	Canadian Bond Rating Service (Canada)	Dominion Bond Rating Service (Canada)	Duff & Phelps (USA)	Fitch Investors' Service (USA)	IBCA Banking Analysis (UK)	Japan Bond Research Institute (Japan)	Japan Credit Rating Agency (Japan)	McCarthy Crisanti & Maffei (USA)	Moody's Investor Service (USA)	Nippon Investor Service (Japan)	Standard & Poor's (USA)
A1+	A1+	R1	Duff 1+		A1+	u/a	J1	MCM1	Prime 1	A1	A1+
A1	A1	R1	Duff 1		A1		J2	MCM2	Prime 2	A2	A1
A2	A2	R3	Duff 1−		A2		J3	MCM3	Prime 3	A3	A2
B1	A3	U	Duff 2		B1		NJ	MCM4	Not prime	B	A3
B2	A3	NR	Duff 3		B2			MCM5		C	B
C1					C1					D	C
					D1						D

Note that these are generally accepted comparisons but will not be the same in all cases.

A money market fund rating is not directly comparable to a debt rating due to differences in investment characteristics, rating criteria and creditworthiness of portfolio investments. For example, a money market fund portfolio provides greater liquidity, price stability, and diversification than a long-term bond, but not necessarily credit quality that would be indicated by the corresponding debt rating. Ratings are not commentaries on yield levels.

A money market fund rating is not a recommendation to purchase, sell, or hold a security inasmuch as it does not comment as to market price or suitability for a particular investor. The ratings are based on current information furnished to S & P by the issuer or obtained by S & P from other sources it considers reliable. S & P does not perform an audit in connection with any rating and may, on occasion, rely on unaudited financial information. The ratings may be changed, suspended, or withdrawn as a result of changes in, or unavailability of, such information, or based on other circumstances.

Standard and Poor's Mutual Bond Fund Rating Definitions
'An S & P rating on the shares of a mutual bond fund is a current assessment of the overall credit quality of the fund's portfolio. Symbols are as follows:

AAAf Funds are composed exclusively of investments that are rated "AAA", and/or eligible short-term investments.
AAf Funds are composed of investments with an overall credit quality of "AA".
Af Funds are composed of investments with an overall credit quality of "A".
BBBf Funds are composed of investments with an overall credit quality "BBB".
Plus (+) *or minus* (−) Ratings from "AAf" to "BBf" may be modified to show relative standing within the rating category.

The rating is based on an analysis of several factors, including, but not limited to, the credit quality of the investments within the portfolio, diversification of the assets, management, liquidity, and investment practices.

A mutual bond fund rating is not directly comparable to a debt rating due to differences in investment characteristics, rating criteria, and creditworthiness of portfolio investments. For example, a mutual bond fund portfolio provides greater liquidity, price stability, and diversification than a long-term bond, but not necessarily credit quality that would be indicated by the corresponding debt rating. Ratings are not commentaries on yield levels.

A mutual bond fund rating is not a recommendation to purchase, sell, or hold a security inasmuch as it does not comment as to market price or suitability for a particular investor. The ratings are based on current information furnished to S & P by the issuer or obtained by S & P from other sources it considers reliable. S & P does not perform an audit in connection with any rating and may, on occasion, rely on unaudited financial information. The ratings may be changed, suspended, or withdrawn as a result of changes in, or unavailability of, such information, or based on other circumstances.

PREFERRED STOCK RATING DEFINITIONS
A Standard and Poor's preferred stock rating is an assessment of the capacity and willingness of an issuer to pay preferred stock dividends and any applicable sinking fund obligations. A preferred stock rating differs from a bond rating inasmuch as it is assigned to an equity issue, which is intrinsically different from, and subordinated to, a debt issue. Therefore, to reflect this difference, the preferred stock rating symbol will normally not be higher than the debt rating symbol assigned to, or that would be assigned to, the senior debt of the same issuer.

The preferred stock ratings are based on the following considerations:

1. Likelihood of payment—capacity and willingness of the issuer to meet the timely payment of preferred stock dividends and any applicable sinking fund requirements in accordance with the terms of the obligation;
2. Nature of, and provisions of, the issue;
3. Relative position of the issue in the event of bankruptcy, reorganization, or other arrangement under the laws of bankruptcy and other laws affecting the creditors' rights.

AAA This is the highest rating that may be assigned by Standard and Poor's to a preferred stock issue and indicates an extremely strong capacity to pay the preferred stock obligations.
AA A preferred stock issue rated "AA" also qualifies as a high-quality fixed income security. The capacity to pay preferred stock obligations is very strong, although not as overwhelming as for issues rated "AAA".
A An issue rated "A" is backed by a sound capacity to pay the preferred stock obligations, although it is somewhat more susceptible to the adverse effects of changes in circumstances and economic conditions.
BBB An issue rated "BBB" is regarded as backed by an adequate capacity to pay the preferred stock obligations. Whereas it normally exhibits adequate protection parameters, adverse economic conditions or changing circumstances are more likely to lead to a weakened capacity to make payments for a preferred stock in this category than for issues in the "A" category.
BB, B, CCC Preferred stock rated "BB", "B", and "CCC" are regarded, on balance, as predominantly speculative with respect to the issuer's ca-

pacity to pay preferred stock obligations. "BB" indicates the lowest degree of speculation and "CCC" the highest degree of speculation. While such issues will likely have some quality and protective characteristics, these are outweighed by large uncertainties or major risk exposures to adverse conditions.

CC the rating "CC" is reserved for a preferred stock issue in arrears on dividends or sinking fund payments but that is currently paying.

C A preferred stock rated "C" is a non-paying issue.

D A preferred stock rated "D" is a non-paying issue with the issuer in default on debt instruments.

NR This indicates that no rating has been requested, that there is insufficient information on which to base a rating, or that S & P does not rate a particular type of obligation as a matter of policy.

Plus (+) or minus(−) To provide more detailed indications of preferred stock quality, the rating from "AA" to "CCC" may be modified by the addition of a plus or minus sign to show relative standing within the major rating categories.

A preferred stock rating is not a recommendation to purchase, sell, or hold a security inasmuch as it does not comment as to market price or suitability for a particular investor. The ratings are based on current information furnished by S & P by the issuer or obtained by S & P from other sources it considers reliable. S & P does not perform an audit in connection with any rating and may, on occasion, rely on unaudited financial information. The ratings may be changed, suspended, or withdrawn as a result of changes in, or unavailability of, such information, or based on other circumstances.

Standard and Poor's Insurance Claims Ratings Definitions

CLAIMS-PAYING ABILITY RATING

DEFINITIONS

A Standard & Poor's insurance claims-paying ability rating is an opinion of an operating insurance company's financial capacity to meet the obligations of its insurance policies in accordance with their terms. Their opinion is not specific to any particular insurance policy or contract, nor does it address the suitability of a particular policy for a specific purpose or purchaser. Furthermore, the opinion does not take into account deductibles, surrender or cancellation penalties, the timeliness of payment, or the likelihood of the use of a defence such as fraud to deny claims. Claims-paying ability ratings do not refer to an insurer's ability to meet nonpolicy obligations (i.e. debt contracts).

The claims-paying ability ratings are based on current information furnished by the insurance company or obtained by S & P from other sources it considers reliable. S & P does not perform an audit in connection with any rating and may, on occasion, rely on unaudited financial information.

The ratings may be changed, suspended, or withdrawn as a result of changes in or unavailability of, such information or based on other circumstances.

The assignment of ratings to debt issues that are fully or partially supported by insurance policies, contracts, or guarantees is a separate process from the determination of claims-paying ability ratings, and follows procedures consistent with debt ratings and definitions and practices.

Claims-paying ability ratings are dividend into two broad classifications. Rating categories from "AAA" to "BBB" are classified as secure claims-paying ability ratings and are used to indicate insurers whose financial capacity to meet policyholder obligations is viewed on balance as sound. Among factors considered in placing insurers within the spectrum of 'secure' rating categories is the time frame within which policyholder security could be damaged by adverse developments. That time frame grows shorter as ratings move down the 'secure' rating scale.

Rating categories from "BB" to "D" are classified as 'vulnerable' claims-paying ability ratings and are used to indicate insurers whose financial capacity to meet policyholder obligations is viewed as vulnerable to adverse developments. In fact, the financial capacity of insurers rated "CC" to "C" may already be impaired, while insurers rated "D" are in liquidation.

Ratings from "AA" to "CCC" may be modified by the use of a plus or minus sign to show relative standing of the insurer within those rating categories.

Secure claims-paying ability

AAA Insurers rated "AAA" offer superior financial security on both an absolute and relative basis. They possess the highest safety and have an overwhelming capacity to meet policyholder obligations.

AA Insurers rated "AA" offer excellent financial security, and their capacity to meet policy holder obligations differs only in a small degree from insurers rated "AAA".

A Insurers rated "A" offer good financial security, but their capacity to meet policyholder obligations is somewhat more susceptible to adverse changes in economic or underwriting conditions than more highly rated insurers.

BBB Insurers rated "BBB" offer adequate financial security, but their capacity to meet policyholder obligations is considered more vulnerable to adverse economic or underwriting conditions than that of more highly rated insurers.

Vulnerable claims-paying ability

BB Insurers rated "BB" offer financial security that may be adequate but caution is indicated since their capacity to meet policyholder obligations is considered vulnerable to adverse economic or underwriting conditions and may not be adequate for 'long-tail' or long-term policies.

B Insurers rated "B" are currently able to meet policyholder obligations, but their vulnerability to adverse economic or underwriting conditions is considered high.

CCC Insurers rated "CCC" are vulnerable to adverse economic or underwriting conditions to the extent that their continued capacity to meet policyholder obligations is highly questionable unless, a favourable environment prevails.

CC,C Insurers rated "CC" or "C" may not be meeting all policyholder obligations, may be operating under the jurisdiction of insurance regulators and are vulnerable to liquidation.

D Insurers rated "D" have been placed under an order of liquidation.'

See also **credit scoring; ratio analysis; z scores**.

credit reference. (i) Third-party endorsement of the ability of a borrower to service additional debts. See **credit rating agency**. (ii) A score or other report providing a measure of **credit risk**. See **credit ratings**.

credit reference agency. An organization specializing in providing **credit references**, usually for trade credit rather than investment purposes. The latter is usually called a *credit rating agency.*

credit referral. The practice of seeking confirmation of a **creditor's credit worthiness** from a third party, often a specialist **credit rating agency** or **credit reference agency** before extending any credit facility or making an investment.

credit risk. The risk that a borrower or issuer may **default** on his obligations or be unable to perform under the terms of the contract (cf. **event risk**). Technically **counterparty risk** is also a credit risk, but the latter is now largely confined to those cases where a positive decision has been made to invest or lend to a particular borrower. Sometimes called *customer risk* or *capital risk* (cf. **settlement risk**). See also **value at risk**.

credit risk insurance. A method of insuring against **credit risk** in other firms (normally taken to be the legal condition when a firm is unable to meet its obligation) (cf. **administration order; chapter 11; insolvency**).

credit risk premium. The difference in yield between **default**-free obligations,such as government **bonds**, and securities issued by private entities or other entities subject to **credit risk**, usually stated in terms of **basis points**.

credit sale agreement. Purchase financing provided by a vendor either directly or through a specialist financing house or bank. Also known as *hire purchase* in the UK.

credit scoring. A **credit** evaluation technique that involves assigning scores to borrowers on the basis of the expectation of **default**. The technique involves a multivariate analysis of significant characteristics such as age, business, size of borrowing, and so forth using prior experience as a guide (cf. **z score**). The approach is also applied to consumer credit applications.

credit sensitive note. An issue of securities with **provisions** designed to adjust the interest rate on the notes in response to changes in the **credit rating** of the issuer. Thus if the issuer is downgraded by a **credit rating agency**, the notes will pay a higher rate to compensate investors for the additional risk and preserve the capital value of the securities (cf. **margin**).

credit spread. (i) The yield differential between different fixed interest securities issued by borrowers with different **creditworthiness** (cf. **default risk**). Also known as *credit risk premium*. (ii) An **options** trading term for the sale and purchase of two options where the **premium** received is greater than that paid (cf. **box spread**). A *debit spread* is the opposite. With a credit spread, the position taker is effectively borrowing; with a debit spread, lending.

credit spread option. **Spread option** aimed at protecting a given **credit spread** relationship between two levels of credit. For instance, an option might seek to protect the buyer against adverse changes in triple-B, the lowest rated **investment grade** securities against government bonds (cf. **benchmark**). If the spread were to widen above the **strike**, the holder would **exercise** the option and receive a cash payment to compensate for the market's adverse assessment of the **creditworthiness** of the triple-B credit **class**.

credit spread swap. See bond index swap.

credit squeeze. Monetary policy measures aimed at reducing economic activity in an economy by directly or indirectly reducing the demand for **credit** on borrowed funds. Indirect measures include raising interest rates, increasing the amount of cash or **reserves** banks need to hold against lending, or other regulatory controls within the powers of the **central bank**. Direct measures involve changes to the amount of lending allowed, increasing the required down payment on any **credit sale agreements**, the borrowing term or other elements likely to affect credit demand.

credit standards. The minimum creditworthiness acceptable in a client or **counterparty** (cf. **investment grade**).

credit standing. See credit worthiness.

credit union (Banking; USA). A non-profit making depository institution operating as a credit co-operative (cf. **savings bank**).

credit watch. A notice issued by a **credit rating agency** alerting the market to a possible revision in a particular **credit rating**. Such notices usually presage a change in status being followed by notice of an upgrade or downgrade in credit rating.

credit worthiness. The measure of a borrower's credit standing. The higher the credit worthiness, the higher the credit standing. See also **credit ratings**.

creepers or **vines.** Informal lines of communication between different parts of a financial conglomerate across **chinese walls**.

creeping acquisition or **creeping takeover** (Mergers and acquisitions). The gradual build-up of a shareholding in a company where the ultimate ambition is to gain a **controlling interest**. This could be achieved by buying shares in the market over a relatively long period of time and attempting to keep the price down; that is, not bid it up in anticipation of a **bid** and premium for control. There are limits to how far such a strategy might work; for example, under UK law once a stake of 30% has been acquired, a formal bid must be made. See also **concert party; dawn raid**.

Crest (UK). The new paperless **settlement** system being developed for the UK market by the **Bank of England** to replace the failed *Taurus* project.

(à la) criée (French). **Open outcry**.

critically undercapitalized (Banking). See **capital-based supervision**.

cross. (i) (Securities) A transaction where a **broker-dealer** acts for both the buyer and seller. (ii) (Forex). **Foreign exchange** transaction which does not involve the US dollar. See **cross-rate**.

cross-asset. Any of a number of cross-market or instrument positions, often created using **derivatives**. For example, **outperformance options; rainbow options**.

cross-asset option. See **spread option**.

cross-border. A transaction where the two parties are domiciled in different countries. Thus a *cross-border loan* or *cross-border swap* has the two counterparties based in different countries.

cross-border listing. Practice by large transnational corporations of obtaining a **listing** or quotation on a **stock exchange** outside the country of domicile. The intention is to make their **common stock** or **ordinary shares** more attractive to international investors. See also **American depository receipt; European depository receipt**.

cross-border one-currency concentration. Cash concentration method involving multinational corporations holding all the balances from one currency in one account in order to be able to benefit from internal offsets and the advantages of aggregated sums. See **netting**.

cross-border one-currency pooling (Banking). Cash pooling service provided by a bank for different subsidiaries of a group which treats all the balances from one currency in whichever account they are held by the different subsidiaries as one account for interest and investment purposes. See **pooling**.

cross-currency. Any of a large number of transactions, instruments, or securities which have an explicit or implicit interchange of payments in more than one currency.

cross-currency basis swap. A cross-currency swap where the two sides of the transaction are **floating rate payers** in their respective currencies (cf. **basis swap**).

cross-currency cap and **floor**. A type of **cap** structure where the seller pays the **spread** between the interest rates of two currencies less a **strike spread**, where this is greater than zero. For instance, an agreement to pay the difference between sterling and Deutschmark **London interbank offered rate** with a strike spread of 3%. If sterling is 10% and Deutschmarks 8%, no payments are made; but if Deutschmarks fall to 5%, then the seller will pay (10% − 5%) − 3% (the strike spread), or 2% of the **notional principal** amount in the settlement currency for the interest period. It is a series of same strike value **forward spread agreements**.

cross-currency coupon swap. A cross-currency swap where one of the payment streams is at a fixed rate.

cross-currency exposure. When a company's liabilities in a particular currency are not adequately covered by the company's earnings in that currency. See **economic exposure**.

cross-currency futures. See **currency futures**.

cross-currency interest rate swap. See **cross-currency swap**.

cross-currency option. A type of **outperformance option** where the difference in two currencies' exchange rates provides the gain. It is possible to have the **premium** in a third currency. See **quantity adjusting option**.

cross-currency settlement risk. See **daylight exposure limit; overnight delivery risk**.

cross-currency spread trading. Buying and selling securities in two currencies based on different interest rate markets, or their **derivatives**, with a view to gaining from a widening or a narrowing of the **spread** or differential between the two markets.

Cross-currency spread trading

If the spread is expected to:	Lower Yielding instrument or underlying	Higher Yielding instrument or underlying
Decrease or narrow	Sell	Buy
Increase or widen	Buy	Sell

See also **rainbow option; spread futures; spread option; yield curve option; yield hedge ratio; yield spread option**.

cross-currency swap (CCS). An agreement between two parties to exchange cash flows in two currencies (cf. **interest rate swap**). Interest on each side may be fixed or floating interest, giving three main types of swaps: fixed/fixed (both sides pay a **fixed rate** to the other) *fixed/floating* (one side pays a fixed rate, the other a **floating**.; also known as a *cross-currency coupon swap*); *floating/floating* (both sides pay a variable rate to the other; also known as a *cross-currency basis swap*. The cash flows can be of any complexity, provided that their **present value** at the time of the transaction is zero. However, the most common type of CCS consists of (*a*) an initial exchange of **principal** amounts (which may be omitted); (*b*) a succession of interest and principal payments, where each party pays only the currency it received in the initial exchange. The sum of the principal payments in each currency will equal the initial principal in that currency and the interest is calculated on the outstanding point at each payment date. Cross-currency swaps normally have three stages:

1. *The initial exchange of principal* (which may be omitted): Party A pays currency A, receives currency B; Pary B pays currency B, receives currency A:

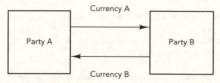
Cross-assurency swap-1

2. *The servicing of each side's respective interest payments*: Party A pays currency B interest, receives currency A interest; Party B pays currency A interest, receives currency B interest:

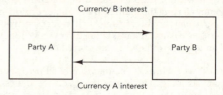
Cross-currency swap-2

3. The re-exchange of principal at maturity: Party A pays currency B, receives currency A; Party B pays currency A, receives currency B:

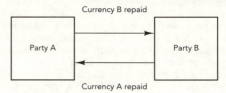
Cross-currency swap-3

The overall liability stream for Party A (B) is now denominated in currency B (A).

In the majority of cases, the initial exchange of principal takes place (1); if not, both parties can use the **foreign exchange spot** market if required to sell the currency. It is necessary to have both parties service each other's liabilities in (2) otherwise the swap would be of more value to one party than the other due to the differences in interest rates between the two currencies. The re-exchange of principal is required in (3) to **close out** their respective **positions** at **maturity**.

Cross-currency swaps allow borrowers to raise funds in markets where they are able to achieve relatively better rates but, at the same time, to convert their liabilities into the currency of their choice. Most CCS have financial institutions as one party only. Cross-currency swaps are also used by asset managers for creating **synthetic securities** which would otherwise be unavailable or for taking advantage of **arbitrage** opportunities. The currency **swaps** market has grown rapidly since its inception in 1981 when the World Bank and IBM made the first such exchange agreement on their respective borrowings and now represents an important technique for currency **hedging** and investment, and **liability management** in the international markets by **treasurers** of corporations, banks, and governments. Also variously known as a *currency swap, currency coupon swap* a *cross-currency interest rate swap*, or a *long-term currency swap*. See **accreting swap; amortizing swap; forward foreign exchange contracts; off-market**.

cross-currency swaption. Swaption allowing one party the right to buy or sell a **cross-currency swap** on a given date under which a pre-agreed fixed or **floating rate** in one currency is exchangeable for a floating or **fixed rate** in another. At the time of entering into the transaction, the amount of final principal is agreed, although initial exchange at the **expiry date** is not mandatory. Such an instrument could be used, for instance, by an issuer to hedge a **dual currency bond** which offered the investor the right to seek repayment or **conversion** in the second currency.

cross-currency warrant. See **dual currency option; rainbow option**.

cross-default. A legal **provision** normally included in most borrowings where a **default** on one debt obligation by a borrower automatically triggers a **default** or **acceleration** clause in another (cf. **covenants**). **Subordinated debt** is normally excepted from the provision.

crossed market. Where one **dealer's bid** price is higher than another's lowest **offer** price, or vice versa. Also known as *backwardation*. Such a situation can arise in a disorderly market, for instance when **index futures** expire and hectic trading is taking place (cf. **triple witching hour**). In practice the condition is unlikely to persist for long since **riskless arbitrage** can take place between dealers.

crossed sale or **trade**. The matching of buyers and sellers in securities without passing them through the market. An unethical and usually illegal practice in most markets.

cross-exchange rate. See **cross-rate**.

cross-forward exchange rate. The forward foreign exchange rate for a **cross-rate**; that is, an **exchange rate** that does not include the US dollar. Also called a *cross-rate forward*.

cross-hedge or **cross-hedging.** (i) The **hedge** of one security, asset, currency, or **commodity** by selling a **forward** or **futures contract** or going **short** in a security, asset, currency, or commodity that is similar to but not identical to the one being hedged (cf. **spread**). The choice of cross-hedge is dictated by the lack of a suitable direct hedge and is predicated on a high degree of co-movement between the instrument being hedged and the availability of a **liquid** hedge instrument (cf. **correlation**). A typical cross-hedge would involve selling long-term **interest rate futures** (on government bonds) to hedge a long position in a corporate bond. The problems with using a cross-hedge are: (*a*) spread or **basis** risk between the two markets or instruments as a result of specific changes in one market, but not the other; (*b*) differences in **liquidity** will cause differences in **short-term** price performance of the two instruments; and (*c*) a difference in **maturity** of the two instruments may lead to performance mis-match. (ii) Used to describe a **futures** purchase or sale intended to reduce price-level **risk** for a financial instrument that is similar to but not the same as that which is deliverable into the futures contract.

cross-holdings. **Equity** investments made by two (or more) companies with a view to establishing friendly ties or as a **takeover** deterrent (cf. **keiretsu; noyaux durs**). Even a relatively small stake in a corporation may be enough to ensure favourable decisions if the issue is finely balanced (cf. **controlling interest**). Also known as *cross shareholdings*.

cross-indexed basis swap (CRIB swap). See **differential swap**.

crossing. The purchase and sale of securities by a **broker** for two different clients. Also known as a *put through*.

cross-over. A **chartist** or **technical analysis** term for the point where two price series intersect. Typically cross-over points arise when an asset price series is being compared to a **moving average** of the same prices or an **index**.

cross-rate (Forex). (i) The **exchange rate** of two currencies that are normally expressed in terms of a third. For example, in the London market, the rate of the yen against the Deutschmark is a cross-rate since they are both normally quoted against the US dollar. (ii) It can also mean an exchange rate quote where neither of the two currencies is the **base currency** of the **market-maker**.

cross-rate option. An **option** offered in a country for two currencies neither of which was the currency of the country in question. Thus a Deutschmark–French franc option in the UK would be a cross-rate option. See also **cross-forward exchange rate**.

cross-rate swap. See **differential swap**.

cross-shareholding. Where two or more **companies** agree to hold **shares** in one another for reasons to do with **cartels** or **collusion** or as means of mutual protection against unwanted **predators**. This practice is commonplace in Continental Europe and Japan, where it is seen as a way of achieving certain longer-term strategic objectives (cf. **noyaux durs**). It occurs much less often in the USA and UK, and when it does appear it tends to be short-lived and intended to achieve specific and limited objectives, such as surviving unwanted challenges to independence or market presence. See **concert party**.

crowd (USA). Term used for concentrations of members undertaking a particular trading activity on an exchange. Hence **active bond crowd**; **cabinet crowd** (cf. pit).

crowding-out. (i) Originally used to describe the perceived adverse effect upon the **liquidity** of the corporate debt market of large and ever increasing government debt issues. The suggestion is that private sector debt is displaced by public sector issues and subsequently more expensive to raise. (ii) Now used to describe the adverse effect on the demand for one type of security by changes in the conditions in the market for another type considered a close substitute.

crown jewels. A defence tactic used in contested **takeovers** based on selling certain high-valued assets or businesses. The intention is to render the **target** company less attractive to the **bidder** by removing such assets (the crown jewels). Under the UK system of **self-regulation** of **mergers acquisitions** such tactics are discouraged once the target company believes a **bid** is imminent. However, the offeree is allowed to state that if the bid fails an asset will be sold in the future. A variation of the crown jewels defence is that, once a company knows it is being bid for (often referred to as being **put-into-play**), it buys assets it thinks the **predator** will not want. See **poison pill**; **lock-ups**; **lock-up options**; **self-uglification**.

crude oil or **crude.** A key basic product in energy **commodities** from which oil products are derived and which tends to be the **benchmark** for other sources of energy (cf. **barrel commodity swap**; **marker crude**). See **Brent crude**; **West Texas Intermediate**.

crude participation. See **equity crude**.

crush margin or **crush spread**. The price difference between soya beans and the products derived from processing (crushing) these, such as soybean oil and soybean meal, or the futures on the above (cf. **crack spread**). It is in effect the processors' margin. See also **commodity swap**; **crack spread swap**.

crush spread swap. See **commodity swap**; **crack spread swap**.

C shares (UK). A temporary special class of common stock or ordinary shares issued by investment **trusts** that is junior to existing shares while the money raised from their issuance is being invested. The intention is to avoid (*a*) the need for a **rights issue** by the trust to existing share-holders when raising new capital and (*b*) the underperformance that results from the trust having a significant cash holding when new funds are received. When the new money has been invested, the C shares are merged with the existing shares and the distinction between the two is eliminated. See also **A shares**; **B shares**.

cum (Latin). Means 'with'; for example, cum div. [**dividends**] and cum **warrants** (cf. **ex**). In market practice, taken to mean that the sale of a security will include the next dividend or **coupon** payment or any other impending capital or income distribution by the instrument.

cum all. Securities which include all potential changes, distributions, or other features.

cum capitalization. The security includes the capitalization issue (cf. **bonus issue**).

cum coupon. The security includes the right to the current **coupon**.

cum dividend. Common stock purchased or sold which is entitled to receive the next **dividend** payment (cf. **ex-dividend**).

cum rights. Shares that are trading with their rights attached. It is often the case that in a **rights** issue the same **common stock** will be traded both cum rights and **ex-rights**. Also reported as *cum new* in the case of a **scrip issue**.

cumulative. A characteristic of certain fixed variable return securities that provides for the carrying forward of **rights** or interest payments until the commitment is met in full should previous payments or purchases not have been made (cf. **arrearages non-cumulative**).

cumulative abnormal return. Econometric model for measuring the value of information in testing for market efficiency and abnormalities (cf. **stock specific risk**). See **event study**.

cumulative adjustment account. A bookkeeping entry used for accounting for the impact of gains and losses arising from **currency** movements (cf. **exchange rate risk**).

cumulative auction market preferred stock (CAMPS). See **auction-rate market preferred stocks**.

cumulative gap. See **gap analysis**.

cumulative option. Type of path-dependent option where the payoff to the holder is cumulated across a number of periods. The basic type is an Asian option, where the daily values of the underlying from the **value date** to **expiry** are averaged, but the period can be any agreed interval, week, month, or year, as desired. Because of the averaging effect, such options are less costly than standard options for the same term. These options appear under a number of different names: an *average-rate option*, *look-back option*, or *path-dependent option*.

cumulative preferred stock or **preference shares.** A type of preferred stock where, in the case the issuer misses paying a **dividend**, the passed dividend cumulates into the future. Normally such issues prevent the payment of a dividend on **common stock** unless the current and all arrears of such dividends on the preferred stock have been made up and paid. When the dividend is in arrears, holders of the notes are often granted special voting rights as if holding common stock. The opposite structure is known as **non-cumulative**.

cumulative provision. A provision in a **preferred stock** issue that prevents **common stock** paying a **dividend** as long as there are **arrearages** on the preferred stock.

cumulative voting. A method of voting that gives a shareholder a number of votes equal to the number of shares held times the number of candidates and which allows the shareholder to allocate them in any proportion, even to the extent of giving all the votes to one candidate (cf. **majority voting**; **supermajority**).

curb (Equities; USA). **Street** name for the **American Stock Exchange**.

currencies. See **world currencies**.

currency. (i) Money. Usually taken to mean notes and coins in circulation. (ii) The legal tender in a country. What constitutes currency (that is, what can be used legally to settle debts) is defined in law as legal tender. (iii) Any instruments which are used as a **medium of exchange**.

currency-adjusted option. See currency protected option (cf. **quantity adjusting option**).

currency availability clause (Banking). A term in a multi-currency **facility** which provides for the lenders to change the currency lent in the event that the currency being provided is no longer freely available.

currency average rate option. See Asian option.

currency band. A method of controlling the value of a currency by setting upper and lower

intervention levels. This is often used for **dirty float** or **crawling peg** type **intervention** and is a central feature of the **Exchange Rate Mechanism** (cf. **divergence indicator**).

currency basket. A group of currencies combined together for trading or valuation purposes. The two best-known currency baskets are the **European Currency Unit** and the **Special Drawing Right**.

currency basket option. (i). An **option** on the **European Currency Unit** or the **Special Drawing Right**. (ii) A tailored **currency option** offered in the **over-the-counter** market on a basket or portfolio of currencies weighted to the requirements of the buyer. Such an option could be used, for instance, to **hedge** an internationally diversified portfolio. In general, the **premium** for such an option will be less than its individual components, the difference depending on the degree of **correlation** between its component currencies. The lower the correlation, the lower the premium relative to the equivalent in single options, since, at any given time, some currencies in the basket option will be moving in an opposite direction. The total volatility of the basket option will therefore be less than that of the single options. See also **rainbow option**.

currency change bond. See **dual currency bond**.

currency clause (Banking). An agreement in a loan facility that the borrower may choose from a given range of currencies to borrow at any rollover date. See also **judgement currency clause**.

currency cocktail. (i). A borrowing which is denominated or lent in a mixture of currencies. (ii) Colloquial term used to describe multi-currency units such as **European Currency Units** or **Special Drawing Rights**.

currency conversion. A bond which offers either (a) the holder the right to receive coupon and/or **principal** in another, usually specified currency; or (b) the issuer the right to vary the currency of payment for the coupon and/or the principal. In the former case, the holder has a currency call on the issuer; in the latter case, the holder has written (or sold) a currency put to the issuer.

currency conversion facility. See **dual currency loan**; **multi-currency clause**.

currency coupon swap. Term used to describe a **cross-currency swap** where one party is paying a **fixed rate** (i.e. **coupon**) and the other a **floating rate**.

currency cross-rate future. Currency future where neither of the currencies is the **base currency** of the country in which the exchange is situated. For example, a currency future between the Deutschmark and the Japanese yen traded in the USA.

currency deposit. Another term used for a **eurocurrency** deposit.

currency exchange. See **foreign exchange**.

currency exchange warrant (CEW). A warrant allowing the holder to benefit from any appreciation of a currency above the **strike price**. Sometimes such warrants are issued as **sweeteners** for corporate issues.

currency forward. See **foreign exchange forward** (cf. **outright forward**).

currency future. A **futures** contract where the **underlying** is a specified foreign currency and amount. By convention all currency futures are quoted in **American terms**, unless a **cross-rate**, when the smaller unit is then used for the quote. With currency futures changes in the dollar (or a cross-currency) cannot take place in isolation; but always in relation to another currency (or group of currencies). Profits and losses on currency futures (and forwards) depend on the *relative movements* of the two currencies. This is different from futures on assets (such as bonds) where these increase or decrease in price. Currency futures are quoted in *American terms*, i.e. in units of currency to the US dollar (except crosses).

Currency future 1

Change in dollar relative to other currencies	Effect on futures quote
Dollar strengthens	*Decreases*: fewer dollars are required to buy a unit of currency
Dollar weakens	*Increases*: more dollars are required to buy a unit of currency

A Deutschmark (DM) contract at $0.5848 = 0.5848 \times DM\ 125,000 = US\$73,100$;

Long position: pays US$73,100; receives DM 125,000;

Short position: pays DM 125,000; receives US$73,100.

Currency future 2

Currency position	Currency Risk	Action in the currency futures market	Effect on futures
Long US dollars/Short currency	Cost more US$ to buy currency	Buy currency futures	Futures increase in value; Sell at a profit
Short US dollars/Long currency	Receive fewer US$ for currency	Sell currency futures	Futures decline in value; Buyback at a profit

currency insurance. A version of **portfolio insurance** applied to managing **foreign exchange rate** risk.

currency interest rate swap. See **cross-currency rate swap**.

currency-linked bond, note or **security.** A **bond** or **note** issue where the interest payments and principal repayment are valued according to one currency but paid in another at the prevailing spot rate. The label includes a number of different structures, including returns linked to other benchmarks, such as indices and so on. See **dual currency bond**.

currency linked outperformance unit (CLOU). A security where part of the return is linked to an **embedded option** that increases the return when the two currencies change in respect of each other. See **outperformance option**.

currency market. The market for the exchange of one currency for another. Financial intermediaries are willing to **swap** one currency for another at an agreed **exchange rate**, both for **spot** or immediate delivery and also via **forward** contracts (cf. **forward foreign exchange**). Also known as the *foreign exchange market*.

currency of denomination. The currency of issue of a security. It may not actually be the currency in which it is repaid (cf. **dual currency bond**).

currency option. An option that allows the holder to exchange one currency for another at a predetermined rate (cf. **option on currency future**). Note that since the option is for an exchange of currencies, a **call option** in one currency is equal to a **put option** in the other currency with the same **strike price** and **expiry** and so the same result can be obtained by buying either the **call** or the **put**. In holding a currency option, it may be optimal to **exercise American-style** currency options before expiry. This is likely to occur in the case of calls on currencies with high interest rates (or the equivalent put on the currency with low rates), since early exercise will allow the holder to reinvest in a higher yielding asset. See also **option pricing**;. They were first traded in the USA in 1982.

currency option bond. See **dual currency bond**.

currency option clause (Banking). A right given in a loan **facility** for the lender to require the borrower to exchange his loan in one currency for a liability in a second currency at a pre-agreed **foreign exchange rate**. In effect, the borrower has written a **currency option** with the lender (cf. **embedded option**). Normally such an agreement will allow the lender to reduce the initial cost of his borrowing, at the potential expense of having the option exercised against him. See also **currency clause**.

currency overlay management. A portfolio management technique that treats **foreign exchange** as a separate asset class to be managed separately from decisions about markets and/or individual sectors or securities.

currency protected. Assets or liabilities in a foreign currency where the **foreign exchange** component has been hedged back into the **base currency**. See also **quantity adjusting option**.

currency protected note. A type of **dual currency bond** where the principal is denominated in one currency and the interest is paid at the rate of a foreign currency. For example, a Deutschmark-denominated **floating rate note** which pays interest at a margin to the **Paris interbank offered rate**, the French franc interbank rate. A number of variations on the structure have been issued which involve a multiple or **leveraged** interest rate spread relationship between the **base currency** of the note and the returns to holders, but at the cost of increasing the **risk** of the instrument.

currency protected option. Option denominated in one currency exercisable into an **underlying** in another currency but paid in the original currency. The original model for this product was an option on the **Nikkei Index index futures** traded on the **Chicago Mercantile Exchange**. They provide holders with exposure to the price performance of the foreign currency underlying without the need to **hedge** their **currency** exposure (cf. **differential swap**). The cost of such an option relative to a package of an option on the underlying and a straight currency option will depend on the **correlation** between the underlying and the currency. Such an option is variously called a *guaranteed exchange rate option* or a *quantity adjusting option* (QUANTO option).

currency protected swap (CUPS). A type of **interest rate** or cross-currency **swap** where one of the payments is denominated in a currency other than the exchanged or **notional principal**. The payments on this part of the swap are calculated against the **base currency** and not the other currency. The instrument is also known as a *cross indexed basis swap* (CRIB), *cross rate swap*, a *diff. swap* or *differential swap* or *difference swap*, *interest rate index swap*, *London interbank offered rate differential swap* (LIBOR differential swap) or a *rate differential swap* or *rate difference swap*.

currency risk. The possibility of loss contingent on a future change in the **foreign exchange rate**. Also known variously as *exchange rate risk* or *foreign exchange rate risk*. See **foreign exchange**; **risk**.

currency selection. See currency overlay management.

currency swap or **exchange**. (i). Term for the simultaneous purchase (sale) of a currency **spot** and the entering into a **foreign exchange forward** contract to sell back (buy back) the same currency (cf. **covered interest arbitrage**). To distinguish from other uses of the term, this is sometimes called a *short-term currency swap*. See **foreign exchange swaps**. (ii) Sometimes used for a cross-currency swap. This may also be known as a *long-term currency swap*.

currency swap option. An option allowing the holder to buy or sell a **currency swap** at a fixed exchange rate.

currency warrant. (i) A separable, tradable option included in a securities issue giving the holder the right to buy additional securities denominated in a currency different from that of the original issue. (ii) A negotiable **currency option**. This is usually an **over-the-counter** instrument offered by a financial intermediary, although **exchange-traded** currency warrants do exist, for instance on the **American Stock Exchange**.

current account. (i) The record of an economy's annual transactions reflecting the **trade balance** and the **invisible balance**. (ii) (Banking; UK) A cheque account held with a **bank** or other depository institution (in the UK these include **building societies**) for immediate withdrawal that pays nominal or no interest. Sometimes includes an **overdraft** facility. In the USA known as a *checking account* (cf. **negotiable order of withdrawal** account).

current assets. Cash and other **short-term** assets of a company; typically stock, debtors and cash (cf. **capital asset; fixed asset**).

current coupon (Bonds). (i) Used in the fixed interest securities market for when a coupon rate approximates current market **yields** for similar securities. Conventional debt securities (cf. 'straights') with current **coupons** have prices close to **par** (cf. **par bond; yield**). (ii) Term used for recent US Treasury issues trading at or near par (cf. **on-the-run**). (iii) Also the term for the coupon that is due on a **floating rate debt** instrument at any point in time. The current coupon will be the interest rate that the holder will receive when interest is next paid (cf. **rollover**).

current day reporting (Banking). Reporting transactions made and the balance held in accounts at a bank or other deposit-taking institution on the same day. The service is either done in batch mode (known as *intra-day reporting*) or, increasingly, as they occur (known as *real-time reporting*).

current delivery (Derivatives). Used in **futures** contracts implying that the **nearby contract** will become **deliverable** during the coming month (cf. **deferred futures; delivery month**).

current issue (Bonds; USA). Market term for the most recently auctioned issues of US Treasuries (cf. **off-the run; on-the-run**).

current liabilities. The **short-term** liabilities of a company; typically trade creditors, tax payable, and **dividend** payable.

current liquidity ratio. See **acid test ratio**.

current maturity. The amount of time to **maturity** remaining to a **bond** as opposed to the **original** maturity (at issue).

current profit. The profit made in the present reporting period.

current ratio. The ratio of **current assets** to **current liabilities** (cf. **acid-test ratio**). See **ratio analysis**.

current yield. Used to assess fixed interest securities (cf. **dividend yield**). Calculated by taking the ratio of the **coupon** on a security to its market price expressed as a percentage. It represents the annual return on the interest only and not on any change in price to **maturity** of the security. Also known as *flat yield, income yield* or *running yield*. See **interest rate calculations; redemption yield**. See also **Japanese Government Bond**.

curve lock. Any **derivative** contract that offers a payoff linked to the price or rate **spread** on two points of the **yield curve**.

curve lock swap. Package consisting of a **yield curve swap** coupled to an agreement to enter into a corresponding swap. The buyer may be attracted by the current differential between the short end of the yield curve and wish to *lock-in* the spread between the short and long rates or prices but not the absolute market level (cf. **backwardation swap; contango swap**). By combining the **curve lock** with a **forward** transaction, the buyer anticipates being able to enter into the combined position at a more attractive rate. Thus a borrower might be attracted by the fact that the six-month **London interbank offered rate** (LIBOR) to the five year **interest rate swap** rate was inverted offering a **spread** of 1% between the two (that is the LIBOR rate was 1% above the five-year rate), but still consider the five-year absolute rate to be too high. By agreeing to enter into a **forward swap**, with the expectation that interest rates will fall between the time the transaction is agreed and the point at which the forward swap takes effect, the buyer is expecting to fix both a lower absolute rate, and the curve lock differential.

curve swap. See backwardation swap; contango swap; yield curve swap.

cushion. See **call protection**.

cushion bond. A high-coupon **bond** that sells at a moderate **premium** because it is **callable** and the call is **in the money**. It will thus be trading on a **yield-to-call** basis. If interest rates should rise, the price fall will be less than that of a comparable non-callable **bond** (due to the **call provision**), hence the cushion this feature provides. See **convexity**.

Cusip Number System (Committee on Uniform Securities Identification Procedures Number System). A standard alphanumeric system used for the identification of individual security issues (cf. **International Security Identification Number**). Cusips consist of a nine-digit code which is permanently assigned to each issue and is displayed on the security (if in **physical** form). The first six digits of the code are used to identify the issuer based on an alphabetic sequence; the next two characters (letters or numbers) identify the particular issue; while the final digit serves as a check designed to ensure the integrity of the entire code sequence.

custodian. The keeper of security **certificates** and other assets on behalf of investors. The custodian usually collects **dividends** and interest and exercises the voting rights of the investor when required. Custodians are common for international investments, known as *global custodians*, since they have experience of **settlement** procedures in the different markets and exchanges. A *local custodian* will be responsible for just one country. Both are common in international investments and may be found in local investment as well (cf. **trustee**).

custody charge or **cost**. Fees payable to a **custodian** for managing securities in its **safekeeping**.

customer business. A securities deal carried out on behalf of a client or non-member of an exchange (cf. **local**). Such business can be transacted with a **broker-dealer** or **agent**, or dealt in directly with a **market-maker** or broker-dealer acting as a **principal**. In the latter case the securities would have been sold or bought to or from the broker-dealer's own **book**.

customer repurchase agreement (customer repos) (Banking; USA). A **repurchase agreement** carried out by the **Federal Reserve** on behalf of foreign **central banks** who hold dollar securities (cf. **desk**).

customization. A feature of the **over-the-counter** markets in that financial contracts can be adapted to the exact specifications or requirements of the two parties. This is generally not possible for **exchange-traded** instruments where standardization is required in order to allow **fungibility** (cf. **flex options**).

custom option. An over-the-counter (OTC) option which has terms is tailored to the requirements of the customer (cf. **exchange-traded**; *exotic option*). Also called a *dealer option*.

customs union. A customs union is set up when two or more countries agree to the free exchange of each other's goods and services such that all tariffs and quotas are removed; and simultaneously establish against non-members a **Common External Tariff** (CET). This contrasts with a free trade area in which in each member state retains its own tariffs against non-members. An example of a customs union is the **European Union** (EU), whilst an example of a free trade area is **North American Free Trade Area**, which covers the USA, Canada, and Mexico. Many believe that such arrangements, especially customs unions, generate economic benefits. Without the distortions imposed by tariffs, trade can be directed towards the producer who has the comparative cost advantage. The argument goes on to claim that as a result of this, world resource allocation is made more efficient. However, the establishing of a customs union can have at least two effects: trade creation and trade diversion. The former effect might be a gain because trade that might not otherwise exist could be induced by lower prices; whilst the latter effect could be harmful, in a global efficiency sense, as higher cost producers within the customs union are protected from relatively more efficient suppliers outside who face the CET. Such effects, however, are only part of the analysis as to whether customs unions are beneficial. Other factors need to be taken into account, such as the effect the removal of tariff barriers has on the **terms of trade** and therefore the relative volumes of different goods and services demanded within individual members. Such action is likely to change the pattern of trade, together with the geographical origins of goods and services traded as in the EU, which seeks to create a *single market*. Whether a group of states will end up in an improved economic position depends on the price and income elasticities of those goods and services. In addition, removing protective barriers can induce improvements in domestic efficiency and enlarging markets can provide the benefits of economies of scale.

cutoff time. Dealing deadline for **clearing** or settlement for a given day.

cycle. See **expiration cycle**.

cyclical stock. A type of **share** that is particularly sensitive to economic conditions. Such **stocks** tend to rise rapidly in periods of recovery, but to fall more rapidly in periods of downturn. In **modern portfolio theory** such stocks would have a higher than average **beta**.

cylinder (Option strategy). A **vertical spread**. The term cylinder is mostly used in the **foreign exchange markets**. It involves the simultaneous purchase of a **put option** (or a **call**) in a currency and the sale of a call option (put) at different **strike prices**. Due to the symmetrical properties of **currency options** (a put is an opposing call in the other currency), the strategy works with buying both puts (for the currency to be sold) or calls (for the currency to be purchased). The apparent inconsistency is due to the call being purchased in order to receive the currency to be held, while the

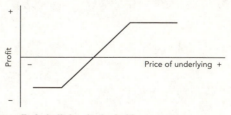

Payoff of a bullish cylinder holder at expiry

put gives the holder the right to sell the currency to the **writer**. A *zero cost cylinder* is where the cost of the **premium** on the purchased side is exactly offset by the income from the sold side. A cylinder allows a purchaser to **hedge the risk** of their exposure at a reduced cost and still benefit from some favourable movements in the currency. Also called a *flexible forward, forward band, minimax currency forward, option fence* or *range forward*. See also **collar**.

D

D. See credit ratings.

Dachgesellschaft (German). Holding company.

daily adjustable tax exempt security (DATES) (USA). Type of **variable rate (demand) note** that is **puttable** to the **remarketing agent** daily prior to a specific cut-off time. Also known as *lower floaters* or *variable-rate demand notes*. See **Master notes**.

Daily Official List (UK). See **stock exchange daily official list**.

daily price limit. The maximum price movement allowed on a **futures exchange** for a particular contract (cf. **down limit; limit; limit up**). See **circuit breaker**.

daily reset paper (USA). **Commercial paper** where the interest rate is reset every day in relation to a **reference rate**, usually the **fed funds** rate.

daily trading limit. A restriction placed on the allowable price movements in many **commodities** markets and some **exchange-traded derivatives** (cf. **limit up; down limit**). Although trading must stop when the limit is reached, if prices subsequently move back within the permitted range, then trading can resume. A daily trading limit cannot prevent a large change in price over several days, during which period it may be impossible to deal in the market. See **cascade theory; circuit breaker**.

daimyō bond (Japan). A type of **foreign bond** issue open to supranational institutions and targeted at the Japanese domestic bond market. It differs from the **samurai** bond in that it is listed outside of Japan, can be settled through the international clearing systems, and has lower issuance fees (cf. **Centrale de Livraison de Valeurs Mobilières; Euroclear**). The bond issuance procedure was developed to address the shortcomings of Samurai bonds, which were costly and lengthy to issue.

daisy chain. (i) A term for the certification process required by **euromarket** transactions in order to comply with US law. (ii) Round tripping trading activity between market participants in order to create the illusion of activity in order to attract investors (cf. **corner the market; ramp**).

damages. Money paid to injured parties to compensate for losses suffered because of the actions of others. In the context of financial markets, such cases are most likely to occur in relation to disputes over the obligations of the various parties to a **contract**. The amounts paid are intended to place the injured party in the position they would have occupied had the wrongful act not taken place. The amount of damages can be *substantial*, paid when an actual loss occurs, or *nominal*, which acknowledges a breach of contract has taken place but no loss has been suffered. See also **liquidated damages**.

dangling debit. Colloquial term for a negative reserve entry used for writing off **goodwill** following a **takeover** or **merger**.

Danmarks Nationalbank (Denmark). The Danish **central bank**.

Dartehen (German). **Loan**.

data. Financial markets are driven by data and information. The significance of information and how it can influence the behaviour of markets, especially with regard to establishing and changing prices, has been captured by the **efficient markets hypothesis**. The role played by data depends upon the type of data available and sought, and the chosen method for analysing the data collected (see, for example, **technical analysis**).

There are several different data types, and as a result a common way of classifying them is often considered desirable in order to provide some consistency in use. This can be particularly desirable when data is exchanged across time periods, or between different **markets** and **traders**. One such method is to regard data as either quantitative, or qualitative, in nature. The former can be seen as numerically based, whilst the latter can be based upon opinions or so-called 'received wisdom' (cf. **market trend; sentiment indicator**). Numerical data is often subdivided into financial or market data (such as, **volatility**), and economic data (such as, the **retail price index**). Individual economic decisions are often added together to calculate broad patterns, a process that creates aggregate economic data (for example, **gross domestic product**). A distinction is also usually drawn between nominal and real economic figures, and between value and volume. This is about distinguishing the effects of **inflation** and changes in the real level of economic activity. Value numbers are calculated as volume multiplied by price, and thereby include inflation; volume numbers are calculated as value divided by price, and hence exclude inflation. Values are in nominal terms at current prices; volumes are in real terms at constant prices (cf. **index construction**).

It is also important to distinguish between trends and cycles, which attempt to differentiate between long-term and short-term movements (cf. **trade cycle**; **trendline**). A **trend** is usually regarded as long-term, although may be used to describe a short-term change that may reverse over the course of a **business cycle**. It is this ability to tell apart which changes are likely to be relatively permanent and which are more temporary that forms the basis for interpreting data. For example, identifying so-called 'turning points' in **chartism** or technical analysis; and cyclical indicators: leading indicators which signal future developments, and lagging indicators which reflect the past (cf. **economic indicators**).

Another important factor in the calculation and evaluation of both economic and financial data is the pattern of **seasonality**. Most figures show a seasonal pattern that is repeated period to period. The most common examples include: the substantial increase in retail sales volume in the period before Christmas; and heavy **securities** trading after markets have been closed for holidays, or at the beginning and end of **account** periods. In such cases data can be subject to **seasonal adjustment** to smooth their pattern over the course of longer time periods and to assist in interpretation. For economic data, a figure for a given month is seasonally adjusted by calculating what percentage of the year's monthly average it represents, and dividing it by the percentage.

Many of the most widely used economic and financial indicators are presented as an **index**, which assumes constant prices from a given date. The reference date is normally arbitrary and provides a convenient benchmark for comparison. What matters is not the index numbers, rather the change from one period to the next. Indices, or indexes, are also used to represent a collection of data in a single number, in an attempt to create order and direction from diversity. This is especially true with financial market indices. Stock market indices, such as the **Dow-Jones Industrial Average**, are designed to collect together the disparate movements of different **share** prices, each responding to a wide range of factors and pressures, in order to discover whether the market, or a part of it, is changing direction. See **fundamental analysis**.

There are several ways of composing equity indices, each with particular characteristics designed to appeal to different user groups (see, for example, **Financial Times Share Indices**). Indices are important **benchmarks** for measuring the performance of **fund managers**. Most will try to outperform the various benchmarks, although some will aim to mirror the rise and fall of certain indices, a practice known as **index tracking**. For corporate managers too, such benchmark data can be important for understanding both the performance of their individual companies and investors' evaluation of their prospects. For example, it is vital to ensure that the company's share price is not seen as underperforming the overall market, perhaps making the management vulnerable to a hostile **takeover bid**. Moreover, many companies are making the share price a key management target through programmes of corporate value creation and value-based management (cf. **shareholder value**).

Beyond the relatively simple establishment of trends and cycles, adjustment for inflation and seasonality, and the interpretation of index numbers exists a much more sophisticated type of analysis known as **econometrics**. One of the most important features of this activity is that it attempts to go on to the next stage: from understanding the sources and possible meaning of quantitative data, to using it dynamically to produce estimates and predictions of market behaviour.

data di maturazione (Italy). Maturity date.

Datastream (UK). A UK proprietary computer-based system for the collection, distribution, and manipulation of financial markets data. Used especially in the analysis of historical movements in securities prices.

dated date. The date from which accrued interest is calculated. A purchaser will reimburse a seller for the interest from the dated date to the **settlement date**. He in turn receives all the interest for the period from the dated date to the interest payment date (cf. **closing date**). Also called the *issue date*.

date d'échéance (French). Maturity date.

date de valeur (French). Value date.

dated securities. Securities which have a fixed maturity date or redemption date (cf. **perpetual**; **one-way stock option**; **undated**).

date of record. The date for establishing the ownership of securities for the purposes of interest or **dividend** payments (cf. **cum**; **ex**; **bearer bond**).

dawn raid (UK). A securities market operation undertaken by a **predator** which involves buying a certain amount of **shares** before withdrawing from the market. It is usually undertaken over a short period and at the beginning of a trading session in order to prevent the victim company, other **shareholders**, and traders from fully realizing that the victim is a **takeover target** and making an appropriate price change. See **putting into play**.

dawn raid rules (UK). Colloquial name for the Rules Governing the Substantial Acquisition of Shares issued by the City Panel on Takeovers and Mergers. (cf. **City Code on Takeovers and Mergers**).

day count. The number of computational days in a given period for establishing the amount of interest due. See **bank basis; bond basis; interest rate calculations; money market basis**.

daylight exposure. See **day trading**.

daylight exposure limit (Forex). Used in the foreign **exchange** market for the limits set by banks on their dealings in a particular currency with an individual customer during any working day (cf. **credit; counterparty; delivery risk**). The limit is set due to the time differences in **settlement** between most currencies which leaves the earlier paying bank with a full principal exposure. Such limits became common after the collapse of the I. D. Herstatt Bank where many counterparties had paid the bank, but were unable to receive payment in return. The problem is increasingly being addressed by banks agreeing to netting arrangements for their respective exposures. Also known as *overnight delivery risk*.

daylight overdraft. An intraday borrowing made on an account, usually for settlement purposes.

day loan (USA). Term for an intraday borrowing to finance securities purchases. Also sometimes known as a *morning loan*.

day order. Instruction that is valid for the trading session; if not executed during the session it is automatically cancelled. See also **good till cancelled**.

days of grace. See **grace period**.

days' receivables. See **ageing schedule**.

daytime trading or **daylight trading** or **day trading.** The practice of opening and closing a position within the same trading day or period. Thus someone who opens and closes a position within a day is known as a *day trader* (cf. **local; position trader**).

day-to-day money. See **call money; overnight deposit**.

dead-cat bounce. Colloquial term for a strengthening in prices after a fall but which is seen as technical and temporary in nature (cf. **correction**). See **bear market; bull market; technical analysis**.

deal. Colloquial term for a **transaction** (cf. **bargain**). Hence, *to deal*, to undertake transactions.

deal date. The date a transaction is entered into.

dealer. A dealer acts as **principal** in transactions by buying and selling for his own account. See **agent; broker; broker-dealer; market-maker; trader**.

dealer agreement (USA). Term often used in the markets for the **selling group agreement**.

dealer loan (USA). A loan made to a dealer to allow the financing of a **position**, usually secured (cf. **repurchase agreement**). See **money broker**.

dealer market. Any market where financial intermediaries purchase and sell for their own account and do not arrange transactions as **agents** for the customer (cf. **broker; direct search market; head-to-head**). See also **market-maker**.

dealer option. An **option** that is offered over-the-counter (cf. **exchange-traded**). The **counterparty**, usually the **writer**, will be the financial institution making the transaction rather than the exchange's **clearing house** (cf. **margin**).

dealer placement. A method for the **distribution** of short-term instruments, common in the **commercial paper** market. Dealers, acting as either **agent** or **principal**, undertake to find investors for issued paper and to maintain a liquid and orderly secondary market. A formal undertaking, called a *dealership agreement*, is made between the dealer, acting for the issuer, and the issuer. This normally limits the number of dealers who can purchase or place paper to named firms. The alternative method of distribution is for **direct placement**.

dealer spread or **dealing spread.** See **bid-asked price**.

dealing. See **deal**.

dealing for new time (UK). See **new time**.

dealing slip or **dealing ticket.** See **ticket**.

dealing within the account (UK). See **account trading**.

dear money. Monetary conditions where interest rates are high and borrowing is difficult (cf. **easy money**). Also called *tight money*.

Death Valley curve. Colloquial term used in venture capital for the reduction in liquidity for a start-up firm as expenses use up available cash. The term derives from being stuck in Arizona's Death Valley and the need to find water before the individual dies of thirst (cf. burn rate; **maximum slippage**).

debenture. (i) (UK) In the UK, a **fixed interest** security secured on **assets** provided by the issuer, which can be for a fixed **maturity** or **irredeemable**. There are two main types: *mortgage debentures*, which are secured against a specific asset of the issuer; and *floating debentures*, which are secured against the entire asset base of the issuer (cf. **asset-backed**). Debenture interest is a **prior charge** and holders rank ahead of **shareholders** in a winding-up. Hence the terms for such issues which are known as *debenture stock* or *loan stock*. A *naked debenture*, by contrast, has no priority over other debts of the issuer and is the same as **unsecured loan stock**. (ii) (USA) In the USA, debenture means an unsecured debt with a fixed **coupon** and where interest is a prior charge. Typically, debentures have **original maturities** of ten years or longer. The security position of a debenture holder in the USA is very much less than the equivalent in the UK market where the US position would be that of unsecured loan stock.

debenture loan. See secured debt.

debenture stock (USA). A type of **preferred stock** which pays a fixed **dividend**.

debenture warrants. A debt issue that has a fixed number of **warrants** attached. Normally the warrants can be detached after a certain date, and separate markets created for the bonds with warrants (**cum warrants**), for the stripped bonds (**ex-warrants**), and for the warrants themselves.

debit. Money paid out of an account.

debit card. A card allowing the holder to make electronic payments which are debited immediately to a bank account. In essence, a kind of electronic **cheque**. It is an **electronic funds transfer at point of sale** instrument, validated by the holder using his personal identification number (PIN number). Also called a *payment card*.

debit cylinder. A type of **option strategy** involving the purchase of a **cylinder** where there is a net **premium** to pay on the purchased and written options (cf. **box spread**; **credit spread**).

debit spread. **Option** combination involving the purchase and sale of two or more options that costs more in **premium** for the purchased options than the premium received on the options that are sold (cf. **holder**; **writer**). See credit spread (cf. **box spread**).

debt. (i) A sum owed by one party to another. (ii) A legally enforceable agreement, expressed or implied, to pay money, to another party. Debts may be secured or unsecured. (iii) General term for securities other than **equity** (cf. **bonds**; **notes**; **paper**). Debtholders normally do not have any claim beyond the nominal **face value** of the debt and any **accrued** and unpaid interest, or as otherwise specified in the terms (cf. **convertible**). A negotiable debt is often called a *debt instrument*; *debt security* is often used for bonds.

debt buy-back. General term for an operation by an issuer to repurchase securities outstanding in the market prior to **maturity**. Usually done when the securities are standing at a large **discount** or where only a **rump** remains (cf. **defeasance**; **redemption**). Sometimes done for tax reasons in order to capitalize a **tax shield**.

debt capacity. Notionally, the amount of debt that a company could raise if it so chose. It is based on the borrower's **credit worthiness**, amount of **reserves**, outstanding **long-term credit** and **leasing** agreements, and existing **capital structure** (cf. **off-balance sheet**). See also **cost of capital**.

debt discounting. See forfaiting.

debt-equity ratio. A measure of the amount of debt in an organization's capital structure. It is found by taking the **ratio** of debt used to shareholders' equity, usually less any goodwill, expressed as a percentage. The basic equation is:

$$\text{Debt} - \text{equity ratio} = \frac{\text{Debt}}{\text{Equity}} \times 100$$

If a firm has £50 in debt and £50 as equity, then the debt-equity ratio is 100%. Note that for the same analysis, the **gearing** ratio would be £50 ÷ [£50 (debt) + £50 (equity)] or 50%. See also **leverage**.

debt-for-equity swap or **debt–equity swap.** (i) In the capital markets, a transaction involving the exchange of a debt instrument for **equity**, or vice versa. Often required when a firm in financial distress needs to rebuild its **capital structure** to reduce **prior claims** on its cash flow. Also sometimes called *debt capitalization* or *debt conversion*. (ii) A way for corporations making direct investments in **less developed countries** to finance their investment. Many countries have put in place debt–equity swap programmes. This involves corporations buying the relevant sovereign debt in the **less developed countries debt market**, usually at a **discount**, and exchanging it for local currency at a favourable rate. This reduces the cost of investment and acts as a subsidy to attract inward investment in these countries while at the same time retiring part of the country's external debt.

debt instrument. See debt security; instrument; money-market instrument.

debt leverage (USA). The use of borrowed money to increase the return to investors in an equity portfolio. See leverage.

debt limitation. A covenant provision that restricts a borrower's ability to incur additional indebtedness (cf. coverage test; leverage).

debt management. See liability management.

debt option. An option on a debt instrument (cf. call; interest rate option; put).

debtor. One who owes a debt to another (cf. creditor).

debtor in possession facility (DIP facility) (Banking; USA). Financing facility available to firms which have filed for Chapter 11 under the US Bankruptcy Code (cf. Chapter 13). Such financings take precedence over debts incurred before the firm sought court protection (cf. prepetition debt).

debt ratio. Ratio of long-term debt to capital. See leverage (gearing).

debt repayable in common stock (USA). A type of borrowing where the proceeds are used by a subsidiary of a corporation to purchase convertible preferred stock in the parent and where the dividend payments are used to service the debt interest. The principal is repaid either by selling the preferred stock in the market, or by converting it into common stock and then selling it and using the proceeds to repay the debt, or where the debtholders receive the equity in consideration directly. Also called a *mandatory convertible*.

debt rescheduling. Any negotiation involving lenders and borrowers aimed at varying the terms of a debt in favour of the latter. It typically involves a range of alternatives: a new-for-old facility, an extension of the maturity or repayment terms, interest deferral, principal forgiveness, or modifications to the contracted arrangements, for instance a debt–equity swap. (cf. kicker; sweetener). Generally the term is taken to mean bank debt or trade creditors since securities are the subject to modification or exchange offer, where new securities are issued for old (cf. waiver). See assented securities; less developed countries debt market; non-assented.

debt security. That class of securities or instruments that require the borrower to repay a fixed amount and usually also periodic interest over the period the security is in existence (cf. straight; plain vanilla). See bond; coupon, zero-coupon bond.

debt service. The payments of interest and principal a borrower is required to make while a debt is outstanding. The ratio of income to debt service is known as the *interest cover ratio*. See also ratio analysis.

debt service ratio (DSR). The ratio of a country's principal and interest foreign debt service to export earnings. The higher the ratio, the more likely the country is to have difficulty in servicing foreign borrowings (cf. country risk).

debt swap. See asset sales; debt–equity swap; sub-participation.

debt-to-asset ratio. The ratio of total debt divided by total assets.

debt warrant. Warrant where the underlying is a bond or other debt instrument. See also bond option.

debt with debt warrants. A debt, or sometimes a preferred stock, issue which has debt warrants entitling the owner to purchase a further debt instrument of the issuer on pre-agreed terms. Sometimes attached to bond issues to make them more marketable (cf. bells and whistles). The debt instrument and the warrants may be detached and traded separately (cf. cum; ex). It is normal for the warrants to have the same expiry date as the maturity of the debt instrument, giving them long lives and therefore, potentially, making them very valuable (cf. option pricing). There exist many variants on the basic scheme, some even allowing the surrender of the debt upon exercise, giving this structure most of the characteristics of a conversion bond. A popular method with issuers for hedging the contingent liability is the harmless warrant. The bond to which a debt warrant is originally attached is known as a *host bond*.

debt with equity warrants. A debt or preferred stock issue which has equity warrants entitling the owner to purchase common stock of the issuer. The debt instrument and the warrants may be detached and traded separately (cf. cum; ex). The two parts may, in fact, appeal to different types of investors. It is normal for the warrants to have the same expiry date as the maturity of the debt instrument, giving them long lives and therefore, potentially, making them very valuable (cf. option pricing). There exist many variants on the basic scheme, some even allowing the surrender of the debt upon exercise, giving this structure most of the characteristics of a **convertible**. The security to which a warrant is originally attached is known as a *host bond*.

debt with mandatory common stock purchase. A debt issue where the holders of the notes are required to purchase a sufficient quantity of the issuer's **common stock** at **maturity** to retire the debt.

debt with mandatory equity conversion. See capital note (cf. **mandatory convertible bond**).

debt with premium put. See put provision.

decision analysis. Techniques, methods, and models used for obtaining optimal strategies in situations involving a range of alternatives and an uncertain or risky set of outcomes (cf. **risk**).

decision tree. Analytic method for optimal problem solving. It involves mapping the alternative courses of action and their consequences using nodes: decision notes are square, event nodes circles from which branches emanate representing the possible courses of action or events that can take place. The value and probability of the different consequences are calculated working backwards from the branch end of the tree to find the best course of action. The standard decision-making criteria is to use *expected monetary value* (EMV), that is, the probability weighted average value of the outcome, although **discounted cash flow** methods can also be incorporated. The decision which leads to the highest EMV (if revenues) or lowest EMV (if costs) is the best solution. One of the advantages of such analytic methods is that decision trees also allow the decision-maker to review the changes to the assumptions or esti-

mates that may lead to an alternative course of action (cf. **sensitivity analysis**). A typical tree might look as in the Figure. The decision is whether to build a factory to take advantage of a product and the resultant EMV from each choice. If demand is high, then there will be ten years of £1m sales, if low £0.5m. There is an 0.6 probability of high demand and 0.4 for low demand. The cost of a small unit is £2.0m, with a capacity of £0.5m; a large unit £3.5m; for £1m and a medium unit at £2.75m with a capacity of £0.75m. If a small unit is built, then a further small unit can be brought on stream after two years (i.e. to last eight years). The choice based on the EMV criterion would be to build big, since this provides an expected gain of £4.5m versus the build small option of £4.2m. See also **binomial tree**.

deck. Colloquial term for the orders held by a floor broker on an exchange (cf. **book**).

declaration. Notice of **exercise** of an **option**, otherwise it is considered **abandoned** (cf. **automatic exercise**).

declaration date or **day.** (i) (Commodities; UK) Term for the **expiry date** or day for an **option** on the **London Metal Exchange**. (ii) (Equities; UK) In the traditional **options market**, the last day the holder had to decide whether to **exercise** his option (cf. **automatic exercise**).

decline guarantee. See put option.

declining call schedule. An issue where the borrower has an **option** to **call** bonds at a **premium**, prior to final **maturity**. The price at which the **bonds** are redeemed falls so as to reach **par** upon maturity (cf. **yield-to-call**). A ten-year ma-

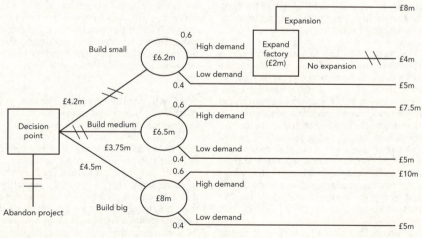

Decision tree

turity bond, callable after the end of the sixth year, might have a call schedule such as appears in the Table.

Year	Redemption Price to par
7	101.50
8	101
9	100.50
10	100

Sometimes known as a 'declining redemption schedule'.

decompounding. Money market technique for establishing the annual rate for interest payments with a greater frequency than one year or a maturity of less than one year. The decompounded rate (DR) is the interest rate required to equate two different maturity instruments. It is derived by:

$$DR\% = \left\{ \left[\left(1 + \frac{i}{n}\right)^{\frac{nt}{Basis}} - 1 \right] \times \frac{Basis}{t} \right\} \times 100$$

Thus a 6% investment per month (n), is decompounded to find what it would equate to as a six-month (180-day) investment (t), expressed as an annual rate (using a 360-day basis):

$$6.06\% = \left\{ \left[\left(1 + \frac{0.06}{6}\right)^{\frac{6 \times 180}{360}} - 1 \right] \times \frac{360}{180} \right\} \times 100$$

dedication. A debt portfolio that is so constructed as to produce a cash flow stream that matches a particular set of maturing liabilities (cf. combination matching; immunization). It is essentially a method of multi-period cash flow matching. An example of such a dedicated portfolio might be that managed by a pension scheme with commitments to existing pensioners. Sometimes called *cash flow matching*.

deed. A legal document which is signed and sealed by the person undertaking it.

deed of arrangement. An undertaking made with creditors over outstanding debts (cf. bankruptcy; default; insolvency).

deed of transfer. A deed evidencing a transfer of property.

deep discount bond. (i) A bond issued at a large discount to par, usually because it pays little or no interest (cf. zero-coupon bond). (ii) It can also mean a bond where the coupon is significantly below the current market rate and therefore stands at a large discount to par (cf. current coupon; on-the-run; par bond). See coupon stripping.

deep discount stepped interest security. See step-up coupon security.

deep gain security (UK). Legal term for an anti-tax avoidance measure introduced in the Finance Act, 1989 to address situations where securities were either converted into **equity** or the redemption amount was not the **par** value.

deep in-the-money option or **deep out-of-the-money option.** Options having strike prices either well below or well above the value of the **underlying**. The option **delta** gives a measure of the degree to which the option has value.

Deep in-the-money/deep out-of-the-money option

	Deep in the money	Deep out of the money
Call	Underlying price *very high* relative to strike price	Underlying price *very low* relative to strike price
Put	Underlying price *very low* relative to strike price	Underlying price *very high* relative to strike price
Delta (δ) (*Hedge ratio*)	high (well above 0.5)	low (well below 0.5)

An option where the underlying was close to the strike price would be **near the money**, and at the strike price, **at the money**.

defalcation. The embezzlement of money held on behalf of others (cf. **commingling**).

default. The failure by a **counterparty** to honour the terms and conditions of a contract. For example, failure to make timely payment of interest or principal on a debt, or failure to comply with some other provision or terms of the **facility** or indenture (cf. **covenants**). Usually an *act* or *event of default* will trigger the obligation to make immediate repayment or otherwise terminate the transaction (cf. **acceleration clause; non-performing assets; technical default**).

defaulted debt. See write off.

default free. Debt where the repayment is certain. This is typically taken to be government debt in the legal tender of the country. See also **risk-free interest rate**.

default premium. See risk premium.

default risk. (i) The risk that borrowers will default (cf. **credit risk**). (ii) The cost associated with a **counterparty** who will not make a payment under an agreement (cf. **cherry-picking; marked-to-market**).

defeasance. (i) The provision found in some debt agreements where the agreement is rendered null and void if certain specified acts are performed (cf. **legal defeasance**). (ii) In the securities markets it usually refers to a **portfolio** that is designed to be **risk-free** in order to produce a certain cash flow to meet the obligations of the holder as and when they fall due (cf. **immunization**). (iii) The case where the issuer of a security cannot be released from any of the obligations under the issue. (iv) Used in the technical sense where the proceeds of an issue are used to buy a portfolio of assets thus removing them from the balance sheet of the seller, who may still service the assets. See **asset securitization; off-balance sheet**. (v) Occasionally used to describe the placement by a **bond** issuer of cash or a portfolio in an **irrevocable trust** for the benefit of the holders of the issue.

defensive securities or **defensive stocks.** Common stocks, ordinary shares, bonds, or notes likely to provide superior performance in a market downturn. Shares in particular sectors bought ahead of recession in the hope that such businesses will suffer less, such as food companies.

deferred. (i) Any element or condition of a transaction which is extended or postponed beyond the market's commonly accepted standard (cf. **forward; straight**): for instance, **coupon** or interest payments, the **settlement**, subordination to another class of security (cf. **subordinated debt**). (ii) (Futures) Another term for **back month** (cf. **position**).

deferred annuity. Annuity which has the start date of payments delayed for a given period.

deferred asset. An asset where the value or realization is deferred to some point in the future.

deferred call provision (Bonds; USA). See **call protection**.

deferred cap. A cap where the start of the protection period is deferred to a future date. Such a structure might be required to match the terms of a bond issue, for instance a **delayed cap floating rate note**.

deferred cap floating rate note (deferred cap FRN). A variation on the **capped floating rate note** issue where the imposition of a maximum **coupon** is postponed to some future date. This might be done so as to improve its marketability with investors (cf. **bells and whistles**).

deferred coupon bond, note, or **security.** A type of **fixed rate, dual coupon bond** which has no **coupon** payments for a predetermined period, usually several years after issue, and then pays interest to **maturity**. When paid, the first coupon is equal to simple interest accrued over the non-paying period. An extreme example is the **zero-coupon bond** where, in effect, all the interest is received at maturity. However, a deferred coupon bond would normally be expected to pay some interest prior to redemption (cf. **Z bond**). Also called a *deferred interest bond, note* or *security.*

deferred equity. Debt instruments on a balance sheet which are expected to be converted into **equity** at some future point, typically **convertibles** and **capital notes**. See also **partly paid**.

deferred futures. In futures trading, it is the more distant **delivery** months (cf. **current delivery; position**). Also known as *back month*.

deferred interest bond. See deferred coupon bond; zero-coupon bond.

deferred interest mortgage (UK). See graduated payments mortgage.

deferred liability. See contingent liability.

deferred months or **deferreds** (Futures). The later delivery months on a **futures contract** (cf. **nearby; position**). Thus, if March is the next contract to **expire**, the June and September contracts would be deferreds.

deferred ordinary share. (i) A type of **ordinary share** often held by founder members of a company which have their **dividends** rights subordinated to other **shareholders**. Such shares often carry a higher rate of dividend payment and may be conditional upon the company achieving some predetermined level of profit or other performance target. (ii) Ordinary share where the right to dividends is deferred for a given period, after which they rank **pari passu** with existing ordinary shares.

deferred payment. (i) Any transaction where the **settlement** is delayed to some later date. See **forward; future**. (ii) Another term for a consumer credit agreement. (iii) Any financial instrument that has payments delayed to a later date.

deferred-payment American-style option. A type of **option** which allows the holder to set the price at which the **exercise** will take place prior to **expiry**. This type of option is far more common with **put options** than **calls** since the **intrinsic value** of the option is not paid out until the option's **expiry date** (cf. **deferred payout option**). The implied **cost of carry** of the **underlying** position is not paid to the holder until expiry; a factor which makes **American-style** options more expensive than their **European-style** counterparts. The deferred payment American option costs approximately the same as a corresponding European option but gives the holder some of the advantages of the timing opportunities of the American-style option. Also called a *deferred payment option* or a *deferred payout option*.

deferred payment bond. (i) An extreme version of a **partly paid bond** where no initial **tranche** is required. While attractive to investors as it provides the equivalent of buying a **bond future**, it exposes the issuer to potential non-payment if interest rates move the wrong way. Generally, such issues require the investor to pay enough in the initial tranche to compensate the issuer for non-payment. However, deferred payment bonds have their uses in **private placements** where the settlement risk is controllable. The attractions to a buyer in such circumstances may be based on the availability of funds, portfolio **immunization**, tax planning, or simply taking advantage of a new issue **window**. (ii) **Eurobond** market term for a partly paid bond. (iii) A bond incorporating a **deferred-payment American-style option** structure (cf. **embedded option**). Such a bond allows the holder to set the **exercise price** at any time prior to **maturity** but with the payment deferred to the **maturity date**.

deferred payment credit. A normal trade credit where the payee has agreed extended **settlement** terms. Sometimes done to increase the attractions of a particular trade since there is an element of hidden discount in such an offer. Obviously, the creditor would want to be satisfied that the debtor would be able to pay when the time came.

deferred payout option. An American-style option which can be exercised at any time during its **life**, although the payout is only made at **expiry**.

deferred premium option. See Boston option.

deferred pricing. A transaction which has been contracted but where the price or value is delayed to a later date. This is notably different to a **forward** transaction since, in this latter case, the price has been agreed, but the execution of the transaction has been delayed to a predetermined time in the future.

deferreds. See deferred months.

deferred shares. See deferred ordinary share.

deferred start option or **warrant.** An option or warrant which is issued (and, possibly, traded) before it is active, for instance a **barrier option** or a warrant incorporating a **trigger** mechanism.

deferred strike price option. A type of option that allows the holder to set the **exercise price** for

a fixed period which is earlier than the **expiry date** of the option but later than the date at which the transaction is agreed. If the holder does not set the exercise price prior to the end of the period then the price is set at the then current **spot** price. Such an option is attractive when the buyer thinks that the current level of **volatility** is low and is expected to rise in the future. The buyer can set all the terms of the option other than the exercise or **strike** **price** to take advantage of the market's current view on volatility.

deferred swap. A type of **interest rate swap** or **cross-currency swap** contract where payments are postponed for a specified time period. The mechanics of deferred swaps are different from those of a **forward swap** since it is only the payments that are delayed, not the start of the swap. Its main use is for tax planning or to meet regulatory requirements. Also known as a *deferred start swap* or *forward swap*.

defered tax. Tax that is due, but not yet paid. There are many reasons why firms may be liable to pay tax, but the actual payment is deffered until some future date. Accordingly, a known tax liability is provided for in the reported accounts of the firm in anticipation of the future liability.

deficiency guarantee (Banking). An arrangement whereby a **guarantor's** obligation in respect to a debt is limited to the loss incurred by a lender when realizing the primary **collateral** supporting the borrowing in the event of **default**.

deficiency letter or **memorandum** (USA). Notice by the **Securities and Exchange Commission** that a **preliminary prospectus** needs revising, amending, or otherwise altering (cf. **cooling-off period**).

deficiency payment agreement. Condition within a **project finance** agreement where one of the parties agrees to make up any shortfall in income.

deficit. Any situation where there is an excess of **liabilities** to **assets**. See also **oversold**.

deficit financing. The use of a fiscal deficit by a government as an instrument of economic policy. The classic Keynesian economic model proposes that governments run deficits in periods of recession counterbalanced by surpluses in periods of high economic activity.

deficit net worth. See negative net worth.

deflation. (i) A fall in the level of economic activity in a country. Lower levels of economic activity as seen in such things as lower rates of increase in wages and prices. It can be induced by **monetary policy** (increasing **interest rates** and restricting growth in **money supply**) and **fiscal policy** (increasing taxes and reducing government expenditure), or both. The aims of deflation might include an improvement in the **balance of payments**, partly achieved by lowering total demand and thereby imports, and partly by **disinflation** and improving exports, by operating upon aggregate demand, to reduce **inflation**. (ii) The adjustment of an economic variable measured in **money** or nominal terms by a price **index** in order to provide an estimate of the change in the variable in **real** terms. See **indexation**.

deflator. The adjustment factor between the real and the nominal estimate of **gross national product**; it is a measure of inflation (cf. **consumer price index; producer prices index; retail price index**).

degearing. See **deleveraging**.

dekidaka (Japan). The **volume** or **turnover** of shares on the exchange.

delay days. Additional days beyond those normally accepted in **settlement** (cf. **forward**). See **delayed delivery** (cf. **fail**).

delayed cap floating rate note (delayed cap FRN). A note with a maximum rate of interest effective only after an initial free floating period. The structure is designed to make the note more marketable to investors. Also called a **deferred cap floating rate note**. See **cap; interest rate cap**.

delayed convertible. A **warrant** or other convertible security that does not allow immediate conversion, but only after a specified future date.

delayed delivery. The practice of deferring securities **settlement** beyond the normal settlement period. In effect it is a **forward** transaction (cf. **roll forward**). The transaction price will normally reflect the opportunity cost involved (cf. **contango market**). Delayed delivery is accepted in new issues.

delayed delivery, delayed settlement. An arrangement that can be made with the **underwriters** of an issue that allows for **delivery** and **settlement** of a new issue to take place on a given date after the original offering. With regard to delaying settlement there are usually regulatory restrictions on the period. Normally the price is adjusted to reflect the interest charges the trader will suffer and **accrued interest**.

delayed LIBOR reset swap. A type of **interest rate swap** or **cross-currency swap** contract where the setting of the **floating interest rate** payment calculation period is delayed until the payment date. Thus in a sterling fixed/floating swap, the sterling **London interbank offered rate** (LIBOR) rate set may be postponed until the first **floating rate** payment is due. It is also known as a *back-end set swap* or *LIBOR in arrears swap*.

delayed opening. The putting back of the scheduled opening of trading in a security (cf. **opening price**). Normally the result of a demand–supply imbalance (cf. **market forces**). See **crash; jumps**.

delayed rate setting (DRS). An arrangement used in a **bond** transaction where the buyer of the bond has the right within a prescribed period to fix the interest rate with the seller at which he bought the security. The parties agree the bond's **spread** above (or below) a **benchmark**, or **reference rate**, at which the investor can then lock in. If rates rise, the transaction is completed at the future prevailing reference rate, plus the agreed spread, giving the investor his required **yield**. However, if rates fall, the investor has to lock in at the then prevailing lower rate. It is equivalent to the buyer selling a **bond future** contract at the same time as buying the bond but without the requirement to provide **margin** and without any **basis risk** (cf. **cross-hedging**).

delayed reset swap. See **delayed LIBOR reset swap**.

delayed settlement. See **delayed delivery**.

del credere. Term for the payment over and above the normal **commission** made to an **agent** who assumes the **credit risk** of a customer.

deleveraged floating rate note (deleveraged FRN). Floating rate note where the reference rate for the **coupon** is a **benchmark** or index of long-term bonds plus a **margin**. Such a note will provide investors with a higher yield than similar securities whose reference rate is a **short-term money market** rate when the **yield** curve is strongly upward sloping (cf. **spread**).

deleveraging. Reducing the ratio of debt to equity in a **balance sheet** in order to reduce the firm's **financial risk**. This can be accomplished by either retiring debt or issuing more **equity**. Known as *degearing* in the UK.

Delhi Stock Exchange Association Ltd, The (India). 3 & 4/4b Asaf Ali Road, IN-New Delhi 110002 (tel. 91 1 3279000; fax 91 11 3326182). See also **Bombay Stock Exchange**.

delinquency (USA). An overdue payment from a debtor which has not yet been **written off** as unrecoverable (cf. **problem asset**). For banks, regulators prescribe any loan with interest overdue more than ninety days as being impaired (cf. **non-performing assets**).

delinquency ratio (Banking; USA). The **ratio** of overdue payments of interest and principal to the total loan book.

delisting. The removal of a security from an exchange (cf. **going private**).

deliverable. A security or **commodity** which meets the requirements for **settlement** of **futures contracts** at **expiry** in terms of quality, maturity, principal amount, and coupon rate and which may be physically delivered to satisfy the contract. Not applicable to **cash-settled** contracts. Increasingly, due to problems with deliveries, futures markets are moving where possible to cash-settled contracts where the futures buyer executes the purchase of the **underlying** for his own account.

deliverable contract. **Futures contract** which is settled by either making or taking **delivery** of the **underlying**.

deliverable grades (Commodities). The range or specification of **commodity** purity or type that is **deliverable** into the **futures** contract. The exchange often allows a range of product to be used, but may impose a price adjustment for such variation (cf. **alternative delivery procedure**). See also **assay**; **contract grade**.

deliverable stock. The quantity of a commodity traded on an exchange that is of the contract quality and in an approved location (cf. **short squeeze**; **warehouse stocks**).

delivery. The settlement of a futures or options transaction (cf. **cash settled**; **clearing**; **deliverable**; **exercise**).

delivery against payment or **delivery versus payment (DVP).** A delivery of securities to a designated recipient only upon receiving payment. The opposite side is **receive-versus-payment** (cf. cash against delivery; free delivery).

delivery basis risk. See basis risk (cf. cheapest to deliver).

delivery date. (i) (Futures) The day, or in some cases days, when the seller of the **futures contract** is obliged to supply the **underlying**. In some cases, the decision to take or make delivery is announced prior to the **expiry** of the contract (cf. **delivery notice**). (ii) (Forex) The payment date or settlement date on a foreign exchange contract. Also called the *settlement date*.

delivery day. The day on which the **short seller** of a **futures contract** is required to make **delivery** of the **underlying** in order to honour his commitments under the terms of the **contract**.

delivery factor. Adjustments to the prices of **deliverable bonds** in **bond futures** contracts. The use of **basket delivery**, allowing different securities to be used to honour the seller's commitment, means that the market prices of these securities will vary in relation to the **underlying notional bond** of the **futures contract**. The amount of the different securities is adjusted to equalize the delivery value of each cash security. To arrive at the adjustment, each security is discounted by the **yield-to-maturity** on the notional bond to arrive at the equalizing price, or conversion factor (CF):

$$CF = \frac{\dfrac{1}{1+\dfrac{C_{nb}}{100}}\left(\dfrac{C_{ab}}{C_{nb}}\left\{1+\dfrac{C_{nb}}{100}\right\}-\dfrac{1}{\left(1+\dfrac{C_{nb}}{100}\right)^{n}}\right)}{100}$$

$$+\frac{\left(\dfrac{100}{\left(1+\dfrac{C_{nb}}{100}\right)^{n}}\right)-C_{ab}(1-f)}{100}$$

where C_{nb} is the coupon rate on the notional bond; C_{ab} the coupon rate on the actual bond for delivery; n the number of remaining whole years from the next coupon date to maturity; f the number of months from the delivery date to the next coupon date, rounded to the nearest whole number of months and divided by 12 (however, if f is zero, then f is set at 1 and n becomes $n-1$).

The above example is based on the **Bundesanleihen** contract traded on the **London International Financial Futures and Options Exchange**. Thus for a 7% coupon government bond with 8.25 years remaining maturity and where the notional bond **underlying** the contract has a 6% coupon, the conversion factor would be:

$$\frac{\dfrac{1}{1+\dfrac{6}{100}}\left(\dfrac{7}{6}\left\{1+\dfrac{6}{100}\right\}-\dfrac{1}{\left(1+\dfrac{6}{100}\right)^{8}}\right)}{100}$$

$$+\frac{\left(\dfrac{100}{\left(1+\dfrac{6}{100}\right)^{8}}\right)-7(1-0.25)}{100}$$

which gives a conversion factor of 1.0155. The **invoice price** is then computed by taking the relationship of this value to the futures settlement price, and including any **accrued interest**:

$$Invoice\ Amount = \begin{array}{c} Exchange\ Delivery\ Settlement \\ Price \times Conversion\ Factor \\ + Accured\ Interest \end{array}$$

Thus, if a bond future is at 98.25, the conversion factor is 1.0155, and the accrued interest per 100 on the bond is 1.75, the cash payment per 100 nominal of the notional bond in the contract is therefore 101.5229:

$$101.5229 = 98.25 \times 1.0155 + 1.75$$

Note that because of variations in the market prices and the delivery factor, this gives rise to a single security which is the **cheapest to deliver**. Bond futures will trade in relation to this cheapest bond, since the short position holder has the right to determine which security will be provided to honour their commitment; he will choose the security which minimizes his loss, or maximizes his gain. The delivery factor is also commonly known as the *conversion factor* or *price factor*. See **exchange delivery settlement price**.

delivery mechanism. The procedure used to fulfil **futures** obligations at the **delivery date**, including **basket delivery**, **cash settlement**, or simple delivery where only one specific asset or instrument can be delivered.

delivery month. A calendar month in which a currently traded **futures contract** will **expire**. For a typical three-month cycle based on March, June, September, and December, if the March and June contracts are active, these would be known as delivery months. Note that some exchanges have a more frequent **expiry cycle**. Also known as a *contract month*.

delivery notice. The notification by the seller to a buyer of a **commodity futures contract** giving the date when the **commodity** is to be delivered (cf. **delivery date**).

delivery option. (i) The ability of a **short position** holder in a **bond futures contract** to decide between several different issues for **delivery** in order to honour his obligations in a **futures contract** (cf. **cheapest to deliver**; **delivery factor**; **notional bond**). (ii) The ability of the short position holder in a futures contract to decide, within specific limits, the **delivery date** in an expiring contract (cf. **wild card option**). The value of the option depends on whether the increase in value of the commodity is more or less than the reinvestment rate available to sellers. If the reinvestment rate is above (below) the increase in value, it is usually optimal to deliver early (at the last possible moment). The futures price will trade on the assumption that the short position holders will seek to

take advantage of the **window** in which they can deliver. Therefore, if it is optimal to deliver early (late), then the futures price should be calculated on the basis of delivery being at the earliest (latest) possible date. Under normal market circumstances, the short would seek the latest possible delivery date. The basic set of options or choices that can be made include:

- *Accrued interest option*: the right of the short position holder to decide when within the delivery month to make delivery of the underlying. This will be determined by the cost of carry; a positive carry situation tending to delay delivery to the last moment; negative carry tending to ensure early delivery.
- *End-of-the-month option*: the ability to make use of the delay in settlement allowed between the exchange's final delivery settlement price set at the expiry of the futures contract and making delivery either to allow the substitution of a cheapest-to-deliver bond or to close out an **arbitrage** position at a profit by buying more cheaply in the cash market.
- *Quality option*: the right of the short position holder to delivery any of the cash bonds in the basket that meet the specifications of the contract. The existence of a quality option makes a long arbitrage position difficult since in setting up the position the arbitrageur does not know which bond will be delivered.
- *Wild card option*: differences between the cut-off time on giving notice of the intention to deliver on any given delivery day within the delivery month and the **exchange delivery settlement price** set at the closing. Differences in the two prices allow an arbitrage that in turn allows either the substitution of an alternative cheapest-to-deliver bond, or the closing-out an arbitrage position at a profit by buying more cheaply in the cash market.

delivery point. The acceptable locations as specified in the relevant contract, as determined by the exchange, where a commodity may be delivered in fulfilment of the short position's obligation (cf. **alternative delivery procedure**; **warehousing**).

delivery price. The price which the **futures exchange** sets for delivery at the **expiry** of the contract. Also known as the *exchange delivery settlement price* (EDSP).

delivery repurchase agreement. Repurchase **agreement** where the securities involved are physically delivered to the buyer.

delivery risk. A term used in the **foreign exchange** markets for the risk that the **counterparty** to a transaction, although willing, may be prevented from honouring his obligations due to, for instance, the imposition of currency controls or quotas (cf. **counterparty risk**). Also called *settlement risk*. See also **overnight delivery risk**.

delivery specifications. The conditions in a **futures**, **option**, or **forward contract** for the type and characteristics of the cash, instrument, or commodity that are required to be provided for **good delivery** in **settlement** at **exercise**, expiry, or settlement. Also known as *contract specifications*.

delivery versus payment or **delivery against payment (DVP)**. A settlement requirement that entitlement to securities is matched with a cash receipt by the vendor. The opposite position is *receive versus payment*.

delta (δ). A measure of **option** value sensitivity that measures the change in the value of the option for a small change in the value of the underlying and which can take a range from 0 to 1. An at-the-money option will have a delta of 0.5; an out-of-the-money option will have a delta below 0.5; while an in-the-money option will have a delta above 0.5. The delta times the value of the underlying gives the **hedge ratio**. The delta of a put is negative it is -1 when the underlying price is at its lowest against the strike price and the option is deeply in the money, and 0 when the underlying price is at its highest and the put is deeply out of the money. The delta is very useful in that it provides the underlying equivalence of the option position. Also known as the *neutral hedge ratio*. See **gamma**; **option pricing**.

delta/gamma hedge. A type of **delta hedge** that eliminates the **market risk** of the **option writer's** exposure to the **underlying**. The **hedge** acts to offset the exposure to the underlying position by matching both the position **delta** and position **gamma** (that is the rate of change in the position delta) over a greater price range. This is a different procedure from that of the delta hedge or **dynamic hedging** since the procedure attempts to replicate the performance of an offsetting option position to the **risk** assumed by taking the **short** option position. That is it aims to behave as if the option writer had purchased an option with the same characteristics as the written option.

delta hedge. A method to **hedge** the change in the price of an **option** due to changes in the price of the **underlying** by buying or selling the underlying in proportion to the option's **delta**. For example, when a **call option** writer has issued an option with a delta of 0.4, he can effect a delta

hedge by buying 0.4 of the total amount of the underlying that must be delivered upon exercise.

A *delta neutral position* (DN) is where the writer delta hedges so that the combined position in options and the underlying is unaffected by small changes in the price of the underlying. However, the option delta will change with changes in the price of the underlying, in its **volatility**, interest rates, and with the reduction in the time to expiry (cf. **time decay**). As a result, the hedge must be frequently re-balanced to maintain a hedged **position** (cf. **dynamic hedging**). Delta hedging will lose money for the **writer** of an option and will make money for the holder of an option. Also known as the *neutral hedge ratio*.

delta negative. The price sensitivity of put options is negative, since with a higher price, the delta of a put will decrease. See **option pricing**.

delta neutral. (i) A position in a **derivative** instrument in which the price **risk** has been neutralized, hedged in respect of market prive movements (cf. **market risk**). This is achieved using a **delta hedge** (cf. **delta**; **delta/gamma hedge**). Because of the dynamic nature of the performance of the derivative, the position is not necessarily also hedged for other sensitivities. See **neutral ratio spread**; **option pricing**; **option strategies**. (ii) A generalization of the hedging process used for derivatives applied to any **position** where the **market risk** has been eliminated (cf. **duration-based hedge ratio**; **tail hedging**).

delta positive. The price sensitivity of **call options** is positive, since with a higher price, the delta of a call will increase. See **option pricing**.

delta shares or **stocks** (UK). Defunct categorization used on the **London Stock Exchange** for the group of **ordinary shares** that were most infrequently traded. Now replaced by the **Normal Market Size**. See **Alternative Investment Market**; **alpha shares**; **beta shares**; **bulletin board**; **gamma shares**; **normal quote size**; **two-way price**.

delta spread. See **neutral ratio spread**.

demain-après (French). **Tom/next**.

demand (i) (Banking) Deposits which may be withdrawn on demand, hence *demand deposits*, or loans where the amount may be varied at the borrower's choice (cf. **demand line of credit**). Also known as *call money*. (ii) (Securities). The investor interest and hence orders for a particular new issue. A new issue would be said to be **hot** if there was excessive demand at the issue price (cf. **blow out**).

demand deposit (Banking; USA). Account held with a bank allowing immediate access to the funds (cf. **current account; call money**). See also **negotiated order of withdrawal account**.

demand line of credit (Banking; USA). A borrowing **facility** that allows a client to borrow on demand or on a daily basis.

demand loan (Banking; USA). A loan of no fixed **maturity** where the lender has the right to ask for immediate repayment (cf. **broker loan rate; call money**).

demand master notes. See **master notes**.

demand shock. A sudden disturbance in an economic system that adversely affects demand. A past example was the sudden increase in the oil price in 1973 which significantly raised energy costs.

dematerialization. Conversion of physical securities into book-entry securities.

demerger. The hiving off a substantial part of a firm to existing **shareholders** by splitting the existing company in two. The logic is both to realize value for shareholders and to provide focus for both firms. Also called a *bifurcation*.

demise hire. See **capital lease; financial lease**.

demutualization. The conversion of a mutual society into a corporate entity. See also **building society**.

denomination. The principal amount represented by a security **certificate** to be paid on redemption (cf. **face value; par value**).

density. See **probability density function**.

Department of the Treasury (USA). The federal state department that handles financial affairs. See **US Treasury**.

depletion (USA). A tax allowance for natural resource companies against the exhaustion of the deposit or oilfield.

depletion accounting. A method of **amortizing** the value of oil reserves based on extraction of the deposit or oil field. See also **depreciation methods**.

depo rate. See **deposit rate**.

déport (French). **Discount** (cf. **backwardation**).

deporto (Italian). Stock lending at the expense of the borrower (cf. **riporto**).

deposit. (i) A sum of money lent to or placed with a financial institution for a set or indeterminate

period. Such lending activities to financial institutions are normally highly regulated and the term *depository institutions* normally implies as much, although deposits are accepted by **brokers** and **broker-dealers** from their clients (cf. **segregation; too big to fail**). Often referred to as a *depo* (cf. **placing; taking**). (ii) A sum provided in good faith as part payment on a transaction (cf. **premium**). (iii) Cash or other negotiable instrument provided as security for losses. See **margin**. (iv) The initial payment on a **consumer credit loan**.

deposit account (Banking; UK). Term account held with a depository institution where withdrawals are subject to notice or an interest rate penalty.

deposit insurance. An insurance designed to protect depositors at a deposit-taking institution in the event of its collapse (cf. **bankruptcy; Deposit Protection Fund**). See **Federal Deposit Insurance Corporation**.

Deposit Insurance National Bank (DINB) (Banking; USA). A banking entity established by the **Federal Deposit Insurance Corporation** to manage the affairs of a financially distressed bank pending a decision to close or sell it to another institution (cf. **capital impairment**).

deposit interest cover (Forex). See **covered interest arbitrage; foreign exchange swap**.

deposit note (USA). Intermediate-term obligations issued by banks. Essentially a type of **medium-term note** (MTN) issued by foreign banks in the US domestic money markets. They differ from normal MTNs in that they are evidenced by a deposit placed with the branch of the bank. They also go by the name of *bank medium term notes* or *certificate of deposit notes*. See also **certificate of deposit; floating rate certificate of deposit; term certificate of deposit**.

Depository Institutions Deregulation and Monetary Control Act of 1980 (DIDMCA) (Banking; USA). Legislation that deregulated activities of deposit-taking institutions, such as ceilings on the interest rates payable on **deposits** and allowing **negotiable order of withdrawal** accounts.

depository receipt (USA). A **certificate** evidencing ownership of a **banker's acceptance** and used to facilitate a secondary market in such instruments. See, for instance, **American depository receipt; global depository receipt**.

depository transfer check (DTC) (USA). Checks used by account holders to move funds from one account to another. They are unsigned and non-negotiable instruments used, for instance, to facilitate **concentration banking**.

Depository Trust Company (DTC) (USA). A central depository institution which holds certificates on behalf of its members and facilitates the transfer of ownership by reducing the transfer of physical certificates between the parties. It is also used by **option writers** as a way of facilitating and guaranteeing delivery of the **underlying** securities if assignment is made, as the DTC will hold the securities for its members.

Deposit Protection Fund (Banking; UK). Insurance fund for depositors in the UK. It is levied on all deposit-taking institutions in the UK and, in the event of a **bankruptcy**, provides reimbursement of 75% on the first £20,000 of any deposit (cf. **moral hazard**). It is operated by the Deposit Protection Board.

deposit rate. The rate achieved by a market participant in the **interbank market**. As the London interbank offered rate is the **asked** or **offer** rate, the corresponding rate is the **London interbank bid rate**.

deposit swap. See **foreign exchange swap**; **covered interest arbitrage**.

deposit-taking institution (Banking; UK). Legal definition for any institution accepting deposits from the public, such as a bank, under the Banking Acts, 1979 and 1987. Such institutions are regulated by the **Bank of England**. Originally deposit-taking institutions were classified as two types: those that could call themselves a *bank* and those, of lesser status, which had to call themselves a *licenced deposit-taker*, although they could use the name 'bank' in their business title. This distinction has now been abolished.

dépôt (French). Deposit.

depreciated cost. The value of an asset less the accumulated **depreciation**. Also known as *written-down cost* or *value*.

depreciation. (i) (Accounting) The recording of an expense to represent the loss of value in a wasting asset over a period (cf. **amortization**). Under the matching concept, depreciation should assign the total loss of value of an asset over its lifetime as expense in the periods when the company benefits from its use. (ii) (Securities) A reduction in **book** or market value. (iii) (Forex) The reduction over time in the value of one currency relative to others (cf. **appreciation**). See **devaluation**; **revaluation**.

depreciation methods (Accounting). The recognition of the fall in value of assets through use and time. Although depreciation is only a book entry item, depreciation is often an allowable charge for tax purposes. Firms may use one form of depreciation for reporting purposes and another for tax offsets. These tax depreciation methods are similar or the same as those used in financial reporting, but are usually called (in the UK) **capital allowances** or (in the USA) cost recovery (cf. **Accelerated Cost Recovery System**). Some of the most common methods of depreciation are given below:

- *Immediate write-off/100 percent allowance*: The purchase price of the asset is written down in the accounting period in which is acquired.
- *Straight-line method*: The asset value is written down in equal proportions over the expected useful life.
- *Sum-of-the-years digits*: Accelerated depreciation method based on calculating the amount of depreciation in any year as the inverse of the number of years from the purchase date to the last year divided by the sum of the number of years for the asset. Thus a five-year asset in year one would have a depreciation of $5 \div 15(5 + 4 + 3 + 2 + 1)$, year two: $4 \div 15$, and so on.
- *Declining balance, diminishing or reducing balance*: Allocates depreciation in a given year by charging a fixed proportion (say 25%) to the written-down proportion in the previous period. Thus an asset worth 100 in year one, would be written down to 75; in year two to 56.25 (75×0.75), and so forth. This is the

Depreciation methods

Year	Immediate write-off Period	Straight-line method Period	Cumulative	Sum-of-the-years Period	Cumulative	Declining balance $(1/5^{th})$ Period	Cumulative
1	1,000	200	200	333	333	200	200
2	0	200	400	267	600	160	360
3	0	200	600	200	800	128	488
4	0	200	800	133	933	102	590
5	0	200	1,000	67	1,000	82	672
	1,000	1,000		1,000		328	

(225)

basic system used for capital allowances in the UK, except that the first-year amount is 40% and subsequent amounts are 20%.

- *150% declining and double declining balance*: A method of depreciation which is one-and-a-half or twice that of the straight-line method.
- *Economic depreciation*: Depreciation is based on the use of the asset over time. Thus if the asset was used in period 1 to make 10,000 units and 20,000 in period two and had an expected life of 100,000 units, the economic depreciation in period one would be 0.1 times the value of the asset in period 1; and 0.2 times in period 2.
- *No depreciation*: There is no writing down of the value of assets (this might apply, for instance, to land and buildings).

An asset is bought for a value of 1,000. The amount of depreciation on the asset will be as in the Table.

depth. The situation in which it is possible to trade large amounts of stock without significantly affecting its price (cf. **liquidity**; **thin**). See **market impact**.

derecognition. See defeasance.

deregulation. Relaxation of the rules governing the conduct and activities permitted by organizations and markets. Regulation can take several forms; for instance, prudential regulation as practised by the bank and securities regulators, price regulation as operated for natural monopolies, and legal restrictions preventing non-authorized businesses from engaging in certain activities (cf. re-regulation). See liberalization.

derivative, derivative asset, derivative instrument, derivative product, or **derivative security**. (i) A generic term for the range of exchange-traded and over-the-counter instruments that have grown up around securities, currency, and commodity markets. They have facilitated investment strategies such as hedging, spreading, and arbitrage (cf. asset allocation). There are four principal classes: forwards; futures; swaps; and options. They are derivatives because their price behaviour comes from the underlying asset's price movements. The price of any derivative is a function of the price or rate behaviour of the underlying and time. Different classes behave differently in relation to the underlying asset and therefore they serve different economic functions. The use of derivatives has been traced back to ancient times (it is believed that there was an active market in silk options and futures in Ancient China). Organized commodities markets evolved in the 19th century, but it was not until the launch of exchange-listed instruments in the early 1970s,

combined with the breakdown in the Bretton Woods Agreement, changes in financial regulation, and developments in information technology, that derivative markets began to be considered a major part of the financial markets. Also known as a *contingent asset* or *contingent claim*. (ii) A contract or instrument, such as a **convertible**, where the value changes in line with changes in the underlying security, future, index, or instrument (cf. **hybrid**).

derivative market. (i) Any of the markets for **derivative instruments**. (ii) Exchanges specializing in the trading of derivative instruments rather than **cash instruments**. See futures; options.

descending tops. A chartist's pattern. See ascending tops.

designated market-maker. See market-maker scheme.

Designated Order Turnaround (DOT) (Equities; USA). The electronic order system used by the New York Stock Exchange for small-sized transactions and **limit orders** allowing them to be sent electronically to the **specialist** on the **floor** of the exchange. DOT is used by **program trading** and other **technical** portfolio management methods to quickly execute orders to buy or sell **stocks**.

Designated Primary Market-maker (DPM). A floor broker who has the responsibility of making a **two-way price** on the **Chicago Board Options Exchange** (cf. **jobber**; **local**; **specialist**).

desk (USA). The name given to the New York Federal Reserve Bank's trading operations; it is the operating arm of the **Federal Open Market Committee** (FOMC). The desk carries out all the FOMC's instructions, buying and selling securities in order to influence the **fed funds rate** and the **money supply**. It also undertakes any currency intervention.

despecialization. The reverse of specialization. A condition where a firm becomes more general in the product or service ranges it offers.

detachable warrant. A **warrant** attached to a debt issue that can be traded separately (cf. **debt with debt warrants**; **debt with equity warrants**).

details. The information required by both parties to settle a transaction.

Deutsche Aktienindex (DAX) (German stock index) (Equities; Germany). Most-watched German **equity index** based on thirty leading **common stocks** quoted on the **Frankfurt Stock Exchange** (cf. **blue chip**). It is a real-time index being updated as transactions are recorded in the **settlement** system.

Deutsche Börse AG (German Stock Exchange) (Germany). Bürsenplatz 4, DE-60313, Frankfurt 1 (tel. 49 69 29977 0: fax 49 69 29977 599). Holding company for the **Deutscher Kassenverein** (the German Central Securities Depository), the **Deutsche Wertpapierdaten-Zentrale** (the German Securities Data Centre) and the **Deutsche Terminbörse** (the German Options and Futures Exchange). The different regional stock exchanges in Germany have an equity participation in the Deutsche Börse (cf. **Finanzplatz Deutschland**). Apart from the **Frankfurt Stock Exchange**, these are the Baden-Württemberg Stock Exchange (Stuttgart), Bavarian Stock Exchange (Munich), Berlin Stock Exchange, Bremen Stock Exchange, Hanover Stock Exchange, Hanseatic Stock Exchange (Hanover), and the Rhineland-Westphalian Stock Exchange (Düsseldorf). The exchanges have combined to provide a centralized market for trading securities.

Deutsche Bundesbank. See **Bundesbank**.

Deutscher Auslandskassenverein AG (AKV) (German Central Foreign Securities Depository) (Germany). See **Deutscher Kassenverein**.

Deutscher Kassenverein AG (DKV) (German Central Securities Depository) (Germany). Centralized securities depository that with the **Deutsche Wertpapierdaten-Zentrale** provides a paperless electronic settlement of transactions undertaken on the various German stock exchanges.

Deutsche Terminbörse (DTB) (Germany). Grüneburgweg 102, D-6000 Frankfurt-am-Main 1 (tel. 49 (0) 69 15303 0; fax 49 (0) 69 557 492). **Derivatives** exchange set up in 1988 and based in Frankfurt. It handles **financial futures** and **options**.

Deutsche Wertpapierdaten-Zentrale GmbH (DWZ). The clearing house for handling securities settlements. In conjunction with the **Deutscher Kassenverein**, it provides a paperless system, involving settlement matching and error reporting. The system allows for **same-day settlement** of transactions. It also includes processing for the **Deutscher Auslandskassenverein**, the Central Foreign Securities Depository.

devaluation (Forex). The reduction of the official rate at which a currency is exchanged for others (cf. **revaluation**). See **depreciation**; **appreciation**.

developmental drilling program (USA). A type of oil and gas exploration **limited partnership** which is of lower risk than an **exploratory** or **wildcat drilling program**.

development capital. Second-stage finance (the first stage being **seed capital**) used to assist established companies in expanding their business.

devisen (Germany). **Foreign exchange**. Hence *Devisenkassamarkt*, which is the **spot** foreign exchange market, and *Devisenterminmarkt*, which is the **forward** foreign exchange market.

devises (French). **Foreign exchange**. Hence *marché à devises*, which is the foreign exchange market.

Dhaka Stock Exchange Ltd. (Bangladesh). Stock Exchange Building, 9/F Moluheel Commercial Area, BD-1000 Dhaka (tel. 880 2 231935; telex 632150 DSE BJ).

diagonal calendar spread or **diagonal spread**. An **option position** or strategy involving contracts with different **strike prices** and **expiry dates** (for instance a purchased and written call on the **nearby** and the **deferred** contracts) (cf. **horizontal spread**; **vertical spread**). Different combinations are possible: *diagonal bear spread* involves the purchase of the longer-dated option and the sale of the shorter-dated option with a lower **exercise price**; the **position** is so designed so as to gain from a fall in the price of the **underlying** within the limits of the purchased and sold options; *diagonal bull spread* involves the opposite set of positions so as to gain from a rise in the price of the underlying within the limits of the purchased and written options. See also **option strategies**.

diagonal straddle calendar spread. A complex option strategy based on relative **volatility** and the **term structure** of **volatility** and the directional view on the **underlying** over the spread period. It involves selling a **straddle** in the short-dated options and buying a straddle in later **expiry** options at a different **strike price**. See also **diagonal spread**.

diff. (i) Quantity adjusting option. (ii) **Difference option**; **differential swap**.

difference account (UK). A rendering to a client by a **broker** on the **London Metal Exchange** of the amount payable when closing a market **position**.

difference clause. An agreement within a contract such as a **forward rate agreement** or an **interest rate swap** where the net difference in payments between the two **counterparties** is paid, rather than the two contractual amounts being exchanged.

difference option or **diff option**. (i) An **option** where the **underlying** is the difference between the price of two assets. Examples include, the spread between **Bundes Bonds** and OATs, or the

S&P 500 and the NASDAQ composite index. The gain from holding the option will depend on the extent the differential between the two assets compares with the differential when the option was written. Thus if the buyer had bought a **call** and the **spread** was 150 **basis points** at **expiry** and the **strike** was set at 140 basis points, the option would expire **out of the money**. If it had been a **put**, the holder would have received 10 basis points times the **nominal amount** according to the payment formula in the contract. Also variously called a *rainbow option* or *spread option*. (ii) Another name for an **outperformance option**.

differential (USA). The higher (lower) price obtained when buying (selling) in **odd lots**.

differential future (USA). A type of **financial future** contract traded on the **Chicago Mercantile Exchange** which has a payment linked to the differences in price performance between two **underlying** assets (cf. **spread**).

differential information. See **asymmetric information**.

differential interest rate fix (DIRF). Any of a range of **derivative instruments** that have a payoff linked to the differences in performance of **underlyings** at different points on the **yield curve** (cf. **term structure of interest rates**). See **curve lock**; **forward spread agreement**; **yield curve swap**.

differentials. (i) Differences in the prices of adjacent quoted contract months for the same **underlying**. (ii) Differences in price between various grades of the same **commodity** (cf. **assay**).

differential swap or **diff. swap**. A special type of **basis swap** in which one party exchanges **floating rate** payments in one currency into floating rate payments in another currency but where the payments are made, however, in the **base currency** of the **notional principal**. It therefore has some of the characteristics of an **interest rate swap** and a **cross currency swap** but where one **reference rate** is the interest rate in the second currency. For example, one party might pay an interest rate based on French franc **London interbank offered rate** (LIBOR) in US dollars against a US dollar LIBOR (in US dollars) plus a **margin** (cf. **spread**). Typically the exposed party will hedge the transaction through a series of **foreign exchange swaps**, but remains exposed to **foreign exchange risk** on the transaction. The result is similar to a series of same-price **forward rate agreements** but where the pricing is based on a fixed-fixed cross-currency swap. The structure is also variously known as a *cross index basis swap* (CRIB swap), *cross rate swap*, *currency protected swap*, *interest rate index swap*, *LIBOR differential swap, LIBOR diff. swap*, or *rate differential swap*.

differential tariff. Variable taxes or duties applied to the same goods or services coming from different countries. As compared with an **Common External Tariff** as used by **customs unions**.

diffition. Option on a **differential swap** (cf. **currency protected swap**).

diggers. See **dragons**.

digital option. A type of **option** where, unlike a normal option, the payout is fixed. There are two types: *all-or-nothing* and *one-touch* options. All-or-nothing will pay out the fixed amount if the **underlying** is above (**call**) or below (**put**) a set value at **expiry**, that is, they are either 'on' (**in the money**) or 'off' (**out of the money**). The one-touch will pay the fixed amount if the underlying reaches a fixed point at any time before expiry. As a result, digital options are sometimes known as *binary options*. The one-touch is the more expensive of the two given the requirement by the **writer** to pay if the underlying should reach the **trigger** at any point. These options have a use in that the **premium** is often much smaller than that on simple options. Where the buyer has a view on the market and expects only a certain movement in the underlying, such options provide a cheaper alternative.

digits deleted (USA). A compression of the price series on an exchange's price indicator in order to speed up the dissemination of the data. Typically, the first digit will be dropped so that a price of $55\,^3/_8$ becomes $5\,^3/_8$.

dilution. The effect on the **earnings** and voting power per **common stock** or **ordinary share** (**earnings per share**) from an increase in the number of shares issued without a corresponding increase in the value of the firm's earnings. When an issue of **warrants** or **convertible bonds** is made, the dilution of existing shareholders' positions is often worked out on (1) a *primary* basis and (2) a fully diluted basis (that is following the **conversion** of the convertible or **exercise** of all the warrants). The amount the new shares thus created affect existing holdings is known as the *dilution factor*. See **fully diluted earnings per share**; **scrip issue**; **split**; **stock**.

Dingo (Bonds; Australia). A **zero-coupon bond** created by stripping a government bond (cf. **separate trading of registered interest and principal of securities**).

dip. A small drop or weakness in prices on an uptrend which is less than a **correction** (cf. **dead-cat bounce**).

direct bid programme. A condition within a tender panel allowing members to make direct, unsolicited bids to the issuer to issue new securities outside the formal tender process.

direct exchange rate (Forex). See **direct quote**.

direct foreign investment. See **direct investment**.

direct hedge. A **hedging** instrument which is the same as the **underlying** being hedged. It could involve, for instance, **futures** purchase or sale designed to reduce price-level **risk** for a deliverable **underlying position** (cf. **consumer's hedge**; **producer's hedge**). See **hedge**.

direct investment. Investment in a foreign country by either setting up a business unit or acquiring a locally based company (cf. **portfolio investment**; **transplant**).

directive. (i) (Banking; USA) An instruction from the **Federal Reserve Open Market Committee** to the operating arm of the **Federal Reserve**, the Federal Reserve Bank of New York (aka the **desk**), to pursue a given **monetary policy** (cf. **open-market operations**). (ii) Legislative order issued by the **European Union**.

direct lease. A type of **lease** where the producer of some **asset** leases it directly.

direct loan. A **loan** made directly by one party to another and taking the latter's **credit risk** (cf. **intermediation**).

director. (i) Individual picked to manage a company or corporation. Directors are elected by the firm's **shareholders** for a fixed term and report to them as their **agent** (cf. **agency theory**; **principal**). They normally are either executive appointments, that is they work full-time for the company, or non-executive, where they attend **board of directors** meetings. This board is led by a managing director or chief executive (CE) under the guidance of a chairman. Firms may give different titles to individual directors depending on their roles on the Board, such as chairman, president, **chief executive officer**, **chief financial officer**, **managing director**, **finance director**, and so forth. The conduct of directors is governed by company law (cf. **Cadbury Committee on the Financial Aspects of Corporate Governance**). There has been controversy over the effectiveness of directors when the roles of CE and chairman are combined. The trend today is for these jobs to be split with the clear implication that the chairman should act as a kind of internal control against executive excesses. See also **corporate governance**. (ii) In the USA, among **investment banks**,

or **merchant banks** in the UK, and elsewhere the term 'director' can be used with reference to any senior manager, not necessarily Board members.

direct paper (USA). Issues made by borrowers directly to investors without a financial intermediary (cf. **direct placement**). See **placement**.

direct participation program (DPP) (USA). A type of financial arrangement which allows investors to participate directly in the cash flows of a business or asset. Most are structured as **limited partnerships**. The rationale is to avoid the double taxation of **dividends** which is a feature of US corporate finance. Although many of the tax advantages of passive limited partnerships have been abolished, the method does allow the recipient to offset some expenses against revenues.

direct pay letter of credit. See **letter of credit**.

direct placement. When a placement **issue** is made directly with financial institutions without using **underwriters** or **dealers** (cf. **private placement**).

direct quotation or **quote** (Forex). The setting of the price of fixed amounts of **foreign currency** in terms of variable amounts of the domestic currency (cf. **indirect exchange rate**). For a German-based investor, the practice of expressing **foreign exchange** between the Deutschmark (DM) and the US dollar (US$) in terms of one US dollar to variable amounts of DM would constitute a direct quote; it is an indirect quotation for a US-domiciled person. Also called *direct exchange rate*.

direct search market. A type of market where buyers and sellers search each other out and transact directly without the benefits of an **intermediary** or **market-maker**.

dirty float (Forex). An informal system of **managed** or **floating exchange rates** where such things as the levels at which **central banks** will intervene to buy own currency (to support value), or sell own currency (to suppress value), remain unstated and unpredictable. See also **crawling peg**; **fixed exchange rate**.

dirty price. The price of a **bond** including accrued interest (cf. **clean price**); the dirty price is the actual price paid when a bond is purchased. Also known as the *full price*.

disagio. (i) The discount necessary to dispose of the goods taken in **counter-trade**. The disagio reflects the marketability of the goods concerned and varies between 2–3% for certain high-quality minerals and **commodities** to as much as 25–30% for low-quality manufactured goods and machinery. (ii) (Switzerland) The **discount to par** on a security (cf. **agio**).

disbursement. (i) (Banking) A payment made under a **facility** or other agreement. (ii) Costs incurred by an **agent** acting on behalf of a **principal** which can be later reclaimed. Also called *expenses*.

disbursement float. The clearing time required for a **cheque** to be drawn on an account (cf. **clearing float**; **float**).

discharge. To release a party from an **obligation**.

disclaimer or **disclaimer clause**. (i) A clause or condition in a contract which limits the obligations of one party. For instance, such a clause might be added to a sale contract to limit the vendor's liability in respect of certain kinds of information provided. (ii) A note attached to a publicly distributed document with the aim of limiting the originator's liability for its accuracy, content or quality. For example, 'The information contained in this report has been obtained from sources which we consider to be reliable. However, we do not guarantee its accuracy and, as such, the information may be incomplete or condensed. All opinions included in the report constitute our judgement as of the publication date and are subject to change without notice. Past performance is not necessarily indicative of the likely future performance of an investment. Any reliance you may place on the accuracy of this information or the validity of our opinions is at your own risk.'

disclosure level. The fraction or percentage ownership in a firm above which the holder has to declare his interest. Typically the level is set at around 3% to 5% of the outstanding **common stock**.

disclosure requirements (USA). The obligation of companies to make known price sensitive information to the market. What is required to be disclosed is governed by the exchange's listing requirements and the **Securities and Exchange Commission**.

discontinuity risk. The risk that price or rates will not follow a continuous path but may 'jump'. Many **hedging** models or strategies require prices to adjust in a continuous fashion so as to eliminate price risk (cf. **break**). A discontinuity may lead to unhedging, and hence losses. Also known as *jump risk*.

discontinuous risks. The risk that price or rate movements will be marked by breaks, that is jump, preventing the maintenance of a neutral

hedge on a complex position. See **binomial jump diffusion process**.

discount. (i) (Securities) When a security is priced below its **par** value. Securities which have a **coupon** which is below the current rate of interest are traded below their par value and are said to be at a *discount to par*. (ii) An offering of 'cheap' securities. It is seen as a way of stimulating investor interest either when the market is thought to be unresponsive to particular types of new issue or when the market is thought to be lacking **liquidity** (cf. **original issue discount**). (iii) (Forex) In quoting **forward exchange rates**, it is the amount added to the spot rate. It implies that the currency being quoted for (purchase or sale) will weaken by the time the contract matures so the currency being exchanged will buy more of the currency being quoted forward. (iv) (Money markets) The amount the **face** or par value of a money market instrument, typically **treasury bills**, **commercial paper**, **banker's acceptances**, or **bills**, is reduced at issue to provide a return to buyers. Discount money market instruments are sold below their par value but repay only par value at **maturity** with no explicit payment of interest. The discount compensates for the missing interest payment. Also known as *bank discount basis*. See also **interest rate calculations**.

Calculating the discount and price on discount instruments with the rate of discount given, where D is the discount from face value; F the face value; d the rate of discount; T_{sm} the days from settlement to maturity; P the price; *Basis* the number of days in the computation year (360 or 365):

$$D = \frac{F \times d \times T_{sm}}{Basis \times 100}$$

Purchase price:

$$P = F - D$$

or can be directly computed by:

$$P = F\left\{1 - \left[\frac{d \times T_{sm}}{(Basis \times 100)}\right]\right\}$$

Calculating the rate of discount on discount securities with the (a) discount amount or (b) price given:

(a)
$$d = \frac{D \times Basis \times 100}{F \times T_{sm}}$$

(b)
$$d = \left(1 - \frac{P}{F}\right)\left(\frac{Basis \times 100}{T_{sm}}\right)$$

(v) The purchase of a (**bill of exchange**) by a third party for an amount less than that party will receive at maturity. Effectively the seller borrows money against the repayment of the bill, the discount representing the cost of borrowing. The amount of the discount varies according to the risk the buyer takes that the obligation will be met and so is influenced by the standing of the **drawee**. Bills are normally discounted with banks and discount houses (forfaiting; without recourse). See also round tripping. (vi) The process of equating a receipt or payment at some future date with to-day's value using the time value of money. Money is given a present value by multiplying its future value by a discount factor for the time and the appropriate rate of interest. (vii) (Equities) Applied to common stock where the market price is below its par value. (viii) (Derivatives) An option which is being traded at less than its intrinsic value. (ix) The amount by which a future trades below its theoretical or fair value. That is the amount of additional basis on the future above and beyond that predicted by the cost of carry model of future values. See price discovery. (x) The amount by which the net asset value of a closed-end fund's shares or units exceeds the market price of the shares or units (cf. investment trust). Also called the discount to net asset value.

discount arbitrage. The purchase of an option which is trading at less than its intrinsic value (that is at a discount) while taking short position in the underlying. The combined position gives the holder a risk-free gain. See option strategies.

discount bond. A bond which is trading below its par value. Also sometimes the name used for a zero coupon bond.

discount broker. (i) A broker that charges commissions that are lower than a full service broker. Typically such a discount broker will not provide any additional services, or, if he does, he charges for these separately. (ii) (UK) Broker active in the bill market (cf. bill broker).

discount certificate of deposit (discount CD). A type of certificate of deposit issued at a discount without a coupon. It is therefore redeemed at par. As such it follows the conventions used by commercial paper issues and the issuing bank ends up receiving less than the face amount, which is not the case with most coupon CDs.

discounted cash flow (DCF). An approach to evaluating alternative investment projects, used by both public and private sector enterprises, based upon a common procedure for reducing a stream of returns to a single value at a particular point in time. This is achieved by using some rate of interest as a weighting device through time (cf. discount factor; discount rate). The two most frequently used DCF criteria are net present value and internal rate of return.

discounted dividend model (DDM). See dividend discount model.

discounted information. Relevant information which does not affect a market price, since the market has already absorbed it and incorporated it into the price. In term of the efficient markets hypothesis, the information is *fully reflected* in the price. The degree to which this occurs is taken as a measure of a market's information processing capacity.

discounted investment in negotiable government obligations (DINGO) (Bonds; Australia). A zero-coupon bond created by stripping the principal and coupons from an Australian government bond.

discounted margin (DM) (Bonds). A measure of excess return from a floating rate note (FRN) relative to its index rate, such as London interbank offered rate (LIBOR), calculated by discounting the future cash flows on a money market basis. For example, a five-year FRN with a semi-annual coupon of LIBOR plus 0.125%, and purchased at 99.75, would have a discounted margin, at a LIBOR rate of 10% of (0.191% basis points) compared to a simple margin of 0.175% (17.5 basis points) (cf. spread-to-maturity; yield-to-maturity.).

discount factor. The present value of a future cash flow of one unit. The formula is:

$$\frac{1}{\left(1 + \dfrac{r_t}{100}\right)^t}$$

where r is the rate of interest per period and t the number of time periods. Where r is the interest rate for annual payments, t is years. When r is the interest rate for semi-annual payments and t is years:

$$\frac{1}{\left(1 + \dfrac{r_t}{200}\right)^{2t}}$$

Sometimes called the *present value interest factor*.

discount house (UK). A UK institution that acts as an intermediary between the Bank of England and the banking system. They underwrite the weekly treasury bill tender, participate in auctions of gilt-edged stock, enjoy lender-of-last-resort facilities with the Bank, and discount bills (cf. eligible bill).

discounting. (i) Reducing the market price of a bond or money market instrument which pays no interest to take account of interest rates (cf. banker's acceptance; bill of exchange; commercial paper; treasury bill; zero-coupon bond). (ii) The act of giving a present value to a future cash flow by applying a discount factor (cf. discounted cash flow).

discounting the news. When the securities price already reflects the publicly available information relevant to a particular issuer or market. According to the **efficient markets hypothesis** any new information, good or bad, should induce a price response, up or down. When there is no such price response the market is thought to have correctly anticipated the information, such that when eventually the announcement is made the current price is left unaffected. See **discounted information**.

discount interest or **discount interest rate** (Money Markets). A method for quoting the annualized return on non-coupon securities, which always sell at a **discount**, in which the amount of the discount represents the investor's income during the life of the securities. Security rates of return quoted on a discount basis are comparable with **interest-to-follow** bank deposits (cf. **London interbank offered rate**). Sometimes known as the *discount-to-yield basis* or *money market basis*.

The purchase price will be:

$$\text{Price} = \frac{\text{Redemption value}}{\left(1 + \dfrac{MMY \times T_{sm}}{Basis \times 100}\right)}$$

Where: *MMY* is the money market yield; T_{sm} the time from settlement to maturity (in days); *Basis* the convention for calculating interest, either 365 days for sterling, or 360 days for most other currencies.

For a 90-day **eurocommercial paper** issue with a rate of 8%, for a value of 5 million on a 360-day basis, the price will be:

$$4,901,960.78 = \frac{5,000,000}{\left(1 + \dfrac{8 \times 90}{360 \times 100}\right)}$$

See also **money market basis**. Not to be confused with the way **discount securities** such as **commercial paper**, **bills**, and so forth are quoted. See also **value of an 01**.

discount market. (i) (UK) The collection of UK institutions and dealers that trade **bills**. The major participants are banks, **bill brokers**, and the **discount houses**. It is usually seen as the short-term money market in the UK, since it is through the discount market that the **Bank of England** effects its **open-market operations** (cf. **band**; **intervention rate**; **London Discount Market Association**). (ii) (Commodities) A situation where the **forward** or **futures** prices for a particular **commodity** is lower than the current cash price (cf. **backwardation**; **contango**; **over futures**; **under futures**). This is unusual since there is a cost to holding the physical commodity and the forward price normally reflects this via the **cost of carry** relationship. Lack of immediate supply is one reason why the term structure for future delivery is negative (cf. **convenience yield**). Also known as *backwardation* or an *inverted term structure* (cf. **premium market**).

discount paper. See **discount**.

discount rate (Money markets). (i) The rate of interest at which a future sum of money is reduced in order to find its **present value**. See **discounted cash flow**; **discount factor**. (ii) It also means the rate at which **bills** are discounted. See **discount**. (iii) The rate at which **central banks** are prepared to lend to the banking system for liquidity purposes. In consequence, it is sometimes referred to as the *official discount rate*. See also **Lombard rate**. (iv) (USA) The rate set by the **Federal Reserve** for member banks to borrow at the **discount window**.

discounts (Bonds; USA). Market term for **pass-through securities** with a **coupon** rate below the current market rate.

discount securities. Typically short-term money market instruments such as **Treasury Bills** or **commercial paper** where there is no interest payable. Instead the security is purchased at a *discount to face value* to reflect the interest that would have been paid on the note. There are two methods of calculating this **discount**: the discount method used for Treasury Bills and a **present value** method used by the money markets. The discount is calculated as follows.

To obtain the discounted amount from face value:

$$\text{Discounted amount} = \frac{\dfrac{\text{Rate of discount(as a percentage)}}{100 \times T_{sm}}}{Basis \times \text{Face value}}$$

Rate of discount (as a percentage) is the percentage rate as an annual rate at which the discount security is reduced from its face value. T_{sm} is the time from settlement to maturity on the security, in days. The basis will be either 360 or 365 days, depending on the currency.

To find the purchase price:

$$\begin{matrix}\text{Purchase} \\ \text{price}\end{matrix} = \text{Face value}\left(1 - \frac{\text{Rate of discount}}{100} \times \frac{T_{sm}}{Basis}\right)$$

Given the price of the discount security, we can find the rate of discount at which it is trading:

$$\text{Rate of discount} = \left(1 - \frac{\text{Price}}{\text{Face value}}\right) \times \frac{Basis}{T_{sm}}$$

To convert the rate of discount on the instrument to an equivalent **money market basis**, *or yield*:

$$\begin{matrix}\text{Money market} \\ \text{interest rate}\end{matrix} = \frac{\dfrac{\text{Rate of discount}}{100} \times Basis}{Basis - \dfrac{\text{Rate of discount}}{100} \times T_{sm}}$$

To convert from a money market basis to a rate of discount:

$$\begin{matrix}\text{Rate} \\ \text{of} \\ \text{discount}\end{matrix} = \frac{\dfrac{\text{Money market interest rate}}{100} \times Basis}{Basis - \dfrac{\text{Money market interest rate}}{100} \times T_{sm}}$$

discount stripped mortgage backed security (Discount STRIP) (Bonds; USA). A stripped mortgage-backed security where the underlying collateral has a higher coupon and therefore a higher expected prepayment rate. Such issues stand at a discount when interest rates are falling, reflecting the higher reinvestment risk. Premium strips are the opposite, with a lower coupon on the underlying. See collateralized mortgage obligation; interest only; principal only.

discount swap. An interest rate swap or cross-currency swap contract where the fixed-rate leg payments are set below the current market rate. The saving in interest by the fixed rate payer is made up in a lump sum at the maturity of the swap: a useful way for companies with negative cash flow to reduce their outgoings in the near term. In effect it is a disguised loan. The floating rate payer will be taking on additional credit risk, the greater the reduction offered on payments. See also low-coupon swap.

discount to the market (Equities). The amount below the equilibrium value by which an issue of new securities should be offered to the market in order to ensure take-up in the primary market and an active after-market. Sometimes just called the *discount*.

discount to yield or **discount yield.** The money market rate equivalent applicable to a discount instrument. See discount interest rate; money market basis.

discount window (Banking; USA). A facility provided by the Federal Reserve enabling banks to borrow reserves against eligible assets. Now also applied to the same activity in other countries.

discrete distribution. A probability distribution where the outcomes can take on only discrete values with a probability for each value. The alternative is for a *continuous distribution* where the outcomes can take any value. See binomial distribution.

discretion. An order giving the broker the authority to use his judgement in executing an instruction (cf. market-not-held order).

discrete jump price generating process. See binomial distribution; binomial option pricing model.

discretionary account (DA). See advisory funds.

discretionary broker or **discretionary manager** (UK). A broker, or manager, who looks after a client's funds and places these at his discretion

in suitable investments. Normally, the overall aims of the portfolio will have been pre-agreed with the client and the broad classes that are deemed suitable agreed. The broker will handle switches to take account of anomalies and changes in market conditions as well as monitoring the individual components of the portfolio.

discretionary order. A transaction order that gives a broker the choice of when and at what price to transact business (cf. at the market). Obviously the giver of the instruction must have trust that this privilege is not abused. One variant allows the broker also to select the security.

discretionary trust (USA). An investment company, such as a mutual fund, where the managers have discretion as to which investments to make.

discriminatory price auction. Auction method, such as the English auction, where the bidder receives the item(s) bid for at the price(s) at which they are bid for (cf. dutch auction; uniform price auction; winner's curse). See auction.

diseconomies of scale. A condition where increased size acts to impair performance. This might happen, for instance, if internal communications break down due to the difficulties of managing a large enterprise.

disequilibrium. See equilibrium.

dishonour. To fail to make or honour an obligation when it is due. Bills of exchange or documentary credits where payment is refused are said to be dishonoured, either by *non-acceptance* (due to some failing in the documentation as presented) or by *non-payment*.

disinflation. The removal or slowing of the rate of inflation in an economy. To this extent it needs to be differentiated from deflation.

disintermediation. The replacement of investment flows through financial intermediaries, such as banks, with direct investments, such as bonds or other securities (cf. intermediation). Disintermediation has occurred because of concerns about the credit worthiness of financial intermediaries and the higher returns available from holding assets directly (cf. securitization). See also globalization.

disinvestment. (i) A partial or total withdrawal from a particular market or geographical area. Usually seen as the running down of capital, taken to be real investments in an activity or economy, by either selling out or not replacing capacity as assets reach the end of their useful lives. See also **mergers and acquisitions**. (ii) Also used for **divestment**.

dispersion. (i) The statistical measure of the degree a data set diverges from its central point. There are a number of different measures of dispersion, the most common being the **standard deviation** or **variance**. (ii) (Bonds) A measure of the variance in timing of a **bond's** cash flow around its **duration** date. A relatively large number means that the cash flow, comprising interest plus principal, is spread out over time. A relatively small number means that most of the cash flow occurs at or near the duration date. A mortgage would normally have a large dispersion, while a **zero-coupon bond** would have zero dispersion. These numbers are used in portfolio management strategies such as **immunization** and **combined matching**. For example, if a **bond** portfolio is being immunized against a single **bullet** liability, the dispersion of the portfolio's assets should ideally match that of its liabilities; that is, have a value close to zero. The dispersion of such a portfolio's cash flows may be regarded as a measure of the **risk** of not being able to reach the target rate of return because of possible changes in the shape of the **yield curve**. See **bond analysis**.

disproportionate voting. A situation where different classes of securities holders have different weights in the final vote tallying. See also **cumulative voting; majority voting; supermajority**.

disregard tape (DRT). A discretionary order allowing the **broker** to use his judgement as to the price at which to execute.

distressed. A condition of a firm when it cannot meet its fixed claims. See **financial distress**.

distributable profits (UK). That proportion of the after-tax earnings of a company that may legally be distributed to **shareholders** as **dividends**. The basic rule is that companies are not permitted to pay out earnings or **distributable reserves** such that **net assets** are less than the combined amount of the **paid-up capital** and undistributable reserves.

distributable reserves (UK). That part of a company's reserve account that may be legally paid out in the form of a **dividend**. Payments to **shareholders** from reserves can be seen as a distribution of **capital**, rather than accumulated profit.

distributed (Bonds; USA). The process of selling US treasuries bought at **auction** to **retail** accounts. When **dealers'** inventories have been sold, the issue is said to have been distributed.

distributed profit. See dividends; payout ratio; scrip issue.

distributing syndicate (USA). See **selling group**.

distribution. (i) The sale of a large block of securities in such a manner as not to adversely affect the price (cf. **Accumulation**). (ii) Any payment to shareholders of profits or retained earnings (cf. **distributable reserves**). In the UK, a **dividend** is known as a *distribution of profits*. (iii) The outcome from any of a number of stochastic processes. See **lognormal distribution; geometric Brownian motion; normal distribution; Wiener process**.

distribution area. A technical analysis term for a price range within which a security trades for a significant length of time. Also called an *accumulation area*.

distribution network. The channels used for distribution. For securities, this can be directly through a firm's own sales force, or via other intermediary firms (cf. **selling group**). See **distributed**.

divergence indicator. A method used by members of the **European Monetary System** (EMS) to track deviations from their central parities against the **European Currency Unit** (ECU). If the currency diverges beyond a given amount (the *divergence threshold*) then the country concerned is expected to take appropriate corrective action. In the first instance this involves official intervention to return the currency to within the accepted bands by either buying or selling the currency; or if this fails, raising or lowering official interest rates. The formula is:

Percentage divergence × permitted margin × (1 − weight of currency in the ECU)

Thresholds are agreed for triggering different kinds of intervention within the EMS.

diversifiable risk. That part of total market risk that can be eliminated by **diversification** (cf. **business risk; residual risk; specific risk; stock specific risk; unique risk**). See also **systematic risk**.

diversification.(i) The reducing of risk in a portfolio by holding different securities. The general rule of thumb is that the more securities in a portfolio and the less they have in common with each other, the more diversified the portfolio is likely to be. Mathematical methods can be used to achieve the best results from a group of securities. See **efficiently diversified portfolio; systematic risk; unsystematic risk**. (ii) Adding a new market, sector, or type of instrument to a portfolio (cf. **correlation**). See also **modern portfolio theory**.

(iii) For firms, to expand products and services into a new market or business segment.

diversified investment company (USA). A closed ended mutual fund that invests in a wide variety of financial instruments. The Investment Company Act of 1940 restricts holdings to the lower of 5% of the funds assets in any security or 10% of voting shares (cf. **holding company**).

divestiture (USA). The selling-off of **assets** or subsidiary businesses (cf. **bifurcation**; **spin-off**).

divestment. The selling-off of **assets** or subsidiary businesses. Also sometimes known as a *divestiture* (cf. **bifurcation**; **spin-off**).

dividend (Equities). That part of a company's earnings which is paid to its shareholders (cf. **common stock**; **preferred**). Many UK companies pay a dividend twice a year: an **interim**, which is paid after the release of the half-year results, and a **final**, which is paid at the end of the company's accounting year. In the USA, dividends are often paid quarterly. See **advance corporation tax**; **dividend policy**; **payout ratio**; **dividend cover**; **dividend yield**; **withholding tax**.

dividend arbitrage. An option and stock combination designed to take advantage of mispricing in the market that involves purchasing the stock and a put which has a **time value** premium less than the expected **dividend**. Also known as *dividend capture*.

dividend clawback. A project finance arrangement where the project's **sponsors** agree to repay any **dividends** (i.e. distributed profits) from the project to cover any subsequent cash flow deficiencies.

dividend cover (Equities). The ratio of a company's available profit for distribution to the total amount of the **dividend**. In **share** analysis it would normally be expected that the dividend cover would considerably exceed one. The larger the dividend cover, the greater the expectation that the company would maintain and even increase the amount of dividends in the future (cf. **price–dividend ratio**). In the USA, it is known as the *dividend payout ratio* or *payout ratio*. See also **earnings analysis**.

dividend discount model (Equities). A method of valuing shares which estimates the return from all future **dividends**:

$$P_0 = \frac{D_1}{(1+r)} + \frac{D_2}{(1+r)} + \ldots + \frac{D_n + P_n}{(1+r)}$$

where P_0 is the current market value; D_1 to D_n the future dividend payments over the holding period;

P_n the selling or exit price for the security at the end of the holding period; and r the required rate of return placed on the investment. See also **Gordon growth model**.

dividend limitation. A covenant provision that restricts a borrower's ability to pay **dividends** (cf. **coverage test**; **debt limitation**; **leverage**).

dividend payout ratio. The percentage of a company's earnings paid out as **dividends**. A high ratio over a number of years tends to indicate a business which is generating more excess cash than profitable opportunities. Also just known as the *payout ratio*. The opposite is called the *retention ratio*, which can be calculated from 1 less the payout ratio.

dividend policy (Equities). The particular strategy pursued by a company to maintain **shareholder** confidence and loyalty, and by extension keep the share price stable or at a level relative to some **index**. The commonest of these strategies is called the intertemporal smoothing of **dividends**, which involves attempting to ensure that the dividend per share remains constant, or increase at a steady rate, over long periods. The claimed attraction with such a policy is that it makes the job of **portfolio** management easier for shareholders, especially the institutional ones. See **clientele effect**.

dividend reinvestment plan. A scheme in which shareholders receive additional **stock** in lieu of cash **dividends**. Not to be confused with a **stock dividend**.

dividend right certificate. Negotiable certificate giving the holder the right to receive a **dividend** (cf. **cum dividend**; **ex-dividend**). See **rights**.

dividend rollover investment. An investment strategy which entails buying and selling **stocks** around the **ex-dividend** period in order to collect the **dividend**. It relies on the stock price recovering from the fall in price after the **ex-date** such that the total gain exceeds the transaction costs. See **dividend arbitrage**.

dividend stripping. (i) (Equities; Germany) Term given to the ability of domestic investors in German-domiciled companies to take advantage of favourable tax treatment of **dividends**. Also sometimes called *dividend washing*. (ii) Another name for **bond washing**.

dividend waiver. Decision by a firm not to pay a **dividend**. That is, the company announces the fact that it will *waive the dividend*.

dividend yield (Equities). The ratio of the **dividend** per share to the market price expressed as a percentage. Used in assessing securities where returns are related to profit (cf. **current yield**). See **earnings yield; price-earnings ratio.**

divisia money. A method for calculating **money supply** using an aggregate of all **monetary aggregates** weighted by the degree of **liquidity**. Therefore, changes in M0, for example, would count for more in the overall measure than would changes in, say, M4. The idea here is to provide a basis for setting **monetary policy** using a measure that reflects accurately changes to the monetary side of an economy.

documentary bill. Attachments to a **documentary credit** including the invoice, bill of lading, insurance, and so forth. These will need to be checked by the accepting bank before it will accept the documentary credit (cf. **banker's acceptance; bill of exchange**).

documentary credit, documentary letter of credit, or **credit** (Banking). An arrangement used mainly in international trade, whereby a bank, acting on behalf of a customer, undertakes to make a payment to a third party or to accept **bills** drawn by the beneficiary upon presentation of specified documents (cf. **banker's acceptance** (BA); **bill of exchange**). It can also be used to authorize another bank to do the same things. It is, after payment in advance, considered to be the safest and fastest way to obtain payment for exports. The term 'documentary' relates to the fact that certain documents must be included with any draft and normally include a Bill of Lading, a Commercial Invoice and, in addition, any of the following: Consular Invoice; Insurance Certificate or Policy; Certificate of Origin; Weight List; Certificate of Analysis; Packing List. The term documentary credit is now used in preference to bills or BAs.

documentation. The legal agreement covering a contract, including all necessary supportive evidence (cf. **bible; conformed copy**).

documented discount notes (Money markets; USA). **Commercial paper** which is backed by a letter of credit. See **letter of credit backed.**

documents against acceptance (D/A). Method of payment used in international trade where the exporter sends the **documentary credit** to a receiving bank in the importing country, which then allows the release of the goods once the credit has been accepted. The opposite transaction is **cash against documents** or *documents against presentation.*

dog. (i) Market term for a new issue which has a poor reception at launch, usually involving losses

by the **underwriters**. It is said of these issues that *once a dog, always a dog.* (ii) Also one of the four types of companies in the Boston Consulting Group strategy matrix. It is a low-growth/low-market-share business. The others are **star; cash cow; problem child.** See **Boston matrix.**

dogs. The currencies of **emerging market** countries.

dollar averaging. See **averaging.**

dollar bond. It can have the following meanings depending on context: (i) A **eurobond** denominated in US dollars. (ii) A **foreign bond** issued in the US domestic market. (iii) In the US domestic market, a **municipal bond** which is traded on a price rather than **yield** basis (cf. **income bond**).

dollar bond index-linked securities (dollar BILS). A type of **floating rate note** that is also a zero-coupon bond in that the amount of interest is determined in arrears based on a pre-set **index**. The notes are primarily used for **asset-liability management** or **immunization** purposes. See also **LIBOR in-arrears swap.**

dollar gap. See **gap analysis** (cf. **maturity gap**).

dollar payer. The party in a **cross-currency swap** involving the US dollar which pays the dollars.

dollar repurchase agreement (dollar repo) (Money markets). A way of borrowing against securities owned similar to a **repurchase agreement** (repo) but which differs with respect to the fact that unlike an ordinary repo, under which the securities are used as **collateral** for the loan, the securities are sold and subsequently repurchased in the dollar repo period. The sale and repurchase prices are agreed at the outset of the repo and for each deal the buyer pays the seller **accrued interest** and retains any **coupon** income; and the securities repurchased need not be the same securities sold but can be equal par amounts of the same issue. See also **buy-sellback forward.**

dollar roll (Bonds; USA). The simultaneous buying and selling of a **mortgaged-backed security** where the security is sold for near month **settlement** and bought back for forward month settlement at a **pick-up** in yield. The price difference between the sale and repurchase of the security, plus the chance to generate a short-term return from the cash released, during the time of the roll, determines the additional income or cost of funds inherent in the deal. Such financial techniques are often used by **savings and loan associations** and as a means of funding **dealers'** inventories. A particular feature of this type of **repurchase agreement** is that the party which provides the securities may receive back a different, but comparable, issue when the transaction is unwound.

dollar stocks. US and Canadian securities, i.e. dollar-denominated. For other currencies which use the dollar, this is indicated by, for instance, *Aussie dollar, New Zealand dollar*, and so on.

dollar-weighted rate of return. See internal rate of return.

domestic cash management. Short-term financial management within the confines of one country. See also **international cash management**.

domestic corporation (USA). A company carrying on business within the state in which it is incorporated. US corporations carrying out interstate commerce are known as out-of-state or foreign corporations.

domestic swap. An interest rate swap or crosscurrency swap between two counterparties domiciled in the same country.

domicile or **domicil**. The state or country of residence of an individual or entity.

Dominion Bond Rating Service Limited (DBRS) (Canada). 200 King Street West, Suite 1304, Sun Life Centre, West Tower, PO Box 34, Toronto, Ontario, Canada M5H 3T4 (tel. (416) 593-5577; fax: (416) 593-8432). Credit rating agency specializing in the Canadian markets. The ratings are shown in the Table.

	Long term[a]	Short term[b]
Highest quality	AAA	R-1
Superior quality	AA	
Upper medium grade	A	R-2
Medium grade	BBB	
Lower medium grade	BB	R-3
Speculative	B	U
Highly speculative	CCC	
In default	CC	
In serious default	C	
Not rated	NR	NR

[a] High (H) and low (L) modifiers indicate relative standing within the rating class.
[b] High, middle, and low modifiers indicate relative standing within the rating class.

domino effect or **dominio effect**. See cascade theory; program trading.

do not reduce (DNR) (USA). A condition attached to a **stop order** not to adjust the price to reflect the stock going ex-dividend.

'don't fight the tape' (Equities; USA). That is, do not try to go against the market **trend** (cf. **market forces**).

don't know or **DK, dked** ('Don't know the trade') (USA). Market expression for inadequate, conflicting, or unknown **confirmation** or settlement instructions (cf. **comparision ticket**).

double or **double option** (DB). Another name for a **choosen option**. Also called *stupid*.

double-auction. Traditional trading method used on **exchanges** for executing transactions. Buyers and sellers both provide prices at which they are prepared to transact. When two such prices are the same, a transaction is effected. Different exchanges employ different approaches to the actual transaction process. Typically in a securities exchange, there will be a **specialist** or **jobber** to intermediate between buyer and seller charged with running an orderly market, managing the **limit order boand**, and intervening to correct temporary imbalances between supply and demand by dealing on his own account. In **futures** and **options** exchanges, brokers deal directly with one another by a process called **open outcry** where buyers and sellers verbally announce their bids and offers and transactions are completed if the two sides match in price and quantity. It is this two-way process, where both sides are in effect auctioning, that gives the process the name 'double auction'. Double auction markets embody one of the key principles of finance, namely that transactions have two-sides. See **auctions**.

double-barrelled (Bonds; USA). A **municipal bond** issue which carries a guarantee from a second party, normally the parent entity to the issuer.

double barrier option. A barrier option which has not one, but two **in-strikes**, **out-strikes**, or **triggers**. Obviously something of a double obstacle to the option being activated/deactivated.

double bottom. A chartist's or technical analysis pattern where there are two lows to the price

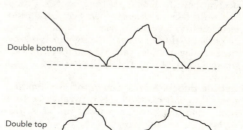

Double bottom

Double top

Double bottom

series. The low points suggest support at that price level. The opposite is known as a *double top*. See W pattern.

double call. See option to double.

double-dated (Bonds; UK). A UK **gilt-edged** term used to describe those issues which have **call** features. Such issues are normally identifiable by the spread of their **maturity** (e.g. Treasury $5\frac{1}{2}$% 2008–12). Also called *double-rated*.

double-declining-balance depreciation. See depreciation methods.

double dip. (i) A type of **lease** designed to take advantage of tax deductions in two countries. For example, a lease written in the UK for a US company where the lessor claims UK capital allowances and the US lessee claims US allowances. (ii) A pattern in a time series where the series has an initial low, it then recovers somewhat, and then returns to the low point a second time. Also known as a *double bottom*.

double drop-lock security (Bonds). A hybrid security which is issued with a **variable rate interest** as a **floating rate note** but will become a fixed-rate **bond** if the reset rate is at or below a pre-set **trigger** rate on two consecutive reset dates. Although it has some of the characteristics of a **bond** with an **embedded option**, the conversion is not at the discretion of the issuer since it forms part of the terms of the issue. Essentially a variation on a **drop-lock security** where the doubling feature aims to prevent a downward **spike** in rates accidentally triggering the feature.

double leverage. The increased **leverage** that is obtained from an **option** on an option (cf. **cacall**; **caput**). See **compound option**.

double option. (i) A two-way **option** giving the holder the right to buy or sell the **underlying**. Effectively a combination of a **call** and **put option** usually with the same **strike price**. It is less flexible than a package of the two options in that the holder does not have the ability to sell one leg of the option play. Also called a *chooser option*. See also **option strategies**. (ii) Sometimes taken to be the same as an **option to double**. That is the right in a **sinking fund** arrangement for the issuer to redeem twice the mandatory amount at his discretion.

double punch. An instruction that is submitted twice for **confirmation**. This is usually due to a transaction being recorded twice by the settlements department.

double-rated (Bonds; UK). Market term for **gilt-edged** securities which incorporate a **call** provi-

sion. The term derives from the calculation of the **gross redemption yield** either to the **call date** or to **maturity** (cf. **yield-to-call**; **yield-to-maturity**). Also called *double-dated*.

double taxation. Tax being levied twice on the same income. It arises principally from the repatriation of foreign profits where the foreign country first taxes the income and then the domestic country also requires tax to be paid (cf. **double taxation agreement**). The effect is to significantly increase the rate of tax on the foreign earned income (cf. **foreign income dividend**). It can also arise in the classical system of company taxation where the company's profits are first taxed, it then pays **dividends** to **shareholders**, and these in turn attract income tax on the recipient (cf. **double taxation of dividends**).

double taxation agreement. A treaty between two countries intended to avoid the double taxation of income. When a taxpayer has tax liabilities in both countries on the same gain, he can credit taxes paid in one country against tax liabilities in the other. When countries have different corporation tax rates or systems, there may not be full double taxation relief. See **unrelieved ACT**.

double taxation of dividends. The problem **equity** investors have when tax is levied twice on **dividends** under classical systems of **corporation tax**. The company first pays corporation tax on its profits and then pays a dividend from those same taxed profits to investors which is subsequently taxed again as income by the tax authorities. This may also apply for cross-border investment where the shareholder may be unable to claim a **tax credit** against any dividends received (cf. **advance corporation tax**; **franked income**; **withholding tax**). Sometimes referred to as *double taxation*. See **imputation**.

double taxation relief. The process of taking into account tax paid in one country when computing the tax liability in another (cf. **franked income**). See **double dip**.

double top. See double bottom; head and shoulders; W pattern.

double-up. See option to double.

double-up swap. Type of **interest rate swap** or **commodity swap** where the **fixed rate** is set below the current market rate at the time the transaction is entered into in exchange for which the **floating rate** has the right to double the **notional principal** amount of the swap if the **spot price** or rate falls below a given **strike** (cf. **embedded option**). The transaction effectively includes a type of **swaption** (cf. **digital option**). The value of the **embeddo** is usually the **discounted** value of the value of the subsidy on the fixed leg of the swap. This is, in effect, the **premium** on the option received by the fixed rate payer.

doubling option. See **option to double**.

doubtful loan. See **charge-off**.

Dow-Jones Averages (USA). The series of indices compiled by Dow-Jones. The most important ones are the Thirty Industrials, Twenty Transportation, Fifteen Utilities, and the Sixty-Five Stocks indices.

Dow-Jones Industrial Average (DJIA; '*the Dow*') (Equities; USA). The earliest US stock market index with a base of 100 in 1928, replacing an earlier index for eleven stocks that had been compiled since 1884. The index is a simple price average based on thirty shares of the most important quoted companies on the **New York Stock Exchange**. It is now largely superseded by wider indices such as the S&P 500 but it is useful for historical interest (cf. **Major Market Index**). It has chronicled the vagaries of the stock market, reaching its low point of 41 on 2 July, 1932, following the **great crash**, but currently stands in the mid-thousand range. The UK equivalent is the **FT Ordinary Share Index**.

Dow-Jones Sixty-Five Stocks Index (Sixty-five stocks) (Equities; USA). A price **index** of the leading US listed company **common stocks** on the **New York Stock Exchange** (cf. **average**). It is made up from three other indices: the Dow-Jones Thirty Industrials ('Thirty Industrials'), the Dow-Jones Twenty Transportation ('Twenty transportation'), and the Dow-Jones Fifteen Utilities ('Fifteen Utilities').

Dow-Jones-Telerate. See **quote vendors**.

Dow-Jones World Stock Index (DJ World Stock Index) (Equities; USA). Capitalization-weighted **index** series that, like the **FT/S&P Actuaries World Indices**, covers the major **stock markets**. The sub-indices cover the Americas (Canada, Mexico, and the USA), Europe-Africa (Austria, Belgium, Denmark, Finland, France, Germany, Ireland, Italy, Netherlands, Norway, South Africa, Spain, Sweden, Switzerland, and the UK), Asia-Pacific (Australia, Hong Kong, Indonesia, Japan, Malaysia, New Zealand, Philippines, Singapore, South Korea, and Thailand). There are also various permutations, such as the World, excluding the USA, Asia-Pacific, excluding Japan, Europe-Africa, excluding South Africa, and so on. The base date is 30 June 1982 for the USA and 31 December 1991 for the rest of the world. The indices provide a performance **benchmark** for in-ternationally diversified investment funds. See also **index construction**.

down-and-in option. A type of **barrier option** which becomes activated if the **underlying** moves through a **trigger** price or rate. Such options are cheaper than the standard type since they only become effective if the price moves beyond the threshold point (cf. **up-and-in option; up-and-out option**). Also called a *knock-in option*. See also **path-dependent options**.

down-and-out option. The type of **barrier option** which becomes deactivated if the **underlying** moves through a **trigger** price or rate. It has the opposite characteristics to the **down-and-in option** (cf. **up-and-in option; up-and-out option**). Also called a *knock-out option*. See also **path-dependent options**.

downgrade. A lowering of a **credit rating** by one of the rating agencies. The opposite is an *upgrade*.

down limit. The maximum fall in price permitted before trading stops on an exchange which operates a **daily trading limit** (cf. **circuit breaker; limit**).

downside or **downside risk**. The disadvantages associated with a particular financial arrangement (cf. **upside**). Usually synonymous with the 'potential losses' from holding a particular **position** or investment strategy.

downsizing. Seen as one of the likely outcomes from business process re-engineering (BPR) which involves a company deciding to operate the various parts of its business differently. This could include no longer having an in-house data processing department, and using an outside agency to undertake all such tasks. The resulting loss of people and function is called downsizing, or more congenially *rightsizing*. See also **bifurcation; divestment**.

downstreaming. A loan provided by a holding or parent company to its subsidiary (cf. **upstreaming**).

down-tick. A transaction effected at a lower price than the preceding one (cf. **up-tick**). See **tick**.

downtrend. (i) A generally falling time series. (ii) A **chartist** or **technical analysis** condition or pattern seen in prices indicating continued selling pressure (cf. **resistance area; seller's over; support level uptrend**).

Dow theory (Equities; USA). A theory of market analysis based on movements in the **Dow Jones**

Industrial Average. If one of the averages making up the index advances above a previous important high, and this is accompanied or followed by a similar advance in another, then the market is said to be on an upward **trend**. When the averages go down below previous important lows then this is seen as confirming a downward trend in prices. It does not attempt to predict how long these trends will continue. See **chart analysis; technical analysis**.

draft. (i) An unconditional written and signed order by one party (*the drawer*) instructing a second party (*the drawee*) to pay a specified amount to a third party (*the payee*) (cf. **cheque**). In foreign trade, a draft is called a **bill** or **bill of exchange** in which case the payee is usually the drawer himself. Where a draft is accompanied with supporting documentation, it is called a *documentary draft*; when without, a *clean draft*. A draft payable on demand is called a **sight draft**; one which can only be cashed on or after a future date, a *time draft*. See **banker's acceptance; documentary credit**. (ii) In the USA, the term for a **bill**. (iii) A preliminary version of a document, report, or set of financial statements (cf. **red herring**).

dragon bond. A foreign bond issued by the People's Republic of China (cf. **yankee bond**).

dragon countries. Those emerging markets on the Pacific Rim, i.e. China, Indonesia, Malaysia, Philippines, Taiwan, and Thailand.

dragons (Australia). **zero-coupon bonds** issued by the Commonwealth of Australia government. Also called *diggers*.

draining reserves (USA). Steps taken by the Federal Reserve to reduce the money supply. These can include (i) **open-market operations**, in which securities are sold for cash; (ii) Alterations to banks' **reserve requirements** requiring banks to hold more **reserves** with the Fed; and (iii) changes to the rate at which banks borrow to maintain reserves (cf. **discount window**). The opposite activity is known as *adding reserves* (cf. **matched sales; repurchase agreement; reverse repurchase agreement**). See also **coupon pass**.

drawdown or **draw** (Banking). When a part of a borrowing **facility** is employed, usually with regard to bank borrowings. Often used in connection with a transaction (cf. **disbursement**).

drawdown period (Banking). The period of time after signing a **credit facility** that a borrower may delay the taking down of funds in full or in part (cf. **rollover**). See **revolving credit facility**.

drawdown swap. See **accreting swap**.

drawee; drawer. The individual, organization, account, or bank who agrees, in the case of the drawee, to make a payment, and in the case of the drawer, to receive it or make it over.

drawings. A method by which some fixed interest securities are redeemed by ballot (cf. **open-market purchases**). See **purchase fund; sinking fund**.

drawn security. A particular **certificate** or registered obligation that has been selected (usually by lot) for repayment according to the terms of the issue (cf. **sinking fund; serial security**).

dressed option. A position for **options** on **futures** where the **underlying futures contract** is held in such a way as to eliminate the **risk** of exercise (cf. **covered call; covered writing; naked call writing**).

drip-feed. Provision of finance in stages, usually on indication of acceptable progress by the borrower (cf. **project finance**).

drop-dead fee (Mergers and acquisitions). A payment based on a contingent funding obligation in a **takeover** where the borrower agrees to pay a fee in the event that the transaction does not go ahead. By structuring the transaction this way, the acquiring company can reduce the costs of obtaining finance and cover itself against the eventuality of failure. Also called a *termination fee*.

drop-lock loan or **security** (Bonds). A hybrid loan or security which is issued with a **variable rate interest**, that is issued as a **floating rate note** but will become a fixed rate **bond** if its **index** or reference rate falls below a predetermined **trigger** rate on a coupon **reset date**. Although it has some of the characteristics of a bond with an **embedded option**, the conversion is not at the discretion of the issuer since it forms part of the terms of the issue (cf. **double drop-lock security**). Floating rate investors can protect themselves from the effects of the drop-lock by agreeing a contingent sale with a fixed rate investor in the event that the security is converted into a **fixed rate bond convertible**. Such a **standby** purchase arrangement normally involves the floating rate investor paying the fixed rate investor a **commitment fee**.

drop-lock swap. A type of **interest rate swap** or **cross-currency swap** where the fixed rate payments may be reset if the **reference rate** used initially to price the swap should change by a pre-set amount and for a given period. For example, if the fixed rate leg was 7% and the variable rate 4% at the onset, if the variable rate were to fall (rise) to, for instance, 2%, then the fixed rate would become 5% (9%). See also **double-up swap**.

dropout option. See barrier option.

dual banking (USA). The US regulatory environment allowing both state and federally chartered banks (cf. **national association**). There are differences in the services each type of bank may offer to customers as well as different reporting and regulatory requirements.

dual capacity (Equities; UK). The ability of a securities firm to act as both **broker** and **market-maker**. Introduced into the UK as a result of the reforms following **Big Bang** in October 1986 (cf. **single capacity**). See **chinese walls**.

dual coupon. Security where the **coupon** is not constant across the **tenor** of the issue. A number of different structures exist:

- *fixed then floating*: issue pays a fixed rate for a predetermined period and then a floating rate to maturity;
- *floating then fixed*: issue pays a floating rate for a predetermined period and then a fixed rate to maturity;
- *step-up coupon*: coupon rate increases towards maturity;
- *step-down coupon*: coupon rate decreases towards maturity;
- *deferred interest or zero-to-full coupon*: issue pays no coupon for a predetermined period and then a fixed rate to maturity.

dual coupon swap. The **interest rate swap** equivalent of a **dual currency bond** position. One of the **counterparties** has the right to receive payments in an alternative **currency** at a predetermined exchange rate. See also **dual currency swap**.

dual currency bond. A security denominated in one currency with interest or **principal** or both paid in another at a pre-agreed rate at issue. The bond has an **embedded option**, a put on the weaker currency. Normally investors are compensated for having sold the **option** by a higher **coupon rate** or other form of **discount** (cf. **reverse dual currency bond security**). Additional features, such as conversion into the issuer's **equity**, have been added in a few cases. These securities also go under names such as *indexed currency option notes* (ICONS), or *principal exchange-rate linked securities* (PERLS).

dual currency loan. A loan where the lender has the right for a predetermined period, at a fixed exchange rate set at the start of the loan, to change the currency borrowed. By agreeing to this arrangement, the borrower has in effect sold (written) a **currency option** to the lender, usually in exchange for improved lending terms. Sometimes also called a *currency conversion facility*.

dual currency option. An option where, at the holder's choice, **exercise** may be into one of two different currencies (cf. **chooser option**). Also called a *two-colour rainbow option*. See **rainbow option**.

dual currency swap. An **interest rate swap** entered into by an issuer of a **dual currency bond** which has the effect of immunizing the issuer from the payments to be made under the terms of the issue. It effectively offers the mirror image to the position created by the security. Since the bond has a written **embedded option**, the issuer can sell on the position, the difference in the value of the **Option** in the bond and the dual currency swap serving to subsidize the issuer's cost of funds.

dual fund. Fund such as the **Americus Trust** where the revenues from the portfolio are split between **capital gains** and income **units** (cf. **split capital trust**). The intention to appeal to investors who have a preference for one type or the other. In some cases there are more than two **classes** of security being issued.

dual listing. A security listed on more than one exchange.

dual option. See outperformance option.

dual option bond. A bond that has its par value expressed in two currencies. The bondholder can select the currency in which to receive interest and principal payments. Sometimes also called a *cross-currency bond*.

dual placing agency. See placing agent (cf. sole placing agent).

dual pricing. (i) Securities which have two prices depending on the market in which they are offered. Such issues violate the law of one price and the differential is a reflection of market impediments or restrictions. See **parallel market**. (ii) (UK). Method used for quoting the value of **unit trust** units with **bid prices** and **offer prices** (cf. **initial charge**). See **single pricing**.

dual purpose fund (USA). A closed-end mutual fund which has two classes of stock. Typically one class receives the **dividends** from the underlying portfolio, the other any realized **capital gains**. The first such fund, *American Dual Vest (ADV)*, was established in December 1966 (cf. **split-capital investment trust**). Also called a *split fund*. See also **dual fund**.

dual strike option. **Exotic option** that offers the holder the better (or worse) of the payoffs from two different **underlyings** which are themselves options. These may be **calls** or **puts** with different strike prices and usually are on different assets. See chooser option; contingent option; rainbow option.

dual trading. An intermediary that undertakes transactions both for clients and itself (cf. **market maker; proprietary trading**).

dual tranche. Issues made at the same time by the same borrower but with differing terms (cf. **serial security**).

due bill. See letter of confirmation.

due date. The date at which something is payable.

due diligence. The detailed investigation of a company by a competent authority to ensure that its condition is satisfactory for the purpose of the envisaged transaction. This involves a detailed examination of the potential borrower's or issuer's ability to service the intended transaction together with the preparation and disclosure of up-to-date information on the borrower's business, financial status, and prospects. The transaction could be an **equity** issue, a **bond** issue, or a **takeover** (cf. **initial public offering; prospectus**). Before an issue is launched, a **lead manager** to a transaction and professional advisers will organize a *due diligence meeting* in which the issue's managers and potential investors have the opportunity to question the issuer's management.

due from/to balance (Banking; USA). See **nostro account; vostro account**.

duet bonds. A structured **bond** issue where the coupon rate is expressed as a difference of amounts between two currencies. It is equivalent to holding a **long position** in a bond in one currency and a **short position** in a bond with the same **maturity** but half the amount (at a given exchange rate) in another. For instance, a sterling bond with a US dollar duet feature set at a £1 : US$1.45 exchange rate on issue, on a £1,000 (US$ 1,450 par amount, would have a coupon of 8% on £1,000, *less* 5% on US$1,450, with redemption of £2,000, *less* US$1,450. Note that the payments will be made at the then future prevailing foreign exchange rate, so investors would be anticipating an improvement in sterling over the life of the issue, or use the structure to hedge against some long-term liability.

Duff & Phelps Credit Rating Company (Duff & Phelps) (USA). 55 East Monroe Street, Chicago, Illinois, 60603 (tel. (312) 263 2610; fax (312) 263 2650). One of the oldest **credit rating agencies** which is active in the USA. The rating scale is shown in the Table.

	Long term		Short term
Highest quality	AAA	Top quality	Duff 1+
Strong protection	AA(+/−)		Duff 1
Average protection	A (+/−)		Duff 1−
Below average protection	BBB (+/−)	Good quality	Duff 2
Below investment grade	BB (+/−)	Satisfactory quality	Duff 3
Below investment grade and risk of potential default	B (+/−)	Not investment grade	Duff 4
Speculative	CCC		
Defaulted	DD	Default	Duff 5
Preferred stock with dividends in arrears	DP		

dumbbell (Bonds). See **butterfly**.

dummy futures. A method used for **interpolating** the value of a **futures** contract for a nonstandard month using the **cost of carry model** (cf. **fair value**).

dumping. Selling large quantities of securities quickly regardless of **market impact** (cf. **accumulation; distribution**).

duopoly. An industry or activity controlled by two firms. An industry controlled by several firms would be known as an oligopoly. See **Cartel Office; mergers and acquisitions; monopolies and mergers commission**.

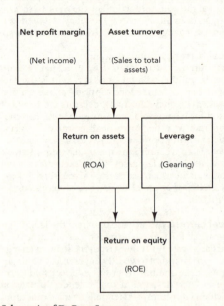

Schematic of DuPont System

DuPont system (USA). A method of evaluating corporate performance named after DuPont which popularized their use. It looks at the component parts of **return on assets** and **return on equity** (ROE) and how they are made up based on four dimensions: **leverage, liquidity, efficiency,** and profitability. See **ratio analysis**.

duration. A measure of a security's tenor that takes into account the size of the periodic **coupon** payments. It is the weighted average maturity of all payments of a security, coupons plus principal, where the weights are the discounted **present values** of the payments. Therefore, the duration is shorter than the stated **term to maturity** on all securities except for **zero-coupon bonds**. Duration is closely linked with modified duration or **bond** volatility (cf. **convexity**).

$$\text{Macaulay's duration} = \frac{\sum_{t=1}^{n} \dfrac{tC}{(1+y)^t} + \dfrac{nM}{(1+y)^n}}{P}$$

where C is the periodic cash payments; M the principal; y the yield; P the security's full price.

Bond duration for a three year annual coupon security (Coupon 10%; current market rate 10%)

(1) Period	(2) Coupon and Principal	(3) PV factor	(4) PV (2) × (3)	(5) Weighted Maturity (4) × (1)
1	10	.9091	9.091	9.0910
2	10	.8265	8.625	16.5289
3	110	.7513	82.643	247.929
			Σ =100.000	273.549

Note: Duration = Sum (5)/Sum (4) = 2.736 years

Bond duration for a ten year annual coupon security (Coupon 10%; current market rate 10%)

(1) Period	(2) Coupon and Principal	(3) PV factor	(4) PV (2) (3)	(5) Weighted Maturity (4) × (1)
1	10	.9091	9.091	9.0910
2	10	.8265	8.625	16.5289
3	10	.7513	7.513	22.5394
4	10	.6830	6.830	27.3205
5	10	.6209	6.209	31.0461
6	10	.5645	5.645	33.8684
7	10	.5132	5.132	35.9211
8	10	.4665	4.665	37.3206
9	10	.4241	4.241	38.1688
10	110	.3855	42.410	424.0976
			Σ = 100.000	675.9024

Note: Duration = Sum (5)/Sum (4) = 6.759 years

Interest Rate effect on Duration (ten-year maturity)

Rate (%)	Price	Duration
5	138.608	7.270
10	100.000	6.759
15	74.906	6.237
20	58.075	5.722
25	46.443	5.231

If different interest rates had been used to calculate the two bonds' duration, we would have had the following results:

Comparison of Duration's of three- and ten-year 10% Bonds

Interest Rate (%)	3-year bond Price	Duration	10-year bond Price	Duration
5	113.62	2.753	138.61	7.270
10	100.00	2.736	100.00	6.759
15	88.58	2.718	74.91	6.237
20	78.94	2.701	58.06	5.722
25	70.72	2.683	46.44	5.231

A bond's duration changes as yields change.

A bond's modified duration or bond **volatility** can be worked out using duration as:

$$\text{Modified duration} = \frac{\text{Macaulay's duration}}{(1+y)}$$

Bond % Change in Price is approximately equal to:

$$-\text{duration} \times (\% \text{ change in } (1 + \text{bond's yield}))$$

For the three-year bond with a duration of 2.736 years, if the yield moves to 15%, then the percentage change in the bond yield = (1.15 − 1.10)/(1.10) = 4.5455%; thus the price change should be approximately −2.735537 × 4.5455% = −12.4343%, or 87.5657% of par (error is 1.0181).

In our examples:

	3-year bond	10-year bond
10% interest rate		
price	100	100
duration	2.7356	6.7590
modified duration	2.4869	6.1446
interest change to 15%		
predicted price change		
using modified duration	−12.4343	−30.7229
predicted price	87.5657	69.2771
actual price	88.58	74.91
error	(1.0181)	(5.6329)

The error from large price/**yield** changes arises due to convexity effects.

Computational formula for modified duration (bond volatility):

$$\text{Modified duration} = \frac{\dfrac{C}{y^2}\left[1 - \dfrac{1}{(1+y)^n}\right] + \dfrac{n(100 - C/y)}{(1+y)^{n+1}}}{P}$$

where the term in square brackets is the appropriate **annuity** formula for the yield (y); (C) the coupon rate; (P) full price (including any **accrued interest**); n the number of periods. Also called the *discounted mean term*. See also **bond risk; dispersion**.

duration-based hedge ratio. The hedge ratio used for hedging **bonds** with **bond futures** contracts. Modified **duration** measures the price sensitivity of the two assets. The hedge needs to match these price sensitivities in opposite directions and thus must take into account the differences in the two assets' modified durations. For bonds, this is given by:

$$\text{Duration based hedge ratio} = \frac{B}{F}\frac{D_B}{D_F}$$

where B is the Value of bond being hedged; D_B the modified duration of the bond; F the price of bond future; D_F the modified duration of the cheapest-to-deliver (CTD) bond underlying the futures contract. Thus if a bond with a modified duration of 6.5 years is being hedged with bond futures, where the cheapest to deliver is 7.5 years and their respective prices are 100 and 95.5, the correct ratio of bond position to the opposing futures position would be:

$$0.9075 = \frac{6.5 \times 100}{7.5 \times 99.5}$$

That is, 91 (90.75) futures contracts must be used to hedge the bond position. With single-period **money market instruments**, the duration should be replaced by the instrument's **term-to-maturity** or **expiry**. Also known as the *price sensitivity hedge ratio*.

duration bogey. The amount of **duration** sought in a **portfolio**. Since the duration represents the discounted term of the future cash flows it is an indicator of the term of the portfolio. The bogey in this context is a numerical standard of performance set up as a target to be surpassed.

duration drift. The problem of matching a constant **maturity** set of **assets** or **liabilities** with fixed maturity liabilities or assets (cf. **asset-liability management**). As time passes, the latter become shorter in remaining life and their duration reduces, while the duration of the constant maturity assets or liabilities remains unchanged. This can arise if, for instance, a car finance **portfolio** with a life of five years and hence an **average** constant maturity of three years is financed with debt with a three-year maturity. Since the assets are replaced,

the duration is unchanged, but as time passes the liability's duration becomes shorter and the position becomes unhedged.

duration-enhanced note. Short-dated security which has a **coupon** which is linked to longer-term rates coupled to a **leveraged** redemption of **principal**. Although the **tenor** of such notes is usually very short, the payment structure means they have the same price performance as much longer-dated fixed rate instruments (cf. **synthetic**).

duration gap. The difference in **duration** between **assets** and **liabilities** (cf. **asset-liability management**).

duration matching. See **immunization**.

duration risk management. Using duration (more normally **modified duration** or **bond volatility**) to control mismatches between **assets** and **liabilities**.

duration-weighted trade (Bonds). A transaction involving a security **swap** or a **switch** which is made on the assumption that the **yield** of the security bought will decline relative to that of the security sold with the nominal values in inverse proportion to the **durations** of the two securities.

Dutch auction. Traditionally a type of **auction** where the asking price is reduced progressively and the first participant to accept the quoted price wins at that price (cf. **English auction**). In the capital markets usually taken to be an auction or **tender** where the securities are allocated to the highest bidders until the total amount on offer is covered; all successful participants pay the lowest price quoted by a successful applicant. Sometimes known as a *unitary price auction*. See also **competitive auction**.

Dutch auction floating rate note. A floating rate note which has the coupon reset by a **dutch auction** process.

Dutch auction preferred stock (Equities; USA). A type of **adjustable rate preferred stock** where the dividend is determined by a **Dutch auction**.

Dutch auction rate term security (DARTS). A variation on the **dutch auction preferred stock** security.

Dutch auction rate transferable note. See **Dutch auction preferred stock**.

Dutch commercial paper (Dutch CP) (Money markets; Netherlands). **Commercial paper** issued by Netherlands entities in Dutch guilders, or foreign issues in Guilders (cf. **sterling commercial paper**).

Dutch rates. Low absolute rates of interest. The phrase stems from the low rates prevailing in the Netherlands due to the good **credit worthiness** of borrowers there.

dynamic asset allocation. See portfolio insurance.

dynamic hedge ratio. The number of **stock index futures contracts** that will duplicate or replicate a put-insured **portfolio**.

dynamic hedging. A program trading method of providing **portfolio insurance** which involves continual adjustment of the **hedge position** in response to changes in market conditions in order to replicate an **option**-like return profile (cf. **replication**). To hedge against a market decline, for instance, the method involves selling **stock index futures** (sometimes via computer-generated buy and sell programmes) on the expectation that gains in the futures will offset losses on the **underlying** portfolio. See **static hedge**.

dynamic overwriting. See overwriting.

dynamic replication. Recreating the performance of a **derivative** by buying and selling the **underlying**. At its simplest it involves, for instance, emulating the payoff of an **option** using the components of an **option pricing model** like the **Black–Scholes Option Pricing Model** which has a **replicating portfolio** made up of a fraction of the underlying and borrowing or lending. Also known as *replication*.

E

each way (USA). When a **broker** acts for both buyer and seller, he is said to earn a **commission** 'each way'.

early bargain (UK). See **after-hours trading** (cf. **kerb market**).

early amortization (Bonds; USA). Earlier than anticipated repayments of principal on **asset-backed securities**. Typically this is a problem with **mortgage-backed** bonds where the expected repayments are accelerated (for instance, due to a significant decline in interest rates, which encourages mortgage holders to refinance at lower rates). See **prepayment risk**.

early exercise. The exercise of an **option** before expiry. This is only possible with American-style or Bermudan-style options which may be exercised early. See entry under **American-style** for conditions leading to early exercise. See also **capped index options**.

early exercise trigger. A condition in **capped index options** where the option is mandatorily exercised if the price of the **underlying** is at or through the **outstrike** price at the **close**. See **trigger**.

early redemption. Terminating a securities issue by repaying it prior to the issue's final **maturity** (cf. **call provision; clean-up call option; early repayment; embedded option; put provision; held-to-call; yield-to-maturity**). This usually involves exercising the issuer's right to redeem the issue, but can also be taken to mean a repurchase of outstanding securities (cf. **tender**).

early redemption privilege. See **call provision; put provision**.

early redemption put option. The right of the holder to seek repayment prior to **maturity**. This may be by **exercise** of a **put provision** or some kind of special **event risk** protection clause; e.g. the put provision may be activated when a firm is taken over (cf. **poison pill**).

early repayment or **early termination.** A condition in a contract that allows parties to cease to be bound by the contract if certain events should occur, most commonly an **event of default** (cf. **acceleration clause; technical default**).

early take-up (Forex). A forward/forward foreign exchange swap designed to shorten an existing **forward foreign exchange transaction**. It is designed so as to have no cash flows at the **maturity** of the original forward transaction. It thus has the effect of shortening the existing forward transaction to the first date of the foreign exchange swap.

earning assets (Banking). That part of a bank's **assets** which earn interest or **fees**. Typically this is loans, securities held in the trading book, and other short-term investments. See **net interest income**.

earnings. Another name for net profit. It is generally taken to be the consolidated profit for the reporting period, after tax, minority interests, extraordinary items, and **dividends** on **preferred stock**. Also called *earnings for common* or *earnings for ordinary*. Note that there are many variations on what constitutes earnings. See following entries.

earnings analysis. A method of assessing securities which measures actual performance in terms of profit and **dividends**. The financial statistics used include: **dividend cover; dividend yield; earnings per share; earnings yield; price–earnings ratio; payout ration**; and **priority percentages**.

earnings before interest and taxes (EBIT). The earnings or profit earned by a firm after taking account of direct costs of production or services and all overheads, except the interest charge and taxes. Regarded as the clearest indicator of the underlying performance of a company, uncomplicated by tax rates and net interest effects. Also called *operating profit*, *trading profit*, and *profit before interest and taxes* (PBIT).

earnings before interest, tax, depreciation, and amortization (EBITDA). A measure of the cash generated by a business or firm which is based on the fundamental operating performance (cf. **cash flow; free cash flow**). It excludes the interest paid, tax, depreciation, and amortization on the grounds that these can significantly distort the underlying performance. In addition, inter-firm comparisons will be greatly complicated if, for instance, **earnings** are measured after including the items since the interest, tax, and depreciation positions of firms may be radically different.

earnings before taxes (EBT). Profit calculated after the payment of net interest but before accounting for taxes. It is the amount of earnings or profit earned by a firm in a given reporting period before taxes. It is similar to **earnings before interest and taxes**, except that it deducts the interest charge. Used to compare company performances, prior to the complication of different tax strategies employed by different companies.

earnings per share (EPS). After-tax accounting profit, less interest on borrowings and **preference stock dividends** divided by the average number of outstanding **shares** or **common stock** for the reporting period (cf. **price–earnings ratio**). In the case where the corporation has a **convertible** and/or **warrants** outstanding, then analysts will also calculate the *fully diluted earnings per share*, based on the full **exercise** of all such **hybrid securities**.

earnings price ratio or **earnings-to-price ratio.** The inverse of the price–earnings ratio. Equivalent to the **current yield** on bonds, since it ignores **capital gains** or **losses**. Useful as an indicator of the relative cheapness/dearness of **stocks** to other financial instruments. Sometimes known as the *capitalization rate* or *earnings yield*.

earnings retention ratio. Retained earnings after paying **dividends**. See also **payout ratio**.

earnings yield. Calculated as the ratio of **earnings per share** to the market price of the stock. Claimed to be a better measure of the return on equity than the **dividend yield** because it is unaffected by distribution policy (cf. **payout ratio**). It is the inverse of the **price–earnings ratio**; that is, it is the earnings-to-price ratio.

earning the points (Forex). The condition when the purchase price in a particular currency on a **foreign exchange swap** is lower than the reselling price. The opposite is known as *paying the points*.

earn out. A method of relating part of the price paid for a business to future profits (cf. **bells and whistles**). See **venture capital**.

ear-stroking (UK). The name given to one of the ways in which the **Bank of England** signals to the banking community what it would like to see happen to, for example, interest rates. Usually used as an informal method of achieving the Bank's objectives ahead of any formal controls. Sometimes called *moral suasion*, it is called *jawboning* in the USA, and *administrative guidance* in Japan.

easy money. Monetary conditions aimed at maintaining a low level of interest rates within an economy. See also **business cycle**.

écart (Equities; Switzerland). The value differential between bearer shares and registered shares (cf. **bearer bond**; **registered security**). Ownership restrictions on the registered shares mean that they tend to trade at a **discount** to the bearer shares. Some Swiss companies also have **non-voting shares** (cf. **participation certificate**; **titre participatif**).

ECOFIN. The **European Union**'s Council of Ministers which handles Economic and Finance and is usually attended by finance ministers or their deputies.

ECO net (Forex). A settlement system for **foreign exchange** allowing participating banks to use multilateral **netting** methods to reduce their **counterparty risk**. The banks pay the net difference between the participating parties and the system resolves the exact amounts to each bank.

econometric model or **modelling.** A method of analysis which seeks to relate a given variable to a series of other economic variables to predict behaviour patterns. Such models are generally used for forecasting the behaviour of an economy, but can be used for valuing securities, **commodities**, **options**, and so forth. There are a number of different techniques, based either on multiple regression techniques or probability forecasting. See also **black box syndrome**; **model risk**.

econometrics. Literally interpreted, it means economic measurement. Although measurement is an important part of the subject of econometrics, its scope is much broader and includes: the application of mathematical statistics to economic data to lend empirical support to the models constructed by mathematical economics and to obtain numerical results; and the analysis of economic phenomena based on the simultaneous development of theory and observation, related by appropriate methods of inference. The use of statistics, at least in the first instance, is about the ways in which numbers on such things as **inflation**, **exchange rates**, **securities** prices, and trading volumes from specific markets are collected and measured. Two types of data are widely collected: time series (changes in one variable measured in aggregate over several time periods, for example, the national rate of unemployment); and cross-sectional (one variable measured in the same time period but across different firms, **agents**, or **traders**, for example, the demand for various types of **bonds**). In such data gathering, some sources are recognized as being more reliable than others; and there is awareness that revisions may be necessary over time as better information becomes available. Data that has been changed in such ways so as to improve its reliability or ability to be analysed with increased levels of confidence can be called 'refined', 'adjusted', or 'smoothed' data. Overall, econometrics can be regarded as an amalgam of economic theory, mathematical economics, and mathematical statistics. Many statements and hypotheses in economics contain references to financial markets, instruments, and dealings systems. As a consequence, with developments in economic theory, higher degrees of analytical sophistication of the behaviour of finance has become possible. Therefore, some appreciation of the rudiments of econometrics is useful as it represents one of the strands of analysis available to professional market analysts and participants: not least because the recent and dramatic emergence of the so-called 'new' financial instruments, such as **derivatives**, emerged partly as a result of such analytics. That is, the development of more detailed ways of modelling the behaviour and likely result from different market outcomes has provided the basis for the design of such **hybrid** products. It also worth remembering that the study of finance itself is a hybrid subject drawing upon the separate disciplines of economics, accounting, mathematics, and statistics.

In considering statements or hypotheses of actions or behaviour most econometric studies will contain the following stages: specification; data collection and refinement; estimation; verification or statistical inference; and forecasting or prediction. There are several ways in which each of these stages can be effected. For example, if the econometric model specified has only one equation (used to express a relationship in mathematical form) then it is called a *single equation model*, whereas if it has more than one equation, it is known as a *multi-equation* or *simultaneous-equation model*. The simplest form for an econometric model can be expressed as:

$$y = \alpha + \beta x \qquad (1)$$

where, for example, y is consumption or expenditure, x is income, and α and β are constants or parameters. The above equation assumes that there is an exact or deterministic relationship between y and x. In practice, economic and financial relationships rarely conform to this assumption. In a sense if they did part of the rationale for financial markets and institutional specialization would be removed. To allow for inexact relationships between the selected variables, the above equation can be modified as follows:

$$y = \alpha + \beta x + \mu \qquad (2)$$

where μ, known as the disturbance, or error, term, is a random (**stochastic**) variable which has well-defined probabilistic properties. The disturbance term may represent all those forces that affect y but are not taken into account explicitly by the equation. Equation (2) is an example of an econometric model. More technically, (2) is an example of a linear **regression analysis** model, which is a widely used model in both economics and finance. The function represented by (2) hypothesizes that the dependent variable y is linearly related to the explanatory variable x, but the relationship between the two is not exact; it is subject to individual variation.

Having specified the **parameters** to be examined in the model (the specification stage), and chosen both a data set and a method for deriving estimates for explanatory variables, such as regression analysis (the estimation stage), what remains in an econometric study is checking the quality of the estimates (the verification stage), which leads on to the level of confidence that can be applied to any forecasts derived from the model. There are several controversies and problems surrounding each of these stages, such as **heteroscedasticity** and **multicollinearity**, which can have the effect of reducing the confidence, and therefore the usefulness, of such studies to the practitioner. However, developments in the fields of both theoretical and applied econometrics have provided a number of 'escapes' from the more serious and pervasive statistical modelling and estimating problems. See, for example, **moving average models**. For additional information on the different aspects of econometrics please refer to the following texts: D. Gujarati, *Essentials of Econometrics* (McGraw-Hill, 1992) (introductory); R. S. Pindyck and D. L. Rubinfield, *Econometric Models and Econometric Forecasts* (McGraw-Hill, 1990) (intermediate); J. Kamenta, *A Textbook of Econometrics* (Macmillan, 1986) (advanced); and P. Kennedy, *A Guide to Econometrics* (MIT Press, 1985) (applied).

economic defeasance. See in-substance defeasance (cf. **legal defeasance**).

economic earnings. Net cash flow from a firm available for distribution to owners in the absence of any change in capacity.

economic exposure. (i) The effects of changes in **macro-economic** variables on the cash flows and value of a firm and, in particular, business exposure to currencies (cf. **systematic risk**). (ii) (Forex) The effects of changes in the value of currencies on the cash flows of a firm (cf. **business risk**; **systematic risk**; **transaction exposure**; **translation exposure**). The exposure may be direct, in that changes in **foreign exchange rates** may directly alter the home currency value of the cash flows, or indirect where competitors or alternative suppliers' costs or prices are affected in different ways. Sometimes also called *operating exposure* or *strategic exposure*. See also **risk**.

economic hedge (Forex). A **hedge** designed to reduce or eliminate **economic exposure**. Typically it involves borrowing in the foreign currency to match cash flow patterns.

economic indicators. Statistics or economic indices produced on an economy on a regular basis. They are important as **barometers** of economic activity and the state of the business cycle. In so far as they relate to government policy and assessment of asset value, they are important new information. Economic indicators are defined as either being *leading, coincident,* or *lagging* indicators. The leading indicators are seen as the most important in terms of new information, the other types of indicators providing confirmation. The most watched key indicators are:

Monthly Series
    Factory orders
    Labour and employment market
    Producer prices
    Consumer credit
    Retail sales
    Inventories
    Industrial production and capacity utilization
    Housing starts (permits), sales, and/or prices
    Personal income
    Durable goods
    Consumer or retail prices
    Trade balance
    Cyclical indicators

Quarterly Series
    GNP (and possibly 'flash' GNP)
    Trade balance (in some countries)

economic life. The expected time frame over which an asset will provide reward to its owner (cf. **depreciation**).

economic order quantity (EOQ). Used in inventory or stock control to measure the amount of something that should be there so as to minimize the costs of ordering, purchasing, and storing. If the rate at which the **commodity** is used is constant, and if reorders can be scheduled to the time when current stock is nil, then EOQ is calculated according to the following:

$$Q = \sqrt{\frac{2sr}{k}}$$

where Q is the economic order quantity; s the quantity used per planning period, usually a year; r the per order cost; k the inventory holding costs per unit per period.

economic rents. The excess of the amount of reward received over and above the return that would be available in the next best use or occupation. See **opportunity cost**.

economic risk. (i) The **risk** in a project that the value of the output will be insufficient to cover the project's operating, maintenance, and debt costs (cf. **project finance**). (ii) The risk arising from changes in **foreign exchange rates**, interest rates, **commodity** prices, and so forth. Also known as *business risk, operating risk,* or *strategic risk*. See systematic risk.

economies of scale. The reduction in average costs of undertaking an activity from increased size or level of production.

EDIFACT. European Union's directive on standard order and invoice formats.

EDGAR (USA). An electronic database of **registrations** and other publicly available filings with the **Securities and Exchange Commission**.

edge. (i) The **spread** between a **bid-offer** quotation. Also called the *dealer's edge*. (ii) The difference in price between the market value of an **option** and the **fair value** derived using an **option pricing model** (cf. **theoretical edge**).

Edge Act bank or **Edge corporation** (Banking; USA). The 1919 Act that allows US banks to undertake foreign lending through federal or state chartered subsidiaries. The legislation also allows domestic banks to own banks outside the USA and to invest in foreign industrial and commercial businesses (cf. **Glass–Steagall Act**).

Effectenclearing (Netherlands). Electronic clearing system used by the **Amsterdam Stock Exchange**.

effective. (i) The adjusted or true payoff, result, or outcome. (ii) The point from which an action commences (cf. **deferred; forward**). (iii) (USA) When the **Securities and Exchange Commission** allows the distribution of a securities offer following the filing of a **registration** statement, it is said to become effective (cf. **cooling-off period**).

effective annual rate or **effective rate.** See annual equivalent.

effective call price. The exercise price of a **call** provision which includes the **accrued interest** to the **redemption** date.

effective date. The date at which a transaction becomes effective. It is normally the date from which interest begins to accrue (cf. **dated date**). For instance, **swaps**, although quoted on a **spot** basis, may have effective **deferred start** dates to meet some **liability**, such as a **bond** issue. In that case, the effective date will be the date the bond proceeds are received. However, the pricing will be adjusted to reflect the delay (cf. **deferred swap**). Also known as the *start date* or *value date*.

effective duration. The proportional change in security value for a very small **parallel shift** in the **yield curve**. See **duration** (cf. **bond risk**).

effective exchange rate. A method used for calculating the impact of changes in currency values of one country by taking into account the relative importance of the trade flows and weighting any changes accordingly. Sometimes called a *currency index*.

effective fed funds (USA). A weighted average of the transactions in the **fed funds** market over a particular period.

effective interest rate. An interest rate calculated one one **basis** expressed in terms of another. See **annual equivalent; interest rate calculations.**

effective net worth. Net worth plus subordinated debt. It is the net worth of a firm from a senior creditor's perspective.

effective rate. (i) The rate of return which takes into account the periodicity of payments and any **premium** or **discount** to **par value** (cf. **nominal rate**). Normally the same as **yield**. See **annual equivalent**. (ii) The **all-in cost** after premiums or **commissions** on a **hedge** are taken into account, less any benefit derived from the hedge itself. Thus the maximum effective rate on a floating rate borrowing of say £100m for five years with an **interest rate cap** of 10% and the premium of 2% would be 10.53%, the extra 0.53% representing the costs of purchasing the interest rate cap.

effective sale (Equities; USA). The price at which a **round lot** has been transacted and which is used to determine the value of an **odd lot** (cf. **differential**).

effective yield. See **realized yield.**

Effektengiro (Germany). Securities clearing system for the German capital market.

efficiency. A securities market is efficient if it can bring together borrowers and lenders at the lowest possible cost and if the securities prices generated adequately reflect the likely rates of return and the degree of **risk** associated with all classes of securities. Other financial trading markets can be similarly defined. See **Capital Asset Pricing Model; efficient markets hypothesis.**

efficiency ratio (Banking). The **ratio** of operating expense to revenue expressed as a percentage.

efficient diversification. A key tenet of **modern portfolio theory** that when creating a **portfolio**, the holder will either seek to maximize returns for a given **risk**, or minimize risk for a given return. In portfolio theory, any portfolio which cannot be bettered as to risk or return is said to lie on the *efficient frontier*. See **Markowitz portfolio model.**

efficient frontier. Those portfolios in a **mean-variance analysis**, as developed by the **Markowitz portfolio model**, which provide the minimum risk for a given level of return (cf. **efficient portfolios**). See also **Capital Asset Pricing Model.**

efficiently diversified portfolio. A portfolio that cannot be changed such that a higher return can be obtained at the same level or **risk** or the same return for a lower level of risk. This concept is central to the **Capital Asset Pricing Model.**

efficient market. A term for a financial market where security prices reflect all available information instantaneously.

efficient markets hypothesis (EHM). This explanation for historical movements in securities prices states that investors cannot earn superior returns by being able to predict winners. Such forecasts are considered elaborate guess-work which, on average, are unlikely to be accurate. All the investor can expect is a fair return, given the **risk** of the security and the costs of becoming informed. The theory does not claim that price randomness is senseless, rather it is the logical result of competition between rational investors seeking **abnormal returns**. This competition is in terms of investment objectives, **yields**, and availability of information. The EMH stresses the role of information, maintaining that prices change only when new information becomes available and current prices reflect all that is known about a particular security. There are three forms of the model: *weak-form efficient market*, which postulates that investors cannot earn abnormal returns from analysing past data; *semi-strong form efficient market*, the weak-form efficient market but also including publicly available information as part of the information available to the market; and *strong-form efficient market*, the semi-strong form efficient market but including all available information, whether publicly available or not. See **Capital Asset Pricing Model; efficiency.**

efficient portfolios. Portfolios which provide a maximum level of return for a given **risk** (cf. **separation principle**). That is they provide the best tradeoff between risk and reward for a given level of risk. They are central to the **Capital Asset Pricing Model.**

either-or facility (Banking). A lending arrangement that allows a borrower to access funds either in the domestic market or in the **eurocurrency** market from one of the lender's foreign branches.

either-or order. An alternative **order** instruction to a **broker** to execute either one instruction or the other at his discretion.

either-way market. Euromarkets term for a **locked market**. That is, one where **bid** and **offer** prices are the same (cf. **backwardation**).

elasticity. (i) An economics term for the responsiveness of one variable to another, for instance price and demand or price and supply. The degree of response can range from *perfect elasticity*, where a change in one variable leads to an infinite change in the other, to *perfect inelasticity*, where a change in one variable has no effect on the other. Most economic effects fall somewhere in between, the degree of elasticity depending on the ready availability of close substitutes. (ii) The change in an **option** price for a given change in the **underlying**. Often equated with an option's **delta** (cf. **neutral hedge ratio**). It is seen as a measure of the option's **leverage** or **gearing**, since the value of the option will change by more than the underlying. (iii) Another term for the **effective gearing** or the **leverage factor** of a **warrant**. It is calculated as:

$$\frac{\text{Warrant's delta}\,(\delta) \times \text{price of underlying}}{\text{price of the warrant}}$$

elasticity of an option. See lambda; option pricing.

elect (USA). Term for a **conditional order** becoming a **market order**. When the price reaches the conditional order price it is elected into a market order and executed. See **limit order**.

electricity forward agreement (EFA) (Commodities). A **forward contract**, similar to a **forward rate agreement** which allows the buyer or seller to fix or receive a guaranteed price for electricity (cf. **commodity swap**).

electric utility bond (Japan). A **bond** issue made by one of the electricity utilities. Such issues are regarded as being in a special category and tend to be more actively traded than corporate or **samurai** bonds.

Electronic Data Gathering and Retrieval (EDGAR) (USA). An electronic database of corporate information maintained by the **Securities and Exchange Commission** (cf. **Form 10-k**).

electronic data interchange (EDI). Paperless system for effecting money transfers either between firms or between banks and their customers. See also **financial electronic data interchange**.

Electronic Data Services (EDS) (UK). London Stock Exchange service providing historical price and turnover or **volume** information.

electronic funds at point of sale (EFPOS). An electronic **settlement** system for retail purchases which allows funds to be moved automatically from a buyer's account to a seller's, the transfer taking place at the time of the transaction.

electronic funds transfer at point of sale (EFT-POS). Paperless system for effecting a bank transfer designed to replace **cheques**. It allows the vendor to request electronically the transfer of funds from the buyer's account to the seller's account. Unlike a credit card, it provides the user with no grace period before payment is due. The attractions are that the vendor is immediately credited with the funds, and it reduces the costs of transactions and the possibility of fraud. Users will have a **debit card** with a personal identification number (PIN number).

electronic funds transfer system (EFTS). A system for moving funds around without the need for any paper records.

electronic purse. A type of **debit card** which has a monetary value held electronically which is then deducted when used to purchase goods and services. The original method was developed for public transport systems allowing users to buy a certain number of journeys which were held on the card and debited as the holder made journeys.

electronic trade confirmation (ETC). Paperless system for advising and confirming transactions. ETC is designed to reduce the processing of transactions and increase operational efficiency by removing the need to punch in transactions at each stage (cf. **comparison ticket; confirmation**).

Electronic Trading System (ETS). Integrated electronic transaction, reporting, and **settlement** system used by the **New Zealand Futures and Options Exchange**.

eligible (UK; USA). Those instruments that are acceptable as collateral by the **Bank of England** in the UK and the **Federal Reserve** in the USA, and called *eligible assets*. Such instruments, the definition of which can change in line with monetary policy, are used as the basis for calculating banks' reserve–assets ratios. See **capital adequacy; reserve requirements**.

eligible bill (Banking; UK). A **bill** that has been discounted by a bank recognized by the **Bank of England** (cf. **ineligible bills**). Eligible bills may be purchased by the Bank of England as part of its **open-market operations** (cf. **intervention rate**).

eligible liabilities (Banking; UK). Those liabilities (principally deposits) which are included in the **Bank of England's** calculation of a bank's **cash ratio**.

eligible list (UK). Those banks in the UK allowed to **discount bills** at the **Bank of England**.

eligible reserves (Banking; USA). **Federal Reserve System** member bank deposits held at Federal Reserve Banks, plus cash.

embedded option or **embeddo.** Those features of the terms and conditions of securities which have **option** characteristics (i.e. the right but not the obligation to **exercise**) but which cannot be **unbundled** to be traded separately. For instance the **call provision** or **put provision** that may form part of a **bond's** terms and conditions (cf. **mortgage-backed securities**). Financial engineering techniques can be used to transform the nature of such embedded options. For example, one way to nullify the effect of a call provision would be to buy a compensating call on a similar instrument. This might be attractive if the security with the undesirable option element was trading at a **discount** to its **fair value**. Note that the term *embeddo* can refer to the option element alone.

embedded risk. Any of a number of **risks** that might be present in a business activity or portfolio as a result of the activities undertaken (cf. **natural option**). For instance *embedded interest rate risk* exists in a loan portfolio if the **assets** and **liabilities** are not matched (cf. **asset-liability management**).

emerging markets. A generic term for developing countries which are attracting foreign portfolio investment capital. The term is generally restricted to portfolio rather than **direct investment** and to those countries with an established market economy and stock market. The investment rationale is that emerging stock markets offer significant investment opportunities due to their high growth rates relative to established markets. According to the **International Monetary Fund** about 85% of the world's population live in emerging markets, but account for only 40% of the world's **gross domestic product** and 12% of the world's aggregate stock market **capitalization**. Individual national markets of emerging countries are likely to be both **illiquid** and highly volatile and are generally considered to be the

domain of the specialist. The term **emerging markets** is increasingly being used as a label by funds specializing in this **sector** (cf. **Latin American fund**).

emerging markets warrant. Warrants issued on securities in emerging markets. The attractions of these instruments is that they provide the holder with the return on the market without directly investing in the securities themselves. In some cases, the **option** writer segregates the holder from undesirable aspects of such investments, such as problems with **settlement**.

employee buy-out. See **management buy-out**.

Employee Retirement Income Security Act of 1974 (ERISA) (USA). The law governing private pension and benefit plans (cf. **individual retirement account**). It is the basic law governing the operation of private benefit and pension schemes. The Act sets guidelines for the management of such schemes (cf. **Pension Benefit Guarantee Corporation; prudent man rule**).

employee share ownership plan (Equities; UK). Scheme designed to increase employee participation in the firms in which they work by setting up a fund to buy **ordinary shares** in the company. The 1989 legislation was modelled on similar schemes in the USA.

employee stock option. An **option** on a firm's **common stock** granted to employees. Typically these are long term, up to five years. They form part of key staff and management incentives designed to align the interests of employees with those of **shareholders** (cf. **agency problem**).

employee stock ownership plan (ESOP) (Equities; USA). A programme that encourages employees to buy **common stock** in the company for which they work. Often the plans are sponsored by the company either to increase employee loyalty or to place **shares** in what are considered to be friendly hands, or as part of some restructuring or rescue package for the firm.

emprunt (French). A **borrowing** or loan. An *emprunt à devise* is a securities issue.

emprunt d'état (French). Government borrowings or securities issues (cf. **obligations assimilables du Trésor**).

emprunt d'état Belge (Belgium). Government bonds.

end-end. The convention used in the eurocurrency markets that investment maturities of a month or more fall within the appropriate month end, regardless of the actual number of days. Thus a sterling (UK-settled) transaction maturing on 29 August (a Saturday) would be treated as ending on the 28th, if the 31st were the August bank holiday, rather than being extended to 1 September. Also known as the *calendar-month convention*.

endigeur (French). **Hedging.** The English word is frequently used, however (a practice known as 'franglais').

end investors. The ultimate buyers of financial instruments. They are usually taken to be institutional investors and **retail**. The market considers there is a significant difference between end investors who are long-term investors and **traders** who will resell at the earliest opportunity (cf. **buy-and-hold; distributed**)

end-of-the-month option. The ability of the **short position** holder in a **futures contract** to make use of the delay in **settlement** that occurs between the exchange's final delivery settlement price set at the expiry of the futures contract and making **delivery** to either allow the substitution of a **cheapest-to-deliver** bond or to close out an **arbitrage** position at a profit by buying more cheaply in the **cash market**. Also known as an *implied put option*.

endorsement. (i) Conferring transferability of a **bill** or **cheque** by signing the reverse. For this to be effective, the cheque needs to be signed by the recipient and include the term *or to order*. Also called *indorsement*. (ii) Another term for a **guarantee**.

endowment mortgage (UK). A type of mortgage which incorporates life assurance. The mortgage is interest only and the life asssurance policy is used to provide a lump sum to pay off the mortgage at **maturity**. The product has been driven by the tax-free nature of premiums on life insurance.

end user. A counterparty that engages in a **risk management** transaction to change its interest rate or currency exposure, thereby becoming the final counterparty, as compared with a trading institution that is likely to be an intermediary (cf. **derivatives; forwards; swaps; options; debt–equity swaps**).

energy futures. Futures contracts on energy products such as crude oil, unleaded gasoline, gas oil, electricity, and so forth (cf. **commodity futures**). The example contract given below is the New York Mercantile Exchange (NYMEX) for sweet crude oil. The **option on the future** is also given for completeness.

LIGHT SWEET CRUDE OIL: FUTURES AND OPTIONS CONTRACT SPECIFICATIONS

- *Trading unit*: Futures: 1,000 US barrels (42,000 gallons) Options: One NYMEX light sweet crude oil contract.
- *Trading hours*: Futures and Options: 9.45 a.m.–3.10 p.m. (New York Time).
- *Trading months*: Futures: 18 consecutive months plus four long-dated futures which are initially listed 21, 24, 30, and 36 months prior to delivery. Options: Six consecutive months plus two long-dated options which are initially listed 9 and 12 months prior to expiration.
- *Price quotation*: Futures and Options: dollars and cents per barrel.
- *Minimum price fluctuation*: Futures and Options: $.01 (1¢) per barrel ($10 per contract).
- *Maximum daily price fluctuation*: Futures: $15.00 per barrel ($15,000 per contract) for the first two contract months. Initial back month limits of $1.50 per barrel rise to $3.00 per barrel if the previous day's settlement price is at the $1.50 limit. In the event of a $7.50 move in either of the first two contract months, back month limits are expanded to $7.50 per barrel from the limit in place in the direction of the move. Options: No price limits.
- *Last trading day*: Futures: Trading terminates at the close of business on the third business day prior to the 25th calendar day of the month preceding the delivery month. Options: Expiration Day is the second Friday of the month prior to the delivery month of the underlying futures contract, provided there are at least five days remaining to trade in the underlying futures contract. Note: Effective 13 July 1992, Expiration Day for all newly listed options contracts is the Friday immediately preceding the expiration of the underlying futures contract as long as there are three trading days left in the futures contract. In the event there are less than three days to futures expiration, option expiration is the second Friday prior to futures expiration.
- *Exercise of options*: By a Clearing Member to the NYMEX Clearing House not later than 6.00 p.m., or 45 minutes after the underlying futures settlement price is posted, whichever is later, or on any say up to and including the option's expiration.
- *Option strike prices*: At all times at least 17 strike prices are available for puts and calls on the underlying futures contracts. The first 11 strike prices are increments of $1.00 per barrel; additionally, three strike prices are offered in the nearest $5 increments above the nearest higher and below the nearest lower existing price strikes. The at-the

money strike price is nearest to the previous day's close of the underlying futures contract. Strike price boundaries are adjusted according to the futures price movements.

- *Delivery*: Free on board (FOB) seller's facility, Cushing, Oklahoma, at any pipeline or storage facility with pipeline access to ARCO, Cushing Storage or Texaco Trading and Transportation Inc., by in-tank transfer, in-line transfer, book-out or inter-facility transfer (pump over).
- *Delivery Period*: All deliveries are rateable over the course of the month and must be initiated on or after the first calendar day and completed by the last calendar day of the delivery month.
- *Alternate Delivery Procedure (ADP)*: An Alternative Delivery Procedure is available to buyers and sellers who have been matched by the Exchange subsequent to the termination of trading in the spot month contract. If buyer and seller agree to consummate delivery under terms different from those prescribed in the contract specifications, they may proceed on that basis after submitting a notice of their intention to the Exchange.
- *Exchange of Futures for, or in connection with, Physicals (EFP)*: The buyer or seller may exchange a futures position for a physical position of equal quantity by submitting a notice to the Exchange. EFPs may be used to either initiate or liquidate a futures position.
- *Deliverable grades*: Specific crudes with 0.5% sulphur by weight or less, not less than 34° API gravity nor more than 45° API gravity. The following crude streams are deliverable: West Texas Intermediate, Mid-Continent Sweet, Low Sweet Mix, New Mexican Sweet, North Texas Sweet, Oklahoma Sweet, South Texas Sweet, Brent Blend, Bonny Light, and Oseberg.
- *Inspection*: Inspection shall be conducted in accordance with pipeline practice. A buyer or seller may appoint an inspector to inspect the quality of oil delivered. However, the buyer or seller who requests the inspection will bear its costs and will notify the other party of the transaction that the inspection will occur.
- *Customer margin requirements*: Margins are required for open futures or short options positions. There is no margin requirement for an options purchaser.

energy mutual fund (USA). An **investment company** which invests solely or largely in the energy sector.

enforcement costs. The costs incurred in ensuring performance under a **contract**. These may be direct costs, such as the cost of legal redress or enforcement, and/or **opportunity costs**.

engineered swap. A type of **foreign exchange swap** where the two legs of the transaction are executed with different **counterparties**.

English auction. A type of unit **auction** where successful bidders receive the quantity bid for at the price bid (cf. **dutch auction**). Where only one item is offered, it is the highest bidder who wins (cf. **winner's curse**). Also known as a *discriminatory price auction*. See **competitive auction**.

enhanced derivative product company (EDPC). A subsidiary of a financial intermediary specifically set up to act as **counterparty** or issuer of **derivative** contracts and benefiting from a high **credit worthiness** reflected in a top quality **credit rating**, typically **triple-A**. The rationale behind such vehicles is to allow customers to transact **over-the-counter** business with the financial intermediary without concern for **credit risk** (cf. **settlement risk**). It is similar to the function performed by a **clearing house** for **exchange-traded futures** and **options** where the method of operation effectively minimizes any credit risk through **collateralization** of participants' positions.

enhanced scrip dividend (Equities; UK). A share alternative method of paying **dividends** by a UK-domiciled company which reduces or eliminates the company's obligation to pay **advance corporation tax** (cf. **unrelieved ACT**). The dividends are paid not in cash, but in the form of additional new shares issued by the company. In addition, to make the transaction more attractive to shareholders, there is normally also a **broker-dealer** who undertakes to purchase, at the prevailing market price, the new shares issued, thus providing holders with a cash alternative. As a mechanism, the enhanced scrip dividend is similar to a **rights issue** in that additional shares are issued by the company. For example: If the share price used for allocating the scrip is 84p and the cash dividend 1.0p per share and the company offers an enhanced scrip dividend of 1.5p, then the new allocation would be one new share for every 56 held (84p/1.5p). For every 1,000 shares held, assuming full election to take up the scrip issue is made, would give:

Entitlement to new ordinary shares, 1,000/56 (rounded down):	£0.17
Enhanced amount on 1,000 shares at 1.5p:	£15.00
Value of 17 new shares at the reference price of 84p each:	£14.45
Residual amount:	£0.55
Balancing cash distribution £0.55/1.5	£0.36

Thus the holder would receive total new shares for a value of £14.45 and cash for £0.36, equal to £14.81.

Normal cash dividend on 1,000 shares
at 1.0p share: £10.00

Tax treatment of the enhanced scrip dividend will depend on the tax position of the recipient: the Inland Revenue will consider the distribution to include a grossing-up element (currently 20%), such that if the market value is 84p on initial trading, then the £14.45 will be grossed up to £18.06, having paid tax on that grossed-up amount (i.e. £3.61 in tax). This compares to the £10.00 cash and £2.50 tax credit for the cash dividend.

Enhanced Structural Adjustment Facility (ESAF). A facility provided by the International Monetary Fund to support long-term, structural, economic reforms.

enhancement of a position. A set of investment techniques, such as covered option writing, designed to increase returns without significantly increasing the risks.

enter open stop (EOS). A trading instruction to a broker to institute a stop order when an earlier instruction has been fulfilled (cf. fill or kill; good till cancelled; stop loss).

Enterprise Investment Scheme (UK). Tax relief provision allowing individuals to invest in small companies giving an immediate 20% up-front income tax relief and also tax-free income and allowing rollover of capital gains. It is an incentive scheme allowing investors to make up to £100,000 investment in a small, unquoted company and to receive income tax relief on the sum at the lowest rate of tax. The scheme replaced the Business Expansion Scheme as an incentive for individuals to back small firms. See also Alternative Investment Market; business angels; equity gap; limited partnership; venture capital; venture capital trust.

entitlement issue. See bonus issue; rights issue; scrip issue.

entrepreneur. Risk-taking individual who undertakes industrial and commercial activities with a view to making a profit (cf. business angels).

environmental risk. The business risk from operating in a given environment or situation. See economic risk.

epsilon (ε). See vega (cf. volatility).

equal variance. See homoscedastic.

equilibrium. A condition under which all forces capable of change are in balance, such that there is no pressure for change. In financial markets, this state would exist if demand is matched perfectly by supply at the ruling price (cf. market forces). If there were dissatisfaction with the price then buyers would try to buy more than is available, or sellers sell more than buyers want at the prevailing price (cf. buyers over; sellers over). To this extent, price is seen as an equilibrating mechanism. Economic models also provide an equilibrium relationship for the activities or relationships being examined. An unstable situation would be known as *disequilibrium*. See also fundamental disequilibrium.

equipment leasing partnership (USA). A limited partnership which acquires assets and leases them to businesses. The partners receive income and tax depreciation on their investment.

equipment trust certificates (ETC) (Bonds; USA). A type of mortgage-backed security used to finance new equipment where the bondholders have the first right to the equipment in the case of default. Ownership of the assets is held in trust and, once the debt is paid off, reverts to the issuer. Such issues have proven popular with transportation companies needing to finance large investments such as ships or rolling stock.

equitable interest. A beneficial interest in an asset recognized by equity but not incorporated in a specific contract. Although there is no contractual arrangement between the parties, the holder of an equitable interest has a claim for their share with the asset's owner.

Equitas (UK). The insurance vehicle used by Lloyds of London to separate old and new years' liabilities in order to cap names' open-ended liabilities for past underwriting losses prior to 1993 (cf. long tail-end liabilities). These uncapped liabilities relate principally to substantial pollution and asbestos-related claims from policies written in the USA.

equitize cash. The purchase of stock index futures, forwards, or stock options contracts from a cash or liquid asset position thus producing a return that is linked to equity performance (cf. covered put).

equity or **equities.** (i) The risk capital of a firm. It is that part of the long-term liabilities used to fund a company that take part in the profits after prior charges have been met or the residual value of the company in liquidation after paying off all creditors. There are many different types of equity: common stock (or ordinary shares), and a wide range of preferred stock (preference shares). The major distinguishing factors between equity and debt instruments (bonds, debentures and loans) are the ownership rights, voting rights, and the tax treatment. Equity receives **dividends** after company or **corporation tax** has been paid and holders of equity sometimes have to pay an additional tax on such receipts under a classical corporation tax system, although with an imputation tax system they may receive a balancing tax credit (cf. **franked income**). From an accounting perspective, retained **reserves** are also **shareholders funds**. (ii) Often used to mean the **common stock** of a company. Sometimes called the firm's *equity capital*, but this may include preferred stock. (iii) The major **class** of security listed on a **stock exchange**. (iv) A holder's stake or contribution to a transaction (cf. **over-collateralized; partnership**). (v) Another term for **net worth**, i.e. total **assets** less fixed **liabilities**. (vi) A beneficial interest in an asset. Hence, an *equity interest*. (vii) The excess **margin** in an account over and above that required to maintain the **position** (cf. **initial margin; maintenance margin**).

equity accounting. Method of treating undistributed **earnings** or profits in an associate or minority investment when consolidating the accounts of the **holding company**. The proportion of earnings attributable to the holding company is shown in the consolidated **profit and loss account**, even though no **distribution** may have taken place. (cf. **consolidated accounts; consolidation**).

equity arbitrage. See arbitrage.

equity buy-back. See stock repurchase plan.

equity capital. See equity.

equity carve-out (Mergers and acquisitions). A type of financing arrangement, short of a **divestiture**, where part of a subsidiary's **equity** is sold to the public (cf. **public offering**). The intention is either to allow the subsidiary to raise further finance from the market at a later date (usually leading to the **dilution** of the parent company's holding) or to prepare the company for full divestiture at a later date.

equity commitment note or **equity contract note** (Bonds; USA). A US **bond** issue in which the borrower sets up a fund to redeem the bonds at **maturity**. The lender is usually a domestic bank and the life-span of such issues is normally twelve years (cf. **mandatory convertible bond**). The fund must hold certain low-**risk** securities and their maturities are specified in strict proportion to the **principal**. The fund is financed by the issuer making periodic sales of **common** or **preferred stock** prior to maturity, thus allowing the commitment note to count as **equity**, or **primary capital** (cf. **defeasance**). See asset-backed; capital note; securitization.

equity contract note. See mandatory convertible bond.

equity contribution agreement. A project finance agreement where one or more parties undertake(s) to contribute more **equity** to a project under certain specific, pre-agreed conditions.

equity convertible. See convertible.

equity crude. The share of the output from an oilfield that is available as product to one or more of the **shareholders**.

equity dilution. Any transaction which raises new **equity** which reduces the ownership rights of existing **shareholders** (cf. **pre-emption right**).

equity enhanced dedication. A type of **portfolio insurance** where the assets of the portfolio are divided between a dedicated part invested in **bonds** and a **risk** part invested in **equities**. The object is to guarantee a certain proportion of the returns of the portfolio through **dedication** while aiming to improve performance via risk-taking.

equity financing. A transaction to raise new **equity**.

equity gap (UK). The alleged difficulty small UK businesses have in raising capital owing to the unwillingness of the capital markets to supply capital below a minimum amount. Such a condition may also prevail in other countries.

equity gearing. See capital gearing; leverage.

equityholder. The owner of an **equity** stake in a firm. See shareholder; stockholder.

equity index. An **index** giving the price or return performance of a basket of equities (cf. **index construction**). Such indices either aim to track the market as a whole or individual industrial sectors. Such an index is monitored to provide an indication of market trends. See stock exchange; stock index.

equity index-linked notes. See equity-linked notes.

equity kicker. An **option** or **right** to acquire **common stock** or **ordinary shares** in a firm at a preferential rate. Equity kickers are normally attached to some high risk financings or as a **sweetener** to make a transaction more attractive (cf. **bells and whistles**).

equity-linked foreign exchange option. See quantity adjusting option.

equity-linked notes (ELN). A set of proprietary vehicle types which have the returns linked to the performance of a particular **common stock**, a stock **index**, or a **basket** of particular stocks. The common feature is a guarantee at **maturity** for the holder to receive back the invested principal. Some have all the returns linked to the performance of the equity instrument; some feature a minimum fixed interest rate, while some have a cap on the possible increase due to the rise in the equity element but equally offer greater participation in the payout range (see diagram) (cf. **cap**; **leverage**). Typically those structures which feature a cap on the equity participation tend to have a higher payout in the participating range. They are essentially a combination of a **zero-coupon bond** or a **deep discount bond** with a purchased call option on the equity instrument. The difference between the value of the zero coupon at issue and the **par value** of the note is used to pay the **premium** on the purchased call. Such one-way bets are attractive to investors who like the possibility of winning on equity investments but are concerned to protect their principal, although investors forgo the interest. In addition, by not investing directly, the holder forgoes any **dividends**. The instruments in all their variety are marketed under many different names: **equity-index linked notes; equity participation notes; guaranteed return index participation securities; guaranteed return on investment securities; guaranteed stock market bond; index growth-linked unit securities; index participation certificate;** money-back; **protected equity note (PEN); protected equity participation; protected index participation; safe return security.**

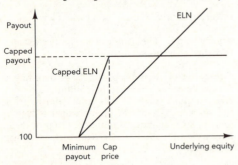

Equity-linked notes

equity-linked swap. A type of **swap** contract, similar to an **interest rate swap** where one leg (or occasionally both legs) of the swap has payments linked to the performance of a **stock index** or a basket of stocks; this is usually the total return, that is the capital appreciation of the index plus the **dividends**. In addition, the swap can be in a single currency or may involve a cross-currency element when it then becomes a **quantity adjusting index-linked swap.**

equity market-maker (UK). A member of the **London Stock Exchange** whose main function is to make **two-way prices** in **ordinary shares** (cf. **gilt-edged market-maker**).

equity note. See capital note.

equity option. Any of a number of **options** on equity instruments, on an individual **stock**, a **stock index** or sub-index, or a bespoke portfolio of stocks. Such options are also offered in securitized form as **warrants**. Also called a *stock option*.

equity participation indexed certificate (EPIC). See equity-linked note.

equity participation note (EPN). See equity-linked note.

equity swap. A type of **interest rate swap** where one party has a payment linked to the performance of a **stock index** and the other pays a **fixed** or **floating rate** (cf. **commodity swap**). Also called an *equity-linked swap*.

equity warrant. A tradable **option** or **warrant** issued by a company that allows the holder to buy shares in the issuer at a predetermined price, the **strike price**, and date. The shares so purchased are normally the **common stock** of the issuer, however *covered warrant writing* involves the **equity** of third party companies. Equity warrants can be issued for **preferred stock**. Sometimes known as a *stock warrant* or *share warrant*.

equity yield-enhanced security (EYES). A type of **equity-linked note** on a single **underlying** stock with a **cap** feature. The structure is designed to increase the return on the instrument compared to the stock throughout the payout range by using the proceeds of the cap to increase the coupon on the EYES above the **dividend** paid on the stock. See preference **equity redemption cumulative stock.**

equivalent bond yield. A measure used to compare the **yields** of **money market discount** instruments and **bonds** with similar **maturities**. It is defined as the **coupon** on a bond with the same maturity trading at **par** which would give the same return as the instrument, assuming a **reinvestment** rate equal to the **coupon** rate. Sometimes known as the *coupon equivalent yield* or *corporate bond equivalent*. See also **interest rate calculations**; **yield curve.**

Equivalent bond yield with no intermediate coupon payments before maturity:

Convert the discount security to its equivalent simple yield, where d is the rate of discount; Y_b the equivalent simple yield; T_{sm} the days from settlement to maturity; *BASIS* the day basis in the computation year (360 or 365); *P* the price.

$$Y_b = \frac{\dfrac{d}{100}\,\text{BASIS}}{(\text{BASIS} \times 100) - (d.T_{sm})}$$

A French **Treasury Bill** with 72 days to maturity offered at a discount of 9.5% (0.095), using a 360-day **basis** will have a simple yield of 9.68%.

Equivalent bond yield with an intermediate coupon payment before maturity:

$$Y_b = \frac{\dfrac{2T_{sm}}{\text{BASIS} \times 100} + 2\left(\dfrac{T_{SM}^2}{\text{BASIS} \times 100}\right) - \left(\dfrac{2T_{sm}}{\text{BASIS} \times 100} - 1\right)\left(1 - \dfrac{1}{P}\right)}{\dfrac{2dT_{sm}}{\text{BASIS} \times 100} - 1}$$

A 270-day US T-bill with an **offered** rate of discount of 4% (a discount of 0.97 to **par value** [for the calculation of how this price is derived, see **discount**]) will have an equivalent US **treasury bond** yield of:

$$Y_b = \frac{\dfrac{2 \times 270}{365 \times 100} + 2\left(\dfrac{270^2}{365 \times 100}\right) - \left(\dfrac{2 \times 270}{365 \times 100} - 1\right)\left(1 - \dfrac{1}{0.97}\right)}{\dfrac{2 \times 270}{365 \times 100} - 1}$$

$$Y_b = 4.14\%$$

See **interest rate calculations** for details of day counts.

equivalent life. A measure of the **life** of a series or issue of securities, taking into consideration any **amortization** provisions (cf. **serial security**). It is defined as the **weighted average maturity**, using as weights the **present values** of the redemption payments discount at the **yield-to-maturity** (cf. **duration**).

equivalent loan. A way of calculating the maximum amount of debt that the payments required under a **lease** could support.

equivalent position. See **synthetic**.

equivalent taxable yield. The yield on a taxable security that would provide an after tax return equal to that earned by a tax-exempt security. See **after-tax basis**.

error account. Accounting or bookkeeping ledger used to record trading mistakes pending their rectification.

escalating principal swap or **escalating swap.** A type of **interest rate swap** or **cross-currency**

swap where the amount of **notional principal** increases towards **maturity**. Also known as a *step-up swap*. See **accreting swap**.

escalating rate swaps. A type of **off-market** swap where the **fixed rate** increases in a predetermined fashion with time. Also called a *step-up coupon swap* or a *step-up swap*.

escalator clause. A term in an agreement allowing increased charges in relation to a specific event or costs, typically inflation.

escrow or **escrow account.** An account relating to a transaction held with a third party, the **custodian**, to be made available to one or other of the contracting parties when certain conditions have been fulfilled (cf. **performance bond**).

escrowed-to-maturity bond (ETM) (USA). Municipal bond where the **coupon** payments and **principal** are backed by an escrowed **pool** of securities, usually federal obligations (cf. **defeasance**). See **in-substance defeasance**.

escrow receipt. A letter from a **custodian** or depository stating that it will ensure **delivery** of assets or securities in the event that an **option writer** is exercised.

estimated total return (ETR). The internal rate of return on a security using an assumed reinvestment rate. See **yield-to-maturity**.

estimation. Used in **econometrics** to describe that stage in a quantitative study of economic or financial market activity that attempts to establish numerical values for those **parameters** considered influential in explaining observed behaviour in the markets under scrutiny. The method of estimation used is likely to be directly related to the type of **model** employed to capture the main characteristics of the market being analysed. Estimated values for these relevant factors are used as the basis for generating forecasts about the future movement of such variables. See **forecasting**.

Euro. Name for the new currency that is due to come into being on 1 January 1999 following European Monetary Union (cf. **Eurofed**).

eurobond. A public bearer bond issued in a euro-currency, usually **eurodollars**. The eurobond market is an international long-term capital market, with maturities out to about fifty years (but also including some **perpetual** issues), which raises finance, in the form of bonds, on behalf of borrowers. In arranging these bond issues the participating banks bring together highly rated borrowers such as governments, government agencies and corporations, and investors, including institutions and **retail investors**. The borrower normally appoints a **lead manager** to arrange the issue and will provide a large proportion of the funds required (cf. **co-lead manager**). **co-managers** will be invited to participate as **underwriters**, share the fees, and purchase a proportion of the issue and a **selling** or **placement group** might be formed to assist in distribution (cf. **International Primary Markets Association**). One feature is the international nature of the **syndicate**. Eurobonds come in two main types: **straights** (either **fixed** or **floating rate**) and **convertibles**, but the market has been tremendously innovative, offering a wide variety of specialized or tailored securities to meet investors' needs. It is usual for **straight bonds** to be of **bullet** type and pay an annual **fixed coupon**. Securities usually have **bearer certificates** or **depository receipts** and are settled via the **Centrale de Livraison de Valeurs Mobilières** and **Euroclear**. There is an associated **euroequity market**. See **interest rate calculations**; **International Securities Markets Association**. Such issues are not **registered** with the **Securities and Exchange Commission** (USA) (cf. **daisy chain**; **distributed**; **seasoned**).

eurobond fees. Although the market is unregulated, there are certain conventions as regards the fees paid on a bond to the **lead manager** and the **underwriting syndicate** (cf. **co-lead manager**; **co-manager**; **selling group**). The traditional fee structure is as in the Table.

Eurobond fees

Maturity (Years)	1–2	3–4	5	7–9	10	10+
Total fee (%)	1	$1^3/_8$	$1^5/_8$	$1^7/_8$	2	2+
Management fee	$^1/_4$★	$^3/_8$	$^5/_8$★	$^3/_8$	$^3/_8$	$^3/_8$+
Underwriting fee	★	$^1/_4$	★	$^1/_4$	$^3/_8$	$^3/_8$+
Selling concession	$^3/_4$	$^3/_4$	1	$1^1/_4$	$1^1/_4$	$1^1/_4$+

★ no accepted split.

There is considerable possible variation in the fee structure. For instance, sometimes a combined **management fee** and **underwriting fee** is paid. Sometimes a **praecipuum** will be taken by the lead manager group out of the management fee. For a **fixed price reoffer** (FPR), the fee tends to be between 0.25% and 0.35%. It is also possible to see the traditional fee structure is combined with that used in an FPR.

eurobond offering. A new issue of eurobonds.

euro certificate of deposit (euro CD) (Money markets). **Certificate of deposit** issued by the branch of a US bank or a non-US bank outside the USA and denominated in a **eurocurrency**. In practice almost all euro CDs are issued in London and therefore fall under the guidelines for issuance set by the **Bank of England** (cf. **London certificate of deposit**). These regulate the currencies that may be issued, (currently **European Currency Units**, (ECU), sterling, Japanese yen, and US dollars) and the **maturity**, which is up to five years (cf. **fixed rate certificate of deposit**; **floating rate certificate of deposit**). In practice most such issues are for short (one- to six-month maturities). Certificates can be issued to pay either interest at **maturity** or on a **discount** basis (cf. **bank basis**; **coupon**; **interest-to-follow**). They rank **pari passu** with (bank) **deposits** made with the issuing institution. See **commercial paper**; **eurocommercial paper**; **euromarkets**; **interest rate calculations**.

Euroclear. A clearing facility and **depository** for euromarket security transactions. It is located in Brussels (Belgium) and is owned by a group of US and European banks who are active in the euromarkets and managed by Morgan Guaranty Trust (cf. **bridge finance**; **Centrale de Livraison de Valeurs Mobilières**; **Clearing House**; **Society for World-wide Interbank Financial Telecommunications**).

eurocommercial paper (ECP) (Money Markets). A generic term used to describe **promissory notes** that are issued in the **euromarkets** without being **underwritten** by a **backstop** (cf. **euronote**; **facility**). See **commercial paper**.

euroconvertible preference share (Equity; UK). A **preference stock** preference share issue made by an offshore subsidiary of a UK-domiciled company, but **convertible** into the **ordinary shares** of the parent. This structure is designed to be tax efficient for the issuer, as well as aimed at attracting foreign investors.

euro CP. See **eurocommercial paper**.

eurocredit (Banking). An **offshore** lending market, forming part of the **euromarkets**, where borrowers can gain access to medium-term bank lending of between one and fifteen years. The major international banks are active participants in this market, which is largely centred on London. Loans can be denominated in one or several **eurocurrencies**, as can be the interest and the **principal**. In the case of a **term facility** there may be a **multi-currency clause** allowing the borrower to select at any interest rate setting period the currency(ies) of choice (cf. **currency availability clause**). The interest rate is normally fixed as a **margin** over some **reference rate**, normally London interbank offered rate. Generally borrowings are at a **floating rate** with a usual period of three or six months in the currency(ies) being borrowed, but may occasionally be on a **fixed interest rate** for the whole loan period. Some lending has used innovative structures incorporating **options** or **drop-locked** interest payments. When a eurocredit is **syndicated** the lending is provided by a group of participating banks (cf. **club deal**). The return to these banks will depend on their amount of contribution. When the eurocredit **facility** is used to **backstop** the issue of **euronotes** (known as a **euronote facility**) which can be resold, the syndicate members are committed to **underwriting** the availability of **funds** by purchasing the notes in the event that these cannot be sold to investors or make advances in lieu (cf. **conditions precedent**; **tender panel**).

eurocurrency. Currency (bank) deposits held outside the country which issued the currency, but not necessarily located in Europe (cf. **eurodollars**). The deposit may be re-lent to another borrower, either directly or after conversion into another currency, or after being deposited via one or more other banks. Although the dominant currency is the US dollar (known as the eurodollar market) for historical reasons, there are active and liquid **euromarkets** in Sterling; Deutschmarks; Belgian, French, and Swiss Francs; Dutch Guilders; yen; and the **European Currency Unit** (ECU). These are referred to as eurosterling, euro-Deutschmarks, and so forth. Most other, freely **convertible currencies** are also traded but the markets in these may be less liquid. The deposit rates (cf. **London interbank bid rate**; **London interbank offered rate**) are important for setting **forward currency** differentials in the **foreign exchange market**. Settlement procedures for eurocurrency are typically carried out by correspondent banks in the currency's domestic market but may differ from those applicable for the same currency traded on a domestic basis; typically eurocurrencies are traded on a **spot** basis for two business days **forward** settlement while most domestic deposits are traded for same-, or next-day settlement. Regular statistics on developments are provided by the **Bank for International Settlements**.

eurocurrency deposits. Short-term wholesale money market deposits made in the **eurocurrency** market. The market is much less regulated than the equivalent domestic money markets and has become a very significant activity for many banks. Interest rates are generally similar but not the same as those prevailing in the domestic market, reflecting the absence of reserve requirements, for instance (cf. **placing**; **taking**). Also abbreviated to *eurodeposit*. See **Interbank market**; **London interbank bid rate**; **London interbank mean rate**; **London interbank offered rate**.

euro-Deutschmarks (Euro-DM). Deutschmarks traded in the **eurocurrency** market. Sometimes referred to as *Euromarks*.

eurodollar bond. **Eurobond** denominated in US dollars.

eurodollar futures. Financial **futures contracts** where the **underlying** is the rate for US dollar deposits based on the **London interbank offered rate**.

eurodollars. US dollars on **deposit** or borrowed from a branch of a US bank or a foreign bank located outside the USA. The name (and that of the **eurocurrency** market) derives from the telex address of the Banque Commerciale pour l'Europe du Nord, which was 'eurobank', the first bank to actively solicit and manage such offshore deposits, hence *eurodollar deposit*.

euroequity. Name given to primary issues of **common stock** on the **euromarket**. The distribution method and participants are the same as for **eurobonds**. The market differs somewhat from the **bond market** in that listing and **settlement** procedures remain those of the domestic market, although increasingly the international clearing houses are being involved. Because of the need for name recognition and the additional costs of such issues, the market tends to be limited to large, well-known corporations. A major milestone in the development of the market was the international syndication of US$ 2.2 billion of Fiat Spa stock following the buy-out of the People's Republic of Libya's 25% stake.

Eurofed. See **European Monetary Institute**.

eurofrancs. Belgian, French, or Swiss francs traded in the **eurocurrency** market.

euroguilders. Netherlands guilders traded in the **eurocurrency** market. A *euroguilders issue* is a guilder-denominated **eurobond**.

euro-issue. Common term for a new issue transaction in the **euromarkets**, used to distinguish it from a domestic issue.

euro lines (Banking). Market shorthand for a banking **facility** based on **eurocurrencies** (as opposed to a domestic **facility**).

euromarkets. A collective term used to describe a series of **offshore**, generally **over-the-counter** (OTC), supranational (stateless) **commodity**, **derivative**, capital, and **money markets** operated by international banks and financial institutions. They comprise the **eurocurrency**, **eurocredit**, and **eurobond** markets as well as the OTC derivatives and commodities markets. In these markets are traded the principal globally important financial instruments with the **Group of Seven** (G7) countries representing the largest proportion.

The unofficial capital of these markets is London but other financial centres in Europe (and increasingly elsewhere) may be the focus for **sectors** of these markets, either for regulatory or for historical reasons (e.g. the euro-french franc market is centred on Paris). While it was once true to consider the euromarkets as pertaining to that region, the market is increasingly taking on a global character and is sometimes used interchangeably with international markets for all cross-border financial activity. Recent trends, following domestic deregulation in the principal countries, have been for national and international markets to converge (cf. **cross-border; globalization**). Information on activity in the euromarkets is compiled and published by the **Bank for International Settlements** and the **Organization for Economic Cooperation and Development**. Good sources of information on the euromarkets are: *OECD Financial Trends*; the **Bank of England**; the **Federal Reserve**; *International Financial Review; Euromoney; Financial Times; Wall Street Journal*. See also **International Primary Markets Association; International Securities Markets Association**.

euro medium-term notes (euro MTN; EMTN). Issues of **medium-term notes** made in the **euromarkets**. Such issues are settled using normal euromarket practices.

euronote. A short-term, fully negotiable, bearer promissory note normally issued at a **discount** and usually of one, three, or six months' maturity when issued. The main difference between euronotes and other **euromarket** instruments, such as eurocommercial paper or **euro certificates of deposit** is that they are backed up by an **underwritten euronote facility** which ensures to the issuer that funds will be available (cf. **borrower's option for notes or underwritten standy; multi-option financing facility; note issuance facility; short-term note issuance facility**).

euronote facility. This allows borrowers to issue short-term **promissory notes** through a variety of note distribution mechanisms, under the umbrella of a medium-term commitment from banks which agree to buy notes at a predetermined rate or a maximum margin, expressed in relation to **London interbank offered rate** (cf. **multi-option financing facility; note issuance facility; short-term note issuance facility**). If the notes cannot be placed with investors at or under the agreed **margin**, then the banks will normally either buy the notes or provide a short-term loan for the same period, known as an **advances option**. An **underwritten** euronote facility requires the bank to provide funds as long as the **conditions precedent** have been met. However, not all facilities are underwritten. See **eurocredits; tender panel**.

European, Australian, Far East Index (EAFE Index). Popular benchmark global **index** which excludes the US market compiled by Morgan Stanley Inc.

European Bank for Reconstruction and Development (EBRD; The European Bank). Modelled on the Bank for International Reconstruction and Development (The **World Bank**) it was set up in April 1991 to provide financial assistance to the former command economies of Central and Eastern Europe. The EBRD provides merchant banking and development assistance to both the private and public sectors with the proviso that 60% of lending should be to the former. It is based in London and has offices in the principal beneficiary nations.

European Coal and Steel Community (ECSC). Forerunner institution to the **European Community** established in the 1950s to regulate the European coal and steel industries. Its activities are now largely under the aegis of the **European Union**.

European Community (EC). The European Economic Community (EEC) was the original designation for the European association formed by the Treaty of Rome in 1958. It then became the EC, and is now more generally known as the **European Union**.

European convention or **European foreign exchange rate quoting basis** (Forex). A practice in the **foreign exchange** markets of quoting currency in relation to US dollar units (cf. **base currency**). Thus quotes, for instance, for French francs, Deutschmarks, or Spanish pesetas are expressed in variable units per dollar. The other common methods are the *American convention*, which expresses currencies in terms of one unit in relation to a variable amount of US dollars, and *cross-rates*, where two non-US dollar currencies are expressed against each other (cf. **direct quote; indirect exchange rate**).

European Currency Unit (ECU). This is a composite (or basket) currency the value of which is given according to a basket of European currencies: Belgian franc, Danish kroner, Deutschmark, French franc, Greek drachma, Irish punt, Italian lira, Luxembourg franc, Netherlands guilder, Portuguese escudo, Spanish peseta, sterling. It is designed as a unit of account for the **European Community/Union** and the **European Monetary System** (EMS) (cf. **divergence indicator**). Distinction should be made between the 'official ECU', which is used by the European Union and in the operation of the EMS and the 'private ECU' which is used for commercial transactions, including bond and **money market** issues. It is in this latter category that it is used as an issuing currency by borrowers in the **eurobond** and **yankee** markets. It is not legal currency, but is settled through ECU accounts where the **Bank for International Settlements** acts as a **clearing house**.

European depository receipt (EDR). A receipt issued by a European bank which holds a foreign security that allows it to be traded in Europe (cf. **American depository receipt**). Also sometimes referred to as a *continental depository receipt*.

European Economic Area (EEA). Integrated trading area formed from the former **European Free Trade Association** and the **European Union** (EU). It provides the advantages of the EU's single market but without participation in the EU's political processes.

European Economic Community (EEC). See **European Community**; **European Union**.

European exercise. Refers to the European-style **option** type that may only be exercised at **expiry** (cf. **American excise**).

European Federation of Financial Analyst Societies (EFFAS). Association of European financial analyst societies which aims to facilitate international securities research (cf. **fundamental analysis**).

European Free Trade Association (EFTA). A grouping of non-**European Union** (EU) nations established in 1960 which aims to promote free trade outside the political structures of the EU. EFTA and the EU have established a pan-European trading zone through the **European Economic Area Agreement**.

European Futures Clearing Corporation (Netherlands). The **clearing house** for futures traded on the **Amsterdam Stock Exchange**'s *Financiel Termijnmarkt Amsterdam* (FTA) and the **European Options Exchange** (EOE).

European Investment Bank (EIB). Established in 1958 as part of the European Economic Community (EEC), now the **European Union** (EU), under the Treaty of Rome, although with a separate legal identity. Its function is to finance major regional, capital investment projects and contribute to a balanced and steady development of the EEC, the member nations' former colonies (Overseas Countries and Territories via the Lomé Convention) and lately to Eastern Europe (cf. **European Bank for Reconstruction and Development**). Its capital base is provided by member states and its reputation allows it to borrow at a **fine rate** (it is triple-A rated by **credit rating agencies**), an advantage it passes on in its lending

activities. It is one of the single most active fund-raising institutions on the international markets and instrumental in developing the **European Currency Unit** market.

European Monetary Institute (EMI). Nicknamed the *Eurofed*, it is based in Frankfurt and has the initial responsibility under Stage 2 of the move towards **European Monetary Union** of coordinating national monetary policies following the Maastricht Treaty in 1991. It is widely seen as the forerunner to a European **central bank**, which would be expected to evolve along the lines of the USA's **Federal Reserve System** with member states' central banks taking the place of the individual Federal Reserve Banks.

European Monetary System (EMS). In March 1979 a group of European countries, comprising Belgium, Luxembourg, Denmark, West Germany, France, Italy, Ireland, and the Netherlands, agreed to maintain their respective currencies within certain defined upper and lower limits in relation to one another. Membership of the EMS, which includes all **European Union** states, does not necessarily mean participation in the **Exchange Rate Mechanism** (ERM). There are two components to the EMS/ERM: the parity grid and the **divergence indicator**. EMS members agree to maintain their respective currencies within the limits set by the parity grid while the divergence indicator acts as a trigger for intervention or other measures, such as a tightening of domestic monetary conditions, to maintain the value of their currency against other members. If the value of one of the currencies is changed, to reflect a fundamental shift in that country's trade position, a realignment within the EMS occurs and all the exchange limits of the currencies are correspondingly adjusted. Sometimes, although rarely now, called *The snake in the tunnel* (cf. **European Currency Unit**).

European Monetary Union (EMU). One of the objectives set by the **European Community** in the Maastricht Treaty of 1991. It involves the creation of a common currency for all member states (cf. **euro**; **European Currency Unit**; **European Monetary Institute**).

European option. See **European-style option**.

European Options Exchange (EOE) (Optiebeurs Groep Amsterdam) (Netherlands). Rokin 65, 1012 KK Amsterdam; postal address PO Box 19164, 1000 GD Amsterdam (tel. 31 (0) 20 550 4550; fax 31 (0) 20 623 00 12). Established in 1978. A derivatives exchange dealing in **options**, whose **settlement** is handled by **Options Clearing Corporation** (OCC) in Chicago (USA). See also **clearing system**.

European Regional Development Fund (ERDF). A part of the integration process within the **European Union** (EU). The ERDF aims at providing funds for infrastructure development in the special need regions of the EU.

European-style option (Derivatives). An **option** which can only be **exercised** at **expiry**. The principal alternative is known as an **American-style** which can be exercised at any time up to and including expiry. Hybrid partial American-style exercise is also possible, for instance, in a **call provision** which can only be exercised on certain (**coupon** payment) dates (cf. **Atlantic-style**; **Bermudan-style**). Sometimes called a *European option* (cf. **European exercise**). See **option pricing**.

European terms (Forex). The quotation of foreign **exchange rates** expressed in terms of how many currency units can be exchanged for one US dollar: that is, the dollar is the **base currency**. For example, DM 1.4532 = US$ 1.00 (Deutschmark/US dollars). Also called the *European convention*. The expression of the exchange rate is often abbreviated in reports. For instance, the rate between the Deutschmark and the US dollar is usually expressed as DM/US$ (i.e. as a **ratio**), although this is not universal practice and some people use the opposite (i.e. US$/DM, that is, a US$ variable amount = £1) for the same method of quoting the exchange rate, so beware.

European Union (EU). New name for the European **Community** following the ratification of the Maastricht Treaty in 1993. The largest and most important of the different European communities, the others being the **European Coal and Steel Community** (ECSC), European Atomic Energy Community (EURATOM). The EU itself comprises a number of different institutions, the European Parliament, based in Strasbourg; the Council of Ministers, the European Commission, both based in Brussels, and the European Court of Justice, in Luxembourg, as is the **European Investment Bank**. In addition, there is the Court of Auditors and the Economic and Social Committee (ESC) which was set up to provide advice on proposed legislation within the EU.

The Commission is the executive arm of the EU with individual Commissioners responsible for one or more *Directorates* which make policy and implement and monitor EU policies and administer EU expenditures within one or more areas. In addition, the Commission is responsible for administering the major funds: the European Social Fund, the European Regional Development Fund, the European Development Fund, and the European Agricultural Guidance and Guarantee Fund. The Council of Ministers is the main decision-making body and is responsible for making policy and is made up of representatives of the respective national governments. Each government normally sends one delegate and the Presidency of the Council is rotated between the member states on a six-monthly basis, to include a summit meeting hosted by the Presidency in his or her country. Qualified majority voting is applied to many issues although states retain a right of veto in a number of crucial areas. In addition to the Council there is a permanent representative body made up of the ambassadors to the EU in Brussels called the Committee of Permanent Representatives (COREPER) (cf. **ECOFIN**).

European Unit of Account (EUA). A composite (or **basket**) currency **unit** using a number of the currencies of member states of the **European Union**. Largely superseded by the **European Currency Unit**.

Euroratings. A credit rating agency set up to rate issues on the **eurobond market**. It is no longer functioning. See **credit ratings**.

eurosecurities. Those financial instruments such as **bonds, commercial paper, common stock, convertibles, floating rate notes, medium-term notes,** and **promissory notes** offered on and traded in the **euromarkets**. Such issues are, in many cases, distinguishable from domestic equivalents by their terms and conditions and **settlement** procedures. Also known as *euro issues*.

eurosterling. Sterling traded in the **eurocurrency** markets. A *eurosterling bond* is a sterling-denominated **eurobond**.

euro-syndicated loan. A facility which makes use of **eurocurrencies**. Typically such facilities will have the **reference rate** tied to the eurocurrency reference rate, which normally will be the **London interbank offered rate**.

Euro-Top 100 Index (Equities; Netherlands). An index of the largest 100 companies in Europe. It forms the basis of a **futures contract** traded on the **European Options Exchange**.

Eurotrack 100 Index (Equities; UK). **Index** of the top 100 European companies, excluding the UK.

Eurotrack 200 Index (Equities; UK). The **Eurotrack 100 Index** together with the **Financial Times-Stock Exchange 100 Index** (FT-SE; Footsie).

euroyen. Japanese yen traded in the **eurocurrency** markets.

euroyen bond. A Japanese yen-denominated **bond** issue in the **eurobond** market. Such issues have terms and conditions in line with other eurobonds, that is annual **coupon** payments and **bullet maturity**, unlike **foreign bonds** issued in Japan, which pay semi-annually and often have a **sinking fund** (cf. **daimyō bond; samurai; shibosai**). The first issue was made by the European Investment Bank in 1977.

euro-warrant. Warrants issued in the euromarkets.

evening up (Derivatives; Futures). Used in the futures markets to describe a buying or selling activity intended to offset an existing **position** (cf. **hedge**).

even lot. See lot (cf. **odd lot; round lot**).

even par swap (Bonds; USA). The sale and purchase of two **bonds** for an equal nominal amount (**par value** or **face value**) without taking into account their market prices.

event. Any news or new information that can affect the value of a security (cf. **efficient markets hypothesis**). See **stock specific risk; systematic risk**.

event of default. An event, or development, in a borrower's condition that puts a debt into **default** and usually allows the debtholder to demand immediate repayment (cf. **acceleration clause; grace period; technical default**). Typically, such events are: failure to pay interest or make repayments of principal, breach of **covenants**, **cross-default**, the **bankruptcy** or **insolvency** of the borrower (cf. **non-performing loans; problem assets**). See **recontracting; workout**.

event risk. The risk a firm loaned to may undergo a sudden and unanticipated downward revision in **credit worthiness** due to some specific event, such as a **takeover**, or loss. Examples include firms which were subject to **leveraged buyouts** and natural disasters or, in the case of Texaco Inc., the requirement to pay massive, punitive damages (cf. **bankruptcy; Chapter 11; insolvency**).

event study. Method used in financial economics to measure the impact or value of information on securities prices (cf. **econometrics**). The **event** or making known the information **triggers** a reaction in securities prices which is then measured (cf. **cumulative abnormal return**). A model predicting the expected market reaction to the information is then compared to the observed result. Many different types of event have been studied in the financial literature. See also **stock specific risk; sytematic risk**.

evergreen credit or **evergreen facility** (Banking). Used to describe a **revolving credit facility**

without a fixed **maturity** that a bank can, normally ever year, choose to convert into a **term credit**.

ex. Without or after; hence ex-**dividend**, ex-**warrants**, and ex-**redemption** (cf. **cum**).

exact interest (USA). The calculation of interest on the actual number of days in a year. Note that **ordinary interest** is calculated on a 360-day **basis**. See **interest rate calculations**.

ex-all. Term for a security traded without any attachments such as **dividends** or **rights**.

ex ante. Before the event (cf. **ex-post**). Hence, for example, *ex ante return*, the expected return before investing.

ex-bonus. A security that is traded without the entitlement to a **bonus issue** attached (cf. **cum**).

ex-capitalization or **ex cap.** Without the **capitalization** or **bonus issue**.

excess (Banking). The **margin** of assets to fixed liabilities (cf. **capital adequacy; equity**). See also **excess reserves**.

excess basis. The difference in **basis** for a **futures** contract between the actual observed basis and the **fair value** of a future based on the **cost-of-carry model**.

excessive trading. See **churning**.

excess margin. The amount of **margin** in a **margin account** in excess of that required.

excess reserves (Banking; USA). A bank's **reserves** held with the **Federal Reserve** in excess of **reserve requirements**. The availability of such reserves (or lack thereof) influences the **fed funds rate**.

excess return. (i) Return generated above some risk-free rate (cf. **market risk premium**). (ii) The return earned beyond that expected for the risk taken. See **risk premium**; also: **abnormal returns; efficient markets hypothesis; Capital Asset Pricing Model**.

excess shares (Equities; UK). Those shares in a **rights issue** which have not been taken up by existing **shareholders** (cf. **pre-emption rights**).

exchange. (i) An authorized market-place or trading mechanism, as in **screen-trading**, for transacting business in financial instruments or other assets, such as **commodities**. Exchanges normally feature regulations covering standard trading contract and **settlement** procedures and restrictions on direct participation by outsiders who normally have to channel transactions through members of the exchange (cf. **over the counter; kerb market**). Sometimes called a *contract market* or *recognised exchange*. (ii) The physical location of an authorized market, such as the **New York Stock Exchange** on **Wall Street**, New York, USA (cf. **floor; pit; screen-trading**). (iii) A type of securities offer where existing, outstanding securities are redeemed in exchange for new securities. (iv) A feature of some securities allowing the holder or issuer to exchange some characteristic of a security, that is *exchangeable*. Also called a *convertible*. (v) An agreement to **swap** an asset or instrument.

exchangeable auction rate preferred stock (Equity; USA). **Auction rate preferred stock** which includes a **conversion** feature to **auction rate notes** at any reset date at the issuer's choice. This allows the issuer to switch the interest payment from being a **dividend** paid after tax to a **coupon** paid from pre-tax income.

exchangeable debt (USA). American term for a **convertible** issue where the **common stock** is not that of the **bond** issuer. See **convertible**.

exchangeable money market preferred stock (EMMPS) (Equity; USA). A type of **preferred stock** issue that after an initial period becomes exchangeable into **money market notes**, which are similar to **floating rate notes**, but in this case the periodic **coupon** rate is set by an **auction** process.

exchangeable preferred stock or **exchangeable preference shares.** Any of a range of **preferred stock** (preference shares) issues which have **conversion** features into other instruments, typically either **common stock** (ordinary shares) or **debt** instruments.

exchange clearing house. See **clearing house**.

exchange controls. Restrictions imposed by a country on the free **convertibility** of their currency usually as a result of shortages of **foreign currency reserves**. Exchange controls can take various forms: one method involves currency permits which are issued by the **central bank** to pay for imports; there may be different markets for commercial and financial transactions, or a dollar pool type of arrangement where a fixed amount of foreign currency is offered to the highest **bidder**; or absolute limits may be imposed on the amount of foreign currency that can be purchased. With the breakdown of the **Bretton Woods** agreement, most countries have moved away from direct exchange controls, preferring to leave the rate to **market forces**, although in many cases **dirty float**

and **crawling peg** exchange rate regimes are used instead.

exchange delivery settlement price (EDSP). Price set by the **derivatives** exchange for **delivery** (cf. **cheapest to deliver**). See also **settlement price**.

exchange distribution (USA). A method of executing a **block sale** on an **exchange** in which a **broker** obtains and bundles together a number of buy orders (cf. **lot**). The transaction is then treated as one trade. See also **odd-lot trader**.

Exchange Equalization Account (EEA) (Banking; UK). British government account holding the country's **foreign currency reserves**. It is managed by the **Bank of England** and is used for currency **intervention** (cf. **Exchange Stabilization Fund**).

exchange for physical (EFP). (i) (Commodities) When a participant in the commodities **futures** markets elects to deliver or receive the **underlying**. Also called *against actuals* (AA) or *exchange of futures for physical* (EFFP). (ii) It can also mean in **cash-settled** contracts an agreement between parties to agree to **deliver** the underlying. The rationale is to allow adjustment to the cash, or physical position, at minimum cost (cf. **bid-offer spread**). (iii) Special concession allowed on the **International Petroleum Exchange** (IPE) whereby participants may enter into transactions outside the **floor**. It allows participants to agree a closing out transaction between the physical product and the futures market which is then confirmed through the exchange at a later stage. This is the only occasion when IPE contracts may be traded off the floor of the exchange.

exchange listed. A security that is quoted on a recognized **exchange** (cf. **over the counter**). Also just called *listed*.

exchange of assets. A type of **merger** where the acquisition takes place by the purchase of the other firm's **assets** by cash or shares. See **merger accounting**.

exchange offer. A proposal made by an issuer to its debt or **equityholders** proposing that existing securities are surrendered in **exchange** for new securities, typically under new terms more favourable to the issuer. Exchange offers are often used in financial **recontracting** as a way of modifying the cash flows of the outstanding debt, usually by reducing the **coupon** rate. In such a situation, holders have an incentive to agree since otherwise the firm might become **bankrupt** (cf. **insolvent**). Typically, holders are offered an **equity kicker** to encourage them to accept (cf. **sweetener**). In the USA many **junk bonds** have been subject to exchange offers in order to allow the issuing, highly leveraged firms to continue in business (cf. assented securities; Chapter 11; exit consent solicitation; non-assented). See cash-for-stock; Trust Indenture Act of 1939.

exchange of futures for physicals (EFFP). See exchange for physical.

exchange of stock. A type of merger where the acquisition takes place by the purchase of the other company's outstanding stock.

exchange option. (i) An exotic type of option allowing the holder to exchange one underlying for another. Typically currency options are exchange options, although technically all options allow the surrender of cash in payment for the underlying (cf. spread option). See outperformance option. (ii) Short for exchange-traded option. This is an option with standard terms and conditions that is traded on an organized exchange. See, for instance, Chicago Board Options Exchange, London International Financial Futures and Options Exchange; Marché des Options Négociables de Paris.

Exchange Price Information Computer (EPIC) (UK). The original system used by the London Stock Exchange to operate its price collection and dissemination activities. See Block Order Exposure System; Small-order Automatic Execution Facility; Stock Exchange Automated Quotations; Teletext Output of Price Information by Computer.

exchange rate. The price at which one currency is traded (exchanged) with another. It is the price of the unit of one currency in terms on another (cf. American terms; base currency; cross-rate; European terms). See foreign exchange.

exchange rate agreement (ERA) (Forex). A type of synthetic agreement for forward exchange developed by Barclays Bank. Unlike the normal forward exchange agreements it makes no reference to the spot rate at settlement. It is designed as an interbank product to eliminate the settlement risk in complex foreign exchange swaps since, unlike other foreign exchange hedging techniques, large sums are not transferred from one party to another and back again. Only the net amount owed at the end of the day is paid. At present a bank wishing, for example, to buy dollars in a month's time and sell them in three months, faces several deals. ERAs are confined to a single transaction and banks trade the difference between the premiums or discounts that one-month and three-month dollars are selling for at a particular date.

Settlement is based on the following formula:

$$\frac{(\text{Margin transacted} - \text{margin at settlement}) \times \text{notional principal}}{1 + (\text{Interest rate} \times \text{number of days in ERA Period} \div 360)}$$

Exchange Rate Index (ERI) (UK). A currency index prepared and published by the Bank of England.

Exchange Rate Mechanism (ERM). The operational part of the European Monetary System (EMS). Currencies within the ERM are expected to remain within given limits of their bilateral central rates compared to other currencies in the European Currency Unit (ECU). The minimum and maximum exchange rate parities are useful predictors of central bank intervention and monetary policy activities (cf. open-market operations). See divergence indicator.

Exchange Rate Mechanism bands (ERM bands). The amount currencies within the Exchange Rate Mechanism are allowed to fluctuate against each other before forcing intervention. ERM currencies are bounded by a high rate, known as the *ceiling* and a low rate, known as the *floor*. Because of the structure of the ERM, these boundaries may force intervention if reached during normal trading hours. See divergence indicator.

exchange rate risk. The risk that the exchange rate will change unpredictably over time (cf. volatility). See foreign exchange rate risk.

Exchange Stabilization Fund (ESF). Government fund available for currency intervention to stabilize the exchange rate.

exchange-traded. Futures and options which are traded on an organized exchange (cf. over the counter). They normally have standard terms and conditions to facilitate trading and participants need to provide margin against their positions (cf. flex options). Sometimes also called *listed*.

Exchequer stocks (Bonds; UK). See gilt-edged.

exclusivity period (USA). The period of 120 days following the filing of an order for relief allowed to a debtor to prepare and present a reorganization plan. See Chapter 11.

ex-coupon. Without the (next or due to be paid) coupon. That is, transactions in a coupon paying security where the buyer does not receive the next due payment (cf. cum). In such cases where the payment date has elapsed the consideration includes a negative interest element.

Sometimes also referred to as *ex-interest*. See **ex-dividend**.

excutory. A contract where performance has not been fully made by the parties bound by the contract.

ex-date. The date at which a security goes ex-dividend or **ex-coupon**. The price will normally fall reflecting the loss of the **dividend** or **coupon** payment.

ex-dividend. Without the (next or due to be paid) **dividend**. A **stock** that is priced on the understanding that it is to be sold without the recently declared dividend. The loss of such a right should be reflected in the price of the security (cf. **common stock; ordinary share; preferred stock**).

ex-dividend date. The date at which a security goes **ex-dividend**.

execute. The process of carrying out a **transaction** or making a trade. *Good execution* is a requirement by intermediaries to carry out a transaction within a reasonable period and price (cf. **fail; overtrade**).

execution. The completion of a transaction (cf. **comparison ticket; confirmation; contract note**).

execution by outcry. See **open outcry**.

execution cost. The direct costs attributable to a transaction. This ignores hidden costs, such as **market impact**. A more comprehensive measure of the cost of dealing are **transaction costs**.

execution-only broker (UK). Securities firm or broker-dealer which only undertakes transactions for clients and does not offer any ancillary services, such as investment advice (cf. **advisory broker**). See also **authorized financial adviser**.

execution risk. The risk that a transaction cannot be carried out at, or around, current market prices on terms acceptable to the party (cf. **forced sale; rollover; unwinding risk**).

exempt securities (USA). Securities exempt from the **registration** requirements of the **Securities Exchange Act of 1934**. The principal categories are: the federal government, **agencies, municipal, commercial paper**, and **private placements** (cf. **Rule 144a**). The rules governing the granting of exempt status are complex. See also **blue sky laws**.

exempt unit trust (UK). Special kind of **unit trust** whose **units** are only available to non-taxpaying institutions. Such trusts are exempt from tax.

exercise. To carry out a transaction, usually applied to the **options market**. For example, to exercise a **call option** involves the holder buying securities from the **option writer** at the **strike price** (cf. **assign; assignment**).

exercise by exception. See **automatic exercise**.

exercise content. Market content of an **equity warrant** adjusted for the **exercise premium**.

exercise cycle. See **expiry cycle**.

exercise date. (i) The date at which an **option** is exercised. (ii) The date at which an option may be exercised. For **American-style** options, this is at any point up to **expiry**; for **European-style** this is at expiry; for **Atlantic-style** or **Bermudan-style** options, there will be specific dates at which exercise is possible prior to expiry.

exercise limit. A feature of **exchange-traded** option markets which sets an overall limit on the number of **options** that can be **exercised** within a given period by one party.

exercise notice. The notification given by option holders of **exchange-traded** options requesting the **delivery** of the **underlying**. The **clearinghouse** will then notify at random one of the **writers** of that **class** of options informing them of the fact and requiring them to make the underlying available at **settlement**.

exercise premium. The **premium**, expressed as a percentage over the current market price, at which an **equity warrant** gives the holder the right to buy the **underlying shares**. (cf. **exercise content; market content**).

exercise price (Derivatives; Options). The price at which an **option** holder may buy or sell the **underlying** as defined in the terms of the **option contract**. As such it is the price at which the **call** holder may buy the underlying, or the **put** holder may sell the underlying. Sometimes the exercise price is called the *strike price* or *striking price*. For an interest rate option, this is called the *exercise rate* or *strike rate*.

exercise value. See **intrinsic value**.

exercising an option. See **exercise**.

ex gratia (Latin; as an act of grace). Payment made by one party to another without any legal liability. Sometimes used to settle a contractual dispute without recourse to the law (cf. **arbitration**).

ex growth (Equities). A type of **common stock** which is generally seen to have ceased to show

above-average growth in **earnings, dividends,** or profits relative to the market or its market sector. See **dividend discount model**.

exhaust price. The price at which a **position** acquired on **margin** is to be **closed out** if additional margin is not provided or is unavailable.

Eximbank. See export-import bank.

ex interest. See ex-coupon.

exit. (i) The method of **closing out** a **position** created by a transaction. (ii) In **venture capital,** the way the financier expects to realize his gain. Sometimes called the *exit route*.

exit bond. A type of **bond** found in **less developed country** (LDC) debt reschedulings which provides a means for lenders to reduce the amounts of their loans to troubled countries. Such issues involve (i) lenders tendering their loans to be retired at a **discount** and receiving (ii) a **variable rate note** at a lower **spread** to the **reference rate** which is **collateralized** through a trust as to **principal** repayment through the purchase, by the obligor, of a **zero-coupon bond** from a highly rated issuer, such as the US government or the **World Bank**. The conversion of existing debt has a twofold benefit to the LDC country: it reduces the amount of debt service required since the existing debt is retired at a **discount** and the new debt has a lower cost since it has been **credit enhanced** through the zero coupon bond. Generally, such bonds are also made eligible for **debt conversion** schemes, to enhance the attractions to the tendering banks. See **Mex-Ex issue**.

exit charge (UK). A fee paid when selling **units** in a **unit trust** (cf. **initial charge; periodic charge**).

exit consent solicitation (Bonds; USA). A method used in **exchange offers** to ensure **bondholders** agree to participate in the restructuring of the **liability** by requesting accepting parties to agree to modify those **covenants** that are *non-core* and therefore can be changed by virtue of a simple **majority** vote (cf. **Trust Indenture Act of 1939**).

ex-legal (Bonds; USA). A description of a **municipal bond** which lacks a legal opinion given by a bond law firm. It is a requirement that buyers are notified of this omission.

ex-new. Security without the right to take up any new entitlements. The opposite would be *cum new*. When the same security is traded both cum and ex, the difference in price reflects the (expected) value of the new entitlement (cf. **bonus issue; rights issue; scrip issue**).

exotic currencies. Any **currency** outside the major traded currencies (cf. **exchange controls**).

exotic option or **exotic(s).** Types of options which have specific features, such as special **strike price** formulae, unconventional **underlyings,** payoffs, or **expiry** conditions. They are used in the situations, shown in the Table for investment purposes.

Applicable exotic option type	Investment activity
Outperformance	Security selection
Path-dependent	Market timing
Rainbow option	Asset allocation
Currency-protected; Quantity adjusting option (QUANTO)	Currency hedging
Barrier option	Portfolio insurance
Binary or Digital option	Asset selection

See Asian option; average rate option; barrier option; Bermuda option; binary option; compound option; contingent premium option; deferred strike price option; digital option; dual currency option; lookback option; options.

expectations hypothesis or **expectations theory of the term structure of interest rates.** A theory that seeks to explain the term structure of interest rates or **yield curve** whereby the current **forward rate** is the expected future interest rate for the relevant period (cf. **liquidity preference; preferred habitat**). Sometimes known as the *pure expectations hypothesis* to distinguish it from other theories of the term structure.

expectations theory of forward foreign exchange rates. A theory that says that the expected **spot foreign exchange rate** at a future point in time is the same as the current **forward foreign exchange rate** for the same **maturity** (cf. **purchasing power parity theory; interest rate parity theory**).

expected. (i) The most likely outcome in a stochastic process (cf. **average; mean; mode**). (ii) The result that is anticipated from a **position** (cf. **downside; upside**). (iii) A valuation process based on probabilities (cf. **expected value**).

expected credit loss. A calculation of the long-term average losses to be anticipated from **defaults** by a particular **class** of **counterparty** to a given transaction (cf. **credit risk**). A lender should include this as well as operating costs and profit in its calculations of the required **margin** or **spread**. Also known as *actuarial loss*.

expected inflation. The amount of future inflation that is discounted in the **term structure of interest rates**. In the UK, and other countries offering **index-linked** securities, it can be estimated by subtracting the **yield** on index-linked government bonds from conventional government bonds (**gilt-edged**).

expected maturity. The date or time in which an **asset-backed security** is expected to be repaid based on the expected repayment of principal (cf. **amortization**).

expected monetary value. See **decision tree**; **expected value**.

expected return. The probability-weighted average of the different possible outcomes. Thus if the value of a security with a current value of 100 has a 0.5 chance of being either 120 or 85 in the next period, the expected return will be:

$$\left[\frac{(0.5 \times 120) + (0.5 \times 85)}{100} - 1 \right] \times 100 = 2.5\%$$

See also **binomial distribution**; **Capital Asset Pricing Model**; **geometric Brownian motion**; **normal distribution**; **volatility**.

expected value. Technically a measure of the value of an uncertain set of outcomes, weighed by the probability of their occurring:

$$E(V) = \sum_{i=1}^{n} p_i v_i$$

where p_i is the probability or likelihood of the ith outcome and v_i is the value and

$$\sum_{i=1}^{n} p_i = 1.0$$

It is used in a more colloquial sense for the expected gain or profit from an investment strategy or transaction where the outcome is not known for certain. See also **normal distribution**.

expected volatility. The subjective estimate of **volatility** that is used to decide a course of action in **risk management** decisions. For instance, options traders will typically sell volatility if the market is overpricing it, and buy volatility if it is underpriced, depending on their view as to what the expected volatility will be over the life of the transaction. See **term structure of volatility**; **volatility cone**; **volatility curve**; **volatility skew**; **volatility smile**; **volatility term cone**; **volatility trading**.

expense ratio (USA). Term used for the recurring annual charge on a **mutual fund**.

experience losses. Losses arising from a divergence between the expected performance and the actual outcome (cf. **analysis of variance**). See **immunization**; **realized return**; **tracking error**.

expert systems. Computerized decision-making system based on the culled knowledge of experts or professionals aimed at replicating human knowledge and behaviour in a given situation. See also **neutral networks**.

expiration cycle or **expiry cycle.** The pattern of expiry dates for **exchange-traded futures** and **options**. In order to facilitate trading, futures and options can expire only on given dates. Most options are traded on a quarterly cycle, so that there are normally three cycles to the year:

1	2	3
January	February	March
April	May	June
July	August	September
October	November	December

Normally only the three nearest to **expiry** contracts are active in any cycle (cf. **nearby**; **position**). If the current time was the end of June, then the July, August, and September contracts would be active. That said, some markets have an extended expiry cycle out to two to three years, or even more.

expiration price. The **outstrike** price in a **barrier option** (cf. **trigger**).

expire. To reach the **expiry date** and time (cf. **wasting asset**). See **mature**; **time value of an option**.

expiry, expiry date, or **expiration date.** (i) The date upon which an **option** or **warrant** contract terminates and thereafter becomes useless. If it is out of the money it is said to *expire worthless* (cf. **automatic exercise**; **cabinet trade**; **exercise**; **wasting asset**). (ii) The last trading day (and time) for a futures contract (cf. **exchange delivery settlement price**). See **delivery**.

expiry cycle. See **expiration cycle**.

expiry day. The last, if **American-style**, or only, if European-style, day on which an **option** can be exercised.

expiry time. The time of day when an **option** ceases on its **expiry date**. Because of the time-dependent nature of many markets, options specify the exact time of day up to when **exercise** can still take place. This is particularly important in markets where there is no official closing, such as **foreign exchange**, and where **intraday** price movements can have a significant impact on value.

ex-pit transaction. See against actuals; exchange of futures for physicals.

exploded tree. See binomial option pricing model (cf. binomial distribution; binomial tree).

exploding option or **explosive option.** Type of option where exercise is automatic if the price or rate reaches the strike (cf. barrier option; knockout option; trigger). Also called a *one-touch option*. See capped index option.

exploratory drilling program (USA). A high-risk, limited partnership set up to invest in unproven oil or gas ventures, better known as *wildcatting*. A *controlled wildcat* is used for drilling around areas of known oil reserves, while a *deep test* involves drilling below known oil reserves.

explosive option. See exploding option.

exponential smoothing. Forecasting technique similar to a moving average or a momentum model which gives greater weight to recent developments. See econometrics.

Export Development Corporation (EDC) (Canada). Canadian government agency charged with providing finance and insurance cover for exports. The agency is an active borrower on the international capital markets (cf. euromarkets).

Export Finance and Insurance Corporation (EFIC) (Australia). Australian government agency which provides finance and insures exports.

Export-Import Bank (Eximbank) (USA). A government agency, set up in 1934, which finances imports and exports, provides export insurance cover, and provides credits to foreign buyers of US products. Overall limits are set by Congress and funds are mostly provided by the US Treasury.

Export-Import Bank of Japan (Japan). Government bank charged with facilitating exports but which also administers the official aid programme to developing countries. The bank raises funds in both the domestic and the international markets.

export letter of credit (export LOC). See documentary credit; letter of credit.

export tender risk avoidance (EXTRA) (UK). The name given to an over-the-counter compound option product developed by Hambros Bank plc. See shared currency option under tender.

ex post. After the event (cf. ex ante). Hence, for example, *ex post return*, the actual return achieved on an investment. This can be quite different from the expected return before the investment was made.

ex post hypothesizing. See econometrics.

exposure. (i) The mismatch between assets and liabilities by currency, maturity, and so forth (cf. value at risk). Exposure is generally calculated as the risk times the amount. (ii) It is also used for the amount of principal at risk to an obligor (cf. credit risk).

exposure management. The process of actively controlling exposures which are at risk. See risk management.

expropriation. To take ownership of assets usually either without payment or for less than their market value against the wishes of the owners.

ex-redemption. When bonds have a sinking fund or drawings, this term describes those bonds traded between the drawing date and the redemption date, which will not be redeemed on the next drawing date.

ex-rights. Shares which are trading without the rights attached. It is often the case that in a rights issue the same common stock will be traded both cum rights and ex rights. In the latter case, the right to subscribe for more shares has been stripped and traded separately (cf. nil paid; preemption rights).

ex-rights date. The date that shares which are eligible for rights go ex-rights.

ex-scrip. Without the entitlement to the new free shares, or scrip issue, being attached. See also ex-date.

ex-stock dividends. Stocks which are trading without the declared stock dividend attached. See also ex-date.

Extel Statistical Services (UK). A UK company that produces information on companies whose shares are traded on the London market as well as major international issuers. The information available details such things as how and when capitalized, recent profit performance, share price history, and any recent acquisitions and disposals. The main two documents produced are the *Extel Card* and the *Extel Book of Prospectuses* (cf. Datastream; McCarthy cards).

extendable bond or **extendible bond** or **note.** A bond or note issue where both the issuer and the holder have one, usually more, simultaneous put and call provisions at the same price (normally **par**) and sometimes accompanied by a provision by the issuer to reset the **coupon** in line with current market conditions. If so, the holder still has the right to **tender** his bonds if he does not like the rate that has been set. In addition, it is often accompanied by a **reoffering facility** to re-market any bonds so offered. See **retractable bond**.

extendable swap. An interest rate swap or cross-currency swap where one of the counter-parties has the right to extend the **maturity** of the swap on the same terms for a predetermined period. It is equivalent to having a straight swap for the initial period and buying a **swaption** for the remaining period, except that the **swaption premium** is built into the cost of the swap (cf. **callable swap**). Also known as an *extension swap*.

extended-term option. A long-dated option with an original **time to expiry** in excess of one year (cf. **warrant**). See **long-term equity anticipation securities**.

extendible. Any issue which features **provisions** to extend the **maturity** of the issue, either by giving the holder the right to **rollover** his investment on agreed terms, such as with the **borrower's option–lender's option** or **lender's option–borrower's option** or other type of **extendable bond**. The effect of the feature is equal to that of a **retractable bond** (cf. **callable**).

extendible swap. An interest rate swap giving one of the **counterparties** the right to extend the **maturity** for a preset period beyond that in the original agreement (cf. **swaption**). See **callable swap**.

extension. (i) An agreement by two parties to lengthen the **tenor** of a maturing transaction. (ii) With **asset-backed securities**, the tendency for repayments from the **underlying** to take place more slowly than anticipated (cf. **prepayment model**).

extension risk. This is the opposite **risk** to **prepayment risk** in an **asset-backed security** where the repayments of **principal** take place later than originally anticipated. See **collateralized mortgage obligation**; **interest only**; **mortgage-backed security**; **prepayment model**; **principal only**.

extension swap. (i) A debt **swap** transaction that lengthens the **maturity** of a position. For instance, selling a five-year **bond** and buying a seven-year bond. (ii) **Forward start swap** designed to extend the **maturity** of an existing swap. If the terms of such a swap are designed to match the existing swap, it is likely that the extension will be an off-

market swap. It is essentially a forward start swap matched to the payments of the existing swap. (iii) A **rollover** of a **forward foreign exchange** position or **swap** (cf. **historical rate rollover**).

external account (Banking). An account held in a country by a foreign person or organization. See also **euromarkets**; **offshore**.

extinguishable option. See barrier options (cf. knock-out; trigger)

extinguishing call or **put.** See barrier options (cf. **knock-out**; **trigger**).

extra dividend. A special one-off **dividend** that may or may not be repeated. Usually the result of some extraordinary cash receipt by the company (cf. **regular dividend**). It is not normally included when computing **ratios**.

extraordinary charge or **extraordinary item.** A one-off income or expense in a **financial statement** that is outside the normal business activity of the reporting entity and is unlikely to be repeated. Although **Generally Accepted Accounting Principles** defines what constitutes an extraordinary item, in practice firms have some discretion over reporting such one-offs. The exact treatment of the item may significantly affect the reported profit (or loss) for the **financial year**. Most analysts would exclude any gains (losses) when evaluating a business. Under the UK's **Financial Reporting Standard 3**, extraordinary items are now subject to severe restrictions.

extraordinary general meeting (EGM). A special meeting of **shareholders** called to approve a special event that requires their approval. While companies are required to hold a shareholders' meeting once a year (the annual general meeting (AGM)), extraordinary general meetings are called by the company's **directors** when immediate approval is required which cannot be deferred to the next AGM. For example, a firm will call an EGM if it wants to make an acquisition or a significant disposal since the decision is of a timely nature.

extreme option. Type of option where the payoff is related to the performance of the **underlying** over the option period (cf. **exotic options**). These include **lookback options**, **lookforward options**, **barrier options**, and **volatility** options. Also called a *path-dependent option*.

ex-warrants. An issue of securities that had **warrants** attached but where subsequently they have been separated. Separating the two (or more) parts of such types of securities is known as *stripping*.

F

face value. The value indicated on a security certificate. See par value; principal value.

facility. (i) (Banking) Generally, a funding arrangement between a borrower and a bank, such as a **loan facility**. (ii) In the international markets often used as a short-hand term for the **backstop** or **underwritten facility**, such as a **note issuance facility, multi-option financing facility**, or **short-term note issuance facility** (SNIF), between an issuer of short-term securities, such as **euronotes** or **certificates of deposit**, and a group of **underwriting** banks which commit to buy such securities at an agreed rate throughout the life of the facility, irrespective of whether notes are issued.

facility fee. The fee paid to an intermediary for extending a **facility**. This is normally paid for a committed or **underwritten facility** (cf. **commitment fee; underwriting fee**).

factor. (i) Selling goods to make a profit (cf. **aval; broker; counter-trade; dealer; trader**). (ii) Specialist trade **receivables** finance house that engages in **factoring**. (iii) A **macro-economic** variable that determines **asset prices** (cf. **factor beta**). See **arbitrage pricing theory**.

factor analysis. Statistical technique used to determine common components or weightings to a multivariate set of data. For instance, time-series data on a number of different types of equity returns might be factored to extract components such as a general market effect, industry effect, and so on. The major problem with the technique is being able to interpret the factors in a meaningful way. The factors themselves can then be used to construct indices for further analysis. See also **arbitrage pricing theory**.

factor beta (factor β). The sensitivity of a firm to a particular economic variable as proposed in the **arbitrage pricing theory** model (cf. **factor model**). See also **risk profile; systematic risk; stock specific risk**.

factor cost. The price of a factor of production, such as land, labour, **capital**, and enterprise.

factoring. Trade creditor financing. Effectively it is a system of raising funding using trade debts (current assets) as security to improve cash flow.

The services offered by banks and other specialist institutions, known as *factors*, include: *sales ledger factoring*, where the factor buys all the firm's invoiced debts and becomes wholly responsible for credit control and collecting debts (cf. **accounts receivable financing; invoice discounting**). *lending*, using future debt settlement as security; and *credit insurance*, whereupon payment of a premium the factor will provide indemnity against up to, for instance, 75% of bad debts by value.

Factoring can be provided on a **recourse basis**, where the **credit risk** remains with the firm; or a **non-recourse** basis, where the factor assumes the risk. In the former case it is a means of raising finance, in the latter also a way of transferring risk.

factor model. A model of securities returns which decomposes the returns into different components. See **arbitrage pricing theory**.

factor sensitivity. See factor beta; sensitivity.

facultative reinsurance. The practice of **reinsurance** of individual risks when the original insurer wishes to reduce the amount of his **exposure**. In the case of facultative insurance, the insurer negotiates the sale of all or part of the **risk** with other parties on a case-by-case basis. In some situations, insurers set up an agreement such that reinsurance of part of any new risk is automatic; a practice known as *treaty reinsurance*.

fail or **failed.** A transaction which does not clear or effect **settlement** is said to fail (cf. **out-trade**). *Fail to deliver* (seller) and *fail to receive* (buyer) are the conditions of the two parties respectively (cf. **aged fail; delivery against payment; free delivery**).

failure. See bankruptcy; crash; default; hammered; insolvency.

fair game. Taken from game theory, it is any situation where there are no winners or losers. When there may be winners, it is known as a *positive sum game*; when only losers can result, a *negative sum game*.

fair-market value or **fair value.** (i) The transaction price for assets or securities in which no ready market exists. The assumption is that both parties know the value of what is bought and sold (cf.

arm's length transaction; open-market value). (ii) The value of a derivative instrument derived from an analytical model.

fair rate of return (USA). The return on capital a regulated utility is allowed to make. This is based on its need to provide services to its customers, maintain its capital stock, and pay interest and dividends.

fair value. A (market) price that is impartial to both buyer aand seller. Such a price is often determined by reference to a model.

fair value of a future. The value of a futures contract implied by the cost of carry and other costs associated with holding or deferring purchase of the underlying. It can be considered the equivalent of holding the underlying for delivery into the contract from selling the future or investing the cash equivalent and purchasing the contract. The return is equal to the time value of money plus holding costs. Any deviation in a futures contract away from its fair value or *carry basis* opens up an arbitrage opportunity since market participants can either hold the underlying and sell the future, or vice versa, and end up making a profit on the transaction without any significant risk (cf. cash and carry). In practice, there is an arbitrage channel which reflects the bid-offer spread in the markets and other uncertainties from such a strategy. The basic model for the fair value is:

Fair value of future = Current value of underlying

$$\times (1 + \text{cost of carry})$$

The cost of carry will vary depending on the type of underlying, whether storage costs have to be included, whether income is earned on the underlying, and, for commodities, the convenience yield. The cost of carry model is only applicable in a contango or premium market (cf. backwardation; discount). See expectations hypothesis.

fair value of an option. The value of an option calculated using an option pricing model. The fair value is the price of the option at which the holder and the writer should both expect to break even on the transaction. It is a calculation of the price at which an option should theoretically trade, not the price at which transactions may actually take place, although many people assume the two are synonymous.

fairway note. See range floating rate note.

fairway swap. See accrual swap.

fair-weather trading. When a market or certain traders are only prepared to make two-way prices

when market conditions are favourable. It is a normal condition attached to becoming a market-maker that they maintain the pricing mechanism under all market conditions. See circuit breakers.

fall-back. A clause within a facility or loan agreement providing for an alternative method of determining the rate of interest in the event of disruption or non-availability of the reference rate.

fallen angel. A borrower or institution whose credit worthiness has significantly declined (cf. rising star). Sometimes used to imply a fall below investment grade (cf. junk bond). See credit rating.

false dawn. When an expected upward movement in security prices, as predicted by chart analysis, does not take place.

false market. A concern of regulators that, due to insufficient information or disclosure, transactions are taking place in the market at uninformed prices (cf. asymmetric information). See also efficient markets hypothesis.

Fannie Mae (USA). See Federal National Mortgage Association.

Far East Stock Exchange (Hong Kong). Small stock exchange based in Hong Kong. See also Hong Kong Stock Exchange.

Farmer Macs (Bonds; USA). Mortgage-backed securities that are pools of agricultural and rural housing loans and largely guaranteed by the Federal Agricultural Mortgage Corporation.

farther out or **farther in.** The relative expiry dates of different options compared to the present or each other. Sometimes expiry dates are referred to as *positions*.

Fast Automated Screen Trading (FAST) (UK). Electronic trading system used on the London Futures and Options Exchange.

fast market. Hectic market conditions characterized by large trading volumes and considerable volatility in prices (cf. sideways moving market). In such cases, price information distribution may not be up to date (cf. disregard tape).

fate (Banking). The outcome of a financial transaction. A correspondent will enquire as to the fate of a money transfer, that is, whether it has gone through or not (cf. aged fail; clearing; dishonour; fail; settlement).

fathers and sons. An issue comprising one or more **tranches**, the original issue being termed the 'the father' and the tranches, 'the sons'. Such issues normally become **fungible** (cf. **serial security**).

fat tails. See leptokurtosis; tail.

federal agencies, federal agency security, or **federal credit agencies** (USA). Agencies or corporations of the federal government of the USA set up to supply credit to various types of institution or individuals. They are major borrowers in the **bond** and money markets and as a group are known as agencies or *agency securities*. The principal agency issuers that have the **full faith and credit** of the US government, or are *de facto* backed by the federal government, are:

Export-Import Bank (Eximbank)
Farmers Home Administration (FmHA)
Federal Farm Credit Bank (FFCB)
Federal Financing Bank
Federal Housing Administration
Federal Home Loan Bank (FHLB)
Federal Home Loan Mortgage Corporation (FHLMC; Freddie Mac), subsidiary of the Federal Home Loan Bank
Federal National Mortgage Association (FNMA; Fannie Mae)
Government National Mortgage Association (GNMA; Ginnie Mae)
Maritime Administration
Private Export Funding Corporation (PEFCO)
Resolution Funding Corporation (REFCO)
Tennessee Valley Authority (TVA)
Washington Metropolitan Area Transit Authority (WMATA).

These agencies issue: (1) **notes**, that is, short-term **promissory notes** with maturities between 7 and 270 days, at a **discount**; these are repaid at **maturity**, similar to **commercial paper**; (2) bonds, with terms between one and forty years; with a fixed **coupon** normally, paid semi-annually, although a number of **zero-coupon bond** issues have been made, and **straight bonds** have been **stripped**; (3) **debentures**, which are secured on specific assets; terms and maturities are similar to bond issues; (4) mortgage participation and **pass-through certificates**, which represent an undivided interest in a **pool** of mortgages or loans held by the issuer. Such issues normally **amortize** as principal is repaid (cf. **mortgage-backed securities; collateralized mortgage obligations; pay-through bond**).

Federal Agricultural Mortgage Corporation (USA). A federal government-sponsored organization set up in 1987 to **securitize** agricultural mortgages (cf. **Farmer Macs**).

Federal Deposit Insurance Corporation (FDIC) (USA). The federal agency established in 1933 which insures deposits of up to (currently) US$100,000 at member banks as well as providing loans and rescue assistance to troubled institutions (cf. **moral hazard; too big to fail**). This insurance is provided by a levy on deposits at institutions. It operates the Bank Insurance Fund. The amount of money held in the fund which the FDIC has to cover claims on insured deposits is known as the *coverage ratio*. This became negative in the early 1990s and fund had to be recapitalized by a loan from the US Treasury as well as a higher insurance charge on deposits. The FDIC is also responsible for supervising those member banks of the FDIC which are not members of the **Federal Reserve System**. See also **Comptroller of the Currency**.

Federal Farm Credit Banks Discount Notes (Farm credits) (Money markets; USA). Short-term **promissory notes** issued by the Federal Farm Credit Bank (cf. **commercial paper; consolidated bonds**).

Federal Farm Credit System. The parent organization to the *Federal Farm Credit Bank*, one of the **federal agencies**, which issues **money market instruments** and *Federal Farm Credit System Consolidated Systemwide Bonds*.

Federal Financing Bank (USA). A US government institution set up in 1973 which lends funds borrowed from the US Treasury to a wide range of federal credit agencies.

federal funds or **fed funds** or just **funds (FF)** (USA). (i) Usually used to describe non-interest-bearing deposits held by member banks at the **Federal Reserve** and actively traded between member banks. Hence **fed funds rate**, which is the interest rate at which these funds are traded, such as when one bank borrows from another. Three types of transactions take place in the market: (*a*) purchase and sale for overnight repayment on an interbank basis where the lender takes the **Credit Risk** of the borrower; (*b*) **collateralized** loans; and (*c*) **repurchase agreements** against a tradable security, such as a **treasury bill, note**, or **bond**. (ii) It can also be used to denote funds that are available immediately in the **clearing** sense, that is cash. See **clearing house funds; same-day funds; money at call; term fed funds; wholesale money**.

federal or **fed funds rate.** The rate of interest banks charge to each other for borrowing or lending **fed funds**. The key rate that the Fed seeks to influence through **open-market operations**. The much-publicized rate refers to the overnight rate. However there is a term market in fed funds called **term fed funds** or *term funds*. See **Federal Open Market Committee**.

federal government bonds (Canada). Bonds issued by the Canadian federal government to raise funds. There are two different types: *savings bonds*, which are targeted at individuals, and marketable bonds, which are actively traded.

Federal Home Loan Bank System (FHLB) (USA). A federal institution that regulates **savings and loan associations**, as the **Federal Reserve** regulates member commercial banks. There is also a system of twelve special banks used for extending secured credit within the system. The governing arm is the Federal Housing Finance Board.

Federal Home Loan Mortgage Corporation (FHLMC; Freddie Mac) (USA). A US corporate body set up in July 1970 to try and increase the supply of housing mortgage finance. It raises its funds by issuing securities backed by pools of conventional mortgages, either **participation certificates** or guaranteed mortgage certificates.

Federal Housing Administration (FHA) (USA). A US federal agency involved in the secondary mortgage market, which guarantees and insures mortgage loans. **Government National Mortgage Association** (GNMA) pools can only comprise loans, guaranteed and insured by the FHA, Veterans' Administration (VA), or Farmers Home Administration. Such loans are also purchased by the **Federal National Mortgage Association** (FNMA). As due on sale clauses are not allowed in FHA/VA loans GNMA **pass-throughs** tend to repay more slowly than FNMA or **Federal Home Loan Mortgage Corporation** pass-throughs.

Federal Intermediate Credit Bank (USA). One of the twelve banks within the **Federal Farm Credit System**.

Federal Land Bank (USA). One of the twelve banks that form the **Federal Farm Credit System**.

federally sponsored agency (USA). See federal agency.

Federal National Mortgage Association (FNMA; Fannie Mae) (USA). A corporation sponsored by the federal government but wholly owned by private shareholders. It buys and sells residential mortgages insured or guaranteed by the **Federal Housing Administration** and the Veterans' Administration, together with conventional mortgages. The funds are provided by the sale of corporate obligations to private investors.

Federal Open Market Committee (FOMC) (USA). The key policy-making committee of the Board of Governors of the **Federal Reserve System**. It is at such meetings that decisions about the conduct of **monetary policy** and the level of interest rates are made.

Federal Reserve, Federal Reserve System or the **Fed** (USA). The central banking system of the USA (cf. **central bank**). It was established by the Federal Reserve Act of 1913 in order to create a decentralized Federal Reserve System. The Banking Act of 1935 reorganized the original system into the structure that exists today. This has twelve regional Federal Reserve Banks, but nearly all the policy-making powers rest with the main Board of Governors in Washington and especially the **Federal Open Market Committee**. This Board has seven members appointed by the President with the approval of the Senate for a term of fourteen years, except for the chairman and vice-chairman whose appointment is for four years only. The Board of Governors is directly responsible to Congress and must make regular reports. In addition, under the Humphrey–Hawkins Act of 1987 the chairman is required to make an annual statement (in February) on monetary policy supplemented by additional testimony in July on any revisions to the original statement.

All depository institutions must hold reserves in the form of interest-free deposits at the **Federal Reserve Banks** or vault cash (cf. **eligible**). These reserve banks can be regarded as bankers' banks and do not transact business outside the banking sector. The Fed also has authority over the activities of the US offices of overseas banks. It shares regulation of the banking system with the **Comptroller of the Currency**, the **Federal Deposit Insurance Corporation** (FDIC), and, for state-chartered banks, state regulators. Note, however, that not all of the regulators will be involved in a given situation.

'Watching the Fed is very easy if one can read. There are sunshine laws available. All one has to read how they go about what they do—and get some experience in watching their little points of finesse such as how they handle customer repo.' (Quoted in Marcia Stigum, 'The Money Market'.

I. FEDERAL RESERVE POLICY

The Fed's long-run policy objectives have remained remarkably constant over time: price stability, high employment, and a stable dollar. The Fed has on occasion departed from its long-run objectives for very valid reasons connected with economic or financial shocks to the system (e.g. the Fed's reaction to the October 1987 crash). However, the Fed has sometimes balked at pursuing one of these objectives (namely translating price stability into zero inflation) at the expense of all others. The Fed's long-term objectives now come under regular scrutiny through the Humphrey–Hawkins testimony, which the Fed Chairman is required to deliver twice a year to Congress and in which the FOMC's policy is laid out.

1(a) How the Federal Reserve determines policy and operating strategy

The Federal Reserve policy-making body is the Federal Reserve Open Market Committee (FOMC) and consists of the permanent members of the Federal Reserve Board of Governors and the Presidents of the twelve regional Federal Reserve District Banks (together making up the Federal Reserve System). Voting, however, is restricted to twelve members: the seven members of the Board of Governors and five of the Presidents. One of the five district name Presidents—the President of the New York Fed—is a permanent voting member of the FOMC. The other four district bank Presidents serve on a scheduled rotation for one-year periods which is now synchronous with the calendar year.

FOMC meetings are held on a regular, pre-announced basis, about eight times throughout the year. All the FOMC members attend meetings and participate in the policy discussions, but only voting members actually vote on the final policy decision. Policy is set for the period between meetings, although *ad hoc* telephone conferences have countenanced a shift in policy emphasis, or sanctioned changes in the Fed funds rate between meetings.

At the meetings, the FOMC uses a broad selection of data describing the current economic and financial condition as part of its decision-making process, including the Fed's own 'Beige Book' (often called 'Tan Book') survey of the US economy. This is prepared by one of the regional Fed banks and is published in advance of the meetings. Federal Reserve Board staffers will also present economic projections, including such models as the P* (P-star) money supply model. After debating the data, the FOMC determines its policy actions in a broad outline form. This forms a 'Directive' to the Manager of the System Open Market Account, known as the 'desk' (which is located at the Federal Reserve Bank of New York). This Directive instructs the desk to carry out its day-to-day open-market operations in a manner consistent with the attainment of the FOMC's broad policy objectives. The Directive will feature some growth rate for reserves, the monetary aggregates (M1, M2, and M3), and a target range for the federal funds rate ('fed funds' or just 'funds') Note that the targets are correlated; an increase in reserves and money supply will decrease the funds rate, and vice versa. The Fed targets a range of variables to allow for changes in their relationship over time. For instance, a rise in interest rates may shift money from the M1 series, which is mostly cash, into M2 and M3, which include interest bearing deposits. In recent years, the Fed has been more concerned to target the latter than the growth in money supply; but see below.

Many commentators have discussed Federal Reserve policy in terms of either interest rates (via a funds target) or the money supply. In the 1980s the Fed has been concerned to control money supply, but it is only under the chairmanship of Paul Volker that this target has been pursued to the exclusion of managing interest rates. More recent behaviour, and certainly that under Chairman Alan Greenspan, has seen a shift to a wider combination of objectives. In fact, under Alan Greenspan the FOMC has, if anything, adopted a more eclectic approach to policy-making and in particular appears unwilling to target any particular economic or financial variable to the exclusion of all others. Present Fed policy appears to target both money supply and interest rate objectives although the latter appears far more important.

1(b) Why the Fed seeks to control money supply

The desirability of controlling the growth in the money supply has strong foundations in economic theory. Advocates of such control have been labelled monetarists in that they concentrate on the relationship between money, its velocity of circulation, and quantities of goods and services and their prices. This is the basic quantity theory of money model:

$$M \times V = P \times T$$

Research based on long-term price/money growth data (see Friedman and Schwartz's monetary history of the USA) shows a consistent pattern that an over-rapid expansion of the money supply (above the long-run growth potential of the economy) leads to a rapid increase in prices. Monetarists make several assumptions in their analysis of the cause of inflation, including a long-run stability of the public's demand to hold money. This translates into a stable pattern for the velocity of money. If the velocity of circulation is not stable or reasonably predictable over long periods, then a policy of controlling money growth would make little sense.

Economists have also disagreed whether the growth in money should be controlled via interest rates or through the physical stock of money (in the Fed's case via bank reserves). The Fed has tried both. In 1979, in response to the high inflation in the US economy, the Fed shifted the emphasis of its control procedures towards a more direct control of bank reserves. Hitherto it had relied more on interest rates as the instrument to control money demand and hence inflation. Following Paul Volker's chairmanship of the Fed, the current FOMC policy-making is, as mentioned above, much less monetarist in outlook, although individual members of the FOMC could still be labelled monetarist.

The principle behind the control of money stock via bank reserves is simple. Banks must hold some level of reserves to support their checking deposits (the key component of money supply). By limiting the growth in reserves, the Fed can limit the growth in deposits and therefore of money.

How does the Fed determine how much growth in reserves to allow? In principle, the problem is simple. The Fed first determines what seasonally adjusted money growth would be necessary to achieve the desired economic goals for inflation, real growth (nominal growth less inflation), and employment. The Fed may also be concerned with the likely level of interest rates required to achieve this, as well as the level of the dollar in the currency markets. After arriving at a target for monetary growth, the Fed translates this into a target for growth in deposits (on a seasonally adjusted basis). The Fed then takes into account the seasonal influences affecting deposit growth in setting its operational target. This will then set a growth path for bank reserves over the target period.

In practice, the Fed's job involves one more step: the Fed must decide how to provide this growth path for total reserves. The Fed can provide reserves either through its open market operations or through the discount window. Recently banks have shown a marked reluctance to borrow from the discount window, so in practice, manipulation of reserves has to be via open-market operations.

1(c) Why the Fed seeks to control interest rates

Currently, as a prime policy tool, the Greenspan Fed has virtually abandoned a money supply target. The Fed remains concerned about the growth (or its recent lack) in money supply (M1, M2, and M3) in reaching its decisions but is now far more concerned to control the overall level of interest rates.

In order to do this, the Fed arrives at a level of reserves required in the system to achieve a given interest rate target. However, unlike the money supply method discussed above, other factors will impinge on the availability of reserves. By seeking to control interest rates, the Fed is attempting to control the demand for money within the economy (and ultimately the level of economic activity and inflation). Unless the demand function for money shifts radically, borrowing activity should rise or fall according to the level of interest rates. By raising rates the Fed hopes to reduce the demand for money and therefore curtail economic activity; and vice versa when it wants to expand activity (e.g. from May 1989 onwards the Fed eased rates).

1(d) Current Fed policy as a synthesis of money supply targets and control of interest rates

There is a good deal of evidence (the minutes of the FOMC meetings which are made public after a 4–6-week delay; public pronouncements by FOMC members; published Federal Reserve research; testimony by Alan Greenspan and other

Fed officials to Congress; and so forth) that points to current FOMC policy-making using a synthesis of both the money supply and interest rate approaches. As such the FOMC appears to adopt a pragmatic approach in analysing the financial condition and the state of the economy when reaching its policy decisions. Fed policy thus steers a path between over-stimulating the economy above the long-term non-inflationary growth path and keeping monetary conditions so tight as to push the economy into an undesirable recession. Note also that the classic twin macro-economic management tools: fiscal and monetary policy have been in imbalance in the USA in recent years, and with a virtual paralysis in fiscal policy, the onus of economic management has fallen on monetary policy—and the Fed.

In setting policy, the Fed will be concerned to try and anticipate the effects of its decisions given the lag between the moment of decision and desired result. Both the growth in money supply and interest rates take some considerable time to affect behaviour in the real economy, although the financial markets are likely to react immediately. As such Fed policy decisions will be forward looking, attempting to evaluate the likely course of the economy over the decision horizon. This accords with the historical observed lag in inflation and movements in money supply. Also, at present, the quality of econometric modelling or forecasting degenerates rapidly with the forecast horizon.

2. POLICY INDICATORS

Fed watchers have to make do with the historical basis of Fed policy in the form of the post-dated releases of the FOMC minutes and the other evidence cited above in order to establish what the Fed is up to.

At present, policy is usually stated in terms of a hierarchy of desirable objectives and either reaffirms them or modifies them in the light of new data. In addition, the Fed may set a series of trigger conditions which may alter the policy stance between FOMC meetings. Up to now, Chairman Alan Greenspan appears to have only changed policy as a result of an *ad hoc* telephone conference with FOMC members.

At present the Fed is targeting a rate for Fed funds with, as a subsidiary condition, a growth path in reserves and hence the economy. Fed watchers will monitor both the changes in reserves and the behaviour of Fed funds.

2(a) Changes in reserves

At present the Fed uses Contemporaneous Reserve Requirement (CRR) accounting over a two-week period starting on a Thursday and ending two weeks later on a Wednesday. When the Fed switched to CRR it initially used a one-week accounting period, but this proved to be very disruptive to the funds market with wide gyrations in funds every Wednesday. As a result, the Fed subsequently adopted the two-week reserve accounting period that is in present use.

As discussed above, interest rates and the growth in money supply are influenced by the availability of reserves. This is controlled by the willingness of the Fed to provide the banking system with additional reserves to accommodate increased loan demand. The following reserve indicators act as a proxy for changes in availability of reserves and may indicate changes in Fed policy. Bank reserve data for each two-week reserve maintenance period are provided every alternate Thursday evening together with a weekly statement of the major factors affecting bank reserves and credit.

Net borrowed (or free) reserves. Net borrowed reserves are defined as the difference between borrowed reserves and excess reserves, which are reserves held in excess of requirements (free reserves are the opposite of net borrowed reserves, i.e. the difference between excess and borrowed reserves). When the Fed tightens, its actions force banks to borrow a larger fraction of their required reserves (to service their loan-making needs). As a result, net borrowed reserves rise. A firmer Fed policy will show up by an increase in borrowed reserves and, if excess reserves do not change, by an increase in net borrowed reserves.

Note that there are dangers in using the above measure as a guide to Fed policy since the net borrowed reserves can change for reasons quite unrelated to Fed intentions. For example, banks may change their holdings of excess reserves, which will directly impact on the reported level of net borrowed reserves.

Non-borrowed reserves. The Fed targets non-borrowed reserves in setting the availability of reserves to their system. However, it may be difficult to interpret the data for non-borrowed reserves since it will require the correct seasonal adjustment to be totally meaningful.

There is a technical reason also for disregarding the data on non-borrowed reserves. When deposits shift from one institution to another, required reserves for the system as a whole may change even though total deposits do not.

Total reserves/monetary base, money supply, etc. The Fed has at various times pursued policies aimed at controlling the level of total reserves, the monetary base, and latterly money supply (as measured by M1, M2, and M3). Currently, the Fed is required to give projections to Congress twice a year under the Humphrey–Hawkins Act of 1978. These include targets for M2 and M3 growth, inflation, and GNP.

2(b) Economic Fundamentals

The Fed looks at a wide range of economic and financial fundamentals when setting policy, although in the final analysis, as described below, the Fed will translate this into an operational directive which includes a growth rate for reserves (and *ipso facto* money supply) and the funds rate.

3. RESERVE REQUIREMENTS AND THE DISCOUNT RATE

The Fed has two additional instruments in addition to open market operations: reserve requirement ratios and the discount rate.

The Fed specifies the ratios of selected categories of liabilities in relation to reserves. Banks must then hold reserves to a minimum of the levels of their liabilities subject to reserve requirements. Once a frequently used policy instrument, changes in reserve requirements have become less important as a policy variable. One reason that reserve ratios are rarely changed is that such changes are a clumsy means of affecting bank reserves and the monetary aggregates. The most common policy use of reserve requirements has been to encourage banks to issue (or discourage them from issuing) particular types of deposit.

Changes in the discount rate are more important and more common than changes to reserve requirements. The degree of ease or restraint that the Fed exercises through its open-market operations has the effect of determining the premium of the fed funds rate over the discount rate that banks are willing to pay to avoid recourse to the discount window. If the Fed limits the availability of non-borrowed reserves relative to required reserves, some banks will be forced to borrow reserves from the Fed. However, before they have recourse to the discount window, the banking system will bid up fed funds relative to the discount rate. This is particularly evident on the last day of the reserve statement period when funds often trade up significantly. Note, however, that recently banks have shown increasing aversion to the discount window and that the spread relationship between funds and the discount rate reached a historical high in May 1989. Since then it has moved back closer to the previous trend.

When the Fed eases by providing a large share of total reserves through open market operations, banks reduce their discount window borrowing. If the Fed tries to increase reserves relative to requirements, banks may not be able to lend the additional funds because credit demand is weak. This may lead the Fed to try to lower interest rates directly (and encourage more bank lending) by lowering the discount rate. Thus, changes in the discount rate tend to be a more important policy lever when the Fed is easing than when it is tightening. When tightening, the Fed can directly impact bank lending by raising the cost of such lending, which will be quickly translated into a higher loan rate. Thus Fed action on lending tends to be asymmetrical in nature, quicker to influence on the upside but requiring the psychological impact of the discount rate cut to favourably influence borrowers' expectations. Indeed, changes to the discount rate have a very strong psychological impact on the market.

4. TECHNICAL OPEN MARKET OPERATIONS

Most of the Fed's daily open-market operations in the markets are predicated on the need to offset some technical swing in the day-to-day availability of reserves. After the Fed has determined the level of reserves consistent with its desired objective (interest rate and monetary growth), it has to take into account a variety of other factors which are likely to exert short-run influences on the availability of bank reserves. These short-run items include items such as Treasury Deposits at the Fed, float, currency in circulation, and so forth.

Having estimated the desired level of reserves consistent with its policy objectives, the Fed must then determine the extent to which it will offset the factors that cause reserves to depart from the desired level. The Fed begins this process by estimating week to week the changes in the 'Factors-Affecting Reserves', or 'adds' and 'drains' in Fed watcher jargon. These terms derive from the type of operation the Fed must execute to counteract their effect, i.e. by adding or draining the reserves available to the banking system.

What the Fed does is to counteract a drain or an addition to reserves by operations on the other side of its balance sheet. The principles of double-entry bookkeeping require that increases in assets must be matched by increases in liabilities or capital. This means that if the Fed wishes to keep the banks' reserve accounts constant when some other liability has risen, it must increase its asset holdings. This is normally achieved by some kind

of open-market operation (by buying, or selling securities the Fed holds on its balance sheet).

If, for example, the public's demand for currency rises, as it does around major holidays as people draw out cash from banks to tide them over the holiday period, banks will need to obtain this cash from the Fed, which will consequently mean a run-down in deposits with the Fed. The Fed will want to do this to prevent abnormal swings in interest rates or loan demand. High volatility in interest rates will send erroneous signals to the market and to borrowers. Equally, wide swings in reserves may impact on the willingness to bank to extend loans. As the Fed wishes to counteract these effects and restore deposits to their previous level so it must buy securities in the open market, for which it in turn credits the accounts of the depository institutions. The Fed can achieve this aim via different means depending on the need for a permanent injection of reserves or merely a temporary addition.

In addition to the Fed, the US Treasury also plays a role. An increase in the Treasury's monetary assets tends to remove funds from the banking system, while an increase in its liabilities provides funds. When the Treasury's deposits at the Fed rise (for instance when individuals and corporations pay their taxes) this causes a rise in Treasury deposits at the Fed and an equal fall in deposits of depository institutions. The Fed normally counteracts this by buying securities in the open market.

Some factors that the Fed has to counteract are of a seasonal nature such as the currency demand over holidays and the change in Treasury balances at the Fed in the tax payment season, and other factors are connected with the operation of the system. These latter are caused by a breakdown in

Balance Sheet of the Federal Reserve System

Assets		Liabilities	
Gold Certificates		Federal Reserve Notes (outstanding)[a]	
Special Drawing Rights		Deposits:	
Coin			Depository Institutions
Loans (to depository institutions		US Treasury	
Acceptances:			Foreign Official
Accounts	Bought Outright	Other	
	Held under repurchase agreements		
Federal Agency Obligations:		Deferred availability cash items	
	Bought Outright	Other liabilities and accrued dividends	
	Held under repurchase agreements		
US Government securities		Capital Accounts:	
	Bought Outright		Capital Paid in
	Bills		Surplus
	Notes		Other Capital accounts
	Bonds		
	Held under repurchase agreements		
Cash items in the process of collection			
Bank premises			

[a] Currency in circulation.

the Fed clearing system (the 'Fed wire') or unexpected movements in float (for instance delays caused by bad weather increasing the amount of transportation float in the system). The Fed normally has a very good understanding of the seasonal factors but little foreknowledge of systemic influences.

The Fed releases a breakdown of the 'Factors Affecting Reserves' each Thursday evening (New York time) which consolidates the Fed's balance sheet and the monetary assets and liabilities of the US Treasury (Form H.4.1). The Fed also holds weekly news conference at the same time to explain the data; and will normally give an explanation for any significant reserve projection misses.

Major factors affecting bank reserves and credit ($ millions)

Data: Week ending 17 January	Wednesday close	Weekly average	Change
Loans to depository institutions	121	197	+61
Includes: seasonal borrowings	40	39	0
Extended credit	26	22	+4
Float	3,649	919	−487
Federal Reserve assets (other)	39,222	39,249	+109
Currency in circulation	256,749	257,350	−1,785
Treasury deposits with Federal Reserve Banks	6,948	4,108	−1,308
Service-related balances and adjustments	2,102	2,102	−117
Other Federal Reserve liabilities and capital	8,692	8,949	+76
Reserve balances with Federal Reserve Banks	35,014	35,087	−1,813
Federal Reserve operations	221,748	222,410	−1,735
Held under repurchase agreements	0	0	0
Federal Agency Issues owned outright	6,525	6,525	0
Held under repurchase agreements	0	0	−285

4(a) How the Fed decides day-to-day intervention
The Factors Affecting Reserves can be seen as a source and use of funds available to the banking system. The Fed determines its need for adding or draining funds from the banking system based on daily updates of each of the factors. The Fed wire, the computerized system used to settle funds trades, will provide the desk with a daily closing statement showing the changes in these factors. Thus the desk has a complete picture of the reserves situation for the previous day and the current bank statement period to date. The Fed's technical open-market operations are designed to offset the effect of these swings on a daily average basis.

In deciding on technical intervention, the Fed determines the volume of reserves that banks are required to post on a daily average basis during the course of the reserve maintenance period. In addition, the desk will estimate the level of excess reserves that banks are likely to hold during the period. The Fed then determines the amount of reserves that banks would need to borrow in order for the Fed to meet the target for non-borrowed reserves. Finally, the Fed estimates the average daily influence of all the factors that affect the supply of funds and which can, as a result, be used to satisfy required reserves.

Each day during the course of the reserve maintenance period, the Fed incorporates new information to recalculate the net effect on reserves of the various operating factors. It knows at the start of each day the previous day's balance sheet, the running totals for the period day's balance sheet, and the running totals for the period to date. It also obtains information about the planned changes in selected balance sheet items. The Fed conducts a conference call with officials from the desk, the Board of Governors, the US Treasury, and Reserve District Bank Presidents. As a result of this information, the desk decides whether to execute technical operations to counteract a drain or addition to funds. The degree to which the desk counteracts these variations in funds will be influenced by any bias in the current FOMC Directive. For instance, the desk, if the Directive has an ease bias, is far less likely to drain a modest surplus in reserves, which is in turn likely to cause funds to trade temporarily below the funds rate target. During the course of the reserve maintenance period, the Fed's estimates of operating factors will converge on the actual values of the operating factors. Thus there may be considerable variability in Fed funds on the last day (Wednesday) of the two-week reserve maintenance period.

5. TYPES OF OPEN-MARKET OPERATIONS
The Fed's decision on what types of operations to execute when intervening is important.

5(a) System matched-sale purchase agreements (adding reserves)
A system repurchase agreement (system RP) is a temporary purchase of securities with dealers in government securities. In a repurchase agreement, the dealer agrees that after some specific time (one day, two days, etc.) he will repurchase the securities from the Fed. When this operation occurs, the Fed credits the dealer's accounts with the proceeds, thus increasing the accounts of banks at the Fed, offsetting the factor(s) which have caused a reduction in reserves. The Fed will use system RPs when its estimates of operating factors dictates that a large infusion of funds is required. Since most changes in Fed operating factors are

seasonal in nature, and likely to be offset in coming weeks by opposite movements, the Fed relies on RPs to inject reserves on a temporary basis. With an RP the injection of reserves lasts only as long as the term of the transaction; overnight RPs being the most common. Under Fed convention, the desk does not disclose the total amount of the system RP it plans to execute.

5(b) System matched-sale purchase agreements (system reverses) (draining reserves)

A reverse RP is just what its name implies: the exact opposite of an RP. In a reverse RP, or matched-sale operation, the Fed sells securities to dealers under an agreement to repurchase them at a specified date. The Fed uses reverses for exactly the opposite reason for doing RPs, to drain funds from the banking system on a temporary basis. Note that the Fed may be more reluctant to use reverses when it is consciously trying to ease policy since a reverse RP may be interpreted by the market as a signal that the Fed wants to firm credit conditions.

The Fed has other means of absorbing reserves. For instance, it can ask the Treasury to increase its deposits with the Fed. The Fed can also arrange to increase its matched sales with foreign central banks.

The Fed has executed both RPs and matched sales in the same statement period. When this occurs it is generally due to a sudden and unexpected event that causes the Fed to revise its estimate of operating factors late in the statement period. Recently, the variability in Treasury Deposits has been responsible for such apparently contradictory operations. In addition, the desk may be concerned that funds do not move significantly above or below its target bands for any length of time. Events such as this should be viewed as purely technical and devoid of policy implications. A major challenge for Fed watchers is to separate those operations which are of just a technical nature and those which signal a change in policy.

5(c) Customer repurchase agreements (adding reserves)

When the Fed does a customer RP it has exactly the same effect on reserves as does a system RP. The 'customers' of the Fed are essentially foreign central banks. The Fed acts as both buying agent and securities custodian for these institutions. Normally, these institutions have surplus cash which they wish to invest. As a result they routinely arrange to buy securities from the Fed. The Fed takes these transactions into account when calculating the extent of its add or drain needs. If the Fed needs to add reserves when it is routinely selling securities under RP to foreign central banks, it may choose to pass this order through to the street. Thus this customer RP injects re-

serves. Had the Fed not passed the customer RP through to the street, it would have had to buy securities from the market instead.

The choice of customer or system RPs will generally be dictated by the amount of additional reserves the desk needs to inject. When the amount is small, the Fed usually will simply pass through some portion of its routine customer transactions to the market. In a customer RP, the Fed always specifies the precise dollar volume of the transaction; the amounts rarely exceed $2.0bn. In contrast, RPs for the desk's system open market account usually inject more than $2.0bn in funds. Since the Fed discloses the amount for customer RPs, but not for system RPs, it can signal to the market more precisely the amount of reserves it wants to add.

5(d) Outright purchase or sale for the system open-market account (permanent addition or draining of reserves)

From time to time the Fed undertakes outright transactions for the system open-market account. This kind of operation is called by the markets a *bill or coupon pass*. The Fed usually executes outright purchases when it determines that, in the weeks ahead, persistent injections of reserves will be required. These 'permanent' injections usually occur when seasonal influences on operating factors combine with large seasonal increases in required reserves to necessitate large additions to reserves. In the past, the Fed's outright purchases have been clustered in April, June–July, and November–December. Outright sales tend to take place in January.

The Fed's decision as to which securities to buy or sell will be determined by references to the Fed's desired maturity of its portfolio. This is not disclosed and thus it is difficult to anticipate the precise timing of an outright purchase/sale. When selling securities, the Fed normally offers short treasuries (two years or less) or bills. However, it may buy across the yield curve. The Fed prefers to enter the market when such activity is unlikely to impact on prices. However, the Fed has in the past used open-market operations to underscore a policy move. It is important that these operations be viewed in the context of the wider events taking place in the money markets and the economy as a whole and in relation to what is known about FOMC policy.

Outright sales by the Fed are much less frequent than purchases. Three reasons probably account for the Fed's limited use of outright sales:

1. A growing economy requires growth in the money supply and, hence, growth of bank reserves and Federal Reserve assets. Any sale of securities would almost of necessity be temporary and shortly thereafter require an offsetting purchase.

2. If the Fed needs to reduce its asset holdings, it can do so by allowing maturing treasury bills to run off as they mature. With a very large portfolio containing billions of dollars of treasury bills and with weekly treasury bill auctions, the Fed can simply choose not to replace its maturing bills. This allows the Fed to reduce its portfolio without recourse to sales to the market.

3. The Fed can in addition buy or sell securities to foreign central banks. The market will not become aware of these transactions until later when the Fed reports its positions.

4. The Treasury's heavy funding demands in the market means the Fed is often having to buy in securities to monetize debt in order to prevent an unwanted decrease in reserves.

5(e) Operations for the account of customers (no reserves effect)

In those transactions the Fed is simply acting as the agent in service to a customer and these transactions have no effect on the reserves position. If the Fed buys (or sells) securities for a customer, the Fed's own portfolio (and balance sheet) is unaffected and only the securities it holds 'in custody for customers' (not a Fed balance sheet item) will rise/fall.

6. THE EFFECT OF TREASURY BALANCES ON BANK RESERVES

Changes in the Treasury balances held at the Fed can exert important short-run effects on reserves. The Treasury holds the bulk of its liquid assets as deposits either with the Federal Reserve Banks or with commercial banks in Tax and Loan (TT&L) accounts. Changes in the Treasury's cash position (Fed deposits, TT&L balances, physical cash) result from the flow of tax collections, funding (bill and bond issues), and government expenditures.

Only changes in the Treasury's balances with the Fed impact on reserves. Accounts held in TT&L accounts in banks do not affect the availability of reserves, but when funds are transferred to the Fed, deposits at commercial banks decline, thereby draining funds.

The Treasury tries to maintain a stable amount deposited at the Fed. However, since it must pay for goods and services only out of its Fed account, it must periodically draw down from the TT&L balances. This potential reduction in reserves is usually matched by the Treasury making simultaneous payments back into the banking system. In order to prevent unanticipated changes in Treasury deposits, the Treasury takes part in the daily telephone conference mentioned earlier.

On occasion, the Treasury will assist the Fed by maintaining higher or lower Treasury balances to compensate for other operating factors. In addition, there are times when the Treasury's daily inflow of tax or funding receipts relative to its outlays is exceptionally large. When this occurs, upward pressure on Fed funds often emerges. As previously mentioned only changes in the Treasury's deposits at the Fed have any effect on reserves. This means that the upward pressure on the funds market is a result of an increase in this component. Normally, the Treasury would transfer money back into the banking system (thus adding reserves and reducing pressure on the funds rate) in TT&L accounts. However, these accounts have to be collateralized and in addition the law requires the Treasury to receive a rate on the TT&L balances which is 25 basis points below the funds rate. Banks may be reluctant to pledge high-grade (US government securities) against TT&L balances when they can earn a wider spread using the same securities in a repurchase transaction with a commercial customer.

Without the availability of collateral for the TT&L accounts, surplus cash is deposited at the Fed. In such circumstances, the Treasury balances held at the Fed will rise above the average level required to support the Treasury's immediate needs, and will be draining reserves from the system.

Although the desk tries to offset this undesirable drain on the system reserves, it may be difficult for the Fed to counteract this on a timely basis, resulting in a temporary upward pressure on the funds rate.

7. FLOAT

In the system of debits and credits in settling transactions within the Fed wire system, the Fed will credit the reserve account held at the Fed by the financial institution at which the cheque has been deposited while at the same time debiting the reserve account of the institution against which the cheque is drawn. Sometimes the reserve credit is made before the reserve debit and this causes a temporary and artificial increase in reserves. This is called float.

Float that is caused by delays in transit due to weather (planes do not fly in fog or hurricanes) in moving cheques from place to place is called 'transportation float'. This is virtually impossible to predict.

8. WATCHING THE FED

Because a change in the Fed funds rate affects all other short-term rates, everyone in the money market has an interest in predicting the next move in the funds rate.

Although there is a month lapse between the FOMC meeting and the release of the minutes, this can be compensated for by an understanding of the overall goals and the way the desk handles day-to-day operations. The key to success in recognizing the Fed's behaviour is to combine the macro factors which go into formulating the Fed's

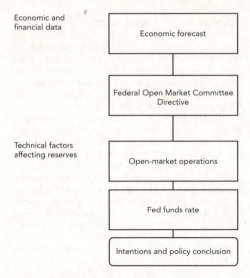

Economic and financial data

Technical factors affecting reserves

Schematic of Fed watching process

own policy Directive with the micro factors of Fed open-market operations.

However, be warned that certainty is impossible until after the event. Conclusions are therefore based on a balance of probabilities weighting the different components of the Fed's decision-making process.

CHIPS: The New York Clearing House's computerized *Clearing House Interbank Payments System*. An interbank clearing system used by banks in addition to the Fed's own wire; often used to clear euro transactions. A failure of the CHIPS system can cause problems in the funds market.

Fed wire: A computer system linking member banks to the Federal Reserve System, used for making interbank payments for Treasury and agency securities and located in Virginia.

Fed funds: (1) non-interest bearing deposits held by member banks at the Federal Reserve; (2) used as a term for 'immediately available' funds in the clearing sense.

Fed funds rate: the rate of interest at which Fed funds are bought and sold by member banks to each other and the rate influenced by the Federal Reserve through open market operations. The usual rate is for overnight borrowing/lending but there exists also a term funds market.

Forward Fed funds: Fed funds traded for future delivery.

Free reserves: excess reserves minus member bank borrowings at the Fed.

Money supply definitions:

M1:   (i) currency outside the Treasury, Federal Reserve Banks, and the vaults of depository institutions; (ii) travellers' cheques of non-

bank issuers; (iii) demand deposits at all commercial banks other than those due to depository institutions, the US government, and foreign banks and official institutions less cash items in the process of collection and Federal Reserve float; (iv) other chequable deposits (OCD) consisting of NOW (negotiable order of withdrawal) and ATS (automatic transfer service) accounts with depository institutions, credit union share accounts, and demand deposits at thrift institutions.

M2:   M1, plus overnight (and continuing contract) repurchase agreements issued by all commercial banks and overnight eurodollars issued to US residents by foreign branches of US banks world-wide. Money market deposit accounts (MMDA), savings and small-denomination time deposits (less than $100,000), and balances in both taxable and tax-exempt general purpose and broker-dealer money market mutual funds. Excludes individual retirement accounts (IRA) and Keogh balances at depository institutions and money market funds. Also excludes all balances held by US commercial banks, money market funds, foreign governments and commercial banks, and the US government.

M3:   M2 plus large-denomination time deposits and term repurchase agreement facilities (amounts over $100,000) issued by commercial banks and thrift institutions, term eurodollars held by US residents at foreign branches of US banks world-wide and at all banking offices in the United Kingdom and Canada, and balances in both taxable and tax-exempt, institution-only money market mutual funds. Excludes amounts held by depository institutions, the US government, money market funds, and foreign banks and official institutions. Also subtracted is the estimated amount of overnight repurchase agreements and eurodollars held by institution-only money market mutual funds.

Monetary base: The monetary base consists of total reserves plus required clearing balances and adjustments to compensate for float at the Fed plus the currency component of the money stock less the amount of vault cash holdings of thrift institutions not having required balances and the excess of current vault cash over the amount applied to satisfy current reserve requirements. Following the introduction of contemporaneous reserve requirements (CRR), currency and vault cash figures are measured over the weekly computation period ending on a Monday. The seasonally adjusted series consists of seasonally adjusted total reserves, which includes excess reserves on a non-seasonally adjusted basis, plus the seasonally adjusted currency component of the money stock plus the remaining items seasonally adjusted as a whole.

Reserve requirements: The percentage of different types of deposits that member banks are required to hold on deposit at Federal Reserve Banks.

See: Marcia Stigum, *Money Market*, (Dow Jones-Irwin, 1990); Milton Friedman and Anna Schwartz, *A Monetary History of the United States 1867–1960*, (Princeton University Press, 1963); Board of Governors of the Federal Reserve System, *Federal Reserve Bulletin* (Washington DC – published monthly).

Federal Reserve Bank (USA). One of the banks forming part of the Federal Reserve System.

Federal Reserve Banks of the Federal Reserve System. District headquarters:
1. Boston
2. New York
3. Philadelphia
4. Cleveland
5. Richmond
6. Atlanta
7. Chicago
8. St Louis
9. Minneapolis
10. Kansas City
11. Dallas
12. San Francisco

Federal Reserve Board (USA). The governing body of the Federal Reserve System, based in Washington, DC.

Federal Reserve Board of Governors. The permanent voting members of the FOMC are the seven governors and the president of the New York Federal Reserve Bank. Under the 1935 amendments to the Federal Reserve Act, the Chicago and Cleveland Banks alternate in a voting seat while the nine other banks rotate, every third year, in three seats. Rotation takes place for the first meeting in the new year.

Federal Reserve float. See float.

federal savings and loan association (USA). A savings and loan association which is federally chartered and a member of the Federal Home Loan Bank System.

Federal Savings and Loan Insurance Corporation (USA). The federal agency providing deposit insurance for savings and loan institutions.

Federal Trade Commission (FTC) (USA). Federal regulator responsible for interstate com-

merce. It was established by the Federal Trade Commission Act of 1914. See also **antitrust laws**.

Fédération des Experts Comptables Européens (FEE). European association of accounting organizations.

Fédération Internationale des Bourses de Valeurs (FIBV). International association of stock exchanges set up in 1961 to compare experiences and as a clearing house for exchanging information (cf. **Group of Thirty**).

Federation of Stock Exchanges in the European Union. A pressure group of the stock exchanges of member countries aimed at representing their interests to the European legislature in Brussels.

fed funds. See federal funds.

fed funds wire transfer or **fed wire** (Banking; USA). Term used for the computer system used by the Federal Reserve to execute the clearing of fed funds and for the settlement of US Treasury and federal agency securities (cf. **Clearing House Interbank Payments System**).

fed wire (Banking; USA). A computer system linking member banks to the Federal Reserve System, used for making interbank payments for Treasury and agency securities. Clearing system is located in Virginia, and can handle a maximum $999,999,999.99 in each trade. An unusual settlement pattern (for instance, the series of payments relating to the $23.5bn acquisition of RJR-Nabisco) can influence the funds rate.

fee. A payment made for services. See also **commission**.

feel. A market participant's expectations and opinions on the tone of a market (cf. **colour**).

Feldmarktbuchforederungen der Bunder (Confederation money market claims) (Switzerland). Negotiable short-term borrowings for up to one year issued by the Swiss federal government and akin to treasury bills in that they are issued at a discount to face value and repay at par.

fence or **fence spread.** An option strategy involving either a purchased call and a written put or a written call and a purchased put for the same expiry date (cf. **conversion; reverse conversion**). Also known as a *combination*. See also **risk reversal**.

Festverzinslich (German). Fixed interest (cf. **coupon**).

FHA experience (Bonds; USA). The prepayment experience of the **federal housing administration** mortgages often used to model the **prepayment risk** of **mortgage-backed** issues in the US domestic market. See **prepayment model**; **Public Securities Association prepayment model**.

fiat money. *Fiat* is a Latin word meaning 'let it be done'. When applied to money it is an instruction issued by the relevant monetary authority that specified **commodities** are to be used as money in order to fulfil its functions as: a store of value; a means of exchange; and a way of settling debt (cf. **specie**).

fiduciary. An individual or trust institution given the power of acting for the benefit of another. Hence *fiduciary issue*, an issue of securities or **promissory notes** by one authority on behalf of another.

fiduciary call and **put.** A method of **collateralizing call** and **put options** by investing the **exercise price** in suitable investments held by a **fiduciary**. This both reduces the **counterparty risk** with the option purchasers and prevents the **writer** from increasing the **leverage** of his **portfolio**. See **covered writing**.

fiduciary deposit (Banking). **Funds** placed with an institution which has discretion in their management.

fiduciary loan (Banking). Lending made on trust, that is without **collateral** (cf. **lien**; **promissory note**). Also known as *unsecured*.

fiduciary risk. The risk of loss from actions taken on behalf of clients.

Fifty Leaders Share Price Index (Australia). Index of the largest fifty companies traded on the **Australian Stock Exchange**. See also **All-Ordinaries Share Price Index**.

figure (Forex). **Foreign exchange** market trading term for a quote where the two smallest digits are '00', the rest of the rate being taken as known to the other side (cf. **big figure**; **handle**). For instance a trader might quote 'eighty/figure' when the French franc rate was 6.6580/6.6600.

figuring the tail. Calculating the **break-even yield** at which a **money market** instrument needs to be sold (purchased) at the end of the initial portion of its life when it is financed with a **term repurchase agreement** (reverse rp).

fill (USA). To carry out a client's order. A *partial fill* is an order that has been carried out in part.

fill or kill (FOK). An **all-or-none** transaction that must be executed immediately in its entirety or it lapses.

film trust (Equities; Australia). A publicly quoted single-purpose trust whose underlying assets are royalties from a film project. The first trust was set up in July 1993 to help finance the film *Lightning Jack* produced by the Australian actor Paul Hogan. The trust, which raised A$35m, receives all income for seven years from the film after initial marketing and sundry expenses are paid initially until the principal is redeemed and then enjoys a 50 : 50 split with Hogan's production company. In addition, trust unit holders will be able to enjoy tax deductions on their investment if held for one or two years.

filter. A system for determining when to buy or sell securities. It depends on the relative price levels of particular securities (cf. **chart analysis**). One of the best known is the 'hatch' method which involves setting a buying or selling price at a certain percentage below or above the ruling price (cf. **trigger**). Only when the security price actually changes by that margin is a transaction executed. See **technical analysis**.

filter rule. Technical analysis and trading decision rule based on a **trigger** point. For instance, a rule that requires a price reversal of say 3% would if from a high trigger a sale, if from a low a purchase. Such rules have much in common with **momentum models**.

final average plan. In insurance, average means losses. Such losses are compensated for and the sharing of these between the insurers involved is a matter of negotiation. See **pure risk**.

final dividend. The dividend paid after the end of the company's financial year (cf. **interim dividend**).

final notice day. The last day upon which notice can be given of an intent to deliver against a **futures contract**.

final salary basis (FSB). The traditional method of calculating pension level according to the salary of the individual at retirement (cf. **money purchase basis**).

final trading day. The last day for trading a particular delivery in the **futures markets** (usually a Wednesday or Friday) (cf. **triple witching hour**).

finance. (i) The study, specialization in, or use of money. Hence *financial officer, financial economics*. (ii) The markets, activities, and businesses involved directly with money rather than real **assets** (cf. **financial institution**). This is an economy's *financial sector.* (ii) **Funds** or a **loan** (cf. **capital**). See **financial instrument.** (iii) Those persons who have specific responsibility for advising about or managing money (cf. **finance director**). Hence a *financial expert.* (iv) Alternative term for capital (cf. **liabilities**).

finance bill. See banker's acceptance; bill of exchange; documentary credit.

finance director. The **director** of a company or other organization who has prime responsibility for managing its **finances**. See **Chief Financial Officer; comptroller; treasurer.**

finance house. A non-bank institution which advances credit, usually on the basis of a **lease** or **hire-purchase** agreement (cf. **consumer credit**).

finance house base rate (UK). The lending rate for a finance house. See base rate.

finance lease. See financial lease.

finance vehicle. (i) An operation involving the setting-up of an offshore subsidiary incorporated by the **parent company** for the purpose of issuing debt and lending the borrowings on to the parent or another subsidiary (cf. **special purpose vehicle**). The parent normally would guarantee the debt issues. (ii) Any **financial package** or operation, usually of a complex nature. See **project finance.**

financial. Relating to **finance** (cf. **money**). This can be any activity directly or indirectly linked to financial activities such as (financial) reporting, (financial) instruments, (financial) transactions, (financial) management, or (financial) regulation or supervision.

Financial Accounting Standards Board (FASB) (USA). The regulatory body which sets accounting standards in the USA (cf. **Generally Accepted Accounting Principles**). The **Securities and Exchange Commission's** rulings on disclosure and accounting treatment can prevail over FASB standards, if it so decides. See **Statement of Financial Accounting Standards.**

financial adviser or **financial advisor.** (i) An individual or institution which proffers investment advice. (ii) A financial intermediary such as an investment bank, merchant bank, or stockbroker which provides assistance and advice on effecting a transaction (cf. **mergers and acquisitions**).

Financial and Operational Combined Uniform Single (USA). See FOCUS report.

financial assets. Claims such as securities or loans on real assets (cf. **derivative; primitive security**). Used in the personal sector to mean all those savings and investment products held in addition to physical assets, such as property. In the corporate sector, it refers to holdings of cash and other assets that are likely to be more liquid that the physical plant, land, and equipment owned by the business (cf. **current assets; fixed assets**).

financial covenant. See covenant.

financial distress. A condition for a firm where it either cannot meet or has difficulty in meeting its fixed charges. See **bankruptcy; Chapter 11; insolvency; workout.**

financial electronic data interchange (financial EDI; FEDI). Computerized link-up between a bank and a customer for the purposes of undertaking financial transactions (cf. **electronic trade confirmation**).

financial engineering. The process of combining, dividing, or otherwise altering existing **financial instruments** to create new financial products (cf. **structured finance; synthetic**). The basic tools or building blocks are **equity; debt; derivatives** (**forwards; futures; options; interest rate swaps** and **cross-currency swaps**).

financial future. A futures contract where the **underlying** is a financial instrument such as a **money-market deposit,** a **bond,** an **index,** or a **foreign exchange rate** (cf. **commodity future**). The first financial futures were established in 1972 by the **International Monetary Market** in Chicago, USA. Most major financial centres now have a financial futures exchange or subdivision of their **stock exchange** devoted to trading such instruments. Financial futures on **money market** instruments are quoted in points of 100 percent (or 100 less the **yield** of the underlying), thus a three-month euro-Deutschmark **future** at 95.10 would imply a deposit rate of 4.9%. The logic is that any decrease in **forward rates** will be counterbalanced by an increase in the value of the future. Financial futures on bonds are quoted in relation to the price of the **notional bond** security which comprises the contract. Financial futures on indices and currencies are quoted directly in terms of the value of the underlying index or the currency. See **bond future; currency future; interest rate future; medium-term interest rate future; spread future; stock index future.**

Financial Futures Exchange (USA). See **New York Cotton Exchange.**

Financial Futures Market Amsterdam (Financiële Termijnmarkt Amsterdam) (Netherlands). Nes 49, 1012 KD Amsterdam (tel. 31 (0) 20 550 4555; fax 31 (0) 20 624 54 016). That part of the

Amsterdam Stock Exchange that trades financial futures.

financial guarantee insurance (FGI). A form of credit insurance used with **asset-backed** securities to provide a **backstop** for payment in the event of default by the **underlying** assets. FGI providers are normally highly rated monoline insurance companies and the provision of the guarantee is one method of increasing the **credit worthiness** of the issue.

financial innovation. The process of developing new securities, financial structures or other innovative solutions to market participants' needs (cf. **financial engineering**). It can involve **derivatives**, tax, accounting, regulatory, or other aspects of the financial environment in value added solutions. A good example of such activity would be the 're-packaging' of **perpetual floating rate notes**, which started with existing issues and then was developed into a structured finance technique in its own right (cf. **instantly repackaged perpetual**). This approach was then adapted and used elsewhere, such as **exit bonds** (cf. **Mex-Ex issue**). See also **exotics**; **hedging**; **packages**; **swaps**; **synthetic**.

financial institution. Those firms whose financial activities are central to their business. Some firms take **deposits** from other firms and the public, others invest funds for the longer term, while yet others act in a transaction or advisory capacity. See also **financial intermediary**.

Financial Institutions Recovery, Reform and Enforcement Act of 1989 (FIRREA) (USA). Legislation aimed at increasing the **capital adequacy** of **savings and loans** associations in response to problems within the industry in the 1980s and giving the **Federal Reserve Board** broad powers of regulation. The act also included changes to the US Bankruptcy Code and placed **netting** agreements on a firm legal basis.

financial instrument. Generic term for those securities or contracts which provide the holder with a claim on an obligor. Such instruments include **common stock, preferred stock, bonds, loans, money market instruments**, and other contractually binding obligations. The common feature which differentiates a financial instrument from a commercial or trade credit is the right to receive cash or another financial instrument from the obligor and/or the ability to exchange for cash the instrument with another entity (cf. **negotiable instrument**). The definition can also include instruments where the claim is contingent, as with **derivatives**.

Financial Intermediaries, Managers and Brokers Regulatory Association (FIMBRA) (UK). A

UK **self-regulating organization** responsible for the conduct of a broad range of financial advisers, usually small independent firms, and accountable to the **Securities and Investments Board** for ensuring adherence to its rule book. Set up following the introduction of the **Financial Services Act, 1986**. It has since been amalgamated into the **Personal Investment Authority**.

financial intermediary. An entity that collects funds and makes loans and which generally facilitates the flow of capital between borrowers and lenders in the economy. The list includes, *inter alia*, banks, securities or brokerage firms, **investment companies**, and **mutual funds**.

financial lease. A type of **lease** contract where the total amount of the payments made by the user of the asset, the lessee, to the owners of the asset, the lessor, covers the initial purchase price of the asset (cf. **capital lease; operating lease**). Such leases must appear on the company's balance sheet. Sometimes called a *bareboat charter, demise hire*, a *finance lease*, or a *full-payout lease*. See **above-the-line activities**.

financial leverage. The use of debt to finance operations (cf. **operating leverage**). See **leverage**.

financial management. Decision-making about the financial aspects of an organization. See **asset-liability management; asset management; cash management; investment manager; liability management**.

financial market. A market in which financial assets are traded (cf. **auction; bazaar; bear market; bull market; market forces; transparency**). See **exchange; over the counter; stock exchange**.

Financial News Composite Index (USA). Stock index on which an exchange-traded option contract is listed on the Pacific Stock Exchange.

financial planning. See **budget; business plan; capital budgeting; financial management**.

financial ratios. See **ratio analysis**.

Financial Reporting Council (FRC) (Accounting; UK). Supervisory entity whose task is to review and regulate financial reporting in the UK. It does this through the Accounting Standards Board and the **Financial Reporting Review Panel**.

Financial Reporting Exposure Draft (FRED) (Accounting; UK). Proposed Financial Reporting Standards issued by the **Financial Reporting Standards Board** for comment and discussion.

Financial Reporting Review Panel (FRRP) (accounting; UK). Executive arm of the **Financial Reporting Council** which has broad investigative and legal powers conferred by the Companies Act, 1989, to enforce proper treatment and disclosure in the reported accounts of UK-domiciled companies in conformity with **Financial Reporting Standards** and **Statements of Standard Accounting Practice.**

Financial Reporting Standard (FRS) (Accounting; UK). Accounting reporting standards for presentation, disclosure, and the treatment of accounts as laid down by the **Accounting Standards Board** which have to be followed by companies preparing their accounts for publication. FRSs have legal status and the ASB may compel compliance (cf. **Generally Agreed Accounting Principles** (USA); **Statements of Financial Accounting Standards** (USA); **Statements of Standard Accounting Practice** (UK). The **Financial Reporting Review Panel** has the legal powers to force companies to restate their accounts in conformity with the standard. *FRS-1* is concerned with 'Cash Flow Statements', *FRS-3* with the presentation of the 'Profit and Loss Account', and *FRS-5* with 'Reporting the Substance of Transactions'. See also FRS-3.

Financial Reporting Standards Board (FRSB) (Accounting; UK). Body set up to report on standards to be set for the disclosure and presentation requirements of **financial** reporting in published accounts. See **Accounting Standards Board.**

financial restructuring. See restructuring.

financial risk. The risk that a firm will not be able to meet its fixed **financial** commitments or prior charges such as interest, **principal** repayments, lease payments, or **preferred stock dividends.** Hence it is the risk arising from the use of **debt** finance which require periodic payments of interest and principal and may not be covered by the operation's cash flows, rather than the firm's line of activities, which is known as **business** or operating risk. See **default risk.**

financials. Shorthand term for a firm's **financial** statements (i.e. **income statement** or **profit and loss acccount, balance sheet,** and **cash flow statements**).

Financial Services Act, 1986 (FSA) (UK). The first attempt to provide a comprehensive statutory-based regulation of UK activity in the **financial** sector. It was enacted in response to the *Gower Report 1982*, and in recognition of changed financial market conditions that rendered the previous *ad hoc* legislation out of date. The guiding principle is one of self-regulation (practitioner-group-

based) within a statutory framework. The Act is largely concerned with protecting the private investor (cf. **self-regulating organization**). Although the investor can still make poor investment decisions, if the Act is effective the investor will not be misled or cheated. The vehicle intended by the Act to establish and oversee the new framework is the **Securities and Investments Board** although the **Bank of England** also shares responsibility for financial regulation. The SIB regulates SROs each of which is responsible for overseeing one or more parts of the market. The Act, which came into force in 1988, is widespread in its effect. It brings under a single framework individual practitioners and large financial institutions with world-wide operations. Many of the latter have not in the past been subject to such extensive regulation in the UK, depending for their exemptions on derivative authorization, for example, as recognized banks.

Financial Services Directive. Directive on the regulation of financial services throughout the **European Union.** Like other directives in the financial sector, it adopts a principle of home country authorization allowing firms to undertake business in other member countries.

financial statement. An organization's balance sheet and **income statement** (profit and loss account).

financial supermarket. See universal banking.

financial synergy. See synergy.

Financial Times Share Indices. A series of UK and world indices compiled by the *Financial Times* *(FT)*, sometimes in conjunction with the Faculty of Actuaries and the Institute of Actuaries, and the **London Stock Exchange,** covering the financial markets. The indices are:

> FT Actuaries All Share Index;
> FT S & P Actuaries World Share Index;
> FT-Actuaries Fixed Interest Indices (made up of eight different subcomponents covering different parts of the market: shorts; mediums; longs; irredeemables; all stocks; short index-linked; long index-linked; all index-linked stocks);
> FT Industrial Ordinary Share Index (FT-30) (cf. **Dow-Jones Industrial Average** (USA));
> FT Government Securities Index;
> FT Fixed Interest Index;
> FT-Stock Exchange 100 Index (FT-100; Footsie);
> FT-Stock Exchange Mid 250 Index;
> FT-Stock Exchange Actuaries 350 Index;
> FT-Stock Exchange Small Cap Index;
> FT-Stock Exchange Eurotrack 100 Index;
> FT-Stock Exchange Eurotrack 200 Index.

financial year (FY). (i) A budgetary or accounting period of approximately one calendar year. (ii) Specific tax year. Also known as the *fiscal year*.

Financiel Termijnmarkt Amsterdam (Futures; Netherlands). See **Amsterdam Stock Exchange**.

financier. A firm or individual who provides finance (cf. **lend**). It tends to be used when a hands-on approach is intended rather than just lending (cf. **venture capital**).

financing gap. See **asset-liability management**.

Finanzierungsschaetze (German). **Treasury notes.**

Finanzplatz Deutschland (Germany). The concept of Germany as an international financial centre for Europe. It has meant developing German financial markets to make them more attractive as a place for international investment activity, including an integrated **stock exchange** to provide a centralized dealing service rather than the previous regional exchanges, better dissemination of information, **settlement**, and fiscal environment.

fineness. The degree of purity in a metal. See **assay**; **contract grade**.

fine rates. Relatively low rates of interest or **margins** over a **reference rate**. Borrowers who can achieve fine rates are usually of very high **credit worthiness**. See also **soft money**.

fine tuning. That part of **demand** management policies involving small corrections in the targets for macro-economic variables, such as **money supply**. Having got an economy moving in the desired direction, in terms of output, expenditure, and employment levels, fine-tuning allows governments to make adjustments to meet more precise outcomes; for example, rather than setting a range for money supply growth it would involve fixing a particular rate for its growth. Some regard fine-tuning as impossible because of **Goodhart's law**; others see it as dangerous for governments to commit themselves to such precise policy objectives because of the **risk** of failure.

FINEX (New York Financial Exchange) (US). 4 World Trade Center, Suite 5572, New York, NY 10048 (tel. 1 212 938 2634; fax 1 212 432 0294). Established in 1985 (as a division of the **New York Cotton Exchange**).

finite life real-estate investment trust (FREIT) (USA). A **closed-end** real-estate investment company that aims to realize its investments within a specified period in order to create **capital gains**.

Finnish Options Index (FOX) (Finland). **Index** of the twenty-five most active **common stocks** on the **Helsinki Stock Exchange**.

Finnish Options Market (FOM) (Suomen Optiomeklarit) (Finland). Keskuskatu 7, 00100 Helsinki. Postal Address: Box 926, 00101 Helsinki (tel. (3580) 13 12 11; fax (3580) 13 12 1211). Established in 1988.

firewall. Arrangements for the financing and ownership structure of a **financial** conglomerate such that problems in one part of the group do not spill over into other parts. Firewalls are required by either law or regulation. Since they require each part of a business to be self-standing, they tend to reduce the attractions of being an integrated financial services group. For instance, a bank with a securities subsidiary may be required to operate the latter in such a way as to have little exposure between the two.

firm. (i) An unconditional order to buy or sell a security that can be carried out without additional confirmation at any time during a mutually agreed period (cf. **subject**). (ii) A **quoted** price or **yield** for a normal amount that may be traded at for some period of time (as in a 'firm price') (cf. **indication**; **level**). (iii) Sometimes used to describe markets where prices are rising. See **strong** (cf. **soft**). (iv) A business unit (cf. **company**; **corporation**; **partnership**).

firm commitment. Binding agreement to enter into a transaction, for instance to lend someone money (cf. **underwriter**).

firm commitment offering or **underwriting.** When an **underwriter** agrees to buy the issued securities (cf. **best efforts**; **purchase and sale**).

firmer. A better **tone** to a market; that is, prices are rising or recovering from a low. See **firm**.

firm hands. Market expression for a **retail** account that will not trade the securities so placed (cf. **buy and hold**; **spectail**).

firm offer. An unconditional offer by an intermediary to undertake a transaction (cf. **best efforts**; **force majeure**).

firm order. An order which is not subject to reconfirmation before the transaction is carried out.

firm price. Price guaranteed by a trader for a given time period (cf. **firm**).

firm quote or **firm quotation.** A price quotation by a **broker-dealer** which is good to be traded on (cf. **firm**; **indication**; **level**).

firm specific risk. See business risk; diversifiable risk; stock specific risk.

First Australia Mortgage Acceptance Corporation (FANMAC) (Bonds; Australia). New South Wales agency set up to securitize mortgages originated in the state (cf. **National Mortgage Market Corporation**).

first board (USA). The dates set by the exchange for delivery when futures contracts are held to expiry.

First Bulgarian Stock Exchange (Bulgaria). 1 'Macedonia' Sq Fl 12, BG—1000 Sofia (tel. 359 2 81 57 11; fax 359 2 87 55 66).

first call date. The earliest date at which an issuer can exercise a call provision. It is used for calculating the yield-to-call.

first class paper. Any security but typically a money market instrument such as a banker's acceptance, bill of exchange, certificate of deposit, or documentary credit which is backed by a bank of the best credit worthiness (cf. **money center bank; triple-A**). Also called *fine paper*.

first line reserves. Liquid reserves held for currency intervention.

first loss guarantee. A technique commonly used in the securitization of assets to provide credit enhancement where a third party agrees to indemnify holders for a given amount or percentage of any losses from the asset pool. See **junior**.

first mortgage bond. A type of mortgage bond which is backed by a lien held in trust on real estate or property.

first notice day. The first date on which notices of intention to deliver financial instruments or commodities against futures are authorized within the delivery month. Under the mechanics of the contracts, a short position holder with an obligation to make delivery would indicate his intention to deliver; a long position holder would receive notice of the short position's intention to deliver.

first preferred stock. A senior class of preferred stock which has prior claim on dividends and in a liquidation of the company (cf. **junior**).

fiscal agency agreement. The agreement covering the duties and responsibilities of a fiscal agent (cf. **trust deed**). Also known as a *corporate trust agreement*.

fiscal agent. (i) An institution, normally a bank, appointed by a borrower as its **agent** under a corporate trust agreement for a new issue of securities when no **trustee** is involved. Its main function is to act as the **paying agent**, but it has none of the **fiduciary** responsibilities of a trustee. (ii) A government agent servicing debt issues.

fiscal drag. As nominal incomes rise over time, a progressive tax system (the higher the income, the more tax is paid) will take an increasing proportion of an economy's income. It occurs whether the rise in nominal income comes from inflation (in the absence of **indexation**), or from improvements in real output per capita, or both. The effects of fiscal drag (on the economy) become less important after the indexation of tax rates.

fiscal policy. Those instruments at the disposal of government to achieve its policy objectives relating to government expenditure, taxation, and budget deficits or surpluses (cf. **monetary policy**).

fiscal synergy. See synergy.

fiscal year (FY). (i) The annual accounting period chosen by an entity. In some jurisdictions this is fixed by law, in others it is a matter of choice. Also referred to as the *financial year*. (ii) The tax year. For the UK, the tax year runs from 6 April in one calendar year, ending on 5 April in the next. This might be written as FY95/96. In the USA, the comparable period runs from 1 July to 30 June. Also known as the *tax year*.

Fisher effect. A relation proposed by the economist Irvin Fisher that there is a positive relationship between interest rates and expected inflation. See also **nominal interest rate; real interest rate**.

Fitch Investors Services, Inc. (USA). Credit rating agency. One State Street Plaza, New York, New York 10004, USA (tel. (212) 908 0500; fax (212) 480 4435). Twenty-four rating categories are used, including relative positions within a class:

Investment grade, top quality	AAA (+/−)
Very high quality	AA (+/−)
High quality	A (+/−)
Good quality	BBB (+/−)
Below investment grade	BB (+/−)
Below investment grade, speculative	B (+/−)
Speculative, best of	CCC
Intermediate	CC
Lowest quality, speculative	C
Default, low value	DDD
Minimal value	DD
Nil value	D

Grades AAA to B have the symbols plus (+) and minus (−) to indicate relative position within a class. Up-to-date rating information is available on electronic data and news systems.

five hundred dollar rule (USA). A condition of **Regulation T** by the **Federal Reserve** which exempts **margin requirements** deficits below that amount from mandatory action by the **broker**.

fix, fixation, or **fixing**. (i) The determination and setting of an interest or **exchange rate**, or security or **commodity** price. Used principally for determining reference rates for **euronotes**, **floating rate certificates of deposit**; **cross-currency swaps**; **interest rate swaps**; **floating rate notes**; **forward rate agreements**; **synthetic agreements for forward exchange**; and commodity and currency-related obligations (cf. **rollover**). (ii) Many countries have an official currency fixing at some point during the trading day to establish a formal rate which is then used in many contractual obligations. See **agent bank**; **gold fix**; **London interbank offered rate**; **tender panel**. (iii) (UK) Term for short selling.

fixed. (i) Contractually determined (as in *fixed interest*). (ii) **Long-term**, stable, or enduring (as with *fixed capital*).

fixed asset. (i) Any of a range of entries on the asset side of a **balance sheet** which are not rapidly turned over in the course of business (cf. **current assets**). Examples of fixed assets include land, buildings, plant and machinery, and other investments. These may be further divided into *tangible fixed assets* and *intangible fixed assets*, the latter being trademarks and patents (cf. **goodwill**). (ii) (UK) An asset of a **company** intended for use on a continuing basis in the activities of a company (cf. **current asset**). (iii) (USA) A fixed asset is a **tangible** asset and capital assets refer to the wider class of assets. Also sometimes referred to as a *capital asset*.

fixed asset turnover ratio. The ratio of sales or turnover to the firm's **fixed assets**. See **ratio analysis**.

fixed assurance note (FAN). See deferred payment bond.

fixed capital. The fixed assets of a **company** or other legal entity (cf. **current assets**; **net worth**; **working capital**).

fixed charge (UK). A **lien** on a specific asset or group of assets. Normally such charges have to be registered to become effective. Also known as a *specific charge* since the lien is registered on specific assets (cf. **floating charge**).

fixed charge coverage ratio. The ratio of earnings before interest and taxes to debt service

interest. Sometimes called simply *times fixed charges*. See **interest coverage ratio**; **ratio analysis**.

fixed commissions. A type of cartel agreement where intermediaries have the right to receive a **commission** that is fixed according to some predetermined schedule. While it was once common for securities exchanges to have fixed commissions, most major markets have now moved to negotiated commissions as a result of pressure by regulators. The current major exception is Japan, where fixed commissions are still in operation.

fixed cost. The total of such costs as rent, debt interest, and management salaries which would remain the same irrespective of activity levels. Also known as *fixed overhead cost* or *fixed expense*.

fixed dates. The standard periods on any day for which **eurocurrencies** and **euromarket money market** instruments are traded. The convention is known as *calendar/month*. Thus a one-month deposit will mature on the same calendar day in the following month, with the following exceptions: a transaction which would mature on a Saturday or Sunday or on any other day (for example a national holiday or bank holiday) which is not a business day will mature on the next business day unless the resultant **maturity** date means that the next business day would be in the following month, in which case the maturity will be the last business day in the month (cf. **broken dates**). See **odd date**.

fixed debenture (Bonds; UK). Equivalent to a **mortgage-backed bond**, since the issue is backed by a **fixed charge** on a specific **asset** or group of assets of the issuer (cf. **floating debenture**; **unsecured loan stock**).

fixed deposit (Banking). A **deposit** with a financial intermediary where there is a **fixed rate** of interest set on the deposit for an agreed period or to **maturity** (cf. **floating rate**; **variable rate**).

fixed exchange rate. (i) Foreign exchange rate that is fixed between two or more currencies (cf. **floating exchange rate**). It can also mean any system where two currencies are kept at a constant parity (cf. **crawling peg**; **currency basket**; **peg**). (ii) The system of fixed exchange rate parities that was operated under the Bretton Woods system, following the Second World War.

fixed exchange rate foreign equity option. See **quantity adjusting option**.

fixed/fixed or **fixed-for-fixed.** Interest rate swap or cross-currency swap where both parties pay each other a **fixed rate** payment. For an IRS this would have to be some form of **spread swap**.

fixed/fixed currency swap. See cross-currency swap.

fixed/floating or **fixed-for-floating.** Interest rate swap or cross-currency swap where one party pays a fixed rate payment while the other makes a payment referenced to a floating rate cost of funds index, such as the London interbank offered rate, or similar.

fixed/floating swap. See interest rate swap.

fixed for floating commodity swap. A type of interest rate swap where one party agrees to pay a floating price on the commodity being swapped, while the other party agrees to pay a fixed price on the swap. Such swaps allow producers and users to fix the price of their product or raw materials over a longer period than is available in the futures markets. The contract would normally specify the amount of the commodity in the swap and they are generally cash settled on the basis of the difference between the two amounts due on the swap.

fixed income. (i) Term debt instruments; this includes bonds, notes, and medium-term notes (cf. equities; fixed interest). (ii) A division of an investment bank, merchant bank, or securities firm that is responsible for transactions involving debt instruments (cf. market-maker; broker-dealer; stockbroker).

fixed income investment. A fixed rate security. It can be, for instance, a fixed rate bond or a preferred paying a fixed-rate dividend.

fixed interest or **fixed rate.** Interest on a security or a loan which is constant over its life (cf. coupon). The opposite type of interest is known as *floating rate* or *variable rate* where the interest is reset periodically in line with market conditions. See also bonds; floating rate note; interest rate calculations; variable rate note; zero-coupon bond.

fixed interest rate short tranche (FIRST) (Bonds; USA). Collateralized mortgage obligation (CMO) which has the first priority for interest and principal repayments. Many CMOs have different series giving different priority to interest and principal. Also known as the *A tranche*.

fixed interest rate substitute transaction (FIRST). A two-tranche issue of floating rate notes (FRN) where the combined cash flows to the issuer constitute a fixed set of payments. This can be created, for instance, by issuing a standard or plain vanilla FRN and a reverse FRN. Since one pays London interbank offered rate (LIBOR) and the other a fixed rate less LIBOR, the two cash

flows equate to the fixed rate, plus any margins (see Table).

Issue	Coupon
(i) Floating rate note	LIBOR
(ii) Reverse floating rate note	12% − LIBOR
(i) + (ii) Combination	12%

fixed operating costs. Those costs associated with production or providing a service which do not vary in line with sales or turnover.

fixed payment bond. A type of mortgage-backed issue where the amortization of the securities is predetermined at the onset, thus reducing the prepayment risk. See collateralized mortgage obligations.

fixed price basis or **fixed pricing.** A securities offer that is at a fixed price (cf. offer for sale). Used when the intention is to encourage all the underwriters to sell the securities at an agreed minimum price. See auction; fixed price reoffer.

fixed price contract. A contract where the provider of the goods or services is paid a sum agreed when the contract was negotiated (cf. cost-plus contract).

fixed price reoffer or **reoffering (FPR).** A type of underwriting agreement where the syndicate agrees to offer securities at a price set by the lead manager (in consultation with the syndicate) until such time as all the securities are distributed or the syndicate is broken.

fixed price tender offer. A tender where the price is fixed. Usually the buyer or seller reserves the right to vary the amount sold or purchased according to the amount tendered. Quite often used by central banks in carrying out open-market operations.

fixed rate or **fixed rate interest.** The interest on a security, debt, or derivative contract calculated as a constant specified percentage of the (notional) principal and paid at the end of stated periods, often annually or semi-annually, until maturity (cf. floating rate interest). Sometimes referred to as *fixed interest*, as in fixed interest securities. See coupon; interest rate calculations.

fixed rate auction preferred stock (FRAPS) (USA). A type of auction rate preferred stock (ARPS) which has an initial period where the dividends are paid at a fixed rate and which then converts to being an ARPS, or may be called.

fixed rate certificate of deposit (fixed rate CD) (Money markets). A term certificate of deposit paying periodic interest on a **fixed rate**. Interest is normally calculated on a **money market basis** (cf. **floating rate certificate of deposit**). See **interest rate calculations**.

fixed rate currency swap. A type of cross-currency swap where the two counterparties agree to exchange **fixed rate** payments on both sides. Also known as a *coupon currrency swap* or a *fixed/fixed currency swap*.

fixed rate instrument. Any security or derivative that has a predetermined and known payoff from its cash flows. Thus a **straight bond** which has a fixed rate **coupon** would fall into this class as would a **cross-currency swap** where both sides paid a fixed rate.

fixed rate loan. A loan made usually by a bank as lender which is on a **fixed rate interest** basis.

fixed rate mortgage. A mortgage where the interest is fixed for the life of the borrowing. It may also have an **annuity** structure, where payments combine both interest and repayment of **principal**. In both cases, the mortgage would have a determinable set of level payments over its life.

fixed rate payer or **fixed payer.** The party to an **interest rate swap** or **cross-currency swap** paying the **fixed rate** (cf. **floating rate payer**). Also seen as the swap buyer or to be **long** the swap (cf. **long funded**). The fixed rate payer is said to *pay fixed*. See **receiver** (cf. **fixed rate receiver**).

fixed rate preferred stock. A type of **preferred** stock or preference share which has a fixed **dividend**. Such dividends are normally paid out of profits and in jurisdictions which have an **imputation** tax system normally are accompanied by a **tax credit** (cf. **franked income**). In a winding-up of the corporation, preferred **stockholders** are normally paid off prior to **common stock** holders. Preferred stock has been issued in many variations; for instance, some fixed rate preferred stock issues have **conversion** rights to common stock.

fixed rate receiver or **fixed receiver.** The party to an **interest rate swap** or a **cross-currency swap** who receives the **fixed rate**. Because it is an exchange of cash flows, the fixed receiver is also the **floating rate payer**. Such a party is considered to be the swap seller or **short** the swap (cf. **short funded**).

fixed rate reset swap. A type of **interest rate** swap or **cross-currency swap** where the fixed rate has periodic reviews.

fixed rate swap. See **coupon swap**; **interest rate swap**.

fixed receiver's swaption. The **option** position in a **swaption** giving the holder the right to pay the floating rate and receive the the **fixed rate**. Also known as a *receiver's swaption*.

fixed-term agreements for long-term call options on Netherlands securities (FALCONS) (Equities; Netherlands). Long-dated **options** traded on the Amsterdam Stock Exchange. They are similar in concept to **long-term equity anticipation securities**. There is also a short-term variety known as **fixed-term agreements for short-term call options on Netherlands securities**.

fixed-term agreements for short-term call options on Netherlands securities (FASCONS) (Equities; Netherlands). Short-dated **options** traded on the Amsterdam Stock Exchange. They are similar in concept to **covered calls**.

fixed-then-floating bond. A type of **bond** which pays a **fixed rate coupon** for a number of years and then switches to pay a **floating** or **variable** rate of interest. Such a structure might be attractive to investors if the **yield curve** was expected to invert at some point in the future. See also **hybrid reverse floating rate note**.

fixed-then-zero coupon bond. A type of **deep discount** security which pays a **fixed rate coupon** for a number of years and then pays nothing until **maturity**. Such a structure might be attractive to investors who wished to receive interest payments for a time and then wanted a guaranteed **yield-to-maturity**. One variant involves the pre-payment of interest in the coupon rate, where the interest rate (**internal rate of return**) is the same as that of a conventional **straight bond**.

Fixed-then-zero coupon bond

	Price \ Years	1	2	3	4	5	6	7
Straight bond	100	10	10	10	10	10	10	110
Fixed-then-zero	76.18	10	10	10	—	—	—	100
Variant	100	19.58	19.58	19.58	—	—	—	100

fixed trust. An **investment company** which has a fixed **portfolio**. Normally such companies are limited to one class of security, but sometimes the content of the whole portfolio is fixed.

fixing. See **fix**.

flag. A chartist's pattern which is a concentration of price movements within a narrowing band. A chartist will monitor a flag pattern to try and identify a **breakout**, which occurs when a resistance line is broken (cf. **pennant**).

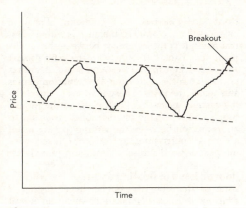

Flag

FLAGS (Bonds). A fixed rate **bearer** instrument created by **repackaging** part of the UK 1996 **floating rate note** (FRN) issue through a special purpose company. The transaction converted a floating rate obligation into a fixed rate synthetic security while maintaining the **underlying** credit through the use of an **interest rate swap**. Another hybrid FRN of UK instruments, based on a 1990/2 **maturity**, was called **bearer eurodollar collateralized securities**. See also **financial engineering**.

flash (USA). (i) A method used for giving participants up-to-date transaction prices for heavily traded securities when the market price reporting mechanism (or **tape**) is running more than five minutes behind time. (ii) More generally an information system method for reporting important news by giving the basic headline.

flash point. See **trigger**.

flat. (i) The quotation of a price excluding the **accrued interest** (cf. **dirty price**; **full price**). See **ex-coupon**; **ex-dividend**. (ii) A **commission** or fee, calculated as a percentage of the **principal** value of an issue of **stock**, which is payable immediately, normally at issue, rather than as a percentage fee payable annually. See **front-end fee**; **front-end loading**; **initial charge**. (iii) The **position** of a **market-maker** which is neither **long** nor **short** (cf. **hedged**; **match**). (iv) The position of an **underwriter** having no outstanding **underwriting commitment**. (v) A condition where there is no **spread** between two or more financial instruments or **commodities**. Hence if all **bonds** irrespective of maturity were trading at the same **yield**, this would be called a *flat yield curve*. (vi) Applied to a market where prices remain basically unchanged over time. See **flat market**.

flat income bond (USA). A US term for a **bond** quoted at a price that includes **accrued interest** (cf. **clean price**; **dirty price**; **ex-coupon**).

flat market. A market where prices are neither rising nor falling (cf. **equilibrium**; **market forces**). Usually the result of either a lack of market activity or the effects of interventions such as **stabilization** (cf. **bear market**; **bull market**).

flat rate. (i) A **bond** quoted with **accrued interest** (cf. **income bond**). (ii) A rate of interest calculated by taking the periodic rate and multiplying this by the frequency of payments. Thus a car loan which repays in monthly instalments with a 2% monthly rate would be expressed as a 24% annual flat rate. The flat rate normally understates the **annual equivalent** rate. Used particularly in consumer credit transactions (cf. **annual percentage rate**; **effective interest rate**). Sometimes called the **nominal rate**. (iii) Another term for **current yield**.

flat rate forward (Commodities). A series of **forward contracts** which have the same differential between the **spot** and the **forward rate**. Also known as an *advanced premium forward* or a *stabilized contango contract*. See **commodity swap**.

flat scale (Bonds; USA). **Municipal bond** market condition where there are similar **yields** for short-dated and long-dated **serial bonds** (cf. **flat yield curve**).

flat yield. See **current yield**.

flat yield curve. Interest rates where all **maturities** are trading at, or near, the same **yield**. Also known as a *horizontal yield curve*.

flex future or **flexible future.** Type of futures contract where the specifications of the transaction can be altered by buyers and sellers. It provides more flexibility than the standardized contract and therefore has some of the advantages of a **forward** but without the **counterparty risk**.

flexible drawdown (Banking). A condition in a facility allowing the borrower to decide when to receive all or part of the loan (cf. **revolving credit facility**; **tranche**). To benefit from such an arrangement the borrower normally pays a **commitment** fee (cf. **standby**).

flexible exchange options. See **flex options**.

flexible forward. See **breakforward**.

flexible swap or **flex swap.** Interest rate swap where one party pays a **fixed rate** and the other party a **floating rate** as long as the **reference rate** less a **margin** is above a predetermined minimum rate; if not, then this leg of the swap becomes a fixed rate at the **strike rate**. In effect, the floating side of the swap has an **embedded floor** position, and the lower margin is the premium from **writing** the **options**.

flexible trombone issue (Equities; UK). See **trombone issue**.

flex options or **flexible options** (flexible exchange options). **Exchange-traded options** which allow institutional investors to customize the terms and conditions of the standard contract, for instance the **strike price**, **expiry date**, whether the **option** is to be an **American-style** or **European-style** exercise, and the type of **settlement**. Each special feature creates a new **series** of options which are then listed on the exchange. Other features are as per the standard contract.

flex repurchase agreement (flex repo) (USA). Arrangement allowing an issuer to re-deposit funds and earn the **repurchase rate** but cancel out part of the agreement when funds are required. Some arrangements have more in common with a **collateralized** loan, as they may extend several years.

flight to quality. A tendency of market participants in times of uncertainty to sell low **credit worthiness** issues and buy high **credit quality** issues (cf. **treasury-eurodollar spread**). For instance, for **bond** investors to sell **corporate bonds** and buy government issues instead. The effect is to depress the price of the low-quality issues and raise the price of the high-quality issues and thereby widen the **spread** between the two. A flight to quality can also take place across different markets. See also **Dow theory**.

flip-flop. A term within a financial instrument that allows the holder to convert back and forth between the original issue and one with a shorter **maturity** usually for some penalty. For example, the Kingdom of Sweden issued a **perpetual floating rate note** (FRN) in 1984 which included a flip-flop that allowed holders to convert or flip into an FRN with a four year maturity at each coupon payment date. See **convertible**.

float (Forex). An exchange rate that is allowed to vary against other currencies. Floating rates may come in different forms: *free float* is when the government of the country allows the supply and demand factors to set the external value of the currency (cf. **market forces**); *managed* or *dirty float* has the government setting a **range** within which the currency may fluctuate before **intervention** takes place; *crawling peg* allows the currency to float within a range, but to ensure that over the longer term the currency either **appreciates** or **depreciates** by a set amount (usually to cover the differential in inflation rates).

float (Money markets). (i) The amount of positive balances that a commercial bank has with its **central bank**. It is the difference between the credits made to a bank's account with the central bank and the debits to the account. Float is always positive because, in **clearing**, the credit sometimes anticipates the debit. These frictions in the **clearing system** mean that float increases the money supply. (ii) The amount of money available to an institution between the writing (paying in) of a cheque and payment (credit). (iii) In securities markets, a shorthand term for **floating supply**.

float an issue or **floating an issue.** The issuance issue of shares to the public; hence *floating a company*. It is usually taken to mean an **initial public offering**, but could refer to additional shares in a company already **quoted** or **listed** on an exchange.

floater. Colloquial term for a **floating rate note** or other instrument with **variable interest** payments.

floating capital. (i) Financial resources available to a firm for its business activities. It generally includes any investments made by the company (cf. **fixed capital**; **working capital**). (ii) Another term used for the **current assets** of a **company**. Sometimes called *circulating capital*.

floating charge (i) (UK) General, unspecific **lien** on a company's **assets** that allows the firm to undertake normal trading activities but crystallizes if certain events should take place (cf. **insolvency**). Agreeing to such a floating charge for smaller firms is often a prior condition for banks agreeing to make a loan. (ii) A form of guarantee offered as a promise to fulfil a **financial** obligation. Usually, such a charge would be against the general assets of a borrower. If the financial obligation is breached, then the lender would be allowed to realize some of the assets to secure repayment. Sometimes called *floating mortgage*. See **fixed charge**; **mortgage bond**.

floating debenture. (Bonds; UK). A type of **asset-backed bond**, where the issue is backed by a **floating charge** on the issuer's assets (cf. **fixed debenture**; **unsecured loan stock**). See **debenture**.

floating debt. (i) Any debt that has a **floating rate** of interest (cf. **variable rate**). (ii) Short-term borrowings with a **maturity** of less than one year. (iii) That part of a country's National Debt that is short term, such as **treasury bills**.

floating eurodollar repackaged assets of the Republic of Italy (FERARI) (Bonds). An issue of synthetic eurodollar securities created by repackaging domestic Italian European Currency Unit bonds. See synthetic security.

floating exchange rate. Exchange rate between currencies that is allowed to be set by market forces. See float.

floating/floating swap or **floating-for-floating swap.** A common term in the euromarkets for a basis swap. It can also mean one of the many exotic swaps which have embedded options.

floating interest rate short tranche (FIRST) (Bonds; USA). The first to repay tranche of a floating rate collateralized mortgage obligation.

floating lien. A type of general lien over a firm's assets or a particular class of asset. See also floating charge.

floating payer. See floating rate note.

floating rate. Any method of paying interest that is periodically refixed in line with the current market rate (cf. margin; reference rate; rollover). See floating rate interest.

floating rate bonds. See floating rate note.

floating rate certificate of deposit (FRCD) (Money markets). A certificate of deposit that pays periodic interest on a floating rate, based on some benchmark or reference rate (cf. London interbank offered rate). Maturities are up to five years under Bank of England rules if issued in the London market (cf. fixed rate certificate of deposit). See interest rate calculations.

floating rate collateralized mortgage obligation (floating rate CMO; FRCMO) (Bonds; USA). A collateralized mortgage obligation which pays a floating or variable rate coupon reset against an index or a reference rate, although there is usually a maximum rate (cf. cap).

floating rate credit rating sensitive note. A floating rate note where the margin relative to the reference rate is determined according to the credit worthiness of the issuer as determined by a credit rating agency's credit rating. Thus a triple-B issuer who received an upgrade to single-A would, with this instrument, be entitled to a reduction in the margin it paid over the reference rate, if this was what was specified in the conditions of the notes. The instrument appeals to those issuers who expect to improve their credit standing in the near term and do not wish to refinance existing borrowings, thus saving on issuing fees. Also known as a *floating rate rating sensitive note.*

floating rate enhanced debt security (FRENDS). Asset-backed security where the underlying is a pool of bank loans. Enhancement comes from over-collateralization where the C and B tranches are subordinated to the A tranche. See securitization.

floating rate interest, floating rate or **variable rate interest, variable rate.** Interest on a security or derivative product that is not fixed for the life of the issue, but which is periodically reset according to a predetermined formula. The rate is usually set at a margin or spread in relation to a specified money market rate, such as the London interbank offered rate. Variations linking the rate to longer-dated securities or other instruments have also been undertaken. See eurocredits; eurobonds; fix.

floating rate note (FRN) (Bonds). A term security paying periodic interest at a floating rate, and where there is often a minimum rate of interest or floor. Because the coupon is reset in line with current market rates, an FRN will normally trade close to its par value. As a result, they often include call provisions and sometimes put provisions since these will have little value as options, but will provide flexibility to issuers and protection to investors. Because the notes normally trade close to par and because the coupon is reset in line with prevailing market rates, FRNs were sometimes considered to be money market instruments. In reality, there is some risk of capital loss if the spread over the benchmark or reference rate required by market participants should rise since the present value of the additional required spread may represent a significant proportion of the par value for a note with a significant term to maturity; or to any put date. On the other hand, the common inclusion of call provisions will usually limit the rise in value much above par. There will also be some fluctuation in price between coupon reset dates in response to changes in short-term interest rates. Known colloquially as a *floater.* See eurocredits; euromarkets; hybrid; mismatch bond; perpetual floating rate note; reverse floating rate note.

floating rate note with issuer set rate. See variable rate note.

floating rate note with variable spread. See variable rate note.

floating rate payer. The party to an interest rate swap or a cross-currency swap who contracts to make variable rate payments. Sometimes known as *floating payer, pay floating,* or *receive fixed* the latter because the floating rate payer will be receiving in exchange fixed rate payments.

floating rate preferred stock (Equities; USA). A type of **preferred stock** issue which pays a dividend in line with prevailing **short-term** interest rates. Variations on the basic formula include auction-rate market preferred stock; **money market preferred stock**, and so forth.

floating receiver. The party to an **interest rate swap** or **cross-currency swap** who agrees to receive the **floating rate** and make **fixed rate** payments. See **floating rate payer** (cf. **fixed rate payer**; **fixed rate receiver**).

floating securities (Equities; USA). The issued stock traded on an exchange. Also sometimes used for that part of a new issue that has not been **distributed** by **underwriters** (cf. **floating supply**).

floating spread (Banking). Term for a **margin** or spread to a **reference rate** in a **facility** where the interest is calculated on a **floating rate** which is itself variable. Thus a facility might have an initial 0.5% margin, but at the point of resetting the interest the banks may be asked to **tender** the rate at which they would be prepared to lend.

floating strike option. See **average strike option**.

floating supply. The amount of an issue in the hands of **dealers** or investors waiting to sell, i.e. that proportion which has not been sold to end investors (that is, is in 'firm hands') and is therefore likely to be resold in the market. A large floating supply would indicate that the upward price potential is limited since considerable added selling would follow any increase in price (cf. **buy and hold**; **firm hands**).

floating-then-zero bond. A variant of the **fixed-then-zero coupon bond**, it is a **floating rate note** which pays all its interest in the early part of its term and then nothing until **maturity**. Such a note might appeal to investors desirous of receiving interest early on at the expense of nothing later.

floor. (i) (Bonds) The minimum coupon rate on a **floating rate note** (FRN). Some issues set a floor for a set period and are known as *initial floor FRNs*. (ii) (Derivatives) A minimum rate on a floating rate of interest. See **interest rate caps** (cf. **collar**). (iii) A position consisting of holding the **underlying** and a purchased **put option**. The combination provides a floor against adverse **downside** price movements. (iv) Also used to mean the place where traders go physically to make transactions on an **exchange** (cf. **pit**). In some markets, trading floors have been replaced by **screen-trading** (cf. **over the counter**).

floor broker. A trader member on an exchange floor who carries out transactions for a **commission** on behalf of customers who do not have access to the trading area (cf. **pit**). See also **commission broker**.

floor-ceiling swap. An interest rate swap where the **floating rate** can only vary between a pre-set upper and lower rate. It is created by buying an **interest rate cap** and selling a **floor**. See also **collar**.

floored put. A type of limited payout **option** where there is a **floor** set on the potential gain from a fall in the **underlying**. It is equivalent to buying a **put** at one price/rate and selling another at a lower price/rate (cf. **bear spread**; **vertical spread**). The **premium** on a floored put should be less than that on an unlimited put.

floorlet. Term used to describe one of the periods in a **floor** contract which is made up of several floorlets (cf. **caplet**).

floor official (USA). An exchange employee who settles transaction difficulties or disputes on the trading floor of an exchange (cf. **out-trade**).

floor rate or **strike.** The strike rate set on an **interest rate floor** (cf. **cap rate**). For instance, it is the minimum interest rate paid or received on an **interest rate collar**, or a **range floating rate note**.

floor ticket. The document used for transactions on an exchange. This is generally a shorter document than the **order ticket**.

floortion or **floption.** An option on a **floor**. The holder has the right to purchase an **interest rate floor** at a set rate at **expiry** (cf. **compound option**; **European-style option**). The other, similar option, is a **caption**, which is an option on an **interest rate cap**.

floor trader. Member of an exchange who trades only for their own account (i.e. as **principal**). Also known as a *local*.

flotation. The bringing of a new issue to market (cf. **initial public offering**; **new issue**; **offer for sale**).

flotation cost. The cost of bringing a new issue (usually **equity**) to market. The term is usually reserved for equity offerings (cf. **all-in cost**). See **float**.

flowback. The sale of **shares**, originally placed with overseas investors, back into the domestic market by those investors. See **global offering**.

flower bond. A low coupon US treasury bond which, when held by the deceased, can be used to pay federal death duties at its **par** value. It is no longer issued.

flow of funds. See **cash flow**.

fluctuation limit. A restriction placed on the movement in **commodity futures** in any one trading session. Once this **limit** is reached, trading ceases for the session (cf. **limit-up**).

flurry. A period of intense market activity characterized by frenetic buying and selling.

FOCUS report (Financial and Operational Combined Uniform Single report) (USA). A statement of condition that **broker-dealers** are required to provide periodically to their **self-regulating organizations**.

follow-up strategies. The actions taken once an **option strategy** has been established based on movements in the **underlying**. These actions can be deemed aggressive, if designed to exploit a profitable position, or defensive, if aimed at limiting further losses.

fonds (French). **Funds**, or securities.

fonds commun (French). **Mutual fund**.

fonds commun de créances (FCC) (French). A type of **money market mutual fund** authorized to invest in short-dated securities and **deposits**.

fonds commun de placement (FCP) (French). Money market fund.

fonds d'état (French). Government **bonds**.

food bills (Money markets; Japan). A type of treasury bill issued by the Japanese government ostensibly to pay for food.

Forbes 500 (USA). An annual listing by the publication *Forbes* of the top 500 US publicly owned corporations, as measured by sales, assets, profits, and **market value**. See also **Fortune 500**.

Forced conversion. (i) The exercise of a **warrant** or **convertible** made necessary by the issuer's decision to invoke the **call provision** (cf. 130 **per cent** rule). Warrants or convertibles are called when the **intrinsic value** exceeds the **call price**. Under such conditions the warrant or convertible holders would incur losses by tendering rather than **exercising** or **converting**. In the case of warrants, by forcing conversion the borrower receives an inflow of cash, the **exercise price**, and eliminates the warrants from the **capital structure**. In the case of a convertible it is a provision of the issue

to remove the administrative inconvenience of a small **rump** remaining when the bulk of the issue has already been converted. (ii) It can also mean the calling of a convertible which is selling above its call price. The investor must convert to **common stock** or **ordinary shares** and take a loss by accepting the call price or sell the convertible.

forced sale. (i) Selling of assets due either to the need to realize cash, as when a company enters into **insolvency** or **bankruptcy** proceedings. (ii) The disposal by a **broker** of a position in the market as a result of the owner failing to meet a **margin call** (cf. **cover**). Forced sale risk is one criteria used by the **Bank of England** in assessing depository institutions' **exposures**.

force majeure (French). Literally, superior force. A term commonly found in most contracts that allows the contract to be terminated or voided if there is a prolonged period of interruption due to fire, flood, storm, war, or some other factors beyond the control of the participants. Although a general let-out clause it is rarely invoked in securities or **derivatives** markets due to the damage to the financial intermediary's reputation.

forecasting. In econometrics, a quantitative guess (or set of guesses) about the likelihood of future events based on past and current information. This past and current information is embodied in the form of a **model**. By extrapolating such models out beyond the period over which they were subject to **estimation**, the information contained within them can be used to make forecasts about future events. Two types of forecasts have been found to be useful: point forecasts predict a single number in each forecast period; and interval forecasts indicate in each forecast period an interval in which it is hoped the actual realized value will exist. Most forecasting tools begin by establishing point guesses, after which interval forecasts, or a **confidence interval**, can be used to provide a margin of error around a point forecast. Such a forecasting sequence can be useful in applying **sensitivity** techniques to various financial problems, such as optimizing portfolios (cf. **modern portfolio theory**; **sensitivity analysis**). See also **hedging**; **risk management**.

forecast volatility. The **expected volatility** over the life of a transaction, determined by forecasting methods (cf. **implied volatility**).

foreign bond. Bond issue made by a non-domestic **obligor** in the domestic capital markets of a country. The markets identify these issues with special names, for instance some of the more common ones are:

Bulldog	UK market
Matador	Spanish market
Navigator	Portuguese market
Samurai	Japanese market
Yankee	US market

Terms and conditions usually conform to those pertaining to corporate issues in the relevant domestic market, such as **coupon** frequency and final maturities, and sometimes include **convertibles, bonds with equity warrants,** and **zero-coupon bonds.** The vast majority, however, tend to be **straight bonds** (cf. **plain vanilla**).

foreign corporation. A company engaging in business in one country but which is domiciled in another country or state.

Foreign Credit Insurance Association (FCIA) (USA). Export finance insurance provided by a group of insurance companies and operated by the **Export-Import Bank.**

foreign crowd. Members of the New York Stock Exchange who trade **yankee bonds** (cf. **active bond crowd; cabinet crowd**).

foreign currency bills. Bills issued in a domestic market in a currency other than the legal tender of that country. Such bills are not eligible for rediscount at the **central bank.** Past issues include some European Currency Unit denominated bills in the US market and US dollar bills in the UK market.

foreign currency bond. (i) An issue where the **coupon** is paid in a different currency from that of denomination and at the then prevailing **foreign exchange spot rate** (cf. **dual currency bond**). (ii) Sometimes used to describe a **foreign bond** issued in a market in a foreign currency (cf. **shogun bond** (Japan)).

foreign currency futures. See **currency future.**

foreign currency interest payment securities. See **foreign currency bond.**

foreign currency option. See **currency option.**

foreign currency payer. The payer of the non-US currency in a **cross-currency swap** against the US dollar.

foreign currency preferred stock or **preference share.** A preferred stock issue made in the domestic market of a country and denominated in a **currency** other than the legal tender. For instance, an issue made in sterling in the US domestic market.

foreign direct investment. A diversification strategy pursued mostly by **multinational corporations** involving the purchase of **assets,** usually associated with manufacturing or distribution facilities, in another country. Often regarded as the second stage of overseas involvement after agency or licensing agreements have been used to establish a market. For the investors in such companies the profits generated from foreign activities can create difficulties regarding the repatriation of profits, not least because of differences in tax systems that may make it more efficient to retain the **earnings** and reinvest overseas, than to bring such earnings home (cf. **double taxation**).

foreign domicile bill (Money markets; UK). A bill which has been drawn and accepted outside the UK.

foreign exchange. The exchange of one currency for another (cf. **foreign exchange forward market; forward exchange market**).

foreign exchange agreement (FXA). See **synthetic agreement for foreign exchange.**

foreign exchange bid rate. The exchange rate at which a **market-maker** will buy the **base currency** (cf. **offer**). See **left-hand side.**

foreign exchange bills (Money markets; Japan). A type of **treasury bill** issued by the Japanese government to fund the purchase of foreign currency.

foreign exchange broker. Broker specializing in transacting **foreign exchange.**

foreign exchange cross-rates. The exchange rate between two currencies neither of which is the US dollar. For currencies quoted in the same way (US terms or European terms), divide one by the other (either way will achieve the same result). For currencies where one is quoted US and the other European, multiply the **spot** of one by the spot of the other. Note: there are market conventions for quoting some cross-rates based on their relative unit values, the heavier currency usually being taken as the **base currency** (e.g. for DM/£, sterling is the base currency).

foreign exchange dealer. Dealer specializing in transacting **foreign exchange** (cf. **principal**).

foreign exchange exposure. (i) The holding of foreign currency which would give the same foreign exchange **risk** as the current position. (ii) The situation of having **currency exposure.**

foreign exchange forward. A forward transaction in **foreign exchange.** Often just called *forwards*. A bilateral contract to exchange a specified amount of one currency for another at a specific future date (cf. **currency futures**). The rate at which the two currencies are to be ex-changed is based on the **arbitrage-free condition** of the two currencies' interest rate differential. The rate at which a contract for a specific future maturity will be undertaken is called the *forward exchange rate*, *forward outright rate*, or *forward rate*. The difference between the forward rate and the spot rate is measured in *swap points*. These are the reported forward rates on information services and in newspapers. Foreign exchange forwards are used to take or reduce risk or to match cash flows. If the currency to be sold has risen when the contract is settled, the seller will have lost; if it has fallen, the seller has gained. Note that the use of forward contracts exposes both sides to **credit risk** or **counterparty risk**. In principle, the only way of closing a forward foreign exchange con-tract is to do the opposite transaction to that already contracted and to pay/receive the differ-ence at **settlement** (cf. **delivery**). See discount; forward exchange rate; forward outright rate; forward regular dates; forward swap points; premium; swap points.

foreign exchange forward market. The mar-ket for **foreign exchange** where **settlement** of transactions is delayed or deferred beyond the normal settlement period (cf. **currency futures**; forward; futures). See appreciation; depreciation.

foreign exchange hedging techniques. Set of cash management techniques designed to minim-ize the impact of expected movements on the value of foreign cash flows. The following tech-niques also go by the colloquial name of *leading and lagging*. The Tables summarize the different approaches commonly used.

foreign exchange intervention. See inter-vention; dirty float.

foreign exchange line of credit. A facility pro-vided to a borrower to meet **foreign exchange** obligations.

foreign exchange long position. A net asset position in a currency. That is, an excess of

Foreign exchange hedging techniques

Depreciation (If the currency to be hedged is expected to *depreciate*)	Appreciation (If the currency to be hedged is expected to *appreciate*)
sell currency forward	buy currency forward
reduce levels of local currency, cash, and marketable securities	increase levels of local currency, cash, and marketable securities
tighten credit terms (reduce receivables)	relax credit terms
delay collection of hard currency receivables	speed up collection of soft currency receivables
accelerate imports of hard currency items	delay imports of soft currency items
increase borrowing in local currency/reduce foreign currency borrowing	reduce local borrowing/increase foreign borrowing
delay payment of accounts payable in the local currency	speed up payment of accounts payable in local currency
speed-up dividend and fee remittances	remittance to parent and fee remittances
speed-up payment of inter-company accounts payable	delay payment of inter-company accounts payable
delay payment of inter-company accounts receivable	speed-up payment of inter-company accounts payable
invoice exports in foreign currency and imports in local currency	invoice exports in local currency and exports in foreign currency

Effects of hedging exposures

Depreciation strategies[a]	Effects: costs and implications
sell local currency forward	a weak currency will stand at a forward discount with the risk of loss on the contract
reduce the level of local currency cash and marketable securities	cash flow and tax problems; opportunity costs from lower interest rates on the hard currencies
tighten credit (reduce receivables)	loss of business if credit terms are non-competitive
delay collection of hard currency receivables	delays must be funded
accelerate imports of hard currency goods	imports must be financed
delay payment of accounts payable in that currency	could affect the firm's credit standing
speed up dividend and fee remittances	increased borrowing costs if funds not already available
speed up payment of inter-company accounts payable	increased borrowing costs
delay collection of inter-company accounts receivable	borrowing costs
invoice exports in foreign currency and imports in local currency	lost sales; forward premium on hard currency import payments

[a] Appreciation strategies are the reverse of strategies for a depreciating currency.

purchases over sales; or an excess of **assets** to **liabilities**. A strengthening of the currency with a **long position** results in a gain; a weakening results in a corresponding loss.

foreign exchange market (FX; Forex). The financial market for the exchange of **currencies** which includes cash or **spot** transactions, **foreign exchange forwards**, **futures**, and **options**. The market is principally **over the counter** between the world's leading banks and their customers, although **currency futures** and **currency options** are traded on a number of exchanges.

foreign exchange offered rate. The exchange rate at which a **market-maker** will **offer** or sell the **base currency** (cf. **bid**). See **right-hand side**.

foreign exchange open position. The existence of a **foreign exchange exposure** that is either a **long** or a **short** position.

foreign exchange rate. The price of one currency expressed in terms of another. It is made up of the *base currency*: the currency against which the value of another is expressed. There are two conventions used for giving the **quote** (cf. **foreign exchange bid rate**; **foreign exchange offered rate**):

American terms: Foreign exchange rates expressed in terms of how many US dollars can be exchanged for one unit of another currency (the non-US$ currency is the *base currency*) eg: US dollars/pounds sterling (US$/£). Also called *US terms*.

European terms: Foreign exchange rates expressed in terms of how many currency units can be exchanged for one US dollar (the US$ is the *base currency*), e.g. Deutschmark/US dollars (DM/US$).

The rate can be either for **spot** delivery (the *spot rate*) or for forward delivery (the *forward outright rate*). See also **swap points**.

foreign exchange rate risk. The risk that the value of an **asset** or **liability**, **portfolio**, or legal entity will change due to the **exchange rate** fluctuating over time.

foreign exchange regular dates. The foreign exchange market is modelled after the eurocurrency market where the regular forward periods are 1, 2, 3, 6, 9, and 12 months and use the **fixed date** and **end–end** conventions. With the **fixed date** method, the **forward value date** for each regular forward period is determined by the (current) **spot date** (cf. **fixed dates**). **Odd dates** or **broken dates** are any non-regular value dates. The end-to-end convention requires that if **spot** is the last day of the month, each forward value date will also be the last day of the month.

foreign exchange reserves. The stock of foreign **currencies** held by countries to finance any obligations that may arise (cf. **Exchange Stabilization Fund**). The extent of these calls depends on the sort of **exchange rate** system operated. For example, if a commitment to maintain a value for its currency comes under pressure the **monetary authority** may have to use such reserves as part of an interventionist policy (cf. **dirty float**). Often, **central banks** will have **swap** lines allowing them to borrow foreign currency in order to be able to defend the exchange rate when a currency comes under market pressure. Also known as *currency reserves*.

foreign exchange risk management (FERM). The methods of managing **foreign exchange rate** risk and **currency exposures** through the **foreign exchange market** (cf. **risk**). This typically involves using **derivative instruments** such as **forwards**, **futures**, **swaps**, and **options**. It also includes wider business strategy decisions such as **foreign direct investment** and **joint ventures** to reduce the magnitude of the exposures. See **risk management**.

foreign exchange services (Banking). The facilities provided by banks for their customers to deal in **foreign exchange**. See also **concentration banking**; **correspondent**.

foreign exchange short position. A net liability holding in a **currency**. That is, an excess of sales over purchases; or an excess of **liabilities** to **assets**. A strengthening of the currency with a **short position** results in a loss; weakening results in a gain.

foreign exchange spot rate. The exchange rate for normal market settlement (cf. **cash**; **same-day delivery**; **spot rate**; **tom/next**). The *spot contract* is a foreign exchange contract in which the value date is the earliest regular value date and the rate is the outright price for that **value date**. The *spot rate* is the **outright exchange rate** which applies to transactions settled on the spot date.

foreign exchange spreads. The difference in price between the **bid** and **offer** within one **quote**.

foreign exchange square position. No exposure to the market and therefore no **currency exposure** and no **foreign exchange rate risk**.

foreign exchange swaps. The exchange and re-exchange of two currencies for different **value dates**. Typically, it is the sale of one currency for another in the **spot market** with the simultaneous repurchase of the first currency in the **forward market**. However, swaps can also be made against two forward rates (cf. **forward-forward**). See also **covered interest arbitrage; cross-currency swaps**.

foreign exchange trading line. A facility allowing the **counterparty** to transact **foreign exchange**. Such trading lines normally include a total exposure limit, a maximum daily exposure limit, and a **maturity** exposure limit.

foreign exchange transaction date. The date on which the terms of a foreign exchange contract are agreed upon by the two parties (cf. **cash market; spot date**).

foreign exchange value date. The date on which the two currencies involved in a foreign exchange contract are settled (the payments date).

Value dates in the foreign exchange market

The value date is	Today	One business day from today	Two business days from today	Three business days or longer from today
Trans-action is: for	cash	tom/next; or spot[a]	spot	forward

[a] spot for Canadian dollars; Mexican pesos against the US dollar

For Islamic countries which have holidays on different days, the following applies:

Transaction date	Settlement date
Monday	Wednesday
Tuesday	Thursday
Wednesday	Non-islamic country: Friday Islamic country: Saturday
Thursday	Monday
Saturday	Wednesday
Sunday	Wednesday

foreign income dividend (FID) (Equities; UK). A method of paying **dividends** on foreign income introduced in the Finance Act, 1993 to cater for those companies which have a large proportion of their profits from overseas operations and are subject to **unrelieved advance corporation tax** (unrelieved ACT). Companies in such a position face a higher rate of effective taxation under the UK's corporation tax laws when **mainstream corporation tax** is insufficient to offset the ACT on dividends. With FIDs, companies can opt to pay a dividend from remitted foreign income which allows the company to avoid paying ACT. A UK-based shareholder who pays tax will still receive a tax credit on the dividend, thus 'grossing up' the payment (cf. **franked income**). The first company to make use of FIDs was BAT Industries. See also **enhanced scrip dividend**.

foreign interest payment securities (FIPS). These are offered, paid for, and redeemed in the same currency, but **coupon** payments are made in another currency at a pre-agreed fixed **exchange rate** (cf. **dual currency bond**). See **foreign currency bond**.

foreign investment. Acquisitions of assets in a foreign country. This may be either by **direct investment**, where a foreign firm either sets up a business in the country or buys a local firm (cf. **foreign direct investment; mergers and acquisitions**). Or it is **portfolio investment**, in which case financial instruments such as **common stocks** or **bonds** are purchased. In the first case, the buying company obtains strategic control over the investment, whereas with portfolio investment the rationale is international **diversification** aimed at improving returns and/or reducing risk (cf. **emerging markets**). See also **global markets**.

foreign property rule (Canada). A law that limits the amount of foreign investment by pension funds to 10% of assets. The rule is gradually being relaxed allowing such funds to invest abroad.

foreign stock index futures, options, and **warrants.** **Derivatives** offered in one country on the stock indices of another. For instance, the **Singapore International Monetary Exchange's** futures contract on the **Nikkei 225** index.

forex. Market acronym for **foreign exchange**.

forex-linked or **currency-linked bond.** A bond issue where the redemption proceeds are linked to the maturity **spot** exchange rate of another **currency** against the currency of denomination. See **heaven-and-hell bond**.

forfaiting. An international trade-based activity where a lender agrees to buy at a **discount** the **medium-term promissory notes** or **bills** issued in payment of goods or services. Normally forfaiting is **non-recourse** and therefore only the best transactions or those which are guaranteed by a bank or state agency are acceptable (cf. **aval; bill of exchange; documentary credit**).

Forfettario (Italy). Flat rate **capital gains** tax on share gains (cf. **analitico**).

Form F-1 (USA) The securities and exchange commission from required to be filed by companies making an **initial public offering** giving details of the securities to be issued (cf. **registration**).

Form 3 (USA). The Securities and Exchange Commission form that is required to be filed by a company giving details of major ownership by shareholders and directors and officers. It is available for public inspection.

Form 4 (USA). The **Securities and Exchange Commission** form that is required to be filed by a company updating details of major ownership by shareholders and directors and officers, that is **Form 3**. It is available for public inspection.

Form 8-K (USA). The **Securities and Exchange Commission** (SEC) form that is required to be filed by a company providing details of any material event and which must be filed within thirty days of the event occurring. In practice, companies tend to issue press releases to comply with disclosure requirements for listing with a subsequent regulatory report. The SEC sets a reasonableness test based on what an average investor would want to know before transacting in the security. It is available for public inspection.

Form 10-K (USA). The annual report form to the **Securities and Exchange Commission** that is required to be filed by a company. It is available for public inspection.

Form 10-Q (USA). The quarterly report form to the **Securities and Exchange Commission** that is required to be filed by a company but which is less comprehensive than **Form-10k**.

formal default. See **bankruptcy; Chapter 11; default; insolvency; technical default**.

Form for Analysing Bank Capital (Banking; USA). A form for the breakdown of a bank's capital position developed by the **Federal Reserve Board** for supervising banks' **capital adequacy** requirements.

formula basis (USA). A method of issuing securities which allows the **registration** statement to become effective based on a formula for the issuing price rather than a fixed price (cf. **shelf registration**).

formula investing. An investment strategy which involves restructuring a **portfolio** according to certain predetermined points in the prices of the various securities. See **program trading; technical analysis**.

formulary tax system. A method of taxing multinational companies operating in a particular tax jurisdiction based on a formula for the consolidated group's profits rather than the **arm's length** tax system which taxes only those profits earned in the particular tax jurisdiction. See also **unitary taxation**.

for the account (Equities; UK). Type of transaction formerly possible on the **London Stock Exchange** (ISE) when it operated the **settlement** on the basis of **accounts** aimed at buying (selling) and selling (buying) within the same account period, thus having to avoid payment (cf. **backwardation; contango; round trip**). The intention to **close out** a transaction within the account period would be notified by marking the **ticket** 'for the account'. The ISE has now instituted **rolling settlement** which precludes this type of activity as previously undertaken (cf. **deferred payment**).

Fortune 500 (USA). A much read annual listing by the publication *Fortune* of the top 500 US industrial corporations, as measured by sales. See also **Forbes 500**.

forum shopping. The tendency for plaintiffs involved in litigation in international transactions to seek the jurisdiction which most favours their case or offers the best redress. To counter this most agreements stipulate the country or jurisdiction of first recourse.

forward. (i) A contract which has its execution or **settlement** delayed until some future date. See **forward contract**. (ii) Any of a number of deferred-start transactions, such as a **forward swap**, where the starting date is delayed past the normal or **regular delivery** date. (iii) The interest rates implied in the current **yield curve**. See **forward-forward**. (iv) The value of an asset, currency, **derivative**, or instrument at some designated date in the future.

fowardation. See **contango; premium market** (cf. **backwardation; discount market**).

forward band. A zero-cost **interest rate collar**, where the **premium** paid for the **interest rate cap** is exactly offset by the premium earned from selling the floor. In the **options** markets this would be known as a **zero-cost option**.

forward book. The combined **positions** of a market-maker who trades in **forwards**, known as a **book** (cf. **limit order book**). See also **gap; ladder**.

forward break. See **breakforward**.

forward cap. An agreement to enter into a specific **interest rate cap** at a pre-agreed date for an agreed **premium** (cf. **deferred swap**).

forward commodity contract. A deferred delivery bilateral contract for the purchase and sale of a **commodity** (cf. **commodity futures commodity swap; over the counter**).

forward contract. A bilateral legally enforceable contract for the purchase or sale of a defined quantity of a given **asset**, **currency**, **commodity**, **deposit**, product, or security at a fixed price at a date in the future. Typically involves the exchange of assets for cash, including the exchange of currencies (cf. **forward foreign exchange contact**), where the parties agree that **delivery** will be delayed until some mutually agreed (forward) date. By extension, includes a **derivative** contract for future **settlement**. It is therefore a transaction where the settlement is delayed until some mutually agreed upon date in the future (cf. **cash delivery**; **spot**). The basic pricing mechanism for forwards is the spot price plus or minus the **cost of carry** for the period of the delay (cf. **backwardation**; **contango**). Notification and many parts of the settlement of such contracts may take place at the time the contract is entered into and the parties may only have to arrange for **good delivery** at the **maturity** of the contract. Unlike a **futures contract**, a forward contract is not usually transferable, its terms are not standardized, and it is not usually **marked-to-market**. Therefore a forward differs from a **future** in two important technical respects: (*a*) it is a bilateral agreement between the buyer and seller and therefore both parties take on **counterparty risk**. As such it may be for any amount and period and have terms and conditions specific to those parties; (*b*) there is usually no **margin** requirement.
The key differences between forward contracts and futures contracts are shown in the Table.

Forward contract

	Forward	Future
Amount	Any	Specific contract amount
Expiry, maturity, or settlement	Any	Specific dates (normally 4 in a year)
Terms and conditions	As negotiated	Standardized by the exchange
Standard or grade	Any	Exchange clearing house
Cancellation	By mutual consent	Has to be sold (purchased)
Margin requirements	None, unless specifically negotiated	Initial and variation margin required

Note: the term forward is often taken to imply a **foreign exchange forward** contract, given the significance of the **currency markets** and the role of the **forward foreign exchange market**. See also **close out**.

forward cover. A method of **hedging** transaction **exposure** where the future cash flows in a foreign currency are known. It involves buying the currency forward in the case of a payable or selling forward in the case of a receivable. See **foreign exchange**.

forward cross-currency swap. A **cross-currency swap** where the start of the swap is **deferred** on terms agreed at the time the transaction is entered into. The deferral is used to allow an issuer, for instance, to match up the cash flows from a **bond** with an **underlying** swap.

forward curve or **forward yield curve.** A graphical representation of the **yield** versus **maturity** of the implied **forward-forward interest rate** that is implicit in the **spot** or current **yield curve**. It is used as an indicator of the market's expectations on future interest rates (cf. **expectations hypothesis**).

forward dated. See **post-dated**.

forward dealing. Forward buying and selling transactions. Also called *dealing forward*. See **forward transaction**.

forward delivery. Contract for the sale or receipt of goods which has a deferred delivery date compared to the normally accepted market settlement (cf. **forward transaction**). Also sometimes called *deferred delivery*. See **cash market**; **spot**.

forward deposit. See **forward-forward contract**.

forward differential. The difference in price between the **cash market** price and that for the same transaction carried out as a **forward transaction**. There will be four main elements which influence this differential: the **time value of money**, **credit risks**, expectations, and market shortages or squeezes. See **backwardation**; **basis**; **cash and carry**; **contango**; **discount**; **forward**; **forward discount**; **expectations hypothesis**; **forward premium**; **premium**; **price discovery**; **term structure of interest rates**; **yield curve**.

forward discount (i) (Forex) A condition for a currency where the **spot foreign exchange rate** is higher than the **forward outright** (cf. **forward premium**; **swap points**). (ii) (Commodities) When commodity prices for deferred **delivery** stand at a price **discount** to **spot** or cash market prices (cf. **backwardation**; **basis**; **contango**). A market where forward prices stood at a discount would be known as a *discount market*.

forward exchange agreement or **forward exchange rate agreement (FXA).** Synthetic agreement for forward exchange product developed by Midland Capital Markets to hedge forward foreign exchange.

forward exchange margin. See **swap points** (cf. **forward outright**).

forward exchange rate. A rate quoted, usually by banks, for **currency** transactions for **forward delivery** at some point in the future and based upon a **premium** (less) or **discount** (more) against the prevailing **spot rate**. The forward exchange rate is linked to the spot rate within **arbitrage** boundaries by the **interest rate parity** relationship. Also sometimes referred to as a *forward foreign exchange rate*. See **foreign exchange forward**.

forward exchange transaction. See **forward foreign exchange transaction**.

forward fed funds. The market in **fed funds** for future **delivery**. Fed funds are normally traded on a **cash settlement** basis. The forward market allows banks to purchase or sell funds for known periods of surplus or deficit and to fix the rate in advance.

forward foreign exchange contract. Forward contract for the purchase and sale of **foreign exchange**.

forward foreign exchange market. The forward **market** for **currencies**. A common method used for hedging **foreign exchange exposure** (cf. **foreign exchange rate risk**). See **foreign exchange risk management**.

forward foreign exchange transaction. A forward transaction in currencies. A common method used for hedging **foreign exchange rate risk**. See **foreign exchange risk management**.

forward-forward (Forex). A **foreign exchange swap** where the start of the swap is delayed to some point in the future. Thus, both the initial exchange and the re-exchange at **maturity** are **foreign exchange forward** contracts. For example, such a transaction might involve a one-month forward sale of sterling against Deutschmarks with a corresponding three-month forward repurchase of the sterling. The effect is to obtain Deutchmarks for two months in one month's time.

forward-forward contract. A loan or deposit that is made where the start date of the deposit is delayed until some point in the future but where the terms are fixed on the **transaction date** (cf. **forward**; **implied forward interest rate**). Sometimes called a *forward deposit*. See **forward-forward interest rate**; **forward rate agreement**.

forward-forward interest rate or **forward interest rate.** The interest rate on a loan that has been agreed but will be disbursed at some spe-

cified future date (cf. **spot rate**). Sometimes known, when inferred from the **yield curve**, as the *implied forward rate*. It is calculated as follows:

$$R_{ff} = \frac{R_2 t_2 - R_1 t_1}{(t_2 - t_1)\left(1 + \dfrac{R_1 t_1}{100 \times Basis}\right)}$$

where R_{ff} is the forward rate of interest; R_1 the interest rate for the period until the start of the deposit; R_2 the interest rate for the period until the end of the deposit; t_1 the days from present to the start of the deposit; t_2 the days from present to the end of the deposit. The basis will be a year of either 360 or 365 days. Also known as a *forward-forward deposit*. See also **forward rate agreement**.

forward intervention (Forex). Currency intervention by a **central bank** made in the **forward foreign exchange market** (cf. **swap**).

forward intrinsic value of an option (FIV). The **intrinsic value** of an **option** plus the **fair value** of the **forward** on which the option is written. Given the **boundary conditions** that apply to options, a **European-style option** should not trade at less than its forward intrinsic value. See **option pricing**.

forward margin (Forex). The amount by which the **foreign exchange forward** rate differs from the **spot rate** expressed in terms of units of currency or as an interest rate (cf. **discount**; **premium**; **swap points**).

forward market. A place where **commodities**, securities, or **currencies** are traded at a fixed price for delivery on a future date (cf. **futures**; **cash delivery**; **spot market**). A forward market is an over-the-counter market which depends on the bilateral transactions of market participants to function efficiently. The **forward foreign exchange market** is probably the most extensive of the forward markets, but there are interesting markets in North Sea oil and **soft commodities** (*softs*) (cf. **Brent crude**).

forward maturities. See **foreign exchange forward**; **swap points**.

forward months. See **deferred**.

forward outright rate (Forex). The quotation of the **foreign exchange forward** rate on the same basis as the cash or **spot market** quote. The exchange rate for a **forward value** transaction; often quoted in terms of the current spot price plus/minus the **swap points**. The underlying principle is that the currency with the *lower* eurocurrency interest rate is expected to be worth *more* in the future; the currency with the *higher* eurocurrency interest rate is expected to be worth *less* in the future. See also **forward points**.

forward plus. See interest rate collar; participating range forward.

forward plus ratio (Forex). Name for a **participating forward**.

forward point agreement (Forex). **Cross-currency swap** where one party agrees to pay fixed forward points and the other party floating forward points in the two currencies (cf. **foreign exchange swap**).

forward points (Forex). A way of quoting the foreign exchange **forward** rate in terms of **foreign exchange** points. Thus a **forward rate** of 65/85 in relation to the current **spot rate** of 1.5500/1.5510 is equal to 1.5500 plus 0.0065 and 1.5510 plus 0.0085. There are rules for deciding whether you add or subtract the forward points to get the **forward outright rate**. If the points are given as 65/85 we would add, if 85/65, we would subtract. The **spread** between the two rates in the forward market should be wider than the spot spread. As with the spot rate, it will be quoted in terms of a **bid rate** and an **offer rate**. The forward points represent the interest differential between the two currencies. See also **foreign exchange swap**.

forward premium. (i) (Forex) A condition for a currency where the **foreign exchange forward** rate is higher than the **foreign exchange rate** at spot (cf. **forward discount**). (ii) (Commodities) When commodity prices for deferred **delivery** stand at a price **premium** to spot or cash market prices (cf. **backwardation; basis; contango**). A market where forward prices stood at a premium would be known as a *premium market*.

forward price or **rate.** (i) The rate, or price, at which **forward** transactions are being made for a forward **settlement date** (cf. **swap points**). See also **forward differential**. (ii) Pricing for forward valuation is also a requirement of purchases and sales of **mutual funds** where the value of the units bought or sold is based on the next **net asset value** calculation. See **forward pricing**.

forward pricing (UK). Transactions in the **units** of **unit trusts** based on the prices to be set on the next valuation (cf. **historic pricing**).

forward purchase or **sale.** See forward transaction.

forward rate (i) (Forex) The **foreign exchange** forward rate at which a **market-maker** is willing to transact for **forward delivery** (cf. **forward outright rate; forward points; swap points**). (ii) An interest rate for a **forward-forward** rate calculated from the current **yield curve**.

forward rate agreement (FRA) (Money markets). A bilateral contract to manage **interest rate risk**. One party pays fixed, the other an agreed variable rate. Maturities are generally out to two years and are priced off the **underlying** (e.g. **London interbank offered rate (LIBOR)**) **yield curve**. It is a **contract for differences**. If rates have risen by the time the agreement matures, the purchaser receives the difference in rates from the seller; if rates have fallen, the purchaser makes the corresponding payment. Sometimes referred to as a *future rate agreement*.

Terminology of the FRA market:

- *'buy' FRA*; *'take' FRA*: pay the fixed rate on the FRA, to be 'long' funded;
- *'sell' FRA*: *'place' FRA*: receive the fixed rate on the FRA, to be 'short' funded;
- *calculation period*: the period over which the FRA interest is calculated;
- *contract date*: the day on which the FRA agreement is made;
- *value date*: start of the calculation period;
- *maturity date*: end of the calculation period;
- *FRA rate*: contract rate — the fixed rate locked in by the FRA and used in the settlement calculation;
- *reference rate*: the variable rate against which the FRA is priced; market convention uses the LIBOR rate for the tenor of the calculation period set at the start of the contract period;
- *settlement rate*: the value of the reference rate at the start of the calculation period; used in the settlement calculation;
- *FRABBA terms*: British Bankers' Association standard terms and conditions for FRA contracts; the accepted market standard.

Note that an FRA is a bilateral agreement for the difference between a fixed interest cost and the actual interest cost at maturity (normally discounted back to the start of the calculation period).

The settlement formula (FRABBA terms) is:

$$\frac{(\text{settlement} - \text{contract rate}) \times \text{calculation period days} \times \text{principal}}{(\text{days basis} \times 100) + (\text{settlement rate} \times \text{calculation period days})}$$

This is equal to the *interest rate differential/discount factor* where:

$$\text{interest differential} = \frac{(\text{settlement} - \text{contract rate}) \times \text{calculation period days} \times \text{principal}}{(\text{days basis} \times 100)}$$

discount factor $= 1 +$

$$\left(\frac{\text{settlement rate} \times \text{calculation period days}}{\text{day basis} \times 100} \right)$$

Day basis: sterling: 365-day year; most other currencies: 360-day year (except for domestic Australian and New Zealand dollars and Belgian francs).

forward rate bracket. See range forward.

forward rate curve. See forward yield curve.

forward regular dates (Forex). The foreign exchange market is modelled after the **eurocurrency** market where the regular forward periods are 1, 2, 3, 6, 9, and 12 months and use the **calendar/month** and **end-end** conventions. With the date-to-date method, the forward **value date** for each regular forward period is determined by the (current) spot date (cf. **fixed dates**). **Odd dates** or **broken dates** are any non-regular value dates. The end-to-end convention requires that if **spot** is the last day of the month, each forward value date will also be the last day of the month.

forward reverse option. See Boston option.

forward spread agreement (FSA). A forward differential contract developed by the Hong Kong & Shanghai Bank (Midland Global Markets) which involves the forward interest rates of two **currencies**. The **settlement** will apply the change in the spread between the two prevailing **London interbank offered rates** less the **strike rate** applied to the **nominal principal amount** of one of the currencies. Like **forward rate agreements** it is possible to take positions on either side, to benefit from a narrowing or a widening of the spread. It is a useful **hedging** or **speculative** instrument when rate differentials are expected to widen or narrow between the two different currencies and as such is indirectly linked to the **foreign exchange forward** market. As an instrument, it is the basic building block of a **currency protected swap**. See also synthetic agreement for forward exchange.

forward spread contract (Forex). Name given to a **cylinder** or **currency collar** by Banque Indosuez.

forward start. Any transaction where the terms are fixed but where the start of the agreement is deferred beyond the standard **settlement** period for that market. Also known as a *deferred start*.

forward start option. A type of chooser option that gives the buyer the right to hold a **call** or **put** option at a future date.

forward swap. An interest rate swap or cross-currency swap contract where the rate is agreed but the period is delayed to a future specified date.

Thus a five-year swap might be agreed to start in one year's time at an agreed rate. It is equivalent to holding a swap with normal settlement and the required characteristics with a maturity that matches that of the delayed start swap and reversing it with another swap with the opposite characteristics for the period of the required delay. Also called a *forward start swap* or a *delayed start swap*, but most commonly known as a *deferred swap*.

forward swap points. The eurocurrency deposit interest rate differential between two currencies for a given forward value date expressed in foreign exchange terms. The formula to derive swap points knowing the relevant eurocurrency deposit rates is.
(*a*) *American terms*:

$$\text{Spot US\$/FC} = \frac{(1 + \text{\$interest rate (days/basis)})}{(1 + \text{FC interest rate (days/basis)})}$$

(*b*) *European terms*:

$$\text{Spot FC/US\$} = \frac{(1 + \text{FC interest rate (days/basis)})}{(1 + \text{\$ interest rate (days/basis)})}$$

where FC is the foreign currency.
A **point** or **pip** is the smallest quoted unit of price, for example in a rate of 1.5273, a pip would be 0.0001.

The rules for adding or subtracting the swap points to or from the spot **foreign exchange rate** are:

American terms: When the foreign currency has a *higher* interest rate, *subtract* the swap points; when the foreign currency has a *lower* interest rate, *add* the swap points.

European terms: When the foreign currency has a *higher* interest rate, *add* the swap points; when the foreign currency has a *lower* interest rate, *subtract* the swap points.

We can use the relationship of the **foreign exchange bid rate** and the **foreign exchange offered rate** in the **foreign exchange swap** market to calculate the **forward outright rates**:

Bid < offer: if the *bid* side of a swap rate is *larger* than the offered side, *subtract* the swap points from the spot rate.

Bid > offer: if the *bid* side of a swap rate is *smaller* than the offered side, *add* the swap points to the spot rate.

Thus if the swap points were 25/30, we would add; if 30/25, subtract.

forward switching agreement (FSA). See forward spread agreement.

forward trade or **transaction.** Any deferred delivery or **settlement** transaction (cf. **immediate delivery**; **spot**). That is, it has a price or rate agreed today but with actual exchange deferred to a specified future date which is greater than the normal market settlement period. A transaction delayed one day beyond the standard settlement is therefore a forward transaction. See also **forward**.

forward value date. The agreed **delivery** date which extends **settlement** beyond the market's norm for cash transactions, or the agreed settlement date in a given **forward** contract. Some markets, such as **foreign exchange**, make a distinction between regular dates for forward delivery and **broken dates/odd dates** in such transactions.

forward volatilities. See **term structure of volatility**.

forward with break option (Forex). See **break-forward**.

forward with optional exit (FOX) (Forex). The name given to a **breakforward** contract by Hambros Bank (cf. **Boston option**).

forward with rebate (Forex). Name given to a **participating forward** by Chase Manhattan Bank.

forward yield curve. A **yield curve** calculated from **forward-forward** rates giving the implied rates for different start and end dates in the future.

for your information (FYI). A condition attached to a **quote** indicating that it is not a transaction price. Such quotes are used for valuation purposes and are therefore sometimes known as *for valuation only*.

founders' shares. See **deferred ordinary share**.

fourchette (French). See **spread**.

fourchette option. See **barrier option**.

fourth market (USA). Term for the direct over-the-counter market between investment institutions, thus saving on brokerage (cf. *Institutional Networks Corporation*).

fourth position. See **expiration cycle**.

fractels. See **chaos theory**.

fractional banking. See **concentration banking**.

fractional discretion order (USA). An instruction that tells the **broker** the amount of discretion on the price (cf. **discretionary order**).

fractional time series. See **chaos theory**.

frais de courtage (French). **Commission**.

franchise. (i) An agreement by one firm (the *franchisee*) to operate a business using the trademarks and patents supplied by another firm (the *franchiser*) for which a **fee** and certain other payments are made. (ii) The competitive advantage or position a firm enjoys in a particular product, market, or service.

franked income or **franked investment income** (FII) (UK). Income that has already been subject to **corporation tax** and is therefore exempt from a further charge of the same tax in the hands of a company or other institution (cf. **dividends**). Sometimes also called a *franked dividend* when related to distributions of profits to **shareholders** (cf. **gross dividend; gross yield**). See **advance corporation tax**.

Frankfurter Allgemeine Zeitung index (FAZ index) (Germany). Key **index** for the German equity market. See also **Deutsche Börse**.

Frankfurt Stock Exchange or **Frankfurt Werpapierbörse** (Germany). Postfach 100811, Börsenplatz 6, 6000 Frankfurt 1, Germany (tel. 4969 2197 398). Established in 1820. See also **Deutsche Börse**.

fraption. Trader term for an **interest rate guarantee**. That is, an **option** on a **forward rate agreement**.

fraud. Criminal activity aimed at obtaining money by deception. See also **front running; misrepresentation; pyramiding**.

fraud risk. The risk that a firm will suffer fraud.

fraudulent conveyance or **conveyancing.** Transaction aimed at removing assets from the reach of **creditors** in the case of a firm in financial difficulties (cf. **bankruptcy; insolvency**). Such sales may be set aside by a court if deemed fraudulent.

fraudulent trading. Operating a business with a view to defrauding **creditors** and investors. See also **misrepresentation; pyramiding**.

Freddie Macs (USA). Colloquial name for mortgage-backed securities issued by the Federal Home Loan Mortgage Corporation.

free box (USA). Jargon for securities safekeeping (cf. **box**).

free capital. (i) That proportion of a company's capital available for trading by the public on a **stock market**. It excludes shares held by the controlling **shareholders**. Known as *free float* in the USA. (ii) Another term used for **liquid assets** (cf. **current assets; quasi-maney**).

free cash flow. As a concept it is used in two main ways: (1) In **capital budgeting** or **project** appraisal it is the difference between the total outflows and inflows associated with the project under assessment. (2) In financial analysis, it refers to **earnings** plus **depreciation** less **dividends** available to **equity** holders. Also known as *net cash flow.* See also **cash flow.**

free collar. A combination of an **interest rate cap** and floor where the **premium** of the purchased **position** is offset by the sold position (cf. **cylinder; zero-cost option**).

free delivery or **free payment.** Delivery of securities not dependent on payment, or payment not dependent on delivery (cf. **certificates; delivery against payment; fail; cash against delivery**).

free depreciation. Method of cost recovery or **depreciation** for tax purposes which allows the company to offset the depreciation expense against profits in any manner advantageous to the business.

freed up (USA). Having broken up an **underwriting syndicate**, members are then 'freed up' to trade the security at whatever price they choose rather than maintaining the **reoffer price** (cf. **stabilization**).

free float. See free capital.

free issue. See scrip issue.

freely callable. A security where the issuer has an immediate **call provision** (cf. **call deferment**).

freely floating exchange rate (Forex). An exchange rate that is allowed to be determined by **market forces** without any state **intervention**. See also **dirty float.**

free of tax to residents abroad (FOTRA) (Bonds; UK). Although **gilt-edged** securities, except War Loan, owned by those resident overseas pay interest net of UK **withholding tax**, some gilt-edged stocks are designated FOTRA and interest is paid gross.

free port or **free zone.** A port or place where imports may be held, and subsequently re-exported, without liability for import duty or excise tax. Once sold into the domestic market the goods become liable for the appropriate taxes. Used to promote business within points of entry as places for transhipment.

free reserves (USA). The sum of the **excess** reserves less member bank borrowings at the Federal Reserve. The term can also be applied to an individual bank's reserves in excess of regulatory requirements.

free rider. A market participant who benefits from other parties' work, such as securities analysis and selection, without having to incur the costs. Hence the *free rider problem* which is the general tendency of participants in an undertaking with a collective benefit to minimize their contribution. See also **front running.**

free riding (USA). (i) The action of an **underwriter** in holding back a portion of his commitment with the intention of then reselling it at a higher price. (ii) The rapid turnround in a **position** such that no funds are required (cf. **daytime trading; position trading**).

freeze (Banking). Colloquial term used to describe a bank's stop on the withdrawal of funds from an account (cf. **frozen assets**). See also **country risk.**

freeze out. Actions taken by a **majority shareholder** against the **minority shareholders** to encourage them to sell out their holdings (cf. **controlling interest; minority interest**).

freight futures. **Futures contracts** where the **underlying** is the freight rate for a given journey. For example, the **Chicago Board of Trade's** Barge Freight Rate Index Future, where the contract is based on an **index** for covered hopper barges for shipment of 1,500 **short tons** of grain on specified stretches of river.

Freimakler (German). An independent **broker.**

French commercial paper (French CP). French franc denominated **commercial paper.**

French treasury bills. See treasury bills.

frequency (i) Statistical term for the relative number of times a given outcome occurs relative to the whole. Hence a *frequency distribution* (cf. **probability distribution**). (ii) The number of interest or **coupon** payments made per annum (cf. **rollover; reference rate**). (iii) The pleonastic history of price or rates used to calculate the payoff for an **Asian option.**

frequency density function. The number of observations at a given point in a **frequency** distribution. It is an indication of the relative likelihood of obtaining a value from that point, or any observation above or below. Density functions can either show the frequency at any point, for instance in the well-known shape of the **normal distribution**, or may be cumulated from the lowest to the highest value, showing the sum of the probability frequency for all observations up to that point.

frogs (Bonds; USA). **Floating rate notes** where the **coupon** is reset in reference to the current thirty year **US Treasury bond** (cf. **benchmark; long bond; reference rate**).

front bond. See **host bond**.

front contract. The futures **contract** nearest to expiry. Also known as the *front month contract* (cf. **back contract; deferred; nearby; position**).

front-door method (UK). Liquidity operations by the **Bank of England** directly with **discount houses** rather than operating through the money market (cf. **open-market operations**).

front-end fee. The **commission** payable at the start of a **financial** arrangement (cf. **management fee; participation fee**). See **flat; unit trusts**.

front-end loading. Where the burden of charges or repayments is at the outset of a **financial** arrangement.

front month. See **front contract**.

front office. The part of a financial firms which deals with clients, investors, and the public (cf. **back office; middle office**).

front running. A trading practice which is generally illegal and which involves the **broker** or intermediary buying or selling ahead of the client in order to benefit from any subsequent price changes (cf. **agency problem**). Generally done when the client is undertaking large orders which are likely to move the market (cf. **market impact**). See also **tailgating**.

front spread. See **credit spread**.

frozen assets. Assets which are blocked so that the owner does not have free use or action thereon. This can arise from government action, when a trade embargo may freeze bank accounts. An example of this type was the freeze on Iraqi accounts at the time of the Gulf War in 1990–1. It can also arise from a court injunction preventing the owner taking any action pending a full hearing or outcome of some dispute.

FRS-3. The **Financial Reporting Standard** introduced for UK reporting companies publishing their annual results as of June 1993. The main changes to company reporting were the requirement to segment the reporting of business activities into on going and discontinued or disposed-of activities, together with effectively doing away with any exceptional or **extraordinary** items; thus reported profits included all one-off gains and losses. The increased volatility of **earnings** under the reporting standard has prompted many analysts and **brokers** to provide their own versions. Companies are also required to provide a **cash flow** statement rather than the previously required flow of funds statement.

FT-Actuaries All Share Index (UK). A **weighted, arithmetic average** of about 750 securities traded on the London market which measures longer-term movements in **share** prices. It is designed to behave like an **efficiently diversified portfolio** so it can be used as a yardstick for portfolio values by professional fund managers. The weights used are linked to initial **capitalization** and subsequent changes in **capital structure** since the base year of 1962. It is a closing index available at the end of each trading day. Its constituents represent about 80% of aggregate **market capitalization**, divided into thirty-four subsections of four sections: Industrials, Oils, Financial Group, and Miscellaneous. See **FT-SE 100 index; FT-SE Actuaries 350 index; FT-SE Actuaries 350 Industry Baskets; FT-SE Mid 250 Index; FT Ordinary Share Index; index construction**.

FT-Actuaries Fixed Interest Indices (UK). A range of price and **yield** indices comprising two sections: a group of nine price indices and a series of fourteen **gross redemption yield** indices. Five of the price indices cover the **gilt-edged** market; one covers industrial **debentures** and loans; and one covers **preference shares**. These price indices are designed to act as a yardstick for portfolio values by professional fund managers in fixed interest securities. Fourteen of the yield indices relate to various segments of the gilt-edged market, hence the Long Gilt Yield Index which relate to **longs**; three cover the debenture and loan markets; and the last one preference shares. The yield indices are used for monitoring the **yield gap** and **bond** market performance (cf. **benchmark; bell-wether; FT-Actuaries All Share Index**).

FT Actuaries Long Gilt Yield Index (UK). See **FT-Actuaries Fixed Interest Indices**.

FT Government Securities Index (Bonds; UK). An **index** of **gilt-edged** securities dating from 1926 (base 100 on 15 October 1926) that, like its **equity** companion, the **FT Ordinary Share Index**, is now chiefly of historical interest. See **index construction**.

FT Industrial Ordinary Share Index (Equities; UK). Former name for the **FT Ordinary Share Index**.

FT Ordinary Share Index (Equities; UK). An un-weighted **geometric average** of thirty securities traded on the **London Stock Exchange** which aims to show short-term movements in share prices. It is a 'real-time' **index** so it is constantly changing throughout the Exchange's opening hours of 9.30 until 15.30 (cf. **after-hours trading**), with a 'closing index' at 16.30. The figure for the index published in the financial press is from the closing index, which is issued at around 5.00 p.m. Until recently the Index had the word 'Industrial' in its title; this has been dropped because the constituent members of the Index are no longer exclusively manu-facturing concerns but include banks and service sector companies. The members of the Index are drawn from so-called **blue-chip**, or front-line, com-panies. The index's significance has largely been superseded by the broader FT-SE series of indices, especially the FT-SE (*footsie*) of the 100 leading companies. It remains of historical importance, for the index series goes back to 1935. See **FT-Actu-aries All Share Index**; **FT-SE**; **index construction**.

FT/S&P Actuaries World Indices. A set of capi-talization-weighted indices for the major **stock markets**. The indices are divided into different categories for the individual national markets, the regional markets, and sum to a world **index**. The values for each of the different indices are calculated daily in US dollars, Deutschmarks, sterling, yen, and the local currency. The indices are designed to provide a comprehensive measure of stock price performance for the major world **stock markets** as well as for regional areas, broad economic **sectors**, and industry groups. The con-cept behind the creation of the series was to pro-vide a broad market coverage of the major securities in each particular market and to approx-imate the **diversification** and **portfolio** holdings of a global investment **fund**. The indices therefore offer a **benchmark** for evaluating the performance of internationally diversified securities portfolios. From the series, an investor is able to determine realized rates of return on about 2,500 individually priced 'globally investable' equities. The computa-tions are made daily, Monday through Friday, by Goldman, Sachs and Company and NatWest Mar-kets in conjunction with the Financial Times, Standard and Poor's Corporation, the Institute of Actuaries, and the Faculty of Actuaries. The base value for the indices is 31 December 1986. For-merly called the FT-Actuaries World Indices.

FT-SE 100 Index (Financial Times – Stock Ex-change; Footsie) (Equities; UK). A **weighted ar-ithmetic average** of the largest, as measured by **market capitalization**, UK companies. It is a 'real-time' continuously computed **index** so there are regular updates throughout the trading day as well as a closing index which is published by the press. It is intended to behave as a typical institutional portfolio as it is assumed that this would contain shares of most, if not all, of the top 100 UK com-panies (cf. **blue chip**). A base figure of 1,000 is used, rather than the more normal 100, in order to make the Index more tradable on the **futures** and **op-tions** markets, as a high base price figure usually produces whole number changes every day. The base date is 3 January 1984 = 1,000.

FT-SE Actuaries 350 Index (Equities; UK). Real-time **index** of the largest 350 companies **listed** on the **London Stock Exchange**. It is the combined FT-SE 100 and FT-SE Mid 250 Index. It has a high degree of correlation with the FT-Actuaries All Share Index.

FT-SE Actuaries 350 Industry Baskets (Equities; UK). The industrial sectors within the FT-SE Ac-tuaries 350 Index. These are; building and con-truction; pharmaceuticals; water; banks, and retail.

FT-SE Eurotrack 100 Index (Equities). A capitali-zation-weighted **index** of the 100 largest **quoted** companies in Europe, excluding the UK; it pro-vides a continuous 'real-time' monitor of the per-formance and direction of Continental European and Irish markets. The index is denominated in Deutschmarks and uses a price feed from the **London Stock Exchange's Stock Exchange Auto-mated Quotations** (SEAQ) and SEAQ Interna-tional, combined with live currency rates.

FT-SE Eurotrack 200 Index (Equities). Real-time **index** of European stock prices based on a weighted combination of the **FT-SE 100 index** for the UK, and the **FT-SE Eurotrack 100 Index** for Europe. The UK index is weighted to ensure that the Index closely follows the behaviour of **benchmark** indices.

FT-SE Mid 250 Index (Equities; UK). Capitaliza-tion-weighted index of the 250 next largest com-panies after those that make up the FT-SE 100 Index that are **quoted** on the **London Stock Ex-change**. It covers medium-sized UK companies and is continuously calculated in real-time during the course of the trading day.

FT-SE SmallCap Index (Equities; UK). **Index** of about 450 companies traded on the **London Stock Exchange** that are ranked in size following the 350 companies that make up the FT-SE 100 Index and the FT-SE Mid 250 Index. It is calcu-lated at the end of the day.

fuefuki (Japan). A temporary halt to trading (lit-erally 'blowing the whistle').

fuel oil. See **energy futures**.

fugit. **Risk**-neutral expected life of an **option**. A case of *tempus fugit*!

fulcrum point (UK). The break-even growth rate required on a **split capital investment trust** portfolio in order to allow redemption of the residual claims holders in full based on the current price of these securities. In essence, it is the market's expected rate of growth in the portfolio incorporated in the current residual claim. See **highly geared income shares**.

full coupon bond. Term for a **bond** issued with a **coupon** in line with current rates for the bond's **maturity** and therefore valued at or close to **par** (cf. **par bond**; **par yield curve**).

full faith and credit (USA). Backing for US government, state, and local municipality debt. It provides for all the revenue-raising resources of the entity to be available to meet the obligation.

full investment note (FIN) Equity-linked security used by **mutual funds** to allow the cash reserves held against possible redemptions to emulate the rest of the fund. It provides the fund with a performance equal to that of being fully invested, but without the costs associated with buying and selling **common stock** to meet day-to-day variations in the fund size.

full listing (Equities; UK). Companies that are included in the Official List of Securities quoted on the London market. Used to describe a company that is **quoted** on the **main market** of the **London Stock Exchange** (cf. **Unlisted Securities Market**). See **Alternative Investment Market**; **listing agreement**; **quoted company**.

full-payout lease. See **financial lease**.

full price. The price of a security, including accrued interest (cf. **clean price**). Also called the *dirty price*. See also **income bond**.

full service broker (USA). A broker-dealer who offers a wide variety of services in contrast to a discount broker who only undertakes trades.

full service lease. A type of lease arrangement where the lessor agrees to meet all incidental costs such as repairs, taxes, and so forth.

full two-way payments clause. An optional condition under the International Swaps and Derivatives Association's master agreement for interest rate swaps and cross-currency swaps where the rights of the two parties are treated as equal, even when one of the counterparties is in default (cf. **limited two-way payment**).

fully diluted earnings per share (eps). A calculation of earnings per share that takes into account commitments to issue near **equity** such as convertibles or warrants as if they had been exercised.

fully distributed (USA). See **distributed** (cf. **seasoned**).

fully invested. A portfolio that has no assets in the form of cash or near-cash instruments.

fully modified pass-through certificates (Bonds; USA). A type of **pass-through certificate** that makes payment of interest and principal on the **underlying** pool of mortgages regardless of whether this has been collected. Modified pass-through certificates are similar, but only the interest is so paid. Unmodified pass through certificates will only pay when both have been received. The fully modified and modified pass through certificates were developed to address the arrearage problem (and hence **coupon** payment indeterminancy) that pass through certificates present. See **asset-backed**.

fully paid. Securities where the issuer has no right to request further payments from the holder (cf. **nil paid**; **partly paid**). See also **contingent liability**; **derivative**.

fully valued. A view about asset prices that takes into account all known fundamental factors. Securities may also be perceived as *overvalued* or *undervalued* in relation to their **fundamentals**.

functional cost analysis (FCA) (Banking; USA). A method of analysing the profitability and resource intensiveness of lines of business based on an **asset** function; that is, the volume of **funds** required to support this activity, and a **liability** function, which is credited with providing funds. The FCA approach assumes that all funds are placed in a **pool** which is then used by the asset function.

fund. (i) Money used for a specific purpose. (ii) Managed **portfolio** of, usually, **financial** assets, such as **common stocks**, **bonds**, **derivatives**, cash, and so forth (cf. **mutual fund**; **venture capital fund**). (iii) To provide **finance**. Hence, to fund a company is to provide **capital** to that company.

fundamental analysis. A branch of market analysis based upon economic modelling, which seeks to relate security value to known asset values. It makes use of factors such as the demand for and supply of raw materials, consumer trends, fiscal and **monetary policy**, as well as company **profit and loss accounts** and **balance sheets** and other company data (cf. **credit analysis**). It is used in **stock** selection based upon company results and the conditions ruling in the markets they operate, rather than on share price movements, and in contrast to **technical analysis**, which is based on market trends and perceptions only. Fundamental analysis can be used to create **ratios** for comparative purposes as well as using a more judgemental approach. Sometimes called *fundamentals*.

fundamental disequilibrium. A condition that can apply to an economy or market where the pressures for change are likely to remain out of balance for long periods of time, or until a major shift in sentiment or operation occurs (cf. **asset bubble**). See also **equilibrium**.

fundamental financial instruments (Accounting; USA). A list of financial instruments by the **Financial Accounting Standards Board** which are deemed fundamental. These include unconditional and conditional payables and receivables, forward contracts, options, guarantees, or other exchanges which have conditional characteristics and equity instruments.

fundamentals (i) An Assessment process that looks at value in absolute terms, rather than **technical analysis**, which uses a comparative or situational analysis. However, in some respects, both the fundamental and technical approaches overlap in their valuation methods. (ii) Shorthand for **fundamental analysis**. An analyst will look at a firm's fundamentals, i.e. the business's financial statements, **cash flow**, business environment, the industrial sector, and economic situation in order to derive a valuation. (iii) The financial statements of a firm. See **annual report**; **balance sheet**; **profit and loss account**.

funded debt. (i) Any borrowing with a **maturity** in excess of a year. Usually represents the interest-bearing **bonds** and **debentures** issued by a company, including **long-term** bank borrowings. It does not include short-term loans or **preferred** or **ordinary shares** (cf. **perpetuals**). (ii) (UK) That part of the UK's government borrowing that it has no obligation to repay (cf. **consols; one-way stock option; perpetuals; irredeem-ables; undated**).

funded pension. A pension scheme where the benefits are paid out of an investment **fund** or **portfolio** built up from contributions by the beneficiaries. The alternative method is an unfunded scheme where beneficiaries depend for their retirement income on current contributors.

funding. Replacing **short-term** debt with longer-term borrowing.

funding gap (Banking). A method of **asset-liability management** which looks at the **mismatch** between the **assets** and **liabilities** in terms of the requirement to obtain new funds. For example, if a bank has assets of 100 with a **maturity** of five

years and has borrowed 100 for three years, there is a funding gap in years four and five.

funding holiday. A moratorium on pension fund contributions allowed when the **fund** is deemed to be overfunded on actuarial grounds (cf. **reversion**).

funding risk. A type of **risk** due to the **mismatch** between the revenues from **assets** and the costs of fixed **liabilities** that arises due to unforeseen costs. The risk may be caused by differences in **maturity**, changes in **credit worthiness**, or a number of other causes. See **asset-liability management; risk management**.

fund manager. Any individual or firm which has responsibility for managing a **fund** or investment **portfolio**. Also called an *asset manager* or *investment manager*. See **investment manager** (cf. **asset manager; liability manager**).

fund of funds (UK). **Unit trust** which has a **portfolio** made up of **units** in other unit trusts. Such an arrangement provides for the maximum possible **diversification** of the portfolio.

funds (i) (Banking) Cash or near cash which is good for settling a transaction. Hence *cleared funds* which have been processed through the **clearing system** and are good to draw upon to settle a debt. Also *federal funds* which are good with the **Federal Reserve System** (USA). See also **liquidity**. (ii) The net working capital used by a firm. It is the difference between the **current assets** and **current liabilities**. Also known as *net current assets/liabilities*.

funds broker (Money markets; USA). A specialist **broker** who acts in the **fed funds** market.

fungible or **fungibility.** Interchangeable. This is a characteristic of most financial instruments and markets, although in some cases fungibility is not perfect. it is the principle by which **futures markets** function, since, with a common **counterparty** in the **clearing house**, all **positions** in the market are interchangeable (cf. **novation**).

fungible issue. An issue of securities that is interchangeable, either at the time of issue or shortly thereafter, with an already **seasoned** issue of the same **obligor**. Sometimes used interchangeably for a new **tranche** of an existing issue made by the same borrower.

fungible securities. These securities are regarded as not being individually recognized or assigned to a particular holder. A large number of **futures** and **options exchanges** offer fungibility where the **opening transaction** can be offset by a closing transaction on the exchange which may ultimately involve two different counterparties (cf. novation). The reason is that the exchange stands as counterparty to all trades and each transaction is matched with an ultimate party, the clearing house netting out the intervening trades (cf. open interest).

furthest month. The longest-dated contract traded on an option exchange (cf. position).

FUTOP (The Danish Futures and Options Market) (Denmark). See Guarantee Fund for Danish Options and Futures.

futsū torihiki (Japan). Regular delivery.

future income and growth securities (FIGS) (USA). See zero-coupon convertible.

future rate agreement. See forward rate agreement.

futures or **futures contract** (Derivatives). An exchange-traded contract to buy or sell a specific amount of underlying for a specific price or rate on a specific future date (cf. expiry date). It is a type of forward contract traded through a futures exchange, nominally for delivery of a fixed quantity of an underlying asset or instrument at a fixed price. The normal price method is determined via an *open outcry* auction. Contracts are held by the buyer or seller against the futures exchange's clearing house and are subject to initial, maintenance, and variation margin requirements (cf. novation). In order to ensure liquidity, the contracts carry standard terms and conditions and are indivisible (cf. fungible). Typically the contract terms specify the asset, commodity, or underlying instrument, the contract size, how prices are quoted, the minimum price movement allowed (known as the tick), where delivery will be made, and how the price paid will be determined (cf. cash settled; delivery factor). Some contracts include alternative assets, grades, or instruments that can be delivered, with a suitable price adjustment (cf. alternative delivery procedure; basket delivery; cheapest to deliver). The key differences between a futures and a forward contract are: (*a*) margining of positions held through the exchange (cf. exchange delivery settlement price); (*b*) contracts are held with the exchange acting as principal; (*c*) the exchange sets the contract specification and settlement; (*d*) contracts are for standardized

Futures contract

Type of futures contract	Nature of underlying	Usual delivery/settlement at expiry
Currency futures	Exchange of two currencies	Give the right to buy and sell a particular currency
Currency index futures	Currency index	Cash-settled exposure into a basket of currencies
Short-term interest rate futures	Treasury bills; bank deposits;	Deliverable into a money market instrument or cash-settled bank deposit equivalent
Medium-term interest rate futures (aka note futures)	Usually bonds or notes with maturities of around 5 to 7 years	Deliverable into an intermediate-term bond or note
Long-term interest rate futures (aka bond futures)	Usually bonds with maturities around 10 years, or longest available in the market	Deliverable into a long-term bond
Futures on an index of interest rate swaps	Index of swap rates from leading interest rate swap intermediaries	Cash-settled
Spread futures	Difference between two market reference points or indices	Cash-settled
Stock futures (on individual stocks)	Single common stock issue	Deliverable stock or cash-settled
Stock index futures (aka index futures[a])	Provide exposure to performance of a stock index	Cash-settled
Commodity index futures	Index of commodities	Cash-settled
Agricultural futures or softs	Perishable commodities	Deliverable into underlying physical commodity
Industrial metal futures	Base metals used in productive process	Deliverable into underlying physical commodity
Precious metals futures	Rare and precious metals	Deliverable into underlying physical commodity
Energy futures	Oil and other energy products	Deliverable or cash-settled, depending on contract
Freight futures	Index of freight costs	Cash-settled
Insurance futures	Index of catastrophic insurance losses	Cash-settled

[a] This term is misleading since it is possible to have indices on other underlyings than a portfolio or index of stocks (e.g. commodities).

amounts for specific expiry dates, usually with four **settlement dates** in the year (for example an **expiration cycle**: March, June, September, December). Trading can be carried out without the need to purchase the underlying using only initial and then variation margin (cf. **close out; leverage**). Exchanges exist to trade futures on **stock indices**, securities, **currencies, and** commodities (cf. **currency futures; financial futures; stock index futures; commodity futures**). Such contracts are usually traded on the **floor** or **pit** of an organized exchange, although **screen-based** systems are operative on some exchanges and transactions are settled through the exchange's clearing house (cf. **globex; margin requirement**). See also **forward rate agreement; forward rates**.

The key features of a futures contract are:

- *asset* or *underlying*: the exact instrument, commodity, or other item that the futures contract can be exchanged for or cash-settled;
- *contract size* or *trading unit*: number of units of the asset or underlying;
- *price quotation*: how the price will be quoted on the exchange;
- *daily price limits* (if any): the maximum price limit allowed in a trading session from the previous day's settlement price; *position limits*: the maximum number of contracts it is permitted for one account to hold on the exchange on one side of the market;
- *expiry cycle*: when in the year the contracts expire;
- *last trading day*: the last day it is possible to trade a particular contract prior to expiry;
- *delivery*: how and where delivery will be made; what options are available to short position holders;
- *notice day*: the day in which the short position holder gives notice of the intention to deliver;
- *alternative procedures*: whether alternative procedures are available as to delivery location, quality, grade, and so forth;
- *invoice amount*: how the price to be paid or received is determined.

The major types of futures contracts are displayed in the Table.

Futures and Options Exchange (FOX) (UK). See **London FOX**.

futures and options fund (FOF) (UK). A type of unit trust which uses **futures** and **options** to generate returns. It is one of two such types of **fund** authorized by the **Securities and Investments Board** (SIB), the other being a **geared futures and options fund**. The latter has more **risk** since it is **gearing** or **leveraging** its **positions** in the futures and options to generate a higher (expected) return. Sometimes referred to as

authorised futures and options funds since they trade with the approval of the SIB.

futures commission agent. An intermediary who acts as an **agent** for transactions on **futures exchanges** (cf. **broker; commission broker**).

futures commission merchant (FCM) (USA). An individual or organization registered with the **Commodity Futures Trading Commission** to undertake trading in **futures** and **options** for others in return for a **fee** (cf. **broker**). The functions they perform are to execute orders on behalf of their clients; guarantee the contracts; arrange **settlement**; service the **margin** accounts; and provide reporting services to their customers. Sometimes also referred to as a *commission house*.

futures delivery. The process of meeting an obligation to deliver or receive securities or **commodities** on a certain date and in a location as given by the terms of the contract.

futures driven. A situation where trading activity in the **futures market** for a particular **underlying** is setting the prices or rates in the **cash market**. This can arise in **thin markets** where the **hedging** requirements from the futures markets are the dominant factor in setting prices. The opposite situation, where the cash market sets prices for **derivatives**, is the more common.

futures exchange. An institution whose purposes is to provide a regulated market for trading **futures contracts** (cf. **spot market**). Different exchanges specialize in different kinds of contracts. Most futures are traded on exchanges with a physical **floor** in special, tiered areas known as **pits** where typically a single type of futures contract is bought and sold, although for different **expiry dates**. Trading is carried out in most cases by a process known as **open outcry**. Futures exchanges also provide a market in **options on futures** and some also in **stock** and other **options**. See **bond futures; commodity futures; currency futures; energy futures; financial future; stock index futures**.

futures fund. **Mutual fund** that invests investors' money in futures contracts. See **futures and options fund; geared futures and options fund**.

futures hedge ratio. The optimal number of **futures contracts** required to **hedge a position** in the **underlying**. See also **dynamic hedging; hedge ratio**.

futures option (USA). An **option on futures**.

futures price. (i) The price at which a long position holder agrees to take delivery of the **underlying**

or the short holder sell the underlying. (ii) The current market price at which **futures contracts** are trading. See **cost of carry; nearby; deferred**.

futures price prediction. See **price discovery**.

futures spread. A **spread** position taken by simultaneously buying and selling **futures contracts**. There are two basic variants: *intra-commodity spread (intra-market spread)*: where the **long** and **short** positions are in the same contract but for different **expiry** months. It is a non-directional position which aims to make a profit when the price spread changes to the advantage of the position, either by widening or narrowing (cf. **basis; turtle spread**). Also known as a *horizontal spread*. See **long the basis; spread futures**. *Inter-commodity spread (cross-asset, inter-market spread)*: where the long and short positions are in contracts on different underlyings. This can be set up either with the same expiry date, or with different expiry dates.

futures-style option. A method applying the **marked-to-market** used for future to **exchange-traded options** which dispenses with the holder paying a **premium** and involves a futures type of **margin** by both buyer (holder) and seller (writer). The maximum margin for the option holder will be capped, however, at the value of the premium that would have been paid.

futures trading. The basic principles of **futures** trading are very simple.

Naked trading or taking a **position**. To take a long (short) **position** in the market, buy (sell) the required. The great advantage of futures is that

(a) Payoff for a long or purchased futures position

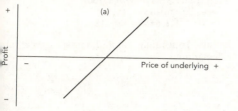

(b) Payoff for a short or sold futures position

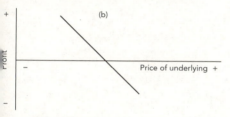

relevant futures contract in whatever amount is they only require a proportion of the total value of the **underlying** to be made available in the form of **margin**. Thus a futures position can be built up with very little original investment (cf. **leverage**).

Hedging a position. Futures are most often used as a hedging instrument. To (basically) hedge a long (short) position in the underlying, do the opposite to the **cash market** position: sell (buy) the futures (cf. **producer's hedge; consumer's hedge; long hedge; short hedge**).

Spreading. Using futures to create relationships between different **expiry dates** or between different underlying assets. An **intra-commodity spread** or **intra-market spread** involves buying and selling futures for different expiry months, the intention being to benefit from any changes in the **spread** between the different dates. The **inter-commodity spread** or **inter-market spread** involves buying and selling futures in two different types of contract. The objective is to profit from changes in their relationship.

Arbitrage. Involves both the underlying and the futures contract. The intention is to benefit from any misalignment between the cash market and the futures prices and involves either: holding the physical asset and taking a short position in the futures and delivering the asset into the contract; or holding a long position in the futures contract and a short position in the underlying. Both arbitrages can be closed out prior to expiry (cf. **cost of carry**).

In practice, a number of factors have to be taken into account with futures which make them less than perfect hedging instruments:

1. The **convergence** of the futures with the cash market as the contract nears **expiry**. As the contract moves closer to expiry, it moves in price closer to the cash market. The ability of the future to provide **price discovery** is reduced and this means that the futures contract behaves more and more like the underlying and ceases to work as a hedge.
2. The effect of margin on the cost/return of taking out the position.
3. The difficulty of matching positions which do not exactly correspond to (*a*) a multiple of the amount of the contract (it is necessary to be over- or under-hedged); and (*b*) a **maturity date** for the underlying that does not meet the exact expiry or **settlement date** of the contract. In this case it is necessary to take out an interpolated position using more than one **maturity** contract and the positions are exposed to possible **rotational shifts** in the **yield curve** (cf. **basis risk**).
4. Some futures contracts allow delivery of the underlying. This must be allowed for if the position is kept to maturity. Otherwise there is **cash settlement** which may involve the

Futures trading

User	Activity or strategy[a]	Application or transaction
Market-makers	Hedging the trading book	Long position: sell futures Short position: buy futures
Traders	Directional view on the market	Buy or sell futures
	Intra-commodity spread	Sell (buy) early expiry contract; buy (sell) later expiry contract
	Inter-commodity spread	Buy (sell) contract on one underlying and sell (buy) another contract on different underlying
	Volatility trade	Combinations using options and futures[b]
Basis trading	View on cash futures basis	Buy (sell) underlying and sell (buy) futures
Long positions in the underlying	Hedging	Long underlying: sell futures
	Investing future cash flows	Buy futures and close position on purchase of the underlying
	Asset allocation	Sell futures on one underlying; buy futures on a different underlying
	Duration adjustment	Buy (sell) futures to lengthen (shorten) duration
Short positions in the underlying	Hedging	Short underlying: buy futures
	Future borrowing	Sell futures and close position when borrowing is undertaken

[a] Not all futures will be used for all these different strategies.
[b] For details see **option strategies**.

problem of acquiring or disposing of the underlying.

5. Although a position will be fully hedged at a given price or rate (a) a shift in the price of the underlying may lead to an imbalance of the two offsetting positions which may require rebalancing; and (b) there is a risk of the price movements of the underlying and the future not moving exactly as intended as expectations move the price of one or the other in different ways. This basis risk means that the hedge may not perform as intended.

6. Hedging a position beyond the expiry date of the longest time to expiry contract requires special analysis (cf. **piled-up rolling hedge**; **strip hedge**).

Some of the uses for futures are shown in the Table.

futures versus options (FO). See **buy-write**.

future value (FV). A method of converting current values or **present values** to a point in the future using the **time value of money**. It is part of the **discounted cash flow** technique which is fundamental to much financial analysis. The basic formula is:

$$FV = PV \times (1 - i)^t$$

where i is the rate of interest and t the number of periods. If the initial investment is 100 and the interest rate 8% for two periods:

$$116.64 = 100 \times (1 + 0.08)^2$$

See also **continuous compounding**; **interest rate calculations**.

G

gamma (γ) (Derivatives; Options). The rate of change of an **option's delta** with respect to the price of the **underlying** (cf. **hedge ratio**). It is the change in delta divided by the change in price of the underlying; it measures the rate of change of delta (the change in option price) in relation to the underlying; it is therefore the second derivative of the option price relative to the underlying. Thus an option with a delta of 0.55 and a gamma of 0.05 would be expected to move to 0.60 or 0.50 given a small change in the underlying. For small changes in delta, gamma is a predictor of the change in delta to be expected. However, as the relationship of delta to the underlying is itself not linear, the gamma of an option will change as the delta changes. It will be highest when the option is at **the money** (i.e. a delta of 0.5), and decline in size the further the option moves either into or **out of the money**. If the option gamma is positive, a move in the underlying will create a higher value for the option than would be predicted by delta alone, that is the position has positive **convexity**. Gamma also increases as the **volatility** on the underlying falls. It also varies depending on whether the option is likely to expire in or out of the money and decreases with **time to expiry**. Also sometimes referred to as an *option's convexity*. See **option pricing**.

gamma distribution. A type of frequency distribution that may approximate the observed pattern of price changes of financial instruments (cf. **lognormal distribution; normal distribution**).

gamma neutral portfolio. A portfolio of options which has a zero net **gamma**.

gamma risk. The risk arising from a **delta/gamma hedge** from the requirement to rebalance the **portfolio** over time or as a result of changes in the price of the **underlying** thus leading to small gains and losses. The risk is greatest for those options which are **at the money** since the **gamma** is highest at this point.

gamma shares (Equities; UK). Defunct categorization of **liquidity** and size of **London Stock Exchange** listed **ordinary shares**. It has been replaced by the **normal market size** method (cf. **normal quote size**). See also **alpha shares; beta shares; delta shares**.

gamma trading. Maintaining a neutral **gamma** in a **portfolio** of **options** by buying and selling options.

gann analysis. A **technical analysis** view of the price cycles seen in financial markets. The model predicts movements based on a ratio or multiple of the number nine: 1/9; etc. See **momentum strategies**.

gap. (i) A break in a security's price series when the range of prices traded on one day does not overlap the next (cf. **jump**). (ii) The **mismatch** between the **maturity** of an asset, or portfolio of assets, and the corresponding liability. The term is often used in a technical sense to describe the relationship of a bank's interest rate sensitive **assets** (loans) and **liabilities** (**deposits** and **borrowings**). Thus a positive gap (or longer maturity liabilities than assets (known as *long funded*) would indicate an increase in **net interest income** if interest rates rose, and a negative gap, the opposite (i.e. *short funded*) (cf. **assets repriced before liabilities; asset sensitive**). See **asset-liability management; gap analysis**.

gap analysis or **gap management.** A methodology for measuring **interest rate risk** of *rate sensitive assets* (RSA) and *rate-sensitive liabilities* (RSL). It consists of making periodic comparisons of the **principal** amounts of maturing **assets** and **liabilities** (cf. **assets repriced before liabilities**). This will provide an indication of the interest rate risk faced by the institution (see Table).

Interest rates	Net interest income (NII) (interest income (RSA) *less* interest expense (RSL))	
	Positive Gap Gap > 0	Negative Gap Gap < 0
Increase in rates	Increase in NII	decrease in NII
Decrease in rates	Decrease in NII	Increase in NII

A more sophisticated version would include calculating the cash flows and **duration** of assets and liabilities and performing **sensitivity analysis** using different interest rate structures. See also **interest rate risk management**.

gapping. The process of deliberately mismatching assets and liabilities in order to benefit from expected interest rate movements (cf. open position). Also known as a *yield curve spread*.

gap ratio. The value of rate sensitive assets divided by rate sensitive liabilities. A positive (negative) gap ratio has the effect of making a bank gain (lose) if interest rates fall (rise).

garage. (i) Used to describe a strategy involving the transfer of assets or liabilities to financial centres for the purposes of benefiting from a tax break. The act of moving such assets is sometimes known as *garaging* or *parking*. (ii) Also the name for an annex of the main floor of the New York Stock Exchange.

Garantifonden for Danske Optioner og Futures (Guarantee Fund for Danish Options and Futures) (Denmark). Kompagnistræde 15, Postboks 2017, DK-1012, Kobenhavn K (tel. 33 93 33 11; fax: 33 93 49 80). The Danish futures and options clearing house.

Garman–Kohlhargen option pricing model (Forex). A model for the fair value of European-style currency options using a modification of the original Black–Scholes option pricing model. The model uses the interest rates of both currencies to price the option. See option pricing.

garnishment. The attachment of earnings to secure the repayment of a debt. Hence a *garnishee order*, which is a court order providing for the enforcement of an attachment.

Garn-St. German Act of 1982 (Banking; USA). Legislation deregulating the rate of interest allowed on bank deposits including the creation of money market deposit accounts. It also permitted savings and loan associations to diversify and simplified the management of failed financial institutions by allowing them to be taken over.

gasoline. Unleaded gasoline is one of a range of energy futures contracts traded on futures exchanges. See also commodities.

gather in the stops (USA). A method of moving the price of a security by triggering stop orders (cf. limit order book).

gaussian distribution. See normal distribution.

geared equity capital unit (GECU). A type of mutual fund which offers the holders a geared return on an equity investment, either via a specific portfolio of common stocks or through exposure to a stock index. The gearing comes from holding more options per unit of

fund (cf. equity-linked note; guaranteed index unit).

geared futures and options fund (GFOF) (UK). A unit trust authorized by the Securities and Investments Board to invest in futures and options as a way of generating income. It differs from the futures and options fund in having a higher exposure to derivatives through greater use of the gearing or leverage effect of options and futures on the underlying.

geared income shares (Equities; UK). A part of a split capital trust which receives the dividend income from the underlying portfolio. The gearing comes from the issue of zero-dividend preference shares, the proceeds of which are used to acquire dividend paying shares. The geared income shares surrender some capital appreciation to redeem the zero dividend preference shares at maturity. An equivalent structure is seen in the USA for prescribed right to income and maximum equity and special claim on residual equity.

geared investment trust (UK). Investment trust which uses debt to increase the risk–reward tradeoff to shareholders (cf. leverage).

geared zero coupon convertible. A type of zero-coupon convertible which offers a geared or leveraged return to the holder over a preset band, coupled to a cap on the payout.

gearing (UK). (i) The measure of the relationship between fixed cost capital, such as debentures, and variable cost capital, such as equity. There are alternative ways of capturing this relationship, which vary according to how the financial obligations issued by companies are defined. It is the UK convention to express the amount of outstanding debt and net bank borrowings, as stated at book value, in relation to shareholders' funds as a percentage:

$$\text{Gearing}(\%) = \frac{\text{Debt}}{\text{Equity}} \times 100$$

Under this definition of gearing it is possible to have gearing levels of over 100%. In the USA, it is more common to express gearing or leverage as it is known, as the percentage of the outstanding debt to the total debt and equity, and usually based on current market valuations (cf. market-to-book ratio). Hence:

$$\text{Gearing}(\%) = \frac{\text{Debt}}{\text{Debt} + \text{Equity}} \times 100$$

If a company had 50 in equity and 60 in debt, the gearing would be 54.5%. The rationale for the measure is that a higher level of debt increases the amount of the fixed charge on income and

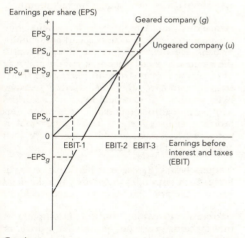

Gearing

the potential for a shortfall (cf. **interest coverage ratio**). Under this definition of gearing the limit to gearing is 100%. Using the US method, the average levels of gearing in the UK is 40%, USA 60%; and Japan 80%. The significance for companies in selecting different combinations of debt and equity can be illustrated in the Figure. If a company has an all-equity or ungeared capital structure (*u*), then the earnings per share (EPS) of the shareholders will be directly related to the earnings before interest and taxes (EBIT). If however, the firm uses financial gearing (US: leverage) by borrowing, then the EPS will be higher as long as the company has an EBIT-3; but lower at EBIT-1 (when the EPS_g of the geared company is actually negative). Depending on the expected future outcome of EBIT, it might be advantageous to shareholders to borrow, since this has the effect of increasing their EPS (or return) for a given level of EBIT. Note also that the relationship of EPS to EBIT of the geared company is steeper than that of the ungeared company. The geared company is more sensitive to changes in the EBIT. For a change in EBIT from EBIT-2 to EBIT-3, the geared company's EPS has increased twice as much as that of the ungeared company.

Gearing is also called the *debt-equity ratio* or *financial gearing* or *financial leverage*. It can also be used to describe the ratio of debt to total profit before interest and tax when it is known as *income gearing*. See also **leverage**; **ratio analysis**. (ii) For **warrants**, the ratio of the **underlying** price divided by the warrant price. Sometimes called the *premium-gearing ratio*.

geisha bond. See **shogun bond**.

Geld und Brief (German). **Bid** and **asked** (cf. **offer**). Abbreviated to G and B in reports.

General Accounting Office (GAO) (USA). The audit and investigation arm of *Congress*.

General Agreement on Tariffs and Trade (GATT). An international organization established in 1947 to facilitate international trade by reducing tariffs and other barriers. It pursues three goals in seeking to liberalize international trade: reciprocal treatment (tariff reductions by one country in favour of another should be matched by the beneficiary); no discrimination (countries should not grant special benefits to particular countries or discriminate against others); and transparent tariffs (rather than non-tariff barriers). Following the conclusion of the Uruguay Round of world trade liberalization, GATT has been superceded by the **World Trade Organization**.

General Agreement to Borrow (GAB). Arrangements made through the International Monetary Fund allowing the **Group of Ten** (the major industrial countries) to borrow amongst themselves (cf. **intervention**).

general average loss. Insurance loss that involves persons other than the insured party.

general cash offer (USA). An issue of securities which is made to all investors (cf. **rights issue**). In some jurisdictions, such **offers** are only allowed for certain types of securities. For instance, in the UK, issues of new **shares** are normally subject to the **pre-emptive rights** of existing holders over a certain percentage of additional **equity** (cf. **vendor placing**).

generalized autoregressive conditional heteroscedasticity model (GARCH model). An econometric **model** for analysing the patterns in time series that allows for the heteroscedastic nature of the residuals. Such models are autoregressive in that they attempt to explain the future behaviour of the time series from past data using a complex fitting equation of lagged variables of past prices. These lagged variables tend to exhibit heteroscedasticity and hence bias models that do not take this into account. GARCH is a generalized version of the **autoregressive conditional heteroscedasticity** (ARCH) model family. Such models are used, for instance, to try and predict the **volatility** of asset prices for the pricing of **options** and other complex **derivative** products (cf. **analytical model**).

general ledger multicurrency system (GLMC) An accounting system used for multi-currency transactions which uses general ledgers in each individual currency and is linked to the **base currency** by conversion accounts.

general loan and collateral agreement (USA). A type of loan made to a **stockbroker** using shares as **security**. See **Regulation U**.

Generally Accepted Accounting Principles (GAAP) (i) (USA) The methods, conventions, and principles for financial reporting in the USA as laid down by the **Financial Accounting Standards Board**. See also **Statement of Financial Accounting Standard**. (ii) The term has come to mean any widely accepted set of accounting conventions that can be taken to have been used to compile any set of **financial statements**. To distinguish the GAAP used in different countries, it is now common usage to refer to the US standards as US GAAP and the UK standards as UK GAAP, and so on.

Generally Accepted Auditing Standards (GAAS) (USA) The standards that cover auditing practice for financial reporting purposes (cf. **Financial Accounting Standards Board**; Generally Accepted Accounting Principles).

general mortgage bond. A bond which has a general rather than a specific **lien** on the issuer's assets (cf. **floating charge**).

general obligation bond or **general obligations (GO)** (Bonds; USA) A **municipal** security based on the borrower's **full faith and credit** and taxing power of the issuer. An alternative structure would pledge specific revenues (a toll or particular tax) to service the obligation. See **limited obligations**; **revenue bonds**.

general partner (USA). A **partner** in a partnership who has unlimited, hence general, liability (cf. **limited partner**). See **limited partnership**.

General Securities Representative Examination (USA). A test of proficiency in investment practice set by the **National Association of Securities Dealers** in order to become a **registered representative** in the US financial markets.

general undertaking (Equities; UK). The **Unlisted Securities Market** equivalent to a **listing agreement** but where the initial and continuing requirements placed on the company, in order to have its shares traded on the London market, are less onerous. See **Alternative Investment Market**; **full listing**.

generic. See **plain vanilla**; **straight** (cf. **exotics**; **bells and whistles**).

generic commodity certificate. See **warehouse receipt**.

generic swap. Any **plain vanilla** interest rate swap or cross-currency swap.

gengetsu (Derivatives; Japan). **Contract month**.

gensaki (Japan). A **repurchase agreement** using Japanese government securities, corporate **bonds**, or bank **debentures**. Before the liberalization of the Japanese financial markets, it was the only way of obtaining a market rate of interest on short-term investments other than buying **treasury bills**. Securities firms would sell (buy) securities with a simultaneous repurchase agreement, thus providing an investment or funds to the **counterparty**. Hence *gensaki market*, the market for such agreements (cf. **money market**).

Genusscheine (Germany). A **participation certificate**. Such instruments typically pay a **dividend** linked to the firm's profit (cf. **preferred stock**).

geometric Brownian motion. Description of the stochastic generating process for a price, or rate, time series. For any two non-overlapping time periods, the changes in price or rate are uncorrelated and, when formulated as a discrete **model**, the variance of the distribution of changes increases by the square root of time. The basic formulation of the model is:

$$\frac{\Delta S_j}{S_j} = E(R_j)\Delta t + \sigma_j \Theta \sqrt{t}$$

where S_j is the jth underlying; ΔS_j the change in price; $E(R_j)$ the expected return; σ_j is its volatility; Θ a random sampling from a standardized normal distribution. The model specifies that it is the changes in the price (ΔS_j) that are normally distributed, not its absolute level (S_j) and that the future value of the price following such a process will have a lognormal distribution. This characteristic of the process makes it a useful description of asset price behaviour and it is the assumption underlying many **analytical models**, in particular the **Black–Scholes option pricing model**. It is also, perhaps misleadingly, called a *random walk*. See also **Wiener process**.

geometric average or **geometric mean.** This is found by taking the nth root of the product of a set of values. For example, the geometric average of the values 2, 2, 4, and 16 is the 4th root of 256, which is 4. The arithmetic average of the same set of values is 6. As a geometric mean can never be larger than the arithmetic mean, indices calculated using the geometric average method are likely to be less volatile, thus tending to understate price rises and price falls. Early indices, e.g. the FT **Ordinary Times Index**, were computed using geometric averages. The formula for a geometric average (GA) is:

$$GA = \sqrt[n]{\prod_{t=1}^{n} P_t}$$

See also **index construction**.

Geregelter Markt (Equities; Germany). Regulated section of the market (cf. **amtlicher Handel**). It is the market for quoted smaller issues (cf. **Alternative Investment Market; National Association of Securities Dealers Automated Quotations**).

Gesellschaft (German). Limited company. There are basically two major categories: *Aktiengesellschaft* (AG), or a joint stock company; and *Gesellschaft mit beschränkter Haftung* (GmbH), or a private limited company.

Ghana Stock Exchange (Ghana). 2nd Floor, Kingsway Building, Kwame Nkrumah Avenue, PO Box 1849, GH-Ghana Accra (tel. 233 21 669908; fax 233 21 669913).

G-hedge (Forex; Belgium). The name for a **range forward** product sold by Generale Bank.

gilt, gilts, or **gilt-edged.** Fixed-interest, sterling-denominated securities issued by the UK government to fund the **public sector borrowing requirement** and forming part of the national debt (cf. **treasury bills**). They derived their name from the gold edge on the original **certificates**, a colour subsequently replaced by green. The market in gilts is divided according to **maturity** dates and type: *shorts* (five years or less); *mediums* (between five and ten years); *longs* (over ten years); *irredeemables* or *undated* (no redemption dates); *index-linked* (with returns linked to the **retail price index** (RPI)); and *floating rate* (which have their **coupons** re-set periodically in line with current **money market** rates). Although most gilts are conventional **straights**, known as *redeemables*, there are a number of **conversion** stocks which allow investors to convert to longer maturity issues and, in addition, there is a significant **index-linked** sector where returns are linked directly to the RPI. Issues are made which carry different names, such as *Exchequer, Treasury*, etc., but these have no significance but help to distinguish the different issues. **Settlement** is carried out through the **Central Gilts Office**. New issues are made via the **Bank of England** in a variety of ways, including **auctions** or **tenders, tap** or **taplet** issues and direct sales to investors (cf. **National Savings**).
  Note that the term *gilt-edged* is sometimes used in the USA for securities of the highest rated (triple-A) borrowers.

gilt-edged bargain (Bonds; UK). See **bargain**.

gilt-edged market-maker (GEMM) (Bonds; UK). A member of the **London Stock Exchange** whose main function is to fix two-way prices in gilts (cf. **equity market-maker**). Authority to become a gilt-edged market-maker rests with the **Bank of England**. This confers some advantages, such as

being able to undertake **repurchase agreements** with the Bank in order to undertake **short sales**.

gilt-edged security. (i) An issue of UK government **bonds**. See **gilt**. (ii) A safe investment.

gilt strip (UK). A **zero-coupon bond** created by stripping a UK government **gilt-edged security**. The market was proposed in consultative document of 25 May 1995 and commenced operations on 2 January 1996. The **Bank of England** controls which issues of gilts may be stripped and acts as the **settlement** agent for all transactions (cf. **reconstitution; separate trading of registered interest and principal of securities**).

Ginnie Mae pass-through (GNMA pass-through) (USA). The market's name for pass-through mortgage certificates issued by the **Government National Mortgage Association** (GNMA). Although such issues tend to have a long **original maturity**, the **amortization of principal** means that they have a much shorter **average life**.

giro. Common term for a **clearing** or **settlement** system, usually used for small transactions (cf. **Effektengiro**).

Giscard bond (France). **Gold-linked bond** offered on the French domestic markets. The timing was perfect since, following the issue, the price of **gold** subsequently rose significantly. In retrospect, probably one of the most expensive *emprunts d'état* (state borrowings) made in recent times.

give-up. (i) The loss of **yield** coming from the sale of securities at one rate and the buying of other securities at a lower yield (cf. **pick-up; switch**). (ii) In some markets, used to describe the practice of a buying **broker** informing the seller of the identity of the buyer so that **delivery** can occur. (iii) (USA) In the securities markets, when a member of an exchange acts for another member by carrying out an order for a third. The first member 'gives up' the second member's name rather than their own in the transaction with the third.

glamor stock (USA). A fashionable **stock** with an investment following.

Glass–Steagall Act of 1933 (USA). The US legislation which prevented commercial banks from owning, **underwriting**, or dealing in corporate shares and **bonds**. At one time the Act debarred all depository institutions from participating in the securities markets but it has been much modified, although not abolished, to allow the full integration of US financial institutions (cf. **universal banking**).

global asset allocation. Internationally diversified **portfolio** management technique which concentrates on market selection and timing. Often the market portfolio is based on a broad **index** or **passive management** approach. **Futures** and **options** may be used to manage **short-term** adjustments because of their low transaction costs and high **liquidity**.

global bank. A bank active in the international markets with activities in more than one country (cf. **money center bank; prime bank**).

global bond. (i) A bond issue that is offered and traded simultaneously in different markets including the US domestic bond market and the **eurobond** market. Since US domestic bonds are **registered** and eurobonds bearer instruments, there need to be special **settlement** arrangements to transfer ownership between markets. See **global bond issue; global offering**. (ii) A temporary certificate representing a whole issue, produced to control the **primary market** distribution of an issue of new securities in order to meet any legal or market restrictions or because definitive **bond certificates** are not available for the present. This arrangement is common in the eurobond market. Sometimes called a *global certificate*. See **lock-up period**.

global bond issue. Bonds where the settlement mechanism allows the transfer of titles between markets (such as the US domestic bond market and the **eurobond** market). See **global offering**.

global commercial paper. A commercial paper (CP) programme that is designed to allow issuance in both the US domestic CP market and the **eurocommercial paper** (ECP) market.

global coordinator. For an issue of securities which is being made in different markets (often called a *global issue*), it is common to appoint a **lead manager** who acts as the coordinator of the entire issue and arranges the amount that will be allocated in each submarket in response to demand. Under the global coordinator, there is usually a regional or national coordinator who has responsibility for the local syndicate. See also **book building**.

global custody. Custodian services that span several markets. Global custodians will normally service the needs of investors in the major markets. Services include **settlement, safekeeping, dividend**, and **coupon** collection and forwarding, **foreign exchange**, tax, and securities valuation.

global depository receipt (GDR). The international markets' equivalent to **American depository receipts**.

global hedge. Hedge that is used to cover all of a particular **risk** exposure. Also known as a *strategic hedge*.

globalization. The trend of major financial markets across the world becoming more interlinked as a result of technological innovations in communications, cross-border investment, and global trading which provides the means for portfolio strategies based upon 24-hour trading. See **global asset allocation; liberalization; program trading; securitization; strategic asset allocation; tactical asset allocation**.

global medium-term note. A medium-term note (MTN) programme that is designed to allow issuance in both the US domestic MTN market and the **euro medium-term note** (EMTN) market. Such an issuance programme must meet **Securities and Exchange Commission** requirements. As a result, notes issued in the EMTN market are resellable into the US domestic market (cf. **flowback**).

global note. (i) A temporary certificate used in **eurobond** issues during the **lock-up** period and held within the **clearing system** evidencing ownership. Once the lock-up period is over, **bearer certificates** are substituted. The use of a global note is designed to prevent sales into the US domestic market and to meet requirements laid down by the USA's **Securities and Exchange Commission**. (ii) A single certificate used in place of definitive certificates in order to cut down on the cost of issuance in **eurocommercial paper** programmes. Such a note has the beneficial owners inscribed on the reverse. One advantage of such a method is to allow for the issuance of odd amounts. Sometimes called a *universal note* or a *grid note*.

global note issuance facility or **global note facility (GNIF).** Permits the issue of **commercial paper** in both the US domestic market and in the **euronote** market at the same time, and is usually **underwritten** by a **syndicate** of banks (cf. **borrowers option for notes** or **underwritten standby; note issuance facility; short-term note issuance facility**. Because of the different settlement arrangements between the euro and the domestic markets, such a facility normally incorporates a **swingline** arrangement.

global offering. A securities issue offered in several markets simultaneously. Usually taken to mean a **bond** or **equity** new issue launched at the same time in the North American, European, and Japanese markets. For such transactions there is normally a global coordinator/**lead manager** responsible for coordinating the placement and for organizing a **syndicate** whose members have specific responsibility for **placement** in the different national markets. Such offerings require special **settlement** and transfer arrangements between the different national markets. For instance, in the case of a **global bond** offering, the ability to convert from US domestic **registered** to international **bearer certificate** modes. The global offering needs to be distinguished from largely domestic transactions with an international element. Because of this, it is largely limited to world class institutions or **transnational corporations**. In 1992, Welcome plc of the UK made a global **seasoned** public offering of **shares** held by the Welcome Foundation where major tranches were placed in Japan, Europe, and North America simultaneously. The World Bank has made several global bond offerings denominated in US dollars which are traded simultaneously in several markets.

global risk management. Multi-centre integrated **risk management** system for international firms. See also **central treasury**; **concentration banking**; **netting**.

GLOBEX. A global, round-the-clock, electronic, screen-based futures trading system introduced by the **Chicago Mercantile Exchange**, **Chicago Board of Trade**, **Marché à Terme Internationale de France** and **Reuters**.

gnomes de l'ombre (French) Literally, gnomes of the shadows. Term used for international speculators against the French franc. First coined by Prime Minister *Alain Juppé* in October 1995 (*FT*, 9 October 1995 p. 23) (cf. **gnomes of Zurich**).

gnomes of Zurich. Often used as a derogatory term to describe the bankers and money managers based in the financial centres in Switzerland. Linked with various financial conspiracies because of the secretive nature of Swiss banking laws, which are designed to protect the true ownership of financial assets held within its jurisdiction. Perhaps most famously applied to international currency speculators responsible for losses of confidence resulting in the need for government action, such as devaluations or exits from currency exchange rate agreements. See **European Monetary System**.

go-around (USA). Market term for the process by which the **Federal Reserve** (Fed) seeks quotes from the **primary dealers** in government securities for **repurchase agreements** (cf. **desk**). This sounding out process normally takes place between 11 and 11.30 a.m. New York time with the results being available to the market shortly thereafter. The resultant transaction, to add or drain **reserves**, is keenly watched to indicate whether it indicates a shift in monetary policy by the Fed since such **open-market operations** are the first indications of changes. See **Federal Reserve System**.

godfather tender offer (Mergers and acquisitions). **Takeover** attempt where the **predator** puts such a high value on the **target** company that the management cannot persuade **shareholders** not to accept (cf. **knock-out**). See also **Two-Tier tender offer**.

go-go fund. A type of **mutual fund** which aims to achieve a higher than average rate of capital appreciation. According to the **efficient markets hypothesis** this would imply taking greater than average **risk** and frequent **portfolio** shifts in order to take advantage of **short-term** changes. See **arbitrage**; **switching**; **transaction costs**. See also **hedge fund**.

going ahead (USA). An unethical practice whereby a **broker-dealer** trades for his own account first in preference to his clients.

going away (Bonds; USA). Term for purchases which are then sold to **retail**. Thus such purchases are 'going away' from the market (cf. **firm hands**; **visible supply**). It can also be applied to heavy purchases of particular maturities of a **serial security**.

going concern or **going concern basis.** (i) Generally, a method of evaluating or valuing an **asset**, **project**, or firm which assumes that the business will continue to operate without impediment. (ii) More specifically, a requirement by an **auditor** to establish that the audited entity is viable as a going concern. In the UK, this requires the auditor to take an active role in arriving at the going concern classification and to register an adverse opinion if he does not agree with the firm's **directors** that the business is a going concern in the foreseeable future (cf. **auditor's opinion**). Qualification of the accounts is required, if in the view of the auditor, the directors have not taken sufficient steps to satisfy themselves that the going concern basis is appropriate (cf. **financial distress**; **insolvency**). Auditors are required to look at all the relevant information available, including taking a **long-term** view.

going-concern value. The value of a firm or project as an ongoing business (cf. **goodwill**). This contrasts with the breakup or liquidation value if the activity was liquidated and the assets realized and used to pay off investors (cf. **asset stripping**).

going long. To take a **long position** (cf. **overbought**).

going private. To de-list a company, normally as the result of its being purchased (cf. **leveraged buy-out**; **management buy-out**).

going public. (i) Market jargon for the process of a company seeking an initial listing on an exchange for its **common stock** (cf. **initial public offering; new issue**). Also known as *floating*. (ii) (USA) The process of obtaining a listing for a company on a recognized exchange and involving **registration** of the securities with the **Securities and Exchange Commission** and the preparation and distribution of a new issue **prospectus** (cf. **red herring**). See **due diligence; flotation; initial public offering; public offering**.

going short. Taking a **short position** (cf. **oversold**).

gold or **gold bullion.** A precious metal **commodity**. Gold bullion is the market in gold ingots or bars, which come in a variety of sizes, but the quoted price is based on the price of one ounce. The gold market also includes gold traded in the form of coins or specie which trade at a premium to the bullion price (cf. **krugerrand; maple leaf; britannias; new sovereigns**). See also **commodities**.

gold bond. A bond issue which is backed by gold (cf. **asset-backed security**). Holders may have the right to exchange their securities for gold. It can also mean a **gold-linked security**. Sometimes called a *gold convertible*.

gold certificate. A statement of current holdings and dealings in **gold bullion** (cf. **warehouse receipt**). Sometimes called the *gold account*.

gold clause. A condition in an intergovernmental loan that repayment must be made in currency linked to the **gold** price.

gold convertible. A bond issue which is exchangeable for gold at a predetermined price.

golden handshake. Compensation for the premature ending of an employment contract, usually paid to company executives ousted as a result of a **takeover** (cf. **golden hello**).

golden hello and **golden hand-cuffs.** Terms used to cover the additional payments made to securities **dealers** in order to attract them away from their present employer or to ensure their loyalty to their existing one.

golden parachute. Generous severance of employment terms put in place by company executives who may be ousted as a result of a take-over.

golden share (Equities; UK). A special **share** retained by the UK government upon **privatization** of previously state-owned enterprises giving the government special blocking powers in certain circumstances, typically a **takeover**. Usually the special share lapses after a given period. The logic is to allow the government to forestall undesirable developments in the initial years following the move of the business into the private sector.

gold exchange standard or **gold standard.** See **gold standard** (cf. **convertibility**).

gold fix (Commodities; Switzerland; UK). The daily setting of the price of gold in London or Zurich. See **London Metal Exchange**.

gold forward rate agreement (GOFRA). A type of financial transaction used by buyers and sellers to set a predetermined gold price for forward delivery in the **over-the-counter** market which is similar to a **gold future** or a **forward rate agreement**.

Gold Franc. (i) A gold coin similar to **krugerrands, maple leafs, new sovereigns**. (ii) An accounting unit used by international telecommunications companies for settling international connection charges.

gold future. A futures contract where the **underlying** is gold.

gold-linked bull-bear. A bond issue in two tranches (a **bull** and a **bear tranche**) where redemption is linked to the performance of the **gold** price over the life of the issue. The bull tranche will provide a higher return if the price of gold rises; the bear tranche the opposite. The issuer is effectively immunized from the movements in the gold price since the total redemption amount cannot be more than the combined value of the two tranches and, likewise, investors can **hedge** themselves from the gold-link by holding both tranches. See **bull-bear bond**.

gold-linked security. A debt issue where the **principal** and/or the interest payments are linked to the price of gold (cf. **gold bond**).

gold loan. (i) A loan of gold. (ii) A loan backed by gold as **collateral**. This is sometimes used in **project finance** to monetize gold deposits in advance of extraction (cf. **commodity swap**).

gold market. The market in gold, a precious metal. The market is in three forms: as bullion, where the **London Metal Exchange** has a predominant role; in gold coins; and the **forward** or **futures market**. There are other precious metals markets in platinum, palladium, and silver. See **commodities**.

gold mutual fund (USA). A **mutual fund** investing primarily in gold mining companies.

gold participation certificate (Bonds; USA). A type of senior **participation certificate** (PC) issued by the **Federal Home Loan Mortgage Corporation** (FHLMC) which features greater security of payment of interest and **principal** than standard FHLMC PCs. The intention was to make such securities more attractive to investors by reducing the uncertainty of the attendant cash flows.

gold pool. Grouping of Belgium, France, Italy, Netherlands, Switzerland, United Kingdom, United States, and West Germany that between 1961 and 1968 acted together to stabilize the price of gold (cf. **Bretton Woods**).

gold reserves. (i) National reserves held in the form of **gold bullion.** (ii) The amount of extractable gold in a gold seam or deposit.

gold shares (Equities; UK). Shorthand for the **ordinary shares** of South African gold mining companies (normally quoted on the **London Stock Exchange**).

gold-silver index. An index of the relative prices of the two precious metals (cf. **spread**). It is used for **technical analysis** of market trends.

gold standard. The setting of the value of a paper currency by reference to and exchangeable for **gold** (cf. **convertibility**). The USA operated a gold standard until 1971 fixed at US$35 an ounce.

gold tranche. Borrowable reserves based on **gold** held by member states at the **International Monetary Fund.**

gold warrant. (i) **Warrant** that is exercisable into gold. Sometimes it is **cash settled.** (ii) A **warehouse warrant** for a given quantity of **gold bullion** in storage.

go my way/go your way (USA). Method of resolving disputes in failed transactions where the **counterparties** mutually agree to change the details of the trade so as to ensure **good delivery** (cf. **out-trade**).

good delivery. A delivery with all conditions satisfied; that is, unmutilated, uncalled securities with unpaid **coupons** that are properly endorsed and for which the **transfer agent** will accept delivery (cf. **bad delivery; fail**). Sometimes called *clean delivery.*

good for the day (GD). An instruction to a **broker** which is valid for the day and the instruction is automatically cancelled if not executed within the time frame indicated. An alternative is known as *good for the session,* which relates to an **exchange-traded** security, where the market

ceases when the exchange closes (cf. **at the close**). See **daytime trading.**

Goodhart's Law. States that the pursuit by a monetary authority of any monetary target renders it completely meaningless for the purpose for which it is sought. It uses the assumption that once a government reveals the basis upon which it measures money supply, attempts will be made to neutralize the controlling effects that might exist.

good money. Term used for the receipt or payment of funds for immediate value. Also known as *good value.*

good names (USA). Recognized names in which US and Canadian shares can be **registered** for delivery without transfer formalities (cf. **street name**).

good this month (GTM). An instruction to a **broker** which is valid until the end of the month. Normally a time limit placed on a **limit** or **stop order.**

good this week (GTW). An instruction to a **broker** which is valid until the end of the week. Normally a time limit placed on a **limit** or **stop order.**

good through. An instruction to a **broker** which is valid for a fixed period or until carried out or cancelled. Normally a time limit placed on a **limit** or **stop order.**

good till cancelled (GTC). An open instruction to buy or sell securities which remains in force until the order is executed or cancelled (cf. **fill or kill**).

good value. Payment by a party to a transaction which the recipient can use immediately (cf. **clearing house funds; regular delivery; town clearing**).

goodwill (i) (Accounting) The excess of purchase price over **intangible asset value** in a takeover. Different conventions apply to the treatment of goodwill. In the USA corporations can opt for immediate **write-off** or include it on the **balance sheet** and subsequently depreciate it over a period of time not exceeding fifty years. In the UK, companies are obliged to make an immediate write-off against reserves. See **merger accounting.** (ii) That part of the value of an asset or business arising from factors not directly associated with the inherent nature of the **asset** or business. Usually a value of business reputation or above-average profits performance or potential (cf. **glamor stock; Tobin's q**). See **market-to-book ratio; price–earnings multiple.**

go public. See initial public offering.

Gordon growth model, Gordon valuation model. A method of common stock valuation based on assumptions about the required capitalization rate or discount rate (r) and the growth rate in the dividend (g). The formula is:

$$\text{Price (value given stock)} = \frac{\text{Current dividend}(1 + g)}{(r - g)}$$
$$= \frac{\text{Next dividend}}{(r - g)}$$

Given historical evidence, or projections, of the growth rate, we can rearrange the basic equation to derive the unknown, required discount rate (r) or the *required rate of return*:

$$\begin{array}{l}\text{Required discount} \\ \text{rate (required rate} \\ \text{of return)}\end{array} = \frac{\text{Current dividend}(1 + g)}{\text{Price of stock}} + g$$

See also **dividend discount model.**

governing law. The jurisdiction in which a security or transaction are subject to legal process and interpretation in the event of disputes.

Governmental Accounting Standards Board (GASB) (USA). Body charged with setting accounting standards for states and municipalities (cf. Financial Accounting Standards Board.

government bond. A bond issued by the state. Government bonds are used to finance fiscal deficits or capital spending. The government bond markets are the **benchmark** against which corporate and financial institutions can issue (cf. **credit risk; credit risk premium; risk premium**). Governments borrow **short-term** in the money markets via **treasury bills** or from the banking sector, or longer term via **bond** or **note** issues (cf. **shorts; mediums; longs; on-the-run issues**). The government may also guarantee issues or provide its **full faith and credit** to its **agencies** and these are variously called the *state sector* or *government guaranteed* issues (cf. **federal agencies; municipalities**). See also **gild-edged; obligations assimilables du Trésor; Japanese Government Bond; treasury bond; treasury note; yield curve.**

government bond market. The financial market in which **government bonds** are traded (cf. **gild-edged market maker; primary dealer**).

government broker (UK). An agent of the **Bank of England** who acted in the **gilt-edged** market by issuing UK government securities and controlling the issue process, including the queue regulating the new issue of corporate debt securities. Traditionally this was the senior partner at the firm of Mullens & Co., who advised the Bank on market conditions and acted as selling agent for new issues of government stocks. However, following the changes instituted by **Big Bang**, the Bank took this function internally. See **auction; tap stock.**

Government National Mortgage Association (GNMA; Ginnie Mae) (USA). A wholly owned federal government corporation set up in 1968 which is designed to provide **secondary-market liquidity** to the market in residential mortgages. It guarantees privately issued securities backed by **pools** of federally insured or guaranteed mortgages. The most common form of GNMA security comprises monthly interest payments and **amortization** prepayments of **principal** on mortgages that are passed through to the holder, known as **pass-through certificates** (cf. **fully modified pass-through**). See **asset-backed; collateralized mortgage obligations; interest only; mortgaged-backed; principal only.**

government obligations or **governments** (USA). Negotiable US Treasury securities and those of federal agencies of the government.

Government Pricing Information System (GOVPX) (Bonds; USA). A real-time price system for the **US treasury market** developed by the **Public Securities Association.**

government securities or **government stock.** Marketable and negotiable debt issued by governments (cf. **gilt-edged**). See **bond; treasury bill; treasury bond; treasury note.**

government securities dealers (Bonds; USA). See **primary dealer.**

Gower Report (UK). A *Review of Investor Protection 1982* prepared by Professor J. Gower, which led directly to the **Financial Services Act, 1986** (cf. **Big Bang**).

grace period. (i) The period between when a debt or security issue is first offered to the market and the start of its **sinking fund** or its **purchase fund** (cf. **call protection**). (ii) (Banking) An initial period included in some loan agreements during which the borrower is not required to make repayments of **principal** but only to keep interest current. See also **repayment period.** (iii) The time allowed to a defaulter to meet the outstanding obligations (cf. **breach of covenant; default**). See **bad debts; non-performing loans; problem assets.**

grades. (i) Quality of assay of a material. (ii) Result of a scoring process (cf. **credit scoring**). See also **credit rating.**

grading. See appraisal.

graduated payments mortgage (GPM) (USA). A type of mortgage where the initial interest payments are insufficient to service the **principal**; but where the payments are increased over time. The **compounded** shortfall is added to the principal balance in the early period thus leading to a higher servicing cost in the later stages. Sometimes called a *deferred interest mortgage* or a *low start mortgage*.

graduated rate security. Applied to a fixed-interest or **variable rate** security which has one or more **coupons** that pay less or more than the first. The structure is commonly used in UK issuances of sterling **mortgage-backed floating rate notes** where the **spread** to the **reference rate** is increased if the note is not called after a given period. It compensates investors for any additional, unanticipated **tenor** and may help initial **marketability** (cf. **bells and whistles**). See **step-up coupon**.

Grain and Feed Trade Association (GAFTA) (Commodities; UK). See **London FOX**.

Gramm–Rudman–Hollings Act of 1985 (USA). Better known as Gramm–Rudman, the act proposed the gradual reduction of the US federal government's budget deficit. Since passing into law, the deficit has not been reduced since there was no real method of enforcing conformity to the targets.

grandfathering. (i) An arrangement or transaction that is allowed to continue when the law or regulations are changed. Hence the concept of *grandfathered issues*. (ii) In the USA the term has a quasi-legal meaning as in (i) above (cf. **safe harbour**). (iii) A provision under UK banking law which allows small banks to retain the name bank in their title.

granny bonds (UK). See **National Savings**.

grant anticipation note (GAN) (Money markets; USA). Short-term instrument issued by a municipality in anticipation of receiving a federal grant (cf. **bond anticipation note; revenue anticipation note; tax anticipation note**).

grant date. (i) The effective date for a deferred start option. (ii) The date from which an employee receives a **stock option** on the firm's **stock**.

grantor (UK). Term used on the **London Metal Exchange** instead of **option writer**. In effect the option writer is granting the holder the choice of whether to undertake the transaction.

grantor trust (USA). A type of trust where federal income tax on the income is levied at the individual level and not on the trust (cf. **limited partnership**).

grantor underwritten note (GUN) (Banking). A floating rate facility, close to a **euronote**, under which a group of banks agree to buy fixed rate notes which investors **put** to them, and then sell them by **auction** (cf. **tender panel**).

graveyard market (USA). Used to describe securities that are infrequently traded either because of the lack of interest or because of a lack of value (cf. **cabinet crowd; thin**). See also **garage**.

grecian bond. Colloquial market term for a bond which has a **maturity** in the year 2000.

Greeks. The sensitivity factors for the value of an **option** derived from an **option pricing model**. See **delta; gamma; lambda; theta; rho; vega**.

green baize door. See **chinese wall**.

Green Book (Equities; UK). Published by the **London Stock Exchange**, it set out the requirements for admission to the **unlisted securities market** (cf. **Yellow Book**).

Greenbury Committee. A group of UK corporate executives established by the Confederation of British Industry to examine the issue of executive remuneration (cf. **agency problem; Cadbury Committee on the Financial Aspects of Corporate Governance**). See **corporate governance**.

green currency. Exchange rates used under the **European Union's** Common Agricultural Policy (CAP) for determining agricultural support levels and based on the **European Currency Unit**. These exchange rates are not market rates, although changes in market rates do mean that the green currency rates have to be changed from time to time. The member currencies are known as *green franc, green pound*, and so forth.

green franc (Belgium; France). See **green pound**.

green inks. See **off-balance sheet**.

greenmail or **greymail** (USA). The acquisition of a large enough stake in a company to be able to influence **board** decisions with the intention of encouraging the **target** company to repurchase the **stock** at a significant **premium** to the current market price. The repurchase offer is not extended to the firm's other **shareholders**. It is often accompanied by a **standstill agreement** between the two parties preventing further share purchases or **takeover** attempts for a given period. Companies surrendering to greenmail were attempting to buy their freedom from a **predator**. See **mergers and acquisitions**.

green pound (UK). An accounting unit used by the **European Union** to calculate agricultural import and export prices between the UK and the rest of the Community under the Common Agricultural Policy (CAP). Also *green franc* etc. See Green currency.

greenshoe. An **option** given by an issuer, normally but not necessarily for an **equity** issue, to the **underwriters** for the issue of additional securities to cover a **short position** generated by overallotting. The name derives from the first company (the Green Shoe Manufacturing Co.) to include such a feature in a **public offering**. See initial public offering; **offer for sale**.

grey book (Banking; UK). The set of regulations issued by the **Bank of England** in its capacity as supervisory institution for the UK banking sector that cover the **over-the-counter** wholesale markets in **foreign exchange**, **interbank** and **money markets**, the **bullion** market, and their attendant **derivatives**.

grey hair investment. A potentially good investment that will take a long time to bear fruit (cf. **lemon; plum**). Thus the investor is likely to be old and grey haired before obtaining the benefit.

grey knight. A second bidder in a contested **takeover** whose intentions are not known. He is grey because he is neither a *white knight* coming to the rescue of the target company, nor a *black knight*, aiding and abetting the **predator**.

grey market. (i) The trading of new issues by dealers on an *if, as and when issued* basis prior to being admitted to the official after-market (cf. **when issued**). Usually, but not always, an 'unofficial' market. Grey markets have evolved as a mechanism for **risk** transfer for participants in auctions; for example the US Treasury when issued market. (ii) In the **eurobond** market, the period during which an issue is traded from the date of its launch until **allotment**.

grid note. See global note.

gross. Before the deduction of taxes (and, sometimes, expenses) (cf. **all-in cost; net**). Hence, a price quoted on a *gross basis* is prior to any deductions.

Grossbanken (Banking; Switzerland). The major Swiss banks, such as Credit Swiss, Swiss Bank Corporation, Union Bank of Switzerland, and others.

gross dividend (Equities; UK). The **dividend** that would have been paid if no **advance corporation tax** (ACT) had been withheld by the company. It is computed by dividing by one minus the ACT

withholding tax rate. The gross dividend is used to calculate the **gross dividend yield** on **shares**.

$$\text{Gross dividend} = \frac{\text{Net dividend}}{(1 - \text{withholding tax rate})}$$

gross dividend yield (Equities; UK). This is the **gross dividend** divided by the current market price expressed as a percentage. Quotations normally reported in the financial press refer to the last full year's **dividend** (i.e. the **interim** and **final dividends**). At times called the *historical gross dividend yield* for that reason. Sometimes the gross dividend yield is calculated on projected or anticipated dividends and is known as the *expected* or *anticipated gross dividend yield*.

gross domestic product (GDP). A measure of the total flow of **commodities** and services generated by an economy over a specified period of time, usually a year or quarter. It is calculated by adding together the market price of all such goods and services. It needs to be noted that in the official statistics it is the value of goods and services in final consumption or investment goods that is used. Therefore, the value of intermediate products are excluded because the value of these goods is included in the price of final goods. In the reported statistic, no adjustment is made for expenditure on replacement capital. The word 'domestic' refers to the fact that income arising from investments and assets owned overseas is excluded. See also **gross national product**.

grossed-up. (i) For **eurobond** issues, the additional payments made by a borrower to compensate for **withholding tax** or other levies which reduce the return. (ii) The implied before-tax return, usually misleadingly (cf. **after-tax**). See **imputation**.

grossed-up net redemption yield (UK). A method used for converting the **after-tax yield-to-maturity** to a pre-tax yield, ignoring income and **capital gains** tax in order to compare different investments.

gross income. (i) Revenues before costs. For businesses this is variously known as **gross sales** or **turnover**, although for accounting purposes trading income is reported separately from investment income. (ii) Total income for taxable purposes before deductions (cf. **net income**).

grossing-up. Calculating the pre-tax return on an investment by notionally adding back any **withholding tax** (cf. **after-tax tasis**).

grossing-up provision. A condition for a **eurobond** issue that requires the issuer to increase the payment to the original cash value in the event that **coupon** interest is subject to withholding taxes, or to **call** the issue.

gross interest. Interest before the deduction of tax (cf. **gross dividend**; **withholding tax**). See also **net interest**.

gross lease. See **full service lease**.

gross loan (Banking). An arrangement in a loan where the borrower is responsible for any **witholding tax** on the interest. Thus the lenders receive interest gross of any tax. However, it is normal in such cases for the lenders to receive any tax credits on this sum (which may be used to offset their own taxable position), which also enhances their returns. The opposite type of transaction where lenders are paid the net amount is known as **tax spared lending**.

gross national product (GNP). This is the gross domestic product plus all income earned by domestic residents from assets held overseas less income paid to overseas residents.

gross national product deflator (GNP deflator). A price **index** number used to adjust money values of the **gross national product** for price changes, in order to identify the variations which have occurred in the physical output of goods and services. See also **index construction**.

gross position. The sum of both **long** and **short positions** even though these might, partially or fully, **offset** one another.

gross processing margin (GPM). The gross difference between a crude product and its refined equivalent. See **crack spread**; **crush margin**.

gross profit. Sales or **turnover**, less the cost of sales (the cost of producing the goods or services), during a particular period, normally a year. Gross profit or **trading profit** captures the profit from selling without deducting selling and administrative expenses.

gross redemption yield. A calculation of the **redemption yield** before tax (cf. **yield-to-maturity**). Also called the *gross yield to redemption*. see **interest rate calculations**.

gross sales. Turnover.

gross settlement. In an agreement where two sets of cash are to be exchanged, as with an **interest rate swap**, the two flows are paid over by both parties. The alternative, and much more common method, is for one of the parties to make a net payment to the other (cf. **net settlement**). See **full two-way payments clause**.

gross spread or **gross underwriting spread.** (i) A fraction of the proceeds from an **underwritten** new issue that is paid as compensation to the **managers** and **underwriters** of the transaction plus any **selling concession**. (ii) For **eurobond** issues, the total of management and underwriting fees plus any selling concession, which is normally expressed as a percentage. See **bid-asked spread**; **discount**; **eurobond fees**.

gross terms. The price and conditions applying to a **contract** before taking into account such things as **trade credit**.

gross yield. The pre-tax return on a security. The after-tax return is known as the *net yield*. See **yield** for different definitions.

gross yield to redemption. See gross **redemption yield** (cf. **yield-to-maturity**).

group accounts. Consolidated financial accounts of a number of companies under common ownership (cf. **holding company**). See also **equity accounting**.

groupement d'intérêt économique (France). A type of **partnership** where the members agree to act together for given business purpose (cf. **consortium**). The best known *groupement* is the four-member Airbus Industrie set up to build commercial airliners and made up of Aérospatiale of France, British Aerospace of the UK, DASA of Germany, and CASA of Spain.

Group of Five (G5). France, Germany, Japan, United Kingdom, and United States. Also known as the *Plaza Group*, following their first meeting, held at the Plaza Hotel in New York.

Group of Six (G6). France, Germany, Italy, Japan, United Kingdom, and United States.

Group of Seven (G7). Canada, France, Germany, Italy, Japan, United Kingdom, and United States. Originally *ad hoc* summits started in the 1970s as a result of world problems, the G7 has evolved into regular summit meetings between the members. The **European Union** President normally attends as an observer.

Group of Ten or **Group of Ten Industrialized Countries (G10).** Belgium, Canada, France, Germany, Italy, Japan, Netherlands, Sweden, United Kingdom, and United States. This comprises the major industrial countries involved in global arrangements to borrow and other financial arrangements(cf. **General Agreement to Borrow**). There are really twelve members since Switzerland and Luxembourg are informally attached to the group, as is a representative of the **European**

Union. It is based at the **Bank for International Settlements**, which provides its secretariat. There are also enlarged groupings with wider aims such as G24, G30, and G77 and narrower groups such as G7. G10 is also known as the 'Paris club' (cf. **London club**).

Group of Thirty (G30). A private sector initiative to develop a common standard for **settlement** and other cross-border securities transactions. The body has set forth a series of 'best practice' proposals for consideration by its membership. G30 recommendations have been implemented in many countries including the UK, where **rolling settlement** has replaced the old **account** system on the **London Stock Exchange**. Settlement in the **eurobond market** has also moved towards the G30 standard by reducing the normal time from five business days ('$T + 5$') to three business days ('$T + 3$').

Group of Three (G3). Germany, Japan, and the United States.

group sale (USA). **Selling group** arrangement where all the members receive a **prorata share** of the amount available for distribution (cf. **club deal**). The alternative method is a designated sale where members receive allocations set by the **lead manager**.

grown-up money. See **serious money**.

growth. (i) Increase in economic output in an economy. (ii) Rise in value of an investment. Hence a *growth stock*, which appreciates rapidly in value relative to the market as a whole (cf. **glamor stock**).

growth and income securities (GAINS) (USA). See **zero-coupon convertible**.

growth fund. A managed **fund** which has as its objective achieving above-average **capital gains** on its portfolio, usually by investing in **growth stocks** (cf. **investment company**; **mutual fund**).

growth industry. A particular industry segment that is expected to show above-average rates of growth compared to the economy as a whole.

growth stock. A common stock that is expected to increase, or has already increased, its **earnings per share** at a rate faster than that for the market as a whole (cf. **glamor stock**; **Gordon growth model**; **high flyer**). See also **capitalization rate**; **price–earnings ratio**.

guarantee. (i) An undertaking by a second party to agree to make good **principal**, interest if the borrower, **counterparty**, or issuer **defaults** (cf.

asset-backed; **collateralized**). (ii) Another term for a warranty.

guarantee amount (Bonds). See **limited guarantee**.

guaranteed bond. A **bond** where the interest or **principal** is indemnified by an authority other than that of the issuer, such as a bank or the issuer's parent or holding company. Such guarantees are quite common in cases where a special issuing vehicle such as an **NV subsidiary** have been used. In the case of a third party guarantee, such as a bank, it may take the form of an irrevocable **letter of credit**. Multiple guarantees have been seen in some transactions, but they suffer from the problem that the value placed on the guarantee will be that of the weakest **credit**. In order to get around this problem, usually one institution will front for the others in the **syndicate** and a series of indemnifications between the parties will be put in place.

guaranteed coupon reinvestment bond. A type of security where the holder has the right to receive additional **bonds** of the same type at **par** in lieu of a cash **coupon** at each payment date. If all the coupons are received in the form of additional bonds, the holder has the equivalent of a **zero-coupon bond**. The bond structure thus guarantees a minimum return, but unlike a zero, if rates rise, the holder may receive the cash and reinvest it at a higher rate in the market (cf. **reinvestment risk**). Such issues are also colloquially known as *bunny bonds*. See also **pay-in-kind bond**.

guaranteed equity bond. A type of bond where the returns are linked to the rise of a stock market **index** but the **principal** is repaid regardless of movements in the index. The bond is in effect a one-way bet or **embedded option** on the performance of the index. The **call option premium** is arrived at by the fact that the forgone interest is used to pay for this since the bond pays little or no interest on the principal. Normally, the bonds have a **zero-coupon bond** structure to ensure the principal can be repaid and where all the gains, if any, are paid back at **maturity**. Some issues feature a *lock-in facility* where any rise in the index over the period is then paid out as interest, regardless of subsequent movements in the market. Note that the holder forgoes the **dividends** by buying an option on the index. See **equity-linked notes**.

guaranteed exchange rate warrant (USA). Warrant on a foreign **stock** or **stock index** which has a fixed **exchange rate** against the US dollar at the time of issue. See **quantity adjusting option**.

guaranteed index unit. Securities which offer an exposure to a **stock index** or **common stock**

and which at the same time guarantee to repay investors the invested **principal** in full. Depending on the type, they may offer a **geared** return, have a **cap**, lock in a guaranteed minimum return, be low or zero **coupon** investments. See **equity-linked notes**.

guaranteed investment contract (GIC) (USA). A type of life insurance contract where the holder is guaranteed a specific return based on the cash flows from a **pool** of **underlying** securities (cf. **synthetic guaranteed investment contract**).

guaranteed mortgage certificate (GMC) (Bonds; USA). A bond issued by the Federal Home Loan Mortgage Corporation (FHMLC) backed by a **pool** of conventional mortgages. It is similar to a **pass-through** except that the FHLMC guarantees that some minimum **principal** will be paid each year. Unlike pass-throughs, GMCs provide interest semi-annually and principal annually. The investor also has the **option** to **put** the remaining principal to the FHLMC at **par** prior to maturity. See **mortgage-backed**.

guaranteed return index participation securities (GRIPS). Type of **equity-linked note** which often has less than full participation in gains from the **index**.

guaranteed return on investment certificate (GROI). Bond or note issue combined with a **vertical spread** position offering the holder a limited participation in the gains and a guaranteed minimum return on their investment. See also **equity-linked notes**.

guaranteed return structures (GRS). A range of **structured** securities which have the common feature of guaranteeing to preserve the initial investment of the holder, plus the opportunity to participate in the gains or returns from the exposure to a **stock**, an **index**, or other variable. A range of different instruments are available which have different features, some incorporate a **ladder option**, others have a **vertical spread**, some

pay a below-market rate of interest, others none at all. See **equity-linked notes**.

guaranteed share. A security, normally a **preferred stock**, where the interest is indemnified by another company.

guaranteed stocks (Bonds; UK). Bond issues by state-owned entities which carry an explicit state guarantee.

guaranteed warrant (USA). **Warrants** issued in the US market by corporations or foreign sovereign entities which offer the holder the exposure to a **stock index** (cf. **covered warrant; guaranteed exchange rate warrant**). See also **quantity adjusting option**.

guarantee fund. A type of offshore fund where the investor's principal is guaranteed via a third party (cf. **Commodity Trading Advisor**).

Guarantee Fund for Danish Options and Futures (Denmark). Kompagnistræde 15, Box 2017, DK-1012 Copenhagen K (tel. 45 33 93 33 11; fax 45 33 93 49 80).

guarantee letter. A letter from a bank undertaking to make a cash payment on the **underlying** in the event that a **put option** is exercised (cf. **covered put**).

guarantor. The party who offers a guarantee to another. In financial markets, there are monoline assurance companies which, for a fee, will guarantee financial transactions.

gun jumping or **jumping the gun** (USA). (i) Trading on **insider information**. (ii) Selling a new issue before the **registration statement** has become effective.

gut or **guts.** **Option** strategy involving the purchase of a **call option** at a given **strike price** and a **put** with a higher strike. See **diagonal calendar spread; horizontal spread; vertical spread**.

H

haircut (USA). (i) The **margin** in a repurchase transaction. This is the difference between the **yield** or price on the **bid** quote and the yield or price used in the **repurchase agreement**. (ii) Calculation of the **discount** to be applied on a firm's inventory of securities used by the regulator to ascertain the capital requirements for **broker-dealers** (cf. **capital adequacy**). See **FOCUS report**. (iii) The capital required by a financial intermediary to support a **position**. (iv) Another term for a **commission** or fee. (v) The **margin** requirement of a member on a **futures** or **options** exchange when undertaking transactions.

haircut finance (USA). Borrowing against pledged **collateral**, usually in the form of securities. It gets its name from the 'cut' made off the value of the securities for the loan by the lender as a precautionary measure. The lender, however, has a **lien** for the entire **asset**.

haitō (Japanese). **Ex-dividend**.

haitō seikō (Japanese). **Payout ratio**.

halal (Islam). Those activities which are permitted under Islamic law (sharia) (cf. **haraam**). See **Islamic banking**; **riba**.

half-commission agent. A broker who is not a member of an exchange but introduces business to an exchange member in return for a split of the **commission**.

half-life (Bonds; USA). Term used to indicate the time until half the principal of an issue of **bonds** has been redeemed. See **amortization**; **average life**; **prepayment model**; **sinking fund**.

half-stock (USA). Term for a stock with half the normal **par value** (cf. **no par stock**).

hammered (UK). Applies when a member of an exchange is unable to meet its obligations.

hammering the market. Colloquial term to describe intense selling by market participants.

Hammersmith and Fulham swaps (UK). The **interest rate swaps** (IRS) undertaken by the Borough of Hammersmith and Fulham for its own and on behalf of other local authorities that were declared *ultra vires*, that is beyond the powers of the Council, by the courts following a challenge mounted by the Audit Commission, the local authority (government) audit and investigative commission, in July 1988. The case eventually ended up in the House of Lords in 1991, when all the swaps were declared to be illegal. At the start of the case, the Borough had oustanding IRS commitments of around £3bn, far in excess of the authority's debt of £390m. Hammersmith and Fulham had agreed to be **fixed receivers (floating rate payers)** and had suffered when sterling interest rates rose from around 7% to over 13%. Following the ruling, the banks sued for restitution of the sums paid under the contracts. The case indicates the dangers of undertaking transactions with governments and states where the law had not been fully tested (cf. **sovereign risk**). See **legal risk**.

handle (USA). Used in US securities markets to indicate the whole number of the price of a **bid** or **offer** of securities. If a price is quoted $95\frac{1}{2} : 95\frac{5}{8}$, ninety-five is the handle. Traders will often make a **quote** leaving out the handle, this being taken to being known by the other party (i.e. in the above just say $\frac{1}{2} - \frac{5}{8}$). See **big figure**.

hand signals. Market standard hand signs used on floor exchanges to overcome the problems of noise when trading is frenetic or **traders** are physically removed (cf. **open outcry**). The signals, which owe a great deal to semaphore, allow the sender to communicate, for instance, whether the transaction is a buy (hand towards sender) or sell (hand away from sender) and by holding the hand to the head for the number and away for the price at which the transaction is to be, or has been, undertaken. The different values are given by holding up the required number of fingers and keeping the hand vertically for numbers zero to five and horizontally for six to ten.

hands-on. Active investment management method where the financier partakes in the direction of the investment (cf. **corporate governance**). See **venture capital**.

Hang Seng index (HSI) (Equities; Hong Kong). Broad market capitalization-weighted **index** of the thirty-three largest and most actively traded **common stocks** or **ordinary shares** on the **Hong Kong Stock Exchange**. The index dates from 1964 when it was originally compiled by the Hang Seng Bank. It is subdivided into finance, utilities, properties and commerce, and industry sub-indices.

haraam (Islam). Those activities which are prohibited under Islamic law (the sharia) (cf. **halal**). See **riba**.

hara-kiri swap. An **interest rate swap** or **cross-currency swap** made without any profit to the party offering the transaction. It derives from the mid-1980s practice of Japanese banks and securities houses offering very low rates in order to obtain business. In Japan, hara-kiri is a form of slow ritual suicide; hence the swaps were dubbed hara-kiri since they are a form of financial self-immolation. In particular, it refers to the provision of a US dollar–Japanese yen cross-currency swap undertaken at a rate below prevailing market conditions or otherwise subsidized by the swap provider. Such swaps have typically been attached to new issues with a view to obtaining a leading **underwriting** position.

hard. A market is said to be 'hard' if prices are rising. A currency can also be so described if there is excess demand and an expectation of a rising value in relation to most other currencies (cf. **soft**). See **foreign exchange; premium**.

hard arbitrage. See **round-tripping**.

hard commodities. Commodities which do not perish when stored, such as aluminium, copper, lead, nickel, tin, and zinc (cf. **soft commodities**). Generally taken to exclude **gold** and other precious metals and oil and other energy products such as gas oil. Sometimes known as *metals*. The most traded commodities are: aluminium, copper, lead, mercury, tin, and zinc.

hard currency. (i) A currency which tends to **appreciate** relative to others over time. The opposite is a **soft currency**. (ii) A currency that may be freely **convertible** is sometimes referred to as hard (i.e. good). Usually taken to be the major traded currencies such as the US dollar, sterling, Japanese yen, Deutschmark, and so on.

hard dollars. Payments for services in the financial services industry. In contrast to **soft dollars**.

hardening or **hardening of the market, rate,** or **price.** Generally taken to be a rise in value or rate.

hard European Currency Unit (hard ECU). A proposal made by the UK in the move towards **European Monetary Union** to change the method of calculation of the European Currency Unit such that it would not be devalued by changes in parities of the components. In the event, the idea was not adopted.

harmless warrant. The name for a type of **warrant** that does not increase the liabilities of the issuer when exercised. When a fixed rate issue of debt has warrants attached they are 'harmless' if the borrower can only **exercise a call provision** of all or part of the **underlying** 'host' or **back bonds** during or at the end of the period during which the warrants can be exercised. Although harmless to the issuer, investors in such bond and warrant packages may not think so.

Hart–Scott–Rodino Antrust Improvement Act of 1976 (Mergers and acquisitions; USA). Changes made to the **antitrust laws** that required pre-**merger** notification to be made to the federal government for **mergers and acquisitions** above a predetermined size (cf. **Clayton Act**).

hatch system. System of automatic investment, governed by movements of a share price **index**. See **filter**.

hazard. Risk management term for a particular **risk** or exposure (cf. **risk factor**). Also sometimes known as a *peril*.

hause des taux (French). A rise in interest rates.

head and shoulders. A chart pattern which approximates to the shape of a person's head and shoulders and which signals a future fall in prices. The head being the summit and the shoulders the lower peaks on either side. For chartists this pattern foretells a **bear** phase, whilst a *reverse head and shoulders* is taken to indicate the start of a **bull** phase. See also **line** and **triangle patterns; chart analysis; technical analysis**.

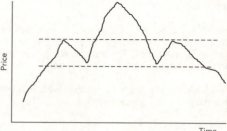

Head and shoulders

head-to-head. Direct trading between **market-makers** without the use of brokers (cf. **inter-dealer broker**).

Heath–Jarrow–Morton option pricing model. **Option pricing model** providing an analytical solution to the pricing of **options** on **bonds** using a **binomial** approach designed to address the observed **mean reversion** in interest rates (cf. **term structure of interest rates**).

heaven-and-hell bond. An issue where the redemption proceeds are linked to the **spot exchange rate** at **maturity** of another currency against the currency in which the issue is denominated. The redemption proceeds are calculated according to the following formula:

$$100 \times \left(1 + \frac{\text{Spot rate at maturity} - \text{rate fixed at issue}}{\text{spot rate at maturity}}\right)$$

Investors gain (lose) if the currency in which the bond is denominated increases (decreases). Also sometimes referred to as an *indexed currency option note* (ICON). See **bull-bear bond**; **dual currency bond**; **embedded option**.

heavy (UK). Used to describe a **share** with a very high price in relation to its **par value**.

heavy market. A market which is falling as a result of selling pressure (cf. **split**).

heavy shares (UK). Units of **ordinary shares** carrying a disproportionate number of **voting rights** compared to other shares. Often differentiated by being called 'A shares', the less ranked shares being known as 'B shares'.

Hebel (German). **Leverage** (cf. **gearing**).

hedge. (i) The taking of offsetting commitments in order to mitigate the effect of undesirable movements or the **risk** in a **position**. A *perfect hedge* will totally eliminate the risk being hedged; an *imperfect hedge* will only eliminate some of the risk, either a particular type of risk like **currency risk** or some of all the risk, leaving some **residual risk**. With a *long hedge* or *buying hedge*, the hedging instrument is purchased; with a *short hedge* or *producer's hedge*, the hedging instrument is sold. (ii) A fixed commitment in a **derivative instrument** or **futures market** that acts as temporary substitute for an intended purchase or sale of a financial instrument for **delivery** and payment at a later date but at the then current market price. (iii) Sometimes used for the action of selling **short** a security to offset the risk of a **long position** in the same or similar security (cf. **cross-hedge**).

hedge account. (i) A reporting account used for booking hedging transactions (cf. **hedge accounting**). (ii) For **futures** transactions, the ability to designate a transaction for a hedge account which allows for a lower level of **margin** to be provided and/or exemption from the **limits** the exchange might set to speculative or **naked positions**.

hedge accounting. An accounting method that treats the **hedge** and the **underlying** as an offsetting package for reporting purposes (cf. **matched book**).

hedge clause. A disclaimer in a published market document disavowing responsibility for the accuracy of the information provided. More commonly known as a *disclaimer clause*.

hedged swap. A term used by **swaps** traders for a **position** taken in a particular swap which has been hedged through the appropriate offsetting transactions with market instruments, typically **futures** or the **cash market** rather than by another swap.

hedged tender. A process involving setting up a **short position** when bidding in a **tender** in order to reduce the **risk**. Such hedges may take the form of **cross-hedging** between markets or participating in the **grey market** or **when-issued** trading.

hedge fund. A type of unregulated investment fund. Typically it is (i) a **limited partnership** or **mutual fund** which is (ii) unregulated and is (iii) allowed to hold **long** or **short positions** in **commodity** and financial instruments, which (iv) may use **leverage** and where (v) management remuneration is linked to financial performance. The first such fund, AR Jones, was set up in the USA in 1949. The name is undoubtedly a complete misnoma since it is generally an **investment company** which takes aggressive **positions** involving significant **risk** in many different markets as its fundamental investment strategy. Managers of such funds are normally remunerated on a percentage of profits and have an incentive to take such risks, which is the opposite of hedging, which aims at risk reduction.

hedge period. The period of time between the initial transaction, which involves creating an **open position**, and the offsetting **derivative** transaction (**forwards**, **futures**, **swaps**, or **options**).

hedger. (i) A person or institution undertaking a transaction in order to **hedge** a **position** (cf. **speculator**). (ii) A **risk-averse** individual or institution concerned to reduce the risks they are taking.

hedge ratio. The amount of **futures**, **options**, **forwards**, or **underlying** purchased or sold against a **position** in the underlying in order to **hedge** the position (cf. **delta**; **gamma**; **delta hedge**). A market participant with a **long** (**short**) **position** in the underlying will want to hold a counterbalancing short (long) position. The extent to which the two cancel each other out will show how effective the hedge is. See **risk management**.

hedge wrap. See risk reversal.

hedging effectiveness. The degree to which a hedging model captures the relationship between the underlying asset being hedged and the hedging instrument. In statistical terms this is the coefficient of determination (r^2; r squared). The higher the r squared, the better the model's fit and the better the expected performance of the hedge.

hedging instrument. Any of a number of securities or financial instruments that can be purchased or sold and can be used to offset a type of risk from another instrument, security, or other transaction. The main kinds are **cash instruments**, **forwards**, and **futures**, **options**, and **swaps**.

hedging models. Models used to balance the amount of a **hedge** required to eliminate the **underlying's market risk**. There are two basic models: (i) the *naïve-hedge model*, which takes as its point of departure the equal behaviour between the two sides of the hedge and can be defined as:

$$N_f = -\frac{V_u}{V_f}$$

where V_u is the value of the underlying and V_f the value of the hedging instrument. The hedge-ratio number N_f gives the number of **futures contracts** of the hedge required to balance the price response of the two positions. (ii) The *price-sensitivity model* takes into account the different price sensitivity of the underlying position and that on the hedge (cf. **cross-hedge**):

$$N_f = -\beta\frac{V_u}{V_f}$$

where N_f is the number of futures contracts (rounded to a whole number) required to hedge the value of the underlying (V) and V_f is the value of the futures contract. β is the price-sensitivity coefficient of the underlying to the contract. For a stock portfolio, this is the portfolio's **beta**; for a bond, the differences in the modified **duration** of the position and the **bond futures**. This is also called the *minimum-variance model* or the *regression hedging model* since it takes as its input the slope of a regression equation between the underlying asset and the hedge (that is the regression's beta (β)) (cf. **hedging effectiveness**). See also **delta hedge**.

hedging pressure theory. A theory of the price behaviour of **futures** that puts forward the idea that if the net demand for **short** hedging exceeds the demand for net **long** speculation, then long speculators will need to be compensated by an additional return **risk premium** to encourage them to balance the excess demand for short hedging (cf. **backwardation**; **contango**).

hell or high water. A condition in **project finance** that requires the buyer of the project's output to make payment regardless of whether the buyer receives the product or not (cf. **take-or-pay contract**).

Helsinki Stock Exchange (Finland). Fabianinkatu 14, PO Box 361, FI-00131 Helsinki (tel. 358 0 173 301; fax 358 0 1733 0399). Principal indices are the Hex index and **Finnish Options Index**.

Herfindahl–Herschman index (HHI) (Mergers and acquisitions; USA). An index of **monopoly** power and market concentration used by the Justice Department for **antitrust law** purposes. See **Clayton Act**.

Hermes Kreditversicherungs AG (Hermes) (Banking; Germany). Export credit guarantee organization.

Herstatt Bank (Banking; Forex; Germany). The name ID Herstatt is a byword for **overnight delivery risk**. The bank was closed in June 1974 by the **Bundesbank** after business hours in Germany as a result of major **foreign exchange** losses made by the bank. In closing the bank at this time in the day, this left many banks who had dealt with Herstatt with significant exposures since, due to the timing of **clearing** or **settlement** arrangements, these banks had paid out Deutschmarks to Herstatt, but its closure prevented them from receiving US dollars in return (cf. **daylight exposure limit**). As a result, the kind of risks created by this kind of **default** is sometimes called *Herstatt risk*.

heterogeneity or **heterogeneous.** The opposite of **homogeneous**.

heteroscedastic or **heteroscedasticity.** See **homoscedastic**.

hidden reserves. Funds owned by an organization but not disclosed in the published **balance sheet**. In some countries, banks are allowed to hold hidden reserves, although the practice is becoming less common. Also called *off-balance sheet* or *secret reserves*.

high. (i) The peak in price or rate for a time series (cf. **spike**). (ii) A rate or price that is above the current market rate (cf. **off-market**).

high coupon bond refunding. The process of replacing a high **coupon bond** with a new issue of lower coupon bonds. Usually a decision that an issuer has to make when he has the choice of **exercising** a **call provision** in a **bond**. He will work out his **break-even** on the refunding, using his **all-in** cost of new funds.

high coupon swap. A swap transaction where the **fixed rate** is above the prevailing market rate (cf. **discount swap**). The fixed rate payer will be taking additional **credit risk** on the **floating rate** payer. Also known as an *off-market coupon swap* or *premium swap*. The opposite is known as a *discount swap* or *low coupon swap*.

higher of proceeds or market (HOPM). A conservative accounting convention applicable to the valuation of **liabilities** that they be recorded in the **balance sheet** at the proceeds received or at the market, whichever has the higher value. For assets, the convention is *lower of cost or market*.

high first coupon bond. A type of **step-down coupon** security which has a large initial **coupon** relative to both market rates and subsequent coupons.

high-flyer. Describes someone destined for the highest reaches of management. It is not always clear what characteristics an individual should display in order to enjoy such an accolade.

high-grade bond. A triple or double-A rated bond (cf. **credit rating; investment grade**).

high leverage (high gearing). See **highly leveraged transaction**.

high-low, closing chart. A chart analysis method of producing price series which plots the day's high, low, and closing prices as a time series. The normal method involves time on the horizontal axis and price or rate on the vertical. The highs and lows are then plotted as a line, with the closing point as a horizontal bar. It is designed to capture the intra-day range and the closing point of the day. See also **candlestick chart**.

High-low, closing chart

high-low floating rate note (high-low FRN). Floating rate note with a large **margin** up to a cap

point on the **reference rate**, after which the note effectively becomes a **reverse floating rate note**. The instrument is attractive to investors who expect short-term interest rates to remain stable over the life of the instrument. In effect, the holders have sold **volatility** by purchasing the instrument (cf. **straddle; strangle**).

high-low option. An option where the payout is the difference between the high and low price or rate of the **underlying** over the tenor of the option times a factor. The same payoff can be created by holding a **lookback option call** and **put**. It is a kind of **volatility** play since profiting from such a position is predicated on the view that the actual volatility over the option period will be higher than the implied volatility in the high-low option package.

highly leveraged transaction (HLT) (Banking; USA). Any transaction with a significantly high **debt–equity ratio**. Bank regulators consider any loan or security holding where the ratio exceeds 75% must be treated as an HLT and recorded appropriately. See **junk bond; leveraged buy-out; takeover**.

high margin security (Bonds). A floating rate note (FRN) which has a **coupon** similar to an ordinary FRN if the **index rate** or **reference rate** lies below the specified level. If the index rate rises above that level then it has a coupon similar to a **reverse floating rate note**. See **high-low floating rate note**.

high premium convertible security. A convertible where the **conversion price** has been set at a high **premium** but where the **coupon rate** is close to the **straight bond** equivalent. Issued mainly as a conventional **bond** with an additional **equity kicker** to increase marketability.

high premium security. (i) A security which is deliberately above **par** in order to attract investors subject to particular tax regimes. (ii) A **zero-coupon** bond which is issued at **par** (100) and redeemed at a large **premium** (cf. **deep gain security**).

high-tech stock. A stock belonging to a high-technology company.

high-tech swap. A complex **interest rate swap** or **cross-currency swap** or series of swaps, often forming part of a funding transaction (cf. **multi-legged swap**).

high-yield bond. Polite term for a **junk bond**.

high yielder (Equities). **Common stock** with an above average **dividend yield**. Typically such securities are high risk, since the higher yield is needed to compensate for the risk of, possibly, **passing the dividend** (cf. **bankruptcy; insolvency**).

high-yield fund. A fixed-interest **fund** or portfolio which invests in high-yielding securities, typically which are below **investment grade** (cf. **junk bonds**).

high-yield security. Polite term for high-risk securities such as a **junk bond,** that is securities below **investment grade** or high **dividend yield common stocks** (cf. **fallen angel; high yielder**).

Hijra years (HY). Years according to Islam. They count from the year of Muhammad's flight to Medina (the Hijra), which in the Gregorian or Western calender is AD 622. The conversion is required because the Islamic calendar is based on a lunar month rather than the solar year, plus the start dates differ. As a result, 33 HYs equal 32 Western years, and we have to add or subtract the differences in the start dates, 621 years, if we want the Western year in which the Hijra year starts, or 622 for the end date. The conversion formulae are:

to convert to Anno Domini (AD):

$$AD = HY - \frac{HY}{33} + 621^*$$

to convert to a Hijra year (HY):

$$HY = AD - 621^* + \frac{AD - 621}{32}$$

*If the end of the year is required, add one to the above.

hike. Colloqiual term for a raise in interest rates.

hike (Japanese). The **closing price** or transaction on the **Tokyo Stock Exchange.** See **ōbike.**

hi-low option. An option strategy which is the combination of two **lookback options** and where the payout is the difference between the high and low points of the **underlying** over the set period. A buyer (seller) would be **taking a view** that the actual **volatility** of the underlying would turn out to be higher (lower) than the **implied volatility** of the two lookback options used to create the hi-low option.

hindsight option. See **lookback option.**

hire purchase. A type of finance where the borrower hires the **assets** from the lender for the term of the agreement. Typically, the user has the right to acquire the asset at the **maturity** of the agreement for a nominal sum. Sometimes called *lease purchase.*

historical cost accounting. The convention of reporting items in a **balance sheet** at their purchase price or cost, less any **depreciation,** without regard to their replacement value. Other methods of reporting would use replacement cost or current cost methods to take account of the changing value of money over time.

historical rate rollover (Forex). An extension to a maturing **foreign exchange forward contract** where the renewal is made at the rate that originally prevailed on the first contract. By using the historical rate, the benefiting party avoids any cash transfers at the **rollover.** The losses or gains from the original contract are thus deferred by being rolled into the new, extending forward contract (cf. **marked-to-market**). It is often done to conceal or defer **foreign exchange** losses (less frequently, gains) by organizations and a number of well-known industrial companies and banks have suddenly become aware of large concealed losses arising from this type of transaction. As a result many foreign exchange **market-makers** will now require special authorization to undertake such business. Some accounting authorities have regulations prohibiting the practice.

historical volatility. The **volatility** of a time series of asset prices based on historical prices or rates. Volatility is one of the pricing variables used in **option pricing models** in order to calculate the **fair value of an option** or its **premium** (cf. **expected volatility; implied volatility**).

historic cost accounting convention. The valuation of **balance sheet** items at their purchase price, or their original, hence historical, cost.

historic pricing (UK). Transactions in the **units of unit trusts** based on the most recent valuation (cf. **forward pricing**).

history-dependent option. See path-dependent option.

hit. (i) To accept a **bid,** as in to *hit the bid* (cf. **lift; take**). (ii) To make a loss on a transaction; hence, *to take a hit.*

hive-down. A technical operation carried out by a receiver which has the effect of 'losing' the busted company's **liabilities.**

hoard or **hoarding.** Holding **assets** in anticipation of a price rise, usually as a result of a shortage or interruption in supply (cf. **ramp**).

Hoare Govett Smaller Companies Index (Equities; UK). Index, rebalanced annually, that tracks the performance of the smallest companies quoted on the **London Stock Exchange.**

Hoekman (Dutch). Specialist.

hold-back. A retention from the price or value in regard to expected or unanticipated future costs (cf. **accrual**; **provision**).

holder. The buyer or purchaser of a **financial instrument** (cf. **long position**).

holder of record. The investor who is **registered** as being the owner of the **asset** or security.

holding. Another term for a **position** or **investment**, usually taken to be a particular security, issuer, or other specific **asset**. Hence *share holdings*.

holding company. A legally constituted company that does not carry on any trade but has a controlling interest in one or more subsidiary trading companies (cf. **consolidated**; **equity accounting**; **parent**).

holding cost. The cost of maintaining a **position** or **investment**, usually taken to include all incidental expenses, such as **safekeeping**, record keeping, and so forth associated with the investment (cf. **all-in cost**; **cost of carry**).

holding period. The time frame within which a market participant expects to keep an investment. This usually implies a period shorter than the **maturity** of the investment and may be measured in hours, days, weeks, or years (cf. **investment horizon**).

holding period return. The expected or actual return over the holding period for an **asset** or security, where the holding period is normally less than the **maturity**. The ex-post return is usually significantly affected by the **market price** at which it can be sold at the end of the holding period, unless this is the same as the **duration** (cf. **immunization**; **total return**).

holdout problem. Difficulties in achieving a reorganization without recourse to the courts to enforce compliance that arise from a firm in financial distress due to **creditors** refusing to endorse any reorganization (cf. **cram down**). Such dissenting creditors are holding out in the expectation of better treatment of their claims as a way of achieving a result (cf. **free rider**).

Ho–Lee option pricing model. A single-factor option pricing model for the **term structure of interest rates** developed in 1986. The **binomial tree** used in the **model** assumes that interest rates recombine over time and that the evolution of **bond** prices is such that **arbitrage** across the term structure is not possible. See T. Ho and S. Lee (1986), 'Term structure movements and the pricing

of interest rate claims', *Journal of Finance*, 41: 1011–29.

home currency (Forex). The currency of account of an enterprise (cf. **base currency**).

homemade leverage. Using borrowed funds to increase the **leverage** of a given **position** (cf. **margin**).

home run (USA). Making a large profit in a short period of time. Derived from baseball, where a good hitter can hit a home run by knocking the ball far enough to allow him to run around all the bases back to his home base, thus winning points for his team.

homoscedastic or **homoscedasticity.** An important assumption for **regression analysis** which is extensively applied in **econometrics**. It is imposed on the disturbances or error term μ_i such that they all have the same variance, little sigma squared (σ^2). If this is not the case, such that the variance of μ_i is little sigma i squared (σ_i^2), indicating that it is varying from observation to observation (note the subscript on little sigma squared) then the situation of heteroscedasticity, or non-constant variance, exists. To illustrate the difference between homoscedasticity and heteroscedasticity, consider the following two-variable linear regression model in which the dependent variable

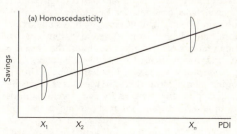

1(a) Homoscedasticity

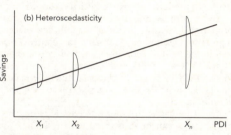

1(b) Heteroscedasticity

S is personal savings and the explanatory variable X is personal disposable income (PDI), or after-tax income. Consider the diagrams, $1(a)$ and $1(b)$. Diagram (a) shows that as PDI increases, the **mean** level of savings also increases but the variance of savings around its mean value remains the same at all levels of PDI $(X_1, X_2, \ldots X_n)$. Remember that **regression analysis** gives the mean value of the dependent variable for given levels of the explanatory variable(s). This is the situation of homoscedasticity. Conversely, in Diagram (b), although the average level of savings increases as PDI rises, the variance of savings does not remain the same at all levels of PDI—here it increases with PDI. This is the situation of heteroscedasticity or unequal variance. In other words, Diagram (b) indicates that relatively high-income individuals save more than lower-income individuals, but there is also more variability in their savings. This conclusion is intuitively appealing since lower-income groups are much less likely to have the opportunity to save. Therefore, in a regression of savings on income, error variances (variance of μi) associated with high-income households are expected to be greater than those associated with lower-income ones. Heteroscedasticity is usually expressed statistically as:

$$E(\mu_i^2) = \sigma_i^2$$

It has been observed that heteroscedasticity is usually found in cross-sectional or panel data, rather than in time-series data. When using cross-sectional data the observations are usually at a given point in time and based on individual agents, firms, or industries. Moreover, these members may be of different sizes, such as small, medium, and large firms. Therefore there is an inherent risk of scale effects and thus the presence of heteroscedasticity. Conversely, when analysing time-series data, the variables tend to be of similar orders of magnitude because the data is normally collected for the same entity over several periods of time: for example, inflation, employment, and GNP rates. It might be expected that any scale effects within such data, and hence heteroscedasticity, can be either adjusted for using devices such as deflators or are not present. However, this neat distinction is not strictly true. In the so-called autoregressive conditional heteroscedasticity (ARCH) models, heteroscedasticity can be observed in time-series data. How this effect is to be handled, whilst retaining the efficacy of the regression technique, remains a controversy within the field of econometrics. For a discussion of the ARCH model, and its more generalized form, GARCH, see G. S. Maddala (1988), *Introduction to Econometrics*, (Macmillan), 218–19. See also **econometrics**.

The significance of heteroscedasticity in the finance area can be illustrated with reference to the levels of brokerage fees charged by London firms since the so-called **Big Bang**. Since deregulation, dealing-only fees have fallen but there have emerged significant differences in the average commissions charged across the various categories of investors. As might be expected, small private investors face a different fee than that offered to large institutional investors. The larger the volume of transactions, the lower the total cost of transacting, and therefore the lower the average cost. Even if there are scale economies in the brokerage industry, why should the variance of the commission rate across the different categories be different? In other words, why is there heteroscedasticity? To attract the business of big institutional investors such as **pension funds**, **unit trusts**, and **insurance companies** brokerage firms compete intensely with one another such that there is little variability in the commission rates charged. Smaller institutional investors may have less bargaining power so there is more variability in the dealing fees they pay.

In attempting to develop a regression model to explain the commission rate as a function of the number of share transactions (and other variables), the error variance associated with high-volume clients would be lower than that associated with low-transaction clients. In order to consider the consequences of heteroscedasticity, how it can be detected, and the remedial measures available, see D. Gujarati (1992), *Essentials of Econometrics* (McGraw-Hill), 324–50.

homogeneous or **homogeneity.** (i) A condition when applied to factors or variables used in **econometrics**. It refers to the degree of similarity (assumed or observed) in the nature or behaviour of such influences. (ii) Applied to a distribution or a data sample which indicates it has been drawn from the same **underlying** population (cf. **jump**). The opposite condition would be known as *heterogeneous* or *heterogeneity.*

homogeneous expectations. A precondition for deriving the equilibrium condition for the value of assets that all market participants have the same view on expected return and risk. See **Capital Asset Pricing Model; risk-neutral valuation.**

homoscedastic. The property of having equal **standard deviations** or **variances**. See **homogeneous.**

Hong Kong Commodities Exchange Ltd (HKCE) (Hong Kong). **Commodities exchange** established in 1977, which deals principally in **softs**, especially sugar.

Hong Kong Futures Exchange (HKFE) (Hong Kong). 5/F, Asia Pacific Finance Tower, Citibank Plaza, 3 Garden Road, Hong Kong (tel. 842 9333;

fax (852) 810 5089; tlx 76375 HKFEG HX). Established in 1976.

Hong Kong interbank offered rate (HIBOR) (Hong Kong). The rate for interbank borrowings charged in the Hong Kong market. Similar to the London interbank offered rate.

Hong Kong Stock Exchange (HKSE) (Hong Kong). 21st Floor, Hutchison House, Harcourt Road, Hong Kong (tel. 5 262697).

horizon analysis. A form of market analysis that considers the total return offered by a security within a given period, based upon normal market conditions and other likely outcomes.

horizontal merger. A type of merger or acquisition involving companies or businesses where the majority of the activity is in the same or similar industry and where they could be regarded as competitors. Such deals can be seen as either *defensive*, that is to protect market share, or *aggressive*, to expand market share.

horizontal price movement. A period when prices do not change much over an extended period of time. Also known as a *sideways price movement*.

horizontal spread. An option position involving buying an **option** (either a **call** or a **put**) while selling another option on the same **underlying** with different **expiry dates** but with the same **strike price** (cf. **calendar spread**). The attractions of such a strategy are that by selling the shorter option and buying the longer, provided the price remains the same, the holder receives the difference in **premiums** and can still sell the longer option when the earlier one expires. The **time decay** on the shorter option will be more rapid than for the longer expiry one. It can also be set up in the opposite fashion, selling the longer-dated and buying the shorter-dated option, when it is known as a *reverse spread* (cf. **credit spread**; **debit spread**). Also called a *calendar spread*, a *horizontal option spread*, or a *time spread*. See **diagonal spread**; **intra-commodity spread**; **vertical spread**; **option strategies**.

hors-côte (French). Unlisted market. See also **Paris Bourse**.

hospital revenue bond (USA). A **municipal bond** issue specifically to finance a hospital or nursing home.

host bond. The name for a **bond** which has **warrants** attached (cf. **debt** and **equity warrants**; **usable security**). The combination of the bond and warrant is known as a *package*. Also some-

times known as the *back bond*. See also **harmless warrant**.

hostile bid or **hostile takeover** (Mergers and acquisitions). **Takeover** attempt that is unwelcome to the **target** company's **board of directors** and, possibly also, its **shareholders**. Also known as a *contested bid*.

hot issue. An issue of securities expected to trade at a significant **premium** to the **issue price** in the **after-market**. Sometimes called a *hot stock*.

hot money. (i) International movements of **short-term** capital, usually of a speculative nature in anticipation of changes in currency values or interest rate differentials. Gives rise to the *hot potato theory of money.* The term is sometimes applied to any volatile deposit liable to be withdrawn at short notice. (ii) Dishonestly acquired money (cf. **money laundering**).

hot potato theory of money. A theory of international capital flows which postulates that money flows around the globe in search of high returns, thus causing sudden shifts and changes to the international markets.

hot stock. Much sought after issue; generally considered to be underpriced and therefore likely to offer an immediate gain. Hot stocks tend to be associated with **new issues**, while **glamor stocks** with fashionable investment sectors or theories.

hot treasury bills. Most recent issues which tend to have the most liquidity (cf. **on the run**).

house. (i) A broker-dealer or **investment banker** firm. (ii) (UK) the **London Stock Exchange**.

house account (USA). Account on which salespeople do not receive a **commission**.

house call (USA). A notification to a client that **maintenance margin** is required to allow the firm to maintain his **position**. If additional funds or **collateral** are not provided, the **broker** will close out the position. See **margin call**.

house fund (UK). Applied to a managed fund that is not a **unit trust** usually operated for 'small' investors of the management institution.

house maintenance requirement. The **margin** requirement set by a firm on a client's **margin** account.

house of issue. The **lead manager** or **underwriter** in a **purchase and sale** transaction.

house paper. A commercial bill of exchange drawn and accepted by companies within the same group or ownership.

house rules. Internal compliance, ethical, and operational procedures for customers and staff. See chinese walls.

house switch. Said to apply to a transaction on a futures exchange where the counterparty to the trade has been incorrectly recorded. Since transactions are settled through a clearing house this will not cause the trade to fail, since the reconciliation of the trading session will cause the clearing house to switch the trade to the correct account (cf. outtrade).

house transaction. A trade or transaction identified as being for the account of the firm's own (presumably risk management) purposes, rather than for customers. Sometimes called a *principal transaction*.

housing bond (USA). A municipal bond issue to finance construction projects (cf. project note).

H shares (Equities; Hong Kong). Common stock of former state-owned enterprises listed in Hong Kong. The first such issue was by Tsing-tao Brewery in July 1993 (cf. A shares; B shares).

Hull–White option pricing model. Option pricing model developed for pricing interest rate options using a trinomial distribution that addresses the observed mean reversion pattern of the term structure of interest rates.

human capital. The idea that investing in people within an organization can be justified in relation to the returns a more effective work-force can bring. Typically, the costs would be seen as training and development expenditure, and the returns in terms of more highly motivated, aware, and flexible employees. Hence the phrase *human resource management* rather than *personnel management*.

humped (Bonds). A description of the yield curve where it initially rises then falls as maturities get longer.

Humphrey-Hawkins Act of 1978 (USA). Technically it is The Full Employment and Balanced Growth Act, but is better known by the name of its two sponsors. The Act requires the Federal Reserve to set annual monetary targets and explain how these targets relate to goals for employment, prices, and economic activity. The Chairman of the Board of Governors of the Federal Reserve is required to make a statement to the House and Senate Banking Committees of Congress in February of each year and a further testimony giving details of any changes or revisions in July. The aim of the act is to make the Fed more accountable to Congress. The testimony provides a guide to the Fed's assessment on the future of the economy and a guide to future monetary conditions (cf. Beige Book).

hung up (USA). The plight of a buyer when the value of his holding falls below his purchase price. He is unable to sell without crystallizing a loss. Also known as *negative equity*.

hurdle rate. (i) The minimum return that is required from taking a position, making an investment, or undertaking a project. The hurdle rate can be expressed in terms of a return or yield which has to be bettered (cf. internal rate of return); or as the discount rate that needs to be applied to cash flows in order to derive their net present value (NPV). It normally is used as a means of filtering different alternatives and, all things being equal, a greater margin over the hurdle rate or a larger NPV is to be preferred. Also called the *cost of capital*, *discount rate*, *opportunity rate*, *required return*, or *risk-adjusted cost of capital*. See also required rate of return; Capital Asset Pricing Model; cost of capital. (ii) (UK) The annual growth rate in the total assets required by an investment trust to offset the annual growth in the prior charges.

hybrid. (i) Any of a class of security whose returns are linked to more than one class of underlying. (ii) Another term for a synthetic. (iii) Complex structures involving more than one type of payoff. For instance, combining an interest rate swap with an interest rate cap.

hybrid debt, instrument, or **security.** Any debt issue or security that combines the features of two or more instruments. Thus a convertible bond is a hybrid instrument, as is a package of a bond with warrants, or any bond which has embedded option features that combine different markets (although generally taken to exclude bonds with put and call provisions). The security will normally include one or more of the derivative product set: forwards, futures, options, or swaps to generate the particular payoff profile of the hybrid.

hybrid derivative. Any derivative incorporating two or more types of risk (cf. embeddo; quantity adjusting option).

hybrid floating rate note (hybrid FRN; hybrid floater). See fixed-then-floating bond.

hybrid reverse floating rate note (hybrid reverse floater) (Bonds). A type of reverse floating rate note (FRN) that has an initial **fixed interest** element before the interest is reset in line with current market terms. The rationale is that the fall in short-term interest rates that is the attraction of the reverse FRN may not be expected for some time when the issue is launched. By including a fixed rate element at the onset, usually with an attractive **margin** to the **reference rate**, investors will be drawn towards the issue (cf. **bells and whistles**). See **financial engineering**.

hybrid split trust (UK). An **investment trust** with two, or more **classes of capital** that are entitled to participate in the growth of the underlying portfolio. See **quasi-split trust**.

hyperinflation. Very high levels of inflation which cause people to distrust money as a store of value and a medium of exchange. Hyperinflationary conditions are noticeable by the flight to physical assets and the use of money substitutes, for instance either via barter or through the use of foreign (non-inflating) money.

hypothecation. (i) The pledging of assets as collateral (cf. **lien**). (ii) In government finance, the pledging of certain taxes or revenues to particular expenditures.

Hypotheken bank (German). A mortgage bank, that is a bank that lends against property (cf. **building society; savings and loan association**). The basic legislation governing its activities is the Hypothekenbankgesetz (HBG) (Mortgage Bank Act) passed in 1900.

Hypothekenpfandbriefe. Pfandbriefe where the **underlying** are residential and commercial mortgages (cf. **collateral; collateralized mortgage obligation; mortgage-backed security**).

I

IBCA Ltd. (UK). Eldon House, 2 Eldon Street, London EC2P 2AY (tel. (44) 171 247 5761; fax (44) 171 247 7665). A **credit rating agency** that, initially, specialized in rating financial institutions, particularly those active in the London market. It now has a much wider remit.

	Long term		Short term
Investment grade			
Best quality	AAA	Best quality	A1+
Good quality	AA	Good quality	A1
Average quality	A	Satisfactory quality	A2
Satisfactory quality	BBB	Adequate quality	A3
Below investment grade			
Best	BB		B
Investment risk	B		C
Speculative	CCC		
Highly speculative	CC		
In default	C	At risk, or in default	D

Note: A plus (+) or minus (−) sign indicates relative position within a rating class.

Ibex 35 Index (Spain). Capitalization-weighted **index** of the thirty-five most liquid **stocks** traded in the continuous market.

Iceland Stock Exchange (Iceland). Kalkofnsvegi 1, IS-150 Reykjavik (tel. 354 1 699 600; fax 354 1 621 802).

idiosyncratic factors. See anomaly; stock specific risk.

ijarah (Islam). Form of financial arrangement allowing the owner of a property to make it available to another party which is similar to a **lease**, but involves both parties sharing the **risks** and offers no fixed reward (cf. **aajir**). This form of association is required because of the ban on interest in Islam and the **joint venture** in which both parties accept a share of the risks and split the rewards complies with Islamic law, the sharia.

ijara-ijara wa iktina (Islam). A form of Islamic finance akin to **lease** financing and therefore allowable under religious law, in accordance with the concept of **risk** sharing by participants.

illiquid. A security or a market that is lacking activity (cf. **liquid**). Sometimes used in the sense

of a market without **depth**. Typically characterized by wide **bid-offer spreads**, difficulties in dealing in **size** on one side and, possibly, lack of adequate information (cf. **bazaar**).

imbalance of orders (USA). A situation where trading in a security has to be suspended because there are not enough offsetting orders to allow a market (cf. **opening rotation**). See **circuit breakers**.

immediately available funds. Funds which have immediate **good value** (i.e. cash). Depending on the market, the term can sometimes be taken to mean funds which are available for immediate settlement, such as **fed funds**.

immediately repackaged perpetual (IRP). See instantly repackaged perpetual.

immediate or **cancel order.** An instruction that any part of the order which is not immediately fulfilled is therefore cancelled (cf. **good till cancelled**).

immunization or **immunize**. A fixed interest portfolio strategy involving the matching of the **duration of bonds** held with a particular **investment horizon** (cf. duration bogey). In **asset-liability management** techniques, the matching of durations is also usually combined with matching of the **present value** of the future liabilities. Immunization is intended to **lock in** a return equal to the initial **yield** on the bonds, although the success of the process is predicated on the assumption of future parallel movements of the **yield curve** (cf. **cash flow match**; **dedication**; **parallel shift**). Also called a *duration-matched hedge*.

immunized portfolio. A portfolio designed to lock in a fixed rate of return over a specific time period. For example, a portfolio can be constructed such that a fixed return of 8% can be generated over a five-year period. This is achieved by setting the portfolio's **duration** equal to the specific time period over which the fixed return is desired.

impact day (UK). The first day upon which an issue of securities may be traded (cf. **preliminary prospectus**; **red herring**).

impact forward. See collar; collared forward; cylinder.

impaired capital. See negative net worth.

imperfect hedge. An attempted hedge which will partly, but not exactly, mirror the change in price of the **underlying** position. It could, for instance, arise through either a favourable or unfavourable change in the **basis** relationship, or through the use of a **cross-hedge**.

imperfect markets. Markets in which participants do not have access to information and/or where transactions may not be executed in the desired size. See **bazaar; efficient markets hypothesis; transparency.**

implied correlation. The interrelationship of two **underlyings** in **rainbow options**. As with **volatility**, it can either be defined by the historical statistical **correlation** between the underlyings, or derived from analytic pricing **models** (cf. **correlation risk**).

implied financing rate. see implied repurchase agreement rate.

implied forward interest rate (IFIR). The rate of interest in the **term structure of interest rates** for a period with a **forward** start date. If the current zero-coupon one-year rate is 8%, and the two-year rate 9%, the implied forward interest rate for one year in one year's time will be:

$$\text{IFIR} = \sqrt{\frac{(1 + 0.09)^2}{(1.08)}} - 1 \times 100 = 10.01\%$$

See **expectations hypothesis; forward-forward interest rate; forward yield curve; strip yield curve; yield curve; zero-coupon yield curve.**

implied futures rate. The rate of interest implied by the price of an **interest rate futures** contract (cf. **strip**).

implied gearing. A measure of the **volatility** of a **warrant** which measures the change in the warrant price given a percentage change in the **underlying** price. See **gearing; lambda; leverage.**

implied put. A feature of some **settlement** arrangements for **derivatives** contracts that the holder of the **short position** has an inbuilt put option as to when to make **delivery** (cf. **delivery options**). See also **embedded option; end-of-the-month-option.**

implied repurchase agreement rate (implied repo rate; IRR). (i) The **interest rate** earned on the funds used to buy the cash security in a cash-

and-carry operation. (ii) The financing rate at which a **long (short)** cash–short (long) **futures** arbitrage transaction would break even (cf. **basis**).

implied volatility (IV). The volatility of the **underlying** determined by using the market prices of traded **options** (cf. **historical volatility**). Since **option pricing models** calculate the 'fair value' of an option, implied volatility is technically the volatility that is required to equate the known pricing variables to the observed option price based on the pricing model. Implied volatility is important since it is the price at which volatility is being exchanged in the market and is often used as a predictor of future market volatility. Increased implied volatility can be taken to be an increase in uncertainty over the future period covered by the options analysed (cf. **volatility curve; volatility skew**). Sometimes called the *implied standard deviation* or *implied variance*. See **term structure of volatility.**

implied yield. A yield predicted on the basis of the current **term structure of interest rates** using the assumption that the **yield curve** is an accurate predictor of the **bond's** return (cf. **expectations hypothesis**). See **efficient markets hypothesis.**

implied zero coupon swap curve. See zero-coupon yield curve (cf. **implied forward interest rate**).

import cover. The ratio of the value of exports to the value of imports. It is the number of times the value of exports exceeds the value of imports. If the country has a deficit in the **trade balance**, then the 'cover' calculation will be negative and, if greater than one, an economy is thought to be a net creditor to the rest of the world. See also **terms of trade.**

import letter of credit (import LOC). See documentary credit; letter of credit.

imputation. A system of **corporation tax**, used in the UK, France, and Australia, involving the provision of a **tax credit** on dividends paid to shareholders on the basis that tax is already paid by the company on its profits. See **advance corporation tax; unrelieved advance corporation tax.**

inactive bond crowd (USA). See cabinet crowd.

inactive post (USA). That part of the **New York Stock Exchange** floor where inactive stocks are traded.

inactive security. A security which is seldom traded and therefore **illiquid** (cf. **lock up**).

in and out. A security that is bought and resold very quickly. Sometimes used to describe quick forays into markets or sectors not normally invested in (cf. **daytime trading**; **scalping**).

in-and-out option. See barrier option.

in-and-out trader. See daytime trading.

in-arrears London interbank offered rate. A method of computing interest rates on a loan or facility where the rate is set at the end of the interest period, that is in arrears, rather than at the beginning.

in-arrears swap. Interest rate swap where the floating rate side of the swap is set at the end of the interest period, that is in arrears, rather than at the start, which is more normal.

in-barrier option. Type of compound option combined into a **barrier option** and where the **premium** is partly reimbursable if the price or rate of the **underlying** does not trade through the **trigger** point (cf. **knock-in**). Such an option is attractive since the cost of protection is reduced if the underlying then does not move above or below a predetermined **limit**.

incentive fee. A payment above the normal remuneration designed to encourage and recompense above-average performance and similar to a profit-sharing incentive.

incentive stock option. See employee stock option.

incentive trade. An agreement between a customer and a **broker-dealer** to share the benefits (or losses) of favourable transaction rates or prices. The incentive means that the **broker** will aim to better the agreed target rate in order to share some of the gains of so doing, thus giving him an incentive to achieve a higher price; equally he is penalized if the target is not met.

incestuous transactions. The mutual purchase of stocks in companies within the same group to gain some advantage (cf. **cross-holdings**; **false market**).

inchoate. A condition where not all the details are provided.

inchoate instrument or **security**. Financial instrument which does not detail all the conditions of issue (cf. **shelf registration**).

income. (i) The revenues generated by a business (cf. **turnover**). The gross income, or sales, is the total revenue received from the business's operations; the net income is the residual for **shareholders** after all costs, including taxes, have been accounted for. (ii) Any distributions from assets such as **dividends**, interest payments, fees earned, sales revenues, and so on.

income and expenditure account. Statement of income and expenditures, similar to a **profit and loss account**, typically issued by a not-for-profit organization.

income and residual capital shares (UK). A class of ordinary shares issued by a **split capital investment trust**.

income bond. (i) (USA) In the USA, a **bond** which is guaranteed as to **principal** but which has interest payments as a contingent liability, based on the earnings of the issuer. The issuer has the right to forgo paying interest without causing a **default**. Such bonds are traded **flat**. (ii) (UK) A type of **National Savings** investment (cf. **gilt-edged**).

income constrained. A fund which has to produce a given level of **income** in order to meet some disbursement objective (cf. **dedication**).

income fund. A portfolio managed to provide a relatively high level of income compared to value growth (cf. **balanced mutual fund**; **growth fund**; **specialized fund**).

income investment company (USA). A mutual fund which aims to provide above **average** income. Such **funds** normally include a proportion of **preferred** and bonds in their portfolios.

income limited partnership (USA). A limited **partnership** which aims to generate high income from the investments made. See **master limited partnership**.

income right. Another term for a purchased **annuity**.

income statement. A report giving the profit (or loss) performance of a firm over a given reporting period (cf. **balance sheet**). See **profit and loss account**.

income stocks or **shares**. (i) That class of common stock or ordinary shares likely to provide the holder with a relatively high rate of **dividends** relative to the market as a whole, but usually at the expense of some **capital gains** (cf. **dividend yield**). Sometimes includes **preferred stocks**. (ii) Any security purchased more for the income or interest earned rather than its growth potential (cf. **growth stock**). (iii) A class of stock issued by **split-level funds** that divide the returns on the **portfolio** into income and capital gains. The income stock holders receive all the income from the portfolio but no appreciation in the portfolio value, the

capital stock holders all the capital gains. Holding both income and capital stocks in equal combinations is like holding the portfolio. By modifying the ratio of the two classes, different combinations of income versus capital gains can be achieved. See also **Americus trust; prescribed right to income and maximum equity; special claim on residual equity.**

income unit. A **mutual fund** or **unit trust**, which distributes all the **income** to holders. See also **accumulation unit.**

income warrant. A **warrant** that pays interest while active based on the warrant issue price. This current income is said to discourage **early exercise** and can be used as compensation for limited exercise rights.

income yield. See **current yield.**

in competition. Used to describe an informal bidding situation where more than one financial intermediary is competing to execute some particular business.

inconvertible (Forex). **Currency** where the holder does not have the right to exchange it for a different currency. Usually called a *blocked currency.* See **convertibility.**

inconvertible paper money. Banknotes that are not exchangeable for **gold.** This is typically the case in almost all countries these days (cf. **fiat money**).

incorporated. In the USA firms which offer **limited liability to stock holders** are designated by *inc.* or *corporation.* In the UK, either *limited,* or *LTD.* or *Ltd.* or *public limited company* or *PLC (plc).*

incorporation. (i) The process of creating a corporation or **company** by carrying out the required legal formalities. Hence, *incorporated.* Usually, but not exclusively, incorporation creates a company which has **limited liability** (cf. **limited company; limited partnership**). In law, a company has a separate and distinct legal status from its owners or **shareholders** (cf. **stockholders**). (ii) The process of changing a **partnership** or **sole trader** into a limited company.

increasing rate note (IRN) (Bonds; USA). A type of **junk bond** where the interest rate is reset at a higher margin to the **reference rate** on a periodic basis. This allows for a lower interest cost in the early period and as recompense for any delay to refinancing. See **step-up coupon.**

increasing rate preferred stock (USA). A type of **preferred stock** issue where the **coupon** rate increases over time, usually in the initial years of issue. Such **prefered stock** are usually issued at a **discount** to compensate investors for the initially below-market interest rate paid.

increasing rate security. A special variant of the **step-up coupon security** where the coupon rate increases several times in steps to **maturity.**

incremental cash flow. Part of the approach used in **capital budgeting** which identifies the new cash flows derived from undertaking an investment or project. See also **discounted cash flow; free cash flow.**

incremental cost of capital. The cost of capital from raising additional **finance.** See **weighted average cost of capital.**

incremental gap. See **gap analysis.**

indemnity. (i) Agreement by one party to another in a transaction to make good losses or any damages arising from a transaction. (ii) A **waiver** provided to a third party for undertaking an action or service for which they might be liable. Often institutions acting as **agents** require the **principals** to provide such an undertaking, to protect the agents from any failure on the part of the principals to meet their obligations.

indenture. The legal document establishing the terms and conditions of a securities issue and the obligations of the **trustee.** See **covenants; trust deed.**

independent (USA). See **local.**

independent broker (USA). A member of the **New York Stock Exchange** who acts for other members of the exchange. That is, he is not the direct contracting party to the transaction, but merely acting as a sub-**agent.** Also known as a *two-dollar broker.*

independent financial adviser (IFA) (UK). A type of financial intermediary defined by the **Financial Services Act, 1986** and authorized to give investors financial advice. Such IFAs must be licensed members of a **self-regulating organisation** or a recognized professional body. The key requirement is to look to the client's interest, which is governed by the **best advice** rule, and requires the adviser to provide the best alternative available in the market (cf. **suitability rule**).

independent venture capital fund. See **venture capital.**

index. Technically an **average** of prices or rates calculated according to a predetermined formula.

The two most common methods are a **geometric average** or a **value-weighted average**, although alternative methods, such as a simple average, can be used. Market indices are used to monitor broad developments in markets, market sectors, or **classes** of **assets**, as **portfolio** performance measures or for determining **asset allocation** strategies (cf. **benchmark**). Some economic variables such as **inflation** are measured by analysing changes in price indices (cf. **consumer price index; producer prices index; retail price index**). See also **index construction; indexing**.

index allocated principal collateralized mortgage obligation (XAC) (Bonds; USA). Collateralized mortgage obligation where the paydown on the security is determined according to the changes in an **index**.

index amortizing rate swap (IAR). Interest rate swap where the **notional principal** is reduced in line with changes (usually declines) to a reference index such as the **London interbank offered rate**. The swaps were developed to allow hedging of mortgages, where the repayment of the principal was linked to changes in interest rates, but have been extended to include any conceivable arrangement.

Index and Options Market (IOM) (USA). A part of the **Chicago Mercantile Exchange**.

index arbitrage. A low-risk investment strategy based upon exploiting the **anomalies** that sometimes arise between the prices of **stock index futures** and the **underlying** stocks (cf. **arbitrage channel**). Such a strategy involves the valuation of the **futures** contract relative to the **cash market** which then **triggers** either the sale of futures, if overpriced relative to the underlying components; or the purchase of futures, if underpriced; or buying or selling a representative sample of the **stocks** that go to make up the **index** (cf. **cash and carry**). Index arbitrage is one component of **program trading**.

indexation. (i) Linking monetary obligations to price levels. See **index-linked**. (ii) A low-cost investment strategy which aims to replicate the performance of a particular **stock index** (cf. **index tracking**).

Index Component Average. A weighted average **index** of European stock markets' leading indices including: France (CAC-40), Germany (FAZ), Italy (BCI), the Netherlands (EOE), Switzerland (SMI), Sweden (OMX), and the UK (FT-SE100).

index construction. There are a number of different ways to construct indices, the most popular being the simple or arithmetic price index, which measures the average change in price across the index constituents. The other major kind is the weighted-average method, where the constituents' market capitalization acts as the weights for the index. This accords more weight to the larger issues and therefore is a value change index.

Average price index:

$$API_t = \frac{BV \sum_{j=1}^{n} P_{jt}}{D_t}$$

where P_j is the price of the jth constituent at time t; BV the base value of the index (for instance 100 or 1,000); D_t the divisor used to adjust for **capitalization** changes in the constituents over time. If a capitalization changes at time t, the index divisor is adjusted to D^*_t by the following formula:

$$D^*_t = \frac{\sum_{j=1}^{n} P^*_{jt}}{\sum_{j=1}^{n} P_{jt}} D_t$$

where D_t is the divisor prior to the change; P_{jt} the price of the jth constituent prior to the change; and P_{jt}^* the jth constituent after the capitalization change.

Weighted-average price index:

$$WAPI_t = \frac{BV \sum_{j=1}^{n} N_{jt} P_{jt}}{\sum_{j=1}^{n} N_{j1} P_{j1}}$$

where N_{jt} is the number of units of constituent j outstanding at time t; BV the base value. This, as with the arithmetic index, needs to be adjusted if there are any capitalization changes between periods to ensure continuity in the series.

Note there are two formulations for a weighted average that economists make use of: the Laspreyes index, which is a base-date weighted basket index, and a Paasche index, which uses current weights. Capitalization-weighted indices for stocks use the latter.

indexed currency option note (ICON). Eurobond issue designed by Bankers Trust where the **principal** repayment of the currency of issue is a variable amount that is directly linked to the **exchange rate** of a second currency at **maturity** (cf. **bull-bear bonds; dual currency bond**). Effectively, the principal repayment is linked to the **foreign exchange forward** for the currency such that the issuer is committed to paying the currency of issue and receiving back the linked currency, which the issuer then resells at maturity for the original currency of issue, which is paid to the noteholders.

The first issue was arranged for the Long-Term Credit bank of Japan and specified a Japanese yen versus US dollar rate of 169 per dollar, at which exchange rate the holder receives the full principal value of the notes; if the rate is below this level it is reduced pro rata until at yen 84.5 and holders receive nothing. The payoff is therefore between 169 and 84.5, adjusted by ({169 ÷ yen–US dollar at maturity}−1). Thus if the rate is 120 at maturity, the payoff per note = US$1,000 × ({169 ÷ 120} −1), or US$408.33.

indexed principal swap (IPS). Interest rate swap which **amortizes** the **notional principal** over the life of the swap based on the movements in some **reference rate**, such as the **London interbank offered rate** with a view to linking the reduction in the amount of principal that is amortized to movements in interest rates. The intention is to match the amount of the swap to the expected reduction of principal of some **underlying** transaction, such as a **mortgage-backed security** (MBS). The most common type of IPS is designed to match the expected repayment profile of an MBS (cf. **index amortizing rate swap**).

indexed security. (i) Where the interest on a security and/or its redemption value is varied according to changes in some agreed measure of price inflation. (ii) It can also mean an **index-linked bond**. See **consumer price index**; **producer prices index**; **retail price index**. (iii) Any of a wide range of securities which have the **coupon** and/or **principal** linked to the performance of a particular price **index**, typically a **stock index** or other reference rate. See **equity-linked note**.

indexed sinking fund security (Bonds; USA). A type of **bond** with a **sinking fund** provision where the repayments of **principal** are linked to changes in a specific interest rate **index** (cf. **constant maturity treasury**). See also **index amortizing rate swap**; **indexed principal swap**.

index fund. A **portfolio** that is designed such that its return and overall behaviour match that of a market index, such as the **FT/S&P-Actuaries World Indices**. Sometimes called *index tracking, tracking,* or *order tracking*. Also known as a *tracker fund*.

index futures. See **commodity index futures**; **stock index futures**.

index growth-linked unit (IGLU). Bond which incorporates a **capped call** on an **index**. Because the structure is equivalent to a purchased option at one price and written option at a higher price, the cost of obtaining the exposure is less and the IGLU normally pays a **coupon** (cf. **vertical spread**). See **equity-linked note**.

indexing. An investment strategy which involves matching the performance of a particular **index**. This is normally achieved by creating a **portfolio** of securities that follow or mimic the behaviour of the index closely. When such a portfolio fails to follow the index this is known as *tracking error*.

index-linked. (i) (Bonds; UK). **Bonds** known as **gilt-edged**, issued by the UK government that have payment of **principal** and **interest** linked to the **retail price index**. The difference between the **yield** on conventional and index-linked gilts of similar **maturity** gives an estimate of the market's concensus of future **expected inflation** over the period. (ii) Similar issues to index-linked gilt-edged issued in Australia, Canada, and Sweden.

index-linked bond. Bond where the interest payment(s) and/or principal repayments are linked to an **index**, for example a **stock market index** like the S&P 500 index. The term **index-linked** is usually taken to mean bonds linked to a stock market index although, in principle, the returns on such bonds could be linked to any type of index or general price series (cf. **commodity-linked bond**; **equity-linked note**; **real yield securities**). The term index-linked bond used to describe the wide variety of such instruments is not exact. See also **bull-bear**; **indexed currency option note**.

index model. The use of a market-wide **index** to represent **systematic** or market effects (cf. **specific risk**). See **Capital Asset Pricing Model**.

index number. A value used in an **index** to represent the changes between the base date, or start of the index, and the current value. Typically indices are either based on 100, or 1,000, at their base date. This may be a specific date (as is usual with stock indices), or an average period (as is often the case with economic indicators).

index option. Option to buy or sell an **index**, or a **stock index future**. Because of the difficulties in delivering the **underlying**, these options are **cash settled**. Also sometimes known as *stock index options* since the vast majority of such index options involve **stock indices**. See **commodity index futures**; **stock index options**.

index participation certificate. A type of **equity-linked note** which has a **leveraged** exposure to an **index** but which may not guarantee to fully repay **principal** at **maturity**.

index participation unit (USA). A retail product designed by the **Philadelphia Stock Exchange** in 1989 to allow individual holders to own a **pro rata** share of an **index**. Legal review determined that such contracts were **futures** and could not be traded on a securities exchange (cf. **Standard and Poor's depository receipts**). See **indexing**.

index price quotation. Method used for giving the value of a financial **futures contract** on interest rates. The value of the contract is based on an **index** which is calculated as 100 less the interest rate. Thus a price of 92.25 corresponds to an interest rate of 7.75%. See also **notional bond**.

index principal return note. See equity-linked note.

index principal swap. See indexed principal swap.

index swap. An **interest rate swap** where the fixed rate payment is calculated on an **index**-linked basis. Such swaps have been executed against **stock**, **bond** or price indices. It is the **derivatives** hedging instrument for an index linked security.

index tracking. (i) The **correlation** between the returns on a portfolio and the **benchmark index** used for performance measurement. (ii) The difference between an indexed portfolio designed to copy the performance of a particular index and the actual result (cf. **tracking error**). See **index fund**; **indexing**.

index warrant (USA). Long-dated **warrants** exercisable for cash where the **underlying** is a **stock index** (cf. **option on futures**). Issuers are typically corporations or foreign sovereign entities.

indicated market. Prices in a market which are not based on actual transactions (cf. **matrix pricing**). Traders will sometimes provide indications which are less precise than **quotes**.

indicated yield. Another term for the **current yield**.

indication. Approximate idea of a security price (cf. **level**). It is not a dealing price (cf. **indicated market**). See also **quote**.

indication of interest. Potential investor interest in a new issue of securities. It is not a firm commitment to purchase since the securities have not been issued as yet. A sophisticated method involves investors indicating prices and quantities at which they would be prepared to buy. Such indications are then used by **lead managers** to build a **book** in order to ascertain the correct issuing price. Also known as *circling interest*.

indication pricing schedule. A set of prices or rates which are **indicative prices** for different transactions. Used extensively in **over-the-counter** markets. See also **scale**.

indicative prices. (i) (UK). Specifically, prices shown on the **Stock Exchange Automated Quotations** system but not taken as **firm prices** at which **market-makers** will deal. It is likely that the prices will vary according to the proposed size of **bargain**. See **marketable quantity**. (ii) Generally, prices based on a dealer's **quote** at or close to which he may be prepared to transact business but at which he is not obliged to transact business. Such quotes are often given for position valuation or information purposes.

indicator. (i) Any price or economic series or **index** which is deemed to provide information about a **sector**, market, or economy. The most watched indicator is usually a key price moving series which can occasion significant market **volatility** when released, especially if it falls outside the market's expectations. See **economic indicator**. (ii) Another term for a **benchmark**, used when pricing new debt issues in reference to the **underlying** government bond market.

indices. See Bell-wether; benchmark; stock indices.

indirect exchange rate or **indirect quotation** (Forex). The quotation of **foreign exchange** rates for foreign currencies in terms of fixed units of domestic currency. Thus the sterling–US dollar rate would be an indirect quote for a UK-domiciled person. The opposite is a *direct quotation*.

indirect investment. Where investors participate in securities markets through an intermediary. See **investment trust company; mutual fund; unit trusts**.

Individual Retirement Account (IRA) (USA). A personal pension plan that has been given US Internal Revenue Service approval and enjoys tax deferment. Set up to help those individuals without a company pension plan.

industrial bank (USA). Bank which specializes in industrial **leasing**. Such banks originated at the turn of the century and were the brainchild of Arthur Morris.

industrial development bond or **industrial revenue bond (IDB)** (USA). A type of **municipal bond** issued by local authorities in the USA and used to finance the purchase of **assets** which are subsequently leased to businesses. The service obligation becomes that of the lessee. Such issues are often used to finance investment in projects which benefit the community. Following the Tax Reform Act of 1986, such issues have to be divided into *public purpose* which are **tax exempt** or *private purpose* activities which are not.

industrial production index. An economic index of manufacturing output. Combined with capacity utilization it provides an indication of the state of the economy. If both the production index and capacity utilization are high relative to trend, it would suggest overheating, bottlenecks, and upward inflationary pressures. See **economic indicators**.

industrials (Equities). The **common stocks** of industrial companies as opposed to financial companies, **utilities**, service companies, and so forth.

ineligible bills. **Banker's acceptances** or **bank bills** which are not acceptable for rediscounting with the bank's **central bank**. Such bills are generally considered to be less creditworthy than **eligible bills**.

inflation. A fall in the purchasing power of a currency per currency unit (cf. **depreciation**).

inflation accounting. Any of a series of methods used in accounting to handle the effect of **inflation** on **asset** values. The principal approaches are *current cost* or *current purchasing power*.

inflation indexed security or **inflation-linked security.** See **index-linked**; **real yield securities**.

inflation risk. The **risk** that the nominal returns on an investment are not sufficient to offset the decline in value of money due to inflation (cf. **real interest rate**). It can be taken as the **opportunity cost** of holding a contract denominated in nominal terms in an inflationary situation (cf. **index-linked**; **real yield securities**).

inflation uncertainty. The fact that future inflation is uncertain. It is one possible explanation for the **term structure of interest rates**.

info rate. Money market rates quoted by **dealers** for information only.

information asymmetry. See **agency problem**.

informm® (USA). Electronic data service provided by **National Association of Securities Dealers Automated Quotations** of current and historical price and other trading information for listed firms.

infrastructure. A term favoured by economists to describe the capital invested by society as a whole in such things as schools, hospitals, and the transport system. More generally, used to mean any support system (for example, distribution network) that must be in place before commercial activity can be started or improved. See **municipal bond**.

Inhaberschuldvarschreibungen (Bonds; Germany). Unsecured bonds.

initial charge (UK). The charge made to buyers of **units** of **unit trusts** (cf. **periodic charge**). Called the *front-end load* in the USA. See **dual pricing**; **no-load fund**; **single pricing**.

initial margin. The amount of **margin** paid on the purchase or sale of **futures** or **exchange-traded options** (cf. **maintenance margin**; **variation margin**). The amount is usually set at a level unlikely to be exceeded by a one-day price movement in the value of the contract (cf. **settlement price**). Exchanges and/or their regulator generally have the right to increase the margin to cover their **risks** in periods of high **volatility**. Also called an *initial performance bond*. See also **limit**.

initial public offering (IPO) (Equities; USA). The first offering to the public of any category of a company's **common stock**. This normally requires the issuer to undergo severe scrutiny through a process of **due diligence** and the preparation of a **prospectus**. See **flotation**; **introduction**; **listing**; **offer for sale**; **placing**; **seasoned new issue**; **tender**.

initial yield. The **yield** available to subscribers at the launch of a new pooled investment vehicle such as a **mutual fund** or **investment trust** (cf. **current yield**).

inland bill (UK). A **bill of exchange** where both parties are within the UK. The alternative, where one of the parties is overseas, is known as a *foreign bill*.

in option. An option that can only be **exercised** if the **underlying** goes beyond a predetermined price or rate (cf. **trigger**). These are also known as *down and in*, *knock-in*, or *up and in options*. See **barrier option**.

inscribed stock. See **registered**.

inside directors. Directors of a firm who are also managers (cf. **non-executive directors**; **outside directors**). Typically, this includes the senior officers of the company. Also called *executive directors*.

inside market. See **inter-dealer market**.

insider. A market participant who has access to proprietary information. Includes the firm's managers, controlling **stockholders**, and any others who may have non-public information about a firm, such as the firm's lawyers and accountants.

insider dealing or **trading.** The trading of securities or **derivatives** on the basis of privileged price-sensitive information, illegal in the USA and UK (by the Companies Securities (Inside Dealing) Act, 1985) (cf. **insider**). See **efficient markets hypothesis; compliance; stock watch**.

insider information. Non-public knowledge that has a bearing on **asset** prices. In most countries it is illegal for **insiders** to take advantage of such information.

insolvency. (i) Another term for **bankruptcy** (cf. **crash**). (ii) (UK) Under the Insolvency Act, 1986, it is taken to be an individual or company that is unable to pay its liabilities as they fall due. For a company, there is an additional criterion of the value of the **assets** to be less than the fixed liabilities (cf. **liquidation**).

insolvency practitioner (UK). Member of the Insolvency Practitioners' Association who is authorized to act in insolvency proceedings (cf. **self-regulating organization**). See **liquidator**.

insolvency risk. See **default risk**.

insolvency test. (i) The inability of a firm to pay out **dividends** when **insolvent**. (ii) (UK) A test of the ability of a company to continue trading. To continue trading while insolvent in the UK is an offence under the Insolvency Act, 1986 and **directors** may be prosecuted for allowing the firm to continue to trade whilst actually insolvent.

insolvent. The legal condition of not being in a position to repay debts (cf. **bankruptcy; financial distress**). See **reorganization; workout**.

instalment. (i) Purchases or sales where the amount is paid in stages which may not be all of the same size (cf. **partly paid**). (ii) Payment made prior to the **maturity** or end of an agreement (cf. **amortization**). See also **annuity**.

instalment credit or **instalment loan** (USA). See **amortization loan; consumer credit**.

instalment option. Type of **Boston option** where the **premium** is paid in a series of payments (cf. **annuity**). The cost can be spread out over time, although the delay means that the cost will be higher due to the **writer** accepting deferred payment. See also **pay-as-you-go option**.

instalment sale or **purchase.** A sale where the buyer makes periodic payments of the consideration (cf. **earn out; partly paid**).

instant call bond or **note.** A bond or note issue where the issuer has an immediate **call provision**. Usually only seen on **floating rate** or **variable rate** instruments. Sometimes referred to as an *immediate call provision*.

instantly repackaged perpetual (IRP) (Bonds). The use of **financial engineering** techniques on a **perpetual floating rate note** at the time of issue which involves (*a*) the purchase of a high-quality **zero-coupon bond** with part of the proceeds to provide a source of redemption to investors at a pre-agreed future date while (*b*) including a clause subordinating the principal but not the interest payments. Holders of the notes are then effectively holding a senior dated instrument with a high **spread**. To make the structure attractive the issuer must be able to capture the cost of the zero as an expense, some of which may be passed to investors as well as to obtain tax reliefs on the interest payments. By adding **interest rate swaps**, investors can convert the asset to **fixed rate** (cf. **synthetic security**). The zero is then used to pay off holders and the issuer is left with the initial sum as a contribution to **reserves**. A variation on the theme has been used in **Brady bonds** to **collateralize** the principal of rescheduling nations (cf. **Mex-Ex issue**).

institutional broker. A securities firm which concentrates on financial institutions, in contrast to a **retail broker** who would service individuals.

institutional brokers' estimate system (IBES) (USA). A survey of **stock analyst** reports which gives the best, worst, and average projection as well as changes in forecasts. Such a database could be expected to highlight changes in the **fundamentals** of firms.

institutional buy-in. See **management buy-in; management buy-out; venture capital fund**.

institutional investor. An organization whose function it is to invest assets on behalf of others (cf. **retail investor**). For example, pension funds, insurance companies, banks, **mutual funds** or **unit trusts**, and **investment trust companies**. Sometimes used to mean *professional investor*.

Institutional Net Settlement service (INS) (UK). Central settlement service offered by the **London Stock Exchange** allowing institutional investors to make or receive a single net payment at the end of the day for transactions and other cash payments.

Institutional Networks Corporation (INSTINET) (USA). A computer-based system for trading large blocks of **shares** in the USA, used by institutional investors, who thus save on **commissions**. INSTINET is registered with the Securities and Exchange Commission as a **stock exchange** (cf. **fourth market**).

institutional pot. See **pot**.

in-strike. The **trigger** price or rate at which a **barrier option** which has a down(up)-and-in boundary becomes a standard option (cf. **knock-in; outstrike**). See **down-and-in option; up-and-in option**.

instrument. (i) A generic term for securities and **risk management** contracts, ranging from debt to negotiable deposits and **bonds** and including **derivatives**. Normally used to describe financial arrangements with short-term maturities, such as *money market instruments*. (ii) An official document. (iii) A means for achieving an end. For instance, manipulating interest rates is the instrument or means for controlling demand in an economy (cf. **open-market operations**).

in-substance defeasance. The placing of cash and securities in an irrevocable trust in sufficient amount to allow a borrower to remove a debt from his balance sheet.

insurable interest. A possession or **asset** that legally can be insured. Only assets over which the insured party can suffer a loss are insurable. This restricts insurance to property and other assets. That said, if an employee or individual has economic value to a firm, this is an insurable interest.

insurable risk. Any type of **risk** where **insurance** can be obtained from a third party, typically a specialist financial institution dealing in **underwriting** such risks. See **pure risk**.

insurance. (i) The purchase of protection against loss by entering into a contract with a third party. The cost of the insurance is called the **premium**. The party benefiting from the insurance is known as the *insured*. (ii) In financial markets, used to indicate a **hedge** or other **risk**-reducing strategy that provides protection against losses but allows participation in gains. For instance, the purchase of **options** is often seen as insurance, since these will be sold or **abandoned** if matters go to plan, thereby losing part or all of the premium, but at the same time allowing the holder to benefit from any favourable price or rate movement. (iii) Investment strategies that replicate the asymmetrical payoff of options. See **portfolio insurance**.

insurance futures. Futures contracts where the **underlying** is an **index** of insurance losses. For example, the **Chicago Board of Trade's** National Catastrophe Insurance Future contract is based on quarterly catastrophic losses for the property/casualty industry covering all fifty states of the USA and the District of Columbia.

insurance options. (i) Options on futures. For example, the **Chicago Board of Trade's** options on their Eastern Catastrophe Insurance Futures where the **underlying** is on futures contract. The contract itself provides exposure to the quarterly catastrophic losses for the property/casualty industry in the twenty eastern US states and the District of Columbia. (ii) **Over-the-counter options** on an insurance **index**.

insurance principle. The law of averages. That is, many trials of a random process will approximate to the average result (cf. **pure risk**). It is a key principle underlying **risk management** activity. Also called the *law of large numbers*.

insured account (USA). A deposit account with a bank or **savings and loan association** which is protected by the **Federal Deposit Insurance Corporation** and **Federal Savings and Loan Insurance Corporation** respectively. Such insurance covers amounts up to US$100,000.

insurer. Organization or individual who **underwrites** an insurance risk.

in syndication. In the process of being **underwritten**. For loans, this involves the **lead manager** or **arranger** soliciting other banks to participate in the transaction by agreeing to lend a fraction of the total amount. With securities, it means the underwriting **syndicate** has not yet been broken.

intangible assets. Non-physical assets of an enterprize such as patents, trademarks, copyrights, establishment expenses, and goodwill (cf. **tangible assets**).

integrated oil company. Oil company which undertakes all the activities required to find, exploit, refine, distribute, market, and sell oil and its direct products. The seven largest oil companies in the world, called the *seven sisters*, are typical examples (cf. **transnational corporation**).

integrated producer. Any company which undertakes the full production process, taking in raw materials and delivering a finished product (cf. **crack spread; crush margin**).

integration. Combining two or more organizations into one (cf. **consolidation**). See **mergers and acquisitions**.

Integriertes - Borsenhandels - und - Informations-System (IBIS) (Integrated Stock Exchange Trading and Information System) (Germany). Computerized trading and reporting system used on the **Frankfurt Stock Exchange** and integrating the regional stock exchanges and the **Deutsche Terminbörse**, providing for best execution in any of the exchanges, as well as providing transparency and liquidity. See also **Börsen-Order-Service-System**.

intellectual property. Any of a number of **intangible** assets such as patents, copyrights, trademarks, and so forth.

inter-account transaction (UK). See account trading (cf. **backwardation**).

Inter-American Development Bank (IADB). A regional international agency set up in 1959 to provide funds to develop Central and Latin America. Shareholders include outside nations such as Japan and members of the **European Union**. See **African Development Bank**; **Asian Development Bank**; **European Bank for Reconstruction and Development**; **World Bank**; **Nordic Bank**.

interbank. Transactions between two banks; hence, the **interbank market** which covers the **money markets**, currency markets, and **over-the-counter derivatives**. Such transactions are notionally different from those with the banks' customers (i.e. not those with end-customers, but some banks are also customers). In practice, larger corporations and institutions will be included in interbank transactions, as are state entities. Interbank transactions provide a way for banks to restructure their **positions**.

interbank currency option market. An over-the-counter market in **currency option** provided by banks active in **foreign exchange**.

interbank deposits. The wholesale **money market** deposit rates as quoted between major banks in a country or in the **eurocurrency** markets. In the latter case these rates are important in setting the **foreign exchange forward rate** differentials (cf. **discount**; **premium**).

Interbanken Information System (IBIS) (Equities; Germany). An automated securities trading system set up in 1989.

interbank fixing. A rate determined for interbank deposits at a specific time of day (cf. **reference rate**). The most important fixing is that which takes place at 11 a.m. London time for **London interbank offered rate** and widely used for determing the **settlement** value of loans and derivative instruments. See also **British Bankers' Association**.

interbank market (Money markets). The wholesale market in **short-term** money and **foreign exchange** between banks but which also includes large companies and organizations. The interbank market is generally distinguished from the money market in that the transactions are non-negotiable deposits and **forward** transactions although it can include **certificates of deposit** (cf. **money market instruments**; **currency futures**).

interbank rate. The interest rate at which banks offer and bid for funds between each other (cf. **placing**; **taking**). See **fed funds**; London inter-

bank bid rate, London interbank mean rate, and London interbank offered rate.

inter-commodity spread (IS). Offsetting positions taken in two different, but usually related, **commodities**. Thus a long position in a gold contract might be matched to a short position in silver. Thus a **long and short position** in different, but related, assets is taken in order to benefit from relative price movements between the two, although the absolute movement is not predicted. Such **spreads** would typically include gold and silver, or oil and natural gas. Called a *cross-asset spread* or an *inter-market spread* in the financial markets. See also **intra-commodity spread**.

inter-dealer broker (IDB) (Bonds; UK). A market participant who trades only with **market-makers** and who does not disclose the identity of his clients, thereby dealing as a **principal** on both sides of the transaction but without taking a **position**. That is, transactions have to be matched between **counterparties**. His function is to increase market **liquidity**.

inter-dealer market. Transactions between dealers for their own inventory. This is required if a dealer becomes overly **long** or **short** in a particular security. Also known as an *inside market* or a **wholesale market**.

interdelivery spread. See calendar spread.

interest. (i) The cost of borrowing or lending money. See **interest rate calculations**. (ii) The wish or indication to buy or sell. See **circle**; **indication of interest**.

interest arbitrage. See covered interest arbitrage.

interest basis conversion. A provision within a **bond** issue which allows either (*a*) the holder or (*b*) the issuer to change the method of computing interest from, say, **fixed rate** to **floating rate**, or vice versa (cf. **drop-lock loan**).

interest bearing eligible liabilities (IBEL) (Banking; UK). Those **liabilities** recognized by the **Bank of England** as being held by banks under its regulation. If required, banks may be asked to hold a proportion as **reserves** with the Bank.

interest bearing liabilities (Banking). Deposits and other borrowed **funds** at a bank on which interest has to be paid.

interest capitalization. An accounting approach to the treatment of interest as a cost of the **asset** being acquired. For instance, a company might build a factory, capitalizing the interest until such time as the factory is turned to productive use. Also called *capitalisation of interest*.

interest coverage ratio. A measure of a borrower's ability to meet interest commitments from future earnings. It is the number of times the interest charge is covered by profits or **free cash flow**. Sometimes called *interest cover* or *coverage* or the *times interest earned*. See credit analysis; ratio analysis; self-financing; self-liquidating loan.

interest-earning assets (Banking). That part of the asset base of a bank that earns income (cf. **net interest income; net interest margin**).

Interest Equalization Tax (IET) (USA). Introduced in 1963 and abolished 1974, it was the 15% tax on foreign investment by US-domiciled persons. The tax is given as one of the main reasons for the rapid development of the **euromarkets** in the 1960s.

interest only and **principal only stripped mortgage backed security (IO; PO; IO strip; PO strip)** (Bonds; USA). Two securities created by separating the interest and principal repayment flows from the **underlying mortgage-backed security** (MBS) (cf. **separate trading of registered interest and principal of securities**). The behaviour of the two securities is **leveraged** against movements in interest rates but in different directions. If interest rates rise, so does the value of the IO since repayments of the **underlying** mortgages will fall and the **present value** of the payment stream will increase, since more payments will be expected prior to the retirement of the MBS. The PO behaves in the opposite manner. The IO and PO combination allows participants in the mortgage-backed securities market to **hedge** themselves by holding the appropriate **position** in either instrument (cf. **planned amortization class**). They have been termed *mortgage derivatives* due to their option-like behaviour in relation to interest rates.

interest only mortgage. A type of mortgage in which the borrower makes only interest payments agreeing to repay the **principal** at maturity or when the mortgage is redeemed. Most such mortgages include the borrower's right to partially pay down the principal before maturity.

interest parity theory of foreign exchange (Forex). See **interest rate parity theory**.

interest payments. The payments to a lender by a borrower in exchange for the loan of money. For computations see **interest rate calculations**.

interest period. On a floating rate or variable rate loan or security, the length of time between each resetting of the interest rate and hence the rate at which interest is charged. Typically this will be one, three, or six months, although other periods can be used.

interest rate. The cost or price of borrowing; or the gain from lending, normally expressed as an annual percentage amount (cf. **continuous compounding; decompounding**).

interest rate calculations. The methods used to calculate interest due can be conveniently divided into three areas: (i) **discount** methods, as per **banker's acceptances, bills of exchange, commercial paper,** and **treasury bills**; (ii) yield-based money market calculations, such as bank **deposits, certificates of deposit,** some kinds of **commercial paper,** and short-dated **bonds** with one or more **coupons** to **maturity**; and (iii) bond market calculations.

The money markets use both methods (i) and (ii) to calculate interest due. Discount methods were favoured given the complications of adding small amounts of interest to a short-term instrument. Selling the instrument below par, using a simple formula was both easier and facilitated repayment at maturity. The discount represented the buyer's interest on his investment. Method (iii) is favoured by the bond markets, although some hybrid instruments such as **floating rate notes** use method (ii).

The difference in approach arises from the **tenor** or maturity of the instruments. It was not quite so important to calculate interest to an exact fraction when the bond has a maturity of ten years, or more. The major complication arises in the exact method used to establish the number of elapsed days of interest in any period, both for determining the amount of coupon, or interest due, and also for secondary market transactions when **accrued interest** has to be included in the **settlement** or **transaction** price. There are a number of ways of accruing interest used by both money markets and the bond markets, but they can be grouped into three methods: an actual day count method, an actual day count method divided by a notional number of days in a calendar year (known as the **basis**), and a fixed day count divided by the basis.

1. *Money markets*: The principal day count methods are: actual/360 and actual/365 (fixed). The basis for calculating interest is therefore a year of either 360 days, or 365 days. The effect of a 360-day year is to increase the amount of interest paid by a factor of 1.013889 over that quoted. The following summarizes the situation in different countries. Basically, the UK and the old Commonwealth or Empire countries use the 365-day basis, the rest of the world, with the exception of Belgium, the 360-day basis (see Table).

Country	Interest basis calculation
Australia	Actual/365
Austria	Actual/360
Belgium	Actual/365
Canada	Actual/365
Denmark	Actual/360
France	Actual/360
Germany	Actual/360
Ireland	Actual/365
Italy	Actual/360
Japan	Actual/360
The Netherlands	Actual/360
New Zealand	Actual/365
Norway	Actual/360, under 1 month; 30/360 over 1 month; also Actual/365 on some money market instruments
Saudi Arabia	Actual/360
Sweden	30/360
Switzerland	Actual/360; federal bills: 30/360
United Kingdom	Actual/365
United States	Actual/360

In the international markets, the domestic market interest calculation methods have been followed, with again the exception of Belgium, where Actual/360 is sometimes used, although Actual/365 is also quoted (cf. **London interbank offered rate**).

The Actual/360 calculation also known as *bank interest basis, certificate of deposit basis, Euro basis,* or *money market basis.* Whatever the maturity, the convention is to quote the interest rate as if for a year and the amount payable is calculated on the actual number of days elapsed in the calculation period multiplied by the interest rate and divided by the number of days in the computation year, which is known as the basis:

$$\frac{Principal \times i\% \times T_{sm}}{Basis \times 100\%} = interest$$

For example, to calculate the interest on a three month (90 actual days) deposit of 5.75% of US$1,000,000 for the period starting on 28 January and ending on 28 April (for calculation purposes, interest is charged from the day following the settlement date up to and including the day on which the payment is due). In the above example this would be:

$$\frac{US\$1,000,000 \times 5.75\% \times 90}{360 \times 100\%} = US\$14,375$$

For the Actual/365 calculation, the interest is also quoted as an annual rate, regardless of the tenor of the transaction, and is calculated on the actual number of days in the period times the rate of interest over a basis of 365. Thus a £5 million sterling certificate of deposit at 6.75% issued on 24 February and maturing on 24 August would pay the following coupon interest:

$$\frac{£5,000,000 \times 6.75\% \times 182}{365 \times 100\%} = £168,287.67$$

If it had been a leap year the interest would have been slightly different, since one day would have been added to the calculation:

$$\frac{£5,000,000 \times 6.75\% \times 183}{365 \times 100\%} = £169,212.33$$

Note that the interest rate for Actual/Actual (see below) is often used, with some confusion, for Actual/365.

2. *Bond markets*: The principal methods of working out interest are: (i) Fixed Coupon; (ii) Bond basis (also called eurobond basis); and (iii) Actual/365 or Actual/Actual.

Fixed Coupon. This method of calculating interest divides the **coupon rate** by the frequency of payments, even though this may lead to differences in the number of elapsed days over which the interest is actually received due to weekends, holidays, or leap years. The interest rate is quoted as an annual rate and is calculated on the years in the period instrument over 100(%).

$$\frac{Principal \times i\% \times f}{100} = interest$$

For example a bond with a fixed coupon of 10% paid quarterly in March, June, September, and December with principal of DM10,000,000, with an interest period running from, say, 31 March to 30 June would pay a coupon of:

$$\frac{DM10,000,000 \times 10\% \times 0.25}{100} = DM250,000$$

Fixed Coupons are used for **eurobonds** (note that the vast majority of eurobonds pay annually).

Bond basis (sometimes notated as *30/360* or *30E/360*). This is the method of day count used in the secondary market to calculate the accrued interest on certain types of **fixed rate** bonds, most notably those traded in the **eurobond market**. The accrued interest is calculated on a computational year of 360 days with each calendar month treated as one-twelfth of 360 days, that is 30 days. For interest purposes each period from a date in one month to the same date in the next or subsequent months is also considered to be 30 days, or multiples thereof. Accrued interest is calculated from, and including the date of, the last coupon date or, in the case of a new issue, from the day interest starts to accrue (the **dated date**), up to, but excluding, the **value date** of the transaction. This is different from the conventions used in the money markets, where the first day is ignored, but the last day is included. Examples of the method showing the difference in day count between actual days, Actual/365, and Actual/Actual are given in the Table.

Interest rate calculations: Bond basis

Interest accrues from coupon date	Value date	Number of days accrued interest		
		Bond basis (eurobond; 30E/360)	Actual/ 365, normal	Actual/ Actual, leap year
Within the year:				
1 Jan.	28 Feb.	57	58	58
1 Jan.	29 Feb.	58	—	59
1 Jan.	1 Mar.	60	59	60
1 Jan.	3 Mar.	62	61	62
1 Jan.	30 Mar.	89	88	89
1 Jan.	31 Mar.	89	89	90
15 Jan.	28 Feb.	43	44	44
15 Jan.	29 Feb.	44	—	45
15 Jan.	1 Mar.	46	45	46
15 Jan.	3 Mar.	48	47	48
1 Feb.	28 Feb.	27	27	27
1 Feb.	29 Feb.	28	—	28
1 Feb.	1 Mar.	30	28	29
1 Feb.	3 Mar.	32	30	31
15 Feb.	28 Feb.	13	13	13
15 Feb.	28 Feb.	14	—	14
15 Feb.	1 Mar.	16	14	15
15 Feb.	3 Mar.	18	16	17
28 Feb.	29 Feb.	1	—	1
28 Feb.	1 Mar.	3	1	2
28 Feb.	3 Mar.	5	3	4
28 Feb.	5 Mar.	7	5	6
28 Feb.	30 Mar.	32	30	31
28 Feb.	31 Mar.	32	31	32
The following year:				
30 Nov.	28 Feb.	88	90	90
30 Nov.	29 Feb.	89	—	91
30 Nov.	1 Mar.	91	91	92
30 Nov.	3 Mar.	93	93	94
30 Nov.	30 Mar.	120	120	121
30 Nov.	31 Mar.	120	121	122
31 Dec.	28 Feb.	58	59	59
31 Dec.	29 Feb.	59	—	60
31 Dec.	1 Mar.	61	60	61
31 Dec.	3 Mar.	63	62	63
31 Dec.	30 Mar.	90	89	90
31 Dec.	31 Mar.	90	90	91
28 Feb.	27 Feb.	359	364	365
28 Feb.	28 Feb.	nil	nil	nil

Note that there are two different forms of the bond basis (*30/360* or sometimes *360/360*, and *30E/360*) which are due to differences in the way the number of days from the last coupon payment to the settlement date are calculated. For 30/360, the 30-day month method involves taking the two dates for accured interest purposes by assuming 30 days in each month using a formula, where the first date is $(MM_1 - DD_1 - YY_1)$ and the later date $(MM_2 - DD_2 - YY_2)$. If DD_1 is a 31-day month, change to 30; if DD_2 is 31, change to 30 if DD_1 is 30; otherwise leave as 31 (this gives a

maximum of 30 days in a month). The number of elapsed days is calculated by:

$$\{(YY_2 - YY_1) \times 360\} + \{(MM_2 - MM_1) \times 30\} + (DD_2 - DD_1)$$

For 30E/360, the calculation is the same as the above, but involves changing DD_1 to 30, if the calendar month has 31 days, and changing DD_2 to 30 days, if 31 days.

For example, a holding of US$500,000 of a eurobond with an annual coupon of 8%, sold for delivery on 3 March, with a coupon payment date of 15 February, would have accrued eighteen days interest:

$$\frac{US\$500,000 \times 8\% \times 18}{36,000} = US\$2,000$$

Note that 30/360 is used in the US domestic market for some US government **agency**, municipal, and corporate bonds; 30E/360 for the vast majority of eurobonds (but excluding floating rate notes, where the accrued interest is calculated on a **money market basis**), German government and agency bonds, and European currency **cross-currency swaps** and **interest rate swaps** which include a fixed rate payment.

Actual/365 or *Actual/Actual*. This method calculates accruing interest by multiplying the principal times the interest rate times the number of days, all divided by 365. With a leap year, it is adjusted so that it is the number of actual days in the period divided by 366. Note that the calculation method takes the day from 31 December to 1 January as part of the earlier year.

Take as an example an 8% coupon US$50,000 Treasury Bond. The period 30 November to 31 March in a leap year would be 122 days. For interest assessment purposes, because US Treasury issues are calculated on an Actual/Actual basis, the calculation has to be split between the normal and the leap year:

Normal year(to January 1)

+ Leap year(from January 1)

The Actual/Actual accrual method is used for US **treasury notes** and US **treasury bonds** and some interest rate swaps denominated in US dollars where interest is paid semi-annually.

Coupon or interest frequency: The great majority of **fixed rate bonds** pay interest (coupons) either once or twice a year (known as *annual* or *semi-annual* basis). Note also that for simplicity of trading, the vast majority of securities issued in a particular market will tend to follow the market's accepted convention for interest frequency. Occasionally, specialized securities may use different methods; for example, **collateralized mortgage obligations** and floating rate notes, which may pay interest quarterly or even monthly.

3. *Yield calculations.* (For money market calculations which use simple interest, see **bank basis; discount; money market basis.**)

Simple, flat, or *income yield*:

$$Y_s = \frac{C}{P - \text{accrued interest(AI)}}$$

Using the US Treasury example given above and if the quoted full price were $98\frac{1}{4}$, we would have:

$$Y_s = \frac{8\%}{98.25 - 2.67} = 8.37\%$$

4. *Redemption yield* (also known as *yield-to-maturity; yield-to-call; yield-to-put,* and so forth). This is the rate of interest at which the total of the discounted values of the future payments of interest and capital are equal to the current price. This is equivalent to:

$$\text{Market full price}_s = \frac{C\left[\dfrac{1 - \dfrac{1}{\left(1 + \dfrac{i}{f}\right)^{n_{cm}}}}{\dfrac{i}{f}}\right] + P(1 + i)^{n_{cm}}}{(1 + i)^{t_{sc}}}$$

where C is the coupon; P the principal amount at redemption, call, or put; i the interest rate as an annual rate; f the coupon frequency; t_{sc} the number of days, expressed as a fraction, from the settlement date to the next coupon date; and n_{cm} the number of periods from the next coupon date to redemption, maturity, call, or put.

The **clean price** is arrived at by deducting the accrued interest.

interest rate cap or **cap.** A bilateral contract for the management of **interest rate risk.** The two parties are known as the buyer and the seller. The buyer pays the seller a fixed **premium** in return for which the seller agrees to refund to the buyer, on agreed calculation dates, the difference between the then current interest rate and an agreed rate and the **strike rate.** Caps are based on a **reference rate,** e.g. **London interbank offered rate** (LIBOR), that is usually refixed every three or six months. If the reference rate is higher than the strike rate, the seller pays the buyer the interest calculated as the difference between the reference and the strike rates on the **notional principal** for the period from the current calculation date to the next. The interest is paid on the next calculation date. If the reference rate is lower than the strike rate, there is no payment. Certain reference rates are more actively traded than others.

Caps are therefore a series of interest rate guarantees allowing the purchaser to take advantage of a reduction in interest rates but to be protected if they rise (cf. **caption** (option on a

cap); **compound option**). They are priced as the sum of the premiums for the individual **option strike prices** for each of the cap/(floor) dates. A one-period cap or *caplet* is almost equivalent to buying a **put option** on a **short-term interest rate future** while a floor is equivalent to buying a **call** on the future (cf. **fraption**). A caplet is therefore effectively an option to buy an asset consisting of floating interest at a strike price consisting of fixed interest (cf. **spread option**). A cap can be seen as the equivalent to the buyer purchasing/selling a series of such options to receive/pay differences between a floating index (LIBOR) and the strike rate.

Strategies with Caps (and Floors): Owning a *cap* sets the maximum cost of a floating rate liability but gives the benefit of interest rate reductions. Owning a *floor* sets a minimum return to a floating rate asset and gives the benefits of interest rate increases.

interest rate ceiling. A guaranteed maximum cost on a debt or security. It is achieved by buying **interest rate caps** (and sometimes to reduce the cost of the purchased option, by selling **floors**) to provide an **interest rate collar.**

interest rate collar (IRC). A **hedging** structure for a **variable rate** borrowing or investment which uses the **premium** received from selling the **floor** (cap) to offset, partially or fully, the cost of purchasing the cap (floor). The result is to fix an upper and lower boundary to the range of the variable rate (cf. **minimax floating rate note; range floating rate note**). See also **option strategies; vertical spread.**

interest rate cycle. Supposedly regular long-term fluctuations in the general level of interest rates in an economy. See **Kondatrieff cycle; monetary policy; term structure of interest rates; trade cycle.**

interest rate differential (Diff). Differences in interest rates in two currencies for deposits or securities of the same **maturity** and **class.** Also sometimes called the *spread.* See **differential future; differential swap; foreign exchange.**

interest rate exposure. The risk of loss arising from possible interest rate movements. See **assets repriced before liabilities; interest rate risk management.**

interest rate floor or **'floor'.** (i) A bilateral **interest rate risk** contract whereby the seller agrees to refund the purchaser the difference between a predetermined interest rate and the actual market rate should this be lower. Floors, like interest rate caps, are based on a reference rate such as six-month **London interbank offered rate.** See **inter-**

est rate cap for additional explanation. (ii) Sometimes used to describe the minimum **coupon** payment allowed on a **floating rate note**.

interest rate futures. Financial **futures** contracts for securities whose prices are determined by interest rates and principally used for **hedging interest rate risk**. There are two principal types:

(*a*) A **short-term** contract based on **money market** interest rates. These are sometimes called the *short-term interest rate futures* or *depo* or *deposit futures*. They are usually given the name of the underlying instrument's **reference rate**, for example T-bill futures, eurodollar futures, euromark futures, and so on.

(*b*) Those based on **bonds**, of which there is an intermediate or **medium-term** contract (for notes or bonds with a 7- to 10-year **maturity**) and a **long-term** contract (for bonds with a 20- to 30-year **tenor**). These are normally called *bond futures* or *long-term (medium-term) interest rate futures*. These often go under the name of the **underlying** market or set of bonds which are **deliverable** into the contract, for instance, gilt futures, Bund futures, JGB futures (Japanese government bond), and so forth.

Contract sizes differ between the exchanges and the type of contract traded. The short-term interest rate contracts are based on a price that is an index set at 100 less the interest rate $(100 - i)$. The minimum price movement tends to be a basis point (0.01%) for short-term futures contracts and fractions of a point for the bond futures. Prices for the bond-based contracts are set by the **yield** on a *notional security* or *notional bond* for that contract and the value of the **cheapest to deliver**. The minimum price movement tends to be equal to that in the corresponding cash market underlying instruments. There are often also **options on futures** on the above contracts traded on the same exchanges. See also **currency futures; stock index futures; tick**.

EXAMPLE OF THE SHORT-TERM INTEREST RATE FUTURE (BASED ON THE CHICAGO MERCANTILE EXCHANGE'S EURODOLLAR CONTRACT):

Three-Month Eurodollar Time Deposit Futures
- *Ticker symbol*: ED.
- *Trading unit*: $1,000,000.
- *Price quote*: IMM Index points.
- *Minimum price fluctuation (tick)*: US $25.00 = 1 IMM Index point = 0.01 or 1 basis point (e.g. from 93.00 to 93.01) $(0.0001 \times \$1,000,000 \times \frac{90}{360} = \$25)$.
- *Daily price limit*: None.
- *Contract months*: March, June, September, December.
- *Trading hours*[1] *(Chicago time)*: 7.20 a.m.–2.00 p.m. Last day: 7.20 a.m.–9.30 a.m.

- *Last day of trading*: Second London business day immediately preceding the third Wednesday of the contract month.
- *Delivery date*: Last day of trading–cash settled.

Trading will end at 12.00 noon on the business day before a CME holiday and on any US bank holiday that the CME is open. This contract also is traded on the GLOBEX system. Contact your broker or the CME for specific GLOBEX trading hours.

OPTION ON FUTURE (ON THE EURODOLLAR CONTRACT ABOVE):

Options on three-month eurodollar futures
- *Ticker symbols*: Calls: CE   Puts: PE.
- *Underlying contract*: One ED futures contract.
- *Strike prices*: $.25 intervals, e.g. 92.25, 92.50, 92.75.
- *Premium quotations*: Total IMM Index points e.g. 0.34 quoted as '34 Index points' or '34 basis points'.
- *Minimum price fluctuation (tick)*[1]: US $25.00 = 1 IMM Index point = 0.01 or 1 basis point e.g. from 0.34 to 0.35 (cabinet = $12.50).
- *Daily price limit*: None.
- *Contract months*: March, June, September, December, and 2 serial months.[2]
- *Trading hours*[3] *(Chicago time)*: 7.20 a.m.–2.00 p.m. Last day March-quarterly expirations: 7.20 a.m.–9.30 a.m.
- *Last day of trading*: March quarterly cycle: second London business day immediately preceding the 3rd Wednesday of the contract month; serial options (January, February, April, May, July, August, October, and November): Friday immediately preceding 3rd Wednesday of contract month.
- *Minimum performance bond*: No performance bond required for put or call option buyers, but the premium must be paid in full; option sellers must meet additional performance bond requirements as determined by the Standard Portfolio Analysis of Risk (SPAN®) performance bond system.
- *Exercise procedure*: An option may be exercised by the buyer up to and including last day of trading. To exercise, the clearing member representing the buyer submits an Exercise Notice to the Clearing House by 7.00 p.m. on the day of the exercise. Any long in-the-money option position not liquidated or exercised prior to termination of trading will be automatically exercised.

Notes
1. A trade may occur at the value of a half-tick (cabinet).
2. Options on ED futures are listed for all twelve calendar months, with each exercisable into the March-quarterly, quarter-end futures contract. For example, January, February, and March options are exercisable into the March futures contract, and the March futures price is relevant for the pricing

of the three sets of options. At any point in time, you can choose from options that expire in the next three calendar months, plus five March-quarterly expirations.

3. Trading will end at 12.00 noon on the business day before a CME holiday and on any US bank holiday that the CME is open. This contract is also traded on the GLOBEX system.

EXAMPLE OF A LONG-TERM INTEREST RATE FUTURE (BASED ON THE GUILDER BOND FUTURE TRADED ON THE AMSTERDAM STOCK EXCHANGE):

Notional Guilder Bond Future

- *Ticker symbol*: FTO.
- *Contract size*: A notional Dutch government bond with a nominal value of Dfl. 250,000 and a 7% coupon.
- *Quotation*: In points per Dfl. 100 nominal.
- *Contract months*: Initial lifetime: 3, 6, 9, and 12 months. Cycle: March, June, September, and December.
- *Trading hours*: 9.00 a.m.–5.00 p.m.
- *Settlement*: Delivery.
- *Minimum premium charge*: 0.01 point (=Dfl. 25 per contract).
- *Clearing organization*: European Futures Clearing Corporation (EFCC).
- *Last day of trading*: The 7th calendar day of the delivery month, provided this is a business day. If this is not a business day, the last day of trading will be the next business day. Trading in the expiring contract will end after a special closing call starting at 4 p.m.
- *Delivery*: In accordance with the delivery procedure prescribed by the EFCC. Delivery shall be made solely on the basis of positions which remain open at the end of the last day of trading. For each open contract delivery is required of Dfl. 250,000 nominal of Dutch government bonds. The seller specifies which bonds will be delivered. These must be Dutch government bonds, selected from public issues with an outstanding amount of at least 1 billion guilders, a single redemption date, and having on the first day of the delivery month a remaining life of at least 8 and not more than 10 years. The delivery obligation arising from a single contract must be satisfied by the delivery of a single issue. Bonds allowing early redemption are not acceptable for delivery.
- *Delivery price*: The delivery price of the bonds is equal to the closing price on the last day of trading, multiplied by the conversion factor for the particular bonds delivered, as published by the FTA plus the accrued interest.
- *Trading break*: If the price of the Guilder Bond Future changes more than 1 point relative to the closing price on the previous trading day, trading in all contracts, with exception of the future with the nearest maturity, shall cease

for a period of 30 minutes. When trading has resumed, there shall be no further break in that day.

- *Initial margin*: Dfl. 4,000   Spreads: Dfl. 2,000.

interest rate guarantee (IRG). A single-period interest rate cap or floor (cf. **caplet**; **floorlet**). Effectively an **option** on a **forward rate agreement** (FRA). As with all option products, buyers have the right but not the obligation to enter into the FRA. The **over-the-counter derivatives** market equivalent to an option on a financial future for a **money market** instrument such as **London interbank offered rate**, or the **treasury bill rate**. Also known as a *fraption* or an *interest rate ceiling agreement*.

interest rate index swap. See differential swap (cf. **currency protected swap**).

interest rate margin. See margin; spread (cf. **reference rate**).

interest rate option (IRO). An option that gives the holder the right to purchase, in the case of a **call**, or sell, in the case of a **put**, a specific debt instrument (cf. **stock option**). Such options are either **exchange-traded**, when they are standardized contracts as to terms and conditions and the **underlying** which is normally a **futures** contract; or **over-the-counter**, where a very great variety of underlying instruments have options written against them (cf. **option on futures**).

interest rate parity theory of exchange rates (IRPT). A model of **foreign exchange** rate pricing that states that the difference in interest rates in two countries should offset the difference between the **spot** rate and the **forward foreign exchange** rate over the same period. Currencies with **high** (low) interest rates will stand at a **discount** (**premium**) to currencies with low (high) interest rates over time. See also **international Fisher effect**; **purchasing power parity theory**; **covered interest arbitrage**.

interest rate reset note. A type of fixed rate security which has a periodic reset of the **coupon** to ensure that they trade at **par** or above in the market (cf. **extendible**; **retractable bond**). See also **floating rate note**.

interest rate risk. The risk that arises from exposure to changes in interest rates. There are several different effects at work from interest rate risk. These are:

(1) *Price risk*: This arises when the valuation of a set of fixed cash flows (as in a **straight bond**) changes as a result of changes in the required **discount rate** at which the market values such

claims (cf. **market risk; parallel shift; rotational shift**).

(2) *Prepayment risk*: This can arise from issuers of securities redeeming these before their due take by exercising an **embedded option** or **call provision**, or by the nature of the **underlying** assets in **asset-backed securities**, principally **mortgaged-backed securities** (cf. **expected maturity**). In these cases, the probability of the security being redeemed is positively linked to changes in interest rates (cf. **negative convexity**).

(3) *Reinvestment risk*: This risk arises from holders of fixed claims not being in a position to reinvest the income stream from the cash flow at the expected rate, which in most cases is the initial **internal rate of return** or **yield-to-maturity** at which the cash flows were acquired.

(4) *Extension risk*: This arises when expected repayments of **principal** are delayed (cf. **mortgage-backed securities**).

See also **basis risk**.

interest rate risk management (IRRM). That function which is concerned with managing the risk arising from movements in interest rates (cf. **interest rate risk**). The process of management involves identifying the risks involved, measuring the possible exposure that results from those risks, and taking the appropriate steps to reduce or control the risk over some predetermined period or investment horizon. See **asset-liability management; gap analysis**.

interest rate sensitive or **interest sensitive.** Any activity, **asset**, or **liability**, whose value is sensitive to changes in interest rates (cf. **interest rate risk**).

interest rate spread (Banking). The **spread** between the average rate on interest earning assets and the average interest rate paid (on an equivalent taxable basis) on **interest bearing liabilities** (cf. **tax sparing**). See also **net interest income**.

interest rate swap (IRS) or **interest rate exchange agreement.** A bilateral contract for managing **interest rate risk** where two counterparties exchange their interest payments on a particular amount of **notional principal** for a specified length of time. In such an agreement no principal payments are exchanged (cf. **cross-currency swap**). Used as a **hedging** technique against interest rate risk and as a means of gaining access to capital markets, or a type of liability or asset profile on terms not otherwise available. There are two principal types of interest rate swaps:

Basis swap: This involves an exchange of two different **floating** or **variable** rate interest payments (for instance, a swap involving exchanging a **London interbank offered rate** flow for one based on US **treasury bills** or US domestic **commercial paper** indices) or tenors (one month versus six months, but using the same **reference rate**) (cf. **cross-currency basis swap**). Also known as *floating/floating swaps* since both payments streams vary over time based on a reference rate (cf. **basis**).

Coupon swap: This involves the exchange of a fixed interest payment for a variable interest payment (cf. **currency coupon swap**). One party will be the **fixed rate payer** (**floating receiver**) and the other will be the **floating rate payer** (**fixed rate receiver**). The swap parties only exchange interest payments, not principal. It is possible to be on either side of the transaction, i.e. fixed for floating (or vice versa). Also known as a *fixed/floating swap*.

The simplest type of interest rate swap is known as a **plain vanilla**. This has a **bullet maturity** on the notional underlying principal and has a fixed and a floating payer. More complex structures are possible, e.g. **amortizing swap** or **accreting swap**, See **commodity swap; differential swap; equity swap; swap assignment; swap reversal; swapping a swap; swap termination**.

interest rate swap future and **option on future.** **Futures** contract (and the **option on future**) where the **underlying** is an **index** of interest rate swaps. For example, the futures contract on the three- or five-year interest rate swap traded on the **Chicago Board of Trade**.

interest reserve ratio. An evaluation of a country's **short-term** ability to service its external **liabilities** calculated by taking the net foreign interest payments divided by **currency reserves**.

interest sensitive. See **interest rate sensitive**.

interest sensitive assets and **liabilities** (Banking). Income-generating **assets** and **interest bearing liabilities** that have their interest rate reset to the current market rate within specific **maturity** buckets (cf. **assets repriced before liabilities**). See **asset-liability management; gap analysis**.

interest-sensitive ratio or **interest-sensitivity ratio.** The degree of interest sensitivity in a balance sheet (cf. **assets repriced before liabilities**). See **asset-liability management**.

interest sensitive stock. A stock which is particularly sensitive to changes in interest rates.

interest sensitivity gap (Banking). See **gap analysis**.

interest-to-follow (ITF) (Money markets). The method used by the interbank markets to pay interest on deposits. Interest is quoted on an annualized basis and is calculated on the actual number of days of the **deposit** or **advance**, excluding the day the deposit is made but including the day the transaction matures, divided by the basis. For US dollars and most other currencies the basis is a 360-day year; for sterling it is a 365-day year. The method is sometimes known as *Actual/360* or *Actual/365*. See **interest rate calculations**.

interest yield (UK). British term for the **current yield**. Also sometimes referred to as the *income yield*.

interest yield equivalent (Bonds; USA). The bond market equivalent **yield** for a security issued at a **discount**. See also **bank discount basis**; **equivalent bond yield**.

inter-exchange transfer. The ability to use transactions in participating **futures** exchanges with similar contracts to **offset** positions. See **mutual offset**.

interface. The ability of two pieces of information technology to communicate with each other.

inter-firm comparison. See **ratio analysis**.

interim dividend. A **dividend** payment which is made part-way through the **financial year** before the final profit is known. Interims are either paid quarterly, as is common in the United States, or semi-annually and are announced after the **interim statement** (cf. **Form 10-q**).

interim report or **interim statement.** An unaudited **financial statement** issued part-way through the financial year, normally quarterly or semi-annually, although other period statements are known (cf. **Form 10-q**).

interlocking shareholdings. See **cross-shareholding** (cf. **keiretsu**; **noyaux durs**).

intermarket behaviour. Cross-asset, or cross-market, relationships (cf. **correlation**; **covariance**; **modern portfolio theory**). These are important if **cross-hedges** are used and for establishing portfolio diversification or for various **spread** type trades across markets (cf. **correlation risk**).

Intermarket Clearing Corporation (ICC) (USA). A part of the **Options Clearing Corporation** that specializes in the **clearing** of **futures** contracts (cf. **clearing house**).

intermarket spread. A transaction involving the purchase (or sale) of a **futures contract** on one **underlying** and the sale (or purchase) of a contract on another underlying (cf. **inter-commodity spread; intramarket spread; spread**).

intermarket spread swap. See **swap**.

Intermarket Trading System (ITS) (USA). A computer link between **specialists** of the major US exchanges (**New York Stock Exchange; American Stock Exchange**; Boston; Midwest; Philadelphia; Pacific) who trade the same securities. The system allows orders to be switched between exchanges in order to provide the best execution price.

intermediaries. Financial institutions which undertake the activity of **intermediation**. See **dealer; broker-dealer; market-maker; principal**.

intermediary. In the contexts of financial markets, normally an **agent, bank, broker-dealer, counterparty, dealer, deposit-taking institution, investment bank, market-maker, merchant bank, securities house, trader,** or other financial institution which facilitates transactions.

intermediate goods. Those goods used in the production of other goods, rather than for final consumption; for example, plastic. Some goods can be both; for example, milk which is consumed and used to produce chocolate.

intermediate-term bonds. Bonds with a **maturity** of between five and fifteen years, or a **duration** between three and six years (cf. **longs; long term; shorts; short term**). Also known as *mediums*.

intermediation. The process undertaken by a financial institution under which it acts as **principal** and introduces its own name and reputation between a lender and a borrower. For example, a bank or **mutual fund** (cf. **dealer; broker-dealer; disintermediation**). Intermediaries can provide diversification to depositors, act as monitors on loans, and provide payment and other ancilliary services.

internal capital generation rate. The rate at which an organization creates **capital reserves** through **retained earnings** (cf. **payout ratio**).

internal finance. Surplus funds generated from a firm's operations after meeting contractual obligations which are used to finance new projects. Also goes by the name of *cash surplus, cash flow,* or *free* or *net cash flow.* Tends to be considered by firms as the major source of funding available for investment projects.

internal rate of return (IRR). A discounted cash flow criterion which determines an average rate of return by reference to the condition that the values be reduced to zero at the initial point of time. As such, it is also the constant **discount rate** that makes equal the **present value** of a future stream of payments equal to the initial investment (cf. **yield**). See **yield-to-maturity**.

internal reserves. See **hidden reserves**.

International Accounting Standards Committee (IASC). International body set up in 1973 and responsible for developing International Accounting Standards.

International Auditing Practices Committee (IAPC). Similar body to the International Accounting Standards Committee responsible for developing a common auditing standard. See **Generally Accepted Auditing Standards; Statement of Auditing Standards**.

International Bank for Reconstruction and Development (IBRD; World Bank). See **World Bank**.

international banking facility (IBF) (Banking; USA). Offshore banking units set up in the USA since 1981 to undertake international transactions on the same basis as the **euromarkets**. Such activities were exempt from **reserve requirements** with the **Federal Reserve**.

international bonds. Term for a **bond** issued outside the country of domicile of the issuer. Such bonds come in two types: **eurobonds** and **foreign bonds**.

international cash management. Short-term financial management of multi-currency and cross-border transactions. This may involve cross-border account management, **netting**, **pooling** arrangements, and **balance concentration** (cf. **centralized treasury**).

International Center for the Settlement of Investment Disputes (ICSID). A part of the International Bank for Reconstruction and Development (the **World Bank**), which provides a forum for the arbitration and resolution of investment disputes between member states and their nationals.

International Commodities Clearing House (ICCH) (UK). The **clearing house** for transactions undertaken on the **London International Financial Futures and Options Exchange** and other **derivatives** exchanges in London.

international debt issue. Debt raised on the international capital markets, either as a loan or as securities (cf. **international bonds; syndicated loan**). See **euromarkets**.

international depository receipt (IDR). A type of a **depository receipt** designed to help facilitate the **global** trading of securities. The **underlying** security is held by a **custodian** and negotiable receipts, providing ownership, are issued. The structure is designed to circumvent problems in holding and trading the original securities. See **American depository receipt; European depository receipt**.

International Development Association (IDA). Part of the International Bank for Reconstruction and Development (the **World Bank**) set up in 1960; the IDA makes concessionary loans to facilitate development projects for the world's poorest countries.

international equity placement. The placement of **equity** on two or more markets, excluding the issuer's domestic market, at the same time. Sometimes known as a *euro-equity placement*.

International Finance Corporation (IFC). The private sector financing arm of the International Bank for Reconstruction and Development (the **World Bank**) set up in 1956. The principles which guide the IFC are similar to those for the World Bank, except that it assists and invests in privately owned businesses in developing countries. It is now a borrower in its own right in the international capital markets.

International Financial Services Centre (IFSC) (Ireland). Based at Dublin's Custom House Dock, the centre benefits from certain tax concessions allowing financial institutions to minimize their tax liabilities (cf. **offshore**). **European Union** investment activities such as the marketing of **undertakings for collective investment in transferable securities** may be operated from the centre, although selling activity to Irish residents is restricted. Colloquially known as *Dublin Dock*.

International Fisher Effect. A theory advanced by Irving Fisher that the difference between the interest rates in two currencies should offset the difference in expected inflation in the two countries (cf. **purchasing power parity theory of foreign exchange**).

international futures. Futures contracts traded on an exchange for an **underlying** that is in a foreign country. These are often settled in the currency of the **futures exchange** in which the trading is undertaken. For example, the **Chicago Mercantile Exchange** has a contract on the **Nikkei 225 Index** that is traded and settled in US dollars. See also **currency protected; quantity adjusting option**.

International Futures Exchange (INTEX) (Bahamas). A computerized financial futures exchange based in Bermuda.

International Institute of Finance (IIF) (USA). A Washington DC based 'think-tank' established by leading international banks following the development of the less developed country debt problems in the early 1980s with a view to providing better intelligence on international financial developments.

international investment bank. Investment bank involved in cross-border transactions (cf. **global bank**).

International Monetary Fund (IMF). Established in 1947 and intended to provide additional liquidity and confidence to the international monetary system. It seeks to encourage the liberalization of cross-border currency and settlement activities. In practice, its role is that of lender to member countries that face trade payments difficulties. The IMF publishes useful surveys of international developments and forecasts.

International Monetary Market (IMM) (USA). A futures and options exchange which is part of the Chicago Mercantile Exchange and allows members to deal in financial futures on foreign exchange, treasury bills, and eurodollar deposits.

International Monetary Market index (IMM index) (USA). The method used for quoting the prices of short-term interest rate futures where the value is 100 less the annual discount yield. Thus if the current discount yield were 8.20%, the value of the futures contract would be 91.80 $(100 - 8.20)$.

international mutual fund. A managed fund that invests in the global market. Returns on such a fund are linked to the performance of the individual markets and changes in foreign exchange rates (cf. **diversification**).

International Organization of Securities Commissions (IOSCO). An institution similar to the Bank for International Settlement's committee on bank regulation, aiming at ensuring harmonization of capital adequacy and other regulatory requirements in different jurisdictions. See also **Group of Thirty**.

International Petroleum Exchange of London Limited (IPE) (UK). International House, 1 St Katherine's Way, London E1 9UN, England (tel. (4471) 481 0643; fax (4471) 481 8485; tlx 927479). An energy futures and options exchange set up in 1980. Best known for trading North Sea oil (cf. **Brent crude; marker crude**).

International Primary Markets Association (IPMA). A professional grouping of euromarket participants, active in **eurobond** new issuance, set up to consider standards and practices for new issues of eurobonds. Membership is restricted to those firms which are active **lead-managers** of issues, having undertaken a minimum of four in the previous two years (cf. **International Securities Markets Association**). See **eurobond fees; fixed price reoffer**.

International Securities Markets Association (ISMA). Formerly the International Association of Bond Dealers (IABD), the Association represents secondary market participants in the **eurobond** market (cf. **International Primary Markets Association**). ISMA is a recognized investment exchange for reporting and self-regulatory purposes under the UK's **Financial Services Act, 1986**. The main aims of the ISMA are to promote an orderly development of the secondary market in eurobonds; to set trading rules; and to provide a forum in which issues relating to the secondary market can be discussed. It also aims to promote the development of the market and act as a pressure group. ISMA operates the TRAX reporting system used for many eurosecurities (cf. **Centrale de Livraison de Valeurs Mobilières; Euroclear**).

International Security Identification Number (ISIN). Identification system developed by the International Organization for Standardization to cover all securities issued in the international markets. The system is based on the CUSIP Number System with the addition of a country code and the numbering agency.

international spread note, option, or **warrant.** A security where the returns are linked to the relationship or spread between two different interest rates (cf. **out performance option; rainbow option**).

International Stock Exchange in London (ISE) (UK). Name given to the London Stock Exchange following **Big Bang** although it now generally goes by its former name. It is the organization which operates the UK's main stock exchange. It trades the issues of domestic and international companies as well as those of UK and Commonwealth governments. The market comprises **main market** and the **Alternative Investment Market** (unlisted securities market). See also **Stock Exchange Automated Quotations**.

International Swaps and Derivatives Association (ISDA). A US-based self-regulatory body responsible for the standardization of some of the technical aspects of **interest rate swap** and **currency swap** transactions, other over-the-counter

(OTC) **derivatives**, such as **interest rate caps and floors**, and **forward foreign exchange** transactions. Publications include a *Code of Standard Wording, Assumptions and Provisions for Swaps*, together with master documentation agreements (*Master Swap Agreement*). Most OTC derivative agreements now conform to the ISDA standard. Formely the *International Swap Dealers' Association*.

interpolation. Estimating intermediate date points on a set of data such as a **yield curve**. There are three basic methods that can be used: *straight-line*—this involves a linear estimate from the two observed points, where the interpolated point, is a time weighted average of the two observed rates; *calendar month convention*—this treats all observations falling within a given calendar month or accepted subperiod as being equal; and *exponential* or *spline*—this involves fitting a best fit curve to the observed points.

interpositioning. Having a second **dealer** between a buyer and a seller, or between the client and the **market-maker**. This might be necessary when transacting in **illiquid** securities or regulated markets. The danger is that double **commission** may be paid, thus increasing **transaction costs**. As a result, in some jurisdictions this is a strictly regulated activity.

interquartile range. One of a number of measures of dispersion or **variance** of a distribution. The commonest measure is the variance or **standard deviation** (cf. **volatility**). The interquartile range, as its name suggests, is the difference in the value between the bottom quarter of the distribution and the top quarter. The advantage of this measure is that it does not make any assumptions about the shape or type of distribution involved. This is especially useful for skewed or other non-normal types of distribution where the use of the variance would be inappropriate (cf. **leptokurtic**).

Interstanza (Italy). Inter-city security **settlement** system operated by the **central bank**, the Banco d'Italia, between the major financial centres in Italy in order to avoid the transfer of **certificates**.

Interstate Commerce Commission (ICC) (USA). The US federal agency charged with regulating interstate commerce and transportation. Although deregulation in the 1970s and 1980s has reduced the importance of the ICC, it nevertheless retains a significant regulatory role in internal US business activities.

interval measure. A **risk** measure that is the number of days that a firm can be self-financing, by drawing down funds, without additional income.

intervention (Forex). Purchases and sales of currency undertaken by a country's **central bank** to influence the exchange rate or to maintain an orderly market (cf. **crawling peg**). Sometimes a number of central banks will act in concert to influence market sentiment or as part of a co-ordinated attempt to squeeze short positions. See **clean float; dirty float; floating exchange rate.**

intervention rate (Money markets; UK). The rate of interest at which the **Bank of England** either rediscounts bills presented to it, or lends to **discount houses**.

in the box (USA). Term for confirmation that securities have been correctly delivered (cf. **bad delivery; good delivery**). It dates from the time when US treasuries were in physical form and were stored in pigeon-holes (cf. **book-entry security**). See **settlement.**

in the money (ITM). (i) Any transaction showing a **profit** (cf. **book gain; mark-to-market**). (ii) Of an **option**, it means it is profitable to **exercise**. A **call** option is in the money if its **strike price** is less than the value of the **underlying** (cf. **intrinsic value**). A **put** option is in the money if the strike price is higher than the the current price of the underlying (cf. **at the money; out of the money**). It comes

(a) For a call option

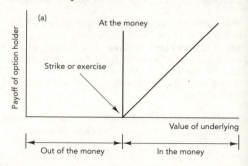

(b) For a put option

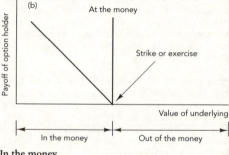

In the money

Intra-commodity spread

	Time spread (bullish)	Reverse time spread (bearish)
t_1 short-dated	Sell (short position)	Buy (long position)
t_2 long-dated	Buy (long position)	Sell (short position)
Rationale: long-dated position more sensitive to price changes in the underlying	Value of underlying rises (bullish), therefore gain in later-expiry contract (t_2) outweighs loss in earlier expiry contract (t_1)	Value of underlying falls (bearish), therefore gain in later-expiry contract (t_2) outweighs loss in earlier expiry contract (t_1)

See also inter-commodity spread.

from the fact that if the holder exercises the option, he will make money.
See also **option pricing.**

in the tank (USA). A term used in the markets to describe a fall in prices.

intra-commodity spread (time spread; reverse time spread) **(SP).** Offsetting positions taken in the same **commodity** (cf. **calendar spread; horizontal spread; intramarket spread**). Also called a *time spread* or *reverse time spread*. The rationale and effect of the two types of intra-commodity spread position can be summarized as in the Table.

intraday. Within a day or trading session. In securities markets, often considered to be the period during the day when the market is open (cf. **day time trading; position trading; scalping**).

intraday limit. (i) A limit on the amount of exposure that is allowed within a given day. See **maximum daylight delivery limit.** (ii) A limit on the price movement that is allowed on an exchange within one day or trading session (cf. **down limit.**

intra-firm analysis. See ratio analysis.

intramarket spread. Another term for a calendar spread where the two **positions** are made on the same **underlying** and the same **futures contracts.**

intrinsic value. (i) The difference between the strike price of an **option** and the current market price of the **underlying** as long as this is positive, that is the option is **in the money.** Although there is no theoretical justification, option prices are made up of a combination of **time value** and intrinsic value. (ii) the value of assets or securities derived by **fundamental analysis** techniques.

intrinsic value of a call. The difference between the **underlying** price and the **strike price** as long as this is greater than zero: max {*Underlying price − Strike price, 0*}.

intrinsic value of a put. The difference between the **strike price** and the **underlying** price as long as this is greater than zero: max {Strike price − Underlying price, 0}.

introduction (Equities; UK). A method of obtaining a price quotation on the **London Stock Exchange** (LSE) which does not involve the issue of new **shares.** The LSE controls the use of introductions, restricting them to firms which are already widely held. It is used mainly by established overseas companies to broaden the market in their **common stock.** See **quotation; initial public offering; listing.**

inventory (USA). In accounting, the items on a **balance sheet** for raw materials, supplies, work-in-progress, and finished goods held by the firm. In the UK known as **stock.** (ii) In trading, the securities held by a **market-maker** or specialist. It can also be taken to mean their net position.

inventory management. The process of managing the trade-off between holding inventory (with its costs of storage, handling, reordering, obsolescence, and wastage) and production scheduling.

inventory turnover ratio. See stock turnover ratio.

inverse floater swap. An interest rate swap where the floating rate has a negative relationship to the **reference rate.** It involves a **fixed rate,** less the reference rate, such that as interest rates fall, the value of the floating rate payments rise. See also **reverse floating rate note.**

inverse floating rate note (inverse FRN; inverse floater). See reverse floating rate note.

inverse yield curve. A yield curve where the short **maturities** have a higher yield than the longer maturities. Sometimes seen as an indication of tight monetary conditions. Also known as an *inverted yield curve*.

inverted curve enhancement interest rate swap (ICE swap). Interest rate swap transaction undertaken when there is an **inverse yield curve** which has a floor on the **floating rate** leg and an above-market fixed rate.

inverted market. A futures market where the nearer months are selling at a higher price than the more distant months. Also known as *backwardation* or a *discount market*.

inverted scale (Bonds; USA). A condition seen in serial bond issues where earlier **maturities** have higher yields than later ones.

invested amount. The principal amount invested, less any repayments and/or **write-offs**.

investment. (i) Buying and holding **assets** to earn income or **capital gain**. Investment may be in physical property, such as **real estate** or collectibles, or in **financial instruments**. (ii) For companies, the acquisition of **capital assets** or allocation of resources to productive use. See **capital budgeting**.

Investment Advisers Act of 1940 (USA). The legislation that requires securities representatives to be registered with the **Securities and Exchange Commission** in order to carry on business (cf. **registered representative**).

investment analyst. Specialist at appraising investments. This can be done via **fundamental analysis** or through **technical analysis**. See also **analyst**; **quant**; **rocket scientist**.

investment appraisal. See **capital budgeting**; **fundamental analysis**.

investment bank (USA). A firm that **originates**, **underwrites**, and distributes new issues, engages in corporate finance or advisory activities, and manages investments (cf. **merchant bank** (UK); **merchant banking** (USA)). A person so engaged is known as an *investment banker*.

investment certificate (IC). See **participation certificate**.

investment club. A pooled **fund** for the purpose of making investments. Such clubs agree to share gains and losses **pro rata** to the amounts invested. Typically, they are groups of private individual investors who get together to **pool** their funds and expertise in an attempt to replicate the benefits of **institutional investors** without the **management fees**. The main advantages of such clubs are seen as the opportunities for **diversification** of the securities holdings, and the control over **transaction costs** which would

be limited to dealing costs. See also **mutual fund**.

investment company (USA). A firm that manages securities investments. There are two basic types of investment companies: open-ended, which are **mutual funds**, and closed-ended or **investment trust companies** (cf. **limited partnership**; **master limited partnership**).

Investment Company Act of 1940 (USA). The legislation that regulates and requires investment companies to be registered with the **Securities and Exchange Commission** (cf. **mutual fund**; **investment trust company**).

investment credit or **investment tax credit** (USA). A tax allowance that has been offered to firms buying certain types of assets, chiefly plant and equipment, from time to time over and above that available from tax depreciation. Thus a 10% allowance would give a firm acquiring a US$100 asset a US$10 credit, plus US$10 say of tax depreciation. The US$10 credit would be set against the business's income tax after tax depreciation was made. Abolished in the Tax Reform Act of 1986. See **accelerated cost recovery system**; **capital allowances**.

investment currency. See **currency overlay management**.

investment grade (USA). A bond rated 'Baa' or above by **Moody's Investor Services** or 'BBB' or above by **Standard and Poor's** or given a similar rating by another US credit rating agency, and as such thought eligible for bank investment under US banking regulations (cf. **junk bond**). See also **credit ratings**; **prudent-man rule**.

investment horizon. The time period over which investors either consider the future or expect to maintain their investment or **portfolio**. The investment horizon may be, and usually is, shorter than the final **maturity** of the investments. Investors do not expect to make significant adjustments to their holdings prior to the elapse of the horizon time period. Sometimes equated with **holding period**.

investment letter (USA). A letter from a purchaser of a **private placement** to the issuer stating that the holding has been acquired for investment purposes and not for resale. Since the issue is not registered with the **Securities and Exchange Commission** such a letter is required as proof that the issuer was not intending to circumvent the registration requirements. See **Rule 144a**.

Investment Management Regulatory Organization (IMRO) (UK). A self-regulating organization established as a result of the **Financial Services Act, 1986** responsible for the conduct of professional fund managers and accountable to the **Securities and Investments Board** for adherence to its rule book. Some of IMRO's activities have now been taken over by the **Personal Investment Authority.**

investment manager. Individual or firm responsible for managing funds for investment purposes. Typically, such a manager will decide day-to-day investment policy within defined limits, administer inflows and outflows from the fund, prepare reports, and advise on investment strategy. Also called an *asset manager* (cf. **liability manager; institutional investor**).

investment memorandum. In venture capital another name for the **subscription agreement.**

investment portfolio. See **portfolio.**

Investment Property Databank indices (IPD indices) (UK). Indices giving details of capital appreciation and rental growth in commercial and industrial property. See **index construction.**

Investment Services Directive. European Union directive dealing with the harmonization of regulation for securities trading. It applies the *passport for Europe* principle using the same approach as the co-ordination of banking legislation, in that securities firms need to have been admitted to securities trading by their home country regulatory authorities before being allowed to operate at a European level, and they will continue to be subject to these as regards regulation. See also **Capital Adequacy Directive.**

investment strategy. Decisions about the allocation of resources. (i) For portfolio purposes, this is a decision on **asset allocation** between different categories of investments in terms of how much **risk** the **investment manager** is required to take and the investment horizon (cf. **diversification; duration bogey; strategic asset allocation; tactical asset allocation**). The four key portfolio objectives (which may not be all achievable simultaneously) are safety of principal, income, growth of income, and capital appreciation. See also **balanced mutual fund; growth fund; income fund.** (ii) For the firm, investment strategy relates to decisions about resource allocation to develop opportunities in the firm's markets, new product development, and the means of achieving corporate objectives arrived at through the strategic planning process.

investment tax credit. The reductions in company taxes given to firms which acquire assets. See **Accelerated Cost Recovery System; capital allowances; tax shield.**

investment trust (UK). A company, usually quoted, which invests in the securities of other, again usually quoted, companies. As an investment vehicle it offers a professionally managed and diversified portfolio to holders of the trust's **common stock** or **ordinary shares.** Investment trusts were established in the nineteenth century in order to facilitate foreign investment. In the USA, known as a **closed-end fund.**

investment trust company. A company whose main activity is to manage **funds** on behalf of its **shareholders.** Its assets are its **portfolio** of securities so that the price of its **shares** is determined by its investment performance. As its capital is fixed by its articles of association it is sometimes described as a **closed-end fund** (USA) (cf. **openend; unit trust**). There may be different classes of stock issued by the company, for instance, capital and income shares (cf. **prescribed right to income and maximum equity; special claim on residual equity**). Also known as an *investment company.* See also **mutual funds; net asset value.**

investment value of a convertible. See **straight value.**

investor base. Market term for holders of a given type of security (cf. **retail**).

invisible asset. See **intangible assets.**

invisible balance or **invisibles.** The difference in value between the export and import of services, interest payments, and profit and **dividends.** See **balance of payments; capital account; current account.**

invisible supply. That part of a new issue of securities held by the **underwriters** but not declared. See **visible supply.**

invitation telex. A telex sent by a **lead manager** or **book runner** inviting participation in a new issue. The use of the telex has been mostly superseded by the fax or electronic data interchange.

invoice. A claim for payment by a **creditor.**

invoice amount. (i) The cash amount in an invoice. (ii) (Futures) The **delivery** amount that the **long** position holder pays the **short** for a bond at the settlement of a **bond future** (cf. **cheapest to deliver; physical delivery**). This will be the bond price times the adjustment factor and any **accrued interest.** For details, see **delivery factor.**

invoice discounting. A method of **receivables** financing where the **creditors** are unaware of the sale of the invoices to a financing house (cf. **asset-**

backed finance). As a result it is sometimes known as *confidential factoring*.

invoice price (Commodities). The actual price paid by a long position holder on the **delivery** of a **commodities future** contract after all adjustments, such as contract specification changes and so forth, have been taken into account (cf. **alternative delivery procedure; cash settled; contract grade**).

Irish Futures and Options Exchange (IFOX) (Ireland). Segrave House, Earlsfort Terrace, Dublin 2, Ireland (tel. 767413; fax 614645). **Derivatives exchange** on Irish government bonds and money market instruments which opened in 1989.

Irish Stock Exchange (Republic of Ireland). 28 Anglesea Street, Dublin 2 (tel. 353 1 6778808; fax 353 1 6719029).

iron butterfly. Option strategy which involves the purchase of a **straddle** and the sale of a **strangle**. For example, it can be set up by selling a **put** at one **strike price**, buying a put and **call** at a higher strike, and selling a call at a still higher strike. The strategy aims to profit from the differences in prices between the near-to- or **at-the-money** options and those which are either **out of the money** or **in the money** (cf. **volatility skew; volatility smile**).

irredeemable (Bonds). (i) A class of UK **gilts** with no final **maturity** but which may be redeemed at any time subject to three months' notice, at the UK government's option. Increasingly being referred to as **undated**. The principal issues are **consols** and War Loan. Sometimes known as a *one-way stock option*. (ii) Any **perpetual bond**, that is a bond with no final maturity.

irrevocable letter of credit or **irrevocable credit** (Banking). A form of **bill** or **letter of credit** (LOC) where the issuing bank is obliged to honour the draft and which can neither be revoked nor amended without the consent of all parties, including the beneficiary (cf. **documentary credit**). The opposite is revocable, where the LOC may be cancelled or modified at any time prior to payment. The revocable LOC is a mechanism for making payments rather than providing security for payments.

irrevocable trust. A trust deed that cannot be altered without the consent of the beneficiary (cf. **fixed trust**). Such trusts are typically used in **asset-backed** or other types of **pass-through** arrangements.

Islamic banking. Carrying on banking activity in accordance with the dictates of the *Koran*. Interest

is forbidden in Islam; however, it is generally agreed that various forms of joint **project** activity which benefit both the provider of **finance** and the recipient are allowed as long as both parties share in the **risks**. The principal arrangements allowed are:

- *ijarah*: joint venture arrangement allowing an owner to engage in property-based activities;
- *ijara ijara wa iktina*: form of banking using risk sharing;
- *ijarawa iktina*: joint venture aimed to recreate a similar position to capital goods leasing;
- *mudaraba*: joint venture financing arrangement, similar to *muqarada*;
- *muqarada*: lenders become joint partners in the project and receive a set proportion of the project or firm's net cash flow which is used to service the obligation as to **principal** and, effectively, interest; and
- *musharaka*: the lender agrees to purchase goods or services from the other party, thus creating an **equity** interest in the transaction, while at the same time agreeing to resell the product or service at a higher price (cf. **forward**).

For year conversion method between Islamic years and Gregorian years, see **Hijra years**.

issue by tender (UK). See **sale by tender**.

issued and outstanding (USA). Authorized **common stock** issued by a corporation. Firms may also have **treasury stock** and/or **unissued shares**.

issue date. The date at which interest on securities begins to accrue. It is not the same as the **allotment** date. Sometimes called the *dated date*.

issued capital or **issued shares.** The amount of a company's authorised capital or **shares** that has been issued (cf. **treasury stock**). Sometimes called *subscribed capital*.

issue price. The percentage of **principal** or **par value** at which the price of a new issue of securities is made. This price may be at par, at a **discount** from par, or at a **premium** over par. The price is normally gross, that is before any **commissions** or other **fees** involved in the issue are deducted (cf. **reoffer price**).

issuer. Another term for a borrower. Tends to be used when the borrower is raising funds through securities issuance (cf. **obligor**).

issuer set margin. A condition of a note issuance facility which allows the issuer to set the maximum **margin** that **notes** can be bid for in a **tender**

which has a **continuous tender panel** arrangement (cf. **tender panel**). The mechanism is designed to limit the margin (and hence profit) at which members of the continuous tender panel have the right to purchase notes.

issuer's option bond. A generic type of **bond** issue which may incorporate any of a range of **options** for the issuer at **maturity** to repay in cash or **common stock**. The most extreme variant is the **mandatory convertible** where the holder receives common stock; other versions include **extendible** or involve partial conversion. See **capital note**.

issuing agent. An institution that acts for an issuer in allocating **certificates** and securities when a **new issue** is launched. See **bearer security; certificate; physical security; registered security.**

issuing and paying agent. A bank in the euromarkets which combines the role of **issuing agent** and **paying agent**, that is, it will arrange for the authentication and **delivery** of **certificates** and their redemption and cancellation at **maturity**. This combination of functions is often seen in **eurocommercial paper** programmes and **note issuance facilities**.

issuing bank. A bank which issues a **documentary credit**. It is normally the purchaser's principal bank or principal international bank.

issuing house. An institution or agency that organizes the arrangements associated with an issue of securities. See **investment bank; merchant banks**.

Istanbul Gold Exchange (Turkey). Physical product exchange for **gold bullion** for the Turkish market set up in July 1995 (cf. **London Metal Exchange**).

Istanbul Stock Exchange (ISE) (Istanbul Menkul Kiymetler Borsasi) (Turkey). Istinye 80860 Istanbul (tel. (90 212) 298 21 00; fax (90 212) 298 25 00). The stock exchange was established in 1985 for **listing** Turkish companies, and trading is divided into a retail and a main market. It has also established an *International Market* section for nonresident issues which benefits from tax-free, offshore status where transactions are made in US dollars.

istituto di credito fondiario (Banking; Italy). A mortgage bank (cf. **building society; savings and loan association**).

ita (Japanese). **Order book** (cf. **saitori member**).

Italian Stock Market (Italy). The combined regional stock **exchanges** of Bologna, Florence, Genoa, Milan, Naples, Palermo, Rome, Triste, Turin, and Venice. Milan is the largest and most important of the exchanges. They are linked together via an Automated Computerized Trading Network, known as the CEDBorsa.

Ito process. See **geometric Brownian motion; Wiener process.**

iyatose (Japan). The custom by Japanese stockbrokers to treat all orders received before the opening as having been given at the same time (cf. **limit order; opening price**). See **opening rotation; open outcry**.

J

Jakarta Stock Exchange (Indonesia). One of the Pacific rim countries and a key **emerging market** exchange, alongside the other **dragon countries**.

Japan Bond Research Institute (JBRI) (Japan). 2–6–1 Nihonbashi Kayabacho, Chuo-ku, Tokyo 103 (tel. (813) 3639 2840; fax (813) 3639 2848). See **credit ratings**.

Japan Credit Rating Agency Ltd. (JCR) (Japan) 14th floor, Shuwa Shibe Park Building B, 2–4–1 Shibakoen, Minato-ku, Tokyo 105 (tel. (813) 3432 9013; fax (813) 3432 9019). See **credit ratings**.

Japanese bills. A market for short-term **bills** along the lines of the US **banker's acceptances** market on which it was modelled. In order to be eligible for rediscount with the Bank of Japan such bills must be related to specific domestic transactions, and the market is therefore more akin to a **forfaiting** transaction than the finance of international trade. Because the bills relate to domestic business, maturities reflect the shorter **tenor** of trade credit.

Japanese government agencies bonds. Bond issues made by an **agency** of the government and guaranteed as to interest and principal repayment by the government. Such issues are priced and traded in the market at a small margin over similar **Japanese Government Bonds** to reflect both the guaranteed nature of the issue and the reduced **liquidity** of such smaller sized issues.

Japanese Government Bond (JGB) (Japan). Bonds issued by the Japanese government and only second in size to the **US Treasury** bond market. Historically there were two types: ordinary government debt and deficit-reducing bonds. Now the distinction is largely lost and the two trade indistinguishably, with new issues being principally of the former type. Currently there are basically two types of new issue: medium-term bonds which have an **original maturity** of up to five years and long-term bonds which are typically ten year **maturity**, and the government may (new issue conditions permitting) offer more than one **tranche** of the same security (cf. **fungible**; **tap**). In addition, occasionally longer-dated issues of up to twenty years have been offered to the market. Each separate issue is numbered sequentially and is identified in the market by these numbers. One of the larger current issue ten-year bonds is given **benchmark** status through a consensus of market participants, given that it best reflects market conditions (cf. **bell-wether**). The benchmark issue tends to be more heavily traded and more liquid than other comparable issues and trades at a **premium**. The market employs a unique method for calculating **yield** based on the **current yield** (or interest yield) and simple appreciation/depreciation of the **discount** or premium. Bonds are traded on a special yield basis. The JGB yield method equals the annualized appreciation (depreciation) to maturity *plus* current yield:

$$\text{Annualized appreciation (depreciation)} = \frac{\text{Par price} - \text{Current market price}}{\text{Number of years to maturity}}$$
$$\times \frac{\text{Par price}}{\text{Current market price}}$$

$$\text{Current yield} = \frac{\text{Coupon rate}}{\text{Current market rate}}$$

JGBs pay interest semi-annually and are quoted on a 365-day year basis. New issue prices (and yields) are determined by negotiation between the Ministry of Finance and the syndicate of **underwriters**, which includes all the major securities houses. When market conditions are adverse, or when the government seeks to use the terms on new issue to signal its wishes on interest rates to the market, both sides can fail to agree terms. Note that **deep discount bonds** are also issued.

Japan premium. The excess interest rate or **spread** that Japanese banks had to pay for borrowing on the international markets that arose as a result of the revelations about fraud losses at *Daiwa Bank*'s New York branch revealed in October 1985 which accumulated since 1984. The cover-up of the information and the evidence of lack of management control led foreign lenders to reconsider the credit risks involved in advancing funds to Japanese banks leading to **premium** being charged for funds.

jawboning. The routine of policy-makers to 'talk up' a situation as an alternative to (painful) concrete actions. This applies particularly to situations such as the **depreciation** of a currency, where governments try to persuade the market that it is wrong (cf. **moral suasion**).

J curve. The short-term worsening of the **balance of payments** resulting from a **devaluation** of the **currency exchange rate**. Such a perverse effect can arise because **currency traders** may believe further devaluations are forthcoming and respond by selling the currency under pressure, or leading and lagging, or both, such that domestic importers will accelerate orders through fear of having to pay more for goods in the home currency later, while foreign importers delay their orders for the exports of the devaluing country in the hope of buying them cheaply later in terms of their own currency. This will cause the volume effect from devaluation, at least in the short term, to be perverse, with the balance of payments deteriorating.

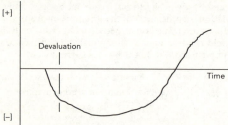

The J curve: devaluation and the effect on the balance of payments

jellyroll. Synthetic futures time spread position created in the **underlying** by holding two offsetting synthetic futures positions in different **expiry** months. One position is a **long** synthetic, created by buying a **call** and selling a **put** at the same **strike price**, while the other is a **written** call and purchased put. See also **box spread** (cf. **horizontal spread**). See also **option strategies**.

jeopardy clause. A condition in **eurocurrency** agreements which specifies that if certain events reduce the lender's operations or the workings of the market then such things as the repayment to the lender involved or the substitution of another agreed rate will take place (cf. **fall-back**). Also known as a *disaster* or a *break clause*.

jikan yūsen (Japan). The time priority rule pertaining to transactions on the **Tokyo Stock Exchange**. If two prices are the same, the earlier transaction prevails.

jika sōgaku (Japan). **Market capitalization** of a security.

jobber (UK). Pre-**Big Bang** term for a **market-maker** on the **London Stock Exchange**. Jobbers acted as **principals**, buying and selling securities for their own account with other members of the exchange, known as stockbrokers. They were for-

bidden by exchange rules from dealing direct with the public.

jobbers' turn (UK). Formerly used to describe a **market-maker's bid-offer spread**.

jobbing. (i) Colloquial **euromarkets** term for an intermediary acting as **principal** in a transaction (cf. **dealer**; **broker-dealer**; **market-maker**). (ii) Buying and selling with a view to taking advantage of **short-term** price movements (cf. daytime **trading**; scalping).

jobbing back. Post-transaction analysis of how an investment or decision turned out. Although post-performance audit of actions taken does explain the result, the key factor in any such contemplation is forward looking. That is, past failure or success should be a guide to the future, not a mechanism for apportioning blame.

job lot. A mixed lot of securities (cf. **basket**; **odd lot**; **block trade**).

Johannesburg Stock Exchange (South Africa). 17 Diagonal Street, Johannesburg 2001; Postal Address: PO Box 1174, Johannesburg 2000, Republic of South Africa (tel. (011) 833 6580; fax (011) 834 3937; tlx 4-87663 SA). It also has a **derivatives** section (cf. **floor**; **pit**).

joint account. An agreement between two or more firms to share the **risk** and funding responsibility in the purchase or **underwriting** of securities.

joint and several liability (UK). A legal liability which is both a joint liability (that is a group have a liability in common) and several (that is a liability as individuals). Each of the parties is responsible for meeting the whole of their collective obligation, while expecting that the others will pay their separate (several) obligations.

joint bond. A bond issue which has more than one obligor. Can also mean a **guaranteed bond**.

jointly and severally (USA). A form of **underwriting agreement** where the **underwriter's** commitment is in relation to the amount of unsold issue regardless of the amount he has **distributed**. Thus an underwriter who had a 10% commitment and had sold 12% of the issue personally would still be liable to take up a further 2.4% if 24% had remained unsold. The opposite type of underwriting agreement is *severally but not jointly*. Also referred to as *joint and several liability*.

joint option. Variation on a **quantity adjusting option** that allows the holder to obtain the benefits of any improvement in the **currency**.

joint stock bank (UK). Traditionally, a bank where the **shareholders** have **limited liability** (cf. **partnership**).

joint stock company. (i) (USA) An unlimited company. That is, one where at least one **shareholder** retains unlimited **liability**. The company issues **shares** which are tradable, like a limited company, but benefits from tax and other treatment like a **partnership** (cf. **master limited partnership**). (ii) (UK) Defunct term for a limited company or a bank with limited liability. See **public limited company**.

joint venture. When a company is owned by two parent firms in equal or unequal proportions. It can also apply to strategic alliances between companies where they agree to collaborate in the development or distribution of particular services or products. Such alliances have been notable amongst financial institutions, especially banks and insurance companies, for crossing geographical (European) boundaries in an attempt to exploit the separately held product or service expertise and local market knowledge and ownership of distribution channels. When more than two businesses are involved the term *consortium* is usually used instead.

judgement currency clause. Used in **eurocredit** and **eurobond** transactions to protect lenders against losses coming from the loan or security being denominated in one currency but where legal decisions may be made in another currency. This arises from the fact that a commercial court can only award settlements in the **legal tender** of the country in which it has jurisdiction.

jumbo certificate of deposit (CD) (Money markets; USA). Term for a **certificate of deposit** which has a **face value** in excess of US$100,000. Such wholesale market instruments do not benefit from deposit insurance (cf. **Federal Deposit Insurance Corporation; retail certificate of deposit**).

jump diffusion process. Description of the stochastic behaviour of security prices proposed by Professor Robert Merton of the Massachusetts Institute of Technology (MIT) involving a two-factor model. The underlying price-generating process is a combination of a jump process and a continuous diffusion process such as the **geometric Brownian motion**. See also **binomial jump diffusion process; option pricing**.

jump process. (i) A combined **distribution** that is used to characterize the movements in financial markets. It consists of a normal diffusion price or rate process over time joined to a second distribution process used to characterize the large price movements recorded in markets from time to time. (ii) The discrete price model used in the **binomial option pricing model**. At its simplest it assumes that the price for any small time interval can only follow one of two paths, either to jump up or jump down in value. Extending the analysis allows the use of a **binomial tree** of price changes. Extensions of the approach include trinomial and higher factor price change models.

jumps. Discontinuities in prices or rates due to extreme market conditions (cf. **break**).

jump Z bond (USA). An accrual **collateralized mortgage obligation** bond that moves ahead in precedence for interest and **principal** if certain specified condition(s) are met. See **Z bond**.

junior or **junior security.** Issues that rank below others in right of payment within a **class** (cf. **pari passu; senior**). See **subordinated debt**.

junior refunding (Bonds; USA). A refunding of maturing **short maturity US treasury notes** with another issue of the same **original maturity**.

junior tranche. A subordinated or deferred element of a transaction where different **tranches** are ranked separately as to their claim on the issuer. Some very complex transactions may have several levels of subordination and are known as A tranche, B tranche, and so on.

junk bond (USA). A **high-yield bond** with a **credit rating** below **investment grade** at issue which has become popular as means of financing corporate **takeovers** and **management buy-outs**. In theory, it differs from the **fallen angel bond** in that the issuer was below investment grade at the time of issue (hence the idea of a *junk bond credit*). The term has come to mean all **speculative grade** bonds whether they were speculative or not at issue. The junk bond market was popularized by Drexel Burnham Lambert and Michael Milken in the USA in the 1970s, although many other securities firms have become active in the market. Milken found when looking at the experience of the fallen angel bond market that the risk (and **liquidity**) spread such issues commanded over investment grade bonds of a similar class were higher than the historical **default** record. Building on this finding, Drexels was able to build up large-scale distribution in such securities to yield-hungry investors. Many innovations have been tried out in an attempt to increase **marketability**, including **pay-in-kind bonds** and **deep discount** issues as well as **step-up** and **convertibles** (cf. **bells and whistles**). Also sometimes called *speculative grade securities* or *non-investment grade securities*.

junk commercial paper (junk CP). Low credit rating and, consequently, high-yielding issues of commercial paper. See investment grade.

jurisdiction. The country, courts, and legal system which arbitrate in any dispute. Most transactions will seek to predetermine the law and place of settlement in the event of a dispute.

jurisdiction risk. See sovereign risk.

justified price. See fair market value.

K

kabu-ka jun-shisan bairitsu (Japanese). Market to book ratio.

kabu-ka shisū sakimono (Japanese). Stock index futures.

kabu-ka shūeki-ritsu (Japanese). Price–earnings ratio.

kabushiki gaisha (KK or **KG)** (Japan). Limited company.

kaffirs (Equities; UK). Colloquial term used to describe shares in South African gold mines.

kakaku yūsen (Japanese). The price priority system operated on the **Tokyo Stock Exchange**. The rule is that a sell (buy) order at a lower (higher) price takes precedence over one at a higher (lower) price.

kamikaze price or **rate** (Japan). Practice of Japanese banks and stockbrokers offering to undertake transactions at very **fine** rates. *Kamikaze* means 'divine wind'; the term, however, relates to suicide bombers of World War II sacrificing themselves, often to no avail (cf. **hara-kiri swap**).

kangeroo bond (USA). An Australian dollar denominated bond issued in the US domestic market (cf. **foreign bond; yankee bonds**).

Kansas City Board of Trade (KCBT) (US). 4800 Main Street, Suite 303, Kansas City, MO 64112 (tel. 1 816 753 7500/5228; fax 1 816 753 3944). Established in 1856. **Commodity** exchange that specializes in grain **futures** and **options**. Kansas is in the heart of the USA's grain belt, the grain-producing region stretching from the Mississippi to the Rockies. Its principal contracts are based on the **Value Line stock index futures** and wheat futures. See also **Chicaco Board of Trade; Chicago Mercantile Exchange**.

Kapitalanlagegesetz (Germany). The law governing investment in securities and real estate investment. First introduced in 1957, it has seen several revisions and updates.

kappa (κ). **Sensitivity** variable for measuring the price response of an **option** to changes in **volatility**. It is the change in the option price in relation to a (usually 1%) change in **implied volatility** (cf. **tau; vega**).

Karachi Stock Exchange (Pakistan). Stock Exchange Building, Stock Exchange Road, PA-74000 Karachi (tel. 92 242 5502; fax 92 1 2410825).

Kassenobligation. (i) (Germany) Three-to five-year securities issued by the federal government or its agencies. (ii) General term used to describe medium-term issues, typically with two-to six-year maturities.

Kassenverein (Germany). Equivalent institution to the **Depository Trust Company** for the German market. See **Deutscher Kassenverein**.

keepwell. Provision made by a parent of a borrowing subsidiary under which the parent specifies that its subsidiary will meet certain requirements, such as solvency, financial ratios, or other agreed conditions. See **letter of comfort**.

kehai (Japanese). A palpable indication or sign. That is, the best **bid** and **offer** price.

keiretsu (Japan). The system of cross-**shareholdings** within an industrial group involving suppliers and customers, and normally centred around a major bank (city bank) and insurance company, designed to show commitment and good faith. It involves small interlocking shareholdings (typically in the 1–3% range) common between the companies as a goodwill and defensive gesture and used to cement special relationships (cf. **noyaux durs; zaibatsu**). See **cross-holdings**.

kengyō (Japan). Non-core activities of financial service companies.

Kenny index (Money markets; USA). An **index** of tax-exempt **municipal notes** computed on a daily basis.

Keogh plan (USA). A tax-deferring personal pension plan for the self-employed, small, and unincorporated business (cf. **Individual Retirement Account**). Such plans were introduced by the Self-Employed Individuals Retirement Act of 1982.

kerb (Commodities; UK). Trading on the **London Metal Exchange** when **open outcry** transaction takes place in all the metals traded on the exchange at the same time. This contrasts to ring trading, which involves each metal being taken one after the other. The two types of trading follow on one from the other.

kerb market or **kerb trading.** Generally, dealing outside the official opening hours of a market. Sometimes called *after-hours* if undertaken after the official close or *sunshine* trading if prior to the official opening. Strictly speaking, the term only refers to such trading in **commodity** markets. It comes from the fact that originally transactions would take place in the street outside the exchange, literally on the kerb or pavement. The term has been expanded to include any unofficial market activity (cf. **grey market**). For many years the **American Stock Exchange** was known as the 'kerb'.

kickback. A bribe used to ensure the award of a contract; normally alleged in international business dealings especially when government contracts are involved. See **soft dollars**.

kicker. Colloquial market term for a condition attached to a security issue to increase its attractions (cf. **bells and whistles**). It takes the form of the **right** to participate in subsequent **equity** or debt issues, for instance a **bond** with **warrants**. Sometimes also called a *sweetener*.

killer bees. Term for those who assist a **target** company in fending off a **predator** (cf. **concept party**).

killing. A highly profitable transaction (cf. **no brainer**).

kingai (Japan). An **investment trust company**.

kisaikai (Bonds; Japan). Bond issuance committee. It regulates new issue processes in the domestic market.

kisei sōchi (Japanese). **Circuit breakers**.

kite-flying. See red herring.

kiting (USA). A series of illegal or unethical practices that are: (i) making use of the payments system to generate **float** by passing cheques between different banks; (ii) altering a cheque illegally; and (iii) buying and selling securities in such a way as to artificially drive up the price (cf. **manipulation; ramp**).

kiwi bond. A New Zealand dollar denominated eurobond.

Knight Ridder Financial. A financial services quote vendor which provides real-time market price and news information electronically.

knock-in or **knock-out option.** Two types of barrier option which become activated if the underlying moves through a trigger price or rate in the case of the knock-in, or deactivated in the case of the knock-out (cf. **down-and-in option; down-and-out option; up-and-in option; up-and-out option**). Such options have different pricing to straight options since they can become valuable or valueless when there is still some **time value** to the option. See also **exotic options; path-dependent options**.

Kobenhavens Fondsbors (Denmark). See **Copenhagen Stock Exchange**.

Kolb-Chiang price sensitivity hedging model. A model for **hedging interest rate sensitive assets** or **liabilities** using **futures**. It uses the price sensitivity of the **underlying** and the futures to provide an optimal hedge against small changes in interest rates. See **bond risk; duration**.

Kommunalobligationen (Bonds; Austria; Germany). **Bonds** issued by a communality (cf. **Bundesobligationen; Länderanleihen**). See also **Pfandbriefe**.

Kondatrieff cycle or **wave.** A long-term trade or business cycle reputed to capture the most protracted of swings in business activity and sentiment. To this extent, it is likely to subsume several other cycles of a shorter or more volatile nature. See **chartism; technical analysis**.

Konkursordnung (Germany). The law covering insolvency. It stipulates a 'cooling off' period during which creditors are enjoined to seek a solution that preserves the enterprise. See **Chapter 11**.

Kontokorrent (Banking; German). Overdraft.

Korea Stock Exchange (KSE) (Korea). 33 Yoido-Dong, Youngdeungpo-ku, KR-seoul 150–010 (tel. 82 2 780 2271; fax 82 2 786 0263). Based in Seoul, a securities exchange originally established in 1911, its current form derives from 1956 and is modelled on US practice. Korea is one of the **dragon countries**, and an attractive **emerging market**.

Kreditanstalt für Wiederaufbau (KfW). Official German development agency. It is owned by the federal and state governments, but borrows its funds from the capital markets.

Krugerrand (South Africa). A one troy ounce gold coin from the Republic of South Africa. One of a number of gold coins which are available to be bought by individuals and actively traded on the **London bullion market**.

Kuala Lumpur Commodity Exchange (KLCE) (Malaysia). **Commodity exchange** specializing in palm oil and rubber, both important products grown in Malaysia (cf. loco).

Kuala Lumpur Options and Financial Futures Exchange (KLOFFE) (Malaysia). 20th Floor, Pernas International, Jalan Sultan Ismail, 50250 Kuala Lumpur (tel. 60 (0) 3 244 6423; fax 60 (0) 3 241 0857).

Kuala Lumpur Stock Exchange (Malaysia). 3rd and 4th Floor, Exchange Square, Off Jalan Semantan, Damansara Heights, MY-50490 Kuala Lumpar (tel. 60 3 2546433; fax 60 3 2557463).

Kurs-Informations-Service-System   (KISS) (Germany). Real-time price information system provided by the **Deutsche Börse**. It can be run off a personal computer (pcKISS) and integrated with the **Börsen-Order-Service-System** for quick execution. The price feed is derived from the consolidated reporting service from all of the German exchanges, known as the **Ticker Plant Frankfurt** (cf. **tape**).

Kursmakler (German). A **specialist** on an exchange.

Kurspflege (Germany). The **Bundesbank's** stabilization of new issues. It aimed at achieving an orderly distribution of new government debt issues and involved the bank allocating control numbers to the securities so as to ensure that the **bonds** were securely placed.

kurtosis. A measure of the shape of a distribution in relation to normal. A *platykurtic* distribution has more observations in the mid-range, with fewer at the mean and the tails; a *leptokurtic* distribution has more observations at the mean and in the tails. The latter is the more commonly observed in financial markets. It has been suggested that the explanation is due to changes in the **variance** of the observed distributions over time and that the mechanism generating the observed dispersion of prices, price changes, or rates is the result of two different processes (cf. **jump diffusion process**; **jump process**). Statisticians measure the extent of deviations by a *kurtosis coefficient* or statistic:

$$Kurtosis = \left[\left(\frac{n(n+1)}{(n-1)(n-2)(n-3)} \right) \sum_{i=1}^{n} \left(\frac{x_i - \mu}{\sigma} \right)^4 \right] - \left(\frac{3(n-1)^2}{(n-2)(n-3)} \right)$$

where σ is the standard deviation; n the number of observations; x_i the value of the ith observation; μ the mean of the total set of observations.

Kuwait interbank offered rate (KIBOR). The rate prime banks lend to each other in the Kuwait interbank market (usually US dollars, to which the Kuwaiti dinar has a fixed link).

Kuwait Stock Exchange (Kuwait). PO Box 22235, KW-Safat, Kuwait 13083 (tel. 965 24 23 130/9; tlx 44015 BORSE).

L

ladder. See **maturity ladder** (cf. **cash buckets**; **gap**).

laddering. A **portfolio** strategy based on **fixed interest** securities under which equal amounts of a broad range of maturities are held.

ladder option. **Exotic option** which provides the holder with guaranteed payouts if the **underlying** trades through a pre-agreed price or rate at a certain point in time, regardless of future performance. If for instance, such an option has a threshold on an index at 3,000, then the holder is guaranteed a minimum payout at that price, even if the option should ultimately expire **out of the money**. Such an option may have more than one threshold level. Such options have been used for **equity-linked notes** to make them more attractive to investors. A ladder option is also called a *cliquet option*, *lock-step option*, or a *step-lock option*. See also **path-dependent option**.

ladder spread. An **option** strategy which involves financing the purchase of a position by selling two **out-of-the-money** options at different strike prices (cf. **seagull**). It can be set up with both calls and puts, depending on the directional view

(a) Payoff of a call ladder spread at expiry

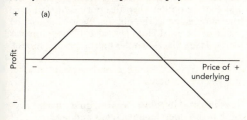

(b) Payoff of a put ladder spread at expiry

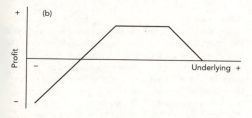

Ladder spread

on the **underlying**. The purchased call (put) at the initial strike is matched to the written second call (put) option at a higher (lower) strike and the third written call (put) option at an even higher (lower) strike.

Lady Macbeth. Ploy used in the **mergers and acquisitions** market where a third party joins in a contested **takeover** appearing at first to be a suitable **white knight** but then sides with the **predator** (cf. **black knight**).

lagging. A tactic in international trade used when a debtor expects the relative value of the **currency** in which the debt is expressed to fall, or when the value of the relative value of the currency to be offered in exchange for the **settlement** currency is expected to rise, thereby making it cheaper to finance the debt than would otherwise be the case. The opposite strategy of accelerating the payments flow is called *leading*. See **foreign exchange hedging techniques**; **leads and lags**.

lagging indicator. See **economic indicators**.

lambda (Λ). (i) A measure of the sensitivity of **option** value when the **underlying** instruments are interest rate sensitive, e.g. **bonds**. The greater option is **in the money**, the nearer lambda moves to unity. See **option pricing**. (ii) Also used for the elasticity of the option price in respect to the underlying.

Länderanleihen (Germany). **Bonds** issued by the various states (Länder) of the Federal Republic (cf. **Bundesobligationen**). See also **Kommunalobligationen**.

Ländesbanken (Banking; Germany). The name given to the twelve **central banks** of the savings banks.

Ländeszentralbank (Banking; Germany). The state central banks that go to make up the **Bundesbank**. Each *Länder* or state has a seat on the Bundesbank's policy-making board.

lapsed option. An option which has reached its **expiry date** without **exercise**, presumably due to being **out of the money** or not activated or having become deactivated (cf. **cabinet trade**; **knock-in option**).

large quote size (LQS) (UK). On the London stock market, the biggest quantity of securities at which at least one **market-maker** is prepared to offer **two-way prices** (cf. **lot**).

last day to register. The last day by which title to securities must be lodged with a **registrar** to qualify for interest, **dividends**, and **rights**. See **cum**.

last notice day. See **declaration date**.

last sale or **last trade.** The most recent transaction in a particular security. Many exchanges operate rules concerning the type of transactions that can be executed which depend on the nature of the last trade. For instance, in the USA, the **Securities and Exchange Commission** stipulate that no **short selling** can take place if the last trade was below the penultimate trade or if the two were the same and the trade before that was above the last two. Such rules are designed to maintain an orderly market and ensure fair market dealing. In connection with the last trade, traders use: *plus tick* (the last trade was *above* the penultimate one); *down (minus) tick* (the last trade was *below* the penultimate one); *zero plus tick* (the last trade was *the same* as the penultimate one, which was itself *above* the one before that); and *zero minus tick* (the last trade was the same as the penultimate one, which was itself below the one before that).

last sale reporting (USA). A stipulation by the National Association of Securities Dealers Automated Quotations that notification of the price and quantity of **shares** traded by a reporting **market-maker** be made within ninety seconds of the transaction taking place.

last trading day. The last day for a **futures** contract to be traded in a particular **delivery month** and in which market participants can **close out** their **positions** by offsetting transactions rather than accepting or making **delivery**, except for those contracts which are **cash settled** (cf. **expiry**). If a contract is still extant after the close of trading, then **physical delivery** is required (cf. **alternative delivery procedure; cheapest to deliver; exchange delivery settlement price**). Note that this does not apply to the cash-settled futures since a cash sum is used to settle up expiring contracts.

latent option. See **embedded option**.

lateral integration. See **horizontal merger**.

latest investment vehicle for ex-warrant swaps (LIVES) (Bonds). An **asset-backed synthetic** security note issue based on repackaging holdings of **ex-warrant** fixed rate bond issues by Japanese corporations and attaching an **interest rate swap** to provide holders of the note with a **floating rate**

coupon. Although the **underlying** corporate bonds were trading at a significant **discount**, buyers of the LIVES notes purchased these at **par**, the differential going to subsidize the **fixed rate** leg of the swap, in order that the notes would pay an on-market rate of interest. Because these repackaged securities were floating rate assets, they were attractive investments for (particularly Japanese) banks.

late tape (USA). Delays in reporting transactions due to heavy trading (cf. **digits deleted; flash**). See **tape**.

Latin American fund. A **closed-end** or **open-ended** fund specializing in investments, usually equity, in the Latin American region (usually taken to mean: Mexico, Central, and South America) (cf. **emerging markets**).

launch date. A **eurobond** term for the day that an **underwriter** is invited to participate in a new issue of securities by either verbal and/or written notification (cf. **closing date**). Often at this stage, the underwriters will not have received a **prospectus** and the **offering telex** (or fax) will contain the essential details of the transaction. The prospectus will normally be available some time after the initial launch.

laundering. See **money laundering**.

law of one price. Principle in economics that two assets which have the same payoffs will have the same value. The law of one price is one of the underlying principles that allowed the development of **option pricing models**. If a **portfolio** can be constructed which replicates exactly the value of an option, then this portfolio must have the same value as the option. By solving for the value of the portfolio, a *fair value* of an option was derived. See **Black–Scholes option pricing model**.

leader. A stock which is indicative of market activity (cf. **barometer**).

leading and lagging. See foreign exchange hedging techniques; lagging; leads and lags.

leading indicator. See economic indicators.

lead manager. The main organizer of a new issue, such as a bank or **broker**, responsible for the overall coordination, distribution, and documents associated with the transaction. Also likely to have the right to appoint **co-managers**, determine initial and final terms of the issue, and select the **underwriters** and the **selling group** (cf. **special bracket underwriter**). In international issues, the title may be prefixed to indicate a geographical responsibility (cf. **global offering**). Sometimes called a *sponsor* or *bookrunner* or if a bank: *lead bank*.

leads and lags. A strategy for the payment and receipt of **foreign exchange**. If it is expected that a currency is going to **weaken**, then payments should be delayed and receipts speeded up. If it is expected that a currency is about to **strengthen**, then receipts should be delayed and payments speeded up. This strategy is intended to maximize the gains or minimize the losses associated with exchanging currencies. See **foreign exchange hedging techniques** for details.

leakage. (i) The prior distribution of information to selected parties prior to it being made generally public (cf. **insider information**). (ii) In the context of asset valuation, any intervening flows, such as **dividends** or interest, that will not accrue to the buyer. Thus in the context of **option pricing**, a dividend paying **stock** will exhibit leakage since, in the normal course of events, the call owner will not receive the dividend, unless the holder can exercise prior to the dividend being paid; and a put writer will only receive the asset once the income is received by the put holder. The opposite condition is known as *zero leakage*.

lean back. Approach to controlling or regulating markets that seeks to delay intervention in the hope that self-regulating behaviour will obviate the necessity for action.

lease. A contractual arrangement by which a lessee has the use of an asset belonging to the lessor in exchange for a series of payments, ranging from an arrangement which is basically rental to a form of hire purchase. There are different types of lease, depending on the needs of the *lessor* (the provider of the asset and grantor of the lease) and the *lessee* (the user of the asset):

- *capital lease*: type of lease which gives the lessor effective ownership of the leased asset and must, therefore, be included on the balance sheet;
- *financial lease*: type of lease contract where the total amount of the payments made by the user of the asset, the lessee, to the owners of the asset, the lessor, covers the initial purchase price of the asset;
- *operating lease*: type of lease contract where the total amount of the payments made by the lessee (the user) to the lessor (the leasing company and owner of the asset) do not cover the initial purchase price of the asset;
- *lease-purchase*: type of lease which allows the lessee to credit payments made under the lease agreement towards the purchase of the asset;

- *sale and leaseback*: transaction where a company simultaneously sells an asset and enters into a lease on the asset.

One of the main functions of a lease is to allow the transfer of the tax benefits of investments between the parties. The process is known as *leasing*.

leaseback. See sale and leaseback.

lease obligation bond (LOB) (Bonds; USA). A **municipal bond** issue used to fund the acquisition of an asset for a municipality where the security is a lease.

lease-purchase agreement. A type of **lease** which allows the lessee to credit payments made under the lease agreement towards the purchase of the asset.

leasing. Either the business of acquiring assets via a **lease**, or the provision of leased assets. The former is a way of borrowing, the latter lending.

least squares regression. A specific method by which the average relationship between two or more variables is quantified (cf. **cointegration**). For example, banks would like to be able to quantify the relationship between individual household disposable income, (Y), and demand for mortgage loans, (L). Intuitively, it might be expected that Y and L would be closely related, and banks would be interested in making quantitative predictions of the consequences of certain changes in Y. Regression analysis begins by measuring, at successive points in time (normally annually), the observed values of L and Y. The following linear hypothesis that $L = \alpha + \beta Y$ is made; that is, household demand for mortgages depends linearly on income. The fundamental questions for regression analysis are: how to find the 'best' values for α and β and then how to decide whether to believe that the relationship holds, using **statistical inference**. If the pairs of L and Y values observed over time were plotted a type of 'scatter diagram' might emerge:

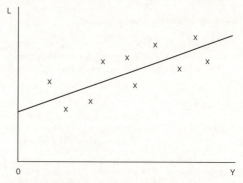

least squares regression: Scatter diagram (1)

If all the data lay along a straight line, regression analysis would be redundant. Given that this will rarely happen, the data can be rationalized by the argument. Although the true underlying relationship is captured by $L = \alpha + \beta Y$, there is a 'random error term', normally denoted by ε, which influences the actual observe value of L, in an unsystematic way, from period to period. Therefore, the actual L, denoted L', is determined by the relationship: $L' = \alpha + \beta Y + \varepsilon$, and hence what must be found is α and β; that is, fit a line to the scatter of points in the above diagram in the best possible way. Least squares is a method for achieving this line of best fit. Any line drawn through the scatter of points implies a particular average relationship between L and Y, and also implies a particular set of differences between L', the actual demand for mortgages, and L, the demand predicted by the fitted line. These differences, $L' - L$, are estimates of ε, the error terms. This can be illustrated by using the second diagram. The least squares approach suggests that the best line to draw is the one that makes the sum of the squares of the differences between L' and L as small as possible. That is, involving the 'least sum of squares'. From all the possible lines that could be drawn, only one has this property, and standard procedures exist for discovering which it is, and which values of α and β are thereby implied.

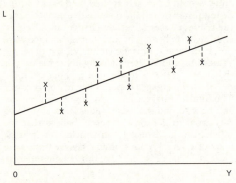

Least squares regression: Diagram (2)

left-hand side (LHS). (i) (Forex) The bid rate at which banks will **offer** or sell a quoted currency or **bid** or buy the **base currency** (cf. **right-hand side**).

For **American terms**, a quote of 1.7070/80 for the US dollar against the Deutschmark (DM/$) would mean it bought the base currency at 1.7070 and sold the base currency at 1.7080. See also **foreign exchange**. (ii) The **assets** side of a **balance sheet**.

leg. (i) One part of a complex transaction or **position**. These may have several 'legs'. For instance, a **straddle** involves two legs each consisting of one **option**. **Closing out** one leg of a position is known as *lifting a leg*. When the transaction does not work, the holder *gets legged* by the position. See also **leg in**, **leg out**. (ii) A leg is also used to describe a trend in prices. Thus one may talk of the *bull leg of a market*.

legal capital. The value of a company's **shares** as recorded on its **balance sheet**.

legal defeasance (USA). A **defeasance** operation where the issuer of a security deposits sufficient cash and securities in an irrevocable trust to fully discharge the debt thus allowing the issuer to strike the item from its accounts (cf. **in-substance defeasance**). By doing so, the issuer has discharged all legal claims on the borrowing. See **asset-backed**; **securitization**.

legal list (USA). See **prudent-man rule** (cf. **investment grade**).

legal reserve (UK). Minimum levels of **liquidity** required to be held by mutual societies (cf. **capital adequacy**).

legal right of set-off (USA). The right under the revised US Bankruptcy Code for parties to net their respective positions (cf. **cherry picking**). See **netting**.

legal risk. The uncertainty over the validity of a given contract or part thereof. It can also include the problems of enforcement and the **risk** attached in going to court. Generally, it can be taken as the risk that a transaction will fall foul of the law. There are two components: (i) that a particular transaction or set of transactions may be declared illegal in court. That is the counterparty did not have the right or capacity (**ultra vires**) to undertake the transaction (cf. **Hammersmith and Fulham swaps**); (ii) the regulatory or legislative risk

Left-hand side

Quotation	Quotation	Bid rate for base currency/offer rate for quoted currency (LHS)	Offer rate for base currency/bid rate for quoted currency (RHS)
American terms	DM/$ 1.7070/80	Buys $; sells DM	Sells $; buys DM
European terms	$/£ 1.5050/60	Buys £; sells $	Sells £; buys $
Cross-rate	DM/£ 2.5220/30	Buys £; sells DM	Sells £; buys DM

that transactions may be deemed unlawful either by regulators or by the courts (cf. **no-action letter**; **safe harbour**).

legal tender. The means of payment for debts which must be accepted by law. In contracts, the question of legal tender can, potentially, become a tendentious issue. For example, if a contract is entered into under US law, it may mean that although the parties may have agreed for payments to be made in Deutschmarks, the court will only enforce payment in the legal tender of the court's jurisdiction, namely US dollars (cf. **judgement currency clause**).

leg in, leg out. To execute one side or **leg** of a complex transaction or **position** at a different point in time (cf. **close out**). Legging-in involves setting up the position; legging-out, unwinding the position.

Lehman investment opportunity notes (LIONS) (Bonds; USA). A negotiable receipt security issued by Shearson Lehman where the underlying are stripped US treasury bond coupons and principal. See **separate trading of registered interest and principal of securities**.

lemon. Slang term for a bad deal (cf. **dog**; **plum**). See **blowout**.

lend or **lending.** (i) To provide money on the understanding, often backed up by a written agreement or contract, that it will be both repaid and that interest will be paid by the borrower (cf. **documentation**). (ii) (Securities) Process by which holders of securities make them available for a fee to market participants who need to provide **certificates** for **settlement** purposes. Taking up a **short position** in securities will require the seller to borrow the securities to make **delivery** (cf. **against the box**). For the lenders it provides an additional return on their **portfolio** since they retain title and all income from the securities. In many cases, the **clearing house** will act as a conduit for such activity. It is also called *securities lending*. The alternative for a short-seller would be to enter into a **repurchase agreement** (cf. **overnight repurchase agreement**; **term repurchase agreement**).

lender liability (Banking; USA). A **risk** that if a lender provides funds to a borrower who then causes pollution, the lender may have a financial liability towards any clean-up if they foreclose and take title.

lender-of-last-resort. A lender, almost always a **central bank**, which provides a class of financial institutions with **funds** when they cannot otherwise obtain them. Central banks perform this function in order to maintain the integrity of the financial system (cf. **systemic risk**). They use their lending rate as a lever to alter the market interest rate or **money supply** (cf. **discount window**; **liquidity**; **squeeze**; **open-market operations**). Such lending is designed to address problems of liquidity and not to act as an automatic bail-out mechanism for institutions (cf. **moral hazard**; **too big to fail**).

lender option. (i) Minimum interest rate on a **floating rate note**. (ii) An **interest rate floor** on a **forward rate agreement**.

lender's option, borrower's option (LOBO) (UK). An issue that provides the holder with the right to choose a new **coupon** rate at any time. The borrower may then decide whether to pay the new rate or redeem the issue (cf. **borrower's option, lender's option**). See **extendible bond**.

lending. (i) (Banking) The process of providing a loan facility to borrowers. Hence a *lending institution*. (ii) (Commodities, UK) The sale or **short position** in a near-dated **futures contract** and a long position in a later-dated futures contract on the London Metal Exchange (cf. **borrowing**; **calendar spread**).

lending culture. See **credit culture**.

lending margin. The difference between the cost of borrowed funds and the rate at which it can be relent (cf. **margin**; **spread**). See **London interbank offered rate**.

lending multiple. The number of times a deposit-taker, such as a bank, can create assets (loans) on the basis of the size of its **liabilities** (**deposits**). The process of credit creation depends upon the rate of interest to depositors being adequate to retain funds in the deposit-taking institution, and borrowers being credit worthy and prepared to offer collateral. The limits to creating advances are influenced by the proportion of deposits that are likely to be 'called' (withdrawn), and the risk–asset ratio specified by the regulatory authority. See **capital adequacy**; **reserve requirements**.

lending securities. A way of obtaining securities on loan to cover a **short position**. Many institutions habitually lend **stock** or **bonds** to **market-makers** or **short sellers** (cf. **against the box**). The lenders are paid a fee for providing the security. The legal position of security lenders is generally different from that arising under a **repurchase agreement** in most countries. Also known as *securities lending*.

leptokurtic, leptokurtosis and **leptokurticity.** Condition of a distribution which has more observations at the mean and in the tails than would be expected (cf. **platykurtic**). It has been suggested the explanation for this effect is due to changes in the **variance** of the distributions over time and/or that the mechanism generating the observed dispersion of prices, price changes, or rates is the result of two different processes. See also **jump diffusion process; jump process; kurtosis**.

less developed countries (LDC). Those countries which are seen as progressing towards but not yet having achieved a high level of development. Not to be confused with the Third World.

less developed countries debt market (LDC debt market). A secondary debt market involving the trading of sovereign debt as between the major lending banks. Recognizing that large parts of such debts will not be readily cleared from their books, banks have sought new ways of liquefying their positions by swapping and selling debts between one another. Loans are traded via **assignment** or **sub-participation**. There is an active secondary market involving **dealers**, traders, **brokers** as **market-makers**, and intermediaries and end-buyers (cf. **debt-for-equity swap**). See **asset sales; bazaar; Brady bonds; buy-back; Mex-Ex issue**.

Less Developed Country Debt Traders' Association. Set up in 1990, this association, which comprises banks and securities firms, aims to promote and improve the secondary market in less developed countries debt market.

less developed country index future (LDCx future). Futures contract traded on the OM London exchange where the **underlying** is an index based on a basket of ten debt issues from less developed countries.

less developed country index option (LDCx option). Option contract traded on the OM London exchange where the **underlying** is an index based on a basket of ten debt issues from less developed countries.

lessee. The user of an asset under a lease. The lessee is contractually bound to make periodic payments to the **lessor** in exchange for the use of the asset (cf. **full service lease**).

lessor. The provider of an asset under a lease.

letras del tesoro (Spanish). Treasury bills.

letter bond or **letter stock** (USA). A private placement of **bonds** or **common stock**. It derives its name from the **investment letter** that the buyer needs to provide to comply with **Securities and Exchange Commission** regulations stating that the **stock** is not intended for resale. Also called *lettered stock*.

letter of allotment. See **allotment**.

letter of awareness. A type of **letter of comfort** from the parent which acknowledges the existence of the transaction.

letter of confirmation. A document which provides evidence of the transfer of ownership and all rights associated with title to a security.

letter of comfort. A document that provides one party's intention to try and ensure that another party complies with the terms of a financial transaction without guaranteeing performance in the event of default (cf. **keepwell**). Also sometimes referred to as a *comfort letter*.

letter of credit (LOC) (Banking). An undertaking by a bank to guarantee payments to the beneficiary, upon fulfilment of stipulated requirements (cf. **guarantee**). The different types are given below:

- *confirmed LOC*: payment is guaranteed by the **correspondent bank**;
- *irrevocable LOC*: cannot be cancelled by the issuing bank or the party which opened it;
- *revocable LOC*: can be cancelled or revoked by the issuing bank of the party which opened it;
- *revolving LOC*: a facility allowing the user to make multiple use of letters of credit;
- *performance LOC*: guarantees the performance of a contract;
- *unconfirmed LOC*: payment is not guaranteed by the correspondent bank.

See also **banker's acceptance; bill of exchange; documentary credit**.

letter of credit backed (LOC backed) (Money markets; Bonds). A guaranteed **commercial paper** or **floating rate note** issue for both interest and **principal**. In the event of **default**, holders have the right of **recourse** to the provider of the LOC for principal and interest.

letter of credit line of credit (LOC line of credit). A borrowing facility using letters of credit as collateral for the loan.

letter of indemnity. (i) A written promise to make good losses or compensate for any damages when an **agent** carries out an act on behalf of a **principal** (cf. **indemnity; waiver**). (ii) A non-legally binding undertaking by one firm that it will make good any faults in what has been supplied. Usually used in export finance to cover faulty packing and loading to achieve a 'clean' **bill of lading**.

letter of intent. A non-legally binding indication by one firm to another of an intention to form a relationship, enter a proposed transaction, or purchase an **asset**, security, business, or company subject to certain conditions being satisfied. Such a letter is not a contract and it may specify prior conditions before the writer agrees to enter into the contract. Its main aim is to assure the recipient of the seriousness of their purpose. See **due diligence**.

letter of licence. See **arrangement**.

letter of moral intent (LOMI) (USA). American term for a **letter of comfort**.

letter of renunciation. See **renounceable documents; renunciation**.

level. A price or yield given by traders for indicative purposes only (cf. **firm quote**). See **indication**.

level payment swap. Interest rate swap used to hedge the cash flows from an **amortizing** instrument, where the **fixed rate leg** matches the payment flows from the instrument. See **annuity**.

level price or **level yield.** A condition where no price or yield **spread** exists between different maturities or market instruments (cf. **flat**). See **backwardation; contango; yield curve**.

leverage or **leveraged.** (i) (USA) The US term for **gearing** or the debt–equity ratio. Also gives rise to the phrase *leveraged buyout* or *takeover* where such transactions are financed mainly or exclusively on the basis of debt (cf. **financial leverage; highly leveraged transaction; operating leverage**). See **ratio analysis** for definition. (ii) Sometimes used to describe a portfolio's exposure to **market risk** (cf. **capital gearing; systematic risk**). (iii) In **margin** purchases and **derivatives**, the **ratio** of the amount of **principal** required to the amount of exposure to the **underlying**. (iv) Any transaction involving **derivatives** where the payoff is greater than the amount of **principal** involved. **forwards, futures**, and **options** all share this characteristic, as do **swaps** to a lesser extent. It can also apply to securities which have **embedded options** or swaps. Sometimes also called *elasticity*. (v) Colloquially used for a transaction allowing the opportunity for large gains at little cost.

leverage capital ratio (Banking). The ratio of tier 1 (**core capital**) to average total-**assets** (cf. **tier 2**). See **Basle Capital Convergence Accord; Cooke ratio**.

leveraged buy-out (LBO) (Mergers and acquisitions). A method of acquiring control of a company where **equity** is largely replaced by various forms of debt. The **buy-out** is normally undertaken by an investment fund or bank which, upon gaining ownership, converts it into an unquoted, private company. The purchaser holds the **equity** and funds the firm's operations using its **debt capacity**. The key difference between an LBO and a normal **takeover** is the degree of **leverage** employed, which is much higher (over 90% in some cases) than that normally found in most **quoted** firms (cf. **gearing**). The rationale is that the **target** firm can be made more efficient through the disciplines imposed by debt and that the acquiring firm can make better use of the cash flow by using the benefits of debt finance, paid out of pre-tax cash flow to fund the firm's operations (cf. **tax shield**). Companies possessing steady cash flows (often linked to mature products) and readily disposable assets are usually considered prime candidates for an LBO (cf. **cash cow**). Following restructuring, the company is subsequently sold or refloated on a stock market (typical **investment horizons** are three to five years), with the expectation of a significant **capital gain** for the fund or bank (cf. **highly leveraged transaction**).

leveraged capped floating rate note (leveraged capped FRN). Floating rate note where the **coupon** is based on a complex formula designed to give a **leveraged** exposure to short-term interest rates as well as a maximum, or capped interest rate (cf. **cap; interest rate cap**). For instance, such an instrument might have a structure offering a coupon with a minimum of the London interbank offered rate (LIBOR) plus 0.50%, or 22% less twice the LIBOR rate. Under such a structure, the holder could, in certain circumstances receive nothing on the coupon payment if 22% minus twice LIBOR exceeded the minimum LIBOR plus 0.50%.

leveraged corporation. A firm which has debt liabilities. The term is loosely applied to firms which have a high **financial leverage**. Sometimes also known as *geared* or *highly geared firms*. See also **highly leveraged transaction; leveraged buy-out**.

leveraged differential floating rate note (leveraged diff FRN). **Leveraged** structure incorporated into a **floating rate note** incorporating a series of **differential swaps** designed to offer a high **coupon** over a given range. For instance, the **coupon rate** might be calculated according to:

$$\{[(6 \text{ month US\$ LIBOR}) - (6 \text{ month Swiss franc LIBOR})] \times 3\} - 0.325\%$$

Thus if the six-month US dollar **London interbank offered rate** (LIBOR) was 5.5% and the Swiss franc rate 3.2%, the payment would be 6.575%. Under such a structure, in some circumstances the coupon could be zero.

leveraged income obligations via new shares (LIONS) (Netherlands). **Zero-coupon bond** traded on the **Amsterdam Stock Exchange** where the repayment is made in **shares** (cf. **zero-coupon convertible**).

leveraged investment company (USA). A type of **split-level fund** with **capital** and **income shares**. The term is also used for a **fund** which has borrowed against its **assets** to increase the returns to **shareholders**. Sometimes called a *leveraged mutual fund*.

leveraged lease, leverage lease, or **levered lease** (USA). A **lease** contract where the **lessor**, the writer of the lease, invests only part of the cost of the **asset** that is being leased to the **lessee**. The balance of the **finance** is borrowed from another source.

leveraged program (USA). A **limited partnership** where debt is more than half of the **finance** raised. Such a **partnership** will be higher **risk** and provide less income to participants since a larger proportion of the cash flow will be used to service the debt. Such a structure would be attractive to participants who are seeking **tax shelters**.

leveraged reverse floating rate note (leveraged reverse FRN). Type of reverse floating rate note where the **fixed rate** is more than twice the market rate at time of issue. This gives the fixed rate **leverage factor**, which is then used to compute the **floating rate**, which is multiplied by the factor minus one (cf. **reference rate**). The structure means the **coupon** on such a note will adjust by more than the change in the floating rate at each reset date, hence the leverage effect.

leveraged securities. Securities purchased on **margin**. It is sometimes applied to **partly paid** instruments.

leveraged swap. Any of a number of different **interest rate swap** (IRS), **basis swap**, or **differential swap** combinations where the payments are levered off the **notional principal** amount. A typical leveraged IRS transaction might involve a floating rate payment by one **counterparty** consisting of a fixed rate (say 20%) and a payment of **London interbank offered rate** (LIBOR) plus 0.50% (50 **basis points**) against receipt of three times the current LIBOR:

Party A pays: Party A receives:
20% + *LIBOR* + 0.50%   3 × *LIBOR*

The well-publicized leveraged swap entered into between Bankers Trust and Procter & Gamble involved a **fixed rate** payment by the bank against a below-market floating rate payment by the company, plus the payment of an additional sum based

on the relationship between the short end and long ends of the US Treasury **yield curve** times a factor (cf. **spread**). If rates remained at or below the values when the swap was entered into, the company made large savings on its interest payments; if the rate rose significantly, the company stood to pay significantly more in interest than the change in interest rates. Also called a *geared swap*.

leverage factor. Price change of an **option** or other **derivative** as a result of a change in the value of the **underlying**. It is equal to:

$$\text{Leverage factor} = \frac{\text{Option delta}(\delta) \times \text{price of underlying}}{\text{Option rate}}$$

The result can be expressed either in per cent or as a multiple. See also **lambda**.

liability. (i) A **payable**. (ii) A generic term for debt. (iii) The right-hand side of a **balance sheet** showing how the entity is funded. (iv) A commitment, as in **unlimited liability**. (v) (Forex) The obligation to deliver a stated amount of a currency to a **counterparty** (cf. **offered price; bid price; overbought; oversold**).

liability management. Any purposeful acts aimed at controlling the effects of **liabilities** on an organization. In most cases, liability management has three purposes: (1) to control the amount of **risk** being taken by the organization; (2) to minimize funding costs; and (3) to ensure sufficient **liquidity** (cf. **contingent liability; current liabilities**). It is often integrated with asset management. See **asset-liability management; assets repriced before liabilities; liquidity risk management**.

liability manager. Generic term for those responsible for managing liabilities (cf. **asset manager; fund manager**).

liability sensitive or **liability sensitive gap.** See **asset sensitive**.

liability swap. A swap that is used to **hedge** liabilities (cf. **asset swap; cross-currency swap; interest rate swap**). See also **risk management**.

liberalization. The trend towards deregulation of the world's money and capital markets. See **deregulation; globalization; reregulation; securitization**.

LIBOR differential swap. See differential swap.

LIBOR eurodollar spread (LED). See spread.

LIBOR in advance swap. Interest rate swap where the **London interbank offered rate** (LIBOR) used as the **reference rate** on the **floating**

rate side of the swap is set one period in advance (except for the first period, where the LIBOR is set conventionally at the start of the period. Thus the three first periods on such a swap would be: for the first period $(0 - T_1)$; second period $(0 - T_1)$ again; and the third period $(T_1 - T_2)$. It is the opposite structure to the **delayed LIBOR reset swap**. Usually the **fixed rate payer** is committed to a lower interest rate in compensation.

LIBOR in arrears swap. Another term for a delayed LIBOR reset swap.

LIBOR function swap. See leveraged swap.

licensed dealer (UK). Dealer who is authorized under the **Financial Services Act, 1986** to undertake securities transactions and give investment advice. Depending on the type of licence, an *execution only dealer* will only carry out transactions for a client and not offer any other advisory services. A *licensed dealer and investment adviser* will offer such ancilliary services. See **Securities and Investments Board**.

licensed deposit taker (Banking; UK). Between 1979 and 1987, financial institutions in the UK which solicited deposits were divided into three categories by the Banking Act, 1979: exempt institutions, institutions which could call themselves banks, and those which were termed 'licensed deposit takers'. This latter group were perceived as having a lower status than the other two categories, even though they could use the title 'bank' in their name. A deposit-taking institution which fell into this category could therefore style itself for trading purposes as 'XYZ Bank plc—Licenced Deposit Taker', the licensed deposit taker being a requirement in the title under the act. Those categorized as banks simply used the title as part of their trading name. The Banking Act, 1987, abolished the distinction between bank and licensed deposit taker.

liée (French). Swap.

lien. A legally enforceable interest in one or more assets given to a lender or creditor (cf. **asset-backed; debenture; hypothecation; mortgage-backed**). It provides the creditor with right of possession over assets belonging to the borrower in the event of **default**.

life. The time between the issue and redemption or expiry of a security (cf. **average life**). Sometimes used interchangeably with **maturity** or **tenor** (cf. **original maturity; current maturity**). Thus *remaining life* is the time from the present to maturity or redemption.

Life Assurance and Unit Trust Regulatory Organization (LAUTRO) (UK). A self-regulating organization responsible for the conduct of practitioners in the life assurance and **unit trust** industries, and accountable for ensuring adherence to its rule book to the **Securities and Investments Board**. Now part of the **Personal Investment Authority**.

lifeboat. (i) (UK) Term for the **Bank of England's** rescue of the secondary banking sector in the 1979 crisis. (ii) Any rescue operation designed to keep a company afloat. (iii) Colloquial name for an investor compensation fund, as operated by most organized exchanges or by regulation (cf. **deposit insurance**).

life of contract. The time period from the start of trading in a particular **futures contract** and its **expiry**. This used to be less than a year, but for some of the more **liquid** contracts, this can now extend up to three years in some cases.

life-to-call. The time period remaining before a **call provision** comes into force (cf. **call protection**).

life-to-put. The time period remaining before a **put provision** comes into force (cf. **call protection**).

lift. (i) To buy a security at a given price (cf. **hit**). Used by market participants to imply a favourable (or unfavourable) transaction as in 'I lifted him at 95.25 when the market was offering 95.32'. (ii) Also used to describe a rise in a market as a result of favourable news. Also called an *uplift*.

lift a leg or **lifting a leg.** An arbitrage or **spread** strategy where part of the transaction (a leg) is **closed out** or cancelled while leaving the other part(s) open. Thus a **long** (**short**) **position** would be the result. Sometimes called *taking off a leg*. See also **leg**.

limit. (i) (Derivatives) In **exchange-traded derivatives** markets, the maximum daily price movement above or below the previous day's **settlement** price allowed on an exchange before trading is stopped for the day or until the price moves back within the permitted range (cf. **limit up/down**). (ii) Used to describe the maximum exposure, or limit, that one party will take on another (cf. **daylight exposure limit**). (iii) A type of order known as a **limit order**. (iv) A restriction imposed by some **derivatives exchanges** on the number of **options** that may be exercised by one party within a given period. (v) A restriction imposed by some **commodities** exchanges on the overall **exposure** or **position** allowed in a particular contract either by size or amount. See **position limit**. (vi) A control placed on a particular risk or exposure by a firm. Hence an *exposure limit*. (vii) A restriction on the freedom of action placed in a contract (cf. **convenant**).

limitation on asset disposal. A covenant that restricts a borrower's ability to sell assets (cf. **negative covenants**).

limitation on consolidation, merger, or **sale.** A **covenant** that restricts a borrower's ability to merge, take over, or in some way consolidate with another firm. The **risk** is that such transactions may lead to a loss of **credit worthiness** of the combined borrower (cf. **negative covenants; event risk**).

limitation on liens. A covenant that restricts a borrower's ability to grant **liens** (cf. **negative covenants**). Such liens would reduce the lender's security.

limitation on sale and leaseback. A covenant that restricts a borrower's ability to enter into **sale-and-leaseback** operations. Such operations would reduce the asset base of the firm and the lender's security or lien (cf. **negative covenants**).

limitation on subsidiary borrowing. A covenant that restricts a borrower's ability to borrow through **subsidiaries** (cf. **negative covenants**).

limit-dependent options. Exotic options where the payoff can be activated or deactivated by the behaviour of the **underlying** between the contract date and **expiry** (cf. **trigger**). See **barrier option; digital option; knock-in option**.

limited by guarantee (UK). A type of company where the **share capital** is not paid up but is guaranteed by **shareholders** in the event of the company being wound up. Such arrangements are often used when the company is set up for, say, charitable purposes. In effect, the shareholders act as guarantors of debts up to the level of their commitments (cf. **limited partnership; partnership**). See also **partly paid**.

limit down. The maximum fall in price allowed during one **session** on an exchange before trading is stopped. See **limit move; limit up.**

limited company (LTD; Ltd.). An incorporated firm where the liability of its owners in respect of its debts is limited. This may take the form of limitation by **shares** or limitation by guarantee. Such firms are said to have **limited liability**. Limited (LTD; Ltd.) is the suffix used for such companies; **public limited company** (PLC, plc) is used for larger capitalized firms in the UK and Ireland.

limited exercise option. See Atlantic-style; Bermudan-style.

limited guarantee. A condition in an **asset-backed security** issue where the originator of the pool of assets undertakes to make repurchases of bad debts up to an agreed amount. Any excess remains with the holders of the security. See **securitization**.

limited liability. A legal limit on the liability of owners to the amount of **capital** provided. The other condition, unlimited liability, allows creditors to have recourse to other assets of the owners in the event of a deficit (cf. **limited company; partnership**).

limited market. (i) Trading conditions for individual securities, sectors, or the market as a whole which are relatively illiquid (cf. **cabinet stock; liquidity; thin**). (ii) Any specialized type of financial instrument which only appeals to a few investors and therefore where demand may be very specific is said to have a limited market (cf. **exotic options**).

limited obligations (USA). **Municipal bonds** which do not carry the full faith and credit of the issuing government and may be subject to annual appropriation; or an addition to **revenue bonds** where the issuing entity adds its moral obligation to top up any shortfall.

limited partner. A partner in an **unincorporated** company or **partnership** whose liability is limited to his investment (cf. **general partner**).

limited partnership (UK; USA). (i) A general term for a partnership agreement by a **limited partner**. (ii) Used to describe special funds set up to hold assets or make investments, either directly or via **pooling** arrangements, where investors participate as **limited partners**. The rationale behind such structures is to allow investors to participate directly in the profits of the investment without the penalty of **double taxation of dividends**. Usually used for investments with predictable cash flows such as **cash cows** or **real estate** but more risky ventures are sometimes financed such as oil and gas exploration.

limited put. See floored put.

limited recourse. A condition attached to a project finance undertaking that allows recourse to the **sponsor** under certain specified conditions or amounts. In project finance, limited recourse is more common than either full **recourse** or totally **non-recourse** conditions.

limited risk. The maximum risk of an option purchase, which is its **premium**.

limited risk differential swap (limited risk diff swap). Reduced-risk version of a differential swap where cross-currency **caps** and **floors** have been used to limit the degree of adverse exposure.

limited tax bond (USA). A **municipal** issue distinguished by the fact that, while a **full faith and credit** obligation of the issuer, the issue has **limited recourse** to the issuer's taxing power or revenues to service the obligation and is limited to a part of the tax base only.

limited two-way payment (LTP). An optional part of the **master swap agreement** issued by the **International Swaps and Derivatives Association** that allows the non-defaulting **counterparty** to cease their obligations to the defaulting party. Such a clause protects the non-defaulting party from additional losses in the event of non-performance of the other party. However, such a condition is not acceptable for **netting** arrangements where **full two-way payment** is required. Also known as a *walkaway clause*.

limit move. Change in price of a **derivative** contract traded on an **exchange** up or down to the limit at which trading will be stopped. See **limit up**.

limit option. See barrier option.

limit order. An instruction to a **dealer** requiring execution to take place at a particular price or better (cf. **at best; fill or kill; market-if-touched**). A buy limit order can be carried out at or below the given price, a sell limit order can be effected at or above the given price.

limit order board. A feature of **derivatives** exchanges where trading is carried out by **open outcry** to allow participants to place **limit orders** (cf. **order book official**). In securities markets there is generally a **specialist** to oversee off-market orders which will be recorded in the specialist's **book**. With open outcry methods, no specialist is involved, so to handle off-market orders, these are recorded on the limit order board and are executed as and when appropriate by a designated exchange official acting on behalf of customers, known as an *order book official*.

limit order book. See specialist; book.

limit order information system (USA). A disseminating service providing subscribers with details of securities transactions, including specialist, the exchange where the security is traded, trade details, and **bid** and **offer** prices.

limit up or **down.** The maximum price movement allowed on a (**commodities**) **futures** exchange for a particular contract during a (daily) trading session. Such restrictions are designed to prevent the **settlement price** moving beyond the amount of daily **margin** provided by participants on the exchange (cf. **circuit breakers**).

line. (i) Large amount of a given security. See **basket; block; lot; odd lot**. (ii) An arrangement, such as a loan. Hence *line of credit*.

linear foreign exchange-linked swap. Cross-currency **swap** where one of the legs has the payments linked to the foreign exchange rate between the two currencies. Such a structure means that the payments increase and decrease in line with the movements in the exchange rate relative to the initial exchange rate used.

linearity. A feature of certain kinds of **derivatives** such as **forwards, futures,** and **swaps** where the payoff has a linear relation to the **underlying**. Also called *symmetrical* since the gains and losses are potentially both the same. See also **asymmetric payoff** (cf. **non-linearity**).

linear programming. A mathematical optimization technique used to establish numerical solutions to particular problems. Such problems involve the search for the 'optimum' value of specified variables, where best usually refers to values which maximize **profit** or minimizes **cost**. An important part of the problem is the existence of constraints on the permitted values of the variables (for example, it may not be possible to have fractional contracts). The objective function (either to maximize gain or minimize loss) is solved in relation to a series of linear constraints, the **model** deriving the best solution given the existing constraints. The solution is based on the best possible values out of those permitted by the constraints, known as the 'feasible set'. For example, the problem of deciding what level of stocks or inventory to be held, given the amount of space available, the discounts available for orders of specified sizes, and the likely levels of demand at particular prices. As the name suggests, all the relationships involved must be linear.

line chart. A method of showing changes in the price of securities or indices, or relative movements, by means of a line joining the observation points on a graph (cf. **candlestick chart; point and figure chart**). See **chart analysis**.

line of credit (Banking; USA). American term for a **credit facility**. Such lines may be **committed**, that is guaranteed to be available, or **uncommitted**, that is available on a best efforts basis at the discretion of the lender. Also termed a *credit line*.

line pattern. A pattern in security price movements identified by **chart analysis**. It is meant to imply resistance to both price rises and falls within relatively narrow limits and indicates that buyers and sellers are fairly evenly matched. Eventually either buyers or sellers predominate and the price moves sharply up or down, known as a *breakaway* or *breakout*. According to chartists the time to buy or sell is when such a breakaway occurs above or below the line (cf. **false dawn**). See **accumulation area; descending tops; flag; head and shoulders; pennant; resistance area; rising bottoms; support level; technical analysis; triangle pattern**.

liquid. Readily negotiable without significant **market impact**, hence a *liquid market*. See also **liquidity**.

liquid assets. Assets which can be sold quickly at close to their mid-market value (cf. **forced sale; liquidity**). Also termed *liquid capital, quick assets*, or *realizable assets* (cf. **acid test ratio**). See **current assets**.

liquidate. (i) Market term used to denote the closing of a **position**. It is normally taken to mean the disposal of the entire position or security rather than just a proportion. (ii) Another term commonly used in the market for **covering** or **offsetting** transactions. Hence a *liquidating transaction*. (iii) The process of winding up a firm. See **liquidation**. (iv) To generate cash.

liquidated damages. Damages stated in a contract payable upon **breach of covenant** or **default**. They must be a fair estimate of the damage likely to be incurred. Amounts which do not appear to be related in any way to possible damages are called *penalties*. Where damages are difficult to assess, what might appear to be a penalty may be adjudged to be liquidated damages, if the court considers that the sum was an attempt to assess the possible loss (cf. **unliquidated damages**).

liquidating dividend. A dividend payment that is a return of **capital** to **shareholders** (cf. **distributable reserves**).

liquidation. The winding up of a business, the disposal of assets, and the paying down of liabilities. Liquidations can be either voluntary, as a result of the owners' decision, or involuntary, as a result of **bankruptcy** or **insolvency**.

liquidation rights. The rights pertaining to a firm's **equity** holders in the event that a company is put into liquidation (cf. **absolute priority rule; bankruptcy; insolvency**).

liquidation value. The value of assets of a business if sold after it has been wound up (cf. **going-concern value**). See **bankruptcy; insolvency; liquidate; winding-up petition**.

liquidator. A person responsible for the winding-up or **liquidation** of a company. In the UK, specialists in this activity are known as *insolvency practitioners* and should be qualified as determined by the Insolvency Act, 1986.

liquid capital. See **current assets**.

liquidity. (i) Of an individual security, the ease with which it can be bought or sold without unduly affecting the price. Factors which might affect liquidity are: the number of securities outstanding in an issue and whether the issue is large or small relative to the market norm; **credit worthiness** of the issuer or **guarantor**; the proportion of the issue that is available for trading and not held by **buy-and-hold** investors; for equities, the number of shareholders; where the security is traded; the number of **market-makers**; the extent to which prices quoted are **firm** or **indicative**; frequency and volume of transactions and the degree of price continuity; the size of the **bid-ask (offer) spread**; the size of the transaction relative to the market; and market participants' subjective perceptions of the security's liquidity. In addition, these factors may change over the life of the security as market participants' views as to what constitutes liquidity change (cf. **buy and hold; on-the-run**). (ii) The volume of trading on an exchange, market, sector, or security. (iii) In a more general market sense, the overall level of funds available for investing or trading (cf. **illiquid; marketability; market impact**). (iv) The ability to turn assets into cash to meet expected and unanticipated obligations or to create **liabilities** to raise **funds** (cf. **acid test ratio; cash equivalents; cash instrument; current assets; liquid assets; standby**). (v) Another term commonly used for **money supply**. (vi) Cash assets. (vii) Cash substitutes; that is, securities or other investments that can readily be converted to **cash** with little **risk** of loss of value (cf. **cash equivalents; cash instrument; forced sale**). (viii) The ability of an entity to meet its cash out flow obligations.

liquidity diversification. (i) A strategy for **portfolio** management which involves holding securities of varying **maturity** and type in order to avoid the **risk** of not being able to realise cash if some markets become **illiquid**. See **marketability**. (ii) Sometimes used in a more general sense of spreading holdings across the **yield curve** to avoid rotational risk.

liquidity preference. (i) A wish to hold more liquid assets at the cost of a lower return (cf. **flight to quality**). (ii) One of the hypotheses used to explain the **term structure of interest rates**. It postulates that investors have to be compensated by receiving a **premium** to extend the **maturity** of their holdings since they are both tying up their money for a longer period and exposing themselves to greater **interest rate risk** by so doing. Liquidity preference thus postulates that the normal shape of the **yield curve** should be **positive**, or upward sloping and that long rates should be higher than the average of expected short rates. See also **expectations theory**; **market segmentation theory**.

liquidity premium. (i) A **yield** premium or value **discount** for securities which cannot be readily turned into cash (for example a **private placement**) (cf. **liquid assets**; **margin**; **spread**). (ii) The difference between the implied **forward** rate of interest and the expected **spot rate** of interest for the same maturity (cf. **liquidity preference**). It is the amount of additional return investors require for buying a security with a longer **maturity**.

liquidity ratio. (i) An accounting **ratio** which measures the ability of a borrower to meet their **short-term** obligations (cf. **current ratio**; **acid test ratio**). Also called the *cash ratio*. See **ratio analysis**. (ii) A measure of a security's **liquidity** in the market. It is generally taken to be the volume of securities traded per 1% change in the price. The higher the ratio, the less price impact a given volume of transaction has on the security's price and hence the greater the market liquidity of the security. Obviously, such a ratio cannot fully reflect the security's liquidity as it does not take into account short-term specific factors which might temporarily affect the liquidity of the market, a sector, or a specific security.

liquidity risk. (i) (Banking) The **risk** that a bank or deposit taking institution will not have enough cash to meet maturing deposits and other obligations (cf. **asset-liability management**). This risk is one of the principal reasons that **central banks** provide a **lender of last resort** facility to banks (cf. **discount window**). (ii) (Securities) The risk that it may prove impossible to sell a security or market sector due to lack of buyers. Liquidity risk is normally seen as a short-term problem, unless a forced seller, although it increases the **market risk** of a **position** (cf. **forced sale**; **value at risk**). See also **liquidity**.

liquid market. Any market where buying and selling is easily accomplished due to the presence of many interested buyers and sellers prepared to trade substantial quantities at small price differentials. Generally liquid markets are characterized by large **marketable quantities**, narrow **bid-offer spreads**, and a multiplicity of intermediaries. See **limited market** (cf. **illiquid**).

liquid ratio. See **acid test ratio**.

liquid yield option note securities (lyons) (USA). See **zero-coupon convertible**.

Lisbon Stock Exchange. See **Bolsa de Lisbon**.

listed or **listed security.** (i) To be admitted for trading on an organized exchange. (ii) A security that is **quoted** and traded on a recognized exchange (cf. **over the counter**). Sometimes called *exchange listed* (cf. **exchange traded**).

listed broker (UK). A broker approved by the **Bank of England** as regulator to undertake broking activities in the UK.

listed company or **corporation.** A company or corporation which has its **common stock** or **ordinary shares** listed on a recognized exchange (cf. **initial public offering**; **quoted**). Also called a *quoted company*.

listed option. Another term used for an **exchange-traded option**.

listing. (i) The process by which an issue of securities is admitted for trading on a stock exchange (cf. **over the counter**). On the London market, companies that have their **shares** listed have to sign a *listing agreement* which provides for the initial and continuing requirements that the company must meet (cf. **general undertaking**). See also **London Stock Exchange**. (ii) Shorthand indicating the recognized exchange on which the security is listed, as in *Luxembourg-listed*, *Tokyo-listed*.

listing agreement (UK). Contract between the **London Stock Exchange** and a company to have its securities **listed** on the exchange.

listing particulars (UK). The **London Stock Exchange's** listing **requirements** as laid out in the **Yellow Book** which require the company to publish information about itself and the securities to be listed. Also known as a *prospectus*.

Listing Particulars Directive (80/390/EC) (European Union). The directive covering the harmonization of listing requirements of companies in member states.

listing requirements. The amount, company size, disclosure, and other requirements that accompany a **listing**. Issues normally have to comply with the conditions applicable to publicly traded securities while individual exchanges set their own complementary standards. See also **registration**.

lists closed (UK). When a new issue of securities is on **offer**, the **sponsor** or **underwriters** will make the issue available to investors for a given period.

However, they have the right to close bids prior to the end of the period. When they do this, the application or the 'lists are closed' (cf. **over-subscription**).

Little Board (Equities; USA). The **American Stock Exchange** (cf. **Big Board**).

Liverpool Cotton Association (UK). Major commodity market in spot wool and wool futures.

living dead. A **venture capital** term for investments which are still in existence but unlikely ever to meet target rates of return for the provider of the funds (cf. **dog**; **lemon**; **plum**).

Ljubljana Stock Exchange Inc. (Slovenia). Ajdovscina 4, SL-61000 Ljubljana. (tel. 386 61 302 019; fax 386 61 301 950).

Lloyd's of London (UK). The London-based market in insurance. It is the world's principal market in marine, aviation, and unique **risks**. Lloyd's organization is complex, involving syndicates of underwriters (made up of *Names*, whose liabilities are unlimited) who are prepared to write most kinds of insurance, although corporate, **limited liability** members have now been admitted. Lloyd's also maintains the Lloyd's Register of Shipping, which sets the standards for construction and operation of vessels which sail on the high seas.

Lloyd's Register of Shipping. A record of all ships at sea kept by **Lloyd's of London**.

load. (i) The initial charge levied by the management of a **mutual fund** to cover marketing, **commission**, and other expenses. Funds which make an initial charge are known as *load funds*, those which do not as *no-load funds*. (ii) (Forex) The difference between the **forward rate** and the contracted rate in a **breakforward**. It is the hidden premium for the **option** in the breakforward contract. (iii) Interest on a **debt**.

load-to-load. Trade creditor arrangement where the customer pays for the last consignment or service when the next one is delivered or undertaken.

loan. The lending of money at a price (interest). Traditionally loans have been advanced by banks to customers, but the term can encompass any sum given to another party where the latter intends to repay rather than exchange for a service or product. Loans can be divided into retail, wholesale, and trade. Retail loans are those made to individuals (usually from a credit granting financial institution, such as a bank) and are usually known as **consumer loans**. The wholesale loan market is made to businesses, while trade loans are extended between businesses (for instance, funds lent from a parent to a subsidiary, or vice versa). See **facility**.

loan-backed or **loan-based securities.** Asset-backed securities where the **underlying collateral** are consumer loans, receivables, or credit card outstandings.

loan broker. A broker who arranges loans with a bank or other lending institution in return for a **commission**.

loan capital. That part of a company's **liabilities** in the form of debt. This can be either **short term**, with a **maturity** of up to one year; **medium term**, where the maturity is over one year and up to seven years; or **long term**, in excess of seven years. It can be at a **fixed rate** or a **floating rate** of interest, and be either in security form or borrowed from a bank. See **bond**; **commercial paper**; **debenture**; **facility**; **unsecured loan stock**. See also **equity**; **share capital**.

loan commitment. See **committed facility**.

loan crowd (USA). **Brokers** on an exchange who borrow or lend securities to provide for **short selling** (cf. **crowd**; **lending securities**).

loan draw down. Borrower calling on funds from a loan or financing facility. Also just called a *drawdown*. See **commitment fee**; **grace period**; **revolving line of credit**; **revolving underwriting facility**; **term loan**.

loaned flat (USA). Securities lending without charging.

loan guarantee. Insurance against **default** on a contract. See also **asset-backed**; **securitization**.

loan loss reserve (Banking). See **reserve for credit losses**.

loan note. **Money market instrument** used to **rollover** a maturing **liability** (cf. **promissory note**).

loan participation. Generally short-term (under one year) **asset sales** to non-bank investors created by reselling loans booked by a financial intermediary. The loan is first financed by the intermediary and then **sub-participated** to other investors. The market has grown significantly in recent years as a substitute for traded **money market instruments**, such as **commercial paper**. The administration is usually simpler for the borrower since the intermediary will normally undertake to lend the money and subsequently re-market the loan. For investors, it offers a higher yield for the same type of **risk** as money market instruments with the same **maturity**, although the participation is **illiquid** in comparison.

loan quality. The degree of lender protection in a loan, either in terms of the **credit quality** of the borrower and/or the amount of **collateral** (cf. **non-performing loans**). See **problem asset**.

loan rate. The rate of interest on a **loan** or **debt** (cf. **interest rate calculations**).

loan review (Banking). Process of reviewing all material aspects relating to a problem loan in order to determine the amount of impairement (cf. **non-performing assets; problem assets**). See also **charge-off**.

loan selling. See **asset sales; loan participation; silent sub-participation; sub-participation**.

loan stock. (i) In the UK, a type of **bond** issued by a company. Typically it is **unsecured** (cf. **debenture**). (ii) Another term for **lending securities**.

loan-to-price ratio (Banking). The ratio of the value of the loan to the expected disposal price on the asset used as **collateral**.

local. Futures trader who deals as a **principal**, that is for his own account. Such **traders** help to provide **liquidity** to the exchange.

Local Authority bills (Money markets; UK). Short-term **promissory notes** issued by the various local authorities and municipalities in the UK. Issued at a **discount**, they are used to provide funds pending the receipt of tax revenues. Such issues are not guaranteed by central government. They are also sometimes known as *corporation, revenue, money bills,* or *local government promissory notes*.

Local Authority Bond (LAB) (Bonds; UK). Bonds issued by UK local government with a maturity in excess of a year. Typically such issues are for a year and six days, and because of this are sometimes known as *yearlings*. However, longer maturities of up to five years are known. They were formerly known as *British Corporation and County Stocks*.

local government promissory notes (Money markets; UK). See **local authority bills**.

lockbox (Banking). An arrangement for the collection of funds where payments are processed locally by a bank which transfers the funds to the company's principle account in another geographical location (cf. **concentration banking**).

locked or **locked market.** Said to occur when a buyer and seller both want to deal at the same

price and neither wishes to pay a commission (cf. **choice**).

locked-in. (i) A **position** which is impossible to unwind or cover. For instance, a **stock** where trading has been suspended. (ii) A guaranteed rate.

lock in. To fix or commit.

lock option. See **ladder option**.

lock-limit. A market situation in which the desire to buy or sell is so great that no one is prepared to take the opposite **position** and where the price movement extends beyond the exchange's permitted price **limit** (cf. **break; crash; jump**). See **circuit breakers**.

lock-step option. See **ladder option**.

lock-up. (i) Securities which are intended to form part of the buyer's core holding. That is, they are unlikely to be traded (cf. **buy and hold**). (ii) A requirement for international securities issues to avoid **registration** with the USA's **Securities and Exchange Commission** that they be traded in such a manner as to avoid being sold to US nationals or domiciled investors (cf. **daisy chain**). See **lock-up period**.

lock-up option (Mergers and acquisitions). A contingent sale contract put in place between a company subject to a **hostile takeover** attempt which is arranged with a friendly company or **white knight** for the former's most desirable assets or business unit(s), known as the **crown jewels**, in order to get the **predator** company to abandon its attempted takeover (cf. **self-uglification**).

lock-up period. The period between the **closing date** of an international issue and when the physical **certificates** are distributed (cf. **bearer participation certificates; seasoned**). During this period the issue can only be traded in electronic form, being evidenced by a **global bond**. This is required for international issues, principally **eurobonds**, which are not registered with the **Securities and Exchange Commission** in the USA and where there is a danger that such issues could be sold to US nationals (in practice this applies to almost all such issues). The reason for such a constraint is to prevent the flow-back of such offshore securities into the US domestic market, or any other jurisdiction in which it is illegal to offer such securities without formal registration (cf. **daisy chain; registration**). After the lock-up period, which is usually ninety days, the securities are exchanged for definitive certificates upon certification of compliance with the restrictions placed on **distribution**. At this point they may be placed in the USA if the issue has a **private placement** exemption. See also **grey market**.

lock-up securities. Negotiable instruments, such as **certificates of deposit** or **medium-term notes** that are issued to buyers on the understanding that they will not be resold or traded. The issuer will normally seek to **safekeep** the securities to ensure investor compliance with the undertaking. Such an arrangement has been frequently used in the **eurocurrency** markets to meet the regulatory requirements of investors who have to hold negotiable obligations. See **private placement**.

loco (location). The place where a **commodity** is being traded. Hence, rubber loco Kuala Lumpur, or copper loco London. Given the cost of shipment from one location to another, this is an important factor in apparent price discrepancies for the same physical commodity in different markets.

logarithmic return. See **continuous compounding**.

logarithmic scale (log scale). A technical analysis or chartist technique used in the compilation of charts, which records proportionate instead of absolute movements in value, size, or number. That is, the price differences are the same magnitude regardless of the price level. This is to iron out the problems that the same price change at one level reflects a different size of movement at another. A 10p movement on a 50p share is very different from the same movement on a 200p share. The log scale provides the correct proportionality. Charts are sometimes seen in *semi-logarithmic form*, where only one axis is so treated (e.g. price on a log scale and time treated as normal).

lognormal distribution. A series of numbers which when transformed to their logarithmic equivalent conform to the logarithmic form of the **normal distribution**. A variable will have a lognormal distribution if the natural logarithm of the variable is normally distributed. The advantage of such (statistical) normality is to allow the use of standard statistical techniques on the data. In the case of **option pricing**, it allows the derivation of the option's **premium** or price (cf. **geometric Brownian motion**). For financial markets, the lognormal distribution is probably a better representation of the likely movement in prices than the untransformed variables, since the log of returns is bounded on the downside at zero.

Lombard rate (Germany). The rate of interest charged on a **collateralized** loan by the **Bundesbank**. The Lombard rate is usually about 0.5%, or so, above the Bundesbank's **discount rate**. Banks prefer to borrow at the Lombard rate rather than

make use of the discount facility because the latter is (informally) rationed by the Bundesbank and frequent use will cause the Bundesbank to investigate (cf. **moral suasion**). The term Lombard comes from the Italian family of the Lombardi, who at the end of the Middle Ages were one of the first international bankers. It is also the **reference rate** for a **collateralized** loan by a German bank.

London and Bishopsgate 100 index (Equities). A component index of 100 large, liquid **common stocks** that forms part of Morgan Stanley Inc's capital international **index**.

London and New Zealand Futures Association (UK). **Commodities** exchange which specializes in New Zealand wool.

London bullion market (Commodities; UK). The physical market in **gold** and silver of a recognized degree of purity. The world market for such metals, usually in the form of bars, is centred in London. The main task is the setting of the price at which gold and silver bars will be traded. Following what is now an archaic procedure, representatives of the main dealers meet twice a day in the same room and set a price on the basis of what is for sale and what is wished to be purchased (cf. **open outcry**). This is known as the *gold fix*; there is also a *silver fix* (cf. **fixing**). There is also local gold-lending activity and a market in gold coins (cf. **krugerrand**; **maple leaf**; **new sovereign**; **specie**).

London Business School Risk Measurement Service. A data service providing **risk** measurement for UK quoted companies.

London certificate of deposit (London CD) (Money markets; UK). Market term for those **certificates of deposit** issued in the London market and complying with the regulations of the **Bank of England**. Such issues normally have physical delivery and for trading within the City of London there are **safekeeping** arrangements and a **clearing system** operated by First Chicago. See also **non-London certificates of deposit**.

London Clearing House (LCH) (UK). The **clearing house** that handles the **settlement** of **derivatives** transactions for the London-based exchanges: **International Petroleum Exchange**; **London Futures and Options Exchange**; **London International Financial Futures and Options Exchange**; **London Metal Exchange**. Prior to 1991 it was the International Commodities Clearing House (ICCH). It is owned by the six largest **clearing banks**.

London club. The name given to the bank lenders engaged in **rescheduling** commercial debt (cf.

Paris club, which is the same for government debt). See also less developed countries debt.

London Commodity Exchange (LCE) (Commodities; UK). See London Financial Futures and Options Exchange.

London daily prices (LDP) (Commodities; UK). Prices as quoted on the London Futures and Options Exchange, formerly the London Commodity Exchange. These are often used for settling many non-exchange contracts between users and producers.

London Discount Market Association (LDMA) (UK). A trade body representing the main players in the London discount market. See also discount house.

London Futures and Options Exchange (London FOX; FOX) (UK). A company responsible for offering services to the soft commodity (non-metal) market in the London market (cf. London Metal Exchange). The exchange makes a market in such commodities as barley, cocoa, coffee, lamb, pigs, potatoes, rubber, soya-bean meal, sugar (raw and white), wheat, in both spot and futures. It is the premier market in many soft commodities and sets world prices. It also has the Baltic International Freight Futures Exchange in freight futures and the *London Grain Futures Market*, *London Meat Futures Exchange*, and the *London Soya-bean Meal Futures Market*. Now merged with the London Financial Futures and Options Exchange.

London Grain Futures Market (Commodities; UK). See London Futures and Options Exchange (cf. Baltic Exchange).

London interbank bid rate (LIBID) (Money markets; UK). The rate at which major banks will bid to take eurocurrency deposits from each other for a given maturity, normally between overnight and five years (cf. London interbank offered rate; Madrid interbank offered rate; Paris interbank offered rate; taking). See basis; interest rate calculations.

London interbank currency options market (LICOM) (Forex; UK). The over-the-counter market between financial institutions based in London and their clients in currency options. The British Bankers' Association has a set of proforma terms and conditions to facilitate a secondary market. See also exchange-traded.

London interbank mean rate (LIMEAN) (Money markets; UK). The average of the London interbank offered rate (LIBOR) and London interbank bid rate (LIBID). Occasionally used as a

reference rate on a floating rate note (FRN). The major eurocurrencies normally are quoted on a 1/8th per cent spread between the bid and offer, therefore LIMEAN is usually 1/16th below LIBOR and the same above LIBID. However it would have an implication for an FRN coupon reset, compared to an FRN with a reference rate based on either LIBOR or LIBID, if the margin were to widen (for instance if there was market disruption). See middle price.

London interbank offered rate (LIBOR) (Money markets; UK). The rate at which major banks will offer to make eurocurrency deposits with each other for a given maturity, normally between overnight and five years (cf. fixing; London interbank bid rate; Madrid interbank offered rate; Paris interbank offered rate; taking). LIBOR is also the reference rate often used for floating rate notes and many over-the-counter instruments such as forward rate agreements, interest rate swaps, cross-currency swaps, interest rate caps, and floors and other interest rate derivatives. See basis; interest rate calculations.

London International Financial Futures and Options Exchange (LIFFE) (UK). Cannon Bridge, London EC4R 3XX (tel. 44 (0) 71 623 0444; fax 44 (0) 71 588 3624). The UK's most prominent financial futures and options exchange, established in September 1982. It initially was a futures market only, but subsequently now also trades options on ordinary shares following the merger with the London Traded Options Exchange (LTOM) in March 1992. It offers futures and options on futures contracts in sterling, Deutschmarks, yen, and Swiss francs, twenty-year gilt stock, and three-month time deposits in Deutschmarks, Lira, and sterling. In 1984 a contract based on the FT-SE 100 Index was introduced. It is one of the largest exchanges of its type by turnover in the world (cf. Chicago Board of Trade; Chicago Board Options Exchange; Chicago Mercantile Exchange; Deutsche Terminbörse; Marché à Terme International de France; Singapore International Monetary Exchange; Tokyo International Financial Futures Exchange).

London Meat Futures Exchange. Now part of the London Futures and Options Exchange.

London Metal Exchange Limited (LME) (Commodities; UK) 56, Leadenhall Street, London EC3A 2BJ (tel. (44 171) 264 5555; fax (44171) 680 0505; tlx: 8951367). Established in 1877, it is one of the world's premier spot and futures markets for dealing in hard commodities, such as copper, silver, tin, lead, and zinc. See also gold fix.

London Metal Exchange (LME) option terms.

Usual option term	LME option term
Holder	Taker
Writer (seller)	Grantor
Expiry day	Declaration day

Note that LME options are **European-style**.

London rules (Banking; UK). Guidelines on market practice and general behaviour with financially distressed borrowers which have been informally sanctioned by the **Bank of England** (cf. **moral suasion**). The key factors are: equality of treatment for all lenders; the Bank of England to act as a neutral arbitrator; standstill on loan facilities, pending agreement; and consideration given to the position of other **creditors** and **shareholders**. The aim is to ensure common action and to prevent precipitate moves to start insolvency proceedings. See also **default**.

London Securities and Derivatives Exchange. See **OM London**.

London Soya-bean Meal Futures Market. Now part of the London Futures and Option Exchange.

London Stock Exchange (LSE) (UK). London EC2N 1HP (tel. (4471) 797 1000; tlx 886557). The market evolved in the seventeenth century around trading activities at New Jonathan's Coffee House. Its origins explain some of its old customs, like 'blue button', the name for messengers on the exchange. In the 1970s it incorporated all the regional exchanges in the UK, to form the Stock Exchange of Great Britain and Ireland, the name being changed to the *International Stock Exchange of the United Kingdom and Ireland* (ISE), following the changes known as **Big Bang** in 1986. These changes brought the abolition of **single capacity** and **screen trading**. It is regulated by the **Securities and Futures Authority**, a self-regulating organization under the auspices of the **Securities and Investments Board**. There are two types of markets, the **main market**, which is **quote-driven**, and a market for small companies shares which has been variously the **unlisted securities market**, the **Bulletin Board**, and, latterly, the **Alternative Investments Market**. Following Big Bang, the **London Traded Options Market** became part of the **London International Financial Futures and Options Exchange** to create the principal securities **derivatives exchange** in the UK, the London Stock Exchange, being restricted to **cash instruments**.

London Sugar Futures Market. Now part of the London Futures and Options Exchange.

London Traded Options Market (LTOM) (UK). The market which used to trade **traditional op-**tions, which became part of the **London International Financial Futures and Options Exchange** in 1992.

long. (i) To own or purchase a security, **stock**, **future**, **option**, or other **asset**, usually in anticipation of selling an identical one at a higher price. Sometimes used simply to describe net buyers of securities (cf. **short**). (ii) For a trader, owning more than one has contracts to deliver. In some markets, such as **foreign exchange**, this is known as *overbought*. (iii) Any **position** that will benefit from a rise in the value of the **underlying**. (iv) Ownership of a security or other asset.

long bond (USA). The **on-the-run** longest maturity **US treasury bond**; at present a thirty year issue (cf. **Resolution Funding Corporation**).

long bonds or **long coupons.** (i) Bonds with a long **current maturity** (over fifteen years). (ii) A bond which has a **coupon** period that is longer than normal or non-standard (cf. **short coupon**). Usually it is the first or last coupon period which is longer than usual market practice.

long bond yield-decrease warrant (Turbo) (USA). **Warrant** allowing the holder to purchase the **US Treasury long bond** at a fixed **yield** (and hence price). It is equivalent to a **put** on the interest rate or a **call** on the bond price. See also **spread future**; **spread option**.

long covering. The selling of a security previously bought **long** in order to **close out** a long position (cf. **flat**; **short covering**).

long-dated. Another term for securities which have a long **maturity** (cf. **short-dated**). See **long bonds**.

long-dated forward. Forward agreement where the **settlement** is more than one year away. Typically these are for **commodities or foreign exchange**.

long-dated forward rate agreement (Long-dated FRA). Forward rate agreement where the **settlement** date is more than one year away at the time of the transaction.

long-dated gilt (long-dated gilt-edged bond) (UK). See **gilt-edged**; **longs**.

long-dated option. Option where the **expiry** date is more than one year away (cf. **long-term equity anticipation securities**).

long-form report (Equities; UK). A detailed report, usually drawn up by accountants, which is intended to provide sufficient information to allow potential investors to make an informed assessment of a company seeking capital on an exchange (cf. **short-form**). Required under a **listing** agreement.

long funded. A situation where the **maturity** of the **liabilities** is greater than that of the **assets** (cf. **assets repriced before liabilities; short funded**). The intention would be to see the assets roll over at a higher interest rate before the liabilities used to fund them, thus allowing a greater **spread** to be earned between the two (cf. **gap; margin**). See **asset-liability management**.

long futures. Owning or holding futures and hence having the obligation to receive **delivery** (cf. **long position; short futures**).

long gilt (UK). See **gilt-edged; longs**.

long hedge. The strategy of buying a **futures** contract or **option** to protect against rising prices of the **underlying** in the **cash market** or to **lock in** the **yield** at which an anticipated cash flow can be invested. Sometimes called a *buying hedge, consumer's hedge,* or a *price fix hedge*.

long interest (UK). Interest on borrowings of more than one year (cf. **short interest**).

long leg. See **leg** (cf. **long**).

long option. To be a buyer or **holder** of an option (cf. **short position**).

long position. To hold a security or derivative contract. It creates a positive exposure to market developments since as the market rises the position improves (cf. **short**). The opposite condition is known as *short position,* which involves selling a security or derivative and benefiting from a decline in the market or **underlying**. See **long**.

Payoff for long asset or purchased futures position at expiry

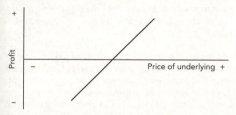

longs (Bonds; UK). In the UK government bond market (**gilt-edged market**), a security with a maturity of more than fifteen years (cf. **mediums; shorts**).

longs or **long bonds** (Bonds; USA). In the US Treasury bond market, a security with a long

maturity (usually up to thirty years). Generally includes those **original maturity** issues of more than ten years. When market participants refer to the 'long bond' they mean the current **benchmark** long bond US Treasury (usually the latest issue). See **on-the-run**.

long straddle. A straddle under which an investor buys **put** and **call options**. The opposite where the position is shorted or written is known as a *short straddle*. See **option strategies**.

long-term. (i) In **bond** markets, **original maturities** of more than seven years (cf. **medium-term; short-term**). (ii) Under **portfolio** strategies, purchasing assets with the intention of realization after at least a year. (iii) In terms of company balance sheets, debts with a maturity in excess of one year (cf. **short-term; medium-term**).

long-term bonds. Bonds which have a current maturity in excess of fifteen years, or durations of six years or more.

long-term currency swap. See **currency swap**.

long-term debt (UK). Securities or debt with a maturity of more than ten years (cf. **redemption**). See also **medium-term; short-term**.

long-term equity anticipation securities (LEAPS) (USA). A type of long-dated, time-to-expiry, index option series offered on the **Chicago Board Options Exchange**. There are three calls and puts: two- and three-year options on the Standard and Poor's 500 Index, the Standard and Poor's 100 Index and the Major Market Index (cf. **special claim on residual equity; prescribed right to income and maximum equity**). In addition, LEAPS are available on some individual common stocks (cf. **stock options**). Each LEAPS contract is worth 100 times one-tenth of the index, or 100 shares. **expiry dates** are set for December in each year. See also **capped index options**.

long-term foreign exchange (LTFX). Forward foreign exchange transactions with maturities beyond a year.

long-term interest rate contract. See **interest rate futures; interest rate options**.

long-term interest rate future. See **bond futures; interest rate futures**.

long-term prime rate (LTPR) (Banking; Japan). A lending rate in the Japanese market which is set at 0.90% (90 basis points) above the new issue rate for five-year **bank debentures** and used as a **reference** rate for long-term lending. Traditionally only the select *long-term credit banks* can issue five-year bank debentures in the domestic market.

long-term rate risk. The interest rate risk from movements in interest rates at the long end of the **yield curve** (cf. **term structure of interest rates**).

long-term volatility. The observed **volatility** for periods in excess of a year. Volatility is seen to change over time, but there is considerable evidence to support a set level of volatility in the market, from which short-run departures appear to take place (cf. **mean reversion**). Long-term volatility can be considered as the market's average volatility. It is used, for example, for pricing long-term **options** on interest rate sensitive instruments where the **expiry** date is measured in years rather than months (cf. **call provision; put provision**). See also **long-term equity anticipation securities; long-term rate risk.**

long-the-basis. Cash and futures or position which involves holding the **underlying** and selling, or going short the future. The opposite is known as *short-the-basis*.

long ton. See ton.

lookback option. A type of **path-dependent** option where the **exercise** or **strike** price is fixed in retrospect, that is at the most favourable price (hence, it 'looks back'), i.e. at the lowest (highest) price of the **underlying** in the case of a **call** (**put**) during the life of the **option** (cf. **average rate option**). It is **European-style**. Also called a *lookback strike option* or a *no regrets option*. See also **Asian option; exotic options.**

lookforward option. A type of European option where the holder has the right to the difference between the **spot rate** at the start and the most favourable price prior to **expiry**. As a result, it 'looks forward' to the highest (lowest) price of the **underlying** in the case of a **call** (**put**) during the life of the **option**. See **exotic options.**

loro account (Banking). Used in banking to indicate the account of a third party. For example, a London bank might arrange to pay an amount to a US bank but where it is credited to the loro account of a French bank held by the US bank. See **nostro account; vostro account.**

lose. To fail to execute a transaction or win a deal.

lot. (i) The basic or market accepted basic trading unit in terms of size. For securities, this tends to be multiples of the issue denomination or **common stocks**; for **futures** and **options** markets, this may be one contract. (ii) (UK) Another term for a **contract**. Hence the *market lot*, i.e. the market

contract (cf. **marketable quantity**). (iii) A random process used to select from a group. Hence, to draw *by lot* securities for **redemption**. See **lottery.**

lot size. See **odd lot** and **round lot.**

lottery. (i) Method of allocation used when a new issue is oversubscribed (cf. **scale down**). (ii) Gambling. Also known as *toto*.

low. The lowest price or rate of a time series over a set period of time. In **technical analysis**, lows are important as indicators of points of **resistance** (cf. **high**).

low-cost option. See **zero-cost option.**

low-coupon bond. See **discount; step-up coupon security; zero-coupon bond.**

low-coupon bond refunding or **refinancing.** The replacement of a low-coupon bond with a new issue of **bonds** with a higher **coupon** (cf. **high-coupon bond refunding**). Usually takes place when a borrower needs to rollover a maturing issue but tax advantages may arise if retiring a **liability** at a **discount** (cf. **debt buy-back**).

low-coupon swap. Off-market interest rate swap or cross-currency swap where one or both legs of the swap are below the current market rate at the transaction date. Such swaps are designed to match off-market cash flows such as subsidized financings, or seasoned investments. There is normally either an interest rate adjustment on the other leg or a lump sum payment in lieu. The opposite is called a *high-coupon swap*.

lower floating rate note (lower floater). See **variable rate demand note.**

lower of cost or market (LOCM). An accounting convention covering the valuation of **assets** or inventory which selects the lower of the purchase cost or the current market value (cf. **marked-to-market**).

low exercise price option (LEPO). A set of options initially issued on the **Swiss Options and Financial Futures Exchange** to overcome **Stamp Duty** on securities transactions. By setting the **exercise price** near zero, the instrument is to all intents and purposes equivalent to the **underlying** security, although holders will forgo **dividends** and voting rights.

low leverage (gearing). (i) A firm where most of the finance is in the form of **equity** (cf. **debt–equity ratio**). (ii) Any security incorporating **derivative** features which leads to the price or rate performance being less than one for one with the underlying.

low-premium options. See zero-cost options.

LTV ruling (USA). Keynote ruling on informal reorganizations for firms in **financial distress** prior to entering **Chapter 11** that **bondholders** who agreed to new terms before the firm entered court protection were only entitled to the **market value** of their **bonds**, and not their **face value**.

Luxembourg Stock Exchange (Bourse de Luxembourg) (Luxembourg). Société de la Bourse de Luxembourg, Avenue de la Porte Neuve 11; Postal Address: B.P. 165, L-2011 Luxembourg (tel. 47 79 36-1; fax: 47 32 98; tlx: 2559 stoex lu). One of the principal exchanges for **listing** securities issued on the **eurobond** market, the other being the **London Stock Exchange**. Although the securities may be **quoted** on the exchange, trading takes place in the **over-the-counter** market for such bonds (cf. **head-to-head**).

M

Macaulay's duration. See duration.

McCarthy cards (UK). Issued by McCarthy Information Ltd. These are collections of newspaper cuttings covering events and announcements related to individual companies.

McRates (Bonds; Canada). Name given to a variant on a **forward rate agreement** developed by McLeod Young Weir based on **long-term** Canadian interest rates. The instrument is designed to allow **bond market** participants to hedge their positions.

macro-economics. That branch of economic theory concerned with explaining and predicting the behaviour over time of broad economic aggregates, such as national income; aggregate saving; consumer expenditure; **investment**; aggregate employment; the **money supply**; inflation; and the **balance of payments** (BOP). It is of particular relevance in the formulation of government **fiscal policy** and **monetary policy** and the extent to which government policy objectives can be met. For example the interplay between the desirable goals of price stability; high levels of employment; positive rates of growth; the removal of regional imbalances; and a stable BOP. Modern macro-economics has been dominated by two schools of thought: those ideas associated with the work of J. M. Keynes, especially *The General Theory of Employment, Interest and Money* (1936); and those associated with **monetarism.**

macro-economic swap. A type of **commodity swap** or **index swap** designed to **hedge** an exposure to some macro-economic variable.

macro hedge. A hedge designed to offset all of a particular type of **risk** in an entity or **portfolio**. It could be considered a 'top-down' method of managing risk. It is in contrast to a **micro hedge** which is designed to hedge a particular **position** or a specific asset.

Madrid interbank offered rate (MIBOR) (Spain). The rate that prime banks lend to each other in the Madrid **interbank** market (cf. **London interbank offered rate**).

Madrid Stock Exchange (Bolsa del Madrid) (Spain). Plaza de la Lealtad 1, 28014 Madrid (tel. 34 (9) 1 589 1106; fax 34 (9) 1 531 2290).

mail float. See float.

main market (Equities; UK). The first tier of the **London Stock Exchange** where the larger, well-established, and most liquid **ordinary shares** are traded (cf. **third market**). See also **Alternative Investment Market; Bulletin Board; listing agreement; Unlisted Securities Market.**

mainstream corporation tax (MCT) (UK). That part of a company's **corporation tax** that is due after deducting any **advance corporation tax** paid on account of **dividends** to **shareholders.**

maintenance bond. A surety used in a contractual agreement to compensate for potential deficiencies by one party or other in the performance of their obligations. Hence often called a *performance bond*. Typically used in construction where the contractor places the bond with a third party to guarantee or compensate for any subsequent defects. Such bonds can be either *conditional*, that is payable if just cause has been demonstrated by the holder of the bond or *unconditional*—payable on demand, without the holder being required to show just cause. Such amounts are repayable in cases where the contractor is not to blame.

maintenance margin. Used to describe the amount by which a **margin** account for a **futures, exchange-traded option**, or **short** security **position** may be reduced by unfavourable price movements before more funds are needed (known as a *maintenance call*) to restore the margin to set up the position (cf. **five hundred dollar rule; variation margin**). Also known as *maintenance requirement* or *minimum margin*. Sometimes called the *maintenance performance bond*. See also **standard portfolio analysis of risk.**

maintenance fee. Servicing fee on an account or facility.

maintenance performance bond. The same as maintenance margin.

maison de réescompte (French). **Discount house**.

maison de titres (French). **Stockbroker**.

major bracket. See bracket; underwriting.

majority shareholder. That shareholder with a controlling interest in a company.

majority voting. (i) (Equities) A system for voting where the shareholder has one vote per member of the board of directors being re-elected (cf. cumulative voting). (ii) In other cases, it can mean (a) in the case of simple majority voting, the right of each security holder to have one vote and for a majority of votes cast to win; or (b) in the case of majority voting by value, the requirement that at least half of the votes by value be cast.

Major Market Index (MMI) (USA). An index based on the performance of 20 blue chip stocks traded on the New York Stock Exchange. It is a simple price index where the weights of the constituents are based on their market price, adjustments being made for splits and stock dividends (cf. capitalization weighted index). It has a similar price performance to the Dow-Jones Industrial Average, which is based on 30 leading stocks.

make a market. (i) To be prepared to quote simultaneously a firm bid and offer price or rate at which a financial intermediary will transact business. A dealer who consistently makes a market in a particular instrument or security is known as a *market maker* (cf. gilt-edged market-maker; specialist). (ii) The bid-offer price at which a market-maker is willing to transact business. (iii) In the euromarkets, the willingness of a broker-dealer to buy and sell a particular issue (cf. head-to-head). Sometimes called *make a price*.

make-up day (UK). The day of the month that monetary figures are compiled by the Bank of England.

making a price (Equities; UK). Two-way quote made by a market-maker on the London Stock Exchange at which he is required to transact. This arises due to the quote-driven methods used on the exchange, rather than the more common order-driven methods used elsewhere.

making-up day (UK). On the London Stock Exchange, the first day of the settlement period. See account.

making-up price (UK). The settlement price at which unpaid for securities were carried forward in to the next account period (cf. contango).

Makler (German). Broker. A *Kursmakler* is a foreign exchange dealer.

Maloney Act of 1938 (USA). The enabling legislation that allowed for the establishment of the National Association of Securities Dealers and

the US domestic over-the-counter markets in securities.

Malta Stock Exchange, The (Malta). Pope Pius V Street, MT-Valletta (tel. 366 244051; fax 356 244071).

mambo combo. Option strategy or combination involving a put and a call, both of which are in the money.

Managed Exchange Rate Insurance Technique (MERIT). Proprietary name for a shared currency option under tender.

managed float (Forex). Method of setting the external value of a currency through intervention to partly or fully counteract market forces by having the central bank buy or sell currency against the market (cf. clean float; convertibility; crawling peg; dirty float).

managed fund. Any of a wide range of funds open to outside investors where the composition of the portfolio and the investment strategy to be pursued are controlled by the fund's managers. This usually allows them some discretion within the fund's objectives to decide the exact composition of the portfolio and timing of investment decisions. The other type of fund, a *fixed fund* where the investments are predetermined and fixed for the life of the fund, is relatively rare. See also investment trust company; mutual fund; open-ended investment company; unit trust.

managed futures fund. Funds which specialize in the use of futures as an investment technique (cf. futures and options fund).

management buy-in (MBI). The purchase of a business by one or more outside managers with the help of a group of financial backers. Buy-ins have evolved as a result of the maturing management buy-out (MBO) market. Recently, the term has been applied to contested takeovers, where the bidder is more of a financier than an operator, as buy-in appears more constructive than raider or predator. Buy-ins are said to enjoy the same benefits arising from devolving decision-making and committed financiers as with MBOs. However, because buy-ins involve an outside management team they are considered riskier, but, if successful, more lucrative for the backers because it is the financier that is likely to have the majority equity stake. When a combination of MBI and MBO is used to effect the purchase of a firm or activity a buy-in and management buy-out (BIMBO) is created.

management buy-out (MBO). The purchase of a business by part or all of its existing management with the help of a group of financial backers; such as, specialist divisions of **commercial banks** or **investment banks** and **venture capital funds**. There are four main reasons why such activities take place: **bankruptcy** of the company or its **holding company** or **parent**, retirement or death of the current owner(s), **divestment** of a subsidiary and **privatization** of a state-owned enterprise. In an MBO, managers provide a relatively small amount of the total **finance** but usually gain a disproportionately large amount of the **equity**. Buy-outs are funded largely by loans secured against the existing assets of the company or business being acquired, usually from **institutional investors**, in the form of **senior debt**. Management buy-outs began in the USA during the 1960s and were known as **bootstrapping operations**. They were used mostly as a way for private companies to raise money by selling activities to managers. The buy-out market has developed differently in the USA compared to the UK or Continental Europe, with no distinction being made in the USA between management buy-outs and other types of **leveraged buy-outs** or **acquisitions** with significant borrowing from third party backers (cf. **highly leveraged transaction**). The rationale for buy-outs can be summarized as follows: (*a*) significant equity ownership by management, coupled with the freedom from constraints of operating as part of a larger group, ought to increase the incentive to perform; and (*b*) the commitment to meeting the cost of servicing outside finance and the control exercised by financial institutions ought to limit management's ability to engage in wasteful expenditure. The beneficiaries of this enhanced performance will be both the managers and the investors once the buy-out company is in a position to be sold on, usually through a **stock market listing** or **trade sale**. Other **exits** include selling to another financier, thereby creating a **secondary market** in MBOs, or the purchase of all the shares by management, known as a **buy-back**.

The formula for success in MBOs appears to rest on management responding to such motivational factors as prestige, money and freedom from bureaucracy, whilst the backers must feel confident in identifying those complete, or part, businesses capable of the growth in cash flow and profits to support the debt servicing and provide attractive prospective **price–earnings ratios**. Given the significant involvement of **venture capitalists** in the provision of equity in MBOs, an annual compound rate of return of around 35–40% would be sought from such transactions. MBOs have become established as a fully-fledged **corporate finance** activity and are regarded as a useful addition to the techniques of financial re-engineering. See also **agency problem**.

management company. Company that manages investments (cf. **holding company**; **investment company**).

management fee. That part of the **underwriting spread** or up-front fee that is paid to the **managers** of the issue or transaction (cf. **arrangement fee**; **arranger**; **lead manager**; **co-lead manager**; **praecipium**; **selling concession**).

management group. A **euromarkets term** for the senior **underwriters** to an issue. The management group consists of the **lead manager**, **co-lead manager**, senior managers, **co-managers**, junior managers and **special bracket**, although not all will be present in any one transaction.

manager. A senior participant in a transaction (cf. **book runner**; **lead manager**; **co-lead manager**). In the **eurobond** market it means an **underwriter**.

managing underwriter (USA). See **lead manager**.

mandate. An authoritization for a financial intermediary to carry out specific or general actions on behalf of a client (cf. **agent**; **lead manager**).

mandatory conversion premium dividend preferred stock (USA). See preference equity redemption cumulative stock.

mandatory convertible bond (USA). Used by US banks in **primary capital** issues, it is a **convertible bond** where they issue new **common stock** on **maturity** in order to provide the cash for redemption. If the **stock** cannot be sold to third parties, then the **bond** holder will receive the stock instead of cash. In some cases the holder may select to receive the stock instead of cash. The attraction for banks is that such issues are treated as primary capital for **capital adequacy** purposes by the regulators. The instrument has also been used on the international capital markets for issuers who would have difficulty issuing a large amount of stock but wish to treat the proceeds as **equity**. Often the security provides a higher yield than the shares and may be denominated in a currency other than that of the issuer's shares.

mandatory quote period (Equities; UK). The requirement on days when dealings on the London Stock Exchange (LSE) take place for **market-makers** to display the prices at which they are prepared to undertake transactions (cf. **normal market size**; **normal quote size**; **two-way price**). Currently the LSE requires for: Stock Exchange Automated Quotations listed securities: 08.00–16.30 (in UK time); Stock Exchange Automated Quotations International: 09.30–16.00.

mandatory redemption. An issue of securities under which the borrower is required to retire part of the issue before **maturity**, either by buying them in the market or by **drawings** at **par** through the use of a **sinking fund** or **purchase fund** (cf. **lot**).

Manila International Futures Exchange, Inc. (MIFE) (Philippines). 7th Floor, Producers Bank Centre, Paseo de Roxas, Makati, Metro Manila (tel. (632) 812 7776, 818 5496; fax (632) 818 5529, 810 5763). Established on 12 October 1984.

Manila Stock Exchange (MSE) (Equities; Philippines). Established in 1927 and modelled on the New York Stock Exchange.

manipulation. Controlling the price of an asset with a view to making a gain (cf. **limit**; **mani-manipulation**; **ramp**).

maple leaf (Canada). A one troy ounce **gold** coin issued by the Canadian Mint. One of a number of gold coins which are available to be bought by individuals globally and actively traded on the **London bullion market** (cf. **kruggerand**).

Marathon bond (Greece). A drachma (Dr) denominated bond issued by a non-resident in the Greek domestic market. The first such issue was launched by the **European Investment Bank** in February 1994. It was for Dr10bn for five years with a **coupon** of 17 1/2%.

marché (French). Market. Thus *marché monétaire* is the **money market**; *marché d'échanges* the **foreign exchange market**; *marché à devise*, the stock market.

Marché à Terme International de France (MATIF) (France). 176 rue Montmartre, 75002 Paris (tel. 33 1 40 28 82 82; fax 33 1 40 28 80 01). Established in 1986, it is the principal **futures exchange** in France.

marché au comptant (French). Cash market.

Marché des Options Négociables de Paris (MONEP) (France). Société de Compensation des Marchés Conditionnels, 39 rue Cambon, 75001 Paris (tel. 33 1 49 27 18 00; fax 33 1 49 27 18 23). Established in 1987 it is the **exchange-traded options market** which is the complement in terms of **derivatives** coverage to the Marché à Terme International de France.

Marché des Valeurs Nouvelles (MVN) (Equities, France). Proposed exchange for small companies to be set up by the Paris Bourse (cf. **Alternative Investment Market**; **National Association of Securities Dealers Automated Quotations**; **stock exchange**).

margin. (i) In the **money markets** and banking, an adjustment, given in **basis points**, which is added to or subtracted from a **reference rate** to provide the **floating rate** or **short-term rate** for a security or loan. See **quoted margin**; **spread**. (ii) In the floating rate note market, a measure of the return computed on the basis of some **reference rate** such as the **London interbank offered rate**. See **discounted margin**; **simple margin**. (iii) For **futures** and **exchange-traded options contracts**, the cash deposit demanded by the exchange (or **broker**) from a market participant to indicate good faith and to minimize its **credit risk** (cf. **guarantee**; **initial margin**; **maintenance margin**; **variation margin**). Also called a *performance bond* and sometimes referred to as *equity*. (iv) In the securities markets, either: that part of the total value of the security price for a purchase of securities on **credit**; or the amount of **collateral** (usually a cash deposit or high-grade negotiable securities) provided against **delivery** by a short seller to a broker. (v) In **repurchase agreements** or **reverse repurchase agreements**, the amount by which the market value of the securities exceeds the funds lent (cf. **haircut**). (vi) In banking, the difference between the loan amount and the market value of **collateral** provided. If the latter exceeds the former, then there is no margin. (vii) In banking, the difference between the cost of funds and the rate at which those funds can be re-lent (cf. **London interbank offered rate**; **London interbank bid rate**; **net interest income**). (viii) Sometimes used in the same meaning as **spread**: the difference between the **bid** and **offer** price quoted or between the yield of two securities of the same **class**.

margin account. An account kept with a **broker** which is used as **collateral** and against which the purchase or **short sale** of securities on **margin** is made, or for recording the margin position in respect to a (usually **exchange-traded**) **derivatives** contract (cf. **hypothecation**; **initial margin**; **maintenance margin**; **variation margin**).

margin agreement. The agreement covering the administration of a **margin account**. Known in the USA as a *hypothecation agreement*.

marginal cost. In economics, the additional costs associated with producing an extra unit of output. In cost accounting, the variable costs used for *marginal cost pricing*.

marginal reverse forex linked bond. See **dual currency bond**.

marginal risk (Forex). See **replacement cost**.

marginal tax rate. The tax rate that would be paid on any additional taxable income. In some cases, this is significantly higher than the tax rate on existing income since lower levels of income can use certain types of fixed deductions or **tax**

shields and may also be taxed at a lower rate. See **tax break.**

margin as a percentage. A type of **coupon** on a **floating rate note** where the **spread** over the reference rate is expressed as a percentage. For instance a note which pays 112.5% of the **London interbank offered rate** (LIBOR). Such a note would have a coupon of 6.75% when LIBOR was 6% (plus 75 **basis points**), but a coupon of 13.5% if LIBOR was 12% (plus 150 basis points). As a result, the spread is a constant fraction of the reference rate. Note that this pricing method is infrequently used due to its complexity and that the amount of spread varies, not with the issuer's **risk** but with interest rates. It might, however, be appropriate for an issuer whose **credit rating** was inversely linked to movements in interest rates.

margin call. (i) Notice issued by a **futures** or **options exchange** or by a **broker** to their clients, instructing market participants to provide more **margin** for their existing open positions in response to adverse movements in the market price or rate in order to maintain the position's **margin requirement.** The amount of new margin required, known as **variation margin,** is calculated from the adverse change in the position from the previous day's close to the current close, less any excess margin in the account (cf. **initial margin; maintenance margin; open interest; settlement price).** Margin normally has to be provided within a specific period following the call. Failure to provide the additional **collateral** required normally leads to the automatic **closing out** of the position, thus safeguarding the position of the broker or **clearing house** (cf. **forced sale; stop-loss).** (ii) Requirement for a buyer of securities on margin to provide additional collateral to the transaction (cf. **five hundred dollar rule; stop loss).**

margin for credit swap. Method used to provide **credit enhancement** to the holder of an asset, loan, or security where, in exchange for an agreed **margin,** the **counterparty** agrees to place a price **floor** on the value at **maturity.** It is equivalent to holding a **put** on the **underlying** at a fixed price and paying the **premium** in instalments (cf. **Boston option).**

margin offset. A reduction in the amount of margin that can be had when a series of **positions** are held in **futures** or **exchange-traded options.** See **standard portfolio analysis of risk.**

margin of profit (USA). A firm's **operating profit** divided by sales or **turnover.** See **ratio analysis.**

margin purchase (USA). The acquisition of an asset or security on **margin,** that is with borrowed money.

margin requirement. (i) The amount of **margin** required by a **broker** for a security purchase made on **credit.** (ii) The amount that regulators require market participants to provide for securities transactions made using margin (usually **short selling).**

margin trading. The practice of buying securities using largely (up to 90%) borrowed funds with the intention of making a **short-term** gain (cf. **leverage).**

margrabe option. See **outperformance option.**

mark (UK). A practice of the **London Stock Exchange** to price and date each transaction for entry into the exchange's publication, the *Stock Exchange Daily Official List.* Marking was required for the **account settlement** system formerly used in the London market.

markdown. Securities **market-makers'** decision to reduce the prices at which they are prepared to transact.

marked-to-market or **mark-to-market.** (i) The revaluation of a security, **commodity, futures,** or **option contract** or other negotiable asset **position** to its current market, or realizable, value (cf. **book cost; book loss).** (ii) For securities which require **margin** payments, a revaluation of the amount of margin owing or owed on a position as a result of changes in their value (cf. **collateral; maintenance margin; variation margin).** (iii) In financial institutions, part of the process of measuring the impact of **market risk** on a position (cf. **hedge accounting; provision; hold back; reserve).** See **value at risk.**

marker crude. Crude oil is not a single product. Each oilfield will produce oil with different specifications and when refined will provide a different mix of the refined products. To facilitate trading in crude oil, it has become customary to reference the different field outputs to a **benchmark** or marker crude. The three most important ones are: Arabian Light (Arabian Gulf), Brent Oil (North Sea Oil), West Texas Intermediate (WTI) (US mainland and Gulf of Mexico).

market. (i) Traditionally, the location where transactions may take place in a particular type or **class** of security or other financial instrument, for instance a **stock exchange.** The term market and exchange have often been used interchangeably. Market is now often used to refer to the process of transactions rather than a particular location. In many instances, such as the **over-the-counter** markets, the market is those who participate actively in transactions rather than a physical location. (ii) The activity in a particular type or class of **asset,** security, **commodity,** instrument, and so on. For instance, the *foreign exchange market*, which is where foreign exchange transactions are undertaken; the *stock market*, the market-place for stocks (cf. **common stock; loan stock; preferred stock**). This can be formal and, often, a physical location, such as an **exchange**, the **floor** or **pit**, or over the counter and hence diffuse. The market in the latter case is more the actions of participants than any bounded organization. (iii) The price or rate at which financial intermediaries are willing to buy and sell. Hence 'at the market'; that is, at the current price or rate (cf. **forward; off-market; spot**). (iv) The trading opportunities provided by a particular group or set of institutions (cf. **crowd; marketability**). See **broker; broker-dealer; market-maker; principal; specialist**. (v) To offer to buy or sell. That is, to 'make a market'. (vi) The demand or supply for a particular asset, security, instrument, commodity, and so on. See **market forces**.

marketability. Often used to describe the ease with which securities can be bought and sold at a particular price. More specifically, used to indicate that large volumes of securities can be traded with little or no effect upon their prices (cf. **market impact; market liquidity risk**). See **liquidity**.

marketability risk. The ability to realize **assets** without loss of principal in the event of unforeseen demands for cash (cf. **liquidity**). See **forced sale**.

marketable eurodollar collateralized securities (MECS) (Bonds; UK). A **synthetic security** created by setting up a **special purpose vehicle** to hold the United Kingdom **floating rate note** due 1996 as **collateral**, together with an **interest rate swap** to convert the **coupon** payments to a **fixed rate**.

marketable quantity (UK). The commitment made by **market-makers** operating on the **London Stock Exchange** following the reforms known as **Big Bang** to buy or sell at certain volumes at their quoted **two-way prices** (cf. **lot**). For **alpha** and **beta shares** this was normally 5,000 and 1,000 shares respectively; for **gamma** and **delta shares** it was 1,000 and 100 respectively; and for **gilt-edged** securities no such requirement was made. It was intended to ensure an active and **liquid market** in those securities in which the market-makers specialize (cf. **fair-weather trading**). It was replaced in 1991 by the **normal market size** method of dealing (cf. **normal quote size**).

market access. The ability of an entity to raise **funds** in a particular market. Whether this is possible may depend on regulations governing a particular market or perceptions as to the entity's **credit worthiness**. Thus, for instance, firms which are below **investment grade** may not be able to issue **bonds** in the corporate bond market since participants would not be prepared to hold such securities (cf. **junk bond**).

market amount. See **lot**.

market analysis. An approach to investment that looks at the behaviour of markets rather than individual sectors or securities. See **asset allocation; efficient markets hypothesis; fundamental analysis; strategic asset allocation; tactical asset allocation; technical analysis**.

market auction rate preferred stock (MARPS) (Equities; USA). Product variation on the **auction rate preferred stock** offering the same **at-the-market** resetting of the **dividend** on the **preferred stock** through an **auction** or **tender** process.

Market-By-Price (Canada). The **Toronto Stock Exchange's limit order** reporting system.

market capitalization. A value for a listed company arrived at by multiplying the outstanding **common stock** or **ordinary shares** by the market price. See **capitalization; market valuation**.

market capitalization rate. The consensus-expected return on a security. It is normally calculated as the reciprocal of the **price–earnings ratio**.

market content. The value of shares that are added to a bond to make up the value of an **equity warrant issue** (cf. **exercise content**).

Market Eye (UK). Real-time market data service from the **London Stock Exchange** provided in conjunction with the British Broadcasting Corporation's (BBC) Datacast service. It covers UK and international **equities**, **gilt-edged** and fixed interest securities, and **traded options**.

market failure. The inability of the market to develop in a competitive way (cf. **cartel**). See also **monopoly**.

market forces. The interactions of supply and demand in a market which then dictates the price and quantity available. Generally an increase in supply will depress prices, an increase in demand will raise them, although every market will have specific characteristics which will add complications.

market for corporate control. See **mergers and acquisitions** (cf. **takeover**).

market gap. The risk arising from discontinuous price or rate movements (cf. **gap; jump**). It is a particular problem for **arbitrage** or **hedging** transactions which depend on frequent rebalancing of the **position** or continuous adjustments of the hedge in response to changes in the market (cf. **dynamic hedging; option pricing**). See **portfolio insurance; program trading**.

market going better (up), market going down (worse). A trader's description of market movements (cf. **bearish; bullish; technical condition**).

market-if-touched (MIT). A type of price **order** which automatically becomes a **market order** if the price is reached and is consequently executed at the prevailing market price even if higher (lower) than the stated price (cf. **limit order; limit order board; stop order**).

market impact. The effect on market prices of a large buy or sell order (cf. **block; lot**). Under the **efficient markets hypothesis**, information is incorporated into prices; a decision to make large purchase or sale is potentially seen by market participants as a significant new piece of information. Large transactions may also temporarily affect the **liquidity** of the market. It can be a significant component of an investor's total **transaction costs**.

market index. A broad price or rate **index** designed to capture the movements of a **market** as a whole. Often called a *composite index*.

market index deposit (MID). Deposits with a financial intermediary where the return is linked to the performance of an **index**, usually a stock index. See **equity-linked note**.

market index target term security (MITT). See **equity-linked note**.

market instrument. See **instrument; money market instrument**.

market letter. Another term for a **newsletter**.

market line. See **Capital Asset Pricing Model**.

market liquidity risk. The risk that positions cannot be sold at the prevailing market price. Also known as *forced sale risk*. See also **liquidity; market impact; market risk**.

market-maker. (i) A financial intermediary who makes a **market** in a security or instrument (cf. **broker-dealer; specialist**). This might be an informal undertaking to transact business, or formally regulated by an agency. For instance, market-makers on the **National Association of Securities Dealers Automated Quotations** have to meet various operational and regulatory conditions. See also **make a market; liquidity**. (ii) (UK)

Specifically a type of broker-dealer at the **London Stock Exchange** who undertakes the making of two-way prices for buyers and sellers in particular securities. Pre-**Big Bang** this role was fulfilled by **jobbers** (cf. **specialists**). See **equity market-maker; gilt-edged market-maker**.

market-maker scheme. A method of providing **liquidity** to a security, a **class** of securities, or a market through a commitment by a **market-maker** to agree to make continuous **two-way prices**. Such schemes are often used with the introduction of a new **future** or **exchange-traded option** contract where the early trading may suffer from a perceived lack of liquidity or two-way demand. In the case of an exchange, such market-makers may commit not only to provide a **bid** and **offered** price on a continuous basis, but also to staff the trading position, or **pit**, at all times during the **session**. Brokers who agree to such conditions are sometimes called a *designated market-maker*.

market microstructure. (i) The processes by which financial instruments are traded (cf. **auction; order**). (ii) The study of intraday trading patterns and the behaviour of financial intermediaries (cf. **broker; broker-dealer; market-maker; specialist**).

market-not-held order. A transaction instruction giving the **broker** the right to use discretion in executing the transaction.

market-on-close order (MOC). A transaction instruction to buy or sell at the **close** of a trading session at the prevailing market price (cf. **limit order**). The close is usually the last five minutes of trading.

market order. Transaction instruction requiring immediate execution at the best prevailing market price (cf. **at best**). See also **good till cancelled; limit order; stop loss**.

market-out clause (USA). See **force majeure**.

market overhang. A theory of market movements that postulates that sellers of securities will hold off making sales because such action would depress prices. Sellers will want to see a firmer tone to the market before making sales. Such a situation means that should prices rise, potential sellers will be tempted into the market, limiting any upward movement. See **accumulation; resistance area; technical analysis**.

market participant. Any institution which is an active buyer and seller in a **market**. This includes intermediaries, lending and investing institutions, as well as borrowers and issuers.

market portfolio. A theoretical concept used in the Capital Asset Pricing Model in order to derive an equilibrium relationship for pricing risk. It is a portfolio that contains every asset in the economy.

market power. (i) The ability of a firm to obtain higher prices for its products. (ii) The ability of a financial intermediary to place large quantities of securities (cf. distribution). See bulge bracket; lead manager.

market price. The last traded price or current good quotes by market-makers. For bonds, it usually excludes accrued interest. See clean price; dirty price; income bond.

market price of risk. The extra return demanded by investors for taking on risk. In modern portfolio theory, it is the reward to risk ratio of the market portfolio.

market profile. A technical analysis or chartist method of evaluating intra-day trading which involves breaking up the period into smaller time spans (say 20 to 30 minutes each) and identifying price patterns within these segments. It is based on views about market participants' behaviour such as the tendency to open positions in the morning, low levels of activity at lunchtime, and the early afternoon followed by closing-out activity prior to the end of the session (cf. day time trading).

market risk. (i) That part of the overall risk of an asset, organization, position, or portfolio which is due to potential changes in their market price (cf. currency risk; market liquidity risk; price risk; interest rate risk; volatility). It can be taken either as an absolute risk, arising from changes in market value, or as a relative risk, due to underperformance against the market (cf. imperfect hedge; tracking error). See also value at risk. (ii) In modern portfolio theory, it is the risk that cannot be diversified away (cf. systematic risk). See Capital Asset Pricing Model.

market risk premium. The additional return market participants require above the risk-free rate for taking on market risk (cf. price risk).

market segmentation theory. (i) A theory about the term structure of interest rates and the structure of the yield curve, which proposes that its shape is determined by the supply and demand for securities within different maturity ranges and which suggests that there is little leakage between maturities in supply and demand. (cf. short-term; medium-term; long-term). (ii) Informally, a view held by market participants that investors will confine themselves to specific parts of a market or markets, thus allowing price dis-

crepancies to develop and permitting arbitrage (cf. anomaly).

market surveillance. See stock watch.

market timer. An investment strategy based on catching changes in the direction of markets rather than the performance of individual securities.

market timing. An investment strategy that involves increasing exposure to the market if the expected return is above holding short-term cash (cf. dynamic hedging; portfolio insurance).

market-to-book ratio. The market value of common stock or ordinary shares divided by the book value (cf. market capitalization; Tobin's q). It can also be worked out on a per share basis. It is also called the *price-to-book ratio* and sometimes the *takeover ratio*.

market tone. The condition or mood of the market is often reported in the financial press. Thus, it can be seen as bullish, bearish, neutral, undecided, hesitant, nervous, patchy, tired, and so on (cf. colour).

market touch (UK). The practice of the Stock Exchange Automated Quotations system of identifying the best bid and offer prices available and displaying this as the yellow strip (cf. blue screen; red screen).

market trend. The general movement in prices or rates that pertain to a market (cf. bear market; bull market; sideways moving market).

market valuation. A measure of the value of a company based upon the current market price of its common stock multiplied by the number of shares issued. Also known as *market capitalization* (cf. capitalization).

market value. Another term for market price (cf. marked-to-market). Also called *open market value*.

market value accounting. A method of reporting assets and liabilities by repricing their value in terms of their current market values (cf. marked-to-market).

market value-weighted index or **value weighted index**. A method of index construction which employs the market capitalization of the securities in the index to determine the relative weights and importance to be attached to each.

marking or **mark** (UK). The recording of a price at which a deal has been struck. See Stock Exchange Daily Official List.

marking name (UK). An institution recognized by the **London Stock Exchange** as suitable for the **registration** of US and Canadian shares in its name, and for the distribution of **dividends**.

marking up/marking down (Equities; UK). Anticipatory changes made to their **quotes** by **market-makers** in the expectation of either increased demand or supply. Market-makers will intepret any news, rumours, or other price-moving events as likely to cause buying and selling and adjust prices accordingly. See also **efficient markets hypothesis**.

Markovian models. Types of **option pricing** models that assume the **underlying** price or rate process follows a **Markov process**. Typically these are **models** for pricing options on interest rates, or the **term structure of interest rates**.

Markowitz portfolio model. A model for portfolio **diversification** based on the **mean** and **variance** of expected return and a key development in the theory of diversification and **asset allocation**. The model assumes that expected returns on a security can be defined by their mean and variance; when two or more securities are combined in a portfolio, the sum of the two returns depends on the **covariance** or **correlation** between the securities' returns. Given suitable combinations of securities, Harry Markovitz demonstrated that by combining securities into portfolios, investors could obtain either significantly higher returns for the same **risk** or the same return with significantly lower risk. His insights led to the development of a theory of asset price formation, the **Capital Asset Pricing Model**, although the original Markowitz model made no assumptions about **equilibrium** prices. See Harry Markowitz (1952) 'Portfolio Selection', *Journal of Finance*, 7: 77–91.

Markov process. A stochastic or random process where only the current value or rate is used for predicting the future. It is assumed that such processes have no memory and that the value or rate in a previous period has no bearing on the current price. The best prediction for the future is the current price plus a stochastic value drawn from some type of probability distribution. This kind of time process has also been called a *martingale* or a *random walk*. See **Brownian motion**; **geometric Brownian motion**; **Wiener process**.

mark-to-market. See **marked-to-market**.

married put. An investment strategy which involves purchasing **put options** and the **underlying** at the same time. The investor is thus protected from any adverse price movements below the **strike** price for the life of the **option**. Another way of achieving this is to buy **calls** on the under-

lying. The rationale for the married put approach rather than holding calls lies in the expected behaviour of the underlying: for instance, where there is some possibility of exceptional payments on the underlying, which would then accrue to the married put holder but not the call holder (cf. **leakage**).

martingale. Type of random diffusion process without a drift or **trend** component. Prices in financial markets are sometimes considered to follow such a process. Also known as a *stochastic process*.

master agreement. An umbrella contract between two parties under which repeated transactions may take place. This is commonly used in the **swaps market** and is becoming usual in other markets such as **foreign exchange** (cf. **netting**).

master limited partnership (USA). A type of publicly held **limited partnership** where the partner's interests are tradable as **depository receipts** (cf. **American depository receipt**; **European depository receipt**). The structure is typically used for **assets** divested from corporations, known as *roll outs* where cash-generating companies have sought to mitigate the effects of double-taxation of **dividends** by their **shareholders**, or previously private limited partnerships where the original partners wanted to sell their stakes. It has sometimes also been used in the **mergers and acquisitions** market to avoid the attentions of a hostile **predator** (cf. **crown jewels**; **self-uglification**).

master notes (USA). Unsecured notes repayable on demand. They can be issued in a variety of forms, either with **fixed rate** or **variable rate** interest, denominated in foreign currency or embody other features, making them a useful mechanism for issuers and investors. The notes have a maximum **maturity** of 270 days but, usually, are **puttable** at will.

master swap agreement. Set of documents covering existing and future **swap** transactions between two **counterparties**. Each new transaction will be made on the basis of the **master agreement**.

master trust. (i) (Bonds; USA). A method used for asset-backed securities, where the **pool** of assets is held in **trust** as **collateral** for the issue (cf. **pay-through**; **put-through bond**). See **mortgage-backed**. (ii) Another name for a **fund of funds**.

matador bond (Spain). A **foreign bond** in the Spanish domestic market (cf. **bulldog bond**; **yankee**).

match or **matching**. (i) Equalizing **assets** and **liabilities** or **long** and **short positions** by time or currency (cf. **asset-liability management; assets repriced before liabilities; flat; matched book**). See **cover**. (ii) In **settlement** a trade is said to match when the details recorded by the buyer and seller are equal and opposite (cf. **bad delivery; comparison ticket; fail; out-trade**).

matched and lost. An explanation as to why an order was not able to be executed. When two orders have identical terms one will receive precedence based on the exchange's rules for deciding the sequence of transactions. Matched and lost refers to a situation when the order either was passed over in favour of an order with a higher priority or, if identical to another order, lost out in being chosen for execution.

matched bargain (UK). **Put-through** transaction involving the simultaneous purchase (sale) and sale (purchase) of a security. See **inter-dealer broker**.

matched book. (i) A **portfolio** or **position** where the maturity of the **assets** is equal to that of the **liabilities**. The converse is called a **mismatched book** or an **open book** (cf. **square**). See also **immunization**. (ii) Applied to a collection of **repurchase agreements** and **reverse repurchase agreements**. Securities acquired by repurchase agreement deals are paired off against reverse repurchase agreements on the same security for the same **maturity**. The manager operating the matched book acts as **principal** in all deals and incurs any liabilities. Sometimes called a *repurchase book*; traders may sometimes call a matched book a *closed book* (cf. **open book**).

matched deal. See **put-through**.

matched funding. The matching of borrowing, or funding, to the **maturity** of the **assets** being funded (cf. **matched book**). See **asset-liability management**.

matched orders (USA). A method **specialists** use for achieving an **opening price** when there is an imbalance between buy and sell orders by finding the nearest price difference.

matched repurchase agreement. A condition said to arise when an intermediary has simultaneously entered into a **repurchase agreement** (RP) and a **reverse repurchase agreement**. Thus, the intermediary has lent a security and borrowed money via the RP and borrowed a security and lent money through the reverse RP, making a spread on the transaction in the middle. As a result, the intermediary is running a **matched book**.

matched sales. (i) The converse of a repurchase agreement; in the context of **matched book** operations it means lending cash with securities as collateral. See also **reverse repurchase agreement**. (ii) (USA) Also describes the process by which the **Federal Reserve** takes in surplus reserves from the banking system by selling securities, technically a *matched sale purchase transaction* (MSP) (cf. **reverses**).

matched swap. Swap where one **leg** of the transaction's cash flows are matched to an existing **asset** or **liability** flow. The effect is to transform the nature of the cash flows, either in terms of **currency** or **interest rate** exposure (cf. **asset swap; liability swap; synthetic**).

match fund or **match funding** (Banking). A banking practice of matching a **loan**, an **asset** from the bank's viewpoint, with a **deposit**, a **liability**, of the same **maturity** (cf. **assets repriced before liabilities**). See **asset-liability management; risk management**.

material adverse change. A provision within a standby facility allowing the **underwriter** or lender to refuse to extend funds in the event of a significant change in the material status of the borrowing entity.

material facts. Information that is required to be disclosed in a **prospectus** or **offer for sale**.

material news. Information of a price-sensitive nature that is normally required to be made immediately public if the firm is **listed** on an exchange. Examples include **acquisitions, dividend** announcements, profits forecasts and warnings, and any other major news such as changes in the directors.

matrix pricing. Method used by financial information providers to provide an estimate of the current market price of **fixed rate** securities. The relevant security is priced in relation to other, more actively traded securities which are matched in terms of **coupon maturity** and **credit worthiness**.

matrix trading. A method of **bond trading** or **risk arbitrage** which involves taking **long** or **short** positions in similar securities which are temporarily mispriced relative to each other (cf. **anomaly; switch**).

mature. The point at which a security or contract ceases to exist (cf. **expiry**). See **maturity**.

maturity, maturity date, or **final maturity.** (i) The period or date when the **principal** or nominal value becomes payable to the holder (cf. **expiry**). When an asset or security has been issued for a period of time, the amount of time still due to elapse before repayment or redemption is known as the **current maturity** or **life** (cf. **life-to-call**). The day repayment is due is known as the *maturity date* or *redemption date*. See **call; extendible; puttable; retractable bond**. (ii) In the **commodities** markets, term for the period when **settlement** can be made by **physical delivery**. That is the time between the **first notice day** (when participants can elect to receive or deliver the **physical commodity**) and last trading day in the expiring **futures contract** (cf. **expiry**). (iii) For **derivatives**, the point of termination of the contractual liability.

maturity adjustable preferred stock (MAPS) (Equity; USA). A type of **floating rate preferred stock** where the **tenor** of the reset period can be adjusted. This is normally done in response to **market** conditions to make the issue more attractive to investors or in response to definite views as to the direction of interest rates by the issuer.

maturity balance (USA). The composition of federal and other securities held by the **Federal Reserve**.

maturity buckets. **Risk management** term for a series of time periods within which **principal** payments are made. Thus maturity buckets might be set for one month, two, three, and six months, and one year, two, three, four, five years, and longer. These buckets are then used to report any **mismatch** between **assets** and **liabilities** (cf. **assets repriced before liabilities; gap analysis**). An extended approach which includes both interest and principal is generally known as *cash buckets*.

maturity date. The date a security is repaid or terminates. In the UK, this is called the *redemption date*. Sometimes it is also applied to **futures** and **options** contracts, but this is technically incorrect for options since these are 'wasting assets' and they **expire** on their **expiry date**, if they are not exercised. See also **maturity**.

maturity factoring. Factoring arrangements which provide for the **factor** to take on the **risk** of non-payment and arrange for collection of the debt.

maturity gap. Method for establishing **interest rate risk** or **currency exposure** by looking at the difference between **assets** and **liabilities** which are repriced within the period or gap (cf. **duration**). The great attraction of the method is its simplicity. To determine the amount of interest rate risk for any given period only requires a knowledge of the **maturity** of the two sides of the balance sheet at the point in time (cf. **assets repriced before liabilities**). The difference is then used to calculate how much risk there is from a given change in interest rates. Each gap period is then summed to provide

an overall interest rate exposure, which is a measure of the magnitude of the **risk** being taken from mis-matching assets and liabilities. A variation on this approach is known as the **funding gap**. See also **asset-liability management**.

maturity gap exposure (Forex; Money markets). The **risk** arising from having an **asset** and **liability** of equal size and of the same currency but with different maturities (cf. **assets repriced before liabilities**). Sometimes known as *refinancing risk* or *refunding risk*. See also **risk management**.

maturity guarantee (Bonds). A method used for asset-backed issues to ensure that at **maturity** there are sufficient **funds** to guarantee **redemption** of the securities. A maturity guarantee normally involves a third party to the transaction agreeing to purchase for cash any **residual** to the **pool** of **assets** that have been securitized rather than having to make good a shortfall in **principal** (cf. **over-collateralized**).

maturity ladder. A report showing the amounts due by **maturity** (cf. **ageing schedule**). It is used for **asset-liability management** purposes to show the **funding gap** that may exist (cf. **mismatch**). An example is shown in the Table. The difference between the maturity of the assets in each period gives the period gap or mismatch between the two positions.

Period	Assets	Liabilities	Assets *less* liabilities (the gap or mismatch)
1	100	350	−250
2	250	150	100
3	150	100	50
4	175	200	−25
5	200	125	75
6	100	50	50
Sum	975	975	0

maturity mismatch risk. **Risk** arising from a cross-hedge that the two sides of the **hedge** may fail to perform in tandem (cf. **basis risk; spread risk**).

maturity value. The maturity value of a security is normally the same as its **principal** or **par value**. This is not always the case: for example, **index-linked bonds** or where the principal is repaid as a stream of redemption payments (cf. **serial securities**). Bonds with call provisions may have a value greater than the **principal** by virtue of a **premium**. Thus an issuer may have the right to redeem the bonds early but must pay, say, 101 of the par value to do so (cf. **declining call schedule; redemption**).

maturity yield. See yield-to-maturity (cf. redemption yield).

maximum capital gains mutual fund (USA). A type of fund which aims to maximize its return through **capital gains**.

maximum daylight delivery limit (MDDL) (Forex). A **limit** for the maximum level of exposure for a **counterparty** allowed during one **delivery** or **settlement** cycle (usually a day) used by institutions to limit their **delivery risk**. A bank's counterparty limit may allow, say, an exposure of 100, but set an MDDL of 20. Limiting the amount of delivery risk is desirable since the risk of loss from yet-to-be settled transactions and those being settled is different. The loss on outstanding **forward** transactions will be the replacement cost (i.e. the difference between the original contract price and the ability of the bank to reconstitute the transaction with another party); while for those being settled it might be the entire principal amount (cf. **Herstatt Bank**).

maximum fluctuation. See price limit.

maximum margin. (i) In the **commercial paper** market, the maximum **margin**, in relation to some interest **reference rate**, at or below which **tender** bids must be made. (ii) Also used to indicate the margin at which **underwriters** commit to buy issues if **tenders** fail to clear the issue at or below the maximum margin (cf. **stop price**). See **multi-option financing facility; note issuance facility; short-term note issuance facility**.

maximum price fluctuation. See limit.

maximum publication level (MPL) (Equities; UK). The point at which the size of a transaction on the **London Stock Exchange's Stock Exchange Automated Quotations** may be subject to a time delay in reporting, currently 90 minutes. Normally the MPL is set at three times a **share's normal market size**. The rationale for the rule is to allow **market-makers** who are **long** or **short** the share time to trade out of the position without the market moving against them (cf. **liquidity**). See **market impact**.

maximum rate note. See reverse floating rate note.

maximum slippage. The longest time a start-up project or business with negative **cash flows** can survive on its own resources. Failure to move into a situation where the enterprise is generating a positive cash flow would signal its death knell. See also **Death Valley curve**.

Maximum Stock Exchange Automated Quotations Execution Facility size (Maximum

SAEF size; MSS) (Equities; UK). The largest-sized transaction that may be put through the **London Stock Exchange's** small order facility (SAEF) in a particular security. This is normally the lower of 10% of a **share's normal market size** or a maximum of 500 shares.

May Day (USA). The day fixed **commissions** were abolished in the US **equity** markets (1 May 1975). See **Big Bang**.

mean. The statistical **average** of a series of numbers. It is the sum of the series divided by the number of observations in the series (cf. **geometric mean; median; mode**):

$$\text{Mean} = \frac{1}{n}\sum_{i=1}^{n} x_i$$

See also **standard deviation; variance**.

mean deviation. The average of the absolute deviations of a series from its **mean**:

$$\text{Mean deviation} = \frac{1}{n}\sum_{i=1}^{n} |x_1 - \bar{x}|$$

The deviations $|x_i - \bar{x}|$ from the mean $\bar{x}$ are calculated ignoring the sign. The result is therefore the average of how much observations deviate from the mean.

mean price. The middle price.

mean reversion. Observed behaviour by which a random process, such as characterizes financial market prices or rates, tends to revert to its **mean** or **average** value over time. Mean reversion appears to be a characteristic of financial market behaviour (cf. **jump process**). In terms of analytical models, failure to incorporate this tendency means that longer-dated **options**, for instance, will be mispriced, since pricing models such as the **Black–Scholes option pricing model** assume a **variance** that is a function of the **tenor** of the option. While this seems to work reasonably well for short-dated options, this is untrue for **long-term** options. Various refinements to the basic Black–Scholes approach incorporate mean reversion into the stochastic price-generating process.

mean reversion investment theory. A quantitative method of investing or **portfolio management** which involves buying those **stocks** which have shown statistical evidence of undershooting their **intrinsic value**. It is based on the statistical evidence of prices being 'mean reverting', that is tending to return to their mean or true value after over- or undershooting over time.

mean-variance analysis. Evaluating uncertain investments in terms of their expected return and variance of outcomes (cf. **volatility**). See also **geometric Brownian motion**; **Markowitz portfolio model**.

median. The statistical number which represents the half-way point between the highest and lowest of a series of numbers (cf. **mean**; **mode**). With n data points, the mean is the $[(n + 1)/2]$th observation. In a distribution which is symmetrical the median is the same as the mean. See **standard deviation**; **variance**.

medium of exchange. One of the functions of money. Money acts as an intermediary depository of value facilitating transactions between different economic agents (cf. **barter**; **counter-trade**; **fungibility**).

mediums (Bonds; UK). A UK government **bond** (**gilt-edged**) with a **current maturity** of between five and fifteen years. Bonds in excess of fifteen years are known as **longs** and less than five years as **shorts**.

medium tap tranche certificates of deposit programme. A method of issuing **certificates of deposit** using the mechanics of the **medium-term note** market. Also called a *medium term tap certificate of deposit*.

medium-term. (i) In **bond** markets, initial maturities of between five and ten years. Definitions will vary between different markets. For **US treasuries**, this will apply to **bonds** with maturities in excess of seven to ten years and less than twenty years (cf. **long-term** and **short-term**). For **euro-bonds** this is two to seven years. (ii) In the money markets, maturities of more than one year (cf. **medium-term note**). (iii) In accounting use, those **liabilities** which are longer than one year, but less than ten years.

medium-term certificate of deposit. See **term certificate of deposit**.

medium-term forecast. A forecast which is made for one to five years, i.e. the typical length of one **business cycle**. A short-term forecast would be concerned with events within a year; a long-term forecast for events beyond five years. Such forecasts are often an integral part of the planning and budgeting process.

medium-term interest rate contract. See **interest rate futures** and **options**.

medium-term interest rate future. An intermediate **financial futures** contract on interest rates somewhere between a **short-term** interest rate future based on money market rates and a long-term interest rate future for **bonds** (cf. **yield curve**). The medium-term future has an **underlying notional bond** that has a **maturity** between these two. Considered in terms of the **US treasuries** market, it can be seen as a contract on US Treasury **note** issues, the short-term contract being on **treasury bills** and the long-term contract being on US Treasury bond issues (cf. **long bond**).

medium-term note (MTN). A debt instrument issued with maturities ranging from nine months up to thirty years. Used in both the US capital markets and the **euromarkets**, where maturities are usually up to five years, to target maturities to the precise requirements of investors. Securities are normally issued in **tranches** under an MTN facility and may be **fixed rate**, **floating rate**, or **zero coupon** in structure, where each tranche may possess a unique **maturity** and **coupon rate**. MTNs are usually placed by an intermediary acting as a **dealer** on a **best efforts** basis who is paid a **flat commission** by the issuer, although direct placement by the issuer is not unknown. Like the **commercial paper** market, from which it gets its issuing mechanisms, MTN issuers are encouraged to post rates at which they would be willing to issue. Although principally a **buy-and-hold** instrument, a **secondary market** for MTNs does exist and dealers are usually prepared to repurchase notes placed by them, as are some issuers. MTNs are sometimes seen as the bridge between the **money markets** and the **bond markets**. US issues of MTNs are registered with the **Securities and Exchange Commission** under Rule 415. See also **deposit note**.

The **settlement** and payment methods used on some MTN issues require that all interest payments take place on a predetermined date, regardless of the tranche's issue date or final maturity. As a result, buyers may need to pay **accrued interest** at issue and receive accrued interest at redemption. See **continuously offered long-term securities**.

meeting of creditors. See **creditors' meeting**.

meltdown. Slang term for an abrupt collapse in prices (cf. **crash**).

member bank (USA). Those banks that are members of the **Federal Reserve System**. This includes all nationally **chartered** banks and state chartered banks which have applied and been allowed to join.

member firm. A brokerage firm that is a member of an exchange. Exchanges may also have individual members. All members get to consult on policy decisions and elect the exchange's executive. To be a member is also to have a *seat on the exchange*.

member's rate. Reduced transaction costs and other charges available to **member firms** of an exchange.

members' voluntary liquidation or **winding-up** (UK). A resolution by **shareholders** to terminate a **solvent** company. The directors of the company must make a *declaration of solvency* prior to the resolution being proposed.

memorandum and articles of association (mem. and arts.) (UK). The legal basis for setting up a limited company in the UK (cf. **charter**). This sets out *inter alia*: the number of **ordinary shares** that may be issued; any transfer restrictions on dealings in the shares; the duties and terms of the **board of directors**; borrowing powers, and other relevant conditions to set up in corporate form (cf. **by-laws**).

memorandum of satisfaction (UK). Notice releasing a **lien**. It is signed by all the parties and lodged with the Registrar of Companies.

Mercado de Futuros Financieros Renta Fija (MEFF-RF) (Spain). Via Laietana 58, 08003 Barcelona (tel. 34 (9) 3 412 11 28; fax 34 (9) 3 268 47 69). See next entry.

Mercado de Futuros Financieros Renta Variable (MEFF- RV) (Spain). Torre Picasso, planta 26, 28020 Madrid, (tel. 34 (9) 1 585 08 00; fax 34 (9) 1 571 95 42). Spanish financial **futures** exchange. It has two parts: MEFF Renta Fija (MEFF-RF), handling **financial futures** and **options**; and MEFF Renta Variable (MEFF-RV), which covers futures and options on **common stocks** and **stock indices**. See also **Madrid Stock Exchange**.

Mercato Italiano dei Futures (MIF) (Italy). Comitato di gestione MIF, Piazza de Gesù 49, CAP 00186 Rome (tel. 39 (0) 6 676 7514, 39 (0) 6 676 7211; fax 39 (0) 6 676 7250). **Financial futures** market set up on 11 September 1992 initially with contracts on the ten-year and the five-year government bonds (cf. **Buoni del Tesoro Poliennali**).

Mercato Ristretto (Italy). **Junior** or second-tier market for **unlisted** securities.

merchant bank (UK). A specialist financial institution that offers a range of services including: advising in the raising of corporate capital; **underwriting** security issues; managing client funds; advising on **takeovers** and **mergers and acquisitions**; **foreign exchange** dealing; and participating in **syndication** (cf. **accepting house**). In the USA known as an *investment bank*. Not to be confused with the US activity of **merchant banking**.

merchant banking (USA). A practice of financial institutions to commit their own **capital** to facilitate a transaction, usually a **merger and acquisition**. The advising institution will provide **funds** from its own resources to assist the **predator** in acquiring a **corporation** with a view to later resyndicating the funding to other **long-term** investors (cf. **bridging finance**). The rationale was (a) to speed up takeovers since third party finance did not have to be put in place at the same time as the acquisition, and (b) to improve the profitability of the transaction to the intermediary. The practice was common in the 1980s but a succession of costly poorly performing transactions has subsequently reduced the appeal of this type of activity. See also **risk arbitrage**; **proprietary trading**.

merger. (i) A combination of two companies in which two firms are absorbed more or less as equals into a new entity (cf. **exchange of assets**; **exchange of stock**). (ii) Used loosely in the **mergers and acquisitions** market to indicate an agreed, or friendly, **takeover** or combination of two companies (cf. **hostile takeover**).

merger accounting. The methods used for the **consolidation** of two companies which are merged. There are basically two approaches: pooling of interests and purchase of assets (cf. **exchange of assets**; **exchange of stock**). With the pooling of interests approach, the two merging companies are grouped via a holding company. With the purchase of assets, one company acquires the other.

Merger Control Directive (EC) No. 4064/89. Regulations established by the European Community to regulate **mergers and acquisitions** within the Community. The criterion for consideration is that (i) the aggregate world-wide turnover of the undertakings involved is more than ECU 5 bn; (ii) the aggregate Community-wide **turnover** of each of, at least two, of the undertakings is in excess of ECU 250 million, unless each of the firms involved achieves more than two-thirds of its aggregate Community wide turnover within one member state.

mergers and acquisitions (M & A). The route by which some firms choose to grow involves getting together with another enterprise and is described using the following terms: **merger**; **takeover**, *amalgamation, absorption, fusion, integration* and *agglomeration* (*uniting of interest*). Analytically, it is possible to distinguish between two main ways that firms can get together and four main types of association. The two methods are: (1) *Takeover*: technically known as an 'acquisition', and where there is a dominant firm and where the owners of the subordinate enterprise give up their interest in exchange for a consideration given by the other enterprise. For example, Firm A takes over Firm B to create an enlarged Firm A. Conventionally, firm A would be the larger of the two, although when this is not the case there occurs what is termed a **reverse takeover**. (2) *Merger*: technically known as a 'uniting of interest' or an 'amalgamation', where two or more companies, of roughly equal significance, agree to transfer their capital to another company newly formed for the purpose and the old company is dissolved. For example, Firm A merges with Firm B to form Firm C.

The four types of M & A are:

1. **horizontal merger** or lateral integration, under which the firms involved are in the same industry and could be regarded as competitors;

2. **vertical merger** integration, under which the firms involved are either suppliers (backward) or customers (forward) of each other;

3. **concentric merger** integration, under which the firms involved share some common expertise that may possess mutually advantageous spin-offs. For example, managerial or technological knowledge that may not be industry or product-based; and

4. **conglomerate merger** integration or **diversification**, under which the firms involved may be unrelated and comprise a holding company and a group of subsidiaries engaged in dissimilar activities. This type of transaction is often regarded as the corporate equivalent to **portfolio diversification**, such that when one activity is facing trading difficulties, the chances are that other activities are doing much better so as to produce a creditable performance overall.

Whatever the motivation, or route taken, the objective of companies engaging in such transactions is to improve **growth**, profits, and the quality of earnings. It would be expected that such improvements in performance would lead to a reduction in the **cost of capital** and an increase in **shareholder value**. The evidence from the UK and USA about the success of such deals in meeting the expectations described earlier is, at best, ambiguous. Many commentators would rate the chances at the time of the merger or acquisition as no more than 50 : 50 of its satisfying the targets set at that time. And even then, the deal would have to possess certain characteristics, such as: it would need to be relatively small in value (the price paid would have to represent less than 10% of **market capitalization** of the bidder); it would have to be in a 'related' industry or technology area; and the acquirer would have to have a 'strong' core business activity. See **cartel office; crown jewels; dawn raid; golden hello; golden parachute; greenmail; insider dealing; killer bees; Lady Macbeth; minority interest; Monopolies and Mergers Commission; Pac-man defence; poison pills; porcupine provisions; putting into play; radar alert; Saturday night special; scorched earth; self-**uglification; shark repellents; shark watcher; standstill agreement; Takeover Panel; takeover ratio; white knight; white squire**.

Mergers Task Force. A part of the European Commission which monitors and acts in regulating mergers within the **European Union** in accordance with Regulation 4064.

Mex-Ex issue. An **exit bond** issue made by the United States of Mexico and led by Morgan Guaranty, Mexico's agent bank. It involved a **tender** by creditor banks of existing Mexican debt at a **discount** and the issuing of new **floating rate** bonds in lieu. These had a lower **margin** and collateralized the repayment of **principal**, and hence the bank's exit, by the purchase of a specially issued US Treasury **zero-coupon bond** which matched the principal amount and would guarantee repayment at **maturity**. As a result, holders of the bonds would only be concerned as to Mexico's ability to service the interest payments. The issue was also **listed** and tradable, allowing banks to sell off their commitment prior to maturity. The Mex-Ex issue method of **credit enhancement** has been widely adopted in other situations.

mezzanine bracket. Second tier **underwriters**. Evidence of being a mezzanine member is found in **tombstone** advertisements recording major financial transactions.

mezzanine finance (Banking).(i) A type of high-yielding debt finance often seen in **leveraged buy-out** transactions and often featuring **bells and whistles** (cf. **equity kicker; kicker; sweetener**). When such finance is in the form of a securities issue it is either called **junior** or **subordinated debt**. (ii) In **venture capital**, the next round of finance after **seed capital** has been provided. Also known as *development capital*.

mezzanine level. Term for the stage of a company's life-cycle just prior to it going public.

MIBTEL General Index (Italy). Principal **market index** for Italian **common stocks**. It is a real-time, continuously updated **capitalization-weighted index**, which will automatically include new issues that are traded on the automated continuous computerized trading system used by the Italian Stock-market, a grouping of all the regional exchanges in Italy. The base date is 16 July 1993 at 10,000.

microbond. A **convertible eurobond** issue small in comparison to the market norm.

MicroCap Index (Equities; UK). An index of the smallest 1% of **listed ordinary shares** by market capitalization (cf. **common stocks**). The index is rebalanced every year so that it includes the smallest 1% of the companies on the London Stock Exchange at the end of December. See size effect.

micro-economics. That branch of economic theory concerned with explaining and predicting the behaviour of particular economic agents. These agents are usually defined as individuals, households, and firms. Special interest is attached to the way such units make buying and selling decisions. In the case of individuals and households what is sold is labour. In the case of firms it is goods and services. Together they form the basis of establishing relative prices of goods and factors of production, and the amounts transacted. The ultimate goal of micro-economics is to understand the mechanism by which the resources in an economy are allocated among alternative uses. One of the key concepts is the **market**, the point of interchange between economic agents for goods and services (cf. **market forces**). The other main branch of economics is **macro-economics**, the differences being to do with different levels of aggregation at which economic activity is being observed. See **opportunity cost**.

micro hedge. Risk-reduction method that matches the **hedge** to individual **positions** or assets rather than hedging the whole in one transaction. It could be considered a 'ground-up' method of managing risk (cf. **macro hedge**; **offset**).

MidAmerica Commodity Exchange (USA). See **Midwest Stock Exchange**.

middleman. See **intermediary** (cf. **agent**; **broker**; **broker-dealer**; **jobber**; **market-maker**; **specialist**).

middle office. The systems support and pricing area for **derivatives** sales and trading combining some of the functions of both the traditional **back office** and the **front office**.

middle price or **middle rate** or **mid price** or **mid rate**. The average of a bid and an offer price for the same security or **yield** (cf. **London inter-bank mean rate**). Also called the *mean price* or *rate*.

midget (USA). Intermediate **maturity** level payment **mortgage pass-through security** issued by the **Government National Mortgage Association**.

midget bond (USA). A **mortgage-backed security** where the **underlying pool** of mortgages have an original term of fifteen years rather than the more common thirty-year term. See **collateralized mortgage obligation**.

Midwest Stock Exchange (USA). One of the nine stock exchanges in the United States. See **American Stock Exchange**; **New York Stock Exchange**.

Milano Indice di Borsa (MIB) (Equities; Italy). Much watched **index** seen as the barometer of the Milan Stock Exchange. The index of the thirty leading **common stocks** on the Milan Stock Exchange.

Milan Stock Exchange (Boursa di Milano) (Italy). Piazza Degli Affari 6, 6–20123 Milan (tel. 392 8534).

mine. Market jargon for accepting a quoted price or rate when buying. The opposite is *yours* when selling.

mini-manipulation (USA). An illegal method of manipulation which involves **leveraging** the effects of changes in prices of securities through holding **derivatives**. Because small changes in the **underlying** significantly change the value of derivatives, a manipulator with a large derivatives position can thus benefit from a small amount of price movement in his favour. See also **position limit**.

minimax floating rate note or **bond**. A type of **collared floating rate note** under which the maximum and minimum **coupons** are close together, thus making it resemble a **fixed rate bond**.

mini-maxi. See **range forward**.

minimax option. An option strategy used in the foreign exchange market involving the simultaneous purchase and sale of options with different exercise prices. See **collar**; **cyclinder**; **straddle**; **strangle**; **vertical spread**.

minimax option strategy. An approach to using **options** for **hedging** which aims to reduce the cost by combining the maximum protection with minimum up-front payments. Typically **option combinations** such as **cylinders** or **vertical spreads** are used, or instruments like **breakforwards**.

Minimum Lending Rate (MLR) (Banking; UK). A method used by the **Bank of England** for setting the minimum rate at which the Bank would lend to the banking system to make good money market shortages. It has largely been replaced by **open-market operations** where the Bank 'signals' its intentions by its activities. Nevertheless, it remains in reserve as a crisis management tool. It was used, for instance, on **Black Wednesday** when the Bank announced the minimum lending rate at which it would advance money on the following day (the Thursday). See also **intervention rate**.

minimum maintenance (USA). The amount of equity or positive **collateral**, after the **position** has been **marked-to-market**, that must be in a **margin account** (cf. **initial margin**; **variation margin**).

minimum payment rate (Bonds). The amount of paydown that a **pool** of **assets** needs to make for there to be sufficient cash available to meet **amortization** or **redemption** of an **asset-backed security** (cf. **maturity guarantee**). The alternative is **minimum rollover period** for quick pay assets such as credit card receivables, where the pool is topped up with new loans prior to the **maturity** of the debt issue.

minimum price fluctuation. Smallest price change allowed on an exchange. See **tick**.

minimum quote size (MQS) (UK). The minimum number of **shares**, for the securities for which they are registered, that a **market-maker** on the **London Stock Exchange** is obliged to display prices for on the **Stock Exchange Automated Quotations**.

minimum rate or **minimum coupon rate.** A condition in a **floating rate note** setting the minimum interest rate or **coupon** that would be payable for any **interest period** (cf. **floor**).

minimum reserves or **minimum reserve requirement** (Banking). The smallest amount of reserves allowed to be held by a bank at the central bank (cf. **reserve requirements**).

minimum-risk hedge ratio. The number of futures or options contracts required to be bought or sold that provides the least possibility of variation in the value of the hedged **position** (cf. **delta hedge**; **hedge ratio**).

minimum rollover period. An undertaking provided in various kinds of **securitization** programmes that for those types of assets, such as credit card receivables, where the paydown is very rapid, the originator will provide similar replacement assets for a given minimum period (cf. **asset backed securities**). This is required to provide a reasonable expected **life** to any issue which otherwise would begin to almost immediately **amortize**.

minimum solvency requirement (UK). Applies to the value of the **assets** held in **pension funds** which must not be allowed to fall below 90% of the **liabilities** of the fund. The liabilities of the fund comprise the current and future pension payments, the latter being subject to **actuarial** assumptions. The assets are likely to comprise both fixed and variable return **securities**. To this extent, the valuation of the assets can also be subject to assumptions about the future. The idea behind this requirement is to encourage **trustees** to better **match** the type of assets held, and the **investment strategy** pursued, to the liabilities of the fund (cf. **immunization**).

minimum subscription. The smallest number of securities that can be **bid** for in a new issue.

minimum-variance frontier. See **efficient frontier**.

minimum variance hedge ratio. The ratio of **futures contracts** to the **underlying** used in setting up a **hedge** that provides the smallest difference in the price behaviour of the two sides (cf. **basis risk**). See also **duration-based hedge ratio**.

minimum yield (Bonds; USA). See **yield-to-operative date**.

mini-tap. See **taplet**.

minor bracket. A term used in **underwriting** to describe a junior class of **underwriter** (cf. **bracket**; **mezzanine bracket**; **senior**; **sub-underwriter**).

minority. Less than 50%. This can apply to a situation such as when only a minority of the firm's **common stock** is available for trading on an exchange, or where a holding company has sold off a portion of the **equity** in a subsidiary. Two firms entering into a joint project may set up a firm held 50 : 50, both would then have a **minority interest** in the venture (cf. **equity accounting**).

minority interest. (i) Usually used to describe the shareholdings of a company that are not owned by the parent of a subsidiary (cf. **equity accounting**). (ii) Also applied to a situation where a company is largely owned, and effectively controlled, by a small number of **shareholders** but where there are other small-scale shareholdings.

minority protection. Any of a number of legal remedies or measures enshrined in a company's **charter** giving additional protection to **minority shareholders**. One of the most effective is to prevent any single shareholder having more than a minority (for instance 15%) vote on company resolutions. Thus even if a **shareholder** obtains a majority of the **shares**, the majority shareholder still needs to get the agreement of a majority of the remaining votes (cf. **controlling interest**).

minority shareholder or **stockholder.** One or more **common stock** holders of a company which is majority owned or effectively controlled by a single **shareholder** or group of shareholders with a common interest, such as a family.

minus tick. See **down tick**.

mirror swap. Swap transaction designed to reverse the cash flows and hence exposure of an existing swap position (cf. **termination**).

misclear. See **fail**.

misfeasance. (i) Negligence or dereliction in the performance of some legal action. It is a ground for civil or criminal proceedings. (ii) Breach of trust by a **director** relating to his stewardship of the company. It can arise in cases of **insolvency** (cf. **bankruptcy**).

mismatch. Any position where the **assets** and **liabilities** are not on the same payment frequency or are of different type, do not have the same **maturity**, are denominated in different currencies, or have different characteristics (such as credit, repayment terms, and so on).

mismatch bond. A type of **floating rate note** (FRN) where the **reference rate** is reset more frequently than the **coupon** frequency. Such a **variable rate security** is attractive at times of rising or falling interest rates since it will effectively protect against increases or decreases in short-term rates. There are two basic types of different types of possible mismatch: *Payment mismatch*— the reset period matches that of the reference rate, but the coupon payments are made at different intervals. For instance, an FRN which paid a coupon at six-monthly intervals using a one-month reference rate: the coupon would be a combination of the six one month rates, and *frequency mismatch*—the reset period is more (or less) frequent than the coupon payment period: for example, a coupon referenced to the six-month interbank rate, but where interest was paid monthly.

It is possible to have a note which combines both the payment mismatch and the frequency mismatch, although these are rare. Also sometimes called a *mismatch floater*.

mismatched book. Used to describe a series of long and short positions that do not complement each other and that would produce a loss or profit if price or yield levels changed (cf. **matched book**; **trading book**). See also **asset-liability management** (cf. **assets repriced before liabilities**).

mismatched collar. Interest rate collar or cross-currency collar where the **maturity** of the cap and the floor differ.

mismatched payment swap. Interest rate swap or cross-currency swap where the two sides' payment flows do not match in time. Since most payments are paid net, there is some increased settlement risk from this structure.

mismatch risk. (i) The risk that two sides of a transaction, or a series of transactions, will not be able to be exactly matched. This is a significant risk if the transaction is either illiquid in nature (i.e. of a bespoke character) or very complex, requiring

rapid execution (cf. **market risk**). See **settlement risk**. (ii) The risk in mismatching the **maturity** of **assets** and **liabilities** (cf. **liquidity risk**; **funding risk**). This typically arises from borrowing short and lending long.

misrepresentation. Providing false or untrue facts or information. If deliberate, it is *fraudulent misrepresentation*; if due to carelessness or lack of diligence, *negligent misrepresentation*; if based on reasonable beliefs about the accuracy of the statement, *innocent misrepresentation*. To avoid such problems financial intermediaries will undertake **due diligence** enquiries before undertaking a transaction and will have proper **rules of fair practice** and ethical guidelines to ensure that their **agents** do not misrepresent a given situation to their clients.

missing coupon security. A type of subordinated issue where the issuer has the right either to pass on the **coupon** payment or reduce the amount paid (cf. **income bond**). As a result it is also referred to as a *reduced coupon security*. Many preferred stock issues have this feature (cf. **cumulative**; **non-cumulative**).

mixed spread. A position which does not correspond to any of a range of accepted categories or strategies.

mixer. See **sweetener**.

mobile home certificate (Bonds; USA). A type of mortgage-backed security issued by the **Government National Mortgage Association** where the **underlying** mortgages are for mobile homes.

mobilisation (France). **Discounting** a security.

mock auction. Corrupt practice used in an **auction** with the aim of encouraging outsiders to bid. Typically it involves collusion between the auctioneer and one or more participants in the auction. Most jurisdictions treat such activity as a criminal offence.

mode. A statistical measure of a series of numbers which represents the most frequent value of the series (cf. **median**). In a symmetrical series, the mode equals the mean.

model. A representation of a real object or situation using a set of simplifying assumptions and relationships. Reality comprises a large number of variables, and a large number of often complex interactions between them. In an effort to identify the most important variables, and understand the most significant relationships, it is important to disregard the less important ones. Although this may render the approach 'unrealistic' it can provide insights into a problem, and far greater predictive ability, than would a less abstract approach that tried to take everything into account. In finance models are extensively used for determining the value of instruments. The best example is undoubtedly the **option pricing model** which, in its many forms, is used to provide an accurate estimation of the value and behaviour of options. Models may have several different forms: *iconic models* are physical replicas of the real thing (for instance a toy); *analogue models* provide a physical representation of the modelled activity (for instance a thermometer); and *mathematical models* use symbols and mathematical relationships to evaluate a situation. These can be further divided into two sub-types: the *analytic* or *deterministic* model which provides a close-form solution to a problem and the *stochastic* or *probabilistic* model where the inputs have a random element. Modelling, either explicit or implicit, is extensively used in financial markets as an aid to decision-making (cf. **chartist; fundamental analysis; technical analysis**). See also **Capital Asset Pricing Model**.

model risk. The risk that a financial pricing or hedging model will not perform as expected.

modern portfolio theory (MPT). A theory which demonstrates an optimal or **equilibrium** relationship between risk and return for a **portfolio** of **assets** under idealized conditions. It considers that the risk and return characteristics of a portfolio are not simply the total of the individual securities held. It postulates that return is directly related to risk, which has two parts: *systematic risk*, which is the portfolio's behaviour as a function of the market's behaviour, also called **beta**; and *unsystematic* or *specific risk*, which is the portfolio's behaviour attributable to the selection of individual securities and not correlated with the market. As the latter can be largely removed by **diversification**, the portfolio will be subject mainly to **systematic risk** (cf. **efficient markets hypothesis**). See also **Capital Asset Pricing Model; Markowitz model; risk–reward**.

modified duration. The sensitivity of the price of a **bond** to changes in **yield-to-maturity**. It is used to assess the price volatility of securities; for example, if a bond has a modified duration of 5 then for every 100 **basis points'** change in **yield** the price would change 5% in the other direction. It is normally quoted in terms of years and is additive (weighted by **present value**) in a **portfolio**. Known also as *bond volatility* in the UK (cf. **unmodified duration**). See **bond risk; duration; immunization**.

modified net present value (modified NPV). The value of an **investment** or project that in-

cludes a value for flexibility (cf. **option**). See also **adjusted present value**.

modified pass-through. A **pass-through** certificate that pays interest whether received from the mortgages or not, but only pays out **principal** when received. It is an intermediate variant between the simple pass-through and a **fully modified pass-through**.

Modigliani–Miller hypothesis (MM). Theory governing the relevance of a firm's **capital structure**, i.e its mix of **debt** and **equity**, in establishing the firm's market value. Prior to the MM hypothesis, the accepted view was that debt was beneficial to firms since it added value; MM demonstrated that in a world without taxes or transaction costs, the actual distribution of a firm's cash flows between different classes of securities did not affect their economic value. This was set out in their Proposition I, which asserted that the market value of a firm was independent of its choice of capital structure (the firm's **leverage** or **debt–equity ratio**). The key determinant for the value of the firm's securities was the economic value of the firm's cash flows or its **assets**. Securities were a convenient conduit for redistributing these cash flows and providing resources for firms to engage in productive activities. Proposition II follows from the validity of Proposition I and put forward the proposal that the cost of equity capital was a linear function of the firm's leverage. This result, albeit based on a world of perfect information, no transaction costs or taxes, made irrelevant the firm's choice of capital structure. The **weighted average cost of capital** of the firm thus remained constant. In addition, investors could achieve the same degree of leverage (or de-leverage) by borrowing or lending on their own account. See Franco Modigliani and Merton Miller (1958), 'The Cost of Capital, Corporate Finance, and the Theory of Investment', *American Economic Review*, 48 (June), 261–96.

momentum indicator. A set of indices which measure the rate of change in a price series. They are normally calibrated to give a range between 0 and 100, with 50 as a neutral point. They are also known as *momentum oscillators*. See **momentum model**. Also called a *Coppock indicator*.

momentum investment strategy. Investment technique which is based on the premiss that rising markets or prices contain an in-built momentum which can be used to advantage (cf. **efficient markets hypothesis**). When prices rise, exposure to the **market** is increased; when they fall, exposure is reduced (cf. **momentum model**). See **portfolio insurance**.

momentum model. A technical analysis method of interpreting the behaviour of a price series by measuring the absolute change in price over different time intervals, typically one, two, or more days/weeks/months. The model is designed to reveal price movement trends in the data indicating supply/demand factors relevant to future behaviour (cf. **market forces**). The best-known model is the **relative strength indicator** (RSI), which aims to find **overbought** and **oversold** conditions (cf. **Dow theory**). The calculation of the RSI involves setting a basis, normally 100 and measuring the upward (U) or downward (D) moves from period to period:

$$RSI_t = 100 - \frac{100}{1 + \text{Relative Strength}_t}$$

where the relative strength is measured by:

$$\text{Relative strength}_t = \frac{\frac{1}{n}\sum_{i=1}^{n} U_{i,t}}{\frac{1}{n}\sum_{i=1}^{n} D_{i,t}}$$

And $U_{i,t} = P_{t-i+1} - P_{t-1}$, if $P_{t-i+1} > P_{t-1}$
$D_{i,t} = P_{t-i} - P_{t-i+1}$, if $P_{t-i+1} < P_{t-1}$

momentum strategies. Technical analysis investment strategies based on the view that market movements once begun tend to persist over a period of time. Various technical indicators are then used to follow the developing **trends** and to time purchases and sales based on the evolving pattern. See **accumulation area; filter; head and shoulders; market profile; resistance area.**

monetarism. The belief that an economy can be effectively managed by using **monetary policy** as the lead set of instruments, with **fiscal policy** playing a secondary or accommodating role. In the USA this school of thought is associated with the economist Milton Friedman; in what has become known as the 'Chicago school'; and in the UK with economists Alan Walters and Patrick Minford. It is a theory or model of macro-economic activity and especially the cause of inflation within a country that is based on the **quantity theory of money**. Simply put, money matters since excessive creation of money or credit within an economy will lead to greater inflation rather than increased employment, unless counterbalanced by real growth. Those who subscribe to the importance of money in economic and policy analysis are known as *monetarists*.

monetary aggregate. One of a series of definitions as to what constitutes the **money supply**.

monetary base. This attempts to measure the liabilities of the **central bank** to the public and the bank system, and as such can represent the basis upon which to direct **monetary policy**.

monetary policy. Those instruments, such as **interest rates, reserve requirements,** and term controls, at the disposal of government for influencing the timing, availability, and cost of money and credit in an economy (cf. **fiscal policy; open-market operations**).

monetary reform. Alterations to a country's currency. It can involve changes to the coinage or simply the creation of heavy units, aimed at restoring the old parities. Recent examples include the UK, which switched from pounds-shillings-pence (£-s.-d.) to a decimal system based on 100 pence to the pound. Australia, which also used the British system, moved to a dollar and cents currency. France, following the Second World War, introduced a new franc, with 1,000 times the value of the old; Poland also has introduced a 'heavy' Zloty, to restore the currency's **exchange rate** to the US dollar to close to where it historically stood. The rationale for reform is to make use of the currency easier or to reduce inflationary expectations. The latter is not usually successful unless accompanied by matching economic policies. In the 1980s Brazil repeatedly attempted monetary reform, but this did not cure the underlying inflationary problem.

monetary unit. The standard unit of currency in a country. See **world currencies**.

monetize. The process of converting assets into cash.

monetization. Extracting the value of an **embedded option** from a security with special features (cf. **call monetization**).

money. Anything which is generally acceptable as a means of settling **debt**. Money is said to have three main functions, being: a store of value; a means of exchange; and a means of debt settlement (cf. **fiat money**).

money-at-call (Banking; UK). UK term for **call money**. Also known as a *discount market deposit*.

money-at-short-notice (Banking; UK). Money on deposit which can be withdrawn by providing notice of the intention to do so. The requirement is usually fourteen days' advance notice.

money-back option. Type of option where the **premium** is returned to the buyer at **expiry** even if the option is not **exercised**. In order to provide the money-back guarantee, the **writer** will blend an option **position** with a **forward** or **future** to create the money-back feature. As a result, the payoff on the money-back option is less **leveraged** than for simple options.

money-back security. See guaranteed return structures (cf. **equity-linked note**).

money-back warrant. An issue of **warrants** where the holder can either redeem the warrant for **cash** at a predetermined price or **exercise**. This allows the holder to reduce his loss in the event of an unfavourable price movement in the **underlying**. Also known as a *puttable warrant*.

money bills (UK). See **local government promissory notes**.

money broker (Money markets). A specialist wholesale market intermediary that arranges for the placement and taking of bank deposits or arranges loans or **repurchase agreements** and helps smooth out cash differences between security market traders by covering their **long** and **short positions** (cf. **inter-dealer broker; placing; taking**).

money center bank, money market bank, or **market bank** (USA). Term for the largest US domestic banks which are active participants in the wholesale **money markets**. The term is also often used for major banks in other countries.

money circulation scheme. See **pyramiding**.

money down. A general feature of **option** type derivatives in that the buyer, given the right not to exercise, has to pay a **premium** for the privilege of being able to walk away from the contract. It should be noted that some free options are touted in the financial markets. These are only free in the sense that the premium is disguised: either paid at the end or incorporated in some other way into the performance of the product (cf. **breakforward**).

money laundering. The process of turning illegitimately obtained cash, usually through crime, into (seemingly) legitimate wealth. The initial stage involves banking the cash then processing it through a large number of accounts, usually in different countries, in order to eliminate the origins of the money. It is then reinvested in legitimate businesses and activities. Many countries have anti-money laundering legislation requiring the accepting institution to make checks on the origins of cash. In the USA and UK for instance, any large cash **deposit** may require the depositor to explain the source of the cash.

money-lender. One whose business it is to lend money. It is generally used in a derogatory sense, implying usurous rates of interest. A tradition of pawnbroking, involving the provision of goods as collateral, has grown up around money-lending activities as well as the suspicion of or actual existence of criminal activity. In the USA, *loan*

sharks lend at very high rates of interest to individuals too poor to borrow from banks.

money market. The short-term market for debt instruments such as **banker's acceptances** (bank) deposits, **commercial paper, certificates of deposit,** and **treasury bills** (T-bills). It is usually used to describe wholesale markets for instruments with maturities of less than one year, but sometimes is used to include longer-term instruments repriced on a money market basis such as **floating rate certificates of deposit** and **floating rate notes**.

money market account. (i) An account held with a deposit-taking institution which pays interest related to wholesale money market rates (cf. **negotiable order of withdrawal**). (ii) An account held with an **open-ended fund** which invests in money market instruments (cf. **money market mutual fund**).

money market basis. The method used to compute **accrued interest** (AI) on bank deposits, **certificates of deposit** (CD), **floating rate certificates of deposit** (FRCD), and **floating rate notes** (FRN) (cf. **bond basis; interest-to-follow**). The rate is multiplied by the number of days elapsed and divided by 360 or 365 depending on the convention in the currency. Sometimes known as *bank interest basis* or *money market yield* (cf. **discount**).

C coupon rate (expressed as an annual rate)
Y_m money market yield (simple interest)
P price
T_{im} days from issue to maturity
T_{is} days from issue to settlement
T_{sm} days from settlement to maturity
AI_{mm} accrued interest on a money market basis
$BASIS$ number of days in the computation year (360 or 365)

To calculate yield given price:

$$Y_m\% = \left[\frac{\left(\dfrac{C_{im}}{BASIS \times 100}\right)}{P} \times \frac{BASIS \times 100}{T_{sm}} \right] \times 100$$

Thus a US dollar CD with a 6% **coupon** offered at a price of 99 with 90 days to run would provide a money market yield of:

$$Y_m = 6.06\% = \left[\frac{\left(\dfrac{6\% \times 90}{360 \times 100}\right)}{99} \times \frac{36,000}{90} \right] \times 100$$

To calculate price given yield:

$$P = \frac{1 + C\dfrac{T_{im}}{BASIS \times 100}}{\left(1 + Y_m\left(\dfrac{T_{sm}}{BASIS \times 100}\right)\right)}$$

To calculate the amount of accrued interest at settlement:

$$AI_{mm} = C\frac{T_{is}}{\text{BASIS}} \times P$$

The amount of principal is therefore:

$$\text{Principal} = P - A_{mm}$$

See also **interest rate calculations**.

money market deposit account (MMDA) (USA). A deposit account that is free of any interest rate controls and pays the current market rate of interest. There are normally minimum balance requirements as well as limits on withdrawals.

money market fund. A managed fund, such as a mutual fund, sociéte & acute; d'investissement collectif à capital variable monétaire (SICAV monétaire) or **unit trust**, that invests entirely in **money market** instruments such as **certificates of deposit** or **commercial paper** (cf. **bond fund**). Also sometimes termed a *cash fund*.

money market hedge. See **interest rate futures**.

money market instruments. Short-term (usually under one year) **assets** and securities such as **treasury bills**, **banker's acceptances**, certificates of deposit, commercial paper, and nonnegotiable bank deposits. See also **money market**.

money market municipal securities (MMMS) (Money markets; USA) See **variable rate demand obligations**.

money market mutual fund (MMMF) (USA). Mutual fund which invests in **money market** instruments and deposits. Some **funds** offer investors a limited **checking** facility, making them akin to a bank account.

money market notes (USA). A type of security where the interest is set by **auction** every thirty-five days. See **money market preferred stock**.

money market optimization. That combination of **money market** instruments that will provide the highest **yield**, given the aims of the investor and **yield curve** predictions.

money market preferred stock (MMP) (USA). A type of **preferred stock** issue that closely resembles a **variable rate preference share**. It is intended to provide **equity** capital to the issuer at money market rates which are either reset at a **margin** to a **reference rate** or by **auction** (cf. **auction rate preferred stock**).

money market securities. See **money market instruments**.

money market swap. See basis swap.

money market yield. See money market basis.

moneyness. See cash equivalent.

money-over-money lease. A lease that is so structured that the total of the lease payments, including any additional obligations the lessee may have at the end of the lease contract, will be sufficient to pay off the original cost and provide the lessor with an interest rate of return over and above the lessor's funding cost. See **operating lease**.

money purchase basis (UK). A method of calculating pension income according to the accumulated value of the contributions made. Under this method the ultimate pension will depend on investment return, the level of the securities market and the **annuity** rate at the time of retirement.

money rate of return. Defined as the annual rate of return as a percentage of asset value (cf. **annual percentage rate**; **effective rate**).

money spread. A type of **option strategy** which involves the purchase and sale of two **options** of the same type (that is either **calls** or **puts**) with the same **expiry date** but with differing **strike prices**. One or other will be further **in the money** or out of the money, hence the expression (cf. **credit spread**; **debit spread**). Also commonly known as a *risk reversal* or *vertical spread*. See also **vertical spread**.

money stock. See money supply.

money supply. Used to measure the total amount of money in circulation within an economy. There are several ways in which this can be calculated, including the following aggregates:

US DEFINITIONS

M1
(i) Currency outside the Treasury, Federal Reserve Banks, and the vaults of depository institutions; (ii) travellers cheques of non-bank issuers; (iii) demand deposits at all commercial banks other than those due to depository institutions, the US government, and foreign banks and official institutions less cash items in the process of collection and Federal Reserve float; (iv) other chequable deposits (OCD) consisting of NOW (negotiable order of withdrawal) and ATS (automatic transfer service) accounts with depository institutions, credit union share accounts, and demand deposits at thrift institutions.

M2
M1, plus overnight (and continuing contract) repurchase agreements issued by all commercial

banks and overnight eurodollars issued to US residents by foreign branches of US banks worldwide. Money market deposit accounts (MMDA), savings and small denomination time deposits (less than $100,000), and balances in both taxable and tax-exempt general purpose and broker-dealer money market mutual funds. Excludes individual retirement accounts (IRA) and Keogh balances at depository institutions and money market funds. Also excludes all balances held by US commercial banks, money market funds, foreign governments and commercial banks, and the US government.

M3

M2 plus large denomination time deposits and term repurchase agreement facilities (amounts over $100,000) issued by commercial banks and thrift institutions, term eurodollars held by US residents at foreign branches of US banks worldwide and at all banking offices in the United Kingdom and Canada, and balances in both taxable and tax exempt, institution-only money market mutual funds. Excludes amounts held by depository institutions, the US government, money market funds, and foreign banks and official institutions. Also subtracted is the estimated amount of overnight repurchase agreements and eurodollars held by institution-only money market mutual funds.

MONETARY BASE

The monetary base consists of total reserves plus required clearing balances and adjustments to compensate for float at the Fed plus the currency component of the money stock less the amount of vault cash holdings of thrift institutions not having required balances, the excess of current vault cash over the amount applied to satisfy current reserve requirements.

Monetary policy in the UK uses instruments, such as **interest rates** and **terms control**, in an attempt to influence the timing, availability, and cost of **money** and **credit**. It is prompted by the setting of particular government objectives, such as, price stability. Putting aside the theoretical controversies regarding the efficacy of **monetary policy**, as compared with **fiscal policy**, the former has now become associated with establishing of targets for the money supply. This is the total amount of money in circulation which can be measured in several ways, including M0 known as *little M0* or the *monetary base*.

UNITED KINGDOM DEFINITIONS

M0

Notes and coins in circulation at the banks *plus* banks' 'operational' (excess) balances with the central bank. Sometimes known as the *monetary base*.

M1

Notes and coins in circulation *plus* private sector sterling sight (current) bank deposits. Usually known as the *transactions balances* as used by consumers and businesses.

M2

M1 *less* private sector non-retail interest-bearing sterling sight bank deposits *plus* private sector holdings of retail building society deposits and national savings ordinary accounts. Sometimes known as the 'quasi-cash' balances.

M3

M1 *plus* private sector holdings of sterling bank **certificates of deposit** (CDs) and all sterling 'time' (deposit account) deposits.

M3(C)

M1 plus private sector holdings of foreign currency bank deposits.

M4

M3 plus private sector holdings of building society shares and deposits and sterling CDs, less building society holdings of notes and coins, bank deposits, and bank CDs.

M5

M4 plus private sector (non-building society) holdings of money market instruments (bank bills, treasury bills, local authority deposits), certificates of tax deposit, and National Savings instruments (excluding certificates, Save-As-You-Earn, and other long-term deposits).

Note that the definitions vary slightly between different countries. Such measures are used by monetary authorities to set targets for monetary growth as part of **monetary policy**. Markets take note of both targets and actuals because they are seen as indicators of government thinking and general levels of economic activity. See also **asset-based monetary aggregate**; **divisia money**.

money-weighted rate of return The rate of **return** realized over a given period based on the initial and final value and any intervening cash flows (cf. **holding period return**; **total return**). It is sometimes used for performance measurement. It is the same as the **internal rate of return** (IRR) over the assessed period. It is calculated as follows:

$$MV_0 = \frac{CF_1}{(1-r_m)} + \frac{CF_2}{(1-r_m)^2} + \ldots + \frac{CF_n + MV_n}{(1+r_m)^n}$$

where MV_0 is the initial value of the fund; CF_t the cash flow at period t; MV_n the final value of the fund; and r_m the internal rate of return that equates the value of the cash flows 1 to m to the current value. Because of the nature of the calculation, the timing and nature of the cash flows affects the results. If we have two funds with an initial value of 1,000 and we are measuring their performance, the effect of different cash flows will distort the result. If they both earn 5% for the first quarter and then one fund receives a cash inflow of 100, the other a cash inflow of 200 at the end of the quarter, then both funds earn 8% in the second quarter, the fund receiving the larger inflow will appear to have outperformed the other one. The IRR of the first fund will be 17% and that of the second fund 27%. The apparent discrepancy is due to the second fund receiving a higher inflow at the end of the first quarter, not the performance of the fund. This cash effect is a serious disadvantage if the money-weighted rate of return is to be used as a performance measure since managers generally have no control over the timing or the magnitude of the intervening cash flows, and these will greatly influence the money-weighted rate of return. For this reason, the **time-weighted rate of return** is a better indication of investment managers' performance.

money yield. The nominal yield on a gilt-edged security, derived by taking all future income payments and redemption proceeds using an assumed rate of inflation (cf. **index-linked; real yield securities**).

monoline financial insurance. A financial guarantee insurance company. See also **securitization**.

Monopolies and Mergers Commission (MMC) (UK). A statutory body with powers to obtain information necessary to investigate alleged monopolies and proposed **takeovers** and **mergers** referred to it by the Trade and Industry Secretary (President of the Board of Trade). It concerns itself with the twin issues of competition and the public interest. Once a **takeover** or **merger** has been referred, the parties are obliged to suspend their plans, and, after reporting, they may find themselves prevented from proceeding. The announcement of a referral tends to dampen down activity in the **shares** of the companies involved. See the **mergers and acquisitions; Takeover Panel**.

Monte Carlo simulation. A mathematical technique for calculating values or sensitivities dependent on future rate or value movements which can be predicted only statistically. For instance, a time sequence of rates is generated using known statistical properties or stochastic processes and a value is calculated. This is repeated many times through a multiplicity of 'trials' of the **model** to determine the range of possible outcomes. Monte Carlo methods are used in a wide range of financial application; for example, in the valuation of some types of **exotic options**, such as **path-dependent options** or to model distributions which incorporate a **jump process**. It is also used for **risk** assessment or project evaluation in the **capital budgeting** process. The method depends critically on both correct model specification and the parameter estimates of the distributions to be used (cf. **model risk**). The name derives from the analogy of generating a sequence of random numbers as if from the roulette wheel at the Casino in Monte Carlo where the result arrives by chance. Sometimes just called *simulation*.

Monte Titoli (Italy). The central securities depository for the Italian market. For government issues this role is undertaken by the **Bank of Italy**.

Montreal Exchange (Bourse de Montreal) **(ME)** (Canada). PO Box 61, La Tour de la Bourse, 800 Square Victoria, 4th Floor, Montreal, Quebec H4Z 1A9 (tel. 1 514 871 2424; fax 1 514 871 3533). Established in 1874, it is Canada's second most important exchange after the **Toronto Stock Exchange**.

Moody's or **Moody's Investor Services** (USA). 99 Church Street, New York, NY 10007 (tel. (212) 553 7135; fax (212) 608 2094). A US credit rating agency (cf. **Standard and Poor's**). See **credit ratings** for details.

mop-up provision. See **clean-up call provision**.

moral hazard. The **risk** that a party to a transaction is not acting in good faith, has provided misleading or inadequate information, or has an incentive to take extraordinary risks aimed at rectifying a desperate position (cf. **due diligence**). See also **agency problem**.

moral obligation bond (USA). A type of **municipal bond** issued by a sub-unit of a state and backed by a moral commitment of the state to honour the obligation in the event of a **default** or inability to pay by the sub-unit. The state's obligation is only moral in that future legislators cannot be bound to make a covering appropriation.

moral suasion. A form of persuasive pressure applied by regulators to firms to adopt a desirable course of action which is not backed up by regulatory authority or law. It works because the regulated firms wish to maintain good relations with the regulators. Sometimes applied to policy objectives. The Japanese have made an art of the practice through *administrative guidance*. Formerly in the UK, the **Bank of England** operated largely through the use of moral suasion.

moratorium. (i) A declaration by a borrower stating his inability to repay part or all debts (cf.

default). (ii) Suspension of **settlement** or **clearing** in a market as a result of exceptional circumstances (cf. **cascade theory; circuit breakers**).

Morgan Stanley Capital International indices (MSCI) (USA). A series of indices for different world capital markets compiled by *Morgan Stanley Inc.* Widely used as a **benchmark** for **asset allocation** decisions and performance measurement. It uses a **capitalization-weighted average** and individual indices are produced for the different countries, by regions, by industry, by economic sector, as well as a complete world index. See also **Dow-Jones World Stock Index; FT/S&P Actuaries World Indices**.

mortality tables. Probability tables for the likelihood of the death of an individual of various ages within a year.

mortgage. Security provided for **funds** advanced, which may either be legal or equitable. The security can be the borrower's **assets**, but is usually taken to mean property even though it can be any pledgeable asset such as ships, **financial assets**, and so forth (cf. **collateral; hypothecation; lien**).

mortgage-backed, mortgage-backed certificate, or **mortgage-backed security (MBS)**. A security issued on the basis of a **share** in a group (or **pool**) of mortgages or trust deeds. Income from the **underlying** loans, secured by property, is used first to meet interest and then **principal** obligations by drawing bonds and redeeming at **par** (cf. **Federal Home Loan Mortgage Corporation** (USA); **Federal National Mortgage Association** (USA); **Government National Mortgage Association** (USA); **pass-through; put-through**). Such issues are normally over-collateralized and thus able to achieve a high **credit rating**. The major distinction between a mortgage-backed and the **collateralized mortgage obligation** (CMO) is that in the latter case, ownership of the mortgages has been sold to investors. The CMO structure also allows the creation of different speed of pay tranches (cf. **interest only; principal only**). See also **asset-backed; structured finance; real-estate mortgage investment conduit**.

mortgage banking. See **building society; Hypothekenbank; savings and loan association; savings bank**.

mortgage bond or **debenture**. A bond issue with a **lien** on property (real-estate), plant, and equipment (cf. **trust deed**). See also **debenture**.

mortgage over Treasury option (MOTO) (USA). **Option** where the payoff is linked to the **spread** between **mortgage-backed securities** and US treasuries. See also **outperformance option, rainbow option; spread option; yield curve option**.

mortgage participation certificate (MPC) (Bonds; USA). Mortgage **pass-through** securities issued by the **Federal Home Loan Mortgage Corporation** and the **Federal National Mortgage Association** The **collateral** is pledged pooled mortgages held by the issuer (unlike, for instance **collateralized mortgage obligations** (CMOs), where the ownership is direct) and is normally included at a **discount** to value in order to over-collateralize the obligation, since the pool is not federally insured (although private insurance may have been taken out) in order to allow the resultant certificates to obtain a high **credit rating**. Also unlike CMOs, there is greater variety in the **underlying** mortgages since they may have different (fixed) interest rates and be on different types of residential property.

mortgage pass-through certificates or **security** (Bonds; USA). A **mortgage-backed security** where the holder has a direct, equitable interest in the **pool** of mortgages and where interest and principal are 'passed through' directly to the holders. See **asset-backed; collateralized mortgage obligations; mortgage participation certificate; put-through**.

mortgage prepayment cap (USA). Cap which is linked to the **prepayment rate** on **mortgage-backed securities** such as to protect the holder from **prepayment risk** (cf. **extension risk**). That is, the payoff on the cap will rise as the rate of prepayment increases to compensate the holder against **early redemption** and having to reinvest returned **funds** in lower-yielding investments.

mortgage real estate investment trust (mortgage REIT) (USA). An **investment company** which provides **funds** for mortgages and real estate development.

mortgage replication swap. Amortizing interest rate swap where the **notional principal** amount is linked to the repayment pattern on a **mortgage-backed security**. See **indexed principal swap**.

mortgage swap. An asset swap for mortgage obligations such as **collateralized mortgage obligations** where the **notional principal** on the swap reduces as the mortgages are paid off. The asset swap converts a **fixed rate** obligation into a floating rate synthetic security.

Moscow Central Stock Exchange (Russia). Ilyinka Street 3/8 Building 3, SU–103012 Moscow (tel. 7 095 229 7635; fax 7 095 291 9391).

most active. Securities in any particular market or sector which have had the greatest **turnover** in a given period such as a day, week, month (cf. **volume**). Typically these are the largest issues or issues subject to special factors, such as a **takeover** or **merger**. Such securities are often reported in the financial press.

moving average. A **technical analysis** or chartist's method for interpreting the significance of movements in a series. The individual series are averaged over a given period (typically a week, month, or year) in such a way as to change the average by adding a new number of the series and by dropping the oldest observation. The principal behind moving averages is to attempt to spot **breakouts** from a trend or major deviations from past behaviour as well as to eliminate random fluctuations in the series which have no significance (cf. **noise; resistance point; support point**). There are various methods of computing this: the two most common are a simple moving average (SMA) and a weighted moving average (WMA) where the weights can be based on some researched criteria or simply an exponential function of time. The formulae are:

$$\text{SMA}_t = \frac{1}{n} \sum_{t=1}^{n} P_t$$

$$\text{WMA}_t = \sum_{t=1}^{n} w_t P_t$$

The exponential moving average (EMA) makes the weights a geometric progression of $1, w, w^2, \ldots w^{n-1}$ backwards over time. Thus, it is calculated by:

$$\text{EMA}_t = \frac{P_t + w P_{t-1} + w^2 P_{t-2} + \ldots + w^{n-1} P_{t-n+1}}{1 + \sum_{t=1}^{n-1} w^t}$$

Where the weights w^t are $1/n$, when n is the number of observation periods chosen for the series, then the reciprocal exponential moving average (REMA) can be simplified to:

$$\text{REMA} = \frac{(1-w)P_t + w \cdot \text{REMA}_{t-1}}{n}$$

This is sometimes modified in practice to:

$$\text{MREMA} = \frac{P_t + (n-1)\text{MREMA}_{t-1}}{n}$$

Analysts will combine different moving averages to provide insights into how persistent price trends are over time, and will seek to determine buy or sell signals from the interactions of the different series. Thus a one-month moving average may be superimposed on a one-week average to portray deviations from the longer-term trend. See also **momentum model**.

moving average models. A family of **models** constructed using stochastic processes as the basis for their specification and with an emphasis upon forecasting. The objective is to develop models that explain the movement of a time series y^t. Unlike the regression model, however, a set of explanatory variables is not used. Instead y^t is explained by relating it to its own past values and to a weighted sum of current and lagged random disturbances. While there are many functional forms that can be used to relate y^t to its past values and lagged random disturbances, the most widely used is the linear specification. The assumption of linearity makes possible quantitative statements about the stochastic properties of the models and the forecasts generated by the models. For example, it makes it possible to calculate confidence intervals around the forecasts. Moreover, such an approach allows the models used to apply to stationary processes and to homogeneous non-stationary processes (which can be differentiated one or more times to yield stationary processes). The models are written as equations with fixed estimated coefficients, representing a stochastic structure that does not change over time. Although models with time-varying coefficients of non-stationary processes have been developed. There are four widely used types of such linear time-series models: (1) Moving average models, where the process y^t is described completely by a weighted sum of current and lagged random disturbances. (2) Autoregressive models, where y^t depends on a weighted sum of its past values and a random disturbance term. (3) Mixed autoregressive moving average models (ARMA), where the process y^t is a function of both lagged random disturbances and its past values, as well as a current disturbance term, such that if the original process is non-stationary, it often can be differentiated one or more times to produce a new series that is stationary and for which a mixed autoregressive moving average model can be constructed. This model can be used to produce a forecast one or more periods into the future, after which the forecast stationary series can be integrated one or more times to yield a forecast for the original time series. (4) Integrated or interactive autoregressive moving average models (ARIMA). This provides a framework for modelling of homogeneous non-stationary time series. When doing so it must first be specified how many times the series is to be differentiated before a stationary series results. In addition, the number of autoregressive terms and lagged disturbances terms to be included in the model of the stationary series needs to be stated. The autocorrelation function can be used to tell how many times a homogeneous non-stationary process must be differenced in order to produce a stationary process. The autocorrelation function can also be used to help determine the number of disturbance terms in the moving average portion and the number of lags in the autoregressive portion of the model.

moving strike option. See path-dependent option.

mudaraba (Banking; Islamic). One method used by banks in the Islamic world to address the prohibition on receiving interest. The bank becomes a joint partner, allowed under Islamic law (the sharia), in the business, project or venture and receives a set proportion of the project's net cash flow, which is used to service the obligation as to principal (and, effectively, interest).

mudarib (Islam). The sponsor or entrepreneur in the joint-venture structure required to comply with Islamic law, the sharia (cf. sahib-al-maal).

multi-asset option. See outperformance option; rainbow option.

multicollinearity. When independent variables in a regression are significantly correlated (cf. correlation). Its presence makes the least squares method of conducting regressions problematical unless certain adjustments are made. Multicollinearity is common amongst variables present in financial markets, and economics more generally, not least because of the way in which the behaviour of market participants and economic agents tend to be inextricably bound together. Nevertheless, it remains useful to attempt to correct for the false validation of competing explanations of market relationships because of the importance attached to forecasting and prediction within, for example, portfolio management techniques.

multi-currency cash concentration. A facility offered by a bank allowing accounts in several different branches and in different currencies to be concentrated at one place (cf. account sweeping). This is a particular useful arrangement for cash management purposes since the surpluses are automatically moved to the central account. Normally in addition, the bank will allow offsets between accounts at different locations which are in surplus and others which are overdrawn. See also single currency cash concentration.

multi-currency clause (Banking). A term within a credit facility that allows the borrower to drawdown funds in a number of different currencies either sequentially or at the same time. Usually a standard part of eurocredit agreements.

multi-currency euronote facility. Euronote facility allowing the issuance of notes in different eurocurrencies. See revolving underwriting facility.

multi-currency revolving credit facility (Banking). A revolving credit facility that has a multi-currency clause.

multi-currency share capital. The denomination of a corporation's share capital in more than one currency. Scandinavian Bank Group, based in the UK, introduced multi-currency share capital to its equity base in order to address the problem of currency movements adversely affecting the bank's capital ratios.

multi-currency swap. See cocktail swap.

multi-factor option pricing model. Refinement to the basic types of option pricing models which involves a two or more factor volatility. Typically used for options on interest rates or the term structure of interest rates or for rainbow options.

multi-factor options. See rainbow options.

multi-index option. See outperformance option.

Multilateral Investment Guarantee Agency (MIGA). A part of the World Bank set up in 1988 to provide political risk and other types of insurance for direct or equity investments in developing countries.

multi-lateral netting (Banking). A type of arrangement used in international money management which involves a firm engaged in foreign transactions using a central entity as an in-house clearing centre for all currency transactions, thus allowing the netting of payments and receipts (cf. reinvoice centre). Only the net remaining position is then hedged in the market, allowing the firm to reduce the amount and number of hedging transactions. It is a technique often used by multinational corporations under which they distribute credits and debits amongst their subsidiaries in different countries, leaving only the balance to be settled, thus reducing the need to undertake foreign exchange transactions with third parties. See also concentration banking.

multi-legged swap. A complex package of interest rate swap and or cross-currency swaps usually involving more than two counterparties. See cocktail swap.

multinational corporation. A company operating in more than one country (cf. global bank; globalization). See transnational corporation.

multi-option financing facility (MOFF; MOF) (Banking). A means of borrowing funds using a variety of funding bases and in acceptable currencies. Normally used in the **euromarket** and for short-term bank advances, although such facilities can include **banker's acceptances, euro-commercial paper, euronote, medium-term note** and **swingline** clauses. Such facilities are usually complex and MOFFs tend to be **syndicated credits**. Other names sometimes used for such a comprehensive loan agreement are *multiple component facility* or *multi-option facility* (MOF), although MOFF is the market standard term (cf. **borrower's option for notes or underwritten standby**).

multi-period option. Refers to several different types of **options** where the payoff depends either on the price or rate of the **underlying** over a period, such as the **Asian-style**, or to a series of same **strike price** options, as typically found in a **cap** (cf. **path-dependent option**).

multiple application. Submitting several bids to a **tender** or **auction**. In some cases this is illegal; in other cases, such as auctions of US **treasuries**, it is standard practice as long as the bidder does not acquire more than a set percentage of the total on offer.

multiple correlation. Concerned with capturing the extent to which one variable is associated with two or more other variables: for example, to discover how much **share** prices are related to current returns in the market, size of each trade, and the overall size of the portfolios held by active investors. A **correlation coefficient**, a number lying between zero and one, expresses how closely share prices vary with current returns, trade size, and portfolio size over the group studied. A value close to one would indicate a very strong association; close to zero, a very weak association. See **correlation; Capital Asset Pricing Model; efficient markets hypothesis; arbitrage pricing theory.**

multiple exchange rate. A form of currency control regime where there are two different markets for the country's currency. Typically it involves a trade exchange rate and separate investment or capital rate. This arrangement might also include a special tourist rate.

multiple listing. Any security or **derivative** which is simultaneously **listed** on more than one exchange.

multiple-option clause. See **cash** or **physical**.

multiple taxation. See **double taxation; unitary taxation.**

multiplier bonds. A bond which gives the holder the right to receive additional bonds of the same type instead of **coupon** payments. It differs from a **bunny bond** in that the holder has the **option** to receive cash or additional bonds. Such a structure gives the holder a guaranteed **reinvestment rate** in the event of a fall in interest rates (cf. **zero-coupon bond**).

multi-purpose facility (Banking). A **facility** provided by a bank that allows the borrower to select different markets or **reference rates** against which to borrow funds. It is the bilateral equivalent of a **multi-option financing facility.**

multi-rate reset swap. Interest rate swap or cross-currency swap where the payment on one or more legs of the swap is more frequent than the market standard.

multi-tranche tap certificates of deposit (MTTCD). A programme designed to issue **term certificates of deposit** using the same methods as for the **medium-term note** market. The difference is that the issuer is a bank and the obligations count as deposits.

multi-tranche tap notes (MTTN). A hybrid **medium-term note** (MTN) issuing system developed by Merrill Lynch to address the problem of a lack of **liquidity** in the **secondary market** in the fledgling market for euro-MTNs. The issuer undertakes to issue a minimum tranche in a given **maturity** and to add further **fungible** notes with the same end date, when there is investor demand (cf. **tap; taplet**). An initial tranche in a given maturity will, as the issue moves towards redemption, then become the issuing tranche in the shorter maturities. Sometimes issuers have run combined medium-term-note and multi-tranche tap note programmes (cf. **maturity ladder**).

municipal bond, municipals, or **muni-bond** (Bonds; USA). Name for term securities issued by state, local governments, municipalities, and their agencies. Such issues generally are **tax exempt** from federal taxes if they are **public purpose bonds**, that is, the funds raised are to be used for infrastructure or other civic purposes (cf. **tax-spared**). Issues for other, for example commercial, purposes, called **private purpose bonds**, are normally taxable but **tax exempt** status may be accorded, if the amount of commercial benefit is small, and these are called *permitted private purpose bonds*. Coupon frequency is semi-annual, like federally issued US **treasuries**.

municipal bond futures (USA). See **municipal bond index futures.**

Municipal Bond Index (USA). An **index** made up of a portfolio of actively traded, high-quality **gen-**

eral obligation or **municipal revenue bonds**. See **municipal bond index futures**.

municipal bond index futures (USA). A range of financial futures contracts where the **underlying** is an **index** of **municipal bonds** (cf. **deliverable**; **notional bond**). The instrument provides a specific hedge for the municipal bond market without any of the inherent problems of **cross-hedging**.

municipal bond insurance (USA). Commercial **default** insurance provided on **municipal bond** issues. It can either be a feature of the issue itself or can be purchased by an investor to cover his holding.

municipal investment trust (USA). A fund which invests in **municipal bonds**. Such funds offer the investor diversification and monthly income. Most are constituted as **unit investment trusts**, that is they have fixed portfolios.

municipal multiplier security (Bonds; USA). **Zero-coupon bond** issued by a state or municipality. Also called a *coupon interest bond*.

municipal note or **muni note** (Money markets; USA). A short-term note issued by US state and local governments in anticipation of future tax, bond issue receipts, or other revenues (cf. **Local Authority Bond**). See also **project note**.

municipal over bond spread (MOB) (Futures; USA). The difference in **yield** between the **futures** contract on **municipal bonds** and that on US treasuries. The **spread** is determined by perceptions of the relative **credit worthiness** of municipals and changes in the shape of the **yield curve** since, on average, municipal bonds have a shorter **maturity** than Treasuries.

municipal revenue bond (USA). A municipal bond where the revenues from a particular infrastructure project are used to cover the repayments on the obligation (cf. **income bond**).

Municipal Securities Rulemaking Board (MSRB) (Bonds; USA). A **self-regulating organization** set up in 1975 by the **Securities and Exchange Commission** to regulate the secondary market in municipal bonds and notes.

municipal swap (USA). Interest rate swap where the **floating rate** payment has a **reference rate** based on an **index** of municipal bond **yields** (cf. **Municipal Bond Index**).

muqarada (Islamic). One of the methods used by lenders in the Islamic world to address the prohibition on receiving interest. While interest is prohibited, providing funds in a venture with a view to turning a profit is allowed under Islamic law. As a result, lenders become joint partners in the project or venture and receive a set proportion of the project or the firm's **net cash flow** which is used to service the obligation as to principal (and, effectively, interest). The structure is similar to **mudaraba**.

murabaha (Banking; Islamic). A common method used by lenders to address the prohibition on receiving interest. In this method, the lender agrees to purchase goods or services from the other party, thus creating an equity interest in the transaction which is allowed under Islamic law (the sharia), while at the same time agreeing to resell the product or service at an agreed higher price (cf. **contango**; **forward**). The difference represents the lender's profit share in the transaction (which is, effectively, interest) (cf. **swap**). The other major method used by lenders to avoid charging interest is **mudaraba** (cf. **halal**).

musharaka (Banking; Islamic). A method used by lenders in the Islamic world to address the prohibition on receiving interest. While interest is prohibited, providing funds in a venture with a view to turning a profit is allowed under Islamic law. As a result, lenders become **equity**-partners in the project or venture and agree to split the profits according to their respective commitments. See **mudaraba**.

mutual fund (USA). A grouping of investors who pool their money in order to act as a single large investor, usually professionally managed (cf. **concert party**; **investment club**; **investment manager**). An *open-ended mutual fund* creates and cancels **units** as required by purchases and sales; a *closed-end mutual fund* has a fixed number of **shares** outstanding which are traded between investors and are usually **listed** on an exchange. See **investment trust company**; **open-ended investment company**; **société d'investissement collectif à capital variable**; **unit investment trust**.

mutually exclusive. A situation where two investment or **project** opportunities cannot both be undertaken.

mutual offset. Agreements between different futures exchanges allowing participants to use **long** and **short positions** in similar contracts on different exchanges to **offset** each other; or to create a position on a given exchange. Such agreements allow trading to be extended across time zones, which means that, for instance, a position could be established or covered in the Far East time zone before trading commenced in Europe (cf. **after-hours trading**).

mutual savings bank (USA). See **credit union**.

mutual-to-stock conversion (USA). The conversion of a mutual society, for instance a savings and loan association, into a joint stock company.

N

Naamlooze Venootschapp (NV) (Netherlands). Limited company. See NV subsidiary.

Nagoya Stock Exchange (NSE) (Japan). 3–17 Sakae, 3–chome, Nakuk-ku, Nagoya 460 (tel. 81 (0) 52 262 3171; fax 81 (0) 52 241 1527). The third largest exchange after the Tokyo Stock Exchange and the Osaka Securities Exchange.

Nairobi Stock Exchange Ltd. (Kenya). Kimathi Street, IPS Building (2nd Floor), PO Box 43633, KE-Nairobi (tel. 254 02 230692; fax 254 02 224 200).

Nakasone bond (Japan). Foreign currency bond issued by the Japanese government from 1982. It is named after the then Prime Minister.

naked. Long or short position in a derivative without an offsetting position in the underlying. Also called *uncovered*. See naked call writing; naked option; naked put.

naked call writing. Writing a call, that is, going short on a call option, without owning the underlying. See also covered call.

naked debenture. See unsecured loan stock.

naked income warrant. A warrant that, until exercised, pays periodic interest. Such warrant issues are normally made to enhance the attractiveness of an issue (cf. bells and whistles). The warrant normally can be exercised into another debt instrument of the issuer. In addition, the strike price on the warrant is normally well out of the money, the interest being designed to compensate the holder for the low probability of its being exercised.

naked option. An option held in its own right and not hedging a position or other options (cf. covered option; embedded option). Sometimes called an *uncovered option*.

naked position. A long or short position not covered by a hedge. It can also mean the situation of an option writer (i.e. seller) which is not covered (cf. covered option; naked option).

naked put. A put held in its own right and not hedging a position (cf. covered put).

naked swap. A swap position entered into without a matching underlying asset or liability. If receiving fixed, it is equivalent to taking a long or bullish position; if paying, it is a short or bearish position.

naked warrant. A warrant not associated with a host bond (cf. cum warrant; ex-warrant). That is, the warrants do not form part of any other financial transaction or package.

name. (i) Colloquial term for a counterparty (cf. marking name; street name). Hence a trader might say to a broker intermediary when offered a trade, 'I'm full up on the name', which would mean the trader had used up all his permitted exposure on the counterparty and did not want to make the transaction. (ii) (UK) An underwriting member of the Lloyd's of London insurance market. Such members are organized into syndicates to spread the risks involved. Traditionally names have assumed unlimited liability, but recent changes to the market have allowed in limited liability capital (cf. partnership).

Namibian Stock Exchange (Namibia). Ground Floor Nimrod Building, Kasino Street, PO Box 1272, NA-Windhoek (tel. 264 61 37477; fax 264 61 227 321).

nariyuki chūmon (Japan). Market order.

narrowing the spread. Increasing the bid price and/or decreasing the offer price (cf. locked). Sometimes called *closing a market* (cf. open-up).

narrow market. Same as thin market.

narrow money. A definition of the money supply which is based on money as a medium of exchange, rather than its broadest economic use (known as *broad money*).

narrow-range securities (UK). That proportion of monies held in trust that can be invested in fixed interest securities with less risk than wider-range securities, as this latter category includes listed stocks and shares.

NASDAQ Composite Index (National Association of Securities Dealers Automated Quatations Composite Index) (USA). A broad market capitalization-weighted index covering all nationally traded **common stock** securities quoted by NASDAQ dealers on the NASDAQ national market and all other domestic common stocks quoted on the NASDAQ **stock market**. There are six sub-indices covering different sectors plus sub-indices set up in 5 February 1971; two newer indices from 1 February 1985 cover the most actively traded stocks, NASDAQ-100, and the financial sector: NASDAQ-financial. See **index construction**.

NASDAQ International. International market service introduced in January 1992 to provide a market in the European time zone for US common stocks quoted on the National Association of Securities Dealers Automated Quotations (NASDAQ) system.

NASDAQ National Market (USA). The major nationally traded securities on the National Association of Securities Dealers Automated Quotations system.

NASDAQ Stock market (USA). See National Association of Securities Dealers Automated Quotations.

National Association (NA) (USA). See **national bank**.

National Association of Securities Dealers Automated Quotations system (NASDAQ) (USA). A US automated securities price collection and dissemination service for **over-the-counter** (OTC) securities traders. Set up in 1971, it was originally very much just an information service for the OTC markets. It is registered with the Securities and Exchange Commission as an exchange and is now generally regarded as a major exchange in its own right (cf. **Stock Exchange Automated Quotations**). The service provides three levels of service: level 1—to NASD members; level 2—to retail dealers; level 3—to other market-makers only.
See also **fourth market**.

National Association of Securities Dealers Inc. (NASD) (USA). A US **self-regulating** organization set up to establish rules for the conduct of securities traders in the **over-the-counter** markets in securities (cf. **Securities and Investments Board** (UK)). Their **rules of fair practice** are normally taken to be the industry standard.

national bank (USA). A federally chartered bank. Such banks are members of the **Federal Reserve System** and **Federal Deposit Insurance Corporation**. They usually have the initials *NA* after their name, which stands for *National Association*. See **charter**; **state bank**.

national debt. The central government debt. Such debt is either in negotiable securities, which are traded in a government debt market; or **savings bonds** sold direct to the public; or foreign debts. See **Bons à Taux Annuel Normalisé**; **Buoni Tesoro Denominati in Euroscudi**; **Buoni del Tesoro Poliennali**; **Bundesbond**; **gilt-edged**; **Japanese government bond**; **obligations assimilables du Trésor**; **treasury bill**; **treasury bond**; **US treasury market**; **treasury note**.

National Futures Association (NFA). Association of firms engaged in futures trading. It sets qualifications, proficiency, registration, financial condition, retail sales practices, and business conduct between professionals in the market and is a **self-regulating organization**.

National Housing Association mortgage securities (Bonds; Canada). Fixed interest, amortizing **bonds** where the **underlying** security is residential mortgages, although they are also guaranteed by the government. Although the interest is credited semi-annually, the securities amortize on a monthly basis (cf. **mortgage-backed**).

national market system (USA). A mechanism for linking the major **stock exchanges** in the USA. A system intended to stimulate competition between US securities markets by providing rapid collection and dissemination of price information across the various markets.

National Mortgage Market Corporation (NMMC) (Bonds; Australia). Agency owned by the government of Victoria set up to assist in the development of a secondary market in mortgages (cf. **mortgage-backed**; **pass-through**).

National Savings (UK). A UK government department that issues savings and investment products through the Post Office and by direct marketing. The range includes: ordinary and investment accounts, income, **index-linked**, deposit, and capital bonds; yearly savings plan, fixed interest and index-linked certificates (sometimes known as 'granny bonds'), and **premium bonds**. Together with new issues of **gilt-edged** and foreign borrowings, one of the three ways the UK Treasury has of financing the **public sector borrowing requirement**.

National Savings Stock Register (UK). Operated by the Department of National Savings, it offers a service for the purchase and sale of gilt-edged securities by post. As such, it represents an alternative to using a **broker-dealer**. It charges commission, the list is limited and unique to the Register, and there is no undertaking to deal **at best**.

National Securities Clearing Corporation (NSCC) (USA). A company set up in 1977 to handle securities transfers for the US domestic market in order to unify the settlement arrangements for the different exchanges (cf. **Crest (UK)**). It is owned jointly by the **American Stock Exchange**, **New York Stock Exchange**, and the **National Association of Securities Dealers**. It acts as a clearing house and provides automated data processing and communications services through the Securities Industry Automation Corporation.

National Stock Exchange (Equities; USA). A small **stock exchange** based in New York that handles dealing in small company **stocks** not transacted on the other eight exchanges.

natural habitat. See market segmentation theory (cf. **liquidity preference**).

natural hedge. Risk management technique for handling **currency risk** which involves moving production, funding, or other revenue stream or expense into the foreign currency with a view to creating natural offsetting cash flows.

natural option. A contractual feature where the buyer or seller has been granted or grants an implicit, embedded option on an **underlying**. An obvious example is the right of an individual taking out a **fixed rate** mortgage to pay back the remaining **principal** prior to the final **maturity** of the loan. Such a borrower is likely to **exercise** this right, or **option**, if interest rates fall and the benefits of refinancing are positive (cf. **extension risk**; net present value; prepayment model; prepayment risk).

natural resources. See commodities.

nearby. In the **futures** market, the contract closest to **expiry** (cf. **position**). Also called *nearby month* or *near month*.

nearest month or **near month.** (i) The exchange-traded option set of contracts on a particular **underlying** which are nearest to their **expiry** date (cf. **furthest month**). (ii) In the futures market the futures contract closest to **expiry**.

nearly perfect swap. Type of interest rate swap where the **floating rate** has a complex in arrears feature linked to the path of the **reference rate** over time. In essence, the floating rate payer is selling **volatility** on the reference rate. See LIBOR in arrears swap.

near money. See quasi-money.

near the money. A situation where the underlying price or rate is close to the **strike price**. See

also at the money; delta; gamma; in the money; out of the money.

Nebenborse (Equities; Switzerland). An **over-the-counter** market in **common stocks** centred in Zurich.

negative amortization. A situation where interest is added to the **principal** of a loan rather than being paid to the lender (cf. **accrual**). See also zero-coupon bond.

negative basis. Where the **underlying** cash or spot price is below the **futures** price (cf. **premium market**). Also known as *under futures*. See **backwardation; contango**.

negative carry. When the interest earned is greater than the cost then there is **positive carry**, and when the cost of borrowing is greater than the interest earned there is a negative carry (cf. **yield gap**). The expectation is that the selling price will be high enough so as to allow the **position** to turn a profit despite the loss arising from funding the position. See also **carry**.

negative cash flow. Either a **payable** or when total outgoings exceed total revenues in a firm or project (cf. **positive cash flow**).

negative convexity. A condition of certain types of bonds where **duration** is inversely, or negatively, linked to interest rate movements. Normal, **straight bonds** have positive **convexity**, but the **call provisions** or other **prepayment** conditions (e.g. in **mortgage-backed securities**) means that the **tenor** of the bond is likely to shorten as interest rates fall, producing the negative convexity condition.

negative covenants. Covenants granted by a borrower to a lender which restrict the former's freedom to take actions which might jeopardize the lender's security (cf. **limitation on asset disposal; limitation on liens**). See positive covenants.

negative equity. See negative net worth.

negative float. Funds tied up in float, and hence not earning interest.

negative gapping. Borrowing short to lend long (cf. **positive gapping**). See asset-liability management.

negative interest. An exceptional condition in a market or with an institution where lenders are penalized. It is used as a tool in currency intervention when the **central bank** wishes to discourage foreign purchases and imposes what amounts to a tax on foreign purchasers. The best-known case is that of foreign holders of Swiss francs who were required to pay negative interest equal to a rate of 40% per annum.

negative net worth. A situation in a business or individual where **liabilities** exceed **assets**. Also sometimes known as *negative equity*.

negative pledge. An undertaking made on a loan or security issue by a debtor that better security will not be offered on other debt during the life-span of the borrowing without this loan or security being given the same protection. Also known as a *covenant of equal value*. See **covenants**.

negatively sloping yield curve or **negative yield curve.** The situation where shorter **maturities** have higher **yields** than longer ones. See **inverse yield curve**.

neglected firm effect. A market anomaly based on the view that investments in less well-known firms offer higher returns without incurring additional **risk**.

negligence. Carelessness due to a breach of duty of care between two parties. Such a duty is owed between **shareholders** and their appointed managers, between financial intermediaries and their clients, and in any other situation where one party relies on the advice or expertise of another (cf. **agency problem; agent; principal**).

negotiable certificate of deposit (negotiable CD) (Money markets; USA). Transferable **certificate of deposit** (CD). The addition of *negotiable* indicates that it may be freely resold to third parties. This is not the case for all CDs in the USA.

negotiable instrument. A document of title that can be freely traded, with transfer of title evidenced by **delivery**, possibly with the endorsement of the seller. Examples include: **bills of exchange** and **promissory notes** (cf. **physical**). The opposite condition is known as *non-negotiable*. See also **assignment; sub-participation**.

negotiable order of withdrawal account (NOW account) (Banking; USA). An interest-bearing bank account upon which cheques can be drawn (cf. **checking account**). Such accounts, which pay a rate of interest linked to wholesale money market rates, emerged as a result of the deregulation of bank interest on the abolition of **Regulation Q** in the early 1980s. Also available in a non-interest-bearing form as a *non-interest-bearing negotiable order of withdrawal*.

negotiated offering, sale, or **underwriting** (USA). A securities offer where the terms of the issue are arrived at by negotiation between the issuer and the **lead manager** and/or the **underwriting syndicate** rather than through competition between rival underwriting syndicates (cf. **competitive bidding**).

negotiation credit (Banking). A **banker's acceptance** or **bill** where payment may be made by banks other than the advising bank.

nehaba seigen (Japan). Price **limits**. The upper limit is known as the *sutoppu-daka* and the lower limit as the *sutoppu-yasu*.

net. Generally the price, value, or residual after deducting expenses, **transaction costs**, or taxes.

net assets. Assets less fixed liabilities. The difference is the **capital**, that is, the **funds** owned by shareholders. See also **net worth**.

net asset value (NAV). This measure of 'worth' of a company is calculated by taking the total **assets**, less all balance sheet **liabilities** and prior **capital**, such as **debentures**, loan stock, and **preferred stock** (cf. **book value**). This residual is divided by the number of shares issued to give the net asset value per share. This computation is particularly significant for valuing the share of **investment trust companies**. Also used to calculate the underlying value for units in **mutual funds** (which may be different from the **bid** or **offered** prices quoted to investors (cf. **loading**)). Sometimes called *net asset worth, net worth*, or *shareholders' equity*, or just *equity*. The *net asset value per share* is the net asset value divided by the number of shares in issue. It is a measure of the surplus based on accounting or current market values that, in theory, would be repaid to **shareholders** in a break-up of the company or **portfolio**. See **asset analysis**.

net book value. The value of an **asset** less any accumulated **depreciation** in a firm's accounts (cf. **marked-to-market**). See **book value**.

net borrowed reserves (Banking; USA). A condition in the banking system where **member banks** as a whole have borrowed more **reserves** than are available. It is usually taken to indicate imminent or actual policy tightening, that is, interest rates will rise (cf. **net free reserves**). See **Federal Reserve; reserve requirements**.

net capital rule (USA). Securities and Exchange Commission rule specifying the minimum **capital** requirements of **brokers** and **dealers**. Compliance is normally delegated to the various **self-regulating organizations** that monitor securities activities.

net cash flow. See **free cash flow**.

net change. The periodic change in a price series, say day to day or week to week, ignoring any fluctuations between the observation points. It is not the same as a range since the price may have moved outside the reported series. See **moving average**.

net charge-offs (Banking). A measure of a bank's **problem assets** due to its lending activities. It is the total of loans that are written off as being unrecoverable less recoveries of amounts previously written off.

net commission or **net of commission** (UK). Transaction undertaken by an intermediary without a **commission** or fee. The intermediary, presumably, earns a return from the bid-offer spread.

net current assets. Current assets less current liabilities from a balance sheet; the amount of uncommitted liquid resources or capital used in the business (cf. **fixed assets**). Also known as *working capital*.

net equity assets. See net asset value; net worth.

net exposure. The residual exposure that exists after assets and liabilities have been netted off, or a position has been hedged (cf. **imperfect hedge**). See asset-liability management.

net dividend. Dividend paid to shareholders after deducting **withholding tax** or, in the case of an imputation corporation tax system, the tax credit (cf. advance corporation tax; mainstream corporation tax; unrelieved advance corporation tax).

net free reserves (Banking; USA). A condition in the banking system where **member banks** as a whole have an excess of reserves with the Federal Reserve (cf. **net borrowed reserves**). It is usually taken to indicate imminent or actual policy loosening, that is, interest rates will fall. See **reserve requirements**.

net income. (i) Income or profit after allowing for the costs of earning it. It can be before or after tax. See also **earnings before tax**. (ii) The income received after tax has been deducted (cf. net interest; net yield).

net income available to common. See net profit.

net income per share (common stock). See earnings per share.

net interest. Interest to lenders paid out net of tax (cf. after-tax basis; net yield).

net interest income (NII) (Banking). The interest earned from lending less the direct costs associated from servicing and borrowing. Equivalent to an industrial and commercial firm's **gross profit**. NII is a key measure of bank profitability since it reflects the difference between the rate a bank can borrow and lend money and the associated costs for doing so. The higher the ratio of NII to assets, the more efficient the bank. Also known as *net interest margin*. See **efficiency ratio**.

net interest margin (Banking). A performance measure that indicates how well a bank uses its earning assets in relation to the cost of funding. It is the **net interest income** divided by the average of the interest earning assets.

net lease. A lease where the lessee, the writer of the lease, retains responsibility for operating costs on the asset, such as maintenance, insurance, taxes, and so forth (cf. **financial lease**).

net liquid funds. See acid test ratio.

net liquidity balance (Banking). The net cash or near cash held by a bank (cf. **liquidity risk**).

net margin. The sum of positive and negative initial or **variation margins** on a complex position. See **Standard Portfolio Analysis of Risk**.

net open position (Forex). The net position of the spot and forward positions in the same currency. Thus a bank could be long at spot but short the forward maturities, the net result being an overall short position. This might arise due to demand and supply factors, or expectations by the intermediary on movements in the currency (cf. **proprietary trading**).

net order. See contingent order.

net position. The overall position of marketmakers: the sum of their long and short positions in a particular issue, maturity, or range of securities.

net present value (NPV). A discounted cash flow criterion which determines the value of a cash flow at an arbitrary point of time by reference to a given rate of interest, the discount rate, or cost of capital, and which takes into account the time value of money. The basic formula is:

$$NPV = \sum_{t=1}^{n} \frac{CF_i}{(1 + r_i)}$$

where CF_i is the cash flow in period i; and r_i the rate of interest for period I. Usually, but not always, this rate is constant for all periods t. The basic premiss is that if the resultant NPV of the cash flow is positive, there is a surplus of gain to cost; if negative, the opposite. This leads to the *NPV rule* where positive NPV projects are accepted and negative NPV projects are rejected. The NPV method is frequently applied to capital budgeting or investment appraisals to determine the economic value of the projects being analysed. See **internal rate of return; yield**.

net price trading. See **all-in cost; clean price; net trade; transaction costs**.

net profit. Profit after interest and taxes and any extraordinary charges or receipts have been included. See also **earnings before interest and tax**. Also called *net income*.

net profit before taxes. See **earnings before taxes**.

net profit ratio. Ratio of net profit to a firm's sales or turnover. See **ratio analysis**.

net realizable value (NRV). The value of an asset if it were sold after all the associated costs of disposal (cf. **hold-back; marked-to-market; provision; retention**).

net redemption yield. See **after-tax basis**.

net return. The return after all the associated costs (cf. **gross**). See **all-in cost**.

net settlement. A method of payment on the two sides of a **swap** which involves only one party making a transfer of the net sum due after deducting the amount they would have received from the other party (cf. **netting**). Also called *net two-way payment*. See **full two-way payments clause**.

net tangible assets. Tangible assets (that is, the total **fixed assets** less any **intangible assets**) less **current liabilities**.

netting. A method **counterparties** use for establishing their respective **positions** where the net value outstanding is paid between those involved (cf. **novation**). Netting is increasing in the **foreign exchange markets** and in the **swaps** markets as a way of reducing **counterparty risk** as volumes increase (cf. **daylight exposure unit**). The legal basis for netting is still uncertain in many jurisdictions; for the United States, the Financial Institutions Reform, Recovery, and Enforcement Act of 1989 (FIRREA) provided a sound legal framework for netting in many situations for US-domiciled entities. There are two basic methods used to net differences: *bilateral netting*, where the two parties agree to make a net payment of the differences between each other over a given period, and *multilateral netting*, where a large group agree to settle net differences between each other over a given

period. This latter method allows all the different positions to be pooled against all the other parties, so that, if in a given situation a given party has a credit with a second party, this may be used to partially or fully offset a debit to a third party. Bilateral netting is commonly used with **over-the-counter** transactions; multilateral netting tends to require a more complicated and formal arrangement with some form of clearing centre. It is used within a group of companies and increasingly also for major participants in markets such as foreign exchange.

netting by novation. A method of **netting** which involves the replacement of existing, outstanding transactions by a new agreement such that the economic, but not the legal, basis of the positions of the parties is altered. For example, two **swaps counterparties** with a large number of mutually outstanding swaps positions could replace the multitude of existing transactions with a new contract with one set of net payments from one party to the other which maintained the current economic position, thus netting by novation. For instance, the firms have two swaps of US$100m, where the **fixed rate** payments mutually cancel each other, but the **floating rate** sides would net to a single periodic payment of 20 **basis points** (BP), then the two current swaps are replaced by a new contract acknowledging that one party would pay a fixed 20 BP on the agreed **notional principal** of US$100m. By netting, US$100m of the notional principal outstanding is eliminated, which reduces the amount of capital required to support the **position**, and the total **counterparty risk** is also reduced.

net trade. Transaction undertaken by a broker-dealer without **commission** or fee. The intermediary, presumably, earns a return from the **bid-offer spread** (cf. **net commission**).

net translation exposure. See **translation exposure**.

net working capital. Current assets less **current liabilities**.

net worth. The total of a company's **share capital** and **reserves**, or the difference between total assets and external liabilities (cf. **negative net worth**). See also **net asset value**.

net writer. A **dealer** who has written or sold more **options** than have been bought (cf. **delta/gamma hedge**).

net yield. (i) (USA) The yield after expenses on a security (cf. **all-in cost**). (ii) Sometimes used for the after-tax yield, that is the yield, net of **withholding tax**.

net yield to redemption (UK). See **after-tax basis** (cf. **gross redemption yield**).

neural networks or **neural net.** A mathematical method of analysis and simulation of complex non-stationary phenomena (cf. **expert systems**). They have evolved as a way of modelling non-linear behaviour in the natural sciences. Since the 1980s they have found increasing use as a way of modelling the behaviour of financial variables. As an analytic tool, they are used to classify observations into two or more sets by training the network via paired explanatory and effect variables. The network will then seek to map the relationship between the explanatory and effect variables based on the initial data provided. This map is then used to provide the best guess effect result when presented with new explanatory variables. For instance, if a net has been trained to associate increased turnover, size of transaction, and inter-market activity with rising volatility, then increased (decreased) volatility estimates would be provided from new explanatory variables. See J. Freeman and D. Skapura (1991), *Neural Networks* (Addison Wesley).

neutral. (i) A view of the market that cannot be equated to either a **bull** or a **bear**. (ii) A **position** that is neither **long** nor **short** (cf. **matched book**).

neutral basis. See basis.

neutral hedge. A hedge intended to provide the greatest protection when the price of the **underlying** remains the same or only moves slightly in price or rate (cf. **delta hedge**).

neutral hedge ratio. The option price sensitivity to a small change in price of the **underlying**. It is the first partial derivative of the option price in respect to the underlying and is known as **delta**. If the delta of an option is 0.5, i.e. **at the money**, then the value of the option price is expected to change by half that of the underlying for a small change in price. Thus if the price of the underlying is 100 and the option price 10, to exactly hedge or offset a price change of one in the underlying, then a hedging position in half one unit of the underlying is required to exactly match the change in price of the option predicted by the neutral hedge ratio of 0.5. The amount of response in the option price, known as **gamma**, will differ depending whether the option is at the money or significantly **in the money** or **out of the money**. Gamma will be highest when the option is at the money. See also **delta/gamma hedge**.

neutral period. Eurocurrency market term for a **placing** that does not start or finish on a Friday or the day before a bank holiday (cf. **broken period; end-end**).

neutral price (Bonds). For **floating rate notes**, the price on the next **coupon** date which will produce a return equal to the **reference rate**, plus the **discounted margin** between now and the next coupon date (cf. **rollover price**).

neutral ratio spread. A delta neutral position involving purchased and written options such that the combined **delta** of the position is zero. If an option is written with a delta of 0.60, and it is to be hedged via purchased options which have a delta of 0.45, then the appropriate ratio of written (short) options to purchased (long) options is:

$$\frac{N(d_1)_s}{N(d_1)_l} = \frac{0.60}{0.45} = 1.33$$

The 0.45 delta long position needs to be held in a ratio of 1.33 to every one of the short 0.60 delta option. This will eliminate the sensitivity of the position to changes in the price of the **underlying** (over small price changes). If the price changed by 1, then the value in the written position would decrease by 0.60, and that of the long position by 1.33×0.45, or 0.60. Note that it may not eliminate other option pricing sensitivities. Also known as a *delta spread*. See also **delta/gamma hedge**.

new issue. (i) The process of creating and issuing new securities. A new issue may have unique characteristics, which is generally the case with debt issues, or in the case of **equities**, be offered to the investing public at large for the first time (cf. **initial public offering; flotation**). (ii) The term can also be used less precisely to describe any new offering of securities, whether already extant or not. Thus a **rights issue** may be called a new issue, as well as a **tap** or **fungible** issue of debt securities. (iii) Any recently issued security (cf. **on-the-run; par bond**). See **seasoned**. (iv) (Money markets) Securities that will be created if purchased by the **counterparty**. That is, they will be issued specifically if the transaction is undertaken.

new issues market. The market in which securities are first offered to investors (cf. **after market; secondary market**). See **grey market; primary market**.

new issue swap. An **interest rate swap** or **cross-currency swap** that is designed to convert the **liability** of the issuer into a different, more acceptable form. Thus an issuer might raise money via **floating rate** or **variable rate** debt and convert it to a more desirable **fixed rate** equivalent obligation by entering into a simultaneous interest rate swap. By allowing borrowers to raise funds in different markets and use the swaps market to convert the liability into a more desirable structure, the diverse currency capital markets are made available to issuers. See **synthetic bond; synthetic floating rate note**.

new money. (i) In portfolio management, funds derived from outside the portfolio but usable for investment purposes. (ii) In company finance, the raising of fresh **capital**, as compared with the restructuring of capital. (iii) In the US Treasury securities market, the amount by which the **par value** of new securities exceeds that of the maturing securities being redeemed (cf. **refunding**).

new shares or **stocks.** New shares issued on a stock exchange (cf. **initial public offering**; **listing**; **offer for sale**).

newsletter. (i) A publication provided by a financial intermediary such as a **stockbroker** or an **investment bank** to its clients on a regular basis keeping them informed of developments in a market, a sector, or economic trends (cf. **disclaimer clause**). Such a publication may also include advice on investment strategy, the impact of new information, and a calendar of forthcoming events. Also called a *market letter*. (ii) A high-priced, subscription-only specialist publication often purporting to provide the recipient with **insider information** or expert advice on investments.

new sovereign (Commodities; UK). A one-quarter troy ounce **gold** coin issued by the Royal Mint. One of a number of gold coins which are available to be bought by individuals and actively traded on the **London bullion market**.

newspaper listings. The price lists of securities reported in various newspapers. Only the largest **quoted** companies are usually reported (cf. **blue chip**).

new time (UK). A London Stock Exchange (LSE) term to describe the now no longer possible opportunity to deal such that the **settlement** was delayed from one **account period** to the next. This was permissible two days before the close of an account period by special arrangement and settled during the following **account**. The effect is to delay payment (cf. **cash and new**; **contango**; **delayed delivery**). The LSE has now moved to **rolling settlement** and this opportunity no longer exists. See also **contango market**; **forward**.

new time dealings. On the London Stock Exchange, those transactions which were made on the penultimate and last days of the **account period** need not be settled, if both parties agree, until **settlement day** of the next account period. Following the move to rolling settlement, this facility no longer exists. See **cash and new**; **contango**.

New York clearing house funds (USA). See **clearing house funds** (cf. **same day funds**).

New York Coffee, Sugar and Cocoa Exchange (NYCSCE) (USA). Soft commodities (*softs*) **futures exchange**.

New York Commodity Exchange (Comex) (US). 4 World Trade Center, New York, NY 10048 (tel. 1 212 938 2900; fax 1 212 432 1154). The New York exchange dealing in gold and silver futures contracts and option contracts in gold futures established on 5 July 1933. Major contracts are gold, silver, copper, and aluminium. There is also a **stock index future** contract on the **Euro-Top 100 Index**.

New York Cotton Exchange (NYCE) (USA). Oldest **commodity** exchange in New York set up in 1870 to trade cotton. It now also trades frozen concentrated orange juice **futures** via the Citrus Associates and financial futures and **options** via the Financial Futures Exchange (Finex).

New York Curb Exchange. See **American Stock Exchange**.

New York Futures Clearing Corporation (NYFCC). The **clearing house** for contracts traded on the **New York Futures Exchange**.

New York Futures Exchange (NYFE) (US). 20 Broad Street, New York, NY 10005 (tel. 1 212 656 4949; fax 1 212 656 2925). A part of the **New York Stock Exchange** opened in 1980.

New York interbank offered rate (NIBOR) (USA). The rate that **prime banks** lend to each other in the New York **interbank** money market (cf. **London interbank offered rate**). See **fed funds**.

New York Mercantile Exchange (NYMEX) (USA). 4 World Trade Center, Suite 744, New York 10048 (tel. (212) 938 2222). Established in 1872, its main area of activity is in **futures** and **options** on energy and precious metals (cf. **marker crude**; **West Texas Intermediate**).

New York Stock Exchange (NYSE) (USA). 11 Wall Street, New York, NY 10006 (tel. 1 212 623 5150). The senior (by size and value) of the two securities markets located in New York. Sometimes called the *Big Board*, it trades shares in large, well-established companies (cf. **American Stock Exchange**; **National Association of Securities Dealers Automated Quotations**). It was established in 1792 and is the oldest exchange in the USA.

New York Stock Exchange Composite Index (NYSE Composite) (USA). Capitalization-weighted index of all **stocks** listed on the New York Stock Exchange (NYSE). Similar in coverage to the **Standard and Poor's 500 Index**, which has

80% of the NYSE by capitalization. The index is computed by the NYSE.

New Zealand Futures & Options Exchange Limited (New Zealand). 10th Level, Stock Exchange Centre, 191 Queen Street, Auckland 1; Postal Address: PO Box 6734 Wellesley Street, Auckland, New Zealand (tel. 9-309 8308; fax 9-309 8817). **Futures** and **options** exchange established in 1984. It is a screen-based market using an Automated Trading System (ATS) computerized trading facility for its members. It is both a commodities and financial exchange, including both short- and long-term interest rate contracts, currency contracts, stock indices, and wool.

New Zealand Stock Exchange (New Zealand). Clatex Tower, 286-92 Lambton Quay, PO Box 2959, NZ-Wellington (tel. 64 4 472 7599; fax 64 4 473 1470).

niche or **niche market.** A part of the market which is the domain of specialists. Niches may include securities with special features, market sectors, or illiquid or poorly researched issuers. The major distinguishing factor is informational or pricing advantages by the specialists (cf. **bazaar**).

nickel (USA). Term used in the US markets for five **basis points** (0.05%). Hence a *nickel spread*, which is a 5-basis points, **bid-asked spread**.

nifty-fifty (Equities; USA). The fifty most popular stocks with major institutional investors (cf. **glamor stock**).

Nigerian Stock Exchange (Nigeria). Stock Exchange House (8th and 9th floors), 2/4 Customs Street, PO Box 2457, NG-Lagos (tel. 234 1 2660 287; fax 234 1 2668 724).

Nikkei calls or **puts.** over-the-counter options written on the Nikkei-225 Index.

Nikkei 225 Index or **Nikkei Index.** A price average index of the largest 225 companies quoted on the Tokyo Stock Exchange. It is equivalent of the FT-SE 100 Index (UK) or the **Standard and Poor's 500 Index** (USA). The base value is 176.21 on 16 May 1947. See also **Tokyo Stock price index**.

Nikkei-linked bond (NLB). Equity-linked note which has an embedded option on the Nikkei 225 Index.

nil paid (UK). Indicates that the rights have not yet been paid for. It is used in the context of a rights issue to indicate that payment on the new issue of shares has not been made (cf. **partly-paid**).

nil shares (UK). New issued **shares** in a company. Such shares can usually be transferred using renounceable documents. See **renunciation**.

nimble dividend (USA). A concession allowed in some states, permitting the payment of a **dividend** from retained **earnings** by a firm which made no **profits**.

Nippon Investors Service Inc (NIS) (Japan). Kojimachi Hiraoka Building, 1–3 Kojimachi, Chiyoda-ku, Tokyo 102 (tel. (813) 3239 5111; fax (813) 3239 5117). One of the **credit rating** agencies in Japan.

N/N (not to be noted). An endorsement added to a **bill** to tell the collecting bank that it should not be noted if the bill is dishonoured by non-payment or non-acceptance.

no-action letter (USA). A letter provided by the **Securities and Exchange Commission** in relation to a transaction stating that the Commission will take no civil or criminal action in relation to the way the transaction has been structured. Such no-action letters typically cover matters where the interpretation of a point of law is somewhat obscure or where precedents do not exist. A body of interpretation has built up over no-action letters and the Commission itself aims for a consistent interpretation of the relevant law.

no-arbitrage condition. (i) The setting of forward or **futures** prices such that it is not possible to make a risk-free profit by either buying (or selling) the **underlying** and selling (or buying) the **derivative** instrument (cf. **cash and carry**; **cost of carry**). Also called *arbitrage-free condition*. See **arbitrage**. (ii) For **options**, see **boundary condition** (cf. **put-call parity**).

no brainer. A transaction so patently favourable that no intelligence is required to enter into it.

noise. (i) In statistics, random fluctuations in a data series which have no explanation. Also called the *error term*. (ii) Market jargon for either **risk**, **uncertainty**, or **volatility**. (iii) Price changes that are not related to new information (cf. **efficient markets hypothesis**).

noise traders. Uninformed market participants.

no-load fund (NL) (USA). A **mutual fund** which does not make a sales charge (cf. **load**).

nominal amount or **nominal value.** Another term for the **principal** or **face value** of a security certificate (cf. **notional principal**).

nominal capital. See **authorized stock**.

nominal exercise price (USA). The **strike price** of an **option** on a **Government National Mortgage Association** (Ginnie Mae) certificate by the **adjusted exercise price**. The adjusted exercise price is a method of varying the **exercise price** to ensure standardization on **put** and **call options** on Ginnie Mae **bonds**. Contracts are traded on a standard Ginnie Mae issue, so that the exercise price is adjusted for different yielding pools of mortgages to give the same **yield** to the holder.

nominal interest rate. (i) The method of computing interest rates. See **interest rate calculations**. (ii) The monetary interest rate earned on an investment. This may be different from the **real interest rate** since the nominal interest rate is not adjusted for inflation. In most cases, the real interest rate is significantly lower than the nominal rate due to a large measure of inflation in an economy (cf. **index-linked**).

nominal owner. The owner of a security in name only (cf. **beneficial owner; nominee**).

nominal price. (i) An insignificant price used in a transaction in order to provide some consideration for the contract (cf. **cabinet trade**). (ii) Sometimes used to describe an estimated price for a security during a trading period in which no deals were struck (cf. **indication; quote**). (iii) The face value or par value of a security. Also called the *nominal value*.

nominal principal or **nominal principal amount.** The theoretical amount that is involved in a derivative contract (cf. **contract for differences**). At the contract's **expiry** or **maturity**, with **cash settled** contracts, only the differences between the initial, contracted amount and the valuation at expiry are then exchanged. With **delivery**, the **underlying** is then bought and sold at the contracted price or rate by both parties. For **interest rate swaps**, there will be periodic exchanges of the net differences in the interest payments and in the case of **cross-currency swaps** an actual exchange of **principal**. Also known as the *notional principal* or *notional principal amount*.

nominal quote. See indication.

nominal rate or **nominal interest rate.** The rate of interest in name only. Interest rates are calculated using different methods and based on different frequency of cash flows (cf. **real interest rate**). It is, however, convention to express all these different rates as an annual rate (cf. **flat rate**). See **annual equivalent; interest rate calculations**.

nominal value. See nominal price (cf. face value; par value).

nominal yield. The stated yield of a bond; that is, the current coupon.

nominated adviser. A representative from a recognized management or financial organization that acts as an internal consultant to a company seeking a **listing** on the **London Stock Exchange's Alternative Investment Market.** The intention is that the adviser should stay with the company for longish periods of time. A sort of hands-on **outside director**.

nominated broker. A member of the **London Stock Exchange** committed to making **two-way prices** in the **shares** of a company **listed** on the **Alternative Investment Market.** The intention is that the **broker** should not only advise on the initial **flotation** but remain interested in the progress of individual companies.

nominative. See registered security.

nominee. When title in a security is held by an individual or organization on behalf of the actual owner, usually to preserve the anonymity of the **beneficial owner**, or for administrative convenience (cf. **proxy**). For instance, traders often hold securities in the name of the market's nominee since this facilitates **settlement** (cf. **street name**).

no money down. A general feature of the **forward, future,** or **swap** type of **derivatives** that the buyer is not required to make any payment until the **expiry** or **maturity** of the contract (cf. **margin**). The exception being cases where the contract is made **off-market** (cf. **off-market coupon swap**). See also **money down**.

non-acceptance. A **documentary credit** which is refused on presentation. Although this would suggest rejection, non-acceptance can, and usually does, arise through a number of technical factors or deficiencies in the documentation which are subsequently rectified and then accepted.

non-accrual (Banking). A situation on an asset where the normal accounting practice of accruing the interest due cannot be reasonably made since there is a chance that interest will not be paid. See **charge-offs; non-performing loans; problem asset**.

non-assented. (i) **Bonds** for which a suggested reorganization of interest and **principal** payments has been rejected by the holders (cf. **assented securities**). See busted. (ii) **Common stock** or ordinary **shares** where the holders have not agreed to accept the terms of a takeover (cf. **tender offer**).

non-borrowed reserves (Banking; USA). The total **reserves** held at the **Federal Reserve** by member banks, less any borrowings made at the

discount window (cf. net borrowed reserves; net free reserves).

non-business days. See bank holiday; business day.

non-callable. An issue of securities where the holders cannot redeem the security before its stated maturity date (cf. straight). Also commonly called a *bullet* (cf. plain vanilla). See call provision; extendible; put provision; retractable bond.

non-call life. See bullet; straight; plain vanilla.

non-clearing member (USA). A New York Stock Exchange firm which has no clearing department and uses the services of another firm or agency instead (cf. clearing member).

non-competitive bid (USA). Bids to purchase US treasuries at auction without any setting price limit. Usually, the total value of the non-competitive bids is limited and they are allotted at the average price. Bidders can normally expect to receive the amounts bid for under this process. See competitive auction.

non-cumulative. The conditions attached to the payment of interest or dividends or to the operation of a sinking fund where if payments are not made when due then they are lost and cannot be carried forward (cf. arrears; arrearages; cumulative).

non-current assets; non-current liabilities. See current assets; current liabilities; fixed assets; liabilities; tangible assets.

non-deposit funds (Banking; USA). Funds borrowed for short periods of time to adjust liquidity. Also called *managed liabilities*.

non-durables. Another name for consumer goods. See economic indicators.

non-executive directors. See outside directors.

non-exempt (USA). A securities issue which for public distribution purposes has to be registered with the Securities and Exchange Commission. Issues by the federal government, states, municipalities, and their agencies are exempted from the registration requirement.

non-interest bearing negotiable order of withdrawal (NINOW). See negotiable order of withdrawal account.

non-linearity. A feature of options in that the payoff is not equal depending on the movements in the underlying. See asymmetric payoff.

non-linear model. Complex mathematical models drawn from chaos theory used to predict price or rate behaviour in the financial markets.

non-London certificates of deposit. (non-London CD) (Money markets; UK). Certificates of deposit (CD) issued by non-UK branches of banks but intended to be traded on the London money market. Such issues are generally of higher risk than London CDs where the Bank of England maintains a monitoring and regulatory role.

non-marketable securities. Financial instruments which cannot be bought and sold in the market (cf. exchange; over the counter). In most cases, they have to be held to maturity or offered back to the issuing entity for repurchase and cancellation (cf. letter bond).

non-member firm (USA). A broker that is not a member of a recognized exchange (cf. self-regulating organization).

non-negotiable or **not negotiable.** When this phrase is attached to a financial instrument it has the effect of removing its negotiable instrument character but does not affect the ability to transfer the instrument from one holder to another. However, if the seller's title to the instrument is in any way flawed, then the buyer takes it subject to the same defect.

non-parallel shift in interest rates. See rotational risk.

non-par swap or **non-par-value swap.** Off-market swap which has a fixed rate either above or below the prevailing swaps market rate. The difference is usually paid as a lump sum adjustment at the start of the swap to the party that would otherwise lose from entering into the transaction. Such swaps are used to hedge seasoned issues or borrowings when interest rates have changed since the time of issue (cf. par).

non-participating preferred stock. A common type of preferred stock which is entitled to a dividend only and does not get a part of the profits (cf. participating preferred stock).

non-pecuniary benefits. Non-cash benefits paid to a firm's management.

non-performing assets (NPA) (Banking). Any assets where revenue recognition has been discontinued or is restricted. The categorization includes non-performing loans, acquired property including other real estate owned, non-accruing interest loans, troubled debt, and restructured loans (cf. problem asset).

non-performing loans (NPL) (Banking). (i) Those assets or loans on which interest income is not being accrued, loans which have been restructured and on which interest payments or repayment have been materially altered as well as real properties which have been acquired through foreclosure (cf. **non-accrual**). See also **charge-off**. (ii) (Banking; USA) A criterion, defined by bank regulators, used to classify problem loans that have stopped earning interest and are likely to **default** on the principal (cf. **non-accrual**; **problem asset**). These are technically defined by bank examiners as loans with interest more than ninety days in arrears. There are four basic categorizations:

- *other loans especially mentioned (OLEM)*: specific problem assets in a bank's portfolio;
- *substandard*: these have inadequate value protection based on the borrower's capacity to repay or the collateral;
- *doubtful*: substandard loans where the repayment is highly unlikely;
- *loss*: uncollectable loans where an actual charge-off is made

non-recourse (Banking). Lending arrangement, usually seen in **project finance** transactions, where the lenders do not have **recourse** to the parent of the entity they are lending to (cf. **limited recourse**; **stand alone**).

non-recourse factoring. A factoring arrangement where the lender cannot seek repayment from the borrower in the event of non-payment by the **debtor**.

non-recurring charge (USA). A one-off revenue loss that is not expected to be repeated in the future (cf. **extraordinary charge**).

non-redeemable. See **irredeemable**; **one-way stock option**.

non-refundable. (i) Debt not redeemable with the proceeds of another debt issue (cf. **rolling debt**). (ii) Debt, usually for a stated period, which is not redeemable with **funds** bearing a lower coupon than that on the outstanding issue (cf. **debt buy-back**). See also **refund protection**.

non-resident. An entity holding assets within a country or jurisdiction which is taken to be not resident for the purposes of tax or other regulatory control (cf. **double taxation**; **offshore**). See **euromarkets**.

non-resident account. Foreign account held by a financial intermediary in a country. Usually the holder gains exemption from local taxes on the interest and **dividends** received (cf. **free of tax to residents abroad**; **withholding taxes**). See **non-resident**.

non-standard option. See **exotic options**; **flex options**.

non-stationarity. An observed characteristic of the **volatility** of financial markets usually attributed to changes in economic factors. Markets tend to have periods of low volatility followed by high volatility which means that pricing options, for instance, need to be able to forecast the volatility over the life of the option (cf. **mean reversion**). See also **binomial jump diffusion process**; **generalized auto regressive conditional heteroscedasticity**.

non-sticky jump bond (NSJ) (Bonds; USA). Collateralized mortgage obligation (CMO) which may change priority to receive **principal** if certain conditions take place (cf. **trigger**). While these conditions are maintained, the CMO 'jumps' to the different priority, but reverts back to its original position once the conditions cease. See **collateralized mortgage obligation equity**; **Z bond**.

non-systematic risk. That part of **risk** in modern portfolio theory that can be eliminated by **diversification**. The risk that cannot be removed from holding a risky asset is known as *systematic risk*. Total risk of an asset will be its systematic risk (measured by its **beta**) and the non-systematic, diversifiable risk. See **Capital Asset Pricing Model**; **residual risk**; **specific risk**; **stock specific risk**.

non-underwritten. Any of a number of transactions where new money is raised and the borrower is willing to dispense with **underwriting** in favour of **best efforts** made to sell the new issue. Many kinds of money market operations are non-underwritten though, given the costs of arranging other types of financing, most issuers prefer the certainty of an underwritten transaction even if they have to pay a **commission** to guarantee the completion of the transaction to a group of **underwriters**.

non-uniformity. The change in the **volatility** of financial markets over time. See **non-stationarity**.

non-voting shares or **non-voting stock.** That part of **equity** that has no formal voting rights, but has the same rights to participate in **dividends** and capital return. Sometimes called *A shares* (cf. **participation certificates**).

no-par stock or **no-par value stock (NPV)** (Equities; USA). It is common for US companies to issue **shares** that have no **nominal value**, the share capital being defined by the number of shares (cf. **par value**). The US commercial code does not require corporations to have a par value on **common stock** although some states may make this stipulation. With NPV stock, proceeds of issues of common stock are therefore credited either to the **capital** account or to the capital surplus account, or split between the two.

no-premium options. See zero-cost options.

Nordic Investment Bank (NIB). A multinational development agency, modelled on the World Bank, that specializes in infrastructure investment in Nordic countries (cf. **European Bank for Reconstruction and Development**).

no-regrets option. See lookback option.

normal backwardation. See backwardation; hedging pressure theory.

normal distribution. One of a number of frequency distributions which can be used to describe the probability density function of occurrences of stochastic processes (cf. **binomial distribution**). The normal distribution has, traditionally, been most commonly used in statistical analysis because it can be described in a relatively simple way and has some desirable properties. In such a distribution, about two-thirds of all observations will fall between minus one and plus one **standard deviation** from the mean; 95% (or 19 out of 20) of observations within plus/minus two standard deviations; while 99% (or 99 out of 100) will fall within plus or minus three standard deviations. A variant on the normal distribution, the **lognormal distribution**, is often used as a good description of the behaviour of financial market prices or rates. The lognormal allows for prices to be bounded by zero on the downside, while still providing the possibility of an infinite rise. It is assumed, for instance, that the lognormal distribution is the random prices generating function for prices in the **Black–Scholes option pricing model**.

normal market. A yield curve which has rising interest rates as **maturities** get longer (cf. **inverted market**). Also known as a *contango* or *premium market*.

normal market size (NMS) (UK). London Stock Exchange classification of different issues by size in relation to the minimum number of **ordinary shares** in which a market-maker will undertake transactions. It replaces the old **alpha, beta, gamma** system. NMS is a value expressed as a number of ordinary shares used to derive the **minimum quote size** for each individual issue. See also **marketable quantity; normal quote size**.

normal quote size (NQS) (UK). On the London Stock Exchange, the usual number of **ordinary shares** assumed in a quote at which the maximum of **market-makers** are obliged to give **two-way** prices.

normal trading unit. See round lot.

normal yield curve. A yield **curve** where the yield on the securities rises with **maturity** (cf. **contango; cost of carry**). See **term structure of interest rates**.

North American Free Trade Area (NAFTA). Grouping of the USA, Canada, and Mexico set up in 1995 to promote free trade (cf. **customs union**). See also **Andean Pact; European Union**.

northbound swap (Forex). A currency swap involving the exchange of US dollars into Canadian dollars. Hence, *southbound swap*, which is the same thing with a different view: the exchange of Canadian for US dollars. It derives from the geographical location of the two countries in relation to each other.

nostro account (Banking). A domestic bank's account held overseas in a foreign bank (cf. **loro account; vostro account**). It is derived from the Italian word for 'our', i.e. our (the bank's) account.

note. (i) Traditionally, a promise to pay rather than an order to pay. See **bill; promissory note**. (ii) Now commonly used to describe any **fixed rate** or **floating rate negotiable** debt instrument, other than a **floating rate certificate of deposit**, regardless of **maturity** (cf. **floating rate note; medium-term note**). (iii) Also used in the US **treasury market** to describe a fixed-rate debt with an **original maturity** of up to ten years. Thus the US Treasury will issue seven-year notes, but thirty-year **bonds**.

note issuance facility (note purchase facility) (NIF) (Banking). A **medium-term facility** allowing borrowers to issue **short-term promissory notes**, normally of three- or six-months maturity, in their own names, often via a **tender panel**. Usually a group of banks guarantees the availability of funds to the borrower by buying any unsold notes at each issue date, or by providing a **standby credit** and agreeing to purchase the notes if investors will not buy them at or below an agreed **margin** over the **reference rate**, usually **London interbank offered rate**. The NIF may or may not include an **advances** alternative for the **underwriting banks**. See **euromarkets; euronotes; multi-option financing facility; revolving underwriting facility**.

note over bond spread (NOB) (USA). The **spread** relationship between the **futures contracts** on the US Treasury ten-year **note** and the thirty-year **bond** contract (cf. **long bond**). Buying one and selling the other is equivalent to a **yield curve** play where price movements reflect a change in the shape of the curve. The same position can be created in the cash market and through **repurchase agreements**.

not held order (NH). A market order where the broker is not held responsible if the transaction is not carried out at the best possible price (cf. **at best**). This caveat is normally provided for large block trades. See **contingent order**.

notice day. In the **futures** markets, the day on which notices of the intent to deliver the **underlying** on an expiring contract may be given. The alternative for a participant is to **close out** their existing **position** by trading in the market prior to the **expiry** of the contract. See also **rollover**.

notice of tender. Written notice given by a **futures** short position (seller) of the intention to make **delivery** against the open, short position (cf. **notice day**).

notional bond. The **bond** against which a **bond futures** contract is priced. If bond futures were based on actual bond issues, it is possible that activity in the futures markets would be so great as to cause problems of **delivery** of the **underlying** bond at expiry (cf. **ramp**; **squeeze**). To avoid this danger of lack of supply, the exchange allows a range of bonds with different **coupons** and **maturity dates** to be delivered to satisfy the obligations of short position holders in the contract (cf. **cheapest to deliver**). When looking at a bond future you are looking at an index price reflecting the prices of all **deliverable** bonds. See **delivery factor**.

notional fund. Fund which is created only notionally to serve as a benchmark for investment performance appraisal. Typically such a fund will have the weights set in such a way as to closely mirror the fund's objectives.

notional principal. The amount of **underlying** used in many **derivatives** contracts for working out payments but not actually exchanged between the parties (cf. **interest rate swap**). Also called the *notional principal amount*.

notional principal contract. Any derivative contract that does not involve the **counterparties** in exchanging the **underlying** principal sum and where the **notional principal** is used purely to calculate the obligations between the two parties. In the UK, this would be known as a *contract for differences*.

notionnel (French). Name for French government bond futures contract traded on the Marché à Terme International de France (cf. **cheapest to deliver**; **deliverable**). See **notional bond**.

not negotiable. See **negotiable instrument**; **non-negotiable**.

not rated (NR). A security or issuer who does not carry a **credit rating**. It can also be applied to a particular security issue by a rated entity where the issue in question has not been assigned a rating.

not to press (NTP). When the **delivery** of certificates will be delayed (cf. **fail**).

novation. A condition where the rights and responsibilities of a contract may be transferred by the substitution of a new contract for the old with the consent of all the parties involved. Effectively, the replacement of one debt instrument with another by consent of both the lender and borrower (cf. **netting**; **netting by novation**). Used significantly in the **swaps** market and the legal basis for a **futures** or **options** **exchange** substitution of the **clearing house** as the **counterparty** to the contract. It can also involve **assignment** to a new counterparty.

noyaux durs (French). Stable or long-term **shareholders** in a company (cf. **controlling interest**; **keiretsu**).

NPV swap. See **concertina swap**.

numbered account. Accounts which can only be identified by numbers. Used to be synonymous with banking secrecy and, in particular, accounts held in a safe haven, such as Switzerland.

number tumbler. Colloquial name for an individual who is good with numbers (cf. **bean counter**; **quant**; **rocket scientist**).

numeraire. A money unit that is not itself tradable but comprises tradable units; for example, **European Currency Units**.

numerical option pricing model. See **binomial option pricing model**.

NV subsidiary. A company set up in the Netherlands Antilles as a wholly owned subsidiary of an overseas parent. Formerly used as a financing vehicle to raise funds either by loan **syndication** or on the **eurocurrency** markets (cf. **special purpose vehicle**). Its main attraction was as a means of exploiting the lack of tax treaties between the Antilles and the countries of the parents, thereby facilitating tax avoidance on international operations.

O

obbligazione (Italy). **Bond**. An *obbligazione a tasso variabile* is a **floating rate note**.

ōbike (Japanese). The **closing price** for the afternoon trading session (*goba*) on the **Tokyo Stock Exchange**. See also **hike**.

obligación (Spanish). **Bond**. An *obligación del estado* is a government bond.

obligation. (i) A promise to pay, bond, or other certificate of indebtedness. (ii) A contractual pledge to repay borrowed money. (iii) Any statutory, regulatory, or other requirement to fulfil certain conditions or meet given criteria. (iv) (French) **Bond**.

obligation bond (USA). A type of **mortgaged-backed** where the issued amount is greater than the **collateral** supporting the issue, the difference being costs incurred by the mortgage originator. See **securitization**.

obligations assimilables du Trésor (OAT) (Bonds; France). A type of French government **bond** which is specifically designed to be **fungible** and issued in **tranches**, normally by **auction** or **tender**. The intention has been to create large, **liquid** issues which are more attractive to investors. Thus a ten-year OAT will normally be issued at the start of the **fiscal year** at a given **coupon** rate and the issue will be added to via regular monthly auctions, the issue price being either at a **discount** or **premium** depending on prevailing market conditions.

obligations linéaires (OLO) (Bonds; Belgium). Government **bonds** modelled after the French **obligations assimilable du Trésor**.

obligations renouvelables du Trésor (ORT) (Bonds; France). A form of government **bond** where interest is rolled up until **maturity** or **redemption** (cf. **zero-coupon bond**).

obligor. One who creates an *obligation*. Usually used for the issuer of a security or other financial instrument requiring the issuer to perform under the terms of the issue. For loans, the term *borrower* is normally preferred.

obrigacâo (Portuguese). **Bond**.

obrigacâo predial (Portugal). **Mortgage-backed security** based on the **Pfandbriefe** model.

ōdai (Japanese). The price level or **range** for a security. Securities have price ranges of 10 yen, called *dai*; the term *odai* denotes a range of 100 yen. A security may have an odai of 700 yen, that is a price range of between 700 and 799 yen. If the price goes from 780 to 810, the price is deemed to have moved to the 800 yen odai; if it falls to 690 yen, it has moved to the 600 yen odai.

odd date. Transactions in the **euromarkets** in currency or deposits for maturities which are different from the standard market convention (cf. **fixed dates**). The normal convention is that transactions are settled **spot** (that is the start value date is two business days forward from the **transaction date**) and the **maturity** is set for the same day in the subsequent calendar months unless it is not a business day, in which case it is set for the following business day (unless such a move would make the maturity fall in the next calendar month, in which case it is the previous business day) (cf. **neutral period**). Any day which does not correspond to one of these days is an odd date. So for a transaction taking place in eurosterling on 24 September (a Friday), the **value date** would be 28 September. The normal **maturity dates** based on the **calendar/month convention** are shown in the Table.

Term	Expected maturity	Adjustment for weekends/ holidays
1 month	28 Oct.	n/a
2 months	28 Nov.	a Sunday, therefore needs to be 29 Nov.
3 months	28 Dec.	a bank holiday (UK), therefore needs to be 29 Dec. for sterling
4 months	28 Jan.	n/a
5 months	28 Feb.	n/a
6 months	28 Mar.	n/a
9 months	28 June	n/a
12 months	28 Sept.	n/a

Dates other than these within the months would be considered to be odd dates. Also known as *broken dates*.

odd lot. Used to describe a block of securities that are bid for or offered in a smaller than normal amount, which is called the **round lot**. Prices for odd lots are usually discretionary; that is, **indicative** only. In some markets, such transactions pay/receive higher/lower prices than a normal amount. See **marketable quantity; large quote size**.

odd-lot dealer. A **broker** who parcels together buy and sell orders for **odd lots** to make up **round lots** in order to transact business.

off. (i) Market term for an uncompetitive price or quote, i.e. it is 'off the market'. (ii) Verbal expression used by traders when cancelling a previous instruction or quote, e.g. 'the deal is off'. (iii) Not recorded, hidden or unseen, as in 'off-balance sheet', 'off-board'.

off-balance sheet (OBS). **Liabilities** that are not required to be reported on a **balance sheet**. Many contingent liabilities such as **swaps** and other **derivatives** are not required to be accounted for on a balance sheet. Note that some reporting practices require the notation of such off-balance sheet liabilities in the notes to the accounts. See **below-the-line activities**.

off-balance sheet financing or **transaction.** A financing or transaction which does not create a **liability** on a **balance sheet**, for example a **sale and leaseback** transaction (cf. **defeasance; in-substance defeasance; leasing; legal defeasance**).

off-balance sheet instrument. Derivative instruments which only have a **notional principal** and therefore do not have to be reported on the **balance sheet**. These are usually reported as a separate item, both in terms of the notional principal and in terms of the net amount at **risk**. See **fundamental financial instruments**.

off-balance sheet reserves. See **hidden reserves**.

off board (USA). A US term used to describe a deal outside a 'recognized' exchange (cf. **Big Board**). See **over the counter**.

Öffentliche Pfandbriefe (Germany). Pfandbriefe covered by loans to the public sector.

offer. (i) The price or **yield** which a seller is prepared to sell or lend a particular security or asset (cf. **ask; bid; London interbank offered rate**). Sometimes known as the *asked-for price*. Hence a price at which a purchase or a sale would be made is known as a *bid-offer quote* (*bid-ask* in the USA) (cf. **quote; spread**). (ii) Another term for a **tender**, or auction (cf. **general cash offer**).

offer by prospectus (UK). One of the ways available to **lead managers** to **offer** securities to the public. See **subscribe**.

offer document. (i) The legal document for an offer for sale transaction (cf. **offering memorandum; prospectus**). (ii) The document giving the terms and conditions of a **takeover** offer by a **predator** and which usually includes some arguments as to why **shareholders** should accept the proposal. See also **tender offer**.

offered market. See **overbought** (cf. **bid only; oversold**).

offered rate. The interest rate at which a financial intermediary will lend funds (cf. **ask; bid; interbank; London interbank offered rate**).

offer for sale. (i) A method of issuing securities to the public by **subscription**. The sponsors of the issue purchase the securities from the issuer and then offer them for sale to investors (cf. **public offering; purchase and sale** (USA)). The offer is advertised, through an offer document or **prospectus**, stating the terms of the issue and the closing dates for applications (cf. **lists closed**). An offer for sale may be on a fixed price or **tender** basis (cf. **placement**). (ii) (UK) One of the ways of offering securities to the public (cf. **introduction; offer by prospectus; placing; subscribe**). It can take two forms: either a fixed price, which is usually known as an offer for sale, or an *offer for sale by tender*, in which case buyers are asked to provide a **bid price** for the securities (cf. **auction; tender**).

offering. A new issue of securities to the public (cf. **public offering**).

offering circular. Another term used for a **prospectus** (cf. **listing particulars; offering memorandum**).

offering date. The date upon which a new issue is allotted.

offering memorandum. A document giving the terms and conditions of securities to be offered in a **private placement** (cf. **placing memorandum**). See **prospectus**.

offering price. (i) The price of a new issue of securities. Sometimes called the *public offering price*. (ii) The price at which **open-ended mutual fund** units are sold to investors. The opposite is the bid price.

offering scale (USA). The schedule of prices for the different maturities of a new issue of **serial securities**.

offering telex. A method of offering participation in a new issue or loan by which the **lead managers** send out a telex detailing the terms of the issue and inviting participation in the **underwriting** and/or **selling group** (cf. **co-manager**). Such a telex normally precedes the preparation and dissemination of the accompanying **prospectus** or **listing particulars**. See also **grey market**.

offer price. See offer (cf. **bid-offer spread**).

offerto (Italian). Offer (cf. **richiesto** (bid)).

offer-to-bid basis. A calculation of performance, return, or cost which includes the **bid-offer** involved in buying and then reselling the investment (cf. **all-in cost; transaction costs; round trip**).

offer to purchase. See takeover.

offer wanted (OW) (USA). Used on security lists when a buyer is looking for a seller (cf. **bid wanted**). Generally such securities are **illiquid** (cf. **direct search market**).

offer yield. See asked; offer.

off-exchange. Securities traded **over the counter** (cf. **kerb trading**).

off-floor order (USA). A transaction that originates with a **broker's** client rather than from a member of an exchange for his own account (known as *on-floor orders*).

Office of Fair Trading (OFT) (UK). The department responsible for regulating anti-competitive behaviour, cartels, consumer credit, **mergers**, monopolies, and restrictive practices. Set up in 1973 by the Fair Trading Act, 1973, it is the body which advises whether any **takeover** should be referred to the **Monopolies and Mergers Commission** for investigation.

Office of Management and Budget (OMB) (USA). The federal agency within the Office of the President responsible for preparing and presenting the federal budget to Congress.

Office of the Commissioner for Securities and Commodities (Hong Kong). Regulator for the securities and commodities markets.

Office of the Comptroller of the Currency (OCC) (Banking; USA). See **Comptroller of the Currency**.

official discount rate. See discount rate.

official intervention rate (France). The floor rate for money market interest rates in France set by the **Banque de France**. If market rates are at or below this rate, the Bank will execute open-mar-

ket operations to drain **liquidity** from the banking system (cf. **discount rate; Lombard rate**).

Official List (Equities; UK). The **London Stock Exchange** list of securities traded on the market (cf. **Yellow Book**). See also **listed; quotation; quoted**.

official rate (Forex). The **foreign exchange rate** set by a government (cf. **convertibility**).

official receiver (UK). Government official who acts in cases of **insolvency** or **bankruptcy** to administer the realization and disposal of **assets**.

official reserves. The holdings of currencies and **gold** retained by governments, managed usually by the appropriate monetary authority, used to support the external value of the currency and other international financial pledges. See **devaluation; International Monetary Fund**.

off-market. A transaction having terms significantly above or below those currently prevailing in the market (cf. **at market**). This can be a legitimate means of manipulating cash flow as with **discount bonds**, where a low **coupon** is matched by a low price. Other times it can be a fraudulent or unethical market practice, for example, where an off-market **transfer price** between two subsidiaries is used to manipulate the allocation of profit for tax purposes (cf. **historical rate rollover**).

off-market coupon swap. Any swap where the agreed **fixed rate** is significantly different from the market rate (cf. **discount swaps; escalating rate swaps; high-coupon swaps; low-coupon swap; zero-coupon swaps**). This will be achieved by modifying the terms on the other side of the swap. Also known as a *new issue swap* or *non-par swap*.

offset. (i) A right in law to set liabilities against assets in any dispute over claims. For instance, where a company runs multiple accounts with a bank, the bank may require the right to offset debits against credits in the **event of default**. Such a *right of offset* substantially reduces the potential **credit risk** of many transactions since only the net **position** need be considered. (ii) Method of **closing out** an existing position by entering into a transaction of the opposite character to the one already taken. If one has a **long** position, it involves selling; if **short**, buying. (iii) Also a method used in **netting** transactions, such as **foreign exchange** or **clearing**. (iv) To liquidate a position in a future or option through a transaction which extinguishes the existing **liability**. Also called an *offsetting order, offsetting purchase, offsetting sale, offsetting trade*, or *offsetting transaction*. See also **buy-in**.

offset hedge (UK). Term used on the **London Metal Exchange** for a **futures** transaction designed to cover an existing **long** (or **short**) cash market **position** (cf. **physicals**).

offsetting order. See **closing transaction**.

offsetting swap. **Interest rate swap** or **cross-currency swap** which cancels the cash flows of an existing swap. Typically to match the cash flows, the new swap is an **off-market coupon swap**. Although the two cash flows are mutually offsetting, the transaction does not necessarily remove all **risks** since **credit** or **counterparty** risk on the two swaps remains. As a consequence, most counterparties would normally agree to the payment of a lump sum to compensate the losing party for the early **termination** of the contract to avoid such problems and free up **capital**.

offsetting transaction. Used in the **futures** and **options** markets to describe a deal that closes out a **position** either **long** or **short**. For example, an opening sale transaction is offset by a closing purchase; and an opening purchase is offset by a closing sale. See **closing transaction**.

offshore. For the purposes of tax or regulatory avoidance, a location where it is possible to effect financial transactions under beneficial regulations, hence *offshore funds*, which are designed to increase after-tax returns. Can also be used to describe any non-domestic siting of funds or transactions, hence *going offshore*. A location having tax advantages is known as a *tax haven*, hence an *offshore centre* (cf. **NV subsidiary**).

offshore banking facility (OBF). A special bank subsidiary allowed to transact business, such as **eurocurrency**, that is normally not permitted to domestic banks (cf. **tax haven**). Such facilities are available, for instance, for the USA and Japan, as a way of allowing domestic banks to compete in the international market.

offshore banking unit (OBU). A bank subsidiary located **offshore** and usually not permitted to engage in domestic activities.

offshore fund. (i) **Funds** managed outside the country of the beneficiary. (ii) (UK) Investment fund based in an **offshore** centre to avoid taxes for the advantage of UK investors. Unlike their domestic counterparts, they are not regulated.

off-the-run issues (Bonds; USA). **Bonds** which have been issued at some time in the past and are less attractive compared to recently issued bonds in relation to amount outstanding, with **coupon** rates which do not reflect current market **yields** and trading at significant **discounts** or **premiums**

to **par**. Such issues could be expected to be less liquid and their prices and spreads would reflect this (cf. **on-the-run issues**; **seasoned**). In **bills** and **notes**, normally only the current issue, i.e. most recently issued, is normally quoted.

oil and gas limited partnership (USA). A type of **limited partnership** specializing in the oil and gas industry. See **master limited partnership**.

oil and gas lottery (USA). A method of allocating drilling rights for oil and gas used by the US Department of Land Management which does not discriminate against small applicants (cf. **winner's curse**).

oil indexed security. A bond where the **coupon** and/or **principal** is linked to an oil price **index** (cf. **Arabian Light**; **Brent crude**; **equity-linked notes**; **embedded option**; **West Texas Intermediate**).

oil price derivative. **Derivative** where the **underlying** is the oil price. To give the contracts a value, there is normally a quantity factor, either barrels or tons, as well as a price. See also **commodity swap**; **energy futures**.

Old Lady or **Old Lady of Threadneedle Street** (Banking; UK). Affectionate term for the **Bank of England**. The Bank is located in Threadneedle Street, and the nickname is attributed to the eighteenth-century playright R. B. Sheridan (1751–1816). The 'old lady' comes from its former nannying approach to regulation (cf. **moral suasion**).

omega (Ω) (i) A measure of the **currency risk** in **options** when the buyer or seller has to report the transaction in a different currency (cf. **quantity adjusting option**). (ii) Third order derivative of the option price against the **underlying** (cf. **delta**; **gamma**). (iii) Sometimes used for an option's sensitivity to **volatility** (cf. **vega**).

omitted dividend. See **passing the dividend**.

OM Stockholm Fond AB (Swedish Futures and Options Market) (Sweden). Brunkebergstorg 2, PO Box 16305, S-103, 26 Stockholm (tel. 46 (0) 8 700 0600; fax 46 (0) 8 723 1092). Established in 1985.

OM London (The London Securities and Derivatives Exchange Limited) (UK). 6th Floor, 107 Cannon Street, London EC4N 5AD (tel. 44 (0) 171 283 0678; fax 44 (0) 171 283 0504). Established in December 1989.

omnibus account. A general account held with a financial intermediary that may be used to **clear** or settle transactions for clients of the account holder. In many cases the financial intermediary may not know the identity of the clients (cf. **clearing house**).

on-balance sheet. Those assets and liabilities that are, by accounting convention, required to be reported on a **balance sheet** (cf. **off-balance sheet**). See also **above-the-line activities**; **fundamental financial instruments**.

on-balance volume. A method of technical analysis which seeks to relate the price movements to trading volumes. By plotting the two together, **breakout** points can be inferred from buying and selling behaviour.

on-demand. A liability that is immediately repayable; for securities, on presentation. Money repayable on demand is termed *on call* or *call money.*

on-demand bond. A performance bond where the holder has the right to demand immediate payment from the issuer or guarantor regardless of justification.

one-cancels-the-other order (OCO order). A type of **alternative order** where the **broker** is asked to execute one of two different trades, the implementation of one automatically cancelling the instruction to do the other.

130% rule (UK). A term included in a **convertible** allowing the **issuer** to **call** the security if the price of the **shares** is trading at a **premium** of 130% to the **conversion price.** Such a rule ensures early conversion if the share price increases rather than allowing the convertible holders to hang on to the, usually higher-yielding, debt instrument.

one-off. (i) Tailored transaction which is unlikely to be repeated in the future. Most company **acquisitions** are customized one-offs since the features of the transaction, or the participants are unlikely to be the same again (cf. **structured finance**). (ii) Transaction between two parties who do not usually do business with each other.

one-man picture (USA). A **two-way price** given by a **broker** where the **bid** and **offer** prices are both from the same source.

one-month money. Deposit with a **maturity** of one month (cf. **call money**; **overnight deposit**).

one-sided or **one-way market.** Where there are only **firm** quotes in one direction (i.e. where in the other direction the market quote is **indicative**). If the market is firm on the **offer** side, it will be indicative on the **bid** side; and vice versa. It often signals that the **market-maker** is only willing to transact on the firm side. Often the sign of a disrupted, **thin**, or **illiquid** market.

one-time put provision. A security with a **put provision** that the holder may only **exercise** at one specific date. At the put date, the **coupon rate** is revised so that the security then becomes a **straight bond** at par at the then prevailing market rate at a preset **spread** to a **benchmark**.

one-touch option. See **digital option**.

one-touch all-or-nothing option. A **digital option** which pays out a predetermined amount if the **underlying** moves above (below) for a **call** (**put**) at any point during the option's **life**.

one-way stock option. Those issues which have no definite date for redemption, but can be redeemed at the **borrowers'** discretion; also sometimes called a *perpetual*. See **consols**; **gilt-edged**; **irredeemable**; **perpetual floating rate note**; **undated**.

one-week money. Money placed on **deposit** for one week (cf. **call money**; **overnight deposit**).

on-exchange. Same as **exchange traded**.

one-year money. Money placed on **deposit** for one year (cf. **call money**; **overnight deposit**).

on-floor order (USA). See **off-floor order**.

on margin. The purchase of a security using borrowed money and **collateral** from a **margin account** (cf. **leverage**).

on stream. A project that has begun to be operational and generate revenue (cf. **sunk cost**).

Ontario Securities Commission (OSC) (Canada). Regulatory body charged with overseeing the operation of the Ontario Securities Act and the principal regulatory body for the **Toronto Stock Exchange**.

on-the-close order. An instruction to buy or sell near the market closing (at the end of the trading session) (cf. **at the close**).

on the money. See **at the money**.

on-the-open order. An instruction to buy or sell near the market opening (at the start of the trading session) (cf. **at the open**).

on-the-run (Money markets). A term for **certificates of deposit** (CD) of a group of similar banks which are treated by market practice as being interchangeable (and therefore priced the same) for trading and investment purposes. There is no legal or regulatory backing to this aggregation of separate issuers; it has developed to provide greater **liquidity** in the CD **market** (cf. **fungible; run; tranche**).

on-the-run issues (Bonds; USA). The most recently auctioned bonds with regard to maturity range. These issues would be expected to be highly liquid, near **par** and **coupon rates** close to current **yields**; and have close **two-way prices** (cf. off-the-run issues; seasoning).

OPD (opening delayed) (USA). A market-reporting mechanism tape symbol used to flag a **delayed opening** or a significant price change at the opening (cf. **consolidated tape**). See **break; jump; opening rotation**.

open. (i) The period at the start of a financial market trading session, hence *opening prices* or *at the-open*. (ii) An instruction that is still valid for execution (cf. **good till cancelled**). (iii) Transactions on a **futures** or **options exchange** which have not been **offset** or **closed out**. See **opening and closing transactions; open interest**. (iv) Any position that creates an exposure that has not been offset or hedged by another transaction. See **open position**.

open account. A form of short-term sales financing where transactions are made with no formal debt contract other than the receipt. Contractual terms are implicit rather than explicit, including the credit period allowed (cf. **creditor**).

open auction. (i) A competitive **auction** or tender which involves the participants actively bidding against one another when they are aware of the values of the competing bids (cf. **English auction; dutch auction; sealed bid auction; silent auction; winner's curse**). (ii) An auction in which anyone can participate without preconditions.

open book. See **mismatched book**.

open contract (Derivatives). **Futures** or **exchange-traded options** contracts which have been bought or sold without the transaction having been completed or **offset** by subsequent sale, purchase, actual **delivery, exercise** or receipt of the **underlying** financial instrument or **commodity** (cf. **cover**). See **open interest**.

open corporation (USA). A company in which anyone is entitled to own **common stock**. The opposite is a **closed corporation** (cf. **controlling interest**).

open-end or **open-ended.** Investment funds, such as **mutual funds** (USA), **société d'investissement collectif à capital variable** (France), and **open-ended investment companies** or **unit trusts** (UK), where the units represent an interest in the assets of the fund (cf. **closed-end fund**). New units can be issued or existing ones redeemed by the fund in line with demand, the managers adding to or liquidating part of the assets as required (cf. **box management**). Unit prices are set by reference to the **net asset value** of the fund.

open-end credit. See **revolving credit facility**.

open-ended investment company (OEIC) (UK; EU). Proposed type of **mutual fund** or **unit trust** designed to meet the requirements of the European Commission's directive on **undertakings for collective investments in transferable securities**. See 'Open Ended Investment Companies: A Proposed Structure (Consultation Document)', HM Treasury, December 1993.

open-end lease. A type of **lease** agreement that provides for additional terminal payments by the **lessee** if the returned asset is below a pre-agreed value.

open-end management company (USA). Company that manages a **mutual fund**.

open-end mortgage. A type of mortgage against which additional debt may be raised (cf. **closed-end mortgage**).

opening. (i) Another term for a **window**. A period when there is an opportunity to undertake a (type of) transaction. (ii) The period at the start of a trading session on an exchange (cf. **opening price**).

opening and closing transactions (Futures). Transactions designed to open or close a **position**. A purchase or sale may *open* or *close* a position, depending on what is required.

	Open	Close
Purchase	No position	Short (sale)
Resultant position	= *long position* (opening purchase)	= *no position* (closing purchase)
Sale	No position	Long (purchase)
Resultant position	= *short position* (opening sale)	= *no position* (closing sale)

An open position is one where rights or obligations are established in the **futures contract**; closing positions extinguish all rights and obligations.

opening only order. See **at the open**.

opening price or **range.** The price or range of prices established at the **opening** of a market or trading in a security at the start of a **session** on an exchange (cf. **bell; rotation**).

opening purchase. Transaction involving the purchase of a **futures** or **options contract** to create a (long) **position** in the market.

opening rotation. Process by which securities or **contracts** on an exchange begin to trade at the opening of a **session**. See **rotation**.

opening sale. Transaction involving the sale of a **futures** or **options contract** to create a (short/written) **position** in the market.

open interest (Derivatives). The net number of **futures** or **option contracts** in existence on an exchange counting a bought contract and a sold contract as one position (cf. **open contract**). It can be either *gross open interest*, which is the sum of all the contracts that have been transacted and which remain to be liquidated by **settlement** or **delivery**; or *net open interest* which is the gross open interest less **matched**, but yet to be settled contracts. It is thus the sum of either the sold or the purchased contracts. The amount of open interest in a particular contract is often regarded as indicative of the amount of uncertainty surrounding price trends in the **underlying** and is used as a measure of the **technical condition** of the market. Sometimes called the *open position* or *uncovered position*.

opening sale. Transaction involving the sale of a **futures contract** to create a (short) **position** in the market.

open market. (i) A market that is open for business. (ii) A market that is open to all participants directly. This is typically the case for **over-the-counter** markets since they involve direct, bilateral transactions between two principals (cf. **direct search market**). Exchanges normally require business to be channelled through members (cf. **broker**).

Open Market Committee (Banking; USA). See **Federal Open Market Committee**.

open-market desk (Banking; USA). See **desk**.

open-market operations (OMO) (Money Markets). The activities of **central banks** in the **secondary markets**, usually money and short-term **bill** and **bond** markets, in order to effect **monetary policy**. These activities involve purchases or sales, often in the form of **repurchase agreements** to control the **money supply** and indirectly interest rates. When the supply of money rises, interest rates will fall and, if this is contrary to the central bank's monetary policy, it will counter this effect by arranging to sell securities, thus draining **liquidity** from the money markets (by so doing raising interest rates) as bank accounts are debited to pay for the securities. The central bank will do the opposite, buying securities and increasing the supply of money to the banking system, if it wants to increase money supply (and so, lowering interest rates). Central banks have to carry out OMOs daily in response to frictions within the payments system as well as to signal changes to monetary policy. See **Bank of Italy**; **Bank of Canada**; **Bank of England**; **Banque de France**; **Bank of Japan**; **Bundesbank**; **Federal Open Market Committee**.

open-market purchase. See **retire** (cf. **purchase fund**).

open-market value. The price that an asset or security would fetch in the open market, that is if generally offered for sale (cf. **marked-to-market**).

open-mouth operations. See **jawboning**; **moral suasion**.

open offer. A securities offer made to all parties (cf. **offer for sale**; **placing**).

open on the print (USA). A situation that arises when a **block** transaction is reported on the tape but where the **broker** has not yet covered his **position**. The **market** as a whole is now aware of the block and may suspect that the broker is long/short and adjust prices accordingly.

open order. An instruction to buy or sell that is valid until executed or cancelled. Also called *good till cancelled*.

open outcry. An auction system used by **futures** and **options exchanges** under which all **bids** and **offers** are made openly by public, competitive, shouted bids and hand signals. The term comes from the fact that the auction process is carried on by **brokers** on both sides of a transaction shouting their bids to one another on the floor of the exchange (cf. **pit**). The method is favoured for **derivatives** exchanges since it allows all concurrent bids and offers to be heard at the same time. A transaction is completed if a buy and sell match in price and quantity. Because trading conditions can be extremely noisy, a system of **hand signals** is also often used. See also **specialist**.

open position or **open net position**. (i) Any exposure to a particular asset or market that has not been offset by a countervailing transaction or otherwise **hedged** (cf. **open book**). (ii) (Forex) A **foreign exchange** dealer's net **assets** or **liabilities** in a particular **currency** (cf. **flat**; **matched book**; **overbought**; **oversold**). If this is not zero, then an open position is said to exist. See **long position**; **short position** (cf. **close**). (ii) (Derivatives) Another term for **open interest** (cf. **open contract**).

open repurchase agreement (Open RP) (Money Markets). A type of **repurchase agreement** (RP) transaction that is made on a rolling day-to-day basis with no final **maturity** and where either the (security) lender or borrower has the right to immediate termination (cf. **call**). The rate paid is likely to be higher than the overnight RP rate and will be subject to change in line with ruling market rates. Used most frequently by money market **dealers** to **fund** inventory or obtain **illiquid** securities (cf. **specific issues market**). Attractive to lenders since it offers a higher rate than overnight repurchase agreements.

open-up. When the **bid-asked spread** (bid-offer spread) of security price quotes widens (cf. **narrowing the spread**).

operating budget. Plan giving expected income and expenditure over a future period (cf. **budget**).

operating cash cycle. The time required for the initial outlays in providing a product or service to be realized in **cash** from sales.

operating efficiency. Measures of how well a firm makes use of its **assets**. See **ratio analysis**.

operating exposure (Forex). See **economic exposure**.

operating lease. A type of **lease** where the total amount of the payments made by the lessee (the user) to the lessor (the leasing company and owner of the asset) do not cover the initial purchase price of the asset. Such leases can have the advantage of not being included as part of the lessee's borrowings as shown in the balance sheet (cf. **capital lease; finance lease; below-the-line activities; off-balance sheet**).

operating leverage or **gearing.** The ratio of fixed costs to total costs in a process. The higher the level of fixed costs, the higher the **risk** since these have to be met regardless of output. Typically capital intensive firms have high operating leverage.

operating profit or **loss.** The accounting profit (or loss) made by a business from its business activities in a given period (cf. **turnover**). This is then further reduced or augmented by adding in the business's overheads and any ancillary investments to give the *profit (Loss) before interest and tax* (PBIT).

operating risk or **operational risk.** The risk inherent in a firm's operations due to **operating leverage** (cf. **business risk**).

opérations de clôture (French). After-hours trading.

operations department (USA). The settlements department of a financial institution (cf. **back office; middle office**).

operative date. The earliest date of repayment of a security. It is used in calculating the **yield-to-operative-date** (cf. call provision).

operative yield. See **yield-to-operative-date**.

operator. (i) A firm which undertakes a given activity. (ii) A firm or individual who behaves unethically. (iii) An old-fashioned term for a **speculator**. The term is still sometimes used for an individual with doubtful credentials. See **pyramid scheme**.

opinion letter. A letter from the **lead manager** or sponsor of a transaction to other involved parties addressing legal questions raised by the actual or proposed deal.

OPM ('other people's money'). Market term for the **leverage** obtained by borrowing money.

opportunity cost. The value given up (the 'lost opportunity') in pursuing the best alternative to the course of action decided upon. It is the return that could have been earned on the next best investment alternative, given the aims of the investor. Thus if two mutually exclusive alternative investments could earn 8% and 8.5% respectively, the opportunity cost is 8%.

opportunity value. See volatility.

optimal hedge ratio. See **minimum variance hedge ratio** (cf. **neutral hedge ratio**).

optimization. See portfolio optimization.

optimized portfolios as listed securities (OPALS) (Bonds; Equities; USA). Proprietary product offered by *Morgan Stanley Inc.* which offers **exchange-traded** securities where the **underlying** asset is an optimized portfolio. It is a tradable **bond–equity** hybrid product which offers investors the equivalent to holding the **stock index** in a specific market. This is achieved by issuing securities and holding a representative basket of **stocks**. The securities have a **maturity** of three years and pay interest semi-annually in the form of **dividends** from the **underlying** portfolio. In addition, holders can exchange the bonds for stock at any time. The advantages of the structure is that it reduces the cost of acquiring a large portfolio to replicate an index in a particular country; because the bonds are exchangeable for stocks, it will not trade at a **discount** to asset value as might a **closed-end** investment company and it also has a final maturity. The product is designed to be attractive to passive investors seeking to replicate a given market exposure but not seeking to pick stocks. OPALS may appeal to investors who cannot buy **stock index futures** or who invest in markets where no futures exist.

option (Derivatives). (i) **call** or **put** option providing the holder, in exchange for the payment of a **premium**, the right but not the obligation to either buy from or sell to the option **writer** a specified **underlying asset**, **commodity**, **currency**, **interest rate**, **spread**, **bond**, **future contract**, and so on. The most common types are **plain vanilla** calls and puts (cf. **chooser option**; **double option**; **option to double**). See also **call provision**; **put provision** (cf. **embedded option**). (ii) A contract providing the holder the right, against the payment of a premium, but not the obligation to obtain the benefits of favourable movements while remaining unaffected by adverse movements on a transaction in an underlying to be undertaken at a future date.

The key factors in options, which are usually specified in any contract are:

- *call*: gives the holder the right to buy; obliges the seller or writer, to sell;
- *put*; gives the holder the right to sell; obliges the seller or writer to buy;
- *underlying*: the specific asset, instrument, currency, interest rate, commodity, or other item that is exchanged if the option is exercised;
- *specification*: the contract quantity, number, quality, grade, cash-settlement terms or other specifics for the underlying;
- *strike price or rate* (or *exercise price* or *rate*): the contracted price or rate at which the right to buy or sell may be made;
- *expiry* or *maturity*: the date (and time) at which the contractual obligations on the writer cease;
- *exercise period*: for American-style options, this can be at any time up to its final maturity; for European-style options, this can only be done at its final maturity; *hybrids* have some aspects of both the American-style and the European-style;
- *premium*: the consideration or fee paid to the writer for the right to exercise the option;
- *payout*: at exercise, the difference between the strike price or rate and the current price on the underlying;
- *exchange-traded*: options which are bought and sold through an organized exchange. These will have standardized conditions as to strike price, expiry date, and the amount of the underlying and settlement through a clearing house;
- *over-the-counter (OTC)*: bilateral contracts between two parties which may be tailored to specific requirements;

- *exotic*: any option with special features (for instance: partial American-style exercise; strike re-sets, and so forth).

Other types of option which are included in the above embrace types such as **Asian options**, **barrier options**; **chooser options**; **digital options**; **ladder options**; **lookback options**, **natural options**; **rainbow options**; (cf. **traditional option**). In some cases, options can be **embedded** within other instruments, for example a **convertible**.

The seller of an option is variously known as the *seller*, *grantor*, or *writer* and is said to be *short the option*. The buyer of the option is variously known as the *buyer*, *purchaser*, *holder*, or *taker* and is said to be *long the option*.

optionable stock. Any security on which options are written.

option-adjusted analysis. A method of modelling the value of a fixed rate security or **portfolio** which contains **embedded options**, typically **call provisions** or **put provisions**, and the potentially positive or negative effect of the option(s) on the return under rising or falling interest rate scenarios. Also known as *contingent claims analysis*.

option-adjusted duration. Method of calculating the **modified duration** of a bond which includes a **call provision** to reflect the expected shortening effect of the issuer exercising his right to call the issue.

option-adjusted spread (OAS) (Bonds; USA). A valuation method used to compute the relative value for the extra **yield** available on **mortgage-backed securities** (cf. **extension risk**; **reinvestment risk**). The OAS takes into account the **prepayment risk** and therefore uncertainty to the holder of the timing of **principal** repayments as opposed to holding a default-free **straight bond** (cf. **plain vanilla**).

option-adjusted yield. Used for valuing bonds with **call provisions**; by adjusting the **yield** for the probability the issuer will **exercise** his right to redeem the issue prior to **maturity**.

optional dividend. A dividend that may be paid in cash or stock. Often called a *cash or scrip*.

optional payment bond. See **dual currency bond**.

optional redemption. See **call**.

optional redemption provision. An issuer's **call provision**; an investor's **put provision**.

option business. See **premium business**.

option buyer. The holder of a **long position** in an **option**. The maximum loss he can make is the amount of **premium** while, theoretically, there is unlimited profit potential. He is buying **volatility** or backing a directional movement in the **underlying**. He is willing to accept a limited loss due to the cost of the premium in exchange for a potentially unlimited gain because he expects the price to move in his favour, that is against the buyer. The motives of a buyer may be to **hedge** an existing position, speculate on developments or as a form of insurance. Also called *option holder, taker,* and said to be *long the option.*

option class. All **options** of the same type on a particular **underlying**. Thus all **calls** on a particular **common stock** would be one **class** (cf. **option series**).

option combination. Position combining two or more **options** of different types. For instance, buying both **calls** and **puts**. Also called *combinations.* See **option strategies**.

option contract (Derivatives). The quantity of the **underlying** represented by an **exchange-traded option**. Standard terms and conditions for buying and selling on the exchange are made available by the exchange. For **over-the-counter options**, a bilateral negotiable agreement gives the terms and conditions for the purchase or sale of an option.

option dated forward. A **foreign exchange forward** contract that allows one of the parties (usually the customer) to choose the exact date of **delivery** between two future agreed dates. This is a helpful flexibility when the exact transaction date is unknown. The **market-maker** offering this type of contract will price the forward rate at the latest or earliest date at which the transaction can be executed, whichever is the most advantageous rate to the intermediary. Such a flexi-dated contract is also known as an *option forward.* A similar result can be achieved by entering into a forward transaction at the latest required date and then **closing out** the unwanted period with an opposite transaction designed to net to zero at the end date.

option dealer. A trader in options (cf. **agent**; **broker**; **broker-dealer**; **dealer**; **market-maker** **writen**).

optioned instrument, security, commodity, or **stock**. The **underlying** that is used in an **option** contract.

option elasticity. The percentage change in an **option's** price for a 1% change in the **underlying** (cf. **delta**). See **lambda**.

option exchange. An organized exchange for trading **options**. Typically contracts will be standardized so as to facilitate transactions. (cf. **flex options**).

option forward or **option forward rate**. A **foreign exchange** market term for the rate at which a **currency** can be bought or sold for **delivery** between two future dates at the discretion of one **counterparty**. 'Option' refers to the choice of timing that is given, and not an optional characteristic of the contract (cf. **option trading**). See also **option dated forward**.

option fund. An investment fund where the returns are derived principally from buying or selling (writing) **options**. The degree of **risk** or **leverage** that the fund adopts will be influenced by its investment strategy. A fund wanting to increase returns to its investors might adopt a policy of **covered call** or **covered put** writing, thus receiving the **premium** income. A more aggressive approach may involve taking a **position** with the use of options either in a **market** (**index options**) or individual **stocks** (**stock options**). Some funds have an aggressive option strategy for part of the fund but guarantee a minimum return by placing the bulk of the invested funds in risk-free assets such as government **bonds** (cf. **equity-linked note**). Many funds deal in a range of **derivatives** (cf. **futures and options fund**).

option hedge. A bearish **volatility** strategy involving the combination of a position in the **underlying** with a **ratio spread**, such that the loss rate is not one for one between the two (cf. **covered call**). The position involves selling more options than underlying owned with a view to making a profit **on the premiums** received. It entails selling **volatility** with a view to making a profit as the maximum profit will be achieved if the price does not change; only if the price moves up or down significantly would the writer make a loss. See also **option strategies**; **ratio spread**; **straddle**; **strangle**; **strap**; **strip**.

option holder. The owner of an **option**. The holder has a **long position** in the option; while the **option writer** has a **short position**. Sometimes called the *option buyer, purchaser,* or *taker.*

option life. See **option period**.

option money. The price or consideration for an option. A call option is known as *call money*; a put option as *put money.* Today more frequently known as the *premium.*

option on a cap or **floor**. See **caption**; **floortion**.

option on an option. See **compound option**.

option on currency future. Exchange-traded option where the underlying is a currency futures contract. See also next entry.

option on futures. An option giving the right but not obligation to buy or sell a futures contract at a fixed price at or before a specific date (maturity). The variables which determine premiums are: time to expiry; strike price; interest rate; volatility; current value of the futures contract. See also option pricing.

EFFECT OF OPTIONS ON FUTURES

Futures transaction	Effect of position	Option on future buy
Buy	Gain if prices rise (rates fall)	Call = receive = buy future
Sell	Gain if prices fall (rates rise)	Put = deliver = sell future

Note to 'write' or sell futures options for a premium is to reverse the above positions, but also to take on unlimited risk. On exercise, the following occurs:

	Call	Put
Holder	Long futures position	Short futures position
Writer	Short/neutral futures position	Long/neutral futures position

There is also a cash payment from the writer equal to the difference between the current futures price and the strike or exercise price in the case of a call (or vice versa for a put).

option on London interbank offered rate (option on LIBOR). A caption or floortion where the reference rate is the London interbank offered rate.

option on options. See compound option.

option on stock index futures. See stock index options.

option on swap. See swaption.

option period. The life-span of an option as stated in the contract and at the end of, if European-style, or within which, if American-style, the buyer may exercise his right to purchase or sell (cf. abandon; Atlantic-style; Bermudan-style).

option portfolio (i) A portfolio of options. (ii) Sometimes taken to mean a covered option position or collateralized written position (cf. fiduciary call).

option premium. (i) The price paid to acquire an option. Often just called the *premium*. (ii) Another term used for the time value of an option.

option pricing. The minimum and maximum value of an option, or its price *boundary conditions*, are as follows:

Minimum value of calls: An American-style *call*: should sell for nothing (i.e. be worthless) or the difference between the underlying price and the strike price, whichever is the greater (it cannot have a negative value).

European-style *call*: should sell for nothing (be worthless), or for the difference between the underlying and the present value of the strike price, whichever is the greater (it cannot have a negative value). If the underlying has leakage (that is, pays a dividend or interest payment) prior to expiry, the European-style call price should be at least zero, or the difference between the underlying, adjusted for the present value of the leakage and the present value of the strike price, whichever is greater.

Maximum value: the value of the underlying.

Time to expiry: the value of a longer-dated American-style call must be at least the same as that of a corresponding shorter-dated American-style call. The value of a longer-dated European-style call must be at least the same as that of a corresponding shorter-dated European-style call as long as the underlying is a zero-leakage asset (that is it has no loss of value through interest or dividend payments). In the case of leakage, this condition does not apply.

Exercise price of calls: the difference in price between two calls that differ only in their strike or exercise price must be less than or equal to the present value of the difference in the exercise price. For American-style calls the difference cannot exceed the exercise price difference.

American-style and European-style calls: an American-style call should sell for at least the same price as a European-style call.

Minimum value of puts: an American put should sell for nothing (be worthless) or for the difference between the strike price and the underlying price, whichever is the greater (it cannot have a negative value). In the case of a zero-leakage asset, a European-style put should sell for nothing (be worthless) or the difference between the present value of the exercise price and the underlying, whichever is the greater (it cannot have a negative value). If the underlying has leakage prior to expiry, then the European-style put price should be at least zero, or the difference between the present value of the strike price and the underlying, adjusted for the present value of the leakage, whichever is greater.

Maximum value of puts: the value of an American-style put should not exceed its exercise price; the value of a European-style put cannot exceed the present value of its exercise price.

Time to expiry: the value of a longer expiry American-style put must be at least as great as that of a corresponding shorter-dated American-style put; for European-style puts no such condition applies (that is, there is uncertainty as to whether a longer-dated put is always more valuable than a shorter-dated one).

Exercise price of puts: the value of a higher exercise price put must be at least the same as the value of a corresponding put but with a lower exercise price. The difference in price between two European-style puts with different exercise prices must not exceed the present value of the difference in their strike price. For American-style puts this difference must not exceed the difference between the two exercise prices.

American-style and European-style puts: an American-style put should sell for at least the same price as a European-style put. For conditions leading to early exercise, see entry under **American-style**.

put–call parity: this condition holds that the price of a European-style call is equal to the price of its corresponding put plus the **spot** underlying price, less the present value of the strike price. That is:

$$\text{Call}_{\text{European-style}} = \text{Put}_{\text{European-style}}$$
$$+ \text{Underlying}_{\text{spot value}}$$
$$- \text{Present Value of Strike Price}$$

Traditional option pricing distinguishes between the **time value of an option** and its **intrinsic value**. The two make up the option value:

$$\text{Option value} = \text{Time Value (TV)}$$
$$+ \text{Intrinsic Value (IV)}$$

where intrinsic value is the positive difference between the market price of the underlying and the strike price for a call, or the strike price and the underlying for a put.

$$IV_{\text{call}} = \text{Market Price} - \text{Strike Price} \geqslant 0$$
$$IV_{\text{put}} = \text{Strike Price} - \text{Market Price} \geqslant 0$$

The time value of an option is calculated by:

$$TV = \text{Option Value} - \text{Intrinsic Value}$$

If the intrinsic value (*IV*) is zero, then all the option value is time value. This is the case if the option is **out of the money**. If the option is **in the money**, it will have both time value and intrinsic value.

BLACK–SCHOLES OPTION PRICING MODEL

This gives the 'fair value' of a European-style call option as:

$$PV \text{ of Call Option Value} = S.N(d_1) - \left(\frac{K}{e^{rt}}\right)N(d_2)$$

Where:

$$d_1 = \frac{Ln\left(\frac{S}{K}\right) + rt + \frac{\sigma^2 t}{2}}{\sigma\sqrt{t}}$$

$$d_2 = d_1 - \sigma\sqrt{t}$$

or alternatively defined as:

$$d_2 = \frac{Ln\left(\frac{S}{K}\right) + rt - \frac{\sigma^2 t}{2}}{\sigma\sqrt{t}}$$

where *N(d)* is the cumulative normal probability density function; *K* the strike or exercise price; *t* the time to exercise date (expiry date); *S* the current price of asset; σ^2 the variance per period of continuously compounded rate of return on the asset; *r* the continously compounded risk-free rate of interest.

The model was originally developed to price European-style options on non-dividend paying stocks. There are six (originally five) pricing variables: asset (stock) price; strike (or exercise) price; time to expiry; risk-free interest rate; volatility; plus **dividends** (or interest payments). When there is no dividend or interest, this is a zero-leakage asset, as in the original model. The model makes the following assumptions about distributions of the pricing variables: the variance (σ^2) is constant over the life of the option; the interest rate is constant; a continuous price exists, that is, there are no 'jumps' in prices; stock returns are characterized by a 'lognormal distribution'; there are no transaction costs. A rearrangement of the basic equation in the model also allows for the calculation of put values (which can also be calculated by using the put–call parity relationship):

$$PV \text{ of Put Option Value} = -S.N(-d_1)$$
$$- \left(\frac{K}{e^{rt}}\right)N(-d_2)$$

The variables being the same as for the pricing of the call option.

A SIMPLE EXAMPLE OF PRICING WITH THE BLACK–SCHOLES MODEL

- *Asset (stock) price (S)*: 145
- *Strike (or exercise) price (K)*: 140 ('in the money')
- *Time to expiry (t)*: 0.5 years
- *Continuously compounded risk-free interest rate (r)* 8%
- Volatility (σ): 0.30 (30%)
- σ^2: 0.09

$$d_1 = \frac{Ln\left(\frac{S}{K}\right) + rt + \frac{\sigma^2 t}{2}}{\sigma\sqrt{t}}$$

$$d_1 = 0.46005 = \frac{0.035091 + 0.04 + 0.225}{0.212132}$$

$$d_2 = d_1 - \sigma\sqrt{t}$$

$$d_2 = 0.247918 = 0.46005 - 0.212132$$

$$\text{Call Value} = S.N(d_1) - \left(\frac{K}{e^{rt}}\right)N(d_2)$$

$$= (145 \times 0.67726) - ((140/1.040811) \times 0.597901)$$

$$= 98.20267 - (134.5105 \times 0.597901)$$

$$= 98.20267 - 80.42397$$

$$\text{Call} = 17.7787$$

The Put-Call parity relationship allows us to price the put option

$$P = \text{Call} - \text{Underlying asset} + PV(\text{Exercise price})$$

$$17.7787 - 145 + 134.5105$$

$$\text{Put} = 7.289219$$

The 'fair value' approach to option pricing works on the principle of replicating the payoff of the option. For a given time period we have the choice of either (i) buying the asset now; or (ii) buying the call option now and investing the difference over the time period. Therefore a way of valuing options is:

1. That combination of the stock and loan that replicates an investment in the option; since the two have identical payoffs in the future, they must have equal value. This is derived from the Black-Scholes model by:

Value of option (call) = [option's delta × share price] − [bank loan]

$$[N(d_1) \times S] - [N(d_2) \times PV(K)]$$

2. Ignore the risks, so the expected return on the stock is equal to the risk-free interest rate. Calculate the expected return on the stock and discount this at the interest rate.

Assume there are only two possible outcomes for the stock in the pricing example given above: a rise to 180 and a fall to 125.5:

Expected return = (probability of rise × rise [%]) + (1 − probability of rise × fall [%])

Expected return = (probability of rise × 24.14) + ([1 − probability of rise] × −13.45)

Expected return = 0.0392% (half year)

Therefore the probability of a rise is 0.4625. If the stock price rises, the option holder will make a profit of 40 (180 less strike price of 140). The payoff is therefore:

(Probability of rise × 40) + [(1 − probability of rise) × 0] = 18.5

$$0.46245 \times 40 + 0 = 18.50$$

We present value the result:

$$\frac{\text{Expected future value}}{(1 + \text{interest rate})} = \frac{18.5}{1.0392} = 17.8$$

Another key aspect of option pricing is the effect on the option value of changes in the pricing variables (see Table).

The variables in the following table, known by the Greek name for the mathematical symbols used to describe the derivation of the basic option pricing formula, indicate the sensitivity of the option value to changes in the option pricing variables.

BINOMIAL OPTION PRICING MODEL

The Binomial model assumes that for a very small time interval (t), the underlying price can only move in one of two directions, either up (u) or down (d) in any given iteration:

Upside change (u): $e^{\sigma_s\sqrt{t/n}}$

Downside change (d): $e^{-\sigma_s\sqrt{t/n}}$ or $\frac{1}{u}$

where $u > r > d$.

The probability of upside change in a risk-neutral world will be:

$$= \rho = \frac{(1+r)^n - d}{u - d}$$

Option Pricing

Increase in	Value of European-style call	Value of European-style put	Value of American-style call	Value of American-style put
Asset (stock) price	+ (plus)	− (minus)	+ (plus)	− (minus)
Strike (or exercise) price	− (minus)	+ (plus)	− (minus)	+ (plus)
Time to expiry[a]	? (indeterminate)	? (indeterminate)	+ (plus)	+ (plus)
Risk-free interest rate	+ (plus)	− (minus)	+ (plus)	− (minus)
Volatility	+ (plus)	+ (plus)	+ (plus)	+ (plus)
Dividends	− (plus)	+ (plus)	− (plus)	+ (plus)

[a] Note that European-style calls and puts do not necessarily become more valuable with time-to-expiry if the asset pays dividends. With dividends, it is not always optimal to hold an American-style option to expiry.

Sensitivity Factors for Pricing Variables

Variable	Name given to Sensitivity Factor	Formulation from Black–Scholes model for calls	Formulation from Black–Scholes model for puts	Relationships	Effect of direction of sensitivity on option position
Asset (stock) price	Delta (δ) (hedge ratio)	$N(d_1)$	$1 - N(d_1)$	Change in option price for a given change in stock price	**Positive delta**: bullish, since price increases are advantageous **Zero delta**: neutral position **Negative delta**: bearish, since price decreases are advantageous
	Gamma (γ)	$\dfrac{N'(d_1)}{S\sigma\sqrt{t}}$	$\dfrac{N'(d_1)}{S\sigma\sqrt{t}}$	Change in delta for a given change in stock price	**Positive gamma** means that if the underlying price increases (decreases), the option delta increases (decreases) **Negative gamma** means that if the underlying price decreases (increases) the option delta increases (decreases)
Elasticity	Lambda (λ) (option leverage or gearing)	$\dfrac{S}{K}N(d_1)$	$\dfrac{S}{K}N(1 - d_1)$	Percentage change in option price for a given percentage change in stock price	The leverage or gearing of an option is at its **highest** when the option is **deeply out of the money**; as the option moves up to and **into the money**, the leverage becomes less
Time to expiry	Theta (θ) (effect of time decay)	$\dfrac{S\sigma}{2\sqrt{t}}N'(d_1) - rK^{-rt}N(d_2)$	$-\dfrac{S\sigma}{2\sqrt{t}}N'(d_1) + rK^{-rt}N(-d_2)$	Change in option price given a change in time until expiration	**Positive theta**: option position profits from time decay **Negative theta**: option position loses from time decay
Risk-free interest rate	Rho (ρ)	$tK^{-rt}.N(d_2)$	$-tK^{-rt}.N(-d_2)$	Change in option price for a given change in risk-free rate	**Positive rho**: option position gains (losses) from an increase (decrease) in interest rates **Negative rho**: option position losses (gains) from an increase (decrease) in interest rates
Volatility	Vega; Kappa; Zeta; Epsilon (ν)	$S\sqrt{t}.N'(d_1)$	$S\sqrt{t}.N'(d_1)$	Change in option price for a change in volatility	**Positive vega**: option position gains from an **increase in volatility** Negative vega: option position gains from a **decrease in volatility**

Where $N'(d_1)$ is: $\dfrac{1}{\sqrt{2t}}e^{-x^2/2}$

where s is the standard deviation of price changes per period; n the number of step jumps per period.

See **binomial distribution**; **binomial pyramid**; **binomial tree**.

option pricing curve. The graphical depiction of the theoretical or **fair value of an option** for a range of prices or rates of the **underlying**.

option pricing models. A number of different models have been developed from the Black–Scholes and the Binomial Option Pricing Models to price different types of options. Many of the models are variations on either the original Black–Scholes model or the Binomial model. They have been developed to provide analytic solutions to different types of options. The main ones are:

- *Barone-Adesi and Whaley model*: An approximation for pricing American-style options.
- *Black's model*: For pricing European-style options on futures.
- *Black–Scholes model*: The original modern option pricing model. Originally limited to the pricing of European options on non-dividend paying stocks (non-leakage assets). Subsequently applied to many other types of underlying asset, with or without dividends or interest (leakage assets).
- *Binomial model*: Model for the fair value of an option based on the binomial distribution and which assumes that the price of the underlying can only take one of two states of nature in any given short time period (an increase, or decrease).
- *Garman–Kohlhagen model*: An exact formula for currency option pricing.
- *Ho–Lee model*: Single-factor option pricing model for the term structure of interest rates developed in 1986.
- *Roll–Geske–Whaley model*: An exact formula method for American options for stocks paying dividends.

option replication. Techniques to recreate the payoffs of an **option** position by dynamically duplicating the price behaviour of an option on an **underlying** (cf. **delta hedge**; **neutral hedge ratio**). They involve taking a combined cash and underlying position such as to emulate the option's behaviour (cf. **dynamic hedging**). There are two different techniques: one aims to create an option position by adjusting an existing underlying position; the other aims to provide a longer **tenor** option by using short-term options. See **portfolio insurance**; **synthetic**.

option right. The right of exercise in an option.

Options Clearing Corporation (OCC) (USA). The **clearing house** formed by the US domestic option exchanges which buys and sells **options** from their holders, thereby removing the **counterparty risk** (cf. **novation**). It clears all options in the US market with the exception of **options on futures**, which are cleared via the respective **futures** clearing houses.

options disclosure form (USA). General health warning required to be issued to all prospective buyers and sellers of **options** about the **risks** involved.

option series. All **options** of a particular **option class** with the same **exercise price** (rate) or **strike price** (rate) and **expiry date**.

options on swaps. See **swaptions**.

option spread. Position combining in two or more options of the same type (cf. **combination**; **option combination**). See **option strategies**.

option strategies. Options may be combined so that their payouts can be tailored to produce a desired **risk** profile given their unique ability in financial contracts to give a one-way bet. A large number of these strategies are trading strategies designed to exploit anomalies in the markets, to hedge, speculate, or to **arbitrage** between different instruments or markets. However combinations of options can be useful for investment and **risk management** purposes in order to pursue a strategy based on a particular view or to surrender some benefit from holding options in exchange for a reduction in **premium** cost. The common option strategies are given below in general rising degree of complexity. Note that the exact effect of the strategy will depend on the terms under which the options are bought or sold.

FUNDAMENTAL STRATEGIES

There are six fundamental strategies from which more complex patterns can be built up. These six strategies involve:

- *long call*: holding the right to purchase an underlying at a fixed price;
- *long put*: holding the right to sell an underlying at a fixed price;
- *short call*: selling the right to purchase an underlying at a fixed price; the vendor has contracted to provide the underlying at the agreed price;
- *short put*: selling the right to sell an underlying at a fixed price; the vendor has contracted to purchase the underlying at the agreed price;
- *short call, plus long underlying*: selling the right to purchase an underlying at a fixed price and holding the underlying in anticipation of having to make the sale;

- *short put, plus short underlying*: selling the right to sell an underlying at a fixed price and being short the same underlying in anticipation of having to make the purchase.

In addition, there are three basic types of transaction that can be set up:

- *directional*: position takes a view or backs a directional movement in the price of the underlying;
- *spread*: position takes a view or backs a relationship movement in the price differentials rather than single movements in the underlying;
- *volatility*: position takes a view on future volatility rather than movement in the underlying.

Note that different strategies can be set up which combine elements of the basic types above.

Generally the following terminology is applied to the different strategies, although it is not used precisely:

- *spreads*: purchases and sales of the same types of options;
- *combinations*: purchases and sales of different types of options;
- *synthetics*: purchases and sales of options to replicate a position in the underlying.

OPTION STRATEGIES IN TERMS OF REPORTED PRICES:

The following price grid is used to explain the various strategies given below.

Option Strategies

Underlying (U) = 98.50	Calls (C)			Puts (P)		
Strike Price	Jan.	Feb.	Mar.	Jan.	Feb.	Mar.
90♠	A	B	C	M	N	O
95♠	D	E	F	P	Q	R
100♥	G	H	I	T	V	W
105♣	J	K	L	X	Y	Z

♠—in-the-money options, if calls; out of-the-money options if puts.
♥—nearest to being at the money.
♣—out-of-the-money options, if calls; in-the-money options, if puts.

SINGLE OPTION STRATEGIES

Buying a call

- Hold (purchase) any of A to L.

A suitable strategy if the holder wants to acquire the underlying at a given price or benefit from an upward movement in the underlying's price or rate. It is also known as *buying volatility* or being *long volatility*, since the holder will benefit from any great movement in the underlying.

- *motivation*: bullish view: calls are bought in the expectation of an upward move in the underlying asset;
- *risk taken*: premium paid (lost);
- *reward*: potentially unlimited.

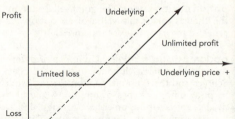

Payoff for holder (buyer) of a call position

Selling a call

- Write (sell) of any of A to L.

Directional play involving selling a call for an upfront premium in the expectation that the underlying will move in a favourable direction, that is against the holder. Hence selling a call is a way of benefiting from an expected fall in the price of the underlying . See also covered call writing below.

- *motivation*: bearish view: calls are sold when the market participant considers that the underlying is unlikely to increase in value. The attraction is that they give the writer the premium up-front with no exercise if the view is correct;
- *risk taken*: potentially unlimited;
- *reward*: limited to the premium received when writing the call.

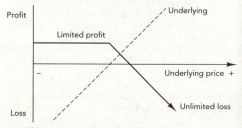

Payoff for writer (seller) of a call position

Note the asymmetric or non-linear risk profile between the purchased (long) call and written (short) call positions.

Buying a Put

- Hold (purchase) of any of M to Z.

A suitable strategy if the holder wants to dispose of the underlying at a given price or benefit from a fall in the underlying's price or rate. As with a call, it is also *buying volatility* or being *long volatility*, since the holder will benefit from any great movement in the underlying.

- *motivation*: bearish view: puts are bought in anticipation of a downward move in the underlying asset;
- *risk taken*: premium paid (lost);
- *reward*: potentially almost unlimited. For most assets, the maximum profit is reached when the underlying asset value falls to zero.

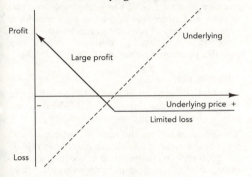

Payoff for holder (buyer) of a put position

Selling a put

- Write (sell) of any of M to Z.

Reverse directional play to selling the call. The writer expects to gain from a rise in the price of the underlying, receiving an up-front premium for taking on the risk of an unfavourable exercise.

- *motivation*: bullish view: puts are sold when the investor feels that the underlying is very unlikely to fall in value. The attraction is that they give the writer the premium up-front with no exercise if the view is correct;
- *risk taken*: almost unlimited. Maximum loss is reached if underlying asset falls to zero;
- *reward*: limited to the premium received when writing the put.

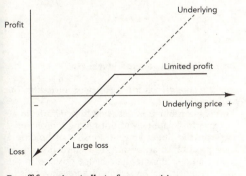

Payoff for writer (seller) of a put position

Note the asymmetric risk profile between the purchased (long) put and written (short) put positions.

Buying and selling options is a speculation on the underlying's value

- *bearish view* on the underlying value: buy calls; or sell puts;
- *bullish view* on the underlying value: buy puts; or sell calls.

The attractions of such strategies is that you do not need to own the underlying to take a view on its future value with options.

Buying versus selling (writing) options

Strategy	Cost/benefit	Risk
Buy (purchase)	premium paid up front	Low risk: maximum loss = value of premium
Sell (write)	premium received up front	High risk: loss = difference between premium and market value of underlying asset and exercise price (C − K, for calls; K − C for puts)

Although the two strategies have different risks, the connecting factor is the likely behaviour of the underlying, which is based on its volatility, which is usually the only unknown pricing variable. Hence to write or sell options is known as *selling volatility* or being bearish on volatility and to buy options as *buying volatility* or being bullish on volatility. This applies to many of the more complex positions where the writer or holder expects to profit from either the price remaining constant or moving significantly, either in a given direction (i.e. bullish or bearish positions) or just away from the current price or strike rate (i.e. non-directional volatility positions).

Summary of risks taken

Position	Risk	Reward
Long call	Limited to premium	Unlimited
Long put	Limited to premium	Almost unlimited[a]
Short (written) call	Unlimited	Premium received
Long (purchased) underlying or *derivative*, e.g. futures	Almost unlimited[b]	Unlimited
Short (sold) underlying or *derivative*, e.g. futures	Unlimited	Almost unlimited[b]

[a] Asset value cannot fall below zero
[b] Underlying or derivative (futures) value cannot fall below zero

Covered call or put writing (fiduciary call or put)

- *Covered call*: buy or hold U (the underlying) and write (sell) any of G to L (Receive premium plus any coupon, dividend or interest, paid before exercise or expiry);
- *covered put*: sell U and write (sell) any of M to R.

A low-risk, income-generating strategy aimed at giving the holder of the underlying additional revenue from receiving the up-front premium from taking a short position in the option. It is equivalent to a subsidy $(P_u - P_c)$ on the purchase price which is, however, capped at the strike price (k), the break-even being the value of the premium $(P_c = \delta . P_u)$. The writer decides the level at which to set the exercise price, depending on their view of the market. If the option is exercised against the writer, the underlying is already held and can be surrendered (and hence is called a *fiduciary call* if the underlying asset is held in escrow to ensure performance). The strategy is even more attractive if the amount of income or dividend from the underlying is unknown, although if the options are American-style, there is the risk that the exercise may be early, prior to any distribution. As a strategy, covered writing is essentially a volatility play, since the writer sells volatility, expecting the underlying to remain within the band set by the strike price.

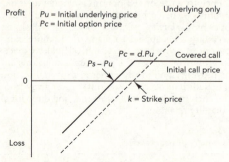

Payoff for the writer of a covered call at expiry

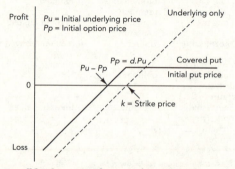

Payoff for the writer of a covered put at expiry

The covered put is similar to the covered call, except that a put is written and the present value of the strike price is invested (hence called a *fiduciary put* if the exercise price is held in escrow to ensure performance). If at expiry the put is in the money, the put holder will exercise, thus delivering the underlying to the covered put writer. This strategy is attractive if the underlying pays no income and the writer is willing to surrender a part of the opportunity to purchase at a lower price $(P_u - P_p)$, although the position will also give the writer an up-front premium.

Protective put

- Hold (purchase) of any of M to R (Receive premium plus any coupon, dividend, or interest, paid before exercise or expiry).

This involves buying the right to put the underlying in the event of a fall in price or rise in rate. It is a protection strategy aimed at securing a minimum value to a long position which is either fully or partially value protected by buying put options at some predetermined level. As a strategy it is functionally equivalent to holding a call on the underlying, except that by owning the underlying asset, holders can receive any coupons or dividends that are paid. This may be particularly valuable where the amount of distribution is unknown (although the put may be priced to reflect this). Since the protective put provides downside cover, it is also known as *portfolio insurance*.

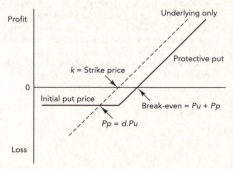

Payoff of buyer of protective put at expiry

Non-directional volatility positions including the underlying

This is a combination designed to benefit from an increase in volatility without taking a directional view on the underlying. It consists of holding a long position in an option offset directionally by taking an appropriate delta-hedge position in the underlying. It can be set up either using calls or puts, either:

Buy call, sell underlying to obtain zero net delta; also known as a *bull straddle*, if undertaken with futures.

Buy put, buy underlying to obtain zero net delta; also known as a *bear straddle*, if undertaken with futures.

Such a position also needs to monitor other factors such as position gamma, theta, and vega, which will change over time.

Two option combinations or spreads

Combination	Term	Effect
Buy and sell calls[a] (puts) with different strike prices	'Bullish call (put) spread', a.k.a. vertical spread; cylinder variation can be horizontal or time spread a.k.a. bearish money spread; back spread	Reduced cost of taking position since pay one premium and receive another; but has a capped profit
Buy and sell puts[a] (calls) with different strike prices	'Bearish put (call) spread', a.k.a. vertical spread; cylinder variation can be horizontal or time spread a.k.a. bullish money spread; back spread	Reduced cost of taking position since pay one premium and receive another; capped profit
Buy call and put with same or different strike prices	'Bullish volatility spread', a.k.a. as bought straddle; strangle	Pay two premiums, the straddle, with same strikes, is more expensive than strangle with different strikes
Sell call and put with same or different strike prices	'Bearish volatility spread', a.k.a. as written straddle; strangle	Receive two premiums, the straddle gives more in premium, but higher risk of exercise; strangle has less risk of exercise, but less premium received
Buy call (put) and sell put (call) with different strike prices	'Combo' or 'splitting the strike', mambo combo, has both positions in the money; surf and turf, has both positions out of the money	Reduced cost of taking position since pay one premium and receive another; potentially unlimited gain (or loss)
Buy call (put) and sell put (call) with the same strike price and buy offsetting position in underlying	'Conversion': sell call, buy put at same strike, buy underlying; 'reversal': buy call, sell future at same strike, sell underlying	Arbitrage which aims to benefit from mispriced options; conversions involve gains from buying underpriced puts or selling overpriced calls; reversals from underpriced calls or overpriced puts

[a] These go by a large number of different names: cylinders; collars; risk reversals.

Bullish call (put) spread

- Call spread: e.g. buy G, sell J; or using puts, e.g. buy M, sell P.

Note given that setting up the position using puts, the premium for M is less than P; the bullish put spread therefore provides a net positive premium when set up (and therefore is also called a credit spread).

The strategy consists of either a purchased call (put) and written or sold call (put). These are variously known as collars, corridors, cylinders, risk reversals, or vertical spreads.

- *Motivation*: moderately bullish view: underlying is expected to rise, but not significantly above the value of the upper, written option strike. The key attraction is that the written position reduces the cost of setting up the position.
- *risk taken*: limited. Profit is capped by upper written position.
- *reward*: limited to the rise in value between the purchased and written positions.

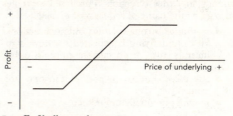

Payoff of bull spread at expiry

Bearish put (call) spread

- *Put spread*: e.g. buy P, sell M; or using calls, e.g. buy A, sell D.

Note: given that for setting up the position with calls, the premium for A is less than D; the bearish call spread provides a net positive premium when set up (and is therefore also called a credit spread).

The strategy consists of either a purchased put (call) and written or sold put (call). It is also variously known as a collar, corridor, cylinder, risk reversal, or vertical spread.

- *motivation*: Moderately bearish view: underlying is expected to fall, but not significantly below the value of the lower, written

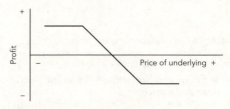

Payoff of bear spread at expiry

option strike. The key attraction is that the premium from the written option reduces the cost of setting up the position.

- *risk taken*: Limited. Profit is capped by lower written position.
- *reward*: Limited to the fall in value between the purchased and written positions.

Bullish volatility combination or spread

- *Straddle*: e.g. buy call G and put T with same strike price;
- *strangle*: e.g. buy call J and put M with different strike prices;
- *guts*: e.g. buy call G and buy put X with a higher strike price.

The strategy consists of a purchased call and purchased put. These are known as straddles (if the two strikes are the same), guts, and strangles (if the put strike and the call strike differ). The strangle is cheaper to set up but depends on the underlying moving some way from the current price or rate, that is it requires more volatility to move into the money in either direction. Purchased strangles also go by the name of *bottom vertical combination*.

- *motivation*: strong volatility but no directional view: underlying is expected to move significantly away from current price in either direction;
- *risk taken*: limited to cost of the two premiums;
- *reward*: potentially unlimited.

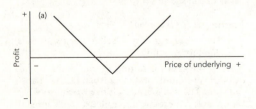

Payoff for straddle holder at expiry

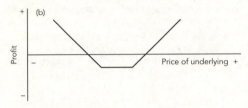

Payoff for strangle holder at expiry

Bearish volatility combination or spread

- *Straddle*: e.g. write (sell) call G and put T with same strike price;
- *strangle*: e.g. write (sell) call J and put M with different strike prices.

These involve selling both calls and puts. The payoff is the opposite of that of the *bullish volatility spread*. The writer expects volatility to fall and depending on the view the straddle gives more premium up-front, although the chance of exercise is higher. The strangle has a lower chance of exercise, but less premium is received. Written strangles also go by the name of *top vertical combination*.

- *motivation*: strong view on falling volatility but no directional view: underlying is expected to remain within a narrow range of the current price;
- *risk taken*: unlimited;
- *reward*: two at- or near-the-money premiums.

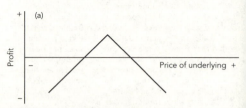

Payoff of writer of straddle at expiry

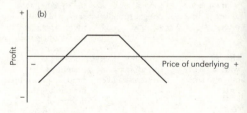

Payoff of writer of strangle at expiry

Note that both these positions can be set up as *calendar spreads*.

Combo or splitting the strike

- *Combo*: sell (write) call at J and buy put at M;
- *mambo combo*: sell (write) call at J and buy put at T;
- *surf and turf*: sell (write) call at D and buy put at M.

A combo involves a written call together with a purchased put at a lower strike price, the written position providing the premium to purchase the put position. Because the written position is in the money, it generates a significant premium which may be more than the cost of the purchased put (i.e. it is a credit spread). A variation on the structure where both the written and purchased positions are in the money, is known as a *mambo combo* and where both options are out of the money *surf and turf*. The structure is also known as *splitting the strike*.

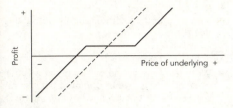

Payoff of a bull combo at expiry

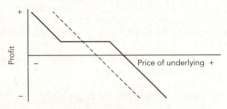

Payoff of a bear combo at expiry

Calendar, horizontal, or time spread

- *Calendar, horizontal,* or *time spread*: e.g. using calls write (sell) G, buy H or I; using puts: write (sell) P, buy Q or R;
- *reverse calendar spread*: e.g. using calls buy G, write (sell) H or I; using puts buy P, write (sell) Q or R.

Either strategy can be set up with a directional view, such that they can also become a *bullish* or *bearish diagonal spread*.

These strategies involve buying (selling) long-dated options and selling (buying) shorter-dated ones with the same strike price. In the case of selling the short-dated option and buying the longer-dated one, the rationale is to benefit from the more rapid time decay of the early expiring option since the intrinsic value of both options will be the same. The reverse calendar spread is predicated on a significant movement in the underlying prior to the expiry of the early-dated, purchased option. That is, the position seeks to profit from an inverted volatility curve, where the near date volatility is higher than the far date. In most cases, the position is closed out prior to expiry once the expected profit is achieved to gain the remaining time value.

Diagonal spreads

- *Bullish diagonal spread*: e.g. with calls write (sell) D and buy H; or with puts: write (sell) P and buy V;
- *Bearish diagonal spread*: e.g. with calls write (sell) G and buy E; or with puts: write (sell) T and buy Q.

The diagonal spread is a variation on a calendar spread, where the strikes of the two options are different. It can be set up with either calls or puts. The rationale is an anticipated directional move-

ment in the underlying, preferably deferred past the expiry date of the written option.

Conversions and reverse conversions (reversals)

- *Conversion*: e.g. buy put at T and write (sell) call at G and be long the underlying;
- *reversal*: e.g. buy call at D and write (sell) put at P and go short the underlying.

Conversions and reverse conversions involve taking long and short positions in options and the underlying. They are a form of arbitrage between option prices and the underlying. They work because they create synthetic positions using the put–call parity relationship. If prices are out of line, the position allows a risk-free profit to be made. For instance, in the case of the conversion above, if the put T was mispriced, this allows the following inequality:

$$-T + G + (K - U) - (U + T - G)(e^{-rt} - 1) > 0$$

where K is the strike price. Since the position involves holding the underlying, it involves borrowing which explains the last term of the equation. If the underlying rises, the call is exercised at G and the position is closed out, the put T expiring worthless; if the price falls, the holder exercises the put T and disposes of the underlying, the call not being exercised. A similar logic applies to the reverse conversion position.

Three-option combinations

Generally these are ratio spreads which involve increasing the leverage of one or other leg of a two-option strategy to increase the potential returns. A variation involves covering one exposed direction by buying an out-of-the-money option at a lower strike price, as with the Tabletop. Because the positions differ on each side, they are partly directional views on the market as well. The strategies are complex and require careful analysis of the market in the underlying, the value of different options, and possible scenarios up to expiry.

Call ratio spread

- Buy i calls and write (sell) j calls at a higher strike price, e.g. two by one ratio call spread, buy one call at G and write (sell) two calls at J.

It is a strategy involving a moderate bullish directional view on the market combined with over-priced volatility. Options are purchased and sold in ratio (i to j) to the expected view and the degree of overpricing. It is often used by market traders as a way of locking in a profit on mispriced options.

- *motivation*: moderately bullish view; mispriced volatility;
- *risk taken*: unlimited, although more on upside than the downside;
- *reward*: limited to net premium received.

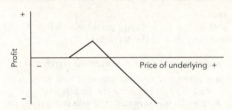

Payoff of written call ratio spread at expiry
(Combination of one purchased call option with
two calls written further out of the money)

Put Ratio Spread

- Buy *i* puts and write (sell) *j* puts at a lower
  strike price, e.g. two by one ratio put spread,
  buy one put at T and write (sell) two puts at P.

It is a strategy involving a moderate bearish directional view on the market combined with overpriced volatility. Options are purchased and sold in
ratio (*i* to *j*) to the expected view and the degree of
overpricing. It is often used by market traders as a
way of locking in a profit on mispriced options.

- *motivation*: moderately bearish view;
- *risk taken*: unlimited, although more so on
  downside than upside;
- *reward*: limited to net premium received.

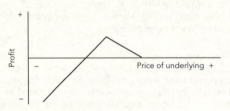

Payoff of put ratio spread at expiry

Call Ratio Backspread

- Write (sell) *i* calls and buy *j* calls at a higher
  strike price, e.g. two by one ratio call spread,
  write (sell) one call at G and buy two calls at J.

The opposite transaction to the call ratio spread.
The position is set up based on a bullish directional
view of the market and an expected rise in volatility. As with the written position, it is also a way
used by traders to lock in mispriced option values.

- *motivation*: bullish view on underlying, plus
  view on rising volatility;

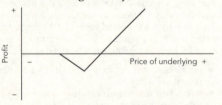

Payoff of call ratio backspread at expiry

- *Risk taken*: limited;
- *reward*: unlimited, although only on the upside.

Put Ratio Backspread

- Write (sell) *i* puts and buy *j* puts at a lower
  strike price, e.g. two by one ratio put spread,
  write (sell) one put at T and buy two puts at P.

The opposite transaction to the put ratio spread.
The position is set up based on a bearish directional view of the market and an expected rise in
volatility. As with the written position, it is also a
way used by traders to lock in mispriced option
values.

- *motivation*: bearish view on underlying, plus
  view on rising volatility;
- *risk taken*: limited;
- *reward*: unlimited, although only on the
  downside.

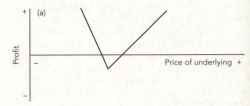

Payoff of put ratio backspread at expiry

Strips and straps

- *Strip*: e.g. buy one call G and two puts T;
- *strap*: e.g. buy 2 calls G and 1 put T.

These are special versions of the straddle where
the puts and calls are purchased in different combinations, usually two to one. They depend on the

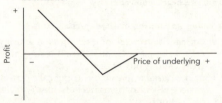

Payoff of strip at expiry

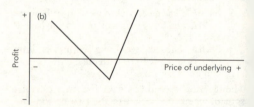

Payoff of strap at expiry

underlying making a large movement, with a slight preference for a bearish outcome (for the strip) and bullish outcome (for the strap).

Seagull

- *Bullish*: buy call G, sell call J and put P;
- *bearish*: buy put T, sell put P and call J.

This is a low- or zero-cost position which involves the simultaneous purchase of a call and writing an out-of-the-money call and put. The aim is to reduce the cost of setting up the position while at the same time providing a suitable degree of gain. To reduce the cost to near zero, it is necessary to write the two options since out-of-the-money options have a lower premium than the near-to or at-the-money option that is purchased. The combination provides that the written call can be further out of the money, since it need only provide part of the income needed to purchase the desired position; the balance coming from the written put. The combination can be structured to allow for different views as to the likely risk of writing the put and the cut-off on the written call.

- *motivation*: moderate directional view on view on underlying, plus view on stable or falling volatility;
- *risk taken*: unlimited on downside;
- *reward*: limited upside gain only.

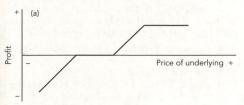

Payoff of bullish seagull at expiry

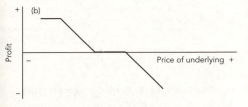

Payoff of bearish seagull at expiry

Ladder

- *Call tabletop*: buy call D, sell calls G and J;
- *put tabletop*: buy put T, sell puts P and M.

This is a low-cost or zero-cost position which involves the simultaneous purchase of a call (put) and the sale or writing of two further calls (puts) at different strikes further out of the money. The tabletop is a variation on a vertical spread where

the cost of setting up the initial call or put position is paid for not by writing one option but two. Thus although the cost is reduced (or eliminated), there is more risk than with the spread positions. The spread can be structured with different strikes to reflect the position holder's views on the potential for losses from the second, further out-of-the-money, written option.

- *motivation*: directional view on underlying, plus view on stable/falling volatility;
- *risk taken*: unlimited above (below) strike of third option;
- *reward*: limited to extent of directional view.

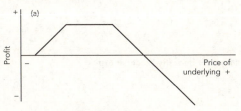

Payoff of a call ladder spread at expiry

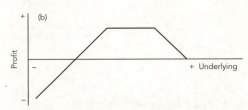

Payoff of a put ladder spread at expiry

Four-option combinations

These are created either by (*a*) purchases and sales of a series of calls or puts; or (*b*) purchases and sales of combinations: for example, purchased at-the-money puts and calls and sale of out-of-the-money puts and calls (as with the butterfly and/or the condor). Generally such positions are the equivalent to a bull spread and a bear spread combined (that is a bullish cylinder and a bearish cylinder). Variations on the strategies are possible using calendar spreads for all or part of the different combinations.

Butterfly and sandwich spread

- *Using calls*: buy D, write (sell) 2 of G, buy J;
- *Using puts*: buy T, write (sell) 2 of P, buy M.

Strategy predicated on expected low volatility to expiry. The price of the underlying is expected to remain close to the written option strike price. The position can be set up using all calls or puts, although there may be a problem in maintaining the position with American-style options, since these could be exercised early against the writer. The written version is also called a *sandwich spread*.

- *motivation*: expectation of limited market movement;
- *risk taken*: limited;
- *reward*: limited to net of premiums received, less paid.

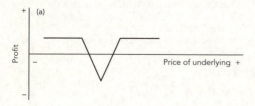

Payoff for butterfly holder at expiry

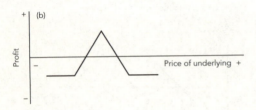

Payoff of sandwich spread at expiry

Payoff of purchased out-of-the-money call (put) and two calls (puts) written near the money and one call (put) purchased in the money.

The relationship between the straddle, strangle, and the butterfly in terms of relative payoffs is shown in the diagram.

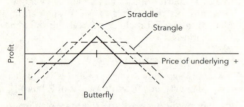

Diagram of straddle, strangle, and butterfly

Iron butterfly
Purchased (long) iron butterfly: combination of:

- *long straddle*: e.g. buy call G and put T with same strike price;

- *short strangle*: e.g. write (sell) call J and put M with different strike prices.

Written or sold (short) iron butterfly; combination of:

- *short straddle*: e.g. write (sell) call G and put T with same strike price;
- *long strangle*: e.g. buy call J and put M with different strike prices.

This is a long (short) position combination of a purchased (written) straddle and a written or sold (purchased) strangle. It aims to benefit from a volatility view, an iron butterfly is written (short) if bullish on volatility and purchased (long) if bearish. The payoff is the same as the Condor shown below.

Condor

- *Long condor using calls*: e.g. buy A, write (sell) D and G, buy J;
- *long condor using puts*: e.g. buy M, write (sell) P and T, buy X.

A long (short) position predicated on high (low) volatility but aimed at reducing the cost of setting up a long strangle payoff, or reducing the risk of the written position. The price of the underlying is expected to move significantly in either direction, but the cost of setting up the position is reduced by selling two options, one in the money and the other out of the money. The position can be set up using all calls or puts, although there may be problems with American-style options, since these could be exercised early against the writer.

- *motivation*: expectation of significant market movement;
- *risk taken*: limited;
- *reward*: limited to difference between purchased and sold options, less net premium.

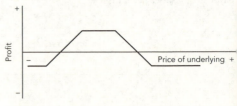

Payoff for iron butterfly or condor holder at expiry

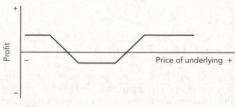

Payoff for iron butterfly or condor writer at expiry

Straddle Calendar Spreads

- *Long straddle calendar spread*: e.g. write (sell) call G and put T; buy call H and put V;
- *long bullish diagonal straddle calendar spread*: e.g. write (sell) call G and put T; buy call K and put Y;
- *long bearish diagonal straddle calendar spread*: e.g. write (sell) call G and put T; buy call E and Q.

To obtain the short position, reverse the held and written options.

This is a position aimed at taking advantage of the differences in volatility between the written contracts and the purchased ones. It can either have a neutral view on the underlying, or incorporate a bullish or bearish view, when it becomes a diagonal straddle calendar spread.

Box Spread

- For example, purchased call D, and written (sold) P and written call G and purchased put T.

The box spread is designed to capture the value of a mispriced option while at the same time eliminating any price risk on the position. It is the all-option counterpart to the *conversion* and the *reverse conversion*, which required a long or short position in the underlying. In the case of the box spread, two pairs of spread transactions effectively cancel each other out such that all that is left is the net premium paid or received. The attraction of the position is that it either allows the position holder to free up cash and reinvest it elsewhere, or to lend out money. The position is attractive if the payoff of the box spread either way is greater than borrowing or lending cash (at the risk-free rate). A more risky version, where the two synthetic positions are for different expiry months, is known as a *jellyroll*.

- *motivation*: locks in an interest rate. With a credit box spread, the position holder receives a positive net sum at initiation, with a debit box spread, a net premium is paid out at initiation;
- *risk taken*: limited;
- *reward*: limited net premium.

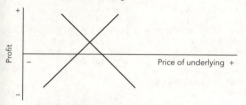

Payoff for box spread holder at expiry

Strategies with more than four options

More exotic option strategies are possible which involve any number of options. At some point this

ceases to be a strategy and instead becomes a portfolio of options.

Option Strategies Including the Underlying

In most cases one part of a strategy can be set up using forwards or futures as one element of the package. This is shown for a vertical bull spread, where the same position can be obtained by holding the underlying, buying a put, for downside protection and selling a call. Such an arrangement might be preferable to the option's only structure, if the underlying was expected to make some form of payout prior to the expiry of the option positions.

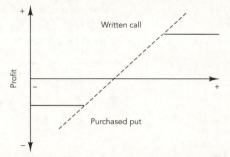

Payoff of a bull vertical spread using a long position in the underlying

Option strategies and market view

The attraction of options, and just one of the reasons they have become so popular, is that overleaf with options many alternative strategies are possible, allowing (*inter alia*) a view on the direction of the underlying, its volatility, whether to pay or receive premium up-front, the exact strike price at which to enter into a transaction, and many other factors to provide a tailored position reflecting the position-taker's specific view. The table overleaf gives the position option pricing sensitivities. Thus for a bullish view on volatility, a positive vega (the position sensitivity to changes in volatility) is required but, depending on the directional view, the delta (position sensitivity to the underlying) could be positive, neutral, or negative.

option swap. A right to enter into a **swap** on or before a particular date. See **contingent swap**.

option time decay. See **time decay**.

option to double. (i) (Securities) A type of security that allows the holder the choice to sell or redeem up to twice the stated contractual principal prescribed for a **sinking fund**, or sometimes a **purchase fund**. Such additional purchases shorten the **average life** of the remaining securities. (ii) See **double option**.

option to purchase. (i) An exclusive right given to a buyer for a specific period to acquire an asset

OPTION, STRATEGIES AND MARKET VIEW

ATM: at the money
ITM: in the money
OTM: out of the money
Long: buy the position
Short: sell or write the position

Market View Volatility (σ) View Option Sensitivity Position to adopt, if	Bearish (market expected to fall)	Undecided (undecided on market direction)	Bullish (market expected to rise)
σ falling	Short call Short two-by-one ratio call spread[a] Short call spread Long put spread Short call volatility trade Long ITM call butterfly Long OTM put butterfly Long ITM call condor Long OTM put condor Long call ladder Ratio put spread[a]	Short Straddle Short strangle Short guts Long ATM call or put butterfly Long ATM iron butterfly Long ATM call or put condor Short ATM calendar spread Short ATM straddle calendar spread Short call or put volatility trade	Short put Short two-by-one ratio put spread[a] Long call spread Short put spread Short put volatility trade Long OTM call butterfly Long ITM put butterfly Long OTM call condor Long ITM put condor Long put ladder Ratio call spread[a]
Delta	−	0	+
Gamma	−	−	−
Theta	+	+	+
Vega	−	−	−
σ undecided	Short underlying or futures on underlying Short call Long put Short call spread Long put or bear spread Long ITM call butterfly Long OTM put butterfly Long ITM call condor Short OTM put condor Long combo	Box spread Conversion Reversal	Long underlying or futures on underlying Short put Long call Short put spread Long OTM call butterfly Long ITM put butterfly Long OTM call condor Long ITM put condor Short combo Bull spread
Delta	−	0	+
Gamma	0	0	0
Theta	0	0	0
Vega	0	0	0
σ rising	Long put Long two-by-one ratio put spread[a] Long put volatility trade Long put spread Short call spread Short ITM put butterfly Short OTM call butterfly Short ITM put condor Short OTM call condor Short put ladder Put ratio back spread[a]	Long straddle Long strangle Long guts Long ATM calendar spread Short ATM call or put condor Short ATM iron butterfly Long call or put volatility trade Long ATM straddle calendar spread Short ATM call or put butterfly	Long call Long two-by-one ratio call spread[a] Long call volatility trade Long call spread Short put spread Short ITM call butterfly Short OTM put butterfly Short ITM call condor Short OTM put condor Short call ladder Call ratio backspread[a]
Delta	−	0	+
Gamma	+	+	+
Theta	−	−	−
Vega	+	+	+

[a] In practice all the ratio spreads and ratio backspreads need careful analysis. Ratio strategies do not fit neatly into a simple market/volatility scenario.

at a set price. Sometimes used in **mergers and acquisitions** by a purchaser being granted the option to allow the acquiring firm time to put in place the financing required for the purchase or to allow a **due diligence** investigation, or other agreed reason. (ii) Another name for the **rights** given to **shareholders** to acquire more **shares** (cf. **pre-emption rights**).

option trading. The buying and selling of tradable options. See **option strategies**.

option valuing models. See **option pricing models**.

option warrant. A type of **warrant** which may be executed into either **stock** or **bonds** at the discretion of the holder. See **compound options**.

option writer. An **option** seller. He receives the **option premium** but is left with a **short position** in the option (cf. **naked option**). He sells **volatility** or backs a directional movement in the **underlying**. He is willing to accept a limited profit from the premium in exchange for a potentially unlimited loss because he expects the price to either move in his favour, that is against the buyer, or to remain unchanged. Written option positions have a positive **theta**, or sensitivity to the **time decay of an option**.

or better (OB). An instruction on an order specifying that the transaction should be made at the stated price, or any better price.

order. An instruction to an **agent** to enter into a transaction (cf. **mandate**). See **limit order**; **market order**; **stop loss**.

order book official (OBO). Exchange employee responsible for administering **limit orders**. Since **futures exchanges** do not have a **specialist** or **market-maker**, the OBO undertakes the **book** activities that would normally be carried out by these intermediaries (cf. **limit order board**; **public limit order board**). Also known as a *board broker*.

order driven (Equities). A type of **share**-dealing system where prices react to orders (cf. **quote driven**). Brokers bid for **stock** around **specialists** who maintain a market in chosen securities by buying and selling on their **own account** or for **commission brokers** acting as **agents**. This system is operated by the **New York Stock Exchange**.

order flow. Purchase and sales transactions, for instance, through an intermediary. A large order flow is seen as desirable as it allows the **dealer** to earn the **bid-offer spread** with little **market risk** or need to **hedge** his **book**, as well as allowing him to judge the state of the market (cf. **box management**). See also **colour**; **tone**.

order for relief (USA). Court order providing protection to a firm from its **creditors** under **Chapter 11** (cf. **debtor in possession**).

order ticket. The written instruction from an order giving transaction details (cf. **comparison ticket**; **confirmation**).

ordinary annuity. See **annuity**.

ordinary capital (UK). Another name for the total amount of **ordinary shares** in issue.

ordinary dividend. See **final dividend**, **interim dividend** (cf. **extra dividend**).

ordinary income. A business's trading income. It excludes **extraordinary items**, **capital gains**, and **asset** disposals.

ordinary interest. Simple interest. In the USA, ordinary interest is used synonymously with **bank basis**.

ordinary least squares regression (OLS) See **least squares regression**.

ordinary shares (Equities; UK). That **class** of **capital** that entitles the holder to company **earnings** and capital after all **prior charges** and claims have been met; and rights to participate in the control of the company through **voting rights** and a distribution of the profits, known as **dividends**. Often regarded as the 'risk-bearing' element of capital and sometimes known as **equity** or, in the USA, as **common stock** (cf. **a shares**; **b shares**; **c shares**; **participation certificate**; **preference stock**). Note that different jurisdictions impose different conditions on shares. For instance, it is possible to issue common stock in the USA without a par value; but an impossibility in the UK. Owners of ordinary shares are known as **shareholders** or **stockholders** (cf. **debt**). See also **preferred stock**.

Organization for Economic Cooperation and Development (OECD). Set up in 1961 and based in Paris, it is an international forum and coordinating agency to advise member governments on economic and other trends and developments and to coordinate assistance to **less developed countries** (LDC). It has specialized Directorates based on the main ministries or departments of member governments and these are responsible for research and policy proposals in different areas of concern to members. The Directorates are:

Economics and Statistics
Environment
Development Cooperation
Trade
Financial, Fiscal and Enterprise Affairs

Science, Technology and Industry
Social Affairs, Manpower and Education
Food, Agriculture and Fisheries
Public Management
Centre for the Cooperation with the European Economies in Transition (established in 1990)
International Energy Agency (IEA)

The OECD produces a range of publications and reports, some of which are published providing details of international trends and comparisons. Membership is nearly the same as the **Group of Thirty**: Australia, Austria, Belgium, Canada, Denmark, Finland, France, Germany, Greece, Iceland, Ireland, Italy, Japan, Luxembourg, Netherlands, New Zealand, Norway, Poland, Portugal, South Korea, Spain, Sweden, Switzerland, Turkey, United Kingdom, and United States.
In addition, under the OECD umbrella there are a number of autonomous or semi-autonomous agencies:

Nuclear Energy Agency
Development Centre
Centre for Educational Research and Innovation (CERI)
Club du Sahel (Interstate Committee for Drought Control in the Sahel) (CILSS)

Organization of Arab Petroleum Exporting Countries (OAPEC). Producer sub-interest group set up in 1968 within the **Organization of Petroleum Exporting Countries** representing Arab producers. It is made up of Algeria, Bahrain, Egypt, Iraq, Kuwait, Libya, Qatar, Saudi Arabia, Syria, Tunisia, and the United Arab Emirates.

Organization of Petroleum Exporting Countries (OPEC). Producer cartel which attempts to set oil prices for the oil market. Its ability to enfore production quotas and set prices has waned in recent years. Its members are: Algeria, Ecuador, Gabon, Indonesia, Iran, Iraq, Kuwait, Libya, Nigeria, Qatar, Saudi Arabia, United Arab Emirates, and Venezuela. Not all producer nations are members.

organized exchange. Normally a securities exchange which has rules governing the conduct and possibly the location, time, and type of business that may be undertaken (cf. **over the counter**). See also **recognized investment exchange** (UK).

organized futures. Organized markets to trade for **forward delivery** were established in the latter half of the nineteenth century in the UK and the USA. However, forward markets for eliminating **risk** date back into antiquity. Various mechanisms for 'selling/buying forward' have been identified in the Middle East as early as the second millenium BC, and in eighteenth-century England contracts were being entered into on the basis of product yet

'to arrive' in the country, i.e. at the terminal, hence *terminal markets*. The development of modern exchanges as we now know them began with the founding of the **Chicago Board of Trade** in 1848. See **forward**; **future** for more details on the mechanics.

organized market. Any market which has specific rules about how and when trading may take place. Organized markets are typically exchanges, involving accreditation and membership (cf. **kerb**; **over the counter**).

origin. (i) The country from which an asset derives (cf. **obligor**). (ii) Another term for **domicile**.

original exposure method (Banking). A standard for assessing the **off-balance sheet** elements of a bank's **assets** under the **Bank for International Settlements** capital adequacy provisions. It is based on the original price of the asset times a **risk** factor designed to create a **credit risk** equivalent **exposure**. See **Basle Capital Convergence Accord**; **risk-adjusted assets**.

original face value. The original issue value of a security, prior to any partical **redemptions** (cf. **amortization**; **average life**; **paydown**).

original issue discount (OID). The difference between the principal amount on **maturity** and its issue price if the latter is less than **par** (cf. **original issue premium**). See **deep discount bonds**; **zero-coupon bond**.

original issue premium (OIP). The difference between the principal on **maturity** and its issue price if the latter is greater than **par**.

original margin. See **initial margin**.

original maturity. The **maturity** of a security at issue. For example a ten-year **bond** would have an original maturity of ten years; but after two years would have a **current** maturity of eight years.

originating exchange. The derivatives exchange where an **open position** is originally set up. Some exchanges (for instance the **Chicago Mercantile Exchange** and the **Singapore International Monetary Exchange** allow the interchange of positions on the two exchanges in certain futures contracts. Hence, the role of the originating exchange where the **open interest** was first established. See **closing transaction**.

origination. The process of creating financial assets.

Osaka Securities Exchange (OSE) (Japan). 8-16 Kitahama 1-chome, Chuo-ku, Osaka 541 (tel. 81

(0) 6 229 8643; fax 81 (0) 6 231 2639). Established on 1 April 1949 it is the second largest exchange in Japan, located in Osaka, transactions include both stocks and **derivatives**.

Oslo Stock Exchange (OSE) (Norway). Tollbugt. 2, PO Box 460 Sentrum, 0105 Oslo 1 (tel. 47 (0) 2 34 17 00; fax 47 (0) 2 41 65 90 tlx 77242). An exchange which acts as a market-place in both securities and **derivatives** on those securities (cf. **floor**; **pit**).

Österreichische Termin-und Optionenbörse (OTOB) (The Austrian Futures and Options Exchange) (Austria). Strauchgasse 1-3, A-1010 Vienna (tel. 43 222 53 165 0; fax 43 222 5329740). Established on 4 October 1991 its major activity is in **stock index futures** and **interest rate futures**.

other loans especially mentioned (OLEM) (Banking). One of the classifications placed on **problem assets** in a bank's loan **portfolio**. The others are: *substandard*: these have inadequate value protection based on the borrower's capacity to repay or the collateral; *doubtful*: substandard loans where the repayment is highly unlikely; *loss*: uncollectable loans where an actual charge-off is made.

other real estate owned (OREO) (Banking; USA). The carried value of **real estate** in a bank's accounts which has been foreclosed. The amount of the **charge-off** is reduced by the appraised realizable value of the real estate held (cf. **lender liability**).

out-barrier option. Type of **compound option** combined into a **barrier option** and where the **premium** is partly reimbursable if the price or rate of the **underlying** extinguishes the option by trading through the **trigger** point (cf. **knock-in**). See also **down-and-in option**; **down-and-out option**; **up-and-in option**; **up-and-out option**.

outcry. See **open outcry**.

out firm (Derivatives). A type of **option** that is operative for a specific period of time, normally measured in minutes rather than hours.

out of line. A security or market which is priced either too high or low in relation to similar securities or markets (cf. **anomaly**).

out of the money (OTM). (i) A **position** standing at a loss due to adverse market, price or rate movements (cf. **book loss**). (ii) An option without **intrinsic value**. A **call option** is out of the money if its strike price is greater than the current price of

the **underlying**. A **put option** is out of the money if its strike price is less than the current price of the underlying (cf. **at the money**; **in the money**; **near the money**). A call option with a strike price of 100 would be out of the money if the underlying price was at 90. It would be considered deeply out of the money if the underlying was at, say, 25; but this would depend to some extent on **volatility**. For instance, a **delta** below 0.30 in this case would suggest it was indeed, deeply out of the money. See also **intrinsic value**; **time value of an option**.

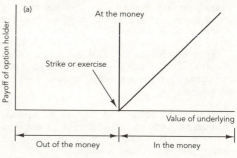

(*a*) For a call option

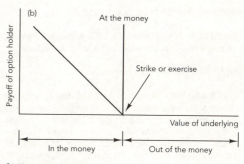

(*b*) For a put option
Out of the money

out of value transaction. See **forward**.

out option. Knock-out option. See **barrier option**.

outperformance option. Option where the **underlying** is the differential performance of two assets, indices, or other measure (cf. **spread**). The outperformance comes from the relative movements in the two. Note that the option is not necessarily directional, since both indices could fall (or rise) over the period, the payoff depending on whether the relationship widened or narrowed. Also known as a *Margrave option*, *multi-index option*, a *relative performance option*, or a *two-colour rainbow option*. See also **rainbow option**.

outright exchange rate (Forex). One method of quoting **forward foreign exchange**. It involves quoting the rate in the same manner as the spot rate, rather than as **swap points** or in terms of a percentage **premium** or **discount**.

outright or **outright forward** (Forex). A term used in the **foreign exchange** markets where a **forward** transaction is effected without a corresponding **spot**, or near-date transaction (cf. **forward outright rate**; **foreign exchange swap**).

outside broker. Broker who is not a member of an **exchange** but acts an intermediary between members and investors.

outside directors. Members of the **board of directors** who are not engaged in the day-to-day management of the firm. Also known as *non-executive directors*.

outstanding contract. A futures or options contract that has not **expired**, been closed by a covering purchase or sale, or in the case of an option, **exercised** (cf. **open interest**).

outstanding issue. See seasoned.

outstanding shares. See issued capital.

outstrike. The value at which a **barrier option** changes the condition of its payoff if **exercised**.

out the window. See blowout.

out-trade. The result of some confusion or error in a transaction where the two reported sides do not match. A situation where both sides thought they were sellers would be considered an out-trade. Normally these need to be resolved as soon as possible since both parties' pre-transaction positions remain outstanding. If the transaction prices do not match, professionals normally agree to split the difference.

over-allocation. A right given to an **underwriter** to over-allot securities in a new issue (cf. **greenshoe**). See also **over-funding**; **stabilization**.

over-and-out option. See barrier option (cf. up-and-out option).

over-and-out warrant. See over-the-top warrant.

overbooked. Another term for over-subscribed.

overborrowed. See asset-liability management (cf. **assets repriced before liabilities**; **long funded**; **short funded**).

overborrowed fixed. A net interest rate swap position which involves paying the **fixed rate** and receiving the **floating rate** (cf. **fixed rate payer**; **floating rate payer**).

overbought or **overbought market.** (i) Generally a market that has risen too rapidly as a result of excessive buying (cf. **bull market**). (ii) Used to describe a **long position** in a market (especially **foreign exchange**). (iii) In the **futures**, **exchange-traded options** (and in purchases (sales) on **margin**), a situation where the margin with the **dealer** or **exchange** does not cover the **position** (cf. **margin call**). (iv) An excessive long position. (v) A state of the market where values have gone beyond those levels which can be supported by **fundamental analysis** (cf. **oversold**). See also **asset bubble**.

over-capitalized. A company having more funds than can be profitably employed.

over-collateralized. A means of enhancing the credit worthiness of a debt by providing **collateral** in excess of the **nominal** or **principal value** of the obligation. The idea is that by providing, say 115% of the debt amount as collateral, there will always be enough good **assets** to meet the obligation. In effect, the difference is the amount of **equity** provided by the vendor from his own resources.

overdraft (Banking; UK). Name for a common form of loan made by a lender which has no fixed **maturity** but which is repayable on demand. The arrangement normally only requires the borrower to pay for the amounts borrowed on a day-by-day basis and, in many cases, allows credit balances to offset the interest charged. The maximum amount that can be borrowed under such an arrangement is known as the *overdraft limit*. See **call**; **demand loan**.

over-funding (UK). (i) An excess supply of **gilt-edged** securities in relation to the **fiscal policy** targets for the **public sector borrowing requirement**. (ii) The situation in which managed **funds**, particularly pension funds, have a surplus amount of income, given their short- and long-term commitments.

over futures. The situation when the cash price is higher than the futures price. Also known as *backwardation* or *discount market*. The opposite condition is called *under futures* (cf. **contango**).

overhang. Blocks of securities or **commodities** that are known to be available for sale (cf. **visible supply**). Such latent selling pressure may prevent prices rising since any firming of prices will encourage holders to sell (cf. **resistance area**).

overheads. (i) Payments or regular allocations from a **subsidiary** company to its **parent** in return for centralized services, such as corporate strategy and marketing expertise. (ii) In production accounting, any cost that is not directly associated with producing merchandise, hence *production cost overhead*. (iii) In non-manufacturing accounting, overhead refers to all costs, excluding the cost of goods traded. (iv) More generally in management accounting, it means any selling or administration cost, including indirect production costs (cf. **fixed cost**; **variable cost**).

overheated economy. Excessive aggregate demand that leads to inflation or excessive imports rather than increased output.

over-investment. Acquisition of **assets** beyond those for which there is ready requirement. For example, ordering a power station in order to generate employment rather than to meet anticipated demand. The result is usually underutilization of the resultant investment.

overlay portfolio management. Method of allocating **assets** to a number of specialist fund managers and the ultimate **asset allocation** decision to a strategic manager. The principle is that the specialist fund managers will outperform in their respective markets or sectors while the overlay fund manager will control the asset allocation in line with the fund's objectives using **derivatives**.

overlay strategy. Fund management method designed to provide a strategic focus to fund objectives which involves uncoupling the traditional connection between investments and return. This is achieved by controlling for different **risks** through the use of **derivatives**. The cherry-picking approach allows the fund to be tactically invested in the best performing markets while strategically hedged against, for instance, adverse currency movements. A variant involves, for instance, covered call writing.

overlent. See asset-liability management (cf. assets repriced before liabilities; long funded; short funded).

overnight delivery risk. The counterparty risk, most noticeable in the **foreign exchange** and eurocurrency markets, where **delivery** of one leg of the transaction is made without **confirmation** until the following day whether **good delivery** has been made on the other side. For instance, a **foreign exchange transaction** booked in London between sterling and US dollars with the dollars settled domestically in the USA, will see the sterling **leg** of the transaction settle before the dollar leg. For sterling, **clearing** will be at the latest at 3 p.m. London time, but for the US dollar not until the same time in the USA (or between 8 p.m. and 9 p.m. UK time).

overnight deposit. (i) (Banking) An amount placed with a financial institution with the intent of withdrawing it the following day. Using such **deposits** banks can create overnight loans used by **brokers** and other **traders** to meet the net obligations arising from each day's activities. From a depositor's viewpoint this type of transaction allows an interest **margin** to be earned without losing the **liquidity** and security uses of the money placed on deposit. Also known as *call money, day-to-day money,* or *overnight money.* (ii) **Euromarkets** term for a **demand deposit** (cf. **call deposit**). Such money is repaid on the following business day.

overnight position. A trader's **position** which is kept overnight, that is for periods when the markets are closed (cf. **daytime trading**; **intraday**).

overnight repurchase agreement (overnight RP). A **repurchase agreement** (repo) that is made for one (business) day. It is typically used by **broker-dealers** as a means of funding their inventories. Securities are temporarily sold to investors with overnight spare cash but the securities are released back to the **dealer** the next day for trading purposes. Longer period repurchase agreements are known as *term repos* (term repurchase agreements), or *open repos.*

overseas investment. See foreign investment.

overshooting. The same as **overvaluation** but applied to the value of a particular currency in the **foreign exchange** markets (cf. **asset bubble**; **purchasing power parity**).

oversold or **oversold market.** (i) A market that is perceived to have fallen too rapidly as a result of excessive selling (cf. **bear market**). (ii) A **short position** in a market (especially **foreign exchange**). (iii) An excessive short position in relation to a **hedging** transaction. (iv) A state of the market or a security where values are perceived to have gone below those levels which could be supported by **fundamental analysis** (cf. **overbought**). See asset bubble.

over-subscribed or **over-subscription.** The case where a new issue has generated applications for securities in excess of the amount available (cf. **subscribe**). Such a situation is likely to mean that applications will be scaled down in proportion to the amount of stock requested (cf. **allotment**; **ballot**). Also known as *overbooked.* The opposite condition, where investors have not subscribed for the entire issue is called *under-subscription* or *under-booked*. See also **book building**.

over-subscription privilege. A shareholder's right to take up any new shares in a **rights issue** that other shareholders have not taken up.

over the bridge. A statement of the settlement of a transaction involving moving the security between a **Euroclear** and a **Centrale de Livraison de Valeurs Mobilières** account. Because of the different processing arrangements of the two clearing systems, it may involve a delay in settlement (cf. **delivery against payment; free delivery**).

over the counter (OTC). Markets or transactions arranged bilaterally between two principals without the participation of an **exchange** (cf. **floor; pit; screen-trading**). Prices in OTC markets are set by **dealer** trading rather than the **auction** system of most organized exchanges (cf. **London Stock Exchange; New York Stock Exchange; Tokyo Stock Exchange**). Some large markets, such as that in US **treasuries** and **foreign exchange** are OTC markets. See **exchange-traded; head-to-head; direct search market; listed; grey market.**

over-the-counter option. Options written by a company or institution and bought by another. Such options provide great flexibility as to amounts, terms, and conditions and type but are generally illiquid since the buyer is taking **counterparty risk** with the seller. In the UK, the **British Bankers' Association** has set standard terms to facilitate a secondary market (cf. **dealer option; London interbank currency options market**). See **exchange-traded.**

over-the-top option or **warrant.** An up-and-out type of **barrier option**.

overtrade or **overtrading.** (i) A method sometimes used in the USA to effect a **discount** on a new issue of securities. It involves a **swap** of existing securities, held by an investor, for the new securities, held by the **underwriter**. The deal is an overtrade if the old securities are valued at less than the new issue. He gains because the loss on the transaction is less than the **underwriting** fee he receives (cf. **spread**). It also has the effect, from the underwriter's perspective, of swapping a new issue for a well-**seasoned** one which may prove easier to sell. (ii) Usually applied to a business that has too large a turnover level in relation to its **working capital** so that too much cash is tied up in inventories and debts, and too little cash is coming through quickly enough to pay creditors

and meet day-to-day expenses. (iii) Can be applied to securities firms trading levels of stock likely to produce difficulties in meeting their obligation. See **hammered**. (iv) Also applied to levels of dealing activity, in particular securities that cannot be supported by **fundamental analysis**. See **asset bubble; overvalued.**

overvalued. Usually used to describe an **asset** or security, rather than a market, whose price is considered to be higher than that supported by **fundamental analysis** (cf. **asset bubble; undervalued**). See **arbitrage; overshooting; overtrading; winner's curse.**

overwriting. Excessive writing of **options** on an **underlying**. The rationale is either that the underlying is mispriced and therefore the **risk** is minimal or that **volatility** is temporarily overpriced. One approach involves writing options with different **strike prices**, with the expectation that relatively out-of-the-money options will **expire** worthless. Another method, involves escalating positions in response to losses. If an initial written option results in a loss, a greater number of new options at the higher price are written, and so on, until the position returns a profit (cf. **mean reversion**). Empirical evidence of the strategy suggests modest profits in most periods countered by exceptional losses from time to time (cf. **jump process**). Since the strategy depends on prices remaining below/above the written strike greater volatility will causes losses. Theory predicts that because the strategy is contrarian, it will dampen the writer's volatility of returns but will not enhance risk-adjusted returns unless there are inefficiencies in the market (cf. **contracyclical trading; efficient markets hypothesis**).

own account. To act as **principal** in a transaction; hence to act for one's 'own account'; literally to book the transaction on the firm's accounts with the **clearing house** (cf. **agent; broker; broker-dealer**).

Own Funds Directive. The regulatory standard for **capital adequacy** laid down by the European Community as regards deposit-taking financial institutions. While generally similar to the **Basle Capital Convergence Accord**, it has some technical differences.

own resources. Internal funds available for investment activities. Thus, to fund a project out of its own resources means a firm has used its internally generated cash flow and/or cash reserves to pay for the investment. See also **new money**.

P

Pacific Stock Exchange (PSE) (USA). 301 Pine Street, San Francisco, CA 94104 (tel. 1 415 393 4200; fax 1 415 393 4202). Established in 1957. Based in California in both Los Angeles and San Francisco. Of the nine exchanges in the USA, it is the only one west of the Mississippi. The others are: the **New York Stock Exchange, American Stock Exchange, National Association of Securities Dealers Automated Quotations, National Stock Exchange, Philadelphia, Boston, Midwest,** and **Cincinnati** exchanges.

packaged equity trust securities (PETS) (Equities). See **short-term equity participation unit.**

packages. Combinations of two or more types of instruments into a single element. Typical packages are **convertibles** and **bonds with warrants.** In the latter case, it is possible to **unbundle** these. See also **exotic options; stapled security; unbundled stock unit.**

package trade. See **basket** (cf. **lot; program trading**).

pac-man defence or **strategy.** A defence strategy in a **takeover** where the target firm retaliates to the aggressor's bid by making its own **bid** for the aggressor (cf. **tender offer**).

pagares de empresa (Spanish). **Commercial paper.**

pagares del tesoro (Spanish). **Treasury bills.**

paid-up capital. The amount of the **authorized stock** of a company, as detailed in the company's **charter** or **articles of incorporation,** that has been paid in or subscribed for by **shareholders.**

paid-up security, stock, or **share.** A security for which the holder has paid the full contractual amount. In some cases, holders may pay only a proportion of the **face** or **par value,** then it is known as *partly paid,* and in some cases, such as a **rights issue,** ownership rights to the new shares are given *nil-paid* to existing **shareholders.**

painting the tape (USA). Above-average reporting of transactions in a particular security as a result of heavy trading. The term is sometimes also used for illegal market manipulation practices involving spurious buying and selling to give the illusion of heavy trading activity.

paired. See **stapled security.**

Panel on Takeovers and Mergers (UK). See **City Code on Takeovers and Mergers.**

paper. (i) **Money markets** term for securities such as **certificates of deposit, commercial paper,** and others. (ii) Used when a **company** issues **stocks** or **shares,** hence to *issue paper;* that is, to raise fresh capital (cf. **certificate**).

paper bid. An offer made by an acquiring company for a **target** company where the consideration is in the form of the acquiring company's own **equity.** Sometimes a partial cash alternative is offered.

paper gain or **profit (loss).** The potential, but unrealized, profit (loss) that would be made if **assets** or securities are sold at ruling market prices, in relation to their purchase prices (cf. **capital gain; capital loss; hold-back; marked-to-market**).

paper trail. See **audit trail.**

par. (i) When used with regard to price it means 100% of the **principal,** usually of a debt. (ii) Used to indicate the **principal amount** or denomination at which an issuer will redeem a security at **maturity** (cf. **market value; redemption price**). Sometimes known as *face* or *principal* value. (iii) With regard to value, it is that price assigned by a company to its **common stock** or **ordinary shares** (cf. **no-par stock**). (iv) An **at-market interest rate swap** or **cross-currency swap.** The alternative is an **off-market swap.**

parallel loan. See **back-to-back loan.**

parallel market. Usually applied to **short-term money markets** that deal in foreign currency deposits and sterling deposits of non-residents, and surplus sterling funds held by domestic banks. As such the term can be applied to the **eurocurrency markets, certificate of deposit** markets, and the interbank sterling market. See **wholesale money.**

parallel shift. A movement in a **yield curve** where yields change by the same amount irrespective of

maturity. Mathematical **risk** measures, such as **duration**, assume that any shifts will be constant across all maturities; stochastic risk models may allow for different behaviour (cf. **rotational shift**). See also **sensitivity analysis**.

parameter. In general use, an alternative for a factor or effect that can influence the behaviour of a market, principal, or agent. Hence, the statement 'The latest balance of payments position is one of the many parameters taken into account when establishing exchange rate forecasts, and an assessment of international asset allocation.' More correctly, used in the statistical sense of items contained within mathematical descriptions of economic or financial relationships. Hence the relationship between the quantity demanded of a good or service and its own price can be stated as follows:

$$Q = \beta_1 + \beta_2 P$$

where Q and P are quantity and price, and β_1 and β_2 are known as parameters of the (in this case linear) function. β_1 is also called the intercept; it gives the value of Q when price is zero. β_2 is also known as the slope which measures the rate of change in Q for a unit (say a £) change in price. It is possible for β_1 and β_2 to take on different values depending on whether Q refers to an individual, household, firm, sector, or an entire economy. Economic theory suggests that it would normally be expected that $\beta_2 < 0$ (that is, negative: the higher the price, the less is demanded); and $\beta_1 > 0$ (demand would be positive if the price was zero).

par banking (USA). Requirement for member banks of the **Federal Reserve System** to honour each other's cheques without deducting a handling charge or transaction **fee**.

par bond. An issue which is selling at **par**, regarded as being consistent with ruling new issues, or where the **coupon** is consistent with prevailing yield levels for the particular **maturity** (cf. **par yield curve**). See also **zero-coupon yield curve**.

parent or **parent corporation.** The ultimate owner of a **subsidiary**. Typically applied to a company with two or more subsidiaries. Usually the source of centralized services, such as corporate strategy and marketing expertise, for which an overhead charge is made. Often such costs are regarded as excessive because it is felt that the contribution made by such services is limited or could be provided more effectively, and cheaper, by management consultants. Also called a *holding company.*

par forward rate (Forex). Foreign exchange rate in the forward market for a range of settlement dates.

par grade. The standard grade of a commodity used in a **futures** contract (cf. **alternative delivery procedure**; **assay**). See also **contract grade**.

pari passu (Latin: equally). Unsecured debt issues which rank equally with each other or with other unsecured debt with respect to payment. A legal term used in a general context to describe securities which are of the same **class** in terms of repayment rights both amongst themselves and in respect to others. Thus all unsecured **bond** and **notes** would rank *pari passu* in any winding up of a corporation and would, in the event of a shortfall, be paid off **pro rata** but ahead of **junior** or **subordinated debt** and **equity**. See **covenants**; **negative pledge**.

Paris Bourse or **Stock Exchange** (Société des Bourses Françaises (SBF); Bourse de Paris) (France). 39, Rue Cambon, F 75001 Paris (tel. (331) 49 27 10 00; fax (331) 49 27 11 71). Since the start of 1991, it incorporates the six provincial stock exchanges of Bordeaux, Lille, Lyons, Marseilles, Nancy, and Nantes, in a national exchange.

Paris Club ('Group of Ten'). The name given to the government lender nations engaged in **rescheduling** official debt (cf. **London club**, which is the same for commercial debt). First established in 1956 to renegotiate Argentina's debts. See **less developed countries debt market**.

Paris interbank offered rate (PIBOR) (France). The rate at which major domestic banks lend French francs to each other in the French **interbank market**. There is also a **bid** rate.

parity. (i) Used in **foreign exchange** markets to describe a predetermined rate around which any given currency may fluctuate (cf. **par**). See **European Monetary System**; **Exchange Rate Mechanism**. (ii) Another term for **par** (cf. **face value**). (iii) The condition when the market value and **intrinsic value** of an **option** are equal. (iv) For **warrants**, the relationship of the warrant value to the **underlying** if exercised. This can be positive or negative. It is thus a measure of how much price appreciation is required to give the warrant intrinsic value.

parity grid. See **European Monetary System**.

parking. (i) A temporary, short-term, low-**risk**, investment made pending a firm decision as to strategy. (ii) A way of disguising ownership by placing holdings in the name of a **nominee**, often with intent to withhold disclosure. See **garage**; **warehousing**.

par priced. A security selling at its **par value** (cf. **face value**).

parquet (French). Slang term for the **Paris Bourse**.

par swap yield curve. The yield **curve** or **term structure of interest rates** constructed from **interest rate swaps** of different **maturity** (cf. **par yield curve**). See **zero-coupon yield curve**.

partial ceiling option. See **range forward**.

partial correlation. An examination of the correlation between two variables which takes into account that one or both of these variables is correlated to (an)other variable(s). Procedures are then employed to eliminate the influence of the other variable(s) from the measure of the two variables under scrutiny.

partial delivery. A delivery that is only made in part. For instance, a **commodity** might be unavailable to the seller or delayed in transportation. Rather than have a totally failed transaction, the seller will deliver in part to mitigate his potential liability from delay.

partial fill plus option swap. A type of **commodity swap** where one side pays (or receives) a high fixed price for the commodity in exchange for a **floating rate** payment. In order to justify the off-market price, the **receiver** gives the payer the right to double the **underlying** amount of the swap, if the price exceeds the fixed rate. The fixed rate receiver has effectively given the **floating rate payer** the **option** to increase the amount and his gain arises if the price exceeds the swap rate. Thus an airline which needs to hedge its fuel exposure might agree to pay the floating rate, knowing that if jet fuel costs rise above the fixed rate, it receives the difference on a larger amount of the underlying commodity.

partial hedge. A position that has been hedged in part and not in its entirety. This will reduce, but not eliminate, adverse movements to the position being hedged. A partial hedge is undertaken if the hedger wishes to still be able to benefit from some **upside** but is concerned about the amount of the exposure being taken (cf. **taking a view**).

partial lookback option or **warrant.** An option or **warrant** in which the **exercise price** is determined on the basis of the most favourable rate to the holder over an initial period. After this initial period, the warrant then becomes like any other warrant with a fixed exercise price and **expiry**, hence the partial lookback feature. Also sometimes called a *reset option* or *warrant*.

participaciones hiptecarias (Spanish). Participation certificates.

participated loan (Banking). A loan where the borrowed amount is resold or **sub-participated** by the front lender to other banks. The lender is often unaware that his loan has been sold to another party. It has a great attraction for banks which are able to generate loans since they are able to sell down these positions and even, in some cases, make a **spread** between the two parties. It is common in most banking transactions today and loan agreements normally include a reselling clause (cf. **less developed countries debt market**).

participating call or **put.** A type of low-cost **call** or **put option** where the holder only gets part of the benefit of any favourable price movement. It is created by blending, to the required proportion, an option and a **forward** or **futures** position. See **option strategies; participating forward**.

participating cap. An interest rate **risk management** contract which can be either (i) a purchased **interest rate cap** on an amount less than the interest rate protection being sought, thus reducing it but not getting rid of the exposure completely; (ii) a combination of cap and **interest rate floor** where the **notional principal amounts** differ (cf. **collar**). Because the strike rate for the floor is **in the money**, and the cap rate **out of the money**, a smaller notional principal on the floor is required than on the cap. As a result, the buyer can still get some benefit from a reduction in interest rates.

participating capped floating rate note. Hybrid form of **floating rate note** (FRN) which is a combination of a **plain vanilla** and a **capped** FRN, the relative proportions dictating the degree of participation. The key feature is that if the **reference rate** moves above the **cap rate**, then the holder still receives some additional interest, thus partially preserving the market value of the note.

participating cylinder (Forex). See **participating option**.

participating forward. A type of **option strategy** which allows the holder to obtain some benefit from a favourable movement in the price of the **underlying** without paying a **premium** and where the cost of buying a **call** (**put**) **option** is offset by the simultaneous sale of a put (call) option with the same **strike price**. The option to be sold is priced **in the money** and those purchased **out of the money**. As a result fewer options need be sold for each one bought. The payoff is less **leveraged** than would be the case if options only had been purchased. It is popular in the **foreign exchange** market since it gives a degree of upside potential for buyers without having to commit to pay a premium, and here it is also known as a *profit-sharing forward* (cf. **cylinders**). The holder can set either the degree of participation, or the level of protection. Setting the one will define the other. See **range forward; ratio spread**.

participating guaranteed investment contract. A guaranteed investment contract (GIC) which is collateralized by a distinct pool of assets. Also sometimes called a *trust account GIC*.

participating interest rate agreement (PIRA). Method of reducing the cost of an interest rate cap to a borrower or investor and which involves combining written and purchased options in different combinations (cf. interest rate collar). For details see participating cap; participating forward.

participating option. An option strategy involving the purchase and sale of options at the same strike price but for a different amount of underlying with a view to reducing the premium cost (cf. participating cap; participating forward; cylinder; ratio spread; zero-cost option). The differences between the two positions allow for a continued, but reduced participation (known as the *buyer's participation rate*) in any gains above (or below) the written option strike price; hence it is participating in the gain but not obtaining it in full.

participating preferred stock. A type of preferred where the holder has the right not only to a fixed dividend but also to share in some part of the remaining profits that are distributed under certain conditions (cf. non-participating preferred stock). For example, such a stock for every 100 nominal may receive a dividend of 5; plus, say, another 2 when the common stock dividend is greater than 3. Known as a *participating preference share* in the UK.

participating range forward. Type of vertical spread or cylinder where the buyer may gain partial benefit from movements in the underlying beyond the bounds of the two strike prices.

participating rate agreement (PRA). A type of interest rate swap with a collar to the floating rate side where the combined premiums paid and received on the cap and floor that make up the collar exactly offset each other. For the floating rate payer, it creates a banded rate.

participating swap. An interest rate swap transaction in which the floating rate payer is hedged against adverse movements through the use of a participating cap structure but can still partially benefit from any reduction in interest rates. Such structures are also available on commodity swaps.

participating swaption. A fusion of a swaption with a participating swap.

participation. (i) (Banking) To provide funds or participate in a syndicated loan (cf. sub-participa-tion). Hence, the bank involved is known as a *participant*. Participation usually involves a junior status, larger commitments or advances usually entail the bank being designated with manager or lead manager status. See invitation telex. (ii) Any transaction offering a share in the outcome, hence a *participating forward* where the customer gets to share any gains from the position. (iii) (French) A shareholding (cf. shareholder).

participation certificate (PC). (i) (USA) In the US secondary mortgage market, this is a transaction where the original grantor of the mortgage retains the first call on the underlying but sells the rights to the cash flow; that is, the interest payments made on the mortgage (cf. amortization; asset securitization; interest only; pass-through; pay-through bond). (ii) An alternative type of equity issued by entities which are unable or unwilling to issue common stock (cf. permanent interest bearing shares; preference stock prefered stock; titre participatif). Normally, the PC has all the benefits of common stock, except voting rights, and in some circumstances may be convertible to common stock. (iii) (Banking) A document providing evidence of part title to a debt. Such certificates are normally provided to members of a syndicated loan or banks who have purchased part or all of a loan from another bank. PCs may be readily negotiable by endorsement, or may require the consent of the borrower. As a practice it is now common for most loans to be in the form of participation certificates, thus allowing the bank to sell some or all of the asset if it should choose to do so (cf. sub-participation; transferable facility). (iv) Sometimes used to describe an equity-linked note.

participation fee (Banking). The fees paid to the participants in a syndicated loan (cf. management fee).

participation note. Bonds where the returns are linked to a specific income stream such as a project or a patent or other asset (cf. film trust). The payment of interest on such bonds is set below the current market rate, but holders also anticipate sharing in part of the expected payments through a *contingent interest payment* clause.

participation rate agreement (PRA). A low- or nil- cost interest rate cap using the same method to reduce the cap option premium as a participating call.

partly paid. An issue of securities where only a proportion of the purchase price or capital due has been subscribed. The balance is usually payable in one or more instalments at predetermined future dates. For partly paid bond issues, the first coupon is calculated using interest accrued on each tranche paid. For partly paid **equity**, the firm's directors normally have discretion as to when to require the payment of additional tranches. The partly paid share mechanism is particularly popular with Australian natural resource exploration companies. It has also been used to provide a **backstop**, as when the Société Nationale des Chemins de Fer Français issued a partly paid **floating rate note** to back up its **commercial paper** programme (cf. **securitized note commitment facility**).

partnership. Association of two or more individuals or firms formed for the purpose of undertaking a business or activity. Since a partnership is not an incorporated company or corporation, it has no stand-alone legal basis and partners are usually liable for any debts incurred, except for **limited partners**, who are only, as with **shareholders**, liable for the investment made. In the USA, because **dividends** end up being taxed twice under the federal tax code, partnerships have been used as a conduit to allow income distribution direct to investors without the use of incorporated companies (cf. **general partnership; limited partnership; master limited partnership**).

par value. (i) The stated or face amount on a security at which it is normally redeemable (cf. **premium**). Also called *nominal value*. See **par**. (ii) The value placed on a unit of **common stock** or **ordinary shares** for regulatory and accounting purposes (cf. **no-par stock**).

par yield curve (Bonds). A type of **yield curve** which is calculated using estimates of **coupon** rates on bonds issued or trading at, or close to, their **par value** for differing maturities (cf. **spot rate yield curve; term structure of interest rates**). Such bonds are likely to be more illustrative of the implicit **discount rates** prevailing in the market than bonds standing at a significant **premium** or **discount** since these may be subject to special factors (cf. **on-the-run**). See also **zero-coupon yield curve**.

passed dividend or **passing the dividend.** See **omitted dividend**.

passif (French). See **actif**.

passing a name. The disclosure of the name of a **counterparty** by one **broker** to another in order to execute a transaction.

passing the book. Term for the activities of global firms where the management of a given trading **position** is transferred with the clock across time zones so as to provide 24-hour active coverage.

passing the dividend (Equities). A company which decides, in view of the adverse trading conditions in a given reporting period, not to pay a **dividend** on its **common stock**. Sometimes, if conditions are very bad, this is extended to **preferred stock** as well (cf. **cumulative; non-cumulative**).

passive bond (USA). A **bond** without a **coupon**. Not the same as a **zero-coupon bond**, but would trade as such. Such securities are issued for good causes or in a financial reorganization. See **income bond**.

passive management. A **portfolio** strategy involving the design of portfolios on a **long-term** basis to reach certain particular returns, such as a target rate of return over a specified period, or the matching of a fixed set of future **liabilities**. Subsequently, little or no **switching** would occur (cf. **active management; dedication; immunization; indexing; portfolio optimization**).

passive portfolio. A portfolio designed to replicate a particular market **index**'s performance (cf. **indexing**).

pass-through or **pass-through security.** A method of asset securitization. A type of **asset-backed** arrangement where the **underlying** comprises pooled debt obligations (for instance mortgages) that have been **securitized** and the payments 'pass through' the originator to the security holders. Used initially in the US secondary mortgage market, it represents ownership of a pool of mortgages or other **assets** (cf. **collateralized mortgage obligation; certificates of automobile receivables; certificate of amortizing revolving debt securities**). The regular interest payments, regular **amortization**, and early **prepayments** of **principal** are 'passed through' to the owner of the certificates by those servicing the mortgage payments. There are three main types of pass-through: *straight pass-through*: where the security holder receives interest and principal when collected; *modified pass-through*: where the holder receives interest whether collected or not and principal as collected; and *fully modified pass-through*: where the holder receives both interest and principal irrespective of whether they have been collected. See **asset securitization; pay-through bond**.

past due loans (Banking). Any loan or debt where interest is more than ninety days overdue. See **charge-off; non-performing assets**.

patent. A legally enforceable right to a process, product, or other piece of intellectual property.

path-dependent options. A range of special feature **options** where the payout on the option is directly linked to the movements in the **under-**

lying during the life of the option. The **lookback option** provides the buyer with chance to buy at the lowest or sell at the highest price. **High-low options** give the buyer the difference between the low and high price over the option's life. The major drawback of these instruments is their cost, which is generally much greater than that of standard **call** and **put** options. **Barrier options** provide protection after or up to a given **trigger** point (or barrier) is reached. There are various kinds, the *down and out* or *up and in* type being the most common (cf. **knock-in**). An **Asian option** (average price or rate option) enables the holder to exercise into the underlying at the average price or rate over the period at the end of the period. Because these provide a limited payoff, they have a lower cost. Such complex options make most sense when there is a distinct **volatility** view over the life of the option. Also called *history-dependent options*.

path-dependent swap. A type of **interest rate swap** or **cross-currency swap** where one of the payment streams has an upper limit on the interest rate at which it can be reset dependent on the level in the previous period. Thus one party might agree to pay the **London interbank offered rate** (LIBOR) but limited to a 40 **basis points** increase at each **rollover** against receiving LIBOR less 0.35%. See also **LIBOR in arrears swap**.

pathfinder prospectus (UK). A preliminary prospectus used in **initial public offerings** to gauge investor reaction (cf. **red herring**).

path integral. The sum of the price or rate movements used for pricing **path-dependent options**. See **average rate option**; **Asian option**.

patterns. A **chartist** interpretation of various price developments in price or rate series in terms of the shapes or patterns that evolve over time. The rationale is that the price series must complete the pattern after the price has broken out of its previous trend. There are two broad classifications of patterns: continuations and reversals. Continuations involve an extension of the price behaviour into the future, examples being **flags**, **pennants**, **rectangles**, and **triangles**. Reversals, as the name suggests, involve a change or reversal in the price behaviour in the future, examples being **double tops** and **head and shoulders**.

pay (USA). Slang term for the currency of denomination of a security.

payables. Trade credit received from suppliers and therefore payable in the future (cf. **receivables**). Hence *accounts payable*.

payable to bearer or **payable to order.** Banker's draft or bill that has no named endorsee or

payee and can be paid to the holder by writing in the holder's name (cf. **bearer bond**).

pay-as-you-go option. Type of **instalment option** where the holder has the right to cancel the contract prior to **expiry** and pay no further parts of the **premium** (cf. **Boston option**).

payback. Financial analytic technique which involves calculating the number of time periods required before the initial investment is returned to the investor (cf. **price–earnings ratio**). The time required to repay the initial investment is known as the *payback period*. A variant involves discounting the future cash flows for the **time value of money**, and is known as *discounted payback*.

paydown (Bonds; USA). (i) A term used in the US **Treasury market** for the amount by which the total value of the maturing securities exceeds that of those sold (cf. **new money**). (ii) Any refunding transaction where the amount of new issue is less than the retired debt. The difference is known as the paydown. (iii) The rate at which a **mortgage-backed security** will **amortize** (cf. **prepayment model**).

payee. The recipient of a payment (cf. **receiver**).

payer. The maker of a payment (cf. **receiver**).

payer's swaption. **Option** on an **interest rate swap** allowing the holder to pay the **fixed rate** and receive the **floating rate**. In terms of interest rate exposure, it is equivalent to owning a **put** on the fixed rate. See also **swaption**.

paying agent. An institution responsible for making **coupon** or interest payments and repayment of principal, on behalf of the issuer, to investors who produce the appropriate coupon or security certificate (cf. **agent bank**; **bearer bond**; **bearer participation certificate**; **fiscal agent**; **talon**). Also known as the *disbursing agent*.

paying banker. The bank that will make the payment on a **bill** or a **cheque**.

paying up. The requirement to pay a **premium** or additional **margin** to be able to undertake a particular kind of transaction. This might arise when a large line of securities is required in an **illiquid** stock, or if there is a large requirement in a **thin** market. A borrower who had failed to raise money at the appropriate time might have to pay up in order to secure **funds** at short notice in order to meet maturing obligations (cf. **backstop**; **swingline**). See **pay-up**.

pay-in-kind bond or **note (PIK bond or note)** (USA). A type of **bond** used in the US **junk bond**

market that pays additional securities in lieu of interest. Some PIK notes are hybrid instruments, initially paying further notes then, after a predetermined period, paying normal interest. Their attraction to issuers is that they delay cash payments to the future (cf. **bunny bonds; multiplier bonds**). The structure has the great advantage for investors of removing **reinvestment risk** on the intermediate cash flows. The ultimate in PIKs is the **zero-coupon bond**.

pay-in-kind preferred stock (PIK preferred) (Equity; USA). A type of **preferred stock** where normally the initial **dividends** are in the form of additional PIK preferred stock (cf. **pay-in-kind bond**). Such items conserve cash for the issuer and have been popular in **leveraged buy-out** transactions.

pay-later options. Options where the holder is only required to pay the **premium** if certain events or conditions are met, although the holder will benefit from any gains whether money has been paid or not. Sometimes called a *contingent* or *deferred premium option*.

payment cap. See **cap; interest rate cap** (cf. **embedded option**).

payment date. (i) The date payments are actually made on securities. This may be considerably later than the **ex-date** for trading purposes. For new issues, this is generally the **closing date**. (ii) Sometimes used synonymously for the **value date** in **settlement**.

payment enhanced capital securities (PEACS) (Canada). A special purpose vehicle designed to maximize the **dividend** paying aspect of **common stocks**. The other part is known as *special equity claim securities* (SPECS). The structure is based on the division of returns principle used in **prescribed right to income and maximum equity** and **special claim on residual equity**.

payment float. Cheques written but not yet cleared by the recipient.

payment in kind (PIK). See **barter; pay-in-kind bond**.

payment netting. See **netting**.

payoff. (i) The value of a financial instrument, portfolio, or a **position** at **maturity, expiry,** or some predetermined date. The **law of one price** predicts that assets with the same risk and other common characteristics will have the same payoffs. (ii) Used colloquially for the expected gain from taking a position, pursuing a strategy, or engaging in a transaction (cf. **risk-reward**).

payout ratio. (i) The proportion of the **underwriting** and **lead manager** fees paid to the **sub-underwriters** and the **co-managers** associated with a **primary market** issue. (ii) Used to describe the proportion of a company's earnings paid out as **dividends**, calculated as the reciprocal of the **dividend cover** (cf. **retained earnings**). See **earnings analysis**.

pay-through bond (USA). A type of **mortgaged-backed** debt where interest and **amortization** are serviced regularly, together with repayment of **principal** from the **underlying** asset. Also known as a *builder bond* since it was developed to facilitate real-estate construction. Although the bond has many of the characteristics of **pass-through** securities, ultimate ownership of the assets is vested with the issuer. See **debenture**.

pay-up. (i) The willingness of a borrower to pay a **premium** to its usual cost of funds in order to raise money. This may be due to a change in perception about the borrower's **credit** or to temporary market **illiquidity** or disruption. (ii) The amount of additional money required when **switching** from lower-priced to higher-priced instruments while maintaining the same **par** amount invested. For instance, in the sale of a **bond** at $95\frac{3}{8}$ and the purchase of another at $95\frac{7}{8}$, the pay-up is $\frac{1}{2}$ per bond.

peak. A high in a time series or economic indicator. Generally, the high point in an economic expansion. The opposite would be a trough (cf. **double dip**).

pecuniary benefits. Employee and management payments in money (cf. **non-pecuniary benefits**).

peg, pegged, or **pegging** (Forex). The fixing of one currency in relation to another or a basket of currencies. Pegs may be fixed or crawling; the latter has the parity adjusted for differentials in inflation between the two countries or the average of the basket (cf. **parity**).

penalty clause. A condition of a contract which stipulates payments or cost reductions (penalties) in the event that certain conditions are not fulfilled (cf. **prepayment penalty**).

penalty interest payment (PIP) (Canada). Penalty interest charged to mortgage takers in the event of **prepayment** exceeding permitted levels. It aims to partially compensate the lender for higher than anticipated **prepayment risk** (cf. **extension risk**).

pennant. A **chartist** pattern of a time series which shows a narrowing price channel over time. When the pattern is complete, the chartist will anticipate a **breakout** (cf. **flag**).

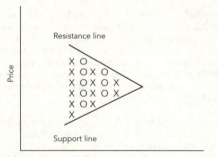

Pennant

penny stocks and **shares** (UK; USA). That group of **ordinary shares** or **common stocks** that are low priced because of the perceived **risks** associated with the companies involved. In the UK shares of less than 50p and in the USA shares of less than $5 are said to qualify for this description. Traditionally such shares have been popular with private investors.

Pension Benefit Guarantee Corporation (PBGC) (USA). A federal agency set up in 1974 which insures defined-benefit pension plans of corporations. It guarantees pensions against certain defined **risks** but excludes fund underperformance.

pension fund. A type of **institutional investor** who administers and invests funds for pension plans.

pension livrée (French). **Repurchase agreement.**

Pensionsgeschaft (German). **Repurchase agreement.**

percentage order (USA). A transaction instruction that becomes effective as either a **limit order** or a **market order** when a given volume has been transacted in the security. The basis of the instruction is to ensure sufficient **liquidity** to undertake the trade.

percentage strike price. An order for the purchase or sale of an **option** which specifies the **strike price** as a percentage of the **underlying**. Thus an order might be placed for a three-month **call** option which has a strike that is 10% out of the money. If, at the time the order is given, the underlying is trading at 267.00, this would translate into a strike at 293.70. If, however, by the time the order is traded, the underlying has moved to 265.25, then the strike is set at 291.78.

percentile ranking. Method of ranking a portfolio's performance against other, similar funds. The highest performing fund in the category is ranked

0, the median performance is 50, and the lowest 100.

per diem (Latin). Per day.

perfected first lien. The recording of a **lien** with the correct registration authority such that the lender is able to act upon it in the **event of default** (cf. **fixed charge**; **floating charge**).

perfect hedge. A **hedge** where the change in the price or rate of the hedging device is exactly contrary to the change in the price of the **underlying**. Every hedger's dream.

performance. A general term for the difference between the return on an asset, portfolio, or **class** against some **benchmark** or reference point.

performance bond. (i) An insurance condition in a commercial agreement used to guarantee compensation in the event of non-performance by the contracted party (cf. **on-demand bond**). (ii) Another term for **margin** (cf. **initial margin**; **maintenance margin**; **variation margin**).

performance bond call. See **margin call.**

performance fee. Another term for an **incentive fee.**

performance fund. See **growth fund.**

performance indexed paper (PIPs). Short-term note issue where the return is linked to an index, exchange rate, or other reference rate. The first such issues took place in the USA with commercial paper issues linked to a currency against the US dollar. Sometimes known as *currency-linked commercial paper.* See also **dual currency bond.**

performance letter of credit (Banking; USA). A **letter of credit** issued by a bank with the same effect as a **performance bond.** Common in the USA, where the issue of bonds by banks is not permitted.

performance measurement. Assessment of the investment performance of a **fund manager** in relation to some **benchmark** or target (cf. **strategic asset allocation**). Typically would analyse separately factors such as: country selection; currency overlay; stock selection; timing; and risk-adjustment.

performance plus shares. Method of providing investors with enhanced returns on **common stock.** It involves an intermediary holding the **underlying** securities and issuing **depository receipts** to investors, which then allows the intermediary to pass on part of the benefits it can obtain from taxes, funding, **leverage**, or other return-enhancing factor. See **equity-linked note**.

performance shares. A way of remunerating management which involves payment of **common stock** or **ordinary shares** if certain performance targets are reached (cf. **agency problem**).

performance stock. See **growth stock**.

performance table. A ranking of the performance by listing the highest to the lowest in a particular category. Sometimes only the best and worst are included. Also known as a *league table*.

peril. See **hazard** (cf. **risk**).

period bill. See **time draft** (cf. **sight bill**).

periodic cap or **floor.** See **variable strike cap** or **floor**.

periodic charge (UK). The management fee deducted from the value of a **unit trust** by its managers. The combined amount that can be charged for this and the **initial charge** is regulated by the Department of Trade and Industry. See **single pricing**.

periodic rate-setting swap. See **periodic reset swap**.

periodic repayment. See **sinking fund**.

periodic reset swap (periodic resetting swap). A type of **swap** agreement where the floating rate leg is reset more frequently than the payments. For instance, such a swap might have a six-month payment, but be based on two three-month interest periods or six one-month periods. Also called a *periodic rate-setting swap*. For details of the different mechanisms see entry under **mismatch bond**.

period of digestion. See **lock-up**; **seasoned**.

period of grace. See **grace period**.

permanent interest bearing shares (PIBS) (UK). Undated, fixed interest paying **shares** issued by **building societies**, which are mutual associations. They are essentially a type of **participation certificate** which is **subordinated** to **deposits** at the society. The issuing society is prohibited from making any payments to PIBS in the event that it fails to meet obligations on its deposits or members' shares or where it might fail to meet the criteria of prudent management. Interest is normally paid semi-annually and they trade at a **spread**, reflecting **liquidity** and **credit risk**, to the relevant **irredeemable gilt-edge** (cf. **consols**).

permission to deal (UK). Application made to the **London Stock Exchange** to allow dealings in a new issue. It is made three days after the issue of a prospectus. See **offer for sale**; **placing**.

perpendicular spread. See **vertical spread**.

perpetual. **Euromarkets** term for an **irredeemable** or **undated** (cf. **consols**; **one-way stock-option**). Normally the issuer has a **call provision** allowing redemption of the issue at some future date. The first such issue in the Euromarkets was made by the National Westminster Bank in 1984. Hence, *perpetual bond*.

perpetual floating rate note. **Perpetual** which has a **floating rate note** structure (cf. **consols**; **flip-flop**; **undated**).

perpetual warrant. A **warrant** which has no expiry date.

perpetuity. A **fixed interest** security that offers a payment for ever (in perpetuity) (cf. **consol**; **irredeemable**; **perpetual**). The market value of a perpetuity is derived from the following formula:

$$\text{market value} = \frac{\text{Periodic payment}}{r}$$

where r is the required return.

per pro (per proc; pp.) (Latin). Actions carried out on behalf of another, that is as their **agent**.

Personal Equity Plan (PEP) (UK). An annual contract under which certain **bonds** and **shares** in UK companies can be bought without liability either to income tax on **dividends** or to **capital gains tax**. Introduced in 1986 and originally designed to encourage individuals to invest in shares for the first time.

Personal Investment Authority (PIA) (UK). The **self-regulating organization** under the **Securities and Investments Board** responsible for overseeing intermediaries selling financial products to individuals. It was formed in April 1993 by merging the Financial Intermediaries, Managers and Brokers Regulatory Agency and the Life Assurance and Unit Trust Regulatory Organization and some of the responsibilities of the **Investment Management Regulatory Organization**.

personal pension or **private pension** (UK). A means for providing income in old age, based on a savings contract between an individual and a financial institution. The agreement is independent of the state and the individual's employer, thereby making it **portable**. The benefits payable on retirement are calculated according to the value of the fund at that time and will be a function of how well the contributions, made during the individual's working life, have been managed. This so-called *money-purchase basis* can be compared with the *final salary basis*, which is used for establishing benefits as a proportion of the salary of the individual at the time of retirement, under company or occupational schemes. The incentives to encourage individuals to save for old age using personal pension contracts, especially those not covered by occupational pension schemes, have recently been improved.

personalty. Personal property, as opposed to realty (real property).

petite bourse (Equities; France). A one-hour session of the **Bourse de Paris** which coincides with the first hour of trading on the **New York Stock Exchange**. This was instituted to allow US investors to trade in French equities in real time at the New York **opening**.

petrodollars. The unused balances of oil-exporting countries placed in US dollar interest-bearing accounts. Refers particularly to the period after the first oil shock in 1974 when the oil price quadrupled and large deposits were made with US and UK banks. These were partially recycled to Latin American and other countries (cf. **less developed countries debt market**). Balances held in other currencies led to the concept of *petrocurrency* or simply *oil money.*

pewter parachute. A less remunerative form of **golden parachute** provided to the lower ranks of an organization subject to a successful **takeover**.

Pfandbriefe (Mortgage bonds). (i) (Germany) Bonds issued by banks to fund mortgage lending with **collateral** based on the mortgages. There are two kinds: *Hypothekenpfandbriefe* (backed up by residential and commercial mortgages); *Offentli-chepfandbriefe* (backed up by public sector loans). (ii) (Switzerland) **mortgage-backed securities** issued by a central mortgage-granting institution to fund lending for home purchase. (iii) (Netherlands) Bonds issued by mortgage banks to fund mortgage lending but also guaranteed by the issuer.

Philadelphia Board of Trade (PBOT) (USA). 1900 Market Street, Philadelphia, PA 19103 (tel. 1 215 496 5025; fax 1 215 496 5653). Established in 1985. It is best known for its **currency options** contracts.

Philadelphia Stock Exchange (PHLX) (USA). 1900 Market Street, Philadelphia, PA 19103 (tel. 1 215 496 5357; fax 1 215 496 5653). Established in 1790, it is one of the nine exchanges in the USA. It is principally involved in trading **currency options**.

Philippine Stock Exchange (Philippines). Unit 2002-C Tektite Tower, 1 Tektite Road, PH-Metro Manila (tel. 63 2 7210286; fax 63 2 7219238). See **Manila Stock Exchange** (cf. **Manila International Futures Exchange**).

physical capital. See **capital**.

physical commodities. The commodities which underlie **commodity futures** contracts. Also just called *actuals*, *physicals* or *spot commodities*.

physical delivery. The settlement of a **futures** or **option** contract at expiry by making or taking delivery of the underlying. The alternative method is for a payment to be made reflecting the value of the contract and known as *cash-settled*.

physical market. The market in **commodities** for immediate delivery. Also called the *cash market*.

physical option. An option where the underlying is a physical good or a **commodity**.

physical price. The price of **commodities** for immediate delivery (cf. **cash market**; **forward**; **future**; **spot**).

physicals. Actual **commodities** rather than futures contracts. Usually taken to indicate the spot purchase and sale of commodities for delivery. Sometimes used for *cash*. Also called *actuals* (see **against actuals**; **exchange for physical**).

physical security. A security issue which is evidenced by **certificates**. These may be either **bearer** or **registered** (cf. **global note**).

physical strip (USA). A type of US Treasury **zero-coupon bond**, where the individual interest payments are separated from the principal, or corpus, thus producing multiple securities. The stripped zeros so created are in **registered** form. (cf. **corpus Treasury receipt**; **coupon Treasury receipt**; **separate trading of registered interest and principal of securities**).

pick-up. The gain made by selling one security and buying another with a higher **yield**, hence *yield pick up* (cf. **give-up**; **pay-up**).

pickup bond (USA). A bond which has an above market **coupon** and is near a **call** date. The assumption is that the buyer will benefit from any call **premium** paid for early redemption if interest rates fall further (cf. **cushion bond**).

picture (USA). Market term for the **bid-asked** price quoted by a **broker-dealer** for a particular security (cf. **one-man picture**). Hence *what's the picture?* (what's the bid-asked?).

piggyback registration (USA). A combined primary and secondary **distribution** of securities. The secondary distribution arises from existing **shareholders** disposing of all, or part, of their holdings. The combined nature of such offerings is detailed in the **prospectus**.

piled-up rolling hedge. A type of **long** or **short hedge** technique used in the **futures** market to cover a **position** which has a longer **maturity** than the future. It involves using the nearest contract to hedge the entire position, rolling it over as required and, as the position is reduced, reducing the hedged amount as appropriate. As such it is an alternative hedging method to a **strip hedge**. It suffers from the disadvantage that the effectiveness of the hedge is affected by changes in the shape of the **yield curve** over the life of the hedge. This can be addressed by simultaneously setting up a **straddle** position in the future by going short on longer maturity future contracts. Also sometimes called a *stack hedge* or a *stack and roll hedge*. See also **rolling hedge**.

Pink Book (UK). The official statistics relating to the UK's **balance of payments**.

pink form (UK). See **preferential form**.

pink sheets (USA). Daily publication by the National Quotation Bureau of securities traded in the **over-the-counter** markets.

pin risk. (i) The **market risk** attached to an **at-the-money option** shortly before **expiry**. A small movement in the **underlying** in the short time left to the option will have a large effect on the payoff value at expiry (cf. **delta**; **gamma**). (ii) The risk in a short **conversion** or **reverse conversion** strategy that if the price at expiry is at or around the **strike price** that one leg of the position might be exercised. In such a condition, the writer does not know whether the **call** will require delivery and whether the **writer** needs to hold the underlying for such a purpose.

pin-stripe pork bellies (USA). Colloquial term used for **stock index futures**. Pork bellies are one of the **commodity futures** contracts traded in Chicago.

pip. 0.01% of the market value of a security (0.0001) (cf. **basis point**). Pips are used to express price differentials. Common in the **foreign exchange market** when quoting currencies, but less so in securities markets (cf. **tick**). See also **big figure**; **point**.

pipeline (USA). Market term for securities ready to be launched and waiting for the appropriate market conditions. Such securities will be pre-registered using a **shelf-registration** with the **Securities and Exchange Commission**. Hence, *in the pipeline* (cf. **calendar**; **visible supply**).

pit. That part of a **floor** of an exchange where trading actually takes place. A pit will usually deal exclusively with one type of security or **commodity**, although on a **futures exchange** it describes a place where different types of contracts may be traded (cf. **crowd**). It derives its name from the generally octagonal stepped area in which the trading takes place, the terracing allowing those at the rear to see and hear the activity in the centre and on the opposite side to facilitate trading by **open outcry** (cf. **auction**). Also called the *trading pit*.

pit broker. Used for a **broker** on a **futures** or **options** exchange; i.e. one who transacts business in a **pit**.

pit trader. See **local**.

place or **placement.** (i) A method of issuing securities, which may be **unquoted** or offered to the public by the **lead manager** (cf. **private placement**). See **placing memorandum** or **circular**. (ii) (UK) A type of listing arrangement allowed on the **London Stock Exchange**. See **placing**. (iii) **Eurocurrency** market term for the making of a **deposit** with a bank. Also sometimes called a *placing*. (iv) The distribution or sale of securities in the **primary market** (cf. **distributed**; **firm hands**).

placement (French). A **short-term** investment.

place on warrant (Commodities). To deliver into a recognized warehouse a quantity of **physical commodity** which is then available to effect **settlement** of contractual obligations (or for lending). Ownership is evidenced by a warehouse **warrant**.

placing. (i) (Equities; UK). A method of offering new **shares** in the UK which involves selling them to a select group of investors (cf. **initial public offering**; **vendor placing**). Because the securities are not distributed to investors at large, the costs can be kept to a minimum, although the success of such a transaction depends critically on the **placing power** of the intermediary (cf. **placing memorandum**). See also **private placement**. (ii) **Euromarkets** term for making a deposit in the **interbank market** (cf. **London interbank bid rate**; **taking**).

placing agent. Financial intermediary who agrees to find buyers or investors for securities issued or sold by an issuer (cf. **dealer**).

placing memorandum or **circular.** A document produced in support of a **placement** or **private**

placement. It is written by the **lead manager** and contains details about the issuer and the transaction (cf. **prospectus**). Also referred to as a *placement memorandum*.

placing power. The ability of a financial intermediary to sell new issues of securities using its own client lists and relationships (cf. **book building; distribution**).

plain vanilla (Bonds; USA). A market term for standard conditions. Thus a plain vanilla **bond** is a bond that lacks any special features, such as a **call provision** or a **put provision**, or has attached **warrants** (cf. **bells and whistles**). It means the same as **straight**.

plain vanilla swap. A plain vanilla **swap** has constant **notional principal** amount and makes the exchange of period **floating rate** payments against periodic fixed interest payments with no other complications (cf. **cross-currency swap; interest rate swap; fixed rate payer; floating rate payer; reference rate**). Also called a *coupon swap*.

planned amortized class bond (PAC) (USA). A class of **collateralized mortgage obligations** (CMO) which is designed to have more predictable cash flows by pre-empting other classes of CMO in the event of unanticipated variability in redemption patterns. CMOs are divided up into different tranches with differing precedence as to interest and principal repayment. The PAC bond is closest in behaviour to a **straight bond** since it is given preference over the other classes (cf. **Z bond**) Also called a *planned redemption obligation* (PRO) or a *stabilized term reduction mortgage obligation* (STRM) obligation).

plan of reorganization (USA). A **reconstruction** plan filed with the court by a firm in **Chapter 11**. The plan includes details of the proposed changes to the firm's financial contracts with **creditors** and the way in which the firm will meet its restructured commitments (cf. **assented securities; cram down**).

platykurtic, platykurtosis, or **platykurtocity.** A description of a frequency distribution curve which is less peaked than a **normal distribution**, i.e. less concentrated around the **mean** than is the case if the distribution was normal (cf. **lognormal distribution**). See **kurtosis; leptokurtic**.

playing the yield curve. Colloquial description of any of a number of **yield curve** investment strategies. These involve basically a **mismatch** between the short and long end of the curve in order to benefit from **spread** income or anticipated changes in the shape of the curve (cf. **spread futures**).

play the market. To speculate (usually taken to be in **equities**).

pledge. (i) A security or **lien** provided by a borrower to a lender (cf. **mortgage**). (ii) An undertaking to enter into a transaction, sometimes with conditions attached. For instance, **shareholders** may pledge their shares in a **takeover**.

pledging. See factoring.

ploughed back earnings or **profits.** See retained earnings.

plowback ratio. See retention rate. (cf. **payout ratio**).

plum. A successful investment (cf. **dog; lemon; star**).

plunger. A reckless trader, investor, or market operator.

plus or **'+'** (USA). (i) (Bonds) A trading convention for quoting the prices of securities. **US treasuries** are normally quoted in 32nd fractions of a **point** (1/32%). To quote a **bid** or **offer** in 64ths (1/64%) a **dealer** will use pluses (+). So a quote of 8+ is equivalent to the **big figure** (or **handle**) and 8/32 + 1/64, which equals 17/64. (ii) (Equities). A transaction reporting sign used on the tape for a trade at a higher price than the previously reported trade. Thus $64 - +$ would indicate that the previous trade was done at $64\frac{1}{4}$ or less. See **up-tick**. (iii) A suffix added to a **credit rating** indicating a superior quality within the grade. For instance, a $AA+$ rating.

plus accrued interest (+AI). Indicates the bond price needs to be adjusted for **accrued interest** when payment is made (cf. **clean price; dirty price; flat rate; income bond; settlement price**).

plus tick (USA). A transaction which is at a higher price than the previous one (cf. **plus**). See **up-tick**.

point. (i) One per cent of **par value** (or 100%). Bond prices are quoted as points and fractions of points. (ii) In **foreign exchange markets** one point equals 10 **pips**. Thus for a quote of 1.7521, the last number (1) is a pip, and the next number (2) is a point. (iii) In the US **stock** markets, equal to US$1. (iv) Used in some markets to indicate a change greater than the minimum price movement allowed (cf. **tick**).

point and figure chart. A type of chart used in **technical analysis** to analyse price movements. Unlike a traditional price graph plotting price against time, the point and figure chart records *X*s when prices rise and *O*s when they fall on the price axis. Each time the price series moves from X to O and back, the columns of price movements are moved to the right, recording the latest price (one above or below the previous column's last entry). By setting a predetermined movement to the price generating the changes in X to and from O, the chart aims to exclude inconsequential price changes to reveal the momentum in the price series.

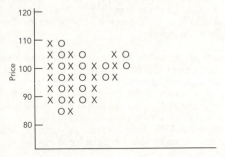

Point and figure chart

poison pill. (i) Specifically, a security that allows a prejudicial action to be taken against the issuer, such as an interest rate penalty or early redemption, should a contested **takeover** succeed. (ii) More generally, in the **mergers and acquisitions** business, any action by a **target** company which is intended to create difficulties for the **predator** company following a contested takeover; for example, the target company could dilute earnings or increase its **gearing** or **leverage** by issuing debt or equity or both. Named after the cyanide pill supposedly carried by secret agents to avoid being taken prisoner. See **crown jewels; greenmail, porcupine provision; self-uglification; white knight; white squire.**

poison put. A **covenant** term that allows the holder to **put** the security in the event of a hostile takeover. Often one part of a **poison pill** defence.

polarisation (UK). A condition of the **Financial Services Act**, 1986 that requires financial intermediaries either to act as vendors of their own financial products and services or to be independent distributors of other producers' products; but not both. Firms which have opted for the latter are generally known as *independent financial advisers.*

polarisation rules (UK). Under the **Financial Services Act**, 1986, any financial organization or individual involved in selling investments, or investment-related products, must be recognized by the **Securities and Investments Board**, via their respective **self-regulating organizations**, as either an 'independent intermediary' or a 'company representative'. The distinction is significant, parti-

cularly for branch banks and building societies, because if they opt for the former status then they are under a legal obligation to offer their clients impartial advice on all available products, rather than simply those offered by their own organization or those companies for whom they may be acting as an agent, as is the case with company representative status.

policy switch. A restructuring of the constituent elements of a **portfolio** in recognition of changing circumstances to achieve the aims of the investor; for example, changes in interest rate levels, **yield curve** structure or **credit rating** (cf. **anomaly; switch**).

political risk. The risk to asset values from a government changing policy, whether the government be changed peacefully or otherwise (cf. **country risk; sovereign risk**). For example, the introduction of a **withholding tax**, or at the extreme, the confiscation of assets. Political risk is sometimes equated with expropriation (with or without compensation), but it includes events like civil unrest, war, restrictions on remittances of profits, foreign, or domestic currency, price controls, fiscal changes, cancellation of contracts, and so on. It can be a direct risk from having operations located in the country, or arise indirectly from **portfolio** investment through having holdings which in turn have assets in the affected country. It can also affect the timing and probability of payments when third-party monies become blocked as a result of government action or embargos. Political risk is a particular problem in international business and finance where different countries operate to different regulatory and ethical standards. Such risks are important in areas of **project finance**, especially when the project relates to large-scale, and therefore high-value, infrastructure schemes, and in **foreign exchange** transactions (cf. **business risk; credit risk; financial risk**).

polynomial swap. Exotic type of **leveraged swap** where the **floating rate** payment is calculated according to a polynomial equation designed to provide significantly enhanced exposure to the **reference rate** over a given range.

Ponzi scheme. See **pyramiding**.

pool. (i) The aggregation of a number of instruments into a single security, usually seen in the mortgage market. See **asset securitization**. (ii) Can also be used for mutual investment funds, for instance investment clubs, which are popular in the United States, place individual resources into a pool for investment purposes. (iii) An illegal form of market manipulation, usually called a **concert party**. (iv) The fees available to the **lead**

managers in a loan **syndication** after the sell-down. Lesser participants are not normally given the full fees and the balance is pooled for distribution to the managers on a pro rata basis. Such fees can significantly increase the returns to the managers. (v) Aggregation of different accounts for **cash management** purposes.

pooling (Banking). A system offered by banks to their larger customers allowing for the balances held in different accounts to be notionally offset in calculating interest or for investment purposes. With pooling, unlike **balance concentration**, there is no commingling of the funds.

pooling of interests (USA). An accounting method used in **mergers** between two companies which is generally tax efficient. The **balance sheet** of the combined entities is arrived at by combining the two sets of accounts.

pop-up option. See **barrier option** (cf. **knock-in option**; **up-and-in option**).

porcupine provision. Anti-takeover defence used in the **mergers and acquisitions** market by potential **target** firms designed to make changes of control difficult. It has much the same effect as a **shark repellent**. See also **poison pill**.

portable pension. A type of pension contract that is not tied to a particular employer or occupation. It is thought to promote occupational mobility and avoid the problems of 'frozen' pension rights.

Portal (USA). System set up in June 1990 by the National Association of **Securities Dealers** to allow trading of **private placements** made under **Rule 144a** by sophisticated investors. The closed nature of the system ensures that only professional investors have access to this particular market.

Porter's competitive forces. A framework used for analysing the strategic environment (cf. **Boston matrix**). There are five competitive forces:

- the threat of new entrants;
- the threat of substitute products;
- the bargaining power of buyers;
- the bargaining power of suppliers;
- the rivalry among current competitors.

portfolio. A combination of financial assets held by an investor for the purposes of achieving particular objectives, such as target rates of return and capital appreciation. The portfolio return is calculated by the weighted average return of its constituents:

$$\text{Return on portfolio} = \sum_{j=1}^{n} X_j R_j$$

The portfolio variance is calculated by:

$$\sigma_p^2 = \sum_{j=1}^{n} X_j^2 \sigma_j^2 + \sum_{j=1}^{n} \sum_{\substack{k=1 \\ j \neq k}}^{n} X_j X_k \sigma_{jk}$$

where X_j is the fraction invested in security j by market value and R_j is the return on security j; σ_j is the variance of security j and σ_{jk} is the **covariance** of returns between security j and k. In a large portfolio, the covariance terms will dominate the individual variance terms on the securities. See **efficient portfolios**.

portfolio beta (β). A measure of **systematic risk** derived from the **Capital Asset Pricing Model**. Beta measures the relative response of the portfolio to changes in the market factor (or market portfolio). A high beta in excess of 1.0 will have more **risk** than the market, a low beta less than 1.0 will have less risk than the market. A portfolio with a beta of unity will have the same risk as the market.

portfolio income note. See **equity-linked note**.

portfolio insurance. Part of a set of investment strategies, known collectively as **program trading**, which involves the allocation of funds between a risky and risk-free portfolio using combinations of **futures**, **options**, and/or other **derivative** instruments. The aim is to artificially reproduce an **option** for **hedging** or **risk management** purposes to guarantee a minimum portfolio value. Also known as *dynamic hedging* or *portfolio protection*.

portfolio management. The process of combining different securities into a **portfolio** to suit the risk–reward preferences and cash flow requirements of the investor; monitoring and evaluating its performance as well as administration (cf. **risk averse**; **utility**). See also **asset management**.

portfolio optimization. The process of choosing securities in order to achieve an aim specified by the investor. This is typically to maximize the outcome in terms of **yield**, **coupon**, **duration**, **convexity**, and the cost of managing the portfolio, and subject to constraints such as **maturity**, **diversification**, and **liquidity** (cf. **duration bogey**). The factors which will influence the degree of concentration or diversification in a portfolio are: (i) size of the portfolio under management; (ii) weightings of the average portfolio position; (iii) maximum ownership limits. The problems to be tackled in achieving optimization include issues such as error maximization, unstable solution portfolios, and extreme solution portfolios (cf. **model risk**). See also **efficient portfolios**; **Markowitz portfolio model**.

portfolio option. See basket option.

portfolio risk. The risk that remains after the benefits of diversification obtained through a portfolio. See systematic risk; residual risk; specific risk.

portfolio swap. Equity swap where the underlying is a specific portfolio rather than a standard market index or sub-index.

portfolio theory. See modern portfolio theory (cf. diversification).

portfolio trade. See block trading.

position. (i) The net holding of an investor or dealer in a security or market; or obligation to take delivery (cf. square). (ii) The amount of securities owned: long position; or owed: short position. (iii) An interest in the direction of the market (cf. taking a view). (iv) The sensitivity of a portfolio to changes in market rates or prices. (v) The relative position of futures contracts in the expiry cycle. Thus first position or nearby contract, second position, and so on.

position clerk. An assistant to a dealer or market-maker who is responsible for the prompt reporting of transactions to a firm's back office (cf. middle office).

position delta. See delta.

position gamma. See gamma.

position limit. (i) A formal limit on the number or amount of a position held one side of the market allowed on an organized exchange by a single participant set by the exchange or by regulation. Such restrictions are more likely to apply to commodities where the supply of the particular underlying may be limited rather than financial markets since there is a stronger possibility that a single party may corner the market (cf. supply squeeze). The limit is designed to reduce the risk of market manipulation (cf. concert party; ramp). (ii) A limit to an exposure to a particular risk set by an organization for internal risk management purposes (cf. credit risk; daylight exposure limit). Also called an *exposure limit*.

position theta or **vega.** See vega.

position trader. A trader in a futures market who holds a position for longer than one session.

position trading. A type of dealing involving the holding of open contracts in futures or options for an extended period of time. Such activity may run to months with the trader rolling over contracts as required. This is in contrast to short-term day trading or scalping.

positive basis. See backwardation; basis; discount market.

positive carry. The book accrual profit earned when the cost of borrowing to finance a position is less than the yield on the securities being funded. See carry; negative carry; yield curve.

positive cash flow. (i) A receivable. (ii) The positive difference between operating revenues less fixed and variable costs in a firm or project (cf. negative cash flow).

positive cash flow collar. See forward band.

positive convexity. See convexity.

positive covenant. A covenant provision that requires certain pre-agreed actions or affirmations on the part of the covenanted (cf. affirmative covenant).

positive float. See float.

positive gapping. Borrowing long and lending short (cf. negative gapping). Such a mismatch presupposes an expectation that short-term interest rates will rise. See asset-liability management.

positively sloping yield curve or **positive yield curve.** A yield curve where yields increase for longer maturities. It is sometimes called a *normal yield curve*.

positive sum game. A game, and by extension an economic relationship, where the net benefits to its participants can increase (cf. zero sum game).

posizione scoperta (Italian). Short position.

post. The place on the floor of an exchange where a security or product is traded. It is at this post that the specialist resides during trading hours.

post-Bang (post-Big Bang) (UK). Refers to the market mechanisms on the London Stock Exchange put in place in October 1986.

post-date or **post-dated.** Putting a date later than the current date on a document (cf. ante date).

posted price. (i) The official price at which an asset or commodity may be purchased (cf. consult grade; marker crude). (ii) The price (or rate) at which securities may be purchased. Typically used for continuously offered securities such as money market instruments or medium-term note programmes (cf. scale). Often the price is quoted as a

margin in relation to a **reference rate** or **benchmark** security.

Post-Market Trading (PMT) (USA). After-hours screen trading system operated by the **Chicago Mercantile Exchange** (cf. **GLOBEX**).

pot (USA). That part of a security issue set aside for distribution to dealers or institutional investors. Once such sales are made, the **lead manager** will announce this to the **underwriting syndicate**, the expression used is *the pot is clean.*

pot protection (USA). An arrangement to ensure that the **pot** occurs. It means assuring an institutional investor of an allocation of securities (cf. **book building**).

pound cost averaging. Investing a fixed amount at regular intervals thereby levelling out fluctuations in price (cf. **averaging up; averaging down**).

power bond. A type of **reverse floating rate note** where the **coupon** is set in terms of a multiple of the **fixed rate** at issue less a multiple of the current **floating rate**. It is achieved by entering into more **notional principal** on the **interest rate swaps** than size of issue.

$$\text{Coupon} = \sqrt{(\text{Fixed rate})^2 - (\text{Floating rate})^2}$$

See also **leveraged swap**.

power of attorney. A legal authorization empowering a person to act for another party for a given period of time either for a specific purpose or in general (cf. **agent**).

power swap. A type of **interest rate swap** where the **floating rate** is a multiple of the **reference rate** (cf. **leveraged swap**). See **power bond**.

praecipium or **praecipuum.** That part of the **management fee** in a **euromarkets** transaction that is deducted by the **lead manager** as a special payment before paying the remainder to the management group.

Prague Stock Exchange (Czech Republic). Na Mustka 3, CS-11001 Praha 1 (tel. 42 2242 19855; fax 42 2421 9187). Principal stock exchange in the Czech Republic based in the capital Prague. It was set up as a result of the move to a market economy following the collapse of communism. Similar exchanges exist in the other former command economies in Central Europe as well as the Commonwealth of Independent States (cf. **Russian exchanges**).

predator or **predator company.** A company which is the initiator of a **takeover** attempt (cf. **target**).

prediction. Another name for **forecasting** (cf. **taking a view**).

pre-emption right. The right given to **shareholders** that their relative claim on the company will be maintained in the event of a further issue of **common stock** or **ordinary shares**. This gives them first right of refusal for any new issue pro rata to their existing holding (cf. **rights issue**).

preference equity redemption cumulative stock (PERCS). A type of **convertible preferred stock** issue with a higher **dividend** than the issuer's **common stock**. The PERC converts into common stock on a ratio of one-to-one as long as the stock is trading below the **exercise price**. If the stock price is above the exercise price, the value is reduced such as to give a fraction of the common stock equal to the exercise price. PERC holders thus receive a higher initial dividend on their stock at the expense of surrendering some of the value increase on the common stock, if the price rises above the exercise price. It is conceptually equivalent to holding the **underlying** stock and writing a **call** at the **exercise** price, except that, with PERCS, holders receive some stock in lieu of cash, if the call is exercised (cf. **covered call; long-term equity anticipation security; special claim on residual equity; prescribed right to income and maximum equity**). Also known as a *mandatory conversion premium dividend preferred stock.*

preference option. Another name for a **chooser** option (cf. **double option**).

preference shares (Equities; UK). See **preferred stock**.

preference stock (USA). A senior class of **preferred stock** which is a **hybrid** with attributes of both **debt** and **equity**. Usually they carry a fixed rate of interest (cf. **bearer participation certificate, ordinary shares; participation certificate**). In most cases, preferred stock has a prior claim for **dividends** before **common stock**. It is sometimes known as *prior-preferred stock.*

preferential creditors. That class of creditors who have first call on the debtor's assets. Such preferential creditors tend to include the tax authority and sometimes employees. Their claims must be met prior to those of other creditors (cf. **absolute priority rule**).

preferential form (UK). Under the new issue rules, companies seeking a **listing** on the **London Stock Exchange** may allocate up to 10% of the issue to preferential investors, either employees of the company or, in the case of a subsidiary, the **shareholders** of the parent company. Because these preferential applications are made on (normally) pink coloured forms, these are also known as *pink forms*.

preferred equity redeemable quarterly-pay shares (Equity; USA). See preference equity redemption cumulative stock.

preferred habitat. See market segmentation theory; term structure of interest rates.

preferred ordinary share (Equities; UK). A class of ordinary shares that ranks between ordinary shares and preference shares issued by some UK companies (cf. common stock; preferred stock).

preferred stock or **share.** A general class of equity capital that ranks ahead of common stock or ordinary shares in respect of dividends and the distribution of assets upon liquidation, but junior to debt and with restricted voting rights. Normally preferred stock has a vote if the dividend is in arrears. Dividends are paid from post-company tax profits and in imputation tax systems, it is taxed income to the recipient (cf. franked income). There are a number of different types of preferred stock issues (cf. participation certificate). The basic types are as follows. Note that in some cases these characteristics are combined in the one issue.

- *Participating*: pays a predetermined dividend and shares in some part of the remaining profits;
- *perpetual*: with no stated maturity (although, usually, includes a call provision);
- *Non-participating*: pays a predetermined dividend only;
- *cumulative*: omitted predetermined dividends have to be made up, usually before common stock dividends may be resumed;
- *non-cumulative*: omitted predetermined dividends are lost;
- *fixed dividend*: the rate of dividend payment is fixed at the time of issue;
- *Variable (or adjustable) rate dividend*: the dividend rate is reset in line with an index or reference rate; sometimes known as *floating rate preferred stock*;
- *convertible*: holder has the option to convert into common stock;
- *Exchangeable*: issuer has the right to convert the issue to common stock or debt of the issuer;
- *Pay-in-kind*: dividends are paid in cash or in additional units of preferred stock;
- *Sinking fund*: redemption takes place according to a sinking fund schedule;
- *Redeemable*: the issuer has the right to redeem the stock via a call provision;
- *Fixed maturity*: has a fixed tenor or life with a predetermined maturity date.

Preferred stock is known as *preference shares* in the UK.

preliminary prospectus. A version of a prospectus often circulated to potential investors prior to a new issue but potentially subject to revision and inclusion of the final terms of the offer (cf. pathfinder prospectus; red herring; registration statement).

pre-market. Transactions made between market participants prior to the official opening of trading on an exchange (cf. after-hours trading; kerb trading).

premi (Italian). Short-dated share options on the Milan Stock Exchange.

premier cours (French). Opening price (cf. opening rotation).

premium (i) (Options) The total price of an option contract. It is the consideration paid by the option buyer to the option seller or writer for the option right. See intrinsic value; time value of an option (ii) (Futures) The difference between the futures price and the cash price of the underlying or another future (cf. cash-and-carry). Sometimes called *contango, positive basis,* or *under futures*. See basis. (iii) (Convertible securities) The difference between a convertible's market price and its conversion value expressed as a percentage over the current equity price. (iv) (Forex) The difference between the forward foreign exchange rate and the spot rate. The foreign exchange market quotes forward rates in terms of points. A currency at a premium implies that the currency being quoted is more expensive forward where the value of the premium is expressed in terms of the forward points (cf. discount). (v) (Securities) The amount by which a bond which is trading in the market above its par value (cf. call premium). (vi) The excess price paid for securities in a tender. (vii) A positive price difference to the offer price of a new issue once trading starts, sometimes called a *new issue premium*. (viii) A fee charged by securities lenders. (ix) A general market term for a security which is expensive or dear relative to others of its class, hence the expression *trading at a premium*. (x) The excess over par that an issuer might have to pay in redeeming securities early (cf. call provision). Normally this is a declining schedule towards maturity (cf. redemption price). (xi) Occasionally used instead of spread or margin. (xii) Any excess paid over current market value on a transaction. For instance, when buying a large or controlling block of stock (cf. mergers and acquisitions). (xiii) When the market price for stock in a closed-end investment company trades above net asset value, the stock is said to be at a premium (cf. discount). (xiv) The excess of the issue price to the security's par value on a new issue. (xv) The fee paid to obtain insurance. (xvi) (USA). An option's time value. Often called *premium* *over intrinsic value.* (xvii) (UK) The amount of loss that would arise from an immediate exercise of a **warrant** which has a **strike price** above the current market price of the security (cf. **parity**).

premium bond. (i) A **bond** which trades at a **premium**. (ii) (UK) A special kind of **National Savings** non-negotiable security issued in the UK where the bond pays no interest but is eligible to win money prizes through a **lottery** mechanism, nicknamed **ernie** (Electronic Random Number Indicating Equipment).

premium business (Switzerland). A type of synthetic **call option** created by means of a **cancellable forward contract** where the buyer has the right to acquire **shares** at a given price, or to annul the contract.

premium currrency (Forex). **Currency** which stands at a **premium** in the **forward foreign exchange** market. Due to the no-arbitrage condition of the forward market, this arises due to a lower interest rate in the quoted currency compared to the **base currency** (cf. **discount**). It is not an expectation that the **spot** exchange rate will rise in the future, although the fact that the quoted currency has a lower interest rate has, in the past, led to a stronger currency in the future. See **international Fisher effect; interest rate parity; purchasing power parity.**

premium-free option. See **zero-cost option.**

premium-gearing ratio (UK). The price or value of an **option** or **warrant** divided by the **gearing** of the instrument. The gearing is the price change in the value of the **derivative** instrument for a given price change in the **underlying** (cf. **delta**). Because it ignores the non-linear response of the option to changes in the underlying, it is not an adequate measure of price sensitivity (cf. **gamma**). See also **lambda.**

premium income. (i) The reward the **writer** of an **option** gets from selling the option. Although he gets up-front income from the contract he is obligated to deliver or take **delivery** of the **underlying** if the option should be **exercised.** (ii) For insurance companies, the revenue earned from underwriting insurance or writing policies.

premium market (commodities). A situation where the **forward** or **futures** prices for a particular **commodity** is higher than the current cash price (cf. **backwardation; contango; over futures; under futures**). This is the expected shape for deferred purchases and sales, since there is a cost to holding the physical commodity and the forward price normally reflects this via the **cost of carry** relationship. Also known as *contango*

or a *positive term structure* (cf. discount market). See *normal market* (cf. *yield curve*).

premium over bond value. The value of the **option** to convert to **equity** in a **convertible.**

premium over conversion value. The amount by which a **convertible** exceeds its **conversion value**. This **premium** may be due to the facts that: (*a*) the convertible offers a higher income than holding the **common stock**, if converted (**yield**-conscious investors will bid up the value of the convertible as a result); (*b*) the lowest value a convertible will take will be as a **straight bond** equivalent, thus giving the holder favourable price protection on the investment; (*c*) the **embedded option** gives the right to convert into the common stock of the issuer at some point in the future (cf. **premium over bond value**).

premium put. Term within a **convertible bond** giving the holder a **put provision** allowing the surrender of the bond prior to the final **maturity** at a **premium** to the **face value**, thus providing the holder with a return more in line with a **straight bond** if the **equity** should underperform. Such issues were common in the **eurobond market** in the late 1980s, especially by UK issuers, but, with the fall in **share** prices following the October 1987 crash, proved in the event to be something of a problem to many issuers, having to be renegotiated with holders due to the unforeseen requirement to redeem the issue from holders who wished to **exercise** their put provision.

premium raid (USA). American term for a **dawn raid**. It derives its name from the willingness of the buyer to pay a **premium** to the market for the acquired securities.

premium stripped mortgage backed security (premium STRIP) (Bonds; USA). A combination of interest and principal payments from a **mortgage-backed security** which has a lower proportion of coupon to principal making up the **underlying collateral** to the issue and thus with a smaller **prepayment risk** (cf. **extension risk**). The opposite applies with a **discount stripped mortgage-backed security.**

premium swap. See **high-coupon swap.**

prepackaged Chapter 11 or **prepackaged bankruptcy** (USA). A means of accelerating a firm's reorganization under **Chapter** 11 to stop a minority of creditors from preventing a **workout**. It involves a majority of the firm's **creditors** accepting a plan to reorganize the firm before filing for court protection and then using the court to enforce a **cram down** on the dissenting minority (cf. **assented securities**). Because the plan has been pre-agreed this greatly decreases the time and cost spent under court protection.

prepaid forward sale. A form of forward contract where the buyer agrees to pay the seller the present value of the price in advance. In effect, the buyer has provided a loan to the seller based on the subsequent supply at the forward date. Such contracts are most commonly used in the **commodities markets**, although not limited to them.

prepaid life (Bonds; USA). An early method of analysing **mortgage-backed bonds** which involves making assumptions about the life of the bond by assuming nil then full repayment of the **underlying** mortgages. The approach has been superseded by more sophisticated techniques for analysing **prepayment risk** (cf. **Federal Housing Administration; FHA experience; prepayment model**).

prepaid swap. See reverse zero-coupon swap.

prepayment. A payment made before the scheduled payment date.

prepayment model (USA). A set of predictive models used in the **mortgage-backed securities** market to calculate prepayment rates; for example, the **conditional prepayment rate model; Public Securities Association prepayment model**. Most active financial intermediaries in this market have their own proprietary models. Such models take account of the past behaviour of mortgage borrowers to prepay due to changed circumstances, such as moving home, as well as predictions of **refinancing** behaviour due to changes in interest rates (cf. **embedded option; FHA experience; negative convexity**). See **prepayment option**.

prepayment option. (i) The right given to people who take out a mortgage to prepay before the final **maturity**. In **mortgage-backed securities** (MBS) it then becomes **prepayment risk** since, if the **underlying** is redeemed, so are the securities (cf. **extension risk**). It is most acute if the MBS is at a **fixed rate**, since prepayments will be highest when interest rates fall (cf. **negative convexity; pass-through certificates; prepayment model**). (ii) Sometimes used to describe the issuer's right to **exercise** his **call provision** in a **callable bond**. Also called the *option to prepay*.

prepayment penalty. A fee paid to compensate lenders for **reinvestment risk**. Early repayments by a borrower in many contracts require the payment of a fee or penalty, often expressed in terms of the interest rate. For instance, a **lease** might require the payment of three months' interest if terminated early. Some agreements allow for a

declining penalty as the transaction nears **maturity** (cf. **declining call schedule**).

prepayment rate. Usually associated with **asset-backed** issues and, in particular, **mortgage-backed securities**, it is the rate at which the **underlying** assets (or mortgages) are repaid by borrowers, and hence paid down to investors in the asset-backed security (cf. **amortization; revolving period**).

prepayment reserve fund (USA). A **fund** designed to protect mortgage investors against early **prepayment** of a significant amount of mortgage **principal**.

prepayment risk. The **risk** that a security will be redeemed or repaid before expected. This is a significant risk for **mortgage-backed securities** and bonds with **call provisions** or redemption schedules linked to mortgage repayments such as **pass-through certificates** (cf. **collateralized mortgage obligations**). It is also connected in effect with **reinvestment risk** (cf. **extension risk**).

prepetition debt (USA). Financial obligations of a firm entered into before the company filed for Chapter 11 protection under the US Bankruptcy Code (cf. **debtor in possession facility**).

pre-refunding. Anticipatory debt raising in advance of a **refunding**. Such activities are designed to take advantage of market **windows** or favourable conditions, such as an **inverse yield curve** where an issuer can sell **bonds** and have **positive carry** until the funds are needed. Sometimes called *anticipatory refunding*.

pre-sale order. A purchase order given in anticipation of an issue being launched. In some regulatory environments, such orders are not allowed or are illegal (cf. **book building grey market; when issued**).

prescribed or **prescription period.** That period determined by law which must elapse before the amount due under a contract, such as a redeemable security, no longer becomes payable. See **redemption**.

prescribed right to income and maximum equity (PRIME) (Equities; USA). A synthetic security, which behaves much like an **option**, created by combining a **stock** and a written option position on an **equity portfolio** where the holder receives the **dividend**, plus a limited amount of **capital gain**. The other part is a pure capital gain instrument, like a **call option** called **special claim on residual equity (SCORE)** (cf. **long-term equity anticipation security; preference equity redemption cumulative stock**). By combining different proportions of the two instruments holders can modify the payoffs of their holding, ranging from being fully invested in the PRIME (high income-generating strategy) to being fully invested in the SCORE (speculative, capital gains strategy), or somewhere between.

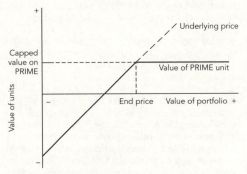

Value of SCORE unit = value of portfolio
– CAP value on PRIME unit

Prescribed right to income

present value (PV). The current worth of a payment or a stream of payments discounted at a given interest rate (cf. **annuity**). The **future value** becomes a present value through the process of discounting (cf. **compound interest**). The formula to calculate the present value of a future value item is:

$$\text{Present value} = \frac{\text{Future value}}{(1+r)^t}$$

where r is the discount rate, expressed in terms of a periodic rate, and t the number of time periods. For a cash stream, the above becomes:

$$\text{Present value} = \sum_{t=1}^{n} \frac{\text{Item at time } t}{(1+r_t)^t}$$

See also **discounted cash flow**; **net present value**.

Presidential Task Force on Market Mechanisms (Brady Commission) (USA). An investigative commission set up to look at the events surrounding the October 1987 crash and to make specific recommendations to improve market mechanisms. The committee, headed by George Brady, then Treasury Secretary, examined the roles of **program trading** and **margin requirements**, and the need for **circuit breakers** (cf. **cascade theory**).

presold issue. An issue of securities that is sold before it is finally priced.

Prestel Citiservice (UK). A private business and financial viewdata service on Prestel (delivered via television).

pre-tax earnings or **pre-tax profits**. Income after interest, but before taxes. See **earnings before taxes**.

pre-tax rate of return. The yield before any taxes on income or **capital gains** on an asset or investment.

prezzo di apertura (Italian). **Opening** price.

prezzo di riferimento (literally, reference price) (Italian). **Closing range** used to determine the **opening price** on the exchange.

prezzo limite (Italian). Price limit.

price. See **clean price**; **dirty price**; **market price**; **par value**.

price–book ratio. See **market-to-book ratio**.

price discovery. An effect of **futures markets** where information on the **underlying**'s future price movements is embodied in the current **futures** price. In principle, **spot** prices should be related to futures prices by the **cost of carry**, that is the **time value of money** (i.e. the futures price should be not be open to **riskless arbitrage**), and therefore give a consensual forecast of the expected spot price to prevail at the contract's **expiry**. However, three extraneous factors might affect the value of futures prices: a term **premium**, a **reinvestment rate premium**, and a **hedging** premium. Fluctuations in these may cause the price movements of futures and spot prices to diverge slightly, a problem known as **basis risk**. See also **basis**.

price–dividend ratio (PDR; P/D ratio). The number of times that a company's **dividends per share** go into the current market price of that share. It is calculated by taking the current price and dividing it by the dividends per share over the latest twelve-month period.

price–earnings multiple or **price–earnings ratio (PE multiple; PER; PE ratio; P/E ratio).** The ratio of the **common stock** or ordinary share price to the **earnings per share** over the latest twelve-month period. The higher the ratio, the higher the market's expectation of future earnings growth. It is sometimes called the *price-multiple*. The reciprocal of the P/E ratio is the *earnings yield*, which is also sometimes called the *capitalisation rate*. See **earnings analysis**.

price factor. The delivery factor for the **notional bond** in a **bond futures contract** used to convert the **deliverable bonds** with their different **coupons** and hence market prices to an approximately equal value (cf. **cheapest to deliver**).

price fix buying or **price fix selling** (UK). Term used on the **London Metal Exchange** for a **Long Hedge**.

price index. See consumer price index; producer prices index; retail price index.

price jump or **gap**. The opening price being outside the trading range of the previous day. For example a jump would occur if the price ranged from $92\frac{3}{4}$ to $95\frac{1}{2}$ during the session and opened the next day at $101\frac{1}{4}$ (cf. limit up; limit down).

price limit. Some exchanges and their regulatory body impose *price limits* on how far the price may move before trading is temporarily suspended:
  up limit: maximum price rise allowed, also known as *limit up*.
  down limit: maximum price fall allowed, also known as *limit down*.
The use of price limits is designed to safeguard the credit standing of exchange. Due to margin requirements; up and down limits are normally set close to **initial margin** put up by participants such that the exchange's **clearing house** remains fully covered by **collateral** for the session (cf. **margin call; variation margin**). See **limit** (cf. **circuit breakers**).

price model. A way of assessing the equilibrium price of **bonds** by deriving discount functions for both **coupons** and redemption values from current market prices (cf. **term structure of interest rates**). See spot rate.

price of non-conformance. A term derived from total quality management (TQM) that measures the costs of not getting it right the first time.

price range. The highest and lowest prices transacted over a given period, typically a day; week; month; year. Sometimes used as a measure of price volatility.

price risk. The risk that a security's price may change due to changed market conditions. See market risk.

price-sensitivity hedge ratio. A hedge ratio used to determine the number of **futures** that must be sold (bought) to **immunize** a fixed rate long (short) position. See duration-based hedge ratio.

price spread. See vertical spread.

price to book ratio. See market-to-book ratio.

price to net tangible assets ratio. See market-to-book ratio.

price value of a basis point (PVBP). See value of an 01.

price-weighted index. A type of index where the weights are determined by the price of the security (cf. **geometric average**).

pricing. The setting of the final terms of a securities issue or loan (cf. **bought deal**).

pricing sensitivities. See option pricing.

primary capital (Banking). That part of a bank's capital that is deemed fundamental by a regulator (cf. **supplementary capital**). See **Basle Capital Convergence Accord; capital adequacy; tier 1**.

primary capital preferred stock (Equities; USA). An issue of **preferred stock** by a bank which at maturity has a mandatory conversion into the common stock of the issuer and thus qualifies as **primary capital** for regulatory purposes. To make the issue more attractive to investors, the bank will normally arrange for a cash alternative by averaging the sale of common stock in the market at, or just before, **maturity**. A debt variant of the above exists, most typically issued as a **floating rate note** and known as a **capital note**.

primary commodities. See commodities.

primary dealer (i). (USA) A trader in government securities who enjoys certain benefits provided by the **Federal Reserve**. It is with these institutions that the Fed conducts its open-market operations. (ii) Reporting **dealer** in the gilt-edged market, reporting to the **Bank of England**. Better known as a *gilt-edged market-maker* (GEMM).

primary earnings per share (primary EPS). See earnings per share.

primary issue. A new issue of securities (cf. secondary issue).

primary market. The market in which new issues are sold or placed (cf. **secondary market**). See new issues market (cf. after-market; grey market; when issued).

primary metals. See commodities.

primary reserves (Banking; USA). The legal minimum reserve requirements that have to be met by banks. See contemporaneous reserve accounting; secondary reserves.

primary securities. See fundamental financial instruments.

primary underwriter. An institution that agrees to underwrite an entire new issue of securities. The primary underwriter may offset its risk through sub-underwriting. (cf. block trade; bought deal)

prime (USA). See prime rate.

prime bank. A bank of high, or best, credit worthness. Such banks command fine rates in the interbank market (cf. money center bank).

prime/London interbank offered rate swap (prime/LIBOR swap). A basis swap between the prime rate and London interbank offered rate (cf. floating/floating swap).

prime paper. Best-quality commercial paper as rated by Moody's Investor Services. It has a *P-1* rating. See credit ratings; investment grade.

prime rate (Banks; USA). (i) The rate at which US banks theoretically lend to borrowers of the highest standing, i.e. their prime customers (cf. base rate (UK). Higher-risk customers pay the prime rate plus a margin, reflecting the credit risk. (ii) It can sometimes be taken to be an average of major banks' prime rates.

prime underwriting facility (PUF). A little-used way of pricing a euronote facility using US domestic market prime rates.

primitive security. Any security or instrument where the payment depends on the financial status or ability to pay of the issuer. Contrast with a derivative, where the price depends on factors beyond the characteristics of the issuer which can be related to the prices of other assets (cf. rainbow option). See also fundamental financial instruments.

principal. (i) A contracting party acting on its own account or through an agent, agency broker, or market-maker. (ii) (Banking and debt markets) The amount of an advance, loan, or debt, excluding any interest that must be repaid. (iii) The amount invested. (iv) Also used as shorthand for principal value (excluding interest and/or any premium).

principal-agent problem. See agency theory.

principal amount. The face value of an obligation. See principal.

principal balance. The amount of principal remaining to be paid back in an amortizing debt or security, excluding interest.

principal exchange rate linked security (PERLS). A variety of currency-linked note.

principal guaranteed bond or **note.** Any of a number of embedded option structures where the interest earned on the invested principal in the bond or note is used to purchase calls (or sometimes puts) on an asset, index, commodity, or currency. The most popular structure relates to equity investment in an index. They are typically constructed by using the present value of the interest forgone to purchase the required options and, depending on the structure, only offer a sub-market rate of interest or none at all to the holders of the notes, although the initial investment or principal is not at risk and is guaranteed to be returned at maturity. See equity-linked note; guaranteed return on investment certificate.

principal only stripped mortgage-backed security (PO; PO STRIP) (Bonds; USA). Part of a combination of cash flows created by separating the interest and principal payments from a mortgaged-backed security (MBS), the other part being known as an interest only stripped mortgage-backed security (IO; IO STRIP). The security is effectively a type of zero coupon but one where the repayment is positively linked to movements in interest rates since a fall in rates is likely to trigger the refinancing of mortgages at a lower rate (cf. extension risk; prepayment risk). The leverage imparted by the structure makes these securities very sensitive to changes in interest rates (about four times as sensitive as the underlying mortgage-backed security), making them attractive instruments in a bull market. Investors can achieve tailored exposures to the MBS market by holding different combinations of IO and PO securities. IOs and POs are part of what are known as *mortgage derivatives*.

principal only swap. See zero-coupon swap.

principal paying agent. The paying agent responsible for managing all the paying agents to an issue or loan. Typically only required in international transactions where the holders may be domiciled in different countries or time zones.

principal protected. Any financial structure or security incorporating option features where the initial investment is not at risk, although the amount of return will be linked to the payoffs from the embedded option. See equity-linked note.

principal risk. The risk of loss to invested principal rather than income (cf. credit risk).

principal stockholder (USA). The Securities and Exchange Commission classifies any shareholder with over 10 % of the voting stock as a principal stockholder and also as an insider.

principal-to-principal. Transactions directly between clients and **market-makers** without the intermediation of an exchange. This is the norm for over-the-counter markets (cf. **direct search market**; **head-to-head**).

principal Treasury receipt (principal TR) (USA). See corpus Treasury receipt.

principal value. The amount stated on the face of a security in the units of value in which the security is issued. It is used to calculate the amount of interest due on the security (cf. **maturity value**). Sometimes called **face value** or *nominal value*. See **par**.

Principles and Practices for Wholesale Financial Market Transactions (USA). Voluntary code of conduct established for the **over-the-counter** wholesale markets in derivatives.

prior charges. (i) The interest obligation on **debentures** and **loan stock** that must be met before distributions to **equity** can occur. (ii) The loan capital, **preferred stock** and other **debt** ranking before **common stock** (**ordinary shares**) for payment of income and claims on the **assets** of the firm in the event of **liquidation**.

prior claim. An overriding obligation that must be met from either **income** or **assets**, or both (cf. **prior charges**). See **junior**; **paripassu**; **priority**; **senior debt**; **subordinated debt**.

priority. The ranking of different claims on a firm. See **class**; **junior**; **secured debt**; **subordinated debt**.

priority percentages. An expression of the **gearing** or **leverage** of a company's profit. Calculated using net profit and the net amount taken up in interest. Then, in order of priority, the cost of interest and dividend payments is compared with this sum. Said to put into perspective the amount of flexibility in the profit figures for the servicing of all the company's obligations (cf. **interest coverage ratio**). This is the proportion of profits or assets needed to satisfy the income requirement or principal repayment of a security. See **earnings analysis**.

prior-lien bond (USA). A bond issue by a corporation which has a first claim on the **assets**, although of the same class as other securities by the same issuer (cf. **pari passu**).

prior-preferred stock. See preference stock.

prior year adjustments (Accounting). Changes to reported accounting items in prior **financial years** to make them compatible with the latest reported year.

private activity municipal bonds (Bonds; USA). See private purpose bond.

private bank. (i) An unquoted bank. (ii) A bank engaged in servicing the needs of high **net-worth individuals**. An activity called *private banking*.

private company. A company which is not a public company and which is usually not allowed to offer its **common stock** or **ordinary shares** to the general public. See also **close company**.

private investor. See retail.

private limited partnership (USA). A limited partnership which is not registered with the Securities and Exchange Commission (cf. **public limited partnership**).

privately held corporation. See unquoted.

private placement or **private placing**. A type of **placement** where new securities are sold by the **lead manager** (often called an *arranger*) to a limited number of investors, usually their own clients, rather than being offered to a wider public. It is private in the sense that little need be disclosed to third parties and usually the securities are not listed, although **back door listing** may take place at a later date (cf. **initial public offer** and **offer for sale**). In the USA such issues do not have to be registered with the **Securities and Exchange Commission** (cf. **Portal**; **registration**; **Rule 144a**; **institutional investor**). In the Swiss market, private placements are quasi-public transactions and reported in the press.

private purpose bond (USA). A type of **municipal bond** where the beneficiaries of the funds raised are private activities and therefore the issue is not federal tax exempt (cf. **public purpose bond**). Such issues are accordingly sometimes called *taxable municipal bonds*.

privatization. (i) The sale by the government of state-owned assets and businesses. The logic of privatization is both to raise funds for the government and to change the mentality and management of the privatized business, the argument being that the private sector is better at running commercial or quasi-commercial enterprises. Also called *denationalisation*. (ii) The introduction of private sector activities into the state sector, either in competition or to supplant current state-provided services. (iii) Contracting out to the private sector of activities previously undertaken by the state.

privileged subscription issue. A rights issue.

privilege money (Banking; UK). An agreement allowing **discount houses** in the London market to borrow overnight funds from certain banks in order to be able to balance their accounts by the 3 p.m. cut-off time for same-day **settlement**.

privileges (UK). Old-fashioned term for an **option**. It is no longer used.

prix limite (French). **Stop out price**.

prize draw account. Deposit account where the interest that could be earned is used instead to pay out a number of prizes as with a **lottery** (cf. **premium bond**).

probability density function (PDF). The area under the curve for a continuous **probability distribution**.

probability distribution. This is a model of an actual or empirically observed distribution of outcomes. It is fundamental to the analysis and pricing of many **derivative** instruments since they depend on the price- or rate-generating process of the **underlying** for their value. The two most common models for such distributions are the **lognormal distribution** used in the **Black–Scholes option pricing model** and the binomial distribution used in the **binomial option pricing model**. In the first case, the distribution is continuous, while in the latter it is discrete. The discrete model is probably more representative of the price-generating process in financial markets but requires a numerical solution, as used in the binomial option pricing model (cf. **geometric Brownian motion**; **Wiener process**).

problem asset, problem credit, or **problem loan** (Banking). An **asset** pledged as **collateral**, an obligation owed by a **counterparty**, and a loan which is non-performing and likely to result in a loss. See **charge-off**; **non-performing loans**.

problem child. One of the four categories in the Boston Consulting Group strategy matrix (cf. **cash cow**; **dog**; **star**). See **Boston matrix**.

processing float. See **float**.

procuration. See **per pro**.

produce. See **commodities**.

produce broker. Another name for a commodity broker. See **broker**; **broker-dealer**; **commission broker**.

producer prices index (PPI) (USA). A measure of costs of wholesale materials used in manufacturing and the price of intermediate goods; that is, not for final consumption (cf. **retail price index**). The **index** provides details of raw materials, inter-mediate goods, and finished products by industry sector.

producer's hedge. See **short hedge**.

product differentiation. The degree to which a product or service has unique characteristics and is distinct from that of competitors.

production payment financing (Banking). A type of **non-recourse project finance** where a part of the income or output from the project is used to service the debt.

production rate (Bonds; USA). The **coupon** rate on a **Government National Mortgage Association** issue.

Professional Standards Panel (UK). A part of the **London Stock Exchange** and the system of **self-regulating organizations** in the UK. The panel investigates allegations of breach of conduct (cf. **conduct of business rules**).

profile options. Any **option** or option-like structure which has a capped return (cf. **cap**). See **collar**; **breakforward**; **digital options**; **range forward**.

profitability index (PI). Used in **capital budgeting** or investment appraisal. It is the ratio of the **net present value** of the project or investment, divided by the total amount invested. Thus it removes the size effect allowing different projects to be compared in terms of the added-value per unit of invested capital.

profitability ratios. See **ratio analysis**.

profit and loss account. Statement of the profit (or loss) in a given period made by a business made up from the business's books. It normally consists of three separate parts: (i) the trading account, showing the total **turnover** or **sales** for the period less the direct costs of making those sales, plus changes in **inventories,** the net position being the gross profit (loss); (ii) overheads required to maintain the business, together with any non-trading income (this gives the net income or net profit); and (iii) the allocation of this profit (or loss) between **dividends,** taxes, and retained profit. Also called an *income statement* or *statement of income*.

profit before interest and taxes (PBIT). See **earnings before interest and tax**.

profit before taxes (PBT). See **earnings before tax**.

profit forecast. Announcement made by the firm's managers as to the profit to be expected in a given period. If profits are likely to be less than generally expected, it is known as a *profits warning*.

profit margin. The ratio of costs or assets to return, usually expressed as a percentage. Also called *return on sales*.

profit participating securities (Bonds). A type of floating rate note which has its **coupon** linked to the profits of the issuer. Typically such payments are bounded and the result is equivalent to a **minimax bond**. A variant has the equivalent but with a reversed linkage on, the principle that a fall in profits increases the **risk,** and hence the holder's required return, on the security.

profit participation certificate. Participation certificate that pays a **dividend** in relation to the stated profit of the issuer.

profit-sharing forward (profit-share forward). See participating forward.

profit sharing option (profit-share option). See participating option.

profit-taking. (i) The selling of an asset or financial instrument in order to realize its **capital gain** (cf. **paper profit**). (ii) Periods in securities markets when the prices of particular **stocks** or securities are considered to have reached a peak and profit-taking selling is putting downward pressure on prices. See also **technical analysis**

pro forma financial statement. A projected financial statement at some future date. Normally used to show a firm's **financial statements** after a transaction has been completed, for instance an **initial public offering**.

programme. An arrangement between a **dealer** or banks and an issuer for the sale of short-term **eurocommercial paper, certificates of deposit,** or **medium-term notes** on a **best efforts basis**. Such arrangements are not **underwritten** (cf. **facility**).

programmed slam. A particular type of program trading under which purchases or sales are automatically executed when the market slips back from a discernible peak.

programme for the issuance of mortgage-backed securities (PIMBS) (Bonds; UK). A type of **mortgage-backed** issue using standard terms and conditions thus reducing **securitization** costs when repeating the same operation. The notes are called *PIMBS 1, PIMBS 2,* and so forth.

program trading. A trading strategy based on automated real-time analysis of market rates and prices intended to exploit periodic anomalies

between the money, capital, **option,** and **futures** markets. There are three basic variants: *index arbitrage*—a purchase (sale) programme designed to exploit anomalies, also known as *buy (sell) programs; portfolio insurance*—transactions are triggered at predetermined price points in order to maintain portfolio returns; *basket trading*—large transactions in **blocks** of **stocks** aimed at changing the portfolio's **market risk** (cf. **block trading**). See also **quantitative analysis; technical analysis**.

progressive tax system. A method of levying taxes where the payment is linked to the amount of taxable income such that the ratio or percentage of tax levied increases with levels of income. The opposite approach would be a flat rate of tax, levied as a fixed percentage of income.

progress payment. Intermediate payment made during the course of a contract or transaction on evidence of progress being made. Thus managers of a project may require reports affirming progress before disbursing funds to pay contractors for work already undertaken.

project. (i) A stand-alone activity. (ii) An investment, usually used in a business rather than a fund management context, involving a medium-to long-term commitment of resources. See **capital budgeting**.

project finance. A form of asset-based financing where the claims of the debtholders are against an **asset** or **project** rather than against the **sponsor** as a whole. The exact terms and conditions vary considerably depending on the degree of **recourse** and the undertakings made by the sponsor of the project. Sometimes referred to as *limited recourse finance*.

project line (Banking). A credit facility provided in connection with a particular project. **Disbursements** under the facility may require documentary proof of the intended use for the funds.

project note (Money markets; USA). An issue by a municipal agency or urban renewal agency of **short-term** notes to finance the construction of a housing project. When the construction is complete, the notes are normally refinanced via a **bond** issue. Project notes and bonds are normally guaranteed by the US Department of Housing and Urban Development and therefore trade like **agencies**.

project pass-through. Pass-through certificate where the **underlying** is a pool of building projects. Tends to have a longer **expected maturity** due to the nature of the **assets** as well as **call protection**.

project sponsor. The originator of a project who has the residual or **equity** claim on the project. See **sponsor**.

promissory note. An unconditional undertaking made by a debtor to pay a certain sum on demand or at a fixed or determinable future date (cf. **bill**; **commercial paper**; **eurocommercial paper**).

promoter. Another name for a **sponsor**.

prompt date or **day** (Commodities). The **delivery date** for the **physical commodity** for transactions on the **London Metal Exchange**. The **settlement price** is set two business days (**spot**) before the prompt date.

pronti-contro-termine (P/T) (Italian). Repurchase agreements.

property bond. An investment scheme offered by insurance companies, usually as a single premium, where the return is linked to the performance of a fund invested mainly in property.

property futures (UK). **Futures contracts** introduced on the **London Futures and Options Exchange** which was designed to hedge property values. The contract was based on an **index** of a large body of property valuations as estimated by Chartered Surveyors. The contract suffered from lack of **liquidity** and evidence of market manipulation.

property income certificate (PIC) (UK). A synthetic property security designed to provide holders with a direct exposure to property returns based on the performance of the Investment Property Databank Indices (IPD Indices). The returns from PICs are based on changes to both the rental income and capital value of the indices.

property investment certificate (PINC) (UK). A tradable entitlement to the **pro rata share** in the rental income from a single property, plus that of the management company running the property. It does not involve the direct ownership of the property and the management company can issue debt so the **equity** investor can benefit from **gearing** or **leverage** effects on returns. The security is designed to allow investors to obtain direct exposure to property without the consequent illiquidity and high transaction costs. PINCs will be limited to a single property to remove the valuation problems inherent in a property portfolio. Investors can diversify their holdings by buying different issues of PINCs. See also **single asset property company**.

property unitization. See **property income certificate**; **single asset property company**; **single property ownership trust**.

proportional representation. A method of allocating votes between **shareholders** in pro-portion to the amount of **equity** held. See **cumulative voting**; **majority voting**; **minority protection**; **supermajority**.

proprietary limited (Pty Ltd.) (Australia). Form of incorporation for **close companies**.

proprietary trading. Own account trading by a financial institution not designed to facilitate customers' transactions but aimed at exploiting anomalies or market imperfections (cf. **scalping**).

proprietorship. A legal form of business organization directly linked to an individual, the proprietor. Also known as a *sole trader*. When more than one party agree to join together for the purposes of conducting a business activity, this creates a **partnership** (cf. **limited partner**). See also **limited liability**.

pro rata (Latin: in proportion). It is the principle of sharing out and involves payments or benefits allocated according to investment or ownership. A *pro rata sinking fund* would thus retire part of the issue proportionally by ownership (cf. **serial amortization**; **sinking fund**).

pro rata stripped mortgage-backed security (Bonds; USA). A **collateralized mortgage obligation** security where redemptions of the principal occur **pro rata** to the paydown of the underlying mortgages (cf. **collateralized mortgage obligation equity**).

ProShare (UK). Organization aimed at promoting wider **ordinary share** ownership, including that of company employees. See **employee stock ownership plan**.

prospectus. A legal disclosure document supporting a transaction circulated at the time of a **new issue** to existing and potential investors which details the nature, price, and timing of the issue of securities to be made and gives financial and other information about the issuer (cf. **pathfinder prospectus**; **preliminary prospectus**). It is usually prepared by the issuer's adviser or **sponsor** and contains a description of the issuer, a historical record of earnings performance, and a forecast of future profit. In the USA, a prospectus must be filed with the **Securities and Exchange Commission** prior to the sale of the new issue (cf. **due diligence**; **red herring**; **registration**). In the **eurobond** market, the prospectus may only become available after the issue has been launched (cf. **offering telex**). For issues admitted to listing on the **London Stock Exchange**, **listing particulars** may substitute for a prospectus. Sometimes called an *offering circular* or *offering memorandum*. See **Extel Statistical Services**.

protect, protection. Market term for a guarantee on price or quantity in a transaction. For example, the **lead manager** or **book runner** in a new issue will offer protection to syndicate members, thus guaranteeing them an agreed amount (which may be more than their **underwriting** commitment in some cases).

protected bear. See covered bear.

protected equity note. See equity-linked note.

protected equity participation (PEP). A type of **equity-linked note** where the **underlying** is a single **common stock** or a small **portfolio** of stocks. They have no **caps** on the upward potential gain from the price appreciation of the underlying.

protected index participation (PIP). Similar to a protected equity participation note where the **underlying** is a **stock index**.

protective covenant. See covenants (cf. **affirmative covenant**; **negative covenant**).

protective put. A protection strategy where the investor's **long position** is fully or partially value protected by buying **put** options on the **underlying**. It is functionally equivalent to holding a **call** on the underlying, except that, by owning the underlying asset, holders can receive any **coupons** or **dividends** that are paid. Also known as *portfolio insurance*.

protest. (i) The situation where a bank refuses to accept or pay a **bill of exchange**. (ii) (USA) In the context of **open-market operations** by the **Federal Reserve**, when **Fed funds** have been giving misleading signals, the desk (the operating arm of the Fed) has undertaken a *rate protest* through its operations to correct the market's impression of its policy intentions.

provincial bond (Canada). A bond issued by one of the provinces of Canada. Coupon interest is paid semi-annually.

provision (i) (Accounting) A sum set aside in the accounts of an organization in anticipation of a future expense and known as a *provision account* or a *reserve account*. Typically banks will make provisions against **bad debts** (cf. **problem loans**). Also known as *reserving*. (ii) A clause or stipulation made in advance within the terms and conditions of a contract usually giving one party a specific right (cf. **call provision**; **clean-up call provision**; **early redemption put option**; **put provision**). See also **covenants**.

provisional allotment letter (UK). The renounceable document received by **shareholders** when a company makes a **rights issue** or **scrip issue**.

provisional liquidator (UK). A court-appointed **liquidator** after the presentation of a petition to wind up a business's affairs, but before the appointment of a liquidator (cf. **administrator**).

provision for bad debts. See bad debts; provision for loan losses.

provision for depreciation. See depreciation.

provision for loan losses (PLL) (Banking). The charge against **earnings** or profit in the **income statement** required to maintain the **reserve for loan losses** at an adequate level to reflect the expected losses inherent in the loan **portfolio**.

proxy or **proxy vote.** Voting rights on resolutions proposed at meetings that are assigned to be voted by another. Proxies are a common feature of most voting arrangements in financial markets. Assignment may be either general, in which case it can be applied at any meeting; or specific to a particular meeting or, indeed, resolution.

proxy contest or **proxy fight.** The use of **shareholders'** votes at company meetings to influence the incumbent management, to make or obtain favourable resolutions, or to take control of the firm by replacing the management.

proxy statement (USA). The information that is distributed on a pending **shareholders'** vote as required by the **Securities and Exchange Commission**.

prudence concept (Accounting). A principle used in the preparation of a statement of financial condition that requires that the statement should be prepared on a conservative basis. The basic principle is to be cautious, to recognize all costs, committed or incurred, but not to recognize revenues or profits until actually received.

prudent-man rule (USA). A criterion for managing money adopted in some states. It requires those entrusted with handling other people's affairs to act as a prudent person would (i.e. conservatively). It is also used to govern the types of investment considered acceptable under the provisions of the **Employee Retirement Income Security Act**. An alternative method used is to prescribe a list of acceptable investments, known as the *legal list* (cf. **investment grade**). Also known as the *prudent expert rule*.

pseudo-American option pricing model. A variant of the **Black–Scholes option pricing model** used to value **options** when the **underlying**

pays a **dividend**. The approach is to value the option (*a*) at **expiry** and (*b*) at the **ex-dividend date**, the higher of the two values derived being used to price the option. This takes into account the value of the **early exercise** right in **American-style** options where the holder can capture the dividend by exercising before expiry (cf. **time value of an option**).

public company (UK). A company whose **shares** are available to be bought by members of the public (cf. **listed; private company**).

public corporation (UK). Name given to state-owned organizations set up to run a particular activity. The best-known example is the British Broadcasting Corporation (BBC).

public float The portion of a firm's outstanding **share capital** that is available to be traded in the market. It excludes **shares** held by the firm's **directors**, officers, or investors with a **controlling interest**.

public housing authority bond (USA). A type of **municipal** issue which is arranged by the US Department of Housing and Urban Development which also guarantees to meet interest and **principal** payments.

public issue (Equities). An offer of **common stock** or **ordinary shares** to the public by subscription (cf. **initial public offering; offer for sale; placing**).

public limited company (PLC; plc) (UK). Company which has over £50,000 in authorized share capital with a minimum of £12,500 paid up. It does not denote a **listed** company (cf. **quoted**). The other, smaller form of company retains the traditional *limited company* definition. Under the Companies Acts, the regulation of plcs is more demanding than that of private companies.

public limited partnership (USA). A type of **limited partnership** that is offered to the public and as a result is registered with the **Securities and Exchange Commission**. Such an investment vehicle is used for specific project investments such as real estate, oil and gas exploration and development, venture capital, leveraged buy-outs, and so forth (cf. **master limited partnership**).

public limit order (USA). Special type of **limit order** where the transaction is carried out by a member of the exchange rather than a **broker**.

public limit order board. A derivatives exchange limit board service for the orders of private customers. It enables **brokers** to leave such limit orders with the exchange for execution.

publicly held or **publicly traded** (USA). A corporation which is regulated by the **Securities and Exchange Commission** and where ownership is usually widely dispersed (cf. **private company**).

public market order (USA). See **order book official**.

public offering (i) (USA) The sale by a firm of **registered securities** to the public. Under US securities laws all securities offered to the public must be registered with the **Securities and Exchange Commission**. The offering may be direct by the firm or, more commonly, through a **syndicate** of **underwriters**. A *public offering price* is the price at which underwriters offer such securities to the public. Offerings are of two types: **secondary** and **primary**. A **secondary distribution** refers to a widely distributed sale of additional new securities of a type already held by investors. Also known as a *registered secondary offering*. A **primary issue** is for securities where there is no previous security which is publicly traded (cf. **initial public offering; private placement**). (ii) In other countries, the term is used for new issues which are simultaneously **listed** on a recognized exchange (cf. **offer for sale**).

public order correspondent member (POCM) (Netherlands). A **broker** member of the **European Options Exchange** who has the capacity to accept trading instructions but has to execute them through a **public order member**.

public order member (POM) (Netherlands). A broker-dealer member of the **European Options Exchange** who may accept trading instructions from clients and who may transact for his own account via **floor brokers**.

public placing. See **placing**.

public purpose bond (USA). A **municipal bond** which meets the federal **tax-exempt** requirements of being primarily used to fund a public good.

public sector. The central, local, municipal, and state-owned companies within a country, i.e. that which belongs to the state or the community. The rest is the *private sector*, that is, privately owned.

public sector borrowing requirement (PSBR) (UK). The annual budget deficit of the UK government and local authorities together with lending to the private sector and overseas which has to be funded by borrowing (cf. **Central Government Borrowing Requirement**. In other countries known as the *public sector deficit*. See **fiscal policy**.

public sector debt reduction (PSDR) (UK). The annual budget surplus of the UK government, together with lending to the private sector and overseas which is used to repay debt. In other countries known as the *public sector surplus*. See fiscal policy.

Public Securities Association (PSA) (USA). Association for dealers in the agency, municipal, and mortgage-backed securities markets.

Public Securities Association prepayment model (PSA prepayment model) (Bonds; USA). A model of prepayment patterns on mortgage-backed bonds prepared by the PSA.

public subscription (USA). See offer for sale (cf. purchase and sale).

public works. Public sector sponsored projects, which may be funded from general revenues or be directly financed through borrowing (cf. municipal bonds).

pulling-in the stops. Refers to a situation where judicious buying or selling which moves the market price can then trigger a significant price movement as the new price activates the outstanding stop orders, which puts further pressure on the price and this, in turn, triggers further stops, and so on (cf. portfolio insurance; tick). See also cascade theory.

pull to maturity or **pull to par.** The trend for a bond to gravitate towards its par value as it approaches maturity. Bonds with a higher than market coupon will lose value as the redemption date approaches; bonds with below market coupons, will rise towards par (cf. accretion; amortization; discount; premium).

pumping in reserves (Banking; USA). See draining reserves.

pump priming. Another name for deficit financing.

punt. Common slang term for speculative trading. Hence, to punt in a stock is to trade speculatively (cf. spectail). See also arbitrage.

punti swap (Italy). Type of open-market operation involving banks tendering foreign currency spot to the Bank of Italy in exchange for repayment in the forward market. It is used both as a flexible means of obtaining currency reserves and to provide liquidity to the money markets.

purchase accounting. See merger accounting.

purchase agent. A financial institution authorized by an issuer with a security with a purchase

fund provision to use its best efforts to buy in outstanding securities.

purchase agreement. (i) In project finance a condition that the project sponsor will purchase an agreed amount of the project's output over a specified period (cf. hell or high water; take-or-pay contract). (ii) In the securities markets, an underwriting agreement. See purchase group agreement.

purchase and sale (USA). An underwritten transaction where a purchase group buys securities from an issuer and sells them to investors (cf. best efforts).

purchased accelerated recovery right (PARR). A financial instrument that holds the rights to any recoveries of previously written off bad debts by banks. The issuer, normally the bank, can exchange an uncertain (and, for regulatory and accounting purposes, valueless) potential gain against a known payment. The buyers expect the value and timing of the recoveries to exceed their purchase price and compensate them for the risk and interest forgone. Buyers must therefore be able to ascertain the likelihood of such recoveries (cf. charge-off).

purchased goodwill. See goodwill.

purchased mortgage servicing rights (PMSR) (USA). Acquisition of the servicing activities and obligations of mortgage lenders (but excluding the credit risk). See mortgage-backed securities.

purchase fund. A form of sinking fund under which the borrower agrees to use his best efforts to buy in the market a pre-agreed amount of an issue per annum in the event that the market price remains below a specified level, usually par. Whereas a sinking fund is obliged to retire a proportion of the outstanding securities and may call part of the issue, a purchase fund is only required to act on a best efforts basis and no repurchases may take place at all. See mandatory redemption; serial amortization; serial bond.

purchase group (USA). An underwriting syndicate which has an agreement among underwriters or a purchase group agreement to buy securities from an issuer and to resell them to investors. The purchase group is distinct from the selling group by underwriting the transaction and sharing in the gross spread (underwriting commission or fee). The purpose of the purchase group is to assure the issuer that it will receive its funds (i.e. they are guaranteeing the issuer the funds regardless of the market reception of the issue) while that of the selling group is to ensure the distribution. In practice many purchase group members will also undertake the latter function.

purchase group agreement. An agreement between the **purchase group** members as to how they will share the **risks** of **underwriting** the issue and the fees, payments, and expenses thereof; the appointment of the **lead manager** as the syndicate's manager and **agent**, and the formation of a **selling group**. Sometimes there are different levels of participation involved (cf. **manager; underwriter; bracket; special bracket**). The purchase group agreement differs from the **underwriting agreement**, which is between the issuer and the lead manager acting as agent for the purchase or **underwriting syndicate**. Sometimes known as the *syndicate contract* or the *agreement among underwriters*.

purchasing power parity theory of exchange rates (PPP). A theory about exchange rates which maintains that the movement in relative value of any two currencies over time is a function of the differential in their inflation rates. It suggests that a long-term equilibrium will adjust exchange rates such that the purchasing power or cost of traded goods and services in different countries will be the same in both countries. See **interest rate parity theory of exchange rates.**

pure arbitrage. A risk-free return made by combining borrowing and a position in a **derivatives** contract and the **underlying** (cf. **quasi-arbitrage**). See also **arbitrage; cost of carry; covered interest arbitrage; synthetic.**

pure discount bond. See zero-coupon bond.

pure jump option pricing model. Another name for the **binomial option pricing model**.

pure play. A market term used for a type of investment that is equivalent to purchasing or selling an **underlying**. For example, a gold-mining company would be seen as a pure play on gold prices since its profits would rise and fall with the gold price, whereas a general mining company would not.

pure risk. An insurable **risk**, that is, one that has a statistical probability of a known loss from which the required **premium** can be derived.

pure yield pick-up swap. See anomaly; swap; switch.

purgatory and hell security. An issue where the redemption proceeds are linked to the maturity spot **exchange** rate of another **currency** against the currency of denomination. The redemption amount is allowed to be between zero and 100% (cf. **dual currency bond; heaven-and-hell bond**).

purpose clause. A clause in an agreement detailing the use to which the borrowing will be put. The most common corporate purpose clause says 'for general corporate purposes'.

pushdown. An accounting term for when a subsidiary revalues **assets** and **liabilities** to the same figures used in the consolidated accounts. This can be significant when a group of companies is considering raising finance, particularly for funding an acquisition which involves the writing off of **goodwill**.

push trade or **transaction.** A trade which should turn a profit, although this is not guaranteed at the time the transaction is entered into (cf. **arbitrage; risk arbitrage**).

put (i) Short for a **put option**. (ii) A provision within a **bond indenture** allowing the holder to resell the security to the issuer, usually on a predetermined date or series of dates (cf. **early redemption put option**). See put provision.

put and call bond. See extendible and retractable.

Put and Call Brokers' and Dealers' Association (PCBDA) (USA). The trade association for firms handling **derivatives**, particularly options.

put an option. The exercise of a put option.

put bond. A bond which has a **put provision** (an embedded option) allowing the holder to redeem the security at **par** (exercise price) on a predetermined date (**expiry date**) prior to the issue's **maturity** (cf. **putholder's option**). Depending on the terms of the provision, such puts may be only exercisable on **coupon** payment dates or at any time; or after an initial **grace period**. Also commonly known as a *puttable bond*.

put buyer. The purchaser of a **put option**. Also called the *holder*.

put-call-futures parity. A condition of the pricing of put and **call options** and related **futures** or **forward contracts** that prevents riskless arbitrage between the different instruments. See also put–call parity.

put–call parity. The relationship that, under ideal circumstances, the values of a **european-style put** and a **call** on the same **underlying** at the same **strike price** and with the same **expiry date** are defined by the identity:

Present value of Exercise Price + Call = Value of Put + Value of Underlying

That is, the present value of the cash required to **exercise** the call option, plus the **premium**, is equal to the value of the put, plus the underlying. This is required to prevent **riskless arbitrage** since the payoffs of both sides of the equation are identical and therefore in an **efficient market** should be valued the same. The put-call parity is normally used to value puts with the **Black–Scholes option pricing model**. Assumptions underlying the relationship include no spread, no transaction costs, the same interest rate for borrowing and lending. In practice put-call parity establishes an **arbitrage** boundary rather than an exact relationship. See also **conversion; reversal**.

put–call ratio. Measure of market activity or sentiment derived by dividing the amount of **open interest** in **call option** positions by **put option** positions. It aims to give the **bull/bear** view of market participants. However, given the ability to create **synthetic options** or positions, if required, the validity of this ratio is somewhat suspect.

put date. The date on which an investor may exercise the right to sell or redeem a security (cf. **expiry rate**). See **putholder's option**.

put guarantee. A notice or affidavit that the writer of a **put option** who is obligated to buy a security if the option is **exercised** holds sufficient cash to cover his commitment (cf. **fiduciary call**).

putholder. The owner of a put option.

putholder's option. An option which allows an investor to shorten the **maturity** of an issue by requiring the borrower to prepay the securities on a certain date or dates (cf. **embedded option**). Sometimes called a *put option*, hence *bond with a put*.

put-of-more option. See **option to double**.

put option or **put.** The right, but not the obligation, to sell an agreed amount of an **underlying** asset, instrument, commodity, or interest rate at a specified price, the **exercise price** or **strike price** or rate, on a specified date, the **expiry date**, or dates, or at any time during a specified period (cf. **call option**). See **American-style; European-style**.

Payoff of put option for holder at expiry

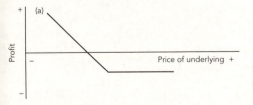

Put option

put premium. The price or **premium** for a put option. Also known as *put money*.

put price (Options). The price at which an **option** to sell may be **executed**. Sometimes called the **exercise** or **strike price**. In the case of **puttable** securities, the price at which the investor can request the issuer to buy back or redeem the security on the **put date**.

put provision. A condition in a security allowing the holder to seek repayment on or after a given date from the issuer prior to the issue's final maturity (cf. **callable; call provision; embedded option**).

put seller. The seller, or more commonly the **writer**, of a put option (cf. **covered put**).

put spread. Bearish **option strategy** based on a **vertical spread** where the cost of buying a **put** is offset by writing a put which is further **out of the money** against it. As with a **call spread**, it could be an attractive means of offsetting the cost of setting up the position if a limited fall in the price of the underlying is expected. It can also be undertaken as a **calendar spread** where the two sides have differing **expiry dates**. It can also be set up using **calls** (cf. **credit spread; debit spread**). Also frequently called a *bear spread*. See also **option strategies**.

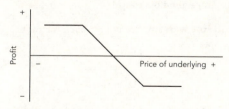

Payoff of put spread at expiry

puttable. A security where there is a provision allowing early repayment prior to the final maturity at the discretion of the holder, that is to *put* the security back to the issuer (cf. **callable; embedded option; putholder's option; put provision**). The

Payoff of put option writer at expiry

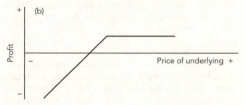

concept has been extended to **common stock** in the USA, where it is known as *puttable common stock* or sometimes *superstock*. See **extendible bond; trust deed.**

puttable common stock (Equities; USA). An issue of **common stock** where the holders have the right to **put** the issue back to the issuer at a predetermined date at a specific price (cf. **European-style; exercise price; strike price**). See also **puttable stock.**

puttable convertible. A **convertible** which has a **put provision** allowing the holder to redeem the issue prior to its final **maturity**. Some issues also featured a **premium** to the **par value** at such a time, giving the issue a higher **yield-to-put** than the **yield-to-maturity** of the issue.

puttable stock. A combined unit of **common stock** and a **put option**, thus giving the **holder** the right to put the **stock** back to the issuer. Special features of the structure include the right of the holder either to redeem the combined unit or to receive additional stock above the contracted amount if the stock price is below the **exercise price** on the put. In terms of payoff it is equal to a **convertible** since the holder participates in the gains on the stock but is protected from any falls through the put option. A number of different variations exist on the basic structure, for instance, limitations on the issuer's right to increase the number of shares in lieu of redemption, or to issue additional debt or **preferred stock.**

puttable swap. An **interest rate swap** where the **fixed rate payer** has the right or **option** to terminate the contract at a specified date before the **maturity** of the swap. It is equivalent to a straight swap for the entire length of the swap together with a **swaption** to receive **fixed rate** at the same **strike rate** but where the **premium** is paid in the form of a higher fixed rate payment on the swap. See also **extendible swaps.**

puttable warrant. See **money-back warrant.**

put-through (Securities markets). The linked sale and repurchase of the same security by a dealer. Sometimes called a *matched deal, matched trade,* or *matched transaction.* See also **bed and breakfast.**

putting into play. Said to occur when a company has been identified as a potential **takeover** target. Usually, this is signalled by increased market activity in the company's **shares,** or by extraordinary investment analysis output (cf. **radar alert**).

put to seller. Term used for the **exercise** of a put option. That is, the **underlying** is delivered (put) to the **option writer** in exchange for cash.

put warrant. A **warrant** that gives the right to the holder to redeem a security at **par.**

pyramiding. (i) A method of embezzlement made famous by Charles Ponzi, and hence often called a *Ponzi scheme,* where receipts from buyers of a scheme are used to fund payments to participants and any early redemptions before the embezzler escapes with the bulk of the funds. Usually the scheme is sold as offering an above-**average** return for no **risk!** It is also sometimes called a *money multiplier.* (ii) Using rising asset values as additional **collateral** for subsequent **margin** purchases. This provides a high degree of **leverage** in a rising market, but exposes the originator to rapid losses in a falling market. Many of the regulatory constraints on purchases on margin are designed to restrict this type of speculative activity. (iii) Building up a succession of controlling interests in larger and larger firms by buying the minimum amount of **equity** to ensure control and then using the controlled firm's resources to buy a controlling interest in the larger firm, which is then used to acquire a controlling interest in an even bigger firm (cf. **cascade shareholdings**).

pyramid scheme. A type of fraudulent **pyramiding** scheme where investors are promised high returns and where the fraudster uses the newly invested funds to pay back any investors wishing to terminate early while the bulk of the funds are stolen.

Q bond (USA). A type of **collateralized mortgage obligation** where the **coupon** is inversely related to the **reference rate**. That is, it behaves like a **reverse floating rate note**.

quadrangle arbitrage (Forex). The process by which the currency markets ensure that the equilibrium forward exchange rate in the **interest rate parity theory of exchange rates** holds. The principle is that the **law of one price** must apply to two portfolios which have the same payoffs or otherwise a **riskless arbitrage** can be undertaken. In order to carry out a quadrangle arbitrage, four transactions are involved: (*a*) **spot foreign exchange** transaction; (*b*) **Forward foreign exchange contract**; (*c*) a **deposit** or **loan** in the **base currency**; and (*d*) a **loan** or **deposit** in the **foreign currency**. Combining any three of the four transactions provides the same outcome as the fourth as shown in the Figure (cf. **replication**).

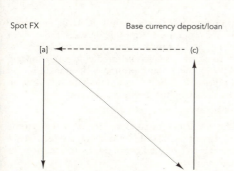

Spot FX   Base currency deposit/loan

[a]   (c)

(d)   [b]

Foreign currency deposit/loan   Forward FX

Quadrangle arbitrage or covered interest arbitrage

If the equilibrium relationship is not maintained and any of the four elements is mispriced in the market, an arbitrage can be achieved after taking into account transaction costs. This is shown in the Table where sterling is traded at $1.50 spot and $1.4815 for six months forward delivery, while the relevant interbank interest rates are 8% in sterling and 6% in US dollars. By engaging in a quadrangle arbitrage, there is a riskless profit of US$0.5 per £100.

Quadrangle arbitrage

Interbank Interest Rates (6 months / 180 days)	%	Foreign Exchange Rates	
		Spot (US$/£)	Forward (US$/£)
Sterling (basis = 365 days)	8	1.50	1.4815
US dollars (basis = 360 days)	6		

	Cash flows			
	At initiation		At termination	
	£	US$	£	US$
Borrow £100 at 8%	100		(103.95)	
Buy US$150 spot	(100)	150		
Invest US$150 at 6%		(150)		154.5
Buy £103.95 forward			103.95	(154)
Net cast flows	0	0	0	0.5

See also **covered interest arbitrage**.

qualified acceptance (Banking). The acceptance of a **banker's acceptance** or bill based on changed conditions to the terms. If the accepting bank refuses to make a qualified acceptance, the bill has to be referred back to the **drawer** and any party that previously endorsed the bill.

qualified institutional buyers or **qualified institutional investers (QIB; QII)** (USA). Sophisticated investors who meet the requirements of the **Securities and Exchange Commission** to participate in **private placements** under **Rule 144a**.

qualified opinion. An auditor's report or letter which highlights limitations or deficiencies in the audited financial statements.

qualified professional asset manager (QPAM) (USA). Securities and Exchange Commission registered professional adviser who counsels funds in **private placements**. See **sophisticated investor**.

qualifying distribution (UK). A payment by a company to **shareholders** that is the subject of **advance corporation tax**.

qualifying stock option (USA). A type of **stock option** scheme for employees that meets criteria set down by the US Internal Revenue Service.

qualitative analysis. Judgemental analysis of the worth of an **asset** or investment which cannot be readily quantified and often used as part of **fundamental analysis** (cf. **quantitative analysis**). Sometimes called *inference analysis*.

quality. In securities markets, applied to the standing of the issue. This is normally a combination of the **credit worthiness** of the issuer or **guarantor**, the degree of investor protection provided, and the seniority of the security in relation to other obligations (cf. **covenants**; **debenture**; **secured debt**; **subordinated debt**). For **equity** it takes in such factors as the stability of **earnings** and **dividends** (cf. **blue chips**). See **credit ratings**; **investment grade**.

quality risk. The risk that arises from using a **cross hedge** where the **underlying** position being hedged is not the same as that used for hedging (cf. **cross-asset**; **inter-commodity spread**; **intermarket spread**).

quality spread. (i) Market term for the difference in **yield** for the same **maturity** between two issuers of different **credit worthiness**. For instance, the difference between supranational institutions, such as the **World Bank**, and **triple-A** or double-A corporate borrowers. As the maturity increases, increased **credit risk** concerns would normally lead to an increase in the **spread** for the lesser rated entity. (ii) An **inter-commodity spread** or **intermarket spread** where the two sides of the transaction have different credit risk. See **treasury-eurodollar spread**.

quant. A type of investment appraisal and strategy that relies on quantitative methods and statistical analysis. The term can be applied to individuals or organizations to reflect their skills or approach (cf. **rocket scientist**). See **quantitative analysis**.

quantitative analysis. A method of appraisal of the worth of an **asset** or investment based on economic, econometric, mathematical, and statistical methods or **models**. Modern quantitative methods have common grounds with **technical analysis** and the two are now often seen as one discipline. A *quant strategy* is an investment strategy which relies heavily on quantitative analysis rather than **qualitative analysis**.

quantity adjusting option (QUANTO). A currency **option** initially issued by Goldman Sachs which allows the holder to vary the amount of **foreign exchange** in the contract but now used generically. It is seen as a useful way of hedging a known exposure with an uncertain foreign currency amount. The amount of currency in such an option will rise and fall in line with movements in the foreign exchange rate and the performance of the **underlying**. For example, an option on the **Deutsche Aktienindex** (DAX index), denominated in US dollars, will pay the total return on the DAX to the holder in US dollars at the exchange rate set at the time of the contract. For the option writer to **hedge** his **exposure** to the currency component of the option requires that the returns from the index be converted back to US dollars at **expiry**. A forward contract, which is for a fixed quantity, cannot be used to eliminate the foreign exchange risk because the value of the index will not be known for certain in advance. The currency element must be adjusted to match the DAX's performance. Thus the index and foreign exchange elements must be taken into account in calculating the writer's hedging element (cf. **correlation**). There will be an additional complication if the **exchange rate** is set at the spot rate when the contract was written as this will be an off-market rate in the forward market (cf. **spread**).

quantity risk. The problem of **hedging** with **exchange-traded** instruments, such as **futures** which have a fixed contractual amount which may not exactly match the amount of the **underlying** to be hedged (cf. **flex futures**; **flex options**).

quantity theory of money (QTM). Economic theory about the relationship between the stock of money and the price level. The model claims that there exists a stable and predictable relationship between the amount of money in circulation and the price level in an economy. It begins with an identity called the 'Fisher equation':

$$MV = PT$$

where M is the the stock of money; V the income velocity of circulation; P the average price level; T the measure of the flow of goods and services, or real income.

The above is known as an identity because the left-hand side captures the total money value of transactions over a particular period; that is, the stock of money multiplied by the number of times it has circulated around the economy financing transactions, while the right-hand side captures the total money value of goods and services sold. Since the total money value of transactions is necessarily the same as the value of goods sold, the two sides of the equation must be the same by definition. However, it is asserted that T is reasonably constant because the economy is normally close to full employment; and V is also reasonably constant, being determined by certain institutional features of an economy, such as the operation of banks, which have a smoothing effect on transactions. Given these two assertions they have the effect of cancelling one another out, leaving *M* to equal *P*, which implies that changes in the **money supply** are associated with proportionate changes in prices. Several important policy implications arise from this postulation. It suggests that **inflation** can be controlled by the monetary authorities through control of the quantity of money in existence. In addition, if a particular rate of growth in real income, *T*, is expected then this can be achieved without inflation by allowing the quantity of money in the economy expanding at the same rate. The QTM model in one of its forms underpins **monetary policy** (cf. **monetarism**).

quantization error. Analytical errors arising in **quantitative analysis**. Examples include errors in the data, programming faults, and reconciliation and compatability problems.

quantize. To denominate a **derivative** instrument in a currency other than that which the **underlying** is normally denominated. Thus a US dollar **interest rate swap** with a Deutschemark rate of interest would qualify. Such derivatives are also known as *diffs*, or *differential forward, future, option,* or *swap.*

quanto option. An exotic option where the strike price is denominated in a currency other than that of the **underlying**. See **currency protected option; quantity adjusting option.**

quanto swap. See **currency protected swap.**

quardi-hasan (Islam). A loan with no interest as required under Islamic law, the sharia (cf. **halal**).

quarter days (UK). The four days each quarter when quarterly rental payments are due (usually on property). The dates are: 25 March, 24 June, 29 September, 25 December in England and Wales and 2 February, 15 May, 1 August, and 11 November in Scotland.

quarterly or **quarterlies.** Financial statements or dividends which are made every three months (cf. Form 10-Q).

quasi-American option. See **Bermuda option.**

quasi-arbitrage. An investment using **futures** and the **underlying** which returns more than an equivalent **risk** position in an **asset** (cf. **synthetic**). See also **covered interest arbitrage.**

quasi-autonomous non-governmental organization (QUANGO) (UK). An agency of government set up to perform specific functions, such as manage the prison service. It is usually constituted with a **board of directors** and managers, rather than run on civil service lines. See also **privatization.**

quasi-money. A type of **asset** that is highly **liquid**; that is, can be turned into cash very quickly without significant loss. For example **certificates of deposit.** Also called *cash equivalents, money substitutes,* or *near money.*

quasi-public company or **corporation.** A profit-making company which is owned by the state or by a state agency. It therefore has some attributes of a sovereign entity. The exact degree of support, however, needs to be carefully established if there is no actual state guarantee on debts as this may significantly affect its value. A number of major international transactions have suffered from this indeterminacy. Obviously the borrower has an incentive to portray itself as much as possible as a sovereign entity to obtain funds at **fine rates** (cf. **ultra vires**).

quasi-split trust (UK). A type of split-capital trust which has geared ordinary shares as well as zero coupon preference shares in its capital structure. Also known as a *highly-geared split trust, hybrid split trust,* or *new split trust.*

quick assets. See quasi-money.

quick ratio. See acid test ratio.

quid pro quo (Latin). Something in exchange for something. A fundamental principle of contracts and financial market transactions.

quiet period (USA). The period when an issuer is undergoing **registration** with the **Securities and Exchange Commission.** The name reflects the general bar on any marketing activity during the period (cf. **cooling-off period**).

quintal. 100 kilograms.

quorum. The minimum number of **directors** or **shareholders** required to attend a meeting to make it binding (cf. **supermajority**).

quota. (i) An agreed share contributed to an undertaking. (ii) A maximum limit on the amount that can be purchased or sold in a particular situation (cf. **cap**). For instance, in US Treasury **auctions**, bidders are limited to a fraction of the whole issue. (iii) Limits placed on exports or imports of a **commodity**, product, or service into or out of a particular country.

quotation or **quote.** (i) The act of making or seeking a price in a security. See **firm quote; indication.** (ii) A **bid** and **offer** given by a **dealer** (cf. **two-way prices**). (iii) The procedure for achieving a **listing** of a company's **stock** on an exchange. Hence, *getting a quote* (cf. **initial public offer**). (iv) The price of a security listed on an exchange. (v) A price or rate indication given by a financial intermediary (cf. **firm quote**; **indication**). (vi) An official or reported price. See **quoted price**.

quoted (UK). The same as **listed**. It refers to those securities that are admitted to the **London Stock Exchange's Daily Official List** and are therefore quoted on the exchange.

quoted company (UK). The same as a **listed company**.

quoted margin (Bonds). Used in the **floating rate note** market to describe the **margin** over the **index** or **reference rate** at which the **coupon** is fixed.

quoted price (i) (USA) Last transaction price in a security. (ii) The officially reported price of a security. See **closing price**; **exchange delivery settlement price**; **price range**; **settlement price**; **Stock Exchange Daily Official List**.

quote driven. A type of share-dealing system where prices are initially determined by **dealers'** or by **market-makers' quotes** (cf. **order driven**). The prices at which securities ultimately settle are determined by the interreaction of **market forces**. This system is operated, for example, by the **London Stock Exchange** and many **over-the-counter** markets. See also **auction**; **head-to-head**; **inter-dealer-broker**.

quote extension time. A period of time that elapses after a **request for quotes** has been made where the **broker** seeks confirmation from the client as to whether to proceed with the transaction or not.

quote vendors. Those firms providing price and other information services via (real-time) electronic distribution mechanisms.

quoting bank (Forex). A bank that makes a price in **foreign exchange** (cf. **market maker**).

Quotron (USA). A proprietary electronic information provider of securities prices providing a **screen-based** dealing facility used by markets to distribute two-way prices thereby allowing traders to make buy or sell decisions. See **Bloomberg**; **Reuters**; **screen-trading**; **Telerate**.

R

radar alert. Company monitoring of buying activity in its **stock** which might indicate an attempted **takeover**.

raider (USA). US term for a **predator**. A raider would attempt to take over a corporation or engage in greenmail. See also **mergers and acquisitions**.

Raiffeisenbanken (Banking; Germany). Agricultural credit banks.

rainbow option. A type of **exotic option** whose payoff is based on the performance of a number of different **assets** (cf. **cross-asset**). There are a number of different types, for instance the **better-of-two-assets option**, the multi-factor option; the **outperformance option** or the **spread option**. The number of **underlyings** that are in the structure are given by the number of colours to the rainbow: a two-colour rainbow having two underlyings; the three-colour, three underlyings; and so forth. See **intra-commodity spread; inter-commodity spread**.

rally. A rise in prices after a fall or **bear market**. The opposite movement to a **reaction** (cf. **technical rally**).

ramp. The process of creating a shortage of supply in order to drive up a price (cf. **churning**). See **corner the market**.

random walk. The predecessor to the **efficient markets hypothesis**. The name derives from the observed price behaviour of financial **asset** prices which followed no predictable pattern. See also **geometric Brownian motion; stochastic process; Wiener process**.

range. The upper and lower bounds of a price series or the **bid** and **offers** over a given period, such as a day, week, month, quarter, or year. Some methods of **technical analysis** attach importance to an asset's range as a measure of **variability** (cf. **breakout; volatility**). See **candlestick chart; point and figure chart**.

range floating rate note (range floater). A type of **floating rate note** (FRN), similar in operation to a **minimax frn** except that the holder of the note receives no **accrued interest** if the **reference** rate is above or below a predetermined **trigger** level. As long as the rate is within the range, the holder receives a significant **margin** over the reference rate. In some structures, the high and low of the range can be reset at the beginning of each **rollover** period. The structure is also known as an *accrual note* or a *fairway note*.

range forward. A type of **option strategy**, particularly used in the **foreign exchange markets**, which involves entering a contract which is a combination made up of purchased **calls** and written **puts**, but structured so that the buyer pays little or no **premium** (cf. **collar; corridor; cylinder; risk reversal; vertical spread**). It is effectively a type of **forward** contract which nevertheless allows the holder to gain some benefit from market movements, hence the title (cf. **put–call parity; synthetic option**). Sometimes called a *partial ceiling option*.

range option. See **barrier option**.

range swap. See **accrual swap**.

range warrant. See **trading range warrant**.

rank or **ranking.** The priority of debt claims in a firm's fixed **liabilities** in the event of winding up. Different **classes** of debt will have different priority in being repaid, the first claims to be met being secured, then senior, then junior or subordinated. One problem of distressed debt restructurings occurs when violations of the absolute priority of different classes takes place (cf. **Chapter 11**). See **junk bond**.

RAROC 2020 (USA) A **risk** assessment system offered by *Bankers' Trust* which aims to measure, evaluate, and set capital requirements for a variety of different financial risks. See also **risk adjusted return on capital; value at risk**.

ratchet. An incentive device used in **venture capital** and **management buy-outs** to allow managers to gain a larger share of the **equity** based on the performance of the firm. See also **agency theory**.

ratchet option. See **ladder option** (cf. **shout option**).

ratchet swap. See **periodic reset swap**.

rate. (i) To provide a credit opinion. See **credit rating**. (ii) Short for *interest rate*. See **interest rate calculations**.

rate anticipation swap. Interest rate swap undertaken in anticipation of unfavourable changes in prevailing interest rates. A borrower might undertake such a transaction ahead of borrowing money in order to lock in existing interest rates before an expected rise.

rate base. See **rate order**.

rate cap. The maximum interest rate that may be charged on a **floating rate** or **variable rate** borrowing (cf. **embedded option**). See **cap**; **interest rate cap**.

rate differential option. See **cross-currency option**.

rate differential swap. See **currency protected swap** (cf. **differential swap**).

rate fixing. The resetting of the **interest rate** on a **floating rate** or **variable rate** obligation or derivative (cf. **fixing**). Also known as the *reset* or the *rollover*.

rate lock. Agreement that allows the holder to lock in a rate for an agreed period from a **forward** date.

rate of discount. See **discount**.

rate of exchange. The price at which currencies are exchanged. See **foreign exchange**.

rate of interest. See **interest rate**.

rate of return. See **after-tax basis**; **all-in cost**; **annual percentage rate**; **current yield**; **dividend yield**; **effective rate**; **interest rate calculations**; **nominal rate**; **real rate of interest**; **total return**; **yield-to-average life**; **yield-to-call**; **yield-to-maturity**.

rate of return ratios. See **ratio analysis**.

rate of turnover. See **sales**; **volume**.

rate order (USA). Regulatory instruction setting the maximum price or rate for utilities' products or services. Hence the *rate base* which sets the schedule of prices.

rate risk. See **interest rate risk** (cf. **assets repriced before liabilities**).

rate sensitive assets and **rate sensitive liabilities (RSA; RSL).** See **asset-liability management**.

rating. (i) The process of obtaining a **credit rating**. (ii) The credit score or rating itself.

rating agency. See **credit rating agency**.

rating sensitive note. (Bonds). See **credit sensitive note**; **floating rate credit rating sensitive note**.

ratio. A measure of the relative size or value of two variables expressed as a proportion. It is usually derived by expressing the top, or first number (known as the numerator) in terms of the bottom, or second (the denominator). Sometimes this is then converted into a percentage by multiplying by 100. See **American terms**; **European terms**; **ratio analysis**; **rights issue**.

ratio analysis. Collective term for analytic methods based on an organization's financial statements and used as indicators of financial position (cf. **DuPont system**; **fundamental analysis**; **Z scores**). It may also be applied to state or other not-for-profit entities.

There are two basic methods of using ratios: *horizontal* and *vertical analysis*. Horizontal analysis looks at the same ratio across time while vertical analysis looks at different ratios at the same time. The ratios so derived are subject to two types of analysis:

Trend analysis. This is to compare the same firm over a number of account periods (normally five years is taken) and to examine the ratios over the resultant period to see if any detectable trends are evident.

Inter-company or *industry analysis*. This compares ratios across different firms and within an industry. This may be combined with trend analysis. With modern database techniques the above methods are readily accessible to most analysts.

Details of the more common ratios used are given below: note that, by the nature of things, ratios indicate but not prove a trend or condition and all the statements below should be read as indicative and not definitive.

ACTIVITY RATIOS

These show how efficient a firm is in using its assets. A good-quality firm will be more effective in its use of its resources than a less well-managed firm.

Average collection period. This measures the average amount of credit extended by a firm to its customers.

$$\text{Average collection period} = \frac{\text{Accounts receivable}}{\left(\frac{\text{Annual sales}}{365}\right)}$$

Stock or *inventory turnover ratio*. This measures the number of times in a year the firm's stock or inventory is turned over.

$$\text{Inventory (stock) turnover} = \frac{\text{Cost of sales}}{\text{Average inventory (stock)}}$$

Fixed asset turnover ratio. This measures how effective the firm is in using its 'in place' assets such as property, plant, and machinery to generate sales.

$$\text{Fixed asset turnover} = \frac{\text{Sales}}{\text{Net fixed assets}}$$

Total asset turnover ratio. This measures how effective the firm is in using all its assets to generate sales.

$$\text{Total asset turnover} = \frac{\text{Sales}}{\text{Total assets}}$$

LIQUIDITY RATIOS

These show the ability of the company to meet **short-term** commitments.

Current ratio. This is the surplus (deficit) of short-term assets to short-term liabilities:

$$\text{Current ratio} = \frac{\text{Current assets}}{\text{Current liabilities}}$$

Quick ratio or 'acid test' ratio. This has a tighter definition of liquidity, or saleability of assets, by excluding stock/inventory from current assets.

$$\text{Quick ratio} = \frac{\text{(Current assets} - \text{stock or inventories)}}{\text{Current liabilities}}$$

MARKET RATIO

These show investors' assessment of the company's performance.

Earnings per share (EPS):

$$\text{Earnings per share (EPS)} = \frac{\text{Profit after tax and minorities}}{\text{Number of shares in issue}}$$

Price to earnings multiple or ratio (PE; PER; P/E ratio):

$$\text{P/E} = \frac{\text{Market price per share (stock)}}{\text{Current earnings per share}}$$

Market (price)-to-book (value) ratio (P/BV). This is the market price of the stock to the book price per share.

$$\text{P/BV} = \frac{\text{Market price per share}}{\text{Book value per share}}$$

Dividend cover. This is the reciprocal of the pay-out ratio.

$$\text{Divident cover} = \frac{\text{Total earnings after tax}}{\text{Total dividend paid}}$$

Dividend yield. This can either be before tax ('gross') or after tax ('net') in jurisdictions with an **imputation tax system**.

$$\text{Dividend yield} = \frac{\text{Dividend per share (stock)}}{\text{Market price per share}} \times 100$$

Net asset value (NAV):

$$\text{Net asset value (NAV)} = \frac{\text{Shareholders' funds}}{\text{Number of common in issue}}$$

OPERATING RATIOS

These assess how well the organization is managing its operations.

Profit margin:

$$\text{Profit margin} = \frac{\text{Trading profit (Sales} - \text{cost of sales)}}{\text{Sales (turnover)}}$$

Net profit margin:

$$\text{Net profit margin} = \frac{\text{After tax earnings}}{\text{Sales (turnover)}}$$

Free cash flow:

$$\text{Free cash flow} = \frac{\text{Depreciation} + \text{profit(earnings)}}{\text{after tax} + (+/-) \text{deferred tax}}$$

PROFITABILITY RATIOS

These show the management's ability to generate profits.

Return on capital employed (ROCE):

$$\text{Return on capital employed (ROCE)} = \frac{\text{Profit before interest charges and taxes}}{\text{Total assets}}$$

Return on investment (ROI):

$$\text{Return on investment (ROI)} = \frac{\text{Profit after taxes}}{\text{Total assets}}$$

Return on equity or to shareholders (ROE):

$$\text{Return on equity (ROE)} = \frac{\text{Earnings after taxes}}{\text{Shareholders' equity}}$$

RISK RATIOS

These show the amount of **risk** taken by the firm in its operations and **capital structure**. They measures the degree of likelihood that a firm will be able to meet its commitments in the future. Generally, the higher the ratio, the more risk taken by the firm.

Debt or gearing ratio. This is the amount of the firm's capital requirements that is provided by lenders.

$$\text{Debt ratio} = \frac{\text{Total debt (short and long term)}}{\text{Total assets}}$$

Debt-to-equity or leverage ratio (D/E):

$$\text{Debt-to-equity ratio} = \frac{\text{Total debt (short and long term)}}{\text{Total equity}}$$

Interest cover:

$$\text{Interest cover} = \frac{\text{Earnings before interest and taxes (EBIT)}}{\text{Interest paid}}$$

Fixed-charge coverage. This is a measure of a firm's ability to meet its fixed obligations. In other words it gives an estimate of the likelihood of **default**.

$$\text{Fixed charge coverage} = \frac{\substack{\text{Earnings before interest and taxes} \\ \text{(EBIT)} + \text{leasing payments}}}{\substack{\text{Interest} + \text{lease payment} + \\ \text{preferred dividends before tax}}}$$

ratio backspread. The sale of an **at-the-money** or **in-the-money** option and the purchase of a larger number of **out-of-the-money** options. The alternative strategy is known as a *ratio forward spread.* See **ratio call spread; ratio put spread; ratio spread.**

radio calendar combination. Any of a number of strategies which involves both **puts** and **calls** in unequal combinations and with different **expiry** dates and **strike prices.** See **ratio spread; ratio time spread.**

ratio calendar spread. See **ratio time spread.**

ratio call spread (Options markets). A low-cost strategy under which a number of **calls** are bought at a lower **exercise price** and more calls are sold at a higher price (cf. **backspread**). The strategy will lock in profits as long as the price of the **underlying** only moves up a limited amount to allow profitable exercise of the purchased options, but not enough to trigger the exercise of the higher-priced written options. Also known as a *variable call spread.* See **option strategies.**

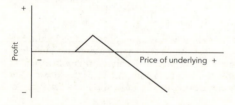

Payoff of ratio call spread at expiry

One call option bought and two calls written or sold further out of the money.

ratio call writer or **writing** (Options market). A strategy involving owning a quantity of the **underlying** and selling **calls** against more than is owned. It will earn a larger profit than a written **naked** or **covered position,** provided the price stays about the same. The *ratio put writer* is the same as the ratio call writer except that the writer stands ready to accept delivery of the underlying. An institution or individual who pursues such a strategy is known as a *ratio writer.* See also **ratio put spread.**

ratio forward. See **participating forward.**

ratio forward spread. The purchase of an **at-the-money** or **in-the-money** option and the sale of a larger number of **out-of-the-money** options. The alternative strategy is known as a *ratio backspread.* See **ratio call spread; ratio put spread; ratio spread.**

rational expectations. An economic theory or description of market participant behaviour that postulates the use of all available information in financial decision-taking so as to avoid systematic errors. In financial markets, if rational expectations hold, then prices will reflect fully all currently available information, such that prices move only when new information becomes available. See **efficient markets hypothesis.**

ratio put spread (Options). A low-cost strategy under which a number of **puts** are bought at a higher **exercise price** and more puts sold at a lower price (cf. **backspread**). The strategy will lock in profits as long as the price of the **underlying** rises or only moves down a limited amount to allow profitable exercise of the purchased options, but not enough to trigger the exercise of the lower priced written options. Also known as a *variable put spread.* See **option strategies; ratio call spread.**

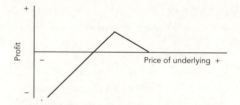

Payoff of ratio put spread at expiry

One put option bought and two puts written or sold further out of the money.

ratio put writer. See **ratio call writer.**

ratio spread (Options markets). Any strategy that involves holding an unequal number of **short options** and **long options,** or **long** positions in the **underlying** (cf. **participating cap, participating forward; participating swap**). As a strategy it is one way of reducing the cost of creating an option position. For the *ratio forward spread,* the purchase of the desired near-to or at-the-money position is financed by selling a greater number of **out-of-the-money** options. Such a strategy has its disadvantages if the **volatility** of the underlying should increase significantly thereby changing the likelihood of **exercise** as measured by the option **deltas.** The opposite transaction is known as a *ratio backspread,* which involves selling the at-the-money option and buying the out-of-the-money options. See ratio call spread; ratio put spread.

ratio strategy. Any option strategy based on holding unequal long and short positions in options and which may also include the underlying (cf. combination). See calendar spread; ratio call spread; ratio put spread; ratio time spread; time spread; vertical spread.

ratio time spread (Option markets). A strategy involving holding an unequal number of short options and long options as in a ratio spread but where the two option positions have different expiry dates. For example, a ratio time spread usually consists of selling more near-term options than later-expiry options that are purchased. The assumption is that near-term volatility will remain the same while over the longer term it will increase. See also calendar spread.

ratio write. See option hedge.

ratio writer. See ratio call writer.

raw material supply agreement. A condition in a project finance agreement that the sponsor will supply an agreed amount of raw material each period for the project.

reaction. A market or security movement in prices as a result of new information (cf. overbought; oversold; rally).

reading the tape (USA). Judging the mood of a market or security by watching the flow and pattern of transactions (which were historically printed on a tape, but are now displayed electronically).

ready market. A liquid market.

real assets. Physical asset items such as land or real estate, buildings, machinery, and equipment used to produce goods and services.

real estate. Land and buildings.

real-estate futures. See property futures.

real-estate investment trust (REIT) (USA). A closed-end investment company which invests predominantly in real estate. *Equity REITs* are those which hold properties as investments; *Mortgage REITs* specialize in funding building acquisition or construction by third parties; some do both. REITs make use of financial leverage to enhance returns to their shareholders. Some REITS have just one property in their portfolio, allowing investors to have exposure to the market but without the problems of being a direct inves-

tor. Many REITs invest in the residual or equity tranche of collateralized mortgage obligations.

real estate mortgage investment conduit (REMIC) (USA) Special purpose vehicle established under the *Tax Reform Act of 1986* to allow the use pass-throughs on multi-class mortgages and which may taken the form of securities, a trust, or a limited partnership. Prior to the legislation, there had been problems in passing interest to holders of such mutiple securities free of tax; the REMIC structure regularized the tax treatment for all mortgage-backed securities and collateralized mortgage obgliations issued after 1 January 1987.

real-estate swap. A type of commodity swap where the returns from a property or real-estate index are exchanged against a reference rate.

realignment. Changes made in the central parity of the European Monetary System's Exchange Rate Mechanism.

real interest rate. The inflation-adjusted rate of interest. Often taken to be the nominal interest rate less inflation. The correct method of calculation is:

$$\left[\left\{ \frac{\left(1 + \dfrac{nominal\ interest\ rate}{100}\right)}{\left(1 + \dfrac{inflation\ rate}{100}\right)} \right\} - 1 \right] \times 100$$

$$e.g. \quad \left[\left\{ \frac{1 + \dfrac{10\%}{100}}{1 + \dfrac{4\%}{100}} \right\} - 1 \right] \times 100 = 5.77\%$$

Inflation can be either the actual or expected rate, depending on the requirement. In the UK, it is possible to observe the yield difference between index-linked gilts and similar maturity gilt-edged paying a nominal rate to infer expected inflation. Also known as the *real rate of return* or the *real yield*. See real rate of interest.

real investment. Investments made in capital assets such as land, buildings, machinery and so forth, rather than financial instruments (cf. capital budgeting; project).

realizable assets. See liquid assets (cf. negotiable instrument).

realized compound yield to maturity (Bonds; USA). See realized yield.

realized profit or loss. The actual ex-post performance on an investment (cf. book profit (loss)). Because most tax jurisdictions distinguish between income and capital, the exact way the loss is derived, whether through a fall in value or through **negative carry**, may determine how it is treated for tax purposes (cf. **capital gain (loss)**). That is, loss of income may be offset against income earned, but not capital gains, and vice versa.

realized return. The actual return on an asset or investment. Also called the *ex post return*.

realized yield. (i) The return on a security over a particular period assuming that the interest income is reinvested at a specified **reinvestment rate**. See also **yield**. (ii) The ex post return achieved on a security, including the reinvestment of any **coupon** interest or **dividends**, when it has been sold (cf. **estimated total return**).

realkredit obligationer (Denmark). Mortgaged-backed security See **Pfandbriefe**.

reallowance (USA). That portion of the **underwriting spread** that an underwriter may legitimately concede when distributing securities to his investor clients (cf. **overtrading**; **selling concession**). The amount of the reallowance is specified at the time the issue is launched. The actual spread obtained by the underwriter will depend on market conditions and demand for the issue. See **discount to the market**.

real market. The market (or market rate) where transactions are actually taking place as opposed to **dealer** or **broker quotes**. The latter may not reflect actual transactions (cf. **killing**; **ramp**). See also **picture**.

real options. These are non-tradable options that arise in the course of business activities. The basic options that arise are:

- *investment timing*: the flexibility to advance or delay the timing of an investment;
- *abandonment*: the ability to discontinue a project;
- *shut down* or *put on hold*: the ability to temporarily cease or shut down or put on hold an activity or the outgoings in relation to a new project;
- *growth*: the ability to make investments which build a platform or the potential for further expansion if the outcome is favourable. Research and development and pilot product are typical examples of such options to grow;
- *design-in* or *innovate*: the ability to modify, expand, or otherwise use an existing product or service in different ways;
- *output flexibility*: the ability to use the output from a project or resource in different ways;

- *expansion*: the ability to add future capacity at a relatively low marginal cost. Such ability may involve modular production design, shell construction of part of a facility, and so on.

real property or **realty.** Class of assets made up of land and buildings. Also called *real estate*.

real rate of interest, real interest rate, or **real rate of return.** A return, **yield**, or interest rate calculated by subtracting the rate of inflation from the **nominal** rate (cf. **money yield**). Also known as the *real yield*.

1. *Components of the* **nominal interest rate**:

$$\text{Nominal interest rate} = \begin{array}{l}(\{1 + \text{real rate}\} \times \{1 + \text{inflation premium}\}) + \text{risk premium over risk} - \text{free rate}\end{array}$$

The **risk premium** is the amount of yield over and above the **risk-free** rate investors require for a particular credit risk.

2. *Actual real interest rate*:

$$\text{Actual real interest rate} = \begin{array}{l}[(\{1 + \text{nominal rate}\} \div \{1 + \text{actual inflation rate}\}) - 1] \times 100\%\end{array}$$

$$\text{e.g.} \quad 3\% = \left[\left\{ \frac{\left(1 + \frac{6.1}{100}\right)}{\left(1 + \frac{3}{100}\right)} \right\} - 1 \right] \times 100\%$$

Where the actual inflation rate is 3% and the expected inflation rate is 4%.

3. *Expected real interest rate*:

$$\text{Expected real interest rate} = \begin{array}{l}[(\{1 + \text{nominal rate}\} \div \{1 + \text{expected inflation rate}\}) - 1] \times 100\%\end{array}$$

$$\text{e.g. } 2.02\% = \left[\left\{ \frac{\left(1 + \frac{6.1\%}{100}\right)}{\left(1 + \frac{4\%}{100}\right)} \right\} - 1 \right] \times 100\%$$

The equation can be rearranged to derive the expected nominal rate given an inflation forecast if the required real rate of interest is deemed to be a constant.

real terms. Time-series adjustment made to assets, indices, returns, or valuations to remove the effects of changes in the value of money, or inflation, on the series. Also called *inflation adjusted*.

real time reporting. A method of reporting that involves the immediate updating of the **positions** as and when trading is undertaken. The alternative method is based of **batch settlement** where the positions are updated at the end of the settlement cycle. Most institutions use real time reporting in order to keep track of **limits** and to control their exposures.

real yield securities (REAL) (Bonds; USA). An **index-linked** issue of **bonds** developed by Morgan Stanley Inc. where the interest rate is set in relation to changes in the **consumer price index**.

rebalancing. (i) The periodic re-optimization of an existing **dedicated** or **immunized** portfolio. It involves selling certain **bonds** and buying others so as to maximize the resulting **yield** or the net revenue from the **swap**. The process should continue to adhere to the constraints such as liability payments or a **duration** target. See **optimization**. (ii) The requirement to alter a **hedge** or **hedge ratio** to maintain its effectiveness due to **time decay**.

rebate. (i) Price or rate reduction provided to buyers, either up-front or after a period of time (cf. **firm hands**). (ii) Return of part of the **premium** which can happen when purchasing a **barrier option**.

recapitalization. Changes made to the **capital** structure or liabilities side of a **balance sheet**. Firms undertake recapitalizations mostly as a result of financial distress or **bankruptcy** problems; however, recapitalization may be a more positive response to changed business or market conditions (cf. **recontracting**).

receivable. Money owed to a firm or individual (cf. **creditor**; **debtor**). Hence *accounts receivable* (cf. **payables**).

receivable pay-through security. An asset-backed security (ABS) where the **underlying** is a pool of **receivables**. Typically such securities, as with credit card ABS issues, involve a top up of the initial pool for a set period in order to allow for a reasonable **maturity** before the **paydown** of the issue begins.

receivables turnover ratio. The relationship between net **sales** and the current value of **trade debtors**. It is intended to indicate the time taken to receive funds from customers; the higher the ratio, the lower it is thought the quality of outstanding debts, because this suggests it takes time to convert sales into cash. See also **ratio analysis**.

receive fixed or **receive floating.** See **fixed rate receiver**; **floating receiver** (cf. **fixed rate payer**; **floating payer**); **receiver**.

receiver. (i) A court- or **creditor**-appointed individual charged with realizing a **debtor's** assets for the benefit of secured creditors in the event of non-payment (cf. **bankruptcy**; **default**; **insolvent**; **lien**; **liquidator**). Hence *receivership*, the state of insolvency of a debtor (cf. **administration order**). (ii) In securities **settlement** the party due to get the securities (cf. **receive-versus-payment**). (iii) The party in an exchange agreement such as an **interest rate swap** or **cross-currency swap** who receives a particular type of cash flow (see Table).

Receiver

	Party who makes the payment	Party who receives the payment
Fixed rate	Fixed payer (fixed rate payer)	Fixed receiver (fixed rate receiver)
Floating rate	Floating payer (floating rate payer)	Floating receiver (floating rate receiver)

receiver's swaption. The **option** position in a **swaption** giving the holder the right to pay the **floating rate** and receive the the **fixed rate**. Also known as a *call swaption* or a *fixed rate receiver's swaption*.

receive-versus-payment or **receive-against-payment (RVP).** A **settlement** instruction that securities (cash) are to be delivered against cash (securities) transfer (**delivery against payment**) (cf. **free delivery**).

recession. A state of an economy when characterized by falling output and employment. Officially, in the UK, a recession exists after four successive quarters of negative growth in **gross national product**. Sometimes called a *depression*, especially when the economic downturn looks persistent.

reciprocal exchange rate (Forex). A quotation of a **foreign exchange rate** using the opposite convention to the market's normal standard. Thus if a currency is normally quoted in **American terms**, a reciprocal exchange rate would have the currency quoted in **European terms**. Thus an exchange rate for sterling against the US dollar which normally has sterling as the **base currency**, would now have the US dollar taking that role. To obtain the rate in terms of the quoted currency as the base involves taking the reciprocal of the normal quote:

Normal quote for sterling (US$/£) $1.7125 = reciprocal quote (US$/£): £0.5839.

Some **currency futures** contracts use reciprocal exchange rates to facilitate **settlement** in the domestic currency (cf. **margin**). For instance, futures traded on US exchanges have European currencies quoted on a reciprocal basis (i.e. in a variable amount of US dollars to one unit of the foreign currency).

reclamation. Recovery of loss due to **bad delivery** (cf. **backdating; partial delivery; purchased accelerated recovery rights**).

recognized clearing house (RCH) (UK). A clearing house authorized by the **Securities and Investments Board** to undertake the **settlement** of transactions under the terms of the **Financial Services Act, 1986**.

recognized investment exchange (RIE) (UK). An exchange authorized by the **Securities and Investments Board** to act as a marketplace for buying and selling financial instruments under the terms of the **Financial Services Act, 1986**.

recognized professional body (RPB) (UK). Professional organization which is registered with the **Securities and Investments Board** to regulate their conduct (cf. **self-regulating organization**).

reconstitution. The reverse process to **coupon stripping**. That is recombining the **coupon** and **principal** elements to recreate a **straight** security.

recontracting. During **bankruptcy** (US) or **insolvency** (UK) a company experiencing **financial distress** may attempt to reorganize its financial claims in such a way as to secure the best use of its assets and its ultimate survival. The formal process by which this can be achieved is called recontracting. It can involve either a private arrangement, negotiated between the company and its creditors, or a court-supervised arrangement as in the USA under the **Bankruptcy Reform Act of 1978** (cf. **workout**). Such arrangements are likely to involve the violation of the claims of **creditors**; for example, a reduction or temporary halt to interest payments or approval for the disposal of assets that had been used as **collateral** for loans. In return for forgoing the original contract, creditors may well safeguard the 'going concern' value of the company, and provide for the eventual satisfaction of at least part of the original claim. The alternative, maintaining the original absolute level of claim, would be likely to lead to a liquidation when creditors may, at best, receive part satisfaction of their claim based on the break-up value of the company. The decision by creditors to enter into a recontracting arrangement will depend upon their assessment of the relative strength of the going concern value, and the ability of the company to continue to operate and meet its reduced commitments, as against the proportion of their claim likely to be satisfied once the assets of the business have been sold. See **covenants; recapitalization**.

reconversion. See **reversal**.

record date. The date at which holders of securities are eligible to receive **dividends** or **coupon** payments, or participate in **rights issues**, **scrip issues**, and so on (cf. **cum; ex**).

recourse. A source of redress should, for example, a **bill** or debt be dishonoured at **maturity**. The holder would have the right of recourse against any of the other parties to the bill or loan, unless expressly negated; that is without recourse (cf. **non-recourse**). See **project finance**.

recovery. A turnaround in prices after a fall (cf. **bear; rally; technical correction**).

recovery fund. A specialized type of investment fund which invests in **recovery stocks** with a view to generating a superior performance. The fund specializes in identifying the appropriate market timing for buying oversold **equities** of cyclical and poorly performing companies.

recovery stock (Equities). Security that is considered to be relatively cheap because of, for example, poor performance but where there is an expectation of some change in the company's **fundamentals** likely to bring about an upward revision in market value. Also used to describe those sectors likely to respond first to positive movements in the **trade cycle**.

red chip (Equities; UK). Name given to a company listed on the **London Stock Exchange** where the controlling interest is a Chinese state-owned entity (cf. **blue chip**).

red clause credit. A condition attached to a **bill** which allows the seller to obtain funds in advance of presenting the documentation. Common in the Australasian wool trade.

reddito alla maturita (Bonds; Italian). **Yield-to-maturity**.

redeemable bond. See **callable**.

redeemable common stock (Equity; USA). Common stock that the issuer may redeem in the future under certain conditions. Such stock is different from common stock repurchased in a stock repurchase plan which then becomes treasury stock.

redeemable preferred stock or **redeemable preference share.** A preferred stock issue that is redeemable. There are a number of alternative types: some have **call provisions**, some call and put provisions, and some are dated liabilities with a final **maturity** and sometimes a **sinking fund** (cf. **irredeemable; perpetual**).

redeemable warrant. See **money-back warrant**.

redemption. The retirement and cancellation of outstanding securities through a cash payment to the holder (cf. **balloon; bullet**). See **call provision; mandatory redemption; prescribed period; sinking fund**.

redemption cushion. The amount, expressed as a percentage, that the **conversion value** on a convertible exceeds the **redemption price**.

redemption date. The date at which the issuer will pay back the **principal** and any outstanding or accrued interest on the security.

redemption price. The price at which a security is, in the case of **mandatory redemption**, or may be, in the case of optional **redemption** or a **put**, redeemed prior to the **maturity date**. Such prices are set at the time of issue and usually at **PAR** or at a **premium**. Thus an issue may have a **call schedule** which indicates the price at which the issuer will redeem the securities, as in the table.

Year	Redemption price
7	$101\frac{1}{2}$
8	101
9	$100\frac{1}{2}$
10	100

redemption yield (Bonds; UK). The **yield-to-maturity** on a fixed rate security, i.e. the yield to the redemption date. See also **gross redemption yield; after-tax yield**.

red herring or **red eye** (USA). A **preliminary prospectus** containing all the information required by the **Securities and Exchange Commission** except the **underwriting terms** (cf. **book building; pathfinder prospectus**). It derives its name from the red dots used to mark the blanks for the market sensitive factors in the terms and conditions on the issue (for instance: the amount of the issue, its price, and its **coupon**.) Although often widely disseminated, it cannot be used to offer securities for sale to the general public. Sometimes called *kite-flying*. See **registration; shelf registration**.

rediscount. Process by which short-term **promissory notes** such as **banker's acceptances** or **bills** which have already been **discounted** at a receiving financial institution are subsequently purchased by another institution. Most **central banks** offer this facility to banks in order to allow them to obtain liquid **funds** (cf. **discount window**).

Rediskontkontingent (Germany). The rediscount quota set by the **Bundesbank** for banks.

German monetary policy is a mixture of official limits and **open-market operations**.

red screen (UK). Where all **market-makers** on the London market are marking their prices down and this shows up on the dealing screens as red strips (cf. **blue screen**). See **screen-trading**.

reduced-cost option. Any of a range of **option combinations** where the cost of the **premium** of the desired **position** is partially **offset** by the selling or **writing** of a corresponding opposite position which pays a premium, thus reducing the overall cost of the option, although the payoff is lower than would be the case with the desired option alone (cf. **cylinder; ratio spread; vertical spread**). A reduced-cost option where the cost of the premium is exactly offset by the value of the premium received is known as a *zero-cost option*. See **option strategies**.

reduced-coupon security. See **missing coupon security**.

reducing balance. See **depreciaton methods**.

reference bank (Banking). A bank whose money market rates are used in determining the settlement interest rate on instruments such as **floating rate notes, syndicated loans**, or **interest rate derivatives**. Hence **reference rate**, for example **London interbank offered rate (LIBOR)**. A number of banks' quotes will usually be averaged. The British Bankers Association collects LIBOR rates for **forward rate agreements**; in this case over a dozen banks' quotes are used in order to get a market average. Some agreements involve a rounding clause where the average is rounded up to the nearest 1/16th per cent.

reference currency. See **European Currency Unit; European Unit of Account; Special Drawing Right**.

reference index. The **index** against which the payments on a **derivative** instrument are calculated. For instance, it might be a **stock index** in the case of an **option** or for an **equity-linked note**; for **commodity-linked** securities, it might be a basket of commodities, a **commodity futures contract**, or a **benchmark** such as Brent Crude (cf. **spread**).

reference rate. (i) (Banking) The rate quoted by a **reference bank** in connection with a **facility** or a **variable rate** instrument such as a **floating rate certificate of deposit** or **floating rate note**. (ii) The **money market rate** against which an instrument or **facility** is priced, for example **London interbank offered rate** or **prime** (USA). (iii) A **foreign exchange** concept for the currency values set for managed exchange rates (cf. **crawling peg**). (iv) The interest rate against which a **derivative** instrument's payments are calculated such as in (ii) above, or other **index** or **benchmark** (cf. **constant maturity treasury; interest rate swap**).

referential bid. (i) A **quote** or price based on a **reference rate**. (ii) In an **auction** or **tender** a bid expressed as a **margin** or **spread** to the highest bid.

refinance credit (Banking). Credit arrangement used in international trade where the buyer uses the facility to pay the seller but still defer payment until the goods are received. It has the same effect as if the seller had accepted a **letter of credit** from the buyer, except that in this case the credit is with the buyer's bank, rather than that of the seller.

refinancing. (i) Raising funds to meet maturing obligations. (ii) Taking advantage of favourable market conditions to retire existing obligations and issue new ones with more favourable terms (cf. **break-even rate**). See also **refunding**. (iii) Used in a more general sense for transactions used to restructure **liabilities** (cf. **recontracting**). Also known as a *restructuring*.

refinancing rate or **refi rate** (Bonds; USA). The rate at which mortgages in a **mortgage-backed security** are re-financed. Because mortgage-borrowers have the right to redeem mortgages before **maturity**, a high-yielding **pool** of mortgages is likely to have a higher refinancing rate than a lower-yielding one, thus reducing the pool. Predicting the rate is difficult since it depends not only on interest rates, but on a combination of natural reductions in the pool as people move homes and the willingness and capacity of individuals to re-mortgage their homes. See **extension risk; prepayment model; reinvestment risk**.

refiner's margin. See crack spread.

reflation. A set of economic policies designed to expand an economy and reverse the effects of recession. Usually involves the use of both monetary and fiscal policies.

refunding (USA). (i) The issuing of new debt to replace existing or redeemed debt. In the USA, most corporate bond issues cannot be called for a period after issue if the funds are coming from fresh issues (cf. **refund protection**). See **rolling debt**. (ii) The US **Treasury's** regular **auction** of new debt, as in *quarterly refunding* (cf. **new money; paydown**).

refunding rate. The saving in interest expense by a debt issuer if debt is refinanced either at **maturity** or by the **exercise** of a **call provision** (cf. **break-even rate**).

refund protection (Bonds; USA). The period between the issue date and the date that the **call provision** can be first exercised allowing the issuer to refund the debt. Refund protection clauses deferring call provisions are a fairly standard feature of US corporate bond issues and are normally five years (ten years for **utilities**). They do not provide complete **call protection** since the issuer may redeem the securities if funds are obtained without the reissue of debt (for instance, by raising **equity**) or making a disposal.

regional bank (Banking). (i) (USA) A bank that operates only in one part of the USA, in either a single state or a group of states rather than nationally (cf. **money center bank**). (ii) Also applied to local Japanese banks, outside the nationally operating **city, long-term**, and **trust** banks.

registered bond. Bond where the issuer or his agent, the **registrar**, maintains records of ownership and interest payment (cf. **book-entry security; physical security**). The alternative condition, where title is transferred by delivering the certificate is, known as a *bearer bond* (cf. **depository receipt**).

registered capital. See authorized stock.

registered commodity (USA). Commodity which is regulated by the federal **Commodity Futures Trading Commission**.

registered competitive market-maker (USA). A **dealer** who is registered with the **National Association of Securities Dealers** as a **market-maker** in a particular security that is traded **over-the-counter**.

registered competitive trader (USA). A New York Stock Exchange member who trades for his own account (cf. **local**). Also known as a floor trader.

registered coupon bond. A registered security for **principal** only. That is, the **coupons** are not registered (cf. **bearer bond**).

registered equity market-maker (USA). An American Stock Exchange member who trades for his own account (cf. **local**).

registered office (UK). The formal address of a company. By law, companies must give this on stationery and any changes registered to the Registrar of Companies.

registered options principal (ROP) (USA). Designated employee who has been registered with the **Securities and Exchange Commission** as to his competence to handle customers' requirements to deal in **options**. Self-policing of such activities is the responsibility of the firm's *compliance registered options principal*.

registered options trader (USA). A floor trader on the **American Stock Exchange** who acts as a **principal** and makes a market in **stock options**.

registered representative or **rep** (USA). An individual who has been authorized to advise on financial investments and has passed the **general securities representative exam** (cf. **advisory broker; agent**). Also called an *account executive*.

registered secondary offering (USA). See **public offering; secondary distribution; seasoned new issue**.

registered security. A security where ownership is recorded by a **registrar** in the name of the holder or a **nominee**. Title can only be transferred with the endorsement of the registered holder. (cf. **bearer security**). Also called a *nominative security*. See **book-entry securities**.

registered shares. See **restricted transferability** (cf. **bearer bond**).

registered trader. Any **trader** who is a member of an exchange, hence registered.

register of charges (UK). Records of any **liens** or prior charges that exist over the **assets** of a company. Such charges have to be registered with the Registrar of Companies, must be kept at the company's registered address, and must be available for inspection by the public.

registrar. A financial institution which maintains records of the issue and holders of securities. In the UK, the title is also used for the recording agency maintaining records of companies: the *Registrar of Companies*.

registration (USA). The process of review by the **Securities and Exchange Commission** of securities to be offered to the public (cf. **exempt securities**). The statement contains detailed financial and other information on the issuer, its management, and the purpose of the offering. Because of the length of time and the delay in reviewing the information, issuers are now largely allowed to use the *shelf registration* method under Section 415.

registration fee. (i) (USA) The fee payable to the Securities and Exchange Commission for registration. Part of the **all-in cost** of an issue. (ii) Fees payable for entering a new owner on a register maintained by a **registrar** when enrolling **registered securities** (cf. **bearer bond**).

registration statement (USA). The **prospectus** and other documents prepared for the **Securities Exchange Commission** and investors in connection with an offering of new securities (cf. **quiet period; red herring; shelf registration**).

règlement (French). Settlement.

règlement mensuel (RM) (French). Monthly settlement (cf. **contango market**).

regression. (i) A statistical approach to examining the relationship between two or more variables (cf. **regression analysis**). In finance, such an examination is important because it allows for the indentification of patterns of behaviour and price relationships in markets. If historical observations suggest certain relationships, then a basis for **prediction** is established. For those interested in the pricing, trading, and issuing of all types of financial instruments, understanding what factors can affect these is important, and the relative significance of these different factors, is regarded a essential for successful market participation (cf. **correlation risk; regression hedging models**). (ii) The tendency for a price or rate series over time to revert towards its long-term mean value or rate. See **reversion to the mean**.

regression analysis. A group of statistical techniques aimed at quantifying the relationship between two or more variables. The purpose of identifying such associations may be to permit quantitative analysis and prediction. This is usually achieved by applying the techniques of **statistical inference** where the main objective is to discover whether variables derived from a population of items are closely related. It also allows various hypotheses about the types of relationship, and the variables to be included in the relationship to be tested for validity. As is the case for **correlation**, regression analysis is concerned with capturing statistical association, and of itself does not imply causation. Regression analysis is frequently used to establish the interaction of different variables in order to determine the **hedge ratio** in a **cross-hedge**; or for pricing, for instance, **rainbow options**. See **autocorrelation; econometrics; heteroscedasticity; multicollinearity; least squares regression**.

regression hedging model. A method of hedging an **underlying** using **derivatives** where the relationship of the price or rate behaviour based on a regression is used to determine the amount of the hedge required. The basic equation is:

$$y_t = \alpha + \beta x_t + \varepsilon_t$$

where y_t is the hedging instrument at time t and x_t the underlying at time t. ε_t is an error term. The regression hedge requires that the two sides be weighted by the regression coefficient β.

regular dates. Same as **even dates.** See also **end-end.**

regular delivery, regular way delivery, or **settlement** (USA). In the US **bond** and **money markets,** the normal method for settling transactions is that **delivery** is made against **fed funds** on the next business day (*T+1*) following the trade (cf. **tom/next**). For **equities** it is five business days (*T+5*), although plans are advanced to reduce this to three business days (*T+3*). See **cash delivery.**

In the stock markets and the **eurobond** market, regular delivery takes place three business days after the transaction is agreed (*T+3*). Regular delivery for the **eurocurrency** market is known as **spot;** two business days after the transaction is agreed (*T+2*).

regular dividend. The **dividend** that a company expects to pay regularly in the future (cf. **extra dividend**). Used to compute the **dividend yield.**

regulated commodities (USA). Those **commodities** where trading is regulated by the **Commodity Futures Trading Commission.**

regulated futures contract (RFC) (Commodities; USA). **Futures contracts** traded on, or subject to, the rules of an exchange designated by the regulatory authority, the **Commodity Futures Trading Commission,** and which use the **market-to-market** method of determining the **equity** stakes of a trader and thus the **minimum margin.** See **maintenance margin.**

regulated market. Any market where there is a degree of supervision concerning either permissible price movements, market behaviour, or other control on the freedom of participants. Regulated markets tend to be organized exchanges.

regulation. Rules governing the behaviour and activities of firms or individuals. See **capital adequacy; compliance; Securities and Exchange Commission; Securities and Investments Board.**

Regulation A (USA). (i) The rules governing the partial exemption from the **registration** requirements for small issues of less than US$1.5 million. (ii) The **Federal Reserve** rules governing the use of the **discount window** by member banks.

Regulation D (Securities; USA). A regulation by the **Securities and Exchange Commission** which gives exemption to high **net worth** individuals from the maximum tally in private limited partnerships. Such individuals are known as **accredited investors.**

Regulation G (Banking; USA). The **Federal Reserve** rules governing the credit providing activities of non-bank institutions.

Regulation M (Banking; USA). The **Federal Reserve** regulation requiring member banks to keep **reserves** against their net borrowings or for **eurodollars** lent by foreign branches to domestic domiciled borrowers from their foreign branches over a twenty-eight-day averaging period.

Regulation Q (Banking; USA). The **Federal Reserve** regulation that limited the amount of interest that banks could pay on retail deposits. Deposits over US$100,000 were exempt. Such limitations were abolished by the Depository Institutions Deregulation and Monetary Control Act of 1980.

Regulation S (USA). **Securities and Exchange Commission** rules governing the offering of securities in the **euromarkets.**

Regulation T (USA). The **Federal Reserve** regulation on credit extended by financial intermediaries for **margin** transactions. The Federal Reserve sets **initial margin** and eligible **collateral** for such activity (cf. **margin requirement**).

Regulation U (USA). The **Federal Reserve** regulation governing the amount of credit that may be advanced by a **bank** to a borrower for the purchase of **listed** **securities** when the loan is to be **secured** by such **stocks** (cf. **collateral**). See **margin; margin call.**

Regulation Z (USA). The **Federal Reserve** regulation governing the application of the Truth in Lending requirement of the Consumer Protection Act of 1968.

regulatory arbitrage. (i) The propensity of financial institutions to structure their operations in such a way as to minimize the impact of regulation, or its burden, on their operations. Thus banks, which are generally highly regulated, have in some circumstances established non-bank affiliates or subsidiaries which have a less onerous regulatory burden to allow them to pursue certain types of business. Since most regulators are committed to the concept of the 'level playing field', such opportunities are likely to decline in the future. However, international harmonization of regulatory standards, such as the **Basle Capital Convergence Accord** or the **capital adequacy directive,** do leave differences in capital requirements between different types of activities, such as lending and trading in securities. (ii) A set of transactions designed to bypass regulatory obstacles to direct investment or ownership. Thus if direct investment is prohibited, it may be possible to set up a **special purpose vehicle** (SPV) which allows an indirect exposure to the **underlying** using the SPV as a **conduit**. Although each step of the process is legitimate, the ultimate aim is to circumvent the regulations.

Regulatory News Service (RNS) (UK). London Stock Exchange information dissemination service used to announce price-sensitive information on **quoted** companies.

rehypothecation. Term used to describe the pledging of securities held in **brokers'** client accounts as **collateral** for the borrowings used to finance the acquisition of securities on **margin** (cf. **margin account**). See **margin agreement**.

reinsurance. The process of subcontracting part of an **insurable risk** to a third party. Hence *reinsurer*, for the party contracting to accept the risk.

reintermediation. See **disintermediation**.

reinvestment. The recycling of **dividend**, **coupon**, interest, and principal cash flows back into the same or similar securities (cf. **roll-up funds**).

reinvestment rate. (i) The rate at which an investor assumes the interest payments can be reinvested. See **realized yield**, **estimated total return**; **discounted cash flow**. (ii) It can also mean the rate at which funds can be reinvested at **maturity**, or when sold (cf. **extension risk**).

reinvestment rate premium. A premium factor affecting **futures** prices due to movements in interest rates (cf. **basis risk**; **price discovery**).

reinvestment risk. The risk that an investor will have to reinvest income at lower interest rates than the **yield** on the original holding, or initially assumed. *Ex ante* **internal rate of return** calculations assume that intermediate cash flows are reinvested at the original rate; if this is not so, the actual outcome may differ significantly from the predicated result (cf. **estimated total return**; **extension risk**; **yield-to-maturity**).

reinvoicing centre. Used in **centralized treasury** management to act as an in-house **clearing** centre for payments between **subsidiaries** (cf. **concentration banking**; **netting**).

related party (UK). Any organization or individual who may exercise significant influence over the affairs of a firm (cf. **controlling interest**).

relationship transaction. See **cash and carry** (cf. **basis transaction**).

relative dividend yield. A method used to compare the attractions of different **common stocks** based on their relative **dividend yields**.

relative gap ratio. See **gap analysis**.

relative performance option. See **outperformance option** (cf. **rainbow option**).

relative strength. A measure of the price or rate performance of an **asset**, an **index**, a particular security, industry, or sector in relation to a **benchmark**, typically a market-wide index. It is not an absolute indication of performance in that it only measures how the security has moved compared to the market or group as a whole. As a tool, its intention is to show relative value (cf. **mean reversion**). The statistic derived from such an analysis is known as a *relative strength indicator*. It can also be viewed as a chart showing the two price series rebased for comparison so as to show the relative performance of the two over time. See also **momentum model**.

relative value. The value of one security in relation to another in terms of **maturity**, **return**, **risk**, or **liquidity**.

re-leveraging. Transaction aimed at significantly increasing the amount of debt (hence **leverage**) in the **capital structure** of a company (cf. **equity buyback**). It is sometimes used as a **takeover** defence. See **refinancing**; **restructuring**; **tax shield**.

remainderman. The individual or organization which is the **principal** or residual beneficiary of a trust when it is dissolved.

remarketed preferred stock (RP) (Equity; USA). A variant of the **money market preferred stock** issue developed by Merrill Lynch that involves reselling the maturing issues. It has the additional feature of allowing the buyer to choose between a seven-day or a forty-nine-day interest fixing period. Such a **preferred stock** issue depends on the ability of the **remarketing agent** to find buyers. Presumably the alternative long or short interest basis is designed to make the security attractive even in a **bear market** (cf. **bells-and-whistles**). Also known as *share adjusted broker remarketed equity security* (SABRES). See **auction rate preferred stock**.

remarketed reset floating rate note (remarketed reset floater). A type of **floating rate note** or a **variable rate note** where the **coupon** rate is determined by a **remarketing agent** in line with current interest rates such that at the rollover; the notes should trade at **par**. In the absence of agreement on the required coupon rate, a predetermined formula or **backstop** rate is imposed;

holders normally have the right to **put** the notes to the remarketing agent at par in this situation. In some issues, the notes are **subordinated** obligations of the issuer. Also known as a *remarketed variable rate note*.

remarketing agent. Term for a **broker-dealer** who is responsible for reoffering securities **put** to an issuer in a **retractable bond** or other type of **puttable** structure and where the issuer does not want to redeem the securities (cf. **variable rate note**).

réméré (French). A type of **repurchase agreement** where the deliverer of the securities or collateral has the right, but not the obligation, to repurchase them at **maturity** (cf. **pension livrée**).

remitting bank (Banking). (i) The bank which sends payments to another bank. (ii) The bank in a foreign transaction which provides the documents in support of a credit due, such as a **letter of credit**, for the collecting bank to obtain payment. This is then sent to the remitting bank in favour of the exporter's account.

remuneration. Payment for services rendered (cf. **management fee**).

rendement (French). **Yield**.

renounceable documents (UK). Temporary proof of ownership of securities used to facilitate transfers pending the receipt of definitive **certificates**. With a **new issue**, this in the form of a **provisional allotment letter**; with a **rights issue**, it is a provisional allotment letter; with a **bonus**, **capitalization**, or **scrip issue** it is a renounceable certificate. They are **bearer securities**, although the definitive certificates that will be ultimately issued are **registered** (cf. **registrar**).

rent. A payment made for the use of an **asset** and usually applied to physical assets such as property. Intangibles normally are *licensed* rather than rented.

rental lease. See full service lease.

Renten-Offerten-System (ROS) (Bonds; Germany). Bond electronic trading system in use for all types of domestic bonds.

rentes (French). Perpetual government bonds. See **consols**; **irredeemable**; **one-way stock option**; **perpetuity**.

rentes sur l'État (France). Government bond. See **obligations assimilables du Trésor**.

renting back. See sale and leaseback.

renunciation (i) (Equities; UK). In the UK, a new issue of **shares** is effected first by a letter of **allotment**, with a *renunciation form* attached. During the renunciation period the **rights** to these shares may be sold. Investors who retain the shares or buy the shares on the **after-market** (and therefore attain title through the renunciation) are subsequently issued with definitive **certificates**. See **grey market**. (ii) (UK). Method of selling **unit trust** holdings (cf. **transfer**). This involves renouncing the units back to the trust managers who then redeem the units for cash.

reoffer price or **yield.** The price or rate (usually the **yield-to-maturity**) at which the **underwriters** offer securities under a **purchase and sale** or a **fixed price reoffer agreement**.

reopen an issue. When an issue sells more of an existing issue rather than offering a new issue. Usually done to assist secondary market **liquidity** or where the old issue is trading close to **par**. The trend in government bond markets (particularly the USA, UK, and latterly France with their **obligations assimilables du Trésor**) in recent years has been to consolidate issuance into large liquid issues where additional **tranches** may be added from time to time (cf. **benchmark**). See **fungible**; **taplet**.

reorganization (USA). (i) The process of financial reconstruction in **financial distress** or **bankruptcy** (cf. **recapitalization**). See **Chapter 11**. (ii) Any capital restructuring which maintains the existing company (cf. **re-leveraging**).

reorganization bond (USA). A security issue made to creditors while a firm is in **bankruptcy** (cf. **assented securities**; **non-assented**). Because of the financial difficulties of the issuer, these normally take the form of **income bonds**.

rep. See account executive.

repackaged perpetual floating rate note. See **instantly repackaged perpetual**.

repackaged security. A new issue of securities made by placing an existing security in a trust and issuing new securities backed up by ownership of the original issue. A form of **financial engineering** designed to change the characteristics of an existing issue (for instance to negate the effect of a **call provision**) and to make the issue more attractive to investors. Repackaging is designed to take advantage of **anomalies** in the market or across markets. Examples include the repackaging of perpetual floating rate notes into **synthetic securities** to provide investors with a final **maturity**, or removing the effect of **foreign exchange** risk from a **dual currency bond**. Sometimes called simply *repackaging*. See **instantly repackaged perpetual; synthetic**.

repatriation. Returning foreign profits and investments to their country of origin. Exchange controls may limit the ability to repatriate funds in some cases. See also **country risk; foreign direct investment**.

repayment. The return of sums borrowed.

repayment period (Banking). The period of a loan after the **grace period** to **maturity** over which **principal** is paid back by a borrower. Thus a ten-year loan with a six-year **grace period** would have a four-year repayment period.

replacement capital. See venture capital.

replacement cost or **replacement value** (i) The cost of replacing an existing asset (cf. **historical cost**). (ii) The loss incurred by having to replace a **counterparty** to a transaction (cf. **counterparty risk**). See **marked-to-market**.

replacement cycle. A period of time over which an **asset** or product would normally be renewed because either it had worn out or it had become redundant according to technology or customer taste. It is regarded as an important consideration in strategic planning as it provides an opportunity to anticipate and plan for changes in industry competitive forces. (cf. **rate options**) Sometimes known as an *asset* or *product life cycle*

replicating portfolio. The portfolio made up of units of the **underlying** and borrowed funds that equals the cash flow of a call on the underlying. It is the **dynamic hedging** model that underlies the **option pricing models** used for deriving the **fair value of an option**. Also called the *duplicating portfolio*.

replication. A dynamic **hedging** or investment strategy that recreates the payoff pattern of an **option** or security with an **embedded option** (cf. **delta hedge**). It is usually undertaken with liquid instruments, such as **futures**, in order to duplicate the **risk** characteristics of a particular, usually illiquid, instrument. Replication forms a key part of many **over-the-counter** hedging practices for **exotic options** or for **portfolio insurance**. Also called *duplication*. See also **option replication** (cf. **synthetic**).

repo rate. See repurchase rate.

reporting deadlines. The requirements of an exchange placed on traders which provide for the time elapse between when a deal is struck and when it must be recorded by the exchange's information systems. The deadlines can differ according to the type of security and the quantities being dealt. Sometimes called *to mark* the transaction. See **tape; consolidated tape; Stock Exchange Automated Quotations**.

reporting dealer (Bonds; USA). See **primary dealer**.

reporting limit. The requirement by **brokers** to report to the exchange **positions** in particular **contracts** when they exceed a certain **limit**. The requirement aims to ensure that no one participant is in a position to influence the market, and to ensure that brokers have sufficient resources to back the positions they have dealt in. See also **disclosure level**.

report of condition. See balance sheet.

report of income. See income statement.

repos. (i) (USA) The term applied to **Federal Reserve open-market operation** transactions where it buys securities and agrees to sell them back at an agreed price and date (cf. **reverses**). By dealing in such **repurchase agreements** the Federal Reserve can smooth out reserve holdings. (ii) **Bank of England repurchase agreements** with **gilt-edged market makers** used to provide securities for **short positions**. (iii) General term for a repurchase agreement.

representations. Information about a transaction made by one party to another in furtherance of the deal. In many cases, representations are limited to information provided in a **prospectus** or **placing memorandum**, the intermediary disclaiming any responsibility for the correctness or accuracy of any other information provided. See **disclaimer**.

representative office. An office of a firm that is less than a full branch or operation.

reprice. Used to describe the situation when **floating rate** or **variable rate** instruments or **deposits** have their interest rates **reset** in line with prevailing market conditions. Such instruments are said to *reprice* at this point (cf. **rollover**).

repriceable assets or **repriceable liabilities.** See gap analysis.

repudiation. A declaration by a debtor giving intent to refuse to service interest or principal on borrowings (cf. **moratorium**).

repurchase. (i) To buy back something previously sold (cf. **cover**). (ii) Any combination of purchase and sale transactions of a temporary nature, treated as a package. See **repurchase agreement; reverse repurchase agreement**. (iii) Operations designed to buy in previously issued securities with a view to cancellation. See **buyback; stock repurchase plan**.

repurchase agreement (repo; RP) (Bonds; Money Markets). An agreement whereby a holder of securities makes a **spot** sale and simultaneous **forward** repurchase for a future date at a preagreed price. The transaction is made up of two simultaneous transactions: (*a*) the buying of securities by a **counterparty** from a bank or **dealer** and (*b*) the commitment by the bank or dealer to buy them back at an agreed price on an agreed future date. The interest rate and term of the loan are pre-agreed, and upon repayment the security is returned. In effect the buyer is lending money to the seller for the period of the transaction and the terms reflect this (cf. **gensaki; overnight repurchase agreement; term repurchase agreement**). It can also refer to a method of borrowing by using a security as **collateral**. The borrower retains possession of the security and continues to receive any interest payments. As a result, the security buyer lends the seller money for the period of the agreement with the security provided as collateral. Repos are extensively used by dealers to finance their **positions** (cf. **open repurchase agreement; term repurchase agreement**). A repo from the viewpoint of the counterparty which provides securities against cash is known as a *reverse repurchase agreement* (cf. **matched sales**). See also **buysellback forward; dollar roll; money broker; pension livrée**.

repurchase book. See matched book.

repurchase rate or **repo rate (RP rate).** The interest rate or **yield** at which the holder of securities will enter into a **repurchase agreement**. Often taken to be a key rate for determining market yields as it enables securities to be converted into cash and vice versa (cf. **conversion; reverse conversion; short position**).

To find the repurchase rate (RP rate):

$$\text{RP rate (\%)} = \frac{\text{Repurchase price} - \text{Sale price}}{\text{Sale price}}$$
$$\times \frac{\text{Basis}}{\text{Days RP'd}} \times 100$$

To find the repurchase price, given the RP rate:

$$\frac{\text{Repurchase}}{\text{price}} = \frac{\text{Sale}}{\text{price}} \left(1 + \frac{\text{RP rate(\%)} \times \text{Days RP'd}}{\text{Basis} \times 100} \right)$$

reputational capital. That part of a company's asset value representing the capitalized value of brand names owned by the business. A reference to the *goodwill* value often said to be embedded in such institutions as investment banks!

request for quotes (RFQ). A method used for obtaining a two-way market price in **flex options** where **market-makers** and other exchange members are notified of a request for the pricing of a flex option. The RFQ specifies the details of the transaction but not whether the intention is to buy or sell. After the appropriate *request response time*, the **broker** seeking the quote will either enter a transaction (via **open outcry**) or seek confirmation from their principal by asking for a **quote extension time**.

required rate of return (RRR). The minimum return for a project to be acceptable. Also known as the *opportunity cost of capital*.

required reserves (USA). The minimum **reserve** requirement necessary for member banks of the Federal Reserve System to support their liabilities. See **reserves**.

re-regulation. The reimposition of previously abolished regulations. The reversal of the trend first established in the 1980s to liberalize the world's financial markets. In effect, this took the form of removing the restrictions on the type of business that could be undertaken by domestic financial institutions. Following some dramatic and significant failures, many of the same regulatory authorities have been looking for ways of updating the rules and supervisory systems. See **Basle Capital Convergence Accord; liberalization**.

rescheduling. The renegotiation of the terms of an existing debt obligation, usually to extend the **maturity** or **amortization** provisions and sometimes as a result of a **default** or **capital reconstruction** (cf. **assented securities; non-assented; repudiation**). In the international markets, the term is often used to imply **sovereign debt** (cf. **London Club; Paris Club**). See **rolling debt**.

rescission. A remedy available from a court of law which restores the condition prevailing before a contract was entered into (cf. **ultra vires**).

research and development limited partnership (USA). A **limited partnership** which invests in research and development projects. The partners expect to get a royalty on any income generated by the projects as well as benefiting from any depreciation allowances.

reserve. (i) (Accounting) An entry that provides for a future liability (cf. **accrual**). Hence, a *loan loss reserve* for future **credit**-related loses from **loans**. Also known as a *provision, provision account*, or a *reserve account*. See also **reserves**. (ii) Funds set aside to meet a future liability (cf. **dedication**).

reserve assets or **funds.** (i) **Funds** or assets held as reserves domestically or internationally (for instance foreign exchange reserves held by a **central bank**). (ii) Technical term for banks' holdings held at the central bank. For instance, US banks' balances at the **Federal Reserve**. These are usually just referred to as *reserves* (cf. **free reserves**).

reserve–assets ratio (Banking; UK). Method of controlling bank lending used in the 1970s in the UK that required banks to maintain a minimum ratio of reserves to **total assets**. It was abandoned in 1981 in favour of a **liquidity** ratio, requiring banks to hold a certain proportion of their assets in **cash** or **cash equivalents**. See **reserve assets**; **reserve requirements**.

Reserve Bank (USA). See **Federal Reserve**.

reserve capital. See **hidden reserves**; **uncalled capital** (cf. **partly-paid**).

reserve clause. A **euromarkets** condition in a borrowing allowing the lender to pass on any unfavourable changes in **reserve requirements** as a cost to the borrower.

reserve currency. Currency held by countries as part of their **foreign exchange** reserves to meet foreign currency payments and manage its trade balance. The principal reserve currencies are the US dollar, Deutschmark, Japanese yen, pound sterling, and the French franc.

reserve for credit losses or **reserve for loan losses** (Banking). A **reserve** held against loans based on the expected **problem assets** or **nonperforming loans** seen to be inherent in the lending process (cf. **retention**). Such reserves take into account the past and predicted future **default** rates on various types of lending based on management's experience. Factors used to establish the appropriate level of the reserve include: trends in **portfolio** size, quality, maturity, and composition, historical loss-rate experience, lending policies, new products, the status and amounts of nonperforming loans and **past due** loans, the adequacy of the **collateral**, and current as well as expected economic and industry-specific conditions that may affect particular borrowers. In addition, management's judgement of volatile **risk** factors such as interest rates, currency movements, and **asset** prices that may significantly affect the potential losses. The reserve also typically includes a further **margin** as an additional buffer against adverse changes in **credit worthiness** or errors in estimating the above factors. Generally, the determination of the adequacy of the reserve is based

on the above and is not specifically applied to individual **loans** or segments in the portfolio. Sometimes the requirement to maintain such reserves is dictated by the regulator. In addition, there can be specific reserves against particular loans or general reserves to cover the expected, but undetected, problem loans that are a feature of any lending. Also called the *allowance for loan losses*.

reserve price. In an **auction** or **tender**, the price under which the vendor is not prepared to sell. In a repurchase tender, it may be a maximum price at which securities can be tendered.

reserve requirements, reserve–asset ratio, or **reserve ratio.** The percentage of different types of deposits or **eligible assets** which member banks must hold with their **central bank**. These deposits often pay no interest and banks therefore compute the amount of interest lost in setting their **bid** rates. Reserve requirements are seen by some central banks as a useful tool for managing **monetary policy**. See **Bundesbank**; **capital adequacy**.

reserves. (i) (Banking). Those assets held in near cash equivalents, such as **treasury bills** or very-short dated securities (cf. **eligible bills**). (ii) (Accounting) Cumulative retained profits. (iii) Sometimes used in the sense of a **provision** (cf. **bad debts**; **problem assets**).

reserves market. See **fed funds**.

reserves multiplier (Banking; USA). The method used by the **Federal Reserve** to determine the amount of **reserves** banks have to keep to support their **liabilities**.

reset. See **reprice**.

reset date. (i) The date at which the **reference** rate on a **floating rate note** or other instrument or **derivative** where the payments are adjusted or reset to the current market rate are made. It is also known as the *rollover date*. (ii) The date on which the **reset option's** exercise price is set.

reset frequency. The time span between adjustments to the interest rate or **coupon** in a **floating rate instrument**, loan, or **derivative** to bring them in line with current market conditions (cf. **reprice**; **reset date**).

reset in-arrears swap. See **LIBOR in arrears swap**.

reset notes. See **extendible bond**; **retractable bond**.

reset option or **reset warrant.** A type of option offering the **holder** an adjustment to the **exercise**

or **strike price** in his favour if, at the **reset date**, the option is **out of the money**. It is a hybrid form of **lookback option**. A **call** would have the strike price reduced, a **put** the strike increased. Different versions may provide full adjustment or partial adjustment to the strike, or may involve general movements in the **underlying** rather than the rate on the reset date. The structure is also known as a *anti-crash option, partial lookback option, step-down option*, or *strike reset option*.

reset period. The time over which a **floating rate** interest payment is calculated. Typically the reset period might be a month, three months, or six months. In some cases, the borrower can choose from a range of periods, allowing a degree of flexibility in response to market conditions.

reset swap or **reset in-arrears swap.** An interest rate swap or cross-currency swap where the **floating rate payment** is set in arrears at the end of the period, rather than at the start. The **floating receiver** will favour such an arrangement when the floating rate is expected to be higher at the end than at the start. Also known as an *arrears swap* or a *back-end reset swap*. See LIBOR in arrears swap.

resident. A legal and tax term for the country of domicile or residence for tax purposes. Thus a UK incorporated company would normally be considered resident in the UK for tax purposes. The rules for residency are complex.

residual. (i) The error term in an **econometric** equation. See **residuals**. (ii) Any remaining value left after prior claims have been met (cf. **equity**).

residual bond. In the context of an **asset-backed security**, a security which has a residual claim on any cash flows once more senior **tranches** of the issue have been paid off (cf. **junior; remainderman**). See **collateralized mortgage obligation equity.**

residual claim. The rights of **shareholders** to the remaining assets once the fixed claims on a business have been met. Since they are owners they are entitled to a pro rata share of any remaining value.

residual risk. (i) In modern portfolio theory, that part of total risk that has not been eliminated by efficient diversification. See **specific risk**. (ii) Non-market risk elements, as in *stock specific risk*. (iii) In hedging, the price or rate variation between the **underlying** and the hedge that is left when the two positions are combined (cf. **basis risk**). See also cross-hedge.

residuals. That part of a regression equation that is not explained by the predictor variables (cf. **specific risk**)

residual security. Any contingent security that may be **converted** or **exercised** for **common stock** (cf. **fully diluted earnings per share**).

resistance area, level, or **point.** A level of prices or rates at which a trend can be anticipated to stabilize or reverse. If the trend breaks past this level a further significant movement in the same direction is expected. See **chart analysis; head and shoulders; line pattern; triangle pattern; technical analysis.**

resolution (UK). A decision placed before **shareholders** at a company meeting in their capacity as its owners. For example, agreeing to the payment of a **dividend** requires a resolution, as does issuing more **shares**.

Resolution Funding Corporation (REFCORP) (Bonds; USA). The funding arm of the **Resolution Trust Corporation** which raises funds on the domestic bond market. REFCORP has issued bonds with an **original maturity** of forty years.

Resolution Trust Corporation (RTC) (USA). The federal agency charged with supervising the reconstruction and bail out of **savings and loan associations** (S&Ls) established in 1989. This need arose due to the general insolvency in the industry and the need to **recapitalize** many S&Ls in the late 1980s. The total cost was considered to be in the region of US$500 billion, spread over half a century. This is being achieved by borrowing large sums in the domestic bond market through the **Resolution Funding Corporation**.

respondentia bond. See **guarantee; hypothecation**.

restricted option or **restricted series.** A condition imposed by a **derivatives** exchange on opening new positions in a particular **option series**. This typically arises if the **option** is deeply **out of the money** with little active trading activity (cf. **illiquid**).

restricted transferability. A condition attached to some securities, typically **common stocks**, which limits the ability of the vendor to freely transfer the securities to any purchaser. Sometimes this is a condition within the **trust indenture** of the securities, or a feature of the law, for instance, the limitation of foreign ownership of common stocks or **ordinary shares** in certain countries. Securities subject to restricted transferability are often called *registered*, since the ability to receive **dividends** and to vote on corporate **resolutions** depends on having the ownership registered with a **registrar** in compliance with the regulations, or sometimes even at the discretion of the issuing firm. The question of restrictions on rights and ownership is a major issue in international investment and **corporate governance**.

restrictive covenants. See **covenants**.

restrictive endorsement (Banking). A limitation imposed by the endorser on the ability of holders to transfer a **banker's acceptance** or **bill of exchange**.

restructuring. Altering the **maturity** of debt by extending the **tenor** or changing its type (cf. **capital restructuring; debt-equity swap; recapitalization; refinancing; rescheduling**).

retail. Market term for individual and small institutional and corporate customers, as opposed to banks and large institutions and corporates. In other words, **end investors** as opposed to middlemen, traders or wholesalers. A financial institution which specializes in marketing to such customers is known as a *retail house*. A *retail investor* is one who invests on his own account and not as a fiduciary for others; this is often synonymous with small orders (cf. **odd lot**). See **institutional investor; Street**.

retail banking. Usually taken to mean providing banking facilities to individuals, as opposed to *corporate banking* which means servicing the needs of firms.

retail certificate of deposit (retail CD) (Banking; USA). **Certificate of deposit** which is US$100,000 or less and thus eligible for **deposit** insurance protection by the **Federal Deposit Insurance Corporation**.

Retail Automatic Execution System (RAES) (USA). Electronic transaction system for public orders designed to match the order flow to the best **offers** and **bids**. See also **Designated Order Turnaround**.

Retail Price Index (RPI) (UK). The UK version of the **consumer price index**; a measure of price changes at the retail level. Used in calculating the values of those **index-linked bonds** issued by the UK government. It has two versions, one which excludes mortgage interest payments (RPIX), since this has the perverse effect of increasing the RPI when interest rates are raised (usually as a way of reducing inflation). The other (traditional) index includes mortgage interest.

retail repurchase agreement (retail repo). A **repurchase agreement** undertaken with a bank.

retained cash flow. Free cash flow less dividends.

retained earnings. That part of a firm's earnings not paid out in the form of **dividends** (cf. **reserves**). The ratio of retained earnings to dividends is called the **payout ratio**. Also called *retained profits*.

retention. That part of an **underwriter's** commitment that is left after the **pot** and the **selling group** allocation has been made. In some markets, the underwriter seeks *protection* from the **lead manager** that he will receive a given amount of securities.

retention money. Funds held in a third party account to cover unforeseen problems on the post-commissioning performance of a completed contract (cf. **hold-back**).

retention rate or **ratio.** The percentage amount of profit retained rather than distributed as **dividends** by a corporation (cf. **payout ratio**).

retire. To remove a debt obligation by **refunding**, a **sinking fund**, repurchase, or exercising a **call provision**.

retractable bond. A bond where the issuer is permitted to reset the **coupon** arbitrarily on the date which the issue is retractable. The investor can choose to **exercise** his **put provision** on the bond or accept the new coupon. In some cases, where investors put the bonds, the issuer may reoffer these via a **remarketing agent**. Sometimes called an *extendible bond*. See **borrower's option-lender's option; retractable maturity**.

retractable maturity. The date upon which the issuer has the right to **call the bonds** and when the investor has the right to **put the bonds** to the issuer at a fixed price (cf. **exercise date**).

retractable preferred stock (Equity). Preferred stock issue where the issuer is permitted to reset the **dividend** at his discretion on the date at which the issue is retractable. Holders may choose either to **exercise** their **put provision** on the preferred stock or accept the new dividend rate. See **retractable bond**.

retractable swap. See **callable swap**.

return. The difference between the initial sum invested and the final value given as a percentage, by convention usually expressed as an annual rate. See **interest rate calculations**.

return of capital. Repayment of equity by a company.

return on assets (ROA). (i) The same as **return on capital employed**. (ii) A method of measuring the earnings from a **eurocredit** derived from the **spread** and fees divided by the average outstanding assets employed.

return on average assets. A measure of performance used for firms which is calculated by dividing **net income** by the **average** of the **total assets** over the assessment period. See **ratio analysis**.

return on capital employed (ROCE). The ratio of profit to the amount of **capital** used during a particular period. Roce can differ because of various interpretations of profit and capital. Usually taken as profit before interest and tax divided by **capital employed** less **intangibles**, such as **goodwill**. In the USA also known as the *return on assets* or the *return on investment*. See **ratio analysis**.

return on common equity (ROCE). The return earned by **common stock** holders in a given period (cf. **earnings per share**). See also next entry.

return on equity (ROE). A measure of the profitability of **equity**, normally taken to mean **common stock** arrived at by dividing profit after interest and tax, less **dividends** on **preferred stock**, by outstanding common stock.

return on investment (ROI). See **return on capital employed**.

return on sales (ROS). The operating profit per unit of sales or turnover. See **ratio analysis**.

return simulation. A method used to predict fixed interest or **portfolio** returns under different projections of future interest rates.

Reuters. Global screen-based information provider initially set up in 1851 as a correspondent news service for newspapers, but now one of many firms providing real-time data on market prices and information. Current systems even allow users to make transactions using the system (cf. **GLOBEX**)

revalorization. The redenomination of a currency, usually as a result of inflation making the value of the old units very small. The French franc was revalorized in the 1960s when new francs replaced old francs at a ratio of 1,000 : 1. Hyperinflating countries such as Brazil have revalorized their currencies several times.

revaluation. (i) Increasing the value of one currency in relation to others. Usually used when the **par value** of a currency is changed within a fixed or administered exchange rate regime, such as the **European Monetary System** (cf. **devaluation**). See **appreciation** and **depreciation**. (ii) Used to describe the **marked-to-market** of a position or

portfolio (and often abbreviated to *reval*). (iii) Changes to **balance sheet** items as a result of changes to their value since being acquired. The most common items to be revalued in this way are land or property, which if left unchanged can seriously distort the interpretation of accounts (cf. **book value**; **historic cost accounting convention**).

revenue anticipation note (RAN) (USA). Short-term **notes** issued by US municipalities and states in anticipation of future revenues (cf. **bond anticipation note**).

revenue bills (Money markets; UK). A type of short-term **promissory note** issued by UK local authorities in anticipation of future tax or grant revenues (cf. **tax anticipation note**).

revenue bonds (USA). A US local government bond secured by income from municipal activities such as renting property (cf. **industrial revenue bond**). Typical examples include bonds for publicly owned utility companies (known as *power bonds*) or to finance housing (known as *housing bonds*).

reversal. (i) A **portfolio** management term to describe a transaction that changes the balance of a portfolio back to a previous position. See also **switching**. (ii) An **options position** consisting of selling a **put** and buying a **synthetic put**. It would involve buying a **call**, selling a put with the same **strike price**, and selling the **underlying**. This is also known as a *reconversion* or a *reverse conversion*. (iii) To reverse the cash flows on a **swap**. That is to enter into an opposing swap transaction to nullify the existing position (cf. **cancellation**; **netting**). See **reverse a swap**. (iv) Covering a **short position** in the **forward foreign exchange** market by buying an **option**.

reverse annuity mortgage (RAM) (USA). A mortgage designed to free up **capital** for senior citizens using their homes as **collateral**.

reverse a swap. (i) The closing-out of a securities **swap position**. (ii) Entering into another and opposite side **interest rate swap** or **cross-currency** swap to close out the original transaction (cf. **assignment**; **cancellation**; **netting**; **novation**).

reverse auction (Bonds; UK). **Tender** used by the Bank of England to buy in **gilt-edged** issues (cf. **public sector debt reduction**). See also **stock repurchase plan**.

reverse calendar spread. A type of **intra-commodity spread** where the longer-dated contract is sold and the shorter-dated contract purchased (cf. **calendar spread**; **inter-commodity spread**; **inter-**

market spread; intra-market spread). The transaction can be set up with either **futures** or **options** and, with the latter, this can have different **strike prices** on the two options (cf. **diagonal spread**). Also known as a *reverse time spread*.

reverse cash and carry. The simultaneous sale of a **cash market commodity** or instrument for physical delivery and the purchase of the same commodity or instrument for delivery at a future date (cf. **cash and carry**). Also used in the securities markets where the sale is financed either by a loan or through a **repurchase agreement**. Also known as *selling the basis*.

reverse contingent premium option. The opposite (reverse) structure to a **contingent premium option**.

reverse conversion. Option strategy designed to lock in a predetermined profit from mispricing between the cash and the options markets; it involves selling the **underlying** and writing a **put** and buying a **call** both with the same **strike price** and **expiry date**. At **expiry**, either the put or call is **in the money** and the position-taker receives the underlying, which is then used to close out the existing short in the cash market. As an option trading strategy it involves creating the equivalent payoff to holding the underlying allowing the trader to **arbitrage** the difference (cf. **conversion**). It involves selling the underlying, purchasing a call and selling the corresponding put (cf. **put–call parity**). The resultant payoff replicates that of the underlying, plus the gain from the option position. The activity is profitable if the underlying and the options are mispriced. For instance, if the underlying is sold for 100 and the call at 105 sells for 3.5 and the put for 9, then the trader sells at 100, buys at 3.5 and receives 9 by selling the put, making a net total of 105.5, a profit of 0.5 on the transaction. In addition, he will be able to get back the underlying at 105 regardless of the prospective market price. If the price is above 105, he **exercises** his call; if below, the put is exercised against him. Note that this strategy can backfire if the underlying pays any intervening cash flows or the options are American-style! The transaction where the underlying is bought rather than sold is called a *conversion*.

reverse dual currency security (Bonds). Type of dual currency issue where the **coupon** is paid in the non-base currency and the **principal** in the base currency.

reverse floating rate note (reverse FRN) or **reverse note.** A **floating rate note (FRN)** where the **coupon** increases when the **reference rate** falls and decreases when it rises. The coupon rate is usually set on the basis of a high, off-market, **fixed rate** less the **variable rate**. For example, such an

issue might pay 15% less six months' **London interbank offered rate (LIBOR)** with a minimum payment of 0%. If LIBOR were 8%, then the note would pay a rate of 7%; but if, at the coupon reset, LIBOR was subsequently 6%, then the issue would pay a coupon of 9%. This particular instrument structure allows investors to benefit from a fall in **short-term** interest rates (cf. **yield curve plays**). As a consequence it is sometimes known as a *bull floater (FRN)* or *yield curve note* (cf. **bear floating rate note**). Created through **financial engineering** techniques by the issuer entering into two **receive fixed interest rate swaps** for twice the FRN principal. These set the fixed rate part of the coupon; the issuer pays one reference rate as his cost of funds while the other is arrived at by deducting it from the coupon. To protect itself from a rise in the two reference rates above the coupon rate increasing its cost of funds, the issuer will also buy an **out-of-the-money interest rate cap** with a **strike rate** at the fixed rate. A variation on the structure where the initial coupon payments are at a fixed rate for a limited period is known as a **hybrid reverse floating rate note**.

reverse floating rate swap. An interest rate swap structure designed to hedge the effects of a **reverse floating rate note**.

reverse floating swap. A type of swap where the floating rate payer's payments vary inversely with interest rates based on a high level **fixed rate** less a variable rate (cf. reverse floating rate note).

reverse heaven-and-hell security. The reverse structure to a **heaven-and-hell** security such that the payments rise when the currency falls and vice versa. In the heaven-and-hell they do the opposite.

reverse hedge. (i) An action involving the buying of **equity** and selling **short** a **convertible** based on the purchased equity. (ii) A type of **simulated straddle**.

reverse index amortizing swap. A type of **interest rate swap** designed to **hedge** against repayments on interest rate sensitive conditionally amortizing securities such as **mortgage-backed bonds**, which increases the floating rate payment if the **reference rate** falls.

reverse indexed principal swap (RIPS). A type of **interest rate swap** where **amortization** is inversely related to interest rates. As interest rates increase, the **notional principal amount** of the swap is reduced. The alternative structure which amortizes as interest rates fall is called an *indexed principal swap*.

reverse interest rate collar. A structure which provides for a fall in interest rates as rates rise and vice versa, within the **interest rate collar** range. It is created by combining a **reverse floating rate note** and the interest rate collar. Its attraction lies in limiting, through the collar, the maximum and minimum rates on the **underlying** asset or liability.

reverse option hedge. A type of **ratio spread** which involves holding a **short position** in the **underlying** and buying more **call options** on more underlying than has been shorted. Such a **volatility** trade increases in profitability, the more the price moves in either direction from the **strike price**. It will lose money if the price does not move significantly. See **option strategies**.

reverse principal exchange rate-linked security (reverse PERLS). The amount of **principal** is linked to a specific **foreign exchange rate** and increases (decreases) as the **base currency** appreciates (depreciates) relative to the specified foreign currency. See **principal exchange rate linked security**.

reverse range forward. A **range forward** contract, but based on **puts** rather than **calls**. That is, the price of the **underlying** is expected to fall rather than rise (cf. **bear spread**; **vertical spread**).

reverse repurchase agreement (reverse RP; reverse repo). The opposite side of the transaction to a **repurchase agreement**. It is used by traders to obtain securities in order to meet **settlement** or **delivery** requirements. Also known as *matched sales*.

reverse risk reversal. The opposite directional view to a **risk reversal** position where the holder will benefit from price falls in the **underlying** (cf. **bear spread**; **vertical spread**). It is created by selling a **put** at a low **strike price** and buying a put at a higher strike price. It can also be created using calls where the strike of the purchased call is higher than the written or sold call.

reverses (USA). Term used to describe a **Federal Reserve** open-market operation which has the effect of increasing bank reserves. That is, the Federal Reserve is injecting money into the system by buying securities for cash (cf. **matched sales**).

reverse spin (USA). A US instrument which has income tied to any fall in Wall Street's main market index, but a principal value that is guaranteed to be repaid in full, with modest interest, after three years. The name derives from the instruments being described as 2% Reverse Standard and Poor's (S&P) 500 **index-linked notes**. It is equivalent to holding cash and buying **put options** on an **index** where some of the principal/income is used to pay for the **premium**.

reverse stock split (reverse split). A reduction in the number of **shares** outstanding by the company recombining them into larger units. Also called a *consolidation*. See **stock split**.

reverse subsidiary merger. The bringing together of two subsidiaries under one operation but where the essence of the new subsidiary owes more to the smaller, rather than the larger, of the two constituent parts.

reverse swap. A **swap** which offsets the **interest rate** or **currency risk** on an existing swap. It can be written with the original **counterparty** or a new counterparty. Used in the secondary swaps market to realize **capital gains**. Most intermediaries will agree to **termination** as adding a reverse swap either creates additional **credit risk** if undertaken with another party or leaves a residual **credit exposure** with the original party, plus the need to service the agreement. Reverse swaps are generally only undertaken if there are specific tax or other costs involved in termination. See **capital adequacy**; **risk-adjusted assets**.

reverse takeover (Mergers and acquisitions). (i) The acquisition of a **listed** company by a private company. (ii) More generally, a smaller company buying a larger one.

reverse time spread. See **reverse calendar spread**.

reverse warrant hedge. A technique involving setting up a **short position** in **warrants** on a company's **shares** and buying shares to hedge or protect the **position**.

reverse yield gap. (i) (Equities; UK) Technically the excess of the interest yield of 2.5% **consols** over the **dividend** yield of the **FT-Actuaries all Share Index** (cf. **yield gap**). In the UK, before the late 1950s, equities were on a higher dividend yield than **gilt-edged** securities, reflecting the perception held then that **equities** were higher risk than **fixed interest** securities. However, it came to be appreciated by the market as a whole that equities, by paying dividends which were approximately linked to the rate of inflation, provided an instrument with a greater certainty of a positive **real rate of return** (cf. **index-linked**) and thus merited a higher price (lower dividend yield) than fixed interest securities where the interest and principal are paid in **nominal** terms. (ii) The situation where fixed interest securities have a higher **yield** than equities (cf. **yield gap**).

reverse zero-coupon swap. A type of **zero-coupon swap** where the **fixed rate** payment is made at the start of the swap. It is equivalent to a loan from the **fixed rate payer** to the **counterparty** and creates more **credit risk** than conventional swaps. Also known as a *prepaid swap*.

reversible swap. A type of **swap** agreement where one party has the **option** to change the payment from fixed to floating or vice versa. This is achieved by the **writer** effectively granting a **swaption** to the holder which is for twice the **notional principal amount** of the initial swap, the first half of which reverses the initial holder's position while the second provides the desired end result. See also **flexible swap**.

reversing trade. A transaction that closes out an existing **position**.

reversion. Repayment of assets from a pension fund when it is deemed to be overfunded on actuarial grounds (cf. **funding holiday**).

reversion to the mean. An observed characteristic of some **asset** prices or rates to return to their long-term average. The implication is that there are short-term deviations from a central tendency as a result of various shocks which are then reversed over time back to the average. Such pricing behaviour is evident in interest rates and the asset price **volatility** observed via **option** prices. Also called *mean reversion*.

revocable letter of credit or **revocable credit** (Banking). A type of **letter of credit** (LOC) that allows the issuing bank to amend or cancel the LOC as long as it has not been endorsed by the **correspondent bank**. See **irrevocable letter of credit**.

revolving acceptance facility by tender (RAFT) (Banking). A facility similar in operation to a **revolving underwriting facility** but where the tendered instrument is a **banker's acceptance** or bill.

revolving credit facility (RCF) (Banking). A loan which allows the borrower the flexibility to **draw down** amounts as required, repay, and draw again up to the limit of the **facility** at its discretion for a set period (cf. **commitment fee; syndicated loan; term loan**). Agreements in the eurocurrency market usually allow the borrower the flexibility of choosing different currencies. A RCF is sometimes called a *revolver* in market parlance; and an *open-end credit* in the USA. See **multi-option financing facility; revolving underwriting facility; short-term note issuance facility**.

revolving letter of credit (revolving LOC) (Banking). Normally a **letter of credit** (LOC) or bill is only valid against one underlying transaction. Some LOCs however are revolving, allowing the beneficiary to draw against an agreed amount for a set period. When revolving two types are used: *cumulative*, where undrawn amounts are carried forward to a future period; and *non-cumulative* where undrawn amounts not used in a particular period may not be carried forward to a future period.

revolving line of credit (Banking). A credit facility where the borrower pays a **commitment fee** and may draw and repay funds according to requirements.

revolving loan commitment (Banking). See **standby**.

revolving period. The period in **asset-backed securities** where the **underlying** has a shorter maturity than the security issue when repayments can be used to acquire additional **assets** to make up the shortfall. Holders of securities such as **certificates of amortizing revolving debt securities** which securitize **credit card receivables** thus have a longer period before the issue begins to **amortize the principal**. Without the inclusion of the revolving period, such an issue would almost immediately begin to repay principal and have a short **average life**.

revolving underwriting facility (RUF) (Banking). A generic term for a **euronote** facility under which an **underwriting syndicate** agrees to purchase **euronotes**. The original RUF agreements, however, allowed for sole placement by the **lead manager**. This proved unattractive to the underwriters, who were unable to make money placing the notes. As a result, facilities usually feature **tender panel** arrangements (which may or may not include members of the underwriting syndicate as well as other **broker-dealer** institutions) for the distribution of such notes. See **multi-option financing facility; note issuance facility; revolving underwriting facility; short-term note issuance facility**.

reward-to-volatility ratio. A measure used in the academic literature on performance measurement based on the ratio of the excess return on an asset or **portfolio** to its **volatility**.

rho (ρ) (Options). The measure of an **option's** sensitivity to changes in interest rates. The risk-free interest rate is one of the five variables used in **option pricing**. For calls rho is positive, for puts it is negative. This is due to the fact that the call holder can defer payment on the **underlying** and invest the **present value** of the **exercise price** in a risk-free asset and earn interest. The opposite situation applies to puts where the sale has to be deferred until **exercise** (cf. **time value of an option**).

riba (Islam). Literally means 'in addition' or 'increase': the prohibition on interest in the sharia, the Islamic law, based on the Koran (cf. **halal**). The principal relevant section condemning the payment of interest as **haraam**, or forbidden, comes in verses 130 to 132, which state that, 'Those who benefit from interest shall be raised like those who have been driven to madness by the touch of the devil; this is because they say "Trade is like interest" while God has permitted trade and forbidden interest'.

rich. (i) Market expression used to describe a high price (or low **yield**) in relation to **fundamentals**. (ii) (*Banking*). Used as a condition of overcharging as in, for instance, the expression *rich pricing*.

richiesto (Italian). **Bid** (cf. **offerto** (offer)).

riding the swaps curve. Taking **positions** due to the shape of the **swaps curve**. For instance, the five-year swaps might pay **fixed** at 5.70% and the seven-years receive fixed at 6.40%. A swaps **dealer** might contract to receive the seven-year and pay the five-year, thus picking up a **spread** of 70 **basis points** with a view to unwinding the position if the spread should move in his favour.

riding the yield curve. Taking **positions** due to the shape of the **yield curve** (cf. **rolling down the curve**; **spread**).

Riegle–Neale Act (Banking; USA). Formally, the Interstate Banking and Branching Efficiency Act of 1994, a key act dismantling interstate banking restrictions which will take full effect in 1997. The act aims to provide for national banking in the USA in order to strengthen the banking system, reduce the problems of banks' reliance on state or regional activities, and allow all banks to compete on the same basis.

rigged market. See **manipulation**.

right or **rights** (Equities). The **nil-paid shares** or **subscription warrant** that are allocated to existing shareholders on a pro rata basis in a **new issue**. They have the same characteristics as a short-dated **equity warrant**. Their theoretical value can be established with the following formula:

$$\frac{\text{Value of one share} - \text{subscription price per share}}{(\text{number of rights to buy one share} + 1)}$$

If a **stock** was trading at 88 and the subscription price is 70 and the rights have been issued at 5 : 1, we have:

$$\frac{88 - 70}{5 + 1} = 3$$

See also **rights issue**.

right-hand side. (i) (Forex) The rate at which a bank will buy a currency against the **base currency**. Thus a foreign exchange **quotation** for Deutschemarks against the US dollar which is quoted in **European terms** would be: DM 1.7450/60. The bank would sell currency/buy dollars at 1.7450, the *left-hand side* and buy currency/sell dollars at 1.7460, on the right-hand side. See also **left-hand side** for additional detail. (ii) The **liabilities** side of a **balance sheet**.

rights issue, rights offer, or **rights offering (privileged subscription issue)** (Equities). An offer of new **shares** to existing **shareholders**, usually in a particular proportion to existing holdings (cf. **pre-emptive right**). To ensure the issue is sold the shares are offered at a **discount** to current market price (cf. **bonus issue**). If the new issue is **underwritten** this is governed by a **standby** or **underwriting agreement**. The transferable entitlement to buy shares given to the existing holders is normally known as *rights* in the UK and *subscription warrants* in the USA. Such short-dated securities have the characteristics of an **option** or **warrant** on the company's stock.

The rights value (RV) can be calculated as follows:

$$\text{Rights value (RV)} = \frac{\text{MV} - \text{SP}}{n + 1}$$

where: MV is the market price of stock or share; SP the subscription price or rights price; n the number of existing shares required for each new share (the ratio of new for old).

If a company with a share price of 210 offers a 1 for 5 rights issue at 180, then:

$$RV = \frac{210 - 180}{5 + 1} = 5$$

See also **scrip issue**; **vendor placing**.

rights-on (USA). American term for a **share** trading with the **rights** attached. In the UK, the expression is *cum-rights* (cf. **ex**).

Riksbank (Sweden). The **central bank**.

Riksobligationer (Money markets; Sweden). **Treasury bills**.

rimawari (Japan). **Yield**.

ring. (i) Another name for a trading **pit**, commonly used on securities or **commodity** exchanges. (ii) Term used for a trading session on the **London Metal Exchange**. It is an abreviation of *ring-dealing session*. (iii) Another term for a **concert party**, that is, a group of investors acting in unison.

ringing or **ringing interest.** The process of establishing investor interest or commitment in a

book building exercise for a new issue. See also **circle**.

ring member (UK). Member of the **London Metal Exchange** allowed to trade in the **ring** and thus participate in the **open outcry** trading sessions (cf. **kerb trading**). See **ring session**.

ring-out. A special regulation on **futures** exchanges allowing the exchange, due to exceptional market circumstances, to set the **settlement** price at the **expiry** of a contract. This may occur due to market disruption or the suspension of trading.

Ringsbanken (Switzerland). A member bank of the **Zurich Stock Exchange**.

ring session (UK). Name for the period of **open outcry** trading that takes place on the **London Metal Exchange** in each metal in turn. This is then followed by **kerb trading**, which is a short period following ring trading involving simultaneous trading in all metals. Inter-office trading takes place prior to and after the ring sessions and kerb trading and can be round the clock.

ring trading. See **open outcry**.

riporto (Italian). Stock lending at the expense of the lender.

rising bottoms. A bullish **chartist's** pattern where lows are at ever increasing prices over time indicating rising support level for the **commodity** or security (cf. **ascending tops**). It would suggest that valuations were being raised over time or more investment interest was being shown (cf. **dips**).

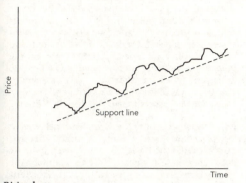

Rising bottoms

rising star. A borrower or institution whose credit ratings have significantly increased (cf. **fallen angel**; **recovery stocks**).

risk. The possibility of large price or rate movements in **assets** or **liabilities**, usually computed using probabilities. Most commentators and market practitioners associate risk with adverse, or the **downside**, effects of price or rate movements (cf. **risk–reward**). The following risk catalogue lists some of the most important categories of risk affecting international financial markets:

CREDIT RISKS

- *Credit risks*: the possibility of the borrower failing to meet interest payments or make repayment;
- *counterparty risk*: the credit risk of creating contractual obligations with other parties;
- *Delivery* or *settlement risk*: the credit risk associated with making or taking delivery of securities, assets, or cash exchange in foreign exchange;
- *settlement risk*: the risk that a transaction will not be settled (cleared) at the appropriate time;
- *industry risk*: the risk associated with a firm within a particular industry or industrial classification;
- *country risk*: the risk of doing business with an entity within a particular country, or from a particular country, or the risk associated with undertaking transactions or holding assets of a particular country; it can also be an *indirect risk* when the impact of such changes affects a third party or the value of securities issued by the country or its enterprises abroad;
- *sovereign risk*: risks arising from sovereign immunity;
- *political risk*: the risk from political change or developments within a particular country, or group of countries;
- *transfer risk*: the risk of the imposition of controls on remittances of interest, dividends, fees, and/or capital to foreign lenders and/or investors;
- *default risk*: the risk that a debtor or counterparty will not honour obligations or contractual commitments;
- *event risk*: the risk that a change in the borrower's situation will impair value.

MARKET RISKS

- *market risk*: the possibility of a change in market prices;
- *interest rate risk*: risks arising from changes in interest rates and in the shape of the yield curve;
- *yield spread risk*: risk arising from non-parallel shifts in the yield curve;
- *net interest risk*: risk arising from parallel shifts in the yield curve;
- *foreign exchange rate risk*: risk from changes in the rate at which two currencies are exchangeable;

- *transaction risk*: risk from buying and selling in a foreign currency;
- *translation risk*: risk from converting assets and liabilities in a foreign currency back into the base currency;
- *commodity price risk*: risk from changes in the price of commodities over time;
- *liquidity risk*: the possibility that the issue will become unsaleable or generate a loss on sale prior to maturity;
- *availability risk*: the risk that new funds will not be made available;
- *cash liquidity*: lack of realizable assets to meet cash outlays;
- *market liquidity*: inability to undertake transactions in the (financial) markets;
- *credit liquidity*: changes in credit quality affecting the liquidity of transactions;
- *forced sale risk*: risk of losses resulting from being a forced seller;
- *reinvestment risk*: the possibility that an investor will have to reinvest cash flow from an issue at a lower rate than the yield on the original investment;
- *extension risk*: the risk that principal will not be repaid when expected;
- *performance risk*: the risk that assets, liabilities, or positions will not perform as intended;
- *prepayment (repayment) risk*: the possibility that an asset will have an adverse pattern of repayments;
- *basis risk*: the risk that the basis between cash and futures markets will change in unpredictable ways outwith the predicted price convergence towards expiry;
- *spread (quality) risk*: risks arising from hedging via cross-market or cross-asset positions;
- *quantity risk*: the risk arising from not being able to match a hedge amount exactly;
- *underwriting risk*: the risk assumed from agreeing to underwrite an issue of securities. The risk is a combination of market risk and investor response to the issue;
- *inflation risk*: risks arising from unanticipated inflation;
- *inventory risk*: the possibility that inventory will become obsolescent or unrealizable at the book price;
- *discontinuity (jump) risk*: the risk that a hedging programme will be be unable to cope with price or rates that do not follow a continuous path;
- *timing risk*: the risk arising from having a mismatch between the maturity of position and that on the hedge.

OPERATIONAL RISKS

- *delivery risk*: the risk that a supplier will not provide delivery as contracted;
- *actuarial risk*: the risk from changes to the assumptions used to value contingent liabilities based on probabilities;
- *fiduciary risk*: the risk of loss from actions taken on behalf of clients;
- *model risk*: risks arising from inappropriate pricing or hedging models;
- *operations risks*: risks arising from undertaking transactions, engaging in business, or otherwise occurred in activities;
- *aggregation risk*: the effect of adding together different risks in a complex instrument;
- *technological risks*: the risk that technologies will change (become obsolescent).

ENVIRONMENTAL RISKS

- *legal risk*: risk arising from legal challenge or from changes in the law;
- *regulatory risk*: risks arising from changes in regulation;
- *political risk*: changes in the political climate or situation;
- *social risk*: changes in social mores, attitudes, or perceptions;
- *direct environmental risks*: those environmental risks that have a direct impact on transactions;
- *indirect environmental risks*: environmental risks that have an indirect impact on transactions;
- *natural risks*: fires, flood, earthquakes and so forth.

BEHAVIOURAL RISKS

- *fraud risk*: the misappropriation of funds and other dishonest deception;
- *errors and omissions risks*: risks arising from human error in undertaking or failing to undertake transactions.

In the insurance market, a risk is *insurable* if it has sufficient past history to provide the basis of a statistical analysis of the likelihood of the occurrence of a claim (cf. **pure risk**). Risk in **modern portfolio theory** can be either **systematic** or **unsystematic** (diversifiable) and is associated with price **volatility** (cf. **specific risk**). Price or rate volatility is more generally applied to any financial arrangement or instrument that is subject to changes in variables, such as interest and currency rates. See also **assets repriced before liabilities**.

risk-adjusted assets (Banking). The 'risk-weighting' placed on a bank's assets for **capital adequacy** purposes that the **Basle Capital Convergence Accord** and the **European Union's Capital Adequacy Directive**, as operated through individual national regulators. It is used to determine how much **capital** is required to support a given level of lending by a bank (cf. **capital impaired**). The system converts all assets, **on-balance sheet** such as loans and securities, and **off-balance sheet items**

Credit type	Government and its agencies			Other banks	Commercial firms
Instrument type					
Cash	0%				
Cash under collection commercial letters of credit	20%				
Secured loans / Standbys	50%				
Other lending / Lending backstops	100%				

Risk-adjusted assets

such as **forward** contracts and **guarantees**, to credit equivalents based on the nature of off-balance sheet items and the **counterparty**. Different categories of **credit risk** are allocated different weights under the system, creating a matrix of categories: sovereign entities and state-owned companies, banks and corporates, matched to asset/instrument type and **maturity**. The adjust-

On-balance sheet risk-weighting

Asset type[a]	Credit type (%)								
	OECD central governments & central bank[a]	Non-OECD central governments & central bank[b] (denominated and funded in local currency)	Primary Dealers	Multi-national development banks	Banks in OECD countries	Banks outside the OECD	Public sector entities in the OECD	Mortgage providers	Non-bank private sector
Loans or claims on	0	0; 100	20	20	20	20	20	50	100
Fixed interest < 1 year		10; 100							
Floating rate (any maturity)	10								
Fixed rate > 1 year	20	20; 100						50	
Loans, guarantees or claims < 1 year		20; 100	20			100		50	
Collateralized loans			10			100			
Cash and other items in process of collection, delivery, or settlement					20	20			
Other assets[d]					100	20			

[a] Cash, gold and bullion held in own vaults or on an allocated basis is 0% rated.
[b] Weighting applies to assets guaranteed by the above.
[c] Applies to assets which are not denominated in local currency and funded locally.
[d] 100% weighting applies to non-OECD public sector entities, premises, plant, equipment, and other fixed assets of the regulated institution, real estate, and other trade investments.

Credit conversion factors for off-balance sheet risk

Conversion factor (%)	On-balance sheet risk
	20% risk weight
50	Transaction-related contingent items (e.g. performance bonds and standby letters of credit)
	Participations with an original matury > 1 year
100	Financial guarantees and letters of credit
	50% risk weight
100	Mortgage commitments
	100% risk weight
0	Unused commitments with a maturity of > 1 year
	Unused commitments which can be unconditionally cancelled at any time
	Endorsement of bills (which have been accepted)
20	Short-term, self-liquidating, trade-related contingent items (e.g. documentary credits and commercial letters collateralized by the underlying shipments)
50	Unused portion of commitments, if unconditionally cancellable involving a separate credit decision before each new tranche
	Interest rate and exchange rate related contracts
100	Direct credit substitutes
	Sale and repurchase agreements and asset sales with recourse where the credit risk remains with the bank
	Forward forward deposits, forward asset purchases, and unpaid partly-paid securities
	Endorsement of bills (which have not been accepted)

ment categories include off-balance sheet items such as derivatives and **foreign exchange**. The basic framework can be illustrated as shown in the figure.

This matrix is then used to derive a bank's risk-adjusted assets against which it is required to be supported by regulatory capital in the form of core capital (**tier 1**) set as a minimum of 4% and supplementary capital (**tier 2**), a further 4%. Further changes divide a bank's activities into a *trading book* and a *banking book*. The capital adequacy directive makes a distinction in the trading book between market-related risks and **credit risks**.

risk-adjusted discount rate. An interest rate adjustment made to the **discount rate** used in analysing cash flows in **discounted cash flow** methods to reflect the **risk** of the future cash flows (cf. **certainty equivalent**). Modern finance theory suggests that all cash flows need to be discounted at an appropriate risk-adjusted rate to reflect their **systematic risk** characteristics (cf. **risk premium**). See **Capital Asset Pricing Model**.

risk-adjusted return. Changes to the expected return on an investment or project to reflect one or more aspects of the **risks** being taken. Risk-adjustments tend to reduce the return or the **present value** of such investments (cf. **risk-adjusted discount rate**). See also **certainty equivalent**.

risk-adjusted return on capital (RAROC) (USA). A **risk**-reward technique initially used by Bankers Trust Inc. and subsequently adopted by other financial institutions to measure its **exposure** in relation to the **return** on a line of business and the amount of the bank's **capital** it needed to (notionally) allocate to each activity. Introduced in

the early 1980s, it has been significantly developed since. The basic concept is to evaluate all of the bank's operations using a common risk method based on **volatility**. This is taken to be the price movement over a **holding period** of a year. Thus a business with little price movement, but equally low returns, would need relatively little of the bank's capital; conversely a highly volatile business would have to have significantly more capital to support its operations (and thereby earn a significantly higher return). The key success of RAROC has been to allow Bankers Trust to see the tradeoff between risk and return in its various businesses activities (cf. **Capital Asset Pricing Model; risk–reward**). See also **RAROC 2020**.

risk analysis models. Any of a number of integrated risk assessemnt **models** aimed at quantifying **risks** and exposures (cf. **RAROC 2020; Risk Metrics**).

risk arbitrage (USA). A financial strategy involving taking offsetting positions in securities as a consequence of a specific event, for example in a takeover, where the resultant price movements are expected to provide a (low-**risk**) profit. Hence *risk arbitrageur*: a person who undertakes risk arbitrage.

risk-asset ratio (Banking). A measure of a bank's exposure under the **Basle Capital Adequacy Convergence Accord**. It is the bank's capital (1 and 2) divided by the total of the risk weighted assets. See **Cooke ratio**.

risk averse or **risk aversion.** The unwillingness of investors to take **risk** unless compensated for additional risk by higher **returns**. The principle of risk aversion is one of the tenets of the modern theory of finance and is generally empirically observable.

Risk averse

	Risk averse	Risk neutral	Risk seeker
Attitude to risk	Requires a risk premium for assuming risk	Looks at expected return	Accepts higher amount of risk without compensating reward
Expected additional payoff	Additional return for assuming risk	None	Lower return for assuming risk

risk-based capital rules. See Basle Capital Convergence Accord.

risk capital. Funds provided for uncertain investments, typically venture capital or risk arbitrage activities usually in the form of equity or equity-equivalents. Such capital is designed to earn a commensurate reward to the risks taken.

risk classes. Assets of comparable risk (cf. credit rating).

risk controlled arbitrage (USA). A form of risk management entered into by mortgage-granting institutions which involves reducing the interest rate risk of granting fixed rate mortgages financed by short-term deposits by using interest rate swaps to hedge the interest rate risk (cf. liquidity risk).

risk conversion. See risk reversal.

risk disclosure statement. Cautionary statement outlining the risks involved in purchasing and selling (writing) of option contracts that has to be signed by a prospective client before dealing may be undertaken.

risk factor. One particular risk element. Thus interest rate risk would be considered a risk factor, as would foreign exchange rate risk.

risk-free asset. Investment that promises a certain return (cf. zero-coupon bond).

risk-free interest rate, risk-free rate or **risk-less rate.** (i) The rate of interest that can be earned for certain (cf. default free). Traditionally government debt has been considered to meet this criteria. Modern portfolio theory requires the existence of a risk-free interest rate in order to allow investors to hold a combination of this safe asset and a portfolio of risky investments. See Capital Asset Pricing Model;. (ii) One of the variables used in option pricing.

riskless arbitrage or **transaction.** Term for an arbitrage transaction where the purchase and sale are simultaneous, hence free of market risk.

risk management. The management of a firm's risk positions. As an activity, it entails using a diverse set of techniques for the assessment, analysis, and control of different types of risks. Typically, risk managers make use of financial analysis, the cash markets, and derivatives to modify and reduce the risks of asset and liability positions. There are three main ways a firm can control its risks, through insurance, via hedging, or by risk-reducing changes in behaviour or activities. See asset-liability management; assets repriced before liabilities; cross-currency swaps; duration; forwards; futures; interest rate swaps; macro hedge; maturity gaps; micro hedge; options.

risk measurement. The process of quantifying risk (cf. exposure; position). See value at risk.

RiskMetrics (USA). A suite of proprietary risk management analytic methods based on, but not identical to, those used by J.P. Morgan and also available to interested parties via the Internet, information providers as well as printed material. The database provides over 300 different time series from the bond and money markets, stock indices, commodities, and foreign exchange. The model proposes two methods of viewing risk: the *Daily Earnings at Risk* (DEAR), which is the amount that can be lost in a 24-hour period; and a longer-term value at risk used for investment purposes.

risk neutral or **risk neutrality.** A condition where investors are indifferent as between different levels of risk on the basis of prevailing returns.

risk-neutral market. A market where investors are willing to accept the same expected return from a risky investment as they would earn for certain from a risk-free investment.

risk-neutral valuation. A valuation which does not depend on the attitudes to risk of market participants. This is true of most analytical models which are used to derive a *fair value* such as the Black–Scholes Option Pricing Model, the Binomial Option Pricing Model, and the cost-of-carry model for futures. Such models work on the concept of replication or duplication of the payoffs from the derivative position, rather than investors accepting a particular risk. The approach means that the valuations derived from the models can be arrived at independently of how investors will view the outcome and that risk-neutral valuations and riskless-arbitrage or arbitrage-free conditions arrive at the same valuation.

risk offset. Any element in a portfolio or set of positions that acts as a **hedge**.

risk preferences. See **risk aversion; risk neutrality; risk seeker.**

risk preferred. Investors that seek out higher levels of **risk** in anticipation of higher **returns** (cf. **utility**). Such investors are also called *risk seekers*.

risk premium. The difference between the expected **return** and interest on the price of the security at the riskless rate. Used generally in financial markets for that part of a price **discount** or **yield premium** seen as relating to the **risk** of the asset over some, normally **default-free**, benchmark such as government bill, bond, or note issues. Sometimes called *abnormal return, excess return,* or *market risk premium*. See also **Capital Asset Pricing Model.**

risk profile. The relationship, and hence sensitivity, of a **position** to a **risk** factor. This can be illustrated graphically by plotting the change in value of the position to changes in the risk. The degree of sensitivity indicates how susceptible the position is to the risk factor (cf. **least squares regression**).

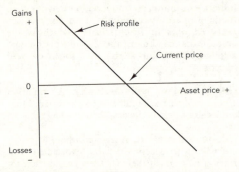

The risk profile or payoff from a short position in an asset.

See, for instance, **beta**.

risk–return tradeoff. The combination of **risk** and return offered by a security. Investors attempt to obtain the most favourable mixture, given their objectives and preferences. Sometimes referred to as *risk-reward*. See **efficiency**.

risk reversal. A **combination** of a purchased **call** (or **put**, if it is a *reverse risk reversal*), and a written call (or put) that is further **out of the money** on an **underlying** (cf. **bear spread; bull spread**). It is essentially a **vertical spread** where, more often than not, there is no up-front **premium** (cf. **zero-**

cost option). The structure or combination is known by many different names in different markets.

Term	Commonly used in the market for
collar (cap and floor combination)	interest rates
corridor (collar on a swap)	interest rate swap;
cylinder	currency
fence or fence spread	
spread (call spread; put spread)	
spread conversion	
conversion spread	
forward rate bracket	interest rates
range forward	currency
tunnel option	
zero-cost option	

See **option strategies**.

risk-reward. The tradeoff between assuming risk and (expected) return in a particular situation. The idea derives from the **Capital Asset Pricing Model**, which proposes a linear relationship between risk and expected return (cf. **market risk premium; risk premium**). The term has entered common usage as a view of the risks being assumed against the suggested potential gain. The better the risk-reward view, the more attractive the proposition (cf. **specific risk; taking a view**). See also **alpha**.

risk seeker. Individual or organization which actively seeks out opportunities to profit from taking on **risk** (cf. **hedge fund**). Such an attitude is often considered akin to gambling or **speculation**.

risk transfer. The use of **derivatives** to change the nature or pattern of **risk** in a **position** (cf. **hedging**). See also **risk management**.

risky. Having **risk** (cf. **risk free asset**).

roadshow. A series of presentations made to investors and other interested parties in advance of a new issue, usually of **equity**. It provides potential investors with an opportunity to meet management and to ask questions (cf. **ringing**).

rocket scientist. A high-powered designer of financial products or innovations (cf. **quant**). Generally refers to experts at **financial engineering**.

roll. (i) (USA) The facility afforded to US **treasury bond** buyers which enables them to exchange previous issues for the new issue (cf. **off-the-run; on-the-run issue**). Also known as *rollover*. (ii) A small **yield** penalty usually paid in order to maintain **liquidity**. (iii) To replace an existing position or transaction with another similar position.

roll date. The date at which a floating rate instrument resets the **coupon** in line with current market rates (cf. **reset date**). See **floating rate certificate of deposit; floating rate note**.

roll-down. An **options market** term for when an **option position** is closed and another is opened at a lower **exercise price** (cf. **roll forward; roll-up**).

roll-down strategy. A follow-up to an existing **option strategy** where existing positions are closed at one **strike price** and reopened at a lower strike.

rolled-up coupon or **interest.** (i) Periodic interest on a loan or a security that instead of being paid to the lender is reinvested by the borrower. (ii) Interest arrears that are added to the principal outstanding on a loan.

roller-coaster swap. A type of **interest rate swap** or **cross-currency swap** with an increasing and decreasing **notional principal** amount. See also **accreting swap; amortizing swap; seasonal swap; step-down swap; step-up swap.**

roll forward. (i) (Futures). The close of a **position** in an **expiring contract** and the simultaneous opening of the same position in a later expiring contract. This is necessary to maintain a **rolling position**. Also known as *rolling over* or *rolling a position*. (ii) (Options market) When one position is closed and another is opened with a longer **time to expiry**. A *roll-up and forward* has both a longer time to expiry and a higher **exercise price**; while a *roll-down and forward* has a longer time to expiry and lower exercise price.

Roll–Geske–Whaley option pricing model. An **option pricing model** for pricing American-style options for **dividend** paying stocks, that is, **options** that allow for **early exercise**. The original **Black–Scholes Option Pricing Model** was for non-dividend paying or zero-leakage assets, and did not extend to providing a solution to the valuation of American-style put options on **leakage-type underlying** assets.

rolling. See **roll**.

rolling call. A call option that may be exercised at any time after a certain date (cf. **American-style; Bermudan-style; European-style; stepped call**). Normally seen as an **embedded option** in a security (cf. **call protection; call provision**). The alternative method is for the call to be exercised only on specific dates when it is known as a *stepped call*.

rolling credit strategy. See **overwrite**.

rolling debt. A general term to describe new issues of debt that have the effect of allowing the redemption of maturing debt. See **refunding**.

rolling down. See **rolling over**.

rolling down the curve (Bonds). The change of yield as a bond approaches **maturity**. With a 'normal' upward-sloping **yield curve**, the yield will fall (the price will rise) even if yield levels remain the same (cf. **dumb-bell; spread**). Sometimes referred to as *playing the yield curve*.

rolling forex (HK). Currency futures that mimic the behaviour of the **spot foreign exchange rate** (cf. **rolling spot**).

rolling hedge. A method of **hedging** interest rate exposures using **financial futures** when the available contracts do not match the **maturity** of the **underlying**. There are basically two alternatives: *simple rolling hedge*, which involves hedging the nearest rollover at the near date contracts but not any subsequent positions; *piled-up rolling hedge*, which involves hedging the entire position at the onset and reducing the amount of the hedge as the **position** itself is reduced over time (cf. **basis risk; rollover lock; strip hedge**). See **piled-up rolling hedge**.

rolling over. The process of **closing out** a **futures** or **option** position at a **near by** date and opening the same position in a more distant or longer **time-to-expiry** contract. The aim is to maintain the effectiveness of the position or to avoid **delivery**. There are a number of variants to the procedure available for options:

- *rolling up*: involves rolling over the position and moving to a higher **exercise** or **strike** price;
- *rolling down*: involves rolling over the position and moving to a lower exercise or strike price;
- *rolling forward*: involves rolling the same position forward in time.

Also known as a *roll over* or *rolling a position*.

rolling position. A position in an asset or liability which is being maintained although the components themselves are changing over time. For example, the trade debtors' or creditors' position may be relatively constant although the identity of the actual outstandings is changing with time. The issue of short-dated **promissory notes** to provide working capital may be continually rolled over at each **maturity** date to provide a continuous supply of funds (cf. **rollover**).

rolling rate floating rate note (rolling rate FRN or **note).** Another term used for a **mismatch bond**.

rolling reset rate swap. Interest rate swap where one of the legs pays either the contractual swap rate or the current market rate, whichever is the lower. See also **interest rate cap (floor)**.

rolling settlement. Method of settling transactions based on a fixed number of days after the **trade date**. In securities markets, current best practice is for payments to occur five business days after the trade date (*T+5*), which is to be reduced to three business days (*T+3*). See also **spot**.

rolling spot (Derivatives; USA). A type of **currency future** offered by the **Chicago Mercantile Exchange** which is similar to the **foreign currency** market's **tom/next** transaction.

rolling the hedge forward. See rollover.

rolling up. See rolling over.

roll-lock swap. See rollover lock.

roll out. See master limited partnership.

rollover. (i) A term used in the **euromarkets** for the resetting of the interest rate in **variable rate** term loans and in the **interest rate swap** markets for the resetting of the variable rate leg of a **swap**. (ii) Used for the reissue or reinvestment of **short-term money market deposits** or instruments on their date of **maturity**. See **rollover certificate of deposit**. (iii) A concession given to borrowers to extend the maturity of debt either as a matter of course or as the result of financial difficulties of the borrower (cf. **refunding**). (iv) Concessions deferring **liabilities**, such as **capital gains** tax, when asset disposals are reinvested in a business. (v) The practice of moving a **position** in a **future** in one expiring contract to a later expiring contract in order to maintain the oustanding position or the effectiveness of the **hedge**. Also known as *roll forward* or *rolling over*.

rollover certificate of deposit (rollover CD; roly-poly CD). A short-term **certificate of deposit** (CD) where the issuer reissues or extends the CD with the same investor but at a new rate of interest. In effect it is a type of informal **floating rate certificate of deposit**. The advantages to the issuer are that neither the interest payment period nor the final redemption period are fixed. Colloquially called a *roly-poly CD*.

rollover lock. Agreement, similar to an **interest rate swap**, where one party pays a fixed **spread** between the nearby, expiring **futures contract** and a later **expiry** one in return for the actual spread. Such an agreement allows a hedger to use a rolling hedge in futures without the risk of a change in the

basis (cf. **basis risk**). Also called a *roll-lock*. See also **backwardation**; **contango**; **piled-up rolling hedge**.

rollover price. Used in **floating rate notes** to denote that price at the next **coupon** date which will produce a return such that the security gives a return at the **reference rate** between now and the next coupon date (cf. **neutral price**).

roll rate analysis (Banking; Bonds; USA). A method aimed at predicting deliquency and **default** in a credit card **portfolio**. Such an analysis is important when **securitizing** receivables (cf. **asset-backed**).

roll-up. Options market term for when an **option position** is closed and another is opened at a higher **exercise price** (cf. **roll-down**; **roll forward**).

roll-up funds (UK). A type of **off-shore fund** that does not distribute income as it arises. Instead the income is rolled up so that it increases the value of the investor's holding (cf. **reinvestment**). Most funds invest in a wide range of **assets**, including **equities** and **commodities**. The advantage comes from the **fund** being taxed on the basis of a (lower) **capital gain** tax rate, rather than a (higher) income tax rate. Recent UK budgetary changes have made all gains on such funds taxed as miscellaneous income.

roll-up option. Variation on a **barrier option** where the **strike price** is raised (with a **call**) or lowered (with a **put**) if the **underlying** moves up through a **trigger** point.

roll-up strategy. A follow-up to an existing **option** strategy where existing positions are closed at one **strike price** and reopened at a higher strike.

roly-poly certificate of deposit (rollover certificate of deposit). A **certificate of deposit** (CD) package comprising, typically, short-term certificates of (usually) six months that will be issued or rolled over for a number of years (cf. **rollover**). The investor buys the package but can sell any of the six-month CDs. There is, however, a commitment to rolling over the CD by redepositing funds to the amount of the next six-month CD. See also **floating rate certificate of deposit**.

rotation. (i) The process by which **contracts** or **securities** to be traded on an exchange are opened for trading at the start of a **session** and, also sometimes at the **close** or if trading has been interrupted for some reason. Also known as the *opening rotation*. (ii) The process of a steepening or flattening of the **yield curve** (cf. **spread**). That is the **yield** differential between maturities changes by a disproportionate amount (cf. **parallel shift**; **spread**).

rotational risk. The risk that the **yield curve** will steepen or flatten in a **rotational shift** (cf. **parallel shift**).

rotational shift. An upward or downward shift in the **yield curve** about a particular **maturity** such that the shape of the yield curve steepens or flattens (cf. **parallel shift**). See **duration; hedging; interest rate risk; risk management**.

rotation of the swaps curve. A change in the shape of the **swaps curve** which is caused by a **rotational shift**.

round lot. The minimum standard trading unit. The size varies across international and domestic markets according to the type of security or financial instrument and the currency of denomination and established market convention (cf. **block; lot; odd lot**).

round trip. The opening and subsequent closing of a **position** such that the initiator is back at his original position before starting to undertake transactions.

round tripping (UK). The condition where a company takes advantage of a **short-term** divergence between the rates at which it can borrow and the rates available for lending, thereby allowing it to make a profit from intermediation. The term is also used when companies switch between **overdraft** and **bill finance** in order to exploit differences in wholesale **money market** interest rates. Sometimes known as *hard arbitrage*.

round trip trading or **round turn trading.** Rapid purchase and sale of securities or **commodities** (cf. **churning; daytime trading; scalping**).

round turn or **trip.** (i) The cost of setting up and then liquidating a **position**, that is, buying and then selling, or vice versa (cf. **bid-offer price; spread**). (ii) Another name for an **offsetting transaction**. (iii) A completed transaction involving opening and then closing a position.

royalty. Fee paid for the use of an **intangible asset**, such as a trademark, name or reputation.

royalty trust (USA). A type of **master limited partnership** for oil and gas reserves which avoids double taxation on cash-generating assets and passes depletion tax benefits to its holders. The concept was first used in the USA by the Mesa Royalty Trust set up by Mesa Petroleum.

Rucknahmepreis (German). **Redemption price**.

Rule 4.2 market (Equities; UK). **London Stock Exchange** small companies market based on rule allowing the matched-bargain transactions in unquoted **shares**. See also **Alternative Investment Market**.

Rule 144a (USA). **Securities and Exchange Commission** regulations issued in April 1990 governing **private placements** by non-US-domiciled entities in the US market as well as the minimum **holding period** requirements for purchasers of such securities. See also **institutional investor**.

Rule 163(2) trading (UK). Under **London Stock Exchange** rules **market-makers** can deal in the **shares** of unlisted companies and in the shares of those listed on markets overseas. Now **Rule 4.2**.

Rule 221. Conditions laid down by the **International Securities Market Association** for the primary **settlement** of securities from one **clearing house** to another (cf. **Centrale de Livraison des Valeurs Mobilières**); **Euroclear**).

Rule 405 (USA). The **New York Stock Exchange's** code of conduct concerning selling investments to clients. The rule basically requires the salesman to know the customer, their prior holdings, and their financial conditions before recommending any particular course of investment and recognizes that what may suit one investor may be inappropriate for another.

Rule 415 (USA). See **shelf registration**.

Rule 535 (UK). See **Rule 4.2 market**.

Rules Governing the Substantial Acquisitions of Shares (SAR; 'dawn raid rules') (UK; Mergers and acquisitions) A set of guidelines issued and administered by the **Takeover Panel**. They are intended to apply during the period leading up to a formal **offer** being made for the purchase of a majority stake (50% plus one share) of the voting capital of a company. These quasi-legal rules are designed to ensure that companies and their **directors** disclose information to shareholders and the **London Stock Exchange** about stake building. By so doing an artificial market in shares should be avoided and the rights of all shareholders can be protected. See **dawn raid**. See **City Code on Takeovers and Mergers**.

rules of fair practice (USA). The **National Association of Securities Dealers'** ethical standards for securities trading.

rump. The residual amount left of an issue after, for instance, the majority of a **convertible** issue has been converted or a **mortgage-backed security** has been paid down (cf. **clean-up call provision**).

run. (i) A **euromarket** and US term for a group of highly rated banks whose **names** are acceptable in the certificate of deposit and bank bill markets. Traders will not concern themselves with the name of the underlying security, as long as the issuing bank is one of the acceptable names (cf. **on-the-run**). (ii) A series of **two-way prices** for different securities or maturities, hence a *run of prices*. Sometimes taken to mean those securities within a **dealer's** inventory (cf. **scale**). (iii) In banking, a sudden demand by depositors for their money, usually in response to some adverse news about the institution.

rundown (Bonds; USA). Amounts and maturities of a **municipal bond** offering (cf. **scale**).

running ahead. See front running.

running broker (UK). Agency broker who intermediates between **bill** holders and banks or the **discount houses**.

running yield. See current yield; interest yield.

runoff (USA). The transmission of closing transactions on the tape after the market has stopped trading.

run the books or **running the books.** The lead **manager's** role in organizing a new issue of securities, keeping both borrower and **underwriters** informed about issue details. Usually implies the senior underwriter in a transaction (as in *bookrunner*).

run to settlement. Holding a futures position to expiry, and hence **delivery** (cf. **exchange delivery settlement price**).

run-up. Period before the official launch of a transaction (cf. **grey market**; **impact day**; **visible supply**).

Russian exchanges. Following the introduction of a market economy in the former Soviet Union, a number of different exchanges have been set up in Russia, notably in Moscow, but also in St Petersburg. The following exchanges have been established: Moscow Central Securities Exchange (MCSE); Moscow International Stock Exchange (MISE); Russian Stock Exchange (RSE); Russian International Money and Stock Exchange (RIMSE); and the Moscow International Currency Exchange (MICEX).

S

safe custody. See safekeep.

safeguard. Investor protection legislation aimed at preventing unethical conduct, fraud, and so on (cf. **insider dealing**).

safe hands. (i) Ownership or possession of securities that is taken to be held by friendly investors. (ii) **buy and hold** investors who are not likely to resell the securities in the short term (cf. **distributed**; **retail**).

safe harbour (USA). (i) Legal concept for compliance with the terms of the law. If a transaction can be shown to comply with a provision of the law, it is said to be in a safe harbour, that is, sheltered from legal challenge. In the securities markets for instance, it is used to describe compliance with known **Securities and Exchange Commission registration** requirements when there could be some doubt as to the legality of a transaction. See **no-action letter**. (ii) Steps taken to avoid legal or financially adverse consequences. (iii) A type of **shark repellent** strategy used in the **mergers and acquisitions** market where a target acquires a heavily regulated business, thus making itself less attractive to a **predator** (cf. **self-uglification**).

safe harbour provision (USA). A ruling by the federal **Commodity Futures Trading Commission** exempting **over-the-counter commodity swaps** from regulation as long as they met certain specific criteria as bilateral transactions and **credit risk management**.

safekeep or **safekeeping.** The service offered by **custodians** to hold **bearer securities** on behalf of their clients. This may involve storing the certificates; **clipping** the **coupons** and presenting for payment at **maturity** (cf. **global custody**; **trustee**).

safe-return security. See equity-linked note.

sahib-al-maal. The financial partner in the joint-venture structures required under Islamic law, the sharia, to avoid the paying of interest or **riba**. Typical structures are **ijarah** and the **mudarabah** (cf. **mudarib**). See also **shirkah**.

saiken sakimono (Derivatives; Japan). **Bond futures.**

saitori member or **saitori kai'in** (Equities; Japan). An **inter-dealer broker** on the Tokyo Stock Exchange (cf. **specialist**). Such members match purchase and sales orders in **common stocks**, **futures**, and **options** and aim to ensure a continuous and orderly market, although they do not take **positions** for their own account. See **sei kai'in**; **tokubetsu sankasha**.

salam contract. A practice of Islamic banking which involves the delayed delivery of a specific asset or **commodity** on pre-agreed terms, somewhat akin to a **forward** contract, but also providing the seller with immediate funds.

sale and leaseback. A transaction where a company simultaneously sells an **asset** and enters into a **lease** on the asset. Usually seen as a method of raising finance from a firm's assets (cf. **mortgage-backed security**; **negative covenant**).

sale by tender. A competitive method of selling an **asset**, **commodity**, or **security**. In the UK used for new issuance on the **London Stock Exchange** where it is known as an *offer by tender* or a *tender offer*. Also called an *issue by tender*.

sale repurchase agreement (sale RP). See repurchase agreement (cf. reverses).

sales. (i) (Securities). That part of a financial intermediary engaged in **distribution**. Hence a **stockbroker** might have an originating group which sourced new issues and a sales group which sold the new issues to the firm's clients (cf. **distributed**; **selling group**). (ii) That part of a financial intermediary involved in selling new products to customers. For example, an insurance company will have a sales department engaged in creating new policies. (iii) The income generated from a firm's main line of business (cf. **turnover**).

Salomon–Russel Global Equity Index (Equities). A performance **benchmark** index for the major stock markets which has the particular characteristic of weighting the value of the stocks in the **index** by the proportion that is considered to be available for foreign purchase. Thus markets which are relatively inaccessible will have a lower weight than in a conventional index.

salvage value. The disposal value of plant and equipment (cf. **sunk cost**). This may be different form the depreciated value in the accounts or for tax purposes. Also known as **residual value**.

same-day delivery. The execution and settlement of a transaction within a working day (cf. **regular delivery**). This is possible if the transaction is made before the **clearing** cut-off **time. See cash settlement**.

same-day funds. Funds which will have good value at the end of the business day on which the order to transfer the funds is made (cf. **clearing house funds**).

same-day settlement. (UK). See **cash** settlement.

same-day substitution. Gains and losses on a **margin** account which offset each other thus maintaining the amount of **equity** or cover in the account.

same day transaction. (i) A transaction that has a **maturity** that is the same as the transaction date (cf. **forward delivery; regular settlement; spot**). (ii) Also used for **daytime trading**.

sample grade. See contract grade.

samurai bond (Japan). A yen-denominated bond issued by a non-Japanese entity in the domestic Japanese capital market (cf. **euroyen; shiboshai bond; shogun bond**). See **foreign bond**.

samurai lease (Japan). A lease for the purchase of Japanese goods by a non-Japanese entity where the interest rate is based on subsidized export-financing rates (cf. **soft money**). The first such lease was undertaken by British Airways in 1978.

sandbag (Mergers and acquistions). Tactic used by the **target** aimed at prolonging negotiations with the **predator** company in the hope that a **white knight** will appear.

S&P—Australian Ratings (S&P-AR) (Australia). 10th Floor, 63 Exhibition Street, Melbourne, Victoria, 3000 (tel. (613) 650 9813; fax (613) 650 4803). See **credit ratings**.

sandwich spread. Option strategy that aims to profit from a lack of **volatility** in the **underlying**. It involves selling both a **put** and **call** which are **at the money** and purchasing an **out-of-the-money** put (with a lower **strike price**) and a call (with a higher strike price). The holder receives the difference between the sold options and the purchased option **premiums**. The holder anticipates profiting from the premium received while the underlying

is expected to remain within the upper and lower price boundaries of the written options. The sandwich spread makes a profit if the underlying remains between the two prices, but the purchased out-of-the-money options provide insurance in the case of significant adverse movements. As such it is the opposite strategy to a long **butterfly spread**, where the holder anticipates significant movement in the underlying although the direction is uncertain (cf. **alligator spread**). It is also called a *written butterfly.* See **box spread; diagonal spread; horizontal spread; option strategies; spread; vertical spread**.

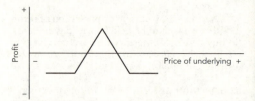

Payoff of a sandwich spread at expiry

sanmekai (Banking; Japan). **Key city banks** who set **short-term** interest rates (cf. **monetary policy**).

sans recours (French). **Without recourse** (cf. **limited recourse**). See also **project finance**.

São Paulo Stock Exchange (Brazil). See **Bolsa de Valores de São Paulo**.

sashine chūmon (Japanese). **Limit order**.

Saturday night special (USA). Refers to an unanticipated **takeover** attempt by a **predator**. A sudden move is required since the alternative of accumulating **stock** in the market to build up a strategic **position** would inevitably disclose such an intention, as holdings over 5% have to be declared and notified to the **Securities and Exchange Commission** (SEC) (cf. **radar alert; Schedule 13D**). The phrase derives from the fact that such offers usually surface over the weekend. The choice of name may also owe something to the fact that a Saturday night special is also a small type of revolver frequently cited as a murder weapon.

Saturne (France). Money markets **settlement** system for **short-term** securities.

saucer pattern. A **chartist's** pattern which is meant to indicate that a price series has bottomed out and is now on a rising trend.

savings and loan association (S&L) (USA). A federally or state chartered institution that takes in deposits and makes loans, usually in the form of fixed rate mortgages or against real estate (cf. building society). In the 1980s S&Ls faced a major risk management problem in that their portfolio of mortgages were at a fixed rate, normally fixed on a margin to the thirty-year long bond while the deposits were both short term and at a variable rate, linked to money market rates (cf. cost of funds index swap). Prior to 1980 deposit interest was capped. The regulator for federally chartered S&Ls is the Federal Home Loan Bank Board, while deposits are insured via the Federal Savings and Loan Insurance Corporation. Also called a *thrift institution* or *thrift*.

savings bank. A type of bank which takes in long-term savings and relends them, often in the form of mortgages. Also known as *thrifts* in the USA, *building societies* in the UK, Australia, and New Zealand, *caisses d'éparge* in French, *Sparkassen* in German, *cajas de ahorro* in Spanish, and *casse di risparmio* in Italian (cf. credit union; Hypothekenbank; savings and loan association).

Savings Bonds (USA). US government debt issues offered directly to the public (cf. National Savings (UK)).

savings deposit (Banking; USA). An account held with a deposit-taking institution that pays interest but with no specific maturity (cf. deposit; term).

saw-tooth swap. An interest rate swap or cross-currency swap where the notional principal changes over the tenor of the contract (cf. accreting swap; amortizing swaps; concertina swap; roller-coaster swap; seasonal swap; step-down swap; step-up swap).

scale (USA). (i) A series of quotes by an issuer for different maturities at which he is prepared to offer paper: for instance, the interest rates that banks will pay on certificates of deposit and commercial paper of differing maturities (cf. run). Hence, *to post a scale*. Sometimes called a *schedule*. (ii) For a serial bond, the terms and conditions applicable to differing maturity tranches. (iii) A transaction instruction that is to be executed in stages in order to average the price. (iv) The scoring range used in credit assessments or credit ratings (cf. credit scoring).

scale down. The process of reducing, usually pro rata or according to a predetermined formula, allocations on an oversubscribed new issue (cf. lot; lottery).

scalper (USA). (i) Market term for a trader acting as a principal on a futures or option exchange who earns small gains by quick in and out transaction (cf. round trip; scalping). (ii) A person intent

on turning a fast profit on an enterprise, sometimes via illegal or unethical means or by overcharging. In investment such activities include front running and price manipulation.

scalping or **scalp.** Trading for small gains over a short period, rather than holding a strategic position. It can involve taking advantage of narrow spreads between market-makers (cf. day time trading; position trading). See arbitrage.

Schatzwechsel (Treasury bills; German). Government short-term treasury bills, usually purchased and resold by the Bundesbank as part of its open-market operations.

schedule. See scale.

Schedule 13D (USA). A submission setting forth ownership required to be made to the Securities and Exchange Commission at the time of acquisition for any holding of a single class of stock by a single issuer in excess of 5%.

scheduled bond (Bonds; USA). A type of collateralized mortgage obligation (CMO) where the redemption of principal is based on an indicated schedule, similar to the planned amortization class or targeted amortization class type of CMOs.

scheme of arrangement (UK). See arrangement.

scheme particulars (UK). The arrangements under which a unit trust has been established.

schlock swap. The market's slang term for an interest rate swap or cross-currency swap which has a high margin to the interbank rate for swaps paid by the counterparty on the fixed rate to compensate for their low credit worthiness. It is the swap market's counterpart transaction to a below investment grade bond issue (cf. junk bonds).

Schuldscheindarlehen or **Schuldschein** (Bonds; money markets; banking; Germany). A unique type of borrowing used in the domestic market where the loans are traded in the form of a promissory letter setting out the terms and conditions of the debt (cf. bond indenture). Although by convention treated by investors as securities, *Schuldscheine* are legally loans and are treated as such by accounting conventions. The primary market involves banks making loans to companies, institutions, the state and central governments, and receiving a certificate which can then be traded in the active secondary market (cf. subparticipation). Interest is paid annually on a 30/360-day year basis.

Schuldverschreibung (Bonds; Germany). Generic term for debt instruments which may include both **money market** and **bond** securities.

sconto (Italian). **Discount**.

scorched earth. Defence tactic in a **takeover** attempt where the **target** company enters into transactions to make itself unattractive (cf. **self-uglification**). See also **crown jewels; poison pill**.

S corporation (USA). Closely held **corporation** with fewer than 35 **shareholders** which can elect under Subchapter S of the Internal Revenue Code to pay taxes as if it were a **partnership** rather than a corporation.

Scottish Financial Enterprise (SFE). A representative organization for almost all firms in the financial sector in Scotland. Acts as a lobby group within the **European Union**: 91 George Street, Edinburgh EH2 3ES (tel. 0131-225 6990; fax 0131-220 1353.)

screen-based. Markets where transactions are undertaken through computer links (cf. **head-to-head**). See GLOBEX; National Association of Securities Dealers Automated Quotations; Stock Exchange Automated Quotations; Stock exchange Automated Trading System.

screening securities. A method of investment analysis which involves selecting securities according to predetermined criteria. Modern database and computer techniques mean that such methods can allow very sophisticated searches which will pinpoint those securities which closely match the investment objective. See also **fundamental analysis; quantitative analysis; technical analysis**.

screen-trading. The replacement of a **physical floor** with the execution of securities deals between traders based on the electronic display of prices and traders' names (cf. **open outcry**). The screens are located in the dealing rooms of individual traders and are all interconnected with one another and the exchange (cf. **over the counter**).

scrip. Share certificates.

scrip dividend. The payment of **dividends** in the form of additional **stock** by the company rather than cash (cf. **enhanced scrip dividend** (UK); **scrip issue**). It is similar to a **rights issue** in that the dividend is capitalized. The disadvantage is that it increases the amount of outstanding stock and can therefore dilute **earnings** (cf. **dilution**).

scrip issue. A 'free' issue of **shares** to existing **shareholders** in some set proportion to their holding. Usually made possible by the **capitalization** of

reserves. It is often done to increase the number of shares outstanding in order to increase the marketability of the stock or to reduce a share price that is considered heavy (in comparison to the market average) (cf. **heavy shares**). Sometimes called a *bonus issue; capitalization issue, free issue* or (USA) *stock split*. The reverse transaction aimed at reducing the number of shares outstanding is known as a **consolidation**. The general formula for calculating the price after the scrip issue is:

$$P_{ex-script} = \left(\frac{n}{n+m}\right) P_{cum-scrip}$$

where P is the price of the security; *ex-script* the expected price after the scrip has been issued; *cum-scrip* the price before the scrip issue; n the number of shares prior to the issue; m is the new shares. Thus the value of a holding where there is a three for two scrip issue which had a price of 450 before the scrip would be:

$$180 = \left(\frac{2}{2+3}\right) 450$$

See also **dilution**.

scripophily. The purchase or collecting of security **certificates** as works of art. While some of the older certificates featured a picture, most modern **bearer** certificates lack such distinction. The craze began in Germany in the 1970s, where the name was coined after a newspaper competition to give a name to the activity.

scrip-settled. Derivative **contract** where the obligation is settled by **delivery** of the **underlying** (cf. **cash settled**). See **exercise notice; notice day; prompt date**.

seagull. Low- or zero-cost **option combination** or **strategy** which involves the simultaneous purchase of a **call** and the sale of an **out-of-the-money call** and a **put** (cf. **zero-cost option**). The intention is to reduce the cost of holding a **position** while at the same time providing a suitable degree of performance. The need to **write** two options is therefore necessary since out-of-the-money options tend to be worth less in terms of **premium** than the near or **at-the-money** option that is purchased.

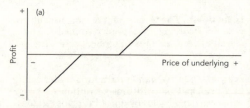

(a) **Payoff of a bullish seagull at expiry**

(b) Payoff of a bearish seagull at expiry

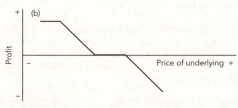

Seagull

The combination provides that the written call can be further out of the money, since it need only provide part of the income needed to purchase the desired position; the balance coming from the written put. The combination can be structured to allow for different views as to the likely **risk** of writing the put and the cut-off on the written call. See **option strategies**.

sealed-bid auction. A competitive **auction** or **tender** where all the bids are submitted simultaneously (in the form of a sealed offer) and where participants are in ignorance of what the value of the other bids are (cf. **open auction; winner's curse**).

seasonal adjustment. A means of adjusting an economic series for seasonal factors; for instance retail sales, for the effect of Christmas.

seasonal cap. An interest rate **cap** where the amount of **notional principal** is varied to take account of the changing hedging needs of the **counterparty** throughout the year. Since a cap is simply a **strip** of short-term interest rate **options**, this is straightforward to implement.

seasonality. Variations in price or performance, return, or other factor due to the changing seasons. Typically, many **commodities** are subject to a high degree of seasonal variation since production and consumption vary throughout the year. Thus for oil, demand is highest going into winter in the Northern hemisphere; **soft commodities** depend on the pattern of harvests, and so forth. Observed seasonality in market prices was one of the reasons for the establishment of **futures markets** in the nineteenth century, to allow producers and consumers to **hedge** against these movements.

seasonal swap. A type of **swap** where the amount of **notional principal** is either zero or the contracted notional principal amount throughout a year (cf. **accreting swap; amortizing swap**). The swap is used to provide a **hedge** for companies with highly variable borrowing needs, such as retailers.

season datings. A method used by seasonal suppliers for spreading the demand of their product by offering extended credit to orders made outside peak demand periods.

seasoned or **seasoned issue.** (i) A Securities and Exchange Commission (SEC) definition for a security that is non-exempt but has been outstanding for a period of ninety days after the **closing date** or after completion of **distribution**, that is up to a year after issue (cf. **unseasoned issue**). Non-exempt securities that have not been registered with the SEC may not be sold until seasoned (cf. **distributed**). See **lock-up**. (ii) A more general description for an issue that has been in the market for a period of time and where the bulk of the issue has been sold to end investors and where the available trading supply is limited. See **buy and hold; ramp**.

seasoned new issue (USA). A new issue of common **stock** for an already **listed** or publicly traded corporation (cf. **rights issue; secondary distribution**).

seat. Market term for the membership rights on an exchange.

secondary bank (UK). Those financial institutions which are licensed under the Banking Act to take deposits but only offer a limited range of banking services. They are also known as *finance houses* if principally engaged in providing **consumer credit**.

secondary currency option or **warrant.** Any of a range of **options** or **warrants** where the currency of issue is different from that of the **underlying**. For instance, in a Japanese company **debt and warrant** package offered in the **eurobond market**, the warrants are usually priced in US dollars, while the underlying **common stock** is traded in Japanese yen. Such secondary currency option structures offer a two-factor payoff, since the gain may come not just from the stock's performance but also through currency effects, although these may equally work against the holder (cf. **compound option; outperformance option; rainbow option**). See also **quantity adjusting option**.

secondary distribution, issue, or **offering** (USA). The sale of **blocks** of already issued securities to investors. This typically occurs when a large holder of a line of securities wishes to dispose of his stake (cf. **block trade; placing; vendor placing**). Such large transactions are sometimes underwritten or carried out on a **purchase-and-sale** basis. The **New York Stock Exchange** has specific rules about the price and distribution methods allowed for such transactions. When an offer is underwritten it may well be registered with the

Security and Exchange Commission. See **block**; **block trading**.

secondary market. The market for already issued securities rather than **new issues** (cf. **aftermarket**; **seasoned**). Conditions in the secondary market (**liquidity**, **yields**, and so forth) will dictate conditions in the new issues or **primary market** (cf. **window**).

secondary reserves (Banking; USA). Near-cash, interest earning **assets** that banks maintain in addition to the **primary reserves** to satisfy their **liquidity** requirements with bank regulators (cf. **reserve requirements**).

Second Banking Directive. Implemented within the **European Union (EU)** on 31 December 1989. It includes **capital adequacy** requirements for banks, the regulatory responsibilities of the home domicile of the financial institution with regard to its role as the prime regulator as well as the role of the regulatory authority in the host country. Financial firms operating in the host country have to conform to that country's regulations when they differ from the home country's. The basic premiss is to provide a level regulatory playing field across the different member countries in the area of financial services.

secondary offering. See secondary distribution.

secondary placement. The sale of already outstanding **shares** to the public (cf. **new issue**). See initial public offering; vendor placing.

secondary warrant. Warrant where the underlying is itself a warrant. See **compound option**.

second bond market (Bonds; Australia). The market for smaller companies securities.

second marché (Equities; France). The market in unlisted stocks.

second mortgage. An additional, but deferred mortgage, secured by a second **lien** made on an asset or property already used as **collateral**. The original lender has a first charge, while the second (and subsequent) lender only has a second charge on the asset or property. The initial lender has to be paid back in full before the beneficiary of the second charge may receive anything (cf. **junior**).

second-mortgage-backed securities (SMBS) (Bonds; USA). A type of mortgage-backed bond where the **underlying** are second mortgages on homes. Such securities are higher risk than conventional **mortgage-backed securities** since the claim on the asset is subordinated to the first mortgage lien. The attractions to investors are

that the **bonds** carry a higher rate of interest to compensate, while historically the **delinquency** rate has been relatively low.

second position. Commodities market term for the **futures contract** which is second in terms of **expiry**. The **nearby** contract would be the first to expire, followed by the second position contract. See **position**.

second preferred stock. A **junior** class of **preferred stock** which ranks behind other preferred for **dividends** and **principal**. Such an issue is, as a result, closer to **common stock**. Often second preferred stock may have **equity kicker** features to make it more attractive (cf. **convertible**; **deferred ordinary shares**).

second price auction. A type of **discriminatory price auction** process where the price paid by the winning bid is the value placed by the second highest bidder. This is done so as to avoid the problems of the **winner's curse** and under-bidding by participants. It is also known as a *Vickrey auction*.

second round. A **venture capital** term for the next step in financing a growing business after **seed money** has already been provided (cf. **development capital**).

second section (Japan). The market for smaller **capitalization** equities listed on the Tokyo Stock Exchange.

second tier market. Market in less active or smaller **capitalization** issues (cf. **Alternative Investment Market**; **fourth market**). See over the counter.

secret reserves. See hidden reserves.

sector. (i) A grouping of assets, activities, securities with common characteristics. For instance, classified by industry, type, **coupon rate**, **maturity date**, or **credit rating**, or a combination of the above. A *sector fund* is an investment **fund** which specializes in a particular sector (cf. **class**).

sector index. An **index** for a part of the market, for instance a particular industry.

secular trend. A **long-term** movement in interest rates or security prices that is unrelated to seasonal or technical factors. Also called a *time trend*.

secured creditor. The holder of a secured debt.

secured debenture. See debenture.

secured debt, liability, or **loan.** Debt backed by particular **assets**, revenues, and/or undertakings of the borrower or **guarantor** which have been provided as security or pledged as **collateral**. In the case of **default** lenders can enforce disposal (or payment by the third party guarantor) so that the obligation can be discharged. Different methods of securing debt can be employed: *direct*—security is provided by the borrower directly (this is usually in the form of a **lien** or **mortgage**); *indirect*—security is provided by a third party, usually in the form of a guarantee; *legal*—the lender has a legal right to take over and realize the value of assets provided as security; *equitable*—the lender can acquire the right to take over and realize the value of assets provided as security by application to the court. See **asset-backed**; **debenture**; **guarantee**; **letter of comfort**.

secured liability. See secured debt.

securities. Tradable claims on a corporation or the state. *Securities* is a generic term for both debt claims, such as **bonds** or **promissory notes** and certificates representing ownership, such as **common stock** or **ordinary shares**, as well as being used for **derivatives** although, in this case, the term **instrument** is to be preferred.

Securities and Exchange Board of India (SEBI) (India). Regulatory body responsible for overseeing the trading of securities on Indian exchanges (cf. **Bombay Stock Exchange**). Its power and functions are modelled on the United States' **Securities and Exchange Commission** and the UK's **Securities Investment Board**.

Securities and Exchange Commission (SEC) (USA). The federal government regulatory agency established by the Securities Exchange Act of 1934 and responsible for investor protection and security market practices and conduct (cf. **Commission des Operations de Bourse** (France); **Securities and Investment Board** (UK)). It has prime responsibility for securities and **options** on securities markets, while the **Commodity Futures Trading Commission** regulates the commodities markets. The Commission is headed by five commissioners who are appointed on a rotating annual basis for five-year terms. The aim of the SEC is to promote full disclosure to protect investors against manipulation and malpractice in the securities markets (cf. **blue sky laws**). Many countries have patterned their regulatory regime on the US model, for instance Japan. See **no-action letter**; **registration**; **registration statement**; **Rule 144a**; **safe harbour**; **self-regulating organization**; **shelf registration**.

Securities and Futures Authority (SFA) (UK). The **self-regulating organization** (SRO) created by merging the Association of Futures Brokers and Dealers (AFBD) and The Securities Associa-

tion (TSA) in 1991. It regulates member firms who are active in transacting in the securities, **futures**, and **options** markets. It sets requirements for **capital adequacy**, based on trading activity, as well as market practices (cf. **rules of fair practice**).

Securities and Futures Commission (SFC) (Hong Kong). Regulatory authority established in May 1989 to oversee the functioning of the financial markets.

Securities and Investments Board (SIB) (UK). The prime regulatory authority for the financial services sector in the UK. A private company, limited by guarantee, responsible together with the **Bank of England** and the **Department of Trade and Industry** for regulating the conduct of financial services businesses operating in the UK (cf. **polarization rules**). Under the **Financial Services Act, 1986** all such business must be *authorized*, replacing the narrow definition of *licensed dealer*, and the SIB lays down the criteria for attaining this status. It oversees a number of agencies or authorities, called **self-regulating organizations** (SROs), that are subordinate to the SIB and handle the detailed self-regulation of the different specialist financial services sectors. See also **capital adequacy**; **Commission des Operations de Bourse**; **rules of fair practice**; **Securities and Exchange Commission**.

Securities Act of 1933 and **Securities Exchange Act of 1934** (USA). Keynote legislation that established the **Securities and Exchange Commission** and set standards for disclosure in the primary and secondary markets for financial instruments and market activities (cf. **Financial Services Act, 1986**).

Securities Exchange of Thailand (SET) (Thailand). See **Stock Exchange of Tailand**.

securities house. A financial institution specializing in the **capital markets**. Typically such firms engage in securities trading as **agents**, **brokers**, **broker-dealers**, **market-makers** and **principals** (cf. **stockbrokers**). Larger firms may also provide **fund management** services, research, advisory, **investment banking**, principally **mergers and acquisition**, and **corporate finance** or other transaction related services (cf. **tender panel**).

securities indexed swap. Any of a range of interest rate swaps where one leg is **indexed** to a market, a sector, **portfolio**, or even an individual security. See **equity-linked swap**.

Securities Industry Association (SIA) (USA). The trade association for the securities industry. It is active in lobbying Congress about legislation. The **Public Securities Association** is the other securities body for **government guaranteed** and **municipal bonds**.

Securities Industry Automation Corporation (SIAC) (USA). A US organization formed by the **American Stock Exchange** and **New York Stock Exchange** to provide: price collection and dissemination; **settlement** services; and communication services (cf. **National Association of Securities Dealers Automated Quotations**).

Securities Investor Protection Corporation (SIPC) (USA). A US mutual insurance fund that protects clients' cash and securities on **deposit** with its members. It is a federally sponsored insurance fund set up in 1970 to protect clients of securities firms. Firms registered with the Securities and Exchange Commission (SEC) and exchange members are required to be participants. It should be noted that it is not part of the SEC.

securities lending. Loaning out securities to short sellers, typically **market-makers** (cf. **borrow; lend**). See **repurchase agreement**.

securities loan. (i) The lending of securities. Short sellers or **market-makers** need to provide securities to ensure **good delivery** when going short. These are borrowed from holders, either from accounts held by the **broker**, from investing institutions direct, or from their **custodians**, who then lend them out for a **fee**. (ii) A loan collateralized with securities.

securities transferred and repackaged (STARS) and **securities transferred and repackaged into pound equivalent securities (STRIPES).** A set of two negotiable **synthetic** securities created by repackaging the Kingdom of Denmark **floating rate note** (FRN) issue, due 1996, by setting up a **special purpose vehicle** to hold the original securities and to act as **counterparty** to two **cross-currency swaps** and issuing bearer participation receipts allowing investors to hold a Deutschemark FRN, in the case of STARS, and a sterling FRN, in the case of STRIPES. See **basis swap; financial engineering; synthetic floating rate note**.

securitization. The process of translating nontradable financial assets into tradable securities (cf. **asset-backed; collateralized mortgage obligations; mortgage-backed; pass-through; pay-through bond**). The benefits to the originator are the ability (1) to remove assets, subject to regulatory and accounting acceptance, from the balance sheet of the originator, thereby improving the return on capital (*ceteris paribus*, a given capital will support a higher level of activity); (2) to diversify the investor base; (3) to set a maximum level of losses (losses above the agreed level are met by

credit enhancers (if any) and investors); (4) to improve asset management and information due to requirements of securitization; (5) to match funding to the maturity of assets; (6) to limit originator's future losses on securitized assets by defeasance; (7) greater flexibility in funding. The benefits to the buyer are (1) it gives a higher yield for an acceptable additional risk; (2) it allows the holding of new asset classes such as mortgages, credit cards, receivables, and so forth, which would be otherwise difficult for most investors. See also **disintermediation; globalization; intermediation; liberalization**.

securitized mortgage. See **mortgage-backed bonds**.

securitized note commitment facility (SNCF) (Bonds). A securitized **note issuance facility** which uses a **partly paid** security issue in the form of a **floating rate note** (FRN) to backstop a **eurocommercial paper** (ECP) issuing programme (cf. **revolving underwriting facility; securitization**). It consisted of a partly paid, floating rate note issued by the Société Nationale des Chemins de Fer (SNCF) as a standby source of finance for their ECP. In the event that the commercial paper market was unable to function, the remainder of the FRN could be called up. The idea behind the issue was to diversify the **underwriting syndicate** away from commercial banks.

securitized option. The combining of an **option** and a debt instrument (cf. **embedded option**). See also **dual currency bond; equity-linked note**.

security. (i) A tradable legal claim upon, or interest in, the **assets** of a borrower which may be in a **bearer** or **registered** form. (ii) Also used to describe a right of **recourse** or claim on a borrower's assets in the case of **default** (cf. **collateral; lien**). See **secured debt**.

security agreement (Banking). A form of lending where the borrower provides physical assets, such as **inventory** or raw materials as a guarantee (cf. **lien**). Also called *chattel mortgage*.

security analysis. See **fundamental analysis; technical analysis**.

securityholders. The owners or holders of securities (cf. **shareholders**).

security market line. The graphical representation of the expected return versus risk relationship, expressed by **beta** or **systematic risk** of the **Capital Asset Pricing Model** (cf. **risk profile**). See also **modern portfolio theory**.

security ratings. See **credit ratings**.

security selection. Investment strategy based on analysing the best individual **stocks**. Also called *stock picking* or *stock selection*. See **tactical asset allocation**.

seed capital or **money.** Money provided by **business angels** or **venture capitalists** to back a new idea or business. It is derived from the idea that seeds then blossom (cf. **development capital**; **second round**).

seed corn financing. See **venture capital**.

segmented market. A business market segment is said to exist if a firm can specialize and gain competitive advantage in a particular arena. It is often, probably wrongly, used to divide up different customer groups. See also **market segmentation theory** and **term structure of interest rates**.

segregated fund. A portfolio which is managed on an individual basis (cf. **pooled funds**).

segregation. Keeping client money and that of the firm separate. It is a legal or regulatory requirement in some jurisdictions, such as the UK.

seigniorage. The return on the monopoly right to print money held by domestic monetary authorities. In the UK, this ability to decide on the charges to be made to the **commercial banks**, and others, for managing the flow of money is held by the **Bank of England**, and in the USA by the **Federal Reserve**.

sei kai'in (Japanese). Regular members of the exchange who trade either for clients or for their own account (cf. **broker; broker-dealer**). See also **saitori member; tokubetsu sankasha**.

selected dealer agreement. See **selling group agreement**.

selective hedging. Setting up a **hedge** only when it is seen as desirable or in response to **taking a view** on market developments (cf. **flat; square**).

self-financing or **self-liquidating.** A loan that is to be used to acquire **assets** that will produce sufficient **return** to meet the interest obligations and repay the principal.

self-funding cap. The application of the **contingent premium option** pricing method to an interest rate cap. See **zero-premium cap**.

self-liquidating loan. A form of finance where the repayment of the **principal** is built in to the transaction. For instance, where the funds are advanced against future known receipts (cf. **factoring; trade credit**).

self-regulating organization (SRO). (i) (USA) An organization which is involved in regulating or supervising business and ethical practices in the financial markets with special regard to investor protection. The organized exchanges such as the **New York Stock Exchange** (NYSE) and the **National Association of Securities Dealers** (NASD) are SROs and have the initial responsibility for regulating their respective markets (cf. **Stock Watch**). (ii) (UK) Licensed by the **Securities and Investments Board** these professional groupings are responsible for their members' conduct and ensuring that there is adequate professional indemnity and compensation available to clients in cases of negligence and fraud.

These SROs were originally: **Association of Futures Brokers and Dealers**, now part of the Securities and Futures Authority; **Financial Intermediaries, Managers and Brokers Regulatory Association; Investment Management Regulatory Organization; Life Assurance and Unit Trust Regulatory Organization; The Securities Association**, now part of the Securities and Futures Authority.

Now the five original SROs have been reduced to the following organizations, which cover the following areas: Investment Management Regulatory Organization, fund management; **Personal Investment Authority**, retail financial products and selling; **Securities and Futures Authority**, wholesale financial market intermediaries.

self-supporting debt. Non-recourse financing where the cash flows from the **project** are anticipated to meet the servicing of interest and **principal**.

self-tender (Equities; USA). Market term for a stock repurchase plan, that is a corporation repurchasing its own stock via a tender. Also called a *stock buyback*.

self-uglification (Mergers and Acquisitions). Steps taken by a **target** in the face of a hostile **takeover** to make itself less attractive to the bidder by changing the nature of the company. This might include conditional sales to parts of the business or the implementation of a **poison pill** (cf. **lock-up option**).

sell and write. See **covered put**.

sell-down. Where a security or **syndicated loan** is offered to an investor outside the **underwriting syndicate**. The sell-down is that part which is taken up by such outside investors. A successful transaction will have a relatively high sell-down and enhances the return to the underwriters (cf. **pool; sub-participation**).

sellers' market. A market condition where sellers are making the prices (cf. **sellers over**). The opposite would be a **buyers' market**.

seller's option. A transaction which, instead of following normal **settlement**, gives the seller the **option** as to the exact **delivery** date over a specified period. Normally, the seller must give notice of his intention to deliver prior to the **expiry date**. The price at which the trade is done will reflect the value of this option (cf. **option dated forward**).

sellers over. A market situation where there is unsatisfied selling pressure (cf. **buyers over**).

selling agent. Any financial intermediary which acts as an **agent** in a financial transaction, such as a **broker**, without assuming any **risk** by purchasing for its own account (cf. **underwriter**). The selling agent's function is to act as a distribution channel and will typically **put through** buy orders received from its clients to the seller without acting as principal.

selling concession. That part of the **underwriting spread** used to remunerate the **selling group** (i.e. to facilitate **distribution**). Calculated as a **flat** percentage of the **face value** of new issues allowed to the selling group by the **lead manager** (cf. **reallowance**). See also **nominal price**

selling group. Members of a new issue **syndicate** who are neither **managers**, **underwriters**, nor **sub-underwriters** in the issue but who are involved in the **placement** due to their ability to **distribute**. They receive a **selling concession** on any securities for which they subscribe and sell to investors (cf. **firm hands**). Sometimes used to describe all those involved in a new issue. Also known as a *selling syndicate*.

selling group agreement or **selling agreement.** A contract between the **managers** of a transaction and each member of the **selling group**. It lays down the terms under which the selling group can purchase securities and details any **selling restrictions** (cf. **prospectus**; **selling concession**). This is also known as a *selling syndicate agreement* or *selected dealer agreement*.

selling group pot. That part of a **new issue** designated for the **selling group**. See **pot**.

selling hedge. When an investor with a **long position** sells a **futures contract** to protect against falling prices and to lock in the **yield** at which an expected cash flow can be refinanced. It is also called a *producer's hedge* or a *short hedge*.

selling off. See **dumping**.

selling on good news. See buy on rumour.

selling out. See sell-out.

selling period. See subscription period.

selling pressure. A situation of excess supply (cf. **market forces**; **thin**; **tone**).

selling price (UK). The price at which a holder can sell **units** back to a **unit trust**. Also known as the *bid price*. See also **single pricing**.

selling restriction. Conditions placed on the **managers** of a new issue regarding where and on what terms the securities may be sold. For instance, most international security offerings are careful to stipulate that the issue is not to be offered to US-domiciled investors since the securities have not been registered with the **Securities and Exchange Commission** (cf. **private placement**; **registration**; **Rule 144a**). See **selling group agreement**.

selling short. See short sale (cf. **bear**).

selling short against the box (USA). A **short sale** made against a security already owned. The **box** in Wall Street jargon is the place where securities have traditionally been kept. Thus a sale against the box is a **covered short**. The motives for such a transaction may be tax driven.

selling the spread. See bear spread.

selling under. See short sale.

sell on fact. See buy on rumour.

sell order. An instruction for an **agent**, **broker**, or other intermediary to make a sale transaction (cf. **buy order**).

sell-out. (i) The sale of a security at market price in order to complete **delivery** on a failed transaction (cf. **aged fail**; **buy-in**). (ii) The liquidation of a **short position** when a **margin call** has not been met. (iii) The completion of **distribution** of a new security. (iv) Sometimes used to describe **shareholder** reactions in a **target** company response to a takeover attempt. Shareholders are said to sell out if they appear to be undervaluing the company. (v) Colloquialism for an issue which has a very positive market reception (cf. **blow-out**).

sell plus (USA). A sale order which is to be carried out only when the price is higher than the previous transaction. Such an instruction would be necessary in a **short sale** to comply with **Securities and Exchange Commission** rules (Rule 10a-1).

sell-stop order. A stop order to sell a security.

sell the book (USA). A transaction instruction to sell as much as possible at the current bid price. The term derives from the book of latent purchases held with a specialist or market-maker which would be activated by the sales order. More generally it refers to any selling instruction which aims to avoid any market impact.

semi-annually compounded yield. The yield on a security which pays interest every six months expressed as an annual rate. See interest rate calculations.

semi-captive venture capital fund. See venture capital.

semi-fixed swap. A type of interest rate swap (IRS) where the fixed rate payer has contracted to pay one of two fixed rates. The rate that is paid will depend on whether the reference rate has moved above a pre-set trigger point, activating the requirement to pay the higher rate. In effect, the fixed rate payer has written a binary option on the floating rate. Such a swap may be attractive to a fixed rate payer who has a more optimistic view of future short-term rates than the market as a whole. Until such time as the trigger activates the option, he gets the benefit of the lower rate.

semi-government securities (semis) (Bonds; Australia). Municipal and local government securities where the principal and interest is normally guaranteed by the state government or security is provided against the borrower's income. They trade at a slight discount to Commonwealth debt of the same maturity. Interest is paid semi-annually and calculated according to a 365-day year basis.

semi-strong form efficiency or **efficient market.** A version of the efficient markets hypothesis that states that investors cannot earn abnormal returns from examining past price data (as postulated in the *weak-form efficient market*) but also goes on to include publicly available information as part of the information set available to the market and therefore priced into market values (cf. chartist; econometric modelling; fundamental analysis; technical analysis).

sender net debit cap (USA). Another term for the daylight exposure limit.

senior, senior issue, or **senior securities.** Issues that rank ahead of all others in right of payment (cf. junior; pari passu). Senior secured means that the debt has first prior claim in the event of default; senior unsecured debt ranks ahead of

unsecured debt in any repayment (cf. unsecured). See subordinated security.

senior participation note. See participation note.

senior refunding (USA). A refunding where the maturity of the new issue is extended from those being retired.

senior registered options principal (SROP) (USA). Designated senior employee at a firm who has been registered with the Securities and Exchange Commission as to his competence to authorize and supervise the opening of new customers' accounts when they wish to start trading in options. Self-policing of such activities is the responsibility of the firm's *compliance registered options principal*.

senior and **subordinated (junior) pass-through certificates** (Bonds; USA). A method of enhancing the credit worthiness of mortgage-backed securities (MBS) where the claims on the pool of mortgages is divided between two sets of securities: a senior and a junior tranche. The senior tranche is given preference for all payments of interest and principal while the junior tranche receives the residual cash flows. The junior tranche acts as an insurance device, taking default and extension risk, allowing the senior tranche to receive a high credit rating. The structure was developed in response to the rising cost of mortgage insurance. The senior-junior tranche method has been extended to many asset-backed issues, such as less developed country debt refinancings.

sensitivity. (i) The degree of interaction between two variables (cf. correlation coefficient; covariance). (ii) In finance, a method used to ascertain the impact of a given input in capital budgeting (or investment appraisal) when using discounted cash flow analysis methods. (iii) A measure of the rate of responsiveness between the value of the option and one or more of the pricing variables in option pricing models (cf. premium). The most important sensitivity measures are delta, delta/gamma, rho, vega. For details, see option pricing. (iv) The effect on the market price of in a derivative or cash position of changes in one of its pricing variables or factors (cf. duration).

sensitivity analysis. An extension to any model or methodology, particularly used with the discounted cash flow technique of investment appraisal, designed to examine the effect of changing the values underpinning the calculation. For example, the effect on the net present value of changing the cost of capital. Intended to indicate how critical the investment decision may be to specific values or estimates of cash flow (cf.

Monte Carlo simulation). See also **risk management**.

sentiment indicator. A scaled response to views on future trends and developments. The indicator usually involves a survey of a representative sample who are polled as to their views about future developments. The results are weighted and then used to create a moving scale showing changes in their views over time. The absolute value of the indicator is generally seen as less important than the trend or the direction of the changes in sentiment that take place. Sentiment indicators attempt to provide insights into market participants' expectations and they are therefore valued as forward looking and as a guide to future intentions. One of the most influential sentiment indicators has been the survey of Purchasing Managers carried out in the USA and released at the start of each month. The results of this survey precede the release of the non-farm payroll and unemployment data on the first Friday of the month; the Purchasing Managers' survey has, historically, provided some guidance as to the likely unemployment data that has been released a few days later.

separate trading of registered interest and principal of securities (STRIPS) (Bonds; USA). US government **bonds** from which the **coupons** have been detached. It can also refer to the coupon itself. **Coupon** stripping is available in physical or certificate form, and produces separately traded securities (cf. **zero-coupon bond**). The remaining part of the bond, called the corpus, can be **callable** and is traded as an individual security (cf. **corpus Treasury receipt, coupon Treasury receipt** and **physical strip**). STRIPS have largely superceded the earlier **certificates of accrual on treasury securities** (CATS) and **treasury investment growth receipts** (TIGERS) issues, as the US Treasury itself separates the coupons and **principal** and acts as the issuer and **registrar**. This has allowed a more liquid market to develop (cf. **reconstitution**).

separation principle. A tenet of modern portfolio theory that the decision on asset allocation can be divided into (i) selecting the optimal risky portfolio, that is one which has the highest return for a given **risk**, or the lowest risk for a given return; and (ii) the allocation of wealth between the optimal portfolio and a **risk-free asset**.

Sequal (UK). London Stock Exchange's electronic **order**, transaction, and **confirmation** reporting system.

sequential expiration cycle. See expiry cycle.

sequential pay collateralized mortgage obligation (SEQ bond) (Bonds; USA). A junior tranche class of **collateralized mortgage obligation** which has the **redemption** of **principal** deferred in favour of more senior tranches, but then has an unimpaired paydown of principal until paid off (cf. **collateralized mortgage obligation equity**).

serial amortization. A feature of some securities where the repayment of **principal**, and hence the amount of interest paid, is amortized over a predetermined period (cf. **purchase fund; serial security; sinking fund**). A ten-year bond with serial amortization might repay in four equal instalments in years seven to ten. If the value of each security was 1,000, then 250 would be repaid at the end of each year, the coupon payment being correspondingly reduced. Serial amortization is not particularly liked by bond investors since it tends to reduce the marketability of the issue.

serial bond. A type of **bond** issue made up of several **tranches** each of a different **maturity** and which may have different **coupon** rates (cf. **amortization**). For example, a bond issue with five, six, and eight-year tranches might have coupons of 6% for the five-year and six-year issue, 6.125% for the seven-year, and 6.25% on the eight-year one. The different bonds would be offered at issue to investors as a package, although holders would then be free to trade the different parts separately. The logic for issuers is to create an amortizing set of cash flows via one transaction rather than have the problem of mounting several different issues. See also **serial security**.

serial correlation. Interdependencies of sequential price changes. This is an observed phenomenon of financial market price changes. It violates one of the assumptions in linear **regression analysis** and has the effect of giving an upward bias to the regression's **coefficient of determination** (r^2). This is important if using estimates of the relationship between two times series for **hedging**. See also **correlation risk; homoscedasticty; regression hedging model**.

serial floating rate note or **serial floater** (Bonds). A **floating rate note** with compulsory **amortization** of **principal** according to a fixed schedule. Unlike a **sinking fund** where securities to be redeemed are drawn by lot or purchased at random in the **after-market**, each note is amortized individually by means of principal repayment coupons (cf. **talon**).

serial forward rate agreements. See strip forward rate agreements.

serial option. Option on a future with an **expiry** date other than that of the **underlying futures** contract. Thus, for a typical **expiry cycle** of March, June, September, and December for the futures, and if the date was May, **nearby** future expiry date in June, the serial options would have expiry dates for August and September. The exchange would also have regular options on futures for the expiry dates in June and September, giving four different dates in all.

serial security. (i) An issue comprising a series of blocks of securities with sequential **maturity**. Each block may have different **coupon rates** and issue prices, but the whole issue is covered by the same **prospectus**. (ii) It can also refer to **bonds** that are partly redeemed on a series of dates according to a predetermined pattern, in which case they are known as *serial sinking fund securities* (cf. **amortization**; **fungible**; **scale**; **tap**). See also **serial floating rate note**.

serial zero-coupon bond. A series of zero-coupon bonds with different maturities issued as a package to investors. Purchasers in the **primary market** subscribe to the complete set of securities, which may be traded individually in the **after-market**. The structure may allow the issuer to generate a series of cash flows which replicate a conventional **straight bond**. The attraction is in the pricing to the issuer as each intermediate maturity is priced off the **yield curve** rather than the longest maturity, which would be the case for a **straight**, giving a lower **all-in cost** or **yield**.

series. Options of the same class (i.e. **puts** or **calls**) with the same **strike price** and **expiry date**.

series of options. Call and put **options** which are in the same **class**, that is options having the same **underlying**, strike price, and expiry date.

series security. A set of securities issued under one **trust deed** or **indenture** (cf. **medium-term notes**; **taps**; **tenders**; **tranches**).

series voting. Voting on company resolutions by class, or type of claim as a separate group. Also called *class voting*.

serious money. Large amounts of cash being used in securities, currency, **option**, and **commodities** trading.

servicer. The entity responsible for collecting and passing to investors interest and principal on **assets**. It is often the orginator of the assets themselves (cf. **pass-through**; **pay-through bond**). See **asset-backed**.

servicing. The payment and management of loans, mortgages, and other financial **assets** or **liabilities**.

servicing a loan. Making interest and, if required, **principal** payments on a borrowing.

session. A period of continuous trading on an exchange. Some exchanges divide the trading day into a morning session and an afternoon session, others trade continuously throughout the day as one session.

set-off. The combining of credit and debit transactions in order to produce a net result. Often used in **settlement** and **clearing systems** and by financial institution regulators for setting prudential limits (cf. **Basle Capital Convergence Accord**). With gross settlement the two parties make payment of the total amount owed from one party to another. With a set-off in place, only one party makes a net settlement of the outstanding difference (cf. **netting**). In some jurisdictions, there are legal restrictions on the right of set-off in the event of **default**.

settlement or **settle.** The exchange of securities or **commodities** for cash or the making of payments under a financial contract. Settlement normally takes the form of an initial notification between the two parties confirming the details of the transaction and the dates and methods that will be used to make the exchange (cf. **comparison ticket**; **confirmation**; **out-trade**). The settlement is then completed on the **settlement date** or **value date** with one or both parties making the required transfers. Most settlement for securities or commodities is carried out through a **clearing house** or through **netting** arrangements. Settlements within a country's banking system of cheques and **bills** is generally called *clearing*. See **bad delivery**; **cash against delivery**; **cash settled**; **counterparty risk**; **delivery versus payment**; **good delivery**; **partial delivery**; **physical delivery**.

settlement committee. The committee charged with establishing and evaluating the **marked-to-market** prices for determining **margin** at the end of the day in **futures** and **options** exchanges. The committee will set the **settlement price** for each contract and expiry which, in some circumstances, may be different from the last reported transaction; for instance for thinly traded contracts (cf. **exchange delivery settlement price**).

settlement date. The day upon which payment is effected and securities are delivered. Markets differ as to the rules governing when this should occur in relation to when the deal was actually struck. Different markets have different conventions as to the time that elapses between the moment the deal is struck and the payments to be made (cf. **cash market**; **spot markets**). The new international standard proposed by the **Group of Thirty** is the **transaction date**, plus five business days (T+5), which will then be further reduced to the transaction date, plus three business days (T+3) when settlement systems can cope. Sometimes called *account day.* See **accounting period; cash delivery; delivery; regular settlement; same-day settlement; skip-day settlement; tom/next; trade date.**

settlement day (UK). See account day.

settlement price. (i) (UK) The price agreed for securities dealt for the **account** on the **London Stock Exchange.** See **accounting period; new time dealings.** (ii) For **futures** and **exchange-traded options,** the price fixed by the **clearing house** at the end of a trading session as the **closing price** that will be used in establishing gains and losses in the **marked-to-market** process for establishing margin balances (cf. **closing range).** See **initial margin; maintenance margin; variation margin.** (iii) The final price set for **futures** and **options** contracts held to **expiry** which have to be delivered. Also sometimes referred to as the *exchange delivery settlement price* (EDSP).

settlement risk. (i) The **risk** that a payment or securities **delivery** will not be made even though payment or delivery has been made to a **counterparty.** It is especially important in **foreign exchange** where the payment of currencies in earlier time zones around the world takes place before the corresponding receipts in later time zones (cf. **daylight exposure limit; Herstatt bank; overnight delivery risk**). See also **netting.** (ii) The risk that a transaction will not be settled (cleared) at the appropriate time due to technical or operational difficulties.

seven-day money. Money placed on deposit or borrowed for a week.

seven-day put security (Bonds; Money markets; USA). A type of long-dated **maturity** security where the **coupon** rate is reset every month and which has continuous **put** and **call** provisions allowing the holder (issuer) to redeem the issue after a seven-day delay after giving notice of exercise. Securities which are put to the issuer are normally redistributed to the market via a **re-marketing agent.** The structure (but not necessarily the reset period) is commonly used for such instruments as **auction market preferred stock.**

Seventh Company Law Directive. A European Union directive relating to the requirement of companies to produce **consolidated accounts** for financial reporting purposes.

severability. The right to separate a **package** of instruments sold as one into their component parts (cf. **stapled security**). An example would be a **bond with warrants** issue where the holder retained the warrants but sold on the related bond. Also known as *detachable.*

several. A form of guarantee in which several parties agree to provide part of the guarantee and in which their contribution is limited to their commitment and they are not required to make good if any other party does not perform.

several liability. See joint and several liability.

severally, but not jointly. A condition of an **underwriting agreement** concerning the commitment of the **underwriters.** Each underwriter is liable for his own proportion of an issue but has no liability towards the performance of any other member. The alternative method, where the underwriter would be required to make good any deficiencies, is known as a joint and several agreement.

Shad–Johnson accord (USA). The agreement reached between the then chairmen of the **Commodities Futures Trading Commission** and the **Securities and Exchange Commission** defining the boundaries of the two agencies' regulatory jurisdiction over the developing **derivatives** markets in **financial instruments** and subsequently incorporated in legislation.

shadow calendar (USA). See **calendar; visible supply.**

shadow director. A person deemed by law to have influence in the direction of a company although not a legally appointed officer of the corporation.

shadow market. See grey market.

shallow discount bond (UK). Name given to a **discount bond** issue by a UK-domiciled entity in order to avoid being treated as a **deep discount** bond for taxation purposes by the Inland Revenue.

share. (i) A **certificate** evidencing ownership rights in a company. See **common stock; ordinary share; preferred stock.** (ii) A beneficial stake in an asset (cf. **equity**).

share account. (i) (USA) An account held with a **credit union.** (ii) (UK) A permanent investment account at a **building society** (cf. **deposit**).

share-adjusted broker-remarketed equity security (SABRES) (Equities; USA). A form of **variable rate preferred stock** with a remarketing feature.

share auction. (i) An **auction** of shares or stock. (ii). An auction of a divisible **asset** or a group of assets, such as a security issue, where the bidders may choose to acquire a part of the whole (cf. **unit**

auction). See **discriminatory price auction; dutch auction; English auction; uniform price auction.**

share broker (USA). A discount broking firm which charges commission based on the number of securities in the transaction, not the amount transacted. The latter is known as a *value broker.*

share buy-back. See stock repurchase plan.

share capital. That part of the capital structure of a company or corporation which is made up of equity rather than debt (cf. **common stock; ordinary share; preferred stock**). See **authorized share capital; issued share capital.**

share certificate. (i) (UK) Document providing proof of ownership to shares (cf. **equity**). See **certificate; bearer security.** (ii) A document representing one or more units of **common stock** (cf. **ordinary shares**).

shared currency option under tender (SCOUT) (Forex). A method developed for reducing the cost of **contingent** foreign exchange protection when making tenders in a foreign currency. Under the scheme, the party seeking tenders buys a **currency option** to cover the expected contractual amount and divides the cost amongst the bidders. After allocating the contract, the successful contender assumes the option to cover the position. The attraction is that all parties gain: instead of all tendering parties taking out cover and adding the cost to the bid, bids are reduced by the amount saved to the benefit of the client and the unsuccessful bidders have had less expense in placing their tenders.

shared option forward agreement (SOFA) (Forex). A **participating forward** product developed by Barclays Bank.

share exchange (Equities; UK). A service provided by **unit trust** managers enabling buyers of **units** to surrender their holdings of **ordinary shares** as opposed to cash. The transaction saves the buyer the cost of disposing of the holding and the **trust** buying new **shares** when the units are issued (cf. **bid-offer spread**).

shared national credit (Banking). See **participation.**

share for share offer. A takeover bid where the predator offers shares in itself as consideration for the acquired company's equity. Also known as an *all equity offer.* The alternative is for an *all cash offer.* Sometimes there is a share-for-share offer which has a cash alternative, or is a partial share offer with a combination of shares, cash, and/or debt. Since selling shares may crystallize a **capital gain,**

such transactions allow tendering holders to roll over their liability into the new holding.

shareholders. Those claim holders who have an equity interest in the firm. Also sometimes called *equityholders* or *stockholders.*

shareholders' equity. That part of the **liabilities** of an organization that, by right, represents the shareholders' interest in the firm. It includes the paid-up shares, the share **premium** account, reserves, and other retained profit items (cf. **debt–equity ratio**).

shareholder value. A precept of **corporate governance** and a criterion of financial management, that decisions should be made with a view to *maximizing shareholder value.* That is, **capital budgeting** and other corporate decisions should aim to increase the value of the stake held by shareholders in the firm by making, for instance, positive **net present value** investments (cf. **risk-adjusted discount rate**). See also **agency problem.**

share premium (Equities; UK). The difference between the **par value** of the **ordinary share** and the price at which it is originally sold. The difference is treated as a special **reserve** on the balance sheet, known as the *share premium account.*

share register. A list giving all the owners of the **common stock** or **ordinary shares** by name and amount (cf. **nominee**).

share repurchase plan. See stock repurchase plan.

shares. Another common term used for **equity,** often taken to mean **common stock** or **ordinary shares** but which is also used, for instance, by **partnerships** in relation to each partners' stake in the firm (cf. **preferred stock**).

shares per warrant. The number of units of **common stock** or **ordinary shares** that can be acquired by the **exercise** of one warrant.

share split. A bookkeeping transaction where the face value of **ordinary shares** or **common stock** is divided to create additional numbers of issued shares. It raises no new capital for the company. The normal reason is to increase the **liquidity** of the market in the firm's shares and to reduce the price, if the shares have become 'heavy', either reason being designed to make the shares more marketable (cf. **heavy shares**). Known as a *stock split* in the USA. The formula for the price after the split is:

$$New\ market\ price = \left(\frac{n}{n+m}\right) Price\ before\ split$$

where *n* is the number of existing shares outstanding prior to the split and *m* is the number of new shares created by the split.

share warrant. See equity warrant.

shark repellent. Changes made to a company's charter or articles of association designed to protect against takeovers (cf. poison pill).

shark watcher (USA). A firm specializing in monitoring company common stock trading for any indication of predator interest (cf. radar alert).

Sharpe index. A measure of the gains from a position or portfolio adjusted for the risk taken (cf. risk–reward). It is calculated by taking the excess return for taking on risk, divided by the standard deviation of return. The higher the ratio, the better the performance for a given risk.

shelf basis. The issuance of securities that were previously registered under a shelf registration.

shelf paper. Any type of security that is continuously issued. The two largest categories are commercial paper and medium-term notes.

shelf registration (USA). An arrangement whereby an issuer of securities can indicate up to two years in advance an intention to issue a given quantity, without revealing the type or timing of the issue. This allows an issuer to respond quickly to advantageous market conditions as new issue registration requirements have been largely completed (cf. window). Shelf registration was introduced by the Securities and Exchange Commission to speed up the process of bringing new issues to the domestic market and reduce the advantages of the eurobond market. Technically known as *Rule 415*.

shell bank. A bank which has no real substance. See next entry.

shell corporation or **company.** (i) A company with few or no assets or business activities. In the UK such quoted companies have been used for reverse takeovers in order to provide a way for a private company to obtain a listing. (ii) A nameplate operation set up in a tax haven to benefit from the advantages of the location but where all activities take place at a different location. If a branch of a bank, this is known as a *shell branch*.

Sherman Act (USA). See Clayton Act.

shibosai bond (Japan). A yen-denominated bond issued by a non-Japanese entity and placed privately in the domestic market (cf. shogun bond).

Typically maturities are for ten years. The shibosai market has been more open to issuers who would not be able to issue on the samurai bond (public) market.

shinkabu hiki-uke ken-tsuki shasai (Bonds; Japan). Bond with warrant package.

shintaka ginkō (Banking; Japan). A trust bank. Such banks accept deposits but also engage in trust business.

shirkah (Islam). A partnership set up to pursue some gainful activity where the risks and rewards are shared and lawful under the shira, Islamic law, which has a prohibition on the paying of interest (riba). See also aajir; mudarib; sahib-al-maal.

shitei meigara (Japanese). Designated issues. Securities so designated are deemed to represent market or sector movements. Such issues are more heavily traded than other securities. See bell-wether; benchmark.

shogun bond. A non-yen denominated issue by a non-Japanese resident on the Japanese capital market. Sometimes known as a *geisha bond*.

shogun lease (Japan). A yen-denominated lease used in international transactions (cf. samurai lease). The attraction is the relatively low interest rates available in yen.

shop (USA). (i) Market slang for a money market or bond dealership. (ii) The name given to the lead manager responsible for a new issue.

shopping or **shopping around.** Getting the best quote by calling several dealers or brokers.

short or **short position.** (i) To sell a security not owned in anticipation of buying an identical one back at a lower price. The gain is the difference between the sale and repurchase prices, less transaction costs (cf. long; margin requirement). (ii) In foreign exchange taken to be an excess of liabilities to assets in a currency. Often called oversold (cf. overbought). (iii) In the bond and money markets, used to describe investments held in short maturity instruments, that is at the near end of the yield curve. (iv) To anticipate a lowering of interest rates and therefore to have an excess of fixed rate assets to liabilities (cf. assets repriced before liabilities; gap). Hence *short funded*. (v) In the futures markets, to sell a future with the aim of repurchasing it at a lower price at a later date. (vi) In the options market, a written option position.

short against the box (USA). See selling short against the box.

short bill. Banker's **acceptance** or **bill** that is due in less than ten days, or on demand or **at sight**.

short bonds (USA). Bonds with a **short term** to maturity (cf. **current maturity**).

short book. See **matched book**.

short coupon. (i) A **coupon** which is less than the normal period for an issue (cf. **long coupon**). That is for a semi-annual payment, less than six months; and for annual payment, less than a year. Such issues may be made where the issuer wishes to match up the **maturity** of the transaction to known payment flows; in this case, an early payment may be desirable to minimize or eliminate reinvestment risk. A short coupon **bond** is not to be confused with an issue where the first payment will be less than the normal for the market but where the buyer pays **accrued interest** and therefore receives a full coupon at the next payment date. This latter method might be adopted by a **tranche** or **fungible** issue where integration with the **seasoned** part of the issue is desirable. (ii) A **bond** with a **short current maturity** (cf. **shorts; short-term**). Sometimes also called a *short bond*.

short covering. The purchase of securities previously sold **short** in order to deliver them and thus **close out** a **short position** (cf. **cover; long covering**).

short-dated or **short dates** (i) (Forex). Foreign exchange transactions with a **settlement** date of less than one week. Sometimes consolidated with **spot** positions for reporting purposes. (ii) (Forex) Transactions for value earlier than spot (cf. **tom/next**). Because spot is typically two (business) days hence, it is also possible to enter into transactions for overnight delivery and even same day. The rate will be adjusted to reflect the earlier **settlement**. Short-dated transactions allow **dealers** to adjust their positions, prior to the settlement of the spot contracts, For example in order to avoid having to borrow in a particular currency by swapping funds through the foreign exchange market. (iii) Securities with only a short term to **maturity** (cf. **long-dated**). Such securities can be either those with a short **original maturity** or long **original maturity** issues with only a short tenor remaining (cf. **current maturity**). (iv) (UK) **gilt-edged** securities with a short remaining **tenor**. Also known as *shorts*.

short-dated swap. An interest rate **swap** or cross-currency swap with an original **maturity** of less than two years. The pricing for such swaps tends to be based on **forward** or **futures** rates rather than on the swap market **yield curve**.

short exposure. The amount at risk from a **short position**. It is computed as the size of the position times the amount by which it can change in value (cf. **downside; upside**).

shortfall constraint (USA). Management objective aimed at ensuring that when **liabilities** are due on a pension fund or other commitment, there is a surplus of **assets** with which to meet the claims (i.e. there is no shortfall) (cf. **duration bogey; immunization**).

short-form (UK). A summary of financial information about a company used in certain types of **prospectus**. Required under a general undertaking (cf. **long-form report**).

short-funded. A situation where the **maturity** of the **liabilities** is less than that of the **assets** (cf. **assets repriced before liabilities; long funded**). The intention would be to see the liabilities rolled over at a lower rate before the assets, thus allowing a greater **spread** to be earned between the two (cf. **gap; margin**). See **asset-liability management**.

short futures. A sold **futures** position. The short futures is obliged to effect **delivery** of the underlying if held to **expiry** (cf. **cash settled**).

short hedge. The sale of a future to **hedge** a long position in the **underlying** in anticipation of a subsequent **cash market** sale (cf. **futures hedge ratio**). Also known as an *anticipatory hedge* when used to cover an anticipated need, and a *producer's hedge* in the commodities markets. See **covered short; hedge; long hedge; ratio hedge; risk management**.

short interest. (i) In the securities markets, the outstanding amount of **short sales**. (ii) Another term used for simple interest, that is one paid over one period (cf. **compound interest**). See **bank basis**. (iii) In the UK, a type of interest on borrowings defined by the Inland Revenue which is not allowable against tax unless paid to a bank, building society, or stockbroker. The other kind of interest which is tax deductible is known as *annual* or *yearly*.

shorting. The act of selling short. See **short sale**.

short option or **short option position.** A written or sold **option**. The option writer or sold option is obliged to perform under the terms of the contract, either agreeing to sell the **underlying** at the **strike price** in the case of a **call option** or receiving the underlying at the strike price in the case of a **put option**.

short position. To sell an asset, security, or derivative contract with the intention of repurchasing at a lower price. It creates a negative exposure to market developments since as the market falls the

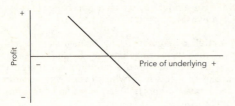

Payoff for short underlying or sold futures position at expiry

short position increases in value (cf. **long**). Going short is often used as a means of **hedging a long position**. The opposite condition, a *long position*, involves buying the asset, security, or derivative and benefiting from a rise in the market or **underlying**. See **short**.

shorts (Bonds; UK). A UK government **bond** with a **current maturity** of less than five years. See also **longs** (current maturities over fifteen years) and **mediums** (current maturities between five and fifteen years).

short sale or **short selling.** The process of selling an asset that one does not own to another party on the expectation of being able to buy it back later at a lower price (cf. **bear**). Short selling (or *selling short* or *shorting*) involves borrowing the asset to be sold, usually via a **repurchase agreement** or a borrowing arrangement. Traditionally, short selling has been seen by regulators as a high-risk activity and is usually circumscribed by heavy regulation, including the setting of minimum **margin** requirements. Many **market-makers** and **traders** are habitually short in their day-to-day activities. An equivalent, but **synthetic** short position can be created by selling a **call option** and purchasing the corresponding **put** on the **underlying** (cf. **put–call parity**). Short selling is also known as a *bearish transaction* or *selling under*.

short sale rule (USA). The conditions laid down by the **Securities and Exchange Commission** (Rule 10a-1) under which a **short sale** may be made. These are that: (i) the last transaction was made at a price higher than the previous one (cf. **up-tick**); or (ii) the last price was the same as the previous price, and the last price change before that was an increase (cf. **tick**).

short squeeze. The requirement to terminate a **short position** due to the inability to continue borrowing securities (cf. **lending**). The short must **close** out the position and return the borrowed securities to the lender (cf. **pulling in the stops**). Sometimes called a *bear squeeze*.

short straddle. A written or sold **straddle** position. It involves selling a **call** and **put option** at the

same strike price (cf. **strangle**). See **option strategies**.

short tendering. Offering more securities in a tender offer than currently owned.

short-term. (i) For **bond** markets, initial maturities of less than two years. (ii) For portfolio strategies, purchasing **assets** with the intention of realization within a year. (iii) In terms of company accounts, debts with a remaining maturity of less than a year (cf. **long-term**; **medium-term**).

short-term appreciation and investment return trust (STAIR) (USA). Income-enhanced stock portfolio created by holding a **long** position in US treasuries and **short** or written **in-the-money puts**. The combination provides the higher income from the bond investment, plus the **premium** on the written **options** but the same price risk as holding the **equity** portfolio. See also short-term equity participation unit.

short-term auction rate stock (STARS) (Equity; USA). A variant of **auction rate preferred stock**.

short-term capital. Funds raised for a short period, usually less than one year (cf. **current liabilities**). See **working capital**.

short-term currency swap. See foreign exchange swap.

short-term equity participation unit (STEP unit) (USA). A variant on the **preference equity redemption cumulative stock** structure, which involves a **package** consisting of a **long** position and a written or **short** position in a **call** on a **stock** portfolio or **index**. The proceeds from the written call are invested in an **annuity** for the life of the unit and are used to provide a higher income than the **underlying** would normally provide. However, the upside **capital gain** is capped by the written call position. When the unit reaches the end of its life, holders have the option of receiving a pro rata share of the underlying portfolio or cash. See also **prescribed right to income and maximum equity**.

short-term facility or **short-term loan** (Banking). A loan that has a **maturity** of less than one year. Also known as an *advance* or a *time loan*.

short-term interest rate futures. See interest rate futures.

short-term interest rates. The rate of interest on money borrowed and lent for a short period (cf. **floating rate**). This is usually taken to be less than one year. Also known as *money market interest rates*.

See also **long-term**; **term structure of interest rates**.

short-term instrument. A negotiable security which has a **maturity** of less than one year (cf. **money market instrument**).

short-termism (UK). The view allegedly taken by UK investing institutions that their investments must perform satisfactorily in the **short term** in order to justify a place in their **portfolios**. Often used, possibly wrongly, as an explanation for the so-called **equity gap** in the provision of fixed capital for UK industry.

short-term note issuance facility (SNIF). Another name for a **note issuance facility** or **revolving underwriting facility** but which tends to be used for **euronote facilities** with a **tender panel**.

short-term volatility. Observed or implied volatility over the short term. This can be a day, week, or month and can be based on expected price movements following the announcement of new information (cf. **mean reversion**). See also **jump process**.

short ton. See **ton**.

shout option. A variation on the **ladder option** allowing the holder of the option to fix a part of the profit at his discretion when the holder thinks it appropriate while at the same time still giving him the right to benefit from any further gains. This flexibility feature is what gives it its name: the holder 'shouts' or indicates his wish to lock in the minimum gain already achieved. This will happen if the holder thinks the market price of a call (put) has reached a high (low) which will not be exceeded before **expiry**. If at expiry, the market has moved beyond the shout strike, the holder can still gain the additional difference. In this respect it differs from the **Asian option**.

show stopper. Steps taken by a **target** in a **takeover** which have the effect of significantly delaying progress and perhaps making an abandonment likely. For instance, actions such as injunctions, lawsuits, or referrals to the regulatory authorities for consideration may mean that the opportunity for the **predator** to proceed lapses (cf. **window**).

Siberian Stock Exchange (Russia). PO Box 233, SU-Novosibirsk 630104, Russia (tel. 7 3832 210690; fax 7 3832 239529).

side-by-side trading. (i) Trading securities and derivatives on the security on the same exchange. (ii) The simultaneous trading of **American-style** and **European-style options** on the same **underlying** on the same **exchange**.

side deal. See **sweetener**.

sideways moving market. A market where prices remain unchanged across time (cf. **bear market; bull market**). See **horizontal price movement**.

sight bill, credit, or **draft.** A bill, **credit** or draft for immediate payment on presentation of the documentation (cf. **time draft**). See also **at sight**.

sight deposit. See **demand deposit**.

sigma (σ). Symbol used in statistics to represent the number of the **standard deviation** or (sigma squared (σ^2)) the **variance** of a probability distribution. The size of the standard deviation determines the degree of spread or dispersion of the observations around the mean. It also indicates how likely an observation is in terms of distance from the mean. For a normal distribution, about 68% of observations will be within one standard deviation of the mean; about 95% within 1.96 standard deviations and 99.7% within three standard deviations. An observation can be combined with a table giving the area under the probability distribution curve to establish the chance of it falling at a particular point from the mean. See also **volatility**.

signalling. A theory of behavioural analysis that actions undertaken by individuals or organizations provide information about their condition. It is based on the view that self-interested behaviour and proprietary information held by the party taking the action will be communicated by the choices made. Thus a firm which raises **equity** rather than debt to finance a new project is signalling to the market its view that the expected gains from the project are less certain or more risky than perhaps already indicated. If it had decided to use debt, then the firm would have indicated that it considered the future cash flows relatively certain. The concept is part of the theory of **asymmetric information**, that is managers have information that investors do not have, and observable actions by firms provide information signals which reduce this asymmetry between the parties. In other words, actions convey information. See also **dividends**.

silent auction. A form of **auction** which consists of an English-style bidding process where participants register their bids in succession over a set time period rather than simultaneously. Each bidder in the auction adds his **bid** to the list as many times as necessary, raising the price each time, until the winner is the last participant to record the highest bid at the end of the bidding period. See **competitive auction**.

silent sub-participation (Banking). A type of loan or **asset sale** via **participation** where the borrower is neither consulted nor, in most cases, informed of the transaction. In practice, most loan agreements allow the assignment of the loan to a third party, although in many cases the borrower has the right to be informed and, in some cases, refuse. See **sub-participation**.

silver. One of the precious metals **commodities**. It is normally quoted in **troy ounces**.

simple hedge. A **hedge** involving one hedging instrument or contract which is based on the **position** to be covered (cf. **multi-legged swap**; **cross-hedge**). Thus hedging a US treasuries position with **futures** on Treasuries would be considered a simple hedge; hedging US dollar eurobonds with the same futures contract would not.

simple interest. The calculation of interest which ignores reinvestment using the formula

$$\frac{P \times i \times t}{100}$$

where P is the principal, i the rate of interest, and t the time period. Money market instruments are all calculated on a simple interest basis (cf. **compound interest**). See also **interest rate calculations**.

simple margin. The annual average cash flow return on a **floating rate note** or **floating rate certificate of deposit** over its life compared with its **reference rate**, comprising the sum of the quoted margin and the straight-line **amortized** premium or discount to par (cf. **discounted margin**; **spread-to-maturity**).

simple option. See **option**; **single option**.

simple yield-to-maturity (SYTM). A measure of the **yield** on a **bond** that assumes that any **capital gain** or loss occurs uniformly over the life of the bond. As such it does not accurately reflect the time value of money (cf. **yield-to-maturity**). This is commonly used in the Japanese bond market. The computational formula is:

$$SYTM = \frac{C}{P} + \left(\frac{100 - P}{P} \times \frac{1}{t}\right)$$

where P is the current price (including any accrued interest); C the coupon; t the outstanding time to maturity (in years).

simulated long position. See **synthetic long position**.

simulated short position. See **synthetic short position**.

simulated straddle. A position with the same payoff as a straddle created by either (*a*) holding the **underlying** and buying two **puts** or (*b*), selling the underlying **short** and buying two calls. The former is also known as a *reverse hedge*.

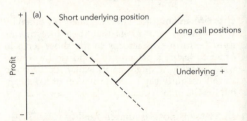

Simulated straddle based on short underlying position and long two calls

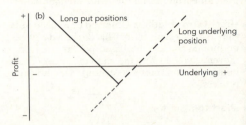

Simulated straddle based on long underlying position and long two puts (reverse hedge)

simulation. A generally multivariate technique for analysing 'what ifs' in a particular situation, project, or other endeavour. There are several types of simulation in use, the most common being known as **Monte Carlo simulation**, although scenario modelling and stress test approaches are also used. Any replication of expected performance based on past data or events can be considered a form of simulation. The main problem is that either the future is not exactly like the past, or the **model** used is unsatisfactory in some way, and thus does not capture some vital factor that may influence the actual outcome (cf. **model risk**). It has the virtue, however, of requiring the analyst to formalize his thinking on the situation or project at hand.

sine die (Latin: without a day). An indefinite adjournment of a process.

Singapore interbank offered rate (SIBOR) (Singapore). The rate at which **prime banks** in the Singapore **interbank market** lend to each other (cf. **London interbank offered rate**).

Singapore International Monetary Exchange (Simex) (Singapore). 1 Raffles Place, OUB Centre No. 07-00, 0104 Singapore (tel. 65 535 7382; fax 65 535 7282). A **derivatives** exchange established on 7

September 1984 to service the Asian–Pacific time zone. It has a **clearing** relationship with the **Chicago Mercantile Exchange** allowing the interchange of **positions** between the two exchanges (cf. **fungible**).

Singapore Stock Exchange. See **Stock Exchange of Singapore**.

single asset property company (SAPCO) (USA). A company that owns a single building. As such, its **asset** base is narrower than a normal property company. Some of the SAPCOs use different **classes** of securities to reflect different risk-return tradeoffs. For instance, there may be a fixed coupon mortgage-backed bond, preferred stock, and **common stock**. In this scheme, the common stock has a residual claim on the asset and benefits from any future increase in rental income. See **property investment certificate; single property ownership trust**.

single capacity. The restriction on a securities firm acting both as **broker** and **market-maker**. Also sometimes used to mean a financial firm acting in a manner that avoids **conflicts of interest** (cf. **chinese walls**). See **dual capacity**.

single currency cash concentration. A facility for a firm operating multiple accounts with a bank to concentrate all cash surpluses at one account (cf. **account sweeping**). See **multi-currency account concentration**.

Single European Act (Europe; UK). The legislation establishing the single European market for goods and services within the **European Union** (formerly the European Community), passed (in the UK) in 1987. The **single market** was due to be established starting on 1 January 1993.

single factor option pricing model. That type of **option pricing model** which has only one unknown pricing parameter: the future price of the **underlying** at **expiry**. Such models make assumptions about other pricing variables such as interest rates, the **term structure of interest rates** or volatility. The original Black–Scholes **option pricing model** is a single factor model. See **multi-factor option pricing model**.

single index model. See **factor models**.

single issue option (Finland). **Option** which has a very low **strike price** and is thus virtually bound to be exercised. Such options are, in effect, surrogate securities, but have no right to **dividends** or to vote. The main attraction is to avoid transaction or capital gains taxes. See also **low exercise price option**.

single market. (i) A term that has become synonymous with removing the most significant tariff and non-tariff barriers that prevent the free movement of goods and services across national frontiers within the **European Union** starting from 1 January 1993. (ii) Any set of diverse **assets** which have a common market dynamic (cf. **market forces**). Thus all corporate bonds would be considered a single market, even if the individual elements are quite dissimilar.

single monthly mortality (SMM) (Bonds; USA). A way of measuring prepayments on **mortgage-backed securities** by taking the percentage of outstanding **principal** which is expected to be prepaid each month (cf. **average life; extension risk; prepayment risk; reinvestment risk**). See **prepayment model**.

single option. A term used to distinguish **calls** and **puts** from more complex combinations, such as **spreads** or **straddles**. Also known as a *simple option*. See **option strategies**.

single payment bond. See **zero-coupon bond**.

single point adjustable rate stock (SPARS). Type of **auction rate preferred stock** which has a reference rate linked to an **index** of **commercial paper** rates, plus a **margin** (cf. **spread**).

single pricing. (i) Method used to calculate the value of **mutual funds** (cf. **undertakings for collective investment in transferable securities; unit trust**). The method uses the last reported transaction price of the securities in the **portfolio**, less administration, management, and sundry fees due to the fund managers, divided by the total number of units outstanding. This gives the quoted price of the units to which are either added (when buying) or deducted (when selling) an entry/exit charge, to give the buying or selling price. (ii) (UK) A proposed method of replacing the current **bid** and **offer** pricing relating to **unit** trusts. Two variants have been proposed: full swing and semi-swing. Full swing involves calculating the net addition/redemption of units and pricing the creation/cancellation price at either the creation value or the cancellation value, including all charges and costs. Full swing avoids dilution of existing holders claims as units will always be created/cancelled at their full cost. Semi-swing is a variant on full-swing pricing, where for normal day-to-day transactions these take place at the mid-price and where the swing only takes place over a threshold in terms of creation/cancellation of units (suggested at 2% of the number of units).

single property ownership trust (SPOT) (USA). A property market term used to describe a **trust**

which owns a single building. Holders of **units** in the trust have the chance of a **share** in the rental income and the profits growth. See **property income certificate**; **real-estate investment trust**; **single asset property company**; **société en commandité par actions de participations immobilières**.

single property trust (SPT) (USA). See **single asset property company**.

single state municipal bond fund (USA). A **bond fund** which invests only in **municipal bond** issues from one of the fifty states of the Union. By investing in **tax-exempt** issues, holders within the state pay no additional tax on income.

sinker. Colloquial term for a security with a **sinking fund**.

sinking fund. A condition within a **bond indenture** or **trust deed** that an issuer will periodically set aside an amount in cash or **eligible securities** to redeem all or part of the **long-term** debt issues (cf. **purchase fund**). Their operation differs depending upon the type of market and the terms of the issue; for example, in the **euromarkets**, the issuer has to meet sinking fund requirements through open market purchases or by redemption of securities drawn by lot, usually at **par**. Sinking funds may be **cumulative** or **non-cumulative** or work on a **best efforts** basis only. See **call provision**; **drawings**; **serial bond**.

size (USA). US term for a large individual transaction or series of transactions (cf. **basket**). More than a **round lot**. Hence expressions such as *dealing in size*.

size effect. Observable differences in **share** price performance between large and small companies in the same industries (cf. **liquidity**). See also **small firm effect**.

skew. See **volatility skew**.

skew-based sentiment indicator. Indicator based on the degree of **volatility skew** observed in the market.

skewness. A statistical measure of the degree of non-symmetry in a probability distribution. A positive skewness indicates there are more observations to the right of the most frequent point, or **mode**, of the distribution, while a negative skewness indicates the opposite. A perfectly symmmetrical distribution will have a skewness of zero. Establishing whether skewness is present is important since the probability of obtaining a given result may differ from the assumption of symmetry. The statistic is given by:

$$Skewness = \frac{n}{(n-1)(n-2)} \sum_{i=1}^{n} \left(\frac{x_i - \mu}{\sigma}\right)^3$$

where σ is the standard deviation; n the number of observations; x_i the value of the ith observation; μ the mean of the total set of observations.

skip-day settlement (USA). The US practice of settling a transaction on the second business day after the **trade date**, rather than the more normal **regular way settlement** which is next day (cf. **same-day settlement**). It provides the equivalent to the international market's **spot** settlement.

SL (USA). Notational shorthand for sold. The opposite is **BOT**, for bought.

SLD (sold last sale) (USA). Abbreviation used on the market transaction reporting mechanism to indicate a significant price difference between the reported trade and the previously reported transaction (cf. **tape**).

sleeper. A security which is undervalued but not recognized as such by the bulk of market participants.

sleeping beauty. A mergers and acquisitions term for a potential **target** company (cf. **putting-into-play**).

sliding parity (Forex). See **crawling peg** (cf. **devaluation**).

sliding peg. See **crawling peg**.

slump. See **recession**.

slush fund. A source of money used to bribe officials or others to undertake particular actions or use their influence to the benefit of the payer. Most infamously used by multinational defence contractors to secure **big ticket** deals to supply governments. Such payments are unlikely to be recorded and properly accounted for and disclosed.

small business investment company (SBIC) (USA). **Fund** which invests **venture capital** in small businesses or start-ups and is authorized by the Small Business Administration (SBA), a federal agency established in 1953.

Smaller Companies Market (SCM) (Equities; Ireland). The **over-the-counter** market for small company **common stocks** (cf. **ordinary shares**). See also **Alternative Investment Market**.

small firm effect. Observation that historically investments in small (quoted) firms have tended to earn abnormal returns.

Small-order Automatic Execution Facility (SAEF) (UK). A service available through the **Stock Exchange Automated Quotations** that will allow subscribers to enter small buy or sell orders into the system for immediate and automatic execution at the best price available. This will save time and keep the dealing fee to a minimum (cf. **Block Order Exposure System**).

Small Order Execution System (SOES) (Equities; USA). **National Association of Securities Dealers automated quotations** computerized small-order transaction system. It is similar in purpose to the **Designated Order Turnaround** system used on the **New York Stock Exchange**, enabling automatic execution of small, retail orders (cf. **lot**; **odd lot**).

smart money. One of the enduring myths of the financial markets is that there is a group of sophisticated investors who are always ahead of the market. Hence, comments like 'that's where the smart money is'. There is precious little scientific evidence to suggest that any group can consistently outguess the market, although some individuals seem better able to gauge trends and avoid some of the fads and excesses that seem to grip markets from time to time (cf. **asset bubble**; **contracyclical trading**; **speculation**).

smokestack industries. Traditional manufacturing industries such as iron and steel.

smoking gun. See **audit trail**.

Snake. Precursor mechanism which operated from 1972 to 1979 to the **Exchange Rate Mechanism** of the **European Monetary System**.

snowballing (USA). The feedback or reinforcing effect of **stop** or **limit orders** on price swings. As the price moves it **triggers** a stop order and limit order, which moves the price further, thus triggering some more, and so forth (cf. **cascade theory**).

snow white. A warrant for debt issued without being part of a bond issue (cf. **bond with warrant**).

Sociedad Anónima (SA) (Spain). Public company.

Sociedade Anónima (SA) (Portugal). Public company.

Sociedad Rectora de la Bolsa de Valores de Barcelona (Spain). Paseo Isabel 11 No. 1, ES-08003 Barcelona (tel. 34 3 401 37 13; fax 34 3 401 37 58).

Sociedad Rectora de la Bolsa de Valores de Bilbao (Spain). José Ma Olabarri 1, ES-48001 Bilbao (tel. 34 4 423 74 00; fax 34 4 424 46 20).

Sociedad Rectora de la Bolsa de Valores de Valencia SA (Spain). San Vicente 23, ES-46002 Valencia (tel. 34 6 387 01 00; fax 34 6 387 01 33).

Società a Responsabilità Limitata (SARL) (Italy). Private limited company.

Società di Intermediazione Mobiliare (SIM). (Italy). Securities market intermediary which may be a joint stock company or limited partnership established following the reforms to Italian securities law that took place in 1991. It is a separate legal category to banks and previously existing stockbrokers.

Società Interbancaria Automatica (Money markets; Italy). Automatic trading and **settlement** system for interbank transactions and government bonds.

Società per Azioni (SpA) (Italy). A limited company.

Société Anonyme (SA) (France; Belgium; Luxembourg; Switzerland). Limited company.

Société à Responsabilité Limitée (SARL) (Belgium; France; Luxembourg). Private limited company.

Société de la Bourse de Luxembourg SA (Luxembourg). 11 Avenue de la Porte-Neuve, BP 165, L-2011 Luxembourg (tel. 352 47 79 36 1; fax 352 47 32 98).

Société de la Bourse de Valeurs (Belgium). Mobilières de Bruxelles SC, Palais de la Bourse–Rue H, Maus No. 2, BE-1000, Brussels (tel. 32 2 509 12 11; fax 32 2 509 13 42).

Société des Bourses Françaises (SBF-Paris Bourse; Paris Bourse) (France). French stockmarket executive body responsible for trading, price dissemination, **listing**, and acting as a **clearing house** for transactions (cf. **Paris Bourse**). Formerly known as the Compagnie des Agents de Change (CAC).

société d'investissement à capital fixe (SICAF) (France; Luxembourg). A closed-end fund.

société d'investissement collectif à capital variable (SICAV) (France; Luxembourg). A **mutual fund** or **unit trust**. A *SICAV monétaire* is a **money market fund**; a *SICAV de capitalisation* allows for the creation of accumulating or growth units which automatically reinvest income. See also **open-ended investment company**; **undertaking for collective investments in transferable securities**.

société en commandité par actions de participations immobilières (SCAPI). A single-purpose investment trust where the shares represent a holding in an office building. Each share represents one square metre of rentable space, and where the rental, after service charges, is paid in the form of a **dividend**. See **single asset property company**.

Société Interprofessionelle pour la Compensation des Valeurs Mobilières (SICOVAM) (France). The clearing house for securities; both bonds and stocks are settled through the system.

Society for World-wide Interbank Financial Telecommunications (SWIFT). A consortium enterprise of the major international banks set up in 1977, based in Brussels, which operates a rapid money transfer notification system for international payments between the leading trading countries. See **correspondent; settlement**.

SWIFT currency codes.

soft. (i) A market is said to be 'soft' if prices are declining (cf. **hard**). (ii) A currency can also be described as soft if there is excess supply and an expectation that its value will fall in relation to other currencies (cf. **hard currency**). See **discount**. (iii) Those perishable **commodities**, such as orange juice, coffee, and so forth. Also called *softs*.

soft arbitrage (UK). **Arbitrage** transactions made between public and private sector issues (cf. **round tripping**.

soft commodities or **softs.** Perishable commodities, typically foodstuffs. These are traded in both the **physical** and the **forward** and **futures** markets. The following example is based on the **Sydney Futures Exchange**.

LIVE CATTLE
- *Contract unit*: 10,000 kilograms liveweight of cattle.
- *Cash settlement*: The Live Cattle Indicator published by Sydney Futures Exchange Limited for the day proceeding the last day of trading, calculated to the nearest 0.1 cent per kilogram.
- *Mandatory cash settlement*: All bought and sold contract in existence at the close of trading in the contract month shall be settled by the Clearing House at the cash settlement price.
- *Quotations*: Prices shall be quoted in cents per kilogram liveweight. (The minimum fluctuation of 0.1 cent per kilogram is equal to $10.00 per contract.)
- *Contract months*: Each successive calendar month up to 12 months ahead.

- *Termination of Trading*: The last business day of each month, except for December, which will be determined by the Exchange. Trading ceases at 4.00 p.m.
- *Settlement day*: The business day following the last permitted day of trading.
- *Trading hours*: Floor—10.30 a.m. to 12.30 p.m.; 2.00 p.m. to 4.00 p.m. SYCOM—4.40 p.m. to 4.00 am.

soft currency. See soft.

soft data. Information held electronically (cf. hard data).

soft dollar services. Brokerage services, such as research on companies, the fees for which are bound up with the dealing costs. Although the term refers to practices in the US markets, it is now used internationally to describe this business practice in the financial services industry. Also sometimes called *soft commissions*.

soft loan. A concessionary financing at below market rates and normally used in the context of subsidized finance provided by export guarantee, financing agencies, or for development assistance, although it can be applied to any cheap rate finance.

soft market. A market where prices are generally weakening (cf. **bear market; hardening market**).

soft money. (i) Usually, the preferential rates of interest offered to developing countries in order to finance large-scale infrastructure projects supplied by developed countries. See **fine rate**. (ii) More generally, any funds that are available at below ruling market rates.

soft sector or **soft spot.** A sector of a market which is not participating in a general market rise.

sold-out market. A condition of **illiquidity** in **commodities futures** markets due to a shortage of **underlying** physical stock and the unwillingness of participants to open positions or engage in transactions.

sole placing agent. A type of **placing agent** arrangement where there is only one intermediary involved. Such a method involves considerable trust between the issuer and the agent.

sole proprietorship. A form of unincorporated business organization where the owner not only has 100% equity but also manages the firm. Sometimes known as *sole trader*. See **company; limited; partnership; unlimited liability**.

solvency. (i) The ability to pay debts when due (cf. **current ratio; net worth**). It is the business and legal condition where a firm is in the position of being able to meet all of the **liabilities** as and when they fall due. See also **liquidity**. (ii) (Banking). The extent to which a bank's **assets** exceed liabilities.

solvency margin. (i) The amount of financial reserves in excess of those required to meet a company's **liabilities**. Often used by bankers and other creditors to assess the terms and conditions of lending arrangements. (ii) (UK). A measure of the financial health of insurance companies based on the extent to which **assets** exceed liabilities. This **margin** or ratio is monitored by the regulator who sets minimum requirements. See also next entry (ii).

solvency ratio. (i) (Banking). The ratio of own funds to **liabilities**. (ii) (UK). Ratio of net assets to non-life premium income used by the Department of Trade and Industry (DTI) to evaluate the financial stability of insurance companies.

solvency ratio directive. European Union directive on the required levels of **capital adequacy** to be maintained by regulated financial institutions which became operative on 1 January 1993. It sets minimum **capital** requirements for depository institutions within the Union which are broadly similar, but not exactly identical, to those of the **Basle Capital Convergence Accord**.

sources and uses of funds statement (USA). Movement of funds breakdown provided in **financial** statements. Normally consists of a list of sources (where cash was generated) and a list of uses (to what uses cash was put). By removing non-cash items, such as **depreciation** it becomes a cash flow statement. Also called a *statement of change in financial position* or *source and application of funds statement* (UK).

South African Futures Exchange (Safex) (South Africa). 32 Diagonal Street, Johannesburg 2001 (tel. 27 (0) 11 836 3311; fax 27 (0) 11 838 4400). **Derivatives** exchange established in 1988.

southbound swap (Forex). A **foreign exchange** or **currency swap** involving the exchange of Canadian dollars into US dollars (i.e. to go south). Hence, *northbound swap*, which is the opposite exchange of US for Canadian dollars (to go north). Note that **spot** transactions between the Canadian dollar, Mexican peso, and US dollar are normally cleared by **regular way settlement**, that is the next business day.

sovereign debt. The loans outstanding of individual countries, usually negotiated by their respective governments. The *sovereign debt problem* is now used as a synonym for default by developing countries. See **rescheduling**.

sovereign immunity. The doctrine that the state or sovereign entity cannot be taken to court. In most countries, the legal fiction of the state's immunity to prosecution has been relaxed when the state acts in a commercial capacity. In many international agreements, the state specifically waives its right to claim immunity.

sovereign risk. The risk that a sovereign borrower may refuse to pay, even though it could. See also **country risk; sovereign immunity**.

special assessment bond or **special district bond** (USA). A type of **municipal bond** issue where the repayment is assured by a special tax on the beneficiaries of the investments made with the proceeds. Holders face the **risk** that the tax base is insufficient to service the obligation. Those securities which carry the **full faith and credit** of the municipality are known as *general obligation bonds*.

special bid. The right of a member of a **tender panel** to place a **bid** which is treated in a different manner to those of other bidders (cf. **non-competitive bid**).

special bracket underwriter. The largest of the **sub-underwriters** in a new issue on a **tombstone**.

special claim on residual equity (SCORE) (USA). A **synthetic option** instrument created by setting up a **trust** to receive all appreciation of the **underlying** above a predetermined value (cf. **Americus trust; capital gain; residual claim**). The counterpart payout vehicle to a **prescribed right to income and maximum equity** issue (cf. **preference equity redemption cumulative stock; long-term equity anticipation security**).

special clearing (Banking; UK). Accelerated **clearing** of a cheque (cf. **town clearing**).

special deposits (UK). A device formerly used by the **Bank of England** to regulate the activities of domestic commercial banks (cf. **reserve requirements**). They are funds required to be placed with the Bank thus reducing the banks' ability to create credit. They pay interest based on the **treasury bill** rate. See **lending multiple; monetary policy**.

special dividend. A one-off **dividend** paid by a company in connection with a **restructuring** or additional cash distribution (possibly from a disposal) (cf. **extra dividend**). See also **bonus issue; scrip issue**.

Special Drawing Right (SDR). A composite currency unit introduced by the **International**

Monetary Fund in 1970 and based upon a standard **basket** system of valuation (cf. **European Currency Unit**). It was originally designed to improve liquidity in international debt **settlement**. Originally expressed in terms of gold, it is now made up of US dollars, Deutschemarks, French francs, Japanese yen, and pounds sterling. It is used as a unit of account by some of the international agencies such as the **World Bank** and the **Nordic Investment Bank**. In addition some security issues have been made in SDRs. It is not a currency and payables must be converted into a currency for **settlement**.

special equity claim securities (SPECS) (Canada). See **payment enhanced capital securities** (cf. **special claim on residual equity**)

special expiration price option. See **barrier option**.

special issue repurchase agreement (USA). **Repurchase agreement** (repo) designed to make available a particular security issue that is in short supply in the repo market. As a result, lenders who make available such securities benefit from a significant reduction in their cost of funds (cf. **implied repurchase agreement rate**).

specialist (USA). A securities market term for a member of an exchange who makes an orderly market in one or more specific issues on a **stock exchange** (cf. **broker-dealer; jobber; market-maker**). The specialist undertakes two functions: (*a*) buying and selling from his own account to meet temporary swings in the two-way flow of transactions and (*b*) executing **limit orders** and **stop orders** placed by **floor brokers** when market conditions are appropriate. Collectively these two accounts are known as a **book**. Exchange rules prohibit the specialist from buying or selling for his own account when there is (i) either a **market order** or (ii) a limit order available at the same price. His main function on an exchange is to provide **liquidity** to the market by committing his own capital when necessary and ensure an orderly market (cf. **auctions**). A *specialist unit* is the term given to members of the **New York Stock Exchange** who are authorized to act as specialists in a security. See also **double auction; head-to-head; open outcry**.

Spécialiste en Valeurs du Trésor (SVT) (France). A **primary dealer** in French government securities (cf. **gilt-edged market-maker**).

specialist quote (USA). See **bid-asked price**.

specialized fund. A type of fund which invests in a narrow range or class of securities. Examples might be the energy sector and financial institu-

tions. They provide exposure and performance related to specific sectors of the market coupled to the managers' specialized knowledge (cf. **emerging markets**). Also called a *sector fund*.

special Lombard rate (Banking; Germany). See **Lombard rate**.

special offering (USA). A type of **secondary distribution** allowed on the **New York Stock Exchange**, which is made during a trading session.

special purpose vehicle (SPV). A legal entity established to facilitate a transaction. Normally such a company will act solely as a single purpose conduit for channelling funds from borrowers to lenders, with its only other activities being the carrying out of regulatory requirements. Such one-function companies are common in **securitization** and are used for **asset-backed** and **mortgage-backed** issues. Normally they are precluded from engaging in activities other than the one intended by the transaction and will immunize the originator from **recourse** by investors. They are also a feature of **project finance** as a legal buffer between the originator or sponsor of the project and its backers (cf. **limited partnership**).

special situation security. Any security where price movements are caused by factors unique to the security and independent of the market as a whole; for instance, such factors could include rumour or actual **takeover** (cf. **abnormal return; residual risk**). See also **stock specific risk**.

special tax bond (USA). A type of **municipal bond** issue which is to be repaid out of a specific, designated tax.

specie. Currency in the form of coins rather than notes or **bullion**.

specific issues market (USA). A particular part of the **repurchase agreement** (repo) or **reverse repurchase agreement** market where the price of the **underlying** security becomes significant. This can be the case where there is a shortage of a particular security. Normally, in repos the underlying security is unimportant. However, if a shortage or a glut of securities by a specific issuer exists, this can have an effect on the rate at which the transaction is undertaken (cf. **implied repurchase agreement rate**).

specific risk. That part of an asset's total **risk** in **modern portfolio theory** that is unique to the asset and can be diversified away by building a **portfolio** (cf. **stock specific risk**). The other element, which cannot be diversified away is known as **systematic risk**. Also known as *unsystematic risk*.

spectail. A **dealer** who does business with **retail** but spends more time on managing his own **positions**.

speculation. The taking of a **position** in a market, instrument, security, or a **derivative** with a view to making a (large) profit from anticipated favourable changes when the position is later unwound (cf. **taking a view**). See also **arbitrage**; **day time trading**; **scalper**; **spreading**.

speculative bubble or **asset bubble**. Any trend in the overpricing of **shares** that is subsequently 'burst' when more realistic views emerge. Financial markets can sometimes be taken over by highly persuasive but erroneous influences that lead some to conclude that a herd instinct or **domino effect** exists. Perhaps the most infamous of these occurred in the UK in 1720 (although similar examples exist for almost all countries), which goes by the name of the South Sea bubble. This extraordinary example of **speculation**, **ramping**, and **fraud** surrounded the shares of a company, South Sea Company, which issued an entirely fictitious **prospectus** but enjoyed massive demand for its shares based on deception and false information about contracts for shipping and 'discoveries' in South America, none of which had the slightest foundation in fact (cf. **pyramiding**).

speculative grade (USA). Those securities which have a **credit rating** that is not **investment grade**, i.e. below that set by the bank regulators as suitable investments, currently Baa (Moody's Investor Services) or BBB (Standard and Poor's) (cf. **junk bonds**).

speculative risk. That category of insurance which is for risks which cannot be determined by probability analysis (cf. **martingdale**). This may be due to the fact that the **risk** is unique or the parameters governing the probability of a claim are unknown or indeterminate. The premier market for handling these types of risk is the Lloyds of London insurance market (cf. **casualty loss**; **hazard**; **pure risk**).

speculator. (i) An investor taking unusually large risks. Hence, *speculative portfolio*; (ii) Taking a risky **position** with the view or hope of making a large profit. (iii) A type of market participant in **derivatives** markets who is not matching his position to an opposite position in the **underlying** (cf. **hedger**; **naked**).

Spezialfonds (Germany). Pooled investment funds only open to incorporated entities. See **investment company**; **mutual fund**.

spike. A short-term upward or downward change in price or rate that is, subsequently, rapidly reversed. Spikes occur in markets due to temporary shortages or abnormal or stressed conditions.

spin-off. The hiving-off of a business or assets of a company either for tax purposes or because it is underperforming or no longer strategic to the business (cf. **master limited partnership**; **royalty trust**). Also known as a *bifurcation* or *demerger* when the spin-off is a publicly listed, stand-alone business in its own right. See **management buyout**.

spiv. A speculator with a very **short-term** view of investment performance (cf. **daytime trading**; **scalper**).

split. See stock split.

split capital investment trust (UK). A managed **portfolio** with more than one class of **capital** and in which the income and capital growth is split into different securities, typically an income **share** and a **zero-dividend preference share** (cf. **zero-coupon bond**). Such trusts have a fixed winding-up date and where the different classes are entitled to different proportions of any surplus assets after meeting the fixed liabilities (cf. **conversion**). Typical trusts comprise a mixture of income shares, capital shares, stepped preference shares, zero dividend preference share, and highly-geared ordinary shares and make significant use of **gearing** (cf. **leverage**). The two principal types are: traditional split capital investment trust and the hybrid or quasi-split investment trust. They are often referred to as *splits*. See also **Americus trust**.

split capital trust (UK). A fixed-life **investment** trust with different categories of **shares** designed to provide either income or **capital gains** (cf. **Americus trust**). Holders of the income shares are entitled to all the **dividends** from the **portfolio** and a predetermined amount of any capital increase. The capital shares are entitled to any increase over and above that required to meet the **liability** on the income shares (cf. **prescribed right to income and maximum equity**; **special claim on residual equity**). The intention is to provide investors with a high degree of flexibility since they can choose the ratio of the types of shares that best meets their requirements. Also called a *split level trust* or a *split trust*.

split cylinder. A time or **horizontal spread** which involves a purchased **option** near to or **at the money** with a written or sold option further **out of the money** (cf. **cylinder**; **risk reversal**). Also known as a *split risk reversal*. See **option strategies**.

split down. A reverse stock split.

split fee. See split spread.

split-level. A type of investment trust company that has more than one sort of share capital, each entitled to different parts of the profits (cf. **prescribed right to income and maximum equity; special claim on residual equity; unbundled stock unit**).

split offering. A securities offering where the offer is not for securities all of one **class**. For instance, a combined **common stock** and preferred stock offering.

split order. Either a transaction instruction that is to be divided between different securities of the same **class** or a transaction instruction where the order amount is to be divided into smaller units to be executed over a period of time in order to avoid **market impact**.

split rating. An issue or issuer which is assigned a different rating by separate **credit rating agencies**.

split risk reversal. See **split cylinder** (cf. **horizontal spread**).

split spread (Banking). A **euromarket** term for a borrower to agree different interest rates during different periods of the life of the loan. Thus a loan facility for five years might have a spread to the **London interbank offered rate** of $\frac{1}{2}$ for three years and $\frac{5}{8}$ for the last two.

splitting the strike. An options **strategy** involving the simultaneous purchase of a **call** with a high **strike price** and a **put** written with a low strike price for the same **expiry date**. It is also known as a *combo*. See also **mambo combo; surf-and-turf**.

Payoff of a bull splitting the strike at expiry

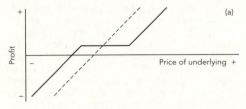

(a)

Payoff of a bear splitting the strike at expiry

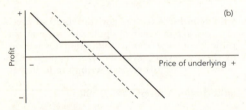

(b)

Splitting the strike

split trust (UK). See **split capital trust**.

split up. To break up a company into its component businesses (cf. **bifurcation; disinvestment; unbundling**).

sponsor. (i) The originator of a deal or project. Also known as a *prime mover* or a *promoter*. (ii) In the UK, used to denote the **lead manager** to a new issue or a **flotation** on the **London Stock Exchange** with special responsibilities for the transaction (cf. **issuing house**). Also called a *sponsoring broker*. See **Alternative Investment Market**.

sponsored American depository receipt (Equities; USA). See **American depository receipt**.

sponsorship (USA). The situation where an important investor in a **common stock**, usually a **stockbroker** of **market-marker** but equally a large investor, provides a favourable opinion on the company's prospects, thus favourably influencing its perception in the market (cf. **greenmail**).

spot. Shorthand for the **spot market** or *spot price* (cf. **cash market**). Frequently used with specific reference to **foreign exchange rate** quotations, although spot is used in other areas, such as the **commodities** markets (cf. **spot commodity**). Also called *cash* or *physicals*.

spot against forward delta hedge. Adjustment made to the value of the **underlying** or the **delta** of a **hedge** to reflect the differences in value between the **spot market** and the **expiry date** of the contract due to the **cost of carry**. Typically, the hedger will either adjust the forward value of the instrument by the carry, or will adjust the delta by the **basis** (Spot × (1 + basis/100)) to work out the amount of **underlying** required to hedge his position correctly.

spot-a-week. A foreign exchange **swap** that is made for a week. The initial transaction is settled on a spot (or in two working days basis and the re-exchange takes place one week from that date. Also called *spot-one-week*.

spot commodity. Commodities traded for actual **physical delivery**.

spot currency. Foreign exchange for immediate (usually two business days) **delivery** (cf. **foreign exchange forward**). See **foreign exchange market**.

spot date. The date for current spot transactions. That is, the current date, plus the standard accepted day's grace before **settlement**. Thus, if spot settlement is two days and the current day is the 4th of the month and a Thursday, the spot date would be the following Monday, the 8th of the month (holidays excepted).

spot deferred. Hybrid type of **forward contract** usually seen in the **commodities markets** in which the implied financing cost is variable and often provides for flexible **delivery** (cf. **rollover; roll forward**). The structure provides a greater degree of flexibility than a traditional **forward transaction** but without the expense of an **option**. See also **breakforward; participating forward**.

spot delivery month. The nearest calendar month in which **commodities** traded in the spot market can be delivered.

spot exchange rate. The price for **spot delivery** in foreign exchange (cf. **forward rate**).

spot foreign exchange. Currency for immediate (usually two business days) **delivery** (cf. **foreign exchange forward**). See also **foreign exchange market**.

spot–futures parity theorem. See cost of carry.

spot market. The market for transactions with settlement at the **spot date**, that is the normal, earliest **delivery date** for that market, which is usually within one, two, or three (business) days. The market price for delivery on the spot date is the *spot price* or *spot rate*. In **futures markets**, the spot price is the current price of the **underlying** in the spot market (cf. **basis; cash price; forward market; futures; regular delivery; tom/next**). Also called the *cash market*.

spot market trading. Term used in the **futures** markets for transactions made in futures which **expire** within the same month.

spot month. (i) **Exchange-traded options** and **futures** contract closest to **delivery** or **expiry**. It draws attention to the fact that delivery may shortly be required in respect of open positions (cf. **notice day**. (ii) The month in which the next **futures contract** will **expire** and delivery will take place. (iii) Another name for the **nearby contract**.

spot-next. Settlement of a **spot market** transaction after the third working day, usually used in currency transactions. Technically it is a **forward transaction** (by one day) and is priced accordingly. Most **market-makers** would include such transactions within their spot positions. Occasionally the term is used for longer transactions, such as *spot-week*, where settlement is deferred for a week after the spot date, and *spot-fortnight*, where the delay is two weeks.

spot position (Forex). The difference between **assets** and **liabilities** expressed in terms of a single currency. A spot position can be a *long position*: assets in one currency exceed liabilities (aka *overbought*); or a *short position*: liabilities in one currency exceed assets (aka *oversold*).

spot price or **spot rate.** (i) The price quoted or transacted in the **spot market** (cf. **forward; future exchange**). Although generally considered to be the cash price, for most markets, these are prices for transactions executed between the spot **settlement date** and the current **transaction date** (cf. **cash settlement; same-day delivery; tom/next**). Thus when spot is two business days, transactions can be made for **same-day settlement** or the next (business) day. Also called *spot goods* (commodities) or the *spot rate* (for instance in **currency** transactions). (ii) For interest rates, the spot rate is the **zero-coupon** interest rate at which a single payment is **present valued** (cf. **discount interest**).

spot rate yield curve or **spot curve.** A yield curve in which every point represents the **yield-to-maturity** of a **zero-coupon bond** from the spot or present date to its **maturity**. See **par yield curve; zero-coupon yield curve**.

spot start. Any **derivative** instrument in which one or more parts commences at the time of the transaction. Since most derivatives involve only exchanges of differences, the start of the exchange can be deferred to the future (cf. **forward start**).

spraddle. Another name for a **strangle**.

spread. (i) The difference between the **bid price** (dealer's buying price) and the **offer price** (dealer's selling price) or **yield** in a **dealer's** quotes. (ii) The difference between the bid and offer price or yields of two securities, used when examining a **switch**. (iii) Often used synonymously for the word **margin**. For instance, **floating rate notes** (FRNs) are sometimes discussed in terms of their 'spread' to the **reference rate**. See also **floating rate** or **variable rate interest**. (iv) The difference between the price or yield of two securities or markets (as in the 'spread between Bunds and OATs'). (v) The difference in yield between different parts of the **yield curve**. Thus the spread between five-year and thirty-year **US treasuries**. (vi) The difference in yield between two securities with the same **maturity** but of different quality (that is a *credit spread*) which represents the discount in valuation representing the differences in **risk**. (vii) (USA). The **underwriting** fee on a new issue (i.e. the difference in price or yield between the issuer and the **underwriter**). Often called the *gross spread*. (viii) Generic term for **option strategies** which involve the simultaneous purchase and sale of options (cf. **vertical spread; horizontal spread;**

ratio spread). Sometimes also called a *combination*. (ix) Old fashioned term for a strangle. (x) Used synonymously for range, the high and low over a given period in a security's price. (xi) (Derivatives). Used synonymously for a straddle. (xii) The difference between the price or rate on securities and that of their derivatives. This is better known as the *basis*. (xiii) Used to denote the difference between the cost of funds and the return on the use of the funds. Thus a bank's net interest margin would be the difference between its borrowing costs (e.g. London interbank bid rate) and its lending rate (e.g. London interbank offered rate, plus any additional rate the bank demanded), its *lending spread* (cf. net interest income). (xiv) A strategy of holding opposite positions in two instruments with a view to benefiting from a change in their spread relationship, which can either widen or narrow (cf. spread futures; spread option). A spread is not concerned with the direction of movement in the two positions, only in the difference in their price or rate. Also known as *spreading*. (xv) The degree of diversification in a portfolio. That is the spread or diversity of investments made (cf. asset allocation).

spread account. See reserve.

spread-adjusted notes. Any type of security where the interest payment is reset in accordance with an auction process relative to a benchmark, index, or reference rate. See, for instance, adjustable rate preferred stock; variable rate notes.

spread conversion. See risk reversal (cf. vertical spread).

spread fund. A guarantee fund used in asset-backed securities for credit enhancement purposes.

spread futures. Futures contract where the payoff is the spread relationship between two underlyings. For instance, the spread between the US Treasury long bond and treasury bills. A long position anticipates a widening of the spread; a short position, a narrowing (cf. yield curve plays; dumb-bell). These are cash-settled contracts. See also note over bond spread; treasury-eurodollar spread.

spread hedge. A form of spreading usually used in the commodities markets designed to protect the relationship between a commodity at different stages of processing. For instance, the spread between crude oil and refined oil products (cf. crack spread; crush spread).

spreading. The buying and selling of different futures or options contracts at the same time. Usually done in anticipation of a narrowing of

the differential between contracts of different maturity. See diagonal spread; futures trading; option strategies; straddle; strangle; time spread; vertical spread.

spread-lock. (i) (USA) In the US bond new issues market a borrower is allowed to fix the spread or margin on its issue over US Treasury securities, and is given the option of establishing the absolute level at a later date. If rates rise, the borrower pays the underwriter a lump sum; if they fall, the underwriter pays the borrower. The underwriter will normally hedge the position by buying the underlying treasury securities, or take the offsetting position in bond futures. See also rollover lock. (ii) Any agreement allowing the holder to fix the relationship between two assets, securities, or indices (cf. spread futures). (iii) (Futures). An undertaking to roll forward a futures position into a later expiring contract at an agreed spread to its fair value (cf. basis; basis risk).

spread-lock option. An option to enter into a spread-lock.

spread-lock swap. (i) A type of swap where the fixed rate payer's payment is made on the basis of a reference rate with an additional spread to a benchmark security. For instance, a French franc swap where the fixed rate is referenced to the ten-year obligations assimilables du Trésor. (ii) An interest rate swap allowing the floating payer to fix the payments at a fixed margin to a reference rate at a future date (cf. swaption).

spread management. See asset-liability management.

spread option or **spread provision.** Option allowing the holder to lock in a pre-agreed spread or margin against a benchmark in a financial instrument such as a bond (cf. call provision; put provision; spread put provision). The call (put) option pays the difference between the strike and the spread at expiry if positive (negative). Sometimes called a *spreadtion* (cf. swaption). See also rainbow option.

spread order. A transaction instruction used in options markets where the client indicates the amount of premium or spread to be paid or received in setting up the trade (cf. margin). See credit spread; debit spread.

spread protected debt securities. A security issue where the put provision is at a spread to a benchmark or reference rate (usually government issues) rather than at a fixed value. The spread element is based on a calculation designed to provide a given present value to the put price based on discounting the future coupon and principal at the benchmark rate (plus spread) at the time the put is exercised. Such a security does not provide the holder with an **option** on interest rates, but a protection against a deterioration in the spread or margin at which the security trades relative to the benchmark.

spread put provision (Bonds). A condition within a **bond** allowing the holder to put the bond back to the issuer at a predetermined **spread** to a **benchmark**, usually a government bond or **index**. The holder is therefore protected against any adverse changes in the spread on the bond against the benchmark, although not against absolute changes in interest rates. The structure has been used to protect investors against the **risk** of a deterioration in the **credit worthiness** of the issuer in the market.

spread rate differential option. See cross-currency option (cf. **quantity adjusting option**).

spread risk. The risk that a spread relationship will not move as predicted. It can also be taken to mean that the behaviour of two different assets does not continue as it has historically (cf. **correlation risk**).

spread-sheet (USA). The final terms on a new security issue decided at the pricing meeting (cf. **terms and conditions**).

spread-to-maturity (Bonds). A measure of return from a **floating rate note** relative to that from its index or **reference rate**, such as **London interbank offered rate**, calculated by **discounting** future cash flows on a **bond basis**. (cf. **discounted margin; simple margin**).

spread trade. Any of a number of securities or derivatives strategies aimed at making a gain from changes in the **spread** relationship between two or more **underlyings**, or in the case of **options** a single underlying (cf. **cross-asset; correlation risk; inter-commodity spread; intra-commodity spread**). See **horizontal spread; spread-lock; spread option; vertical spread**.

spread warrant. See spread option.

square. A position in a security, currency, or commodity that is neither **long** nor **short** (cf. **flat; hedge**).

square mile (UK). Colloquial name for the City of London, the financial, banking, and insurance centre of London (cf. **Bay Street; Wall Street**). Also referred to as the 'City'.

square root law. The mathematical principle that the dispersion in a diffusion process increases

with the square root of time. See **volatility** (cf. **Markov process**).

squeeze. A condition which involves a shortfall in supply or demand. Thus a *long squeeze* occurs when long position holders refuse to sell to those who have gone short. A *short squeeze* occurs when **short position** holders cannot borrow securities with which to execute the short and therefore have to close out their position.

stabilized contango. See flat rate forward.

stabilization. (i) The way in which a **lead manager** supports the market performance of a new issue. This may be done by over-allotting securities, going **short**, and covering the shortage of the issue through **after-market** or **grey market** purchases. Such support can also involve going **long**, with the surplus being sold subsequently in the after-market. Usually there is a time limit placed on such activities which is given in the **prospectus** or by market regulations (cf. **manipulation**). (ii) Transactions by market participants aimed at dampening down price movements: buying after price falls and selling after price rises (cf. **circuit breakers**). (iii) Sometimes the term stabilization is used with reference to the government objective of achieving price stability, control over price inflation, the external value of the currency, using **monetary and fiscal policies**.

stabilizing bid. A conditional purchase order by a **lead manager** of a new issue used to set a **floor** on the price in order to stabilize the **after-market** (cf. **grey market; stabilization**).

stack hedge or **stack and roll hedge.** Rolling short-term **derivatives** positions to hedge a longer term exposure. See **piled-up rolling hedge** (cf. **rolling hedge**).

stag (UK). An investor or **speculator** who specializes in new issues, usually for **equity**, and tries to assess which issues are likely to be **over-subscribed** with the intention of selling for a **short-term** profit, usually on the first trading day (cf. **bull; bear; spiv**). Hence *stagging*, the short-term purchase of new issues with a view to making a dealing profit. See grey market; offer for sale; profit taking.

staged drawdown swap. Another term for an accreting swap.

stagflation. A combination of economic *stagnation* with high inflation.

staggered board provision or **staggered directorships.** A defence used against takeovers which involves arranging that the re-election of

directors to the company be spread out over time and have service contracts which preclude removal without due cause. It means that although a **predator** can acquire voting control, it will be some time before the acquiring company gains control of the **board of directors**. See **poison pill**.

staggering maturities. See **amortization**.

stake. Colloquial term for a holding or investment in an asset, business, security, and so forth. It is usually taken to imply a large **position** or investment or an interest in the outcome of any event having an impact on the value of the holding.

stakeholder. Any individual or organization that has an interest, pecuniary or otherwise, in a company. It would include: customers; employees; suppliers; distributors; joint-venture partners; the local community; bankers; and **shareholders**. The suggestion is that all such people have a right to influence the decisions of the company. Sometimes used by firms to help in drawing up a mission statement. See **corporate governance**; **business ethics**; **shareholder value**.

stale. (i) A market where price movements have not behaved in the way expected, hence *stale bull* and *stale bear*. Sometimes used to describe the reaction of the market to a new issue that has not sold but where the **subscription period** has not yet expired (cf. **dog**). (ii) Also used to denote an out-of-date **bill**.

Stamp Duty (UK). A UK tax on the buying of shares and other assets, such as houses, evidenced by the exchange of documents. The amount of tax is based on a percentage of the value of the transaction. A variant, known as Stamp Duty Reserve Tax was introduced in the Finance Act, 1986 and applied to written agreements to transfer securities. It is currently $\frac{1}{2}$% on shares and 1% on property. See **transaction costs**.

stamp tax. Tax on the issue of new securities.

stand alone or **stand alone credit.** A type of financing where the lender or noteholder has **no** recourse to the sponsor. A limitation often seen in project finance (cf. **special purpose vehicle**).

standard amount. The round lot amounts set by market convention and practice for trading (cf. **marketable quantity**; **odd lot**). Usually the standard amount is not a legally binding condition, although professional traders will normally agree to make markets for these amounts. Standard end dates are also set for term transactions (cf. **broken dates**; **calendar/month convention**; **odd date**; **regular dates**).

Standard and Poor's Corporation (S&P) (USA). 25 Broadway, New York, NY 10004, USA (tel. (212) 208 8000; fax (212) 208 1500). A US credit rating agency. See **credit ratings** for detailed analysis.

Standard and Poor's—Agence d'Evaluation Financière (ADEF) (France). Subsidiary of Standard and Poor's Corporation's set up to rate Continental European firms.

Standard and Poor's depositary receipts (SPDRs; spiders). An investment trust vehicle, launched by the **American Stock Exchange**, which holds the principal stocks in the **Standard and Poor's 500 Index** and allows investors to track the performance of the index (cf. **indexation**).

Standard and Poor's 500 Stock Index or **Standard and Poor's index (S&P 500)** (Equities; USA). The leading US index made up of the largest 500 **New York Stock Exchange** (NYSE) listed companies weighted by **capitalization** (cf. **FT-Actuaries All Share Index**). It consists of **stocks** of the leading 400 industrials, 40 utilities, 20 transportation, and 40 financial institutions. It represents about 80% of the capitalization of the NYSE. See **index construction**.

Standard and Poor's 500 Index-Linked Notes (SPINS) (USA). An **equity-linked note** issue where the **maturity** proceeds are linked to the performance of the **Standard and Poor's 500 stock Index**. It has an **embedded option** giving a call on the **index**.

Standard and Poor's 100 Stock Index (S & P 100) (Equities, USA). A broad market **index** of 100 **common stocks** made up of 40 companies involved in finance, 20 transport, and 40 utilities.

Standard and Poor's MidCap 400 Index (S & P MidCap) (Equities; USA). An **index** of the second tier, or middle capitalization stocks.

standard basket. A method of valuing a **composite currency** where the value of one unit is deemed to be equal to the sum of the values of certain amounts of the stated currencies. See **European Currency Unit**; **Special Drawing Right**.

standard deviation. A measure of the dispersion of a distribution and therefore a useful measure of its **risk**. The square root of the **variance** is more intelligible than the variance since it is expressed in the same units as the distribution. If the data is normally distributed, then two-thirds of the observations will lie within plus or minus one standard deviation of the mean; and 99.7% within plus or minus three standard deviations. The general formula is:

$$\sigma = \sqrt{\sum_{i=1}^{n} \rho_i (x_i - \mu)^2}$$

where σ is the standard deviation; n the number of observations; ρ_i the probability of the ith observation; x_i the value of the ith observation; μ the mean of the total set of observations.

In most cases, each observation carries the same weight, so the calculation becomes:

$$\sigma = \sqrt{\frac{1}{n-1} \sum_{i=1}^{n} (x_i - \mu)^2}$$

standard deviation of returns. A measure of a security's or a portfolio's **volatility**.

standard error. A statistical measure of the estimated 'goodness of fit' of the estimated standard deviation of a sample. See also **least squares regression**.

Standard Industrial Classification Code (SICC). A method of classifying companies and their subsidiaries according to their line of business or activities as defined by Standard & Poor's Compustat Services Inc. (USA). It uses a four-digit classification system for companies by industry. For instance, the code 2800–2899 includes firms classified as *chemicals and allied products* while 2900–2999 is for firms in *petroleum and coal products*.

standardization. A condition of futures contracts allowing interchangeability between market participants (cf. **fungibility**).

standardized. A feature of contracts traded on **futures** and **options** exchanges where the details of the contract are defined in the contract specification: the unit, month, cash settlement, delivery, and price calculations (cf. **tick**).

standard option. Straight or simple **option** without any features likely to complicate its valuation (cf. **exotic options**).

standard portfolio analysis of risk (SPAN). A method used for working out the amount of **risk** and hence **margin** required for open short (written) positions in **exchange-traded options**. The method was developed by the **Chicago Mercantile Exchange** and is used widely, for instance, by the **London International Financial Futures and Options Exchange**. The system uses a scenario building method to work out a range of possible adverse outcomes for option values against which writers have to provide margin. SPAN takes entire open position (in a single option **class**) and treats it as a single **portfolio** of positions. Factors influen-

cing option prices (or option values) such as the price of the **underlying**, time to **expiry**, and **volatility** are used to calculate the scanning loss. The method uses historical data to calculate the largest probable one-day change in price: then calculates the effect of a variety of changes in price and volatility on the portfolio. Thus SPAN calculates the potential worst case risk in the portfolio across a number of changes in price and volatility to arrive at the required margin for option writers on a worst case basis. SPAN does not apply to option buyers whose risk remains the loss of the **premium** paid.

standard prepayment assumption (Bonds; USA). Historical estimates of mortgage prepayment rates published by the **Public Securities Association**. These rates are based on expected prepayments for factors such as selling, divorce, death, and so forth but not on refinancing due to lower interest rates. It is also known as the *Public Securities Association prepayment model*.

standby. A contingent agreement which depends on certain events to become effective normally against payment of a **commitment fee** (cf. **contingent**). For instance, an agreement concerning a **drop-lock security** (this is a **floating rate note** which has mandatory **conversion** into a **fixed rate bond** if the **reference rate** falls below a preset level) for the holder to sell it to another party on pre-agreed terms in the event that the drop-lock feature becomes effective.

standby agreement or **commitment** (USA). Term for an agreement to **underwrite** a **rights** issue or a **forced conversion**. Effectively a **put option** by the issuer on the **underwriter** for any **stock** not taken up by investors. Hence, the term *standby underwriter*.

standby credit. See standby letter of credit.

standby facility. (i) A contingent funding arrangement, the main purpose of which is to provide **liquidity**, for instance, to back up the issue of **commercial paper** in the event that the issuer cannot **rollover** maturing issues (cf. **liquidity risk**). (ii) More generally, any pre-agreed line of credit normally supplied by a bank but not expected to be drawn other than for exceptional purposes (cf. **commitment fee; standby fee**). (iii) A contingent undertaking to purchase or **fund** a **counterparty**. See **letter of moral intent**.

standby fee. The fee paid on a standby agreement.

standby offering (Equities; USA). An **underwriting agreement** for a **rights** or **privileged subscription issue** where the **underwriter** agrees to purchase any **stock** which is not acquired by existing **shareholders**.

standby letter of credit or **standby trade credit** (Banking; USA). (i) Used in the USA by banks in trade finance or to provide an undertaking in lieu of a guarantee which they are prohibited from giving by law. (ii) Also used to provide **credit enhancement**. See **letter of credit backed**.

standstill agreement. (i) An agreement by a **raider** or **predator** following a **greenmail** attempt in which he promises not to buy **stock** in the **target** for a set period. (ii) In banking, an agreement between **creditors** with outstanding facilities to a borrower facing financial difficulties not to precipate any action to place the company into **bankruptcy** or **insolvency** proceedings without the consent of the other parties (cf. **London rules**). See **event of default**.

Stansa di Compensazione (Italy). Clearing house.

stapled security. Two securities by different issuers which are traded as one indivisible package. Such securities normally have the two **certificates** printed back to back. Also known as *Siamese securities* or *paired shares*.

star. A highly successful performing investment (cf. **dog; problem child; Boston matrix**).

start date. The date at which a **derivatives** contract becomes operative (cf. **deferred start; spot start**). The contract is negotiated on the **trade date**, but the implementation may be deferred to a mutually agreed time. For simple contracts like **forwards** the operative date is generally the same as the **maturity** when both sides are required to honour their obligations under the contract. For more complex transactions such as **swaps**, the start date will create an effective period between the transaction being agreed and maturity involving commitments by both **counterparties**.

Star Trek (USA). A new issue where the pricing is in undiscovered country. That is the price or yield breaks new ground in relation to some benchmark, **spread** or **maturity**.

start-up. See **venture capital**.

Stasskulväxlar (Money markets; Sweden). **Treasury bills**.

state and local government series (SLGS) (USA). Non-tradable federal debt issued to states and local governments. These are used to invest surplus funds from local government. The interest rate is set so as to prevent **arbitrage** between taxable and tax-exempt interest.

state bank (Banking; USA). A bank which has a state charter and is state regulated. Federally chartered banks are known as **national banks** (cf. **chartered bank**).

stated interest rate. See **flat rate; nominal interest rate**.

stated maturity. The last date on which a debt obligation can be still outstanding. The implication is that the obligation will be **amortized**, have a **purchase** or **sinking fund**, or feature an early **call provision** such that the stated maturity is longer than the **average life** or expected term.

stated maturity surety security. A form of financial guarantee on a security that undertakes to provide sufficient funds to ensure repayment of the issue at the **stated maturity**.

stated rate auction preferred stock (STRAPS) (USA). A hybrid variant of **dutch auction preferred stock** that has an initial period, usually of several years, when the **dividend** is at a **fixed rate**, after which the dividend then becomes **variable rate**, reset by a **dutch auction** process every forty-nine days.

state immunity. See **sovereign immunity**.

statement of affairs. A schedule that lists **assets** and **liabilities** of a **bankrupt** or **insolvent** party. Also called a *statement of condition*.

Statement of Auditing Standards (SAS) (UK). A set of standards of good practice for **auditors** when examining a set of accounts.

statement of changes in financial position. See **sources and uses of funds statement**.

Statement of Financial Accounting Standards (SFAS) (USA). The rules governing financial reporting as laid down by the **Financial Accounting Standards Board (FASB)** in respect of the treatment of a particular accounting entry, item, or category. Such rules then form part of the **Generally Accepted Accounting Principles** used by firms making statutory reports. The FASB will issue a statement to clarify the treatment of an accounting item and to increase the disclosure requirements of firms. Each new statement is sequentially numbered and details the nature of the proposed new change, for instance, SFAS No. 118, 'Accounting by Creditors for Impairment of a Loan—Income Recognition and Disclosures'.

statement of income. That part of the financial condition of a firm which reports the income and expenses over the accounting period, typically a year, a half-year, or a quarter (cf. **balance sheet**). Also known as an *income statement*.

Statement of Recommended Practice (SORP) (UK). Best-practice, but non-compulsory, standards for financial accounting and reporting as proposed by the **Accounting Standards Board**.

statement of retained earnings (Accounting). A statement that reconciles the opening balance of retained earnings or reserves with the balance at the end of the period.

statement of source and application of funds. See sources and uses of funds statement.

Statements of Standard Accounting Practice (SSAP) (Accounting; UK). Proforma methods of accounting treatments (cf. **Generally Accepted Accounting Principles** (USA)). See also **Financial Reporting Standard; Statement of Auditing Standards**.

static hedge. A **hedge** that is put in place but not adjusted or rebalanced over its life (cf. **dynamic hedge**). A **forward** contract would be a static hedge in that the protection it afforded would not change over time.

statistical inference. A part of statistics that attempts to postulate general propositions about a set of observations or 'population' of items, in the absence of perfect or complete information. For example, company **directors** may be interested in learning how **shareholders** might react to a dramatic change in **dividend** levels. By taking a **random sample** of investors, it will be possible to obtain information about potential reactions to such a policy, but it is incomplete since it will not describe the reaction of all investors. Nevertheless, it is possible to generalize about the population on the basis of this sample. Statistical inference techniques concentrate upon the issue of the degree of confidence which can be placed on the generalizations and the margin of error involved. This is achieved mainly by using the methods of probability theory. Owing to the importance in finance attached to testing hypotheses, examining relationships, and deriving measurements, statistical inference is a primary analytical device despite the constraint of incomplete information.

statutory merger (USA). See **pooling of interests**.

step down. To reduce by a predetermined amount at specific points in time (cf. **amortization; step-up**).

step-down cap. An interest rate cap that has a **strike rate** that decreases with time. The opposite structure, a *step-up cap* also exists.

step-down coupon security. A security where the **coupon** rate is reduced at some point in the future. Such issues might be attractive to an investor seeking current income or for tax or regulatory reasons. At issue, the overall **yield** is equivalent to the market rate on a **straight bond**, but the initial coupons are above the market rate, while the coupons paid after the step-down takes effect are below the market rate. The alternative structure where the coupons are stepped-up also exists. See **dual coupon; step-up coupon security**.

step-down floating rate note. A floating rate note where the **margin** over the reference rate decreases over time.

step-down option or **warrant.** See reset option.

step-down spread. A borrowing where the margin to the reference rate decreases towards maturity. In some cases, the step-down is conditional on certain events, such as an increased **credit rating** by the borrower (cf. **split spread**).

step-down swap. (i) An **interest rate swap** which has a reduction in the **fixed rate** payment. Such a swap might be used to **hedge** the fixed rate on a **step-down coupon security**. (ii) **euromarkets** term used for an **amortizing swap**.

step-function. Condition in certain types of **exotic options** which defines the payoff if the **underlying** goes through a given price or rate point (cf. **trigger**). See **barrier option; digital option**.

step-lock option. See ladder option.

stepped call. A call provision in a bond that may be **exercised** only on **coupon** days, following the initial first **call date** (cf. **rolling call**). See **Atlantic-style; Bermudan-style**.

stepped interest. An interest rate, or **margin** over a **reference rate**, that is increased periodically over the term of the transaction. See **step up; step down**.

stepped preferred stock or **preference share.** **Preferred stock** with a fixed **dividend** that has a predetermined increase over time. See **step-up coupon security**.

Step Tax-exempt Appreciation and Income Realization Security (STAIRS) (USA). Municipal bond which has a **dual coupon** structure. Normally it pays no interest for a predetermined period and then a fixed rate to **maturity**.

step up. To increase by a predetermined amount at specific points in time (cf. **accrual; step down**).

step-up cap. An interest rate cap that has a strike rate that increases with time. The opposite structure, a *step-down cap* also exists.

step-up capped floating rate note (step-up capped floater). A capped floating rate note where the cap rate increases with time. Such an arrangement might be more attractive than the simple capped structure if holders were concerned about rising interest rates in the future.

step-up coupon security. A security where the coupon rate is increased at some point in the future. In cases where the original coupon rate was in line with the market at issue there is usually a **call provision** at the step-up point. The structure is designed to facilitate distribution of securities where there may be some medium-term doubt as to the **credit worthiness** of the issuer and the step-up is designed to compensate investors for this fact (cf. **bells and whistles**). Alternatively, it may be used where the investor is required to hold the security for a longer period than anticipated (cf. **extension risk; step-down coupon security; step-up floating rate note**). See **dual coupon**.

step-up floating rate note. A floating rate note (FRN) where the **margin** over the **reference rate** increases over time. Issuers normally have the right to redeem the issue in full or in part at the point(s) where a step-up in margin occurs through a **call provision**. Step-up FRNs have been used in mortgaged-backed or **asset-backed securities** where the final **maturity** is uncertain. Investors are therefore compensated for any additional term beyond that anticipated at issue (cf. **extension risk**).

step-up option or **warrant.** An option or warrant which has one or more timetabled increases in the **exercise price** prior to **expiry**. See **reset option**.

step-up or **step-down puttable security.** A variant on the step-up or step-down coupon security where the holder has a **put provision** at each step-up (down) point during the life of the security.

step-up recovery floating rate note (SURF). Type of **floating rate note** where the coupon has a **reference rate** which is based on an **index** of bonds.

step-up swap. (i) Euromarkets term for an accreting swap. (ii) An **interest rate swap (IRS)** or cross-currency swap where the fixed rate payer's crate is increased over the tenor of the transaction

(cf. **step-down swap**). Such swaps might be designed to match the **coupon** payments on a step-up security.

sterilization. That part of **monetary policy** usually designed to neutralize the effects of shocks to the domestic monetary system from international sources. See **open-market operations**.

sterling (UK). The name given to the currency of the United Kingdom (cf. **cable**). Also called *pound sterling* or *pounds*.

sterling commercial paper (sterling CP) (UK). Issues of sterling-denominated **commercial paper** in the UK market. Though a domestic market where the transaction is normally settled the same day, such paper is also sold on the **eurocurrency markets** for **spot settlement**.

sterling medium-term notes (sterling MTNs). Issues of **medium-term notes** in sterling either for the UK domestic market or internationally.

sterling mortgage-backed floating rate note (sterling mortgage-backed FRN or floater) (UK). Common form of **mortgage-backed security** in the UK market. Most UK residential mortgages are of the **variable rate** type and a **floating rate note** structure provides a good interest rate match to the **underlying** assets' income. Such issues generally have a long **maturity** to match the life of the **pool** of mortgages, although in practice the **average life** is much less. To compensate holders in case there is a longer than expected tenor, there is normally a **step-up** provision to the **margin** after a predetermined period (cf. **extension risk**). Equally, there may be some initial topping up made to the pool of mortgages in the early years if there is above expected redemption to the pool (cf. **prepayment risk**).

sterling transferable accruing government securities (STAGS) (Bonds; UK). Zero-coupon receipt securities offered by Quadrex Securities created by **stripping** UK government bonds (GILTS). See zero-coupon eurosterling bearer or registered accruing certificates (zebras).

sterling warrants into gilt-edged stock (SWING) (UK). A custom-made **option** to buy or sell a specific **gilt-edged** security.

sticky deal. A transaction that will be difficult to realize at a profit (cf. **dog**).

sticky-jump bond (USA). A type of **collateralized mortgage obligation** where the bond's right or precedence to repayment of **principal** changes if certain trigger events should occur. Unlike the **planned amortization class bond**, the new advantage is maintained for the security's remaining **term**.

Stillhalter (Switzerland). **Covered call**; a *stillhalter* warrant is a **covered warrant**.

stochastic error. Estimation error in a **model** that arises from the exclusion of an important explanatory variable or due to incorrect specification of the relationships being examined (cf. **model risk**).

stochastic process. Any price or rate series that varies over time in an unpredicatable way is said to follow a stochastic process. This can either be in discrete time, i.e. where the value can only change at certain fixed points, or be continuous where the process can change at any time. In the continuous process the variable can take any value within a certain range, while for discrete processes, only certain discrete values are possible (cf. **binomial option pricing model**). See **arithmetic Brownian motion**; **binomial distribution**; **geometric Brownian motion**; **Markov process**; **normal distribution**; **Wiener process**.

stochastic variables. When using regression **analysis** it is assumed that a relationship exists between the dependent variable (stated as the left-hand side of the model) and the explanatory variables (expressed on the right-hand side of the model). A stochastic or random variable is one where its value is determined by some chance mechanism or process according to some given **probability distribution**. To argue that an explanatory variable is non-stochastic implies that its values are not randomly determined, rather that they are chosen or fixed beforehand by the investigator (usually to suit the particular objectives of the research). No such control is assumed over the values of the dependent variable. These values will be given as a result of not only the independent variables but also the so-called random disturbances; that is, all of those things that could influence the relationship being studied but not specifically accounted for. These disturbances are usually assumed, under this kind of procedure, to be 'normally distributed'. Therefore, having chosen the explanatory variables, the values for the explained variable can be observed which result from the combined influences of the explanatory variables and the disturbances. The explained variable values are thus unlike the explanatory variables and are stochastic, deriving their randomness from the random nature of the disturbances.

stochastic volatility. A feature of some **option pricing models** aimed at capturing the observed behaviour of **volatility** in the markets. See also **multi-factor option pricing models**.

stock. (i) Strictly speaking, a collection of securities that have been bundled together to make their trading easier (cf. **block**; **line**; **lot**; **odd lot**). (ii) (US). The name for a **share** (cf. **common stock**; **preferred stock**). (iii) (UK). Used to describe **equity**, **gilt-edged**, or **bond** issues. For example, *a company's loan stock* (cf. **unsecured loan stock**), an *auction of gilt-edged stock*. (iv) (UK). In the local government **bond** market, issues with an initial **maturity** of more than five years. (v) An accounting entry for a business's stock-in-trade; in the USA called *inventory*. (vi) Also used for the **fixed assets** of a business (cf. **current assets**).

stock ahead (USA). Market term for an order which was not completed due to other trades taking precedence under market procedures. That is other orders were traded ahead or in front of the order, thus rendering it impossible to execute.

stock appreciation rights (SAR) (USA). An employee **stock option** used as a management incentive that either allows the holder to receive the difference between the market value of the **stock** and the **strike price** as payment, or allows for exercise into the stock.

Stock Borrowing and Lending Committee (SBLC) (UK). A market practices committee set up by participants to lobby for changes in the law relating to securities lending, in particular clarification of the tax and legal positions of both parties (cf. **repurchase agreement**; **short sale**).

stockbroker. A firm or individual whose business is dealing in securities (cf. **dealer**; **broker-dealer**; **jobber**; **market-maker**; **specialist**). Also just known as a *broker*, although this may lead to confusion since there are **commodity** brokers, **foreign exchange** brokers, **money market** brokers, and so forth. In the USA a stockbroking firm may be known as a *securities firm* or *securities house* and the individual as a *securities broker* or *securities dealer*.

stock buyback. The repurchase of **common stock** or **ordinary shares** either by purchases in the market or by **tender**. See **stock repurchase plan**.

stock dividends. Dividends paid in the form of additional issues of stock (cf. **scrip issue**).

stock equivalent. Any of a number of ways used to replicate the price performance of holding **common stock** or a **stock index** using **derivatives**. The principle involves the creation of **synthetic** positions by buying and selling combinations of **options** together with cash investments. A variant involves written option positions and a combination of cash and stock investment to replicate the price performance of the option (cf. **delta hedge**).

stock exchange, stock market or **bourse.** An organized market for the buying and selling of securities (cf. **over the counter**). The first stock exchange was established at Amsterdam in the Netherlands in 1602 to trade **shares** in the United East India Company. The key functions of an exchange are: the creation of a regulated, central market; provision of **liquidity**; fairness of the pricing or **auction** process; the management of **risks** in **settlement**, **delivery**, or **clearing**. Members who transact business on an exchange are known as **brokers** (or stockbrokers) who act as **agents** for buyers and sellers as well as **dealers** or **traders** who may be acting for their own account as **principals** (cf. **local**; **floor trader**). In addition, most exchanges maintain a system of **market-makers** or **specialists** who may also be known as **jobbers**. Key factors in an exchange are a designated or physical market-place, the **floor**, and the requirement that securities traded on the exchange have gone through a vetting procedure to obtain a **listing** or **quote**. Transactions are either of a primary nature, that is new capital is being raised, or are of a secondary nature, that is existing claims are being traded between market participants (cf. **initial public offering**). **Secondary market** trading accounts for most of the **volume** or activity on exchanges.

Some of the more important exchanges are:

American Stock Exchange (Amex; ASE) (USA)
Amsterdamse Effectenbeurs (Amsterdam Stock Exchange) (Netherlands)
Athens Stock Exchange (Greece)
Australian Stock Exchange (ASX) (Australia)
Bangalore Stock Exchange (India)
Basel Stock Exchange (Switzerland)
Bolsa de Bogota (Colombia)
Bolsa de Comercio de Santiago (Chile)
Bolsa de Medellin (Colombia)
Bolsa Mexicana de Valores (Mexico)
Bolsa Nacional de Valores (Costa Rica)
Bolsa de Valores de Lisboa (Portugal)
Bolsa de Valores do Porto (Portugal)
Bombay Stock Exchange (India)
Bourse de Genève (Switzerland)
Bourse des Valeurs Abidjan (Ivory Coast)
Bourse des Valeurs Casablanca (Morocco)
Bratislava Stock Exchange (Slovakian Republic)
Budapest Stock Exchange (Hungary)
Colombo Stock Exchange (Sri Lanka)
Consiglio Di Borsa (Italy)
Copenhagen Stock Exchange (Denmark)
Delhi Stock Exchange (India)
Deutsche Börse (Germany)
Dhaka Stock Exchange Ltd (Bangladesh)
First Bulgarian Stock Exchange (Bulgaria)
Frankfurt Stock Exchange (Germany)

Ghana Stock Exchange (Ghana)
Helsinki Stock Exchange (Finland)
Hong Kong Stock Exchange (Hong Kong)
Iceland Stock Exchange (Iceland)
Irish Stock Exchange (Republic of Ireland)
Istanbul Stock Exchange (Turkey)
Johannesburg Stock Exchange (South Africa)
Karachi Stock Exchange (Pakistan)
Korea Stock Exchange (Korea)
Kuala Lumpur Stock Exchange (Malaysia)
Kuwait Stock Exchange (Kuwait)
Ljubljana Stock Exchange Inc. (Slovenia)
London Stock Exchange (ISE) (UK)
Luxembourg Stock Exchange (Luxembourg)
Madrid Stock Exchange (Spain)
Malta Stock Exchange (Malta)
Milan Stock Exchange (Italy).
Montreal Exchange (ME) (Canada)
Moscow Central Stock Exchange (Russia)
Nagoya Stock Exchange (NSE) (Japan)
Nairobi Stock Exchange Ltd. (Kenya)
Namibian Stock Exchange (Namibia)
New York Stock Exchange (NYSE) (US)
New Zealand Stock Exchange (New Zealand)
Nigerian Stock Exchange (Nigeria)
Osaka Securities Exchange (OSE) (Japan)
Oslo Stock Exchange (OSE) (Norway)
Pacific Stock Exchange (PSE) (US)
Paris Bourse or Paris Stock Exchange (France)
Philadelphia Stock Exchange (PHLX) (US)
Philippine Stock Exchange (Philippines)
Prague Stock Exchange (Czech Republic)
Sociedad Rectora de la Bolsa de Valores de Barcelona (Spain)
Société de la Bourse de Valeurs (Belgium)
Stock Exchange of Mauritius (Mauritius)
Stock Exchange of Singapore (SES) (Singapore)
Stock Exchange of Thailand (Thailand)
St Petersburg Stock Exchange (Russia)
Swedish Stock Exchange (Sweden)
Swiss Stock Exhange (Switzerland)
Sydney Stock Exchange Limited (Australia)
Taiwan Stock Exchange (Republic of China)
Tehran Stock Exchange (Iran)
Tel-Aviv Stock Exchange (Israel)
Tokyo Stock Exchange (TSE) (Japan)
Trinidad and Tobago Stock Exchange (Trinidad and Tobago)
Vancouver Stock Exchange (VSE) (Canada)
Warsaw Stock Exchange (Poland)
Wiener Börsekammer (Austria)
Zagreb Stock Exchange (Croatia)

In addition, most other countries have one or more exchanges devoted to trading equities.

Stock Exchange Alternative Trading Service (SEATS) (Equities; UK). **London Stock Exchange market-making** system designed to facilitate the trading of small capitalization issues. Unlike the **Stock Exchange Automated Quotations**, which is a quote-driven system, SEATS also includes unfilled **orders** (cf. **limit order**; **stop-loss order**). It replaced the earlier **Company Bulletin Board Service** in November 1992. See also **Alternative Investment Market**.

Stock Exchange Automated Quotations (SEAQ) (UK). The continuous 'real-time' computer-based price collection and dissemination system operated by the **London Stock Exchange** which is the basis of **screen-trading** of securities in the UK. It provides details of **market-maker's bid** and **offer** prices for individual issues. The best **quote** given in the market for each security is reported in yellow (called the yellow strip). When prices are rising they are reported in blue and red when falling. See **mandatory quote period**; **small-order automated execution facility**.

Stock Exchange Automated Quotations International (SEAQI) (UK). Reporting system used for trading securities in the UK but which are quoted outside the UK. See **mandatory quote period**.

Stock Exchange Automated Trading System (SEATS) (Australia). Screen-based system used to trade securities, linking all exchanges in Australia, which largely replaces **floor** trading operated by the **Australian Stock Exchange** Limited. It went into service on 19 October 1987, the day of the October Crash! Settlement is carried out by the Flexible Accelerated Security Transfer (FAST) system.

Stock Exchange Committee (Cyprus). Cyprus Chamber of Commerce and Industry, Chamber Building, 38 Grivas Dhigenis Av & 3, Deligiogis St, PO Box 1455, Cy-Nicosia (tel. 357 2 449 500; telex 2077 CHAMBER CY).

Stock Exchange Daily Official List (SEDOL) (UK). A daily publication of the **closing prices** of most of the securities **listed** on the **London Stock Exchange**. The first issues date back to 1698. Listed securities also have *SEDOL numbers* for identification purposes.

Stock Exchange Money Brokers (SEMBS) (UK). Inter-**dealer** brokers who match up interbank transactions and arrange the loan of securities to **gilt-edged market-makers** in the gilt-edged market (government **bond** market).

Stock Exchange of Hong Kong (Hong Kong). 1st Floor, One and Two, Exchange Square, 8 Connaught Place, PO Box 8888, HK-Hong Kong (tel. 852 522 1122; fax 852 868 1308).

Stock Exchange of Mauritius Ltd (Mauritius). 6th Floor 'Les Cascades' Building, 33 bis Edith Cavell Street, MU-Port-Louis (tel. 230 212 9541; fax 230 208 8409).

Stock Exchange of Singapore Ltd (SES) (Singapore). 20 Cecil Street, #26-01/08, The Exchange, SG-Singapore 0104 (tel. 65 535 3788; fax 65 535 2231). The main market for dealing in **shares** in Singapore, together with the **Singapore International Monetary Exchange** (SIMEX), offering international investors considerable attractions for dealing. The exchange is a screen-only market in line with, for instance, the **London Stock Exchange** and is regulated by the Monetary Authority of Singapore. It also manages the Stock Exchange of Singapore Dealing and Automated Quotations System (SESDAQ), a second-tier market modelled on the USA's **National Association of Securities Dealers Automated Quotations** (NASDAQ) system.

Stock Exchange of Singapore Index (SESI). The **Stock Exchange of Singapore's** own market **index**. It is less commonly followed than the **Straits Times (Industrial) Index** of leading **shares**.

Stock Exchange of Thailand (Thailand). Sinthon Building, 2nd Floor, 132 Wireless Road, TH-Bangkok 10330, Metropolis (tel. 66 2 254 0960 9; fax 66 2 254 7120).

Stock Exchange Pool Nominees Ltd (SEPON) (UK). The nominee company owned by the **London Stock Exchange** which holds all **shares** during the course of **settlement** and is designed to ensure the smooth transfer of ownership. See also **Crest**.

Stock Exchange Surveillance Commission (Japan). Regulatory body for overseeing securities origination and trading.

stock futures. Financial futures contracts where the **underlying** is a specific **security** rather than an **index**. Also, sometimes, wrongly used for **stock index futures**.

stockholders. Those claim holders who have an **equity** interest in the firm. Also sometimes called *equityholders* or *shareholders*.

stockholders' equity. See net worth.

stockholder value. See shareholder value.

Stockholms Fondbörs (Stockholm Stock Exchange) (Sweden). Postal Address: Box 1256, 11182 Stockholm (tel. 08-14 31 60; fax 08-10 81 10; tlx 13551 BOURSE S).

stock index or **indices** and **averages.** Stock exchange indicators and performance measures. There are two principal kinds: the stock price

Stock indices

Country	Indices	Type
Argentina	Merval index (29/12/77)	
Australia	All Ordinaries (1/1/80; base = 500)	WA: leading stocks
Australia	All Mining Index (1/1/80, base = 500)	
Austria	Credit Aktien (30/12/84)	
Austria	Traded Index ATX (2/1/91, base = 1,000)	
Belgium	BEL-20 (1/1/91, base = 1,000)	leading stocks
Brazil	Bovespa index (29/12/83)	
Canada	TSE 300	WA: broad index
Canada	Composite (1975, base = 1,000)	
Canada	Portfolio (4/1/83, base = 1,000) (Montreal Exchange)	
Chile	IPGA General (31/12/80)	
China	Class A index	Foreign investment
Cross-border	Barings Emerging Markets (7/1/92)	
Cross-border	J. Capel Drgns (31/12/88)	
Cross-border	FT-SE Eurotrack 100 (26/10/90)	WA: leading stocks
Cross-border	Eurotop 100 (26/6/90, base = 1,000)	
Denmark	CSE (3/1/83)	
Denmark	KFX Index	
Europe	FT-SE Eurotrack 200 (26/10/90)	WA: leading stocks
Finland	HEX General Index (28/12/90, base = 1,000)	
France	CAC-40 index (31/12/87, base = 1,000)	WA: leading stocks
France	SBF 250 (31/12/90, base = 1,000)	WA: broad index
Germany	Commerzbank (1/12/53)	
Germany	DAX (30/12/87, base = 1,000)	WA: broad index
Germany	FAZ Aktien (31/12/58)	
Greece	Athens SE (31/12/80)	
Hong Kong	Hang Seng Index (31/7/64)	WA: leading stocks
India	Bombay Stock Exchange: BSE-30 Index (1979)	
Indonesia	Jakarta Composite Index (10/8/82)	broad index
Ireland	ISEQ Overall Index (4/1/88, base = 1,000)	
Italy	Banca Commercial Italia (Comit) (1972)	
Italy	MIBtel Index (base = 1,000)	WA: broad index
Italy	MIB General (2/1/95, base = 1,000)	
Japan	ISE/Nikkei 50	
Japan	Nikkei 225 (16/5/49)	AV: leading stocks
Japan	Nikkei 300 (1/10/82)	broad index
Japan	OSE Average	
Japan	TOPIX (4/1/68)	
Japan	Tokyo Stock Exchange 2nd Section (4/1/68)	second tier
Malaysia	KSLE Composite (4/4/86)	broad index
Mexico	IPC index (Nov. 78)	
Netherlands	AEX Index	WA: broad index
Netherlands	CBS TRG (end 83)	
Netherlands	CBS All Share (end 83)	
New Zealand	NZSE-40 Index (1/7/86)	
Norway	OSE Total Index (1/1/83)	broad index
Pakistan	Karachi 100-share index	
Philippines	Manila Composite (2/1/85)	
Portugal	BTA (1977)	
Singapore	Straits Times Index	
Singapore	SES-All Singapore (2/4/75)	
South Africa	JSE All Industrial Index (28/9/78, base = 264.3)	WA: broad index
South Africa	JSE Gold Index (28/9/78, base = 255.7)	
South Korea	Korea Composite Exchange (4/1/80)	
Spain	Madrid SE General Index (30/12/85)	
Sweden	Affaersvaerlden General (1/2/37)	
Sweden	OMX index	
Switzerland	Swiss Bank Industrial Index (31/12/58)	
Switzerland	Swiss Bank General (1/4/87)	
Switzerland	SMI	
Taiwan	Taiwan Weighted Price (30/6/66)	WA:
Thailand	SET Index (30/4/75)	
Turkey	Istanbul Composite Index (Jan 86)	
UK	FT-SE 100	WA: leading stocks

Country	Indices	Type
UK	FT-SE Mid 250	WA: second tier
UK	FT-SE-A 350	WA: broad index
UK	FT-SE-A All Share	WA: broad index
UK	FT-SE SmallCap	WA: small companies
UK	FT Ordinary Index	GA: leading stocks
USA	Amex Market Value	
USA	ASE Composite	WA: broad index
USA	Dow-Jones Industrial Average	AV: leading stocks
USA	Dow-Jones Sixty Five Stocks	
USA	Dow-Jones Transport	sector index
USA	Dow-Jones Utilities	sector index
USA	Major Market Index	AV: leading stocks
USA	NASDAQ Composite	WA: broad index
USA	NASDAQ National Markets Composite	
USA	NYSE Composite	WA: broad index
USA	Russell 2000	small companies
USA	Standard & Poor's 100 Index	WA: leading stocks
USA	Standard & Poor's 500 Index	WA: broad index
USA	Standard & Poor's 600 Index	WA: small companies
USA	Standard & Poor's Composite	WA: broad index
USA	Standard & Poor's Financial	WA: sector index
USA	Standard & Poor's Industrial	WA: sector index
USA	Standard & Poor's MidCap	WA: sector index
USA	Value Line Index	GA:
USA	Wiltshire 5000 Equity	
World	Dow-Jones World Stock Index (US: 6/30/82; World: 31/12/91)	WA
World	Morgan Stanley Capital International (1/1/70)—US dollar based	WA
World	Salomon–Russel Global Equity Index	WA (uses special weights, see entry)
World	FT-Actuaries/Standard & Poor's World Indices	WA

average index, which is an arithmetic average of the component prices, or a capitalization-weighted index which captures changes in value since the larger issues count for more in the calculation of the index value. Such indices can be either leading stocks, sectors (by type or activity), or broad or composite indices aimed at capturing the performance of the market as a whole.

The major stockmarkets have one or more index; the list above gives those which are reported internationally and is, by no means, a full list. The term 'leading stocks' means it aims to measure market leaders (normally the largest companies traded on a particular exchange or market); 'broad index' means it is a general index covering most or all of a particular market; in addition there are a number of specialized indices, for example those covering small companies or stocks available to be purchased by foreigners. The abbreviation WA stands for weighted-average, that is the index is capitalization-weighted; AV means a price average index; GA is a geometric average. The base date from which the index has been constructed is also given. For a detailed methodology on compilation, see **index construction.**

stock index futures. Futures contract based on stock indices, normally settled by paying differences in cash. As a result such a contract is an agreement to buy or sell at a future date the equivalent cash value of the index. A number of important differences should be noted between buying a stock index future and holding the **underlying:**

1. The future buyer will not receive any **dividends** paid on the underlying **stocks**. As a result, the forward value of the index future will be reduced by the anticipated dividends to be received.

2. A futures contract offers an opportunity to buy on **margin** without having to commit all the funds immediately. As a result, higher interest rates and a longer **expiry** period will raise the forward value of the contracts.

3. The index reflects a holding of a certain number of stocks. The higher the index, the greater the purchase cost of the basket and so the greater the carrying cost of the underlying **position.** This will be reflected in a fair value premium which rises with the index level.

A 'fair value' of such a future can be calculated as follows:

$$F_{si} = \frac{C \times 1 + (T_{sm} \times r \times M_c) - D + m + t}{365}$$

where F_{si} is the value of future; C the cash value of the index; T_{sm} the number of days from settlement to maturity; r the rate of interest; D the expected dividends, expressed in index points; m the transaction cost differential; M_c the adjustment for loss of interest on initial margin; t transaction fees.

The fair value is basically arrived at by taking the interest that could have been earned by holding the future less the forgone dividends (cf. **cost of carry**). Because interest rates are normally higher than **dividend yields** stock index futures tend to trade at a **premium** to the underlying. This is a best estimate of what the future should trade at but different participants will hold different views as to likely dividends and will have made alternative cost of money assumptions. Normal supply and demand will also affect whether a stock index future stands above or below its fair value, which is known as the *value basis* (cf. **basis**). The following contract specifications are taken from the stock-index future contract on the **FT-SE 100 Index** traded on the **London International Financial Futures and Options Exchange** (LIFFE). For completeness, the option contracts are also given.

FT-SE 100 INDEX FUTURE

- *Unit of trading*: valued at £25 per Index Point.
- *Expiry months*: nearest three months of March, June, September, and December.
- *Settlement day*: First business day after the Last Trading Day.
- *Last trading day*: 10.30; third Friday of the delivery month.
- *Quotation*: Index points.
- *Minimum price movement (tick size)*: 0.5 (£12.50).
- *Trading hours*: 08.35 to 16.10.
- *APT trading hours*: 16.32 to 17.30.
- *Contract standard*: cash settlement at the Exchange Delivery Settlement Price.
- *Exchange delivery settlement price*: the EDSP is based on the average level of the FT-SE 100 Index between 10.10 and 10.30 on the last trading day.

Note: APT is LIFFE's Automated Pit Trading System. APT operates for many LIFFE futures contracts after the close of floor trading.

FT-SE 100 INDEX OPTION (ESX) (EUROPEAN-STYLE EXERCISE)

- *Unit of trading*: valued at £10 per Index Point.
- *Expiry months*: March, June, September, and December plus such additional months that the three nearest calendar months are always available for trading.
- *Exercise/settlement day*: Exercise by 18.00 for expiring series on the Last Trading Day. Settlement Day is one business day after the Last Trading Day. (An option can only be exercised on the Last Trading Day).
- *Last trading day*: 10.30; third Friday of expiry month.
- *Quotation*: Index Points.

- *Minimum price movement (tick size)*: 0.5 (£5.00).
- *Trading hours*: 08.35 to 16.10.

FT-SE 100 INDEX OPTIONS (SEI) (AMERICAN-STYLE EXERCISE)

- *Contract standard*: Cash settlement based on a daily settlement price for non-expiring options or the exchange delivery settlement price of a particular expiry month.
- *Daily settlement price (American-style option)*: The daily settlement price is the equivalent of the FT-SE 100 Index level at 16.10.
- *Exchange delivery settlement price*: The EDSP is based on the average level of the FT-SE 100 Index between 10.10 and 10.30 on the Last Trading Day.
- *Option premium*: Option Premium is payable in full by the buyer to the seller on the business day following a transaction.
- *Exercise price and exercise price intervals*: American-style option: Index Points e.g. 2000, 2050. The Interval between strike prices is determined by the time to maturity of a particular expiry month and is either 50 or 100 Index Points. European-style option: Index Points e.g. 2025, 2075. The interval between strike prices is also 50 or 100 Index Points and is determined by the time to maturity for expiring options.
- *Introduction of new exercise prices*: Additional exercise prices will be introduced on the business day after the underlying Index level has exceeded the 2nd highest, or fallen below the 2nd lowest, available exercise price.

FT-SE 100 INDEX FLEX OPTIONS (EUROPEAN-STYLE EXERCISE)

- *Contract standard*: Cash settlement based on the exchange delivery settlement price of a particular expiry date.
- *Daily settlement price (European-style option)*: The daily settlement price is the equivalent of the FT-SE 100 Index level at 16.10.
- *Exchange delivery settlement price*: The EDSP is based on the average level of the FT-SE 100 Index between 10.10 and 10.30 on the Last Trading Day.
- *Option premium*: Option Premium is payable in full by the buyer to the seller on the business day following a transaction.
- *Exercise price and exercise price intervals*: FLEX Option: Exercise prices for FLEX are specified by the user and can be any whole number of Index Points e.g. 2000, 2010.
- *Exercise price and expiry day*: A FLEX option cannot be introduced with the same expiry day and exercise price as an existing European-style Index Option (ESX) series and when an existing ESX contract is listed with the same Exercise Price and Expiry Date as an existing FLEX series, the existing FLEX

series will be converted into the corresponding ESX series.

stock index future options or **options on stock index futures.** Option contracts that give the holder the right to buy (**call**) or sell (**put**) **stock index futures.** Confusingly these are sometimes referred to as *stock index options* (cf. **stock options**).

	Stock index futures: position desired (if exercised)[a]	Underlying index: position to be hedged
Buy Index option Call	Long	Short
Buy Index option Put	Short	Long

[a] Plus a cash payment for the difference between the current stock index futures value and the **strike price**.

stock index growth note (SIGN) (USA). A **Zero-bond coupon bond** where the redemption value is linked to the performance of the **Standard and Poor's 500 Index**.

stock index options. (i) An exchange-traded option on a stock index. See entry on **stock index futures contract** for example of contract specifications (cf. **flex options**). (ii) **over-the-counter** (OTC) **option** contracts that give the holder the right to buy or sell a stock index at an agreed level (**strike price**) and **expiry date**. These are cash-settled agreements. These OTC products are not to be confused with similar options which are exchange-traded. (iii) Another (misleading) term for **stock index future options**.

stockjobber (UK). Old term used for **market-makers** on the **London Stock Exchange**, prior to the mid-1980s' reforms known as **Big Bang** (cf. **specialist**). Up to that point, the London Market had operated a system of **single capacity** separating the functions of market-makers from **brokers**. This was then replaced by a system of **dual capacity**, with the vast majority of stockjobbers becoming part of integrated dealing operations.

stock lending. The practice of providing securities to market participants in return for a fee in order to allow **short selling** or to facilitate **delivery** or the **settlement** of transactions. It differs from a **repurchase agreement** in that the lender retains all the rights and obligations of the security.

stock liquidity ratio or **stock trading liquidity ratio.** A measure of a stock's **liquidity** given by:

$$\frac{\text{average volume during period } t}{\text{average price trend during period } t}$$

A high ratio indicates that the stock is liquid; a low ratio illiquid. That is, transactions create price **volatility**.

stock margin trading. Purchase or sale of common stocks on **margin** with a view to making a **leveraged** profit on the holding (cf. **margin requirement**). Such activity is generally now largely carried out on **futures** and **options** exchanges, where the amount of margin is less than that for the corresponding securities purchases.

stock market. See **stock exchange**.

stock option. (i) An **option** giving the holder the right to buy in the case of a **call option** or sell in the case of a **put option** a given **common stock** at a set **exercise price** and **expiry date**. (ii) Also common term in the USA for an employee **stock** incentive ownership plan.

stock-over-bond warrant (SOB warrant). Outperformance option where the payoff is the change in a **stock index** less that of a bond index. The opposite structure is a *bond-over-stock option* or *warrant*.

stock performance exchange-linked investments (SPEL) (USA). A security issue arranged by and traded on the **American Stock Exchange** where the redemption value is linked to the performance of the **New York Stock Exchange composite index** although holders are guaranteed to receive back as a minimum their original investment. See also **Standard and Poor's Index Notes**.

stock repurchase plan. A plan, approved by **shareholders**, for a corporation to repurchase its own **stock** in the market. Such a plan can be seen as a tax-efficient means of returning **capital** to shareholders; using up surplus cash when there are insufficient attractive investments to be undertaken and/or as a way of increasing **financial leverage**. Companies undertake such actions when their **common stock** is perceived as underpriced or underperforming.

stock sales ratio. The number of times a firm's stock or inventory is turned over in the financial reporting period. Also known as the *stock turnover ratio*.

stock selection. Active fund **management** approach that focuses on selecting individual securities rather than on broader asset allocation decisions.

stock specific risk. That element of **price risk** in a security that is unique to the security and not the result of changes in the overall market. In **modern portfolio theory**, risk is divided into **market risk** or **systematic risk** and residual or **specific risk**. See also **Capital Asset Pricing Model**.

stock split. An increase in the number of issued shares by dividing each existing share into two or more **shares** with a proportionately smaller **nominal value** (cf. **consolidation**). Normally done to decrease the individual share price when a stock gets what is known as 'heavy', i.e. expensive, in order to increase the stock's **marketability** since the split will increase the number of outstanding shares available. It will not raise any new capital for the company undertaking the operation, although, in some cases, stock splits have been combined with other transactions, such as a **rights issue.** Called a *scrip issue* in the UK. See **dilution**.

stock swap. See debt–equity swap.

stock symbols. Unique abbreviations or acronyms used to identify company **stocks** for reporting or database purposes. Different systems may use different combinations of letters and numbers. A standardized system is available called **CUSIP numbers.** Such stock symbols are not to be confused with the company nicknames used by the market (cf. **Standard Industrial Classification code; Stock Exchange Daily Official List** (SEDOL numbers)).

stock turnover ratio. The ratio of the cost of goods sold to average **inventory** or stock-in-trade held.

stock warrant or **common stock warrant.** See equity warrant; warrant.

Stock Watch (USA). That part of the **Securities and Exchange Commission** that monitors **share** dealings in the USA. Its primary role is to identify unusual or unexpectedly large transactions, particularly ahead of **takeover** activity, as an indication of possible **insider dealing.** Individual **stock exchanges** participate in this surveillance activity. In the UK this function is performed by the surveillance department at the **London Stock Exchange.** See **chinese walls; compliance officer.**

stock watering. See dilution.

stock with attached put or **stock with married put** (Equities; USA). See **superstock.**

stop-limit order. A variation on a stop order which combines a contingent transaction instruction (the stop order) with the execution of the transaction at another price (the **limit order**). It is activated when the price or rate **triggers** the stop and is executed at no worse than the stated price or rate. The instruction avoids having the stop order automatically become a **market order** if the price is reached. The disadvantage is that there is a **risk** of not having an execution if the price then moves above/below the limit order before a transaction

can be carried out. The risk is that such an order can be superceded by volatile market movements, thus nullifying the intentions of the instruction.

stop loss. A means of **risk management** of positions which involves giving contingent instructions to buy or sell in the event of unfavourable price movements. The most common is the **stop order,** but other instructions which have their uses are: **limit order; good till cancelled; good for the day; good this week; good-this-month.**

stop order. An instruction to buy or sell that becomes operative once a certain price is reached. When the stop price is reached or passed, the stop order becomes a **market order** (cf. **market-if-touched**). There are two kinds: *buy stop* and *sell stop.* Sometimes called a *stop-loss order.*

stop-out price, stop price or **stop-out rate** (USA) (i) The lowest accepted price (or highest **discount** rate) on an **auction** of treasury bills. The equivalent for **bonds** or **notes** is the **tail.** (ii) Also used in the same sense for the **Federal Reserve's open-market operations** (FOMC) during the **desk's go-round.**

stopping curve. A term for the refunding or reinvestment rates across time, which give the break-even rates at which the issuer or investor is indifferent as to whether to **call** or **put** an issue.

stopped stock (USA). A trade with a **specialist** where the transaction price is guaranteed for a given period to be the more favourable of (*a*) the best currently available in the specialist's **book**, or (*b*) an improved price during the guaranteed period.

stop price or **stop-out price** (i) (Bonds; USA). A US Treasury Auctions term for the lowest price accepted on a new issue (cf. **tail**). (ii) The price at which a **stop order** is given.

stoption. See barrier option.

storage costs. Costs of storing a given asset for a set period. In the case of **commodities** a significant factor in setting forward or futures prices (cf. **convenience yield**). See also **cost of carry.**

story stock or **story book stock** or **story paper.** A **stock** or security where the attractions have to be explained by the salesman as a narrative rather than through appeal to fundamental value.

St Petersburg Stock Exchange (Russia). Skorohodova 19-Room 313, SU-St Petersberg 197061 (tel. 7 812 238 3384; fax 7 812 232 1886).

straddle. (i). An **option strategy** that is a **combination** of a **put** and a **call,** either purchased or sold, on the same **underlying** at the same **strike price** for the same **expiry date** (cf. **strangle**). If the market moves significantly in either direction, the profit on one **leg** will be greater than the **premium** lost on the other (cf. **lifting a leg**). If the market does not move, both **options** expire at a loss. A **long** straddle involves purchasing the put and call, a **short** straddle involves selling (or writing) the options. It can also be created either by holding the underlying together with holding two puts; or by holding two calls and a short position in the underlying. The position is also known as a *volatility spread, play* or *trade* or *vertical combination*. See **diagonal spread; horizontal spread; option strategies; ratio spread; straddle calendar spread.**

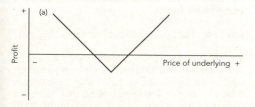

Payoff of a long straddle at expiry

This is also known as a *bottom straddle* or a *straddle purchase.*

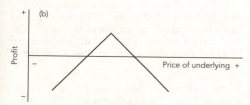

Payoff of short straddle at expiry

This is also known as a *top straddle* or *straddle write.*

(ii) A **futures position** based on any combination of **long** and **short** positions in **contracts** of the same **underlying** for different delivery months or the purchase and sale of contracts with different **expiry dates**. For example, the purchase of June contracts and the sale of September contracts (cf. **strangle** and **strap**). The expectation is:

Purchase early expiry, sell later expiry: spread expected to widen (early *less* late)

Sell early expiry, purchase later expiry: spread expected to narrow (late *less* early)

Confusingly, people sometimes refer to futures straddles as **spreads** and vice versa. See also **cash and carry; intra-commodity spread; intra-commodity spread.**

straddle calendar spread. An option strategy which involves selling or writing a straddle for a

near to **expiry** position and buying a straddle with a later expiry. The rationale is to take advantage of the **implied volatility** inherent in the **term structure of volatility** where near-date volatility is low compared to volatility further out along the curve. The written straddle is used to subsidize the cost of setting up the longer-dated long straddle position. See also **diagonal straddle calendar spread.**

straight. Term in widespread use in the **euromarkets** for a fixed-income, **coupon**, or **fixed rate** security with a **bullet maturity**. In the USA known as a *plain vanilla* issue. Both terms are commonly used. See **bond value.**

straight cancel (CXL). Instruction to terminate the execution of an existing order, which is not replaced by another. See also **one-cancels-the-other order.**

straight line method. (i) A method of calculating **depreciation** where the cost or agreed value of an asset is written off over its expected life by charging equal amounts against profits each year. See **depreciation methods.** (ii) A method of measuring the return on a **floating rate certificate of deposit** (FRCD) or a **floating rate note** (FRN). It takes return as a **margin** over the **reference rate** by adding the quoted margin to the straight line amortization over time of the **note's premium** or **discount** to **par.**

$$\text{Simple margin} = \frac{100 - (FR + (R - T_{SNC} + margin - current\ coupon\ rate) \times (T_{SNC} \div basis))}{\text{Remaining term to maturity}}$$

Where *FP* is the flat price (i.e. excludes accrued interest on the note); $R - T_{SNC}$ the reference rate from the settlement date to the next coupon date; margin: the coupon margin over the reference rate; T_{SNC} the term from settlement date to the next coupon date; *basis* the number of days in the year (either 360 or 365). See also **discounted margin.**

straight loan (Banking). Another term for a **bullet** loan. That is, there is no **amortization** prior to **maturity.**

straight value. The price or value that a security would have if any special features, such as a **call provision** or a **put provision**, had been removed (cf. **benchmark; embedded option; yield-to-call; yield-to-maturity; yield-to-put**). The difference between the market price including the features and the security's straight value represents the value differential created by the embedded feature (cf. **premium; discount**).

Straits Times Industrial Index (STI) (Singapore). Principal index consisting of thirty large industrial companies used to track the performance of shares listed on the **Stock Exchange of Singapore.**

strangle. An options strategy involving buying a put option with a strike price below that of the underlying, and a call option with a strike price above that of the underlying (i.e. they are both out-of-the-money). As a consequence the cost is lower than that with a straddle and the payoff requires a greater movement in the underlying before expiry. As a result, if the market is over-estimating volatility, a strangle should be sold (cf. strap; strip). Also known as a *bottom vertical combination* when purchased and a *top vertical combination* when written.

Payoff for strangle holder at expiry

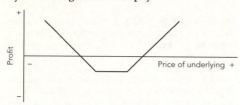

Payoff for strangle writer at expiry

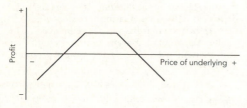

Strangle

See also **diagonal spread**; **straddle**; **spread**; **straddle calendar spread**.

strap. An options strategy which is a mixture of a long position of two calls and one put on the same underlying at the same strike price for the same expiry date. The corresponding bear position is known as a strip (cf. **straddle**; **strangle**). Sometimes called a *ratio spread* or a *triple option*.

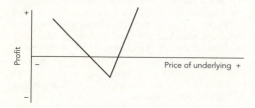

Payoff of Strap at Expiry

strategic asset allocation (SAA). The fundamental criteria for deciding on investment objec-tives. These need to take into account *inter alia* the desired return on the **portfolio**, the risk tolerance of the ultimate owners, the time horizon, and known and anticipated income and expenditure flows into and out of the portfolio. In practice such decisions need to be made in conjunction with the **liabilities** that are to be matched against the **assets** in the portfolio (cf. **asset-liability management**). See also **tactical asset allocation**.

strategic planning. Long-range planning of a firm in relation to its market, competitors, technology, management, resources, funding, and so on. The result is usually the preparation of a strategic plan or **business plan** covering the medium and long term. See **Boston matrix**; **Porter's competitive forces**.

strategic risk. Another term for **economic risk**.

streaker. A zero-coupon bond issued at a deep **discount** to produce on **maturity** a known interest rate when redeemed at **face value**. Sometimes used to describe a **stripped bond** that has been converted into a zero coupon bond. In the USA, such zero coupon bonds are also called *money multipliers*.

Street (i) (USA). New York financial institutions that are considered to be close to markets and therefore best informed, such as **brokers dealer**. Also known as **Wall Street**. (ii) Sometimes also used as a shorthand description of the market. The term 'Street' is used to indicate those who might be in the know, as in 'the Street says . . .' (cf. **smart money**).

Street name (USA). Bonds and stocks where the registered owner is a **broker** or **dealer** (cf. **marking name** (UK); **nominee**).

Street practice (USA). A term that refers to generally accepted conventions in the financial community, including the allusion to Wall Street, the financial district of New York. These include conventions for calculating prices and yields and for generally accepted behaviour (cf. **rules of fair practice**; **Street**).

strengthening of the basis. A move in the relative prices (or rates) between the **cash market** and its related **futures** in which the **spot market** price increases by more than the futures price (cf. **backwardation**; **basis**; **basis risk**; **contango**; **convergence**; **cost of carry**; **price discovery**; **weakening of the basis**).

strengths, weaknesses, opportunities, threats (SWOT). Framework often used for evaluating the business environment of a firm which seeks to compare its internal and external advantages and disadvantages. See **Boston matrix; Porter's competitive forces**.

stress. (i) Any abnormal condition in a market, such as very large price movements and/or transaction volumes (cf. **triple witching hour**). (ii) A situation where conditions are stretched beyond the normal bounds to crisis point. See **stress test**.

stress test. (i) A worst case scenario approach to assessing the potential risks in a **position** or a **portfolio**. Typically it is combined with the expected loss framework of the **value at risk** methodology to show the extreme behaviour of the position being modelled. Also sometimes referred to as the *stressed case loss*. (ii) An evaluation method used by **credit rating agencies** when assigning **credit worthiness**. Typically, it involves a scenario method of **credit assessment** used in **risk management** to determine the vulnerability of the position or obligor to adverse business and/or economic conditions. For instance, the rating agencies consider conditions similar to those at the time of the Great Depression as being the appropriate conditions for stressing the credit. See also **simulation**.

strike premium. The premium to be paid on exercise on the second **option** which is the underlying in a **compound option**.

strike, strike price, strike interest rate or **strike rate**. (i) The price or interest rate at which an **option** may be exercised (cf. **adjusted exercise price; call price; exercise price; expiry date; expiry time; put price**). That is, it is the price or rate at which the holder may buy or sell the **underlying** (cf. **in the money; intrinsic value**). Note that the actual strike may be adjustable in certain circumstances. Also commonly known as the *exercise price*. (ii) The price at which bidders in an **auction** will receive securities. The exact price may differ depending on the type of auction mechanism used (cf. **dutch auction; English auction**).

strike price interval. The price gap between different exercise prices or strike prices for exchange traded options. This is normally a function of both the price of the **underlying** and its volatility.

strike reset option or **warrant**. See **reset option**.

striking price. The price or rate at which a **dutch auction** tender price is established.

strip. (i) In the futures, forward rate agreement or options markets, a succession of **contracts** with adjacent **expiry** or **maturities** (cf. **strip yield curve**). (ii) An **option** strategy consisting of the purchase of two **puts** and one **call option**. The

opposite, two calls and one put is known as a **strap**. Also known as a *ratio spread* or a *triple option*; (iii) An investment strategy which involves buying securities just prior to the **ex-date** with a view to receiving the **dividend** or **coupon** (cf. **dividend rollover investment; dividend stripping**). (iv) A **bond** that has been separated from its coupons and where the components are traded separately. The holder receives only the **face value** of the bond or coupons at maturity (cf. **zero-coupon bond**). See **certificates of accrual on Treasury securities corpus Treasury receipts; separate trading of registered interest and principal of securities**.

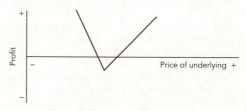

Payoff of strip at expiry

strip forward rate agreements (strip FRAs). A series of forward rate agreements (FRAs) designed to create a continuous **strip yield curve**.

strip hedge. Using a series of **futures contracts** with different **expiry dates** to match and hence hedge a cash position (cf. **piled-up rolling hedge**). For instance, an oil producer might use the crude oil futures to lock in his selling price for the next twelve months by selling futures of the four different contracts which expire over this period. Since demand for oil is seasonal, he may choose to sell more of the September and December contracts to reflect the expected higher demand going into the winter.

stripped bond. A bond which has had its **coupon** and **principal** components made into a series of zero-coupon bonds (cf. **strip**).

stripped mortgage-backed securities (MBS strip) (Bonds; USA). These are tertiary securities, similar to US Treasury issued **separate trading of registered interest and principal of securities** (STRIPS), involving repackaging the interest and principal components of **mortgage-backed securities**. The holder can select a combination of principal and/or interest payments that typically provides: *discount strips*—these have a predominance of interest payments and therefore have a higher **prepayment risk**; *premium strips*—these have a predominance of principal repayments and therefore have a lower pre-payment risk; *interest only strip (IO), principal only strip (PO)*—these are created by separating the cash flows from principal and interest into two different securities. The two securities provide a **leveraged** or **geared** exposure to the market. Because of the nature of the **underlying** mortgage-backed issue, IOs appreciate in value if interest rates rise since the cash flow rises, because there will be a less prepayment. POs tend to be speculative instruments. See also **real-estate mortgage investment conduit**.

stripped Treasury certificates. See separate **trading of registered interest and principal of securities**.

stripping. The act of unbundling the cash flows from **straight bonds**. Typically, two types of securities are created: those with an **annuity** type structure and **zero-coupon** instruments with a single cash flow at **maturity**.

strips program (USA). See **separate trading of registered interest and principal of securities**.

strip yield curve. A yield curve generated by a strip of **futures contracts**. It is the implied yield curve calculated from the different outstanding contracts. It is calculated by recognizing that the rates on the futures contracts are implicit **forward rates**, so that the **underlying** cash yield is computed by working backwards from the near end of the cash market and the next **futures contract** and so on to the next **contract**. This may differ from a yield curve calculated from the **spot rate yield curve** due to slight differences between the two markets (cf. **basis**; **basis risk**). See **arbitrage**; **price discovery**.

The formula for calculating the strip involves repeated calculations of the futures from using the following formula:

$$Y_2 = \left(\frac{Basis}{M_2}\right)\left\{\left(F_i\left[\frac{M_2 - M_1}{Basis}\right] + 1\right)\left(1 + \frac{Y_1 M_1}{Basis}\right) - 1\right\}$$

where Y_1 is the known or calculated yield on a short-dated instrument; M_1 the maturity of a short-dated instrument; M_2 the maturity of a longer-dated instrument; F_i interest rate on futures; $Basis$ the number of days in a computational year (either 360 or 365).

For example, if the expiry date on the futures contract is 75 days and the futures price implies an 8.12% rate of interest, and there is an interbank deposit rate for 60 days hence of 8%, the strip yield is 8.05%.

$$Y_1 = 8.0457\% = \left(\frac{360}{75}\right)\left\{\left(0.0812\left[\frac{75 - 60}{360}\right] + 1\right)\left(1 + \frac{0.08 \times 60}{360}\right) - 1\right\}$$

If the next futures contract with 165 days to expiry is trading at an implied interest rate of 8.22%, the second strip yield (Y_2) is:

$$Y_2 = 8.2159\% = \left(\frac{360}{165}\right)\left\{\left(0.0822\left[\frac{165 - 75}{360}\right] + 1\right)\left(1 + \frac{0.08046 \times 75}{360}\right) - 1\right\}$$

Continuing the process, if the contract with 255 days to expiry has an implied interest rate of 8.35%, then the Y_3 strip yield is 8.3742%.

strong. A description of **market tone** (cf. **weak**). See **firm**.

strong-form efficiency or **strong-form efficient markets hypothesis**. A version of the efficient markets hypothesis that states that investors cannot earn abnormal returns from examining past price data (as postulated in the *weak-form efficient market*). It goes on to include publicly available information as part of the information set available to the market (as postulated by the *semi-strong form efficient market*), but then also includes all proprietary information as being fully reflected in securities and therefore priced into market values (cf. **chartist**; econometric modelling; fundamental analysis; insider; insider dealing; technical analysis). This version of the EMH model is the least likely to be valid given the availability of 'inside' information (cf. **tip**). See also **asymmetric information**; **signalling**.

Structured Enhanced Return Trusts (steers) (USA) A grantor trust designed to act as an issuer of a series of **structured note** issues.

structured finance. Either of (i) the process of turning assets into negotiable securities (cf. **asset-backed**); (ii) packaging straight debt with derivatives (cf. **bells and whistles**; **embedded option**; **hybrid security**). The results are often known as *structured products*. See also **financial engineering**.

structured note. Non-standard securities incorporating one or more **embedded derivatives** providing the holder with exposure to interest rates, foreign currencies, a commodity, or and index. See **commodity-linked note**; **equity-linked note**; **reverse floating rate note**; **yield curve note**;

structured receivable finance. See **asset-backed**.

stub or **stub equity**. The residual equity left from a major re-**capitalization** of a firm's balance sheet (cf. **leveraged buy-out**; **management buy-out**; **vendor finance**). Sometimes used to describe the shares left in the market after the majority have been purchased in a **takeover** (cf. **rump**).

stub period. (i) The period between when a **bond** is purchased and the next **coupon** date, when this is shorter than the later coupon periods (cf. **accrued interest**). Some bonds issued to be **fungible** have stub periods (cf. **long; short coupon**). See also **interest rate calculations**. (ii) Any non-standard period in a transaction. Thus an initial interest period that was shorter than the remaining periods would be known as a stub period.

stub security. The residual security left after having been separated from a package, normally taken to mean the less desirable part of the original whole. Thus the **bond** left after detaching a **warrant** in a **bond with warrants** package would be known as the stub security. Such a bond is likely to have a below-market **coupon** rate and thus is seen as less desirable than the warrants.

Student Loan Marketing Association (SLMA; Sallie Mae) (USA). A US institution responsible for guaranteeing loans made on behalf of college students and acting as administrator and intermediary. It raises funds on the debt markets.

stupid. See **double**.

Sub Chapter S. See **S corporation**.

subject. A qualification to a **bid** or **offer** meaning it is not a firm quote. It is an abbreviation of *subject to confirmation* or *subject to prior sale*. It is stronger than an **indication** or a **level**.

- *subject bid or offer*: a set price or rate, subject to the buyer's acceptance of the counterparty's credit;
- *bid or offer subject*: the price or rate at which the buyer is willing to pay but which is not a firm quote.

subordinated debt, loan, or **security**. An issue or debt that ranks below other debt in right of payment in liquidation and interest (cf. **debenture** and **unsecured debt**). Holders are recompensed for the additional **risk** through higher interest. Also known as **junior** debt if it ranks behind other issues of the same **class**. Often referred to as *subordination*. See **pari passu; senior**.

sub-participation (Banking). The process of assigning the rights and obligations of a bank loan, or part thereof, to a third party. Sub-participation is also known as an *asset sale* and may be either silent, where the borrower is unaware of the transfer of the obligation, or **participated**, where one bank engages to provide funds but informs the borrower of its intention to sell down the transaction. The attraction to both lenders and borrowers is that it increases the **pool** of available funds. Financial institutions which originate loans can increase their lending activities, keep their sales

network, and redistribute the **credit risk** to banks which have neither the ability nor the resources to seek out borrowers. The originating bank makes fee income on the transaction. The sub-participant is able to book a loan from a credit which in the normal course of business would not be available to him. At times the process has been criticized since the selling bank is able to exit its legal obligation to the borrower by selling off its commitment.

subrogation. A legal method of acquiring ownership of **assets** available in certain jurisdictions as an alternative to **assignment** (cf. **novation**).

subscribe. To buy. Usually used in the context of new offerings; e.g. *to subscribe for a rights issue*.

subscribed. See **over-subscribed** and **undersubscribed**.

subscribed capital. See **issued capital**.

subscription agreement.(i) Eurobond market term for the **purchase group agreement** (that is the contract between the **managers** and the issuer). It is also called the *agreement among underwriters* or *underwriting agreement* in some cases. (ii) Used in **venture capital** to describe the terms and conditions upon which the **equity** and often debt-based investment is to be made in a business.

subscription period. The time period which the issuer and his **manager** have given the investor the **option** to subscribe.

subscription price. The price at which the buyer has the right to suscribe (cf. **after-market**). Normally a **primary market** price which may or may not include additional **sweeteners** (e.g. additional **subscription rights**) (cf. **equity kicker**).

subscription ratio. The number of new shares that may be obtained for existing ones. The ratio is normally expressed in terms of the number of old shares required to obtain one new share. A ratio of 1 : 1 would indicate one new share for each existing; a ratio of 4 : 1 would be one new share for each four already held.

subscription rights. (i) The right, but not the obligation, to subscribe (cf. **option**). These are rights usually pertaining to existing **shareholders** in a corporation giving them first refusal for any new **equity** issued. (ii) Also used for a **right** or a **pre-emptive right** allowing shareholders preferential treatment in purchasing new **common stock** issued by a company. See **subscription warrants**.

subscriptions. In a new issue, that part of the total that is bought by the **managers**, **underwriters**, or **selling group** members (cf. **protection**). See pot.

subscription warrants. (i) A warrant issued by a company to buy **stock** in the company. Such warrants, if exercised, will increase the amount of stock outstanding (in other words, they are dilutive) (cf. **dilution**). (ii) {USA} The tradable instrument given to **stockholders** in a **rights issue**. To avoid confusion with definition (i), these are normally known as *rights*.

subsidiary. A company which is controlled by another. Technically a company owned 51% by another; in practice effective control dictates what might be a subsidiary (cf. **controlling interest**; **equity accounting**).

subsidiary merger. A merger in which the surviving entity is a subsidiary of the acquiring firm.

subsidiary undertaking (Accounting; UK). The requirement for companies to consolidate their subsidiaries when reporting their results (cf. **equity accounting**).

subsidized interest rate. A feature of many export financing or special assistance schemes where the rate of finance is set below prevailing market rates, the lender effectively subsidizing the borrowing.

substandard loan (Banking). See **charge-off**.

substitution swap. The exchange of one security for another with, generally, identical features (cf. **fungibility**; **novation**). See **swap**; **switch**.

sub-underwriter. A member of a new issue **syndicate** who agrees to buy a certain proportion of the issue from the **managers** should the issue be **under-subscribed**. He receives an **underwriting fee** and a **selling concession** on the principal amount of the securities for which he may subscribe. Confusingly, in the **euromarkets**, sub-underwriters are called 'managers' while **underwriters** are called **lead managers**. See **bracket**.

sufficient and relevant. A principle of reporting accounting information that requires the disclosure of financial information to be sufficient in scope and relevant to assessing the financial condition of the reporting entity.

suitability rule (USA). A requirement by the **Securities and Exchange Commission** that vendors of **options** consider the appropriateness of the purchaser's position to engage in this type of investment. Criteria such as wealth, previous experience and so forth have to be met before such individuals may be solicited.

Summary of Activity (USA). A market report provided monthly to firms quoted on the **National Association of Securities Dealers Automated Quotations** system giving details of prices and trading volume, the stock's **market-makers**, and other relevant market information.

sum of the year's digits or **sum of digits (SOYD).** A method of calculating **depreciation**. See **depreciation methods**.

sunk cost. Irrecoverable costs involved with an investment that are therefore irrelevant to subsequent decisions. Although sunk costs should be ignored, many decisions are made which include these in the justification.

sunrise industries. New emerging industries, such as virtual-reality or bio-technology.

sunshine laws (USA). The legal requirement that regulators hold meetings in public and disclose the methods used to arrive at decisions.

sunshine trading. The giving of advance notice by **futures dealers**, to their exchange, of the futures and **option contracts** they intend to trade once the market opens. Viewed as an attempt by a trader to extend the trading period of the exchange (cf. **GLOBEX**). See **kerb market**.

Super Designated Order Turnaround (DOT) (Equities; USA). See **Designated Order Turnaround**.

superfloater interest rate swap. An interest rate swap where the **floating rate** payments are linked to a **bear spread** position, such that the floating rate payer doubly benefits from any fall in interest rates, hence the superfloater label (cf. **reverse risk reversal**).

super liquid yield option note (super LYON). See **zero-coupon convertible**.

supermajority. A provision in a corporate **charter** or **articles of incorporation** requiring a large majority (two-thirds to 90%) for approval to certain changes. Sometimes seen as a **takeover** defence.

super-NOW accounts (Banking; USA). A variant on the **negotiable order of withdrawal account** designed to attract funds from the corporate sector by paying a rate comparable to that in the wholesale money market for large deposits.

super premium notes (USA). An intermediate-term, typically one-to three-year **maturity**, note issue with an above-market **coupon** issued at a significant **premium** to **par value** or **face value**.

Such notes are attractive to **funds** which want a high income and do not have to **amortize** the premium over the life of the issue.

superpriority. See debtor in possession facility.

supershare options. A type of **option** popularized by Drexel Burnham Lambert where the option has a binary payout (cf. **all-or-nothing option; binary option; digital option**). The option will pay a predetermined amount if the **underlying** expires at exactly the **strike price** or, if not, nothing. Combinations of supershare options with different strike prices allow holders to create exactly the payoffs they desire. See also **superstock**.

supershares (Equity; USA). A series of instruments designed to provide targeted payoffs on a **stock index**. The original idea was conceived by Leland O'Brien, Rubinstein Associates Supershares Service Corporation and uses the insights provided by **option** theory to divide the expected returns according to individual preferences. Since it is possible to create a **vertical spread** which involves purchasing an option with a given **strike price** and selling another with a higher strike, it is in theory possible to create packages of options which provide a wide range of different payoffs depending on investors' preferences. The **trust** held a portfolio consisting of a holding in a **stock index** and **treasury bills** against which four tertiary securities were issued: (a) *Priority SuperShares*, which received the **dividends** from the **underlying** securities, plus a limited amount of any capital appreciation; (b) *Appreciation SuperShares*, which provided a **capital gain** above the **cap** on the priority units; (c) *Protection SuperShares*, which provided an increase in value for any decline in the portfolio, which behave like **portfolio insurance**; and (d) *Money Market Income SuperShares*, paid out income from the Treasury Bill element of the portfolio after the Protection units had been paid. A similar, but simpler, structure was used in the **Americus** trust division of a portfolio's returns into **prescribed right** to income and maximum equity and special claim on residual equity elements.

super sinker bond. A bond with a long final maturity but where **principal** redemptions commence very early on and/or be very substantial, leading to a short **average life**. Some asset-backed securities embody this feature (e.g. credit card receivable financings).

superstock (Equities; USA). A variety of **common stock** with an attached **put option** marketed by Drexel Burnham Lambert. See **puttable stock**.

superunits (Equities; USA). Name given to the shares issued by the Supertrust Trust for Capital Market Fund, Inc. Shares, a **mutual fund** (cf. **units**). There are two kinds, shares where the returns are linked to the **Standard and Poor's 500 Index** and a US treasuries series, where the returns are linked to short-term US treasuries.

supervisory analyst (USA). An **analyst** who has been examined by the **New York Stock Exchange** (NYSE) and is seen as qualified to endorse publicly distributed research material (cf. **newsletter**).

supervisory board (Germany; Netherlands; Scandinavia). Normally elected by a combination of **shareholders** and trades unions they have the responsibility for the appointing and dismissing of the company's executive board. The supervisory board will also exercise a duty of general monitoring of company's behaviour. See also **corporate governance**.

supplementary capital. The capital defined as tier 2 in the Basle Capital Convergence Accord.

supplier credit. A method of international trade finance involving a loan **facility** made to the exporter. The credit is normally guaranteed by an export credit guarantee scheme or insurance.

supply and demand. The balance of sell (supply) and purchase (demand) orders over a given period which creates **market forces** (cf. **liquidity**).

supply squeeze (Commodities). A supply shortage that has the effect of driving up prices (cf. **short squeeze; ramp**). Also called a *short squeeze*.

support level or **point**. (i) Used in **technical analysis** to describe when a price series has repeatedly fallen to a certain price level, but has then recovered. The fact that the price has not breached this level is seen as providing support (i.e. buyers will enter the market to support the price). The opposite condition when the price series is unable to rise above a given point is known as the *resistance level*. (ii) Also used in managed or administered exchange rate regimes for the currency rate at which official intervention takes place (cf. **divergence indicator**). See European Monetary System.

support tranche (Bonds). See **collateralized mortgage obligation equity**.

supranational institution. A multi-governmental organization such as the **World Bank** or the **European Bank for Reconstruction and Development**.

surety. Another term for a **guarantee** (cf. **performance bond; standby letter of credit**).

surety bond. See credit enhancement; performance bond; tender bond.

surf-and-turf. Market term for a **strangle** where both the **strike prices** are **out of the money**. The strangle involves purchasing a **call** and a **put option** with a view to benefiting from significant price movements before **expiry**. When the strikes on the strangle are **in the money**, this is called a *mambo combo*.

surge option. Option where the **exercise price** is reset daily in relation to a moving average of the price or rate of the **underlying**. The **call** (put) would be **in the money**, if the price of the underlying was above (below) the moving average price by a pre-agreed **margin**. Due to the changing nature of the payoff, the structure is designed to provide a **hedge** against rapid price changes rather than absolute price or rate protection. Such options are popular in **commodities markets** since they provide protection against **spikes** in prices and cost less than standard options.

surplus. (i) Excess of income to expenditures. (ii) Another term for gain or profit. (iii) The net amount after financing costs.

surplus advance corporation tax (surplus ACT). See unrelieved advance corporation tax.

survivor bias. The problem of analysing historical **data** where the failures are eliminated from the data set. It can be very misleading if – usually poorly performing – **assets** or firms are removed from the data as it gives an erroneous impression of the average result. For instance, many aspects of **fund** performance can be massaged through survivor bias if medians are used.

sushi bond (Japan). An issue made in any capital market by a Japanese obligor which is not denominated in yen. Such issues are typically sold to Japanese investors since they are not considered to be foreign assets.

suspension, suspended share, or **trading**. An exchange's decision to stop trading in a security or a market. The reason is to promote an orderly market or to prevent a false market developing. Events such as **takeovers** or **mergers** or other major specific events may lead to temporary imbalances of orders and an inability of the exchange to maintain a proper market (cf. **event risk**). At the market level, a suspension of trading is a form of **circuit breaker** designed to allow investors a cooling-off period during periods of heightened uncertainty (cf. **cascade theory**). Many exchanges introduced these following the events of the October 1987 stock market crash (cf. **limit**).

Svensk Exportkredit (SEK) (Sweden). Official export agency set up in 1962 and jointly owned by the state and Swedish banks. It is a major borrower on the international capital markets.

swap. (i) In the securities markets, the sale of one security to purchase another (cf. **bond swap**). Also known as a *switch*. (ii) In **foreign exchange**, the purchase or sale of a currency combined with a simultaneous trade in the opposite direction for a later **maturity** date (cf. **covered interest arbitrage**; **foreign exchange swap; forward; forward-forward; spot**). The initial exchange may be a **spot** transaction or itself a forward, the re-exchange having a later maturity than the initial exchange. The effect is to borrow and tend in the two currencies. (iii) (Derivatives). The exchange of one type of cash flow for another. See **commodity swap; cross-currency swap** (a.k.a. currency swap); **interest rate swap**; (iv) (Commodities). The spot purchase or sale of a commodity combined with the simultaneous opposite **forward** or **futures contract** for the same amount (cf. **borrowing; lending**). (v) An agreement between **central banks** allowing them to borrow currency from each other in order to intervene in the **foreign exchange** market. The context normally makes clear which use is involved.

swap arranger. Intermediary who brings two parties together to allow them to undertake a **cross-currency swap** or **interest rate swap**. Unlike a **market-maker**, the arranger is unlikely to act as intermediating **counterparty** to both sides.

swap assignment. A way of unwinding an **interest rate swap** or a **cross-currency swap** where a cash payment is made for current market values but the original swap remains intact for one **counterparty**, with a new counterparty stepping in to the assignor's position (cf. **credit risk**). Now largely superseded in market practice by **swap termination** or **cancellation**.

swap bid rate. The rate at which the **swap market-maker** will receive the fixed rate and pay the **floating rate** (cf. **fixed rate receiver; floating rate payer**).

swap buyer. See fixed rate payer (cf. floating rate payer).

swap curve. The term structure of interest rates obtained by plotting the **fixed rate** side of **interest rate swap** rates against **maturity** (cf. **yield curve**). See **par swap yield curve; zero-coupon swap**.

swap de taux d'intérêt (French). Interest rate swap.

swap differential agreement (SDA). Basis swap designed to fix the differential between a swap rate and the yield on a security of the same maturity.

swap driven. New issues of debt that come to the market because there are attractive, or cost-reducing, opportunities for the issuer to use the interest rate swap and cross-currency swaps markets to alter the risk profile of the issued liability to a more desirable form. The idea that issuers come to the market when the swaps market is attractive is seen by the bond markets as one of the less desirable consequences of swaps, since the issuer will be looking at the attractions of the package and not necessarily at the conditions in the primary market. The choice of markets and maturities of issuance is driven by the two parts of the transaction (debt issue and swap availability) and the package's relative cost to the issuer. As a result, for major world class borrowers, the principal bond markets are interlinked as long as there exists attendant swaps markets.

swap line. Agreements between central banks allowing them to borrow each other's currency if required. Swap lines are typically used when one country needs to defend the value of its currency when it comes under selling pressure. They are known as swaps since the borrower agrees to repay the borrowing, usually within three to six months. Because the facility can be called upon at any time, central banks may find that providing assistance to a troubled currency affects domestic monetary conditions (cf. sterilization).

swap market-maker. An institution that is willing to act as a counterparty or as principal to an interest rate swap or cross-currency swap transaction. Such market-makers will be active in a wide variety of swaps and will quote two-way prices and be willing to enter into swaps without a commitment to unwind their positions on the opposite side. They will warehouse or hedge their exposures in a variety of financial instruments before finding a suitable swap to partly or fully match the existing positions they have entered into.

swap offer rate. The rate at which the swap market-maker will pay the fixed rate and receive the floating rate (cf. fixed rate payer; floating rate receiver).

swap offset agreement. Netting agreement designed to reduce the counterparty exposure and hence the credit risk of both parties.

swap option. See swaption.

swapping a swap. A way of adjusting a cross-currency swap or interest rate swap position that preserves the user's original objective of entering into the transaction. For example, the holder of a long position of a swap which is out of the money (current market value less than par value) can exchange the existing one with a dealer for a new swap with a longer maturity and spread the loss over a longer period. This is known as *stretching* or *underwater swapping*.

swap points. The foreign exchange forward differentials used to create a foreign exchange swap, hence the term, but also used for a forward outright transaction and therefore also commonly known as *forward points*.

swap rate (i) (Forex). The difference between the spot market rate and the forward rate at which a currency is traded, normally expressed in terms of swap points (cf. forward differential). (ii) (Derivatives). The fixed rate paid on an interest rate swap (cf. coupon swap).

swap rate lock. A future start interest rate swap or cross-currency swap where the fixed rate is predetermined (cf. swap spread-lock).

swap reversal. A way of unwinding a cross-currency swap or interest rate swap where the original swapholder executes a new swap with opposite effect to the original; i.e. if the original swap was to pay fixed, then the new swap will be to receive fixed, thus cancelling out the effect of the original swap. Used as a means of locking-in a profit or closing a position (cf. swap termination).

swap sale. The sale and transfer of the rights and obligations of a swap agreement to a third party for a consideration. The buyer then assumes the credit risk of the remaining counterparty. Both the remaining and the new party must be satisfied as to their respective credit worthiness. As a means of removing obligations, this has given way to swap termination.

Swaps Depository Trust (USA) Clearing system offered by the Chicago Mercantile Exchange for over-the counter transactions in swaps (cf. clearing house)

swap seller. See floating rate payer (cf. floating receiver).

swap spread. (i) The difference between the quoted swap rate and some underlying benchmark, such as a government bond (cf. yield curve). The difference represents the credit risk or default risk of the commercial participants in the swaps market. (ii) The difference between the quoted swap rate by swap market-makers and the rate obtainable by a particular counterparty. For instance, if the counterparty has a better (worse) credit **standing** than the market-makers, this would involve a reduction (increase) in the **fixed rate** to be paid or an increase (decrease) in the fixed rate to be received by this party (cf. **schlock swap**).

swap spread-lock. A future start **interest rate swap** that has a guaranteed maximum (minimum) **spread** over a **benchmark** bond for the **fixed rate payer** (fixed rate receiver). This means the absolute rate on the swap is not fixed, but is measured against actual interest rates, although the **swap spread** is predetermined. The party offering the transaction could lose if the swap spreads were to widen before the spreadlock was exercised.

swap tender panel. A feature in a **credit facility** (or other financing facility) allowing the borrower to seek competitive **tenders** for **interest rate** (**swap**) or **cross-currency swaps** linked to **drawdowns** or security issues (cf. **medium-term notes**).

swap termination or **close-out**. A way of extinguishing all the obligations under a **cross-currency swap** or **interest rate swap** completed upon a cash settlement between the two counterparties. This termination value is equal to a compensating amount at which the counterparties would be willing to give up the transaction and enter into a new swap at current market value without being any worse off (cf. **marked-to-market**).

swaption, swap-option, or **option on a swap**. Because an **interest rate swap** or a **cross-currency swap** is an exchange, there are two possible swaption **positions**: a *payer* (or put) *swaption* gives the buyer the right to be a **fixed rate payer**; while the *receiver* (or call) *swaption* gives the buyer the right to receive fixed (or be the **floating rate payer**). Most swaptions offer **European-style exercises**, although **American-style** are available. Swaptions are also available on the more exotic swap structures (cf. **quantity adjusting option**).

	Buyer	Writer
Payer swaption (put swaption)	hedges against rise in interest rates	anticipates fall in interest rates
Exercise results in:	pays fixed rate	pays floating rate
Receiver swaption (call swaption)	anticipates fall in interest rates	anticipates rise in interest rates
Exercise results in:	pays floating rate	pays fixed rate

Note that in practice most swaptions are **cash settled**.

Swaptions are complicated for two reasons. First, there is the payoff which, unlike many other kinds of **underlying**, is convex in nature due to the compounding effect on the present value of the underlying swap. This is true of **bond options** as well, which they resemble. Second, the value of the underlying is based on the shape of the **yield curve** and consequently may be influenced by all those factors which affect the **term structure of interest rates**.

Swaptions are used for **hedging** purposes in a number of different ways. If a **fixed rate bond** issuer is unsure about the future course of interest rates, he might buy a receiver swaption so as to benefit from any subsequent fall by either selling back the swaption at a profit or exercising it to pay a **floating rate**. Contingent liability costs can also be fixed by the use of swaptions as when a company is tendering on a project and wants to fix the cost of any future borrowings. It is also used to **arbitrage** between two different markets. A **bond** issue can be made with either a **call** or **put provision** and the issuer can then attempt to capitalize on these by either reselling the **embedded option** or hedging it in the swaptions market. Differences in the two markets' perception of the value of what are effectively the same option may allow the issuer to reduce the cost of borrowing. There may also be tax benefits to this type of transaction, plus the ability to trade in or out of the swaption at a later date.

swap warehouse. See **warehousing; swaps**.

swap warrant. Warrant allowing the holder to enter into a **swap** (cf. **cross-currency swap; interest rate swap**).

swap yield curve. The **term structure of interest rates** at which market participants in the **interest rate swaps** market enter into transactions. Such a curve has a **bid** and an **offered** side, like the **interbank market** (cf. **yield curve**).

Swaziland Stockbrokers Ltd (Swaziland). MBABANE. (tel. 268 46163; fax 268 44132).

Swedish Stock Exchange (Sweden). Box 1256, S-111 82 Stockholm (tel. 468 143160).

sweep arrangement (Banking). A service provided to bank customers that automatically transfers surplus funds on a **current account** into an interest bearing account, so as to maximize the amount of interest earned by the depositor.

sweetener. (i) A high-yield security included in a portfolio in order to increase the overall return. Usually used in a new issue or exchange offer. Sometimes called a *mixer*. (ii) A feature or addition to a security, such as an **equity kicker**, in order to increase its attraction to investors. The terms sweetener and *kicker* are generally interchangeable.

SWIFT currency codes See Society for World - wide Interbank Financial Telecommunications.

swingline (Banking). Term used to describe a standby facility, usually committed, that can be activated at very short notice and provide funds to make up an unanticipated shortfall due to the inability by the borrower to raise money by the usual means. Often used in the US domestic commercial paper (CP) and eurocommercial paper (ECP) markets to provide a means of honouring maturing issues in the event of market disruption.

Swiss Market Index (SMI) (Equities; Switzerland). An index made up of the largest turnover stocks in the Swiss equity market.

Swiss Market Index Liierte Emission (SMILE) (Bonds; Switzerland). A bond issue where the coupon payments are linked to the performance of the Swiss Market Index. See equity-linked note.

Swiss Options and Financial Futures Exchange (Soffex) (Switzerland). Neumattstrasse 7, CH–8953 Dietikon. (tel. 41 (0) 1 740 3020; fax 41 (0) 1 740 1776). Established in 1988. Trades futures and options on Swiss financial instruments. See low exercise price option.

Swiss Performance Index (SPI) (Equities Switzerland). A capitalization-weighted, broad market index of Swiss stocks or shares, including some traded over the counter.

Swiss Stock Exchange (Switzerland). The Association of Swiss Stock Exchanges, Seinaustrasse 32, CH–8021 Zurich (tel. 41 1 229 21 11; fax 41 1 229 22 33).

Swissy or **Swissies**. Market jargon for Swiss francs (cf. eurocurrency).

switch or **switching**. (i) A method for restructuring a portfolio by replacing one specific security, or a group of securities, with another. This is usually prompted by a change in the objectives of the portfolio or a change in market conditions (cf. churning). See anomaly; policy switch; tax switch; yield; yield cap. (ii) (Forex; UK) Foreign exchange swap. Also often called a *deposit swap*. (iii) (Futures) The simultaneous sale and purchase of contracts with different expiration dates. Thus a switch might involve selling the near-dated contract and buying a later expiry one. This is required in order to rollover positions as the future nears expiry (cf. convergence). See also intra-com-

modity spread; rollover. (iv) Used in the sense of a swap (cf. bond swap). (v) In commodities, to move ownership from one location to another (cf. warehouse warrant).

switchback option or **warrant**. A complex combination of a capped call (floored put) and an up-and-in put (down-and-in call) barrier option. In most cases, the instrike of the barrier option is set equal to the capped or floored strike price. If during the life of the option, the value of the underlying touches the capped or floored level, the options are automatically exercised, which at the same time activates the barrier option leaving a standard put or call for the remainder of the life of the option or warrant. The investment strategy surrounding these instruments is that the buyer sets the strike near a high (low) for the underlying, thus the option then gains in value as the price reverses from this point (hence the switchback label).

switches department. A unit within a bank for managing the nostro accounts with correspondent banks.

switching discount (UK). A reduction in the fees payable for holders of units in a unit trust who switch holdings between different trusts under the same management.

switch option. See as-you-like option (cf. chooser option).

switch reversal. See reversal (cf. switch).

sycurve option. An outperformance option or spread option on the shape of the yield curve. A call will increase in value if the difference between the two reference rates on the curve widens, while a put will increase in value if the spread narrows.

Sydney Computerized Overnight Market (SYCOM) (Futures; Australia). Screen-based trading system operated by the Sydney Futures Exchange (SFE). It allows out-of-hours electronic late trading of SFE contracts into the European time zone.

Sydney Futures Exchange Limited (SFE) (Australia). 30–2 Grosvenor Street, Sydney 2000 Australia (tel. (02) 256 0555; fax (02) 256 0666; tlx AA126713). Established in 1960, it is a commodities and financial futures and options exchange and offers an after-hours screen-dealing service, the Sydney Computerized Overnight Market (SYCOM). Settlement is carried out by the Sydney Futures Exchange Clearing House (SFECH). *Inter alia*, the contracts traded include: 90-day Bank Accepted bills; 3-year Treasury Bonds; 10-year Treasury Bonds; All Ordinaries Share Price Index (AOI; SPI); Fifty Leaders Share Price Index

(FLI), wool and live cattle. See **commodities futures; interest rate futures; stock index futures.**

symmetric distribution. A description of a frequency distribution where the probability of a value is equally likely below and above the **mean**. That is, the distribution is not skewed in any way. An example of such a symmetric distribution would be the **normal distribution.** See **skewness.**

symmetric payoff or **risk profile.** A feature of certain types of **derivatives**, such as **forwards, futures,** and **swaps** that they offer equal opportunity for gains and losses. Also called a *linear payoff.* See **asymmetric payoff.**

syndicate. (i) (UK) A grouping of Names in the Lloyd's of London market to **underwrite** insurance business (cf. **pool**). (ii) (Securities) Normally comprises three groups of securities **dealers** with different responsibility for the underwriting and distribution of new issues: the **managers; underwriters;** and the **selling group.** Note these three groups may be called by different names in different markets. Also known as a *purchase group.* (iii) (Banking) Used in a similar sense to (ii) in the **syndicated loans** market for banks accepting a part share of a loan commitment. (iv) To distribute or allot securities. (v) A group working in concert for a particular, usually short-term, purpose (cf. **investment club**). Hence, a bidding syndicate formed to purchase an asset or business, or tender for a contract.

syndicate agreement. See underwriting agreement.

syndicated loan or **credit** (Banking). A loan which is distributed amongst banks and other lenders as a method of sharing **risk.** Normally arranged by one or more **lead managers** who will retain a part of the loan itself and offer the rest to a large number of banks who will be asked to participate for different commitments which will be reflected in their status, and the fees they receive (cf. **bracket; co-manager; manager; participant**). The borrower will be aware of the participating lenders (cf. **tombstone**). Such loans will normally be **floating rate,** at a predetermined **margin** over **short-term** interest rates (cf. **club deal; revolving credit facility; term loan**). The costs of the loan may involve (i) the margin to the **reference rate;** (ii) a **commitment fee,** if part of the loan remains undrawn; (iii) a **management fee;** and (iv) an **agency fee.** Such loans are also sometimes known as *consortium loans.* See also **sub-participation.**

syndicated loan synthetic securities. Synthetic securities created by combining **interest rate swaps** or **cross-currency swaps** to part of a syndicated loan. Such securities enable lenders to resell parts of such loans to investors who seek a particular cash flow generated through the swap.

syndicated swap. A large **interest rate swap** or **cross-currency swap** where a number of **counterparties** form a **syndicate** to provide the other party with the transaction.

syndicate manager. See lead manager.

syndicate release. See breaking the syndicate.

syndicate restrictions. The restrictions found in an **underwriting agreement** or placed on a **syndicate** in relation to the offer (cf. **fixed price reoffering**).

synergy. When two and two makes five. Often used to justify **mergers and acquisitions** and sometimes called *business fit.* Convention suggests three different types of synergy: (*a*) universal synergies which are available to any logical acquirer; (*b*) endemic synergies which are only available to particular companies that may have specific weaknesses or opportunities to exploit new areas; and (*c*) unique synergies which can only be utilized by a specific acquirer; equally such synergies may only be available to the firm about to be taken over.

synthetic. Any of a range of combinations of cash and **derivative** instruments designed to mimic the performance of another type of financial instrument. Also sometimes called *duplication* or *replication.* See, for instance, **synthetic call; synthetic option–futures combinations; synthetic put.**

synthetic agreement for forward exchange (SAFE). The generic term for **exchange rate agreements** (ERA) and **forward exchange agreements** (FXA). Originally a type of **foreign exchange forward** developed by Barclays Bank and Midland Montagu in response to the requirements imposed by **capital adequacy** guidelines. SAFEs are **notional principal** contracts and are treated as interest rate products from a **Bank for International Settlements** standpoint and therefore require a lower level of committed capital. The **British Bankers' Association** formula for calculating the settlement amount is as follows:

$$\left(A_2 \left[\frac{(OEX_{c1/c2} - BBASSR_{c1/c2}) - (FS - BBASFS_{c1/c2})}{1 + \left(\frac{BBAIR_{c2} \times T_{sm}}{Basis \times 100} \right)} \right] \right)$$
$$- (A_1 \times [OEX_{c1/c2} - BBASSR_{c1/c2}])$$

where C_1 is the first currency; C_2 the second currency; A_1 the first amount in the SAFE contract; A_2 second amount in the SAFE contract (for

ERAs, $A_1 = A_2$); $BBASFS_{c1/c2}$ the British Bankers' Association settlement rate for the forward spread; $BBASSR_{c1/c2}$ the British Bankers' Association spot settlement rate (for ERAs this is zero); $BBAIR_{c2}$ British Bankers' Assocation interest rate for the second currency for the period T_{sm}; FS the forward spread contracted in the SAFE; $OEX_{c1/c2}$ the outright exchange rate (this is nil for ERAs); T_{sm} the time from settlement to maturity (for the ERA this is the swap period); *Basis* the number of notional days in the year, either 365, for sterling, or 360 for most other currencies.

An example of the settlement price on such an agreement would be a Deutschemark/US dollar FXA for US\$10 million:

C_1: US dollars (first currency); C_2: Deutschemarks (second currency); A_1: US\$10,000,000 (first amount in the SAFE contract); A_2: US\$12,000,000 (second amount in the SAFE contract); $BBASFS_{c1/c2}$ 50; $BBASSR_{c1/c2}$ 1.4650; $BBAIR_{c2}$ 8.5%; FS: 75; $OEX_{c1/c2}$ 1.5240; T_{sm} 90 days; *Basis*: 360 for Deutschemarks.

$$DM\$73,892.29 =$$

$$\left(US\$10,000,000 \left[\frac{(1.5240 - 1.4650) - (0.0075 - 0.0050)}{1 + \left(\frac{8.5\% \times 90}{360 \times 100} \right)} \right] \right)$$

$$-(10,000,000 \times [1,5240 - 1.4650])$$

synthetic bond. A synthetic security which gives the holder the equivalent **position** to holding a **fixed rate bond**. It can be created, for instance, by combining a **floating rate note**, or loan, with an **interest rate swap** where the investor receives the **fixed rate**, or by investing in **money market** instruments and taking a position in **bond futures**.

synthetic call. A dynamic **hedging** strategy that replicates the payoff of a **call** option. For instance, holding the **underlying** and buying a **put** option has the same payoff as a call (cf. **put–call parity**). Sometimes called a *synthetic purchased call*. The opposite transaction is to **write** the position, which is known as a *synthetic written call*.

synthetic convertible. Debt and warrant package or **equity-linked note** designed to behave like a **convertible**. This can be achieved, for instance, by allowing the warrant holder to tender the debt as payment when the warrant is **exercised**. Some issues of synthetic convertible allow the holder to unbundle the components to allow separate trading.

synthetic equity. A debt plus **derivative** package that replicates the price performance of holding **common stocks** or a **stock index**.

synthetic fixed rate bond (synthetic bond). A long position in a **floating rate note** combined with a **receive fixed** rate position in an **interest rate swap**.

synthetic floating rate note (synthetic FRN). A **synthetic security** which gives the holder the equivalent **position** to holding a **floating rate note**, made up by holding a **long** position in a **straight bond** combined with a **floating rate receiver** position in an **interest rate swap**.

synthetic foreign currency bond. A long position in a **fixed rate** or **floating rate** security in one **currency** combined with a **cross-currency swap** to receive a fixed rate in another currency.

synthetic forward contract. A long (short) position in a **call** with a **short** (long) position in a **put** with the same **strike price** and **expiry date**, where both options are European-style. The payoff is equivalent to a long (short) position in the **underlying** with a **forward** transaction date. If the underlying is above the strike price, the call is **exercised** and the put expires worthless; if below, the put is exercised against the holder and the call is worthless. Synthetic forwards are used to create forward style contracts where none exist or to **arbitrage** price differences (cf. **put–call–futures parity**).

synthetic futures. A **synthetic security** that replicates the performance of a **future**. Synthetic futures can be constructed using **options on futures**, to create a **long** (short) **position** by simultaneously buying (selling) a **call** option and selling (buying) a **put**.

synthetic	action
long synthetic future	sell put, buy corresponding call with the same exercise price and expiry date
short synthetic future	sell call, buy corresponding put with the same exercise price and expiry date

synthetic gold loan. A form of collateralized borrowing against gold that does not directly involve the monetizing of the **physical commodity**.

synthetic guaranteed investment contract (synthetic GIC). A type of **guaranteed investment contract** where the holder has a lien on the assets together with an additional guarantee by the issuing institution.

synthetic high-income equity-linked debt (SHIELD) (UK). Proprietary name for an **equity-linked note** issue by S. G. Warburgs.

synthetic long position. A purchased **call** option and short position in a **put** at the same **strike**

price and for the same **expiry date**, plus a cash investment equal to the **present value** of the strike price. See **synthetic forward**; **synthetic futures**.

synthetic option. Any of a number of replication strategies designed to emulate the behaviour and payoff of an **option** position (cf. **duplication**; **dynamic hedging**; **replication**). This is most commonly done with **futures** (cf. **portfolio insurance**).

synthetic options–futures combinations. These are replicating strategies designed to provide the same payoffs as holding an **option** on a position. The following are the basic methods:

Synthetic	Combination required to replicate payoff
long future	call − put
call	put + futures
put	call − futures
short futures	put − call
short (written) call	− put − futures
short (written) put	− call + futures

synthetic position. An **option** or futures position that has the same **risk–return** characteristics of other **positions**. For example, the buying of a **call** and selling a **put** with the same **expiry date** and **strike price** is the same as a **forward** purchase of the **underlying**.

Synthetic	Combination required to create position
long call	long underlying position plus long put
long put	short underling position plus long call
long underlying	long call position plus short put position
short underlying	short call position plus long put position
short call	short underlying position plus a short put position
short put	long underlying position plus a short call position

synthetic put. A combination of assets that replicates the payoff of a **put option**. See **synthetic call**.

synthetic security. A security formed by repackaging an existing **asset** in the secondary market. For instance by combining an **interest rate swap** with a **fixed rate bond** an investor can produce a synthetic **floating rate** payments flow. The resulting security is artificial because its terms might not have otherwise been available in the market. The term is used interchangeably for a **repackaged security** where a new issue is made of the synthetic security using the **underlying** security as **collateral**. There is an important technical difference between a repackaged security and a synthetic in that the latter may have some elements, such as a **swap**, that are bilateral in nature and cannot readily be traded.

synthetic short position. A purchased **put** option and **short** position in a **call** at the same **strike** price and for the same **expiry date**, plus a cash investment equal to the **present value** of the strike price. See **synthetic forward contract**; **synthetic futures**.

synthetic short call. A combination of **assets** that replicates the payoff of a **call option writer** (or seller). Also known as a *synthetic written call*. This can be created by, for instance, selling a **futures contract** and writing the corresponding **put** option on the future.

synthetic stock. Either synthetic long or synthetic put positions where the **underlying** is a common stock (cf. **stock equivalent**).

synthetic variable rate note (synthetic VRN). See synthetic floating rate note.

synthetic zero-coupon convertible. A synthetic **convertible** where the debt is a **zero-coupon bond**. Also known as a *super liquid yield option note*. See **liquid yield option notes**.

systematic risk. (i) A modern portfolio theory term for that part of an asset's **risk** that is due to the market factor. Sometimes called *market risk* (cf. **residual** or **unsystematic risk**). The asset's systematic risk is measured by the asset's **beta**. (ii) General term derived from (i) used to denote that proportion of the **asset**, instrument, or security's overall **risk** due to market movements (cf. **market risk**). See **specific risk**; **stock specific risk**.

systemic risk. The **risk** of failures within the financial system either through problems with payments or **settlement** or a major **default** by a financial institution (cf. **too big to fail**). The dangers of systemic risk seem a major preoccupation of regulators. A type of risk faced by domestic monetary and financial systems, and when combined together to form the international monetary system. This type of risk is associated with the mechanisms of finance, as compared with risks associated with particular transactions or products. The risk comprises those factors capable of causing a loss of confidence in an entire country's monetary and financial fabric, which is made of many different kinds of institutions and markets. Ultimately, leading to the default of all **liabilities** held within the system, an outcome which has the potential for causing the complete breakdown in the world's mechanisms for debt settlement and storing value using financial instruments. For example, the stock market crashes of 1929 and 1987 had such a potential (cf. **cascade theory**). The fact that the knock-on effects were contained was probably as a result of safeguards already in place, especially within international banks, but also because of specific assurances provided by key central banks; such as the honouring of all counterparty obligations. Also known as *aggregation risk* or *interconnection risk*.

system meigara (Japan). Those securities traded by the **Tokyo Stock Exchange's Computer-assisted Routing and Execution System**.

system repurchase agreements (system repo) (USA). **Open-market operations** where the **Federal Reserve** (the Fed) buys securities from **dealers** for its own account, thereby crediting their accounts and adding to the **money supply** and hence lowering interest rates. The Fed also undertakes customer repurchase agreements when acting as agent for funds held by foreign institutions.

T

table top. See ladder spread.

T-account (Accounting). A device used in double-entry bookkeeping to record transactions. The two sides of the account record credits and debits, the balance at any time being determined by adding the two columns and finding the difference, if any (cf. balance sheet).

tachiaijō meigara (Japan). Floor transactions on the Tokyo Stock Exchange. The exchange allows either direct broker execution of the order with the specialist or for transactions to be made via the Computer-assisted Order Routing and Execution System.

tactical asset allocation (TAA). A method of allocating assets within a portfolio to take advantage of short-run expected changes in markets, sectors, or instruments. There are many different approaches to TAA. It can include: contrarian investment, fundamental value, relative value, and technical approaches. Where tactical asset allocation stops and strategic asset allocation starts is somewhat vague. Some practitioners discuss tactical asset allocation in ways that correspond with other practitioners' views on strategic asset allocation.

Tagesgeld (Money markets; Germany). Overnight money. Call money is called *tagesgeld bis auf weiteres*. Rolling deposits are known as *taglishes geld*.

tail (Bonds; USA). (i) In US Treasury security cash-based auctions, the difference between the average issuing price and the stop price. (ii) In the repurchase agreement (RP; repo) market, funds obtained via a RP may be re-lent by a means of a reverse repurchase agreement (reverse repo). A tail is established by making the reverse repo maturity longer than the original, in the expectation that interest rates will fall in the intervening period so that a new repo can be set up to meet the reverse one; but at a lower rate. (iii) The decimals or fractions of a quote (the figures or fraction on a quote to the right of the decimal place) (cf. big figure; handle). (iv) A change in a bid or offer instruction to avoid a tie (cf. matched and lost). (v) That part of a probability distribution where the likelihood, but not the magnitude, of an occurrence is small (cf. standard deviation; variance).

(vi) The residual to a pool of assets in an asset-backed security at maturity (cf. run off). (vii) The change in a futures position used for hedging because of changes in margin (cf. variation margin). (viii) The excess in futures contracts after undertaking a basis transaction. (ix) A bond with only a short time to maturity or redemption.

tailgating (USA). An unethical practice similar to front running where an intermediary executes a trade immediately after the customer's order in order to take advantage of the market impact of the client's trade.

tail hedging (Futures). Adjustments required to a futures position used for hedging as a result of changes in the amount of margin required on the position. This arises from the daily marked-to-market of the futures position and the requirement to provide or to receive variation margin on the account. Also called *tailing the hedge*.

tail of the arbitrage. See delivery options; end-of-the-month option; wild card option.

tailored swap. An interest rate swap or cross-currency swap where one or more features are designed to match one of the counterparty's cash flow requirements. See accreting swap; amortizing swap; deferred swap; roller-coaster swap; seasonal swap.

Taiwan Stock Exchange Corporation (Republic of China). City Building, 85 Yan-Ping, South Road, TW-Taipei, Taiwan ROC (tel. 886 2 311 4020; fax 886 2 311 4004). Principal stock exchange situated in Taipei, regulated by a Securities and Exchange Commission based on the US model. One of the more important emerging markets. Taiwan is one of the Pacific tigers, that is, fast-growing nations of the Pacific rim.

take. (i) To agree to buy at the quoted offer price (cf. hit; lift; lose). (ii) In the euromarkets used to describe the acceptance of deposits, hence *to take deposits* or a *taking* (cf. place).

take a bath. To lose a substantial sum of money (cf. toasted).

take a flyer. To take a speculative position (cf. taking a view).

take a hit. To take a loss on a transaction.

take-and-pay contract. A variant on the take-or-pay contract used in project finance where the buyer is only committed to purchasing output if produced. It is a lesser guarantee than the take-or-pay agreement. Sometimes called a *take-if-delivered* agreement.

take a position. To buy or sell in such a way as to become **long** or **short** (cf. **position**).

take back. The return to the **lead** or **syndicate manager** involved in a new issue of securities that have been allocated to **underwriters** or the **selling group**, but not yet been sold or definitely alloted to them (cf. **circle; protection**).

take delivery. (i) In **derivatives** markets to receive the **underlying** at **expiry** or **exercise**. The alternative is to have a **cash-settled** contract where the holder is left to acquire the underlying in the market. (ii) In securities markets, to receive **certificates** in the settlement of a transaction (cf. **cash against delivery; delivery versus payment; free delivery**).

take down. (i) (USA). An **underwriter's** share of an offering. Hence, *take down price*, which is the price at which such securities are received by the underwriter (that is, net of his **spread**). See **take back**. (ii) Drawing funds from a lender. This is also known as a *drawdown*. (iii) The ratio of **funds** borrowed to available **credit lines**.

take-or-pay contract. A project **finance** condition where the buyer(s) of the project's output are required to purchase an agreed amount in a specific period if produced. See **take-and-pay contract**.

take out. (i) Cash generated by selling one block of **bonds** at a price higher than that paid for the replacement block (cf. **pay-up**). (ii) Market expression for a **bid** made to a seller to 'take out' his **position** (cf. **lift**). (iii) Creating a position in **derivative** instruments which provides a net up-front income (cf. **credit spread; debit spread**).

takeover. The process by which one company tenders for the **common stock** or **ordinary shares** of another in order to gain control. A takeover is usually taken to be of hostile intent, while a merger involves a pre-agreement or the consent of the target company. See **mergers and acquisitions**.

takeover accounting. See **merger accounting**.

takeover battle. A contested **takeover**, where the **target** company resists the approach of the bidder.

takeover bid. Market colloquialism for a **tender offer** for another company's **common stock**. Also known as an *offer to purchase* or a *tender to purchase*.

takeover market. See **mergers and acquisitions**.

Takeover Panel (UK). Independent panel set up with responsibility for implementing and monitoring the **City Code on Takeovers and Mergers** and the **Rules Governing the Substantial Acquisition of Shares**. In particular, it has been used as the arbiter in disagreements about the tactics and methods used in contested **takeover bids** and has recommended, for example, the withdrawal of advertising and the changing of offer documents. Any party judged to have breached its rules can receive a private or public reprimand; or be reported to the **Securities and Investments Board**. See **City code**.

takeover ratio. The relationship between the book values of a company's assets, historic cost less depreciation, and the market value of the company (cf. **market-to-book ratio**). If the numerical value of this ratio is greater than one, then the company is said to be a likely target for **takeover**. See also **Tobin's q**.

taker. (i) Sometimes used for borrower. (ii) (UK) The holder or buyer of an **option** on the **London Metal Exchange**.

take-up fee. A form of additional remuneration to **underwriters** who are obliged to take up any unsold securities in an offering. It usually allows the issuing entity to reduce the initial **underwriting commission** (cf. **gross spread; standby fee**) at the expense of greater cost should a large proportion of the issue remain with the underwriters. It is mostly used with **rights issues** where a large degree of take-up by existing **shareholders** is to be expected.

taking (Banking). Accepting or soliciting a (usually short-term) **deposit** (cf. **placing**). See **take** (cf. **lift**).

taking a view (UK). The process of forming an opinion on the likely course of the market and taking the corresponding **position** to benefit most from the expected outcome (cf. **flat; neutral; square**).

talon. A detachable part of a **bearer security** used to claim fresh **coupon** vouchers. Required when a security has a very long **maturity** or is a **perpetual**.

Tan Book (USA). See **Beige Book**.

tandem or **tandem options (TE).** A package of same-type, **call** or **put**, **options** which may have different **strike prices** and where the **expiry**

dates are usually for non-overlapping periods (cf. strip).

tangible assets. The physical assets of a business, including financial instruments, but not patents, trademarks, etc. (cf. **intangible assets**). By definition, those assets which can be readily sold for cash. Sometimes they are known as *tangible fixed assets* to differentiate them from the **current** assets of a business.

tangible net worth. Net worth excluding any **intangible assets**. A conservative asset-based valuation which assumes that assets are realizable at or close to their book values (cf. **sunk cost**). See **fundamental analysis**.

tankan (Japan). The Bank of Japan's survey of the Japanese economy, published every three months.

tanshi (Money markets; Japan). Short-term money. A *tanshi company* is a money market brokerage firm.

tap. (i) To raise funds in a market (*to tap the market*). (ii) A means of controlling the new issue of a security by ensuring supply roughly matches demand at the given price at a particular time. Supply of the security can thus be turned on or off depending on market conditions without the need for large movements in price (cf. **medium-term note**). Used in the UK as a method of issuing gilt-edged (cf. **auction; taplet; tender; tranche**). An offering sold in this way is known as a *tap issue*.

tap certificate of deposit (tap CD) (Money markets). **Certificates of deposit** available by a bank to be issued when required (cf. **tranche**).

tape (Canada; USA). The stock market's transaction reporting system. Formerly known as the *ticker tape* from the noise made by the mechanical device used to print the stock price information. Also taken to mean the **consolidated** or *broad tape* computer-based information systems used for reporting market activity and other news. Reading the tape, which is normally projected electronically onto a screen, requires an understanding of the shorthand used to compress the information. A simple stock transaction may look like:

tape 1

Which means that ABC stock has just traded fifteen **lots** or board lots at 75. If the ticker had shown:

tape 2

this would have been a transaction for just one lot at 75. For odd lots or blocks, the ticker would include an additional symbol S, such as:

tape 3

It could also include the **bid** and **offer** (**ask**) price of the stock:

tape 4

Exchange-traded options data would include the stock symbol (ABC), **expiry** month (MY), **strike**

tape 5

price (70), number of **contracts** traded (5), and the **premium** (145):

If the option had been a **put**, rather than a **call**, the ticker would have read:

ABC♦MY..P

.

. . . . . .70♦5s8

5

tape 6

the P standing for put.

taplet. Small **tap** issues. Also known as a *mini-tap* or *tranchette*.

tap stock (Bonds; UK). An issue of **gilt-edge** via a tap mechanism. This can be either a new issue, where the **Bank of England** as the Treasury's agent holds unsold portions of a recent issuance which it then offers out as and when there is demand, or additional amounts of an existing one (cf. **taplet**). The term can be used either for gilt-edge obtained via the tap mechanism or for the issue trading in the market. Tap stocks are expected to stand at a **discount** to the market due to selling pressure (cf. **yield curve**).

target. (i) A company which is the objective of a **takeover**. (ii) An objective or desirable level.

targeted amortization class (TAC) (Bonds; USA). A similar **collateralized mortgage obligation** structure to **planned amortization class** issues except that with TACs holders are not protected against unexpectedly high prepayments.

target payout ratio. The desirable balance between retained **earnings** and **dividends** by a company over time.

target price. (i) A forecast price at some point in the future. (ii) The price of the **underlying** on an option at which, after taking into account the **premium** paid, it would be profitable to **exercise** (cf. **break-even point**).

tariff. Taxes levied on imported goods and services.

tasso di base (Italy). Italian equivalent to base rate or **prime rate**.

tasso fluttuante or **tasso variable** (Money markets; Italy). Floating rate or variable rate interest.

Tasso Sulle Anticipazioni Straordinarie (Lombard rate) (Banking; Italy). The upper bound to official interest rates. The **Bank of Italy** will provide **collateralized** repurchase facilities for banks at this rate for **liquidity** purposes, known as anticipazioni a scadenza fissa o straordinarie.

Tasso Ufficiale di Sconto (TUS) (official discount rate) (Banking; Italy). The lower bound to official interest rates. The **Bank of Italy** extends a fixed credit line for funds available based on the TUS rate.

tategyoku (Japan). **Open interest.**

tau (τ). A measure of **option** price sensitivity to changes in **volatility**. It is normally the unit change in the option price for a percentage point change in the **standard deviation** of the **underlying** asset. Better known by other names such as *epsilon*, *kappa*, or *vega*.

taux annuel glissant (TAG) (France). Variable annual rate of interest.

taux annuel monétaire (TAM) (France). An **index** of the official overnight money market rate used as a **reference rate** for some **floating rate** or **variable rate** loans or securities.

taux d'escompte (French). The **discount** rate.

taux des pensions sur appels d'offres (France). The lower bound set for short-term interest rates established via **open-market operations** by the **Banque de France** via official **repurchase agreement** transactions.

taux d'intérêt (French). Interest rate.

taux mensuel obligatoire (TMO) (France). The average rate for recently issued government debt over the last twelve months. Each month uses the **settlement** price for newly issued securities.

taux moyen mensuel du marché monétaire (TMMMM) (France). The average monthly money market rate based on the daily rate.

taux moyen pondéré (TMP) (France). The **fixing** rate set daily by the **Banque de France** at 11.30 a.m., Paris time, based on the average of interbank transactions (cf. **Paris interbank offered rate**). Used as a **reference rate** in many financial transactions and legal agreements.

taxable capacity. The maximum amount of profit that can be rendered free of tax, or charged at a lower rate, by using a **tax break**. Tax breaks that exceed the profit available or earned for tax offsetting purposes are of limited attraction. Hence the term *tax exhaustion* where the total amount of the tax break exceeds taxable profit. Sometimes this excess taxable capacity can be passed on through financial transactions, such as **wrap leases** (cf. **depreciation methods; depreciation**). See **tax shield**.

taxable equivalent income. Adjusting tax-free income to the level that allows it to be compared to taxable income before any taxes are deducted (cf. **earnings before taxes**). See **taxable equivalent yield**.

taxable equivalent yield (USA). The **yield** on a **bond** producing taxable income which would be needed to equal the yield on a **tax-exempt bond** (cf. **corporate tax equivalent**).

taxable income. That proportion of income subject to tax after any allowances, such as **capital allowances** or **depreciation** or other tax breaks, have been deducted.

taxable municipal bond (USA). A **municipal bond** issue where the private use exceeds that required for a **public purpose bond** (cf. **private purpose bond**).

taxable transaction. A transaction which is not tax-free to the parties. In such cases, the appropriate valuation method should be on an **after-tax basis**.

tax and loan account (USA). A US Treasury account held with a deposit-taking institution. Such accounts facilitate the Operations of the **Federal Reserve's Open-Market Committee** as they reduce the wide swings in **reserves** occasioned by tax payments or by the federal government.

tax anticipation bill (TAB) (Money markets; USA). Special issues of **short-term treasury bills** auctioned by the US Treasury in anticipation of future tax revenues and which can be used by corporations to pay their taxes. They normally mature within a week of the end of the quarterly due dates for corporate income tax, but holders can surrender them on the due date at **face value** without giving up income to meet their tax liabilities (cf. **cash management bill**).

tax anticipation notes (TAN) (Money markets; USA). Short-term securities issued by US local authorities and states to raise funds in anticipation of future tax revenues (cf. **bond anticipation note**).

tax arbitrage. Transactions designed to reduce the tax position of a firm or individual (cf. **instantly repackaged perpetual**).

tax avoidance. Legally acceptable arrangements designed to reduce the tax burden on an individual or organization. Most organizations aim to arrange their affairs so as to minimize their tax position, a proposition accepted in law. It may involve simple steps such as deferring income from one fiscal year to the next, or sophisticated structures designed to exploit loopholes or concessions offered in the tax laws. It is also known as *tax planning*. The illegal route is known as *tax evasion*.

tax base. The activity or area upon which a tax is levied. It can also mean the amount of tax that can be raised from a type of tax.

tax break. A generic term for specific financial arrangements or instruments that attract an exemption or reduced liability from different forms of taxation (cf. **tax shield**).

tax burden. The amount or rate of tax that a particular organization has to pay. Theories about efficient taxation require that any tax burden not act as a disincentive or create behaviour which is uniquely motivated by **tax avoidance** considerations.

tax clawback agreement. A project finance condition where the **stakeholders** agree to provide additional finance to the extent of the value of any tax benefits derived from the project in the event of a cash-flow shortfall.

tax clearance (UK). Prior recognition by the Inland Revenue that a transaction will not be taxed in a way harmful to the outcome (cf. **safe harbour**). Typically, major reorganizations of company affairs obtain prior approval from the Revenue that any scheme will not be challenged (cf. **tax avoidance**).

tax credit. A tax allowance or payment that can be used to offset an existing or future liability to pay taxes (cf. **franked income**).

tax deductible. Any payment or cost that can be used to reduce taxable income. For instance, life assurance payments may be offset against taxable income in some instances.

tax deferred. An instrument where the payment of tax is deferred to **maturity**. A zero-coupon bond might qualify if holders were able to defer liability to redemption or sale and then be taxed at their prevailing marginal tax rate (cf. **tax avoidance**).

tax deposit certificate (UK). An advance deposit that can be made to the Inland Revenue and used to settle a tax liability in the future. Such certificates are interest bearing. See **tax anticipation bill**.

Taxe (German). Quote.

tax evasion. See tax avoidance.

tax-exempt bond or **security.** A bond where the **coupon** payments are exempt from income taxes in the jurisdiction in which they are issued. Normally issued by government, state, or municipal authorities. In the USA, there is a large market in such issues (cf. **municipal bonds**). Sometimes known as a *tax-spared* instrument.

tax-exempt commercial paper (TECP) (Money markets; USA). **Commercial paper** issues by local authorities, municipalities, and states which are exempt from income taxes. (cf. **tax sparing**).

tax-exempt swap. A type of **swap** used to hedge a **long position** in bonds that are exempt from income taxes (cf. **municipal bond**).

tax-exempt yield. The yield on a tax-exempt bond. See **interest rate calculations; yield-to: -average life; -call; -equivalent life; -operative-date; - maturity; -put**.

tax-free. See items under **tax-exempt**.

tax haven. See offshore.

tax holiday. A concession granted to companies, setting up either in a particular country and/or within a particular industry and/or region, where the liability for income or profits tax is either reduced or excused for a given period. It is provided as an incentive to firms to set up in particular countries or to undertake certain types of projects where the economic gains of the activity outweight the forgone tax collected. Many developing countries offer such tax holidays as well as being a part of regional development assistance plans within countries. The attraction for governments is that the cost is hidden, since the revenue is forgone rather than a subsidy or grant having to be paid out.

tax loss carryback and **carryforward.** See carryback and carryforward.

Tax Reform Act of 1986 (USA). General reform of US taxation aimed at simplifying the US Tax Code by reducing the number of concessions and **tax breaks** available while at the same time lowering the general tax rates payable. Many concessions were abolished at the time and the legislation also aimed at regularizing foreign sourced income.

The twin objectives of simplification and lower rates have been partially reversed in subsequent legislation.

tax relief. Statutory concessions against a tax liability provided by a country's tax code or laws. These are initially formulated as special concessions aimed at securing a desirable economic or social objectives but then become part of the general pattern of **tax avoidance** or **tax breaks**.

tax revenue anticipation note (TRAN) (Money markets; USA). See **revenue anticipation note; tax anticipation note**.

tax shield or **tax shelter.** The reduction in tax paid that arises from using allowable deductions from overall taxable income. Typically **debt, lease**, and other costs of running a business or profession (cf. **taxable capacity; tax break**).

tax sparing. A debt that is covered by a double exemption from **withholding tax**, thus enabling lenders to offer narrow (sometimes negative) margins over the **reference rate**. Lenders receive two sets of tax credits. It works as follows. Assuming a 20% witholding tax rate in country A and a 30% tax rate for the banks:

Interest on loan	100
Grossing up amount at 20%	20
Subtotal	120
Less cost of funds	90
Taxable profit	30
Tax at 30%	10
Credit for withholding tax	20
Net gain	10

The bank has ended up with a tax credit of 10. Note that timing differences on the credit and tax payments by the bank may reduce the net gain.

tax straddle. Any transaction aimed at manipulating cash flows such that they fall in a particular **financial year** or **fiscal year** in order to take advantage of various deductions or tax-minimizing opportunities.

tax swap. The exchange of two securities to create a tax benefit.

tax switch. A restructuring of the member elements of a **portfolio** in recognition of a changing tax environment, as a result of changes in tax law or of the status of the investor (cf. **anomaly; policy switch**).

tax timing option. The ability to realize or defer gains or losses between one tax assessment period and another.

tax year. See fiscal year.

teaser rate (USA). A low initial rate offered on **adjustable rate mortgages** to attract buyers. The cost to the issuer will be made up by a higher **floating rate** in later periods.

technical analysis. A branch of market or security analysis based upon the study of price movements and trading volume and the forecasting of future movements from past movements (cf. **fundamental analysis**). It seeks to gather insights about price trends due to demand and supply and behavioural characteristics of markets which can be used to make predictions about future behaviour. Such analysis relies on many different approaches, the following being the most common: **volume** and **open interest**, trends, price patterns, relative values (such as **price–earnings**, relative **yield**), reversals, sentiment, continuation and **momentum models**, gap theories, mean reversion, mathematical and statistical models such as **relative strength**, trading rules, **seasonality**, the Elliot wave, and other **anomalies**. Such research relies heavily on **quantitative** methods using high-capacity computers or charts, this latter approach being also known as **chart analysis** or *chartism*. As such, the techniques are not directly concerned with the **fundamental analysis** of the **underlying**. The results lead to investment strategies such as **index arbitrage** or **program trading**, which is a form of applied technical analysis aimed at exploiting the observed short-run price differences between markets. A person who makes predictions based on the techniques is known as a *technical analyst* (cf. **quant**).

technical barrier. See resistance area.

technical buying or **selling.** Transactions based on a **technical analysis** view of the market, sector, or individual security or **derivative**.

technical condition. The demand and supply situation affecting the state of a market, i.e. whether it is **overbought** or **oversold**.

technical correction. Price changes attributed to changes due to the **technical condition** of the market, that is, a reduction in the trading positions held by market participants.

technical decline or **rally.** A price movement that has to do with the **overbought** or **oversold** condition of the market and not **fundamental analysis** (cf. **liquidity**). In financial economic theory, price changes would not be due to new information.

technical default. A breach of the terms and conditions on a debt by a borrower which is of minor effect, such as failure to provide information or to comply with one or more of the **covenants** in the terms. While in principle the whole borrowing is thus in **default** (and usually immediately repayable) it is usual to give the borrower some leeway to put matters right (cf. **acceleration clause; waiver**).

technical rally. A rise in prices in a general downtrend due to investor support at a given price level (cf. **support level**).

technical reserves. Assets held by an insurance company against future claims by policyholders.

technical risk. The risk arising from technical factors in the market. For example obtaining an exact match of the cash and **futures** positions at the **expiry** of a contract (cf. **pin risk; witching hour**). For example, the **London interbank offered rate** (LIBOR) used to establish the closing **settlement** rate for the **Chicago Mercantile Exchange's** short-term interest rate contract on the three-month **eurodollar** deposit future uses rates from banks in Europe and the USA which are established at different times of day. A firm operating in the European time zone may find that the LIBOR rate may not correspond to the expected rate if there is a change in US dollar interest rates in the US time zone prior to the contract expiring.

teddy bear hug. A form of **bear hug** takeover where the **target** company is not unreceptive to the offer, but wishes to obtain a higher price. See also **mergers and acquisitions**.

Tehran Stock Exchange (Iran). 228 Hafez Avenue, PO Box 11355-399, IR-11389 Tehran (tel. 98 21 670309; fax 98 21 672524).

Tel-Aviv Stock Exchange Ltd. (Israel). 54 Ahad Ha'am Street, IL-Tel-Aviv 65202 (tel. 972 3 567 7411; fax 972 3 510 5379).

Telefonverkeh (Germany). **Over-the-counter** trading.

telegraphic transfer (TT) (Banking). Derived from the practice of using the telegraph to affect a foreign money transfer (cf. **cable**). Now it is more usual to use a datalink or the telephone to affect transfer (cf. **Society for World-wide Interbank Financial Telecommunications**).

Telerate (USA). Financial information provider for market prices and news information owned by Dow-Jones Inc.

Teletext Output of Price Information by Computer (TOPIC) (UK). A viewdata system used by the **London Stock Exchange** to disseminate

Stock Exchange Automatic Quotations to the dealing rooms of its members. It also distributes financial data about, for example, exchange rates and **option** prices.

tender. (i) A competitive method of offering or purchasing **assets**, contracts, or securities where allotment takes place according to the highest (or average of the) bids received (cf. **tender offer; winner's curse**). See **auction.** (ii) To bid for securities at a tender. (iii) To offer securities in a tender offer (cf. **reverse tender**). (iv) The intention by the **short position** holder to **deliver the underlying** commodity in a **commodities future** contract or a financial instrument in a financial futures (cf. **physical delivery**). This is done via a *notice of tender.* (v) Used interchangeably for an auction. Technically there is a difference since an auction is a public event open to anyone, a condition which does not necessarily apply to a tender.

tenderable grades. The range of **commodities** that are allowable or specified in a **commodities futures contract** and are thus eligible for **delivery** (cf. **alternative delivery procedure; assay; contract grade; tender**).

tender acceptance facility (Money markets). Facility for the issuance of **banker's acceptance** similar in method of operation to a **revolving underwritten facility.**

tender bills. See **treasury bills.**

tender bond. A type of guarantee used in competitive bids where the bidders are required to post an undertaking that the winner will enter into a full contract. The tender bond is designed to ensure that the bidder does not withdraw if conditions should move against him.

tender offer. (i) A general, or two-part, offer (known as a *two-tier tender offer*) by a company to purchase its own **liabilities** or, in the context of a **takeover** attempt, those of another company, for cash and/or new securities. (ii) Another name for an **auction** of new securities. See **dutch auction; English auction.**

tender panel. A type of issuing or loan **facility** arrangement where a predetermined group of banks and/or **broker-dealers** agree to try and place securities, typically **promissory notes**, or make loan **advances** on a **best efforts** basis. The tender panel system normally involves a formal method for participants to receive notification of tenders, provide bids, and receive an allocation, if successful. A similar mechanism has been used for new issuance in the **bond** market and, in a modified form, for **equity**. It is similar in method to an **auction** (e.g. those in common use in government bond markets) but differs in that participation is restricted to members selected by the issuer. The tender panel attraction to an issuer is that it increases competition; the disadvantage is that it may lead to a disorderly **after-market**. Hence *tender panel agent*, the party responsible for organizing the tenders on the issuer's behalf.

tender rate guarantee (Banking). A technique used to manage **foreign exchange rate risk** on a tender which guarantees a set exchange rate to the successful party (cf. **tender-to-contract**). See **shared currency option under tender.**

tender-to-contract (TTC) (UK). A method of handling the **contingent** foreign exchange exposure created by bidding on a contract denominated in a foreign currency. The product, developed by the Export Credit Guarantee Department (ECGD), allowed firms to pay only a small fraction of the total cost of buying a **currency option** which would **hedge** their position. See **shared currency option under tender.**

ten K; ten Q (10 (K); 10 (Q)) (USA). The set of financial statements filed with the **Securities and Exchange Commission**. The 10K refers to the annual report, the 10Q to the quarterly reports.

tenkan shasai (Japan). **Convertible.**

tenor (USA). Another term for **maturity** or **term**. Also the time period from the issue of a security to maturity (cf. **current and original maturity**).

ten widows (China). The ten state entities given approval for foreign borrowing:

> Bank of China
> Bank of Communications
> China Investment Bank
> China International Trust and Investment
>   Corporation (CITIC)
> Dalian International Trust and Investment
>   Corporation
> Fujian Investment and Enterprise Corporation
> Guangdong International Trust and Investment
>   Corporation (GITIC)
> Hainan International Trust and Investment
>   Corporation
> Shanghai Investment and Trust Corporation
>   (SITCO)
> Tianjin International Trust and Investment
>   Corporation (TITIC)

term. (i) The time before **expiry** or **redemption** (cf. **maturity; term-to-maturity**). (ii) Conditions or provisions within a contract.

term bonds (USA). An issue with a **bullet maturity**.

term certificate of deposit (term CD). A certificate of deposit (CD) with an original maturity of more than one year. Such instruments may have a fixed rate coupon, when they are also known as *fixed rate CDs*, or a variable rate coupon, when they are known as *floating rate CDs* or FRCDs. A term CD is sometimes called a *term certificate*.

terme (French). Means 'period'. The French for a futures market is *marché à terme d'instruments financiers*. The foreign exchange forward market is *changes à terme*. A forward outright is a *terme sec*.

term fed funds (Money markets; USA). Fed funds which are bought and sold for maturities longer than overnight.

terminal contract. See forward; future; swap.

terminal date. See expiry date.

terminal market. Another term for a futures market (cf. Deutsche Terminbörse). It derives its name from the commodities markets that evolved in the major trading centres rather than at the point of production.

termination. The ending of an agreement or transaction on pre-agreed terms (cf. cancellation). Normally agreements include a *termination clause* giving the terms and conditions on which the agreement can be ended. The *termination date* is the date at which such a termination becomes effective (cf. maturity date).

termination claim (USA). The ending or exercise value of a unit in the Americus trust (cf. prescribed right to income and maximum equity; special claim on residual equity).

Termingeld (Germany). Money market transactions of with maturities of more than one month. Fixed-term transactions of less than one month are called *terminiertes tagesgeld* (cf. Tagesgeld).

term loan or **term credit** (Banking). A bank advance that is for a specified period of time. A term loan is usually taken to mean more than one year (cf. committed and uncommitted facility). See short-term.

term premium. A premium factor in futures prices that is due to liquidity preference in the term structure of interest rates (cf. market segmentation theory). See also price discovery.

term repurchase agreement (term RP; term repo). A repurchase agreement with a maturity longer than overnight. Maturities are typically those common in the money markets. The more

usual kind of repurchase agreement is known as an *overnight repo*.

terms and conditions. The specifications of a security or other transaction, such as the coupon or interest rate, maturity, amount, protection, and so forth (cf. contract; covenants). See trust.

terms control. That part of monetary policy aimed at influencing consumer credit activity by setting minimum deposits and maximum payback periods.

terms currency (Forex). The currency in which an exchange rate is quoted. The opposite is known as the base currency. See European convention.

terms of trade. The ratio of the index of export prices to the index of import prices. If export prices rise at a faster rate than those of imports, then an improvement in the terms of trade are said to have occurred. A change in the terms of trade is of importance in assessing the credit risk of individual countries.

term stock or **term shares.** Securities that cannot be sold for a predetermined period.

term structure model. A model of the term structure of interest rates used to explain the behaviour of the yield curve (cf. model; stochastic process). See whole-term structure of interest rates option pricing model.

term structure of interest rates or **term structure.** An explanation of the framework for establishing money market interest rates based upon cash flows and maturity or holding periods (cf. yield curve). The key theories can be summarized as follows:

Expectations theory	Preferred habitat theory	Liquidity preference theory
Borrowers and lenders are risk neutral	Borrowers and lenders are risk averse	Borrowers prefer long maturities; lenders prefer short
Securities are perfect substitutes	Securities are substitutes at the market price of risk	Liquidity premium increases with maturity

Also called the *yield curve*. See expectations theory; liquidity preference market segmentation theory.

term structure of volatility. A graph or tabulation of the implied volatility of options with different expiry dates. The relationship tells participants something of the degree of uncertainty expected in the **underlying** in the future. As with the **term structure of interest rates** or the **yield curve**, there are four distinct patterns that can be observed. The term structure of volatility shows evidence of **mean reversion** with longer periods having less volatility than shorter ones, with the short period volatility tending to move back towards the longer term average.

Term structure of volatility

Months	£/$	$/DM	$/Sfr.	$/yen	DM/yen	£/DM
1	10.30	14.30	16.20	13.10	11.50	12.00
3	10.80	13.90	15.50	13.20	11.60	10.90
6	11.20	13.00	14.30	13.20	11.50	10.20
12	11.55	12.70	13.80	13.35	11.40	9.80

term TED spread. This is the implied **spread** between a **bond** and the **London interbank offered rate** (LIBOR) curve (cf. **treasury-eurodollar spread**). It is the spread above or below LIBOR obtainable on a bond. It is created by buying (or selling) a particular bond either outright or through a **repurchase agreement** and selling (buying) a **futures strip**. The position is laid on at a particular spread and when this level changes, the transaction is unwound.

term-to-maturity. Another word used to describe the **life** of a security or financial instrument (cf. **current maturity**; **original maturity**).

tesobonos (Money markets; Mexico). Mexican peso–US dollar linked **treasury bills** issued by the United States of Mexico and sold to international investors, particularly US investors. The redemption amount is paid in pesos, but linked to the prevailing peso–dollar rate at maturity. See also **dual currency bonds**.

test or **testing.** A description of price movements near known **resistance** or **support levels**.

Texas hedge. (i) A misnomer, used to describe a market **position** that increases **risk**. Such a position is certainly not **hedged**. It is an allusion to the reputation that Texans have of being naturally gifted gamblers which means, in a financial markets context, they have no need to hedge their positions (cf. **naked position**). See **hedge fund**. (ii) A double-or-quits strategy used by bankrupt Texan **savings and loan associations** to recoup solvency or go down gloriously.

Thailand Stock Exchange. See Stock Exchange of Thailand.

theoretical value. The price or value derived from a pricing **model** rather than observed in the market. If the model is correctly specified and the

market is efficient, the two should be approximately equal. Also known as *fair value*.

theoretical value of a right. See **rights**.

The Securities Association (TSA) (UK). The largest of the **self-regulating organizations** which was responsible for the behaviour of all the professional users of the **London Stock Exchange** and the conduct of securities traders in particular. It was accountable for ensuring adherence to its rule book to the **Securities and Investments board**. Now merged with the Association of Futures Brokers and Dealers to become the **Securities and Futures Authority**.

theta (θ). An **option's** sensitivity to passing time, that is **time decay** (cf. **time value of an option**). The behaviour of theta is non-linear in that value decreases fastest as the option approaches its **expiry date**. In addition, the more the price of the **underlying** and the **strike price** diverge, the less effect it has on option value. This is because with a long time to expiry, there is considerably more chance that the option will be exercised and have value. That means deeply **out-of-the-money** or **in-the-money** options will have lower thetas than an **at-the-money** option. Note that when an option has a positive **gamma** (the rate of change of an option's **delta**) one would expect a negative theta; and vice versa. It can be considered a measure of the *wasting asset* quality of options. A theta of 0.065 means that the option will fall in value by that amount per day. Theta works in favour of option **writers** (sellers) and against holders (buyers). See **option pricing**.

thin. A market with low trading volume and poor **liquidity** usually characterized by wide **bid-offer spreads** (cf. **tight**).

thin capitalization. A condition determined by tax authorities where the ratio of **equity** supporting a given level of debt is deemed to be too small for the activities undertaken. The taxing agency will treat some of the debt as if it were equity. Such a situation may typically arise with a foreign subsidiary, funded by a parent company, where there is some suspicion that high levels of debt are being used to reduce the amount of tax on the subsidiary's profits (cf. **tax shield**).

thinly traded. Securities which are infrequently traded.

third country acceptance. A banker's acceptance or **bill of exchange** where the **drawer** is not domiciled in the exporting or importing country.

third market (Equities). (i) (UK) Former official **London Stock Exchange** regulated market intended to offer access to **equity capital** to companies that are likely to be considered too young or too risky, or both, for either the **main market** or the then Unlisted Securities Market. See **Alternative Investment Market**. (ii) (USA). Exchange-listed securites which are traded **over the counter** (cf. **block; National Association of Securities Dealers Automated Quotations**). See also **fourth market**.

third party warrant. See **covered warrant**.

third position. See **position**.

thirty per cent rule (USA). Tax regulation covering **open-ended investment companies** concerning the treatment of gains on disposals that have been held for less than three months which disqualifies the tax pass-through status of such gains if they exceed 30% of gross income. The rule is aimed at discouraging active trading by **mutual funds**. Also sometimes referred to as the *short-short rule*.

threshold option. See **ladder option**.

threshold price. See **trigger**.

thrift institution or **thrift** (USA). A class of financial institutions in the USA which accept deposits but are not commercial banks: it includes **savings and loan associations** and savings banks.

throughput (Banking). A type of credit arrangement used in **project finance** based upon the output performance, such as the production of gas or oil, by the project. The revenue generated should be enough to meet the debt obligation, which means the lender has to be concerned about the value of the output. Sometimes called a *deficiency agreement* because any shortfall in the revenue has to be met by the borrower on demand. See **self-financing**.

throughput agreement. A project finance condition that requires the sponsors to the transaction to agree to use or process a specified amount of material in the project in a given period (cf. **take-or-pay contract**). Typically such agreements are used in gas and oil pipeline projects or other distributional investments.

through-the-market. (i) A bond that has a yield-to-maturity less than that of comparable bonds. See **trading through the curve** (cf. **trading over the curve**). (ii) A market condition where one dealer's bid (offer) is higher (lower) than another's offer (bid) (cf. **triple witching hour**). Also sometimes called *backwardation*.

through Treasuries (Bonds; USA). A **bond** which is issued or is trading at a **yield** less than that of

comparable US Treasuries. See **trading through the curve** (cf. **trading over the curve**).

thundering herd (USA). Used to describe Merrill Lynch, the US brokerage group. When this finance house adopts a position in the markets others take note. See **domino effect**.

tick. The smallest price change in the market price of a security or **derivative** contract (cf. **pip; point**). Typically ticks are either fractions or **basis points**, except in **foreign exchange** where most currencies are quoted to two or four decimal places. Also known as the *minimum price fluctuation*. See **down tick; tick size; up tick**. (ii) The net number of securities in a sector, group, or market that have a common price movement. Thus if there are a dozen securities in the sector and eight have seen a price increase and four a decrease, the tick is plus four ($+4$).

ticker. A mechanical device used for printing out security price information, hence *ticker-tape*. Now largely superseded by electronic displays. See **stock symbols; tape**.

Ticker Plant Frankfurt (TPF) (Germany). Real-time, integrated stock price dissemination service for all transactions made on the German stock exchanges (cf. **consolidated tape**). See also **Börsen-Order-Service-System; Kurs-Informations-Service-System**.

ticket. A record of a transaction used for settlement and control purposes. Also called a *dealing slip*.

tick size. The change in a **futures contract** or an **exchange-traded option** caused by the smallest price change in the market price. If a contract has a value of £50,000 and the tick is a 1/32nd, then the tick size is £50,000 × 1/32, which is £15.625.

tick value. The change in value of a **futures contract** or an **exchange-traded option** when the price changes by a **tick**. Thus for a short interest futures contract with a nominal value of US$1m, a one tick change in price will change the value by US$25. See **value of an 01**.

tied loan. A loan made by one party to another (usually by and to a government or its agencies) which stipulates that the funds are used in specified ways. In the case of loans made by government, in purchasing goods or services from that country.

tie-in. An agreement that a **subsidiary** or associated company will purchase an agreed amount from the parent. Also used in **project finance** to force the **sponsor** to buy from the project (cf. **take-or-pay contract**).

tier 1 capital (Banking). Defined as (i) common stockholders' equity and retained profit or earnings; (ii) qualifying non-**cumulative preferred stock** (up to a maximum of 25% of total tier 1 capital); and (iii) **minority interests** in equity accounts of consolidated subsidiaries. The minimum requirement is 4% of **risk-adjusted assets** under the **Basle Capital Convergence Accord** as operated by most domestic regulators. Tier 1 capital is also sometimes called *core capital*.

tier 2 capital (Banking). Defined as (i) reserves for loan losses (this item may not exceed 100% of **tier 1 capital**); (ii) perpetual preferred stock not qualified to be in tier 1; (iii) hybrid capital instruments and **mandatory convertibles**; (iv) **subordinated** debt; (v) **preferred stock** with medium-term remaining **current maturity**. The minimum regulatory requirement for tier 1 and tier 2 combined, less any deductions, is 8% of **risk-adjusted assets**. Deductions have to be made in respect of the following: (*a*) unconsolidated investments in subsidiaries; (*b*) holdings in other **deposit-taking** institutions' capital; (*c*) any other deductions imposed by the regulator (cf. **non-performing loans**; **problem assets**). Tier 2 capital is sometimes referred to as *supplementary capital*.

tiger countries or **tigers.** Colloquial term for the four fastest-growing Pacific rim countries, excluding Japan. These are Hong Kong, Singapore, South Korea, and Thailand (cf. **dragon countries**).

tight. (i) In financial markets, heavy trading and narrow **spread** conditions (cf. **thin**). (ii) In monetary policy, strict control over monetary aggregates; usually equated with high interest rates. Hence *tight money.*

time bargain. A forward or futures position which involves an obligation to make delivery (cf. **short**).

time bill. A banker's acceptance or bill of exchange that is not payable until some specific future time. Contrast with a bankers's draft or sight bill which is good for immediate payment (cf. **after date; after sight; at sight**). See also time draft.

time box. An option strategy better known as a jellyroll (cf. **box spread; horizontal spread**).

time decay. The loss of time value of an option or a future as it moves closer to its expiry date. In the case of a future, this is generally known as convergence (cf. **basis**). See theta.

time-dependent option. Any of a number of exotic options which have special features. For example, an option which is initially European-style and then, after a predetermined time, becomes Bermudan-style or an option with an escalating **strike price** after an initial period. See also **path-dependent option**.

time deposit (USA). A fixed-term interest-paying account at a deposit-taking institution (cf. **call; checking account; deposit account; negotiated order of withdrawal**).

time draft. A demand for payment on a specified future date (cf. **banker's acceptance; bill; sight draft**).

time hedge. See option hedge.

time option (Forex). See **break forward**.

time order or **time limit order.** A transaction instruction that has to be executed within a specific time otherwise it will lapse (cf. **good till cancelled; good for this week; good for this month**).

times common covered ratio. See dividend cover.

times covered. See interest coverage ratio.

times interest earned. Profitability ratio, that is, the **earnings before interest and taxes** divided by the interest charge. Also called *interest cover* in the UK. See ratio analysis.

time spread. An option strategy involving selling a **call** or put and buying another with a longer expiry date but with the same **strike price** (cf. **horizontal spread**). The sale reduces the **premium** cost of the later maturing **option** purchased. The implicit assumption is that short-term **volatility** is overpriced. Sometimes called a *calendar spread*.

times preferred coverage ratio. The number of times net profit covers the dividend on preferred stock. See ratio analysis.

time swap. See accrual swap.

time to expiration, expiry, or **maturity** or **time until expiration, expiry,** or **maturity.** The time that remains before a security matures or expires (cf. **current maturity; original maturity; life; tenor**).

time value. (i) A means of comparing cash flows at different points in time. See discounted cash flow; net present value; present value. (ii) That part of an option's value represented by the difference between its **intrinsic value** and the market price. See **time value of an option**. (iii) When discounting, the difference in the value arising from the separate timing of cash flows. See **time value of money**. (iv) The value that is gained (lost) from deferring a transaction to a future date (cf. **cost of carry; forward; future**).

time value decay. The loss of value of an option as it moves towards **expiry** (cf. **theta**).

time value of an option. The value of the **time to expiration** of an **option**, taken as the difference between the option **premium** or price and the **intrinsic value** when this is positive (cf. **time decay**). It represents the probability that the option may come **into the money** at some time before **expiry** and is therefore closely linked with the option's **volatility**. The higher the volatility, the greater the time value. It can normally be assumed that the time value decreases (asymptotically) as the **expiry date** comes nearer since the likelihood of an **out-of-the-money** option subsequently moving into the money is reduced, although variations in the price of the **underlying** will cause changes to the time value for out-of-the-money (low **delta**) options. The reduction in value of an option as it approaches expiry is known as *time decay*. See also **theta**, which is the measure of the price sensitivity of an option to a change in time to expiry. Also called the *time value premium* or just *time value*.

time value of money. The principle of finance that money received or paid in the future is worth less than money today, that is, future cash flows are **discounted** to give a **present value**, from which the **interest rate** is observable in the market for funds: the money and capital markets (cf. **yield curve**). As such it is an **opportunity cost** and sets minimum required rates of return on investments.

time value premium. The difference between an option's price and its **intrinsic value**.

Time value premium = option value − intrinsic value

See **time value of an option**.

time-weighted rate of return. A rate of return calculation used in performance measurement which gives equal weight to each period and eliminates the effects of cash flows into and out of the fund (cf. **dollar-weighted rate of return**). As a measure of performance it includes the effects of the amounts and timings of inflows and outflows to the fund and measures the compound rate of growth of the fund, unlike the **money-weighted rate of return** (cf. **internal rate of return**). It is the geometric rate of return and is found by calculating the value of each periods' return, including any intervening cash flows:

$$(1 + \text{twr}) = \frac{MV_1}{MV_0} \times \prod_{t=2}^{n} \frac{MV_t}{MV_{t-1} + CF_{t-1}}$$

Where *MV* is the market value of the fund and time 0 to time *n*; CF_t is the cash flow at time *t*; and *twr* is the time-weighted rate of return for the period. For example, if we have a fund with an initial value of 1,000 and it has a cash inflow of 100 at the end of the first quarter when the fund value is 1,050, it has a cash outflow at the end of the second quarter of 120 when the fund has a value of 1,250, and the fund has a value of 1,180 at the end of the third quarter; the time-weighted rate of return for the three-quarters of the year is 19.18%:

$$\frac{1,050}{1,000} \times \frac{1,250}{1,050 + 100} \times \frac{1,180}{1,250 - 120}$$
$$= (1.05)(1.09)(1.04) = (1.1918)$$

Note that the money-weighted rate of return (or internal rate of return) for the same fund would be only 5%, illustrating the large discrepancy that arises due to the nature and timing of the cash flows.

timing option. A right in some **futures contracts** allowing the **short futures** position holder to determine when he will **deliver** the **underlying** to the **long position** holder (cf. **cheapest to deliver; wild card option**). The result of this option is to make the futures price trade to the most probable delivery date, that is, the one which is most attractive to the short position with their obligation to make delivery. Factors likely to influence the choice will be whether the underlying is in short supply or earns interest at a rate above or below the allowable timing differences. See **delivery options**.

timing risk. The risk of loss arising from using a hedge which has a different expiry or end date to the **underlying** being hedged. This typically arises in the futures markets where the fixed **expiry** dates do not correspond to the hedging period (cf. **basis; basis risk**).

timing swap. An interest rate swap or cross-currency swap entered into for asset-liability management or hedging purposes. The swap is contracted to be entered into at a predetermined future date. See **deferred swap; forward swap**.

tip. Information.

tip off. To give privileged information expecting this knowledge to be exploited (cf. **insider information**). See **insider dealing**.

titre de créance négociable (TCN) (French). A transferable debt certificate or instrument (cf. **Pfandbriefe**). See **sub-participation**.

titre participatif (Equities; French). Non-voting but profit-sharing securities issued by state-owned firms in France. They have some features in common with **participating preferred stock**.

titresation (French). **Securitization**.

titre subordonné à durée indéterminée (French). An **instantly repackaged perpetual**.

toasted. Slang for losing money. To lose a lot is to be *toasted black*. Also called *taking a hit*.

to bearer. Indicates title passes with presentation of the certificate (cf. **registered security**). See bearer.

Tobin's q. An economic assessment, proposed by James Tobin, that over time the ratio of market value to replacement cost of assets should be equal. See **market-to-book ratio**.

toehold (USA). A strategic stake in a company built up by a **predator** which is less than the 5% required to trigger disclosure and filing with the **Securities and Exchange Commission**.

tōgiri (Derivatives; Japan). **Nearby contract**.

tokkin (Japan). Common **funds** set up to manage the cash surpluses of industrial and commercial corporations with a view to maximizing their returns (cf. **zaitech**). See **mutual fund**.

tokubetsu sankasha (Japan). Special members who have bond dealing permits and are allowed to engage in **bond futures** transactions on the Tokyo Stock Exchange.

Tokyo Commodity Exchange for Industry (TOCOM) (Japan). Tosen Building, 10-8 Nihonbashi Horidomecho 1-chome, Chuo-ku, Tokyo 103 (tel. 81 (0) 3 3661 9191; fax 81 (0) 3 3661 7568, 81 (0) 3 5695 6059). Established on 1 November 1984. Commodities exchange dealing principally in **hard commodities**.

Tokyo Grain Exchange (Japan). Commodity exchange dealing, principally in rice and maize futures.

Tokyo interbank offered rate (TIBOR). The interbank market in Tokyo (cf. **London interbank offered rate**).

Tokyo International Financial Futures Exchange (TIFFE) (Japan). 2-2-2 Otemachi, Chiyoda-ku, Tokyo 100 (tel. 81 (0) 3 3275 2111; fax 81 (0) 3 3275 4840). Established on 25 April 1989.

Tokyo Stock Exchange (TSE) (Japan). 2-1 Nihombashi-Kabuto-cho, Chuo-ku, Tokyo 103 (tel. 81 (0) 3 3666 0141; fax 81 (0) 3 3639 5016). Principal stock exchange in Japan, the other major exchange being the **Osaka Securities Exchange**; it is divided into a first and second section. First section **listed** companies are the largest and market behaviour is measured by the **Nikkei 225 Index**. It also has a derivatives annex for trading Japanese government bond futures and options.

Tokyo Stock Price Index (TOPIX). Capitalization-weighted **index** of all the **common stocks** traded on the first section of the **Tokyo Stock Exchange**. See also **Nikkei 225 Index**.

tolling agreement. A project finance condition that requires one of the parties to the transaction to put a specified amount of material in a set time through the project, thus contributing to the project's revenues (cf. **throughput agreement**).

toll revenue bond (USA). A **municipal bond** where the **principal** and **coupon** are serviced via a toll on the assets built with the funds raised (cf. **revenue bond**). See **moral obligation bond**.

to mark. See **reporting deadlines**.

tombstone. An advertisement that reports a financial transaction. It normally states the borrower's or principal's name and certain terms of the transaction and lists the **managers** and usually the **sub-underwriters**. It does not represent an offer to buy or sell securities or an invitation to participate but is published in order to record the completion of the transaction. It derives its name from the tombstone-like format of the advertisement.

tom/next (tomorrow to the next (business) day). For the **eurocurrency** markets a transaction that has a start date of the next day and a **settlement date** the following day (or the next business day), as opposed to **spot**, which (usually) starts in two business days. A transaction which can be entered into prior to and matures on the same day as spot transactions is useful for adjusting spot **positions** the day after. Since most foreign exchange is quoted for spot settlement, the rate has to be adjusted for the earlier payments; these are called *short dates*. If the US dollar/sterling rate is US$1.4772 and the tom/next quote is at a two point **premium**, then the transaction rate is US$1.4774. Tom/next is sometimes referred to as *tom/spot*, since for transactions involving the Canadian dollar, Mexican peso, and US dollar, the standard settlement date is one business day.

ton. (i) (USA). US$100 million. (ii) Measure of weight. There are various definitions as to what is a ton:

- *long ton*: 2,240 lbs (1,016.046909 kg);
- *short (net ton)*: 2,000 lbs; (907.184 kg);
- *metric ton*: 1,000 kg;
- *freight ton*: usually 40 cubic feet; 1 cubic metre or 1,000 kg;
- *shipping ton*: 40 cubic feet.

tone or **tone of the market.** Participants will want to know the tone of the market in order to best take advantage of trading activity. The market tone may be **firm**, **soft**, **strong**, or **weak** (cf. **colour**).

tontine annuities. A type of closed lifetime annuity structure where the surviving members receive the full interest on the loan pool until the last subscriber is dead. Thus, as members of the scheme die, the amount per subscriber rises.

too big to fail. The existence of an implicit, and sometimes explicit, undertaking by a country's **central bank** that certain of its major financial institutions will not be allowed to become insolvent. The rationale for central banks to provide funds, or compel or persuade other institutions to buy out failing institutions, rests on the difference between the costs of failure and the costs of rescue. The fact that any loss of confidence in a particular institution may spread throughout an entire financial system could prompt central banks to take the view that such key players are worth saving at almost any cost. The difficult judgement to be made, by both the central bankers and those entering into **counterparty risks** with specific institutions, is which banks to protect and which could be let go. This decision would rest on an assessment of whether the damaging side-effects could be contained, or whether the chances of systemic collapse were unacceptably high. The US monetary authority, the **Federal Reserve**, has taken the implied indemnity described so far one stage further and specified a list of institutions it would not be prepared to see fail. This has created a situation in which those banks included in the list said to number eleven, could be tempted into taking types and levels of risk not otherwise contemplated, safe in the knowledge that if things went wrong the institution would not be allowed to collapse. One effect of this could be to distort the stock prices of the 'protected' banks. They would be seen by the market as having a sort of guaranteed minimum **capital** value, such that all the risk would be centred upon the variability of the **dividends**, as compared with the share prices of the banks not included in the list, which would be expected to be depressed because they would bear the sector **business risk**. It is probably reasons such as the fear of systemic failure, and the associated costs of recovery, that have prompted some regulatory authorities to consider **reregulation**. See also **systemic risk**.

top-down investment strategy. See strategic asset allocation.

top out. The state of a market after a bull run. At this point securities are fully valued, or even overvalued, (using) **fundamental analysis** (cf. **full price**).

topping up. A feature of some types of asset-backed securities where the pool of assets may be subject to replacement in the early stages of the life of the security. This arrangement is designed to prevent a too rapid **amortization** of the **principal** that would otherwise take place. See, for instance, **certificates of amortizing revolving debt securities**.

top straddle. See straddle.

top vertical combination. See strangle.

torihiki posts (Japan). Trading posts on the **Tokyo Stock Exchange**. See **specialist**.

Toronto Futures Exchange (TFE) (Canada). The Exchange Tower, 2 First Canadian Place, Toronto, M5X 1J2 (tel. 1 416 947 4487; fax 1 416 947 4772). Established in 1984 (it had operated as a division of the **Toronto Stock Exchange** since 1980).

Toronto Stock Exchange (TSE) (Equities; Canada). The Exchange Tower, 2, First Canadian Place, Toronto, M5X 1J2 (tel. (416) 947 4700; fax (416) 947 4662). It is the largest exchange for Canadian **equities** (cf. **Montreal Exchange**; **Vancouver Stock Exchange**). The key market indices are the Toronto-35 Index and the TSE 300 Composite Index. The exchange has a cross-border link with the **American Stock Exchange**.

Toronto Stock Exchange 300 Composite Index (TSE Composite) (Equities; Canada). Index providing broad market or composite indication of market trends. It is a **value-weighted average** of the largest 300 companies quoted on the **Toronto Stock Exchange** (cf. **New York Composite Index**).

Toronto-35 Index (Equities; Canada). An **index** of the largest, most **liquid**, and most important thirty-five companies quoted on the **Toronto Stock Exchange**. It is used as the **underlying** for **stock index options** and **stock index futures** contracts (cf. **FT-SE 100 Index**).

Toronto 35 Index Participation Units or **Toronto Index Participation (TIPs)** (Canada). Participation **certificates** designed to allow retail investment in a fund designed to track the Toronto-35 Index. In effect a basket stock unit representing a diversified portfolio made up of the components of the Toronto-35 Index. The underlying securities are held in a trust. Options on TIPs are also traded on the **Toronto Stock Exchange**. See also **index tracking; Standard and Poor's depository receipts**.

tosho kabu-ka shisū (Equities; Japan). See **Tokyo Stock Exchange Price Index**.

total asset turnover ratio. The sales or turnover to total assets. See **ratio analysis; current assets**.

total capitalization. See **capitalization; market capitalization**.

total return. The aggregated **coupon** or **dividend** stream, plus reinvested income and change in the market value of a security over a particular period. It is usually divided by its initial price and expressed as an annualized percentage rate of return (cf. **capital gain; interest; yield**). See **estimated total return**.

total return optimization. A portfolio designed to achieve maximum **total return**, subject to constraints such as credit and uncertainty, and **yield curve** projections. See **portfolio optimization**.

total return option. An option which includes provision for the intermediate interest or **dividends** or other value **leakages** to the **underlying** over the life of the option. The payoff **for calls** will include any distributions, that for **puts** will be deducted.

total risk. Systematic risk and **unsystematic risk**. See **modern portfolio theory**.

total volume. The amount of securities traded in a given period. For **technical analysts** this is an important indicator of trends. A price rise (fall) accompanied by a large total volume is more significant than the same price change with low volume (cf. **thin**).

to the buck (USA). In the securities markets a price quote where the offer (asked) price is the next whole number; i.e. $95\frac{31}{32}$ (bid) – 96.00 (offer). A dealer will thus give the quote as *31 to the buck*.

touch. The difference between the best **bid** and best **offer** price amongst all **market-makers** quoting for a particular security (cf. **spread**).

touch option. Type of **barrier option** which is activated/deactivated if the **underlying** touches the **trigger** price or rate.

touch price. The best **bid** and best **offer**.

tout. The process of promoting a security. The need to tout a security suggests it is a difficult sell (cf. **blow-out; story paper**).

town clearing (UK). System allowing same-day or late processing of large commercial payments between selected banks in close proximity (hence the town aspect) beyond the normal cut-off time set by the **clearing** system. Branches which are town clearers have a capital T suffix after their sorting codes.

tracker fund. A fund that is designed to emulate the performance of an index or particular **benchmark** (cf. **indexation**). The term is also used for a notional fund designed to act as a reference point for investment performance evaluation (cf. **duration bogey; strategic asset allocation; tactical asset allocation**). Also known as an *indexed fund*.

tracking. Another term for **index tracking**.

tracking error. (i). The deviation of an **index** fund from the **benchmark** or **index** it is designed to replicate. (ii) Any deviation of a **hedge** from its anticipated performance (cf. **basis risk**).

tradable amount. See **marketable quantity**.

tradable contract. See **exchange-traded; negotiable instrument; novation**.

trade. (i) Colloquial term for a **transaction** (cf. **deal**). (ii) A business or profession. (iii) Another term for commerce. (iv) An exchange.

trade acceptance (USA). A **bill** drawn by one company and accepted by another company which thus undertakes to pay a given sum at a specified future date (cf. **banker's acceptance**). In the UK called a *trade bill* (cf. **credit**).

trade balance. Normally, the difference in value between merchandise exports and merchandise imports (cf. **invisible balance**). Also called the *balance of trade*.

trade bill. See **bill; trade acceptance**.

trade credit. Extended payment terms given by one company to another when selling goods or services; the convention between wholesalers, retailers, and manufacturers of allowing a specified period of time for the **settlement** of a debt after the goods or services have been provided. Normally, 30, 60, or 90 days are the sort of periods of credit agreed. Because the vendor has deferred receipt of payment for a set period (usually 30 days), the company faces a potential **credit risk**. Such exposures need to be managed to avoid overexposing the company to bad debts and to preserve **working capital** (cf. **ageing schedule; trade debt**). Firms which are owed money in this respect are called *trade creditors*. See **supplier credit**.

trade cycle. Regular fluctuations in the level of business activity over a period of years. Expectations about the length of the cycle and whether an economy is on the upward or downward part of the cycle are used in **fundamental analysis**. Also known as the *business cycle*. See **Kondatrieff cycle**.

trade date. The day upon which a deal is made (cf. **settlement date**). Settlement then normally follows the market norm (cf. **delayed delivery; forward**). Also called the *transaction date*.

trade debt. Debts incurred during the normal course of receiving credit when buying raw materials and other inputs into a firm as opposed to money raised to help fund the business, such as loans, bonds, or other fixed claims (cf. **trade credit**). See **accounts receivable**.

traded months. The futures or exchange-traded **options** contract months which are actively being traded (cf. **nearby; furthest month; position**). See **expiry cycle**.

traded option. An option that is itself tradable like a security but on a separate market from its **underlying** (cf. **exchange-traded option**). Such options will have standard terms and conditions in order to improve **liquidity**. See also **warrant**.

trade draft. See **documentary credit**.

trade house or **trading house**. A firm which specializes in middleman trading activities, **turnkey** contracts, and other trading activities rather than manufacturing. Such firms are often active in international trade providing economies of scale for exporters and importers and assuming many of the **risks**.

trade investment. Equity or debt investments made in other companies with a view to accommodating commercial transactions.

trade on top of (USA). Market expression for a **swap** transaction (the sale of one instrument and the purchase of another) at a narrow or nil **basis points** spread.

trader. (i) Strictly speaking, an individual or entity that seeks profit by buying and selling securities rather than holding them for investment purposes. Normally known as a *speculator*. (ii) More generally used to describe a professional market participant who actively facilitates transactions rather than holding investments in his own right. See **market-maker; dealer; specialist; Street**.

trade sale (Mergers and acquisitions). The sale of a company to another firm in the same or related industry (cf. **float**). The trade sale is a common method of exit for **venture capital**-backed firms.

trade-weighted exchange rate. See **dirty float** (cf. **index**).

trade weighting. A technique used in **portfolio** management to ensure that the probability that factors other than the **yield spread** will affect a particular **switch** is minimized. For instance, one result of weighting transactions would be to maintain a constant **duration** for the portfolio.

trading book. (i) The securities held in inventory by a financial intermediary and available for sale to customers; (ii) (Forex). The total long and short positions held by a **market-maker** (cf. **overbought; oversold**). (iii) (Banking). That part of a bank's **asset** portfolio that is expected to be realized over the **short term** and, under banking regulations, has to be **marked-to-market** for **capital adequacy** purposes. The other part is the banking book, which is deemed to be held to **maturity** (cf. **credit equivalent**).

trading dividends (USA). An investment strategy by a corporate entity designed to take advantage of double taxation relief on **dividends** from other companies. It involves buying **stocks cum dividend** and reselling them shortly thereafter when they go **ex-dividend**.

trading floor. See **floor; pit**.

trading halt. (i) A suspension of trading due to the implementation of a **circuit breaker, limit**, or, possibly, some technical breakdown. (ii) The suspension of trading in a particular security as a result of a news announcement to prevent the development of a **false market**.

trading limit. See **limit**.

trading market. See **two-sided market**.

trading models. See **fundamental analysis; program trading; technical analysis**.

trading over the curve (Bonds; USA). Securities that display **yields** above that offered on the US Treasury yield curve (cf. **trading through the curve**).

trading paper. Those **money market** instruments placed with investors who are likely to resell, or trade, any purchased instruments for short-term gains (cf. **profit-taking; spectail**).

trading pattern. The time-series price behaviour of a security, important in **chart** or **technical analysis**. A rising (falling) **trend** would suggest a continuing reappraisal of the value of the security by investors (cf. **resistance** and **support level**). Patterns, such as **flags**, may also be part of the observed behaviour of the series.

trading pit. See pit.

trading post. Position on the floor of an exchange where a **specialist** or **market-maker** stands and securities are traded (cf. **jobber**). Such positions in **exchange-traded options** and **futures** exchanges which use **open outcry** are known as *pits*.

trading profits. (i) (USA). The profits generated by a securities firm from buying and selling securities. They are distinguished from income generated between the cost of funds and the return from holding securities (cf. **net interest income**; **positive carry**). (ii) (UK). A type of profit as defined by the Inland Revenue for taxation purposes. The Revenue divides profits into different Schedules and Cases which affect their tax treatment. Thus Schedule D Case I is profits generated by a firm in the course of its normal activities, while Case VI handles sundry items, such as royalties. Gains from disposing of **assets** are not considered trading profits for tax purposes and fall into Schedule 6. The distinctions are important since the Revenue limits types of offsets that can be claimed against profits not generated in the course of trading. (iii) Profits generated in the normal course of business activity and before certain costs, such as interest, directors' remuneration, audit fees, and so on. See **gross profit**.

trading range. See **price range**.

trading range warrant. A warrant that provides a payoff within specific price or rate parameters or range and nothing if the **underlying** trades outside these limits (cf. **all-or-nothing option**; **digital option**). It is equivalent to a written **condor** where the limiting purchased option positions are set to provide a fixed loss no greater than the purchase price of the package.

trading rotation. A procedure used on exchanges to ensure an orderly market. Normally the procedure is used for establishing the **opening price** of a security or instrument, but it can be used sometimes in volatile market conditions to re-establish the market price after a **limit-up** or **limit-down** has been reached and if activity is very heavy, also at the **close**.

trading the skew. See **volatility skew**.

trading through the curve (Bonds; USA). Securities that display **yields** below that offered on the US Treasury **yield curve** (cf. **trading over the curve**).

trading unit (USA). The number of securities that makes up a **round lot**.

traditional option. Old-fashioned term for **options** which are bilateral contracts between the option buyer and the option **writer**. Generally now referred to as **over-the-counter** options.

traditional split investment trust (UK). See **split investment trust**. Also called a *conventional split investment trust*.

tranche. (i) An additional issue of an existing security which will become **fungible** with the existing security at issue or at a future date (such as the first **coupon** payment date) (cf. **tap**; **taplet**). (ii) Used to describe one part of two or more market operations which have a common **prospectus**, but may differ in detail, such as currency denomination or area of placement (e.g. *international tranche* of a **public offering**), but often offered as a package to investors (cf. **serial security**). (iii) In **certificate of deposit** (CD) and **floating rate certificate of deposit** issues, the term is applied to those issues with identical terms in large blocks of small denominations and distributed world-wide to **retail** or 'small' investors. Sometimes called a *tranche CD*. (iv) A part of a loan or other debt facility which partakes of the same characteristics. (v) An individual advance from a facility which is made available in stages, perhaps when certain conditions have been fulfilled such as the completion of parts of a project or by meeting performance targets. (vi) (Bonds; USA) The name given to the different types of **collateralized mortgage obligations**.

tranchette. A small **tranche**; another word for **taplet**. Also known as a *mini-tap*.

transaction. A purchase or sale made in the markets. This includes the original order by the client, the actual execution by the **broker** or **market-maker**, the subsequent **confirmation** of the details of the order once executed, to be followed on the **value date** by the **settlement** or **clearing** of the payments and transfer of securities or entitlement between the two parties. Also known colloquially as a *deal* or *trade*. See **bad delivery**; **comparison ticket**; **delivery**; **delivery versus payment**; **fail**; **free delivery**; **out-trade**; **partial delivery**; **receive versus payment**; **regular delivery**; **rolling settlement**; **settlement**; **spot settlement**.

transaction costs. Explicit and implicit costs associated with executing a securities transaction.

Explicit costs include **brokerage**, taxes, margin requirements, and so forth. Implicit costs include the costs of research in support of security selection, **risk**, **market impact**, as well as any **opportunity costs** (cf. **free rider**).

transaction date. The date on which a transaction was struck. This will normally be close to or the same as the date on which the transaction was confirmed to the other party, but may be significantly in advance of the actual **settlement date** in the case of **forward** transactions (cf. **comparison ticket**). Also known as the *trade date*.

transaction exposure (Forex). The **risk** that future cash transactions in a currency other than the home currency may be affected by changes in the value of the currencies (cf. **foreign exchange rate risk**).

transaction netting. See **netting**.

transaction risk (Forex). The **currency** or **foreign exchange rate risk** arising from the mismatch in timing between the points when a firm or individual in one currency makes commitments in another currency and payment is made in that currency and when the money is paid or received in the **base currency** (cf. **economic risk**; **translation exposure**).

Trans Canada Options Inc. (TCO) (Canada). **Clearing house** equally owned by the **Montreal Exchange**, **Toronto Stock Exchange**, and the **Vancouver Stock Exchange**.

transfer. (i) Process of moving money from one account to another. Also called *money transfer*. See **clearing**. (ii) (UK). The form signed by a seller giving authorization for the deletion of his name from the security's register and the substitution of that of the buyer (cf. **settlement**).

transferable. See **negotiable instrument**.

transferable credit. A **letter of credit** (LOC) which allows payment to be made to more than one beneficiary. In cases where an agent has acquired goods on behalf of a client, payment must be made to both the supplier and the agent. The transferable letter of credit allows the supplier to be paid against presentation of documents evidencing shipment. These LOCs are sometimes wrongly described as 'divisible', 'assignable', 'fractionable', or 'transmissable'. See **documentary credit**.

transferable loan facility. A clause or method in a loan agreement allowing the lender to transfer the rights and obligations to a third party. The exact conditions under which transfer can take

place may differ, depending on the agreement: some require the consent of the borrower (*transferable loan certificate*); others give full rights of transfer to the lender. In the latter case the loan is normally made with *transferable loan instruments* (TLI) which can be readily negotiated. See also **asset sales**; **participation**; **sub-participation**.

transferable participation certificate. A hybrid method of making **asset sales** incorporating features from both the **transferable loan facility** and **sub-participation** methods.

transferable put right (USA). A tradable right that allows the **stockholder** to put common stock to the issuer on pre-agreed terms. See also **super-stock**.

transferable revolving underwriting facility (TRUF) (Banking). A **revolving underwriting facility** which allows the lenders to transfer their obligations in a manner similar to a **transferable loan facility**. In this case, since no **funds** have been advanced, borrowers have had natural concerns as to the standing of the purchaser of the commitment.

Transfer, Accounting, Lodgement for Investors, Stock Management for Jobbers (TALISMAN) (UK). The automated settlement procedure operated by the **London Stock Exchange** which covers most UK **registered securities**. See **Stock Exchange Pool Nominees**.

transfer agent. See **registrar**.

Transfer and Automated Registration of Uncertificated Stock (TAURUS) (UK). A projected computerized **stock settlement** system for the UK market. The project was abandoned as a result of significant cost overruns and developmental difficulties. See **Crest**.

transfer deed or **form.** Legal document in the form of a deed that transfers ownership from one party to another.

transfer price or **transfer pricing.** Intra-group prices for goods or services. The term is normally applied to cross-border transactions where the relevant tax authorities carefully monitor the prices. The reason is that it is possible for an organization to move profits from a high-tax country to a low-tax country by altering the internal prices of the goods so as to move the value added to the low-tax area. See **unitary taxation**.

transfer risk. The risk from difficulties or restrictions that might arise in seeking to transfer funds from one country to another (cf. **country risk**; **settlement risk**). It is that part of country risk which is concerned with the imposition of **ex-change controls** in a country thus preventing the movement of funds out of a particular country. This risk might be indirect in that it may also apply to foreign currency deposited in the country in question.

transfer tax. See Stamp Duty.

translation exposure (Accounting; Forex). The foreign exchange rate risk associated with having items in a company's **balance sheet** denominated in a foreign **currency** and converting them into the **base currency** for reporting purposes. This is usually associated with the consolidation of foreign subsidiaries in the group accounts of the holding company. The current US standard is Statement of Financial Accounting Standard (SSAP) 52, for the UK, Statement of Standard Accounting Practice (SSAP) 20, and internationally, International Accounting Standard (IAS) No. 21 issued in November 1993.

transnational corporation (TNC). A firm which has global presence, range of markets, production, and/or subsidiaries. See also **multinational corporation**.

transparency. (i) A condition of the markets as to the availability and timely dissemination of price and other relevant information to market participants. The opposite would be *opaque* (cf. **bazaar**). See **efficient markets**. (ii) A feature of organized exchanges where their regulated methods of matching and reporting transactions ensure that market participants have accurate information on market prices (cf. **tape**). See **market-maker; limit book; limit order board; open outcry; opening rotation; over the counter; specialist**.

transplant. Factory or production unit set up by a parent company in a foreign country to manufacture the same items as in its domestic market. Firms set up such satellite units for a variety of reasons; to improve competitiveness, to overcome tariff barriers, to ease trade frictions, and/or to reduce a variety of business exposures or risks.

transportation costs. A factor in futures pricing involving the cost of assuring **physical delivery** of the **underlying** to the contract. In most financial futures markets other than **commodities** it is not a material factor in setting prices. See **cost of carry**.

treasurer. The individual in an organization with designated responsibility for managing the **financial** aspects of the organization. Smaller firms may combine the management position of Finance Director with that of Treasurer, larger firms

would split these responsibilities, with the Treasurer responsible for day-to-day activities and the Finance Director for policy.

treasurer's check (USA). A cheque issued by a bank to make a payment (cf. **banker's draft**).

treasuries (USA). Generic term used for traded federal government debt backed by its **full faith and credit**. There are three principal categories:

- *Treasury bills*: Discount securities with maturities of up to one year. Interest is calculated on a 360-day year. Prices are quoted on a **discount** basis.
- *Treasury notes*: Coupon securities with original maturities between one and ten years. Typical issue maturities are two, five, and seven years.
- *Treasury bonds*: Coupon securities with original maturities in excess of ten years.

For both **bonds** and **notes**, interest is calculated semi-annually on an actual/actual basis (cf. **interest rate calculations**). In the secondary market, prices are quoted in relation to **par**, with quotes going as fine as $\frac{1}{64}$th of 1%. See also **US Treasury market**.

Treasury, The (UK). The department of state, headed by the Chancellor of the Exchequer, responsible for the government's finances, including setting the annual **budget** and any borrowing (cf. **public sector borrowing requirement**).

treasury bill (T-bill) (Money markets). A government **short-term** non-interest debt instrument, normally issued at a **discount**, which can have different methods of issue; for example **tender** and **auction**. Maturities are normally less than one year. In some cases, for instance the US T-bill market, new issues are normally made **fungible** with existing **seasoned** supply issued with a longer **original maturity**. Central banks often use T-bills to undertake **open-market operations**. See **bill; commercial paper; promissory notes; US Treasury market**.

treasury bill futures (USA). Short-term interest rate futures contract where the **underlying** instrument is a US government **treasury bill** with a 90-, 91-, or 92-day **maturity** and a face value of US$1 million.

treasury bill option (USA). An **option** that gives the holder the right to buy, if a **call**, or sell, if a **put**, a US government **treasury bill** with a 91-day maturity and a face value of US$1 million at a specific price.

treasury bill rate. The interest rate obtained by buying a treasury bill and holding it to **maturity**. It is seen as the safest short-term investment that can be made. In times of financial crisis, there may be a **flight to quality** which can be seen in a widening of the **spread** relationship between treasury bills and commercial obligations, such as **interbank deposits** (cf. **treasury-eurodollar spread**). See **risk-free rate**.

treasury bond. (i) (UK). Some **gilt-edged** securities have this in their title but it has no significance for the investor. (ii) (USA). A **bond** issued by the government with an original maturity of ten years or longer (cf. **treasury bill; treasury note**). See also **US Treasury market**.

treasury bond futures (USA). Long-term interest rate futures contract where the **underlying** instruments deliverable into the **contract** are US government **treasury bonds** (cf. **options on futures**).

treasury bond option (USA). An **option** giving the holder the right to buy, if a **call**, or sell, if a **put**, a **treasury bond**.

treasury certificate (USA). Used by the **Federal Reserve** and issued to member banks to signify surplus balances held by the US **central bank**. Such certificates are **eligible**. Sometimes referred to as a *certificate of indebtedness*.

treasury-eurodollar spread (TED Spread) (USA). (i) The **spread** relationship between the **treasury bill futures contract** and the same **expiry** futures contract traded on **eurodollar interbank deposits**. The differential reflects market participants' views and concerns about the relative attractions of commercial versus default-free assets (cf. **flight to quality**). (ii) It can also be taken to be a **spread** strategy involving a long (short) position in one **contract** held together with a short (long) position in the other aimed at making a profit on a change in the relationship between the two (cf. **inter-commodity spread**).

treasury-indexed notes (Bonds; USA). A synthetic **security** offered by Morgan Stanley which offered an **index-linked** return and was collateralized by US **treasury bonds**.

treasury investment growth receipt (TIGER; TIGR) (Bonds; USA). A form of **strip** where the **coupon** payments and **principal** on a US Treasury security were repackaged by Merrill Lynch to trade as separate **zero-coupon bonds** (cf. **certificates of accrual on Treasury securities; zero-coupon eurosterling bearer or registered accruing securities**). Now largely replaced by the more liquid **separate trading of registered interest and principal of securities** issued by the US Treasury itself. Also known as *money multipliers*. See **corpus**

Treasury receipts; coupon Treasury receipt; physical strip; reconstitution.

treasury management system. A position reporting and transaction tracking system used for treasury management purposes to monitor positions and report exposures. Such systems can also be linked to the firm's accounts via **real-time** reporting.

treasury note (Bonds; USA). A US government **coupon** security with a maturity of not less than two years or not more than ten years (cf. **treasury bill; treasury bond**). See **US Treasury market**.

treasury note futures (USA). Intermediate interest rate futures contracts where the **deliverable** securities are US government **treasury notes**, that is securities with between a two-and ten-year **maturity**.

treasury receipt (TR) (Bonds; USA). A **zero-coupon** certificate issued in respect of **principal** payments on particular **US Treasury** securities and as such a direct obligation of the federal government. No payments are made on TRs before the **maturity** of corresponding principal or **coupon** payments on the **underlying** Treasury security. See **corpus Treasury receipt; coupon Treasury receipt; physical strip; separate trading of registered interest and principal of securities; zero-coupon bonds**.

treasury stock or **treasury shares.** (i) (USA). The name given to **issued shares** held by a company but not cancelled as a result of a **share repurchase**. Such stock is available for reissue or to service the **exercise** of **warrants** of executive **stock option** plans. While held by the corporation's treasury, such **stock** receives no **dividends**, carries no votes, and is excluded for **ratio analysis** purposes. (ii) In the UK, one of the terms for **gilt-edged** issues. The other is *Exchequer*. The titles have no special significance other than helping to distinguish the different issues.

treasury tax and loan account (TT&L account) (USA). An account held by the US Treasury with a commercial bank. The Treasury has an account with the **Federal Reserve**, but to avoid disruptions to the money supply, the Treasury holds some of its balances with commercial banks.

Treaty of Rome. Legal basis for the setting up of the **European Community** (now the **European Union**).

trees. See **binomial tree**.

trend. The general behaviour of a security price or market. A rising (falling) trend is the same as a bull (bear) market, although the latter is generally reserved for longer-term overall market conditions and individual **asset** prices usually are said to follow trends.

trending quotes. Anticipatory changes in a dealer's **quote** to reflect expected changes in the **asset**, instrument, security, or **commodity's** price trend.

trendline. A chart or **technical analysis** method used to plot **resistance** or **support level** points over time within a **trend**. It involves a line on a chart showing the direction of movement in the asset or rate, drawing lines from the high and low points of the series. It is drawn under a rising price trend and above a falling one at the lowest or highests points respectively. From the chartists' point of view, it needs to have a minimum of three points to count (cf. **rising bottoms**). Any behaviour which does not conform to the expected pattern is deemed to be significant.

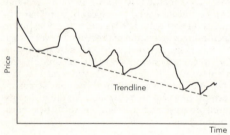

trendline

See breakout; momentum indicator; moving average.

Treuhandanstalt or **Treuhand** (Germany). Federal agency charged with the privatization of the former East German state industries.

Treuhandler (German). Trustee.

Treynor index. A measure of the return earned for assuming risk (cf. **risk–reward**). It is the asset's excess return above the **risk-free rate** divided by the asset's beta (β_a):

$$TI = \frac{(R_a - R_f)}{\beta_a}$$

where R_a is the rate of return on the individual asset; R_f the risk-free rate.

triangle pattern. A pattern in security price movements identified by **chart analysis**. It implies that movements are initially fairly **volatile** but subsequently buyers and sellers become more evenly matched. Chartists claim that the price is likely to move violently up or down. See **flag**; **head and shoulders**; **line patterns**; **pennant**.

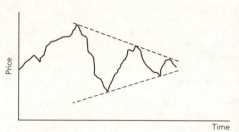

Triangle pattern

triangular arbitrage (Forex). A three-way transaction in currencies designed to exploit misalignments between currencies and their **cross-rates**.

triangular transaction. (i) (Forex). The purchase of one currency by trading two others. This is common for less liquid currencies where, for instance, a transaction between French francs and Chilean pesos would involve first an exchange of francs for US dollars and then the re-exchange for pesos. Also known as a *cross-trade*. (ii) A commercial transaction which involves an exchange between party A and party B, who trades then with party C, who in turn trades with A.

trigger. The event which will bring a **contingent** instrument, provision, or condition into (or out of) effect (cf. **event of default**). See **knock-in**.

trigger option. See **barrier option** (cf. **digital option**).

trigger price. The price at which a **barrier option** is either knocked in or knocked out.

trigger rate. The rate stated in a **drop-lock** issue to which the **reference rate** must fall before the issue becomes **fixed rate**.

trigger swap. See **curve-lock swap**.

Trinidad and Tobago Stock Exchange (Trinidad and Tobago). 65 Independence Square, Port of Spain, TT-Trinidad WI (tel. 1 809 625 5107; fax 1 809 623 0089).

trinomial tree. A variation on the **binomial distribution** which provides for three possible outcomes: unchanged, a rise, or a fall. Such refinements are used for determining the probability distributions of **exotic options**.

triple-A. (i) An entity awarded the highest available **credit rating**. (ii) General term derived from the credit rating scale applied to entities with a very high **credit worthiness**, although these entities do not have a formal rating.

triple nine (Commodities). 99.9% purity (cf. **assay**). See **contract grade**.

triple tax exempt (Bonds; USA). Exemption from federal, state, and local taxes on **municipal bonds** by persons domiciled within the jurisdiction of the issuer. Note that exemption from federal taxes is available to all holders, regardless of geographic location, if the issue is a **public purpose bond**.

triple witching hour (USA). The highly volatile and abnormal trading conditions that occurred when **stock index futures**, their related **options**, and exchange-traded **stock options** all **expired** at the same time during the last hour of the trading session (cf. **backwardation; crossed market; double witching hour**). This happened every third Friday of March, June, September, and December. The **expiry dates** of stock index contracts were adjusted to reduce the impact of this triple expiry on the **underlying** cash market.

troc (French). **Foreign exchange swap**.

trombone issue (Equities; UK). Name given to a two-stage, flexible **rights** issue by British Aerospace as part of its contested **takeover bid** for VSEL. It differs from a conventional rights issue in two respects. First, there is a fixed minimum amount that will be raised via the rights offer; second, after approval by shareholders, the company will be able to raise a further amount up to a predetermined total. This slide (or trombone) quality to the rights issue allows the company the flexibility to raise sufficient funds to negotiate the takeover successfully without having to return continually to **shareholders** to obtain permission for further **share** issues.

trough. A low in a price series (cf. **peak**). In the business cycle the point between recession and recovery.

troy ounce (Commodities). The weight unit for precious metals, particularly gold. Prices of these **commodities** are reported in relation to one troy ounce. It is equal to 31.1035 grams. It is also 480 grains, each grain being 0.0648 grams.

true and fair view. A requirement in an auditor's report that the set of accounts or **financial statements** are true, in that there are no falsehoods, and fair, in that the result accurately reports the condition it wishes to portray.

true lease (USA). A lease agreement that is accepted by the US Internal Revenue Service and where payments are deductable for tax purposes (cf. **tax shield**).

trust. (i) An agreement by which a **trustee** is appointed by a borrower for its issue of securities in order to interpose a neutral third party between it and the security holders, and which sets out the terms of the securities, the powers of the trustee, and provides for the holding of meetings. In the US it is known as an *indenture.* Typically the document will specify: type and amount of the issue; **collateral**, if any; **covenants**; features of the issue, such as **put** or **call provisions; redemption price; sinking fund**, if any; and other material facts. The document drawing up the trust is called the *trust deed.* (ii) A legal arrangement allowing **assets** to be held by one person, known as the *trustee* on behalf of some other entity, person, or persons, known as the *beneficiaries*, for their benefit. Under trust law, the trustee is the legal owner of the property but the beneficiaries have an equitable interest in the assets. Trust arrangements are common where it would be inappropriate (for instance in a family trust where the beneficiaries are minors) or unwieldy (as with a company pension scheme) for the beneficiaries to hold the assets direct (cf. **unit trust**).

trust account guaranteed investment contract. See **guaranteed investment contract**.

trust bank (Japan). A category of bank in Japan which acts both in a commercial capacity and also as a **trustee**. Typically **bond** issuers will appoint a trust bank to advise on an issue.

trust corporation (Banking; USA). State-chartered financial institution that can undertake banking activities. Sometimes called a *non-bank bank*.

trust deed. The document setting out the terms under which a **trust** is established.

trustee. (i) An individual or institution appointed by a borrower or security holder to represent his interests. See **covenant; indenture**. (ii) The manager of a trust.

trustee status (UK). Those securities which meet the requirements of the 'wider range' investments as defined by the Trustee Investments Act, 1961. See also **investment grade**.

trust fund. A fund which holds the assets of a trust (cf. **portfolio**).

Trust Indenture Act of 1939 (USA). Principal legislation governing the role and process for trustees in the United States. Most **bond** issues use a trustee and therefore come under the conditions of the legislation. For instance, changes to core conditions of bonds may require the consent of all bondholders, although a simple **majority** is needed to modify 'non-core' protective **covenants** (cf. **exit consent solicitation**).

trust letter (Banking). A document which makes over **assets**, typically saleable goods or finished inventory, as **collateral** to a loan (cf. **lien**). See **trust receipt**.

trust obligation participating securities (TOPS) (Bonds). A **synthetic security** issued in 1987 in the form of a **floating rate note**. This was created by holding in a **special purpose vehicle** (SPV) Kingdom of Denmark fixed rate bonds as **collateral** and to provide the fixed rate payment flow on an **interest rate swap** in which the SPV paid fixed and received floating.

trust obligation participating securities 2 (TOPS 2) (Bonds). A similar structure to TOPS, except that the **underlying** were **ex-warrant** Japanese corporate, bank-guaranteed **bonds** with (equity) warrant issues.

trust receipt. A form of commercial guarantee promissory note provided by a firm to a bank in order to have the documents of title, held by the bank as surety, released, so that the goods may be received into the firm's possession without it paying for them. Typically this may happen if the firm needs to warehouse the merchandise but cannot repay the credit that is financing the purchase. It is also called a *letter of hypothecation* or *trust letter*.

Truth in Lending Act of 1969 (USA). Consumer protection legislation which provides *inter alia* a **cooling-off period** for any agreements and details of interest and other charges as well as the **annual percentage rate** that is applicable.

tunnel. An alternative term for a **vertical spread**, usually applied to **interest rate caps** and **floors** (cf. **cylinder**).

tunnel option. Interest rate collars with the same **strike price** and non-overlapping periods on the **underlying** interest rate.

turbo. See **long bond yield decrease warrant** (cf. **spread**; **sycurve option**).

turkey. Market jargon used to describe a poorly performing investment (cf. **dog**; **taking a bath**; **taking a hit**). (ii) A poorly performing business unit or firm which is restructured so as to make it an attractive buying opportunity.

turn. The difference between the **bid** and **offer** prices quoted by an individual **market-maker** (cf. **spread**). See **touch**.

turnaround. (i) Used to describe the purchase and sale of securities with **settlement** taking place on the same day (cf. **daytime trading**; **scalper**). (ii) The restoring to health of a company which has been making losses or is performing badly. A **stock** of such a business is known as a *recovery stock*.

turnkey. (i) An event or specified clause that will **trigger** the start or the next state of, for example, a **project finance** transaction. (ii) Where the involvement of a **name** in a transaction is required before others are prepared to participate. See **lead manager**.

turnover. (i) In **portfolio management**, the amount of trading relative to the value of the portfolio. (ii) In market terms, the **volume of business** in a security or the whole of the market, or the number of securities or contracts that have been dealt in on a given day or period. Sometimes computed as the number of items transacted times their value. Also known as *trading volume*. (iii) In the UK, the total sales by a business during the reporting period. Also known as *sales*.

turnover ratio. (i) Total sales to **net worth**. (ii) **total volume** to total market capitalization.

turnround rate. The cost of a **round trip** in the **commodities markets**, including both **brokerage** and **clearing** fees.

turtle spread (USA). A type of **arbitrage** using **futures** based on taking opposing positions in two different **expiry date treasury bond futures** contracts and a position in a **Treasury Bill Futures** contract. The rationale is that the two bond futures contracts are misaligned and therefore provide a **risk-free** gain, while the T-bill future locks in the implied forward rate, thus guaranteeing the arbitrage.

twenty-day period (USA). See **cooling-off period**.

twenty-four-hour trading. A practice of some markets, such as **currencies**, to be open to transactions round the clock. As the day progresses, different time zones become the centre of trading and the centre of activity moves around the globe, providing active markets throughout a twenty-four hour period. In practice, trading is centred on three areas: the Pacific rim, in particular Tokyo, Hong Kong, and Singapore, then Europe, and finally the USA; the Far East then starts the cycle again. Major financial institutions will have offices in these centres and arrange for their clients to be able to transact business at any time of the day by contacting the appropriate office. In addition, such firms will arrange to pass orders and positions from one centre to the next.

Twin Cities Board of Trade (TCBOT) (Commodities; USA). Joint Minneapolis and Minnesota exchange founded in 1988 by the then Minneapolis Grain Exchange.

twisting (USA). Term for getting a client to make unnecessary trades in order to generate **commissions**. When the **broker** has discretion on the account, it is known as *churning*. Such a practice is unethical and, sometimes, illegal.

two-dollar broker (USA). Name for a **floor broker** who executes transactions for other **brokers**. A rough equivalent to an **inter-dealer broker**.

two-sided market or **two-way market.** (i) A market where **two-way** prices are quoted (cf. **buyers over; sellers over**). (ii) Sometimes taken to mean a market where there is a good flow of buying and selling activity (cf. **overbought; oversold**). (iii) An obligation on **market-makers** or **dealers** on some exchanges to make two-way quotes during market hours in a minimum quantity of the securities for which they are registered to act as market-makers.

two-state option pricing model. See **binomial option pricing model; option pricing**.

two-tier market. A type of **foreign exchange** or interest rate system operated in some countries where the rates depend on the end use or activity. For instance, there may be a tourist and a commercial **exchange rate** in force in some countries, or a financial and commercial rate. Usually one is a free market, while the other is subject to official intervention or regulation. Belgium operated such a system with commercial and financial Belgian francs having different exchange rates, likewise South Africa, with a commercial and a financial rand rate.

two-tier tender offer (USA). A type of **takeover** where **shareholders** are made an initial offer for a (usually) controlling interest in the **target** together with a second offer for the remaining **minority interest**, usually on inferior terms (cf. **two-tier tender offer**). Shareholders are encouraged to accept the first **bid** rapidly by the threat of only being part of the second offer. It is an illegal method of bidding for a company in some jurisdictions (for instance, the UK). See **mergers and acquisitions**.

two-tone preferred stock. A type of **convertible preferred stock** which is convertible into the **common stock** of a different company.

two-way margining. A system of collateralizing **positions** at a **clearing house** or with a **counterparty** where both sides agree to add **margin** to the position if the **marked-to-market** value should move against them (cf. **initial margin; maintenance margin**). This reduces **credit risk** in that the **replacement cost** of the position is largely eliminated since, if one party fails to perform, the counterparty can use the **collateral** from the margin account to offset losses incurred from replacing the position. A variant of the process has one side, the lesser credit, provide collateral to the higher credit quality counterparty and is known as *unilateral margining*.

two-way market. See **two-sided market**.

two-way price. Where **market-makers** quote both **bid** and **offer** prices or rates for immediate execution and in **marketable quantities**.

type of option. The distinguishing characteristics of an **option**, such as whether it is a **call** or a **put**, **American-style** or **European-style**, and so forth.

U

uberrima fides (Latin: in utmost good faith). A condition of certain types of contract, for instance, the provision of insurance cover. The benefiting party is required to disclose all material facts that may affect the value of the contract, whether requested to or not. Failure to supply such information or the provision of false information may nullify the contract.

ultimo. The end of the month or end of the year.

ultra vires (Latin: beyond the powers). Literally, outside authority. Term used for actions or contracts made by individuals, officials, and corporations for which there is no authority and which are outside their legal power, which may render them null and void (cf. **safe harbour**). See **Hammersmith and Fulham swaps**.

umbrella fund. See fund of funds.

unamortized discounts (Bonds; USA). The difference between the **par value** or redemption amount and the amount received on the security when issued. A **discount** has to be **written off** as a cost.

unamortized premiums (Bonds; USA). The difference between the **par value** or redemption amount and the amount invested in a security when purchased. A **premium** has to be **written off**.

unbundled stock unit (USU) (Equity; USA). Proposal by Shearson Lehman to disaggregate the returns on **common stocks** into three components: a **bond** with a **coupon** equal to the current **dividend**; a **preferred stock** which would pay out in dividends any increases in the firm's dividend flow; and a **warrant** on the capital value of the stock. The idea was to allow holders of the original stock to choose which elements of the package to invest in, investors seeking capital growth selecting a greater weight in the warrants while investors seeking immediate income would seek a larger proportion in the bond units. The concept was never put into practice due to regulatory objections. The concept is seen in modified form in **equity-linked note** structures.

unbundling. (i) To take apart the components of a position, security, or other asset, usually with the intention of disposing of part or all the parts separately at a higher price than the whole (cf. **stripping**). (ii) Selling off non-core activities of a business with a view to increasing the focus or profitability of the retained portion. This is also known as *bifurcation*. When this is the result of a **takeover**, it is also called *asset stripping*.

uncalled capital. Stocks or shares that a company is allowed to issue, but has not. Can sometimes mean the unpaid portion of **partly paid** stocks. Also known as *reserve capital*. See **authorized capital**.

uncertainty. Arises when decisions have to be made about the future where it is not possible to assign probabilities to the various outcomes. Often used as a synonym for **risk**.

uncertificated. See book-entry securities.

uncommitted. Any facility or transaction that is of a **best efforts** nature only. With such an arrangement the party due to perform under the agreement is not legally obligated. Uncommitted facilities are common in banking where a bank is interested in demonstrating a willingness to undertake transactions with a potential customer (cf. **advised line of credit**). They also exist in securities markets where **dealers** and **agents** are willing to search out customers but offer no guarantee that transactions will actually take place (cf. **commercial paper**). See also **committed; line of credit**.

unconditional. The situation in a **takeover** where the acquiring company has over 50% of the **acceptances** from **shareholders**.

unconfirmed. (i) A banker's acceptance, bill of exchange, documentary credit or letter of credit which has yet to be confirmed by the accepting bank (cf. **acceptance**). See **confirmed and irrevocable**. (ii) A transaction due for **settlement** or **delivery** where the details have yet to receive **confirmation** from the **counterparty** or the **clearing house** (cf. **comparison ticket; fail; out trade**).

unconfirmed letter of credit or **credit** (Banking). See confirmed letter of credit.

uncovered call. See naked call writing.

uncovered interest arbitrage. A form of arbitrage involving switching funds through the foreign exchange market from a currency with a low interest rate to one with a higher interest rate without doing the corresponding reversing forward transaction. When this forward is undertaken, the technique is known as **covered interest arbitrage.**

uncovered option. See naked option.

uncovered position (Forex). A long or short position in a currency where no offsetting transaction has been made. Also called a *naked position*. See also foreign exchange rate risk; open interest.

uncovered put. See naked put.

uncovered sale. See naked option.

uncovered writer. See naked option.

undated. A security which has no definite maturity date, but may be redeemed at the discretion of the issuer. Sometimes undated issues can be converted into a redeemable or fixed maturity issue by the holder subject to some penalty, usually a lower coupon and a delay in redemption (cf. remarketing agent). Often known as *irredeemables* or *perpetuals*. See one-way stock option.

underbanked (Bonds; USA). A situation where a lead manager has difficulty in putting together an underwriting syndicate (cf. bought deal).

underbooked. A condition of a new issue when there is little investor interest. That is, the lead manager is having difficulty building a book (cf. book building; circling; ringing interest).

undercapitalized. (i) A company whose assets are considered to be worth less than its issued capital. (ii) A company that cannot generate enough earnings to meet its debt commitments or fixed charges (cf. financial distress; restructuring). (iii) A condition where a firm is thought to have insufficient capital of all types. It may need fresh injections of both working capital and fixed capital. See overtrading.

under futures. The situation when the cash price is lower than the futures price. Also known as *contango* or a premium market.

underlying or **underlying asset, commodity, future,** or **security.** The asset that an option, forward, future, or warrant has the contractual right to buy or sell (cf. derivative). Sometimes called *cash* or *cash instrument*, hence *underlying cash instrument*. For exotic options, it can be the relationship between two or more assets times a

notional factor (cf. rainbow option). See also cash-settled; notional principal.

underlying debt (Bonds; USA). A municipal bond market term for the responsibilities of a superior authority towards the indebtedness of sub-authorities within their jurisdiction.

underlying equivalent. See synthetic.

underlying tenor. The interest period in an agreement. Typically, this follows money market practice.

underpricing. The issuance of securities below their market value (cf. discount).

under reference. A transaction between two counterparties which cannot be agreed until the terms and conditions are referred back to one of the party's principals for acceptance.

under-subscribed or **under-subscription.** When a new issue or auction of securities fails to attract enough buyers in the primary market to sell all the securities on offer (cf. allotment; initial public offer; scale down; secondary distribution; tender). See underwriting.

undertaking for collective investments in transferable securities (UCITS) (Europe). An open-ended collective investment vehicle, established by a European Community Directive in December 1985 (cf. fonds commun de placement; mutual fund; open-ended investment companies; société d'investissement à capital variable; unit trust). In order for such funds to raise money from the public they must be authorized by the relevant regulator in the country in which they are based. UCITS must invest the bulk (90%) in quoted securities, or new issues which will be quoted within the next twelve months. In addition, the bid and offer price for units must not diverge significantly from the net asset value of the fund (cf. single pricing).

undervalued. Usually used to describe a security, rather than a market, whose price is considered to be lower than that indicated by fundamental analysis (cf. overvalued).

under water. A transaction showing a loss when compared to market values (cf. book gain; marked-to-market).

underwrite. (i) (Securities). An undertaking to buy unsubscribed securities on a given date at a particular price, thus guaranteeing the full proceeds to the borrower, less transaction costs, including an underwriting fee paid to the underwriter (cf. best efforts; bought deal; sub-underwriter). (ii) (Insurance). An agreement to provide an insurance policy against a **risk** for a **fee**, known as a **premium** (cf. **pure risk**).

underwriter. (i) Generally, a member of a new issue **syndicate** who is invited to **sub-underwrite** the issue but does not participate as a **manager** (cf. **primary underwriter**). In the **euronote** and **certificate of deposit** markets, applied to those banks and institutions that undertake to buy such instruments throughout the life of the **facility**. Underwriters receive a **fee**, irrespective of whether they are required to buy securities, and if they do take securities it is usually at a **discounted** price. This is said to be needed in order to ensure an **aftermarket** for the securities. (ii) A person willing to assume a **risk** in exchange for a **premium**. Hence a *writer* of an **option**, that is, the person who sells the option and therefore assumes the risk that it will be **exercised**. (iii) In the insurance market a party which accepts an insurance risk in exchange for a premium. The term is derived from this insurance use and comes from the practice of the party accepting the risk writing their name (thus entering into the contract) under the amount they insured.

underwriting. (i) The process of providing a purchase guarantee in a financial transaction. Typically, the transaction is a major undertaking such as a **new issue** or an **initial public offering** where the issuer is concerned about the reception of the issue and obtaining the required funds (cf. **best efforts**; **seasoned new issue**; **secondary distribution**). The issuer pays a fee to the **underwriters**. (ii) Providing insurance against loss (cf. **pure risk**). (iii) (Banking). Any **facility** which has a commitment to advance funds to a borrower, hence an *underwritten facility* (cf. **loan facility**; **note issuance facility**). Also known as a *committed facility* (cf. **uncommitted facility**). (iv) Taking a **risk** in return for a payment (cf. **premium**).

underwriting agreement. The contract between the **underwriters** or **managers** and the issuer giving the terms of the issue and stating the legal and commercial obligations of each of the underwriters or managers of the issue (cf. **purchase agreement**). Also called a *subscription agreement*. See also **selling group**.

underwriting commitment. The portion of an issue that an **underwriter** has agreed to underwrite (cf. **severally but not jointly**; **jointly and severally**).

underwriting fee or **underwriting commission.** The fee for **underwriting**, calculated as a flat percentage of the amount of securities or funds underwritten, to which **underwriters** are entitled pro rata to the nominal amount they

underwrite (cf. **management fee**; **participation fee**). Known as the *gross spread* in the USA.

underwriting premium. The payment received by an **underwriter** when providing an insurance policy (cf. **premium**).

underwriting risk. The risk that an **underwriter** will be required to perform when **underwriting**. If the underwriter is called upon, then it means that the risk has not paid off since the transaction, if securities, has failed in the market-place or, if insurance, a loss has been sustained. Establishing the risk of loss is a key requirement for any underwriter.

underwriting spread. See **underwriting fee**.

underwriting syndicate. A group of institutions that act together to share, or syndicate, an **underwriting risk** (cf. **purchase agreement**). See **underwriting agreement**.

underwritten enhanced scrip dividend alternative (UESDA) (Equities; UK). Structure first used by Cadbury Schweppes to reduce the cost of funding in an acquisition. See **enhanced scrip dividend**.

underwritten facility (Banking). A funding method where the lending institution is only expected to provide funds if the borrower cannot raise funds elsewhere (cf. **multi-option financing facility**; **note issuance facility**; **revolving underwriting facility**; **short-term note issuance facility**). See **committed facility**.

underwritten offering. See **purchase and sale**.

undigested (USA). Market term for that part of a new issue remaining with the **underwriters** and thus not **distributed** (cf. **visible supply**). See **seasoned**.

undistributable reserves. See **capital reserves**.

undistributed profit. See **retained earnings**.

undiversifiable risk. See **market risk** (cf. **nonsystematic risk**; **residual risk**; **specific risk**; **stock specific risk**; **unique risk**).

undo. To reverse a transaction or unwind a position.

undue influence. Pressured selling or persuasion on a party to enter into a contract which is not in their best interests and, if properly counselled, would not be entered into. Many of the provisions of regulation in the financial sector aim to prevent such an approach leading to individuals making unsuitable investments (cf. **widows and orphans**). See **rules of fair practice**.

unencumbered. An asset which has no lien.

unfranked income. See franked income (cf. **fixed charge; floating charge**).

unfunded debt. Debt with a **maturity** of less than one year (cf. **current liabilities**).

Ungeregelter Freiverkehr (Germany). Literally unregulated and free market. The unofficial market for non-quoted securities.

unified budget (UK). Name given to the new-style **budget** in which both the income and expenditure elements are laid out, which is, presented in the autumn of the year prior to the start of the new fiscal year in the following April.

Unified Clearing Group (USA). Association of major exchanges set up to share information about major exposures in their respective markets designed to avoid **systemic risk**.

uniform customs and practice for documentary credits (Banking). A standard code of practice for **documentary credit** business prepared by the International Chamber of Commerce, Paris. See also **banker's acceptance; bill; letter of credit**.

Uniform Partnership Act (USA). The legal rules governing the formation and management of partnerships. See **general partner; limited partner; master limited partnership**.

uniform practice code (USA). Transaction and settlement standards and rules for the **over-the-counter** market as laid down by the **National Association of Securities Dealers**.

uniform price auction. A type of **dutch auction** in which all the bidders receive an allocation at the same price. Bidders make competitive bids aimed at securing the best price, but the securities are allocated on the basis of the clearing price required to fill the last bid needed to have the issue fully subscribed. All bidders who tendered above the cut-off point are allocated securities pro rata to their bids, irrespective of the price or rate at which they bid, as long as their bids fall within the parameters of the accepted bids. For instance, in the dutch auction, all bidders who bid above the level required to satisfy the amount on offer will receive their allocation at the lowest price required to cover the offered amount. Any excess of bids at the minimum price is appropriately scaled down in proportion to the amount bid. Some auction processes, such as new issues or bond issues, further require that any single bidder be limited to a maximum percentage of the total amount on offer. See also **auction; competitive auction; English auction**.

uniform securities agent state law examination (USA). A test of proficiency in investment required to be passed to become an **account executive** in many states (cf. **General Securities Representative Examination**).

unilateral margining. A requirement by a low credit standing party involved with an **over-the-counter derivative** contract to provide **margin** to the **counterparty** to **collateralize** its performance under the agreement (cf. **two-way margining**). The margining system involves the **marked-to-market** of the value of the contract to the counterparty and a payment into an account, as with exchange-traded **futures**, to cover any potential losses through **default**.

unilateral relief. Reduction in the tax burden by one tax authority from foreign sourced profit which has already paid tax even if there is no tax treaty with the foreign country. See **double taxation** (cf. **unrelieved advance corporation tax**).

unincorporated. A form of business organization which is not in corporate form. This can either be a **sole proprietorship** or via a **partnership** (cf. **limited partner; master limited partnership**). See also **unlimited company; unlimited liability**.

uninsurable risk. A low-frequency but potentially high-loss situation where the insurance underwriter is unable to determine the probability of loss and therefore is unwilling to write such a policy. Traditionally, Lloyd's of London has specialized in extending cover to risks the general insurance market has considered uninsurable. Sometimes also called a *unique risk*. See **pure risk**.

unique risk. Risks pertaining to an asset, security, or firm that are diversifiable. See **market risk; modern portfolio theory; specific risk; stock specific risk; unsystematic risk**.

unissued stock or **unissued shares.** Shares that have been authorized but which have not been issued by the company. Not to be confused with **treasury stock**. It is the amount of **equity** that a company is **authorized** by its **charter** or **articles of incorporation** to issue but has not issued (cf. **issued shares**).

unit. (i) (UK). A share in a **portfolio**. See **unit trust**. (ii) Any of a range of financial instruments where the issuer is not itself the end user of the funds or the **underlying** assets have been modified in some way, or are held in trust for the (unit) holder. Also known as a *receipt* or a *certificate*. See, for instance, **American depository receipts**; **repackaged security**; **synthetic security**. (iii) A package of securities sold as one. The components of the package may be later unbundled in most cases (cf. **stapled security**).

unitary pricing. See **single pricing**.

unitary taxation. A method of assessing the activities of international firms operating in a tax jurisdiction which apportions the taxable liability on profits on the basis of their whole operations rather than restricted to the subsidiary or activities within the tax jurisdiction. The unitary tax approach seeks to relate the amount payable to the ratio of factors such as assets, turnover, employees, and so forth within the jurisdiction rather than the declared profits. Proponents of unitary taxation believe that this system means that international firms cannot manipulate their tax liability via transfer pricing strategies. Unitary taxation is sometimes known as *world-wide combination taxation*.

unit auction. Action of a specific asset, for instance a company, a concession, or other indivisible item (cf. **share auction; winner's curse**).

unit banking. A legal requirement that a bank may only have one physical location and is not allowed to open other branches. The requirement has generally fallen out of favour with regulators. The collapse of Continental Illinois Bank based in Chicago which was subject to unit banking regulations was widely seen at the time as partially precipitated by the lack of a branch network to provide retail **deposits** (cf. **core deposits**). The bank had become one of the largest in the USA and the world and was largely funded by **interbank deposits**. When the bank got into difficulties, these evaporated and created a severe **liquidity** crisis. Similar problems at Bank of America, based in California, which allowed branch banking, although severe did not ultimately lead to the collapse of the bank.

United Currency Options Market (UCOM) (USA). A method of trading **currency options** on the **Philadelphia Stock Exchange** that allows considerable flexibility in the choice of currency pairs, the size of the contract, and the **expiry date** (cf. **flex options**).

United States government guaranteed (USGG) (USA). An issue or institution carrying the **full faith and credit** of the US government. Better known as **agencies**.

United States government securities (USGS) (USA). Direct debts of the federal government carrying its **full faith and credit**. Includes US **treasuries** and non-marketable issues such as **savings bonds** and state and local government series (SLGS). See also **agencies**.

unit investment trust (USA). A fixed investment fund where the proceeds of the sale of **units** are used to purchase **underlying** securities which are held for the life of the trust. It has no flexibility to adjust the **portfolio** as would a **mutual fund** and the income and capital are passed back to investors as they are received.

unitization (UK). Converting an **investment trust** into a **unit trust** (cf. **mutual fund**).

unit-linked (UK). A financial arrangement the performance of which is connected to a **unit trust**. Usually found in certain types of insurance contracts.

unit of account. (i) One of the functions of money (cf. **accounts**). (ii) A country's currency (cf. **legal tender**). (iii) A currency basket. See **European Currency Unit; Special Drawing Rights**.

unit of trading. See **lot** (cf. **basket; odd lot**).

unit priced demand adjustable tax-exempt securities (UPDATES) (USA). See **variable rate demand obligations**.

unit share investment trust (USIT) (USA). The issuing entity for **prescribed right to income and maximum equity and special claim on residual equity** (cf. **Americus trust**).

unit trust (UK). An **open-ended** fund set up to offer 'small' investors the benefits of pooled **risk**, through **diversification**, and professional **portfolio** management that would otherwise be beyond the scope of the size of their individual investment holdings. It is established by a **trust deed** and has a **trustee**, who holds the securities purchased, and **investment managers**, who decide investment strategy and buy and sell the 'units' in the fund, which normally makes an initial charge or fee and an annual charge payable to the managers (cf. **front-end load; back-end load**). The units are not tradable on the securities markets, rather they are bought from, and sold back to, the **fund**. The terms under which this is effected, the **fees** chargeable, together with restrictions on **assets** that can be bought, are regulated in the UK by the *Department of Trade and Industry* (DTI). DTI regulated unit trusts are known as *authorized*, which means the units can be marketed to the general public and the trust enjoys certain tax advantages (cf. **load; net asset value**). Unauthorized unit trusts can invest in a full range of assets and instruments, including property and commodities, but are restricted in advertising and suffer a tax penalty. See **balanced mutual fund; box management; futures and options fund; growth fund; investment trust companies; mutual fund; sector; split capital investment trust; single pricing**.

unity bonds (Germany). **Bonds** issued by the federal government to fund the costs associated with the unification of East and West Germany.

universal banking. The trend towards financial institutions offering the widest possible range of services to both their private and corporate customers. Such services would include: money transmission; secured and unsecured lending; insurance; share and bond issuing and placement; syndicated lending; euromarket transactions; and foreign exchange contracts. Sometimes called *financial agglomeration* because it represents an erosion of the traditional distinction between institutions such as **investment banks** and **commercial banks** (at least for the time being) (cf. **Allfinanz; bancassurance**). Universal banks are common in many European countries but are prohibited in Japan and the United States (cf. **Glass–Steagal Act**).

universal bond. A bond issue that is made on a domestic market and the **euromarket** at the same time. See **global bond issue**.

universal note. A variety of **global note** arrangement allowing an issuer to make issues in a wide range of denominations and where the **clearing system** holds non-definitive **bearer certificates** evidencing ownership. Only if the owner requires **physical delivery** are definitive notes produced. The structure was designed to allow issues 'to the buck' at an acceptable cost. See also **grid note**.

universe. The totality of **assets**, securities or, for instance, managed funds in a particular **class**.

unleveraged program (USA). A **limited partnership** where debt is less than half of the finance raised. Such a **partnership** will have less **risk** and provide higher incomes to participants but, potentially, less **capital gains**.

unlevered firm. A firm with no debt in its **capital structure** (cf. **adjusted present value; tax shield**). Sometimes called an *all-equity firm*.

unlimited company. Uncommon form of incorporation where the company's owners have not limited their liability. When joint-stock companies were first created, owners were in effect partners since they were liable for any debts incurred by the company. See **partnership**.

unlimited liability. (i) The requirement by owners to meet all the debts of a business, whatever the investment made. **Sole proprietorships**, names underwriting insurance at Lloyds of London, and **partnerships** fall into this category since the individuals who make up the businesses are required to make good on any debts incurred that cannot be met from revenues (cf. **bankruptcy; limited partner**). (ii) A lending situation where creditors have recourse to the personal assets of the owners, as well as the funds of the business.

unlimited tax bond (USA). A type of **municipal bond** where the issuer has agreed to raise taxes to whatever level required to service the **principal** and **coupon** payments (cf. **moral obligation bond**).

unliquidated damages. Liabilities for **damages** as assessed by a court of law (cf. **liquidated damages**).

unlisted. A security not **listed** on a recognized exchange. Also sometimes called *unquoted*. See **unquoted securities**.

Unlisted Securities Market (USM) (Equities; UK). The former second tier of the UK capital market for **ordinary shares** designed for companies that are not considered, for reasons of size or length of existence, eligible for the **main market**, the so-called first tier (cf. **National Association of Securities Dealers Automated Quotations**). The USM itself has been replaced by the **Alternative Investment Market**. The third tier known as the **third market** was abolished in 1990 and incorporated into the, then still extant, USM. The idea behind the different markets was that the costs of raising fixed capital on each of these 'tiers' was intended to be in proportion to the initial and continuing requirements placed on the issuers of **equity**. The percentage of **issued shares** that is required to be made available was lower than in the main market. Variations on such 'unlisted' markets exist in many other countries, sometimes being called second-tier or restricted markets. See also **general undertaking; London Stock Exchange; listing agreement**.

unload. A market term for selling in the expectation of falls in prices. Also known as *dumping*.

unmatched or **unmatched book.** A portfolio of **assets** and **liabilities** where the **maturities** are unequal (cf. **matched book**). Sometimes called *mismatched* or *open book*. See also **asset-liability management**.

unmatched swap. An interest rate swap or cross-currency swap where there are no **underlying** cash flows by the end user of the swap. In most cases a **swap market-maker** will initially enter into unmatched (but not unhedged) swaps with a **counterparty**. Also called a *naked swap*.

unmodified duration. Another name for Macauley's **duration**.

unquoted securities. Securities which are not quoted on a recognized exchange (cf. **over the counter**). Sometimes assumed to imply illiquidity, although the biggest single market in securities, that for **US treasuries**, is an unlisted market. See **Rule 163**.

unrealized profit or **loss**. A position or holding which stands at a profit or loss if sold and is therefore not yet fixed since subsequent price changes could increase or decrease the result. See **book gain**; **marked-to-market**.

Unrelated Business Income Tax (UBIT) (USA). A tax imposed on the commercial activities of tax-exempt entities in the United States in order to provide a level playing field for commercial, and hence taxable, organizations involved in the same line of business. There has been some debate as to whether new financial instruments fell under the UBIT provisions.

Unrelieved Advance Corporation Tax (Unrelieved ACT) (Equities; UK). The problem created by UK-domiciled companies paying **dividends** on income from foreign sources without sufficient domestic taxable profits to cover **mainstream corporation tax**. This arises due to the particularities of the UK's **imputation system of taxing company** profit where **advance corporation tax** (ACT) payments can only be set against mainstream corporation tax generated in the UK. A simple example will illustrate the problem. The hypothetical company shown in the Table has paid a (gross) **dividend** of £20m in the previous financial year; it plans to maintain its **dividend** this year.

Unrelieved Advance Corporation Tax

	UK operations (£m)	Overseas operations (£m)	Consolidated position for UK tax purposes (£m)
Profit before tax	10	30	40
Local tax @ 40%		(12)	(12)
Mainstream corporation tax (@ 30%)	(3)	(9)	(3)
Less ACT paid	4		4
Profit after tax	6	18	24
Effective tax rate	40%	40%	40%

Proposed dividend: £20m; ACT due on dividend: (20% of £20m = £4m).

The unrelieved ACT is £1m for this company. The company can carry this forward to future years, but the problem will compound if the company does not generate additional UK mainstream profits. The result is that the company is paying more tax by distributing profits to **shareholders** and the effect is to raise its effective tax rate from 37.5% to 40% (cf. **enhanced scrip dividend**). The problem has been addressed by the **foreign income dividend**.

unseasoned issue. The issuance of a security for which there is no current market (cf. **seasoned issue**). See also **initial public offering**; **lock-up**.

unsecured creditor. A creditor who has no special claims on the debtor and would rank **pari passu** with other claimants (cf. **secured creditor**).

unsecured debenture (Bonds). Bond issue which, although termed a **debenture**, has no specific asset or pool of assets allocated as **collateral** (cf. **junior**; **pari passu**; **senior**; **subordinated**).

unsecured debt, credit, or **security.** Debt that has no specific **collateral** or guarantee other than the credit **worthiness** of the debtor (cf. **pari passu**). That is, it provides no specific **recourse** to designated assets in the case of **default** and the holder ranks as a common creditor (cf. **asset-backed**). See **debenture**; **lien**; **subordinated**.

unsecured loan stock (ULS) (Bonds; UK). An unsecured issue of **bonds**, known as loan stock in the UK. In Australia, such issues are known as *unsecured notes*. See **debenture**; **subordinated**.

unsponsored American depository receipt (unsponsored ADR) (Equities; USA). An American Depository Receipt programme which is instigated by a financial intermediary in response to demand but without directly involving the company, although it has to give its permission. It is more common for such programmes to be backed or 'sponsored' by the company against which the ADRs have been issued.

unsystematic risk. The risk that is not **market risk** or **systematic risk** in **modern portfolio theory**. It is the individual characteristics of the asset which can be **diversified** away by holding a portfolio. Sometimes called *residual risk*, *specific risk*, *specific stock risk*, or *unique risk*.

Unternehmensbeteiligungsgesellschaft (Equity; Germany). A type of **closed-end investment company** which specializes in unquoted investments.

Unverzinsliche Schatzanweisungen (U-Schätze) (Money markets; Germany). Short-term, with original maturities of up to two years, discount securities issued by the federal government and its agencies. See **treasury notes**.

unwind or **unwinding.** The process of reversing an existing **position**, either by selling or by making offsetting transactions in the opposite direction (cf. **close out; futures; options; undo**).

unwinding a swap. See **cancellation; termination**.

unwinding risk. The risk attached to reversing or dismantling a **position**. It is the risk that the sum of the parts ends up as less than the whole. This can arise through the timing of transactions and market movements as well as general **transaction** costs (cf. **bid-offer spread**).

up-and-away option. A type of option which has an early **exercise** if the **trigger** price or rate is reached (cf. **quasi-American option**). See **capped index options**.

up-and-in option. A type of **barrier option** where the **option** only becomes valuable if the **underlying** trades up through a **trigger** price or rate, thus making the option come into effect (cf. **down-and-in option; down-and-out option**). Such options are also called a *knock-in* since they have to be activated by a specific event. See also **exotic option; path-dependent option**.

up-and-out option. A variety of **barrier option** where the option becomes worthless if the **underlying** trades up through the **trigger** price or rate (cf. **down-and-in option**). Holders are therefore anticipating either limited movement or that, in a **put** for instance, the price will move in the desired downward direction without appreciating to the trigger point. Such options cost less than simple ones since they need to be activated by a move in the underlying. The up-an-out is the counterpart to the **up-and-in option**, the two together equalling a standard option. The up-and-out and **down-and-out** options are also called a *knock-out* since they have to be deactivated by a specific event.

U pattern. A chart pattern in the form of the letter U which is believed by **chartists** to indicate that prices have bottomed out and are on a **bullish**, rising trend. See also **saucer pattern; V pattern**.

uplift. Information that leads to a rise in price(s). See **economic indicators**.

upside. Positive changes in asset prices. Market participants will talk of an asset's *upside potential* which is the expected increase in value over the

investment horizon. The **risk** of the opposite (prices falling) is known as the *downside*. See **risk–reward**.

upside capture. That part of an insured **portfolio's** increase in value in a rising market above that anticipated by the **portfolio strategy**. See **program trading; portfolio insurance; protective put**.

upstairs market (USA). The process of matching two-way orders within a brokerage firm. Such transactions are closely regulated by exchanges and the **Securities and Exchange Commission** to ensure prices are comparable with those on the exchange.

upstairs trader. A trader who operates away from the **floor** of the exchange (cf. **floor broker; floor trader; local**).

upstreaming. A loan provided by a **subsidiary** to its **parent** (cf. **downstreaming**).

up-tick. (i) An increase in price equal to a **tick**. (ii) A transaction, normally on the **commodities** market, at a higher price than the preceding deal (cf. **down-tick**).

up-tick rule (USA). See **short sale rule** (cf. **tick**).

uptrend. (i) A generally rising time series. (ii) A **chart** or **technical analysis** pattern believed by **chartists** to indicate rising **support levels** (cf. **downtrend**).

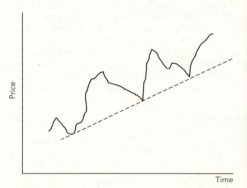

Uptrend

usable security. A security that can be used when exercising a **warrant**. Normally a warrant has to be exercised for cash, but, in some instances, securities of the issuer may be tendered at a pre-set price instead.

usance (Banking). The traditional time for **bills** between two countries. For instance, between the UK and Australia a ship might take 8–10 weeks to make the trip, so a bill would need a **maturity** longer than two months in order to be useful. It also has an ancient usage as the interest rate on a loan.

U-Schätze (Germany). **Unverzinsliche Schatzanweisungen.**

US Dollar Index (USA). Geometric trade-weighted **index** of the external value of the dollar against a basket of ten currencies compiled by the **Federal Reserve**. The base of 100 was set in March 1987 and the currency weights are based on the country's contribution to international trade by value. It forms the **underlying** for a **futures** contract traded on the **New York Cotton Exchange**.

U shaped volatility curve. See volatility smile.

US private placement (USA). See **Rule 144a**.

US Treasury (Department of the Treasury) (USA). The department of state responsible for the federal government's finances and responsible for tax policy, collecting revenue (via the Internal Revenue Service), debt management, and some aspects of financial regulation. Both the US Treasury and the **Federal Reserve** share some role in foreign exchange intervention. The Treasury operates the **Exchange Stabilization Fund**. Federal government debt in the form of **bills, bonds,** or **notes** is known collectively as *US treasuries*. The office of the **Comptroller of the Currency** is also part of the Treasury Department. See also **agencies**.

US Treasury market (US). The market in which US Treasury securities are traded. This is the largest securities market in the world and is an **inter-dealer over-the-counter** market. See also **auction; bell-wether; benchmark; primary dealer; refunding**.

usury. Charging excessive or exorbitant interest. Often combined with illegal lending activities, known as *loan sharking*.

usury laws. Laws governing the maximum permitted rate of interest that might be charged. These are typically ancient laws aimed at curbing usurous practices such as loan sharking rather than recent legislation. Modern regulations on lending practices aim at informing borrowers of the costs and consequences rather than restricting the rate at which lenders can advance sums.

utilization fee. An amount paid to lenders, over the interest rate, based on the average level of use of a **facility** during a certain period. It has the effect of increasing the return to the lender and is often applied to **drawdowns** in excess of a predetermined percentage of the facility amount.

utility. (i) A business involved in manufacturing, distribution, and/or retailing basic services or products such as gas, electricity, water, sewerage, telephone, and so forth. They normally have signi ficant **fixed assets**, long investment horizons, and benefit from significant economies of sale. As a result, such firms generally have natural monopolies and are, in consequence, heavily regulated. (ii) In economics is a measure of welfare or satisfaction. See **utility theory**.

utility revenue bond (USA). A type of **municipal bond** issue used to finance **utility** investment (electricity, gas, sewerage, water, etc.). The project's revenues are used to service the issue's **principal** and **coupons** payments.

utility theory. That part of micro-economics that deals with the analysis of how goods and services provide satisfaction and therefore create demand. It provides a useful set of analytical devices which helps in the building blocks of **modern portfolio theory**, especially the idea that investors may be indifferent as between financial instruments that provide the same kinds of return but in different ways. See also **risk neutral**.

utility value. The welfare or satisfaction given by a particular combination of **risk–reward**.

utmost good faith. See uberrima fides.

V

valeur compensée (French). Literally compensation value. Used for transactions where payment is made by one party at one point of **settlement** and by another party at a different point of settlement (cf. **netting**). This is typical of the **currency** markets and **foreign exchange** where the payments are made in different countries.

valeurs en dépôt (French). A **trust fund**. See **société d'investissement collectif à capital variable**.

valium holiday or **picnic**. Colloquial term for a market holiday (cf. **business day**).

valorization. The attempt to give an arbitary market value to an **asset**, **commodity**, or **currency** usually through government intervention. For instance, by setting up a **fund** to buy up surpluses (cf. **Exchange Stabilization Fund**). See **intervention**.

valuation. The capitalization of the future cash flows from an **asset**.

valuation risk. The risk that the price put on an asset or financial instrument is correct. The problem of accurate valuation is acute in **mergers and acquisitions** and in some complex **derivative** instruments. In the latter case, valuation depends on sophisticated mathematical and statistical models (cf. **Black–Scholes option pricing model**; **option pricing**). See also **winner's curse**.

value added. The difference in value between the inputs to a process and the resultant value of the output (cf. **gross profit**; **net profit**).

value added tax (VAT). A form of indirect taxation aimed at taxing the value added by production or service activities. The original idea was developed in France and has been adopted extensively by other countries. VAT is attractive to tax authorities in that firms do not just report the output value but seek to lessen the burden by claiming back the tax on inputs (other than wages and salaries). Since it is levied by all registered economic agents, it provides the taxing authority with considerable insight into the performance of different sectors of the economy and lessens the scope for evasion. Economically, since the cost is paid ultimately by the final consumer, it is equivalent to a sales tax, but administratively more complex.

value at risk (VAR). **Risk management** measure of the position risk from a transaction or a trading position used by financial intermediaries to monitor their exposures. It measures the potential amount of value that can be lost (or gained) from changes in the price or rate before it can be closed out, showing the amount of a firm's capital at risk from the **positions** held. Also called *earnings at risk*. See **RiskMetrics**.

value broker (USA). A discount broking firm which charges **commission** based on the value of the transaction, not the number transacted. The latter is known as a *share broker*.

value date. The day upon which payment is made to settle a transaction. Such dates vary between markets; for example, **foreign exchange** spot deals are usually settled two working days ahead (T+2) except the US and Canadian dollar and the Mexican peso for which the standard is one working day (T+1), while **eurobond** deals are normally settled within three business days (T+3) (cf. **spot- next**). In the US markets, **stock**

Value date

Instrument	Market	Standard settlement	
Commodities	Spot (cash)	Up to a month	
Foreign exchange	Eurocurrency spot	2 business days	T+2
except	US, Canadian dollar and Mexican peso spot	1 business day	T+1
Eurobonds	International bonds	3 business days	T+3
Eurodeposits	Eurocurrency	2 business days	T+2
Common stocks	USA	5 business days (moving to 3)	T+5/T+3
Domestic interbank		Same day, until clearing cut-off, then next business day	T/T+1

transactions normally settle five business days later (T+5), but **bonds** are traded for **regular way delivery** (cf. **accrued interest**). Value date is sometimes used interchangeably for the *transaction date*, if the two are the same. See **accounting period**; **rolling settlement**; **settlement**.

Value Line Composite Average (VLCA) (Equities; USA). Broad market index using a **geometric average** of **common stocks** traded on the **New York Stock Exchange**, the **American Stock Exchange**, and the **NASDAQ national market**. See **Kansas City Board of Trade**.

Value Line index (Equities; USA). See **Kansas City Board of Trade**.

value of an 01. A measure of price sensitivity of different debt instruments to 0.01% (one hundredth of 1%) change in the interest rate. Traders use the cash value of an 01 to work out the gain or loss from undertaking different transactions (cf. **duration**). It is normally expressed as the value change for a unit of 1 million over a given number of days (see Table). Also known as the *price value of a basis point* (PVBP) or the *value of a basis point*.

Value of an 01

Days	Price value per 0.01 (1 basis point)
1	0.277778
7	1.944444
30	8.333333
60	16.66667
90	25
180	50
270	75
360	100

value spot. The **cash market** price for immediate delivery (cf. **forward price**).

value to business. The replacement cost of an asset. See **book value**; **replacement cost**.

value-weighted average. The average where the components are weighted according to their value. It differs from the normal average which assigns the same weight to each observation in that the significance accorded to each observation is based on its contribution to the total. Value-weighted averages are frequently used to create indices since the changes in the market values of the constituents will then be incorporated in the changes to the **index**. A **stock** index using the value-weighted approach is often referred to as a *market-weighted index* whereas the simple average index is called a *price index*. See **index construction**.

Vancouver Stock Exchange (VSE) (Canada). Stock Exchange Tower, PO Box 10333, 609 Granville Street, Vancouver, BC V7Y 1H1 (tel. 1 604 689 3334; fax 1 604 688 6051). Established in 1907. One of the three major **stock exchanges** in Canada, the others being the **Montreal Exchange** and the **Toronto Stock Exchange**. It specializes in the **listing** of international venture-type companies. See also **VSE index**.

vanilla issue. See **plain vanilla** (cf. **bells and whistles**).

vanishing option. See **barrier option**.

variable cost. Costs of a company that vary directly with the level of output. The other components of total cost are **fixed costs** and **overhead**.

variable coupon renewable note (VCR) (Bonds; USA). A type of **floating rate note** where the **coupon** rate is reset weekly, but paid quarterly, at a fixed **spread** to the **reference rate** (typically, the 91-day **US treasury bill** rate) with an advance **put provision**, excercisable at each refixing, allowing the noteholder to put the notes to the issuer at **par** on coupon dates, although at a lower spread to the reference rate. See **variable rate demand note**.

variable cumulative preferred stock (USA). See **adjustable rate preferred stock**.

variable duration notes. See **pay-in-kind bond**.

variable hedge. See **option hedge**.

variable interest rate or **variable rate**. See **variable rate interest**.

variable margin call. See **variation margin**.

variable maturity swap. Certain kinds of interest rate swaps and cross-currency swaps where the **maturity** is indefinite but falls within a known lower and upper band. For instance, a swap where the floating rate payments are adjustable would have this characteristic. Pricing for such swaps is always based on the most likely end date, which benefits the party able to set the **reset period** on the floating rate side. See also **index amortizing rate swap**.

variable rate (USA). Any feature on a debt, instrument, or **security** where the interest rate, **coupon**, or **dividend** is periodically reset in line with market conditions. The usual mechanism is for the payment to be repriced in line with current market rates (plus any required **margin**) at the **rollover** date based on a predetermined **reference rate**. That said, the term 'variable rate' is used for types of mortgages which contain embedded caps on the amount by which the rate on the mortgage can be changed at each reset period. An alternative method of repricing is provided by the auction rate mechanism where investors set the required margin on the securities. Confusingly, these can also be called variable rate notes! Note that the international markets generally refer to variable rate as *floating rate*, although the term 'variable rate' is also sometimes used.

variable rate certificate of deposit (variable rate CD) (Money markets; USA). A type of certificate of deposit with a longer maturity but where the coupon rate is reset periodically in line with some reference rate. The attractions of these instruments, first issued in 1975, are to give banks greater surety of funding while, like a floating rate certificate of deposit, ensuring that the instrument remains close to par throughout its life. By encouraging an active secondary market, such CDs become close substitutes for the traditional kind.

variable rate demand note (USA). Type of demand note which has the interest reset periodically in line with prevailing market rates and is usually puttable back to a remarketing agent. The demand element requires the issuer to redeem the notes on demand or at pre-set intervals at par, plus accrued interest. Also known as a *daily adjustable tax exempt security* or a *lower floater*.

variable rate demand obligations (VRDO) (USA). Securities with a long final maturity and which pay floating rate interest which is reset either daily or weekly in line with the prevailing market rate. In addition, the holders have a put provision allowing the securities to be redeemed by the issuer with seven days notice at par plus any accrued interest. The effect is to provide the investor with a short-term instrument similar to commercial paper. Such issues go by a variety of different proprietary names, such as *bond interest term securities, demand master notes, money market municipal securities*, or *unit priced demand adjustable tax-exempt securities*.

variable rate interest (USA). A rate of interest that is repriced periodically in relation to a reference rate. It means the same as floating rate interest, hence: *variable rate loan; variable rate security*, and so forth. Sometimes used interchangeably for *adjustable*. See also interest rate calculations.

variable rate mortgage. A mortgage where the interest rate is adjusted by the lender in full, or in part, in line with prevailing market rates (cf. reference rate). Also known as a *floating rate mortgage*. See also adjustable rate mortgage.

variable rate note (VRN) (Bonds). A type of floating rate note which has a margin to the reference rate that is not fixed. Various mechanisms have been developed to determine the market clearing margin at which the notes have to be set, including soundings, negotiation, and an auction process. They may also include a remarketing agent for notes which are not taken up by investors. In addition, VRNs typically have a backstop rate in the event that market clearing is impossible, which sets the highest possible cost of funds to the issuer.

variable rate preferred stock (VRP) (Equities; USA). A type of preferred stock which has the dividend periodically reset in line with an index or a reference rate. See adjustable rate preferred stock.

variable rate renewable note (Bonds; USA). A type of variable rate note with an evergreen maturity where the holder has the right to demand redemption on the (quarterly) coupon payment dates; otherwise he continues to hold the note for the next period (cf. put provision).

variable rate repurchase agreement (Germany). A repurchase tender undertaken by the Bundesbank where tendering banks must quote the rate and amounts of securities they are willing to offer. Normally used for longer maturity repurchase agreements, typically twenty-eight days, and when interest rate policy is easing or seen as uncertain by the market. Differs from a fixed rate repurchase agreement where the Bundesbank sets the rate at which it will transact and banks tender the amounts they are willing to offer.

variable rate security. Any of a number of money market or quasi-money market instruments which have the coupon adjusted in line with the prevailing market conditions.

variable redemption bond, note, or **security.** An issue where the principal at redemption or maturity is allowed to vary, depending on the performance of some index, commodity, or currency. See commodity-linked bond; dual currency bond; equity-linked note; heaven-and-hell bond.

variable spread. See ratio spread.

variable strike cap or **floor.** Interest rate cap or floor which reduces the up-front premium by resetting the cap or floor rate (cf. exercise price; strike rate). The reset is made at a pre-agreed spread to the reference rate for each period (cf. caplet). Since the strike rate is not fixed, the holder of a variable rate cap will not get the same absolute protection as with a normal cap. Also called a *periodic cap* or *floor* or a *periodic reset cap* or *floor*. See also **ladder option**.

variance (Statistics). A measure of the dispersion of a distribution from the mean, where the **underlying** variable is a market rate or price, and useful as a **risk** measure. It is calculated by taking the squared differences between the individual observations and the **mean** times the probability of their occurence.

$$\sigma^2 = \sum_{i=1}^{n}(x_i - \mu)^2 \rho(x_i)$$

where σ^2 is the variance; x_i the ith observation of the data set; μ the mean of the observations of the data set; $\rho(x_i)$ the probability of obtaining the ith observation.

Typically each observation is given equal weight and the computation then becomes:

$$\sigma^2 = \frac{1}{n-1}\sum_{i=1}^{n}(x_i - \mu)^2$$

the $n - 1$ adjustment being made in order to improve the accuracy of the observed variance from a sample.

The larger the variance, the greater the degree of dispersion around the mean. The square root of the variance, the **standard deviation**, is more often quoted as it is in the same units as the underlying variable (cf. **correlation**; **covariance**; **variance-covariance matrix**). See also **Markovitz portfolio model**.

variance analysis. An ex-post auditing of the actual performance or outcome against that predicted or budgeted for in advance. Also called *analysis of variance*.

variance-covariance matrix (VCV matrix). The basic matrix of the **variances** and **covariances** of securities, sectors, or markets used in estimating efficient portfolios in the **markovitz portfolio model**. These may be simply based on historical data, modified via other assessments (such as estimating the expected degree of future **mean reversion**), or created through other econometric techniques (cf. **historical volatility**; **implied volatility**; **volatility**). See also **strategic asset allocation**.

variation call. A notice by an exchange's **clearing house** or a **broker** for a market participant to provide more margin to top up their **margin account** due to adverse price changes affecting the balance in the account (cf. **maintenance margin**).

variation margin. Generally, the funds required to bring the **equity** in an account back up to the **initial** or **maintenance margin** level. Used for **futures** and **exchange-traded options** where

margin trading is permitted, but if the market should move against the **trader** an additional margin has to be paid to maintain the equity stake (cf. **marked-to-market**). The system ensures that the obligations of participants in the market are always covered by **collateral** at the exchange's **clearing house**. The system is also occasionally used in the **over-the-counter** markets in **derivatives**.

Varvepappier Centralen (Sweden). Central securities **depository** for the Swedish market.

vault cash (Banking). Notes and coins held by the bank to meet cash withdrawals (cf. **cash equivalents**; **deposit**).

vega. The measure of the change in an **option's** value with respect to changes in the **volatility** of the **underlying**. The vega will be greatest when the option is **at the money** and it will decrease as the price of the underlying diverges from the **strike price**. When two options are the same, except for their **expiry dates**, that with the longest **expiry time** will have the greater vega. An **option position** with a positive vega will also generally have a positive **gamma** (the rate of change of an option's **delta**). Also known as *epsilon*, *eta*, (wrongly as) *lambda*, *kappa*, or *tau*.

vega spread. A type of **volatility trading** where two **options** with different **vegas** are held in order to capitalize on changes in **volatility**.

velocity. (i) The number of times any given level of **liquidity** supports security transactions. See **turnover**. (ii) The speed at which money circulates within an economy. The *income velocity of circulation* is derived by dividing **gross national product** by the amount of money in circulation; the *transaction velocity of circulation* is the total spent on sales and services divided by the amount of money in circulation. See also **quantity theory of money**.

vendor finance. Funds provided by the seller in a disposal of a business by deferring payment. Typically such vendor finance may form part of the financing of a **management buy-out** (cf. **management buy-in**). Such finance is sometimes linked to an **equity kicker**, the idea being that the selling company may partially benefit from the efforts of the management team.

vendor placing (Equities; UK). A **secondary offering** of stock by a company as the result of receiving **shares** as consideration for the sale of a business to another company (cf. **initial public offer**; **rights offer**). Because the seller does not wish to hold the securities, these are immediately resold to the market by an **underwriting syndicate** by pre-agreement.

vendre au comptant (French). A cash transaction (cf. **spot**).

venture capital. (i) A specialist form of **equity** finance provided to new, young, small, or risky unquoted firms by **institutional investors**. The **funds** can be channelled in three main ways: (*a*) directly by venture capital funds raising money in the capital markets as *independent* entities; (*b*) by institutions owning such funds and making a capital allocation to the activity in the same way as allocating **assets** to other sectors, such as the quoted equities market (such funds are known as *captives*) and (*c*) by some combination of direct market participation and internal allocation. These funds are called *semi-captives*. In all cases the investors are relying on professional investment selection and management for the equities of companies not **listed**. Given the involvement of banks in the funds it is not surprising to find that when deals are structured they include **debt**. Two main types of debt are used: (*a*) **secured** or **senior** and (*b*) **unsecured**, **junior**, or **mezzanine**. The **fund managers** may also offer advice, expertise, and industry contacts to the investee firms. They may also take on an active role in running the firms in which they have invested. This practice is known as *hands-on* venture capital behaviour, and is compared with those venture managers that stay away, *hands-off*. The return to investors comprises **dividends**, often forgone in the early periods of the investment (hence *carried dividends*), and the anticipated capital appreciation from the increase in the value of the equity stake when the investor exits from the transaction. The **exit**, which is likely to occur after a period of between two to five years, may take several forms: **trade sale**; **flotation**; sell-back to the management; or sell-off to another venture capital house. Most venture capital fund managers would expect an annualized rate of return on equity of between 30 and 50%. Clearly, such rates of return on equity, with the help of **leverage** (**gearing**) effects, are available because of the risks being taken. However, the level of **risk** taken can vary according to the stage at which the investor becomes involved. The different stages of venture investment are usually divided up as follows:

1. *start-up, seedcorn* or *cornerstone*;
2. *early stage*;
3. *expansion* (also called *mezzanine*);
4. *management buy-out* or *management buy-in*;
5. *refinancing* or *replacement*;
6. *secondary purchase*.

Categories (1), (2), and (5) are seen as the higher-risk areas and are, as a consequence, often referred to as pure venture capital, as compared with categories (3), (4), and (6), which are seen as relatively safer, albeit at high absolute levels of risk, and are called **development capital** or generic venture capital. In addition to the dividend and **capital gain** expectation, the venture managers will charge set-up and annual fees paid by the investee firms. Hence the description **vulture capital**. The main controversy surrounding venture capital operations is the extent to which such relatively attractive rates of return can be justified. This has prompted some to argue that (ad)venture is a misnomer, given that most of the investment occurs at the **management buy-out** stage. In other words, such businesses are likely to be established with proven management so the amount of risk being taken by the investor is overstated. Whilst it is true that there have been some large and 'safe' deals done most venture transactions are highly geared with a short period for the management to deliver the expected returns. It must also be remembered that the funds themselves have to justify an existence, in relation to returns available in other markets and financial instruments where the **due diligence** costs and **agency** costs are smaller. Moreover, the evidence suggests that only one from every three transactions will produce the expected return. In addition, venture fund managers sift through ten **business plans** to find one deal that they feel can be done. Once they have become involved, if things go wrong, they cannot simply walk away by selling the investment, as there is a very limited secondary market. Therefore, they are required to spend time with the management, and possibly inject more funds, in an attempt to help the company through difficult times. Against this, of the successful investments a number will be blockbusters, producing returns greater than expected by a factor of ten or more. See also **corporate venturing**; **downside**; **lemon**; **plum**; **risk-reward**; **upside**. (ii) Another term for risk capital.

venture capital holding company. A company established by a **venture capital** fund in order to place its **equity** stakes for all those firms in which it has an investment (cf. **pool**; **portfolio**). It would result in the name of the venture capital holding company appearing as the owner of the **stock** or **shares** in the investee firms, although the ultimate beneficial ownership of the stake would rest with the owner(s) of the venture fund.

venture capital investment company. A type of **investment trust company** set up with the express intent to form or provide finance for **venture capital** funds. **Shares** in such companies could be **listed**, or be privately owned by other companies or financial institutions.

venture capital limited partnership (USA). A **limited partnership** set up to provide **venture capital**.

venture capital trust (UK). A tax relief provision of the Finance Act, 1994 aimed at increasing the flow of **seed capital** in start-ups and high-risk new businesses. It allows the setting up of special **venture capital** trusts for private investors who can obtain an immediate 20% up-front tax relief and tax-free income and **capital gains** from the investment.

Verfall (Germany). The **Maturity date** or **redemption date**.

vertical cap. See **corridor**.

vertical line chart. See **high-low closing chart**.

vertical merger. A takeover or merger where the two companies coming together are from the same industry but different parts of the production cycle (cf. **conglomerate merger**; **horizontal merger**).

vertical option spread. See **vertical spread**.

vertical spread. (i) The simultaneous purchase and sale of the same **class** of **options** which have the same **expiry date**, but different **strike prices**. The idea is to benefit from any directional change in price but to reduce the cost by selling another option, thus capping the total gain. Since the initial position has a greater probability of making a profit, the range within the **spread** should capture most of the potential gains, if the price of the **underlying** moves by the predicted amount. There are essentially two different strategies:

- *Vertical bear spread*: this involves purchasing a **put** and selling another one which is further **out of the money**. Holders would anticipate a fall in the price of the underlying within the range of the spread. Also called a *put spread*.
- *Vertical bull spread*: this involves purchasing a **call** and selling another one which is further out of the money. Holders would anticipate a rise in the price of the underlying. Also called a *call spread*.

Such spreads go by a wide variety of names, both proprietary and as used in different markets:

Term	Commonly used in the market for
collar (cap and floor combination)	interest rates
corridor (collar on a swap)	interest rates
cylinder	currency
fence or fence spread	
risk reversal	
reverse risk reversal	
spread (call spread; put spread)	
spread conversion	
conversion spread	
forward rate bracket	interest rates
range forward	currency
tunnel option	
zero cost option	

See also **calendar spread**; **horizontal spread**; **option strategies**; **straddle**; **strangle**; **strap**; **strip**.
(ii) An **option strategy** which creates a **delta neutral** position involving both **long** and **short** positions where there are more written than held options.

vested interest. An stake in a project, enterprise, or position, usually with a view to making a profit (cf. **contingent interest**).

Veterans' Administration (VA) (USA). See **Federal Housing Association**.

Vickrey auction. See **second price auction**.

vines. See **creepers**.

Vinkulierung or **Vinkulierungspraxis** (Equities; Switzerland). Literally, restrictive practice. It refers to the right of Swiss companies to refuse to register undesirable **shareholders**, thus depriving them of their rights.

virement (French). **Clearing** or **settlement**.

virgin bond. Another term sometimes used for the **back bond** in a **bond with warrant** package.

visibles. See **trade balance**.

visible supply. (i) In the securities markets, the new issues known to the market and expected to be offered within a known time span. For instance, **auctions** of government or state sector securities announced but not actually offered (cf. **calendar**). (ii) In **commodities** markets, the amount of a commodity known to be available because it is either in the exchange's warehouses or entering the market (cf. **warehouse receipt**). A commodities **analyst** will track supply very carefully since an overhang will tend to depress the **cash market** while a shortage is likely to push up prices.

volatile. A description of a market or security with large and rapid price changes. Hence a *volatile market* (cf. **whipsawed**). See **market risk**; **price risk**; **standard deviation**; **variance**; **volatility**.

volatility. (i) The variability of movements in an asset's price or that of a group of similar assets, or for market prices as a whole. (ii) The **sensitivity** of an asset's price to a particular variable, such as changes in interest rates or **yield**. Also known as *modified duration*. See **bond risk**. (iii) One of the variables used in **option pricing**. This is defined by a specific statistical formula, namely:

(*a*) The continuously compounded return from each observation period (transaction, hour, day, week, month, year):

Continuous return for period $t = r_t = \ln\left(\dfrac{P_{t+1}}{P_t}\right)$

Where P_i is the price at time i, and m is the number of observations, the standard deviation of returns is calculated by:

$$\sigma = \sqrt{\dfrac{\sum_{t=1}^{m}(r_t - \bar{r})^2}{n - 1}}$$

(*b*) Volatility is expressed as an annual rate (as with interest rates), and needs to be annualized by the ratio d/t, where d is the number of days in the year (actual or traded):

$$\text{Variance} = \sigma^{d/n}$$

Volatility is thus the **standard deviation** of continuously compounded returns per period, expressed as an annual rate:

$$\text{Annualized standard deviation} = \sigma_p \sqrt{t}$$

or

$$\text{Annualized variance} = \sigma_p^2 \cdot t$$

If the volatility per day was 0.15, and we assume 250 trading days per annum, then the annualized standard deviation would be 2.3717:

$$2.3717 = 0.15\sqrt{250}$$

There are two ways of working out volatility: historical and implied.

Historical volatility is the change in underlying price that has been observed over a given period in the past (hence historical). It is calculated by taking the annualized variance of the return on two successive prices. If daily prices are observed for a month, then the monthly variance is multiplied by twelve (months) to annualize it. This assumes that the underlying's price continues to fluctuate on non-trading days. If this assumption is unreasonable, then the volatility estimate needs to be based on the actual trading days in a year. Empirical studies indicate that trading days data should be used and non-trading days ignored, if daily data is being analysed. In addition, judgement has to be used as to what should constitute the correct historical period. In general, more data are preferable since this leads to more accuracy. However, volatility may change over time and the older the data the less relevant they may be to predicting future behaviour. Typically data over the last 90 to 180 days are used, unless the estimate is designed to capture an average over a long period, when very long estimates are more appropriate. Sophisticated methods of assigning more weight to recent observations can also be employed. Typically short-run measures of volatility are used for pricing and trading purposes and longer-term estimates for measuring strategic exposures.

Implied (market) volatility is derived by using an **option pricing model** where the unknown variable is the **option's** volatility. This is an iterative procedure that is standard in most option pricing software. Implied volatility assumes the option pricing formula correctly identifies the pricing factors and assumes a lognormal stochastic price-generating distribution (cf. **geometrical Brownian motion**; **Wiener process**).

Volatility has a positive effect on option prices: the higher the volatility, the higher the option price. It is also the major factor in the differences in option prices quoted by different **market-makers** since the prices of the other variables are known to all market participants. Whether or not an option is considered to be cheap relative to its **fair value** or theoretical value will depend on the volatility that has been assumed or implied by the option pricing model.

volatility autoregressive integrated moving average (VARIMA). Econometric **model** used for modelling the mean-reverting behaviour of **volatility** over time.

volatility cone. A **technical analysis model** of the expected upper and lower boundaries of the **term structure of volatility** used for analysing **option** values.

volatility curve. The graphing or computing of implied **volatility** of different **option** prices against time. Changes in the level and shape of the implied volatility curve are often used as a measure of the future uncertainty in the option's **underlying**. See **term structure of volatility**.

volatility point. Equal to 0.01% of the annualized **volatility**. Many **over-the-counter options** are quoted in terms of a **bid-offer** rate expressed in terms of volatility rather than option price (cf. **premium**). Also known as a *vol point*.

volatility quotation. A method of quoting the price of **options** that gives their **premium** or price in terms of the **volatility** at which they will be purchased or sold (cf. **bid**; **offer**).

volatility rate agreement (VRA). Derivative instrument which allows the purchase or sale of **volatility** rather than requiring the holding or selling of **options** or option-like instruments. See **forward rate agreement**; **synthetic agreement for forward exchange**.

volatility ratio. Not to be confused with **volatility**. This is a measure of relative price change over a particular period. Calculated by taking the difference between the highest and lowest price, for a given time period, and dividing it by the lowest price.

volatility risk. The risk to a position from changes in **volatility**. The gain or loss will depend whether the position is **long** or **short** volatility. A written **option** would leave the **writer** with a short volatility position; a purchased option would give the holder long volatility. The writer will gain if the **underlying** does not change in value over time since the likelihood of the option being **exercised** is reduced. The opposite is the case for the holder. Many other financial or **derivative** instruments create similar volatility positions and hence risk. See **vega**.

volatility skew. The difference in the **implied volatility** of similar **out-of-the-money calls** and **puts**. It is observed that the implied volatility for calls is lower than for puts, a factor attributed to **market forces**. Option traders talk of *trading the skew* as a way of making a profit from changes in the shape of the implied volatility curve and positioning themselves accordingly. When the implied volatility curve is positive (negative), this implies a positive (negative) **skewness** to the probability distribution of the **underlying**.

volatility smile. A tendency for the **implied volatility** for **options** to be lowest near to or **at the money**, and higher the further **out of the money**. This reflects the market's perception that the **premiums** received for **writing** such options do not fully compensate for the **hedging** costs involved. Hence the higher observed implied volatility since the **writer** is adding such costs onto the option's premium.

volatility spread. The purchase of a **call** and a **put option** on the same **underlying** with the expectation that the price will move significantly before their **expiry**. See **option strategies**; **straddle**; **strangle**; **strap**; **strip**.

volatility subsidized swap (VSS). Interest rate swap or **cross-currency swap** where the **fixed rate payer** has a lower fixed rate in return for taking a **short position** in an **interest rate cap** with the same tenor as the swap. Thus the fixed rate payer has a lower payment as long as the floating rate remains below the strike. As long as the floating rate remains below the **cap rate**, the fixed rate payer only pays the fixed rate; if, however, the floating rate is above the cap rate for the period, then the fixed rate payer pays the fixed rate plus the difference on the cap. The volatility subsidy element arises from receiving the premium (in the form of a lower fixed rate payment) by selling volatility and hence receiving the premium as a subsidy.

volatility term cone. A bounded estimate of the likely movements in **volatility** over the **time to expiry** of an **option** (cf. **term structure of volatility**).

volatility term curve. See **term structure of volatility**.

volatility test. The evaluation of the risk of a complex **option** position or portfolio by varying the **volatility**. See **standard portfolio analysis of risk**; **stress test**.

volatility trading. **Option strategies** based on expectations about future **volatility** compared to the current **implied volatility**. A trader will **take a view** that this is either too high (the trader will **write**, or sell **options**) or too low (when the trader will buy) on the expectation that the trader can either buy back or resell the **position** at a profit. The trader will use **delta hedging** to remove the **price risk** of the **underlying**. Hence an option trader will talk of *buying (selling) volatility* when buying (writing/selling) options. Volatility trades can also be put on using **vega** (the sensitivity of option value to changes in volatility) by setting options with different vegas against each other. Traders can also profit by anticipating changes in the **term structure of volatility** by buying and selling options with the appropriate **expiry date**. Total exposure to volatility will depend on vega: a positive (negative) vega is required to profit from a rise (fall) in volatility.

volatility value. See **time value of an option**.

Volksbank (Banking; Germany). A co-operative bank.

volume. The number of transactions on a particular market or a security or **commodity** during a specific time period, usually a trading session, but it can be any period—a week, a month, and so forth. See **turnover**; **velocity**.

volume deleted (USA). A rider on the consolidated **tape** reporting market transactions indicating that, due to late running, the **volume** information on small securities transactions will be omitted and only price information will be provided. See **tape**.

voluntary arrangement (UK). A procedure allowed under the Insolvency Act, 1986 for a financially distressed company to resolve its difficulties and pay off its debts. The intention of such an arrangement is to avoid a winding-up of the company or having to place the company into **liquidation**. The company's **directors**, a court-appointed **administrator**, or an **administrative receiver** to the company may propose such a scheme at a meeting of the company's **shareholders** and **creditors**. If accepted, it is binding on all parties and, if court supervised, may involve a court order.

voluntary liquidation or **winding-up** (UK). The winding-up of a company's affairs by special resolution. If the company is insolvent, then it will be a *creditors' voluntary liquidation*, if solvent, a *members' voluntary liquidation*.

voluntary swap termination. See swap termination.

Vorbörse (Equities; Switzerland). The market for non-listed companies which takes place through an exchange.

vostro account (Banking). A banking term used to describe an account held by one bank on behalf of another, usually a **correspondent**. One bank's vostro account will be the other bank's **nostro account** (cf. **loro account**).

voting right certificate (VRC) (Equities). See voting trust certificate.

voting rights. The rights of securities holders to vote on matters that are put to the owners. Usually refers to the voting rights of **common stock**, but can apply to **bondholders** in a **default** situation or **preferred stockholders** in a **takeover**, for instance.

voting shares or **stock**. Stock which has the right to vote on company **resolutions** and at annual and extraordinary general meetings.

voting trust certificate (Equities; USA). A type of receipt which represents all the rights of **common stock**, except the right to vote. Normally such receipts are issued as the result of a reorganization of a corporation and where it was felt necessary to consolidate the voting power of the common stockholders. Such power is exercised by *voting*

trustees on behalf of the **shareholders**. The rationale is to provide effective control over managements in, for instance, a recovery situation.

V pattern. A **chart** pattern in the form of a a letter V which is believed by **chartists** to indicate that prices have bottomed out and are on a **bullish**, rising trend. See also **saucer pattern**; **U pattern**.

V rating (Bonds; USA). A ranking of **collateralized mortgage obligations** according to their **volatility** (hence the V). See **duration**.

VSE Index (Canada). Set of **indices** maintained by the **Vancouver Stock Exchange** . It is made up of a Composite Index which is in turn made up of three sub-indices: Commercial/industrial index; Resource index and Venture index. They are all based at 1,000 in January 1982, and are capitalization-weighted price indices. The venture sector is due to the fact that the VSE specializes in listing venture companies.

vulture capital. A derogatory term to describe those **venture capital** fund managers that extract what the managers and co-owners of the business regard as excessive **rates of return**. This view probably comes about because of the way in which the deals are structured. In particular, the priority that venture capital investors enjoy in terms of receiving interest on **debt**, and the penalties applied should the business underperform. For example, owner-managers run the **risk** of having their **equity** stakes diluted, or confiscated entirely, if they fail to meet the profit targets set by the venture capitalists.

vulture fund. A type of fund which specializes in investing at low prices in depressed or forced sale assets.

W

WABO. Indicates *we are buyers of*. See **bid price**.

waiting period (USA). The twenty-day time delay required by the **Securities and Exchange Commission** between **registration** and the offering of new securities. See **cooling-off period**.

waiver. (i) Any change in conditions of a contract or binding undertaking. It is used to describe the assent provided by a lender to the modification to the terms and conditions of a loan in the borrower's favour. For instance, a reduction in the **interest cover** required by the borrower would require a waiver (cf. **amendment**; **covenants**; **default**; **technical default**). (ii) An indemnity or agreement either to forgo the right to some action or to protect an **agent** from the consequences of actions carried out on the **principal's** behalf.

walk away clause. A condition in a **derivatives** contract that allows one of the parties to terminate a contract without compensation in the event that the other party is not of good standing or goes into **default**.

wallflower (USA). A previously attractive **stock** which has become unattractive to investors. Such stocks would have been recommended to investors as attractive opportunities, but subsequent events or developments will have shown such expectations to be unfounded (cf. **glamor stock**; **nifty fifty**).

Wall Street (USA). (i) The financial district of New York. See **Street**. (ii) The street where the **New York Stock Exchange** is situated. (iii) Sometimes used as a synonym for the New York Stock Exchange.

Wall Street refiners (USA). Reference to the key role of **Wall Street** financial institutions in trading derivatives on energy products in the **commodities** markets (cf. **pin-stripe pork bellies**).

war babies or **brides** (USA). Market jargon for the **common stocks** of defence contractors.

warehouse receipt or **warehouse warrant.** Certificate evidencing the deposit of goods in a warehouse. For the **commodities markets**, the change of ownership usually involves the exchange of the **warrant** rather than **delivery** of the item itself. Most commodities exchanges designate warehouses which are acceptable delivery points in **settlement** of transactions.

warehouse stocks. **Commodities** held in exchange warehouses and available for making **delivery** against a short position in a **futures** contract. See also **against actuals**; **alternative delivery procedure**; **cash market**; **exchange for physical**; **physicals**.

warehousing. (i) Another term for **garage**. It is longer term than holding a trading position, but less than an investment. For example, a transaction may be temporarily warehoused if market conditions do not allow for the smooth unwinding of a **position**. (ii) Also used to describe the buying of an **equity** stake in a company, through **nominees**, in anticipation of a **takeover**. Small purchases are made and split between different nominees with a view to avoiding the 3% disclosure requirement on the holding. (iii) (US) Borrowing of **short-term funds** by a mortgage company from a bank using its mortgage loans as **collateral**. (iv) Sometimes taken to mean holding a **position** to facilitate transactions (cf. **book**). **Interest rate swaps** and **cross-currency swaps** are often warehoused by intermediaries before a matching **counterparty** is found.

warrant. (i) An **option** in the form of a security, usually of a medium-to long-term character. (ii) (Securities). A certificate, usually attached to a financing, such as an issue of debt, which allow the holder to buy a number of **shares**, or **fixed rate** or **floating rate bonds**, of the issuer at a stated price (cf. **convertible**; **naked warrant**). This right is valid for a given period, the terms of **conversion** may vary depending upon when it is exercised, and it may **expire** either before or, in the case of warrants to buy shares, on or after the **maturity** of the **underlying** financing. Warrants are normally separable and may be traded independently of the debt instrument and be **listed** in their own right (cf. **stapled security**; **unbundling**).

One of the principal attractions of warrants is that they offer a geared or leveraged **position** in the underlying (cf. **leverage**). If the underlying is at 60 and the warrant can be exercised for 55, then the warrant is worth at least 5. If the underlying rises to 70 (an increase of 16.7%), then the warrant will rise to 15 (an increase of 200%).

Warrants on securities differ from **options** into the same instrument in that in the former case, the issuer will be issuing additional or new claims upon **exercise** and therefore warrants will feature a **dilution** effect on the underlying. However, in the case of **foreign exchange** or **commodity** warrants, the dilution effect is nil and they are virtually equivalent to **exchange-traded options**, except that the **counterparty** will be an issuing institution, such as a bank, rather than a **clearing house**. See **contingent claim; cum; ex,** and **option pricing.**

(iii) (Commodities). Title to **physical commodities** held in storage. Exchanges of physical commodities normally involves the seller providing a warrant to the buyer rather than actually providing for **delivery** (cf. **physical delivery**). Also called a *warehouse warrant* since it gives entitlement to a quantity of a commodity held in one of the exchange's approved warehouses. See also **against actuals; alternative delivery procedure; cash market; exchange for physical; physicals.**

warrant-driven swap. A term used for what is an **extendible swap** or a **swaption** when the extension or increase in **notional principal** is dependent on the **exercise** of **bond warrants** against the issuer on the **underlying** liability.

warrant hedge. A position involving buying a warrant for equities and taking a **short** position in the **underlying** (cf. **long hedge**). See **option strategies.**

warrant into a back bond. Term used to describe a debt **warrant** that is exercisable into a new bond from the issuer as opposed to a *warrant into the host bond* which allows the holder to purchase additional amounts of the same issue. The back bond may have significantly different terms and conditions from the original host bonds which were issued with the attached warrants.

warrants into negotiable government securities (WINGS) (USA). A special type of **warrant** which gives the holder the right to buy US treasury **bonds** within a certain period at a set price. See **bond option.**

war risk. A condition of insurance that provides for compensation in the event of loss arising from war. Normal insurance conditions except the eventuality of war from their policies. However, parties risking assets in a potential or close to an actual war zone may, in payment of additional **premium**, secure coverage against loss from this cause.

Warsaw Stock Exchange (Poland). Nowy Swiat 6/12, PL-920 Warszawa (tel. 48 2 628 32 32; fax 48 2 628 81 91). Set up in April 1991, the exchange

trades both **debt** and **equity** instruments. The trading system uses a **specialist** exchange **broker** responsible for an individual issue and uses a computer-based **order-driven** system for transacting business. When initially established, the exchange was open three days a week, although it is anticipated that, as the **privatization** programme increases the number of securities available, this will gradually be extended to a daily trading session.

washing. See **bed and breakfast; bond washing; money laundering; wash sale; wash trade.**

wash sale (USA). Term for selling a security and buying a similar one within a given period as a means of establishing a tax loss (cf. **bed and breakfast**). The US Internal Revenue Service will disallow the deduction in most cases. It can be used as a form of market manipulation designed to give the impression of an active and by implication liquid market (cf. **ramp**).

wash trade or **wash transaction.** The purchase and sale to order of a security or other instrument or **asset** at the same price (cf. **flat; matched sale; put-through**).

WASO. Indicates *we are sellers of.* See **offer.**

wasting asset or **security.** An asset or security which, at the end of its life or term, has no redemption value. Typically **leases** or **options** are wasting assets; in the latter case, if they are not **exercised** they **expire** worthless (cf. **abandonment; cabinet trade**).

watch or **watchlist.** Those securities marked out by research or potential events for special attention by investors and/or regulators (cf. **nifty fifty**). For instance, Creditwatch is an overview of potential **credit rating** changes published regularly to alert investors to possible changes in ratings. Also known as *red flagging.*

weakening of the basis. A move in the relative prices (or rates) between the **cash market** and its related **futures** in which the **spot market** price changes by less than the futures price. See also **backwardation; contango; convergence; cost of carry; price discovery; strengthening of the basis.**

weak-form efficient market. A version of the **efficient markets hypothesis** which postulates that investors cannot earn abnormal returns from analysing past price data (cf. **chartism; technical analysis**).

weak market. A market condition with declining prices (cf. **bear market; strong**).

wedding band swap. A type of **interest rate swap** where the payments are linked to an upper and lower band of interest rates but where payments are leveraged if the rate moves outside the bands.

wedding warrant. A **warrant** issued with a **callable host bond** which may be exercised into a **bullet back bond**, with the same **coupon** and final maturity date as the **host bond**. They expire on the **maturity date** of the bonds. From issue until the first **call date** of the host bond, the warrant may be exercised only by giving up the host bond. After the call date the warrants may be exercised with cash (cf. **harmless warrants**).

wedge pattern. A chartist pattern which shows a time series confined within two narrowing bands. It differs from the similar **triangle pattern** in that the **resistance** and **support lines** are both positive, in the case of a rising wedge, or negative, in the case of a falling wedge. Wedges tend to be identified as temporary aberrations in the price behaviour within a longer trend. That is, a rising wedge will be identified within a bear trend and vice versa.

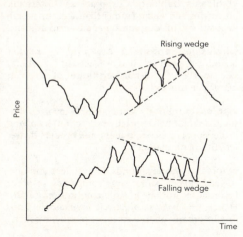

wedge pattern

weekend (Forex; Money markets). A **deposit** or **foreign exchange swap** designed to start on a Friday and mature on the following Monday (or next business day).

weekend effect. Observable market **anomaly** that **common stocks** on average have a negative return over the weekend period.

weighted average. An arithmetic average adjusted to reflect the relative importance of a particular quantity relating to the items being averaged. Used in calculating stock market indices,

where the 'weighting' is based upon **market valuation**. If 100 **shares** comprise an **index** and a weighting of five is given to one share, as it represents 5% of market valuation, then changes in the price of that share will be given five times more importance than those of a share with a 1% valuation. The resulting index will measure changes in market valuation. If all shares had equal weighting, the index would measure changes in the average price, which is not the same. The basic formula to calculate a weighted average is:

$$\text{weighted average} = \sum_{i=1}^{n} w_i x_i$$

where w_i is the weight of the ith observation and

$$\sum_{i=1}^{n} w_i = 1$$

See **index construction**.

weighted average cost of capital (WACC). A calculation of the average cost of funds used by an enterprise, based upon the ruling interest rates for debt, the normal **yield** or **capitalization rate** on **equity**, and the **debt–equity ratio**. Used by firms for setting an appropriate project cost of capital and in explaining alternative corporate capital structures. See **capital budgeting**; **cost of capital**; **discounted cash flow**.

weighted average coupon (WAC) (Bonds; USA). The average fixed interest rate in a **pool** of mortgages weighted by the outstanding principal balance. The higher the WAC, the greater the **prepayment risk** on the pool.

weighted average life. The average life of a portfolio weighted by its constituents according to their share of the portfolio's value and their term to maturity.

weighted average maturity (WAM) (Bonds; USA). See **average life**.

weighted average rate option. A type of average rate option where the average is weighted according to a set formula. Thus it is able, for example, to replicate an **accretion** or **amortization** schedule on the **underlying**.

weighted ballot. A method of reconciling the demand for a new issue of securities which is **oversubscribed**, which involves weighting the scaled back **allotment** by the amounts **tendered** for by the individual parties. Thus those offering to purchase a larger amount end up with a stake in proportion to their original requirements.

weighted collar. A collar where the amount of the **floor** and the **cap** are not the same. In order to obtain a **zero-cost collar**, more floor has to be written than purchased cap. Alternatively, a smaller floor will allow the holder to obtain some benefit from falling interest rates while maintaining full protection from the cap, but at a somewhat reduced price. See also **ratio spread**.

weighted hedge or **hedging.** When **hedging** a cash market **position** with a **futures** position which is not an exact match of the **underlying** (cf. **interpolation**). For example, in trying to hedge a holding of a **certificate of deposit** (CD) with a thirty-day **maturity** while the only futures contract available might be for a ninety-day underlying. To effect a hedge which balances the two exposures, approximately one-third the weight of the value of the futures position would be sold in order to fully hedge the cash position. This is because for any change the impact on profit is three times greater on a ninety-day than on a thirty-day contract. The hedge is only approximate because of **basis risk** and the **risk** of a **rotational shift** in the **yield curve** (and present valuing on the CD) as well as a fixed contract amount for the future. See also **duration-based hedge ratio; value of an 01**.

well capitalized (Banking). A definition of a bank's regulatory **capital adequacy** which is seen by the regulator as being above the minimum standard and therefore not a concern. See **capital-based supervision**.

well-diversified portfolio. See efficient portfolio.

West Texas Intermediate (WTI) (Commodities). The **benchmark** crude oil price in the US domestic market and the basis for most **derivative** contracts on US oil. Other benchmarks are **Brent oil** and **Arabian Light**. See **marker crude**.

wet lease. A type of operating **lease** contract where personnel to operate the equipment being leased are provided by the lessor, rather than the user, the lessee.

when issued; when, as and if, issued (WI). Conditional transactions in a security yet to be issued (cf. **WIWI**). Common in the US Treasury market since it allows **dealers** to hedge their **risk** going into the **auction**. The securities are not deliverable and are subject to the issue actually being made. In effect, the transactions have some features in common with **futures** (cf. **forwards**). See grey market.

whiplashed or **whipsawed.** To be caught out by sudden reversals in price trends. Usually associated with a **volatile market**.

white goods. Consumer durable items, such as washing machines and refrigerators (cf. **brown goods**).

white knight (Mergers and acquisitions). A company that is invited to bid for a **target** company in an ongoing hostile **takeover bid** situation to save the target from the hostile **raider** (cf. **black knight**). The white knight is usually chosen by the potential victim as a means of frustrating the overtures of the **predator** (cf. **greenmail; poison pill; white squire**).

white squire. Either one or more companies acting together, or in support of a **white knight**, in order to prevent a bidder for a **target** company in a contested **takeover** or **shareholders** who have agreed not to sell to a corporate **raider**. The company would not acquire a **controlling interest** in the target.

whole loan (USA). A **mortgage-backed** market term used to distinguish a security which has a direct **lien** on the **underlying** as opposed to a pooled or **pass-through** arrangement.

wholesale banking. Corporate and **interbank** borrowing and lending rather than accepting retail **deposits** and making consumer advances or loans.

wholesale deposit. A large, money market quantity, **deposit** solicited or placed in the **wholesale market** (cf. **retail certificate of deposit; wholesale money**).

wholesale market. Market which involves substantial amounts in each transaction involving professional investors, **traders**, and **brokers-dealer** (cf. **interbank market**).

wholesale money. Funds that are lent and borrowed between banks, large companies, or other financial institutions in large amounts (cf. **retail**). Hence, *wholesale rate of interest*, for example: London **interbank offered rate**. See **parallel market**.

wholesale price index. See economic indicators; producer prices index.

whole-term structure of interest rates option pricing model. Method of assessing the sensitivity of **options** on interest rate instruments designed to allow the aggregation of exposures at all points on the **yield curve** (cf. **term structure of interest rates**).

Whoops (Washington Public Power Supply System) (USA). The large-scale **municipal bond** default that occurred when the **underlying** contractual arrangements, and hence **bond** security, were declared invalid (cf. **ultra vires**).

wider-range securities (UK). That proportion of monies held in trust that can be invested in securities with a higher risk than **narrow-range securities**, which is largely confined to **fixed interest securities**.

widows and orphans. Safe investments; and hence suitable for those who could be deemed to have no knowledge of investing, such as widows and parentless children. See **investment grade; prudent-man rule; rules of fair practice.**

Wiener Börsekammer (Vienna Stock Exchange) (Austria). Wipplingerstrasse 34, AT—1011 Wien 1 (tel. 43 1 534 99 0; fax 43 1 535 68 57).

Wiener process. A model for the stochastic price-generating process for securities (cf. **Brownian motion; Markov process**). The process is characterized by the fact that at any time interval (*t*), the increase in value of a series that follows a Wiener process will be normally distributed with a mean of zero and a **standard deviation** of the square root of *t*. The uncertainty of the value therefore increases by the square root of the time interval into the future we are examining. In a generalized Wiener process, both variations in the mean through a trend and the **variance** can change over time. This is also known as *geometric Brownian motion* and is the price diffusion process in, for instance, the **Black–Scholes option pricing model.**

wild card option or **play** (USA). Term given to the **short position** in a **Chicago Board of Trade** treasury bill or **bond futures** due to the **delivery** methods for the **underlying.** The short is obliged to deliver securities at the **expiry** of the contract, but can select a date within a set period in the **delivery month** to their own advantage as well as being able to take advantage of the fact that the notice stating the intention to deliver can be made after the close of the **session**, effectively giving the short an **option** on the Treasury market for that period. See **delivery option.**

wildcat drilling (USA). A high-risk, but potentially high-reward, **limited partnership** which prospects for oil and gas in untested areas.

Wiltshire 5000 (USA). Broad **index** of companies traded through the **National Association of Securities Dealers Automated Quotations** market. It is an indicator of **over-the-counter** securities covering a wide range of different sectors and is widely used as an indicator of **market tone** about investment in small firms.

Wiltshire Small Capitalization Index (WSCI) (Equities; USA). Capitalization-weighted **index** of 250 **common stocks** from the small **capitalization** sector.

windbill. See **accommodation bill.**

wind down (a position). Decreasing the exposure to a market by buying or selling securities to reduce a position (cf. **cover**).

windfall. Unexpected profit.

winding-up. See **liquidation** (cf. **bankruptcy; insolvency**).

winding-up date (UK). The final date in which the shareholders of a **split-capital investment trust** will decide whether to wind up the company.

winding-up petition (UK). A request presented to a court ordering the termination of a business's activities. Such a petition is normally sought by creditors to the business as a result of non-payment. When the petition is accepted by the court, a *winding-up order* is issued (cf. **default; liquidation**).

window. (i) A time during which certain deals can occur because of particular market conditions; for example, it may be possible to issue certain types of securities because of ruling investor sentiment that is not expected to last. (ii) Also shorthand for the US **Federal Reserve's discount window**. Hence *borrowing at the window*. (iv) The business hours during the day in which **clearing** and **interbank** transfers may be carried out (cf. **town clearing**). (iii) A deferred or restricted opportunity in securities, as with a **window warrant** (cf. **put provision**).

window dressing. (i) The practice of raising funds at certain critical disclosure times, such as financial year-ends, to indicate high **liquidity** or otherwise disguising or improving the look of the accounting numbers by **short-term** transactions. (ii) Creative accounting practices used to dress up the financial statements to make them look more favourable than they would otherwise be (cf. **depreciation; off-balance sheet; revaluation**). See **true and fair view.**

window reset. A feature found on a number of **interest rate swaps** giving the **floating rate payer** the right to reset the **reference rate** at any point within the **reset period** (cf. **embedded option**). This provides the payer with the opportunity to take advantage of falls in interest rates.

window warrant. A type of **warrant** that can be exercised only within a certain future period.

Windsor Declaration. Set of principles published on 17 May 1995 setting out how regulators will cooperate to prevent **systemic risk**, using bilateral and multilateral information sharing arrangements for large **exposures** (cf. **market risk**).

wind up (a position). Increasing the exposure to a market by buying or selling securities to increase a position (cf. **opening transaction**).

winner's curse. The problem of overbidding in a competitive auction. This is the danger that the winner in a fair, discriminatory (i.e. English style) price auction has overvalued the benefits, i.e. the winner has been over-optimistic in assessing the value of the business, asset, or security. Typically such situations arise when looking at complex or difficult to price decisions (the original research was done on oil and gas **lease** tenders) although it exists in any competitive bidding situation. The corollary to the theory adds that the second bid is more likely to have established the correct valuation.

wire house (USA). A large national and international financial intermediary.

witching hour (USA). (i) The last hour of trading each month when **exchange-traded stock options** expire. Hedging activity causes significant volatility in the market. A worse condition of the same phenomenon, now corrected, was known as **triple witching hour**, when **stock index futures and options** all expired together. (ii) (UK) The one-hour period when the stock index futures and **options stock index** on the **FT-SE 100 Index** all expire at the same time (cf. **backwardation**).

with dividend. Same as **cum dividend** (cf. **ex**).

withholding tax. A tax levied by a country at source on, for example, interest payments or **dividends** paid on securities issued or debt. By withholding part of the payment this tends to (*a*) raise the cost of **funds** for that country, because (*b*) it discourages foreign investors because, even if they can offset or reclaim the tax because of **double-taxation** treaties, they are still obliged to undergo certain formalities in order to benefit from such exemption (cf. **free of tax to residents abroad**). In addition, in most cases, even where double-taxation relief is available, the investor has lost the use of the proceeds in the interim. Where no such exemption exists, such as when an investor is operating **off shore** and has no tax to offset under the double-taxation system, the after-tax return is significantly reduced. Such a tax can act as an important determinant of the competitiveness of a financial centre, especially in terms of capital mobility and market **liquidity**. It can also have the effect of increasing the **yield** on securities such as to create **arbitrage** possibilities. An example was the ability of foreigners to buy domestic Italian government **bonds**, hedge these into their own or desired currency, apply the withholding tax against their own domestic tax liability, and end up with a higher after-tax yield than would be possible if investing directly in Republic of Italy tax-free **eurobonds** (cf. **tax sparing**).

without (USA). A trader's expression for a **quote** in a **one-sided market** where the trader is willing to transact only on the side quoted. Hence a quote for a **treasury bond** such as '22 plus **bid** without'. The bid has been given, but the trader is unwilling to make an **offer** price. The price quoted is 22/32, plus 1/64, or 23/64th at which he will buy. As would be normal practice, he has given the bid without giving the **big figure** or **handle**, which is presumed known.

without recourse. (i) A type of financial arrangement that limits the debtholders' rights to seek repayment from the parent obligor to a transaction often used in **asset-backed** or **project finance** arrangements. The degree of non-recourse may vary, depending on the exact contractual agreement between the parties (cf. **fraudulent conveyancing**). (ii) A condition attached to a **banker's acceptance** or **bill of exchange** restricting the holder's recourse to the **drawer** at **maturity**.

with rights. Same as **cum rights** (cf. **ex**).

WIWI (when issued, when issued) (USA). A term for **treasury bills** (T-bills) that are traded before they are even auctioned (cf. **when issued**). This is possible because the US **treasury** arranges a timetable of issuances in advance with standard terms. In effect, this produces a **financial futures market** in US treasury bills, but outside a normal **financial futures exchange**.

working capital. The capital needed by an enterprise to support its day-to-day activities. Conventionally defined as the difference between **current assets**, such as cash, marketable securities, debts, and inventories, and **current liabilities**, which comprise financial obligations falling due within a year. Also known as *working assets*. See **current ratio**.

working capital acceptance (Banking; USA). A type of **banker's acceptance** that is not backed by a trade transaction and where the funds are for working capital purposes (cf. **accommodation paper**). Such bills would not be **eligible** for **discount** at the **Federal Reserve**.

working capital management. Decisions involving the control of **short-term assets** and **liabilities**.

working control. See **controlling interest**.

working interest (USA). A member of a partnership who has **unlimited liability**. Passive investors may take advantage of a limited **partnership** where their exposure is limited to the amount invested.

work in process or **work in progress (WIP).** That part of a firm's production or contracts that have been partly completed. The raw materials have been partly processed, but have not been finished and therefore cannot count as **inventory** or completed **stock**. For uncompleted service contracts of a long-term nature, the item may include an element of profit.

workout. (i) An informal process of financial reconstruction for companies in **financial distress** where **creditors** agree to suspend or modify their claims on a firm in order to allow it to trade out of its difficulties. It may involve the reconstruction of a business with new management and strategies, together with any additional finance, conversion of existing claims, or deferral of repayment that may be required, thus allowing the firm to recover from its problems (cf. **debt–equity swap**). See Chapter 11. (ii) Another term for **best efforts.**

workout market. **Thin** or **illiquid** market where the **dealer** may only be willing to execute transactions if he can find a **counterparty** on the other side (cf. **cabinet crowd**). He will thus work out the trade by finding the other party. Generally, in these conditions, transactions take more time to be completed and are subject to significant **market risk** or **price risk** (cf. **direct search market**).

workout period. (i) The time taken for a firm to overcome its financial difficulties. (ii) In markets, the period of time required for a pricing or rate anomaly to reverse itself.

World Bank (or International Bank for Reconstruction and Development). An international provider of **funds** to **International Monetary Fund** member countries that may be experiencing difficulties in raising capital for long-term projects. Its capital base is provided by members' subscriptions and its reputation and ability to collect preferentially from debtor nations allow it to borrow at **fine rates**, an advantage it passes on to its borrowers. It is an important and innovative borrower on domestic and international capital markets, pioneering such transactions as **cross-currency swaps** and **global bond issues**. The World Bank 'group' of multilateral development agencies includes: *International Development Agency* (IDA) (soft loans); *International Finance Corporation* (IFC) (private sector lending); *International Centre for the Settlement of Investment Disputes* (ICSID) (arbitration); *Multilateral Investment Guarantee Agency* (MIGA) (guarantees).

world currencies.

COUNTRY	CURRENCY	SWIFT Code
Afghanistan	afghani	AFA
Albania	lek	ALL
Algeria	Algerian dinar	DZD
Andorra	French franc	FRF
	Spanish peseta	ESP
Angola	New kwanza	AOK
Antigua	East Caribbbean $	XCD
Argentina	Argentinian peso	ARS
Armenia	dram	
Aruba	florin	AWG
Australia	Australian $	AUD
Austria	schilling	ATS
Azores	Portuguese escudo	
Bahamas	Bahama $	BSD
Bahrain	Bahrain dinar	BHD
Balearic Is.	Spanish peseta	
Bangladesh	taka	BDT
Barbados	Barbados $	BBD
Belarus	Belarus rouble	SUR
Belgium	Belgian fr.	BEF
Belize	Belize $	BZD
Benin	Communauté Financière Africaine fr.	XAF
Bermuda	Bermudian $	BMD
Bhutan	ngultrum	BTN
Bolivia	boliviano	BOB
Botswana	pula	BWP
Brazil	real	BRR
Brunei	Brunei $	BND
Bulgaria	lev	BGL
Burkino Faso	Communauté Financière Africaine fr.	XAF
Burma	kyat	BUK
Burundi	Burundi fr.	BIF
Cambodia	riel	XAF
Cameroon	Communauté Financière Africaine fr.	XAF
Canada	Canadian $	CAD
Canary Is.	Spanish peseta	
Cape Verde	Cape Verde escudo	CVE
Cayman Is.	Cayman Island $	KYD
Cent Afr. Rep.	Communauté Financière Africaine fr.	XAF
Chad	Communauté Financière Africaine fr.	XAF
Chile	Chilean peso	CLP
China	yuan	CNY
CIS	rouble	
Colombia	Colombian peso	COP
Comoros	French fr.	KMF
Congo	Communauté Financière Africaine fr.	XAF
Costa Rica	colon	CRC
Côte d'Ivoire	Communauté Financière Africaine fr.	XAF
Croatia	kuna	
Cuba	Cuban peso	CUP
Cyprus	Cyprus £	CYP
Czech Republic	koruna	CZK
Denmark	Danish krone	DKK
Djibouti Rep.	Djibouti fr.	DJF
Dominica	East Caribbean $	XCD
Dominican Rep	Dominican Rep. peso	DOP

COUNTRY	CURRENCY	SWIFT Code	COUNTRY	CURRENCY	SWIFT Code
Ecuador	sucre	ECS	Malaysia	ringgit	MYR
Egypt	Egyptian £	EGP	Maldive Is.	rufiya	MVR
El Salvador	colon	SVC	Mali Republic	Communauté Financière Africaine fr.	XAF
Equatorial Guinea	Communauté Financière Africaine fr.	XAF	Malta	Maltese lira	MTL
Estonia	kroon		Martinique	local fr.	FR.F
Ethiopia	Ethiopian birr	ETB	Mauritania	ouguiya	MRO
Falkland Is.	Falkland Is. £	FKP	Mauritius	Mauritius rupee	MUR
Faroe Is.	Danish kroner	DKK	Mexico	Mexican peso	MXP
Fiji Is.	Fiji $	FJD	Miquelon	local fr.	
Finland	markka	FIM	Monaco	French fr.	FRF
France	French fr.	FRF	Mongolia	tugrik	MNT
Fr. Central Africa	Communauté Financière Africaine fr.	XAF	Montserrat	East Caribbean $	XCD
Fr. Guiana	local fr.	FRF	Morocco	dirham	MAD
Fr. Pacific Is.	CFP fr.		Mozambique	metical	MZM
Gabon	Communauté Financière Africaine fr.	XAF	Namibia	South African rand	ZAR
			Nauru Is.	Australian $	AUD
			Nepal	Nepalese rupee	NPR
Gambia	dalasi	GMD	Netherlands	guilder	NLG
Germany	mark	DEM	Netherlands		
Ghana	cedi	GHC	Antilles	Antilles guilder	ANG
Gibraltar	Gibraltar £	GIP	New Zealand	New Zealand $	NZD
Greece	drachma	GRD	Nicaragua	gold cordoba	NIO
Greenland	Danish krone	DKK	Niger Rep.	Communauté Financière Africaine fr.	XAF
Grenada	East Caribbean $	XCD			
Guadeloupe	local fr.	FRF	Nigeria	naira	NGN
Guam	US $	USD	Norway	Norwegian krone	NOK
Guatemala	quetzal	GWP	Oman	rinai Omani	OMR
Guinea	local fr.	GNF	Pakistan	Pakistani rupee	PKR
Guinea-Bissau	GB peso	GWP	Panama	balboa	PAB
Guyana	Guyanese $	GYD	Papua New Guinea	kina	PGK
Haiti	goude	HTG			
Honduras	lempira	HNL	Paraguay	guarani	PYG
Hong Kong	HK $	HKD	Peru	new sol	PEN
Hungary	forint	HUF	Philippines	Philippines peso	PHP
Iceland	Icelandic krona	ISK	Pitcairn Is.	£ sterling	
India	Indian rupee	INR		New Zealand $	NZD
Indonesia	rupiah	IDR	Poland	zloty	PLZ
Iran	Iran rial	IRR	Portugal	escudo	PTE
Iraq	Iraqi dinar	IQD	Puerto Rico	US $	USD
Irish Republic	punt	IEP	Qatar	Qatar riyal	QAR
Israel	shekel	ILS	Reunion		
Italy	Italian lira	ITL	Is. de la	French fr.	FRF
Jamaica	Jamaican $	JMD	Romania	leu	ROL
Japan	yen	JPY	Rwanda	local fr.	RWF
Jordon	Jordanian dinar	JOD	St Christopher	East Caribbean. $	
Kenya	Kenya shilling	KES	St Helena	£	SHP
Kiribati	Australian $	AUD	St Lucia	East Caribbean. $	XCD
Korea North	won	KPW	St Pierre	French fr.	FRF
Korea South	won	KRW	St Vincent	East Caribbean. $	XCD
Kuwait	Kuwaiti dinar	KWD	San Marino	Italian lire	ITL
Laos	new kip	LAK	São Tomé	dobra	SUR
Latvia	lats	LVL	Saudi Arabia	Saudi riyal	SAR
Lebanon	Lebanese £	LBP	Senegal	Communauté Financière Africaine fr.	XAF
Lesoto	maluti	LSL			
Liberia	Liberian $	LRD	Seychelles	Seychelles rupee	SCR
Libya	Libyan dinar	LYD	Sierra Leone	leone	SLL
Liechtenstein	Swiss fr.	CHF	Singapore	Singapore $	SGD
Lithuania	litas	LTL	Slovakia	koruna	SKK
Luxembourg	Luxembourg fr.	LUF	Slovenia	tolar	SIT
Macao	pataca	MOP	Solomon Is.	Solomon Is. $	SBD
Madagascar	Madagascar fr.	MGF	Somali Rep	Somali shilling	SOS
Madeira	Portuguese escudo		South Africa	rand	ZAR
Malawi	kwacha	MWK	Spain	peseta	ESP

COUNTRY	CURRENCY	SWIFT Code
Spanish ports in N. Africa	Spanish peseta	ESP
Sri Lanka	Sri Lankan rupee	LKR
Sudan Rep.	Sudan dinar	
Surinam	Surinam guilder	SRG
Swaziland	lilangeni	SZL
Sweden	Swedish krona	SEK
Switzerland	Swiss fr.	CHF
Syria	Syrian £	SYP
Taiwan	Taiwan $	TWD
Tanzania	Tanzanian shilling	TZS
Thailand	baht	THB
Togo Rep.	Communauté Financière Africaine fr.	XAF
Tonga Is.	pa'anga	TOP
Trinidad and Tobago	Trinidad and Tobago $	TTD
Tunisia	Tunisian dinar	TND
Turkey	Turkish lira	TRL
Turks and Calcos	US $	USD
Tuvalu	Australian $	AUD
Uganda	new shilling	UGX
Ukraine	karbovanets	SUR
UAE	dirham	AED
United Kingdom	£ sterling	GBP
United States	US $	USD
Uruguay	peso Uruguayo	UYP
Vanuatu	vatu	VUV
Vatican	Italian lira	ITL
Venezuela	bolivar	VEB
Vietnam	dong	VND
Virgin Is. – British	US $	USD
Virgin Is. – US	US $	USD
Western Samoa	tala	WST
Yemen (Rep. of)	Yemeni rial	YER
Yemen (Rep. of)	Yemeni dinar	YED
Yugoslavia	new dinar	YUN
Zaire Rep.	zaire	ZRZ
Zambia	kwachal	ZMK
Zimbabwe	Zimbabwe $	ZWD

worldscale (world-wide tanker nominal freight scale). Index of tanker freight rates denominated in US dollars. It is based on key shipping routes for a 'standard' voyage. See also freight futures.

World Trade Organization (WTO). Successor organization to the General Agreement on Tariffs and Trade, responsible for handling international trade and intellectual property rights disputes.

world-wide combination taxation. See unitary taxation.

worst of two assets option. See rainbow option.

W-pattern. A chartist's pattern in the form of a 'W'. See double bottom.

wrap around. Insurance on a financial transaction, usually a securities issue, which covers 100% of the amount. In most cases credit enhancement in asset-backed transactions can achieve high credit worthiness by just insuring the expected losses plus some additional contingency reserve.

wrap lease. A type of lease contract involving a third party that buys the asset to be leased, leases it to the leasing company, who then on-leases it to the user. Used when the initial leasing company has limited taxable capacity.

wrinkle. Any innovative variation on a standard security issue's terms and conditions which may make it more attractive to buyers. Wrinkles tend to follow fashion or respond to specific market conditions (cf. window). Often they only appear once. Successful wrinkles tend to evolve into a niche product or a class of their own.

write. (i) To create and sell an option. This is equivalent to taking a short position in the option. Writing options is potentially a high-risk activity since the value of the underlying can rise significantly above the strike price (in the case of a call) or be worthless (in the case of a put). Often option writers will hedge their position or undertake covered call (put) writing (cf. delta hedge). The person who writes the option is called the *writer*. (ii) In the insurance market, it means to accept an insurance risk (cf. pure risk; unique risk). In the financial markets, it is also sometimes used to mean writing in the insurance sense by providing a guarantee. *Writer* is also used in the insurance market for individuals and firms who sell insurance.

write-buy. See buy-and-write.

write down. (i) To reduce the value of an asset or holding in the balance sheet to its economic worth or realizable value, taking the reduction as a loss (cf. charge-off; marked-to-market). (ii) An accounting action reducing the book value of an asset by the amount of depreciation.

write off. To remove an asset or holding entirely from a balance sheet taking the reduction in value as a loss (cf. default). See also charge-off.

write out (USA). Term used for a transaction between a broker and a specialist when the source or destination of the transaction is the specialist's own account rather than another trade with a broker (cf. book).

writer. The seller or short position holder in an option. The writer is contractually obliged to fulfil the obligation of the option contract if exercise should take place. In the case of a call option it is to sell the **underlying** at the agreed price or rate; in the case of a **put option**, to buy the underlying at the agreed price or rate. See **write**.

write tickets. Market term for doing business, that is, undertaking transactions (cf. **deal**).

writing cash-secured puts. See cash-secured put; fiduciary call.

writing naked. See naked option.

writing puts to receive securities. A method of acquiring securities where the writer also receives a **premium** for so doing. The writer can decide what **exercise price** to set, even writing an **in-the-money put** in order to secure the security. The premium is a bonus, as it were. Also known as *covered put writing*.

written-down value (WDV). The current book value after depreciation or capital allowances on capital investment.

wrongful trading (UK). If a company, to continue trading when it has no reasonable prospect of avoiding becoming insolvent (cf. **fraudulent trading**).

Y

yakujo nedan (Japan). Contract price. See yonhon ne.

yakusoku tegata (Money markets; Japan). Promissory note.

yankee (USA). A foreign issue in the US domestic market.

yankee banker's acceptance (yankee BA) (Banking; USA). US dollar denominated banker's acceptance issued in the domestic market by foreign domiciled issuers.

yankee bond (USA). A bond issued in the US domestic market by a non-US-domiciled borrower denominated in US dollars. Unlike eurobond issues yankees pay interest semi-annually, rather than annually (cf. bulldog bond; matador bond; samurai bonds). Such issues are registered with the Securities and Exchange Commission (cf. registration).

yankee certificate of deposit (yankee CD) (USA). A certificate of deposit issued in the US domestic market by a branch or subsidiary of a foreign bank based in the USA (cf. euro certificate of deposit).

yard. (i) A quantity of 1,000 million, a milliard. In the USA, a billion (and now commonly in the UK). (ii) (USA) Colloquial term for US$100.

Y-bond (USA). A class of collateralized mortgage obligation (CMO) which has a predetermined sinking fund schedule and, therefore, has the same behaviour as a similar corporate bond issue (cf. amortization). As such it has precedence for the cash flows over all other classes of CMOs (cf. Z bond). See also planned amortization class bond.

yearling (UK). A UK local government bond issue of maturities of between one and four years, traded on the gilt-edged market or the discount market. The name yearling comes from the fact that the vast majority of such bonds have maturities of just over a year.

year of assessment. See fiscal year.

Yellow Book (*Admission of Securities to Listing*) (UK). A London Stock Exchange publication that lays down the requirements for being admitted to a listing and the subsequent procedure for reporting (cf. Green Book). It derives its name from its yellow colour. See also Alternative Investment Market; main market.

yellow sheets (USA). A daily publication by the National Quotation Bureau for over-the counter traded corporate bonds (cf. pink sheets). Provides more extensive coverage than that published in newspapers.

yellow strip (Equities; UK). The name given to the reporting system used by the Stock Exchange Automated Quotations to identify the best bid and offer prices being quoted by market-makers. It derives its name from the yellow colour used by the Teletext Output of Price Information by Computer (TOPIC) to indicate the touch (cf. spread).

yen bond or **yen-denominated bond.** In principle any bond denominated in yen; but in practice, usually taken to imply a eurobond (cf. Japanese government bond; samurai bond; shibosai bond).

yield. The annualized rate of return of a security or asset expressed as a percentage. There are a number of different types of yield, and different methods of computation, but six main groups can be identified: (i) simple yield calculations as used in the money markets (i.e. which ignores compounded value) (cf. annual equivalent); (ii) those using only current income, known as current, earnings, flat, interest, or running yield; (iii) those using a bond basis, (cf. equivalent yields bond; discount-to-yield); (iv) those allowing for capital gain/loss over some stated life, such as the full maturity period, or some shorter period like the first call or put date (cf. gross redemption yield; after-tax basis; yield-to-average life; yield-to-call; yield-to-maturity; yield-to-operative date; yield-to-put; (v) nominal yield, the cash return on a security (usually expressed as an annual rate); (vi) real rate of interest, or real yield, which is the return above inflation.

Additional adjustments can be made to yield calculations to reflect company tax, such as corporate tax equivalent, and for reinvestment income, such as realized compound yield-to-

maturity and total return. Note that yield calculations in Japan for bonds follow (ii) above rather
than (iii), which is common in other bond markets. See also discount; interest rate calculations;
yield curve; yield margin; yield pricing.

yield advantage. The amount of **pick-up** in
yield obtained by purchasing a **convertible** rather
than a company's **shares**.

yield analysis. A method of assessing securities
which attempts to relate actual performance to the
operation of the market. See **yield**.

yield auction. See auction (cf. tender; yield tender).

yield basis. A method of expressing the value of a
financial instrument where the **dealer** gives both a
bid yield, meaning a purchase price that will produce that **yield**, and an **offer** yield, meaning a
selling price that will produce that yield (yield-
to-maturity) for the buyer. Yield basis is a common method of **quoting** in the **money markets**,
but relatively rare in the **bond market** (cf. **discounting**). The other method is to quote bid and
offer prices. See basis price.

yield curve. A graph that shows the relationship
between **yields** and **maturities**, for a set of similar
securities or **wholesale money** deposits (cf. **strip
yield curve**). Another approach which has not
caught on has been to plot the yield against **duration**. Four shapes of yield curve can be commonly
observed:

Upward, positively sloped, or *normal*, indicating
interest rates rising as maturities lengthen, that is,
shorter maturities have lower yields than longer
ones (cf. **contango**). Usually taken as a sign of
aversion to the uncertainty resulting from the
increased price **volatility** and inferior liquidity of
long-term issues, or investor expectation of higher
rates in the future, or both (cf. **liquidity preference**).

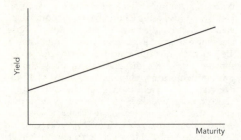

Upward yield curve

Horizontal or *flat*, indicating similar yield levels
for all maturities. Usually taken as investor indifference to **maturity mismatch risk**.

Horizontal yield curve

Downward or negatively sloped, or *inverted*,
indicating interest rates falling as maturities
lengthen (cf. **backwardation**). Usually taken as a
sign that **short-term** interest rates are expected to
fall in the future.

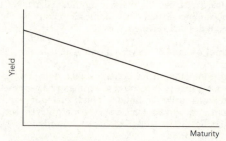

Downward yield curve

Humped shaped, showing bulges in the yield
curve with lower yields on either side. The bulges
are normally the result of excess supply in a maturity area or fragmentation of investor maturity
preference (cf. **segmented market theory**).

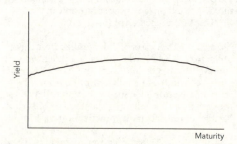

Humped yield curve

See also **forward yield curve; term structure of
interest rates; zero-coupon yield curve**.

yield curve adjustable notes (YCAN) (Bonds).
Another term for a reverse floating rate note.

yield curve floating rate note. See mismatch
bond.

yield curve note. Another name for a **reverse floating rate note** commonly used in the USA (cf. **bear floating rate note; bull floating rate note**).

yield curve option. A type of **rainbow option** where the payoff is a function of either the reduction or the increase in **spread** between different points of the **yield curve**, e.g. the short and long ends, where the payoff depends on either a flattening or a steepening of the yield curve relationship. A yield curve **call** gains if the curve flattens; a **put**, if the curve steepens. See **spread option; sycurve option**.

yield curve plays. A set of investment strategies which seek to make a profit on either a steepening or a flattening of the relationship between the short and long ends of the **yield curve** (cf. **yield curve swap**). This can be accomplished either by **long** and **short** positions in two instruments of the required **maturities** or through positions in **derivative** instruments, for example by taking a short position in the US **treasury bill future** or US **treasury note future** and a long position in the **treasury bond** future (cf. **spreading**). See **outperformance option; spread future; spread option; sycurve option**.

yield curve spread. Holding a **long-term** instrument and financing it with **short-term** borrowings in order to earn the **positive carry** between the two positions (cf. **gapping; spread**).

yield curve swap. (i) (Derivatives) A **swap** contract where the two payment streams are referenced to two different points of the **swap yield curve** (cf. **constant maturity treasury**). For example, one party might pay a five-year rate, and the other a ten-year rate (cf. **differential swap**). There is gain or protection from changes in the shape of the yield curve. See also **backwardation swap; contango swap**. (ii) (Securities) Another term for a *barbell*.

yield decrease warrant (USA). **Warrant** where the payoff is linked to the increase in price (or fall in **yield**) of the **long bond** relative to a fixed **strike** or **exercise price** or rate.

yield differential. See yield spread.

yield enhanced security. Any of a set of proprietary offerings aimed at increasing the **dividend yield** on **common stocks**. See, for instance, **preference equity redemption cumulative stock**.

yield enhancement. Any set of strategies designed to provide additional **yield**, that is increased **dividends** or **interest** to holders of a **position** or instrument. Typically such strategies surrender

capital gain potential for immediate income through selling options or surrendering some future return. See **equity-linked notes; preferred right to income and maximum equity; special claim on residual equity**.

yield equivalence (USA). A US term for the **gross yield** on a **tax-exempt bond**. Calculated by dividing the **tax-exempt yield** by one less the tax rate. For example an 8% tax-exempt yield would, for a person paying income tax at 30%, be equal to a gross yield of 11.43% {8% ÷ (1 − 0.30)} (cf. **taxable equivalent yield**).

yield gap. (i) The difference between **yields** on **common stocks** and **fixed interest** securities. Usually used as a guide to market rates in making valuations or in setting the terms for new issues (cf. **reverse yield gap**). (ii) (UK) The excess of the **dividend yield** on securities making up the **FT-Actuaries All Share Index** over the interest yield of 2.5% **consols**.

yield maintenance (Bonds; USA). The price adjustment upon **delivery** of a **Government National Mortgage Association** (GNMA) or other **mortgage-backed security** purchased under a **futures contract** or **standby commitment**, in order to provide the same **yield** to the buyer that was specified in the original agreement. The adjustment is needed when the **coupon** on the GNMA that is delivered is different from the coupon that had been expected at the time the deal was made.

yield margin (Bonds; UK). A method of setting price based on a **yield** return above some **reference yield** in the **gilt-edged** market. Used, for example, in the **bulldog** market (cf. **yield spread**).

yield margin tender. A method of inviting **bids** for **bond** issues based upon a **yield margin**. A **margin** would be guaranteed by an **underwriter** and investors would be asked to **tender** at this yield or lower.

yield pricing (Bonds). A method of issuing **bonds** on a **yield basis** comparable to ruling **after-market** yields. Rather than indicating the **coupon** in advance, leaving the issue price to be established at the time of the issue, yield pricing gives increased flexibility since both the coupon and price can be adjusted.

yield spread. The difference in **yield** between two debt securities. This difference can be: **credit worthiness; maturity; bond** features (such as **call provision** or **put provision**); types or classes of instrument (eg on **preferred** and bonds, or **senior** and **subordinated**). Often just called *spread*. See also **cross-currency spread trading; margin; spread**.

yield spread hedge ratio. This is the ratio required to **hedge** opposite exposures on two instruments. For a single currency, we need to establish the ratio of the two instruments' **modified duration** or bond volatility. If it is a cross-currency **spread**, we need not only to establish the two securities' modified durations, but also to adjust for the **foreign exchange rate** between the two currencies. For example, if we wished to set up a spread between UK government bonds (**gilt-edged**) and German government bonds (**Bunds**) and the modified durations of the two securities were 6.25 and 6.85 respectively and the exchange rate was 2.50, the correct hedge ratio between the two would be:

$$\text{Cross-currency held ratio}\left(\frac{\text{Gilts}}{\text{Bunds}}\right) = \frac{6.25}{6.85}$$
$$\times 2.50 = 2.28$$

That is, to be correctly hedged, every pound in gilts needs to be balanced by DM 2.28 worth of the appropriate Bund. This type of transaction can also be set up using **derivatives**. See **bond risk; cross-currency spread trading; rainbow option; spread futures; spread option; yield spread option.**

yield spread option. An option designed to provide a payoff based on changes in the relationship between two yields. See also **rainbow option; yield curve option; yield spread hedge ratio.**

yield tender. A tender made by bidding on the basis of **yield** rather than price.

yield-to-average life (YTAL). The yield produced when the **average life** is substituted for the maturity of the issue by assuming that the security is redeemed in accordance with the **amortization** schedule. See **interest rate calculations.**

yield-to-call (YTC). The yield produced by assuming that the **maturity** will be the first call date and that the issue will be redeemed at its **call price** (cf. **declining call schedule; discount; par value; premium**). See **convexity; duration; interest rate calculations.**

yield-to-equivalent life (YTEL). The yield calculated for issues with an **amortization** schedule. The resulting cash flows can be calculated assuming that the issue will be redeemed according to the schedule and, as such, can be taken as the **internal rate of return** of the cash flows. Normally close to the **yield-to-average life.** See **interest rate calculations.**

yield-to-maturity (YTM). The return on a security if is held until **maturity**, which will be a function of: **coupon** rate; **reinvestment rate;** and accrual of discount or amortization of premiums. See **interest rate calculations.**

yield-to-operative date or **yield-to-operative life (YTOD)** (USA). A measure intended to indicate the **yield** of the shortest possible life of a **bond**. It is taken as the higher of the **yield-to-put** or **yield-to-maturity** (or **yield-to-call**, if applicable, and the **embedded option** is **at the money** or **in the money**). It assumes the operation of maximum **sinking fund** and the **exercise** of a **call provision** in the bond as early as possible. Sometimes called *yield-to-worst, yield-to-adjusted-minimum maturity,* or *yield-to-crash.* See **interest rate calculations.**

yield-to-put (YTP) (USA). A US term for a measure of the return on a **bond** assuming it is held until a particular date and sold to the issuer at a specific price. It represents, therefore, the **internal rate of return** of the security assuming that the **put provision** is **exercised** at the **put price** (cf. **yield-to-call**).

yield-to-redemption (UK). See **redemption yield** (cf. **yield-to-maturity**).

yield-to-worst (YTW). A pessimist's calculation of the **yield** based on the worst outcome that could happen to a particular security. Typically, if the current market rate is above the **coupon** rate, it would assume the **yield-to-maturity;** if rates were below the coupon, it would assume the **yield-to-call.**

yonhon ne (Japan). The four key prices during a trading **session**. They are: *hajime ne* (the opening price); *taka ne* (the highest price); *yasu ne* (the lowest price); *owari ne* (the closing price). See also **candle stick chart; range.**

yoritsuki (Japan). The opening transaction on the **Tokyo Stock Exchange.** The price at which this takes place is called the *hajime ne,* the second session opening goes by the name of *gobayori.*

you choose option or **warrant.** See **as-you-like option** (cf. **chooser option**).

yours. Colloquial term for accepting a **bid,** or to make a sale (cf. **mine**).

yo-yo security (USA). A security with a high **volatility.**

yūsen kabu (Equities; Japan). **Preferred stock.**

Z

Zagreb Stock Exchange (Croatia). Ksaver 208, Croatia-Zagreb 41000 (tel. 38 41 42 84 55; fax 38 41 02 93).

zaibatsu (Japan). Name given to informal ties between companies in different industries who often share similar names (eg Mitsubishi, Sumitomo, etc.) and usually centred on one of the City banks. They are the successor firms to **conglomerates**, which were disbanded in 1947, but which have since retained a close association, assisted by a system of cross-shareholdings (cf. **cross-holdings**). See keiretsu.

zaitech (Japan). Literally means financial engineering. The word is used to denote active **asset management** policies by companies, including a degree of speculation.

zaraba hoshiki (Japan). The two-sided **auction** part of trading on the exchange. Opening transactions use a supply and demand method to determine the initial price, called **itayose** (cf. **opening rotation**). The flow of orders then determines the subsequent price movement.

Z bond or **tranche.** Collateralized mortgage obligation (CMO) tranche which has some of the characteristics of an **accrual bond**. Until earlier tranches of the CMO are redeemed, the Z bond pays no interest (it is in effect a zero-coupon security). Once the senior tranches have been redeemed, the Z bond pays interest and principal on the accrued amount, the original principal, and the compounded, accrued interest (cf. **collateralized mortgage obligation equity**). Such CMOs are also known as *accretion* or *accrual bonds* or *ABC bonds*.

Z certificate (UK). A type of certificate issued by the Bank of England to **discount houses** indicating **gilt-edged** holdings, thereby allowing rapid trading in **shorts**, that is, bonds with maturities up to five years.

zero collar or **zero-cost collar.** An interest rate collar where the **premiums** on the purchased **interest rate cap** and the written or sold floor exactly offset each other. See **forward band**.

zero-cost option. An option strategy where the cost of the purchased **option position** is offset by the income from the sale of one or more **options** (cf. **collar**; **cylinder**; **ladder spread**; **participating forward**). Also called a *zero premium option*.

zero-cost ratio option (ZECRO). A **participating forward** product developed by Goldman Sachs.

zero-coupon. A type of term instrument with only one cash flow which is paid at **maturity** or **redemption**. The instrument is issued at a **discount** to its **face value** and protects the holder against having to reinvest intermediate cash flows (cf. **interest rate risk**; **reinvestment risk**). Many different categories of zero-coupon securities exist, such as **bonds**, **notes**, **convertibles** and **asset-backed**. The zero-coupon structure whilst the exception in the capital markets, is the norm in the money markets.

zero-coupon bonds or **zeros (ZCB)** (Bonds). Securities which pay no interest until **maturity** in order to offer a guaranteed **yield** to both lenders and borrowers; this is often to exploit tax advantages (cf. **reinvestment risk**). They are more **volatile** than other, interest bearing, securities of the same maturity because the rolling up of the implied interest increases the **risk**. The **duration** of a zero-coupon is equivalent to its maturity, but for **coupon**-paying bonds, the duration will always be less than maturity. ZCBs have some tax advantages in some countries, such as the UK, where corporate issuers can set the implied interest against their current profits while holders defer the tax liability until the sale date or maturity. Zero-coupon issues have been used to **collateralize** the principal of security issues, such as the so-called **Brady bonds** (cf. **Mex-Ex issue**). See also **coupon stripping; reconstitution**.

zero-coupon convertible (USA). (i) A zero-coupon bond which is **convertible** at some point prior to **maturity** into another type of **bond**, usually interest paying. Seen most frequently in the **municipal bond market** Also known as *future income and growth securities* or *growth and income securities*. (ii) A zero-coupon bond which is convertible into the **common stock** of the issuer (cf. **liquid yield option note securities**). As with conventional convertibles they trade at a lower **yield-to-maturity** than straight zeros and at a small **premium** to **conversion value**.

zero-coupon eurosterling bearer or **registered accruing securities (ZEBRAS)** (UK). A gilt-edged security from which the coupons have been stripped. The issuer, usually a bank, buys a quantity of gilt-edged and issues receipts denominated in sterling (which are then tradable in the euromarkets) against every interest payment and repayment of principal. These receipts are sold for the present value of the payments they evidence thus creating a series of zero-coupon bonds, maturing on every coupon date and on the principal repayment date. The effect is to create an interest stripped capital appreciation-only security. As such, it is the UK equivalent of the certificate of accrual on Treasury securities and treasury investment growth receipts.

zero-coupon swap. A type of swap contract where the fixed rate payments are all made at maturity. Used sometimes to hedge the liability from a zero-coupon bond or to match some underlying cash flow liability where revenue is deferred, such as the construction and subsequent sale of a property. Due to the structure it is tantamount to making a loan. The disadvantage is that the party making the payments prior to maturity has increasing credit risk over the life of the swap. See also reverse zero-coupon swap.

zero-coupon yield curve. (i) A yield curve constructed by plotting the return for zero-coupon bonds against time (cf. separate trading of registered interest and principal of securities). (ii) A yield curve of zero-coupon interest rates derived from the yield curve of straight bonds by bootstrap methods (cf. forward yield curve).

zero-dividend preference share (Equities; UK). A type of preference share which pays no dividend but provides a return via capital appreciation in the same manner as a zero-coupon bond. These are most commonly used as part of a split capital trust where the zero-coupon preference shares are used to enhance or gear up (leverage) the dividend stream from the portfolio to service the geared income shares. These in turn surrender some capital appreciation to redeem the preference shares at the maturity of the trust. An equivalent structure is seen in the USA for prescribed right to income and maximum equity and special claim on residual equity.

zero-investment portfolio. A position created by purchases and short sales where there is no cash invested (cf. repurchase agreement).

zero-leakage option. An option on an underlying where there is no distribution of income or capital during the life of the option (cf. leakage).

zero minus tick (USA). A trade which is at the same price as the last transaction, but which is lower than the previously transacted different price. The opposite is a zero plus tick. See tape.

zero-premium cylinder (Forex). A zero-cost cylinder.

zero-premium cap or **floor.** Interest rate cap and floor versions of the contingent premium option. Also known as a self-funding cap or floor.

zero-premium option. Any of a number of option strategies where the written option cancels the cost of the purchased option. See also Boston option; reduced cost option.

zero strike price option (Zeds). A tax avoidance, surrogate ownership, or settlement facilitating structure used in countries where there is a tax on securities transactions, restrictions on (usually foreign) ownership, or difficulties in affecting settlement. By setting the option strike price at, or close to, zero the option is effectively equivalent to the underlying asset. See, for instance, low exercise price options.

zero sum game. A situation where the winning participants can only gain at the expense of the others involved (cf. positive sum game).

zero suppression. The removal of noughts from the display of financial information, particularly in large-scale funding or security deals. See tape.

zeta. See vega.

zipper. An issue of a package of securities where each part has individual special features. For instance an issue which combined a fixed rate bond and a floating rate note.

zombie. A company more dead than alive. Such a company is only kept alive by the goodwill and support of creditors, especially lenders. See bankruptcy; financial distress; insolvency; restructuring.

zoo. The tendency for new derivative securities or structures to have exotic animal names such as CATS, LYONS, STAGS, TIGERS, ZEBRAS. In the world of new financial instruments, it is a zoo out there.

Z score. A method of assessing the credit worthiness of firms upon a model that predicts the likelihood of default or bankruptcy. The larger the Z score, the less likely it is that the business will fail; and a negative score is associated with a failed business. The Z value is a function of several variables, including, typically, the following ratios:

earnings before interest and taxes to total assets; earnings before tax and interest to total interest payments; retained earnings to total assets; market valuation to total capital; and the current ratio. It uses a multivariate statistical technique called discriminant analysis to establish the relationship between firm performance and the predictor variables. The model is based on a (historical) data set of failed firms and healthy firms where the discriminant function seeks to explain the differences in the two types. Further firms are then compared to the existing model's parameters and assigned to one of the two types (that is either healthy or resembling a previously bankrupt firm), Z-scores also go under the name of *bankruptcy prediction models*. See also **credit ratings**; **ratio analysis**.

Z tranche. See Z **bond**.

Zürcher Börse (Zurich Stock Exchange) (Switzerland) Selnaustrasse 32, CH-8021 Zürich (tel. 01 229 21 11; fax 01 229 22 33).

Zusammenschlüsse (Germany). **Mergers and acquisitions**.